RIO.

Nova zemla.

Tazata

Taingin Mongol.

Islant · Noruegia
Suedia
Bergen
Or Nougrod
Gallia

Tartaria

EVROPA · Russia
Mosco.

ASIA

Naiman
Mongul

Cattigara
Tendue.

Carthaio

China

Turcheltan
Samarchand
Voci am Iaci China.

Miaco.

Natolia
Soria.
Persia

Coraian

India orien talis.

Iapan.

AFRICA
Agisymba

Nubia

Arabia.

Guzarate

Aegyptus

Abissini

Zeilan

Manicongo.

Melinde.

Vasco de Acuña

Gissam
Due Compagne.

Iana ma ior.

OCEANVS AE
THIOPICVS.

Don Garçia
Poueada fona

Lantchidol mare.

BEACH

Mar di India

LYCACH

Iaua minor.

MALETVR

Vastissimas hîc esse regiones ex M. Pauli Ven: et Lud: Vartomanni scriptis peregrinationibus constat.

Psitacorum regió,
sic à Lusitanis appellata ob incredibilé earum auium ibidem magnitudinem.

20 30 40 50 60 70 80 90 100 110 120 130 140 150 160 170 180

IES.

BVS HVMANIS, CVI AETERNITAS
A SIT MAGNITVDO. CICERO:

HISTORICAL
ATLAS
OF THE WORLD

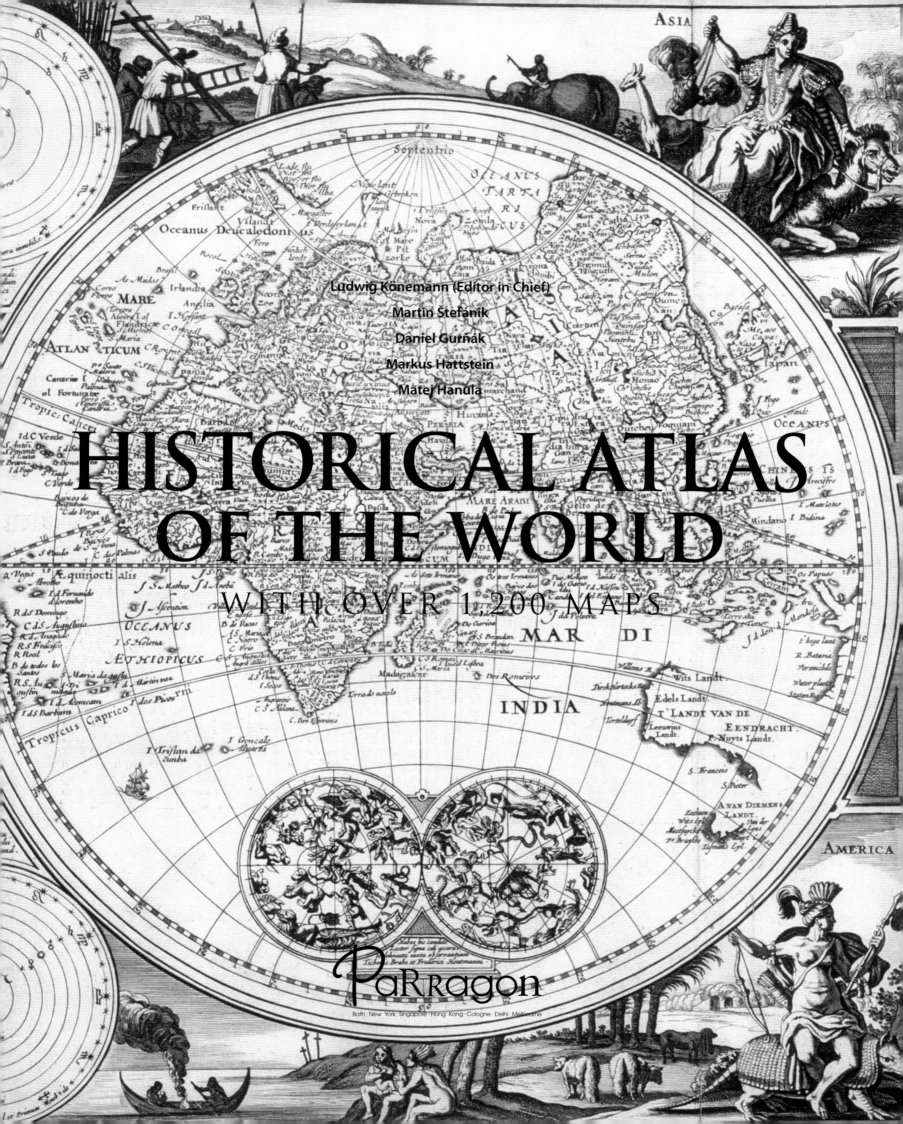

Ludwig Könemann (Editor in Chief)

Martin Štefánik

Daniel Gurňák

Markus Hattstein

Matej Hanula

HISTORICAL ATLAS OF THE WORLD

WITH OVER 1,200 MAPS

PaRragon

Bath · New York · Singapore · Hong Kong · Cologne · Delhi · Melbourne

Contents

7 Foreword

8 An Unimaginably Large Space
over an Unimaginably Long Time

10 Our Picture of the World

AN OVERVIEW OF WORLD HISTORY

16 THE WORLD: AN OVERVIEW

20 The Most Important Sites Where Traces
of Human Ancestors Have Been Found

22 The First Empires

24 The Civilizations of Antiquity,
1000 BCE–500 CE

26 The World in the Middle Ages, 500–1450

28 The World ca. 1450

30 European Exploration of the World

32 Early Modern Times, ca. 1500–1776

34 Moving Toward Modernity, 1776–1913

36 World War I and the Interwar Period,
1914–1933

38 Nazi Dictatorship, World War II
and the Postwar Period, 1933–1949

40 World War II

42 The World, 1949–1990

44 The World Economy

46 Hunger and Poverty, Overpopulation,
Terrorism, Climate Change and
Natural Resources

48 World Religions

50 The United Nations

52 The Nobel Peace Prize Laureates

54 The World Since 1990

EUROPE

58 EUROPE: AN OVERVIEW

62 THE CRUSADES, 1096–1270

64 EUROPE: AN OVERVIEW

70 EUROPE IN DETAIL

70 Mesopotamia and the Near East
Until 330 BCE

72 Ancient Greece

76 THE ACHIEVEMENTS OF ANTIQUITY

78 Ancient Rome

82 ROMAN PROVINCES AND TRADE ROUTES

84 BIBLICAL TIMES UNTIL 70 CE

86 JUDAISM

88 CHRISTIANITY

90 Northern Europe Before the
Barbarian Invasions

92 The Barbarian Invasions, 350–568

94 THE LEGACY OF ANTIQUITY (SELECTED EXAMPLES)

96 The Frankish Empires, 482–887

98 THE MOST IMPORTANT ROYAL HOUSES OF EUROPE

102 MEDIEVAL CASTLES

104 MEDIEVAL RELIGIOUS ORDERS AND MONASTERIES

106 The Late Middle Ages

108 THE GREAT EUROPEAN UNIVERSITIES
OF THE 13TH–15TH CENTURIES

109 THE PLAGUE IN THE 14TH CENTURY

110 The Early Modern Era and Reformation

112 The 16th and 17th Centuries

114 The French Revolution and
Congress of Vienna, 1789–1815

116 The Industrial Revolution and
the 19th Century

118 SIGNIFICANT WARS AND BATTLES
IN EUROPEAN HISTORY

120 The Great Powers Around 1900

122 World War I, 1914–1918

124 Between the World Wars, 1919–1939

126 World War II, 1939–1945

130 War Damages and
Postwar Order

132 NATO, the Warsaw Pact and
the European Union

134 The Dissolution of the Eastern Bloc

136 Today

138 Scandinavia

142 England, Wales, Ireland and Scotland

156 The Low Countries

162 Germany

182 Switzerland and Liechtenstein

186 CENTRAL EUROPE:
AN OVERVIEW

192 Austria

196 Hungary

200 Czech Republic and Slovakia

204 Slovenia and Croatia

208 Poland

212 Estonia, Latvia and Lithuania

214 Russia and the Soviet Union

226 Russia, Ukraine and Belarus

230 France

244 Spain and Portugal

252 Italy

264 THE POPES

266 SOUTHEAST EUROPE – BYZANTIUM:
AN OVERVIEW

270 SOUTHEAST EUROPE – THE
OTTOMAN EMPIRE: AN OVERVIEW

274 Serbia and Montenegro

278 Serbia and Yugoslavia

280 Bosnia and Herzegovina,
Macedonia

282 Albania

284 Bulgaria

288 Romania and Moldova

292 Greece

296 Turkey, Cyprus and Malta

AFRICA

302 **AFRICA: AN OVERVIEW**
304 EUROPEAN EXPLORATION OF AFRICA AND THE SLAVE TRADE
306 **AFRICA: AN OVERVIEW**
308 Ancient Egypt Until 395 CE
310 The Maghreb
312 Libya and Egypt
314 Western and Central Africa
316 Eastern Africa
318 Southern Africa
320 CURRENT ISSUES ON THE AFRICAN CONTINENT

ASIA

324 **ASIA: AN OVERVIEW**
332 **THE ARAB WORLD: AN OVERVIEW**
336 THE HISTORY AND EXPANSION OF ISLAM
338 Israel and Palestine
342 The Levant: Syria, Lebanon and Jordan
346 The Arabian Peninsula
348 OIL AND ENERGY
350 Iraq and Kuwait
354 Persia / Iran
356 Transcaucasia
358 Central Asia
360 Siberia and Mongolia
362 India, Pakistan and Bangladesh

366 Tibet and Bhutan / Buddhism and Hinduism
368 China
376 Korea
378 Japan
382 Vietnam, Laos, Cambodia, Thailand and Myanmar
386 Malaysia, Brunei and Singapore
388 The Philippines
390 Indonesia

AUSTRALIA AND OCEANIA

394 Melanesia, Micronesia and Polynesia
396 Australia
399 Aborigines / Papua New Guinea
400 New Zealand

NORTH AMERICA

404 **NORTH AMERICA: AN OVERVIEW**
406 Indigenous Peoples of North America
408 Canada and Greenland
412 The United States of America
415 THE FIFTY STATES
420 IMMIGRATION AND SETTLEMENT OF THE USA
422 THE UNITED STATES BECOMES A WORLD POWER
424 The Caribbean

CENTRAL AMERICA

428 Mexico
432 Central America

SOUTH AMERICA

436 **SOUTH AMERICA: AN OVERVIEW**
439 20TH CENTURY: A HOTBED OF POLITICAL UNREST
440 Venezuela
442 Colombia
443 Ecuador
444 Guyana, Suriname, French Guiana
445 NATURAL RESOURCES IN SOUTH AMERICA
446 Peru
448 Bolivia
449 INDIGENOUS PEOPLES OF SOUTH AMERICA BEFORE SPANISH COLONIZATION
450 Brazil
454 Uruguay
455 Paraguay
456 Chile
458 Argentina

ISLANDS AND POLAR REGIONS

462 Atlantic Ocean
465 Indian Ocean
468 Pacific Ocean
470 The Arctic Region
472 The Antarctic Region

APPENDICES

474 Countries of the World
504 Index
512 Acknowledgments, Picture Credits

2707 BCE 1050 BCE 814 BCE 333 BCE 323 BCE 264 BCE 241 BCE 216 BCE 211

31 BCE 27 BCE 4 BCE 14 37 64 68 70 79 98 117 138 161 180 193 211 222

498 511 526 527 565 610 622 632 732 768 787 800 814 843 855 911 919 936 962

1197 1215 1226 1250 1273 1303 1347 1356 1378 1415 1440 1461 1477 14

1608 1612 1618 1620 1631 1632 1634 1640 1643 1648 1658 1688

1765 1776 1789 1790 1793 1794 1796 1799 1804 1805 1806 1812 1814 18

1837 1848 1849 1853 1859 1861 1864 1866 1868 1870 1871 1881 1

1898 1900 1901 1902 1904 1905 1908 1911 1914 1916 1917 1918 1919 1922 1923 1

1933 1936 1938 1939 1940 1941 1942 1943 1944 1945 1948 1949 1950 1

1959 1961 1962 1963 1964 1967 1968 1969 1970 1973 197

1985 1986 1987 1989 1990 1991 1994 1995 1997 1999 2001 2003 2004 2005

Foreword

This book is an encyclopedic textbook of world history.

More than 1,200 historical maps, all newly created for this book; over 300 chronological tables and some 20,000 historical facts convey the history of the world from a global perspective using a visual, graphic and educational approach.

Clarity is the foremost consideration for the historical maps. The entries have been optimized so that they are unambiguous, readily understood and easy to remember.

The short entries in the chronologies focus on important historical events. When necessary, the context and interrelationships are explained in a short glossary on the same two-page spread. The maps relate directly to the timelines and vice versa. The maps, timelines and glossaries are in constant dialogue with one another.

Each two-page spread is a little history lesson in itself. If you spend about twenty minutes on each of the 230 spreads, in approximately eighty hours you will have a far deeper understanding of world history. And hopefully you will agree with us: seldom has history been so entertaining.

A word about the organization of the book: dividing history into epochs such as early times, first empires, antiquity, the Middle Ages, the modern era and the present may work well for Europe. But in other cultures, the Stone Age lasted into the 20th century, and those societies basically skipped four epochs in order to arrive directly in the global present.

A geographical breakdown is also problematic. The empires of the past did not abide by continental divisions. The Middle East and northern Africa were decisive for European history throughout antiquity, for example. And with the spread of Islam in the 7th century, a cultural continent arose that not only encompassed northern Africa and central Asia, but proceeded to influence the history of much of Southeast Asia and even Spain and parts of the Balkans.

We have therefore opted for a functional structure. First, the history of the world is presented in a rapid overview. This is followed by each of the continents, including their empires and nations or groups of states, even if the assignments to a continent are not entirely unambiguous. This approach inevitably leads to some repetition of facts, but corresponds most nearly to historical reality.

Ludwig Könemann (Editor in Chief)

An Unimaginably Large Space over an Unimaginably Long Time

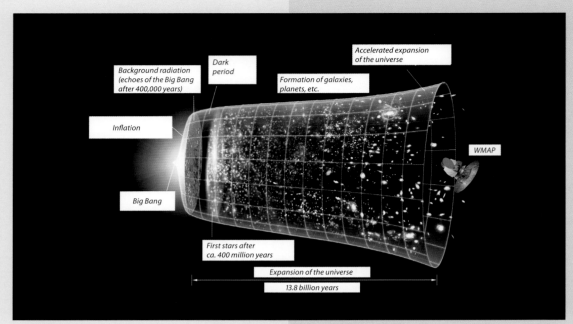

The Big Bang

13.8 billion years condensed into one year

Let's imagine that the entire history of the universe had taken place in one year, and the Big Bang occurred at midnight on January 1. That dates back about 13.8 billion years.
The following times would thus represent:

1 day	37,800,000 years
1 hour	1,575,000 years
1 minute	26,250 years
1 second	437.5 years
1 human life span	ca. 0.15 seconds

This is how the calendar would look:

Jan. 1   0:00:00 hours
13,800,000,000 years ago

The Big Bang: matter, space and time came into existence. It was inconceivably hot; the temperature after one second was still ca. 18 billion °F (10 billion °C). The universe has expanded continuously ever since and cooled considerably.

0:15:15 hours
13,799,600,000 years ago

The temperature was still ca. 4,890°F (2,700°C), or about half that of the sun's surface. Atoms came into being.

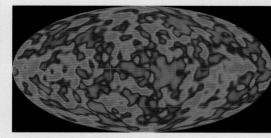

NASA image of background radiation

Jan. 10   13,400,000,000 years ago

The first stars were formed.

Aug. 1   4,600,000,000 years ago

Our solar system emerged out of a gigantic solar nebula, a mixture of 99 percent hydrogen and helium. The first planets formed and circled the sun in elliptical orbits.

Aug. 22   3,800,000,000 years ago

The temperature of the Earth's surface dropped below 212°F (100°C). A solid crust developed, and the Archean eon began. Unicellular life began.

Oct. 25   2,500,000,000 years ago

The Earth's atmosphere became capable of supporting life. Beginning of the Proterozoic: the first multicellular creatures appeared.

Dec. 16   540,000,000 years ago

The Cambrian explosion: rapid appearance of the first vertebrates.

Dec. 19   435,000,000 years ago

The first land plants emerged in the Silurian period.

Dec. 24   250,000,000 years ago

Triassic period: the first dinosaurs walked the Earth.

Dec. 26   203,000,000 years ago

The first birds appeared; the famous fossil *Archaeopteryx* dates from this period.

Dec. 30   05:00 hours
65,000,000 years ago

A mass extinction took place at the end of the Cretaceous period, to which the dinosaurs also fell victim.

Dec. 31   20:50 hours
5,000,000 years ago

The first ancestors of human beings walked the earth.

Dec. 31   22:00 hours
3,200,000 years ago

The *Australopithecus afarensis* named "Lucy" died in eastern Africa at the age of twenty-five. Her discoverer named her after the Beatles song "Lucy in the Sky with Diamonds."

Dec. 31   23:55:12 hours
126,000 years ago

Modern humans, *Homo sapiens*, lived in Africa. They would soon begin their great migration to and conquest of all the continents.

Geological Time Scale

The Cambrium through Permian periods comprise the Paleozoic era, followed by the three periods of the Mesozoic era. Within the current Cenozoic era, we are currently in the Quarternary period, which began only 1.8 million years ago.

	million years ago
Cenozoic era	65
Cretacious period	145.5
Jurassic period	199.6
Triassic period	251.0
Permian period	299.0
Carboniferous period	359.2
Devonian period	416.0
Silurian period	443.7
Ordovician period	488.3
Cambrium period	542.0
Proterozoic eon	2,500.0
Archean eon	4,000.0

Dec. 31   23:57:09 hours
75,000 years ago

Eruption of the Toba Volcano in Sumatra. Worldwide, between one thousand and ten thousand people survived the disaster. Since then, the world's population has multiplied thousands of times over.

Satellite image of Lake Toba, Sumatra, Indonesia

Dec. 31   23:59:00 hours
26,000 years ago

Neanderthals died out one minute before the end of our calendar year; *Homo sapiens* were the only human life form to survive. The first works of art—carvings and cave paintings—appeared.

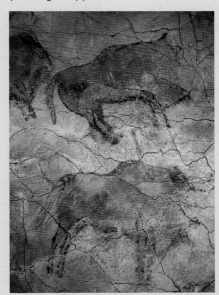

Cave painting, Altamira, Spain

Population Growth

Population in millions

[line graph showing population from -5000 to 2020, with values on y-axis: 0, 500, 1000, 1500, 2000, 2500, 3000, 3500, 4000, 4500, 5000, 5500, 6000, 6500, 8000; and x-axis years: -5000, -2000, -1000, -800, -600, -400, -200, 0, 200, 400, 600, 800, 1000, 1200, 1400, 1600, 1800, 2000 ... (year)]

Dec. 31   23:59:37 hours
10,000 years ago
23 seconds before midnight

The Neolithic revolution began. Humans established permanent settlements, planted crops and raised animals. About 5 to 10 million people were living in the world.

Dec. 31   23:59:48 hours
ca. 5,000 years ago

The Sumerians invented writing, and the Egyptians built the first pyramids.

Pyramid of Djoser in the Saqqara necropolis, ca. 2650 BCE

Dec. 31   23:59:56 hours
ca. 2,000 years ago

Life of Jesus of Nazareth. Some 300 million people lived on earth. About half the world's population resided in the Roman or Chinese empires.

Dec. 31   23:59:59 hours
ca. 500 years ago

Columbus discovered the Americas on behalf of Spain. Of the first 500 million people, about one-fifth were native peoples.

Dec. 31   23:59:59 hours
in the last 100 years

Within the last century, people have invented the automobile, the airplane, television and the Internet. We have traveled to the moon and discovered the farthest reaches of the universe. We navigate using space satellites and produce pictures of the universe as it was 13.8 billion years ago using background radiation. We build atomic and hydrogen bombs whose explosive force can annihilate Earth many times over. About 150 million people died under Hitler, Stalin and Mao; that was half the population at the beginning of the Common Era. World population is approaching 7 billion and growing rapidly. Of all the human beings who have ever lived, over 10 percent lived during the 20th century, i.e., during the last one-tenth of a second of the history of the universe.

The Sizes of the Universe

Filaments and voids (example: Great Wall or Coma Wall, ca. 1 billion light-years in diameter)
Superclusters (example: the Virgo Supercluster, ca. 200 million light-years in diameter)
Galaxy clusters (example: local groups, ca. 10 million light-years in diameter)
Galaxies (example: the Milky Way, ca. 100,000 light-years in diameter)
Star clusters (globular clusters, open star clusters: dozens to hundreds of light-years in diameter)
Planetary systems (example: our solar system, ca. 41 light-hours in diameter)
Stars (example: the Sun, ca. 864,743 miles or 1,392,500 km in diameter)
Planets (example: Earth, ca. 8,000 miles or 12,756 km in diameter)
Moons (example: the Earth's moon, ca. 2,160 miles or 3,476 km in diameter)
Asteroids, comets (a few to several hundred kilometers in diameter)
Meteoroids (range from millimeters to meters in diameter)
Dust particles (from a few molecules to 0.1 mm)
Molecules, atoms, elementary particles (example: the radius of a helium atom is 32 pm)

If we assume that a filament were equal to the circumference of our equator, then the Milky Way would be about 2.5 miles (4 km) wide, and our solar system would be a minute 0.2 mm.

If our solar system was reduced to the circumference of our equator, the Sun would be 3¼ feet (1 meter) in diameter and Earth just ⅜ inch (1 cm).

If the equator's circumference equaled a filament, Earth would have a diameter of 0.000000005 mm, and would be approximately the same size relative to the universe as an atom is to the Earth.

Or are there multiple universes?

In recent years, a new theory seems to have confirmed that there have indeed been many universes. In their calculations concerning the Big Bang, researchers ran into a phenomenon: when the concentration of stars reaches several billion per cubic centimeter, the mass begins to expand again. From this they inferred that a great implosion preceded the Big Bang.

Like a string of sausages, the universe expands explosively from a certain point in time and grows continuously; when it extends to a certain point, it will again contract and implode in a Big Crunch. Incredible as it may seem, this theory suggests there may have been billions of universes before ours, and not one, but many, recurring "creations" and new beginnings. This theory may generate renewed interest in cyclical models of the origins and ends of worlds, such as those known to the early Hindus.

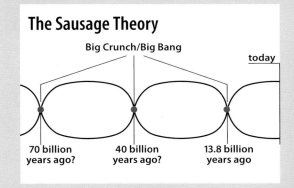

The Sausage Theory

Big Crunch/Big Bang

today

70 billion years ago?   40 billion years ago?   13.8 billion years ago

Our Picture of the World

From the very beginning, human beings have tried to understand themselves and the world in which they lived. Initially, their interpretation was magical in the sense of attempting to exert an influence on nature and assert the self; later, it was primarily religious, as people saw themselves and the world as part of a universe created and controlled by the gods. As the world continued to be discovered and explored, philosophical questions dealing with space, time, existence and change yielded to a scientific worldview that included the entire cosmos.

Perhaps the greatest paradigm shift was the transition from Ptolemy's geocentric cosmology, in which Earth was at the very center of the universe, to Copernicus's heliocentric model that recognized that Earth and the other planets circle the sun, thus making way for the discovery of other solar systems.

Prehistory and Protohistory

ca. 6200 BCE

As early as the Paleolithic or **Late Stone Age** (ca. 40,000–10,000 BCE), humans tried to draw images of distinctive geographic features. The oldest "map" of an area was found in Çatalhöyük in Central Anatolia and is dated at 6200 BCE. It is a wall painting that depicts the houses of a village and the twin peaks of the nearby volcano Hasan Dağı.

Wall paintings (for example, those in the Lascaux Cave) depicting the stars of the zodiac and other constellations indicate that prehistoric people observed celestial bodies. In the Late Stone Age, a calendar that required knowledge of celestial phenomena took on vital importance for agricultural cultures. Knowing about significant annual celestial events made planning possible.

The Cave of Lascaux / Montignac, France

The **Goseck circle** in Saxony-Anhalt, Germany, is considered to be the oldest solar observatory in the world; it was erected approximately 7,000 years ago. Perhaps the most impressive prehistoric ritual site in Europe is **Stonehenge**, in England. No information has been passed down about the cultic practices that were performed there, but the geographic siting of the monument strongly suggests an astronomical connection.

Era of the Ancient Civilizations

ca. 3800 BCE

Highly diverse cartographic evidence from ancient **Mesopotamia** has been preserved. The clay tablet of Nuzi (Ga-Sur, Iraq) was inscribed around 3800 BCE. The 2¾ x 2¾ inch (7 x 7 cm) tablet is incised with a map showing mountains, rivers and cities of northern Mesopotamia.

ca. 2000 BCE

Increasingly precise maps were developed in **China** and **Egypt** as well. Regions were systematically surveyed, initially to create local and regional maps.

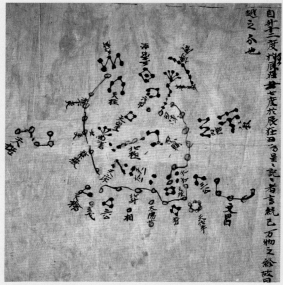

Graphic representation of the stars, scroll, China, ca. 618–906

ca. 1500 BCE

In **Babylonia**, a 8¼ x 7 inch (21 x 18 cm) clay tablet was inscribed in Sumerian cuneiform script with a map of the city of Nippur, showing the city gate, various buildings and the Euphrates River.

ca. 1300 BCE

A papyrus map of the Nubian gold mines from **Egypt** has been preserved. It represents the basin east of Coptos with a main road and the Temple of Ammon.

ca. 500 BCE

The oldest surviving map of the world—called the Babylonian world map—dates from the 6th century BCE.

Europe in the Bronze Age

between 1800–1600 BCE

The discovery of the **sky disk of Nebra** in Saxony-Anhalt, Germany, in 1999 caused an archaeological sensation. It was created sometime between 1800 and 1600 BCE.

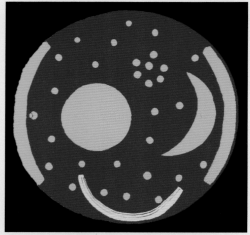

The Nebra sky disk is considered the world's oldest concrete representation of the cosmos.

ca. 1500 BCE

Rock carvings (petroglyphs) created in this period can be seen in Italy at Capo di Ponte in the Camonica Valley. One of them measures 13⅔ x 7½ feet (4.16 x 2.30 m) and shows topography, animals and people.

Antiquity

6th–5th centuries BCE

Hecataeus of Miletus (ca. 560–ca. 485/475 BCE)

Around 500 BCE, Hecataeus of Miletus used the world map of **Anaximander of Miletus** (ca. 611–546 BCE, map ca. 600 BCE, now lost) for his historical and geographical studies. A contemporary text by Herodotus (490/480–ca. 425 BCE) includes a detailed description of how a world map should be drawn.

Hecataeus wrote the first geographically and historically accurate travel account (*periegesis*) of the known world, including the first mention of the Celts.

For Hecataeus and Herodotus, the borders of the world were northern Europe (Hyperborea), the Caspian Sea, western India and the Sahel Zone.

Anaximander, a contemporary and student of **Thales of Miletus**, postulated a **geocentric cosmology**; he was the first to describe the sky as a sphere with the Earth at its center. Earlier cultures perceived the sky as a semisphere above the flat disk of the Earth.

4th century BCE

Pytheas of Massilia (Marseilles) (ca. 380–310 BCE)

One of the great explorers of antiquity was Pytheas, who traveled to the western and northern coasts of Europe. He explored Britain (mentioning its triangular shape) and possibly traveled as far as the mouth of the Elbe River. He mentions being told about Thule (Iceland) and the land of amber.

Pytheas created a grid map of the ancient world with degrees of latitude and longitude.

Using the differing length of shadows cast by a sundial, he calculated the distance from the northernmost tip of Scotland to his home port of Massilia as 1,056 miles (1,700 km). The actual distance is 1,123 miles (1,815 km)!

Pytheas observed the phenomenon of the tides, previously unknown to the Greeks, and was the first to connect them to the phases of the moon. He was also the first Greek to see drift ice, the northern lights and the midnight sun!

3rd century BCE

Aristarchus of Samos
(310–230 BCE)

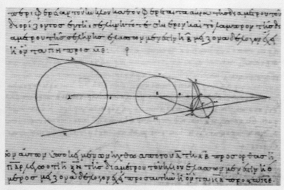

Sketch of the hypothesis of Aristarchus

Aristarchus was one of the first to assert that the Earth and Sun are not at the center of the universe.

He observed how the moon moves across Earth's shadow during a lunar eclipse, concluding that the Earth's diameter is three times that of the moon.

He developed a cosmology in which the Sun is at the center (heliocentric cosmology).

While Aristarchus's estimation of the distance to the Sun using the distance he had calculated to the moon is inaccurate, the method itself is correct.

It was not until almost two thousand years later that his theory of heliocentric cosmology was rediscovered and revived by Copernicus.

3rd–2nd centuries BCE

Eratosthenes
(ca. 276–194 BCE)

Eratosthenes drew a world map and was the first to calculate the circumference of the Earth.

He declared the Earth a sphere! His calculation of Earth's circumference, made in 225 BCE, is almost consistent with the actual circumference.

Eratosthenes coined the term "geography."

The world map of Eratosthenes

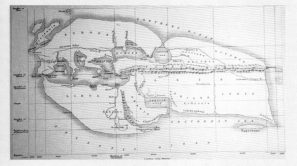

2nd century BCE

Hipparchus of Nicaea
(ca. 190–120 BCE)

Hipparchus of Nicaea was the most important Greek astronomer of his time.

With great precision, Hipparchus perfected the methods of calculating the seasons, which were already known to the Babylonians, as a basis for determining exact geographic positions using the path of the sun (he introduced the astrolabe, also called an armillary sphere).

He catalogued and calculated the brightness of more than 800 stars and drew a star map.

His calculation of the tropical year, that is, the length of the year as determined by the seasons, is within 6.5 minutes of modern measurements!

In addition, he calculated the distance between the Earth and Moon to be almost exactly thirty times the circumference of the Earth (for a total of 238,600 miles or 384,000 km). **Ancient Rome** has yielded only a few cartographic documents, one of them being the **Forma Urbis Roma**, a monumental map of Rome that is dated to ca. 203–211 CE. Only later copies of the **Tabula Peutingeriana** have survived. This is a map with distances given in miles showing the network of roads in the late Roman Empire (from the British Isles to the Mediterranean and the Near East, to India and the Ganges, to the island of Sri Lanka in the Indian Ocean and to China).

The Common Era
~0

Strabo
(ca. 63 BCE–ca. 23 CE)

Strabo wrote a seventeen-volume *Geography* that contains a map of the world. In his lifetime, the work remained unknown; it was not discovered until the 5th century. In the European intellectual canon, Strabo became the "prototype" of the geographer.

2nd century CE

Claudius Ptolemy
(87–150 CE)

Based on works that existed in his day (by Hipparchus and others), Ptolemy developed the cosmology that bears his name and that became the pinnacle of ancient astronomy. His *Almagest* became the standard work of astronomy, and astronomers up to and beyond the Renaissance relied on its catalog of stars.

His vast geographical works also brought him fame in posterity: he wrote a geographical treatise in which he described the known world and its inhabitants, and drew numerous maps of the world, of continents and of countries.

He understood the Earth to be a sphere, but located in the center of the solar system.

The **geocentric Ptolemaic cosmology** dominated the entire medieval period in Europe and was not overturned until the modern era by Nicolaus Copernicus (1473–1543), Johannes Kepler (1571–1630) and Galileo Galilei (1564–1642).

Middle Ages
~6th–15th centuries

During the Middle Ages, the **Arabs** were in the forefront of cartography. In the 9th century, they calculated the circumference of the Earth even more precisely than Eratosthenes had. Due to their trading activities and the expansion of their empire, they needed good maps, and they produced them in large numbers.

In **Europe**, cartographic knowledge from antiquity was lost. Drawing maps became the purview of monks, and their maps mirrored Christian cosmology, as seen for example in the **mappae mundi** (8th–15th centuries). Contemporaneously, two independent cartographic traditions developed: portolan charts and Ptolemaic maps.

Fra Mauro's world map, 15th century

The end of medieval cartography: people called cosmographers began to add new maps (tabulae novae) to Ptolemy's *Geography*. Ptolemaic atlases (16th century) bear witness to the shift in the world-view at the end of the Middle Ages. One of the most famous cosmographers was Sebastian Münster (1488–1522). The continents of America and Australia are still missing on the oldest surviving globe— Martin Behaim's *Erdapfel* ("potato," literally "earth apple"), dated 1492.

Mappae mundi were usually illustrations of theological works. They are not oriented to the north but instead toward the east, with the holy city of Jerusalem at the center. The most frequent type was T-O maps (wheel maps), where the Don and Nile rivers created a "T" that divided the known world into three continents. The "O" symbolizes the ocean—the boundary of earthly space.

Portolan charts: The term "portolan" (from the Latin *portus*, or port) originally referred to a book with nautical information (first chronicled in 1285); from the 16th century on, the term is also used for nautical charts. These maps are covered by a web of criss-crossing lines originating from compass roses and show coastlines, ports, cliffs and shallows, providing all the necessary information for navigation.

Ptolemaic maps: From the 14th century on, many copies of Ptolemy's *Geography* existed and its authority was initially accepted without criticism. The book was very widely disseminated after the advent of the printing press (from 1450 on).

Our Picture of the World

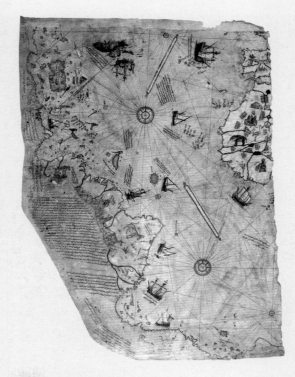

Piri Reis map, 1513, Turkey

Ancient scholarship continued to be fostered in the Islamic world, whose knowledge of cartography and mathematics was later groundbreaking for European cartography during the Renaissance. European discoveries during the modern era were also based on **Arab cartography**. The **Ptolemaic maps** were very popular and considered an improvement over the *mappae mundi*, but they were not more precise than the **portolan charts**.

It was not until **seafaring** became prevalent worldwide **around 1500** and cartographers adopted new and critical methods that cartography became more realistic and accurate.

Cosmic globe, Gerardus Mercator, 1551

Modern Era

from ~16th century

The **Renaissance** was the period when classical astronomy flourished as *the science of the geometric model of the universe*, a science dedicated—initially only rudimentarily—to the exploration of physical aspects of the movement of the stars.

As a result of scientific research, the old worldview came under pressure; in addition, the expansion of seafaring (exploration voyages by the Portuguese, Spanish, Dutch and English) required good, precise maps. Cartography experienced a surge due to the invention of the printing press, which enabled mass dissemination.

Nicolaus Copernicus
(1473–1543)

Emancipation from Ptolemaic cosmology: Nicolaus Copernicus initiated a new era of astronomy. His work *De revolutionibus orbium coelestium* appeared in 1543. He questioned the Ptolemaic (geocentric) model by mathematically proving—as the ancient astronomers had done before him—that celestial phenomena can be accurately described within the heliocentric system by way of planetary motion.

In 1507 Martin Waldseemüller, together with Matthias Ringmann, produced a globe, a world map and the treatise *Introduction to Cosmography*. This map, for the very first time, contains the continent labeled "America," which Ringmann or Waldmüller derived from the first name of Italian explorer and geographer Amerigo Vespucci (1451–1512).

The early modern era also saw the introduction of maps that were of practical benefit to travelers and merchants: travel maps (predecessors of the road atlas), miles disks (an early form of the distance table) and city maps, as well as bird's-eye city views.

Globe of the Earth with zodiac signs, 1660

Gerardus Mercator
(1512–1594)

Mercator invented the "Mercator projection," which preserves angles on a map but distorts area and distance; it remains important for nautical and aeronautical navigation. In 1569 Mercator published the first world map that correctly preserves angles, entitled "Nova et aucta orbis terræ descriptio ad usum navigantium emendate accomodata."

Maps of all regions of the world in a uniform format: Abraham Ortelius (1527–1598) was the first to publish an atlas of Earth (*Theatrum Orbis Terrarum*, 1570). It is Mercator, however, who first used the term "atlas" for his epoch-making book, *Atlas sive Cosmographicae meditationes de fabrica mundi et fabricati figura*.

Galileo Galilei
(1564–1642)

Galilei defended Copernicus's model and provided scientific proof for the theory of a heliocentric planetary system, in other words, one that revolves around the Sun. This helped advance the "Copernican shift" in our worldview, our

understanding of humankind and the philosophy of science in the early modern era.

Among Galilei's discoveries are the moons of Jupiter and Saturn's ring.

The invention of the telescope in 1608 by Dutch lensmaker Jan Lippershey was crucial for Galilei's discoveries and the proof he collected.

Johannes Kepler
(1571–1630)

Kepler and Brahe, ca. 1600 (painting dated 1870)

In his book *Astronomia Nova*, Kepler described his laws of planetary motion around the sun.

Kepler's model of the solar system

Satellite image of the Earth

Additional Significant Developments of the Modern Era

17th–18th centuries

The Cassini Family
France was particularly active in the development of land surveying (triangulation). Between 1750 and 1793, Jacques and César Cassini de Thury completed their great survey and detailed mapping of France. This was the start of modern, topographical mapping.

1793

The culmination of the Cassinis' work, the **Carte de Cassini**, is the first precise map of all of France. It is considered the prototype of the topographic map, in which every detail (cities, roads, villages, buildings, bodies of water, vineyards, etc.) is represented.

19th century

The first official topographic maps were created in Prussia, Austria and Switzerland.

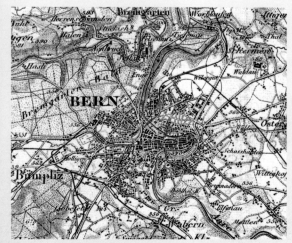
Dufour map of Berne, Switzerland (1907 edition)

Initially, the copper engraving process was used; later the invention of lithography revolutionized the reproduction technology used for maps and enabled cost-effective color printing.

20th century

In 1913 specifications were determined for an international world map (scale of 1:1 million). The project suffered a serious setback due to World War II; the United Nations continued the project in 1953. Although it has never been completed, this cartographic work contains all the most important landmasses of the world.

The importance of the project lies primarily in the attempt to achieve a worldwide standardization of maps and in the joint work conducted by institutions from many countries.

World Wars and the Postwar Period

Due to military requirements during the two world wars, many new technologies and innovations were developed in cartography and in production technology, which became established during the 20th century. Since 1920 aerial images have been used in cartography (stereo photogrammic analysis).

From 1960 to the 1990s

Digital cartography: From the first tentative use of computers in cartography in the 1960s through to the 1990s, cartography experienced a technical revolution that replaced practically all the previous cartographic methods.

Since the 1990s, **geographic information systems (GIS)**, which combine remote sensing data and data that has been cartographically processed, have become common in Europe and the United States. Satellite cartography systems use computers to convert data and images of the Earth to three-dimensional maps.

Contemporaneously with the introduction of computer technology, the shift in cartography accelerated dramatically due to the availability of **satellite images** (spy and Earth observation satellites). Even the most inaccessible and remote parts of the planet can be observed and the observations continually updated.

21st century

Route planners on CD-ROM or as an online service have become commonplace.

The use of satellite-based navigation systems (**GPS – Global Positioning System**) and 3-D map images with "Google Earth" are an everyday part of modern life for many people.

Every single day, a greater number of (interactive) maps are created on the Internet than had been created in all the previous centuries combined!

Navstar 2 (GPS-2) satellite

13

AN OVERVIEW OF WORLD HISTORY

In **pre- and protohistory**, early humans were organized in families and clans. They lived as hunters and gatherers in a constant fight for survival. It was not until the Neolithic revolution that human beings created permanent settlements, began to cultivate crops and domesticate animals, and lived in small communities whose members were not all closely related. However, competition for land, possessions, and resources brought with it new potential for conflict. For a long period, the distinction between farmers and nomads played an important role.

Soon larger settlements developed into the first (city) states. Egyptians, Mesopotamians, Indians and the Chinese established the **first empires** independently and probably without any knowledge of one another. Highly developed state entities arose, with water supply systems, central inventory management and controlled markets, armies, hierarchies and bureaucracies. Writing was invented, and with it recorded history began.

Antiquity saw the emergence of the first world empires. One after another, the Persians, Greeks and Romans conquered what was known to them and seemed to be strategically significant. The first of the current world religions were established: Judaism, Christianity, Hinduism and Buddhism.

The barbarian migration into the lands of the decaying Roman Empire marked the beginning of the **Middle Ages**. In Europe, the states that still exist today began to be established, the Mongols built a world empire, Central American civilizations experienced their zenith, and the last of the world religions, Islam, conquered large parts of the then-known world.

Revival of the ideals of antiquity (the Renaissance), printing, technical innovations and the Reformation (religious schism in Christianity) triggered the advent of the **modern era**. Larger ships, cannons and other weapons enabled the great European powers not only to discover "new" worlds previously unknown to them, but also to conquer them and destroy the existing civilizations or force them into submission. Portugal and Spain, and later England, France and the Netherlands, divided the western, southern and southwestern world (including Australia) among themselves. Russia advanced through Siberia as far as Alaska, and the Ottoman Empire controlled the Islamic world. Only the Orient took almost no part in the conquests; on the contrary, it walled itself off culturally from the rest of the world.

The American War of Independence initiated the **age of the great revolutions**. The French Revolution followed, transforming Europe, South America and Russia in its wake. The Meiji Restoration brought radical change to Japan, and imperial rule ended in China. Aristocratic absolutism now became a thing of the past, and the middle class, already the leading economic force, took over political power as well. The new human rights, however, only applied to people with white skin. The rest of the world was colonialized and/or enslaved. Even when the former Ottoman Empire collapsed, it was carved up between the English, Italians and French.

The era of the globalized **present** began with devastatingly destructive world wars and totalitarian regimes of different stripes. In their wake, two competing systems, capitalism and communism, have contended for world supremacy. The third world is mired in chaos, poverty and famine. The global community searches for solutions, but its historical legacy makes progress difficult. The root of many of today's problems lies in the past. The only solution would be a peaceful coexistence of all peoples, with equal rights for all, and a just distribution of land, riches and resources. National thinking will have to yield to a global approach. This is the great historic task for a shared future of the world.

Mappe-monde Géo-Hydrographique ou Description Générale du Globe Terrestre et Aquatique en Deux-Plans-Hémisphères, Gerard Valck, Amsterdam, undated

The World: An Overview

Until 13,000 BCE: The First Humans and Prehistory

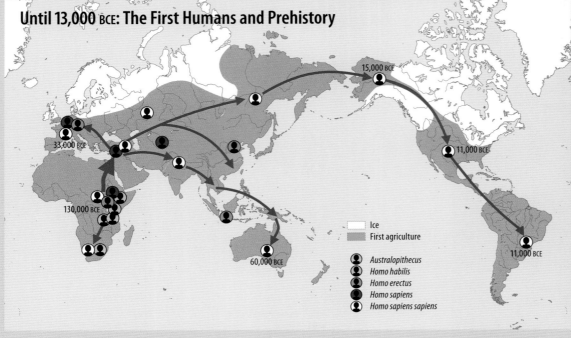

15,000 BCE

33,000 BCE

130,000 BCE

11,000 BCE

60,000 BCE

11,000 BCE

Ice
First agriculture

Australopithecus
Homo habilis
Homo erectus
Homo sapiens
Homo sapiens sapiens

4000–1000 BCE: Beginnings of Agriculture and the First Empires

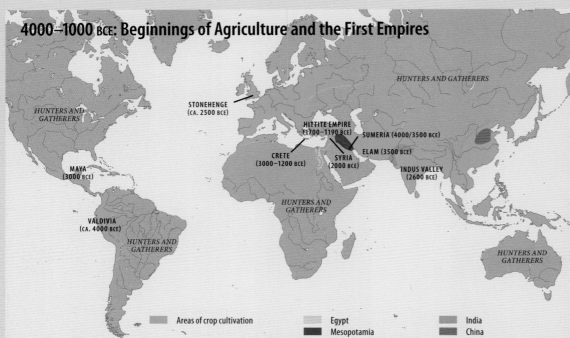

HUNTERS AND GATHERERS

STONEHENGE
(CA. 2500 BCE)

HUNTERS AND
GATHERERS

HITTITE EMPIRE
(1700–1190 BCE)

SUMERIA (4000/3500 BCE)

CRETE
(3000–1200 BCE)

SYRIA
(2000 BCE)

ELAM (3500 BCE)

MAYA
(3000 BCE)

INDUS VALLEY
(2600 BCE)

VALDIVIA
(CA. 4000 BCE)

HUNTERS AND
GATHERERS

HUNTERS AND
GATHERERS

HUNTERS AND
GATHERERS

Areas of crop cultivation

Egypt
Mesopotamia

India
China

1000–250 BCE: Early Antiquity

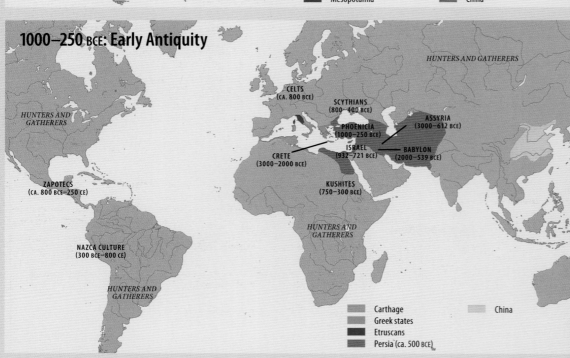

HUNTERS AND GATHERERS

CELTS
(CA. 800 BCE)

SCYTHIANS
(800–400 BCE)

ASSYRIA
(3000–612 BCE)

PHOENICIA
(1000–250 BCE)

HUNTERS AND
GATHERERS

ISRAEL
(932–721 BCE)

BABYLON
(2000–539 BCE)

CRETE
(3000–2000 BCE)

ZAPOTECS
(CA. 800 BCE–250 CE)

KUSHITES
(750–300 BCE)

NAZCA CULTURE
(300 BCE–800 CE)

HUNTERS AND
GATHERERS

HUNTERS AND
GATHERERS

Carthage
Greek states
Etruscans
Persia (ca. 500 BCE)

China

3,500,000–2,500,000 BCE East Africa The cradle of humankind: the oldest human remains have been found in the Olduvai Gorge.

2,400,000–1,900,000 BCE Europe *Homo erectus*, a species credited with the controlled use of fire, populates Europe.

150,000–30,000 BCE Europe Inhabited by Neanderthals before the beginning of the last ice age

40,000–10,000 BCE Australia and the Americas Humans populate the rest of the world.

8000–5000 BCE Ancient Anatolia and the Fertile Crescent Beginning of crop cultivation; later pottery and weaving appear.

4000–1000 BCE Mesopotamia Sumerian-Akkadian civilization; the first cities, states and empires arise, and writing is invented.

3000–1200 BCE Crete Development of the oldest European civilization (the Minoan civilization), palace cities

3000–1000 BCE Egypt Empire of the pharaohs in the Nile Valley; monumental architectural structures and pyramids are constructed.

3000–1000 BCE China Development of crop cultivation; the first cities and states arise.

3000–1000 BCE Europe Bronze Age; huge megalithic monuments such as Stonehenge are built.

3000 BCE–250 CE Americas Pre-classic period of the Mayan civilization

2600–1800 BCE India Advanced civilization in the Indus Valley and the cities of Mohenjo-daro and Harappa develop.

1050–700 BCE China Establishment of a centralized government and highly developed cities

1000 BCE–500 CE Arabia Ancient Arabic empires flourish in the south.

814 BCE Mediterranean Phoenician settlements and the empire of Carthage in northern Africa; Etruscan civilization in Italy

from 800 BCE Europe The Celtic culture spreads throughout the continent.

800 BCE–250 CE or later Mesoamerica Zapotec civilization

750–300 BCE Africa Early kingdom of the Kushites in Nubia (Napata)

700–146 BCE Greece Cradle of European civilization; withstands attacks by the Persians; polis culture and rivalries between the city-states

550–330 BCE Persia The largest empire in the Middle East is ruled by the Achaemenid dynasty, with modern public administration and magnificent buildings.

~330 BCE Greece The Greek empire attains its greatest extent under Alexander the Great.

320–185 BCE India Development of the first major Indian empire (Maurya); spread of the Buddha's teachings

300 BCE–800 CE Americas Nazca culture in today's Peru

247 BCE–224 CE Persia Parthian empire, the most dangerous rival of the Roman Empire

221 BCE–220 CE China Unification under the leadership of Qin Shihuangdi; the country begins to prosper under the Han dynasty.

200 BCE–600 CE Mesoamerica Civilizations develop in western Mexico (Teotihuacán), the Yucatán Peninsula (Maya) and Peru (Moche).

185 BCE–80 CE India The Mauryan empire dissolves into smaller states.

50 BCE–430 CE Europe Celtic civilization declines; Germanic tribes dominate.

ca. 1 CE Roman Empire Zenith of classical antiquity in the largest empire in the Mediterranean region; Octavian Augustus becomes the first Roman emperor.

1–842 Africa The Aksumite empire prospers.

321–1000 India Gupta empire and its successor states; Buddhism takes root in the north, while Hinduism remains dominant in the south.

476 Europe The Western Roman Empire ends when Romulus Augustulus, the last Roman emperor, is overthrown by Odoacer.

527–1071 The Byzantine Empire defends itself successfully against Arabs and Slavs; the empire flourishes.

600–900 Mesoamerica Classic period of the Mayan civilization; Tiwanaku empire in the Andes

618–907 China Cultural blossoming during the rule of the Tang dynasty

630–750 Arab world Early triumphant successes and rapid spread of Islam

750–861 Islamic Empire The Abbasid caliphate is at the height of its glory; the empire gradually breaks up after 800.

768–880 The Carolingian dynasty attains the height of its power under Charlemagne and his successors as the "empire of the West."

793–1066 Europe Viking invasions; emergence of the medieval states

843 Europe Division of Charlemagne's empire; emergence of France and Germany in 875

850–1300 Europe Rise of the medieval states and centralization in France and England; feudalism emerges and the Holy Roman Empire of the German Nation is established in 962.

1096–1254 Europe and the Near East Era of the Crusades; the Crusader states are founded.

1113–1220 Southeast Asia Zenith of the Khmer kingdom of Angkor

1200–1550 Meso- and South America Destruction of the major ancient civilizations; only minor states survive; rise of the Inca empire in Peru

1205–1526 India The Muslim sultans of Delhi firmly control the northern areas of the country; Hinduism is in retreat.

1206–1368 Mongolia Peoples of the steppes are under the leadership of Genghis Khan and his heirs; the Mongols build a world empire.

1245–1433 Africa Rise of Great Zimbabwe and the Mali empire; many Arab cities are established on the east coast of the continent.

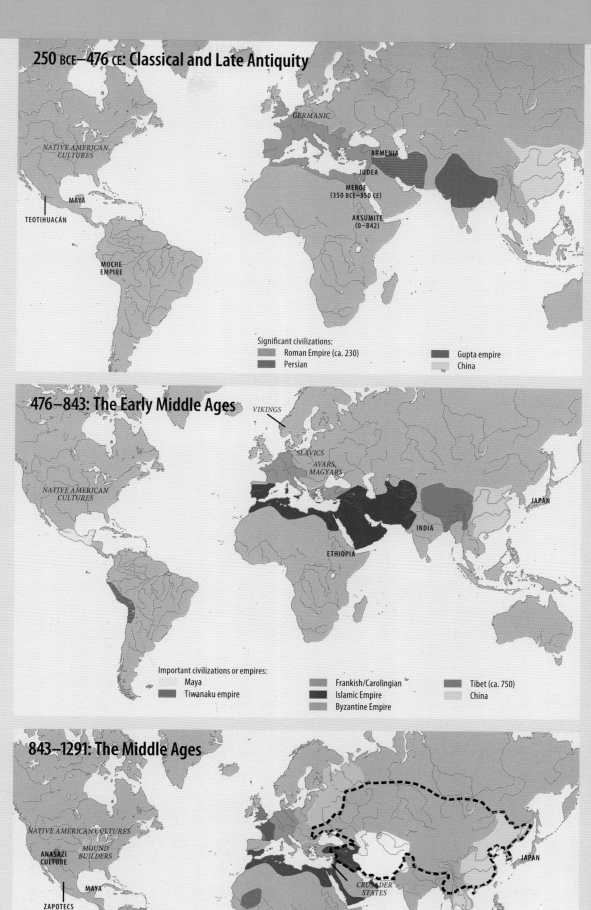

250 BCE–476 CE: Classical and Late Antiquity

GERMANIC

NATIVE AMERICAN CULTURES

ARMENIA

JUDEA

MEROE (350 BCE–350 CE)

TEOTIHUACÁN

MAYA

AKSUMITE (0–842)

MOCHE EMPIRE

Significant civilizations:
- Roman Empire (ca. 230)
- Persian
- Gupta empire
- China

476–843: The Early Middle Ages

VIKINGS

SLAVICS

AVARS, MAGYARS

NATIVE AMERICAN CULTURES

JAPAN

INDIA

ETHIOPIA

Important civilizations or empires:
- Maya
- Tiwanaku empire
- Frankish/Carolingian
- Islamic Empire
- Byzantine Empire
- Tibet (ca. 750)
- China

843–1291: The Middle Ages

NATIVE AMERICAN CULTURES

ANASAZI CULTURE

MOUND BUILDERS

JAPAN

CRUSADER STATES

MAYA

ZAPOTECS

ETHIOPIA

ARAB STATES

SRIVIJAYA

CHIMÚ EMPIRE

GREAT ZIMBABWE

Important empires:
- England
- France 875
- Holy Roman Empire 962
- Russia
- Byzantine Empire
- Arab and Turkic states
- Ghana (Mali)
- Khorasan ca. 1200
- Delhi sultanate
- Khmer kingdom
- China
- Mongolian Empire ca. 1260

The World: An Overview

1490: Early Modern Era

- Holy Roman Empire
- Portugal
- Spain

1600: The Early Modern Era

- Spanish-Portuguese empire
- Holy Roman Empire

1700: The Modern Era

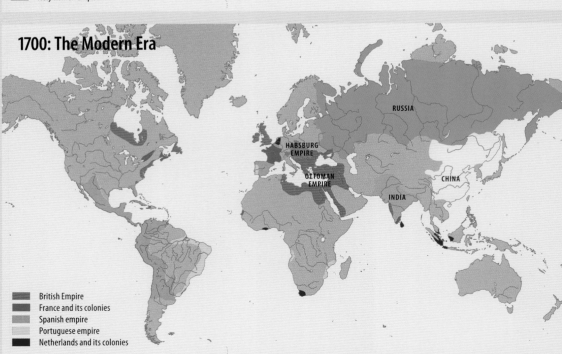

- British Empire
- France and its colonies
- Spanish empire
- Portuguese empire
- Netherlands and its colonies

after 1450 **Europe** The printing press is invented.

1453 **Europe** The fall of Constantinople (Istanbul): Ottomans conquer Constantinople, bringing the Byzantine Empire to an end.

1492 **Americas** Christopher Columbus undertakes his first voyage and reaches the Great Antilles.

1501 **Africa** Shah Isma'il I establishes a new empire in Iraq and Iran; Persia is under the leadership of the Safavid dynasty.

1511–1539 **Americas** The Spaniards conquer the flourishing empires of the Aztecs and Incas.

1517 **Europe** Beginning of the Protestant Reformation; religious wars and creation of nation-states.

1526 **India** The Mughal Empire is established.

1534–1563 **Europe** Beginning of the Counter-Reformation within the Catholic Church

1574–1603 **East Asia** Era of the three Great Unifiers in Japan

1591 **Africa** Morocco annexes the Songhai empire.

1607 **Americas** The British colony of Virginia is founded at Jamestown.

1618–1648 **Europe** The Thirty Years' War, conflict over European hegemony and religious war, which finally ends with the Peace of Westphalia

1644 **China** End of the Ming dynasty (which had ruled since 1368) and formation of the final regime, the Qing dynasty (also called Manchu dynasty).

1683 **Europe** Ottoman forces are turned back at the gates of Vienna; ongoing wars with the Turks begin to turn in favor of the Habsburg Empire.

1703 **Russia** Peter I the Great founds St. Petersburg and models his reforms and modernization program after those of western Europe.

1715 **France** The absolutist Louis XIV, the Sun King, dies. His reign of seventy-two years (from 1643 to 1715) is the longest in European history.

1720 **Asia** China drives the Mongols out of Tibet and occupies the country.

1756 **India** The British East India Company subjugates large parts of India.

1763 **America** The British defeat the French in the war for control of Quebec.

1765 **Europe** Invention of the steam engine

1776 **America** The United States declares its independence from England; Revolutionary War

1789 **Europe** The French Revolution

1815 **Europe** Napoleon meets his final defeat at the Battle of Waterloo.

after 1817 **Americas** The countries of Latin American gradually attain independence.

1830 **Europe** The first railroad is built in England; July Revolution in France.

1848 **Europe** *The Communist Manifesto*, by Karl Marx and Friedrich Engels, is published in London.

from 1848 Europe A wave of revolutions take place.

1853–1856 Europe In the Crimean War, Russia fights the Ottoman Empire and its allies, particularly England and France, for control of the Balkan territories.

1854 Japan End of isolation; an American military mission opens trade with Japan; after 1868, emerging national consciousness during the Meiji Restoration

1861 Russia Serfdom is abolished.

1865 United States Slavery is abolished and the American Civil War ends.

1871 Europe Unification of Italy and Germany (founding of national states)

1914–1918 Europe World War I

1917 Russia Bolshevik Revolution led by Lenin

1922 Italy Coup by the Fascists under Benito Mussolini

1933 Germany Adolf Hitler becomes chancellor.

1937–1945 Asia Sino-Japanese War

1939 Europe Beginning of World War II

1945 Germany and Japan are defeated by the Allied forces, ending World War II.

1945–1948 Europe Communists seize power in Central and Eastern Europe.

1947 Beginning of the Cold War between the two superpowers, the United States and the USSR

1950–1953 Korean War between the Democratic People's Republic of Korea (communist) and the Republic of Korea (pro-Western)

from 1957 Africa Most of the former colonies win their independence.

1961 Germany The Berlin Wall is built, separating East and West Germany.

1962 Cuba The Cuban missile crisis brings the world to the brink of nuclear war.

1964–1975 Asia Vietnam War; Western involvement provokes protest movements in the West.

1965 Europe The European Community (today European Union) is founded.

1967–1970 Africa Biafra experiences war and famine after it declares independence from Nigeria, its parent country.

since 1980 Middle East Wars in the Persian Gulf

1989/1990 Europe Fall of the communist regimes in Central and Eastern Europe, reunification of Germany

1991 Russia Breakdown of the USSR into the Commonwealth of Independent States (CIS)

1991–1995 Europe Wars in Yugoslavia; several republics declare independence and new states are formed.

1994 Africa Genocide in Rwanda

as of 2001 Asia After terrorist attacks in the United States, wars in Afghanistan and Iraq

1850: The Industrial Revolution

- British Empire
- Independent countries of Latin America
- France
- Germany
- Italy

1930: Modern Times

- United States
- British Empire
- France and its colonies
- Germany
- Italy and its colonies
- USSR and dependencies
- Japan and dependencies

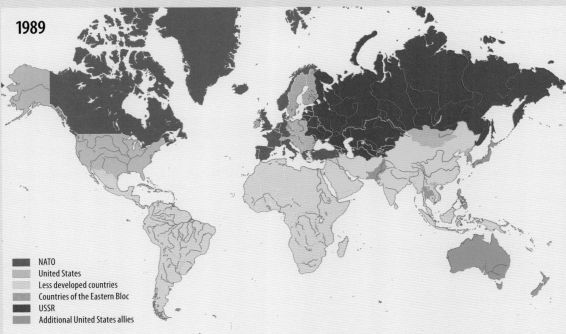

1989

- NATO
- United States
- Less developed countries
- Countries of the Eastern Bloc
- USSR
- Additional United States allies

The Most Important Sites Where Traces of Human Ancestors Have Been Found

Africa

Moroto (Uganda) Remains found of *Morotopithecus bishopi*, a primate that lived 20.6 million years ago and is considered the oldest common ancestor of humans and apes.

Tugen Hills (Kenya) Discovery of thirteen bone fragments of *Orrorin tugenensis*, which lived about 6 million years ago and is known as "Millennium Man" because it was discovered in the year 2000

Aramis (Ethiopia) *Ardipithecus ramidus* remains found; lived about 4.4 million years ago

Hadar (Ethiopia) Skeleton of an *Australopithecus* woman dubbed "Lucy" who probably lived 3 million years ago

Koobi Fora (Kenya) Lower jaw and later additional skull fragments of *Homo rudolfensis*, which lived about 2.5 to 1.8 million years ago

Taung (South Africa) Complete skull of the "child of Taung," *Australopithecus africanus*, which lived about 2.4 million years ago. This first hominid find in Africa (1924) triggered a debate on where the *cradle of humankind* is located.

Swartkrans (South Africa) Fossil findings of *Homo erectus* and *Paranthropus*, a genus of *Australopithecus*. The use of fire in Swartkrans has been dated to 1 million BCE.

Klasies River Mouth (South Africa) Some of the oldest remains of modern man. The *Homo sapiens* here probably lived as long as 125,000 years ago.

Olduvai (Tanzania) Numerous Pleistocene fossils of hominids and especially Old Stone Age tools. The Olduvai Gorge is regarded as the *cradle of humankind*.

Europe

Swanscombe (England) Fragments of a skull of *Homo sapiens*, 200,000 years old, as well as bone fragments and tools

Neanderthal (Germany) Bones found and dubbed Neanderthal man, dating from 130,000–30,000 BCE

Heidelberg (Germany) Lower jaw, and later additional bones, of *Homo heidelbergensis*, which lived 600,000 to 200,000 years ago

Caves of Lascaux (France) Some of the oldest known representational artworks in human history (17,000–15,000 BCE) are here, mainly realistic depictions of large animals and human hands.

Cro-Magnon (France) Fossil remains of *Homo sapiens* of the Cro-Magnon species, around 25,000 years old

Le Moustier (France) Site where prehistoric artifacts were found lent its name to the Paleolithic Period from 100,000–35,000 BCE—the Mousterian

Altamira (Spain) Spanish caves known for Paleolithic paintings of animals and human hands (16,000–11,000 BCE)

Mladeč (Czech Republic) The oldest directly dated remains of modern man. According to carbon-14 dating (see box opposite), the fossils found here are 31,000 years old.

Dolní Věstonice (Czech Republic) Venus—female ceramic figure (25,000–29,000 years old)

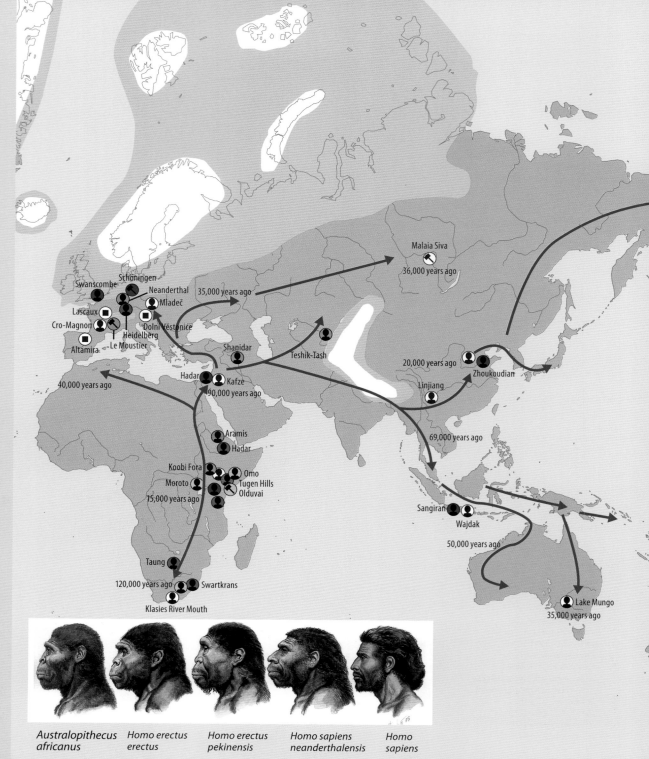

Australopithecus africanus — *Homo erectus erectus* — *Homo erectus pekinensis* — *Homo sapiens neanderthalensis* — *Homo sapiens*

Asia

Shanidar (Iraq) Oldest Neanderthal skeleton (60,000–80,000 years old); over time the remains of nine individuals have been found.

Sangiran (Java/Indonesia) Some of the oldest fossils of the genus *Homo erectus* outside Africa

Wajdak (Java/Indonesia) Java man, of the species *Homo erectus*

Majuangou (China) Remains found of 2-million-year-old hominids and tools, calling into question the thesis of eastern Africa as the sole *cradle of humankind*.

Zhoukoudian (China) Peking man, a later *Homo erectus* than Java man, lived between 600,000 and 420,000 years ago.

The Americas

Clovis (New Mexico, USA) Skeleton, around 11,000 years old

Stone Age

Paleolithic Period (Old Stone Age, 2.5 million–8000 BCE)
- Hunters and gatherers, no food production
- Remains of earliest forerunners of modern man found in Africa and Java
- Around 600,000 BCE *Homo erectus*
- Used stone and bone tools (hand axe, scraper)
- Around 150,000 BCE Neanderthal man; died out around 30,000/24,000 BCE
- Around 40,000 BCE *Homo sapiens sapiens*

- Use and mastery of fire
- Around 11,500 BCE, settlement of the American continents
- Wall paintings
- Probably mother and fertility cults; Venus statuettes

Mesolithic Period (Middle Stone Age; 8000–4500 BCE)
- In the Middle East the Paleolithic segues directly into the Neolithic Period; in regions where farming spread later, we speak of the Mesolithic Period.

Neolithic Period (New Stone Age; 6000–2000 BCE)
- Farming and raising livestock; domestication of animals

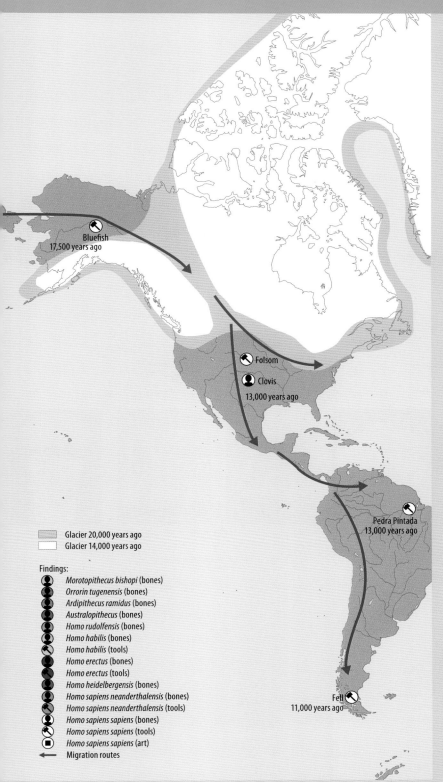

Bluefish
17,500 years ago

Folsom

Clovis
13,000 years ago

Pedra Pintada
13,000 years ago

Fell
11,000 years ago

Glacier 20,000 years ago
Glacier 14,000 years ago

Findings:
- Morotopithecus bishopi (bones)
- Orrorin tugenensis (bones)
- Ardipithecus ramidus (bones)
- Australopithecus (bones)
- Homo rudolfensis (bones)
- Homo habilis (bones)
- Homo habilis (tools)
- Homo erectus (bones)
- Homo erectus (tools)
- Homo heidelbergensis (bones)
- Homo sapiens neanderthalensis (bones)
- Homo sapiens neanderthalensis (tools)
- Homo sapiens sapiens (bones)
- Homo sapiens sapiens (tools)
- Homo sapiens sapiens (art)
→ Migration routes

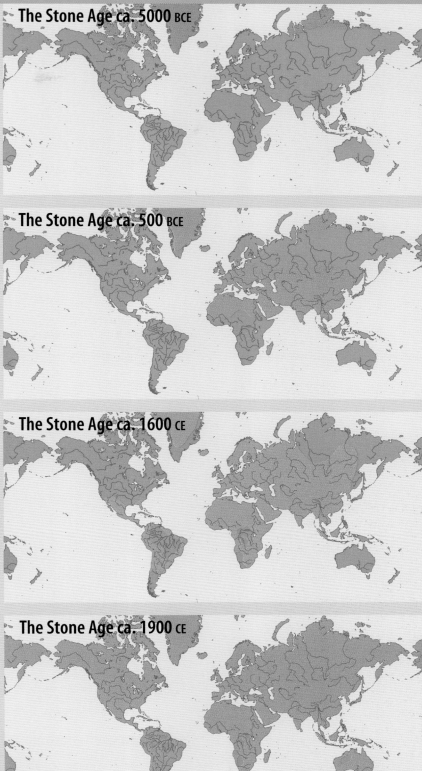

The Stone Age ca. 5000 BCE

The Stone Age ca. 500 BCE

The Stone Age ca. 1600 CE

The Stone Age ca. 1900 CE

Even in the 20th century, some tribes in remote regions of the world still lived at the Stone Age level.

- Rapid population growth
- The beginnings of metallurgy
- First major settlements
- Death and animal cults
- Megaliths built in western Europe

Bronze Age (3000–1000 BCE in the Middle East, 1800–800 BCE in Europe)
- The knowledge of how to make bronze spreads from the Middle East.
- Dead not buried but burned (urnfield culture)
- Crystallization of social differences
- Population growth leads to conflicts.
- First fortified towns develop from hill settlements ("tell" cultures).

Iron Age (1200–450 BCE in the Middle East, 800 BCE–beginning of Common Era in Europe)
- Agriculture is increasingly effective; new forms of grain are cultivated.
- Wealth in the hands of tribal chieftains and clan leaders
- 750–400 BCE Celtic Hallstatt period (named after finds in Hallstatt, Austria)
- Artifacts of high artistic value
- First evidence of ethnic divisions
- 400–50 BCE Celtic La Tène culture (named after finds in La Tène, Switzerland)

Methods of Radio Carbon Dating

Radio carbon dating (the C-14 method or **radio carbon method)** is a way of radiometrically dating materials that contain carbon, primarily organic, as far back as about 50,000 years. The technique is based on the radioactive decay of the carbon isotope ^{14}C and is used especially by archaeologists to determine the age of remains and fossils. The decay of radioactive carbon begins at the death of an organism. The half-life of ^{14}C is around 5,000 years. Thus, if the fossil still has 25 percent radiation, it is 10,000 years old; if it has 12.5 percent of its original radiation, it is 15,000 years old. After 60,000 years the radiation is only about one-thousandth as strong and measurement becomes difficult.

The First Empires

Empires

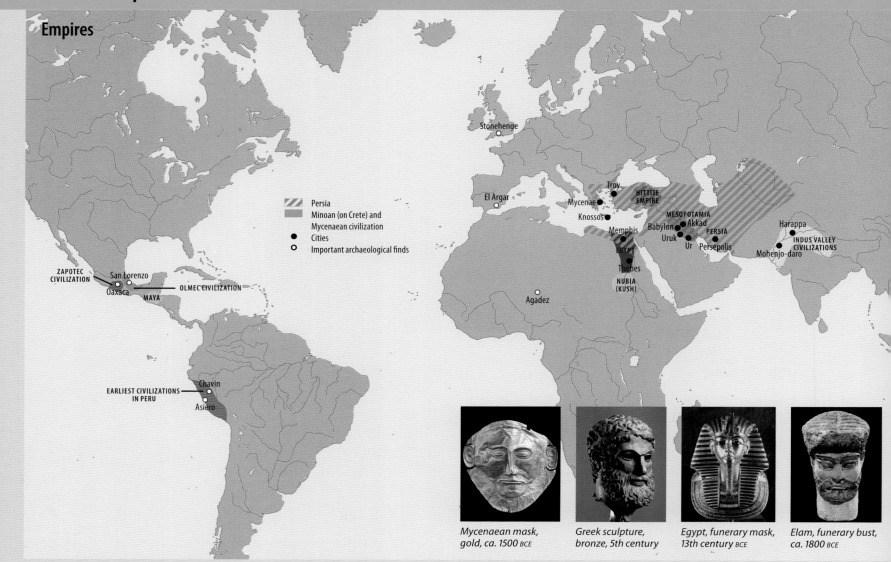

Persia

Minoan (on Crete) and Mycenaean civilization

● Cities

○ Important archaeological finds

Mycenaean mask, gold, ca. 1500 BCE

Greek sculpture, bronze, 5th century

Egypt, funerary mask, 13th century BCE

Elam, funerary bust, ca. 1800 BCE

Sumer 2500 BCE

Akkad 2300 BCE

Akkadian empire (ca. 2300 BCE)

The World 3000–100 BCE

Larger, well-organized communities were necessary to build irrigation and drainage systems as well as to gain alluvial soil to be used for agriculture. This is the origin of the first city-states in Mesopotamia, Egypt, India and China.

Ancient Anatolia

The hilltop sanctuary of Göbekli Tepe (ca. 9500 BCE) and several large settlements such as Çatalhöyük (ca. 7400–6200 BCE) were first discovered and excavated only in the 20th century. These structures are the first traces of the shift from small communities to larger ones organized something like cities. Starting around 1700 BCE, the Hittites with their highly developed culture dominated the Anatolian area. Around 1355 BCE their culture evolved into a large empire, dominating the Hurrian empire of Mitanni and competing on equal footing with the Egyptians and Assyrians for dominance of the Near East. Finally, around 1190 BCE, their empire collapsed under the attacks of the Sea Peoples.

Babylon 1750 BCE

Empire of Hammurabi (1750 BCE)

Egypt

The yearly flooding of the Nile River deposits enough mud to turn the land alongside the river into an extremely fertile arable area, the only place to plant sufficient amounts of food. The land was unified around 2900 BCE by the lord of Upper Egypt, King Menes. Approximately 400 years later, during the Fourth Dynasty, the country experienced its first heyday, during which the great pyramids of Giza were built.

Egypt 2500 BCE

Old Kingdom (ca. 2500 BCE)

▲ Pyramid

Mesopotamia

The region between the Euphrates and Tigris rivers has always been highly fertile (it is sometimes called the Fertile Crescent). The societies that flourished there early on united to form city-states such as Uruk or Sumer, all of which tried to expand their territories beyond the area bounded by the two rivers. The first dynasty to form in Mesopotamia, Akkad, came into existence around 2300 BCE. Sargon the Great is considered to be its founder. In the course of the following millennia, the civilizations of Babylon and Assyria often vied with each other for dominance of this important region.

forming the last great empire of antiquity. The Persian Empire proved to be progressive both economically and culturally. The Persians conquered many peoples, but allowed them relative freedom by embedding their elites into the regional administration (satrapies). During its heyday around 400 BCE, the Persian Empire stretched from Egypt on its southern end to India in the east. It was Alexander the Great who conquered and demolished the Persian Empire in 330 BCE.

Origins of Greek Culture (Minoan and Mycenaean)

Early Greek civilization is considered the first high culture of the Western world. At its dawn was the Minoan civilization, which built palaces on Crete. The Minoans lived peacefully for the most part, living from fishing and trade. They worshipped mother goddesses and the symbol of the bull. The Mycenaean culture, which developed on the Greek mainland somewhat later than Minoan culture, is characterized by fortified castles and cities, chariots and weapons. These two realms ("kingdoms") existed in a state of continual competition and frequent war; Homer's record of the Trojan War testifies to that.

India

Development in India was marked from its inception by the influences the various languages and ethnic groups wielded over each other. While agrarian techniques appeared as late as ca. 7000 BCE, the culture on the shores of the Indus River nevertheless gave rise to bustling large cities (Harappa, Mohenjo-daro). Between 1500 and 600 BCE, Indo-European tribes from the north (Aryans who already lived in a social caste structure) immigrated to India, pushing the indigenous Dravidian people toward the south of the Indian subcontinent.

China

The traces of the first societies in China displaying well-developed cultural traits date back as far as the third millennium BCE, and over the next thousand years developed into a highly refined state. This was followed by a period of cultural blossoming and important inventions, including the creation of porcelain and raising silkworms to produce silk. In the course of the 8th century BCE, the empire split into various independent states.

Mexico

One of the oldest known civilizations of North and Central America is the Olmec culture that appeared along the Gulf of Mexico around 1500 BCE. Around 1200 BCE the smaller societies joined forces and formed larger population centers. The Olmec culture is marked by its characteristic artistic production. As early as 3000 BCE, the Maya formed the first city-states, which competed with each other, and beginning in 1200 BCE founded settlements on the Yucatán Peninsula.

South America

The Valdivia culture in Ecuador, dating back to the fourth millennium BCE, is considered the oldest American civilization. The most famous relic of this culture is the small Venus of Valdivia. The Chavin civilization originated 3,000 years ago in Peru and was later supplanted by the Moche culture.

Persia

The empire of Elam arose as another competitor for power in Mesopotamia around 2500 BCE. Later the Medes, an equestrian people, took over leadership in the region. The Persians, led by Cyrus the Great (559–529 BCE), shook off the yoke of the Medes and began conquering Persia and Mesopotamia starting in 550 BCE,

Crete and Mycenae 1550 BCE

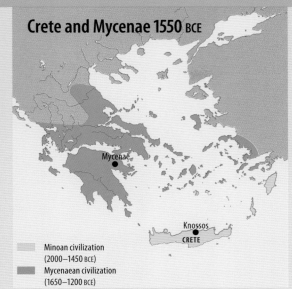

Minoan civilization (2000–1450 BCE)

Mycenaean civilization (1650–1200 BCE)

China 1700–100 BCE

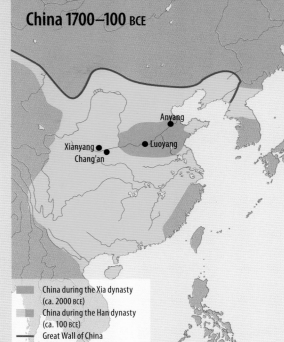

China during the Xia dynasty (ca. 2000 BCE)

China during the Han dynasty (ca. 100 BCE)

Great Wall of China

Mexico, ca. 500 BCE

South America, ca. 400 BCE

India 1500–250 BCE

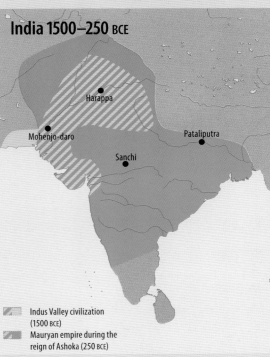

Indus Valley civilization (1500 BCE)

Mauryan empire during the reign of Ashoka (250 BCE)

Persia 512 BCE

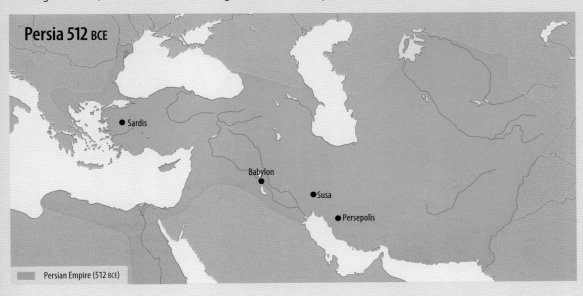

Persian Empire (512 BCE)

23

The Civilizations of Antiquity, 1000 BCE–500 CE

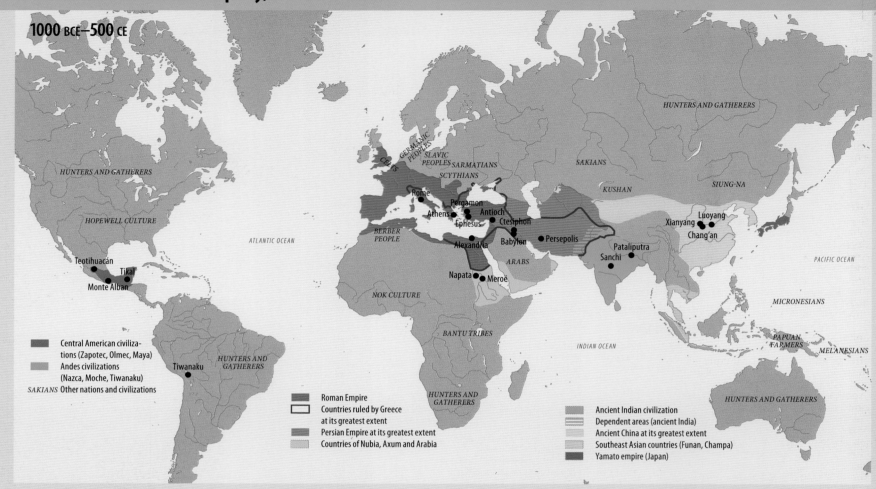

1000 BCE–500 CE

HUNTERS AND GATHERERS

GERMANIC PEOPLES
CELTS
SLAVIC PEOPLES
SARMATIANS
SCYTHIANS
SAKIANS
KUSHAN
SIUNG-NA

Rome
Pergamon
Athens
Ephesus
Antioch
Ctesiphon
Babylon
Persepolis
Alexandria
Luoyang
Xianyang
Chang'an

HUNTERS AND GATHERERS

HOPEWELL CULTURE

ATLANTIC OCEAN

BERBER PEOPLE

ARABS

Napata
Meroë

Pataliputra
Sanchi

PACIFIC OCEAN

Teotihuacán
Tikal
Monte Alban

NOK CULTURE

BANTU TRIBES

INDIAN OCEAN

MICRONESIANS

PAPUAN FARMERS
MELANESIANS

HUNTERS AND GATHERERS

Tiwanaku

SAKIANS

HUNTERS AND GATHERERS

HUNTERS AND GATHERERS

- Central American civiliza-tions (Zapotec, Olmec, Maya)
- Andes civilizations (Nazca, Moche, Tiwanaku)
- *SAKIANS* Other nations and civilizations

- Roman Empire
- Countries ruled by Greece at its greatest extent
- Persian Empire at its greatest extent
- Countries of Nubia, Axum and Arabia

- Ancient Indian civilization
- Dependent areas (ancient India)
- Ancient China at its greatest extent
- Southeast Asian countries (Funan, Champa)
- Yamato empire (Japan)

The Civilizations of Antiquity 1000 BCE–500 CE

The civilizations of the "Old World" entered the Iron Age. Large empires arose quickly and made rapid devel-opments in the arts and sciences, economy and the art of war. At the end of the age of antiquity there were first signs of decay and disintegration, and most of the great empires fell. But the cultural heritage of the era remained highly influential, particularly in the guise of the great world religions: Judaism, Buddhism, Confucianism and Christianity.

Near and Middle East

Assyrians A Semitic people in northern Mesopotamia founded its empire after 1800 BCE and lived in constant war and strife with the Babylonians—without decisively winning or losing. The Assyrians were feared for being merciless warriors and are considered the first military power in history. After 883 BCE they finally dominated the regions of Mesopotamia as well as modern-day Syria and Palestine; they levied tributes and deported entire ethnic groups to serve as slaves within their empire. In the year 612 BCE, they finally succumbed to the assault of their constant adversaries, the Babylonians and Medes.

Babylonians A Semitic people (also known as the Amorites) who came from what is now Syria to invade Mesopotamia at the beginning of the second millennium BCE. Babylonian culture and scientific knowledge were more advanced than that of any of their neighbors in the Near East and influenced many other peoples.

After the fall of the first Babylonian empires, the Chaldeans managed to reestablish the empire one last time in its ancient splendor between 626 and 539 BCE, and again made it the leading power of Mesopotamia. The structures built by King Nebuchadnezzar II bear witness to their power.

Persians These people are the indigenous population of Iran. The Achaemenid kings first subjugated the dominant power in the region, the

Medes, and enlarged their empire by acquiring the lands of many peoples so that in the end, the majority of their subjects were non-Persians. The tightly organized empire was navigable via a system of safe streets and trade routes, called royal roads, and is considered the last large Eastern empire of antiquity. Its heirs—the Seleucids, Parthians and Sasanians—proved to be worthy successors as formidable opponents of Rome and Byzantium until the 7th century CE.

Phoenicia, Carthage

This semitic people hailed from the area of modern-day Lebanon. The Phoenicians were master seafarers and dominated maritime trade throughout antiquity. They established colonies throughout the Mediterranean region, most famously Carthage in 814 BCE, and thus spread their culture. They were organized in competing city-states, monopolizing the trade in cedar wood and purple dye.

Mediterranean Region ca. 800 BCE

Tanais
Olbia
Chersonesos
Sinope
Trapezus
Odessos
Mesembria
Massalia
Volaterrae
Byzantium
LYDIA
Rome
Apollonia
Gordium
Neapolis
Taras
Pella
Ephesus
Soluntum
Gadir (Cádiz)
Palma
Karalis
Corinth
Athens
Miletus
Aspendos
Aradus
Panormus
Sparta
Salamis
Byblos
Syracuse
Tyre
Carthage
MEDITERRANEAN SEA
Cyrene
Memphis
Barqah
Leptis Magna
EGYPT

- Phoenician territory
- Greek colonies
- Etruscans
- Greece
- + Phoenician city
- ○ Phoenician colony
- ○ Greek colony
- ● Greek city
- ● Other city

Carthage emerged as a power in its own right from around 600 BCE, relying not only on a large trade fleet, but also building an enormous naval force that ruled the western Mediterranean. Carthage was in constant conflict with the Greek colonies on Sicily and challenged Rome in the Punic Wars in the 3rd century BCE. The success of the ingenious general Hannibal turned into a nightmare for the Romans, ultimately leading to the destruction of Carthage in 146 BCE.

Greece

Greeks Indo-European people who inhabited the Peloponnese. The oldest Greeks were Mycenaeans. Additional Greek tribes—the Achaeans, Ionians and Dorians—reached modern-day Greece and soon intermingled with the Mycenaeans. Greek civilization had a profound impact on the cultural development of all Europe.

The competing city-states or *poleis* united their forces to fight off tyrants and defend themselves against Persian attacks, and developed a unique culture and civilization in almost all artistic and academic fields. The hegemonial aspirations of the two most powerful cities, Athens and Sparta, led to the Peloponnesian Wars in 431–404 BCE, which weakened the Greeks and enabled the ascent of Macedonia under Philip II and Alexander the Great, who gained control over the Greek world. They initiated the era of Hellenistic civilization that would deeply shape Rome, as well, when it assumed power in the region in the course of the 2nd century BCE.

Rome

Romans Inhabitants of the Roman Empire. Originally the term applied only to citizens of Rome, then expanded to include the Italic people and later other peoples within the empire. The Romans are renowned for their soldiers and for developing a centralized administration of their empire as well as an excellent infrastructure, including cities, roads, markets and public baths. After the rule of Etruscan kings, Rome became a democracy in 510 BCE, with strict controls on the most powerful positions, such as adherence to a double consulship with a term limited to one year at a time. In the first century BCE, social discrepancies led to an era of civil wars and the downfall of the republic, caused by various generals' grasping for power. After the assassination of Julius Caesar, Augustus established imperial reign in Rome after 27 BCE, which remained in place in the western half of the empire until 476 CE and in the east as Byzantium until 1453. Rome remained a world center until the 4th century CE, and its political structures formed the basis of those of the entire Occident, particularly after Christianity became the state religion in 312.

India

Indians Term used for diverse peoples populating the Indian subcontinent. The rise of the Indus civilization in the third millennium BCE is considered to mark the historical beginning of the Indian peoples. Later on, Aryan peoples from northwestern Asia immigrated

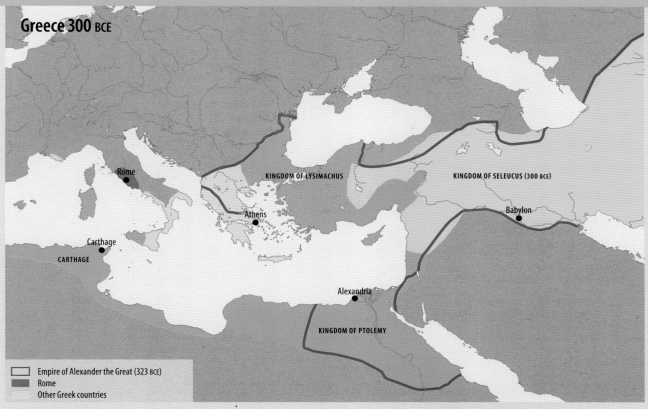

Greece 300 BCE

KINGDOM OF LYSIMACHUS
KINGDOM OF SELEUCUS (300 BCE)
Rome
Babylon
Athens
Carthage
CARTHAGE
Alexandria
KINGDOM OF PTOLEMY

Empire of Alexander the Great (323 BCE)
Rome
Other Greek countries

and effectively became the bearers of cultural developments that took place after 1500 BCE (the Vedas, castes, Hinduism). After the Indian expedition of Alexander the Great in 321 BCE, the Maurya empire ruled almost all of the subcontinent; Emperor Ashoka the Great (272/268–232 BCE) fostered the expansion of Buddhism, which increasingly pushed Hinduism toward the south until around 650 CE. The second large political entity, the Gupta empire (320–ca. 550 CE), led to a cultural golden age in India and sought to mediate between the different religions. After 650, India dissolved into several competing regional empires.

China

Chinese The largest group of Asian peoples who formed some of the oldest civilizations. The Han Chinese established themselves as the dominant group. They saw their empire as the center of the world ("Middle Kingdom" or "Central Kingdom"), surrounded by barbarian peoples to the west and north who needed to be fended off. Around 1066 BCE, the Western Zhou founded a small but powerful empire that split after 771 BCE (Eastern Zhou). The "Warring States Period" (480–221 BCE) became a time of cultural blossoming during which the main Chinese schools of thought developed. In 221 BCE, Qin Shih Huang-di united China under his tight control as the first emperor and established a uniform administration under his rule. It was further developed and refined during the Han dynasty (206 BCE–220 CE) and its successors.

Southeast and East Asia

The first empires that can be historically documented formed on the Korean peninsula in the course of the first century BCE. These empires coexisted for a long time in a balance of power. In Japan, it was not until 300 CE that

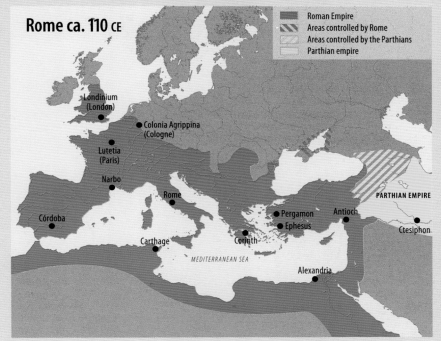

Rome ca. 110 CE

Roman Empire
Areas controlled by Rome
Areas controlled by the Parthians
Parthian empire

Londinium (London)
Colonia Agrippina (Cologne)
Lutetia (Paris)
Narbo
Rome
Córdoba
Carthage
Corinth
Pergamon
Ephesus
Antioch
Ctesiphon
PARTHIAN EMPIRE
MEDITERRANEAN SEA
Alexandria

regional rulers joined forces to form a unified country around the emperor (tenno), who was considered to be divine. Around 50 CE, Funan emerged as the first empire of Southeast Asia and was followed around 200 by the kingdom of Champa in Vietnam.

Africa

In the course of the 8th century BCE, the kingdom of Kush in Nubia, with its capitals Napata (until 350 BCE) and Meroë (until 350 CE), became an influential political power. Its rulers, called the "black pharaohs," soon conquered the throne of Egypt. The Kushites built numerous pyramids in the desert and remained in bitter resistance against the Romans. Around the year 1 CE, the kingdom of Aksum arose in Ethiopia, monopolizing trade in Africa and taking part in the power

struggles in southern Arabia. King Ezana of Aksum accepted Christianity around 350.

Americas

The Mayan civilization experienced the later periods of its preclassic era starting in 900 BCE, moving on to its classic era in approximately 250 CE. The decline of the earliest highly developed cultures and civilizations in the Americas—those of the Olmecs— around 400 BCE created the conditions necessary for the rise of the Aztecs in the area around Monte Alban as well as the larger city-states of the Mayas. All the cultures in this region established large cities and built pyramids and temples. Between 200 and 600 BCE, the enormous and still cryptic landscape images called the Nazca lines originated in southern Peru.

The World in the Middle Ages, 500–1450

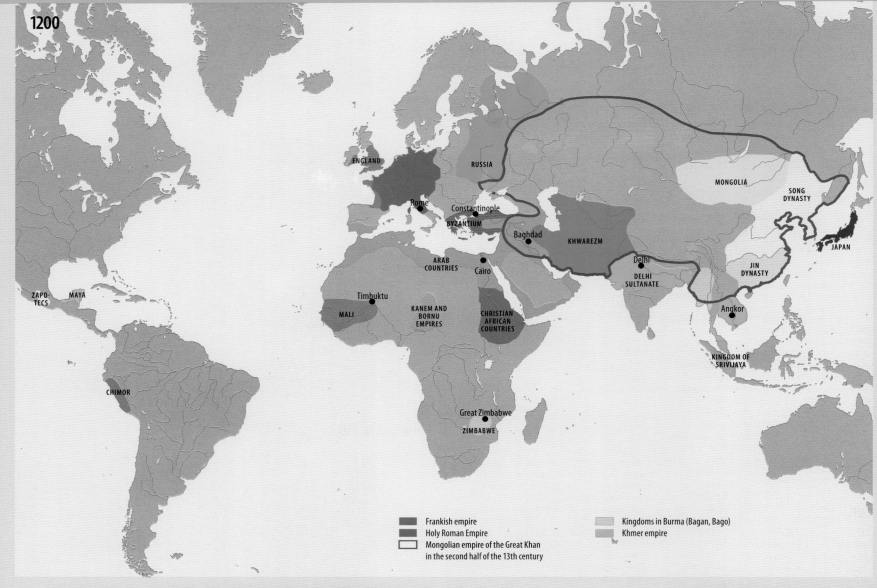

1200

ENGLAND
RUSSIA
MONGOLIA
SONG DYNASTY
Rome
Constantinople
BYZANTIUM
Baghdad
KHWAREZM
JIN DYNASTY
JAPAN
ARAB COUNTRIES
Cairo
Delhi
DELHI SULTANATE
ZAPO-TECS
MAYA
Timbuktu
MALI
KANEM AND BORNU EMPIRES
CHRISTIAN AFRICAN COUNTRIES
Angkor
KINGDOM OF SRIVIJAYA
CHIMOR
Great Zimbabwe
ZIMBABWE

■ Frankish empire	■ Kingdoms in Burma (Bagan, Bago)
■ Holy Roman Empire	■ Khmer empire
□ Mongolian empire of the Great Khan in the second half of the 13th century	

Europe ca. 500

SLAVIC PEOPLES
FRANKISH EMPIRE
Paris
OSTROGOTHIC KINGDOM
VISIGOTHIC KINGDOM
Ravenna
Constantinople
PERSIAN EMPIRE
Rome
BYZANTINE EMPIRE
Toledo
Carthage
VANDAL KINGDOM

Europe ca. 800

ANGLO-SAXON KINGDOMS
London
Aachen
KHAZAR KHAGANATE
SLAVIC PEOPLES
Paris
EMPIRE OF CHARLEMAGNE
BULGARIA
ASTURIAS
Preslav
Constantinople
Cordoba
Rome
BYZANTINE EMPIRE
Baghdad
Damascus
ARAB EMPIRE
ARAB EMPIRE

Europe ca. 1200

ICELAND
NORWAY
SWEDEN
Novgorod
VOLGA BULGARIA
SCOTLAND
DENMARK
RUSSIAN DUCHIES
ENGLAND
London
POLAND
Kiev
Paris
FRANCE
HOLY ROMAN EMPIRE
HUNGARY
LEON
PORTUGAL
CASTILE
ARAGON
Rome
Constantinople
BULGARIA
Toledo
KINGDOM OF SICILY
BYZANTINE EMPIRE
CRUSADER STATES
MUSLIM STATES
Cairo

Europe

European history of the Middle Ages begins with the Migration Period and the emergence of various Germanic kingdoms, pushed westward by the onslaught of the Huns, atop the ruins of the Roman Empire. These kingdoms were all doomed to disappear or be annexed by their neighbors in countless wars. In the year 800 a new (Roman) empire arose under the leadership of the Frankish king, Charlemagne. In 962, this spawned the Holy Roman Empire, which dominated the history of large portions of Europe for centuries to come. Christendom spread throughout Europe and fought the expansion of Islam on the Iberian Peninsula as well as later

The Muslim World ca. 1100

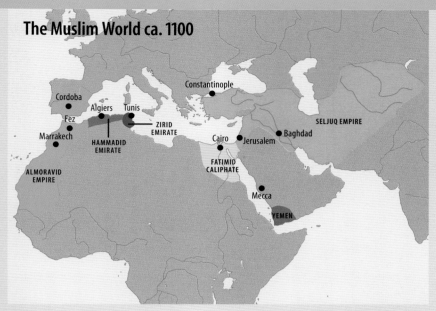

Cordoba
Fez
Marrakech
Algiers
Tunis
ZIRID EMIRATE
HAMMADID EMIRATE
Constantinople
SELJUQ EMPIRE
Cairo
Jerusalem
Baghdad
FATIMID CALIPHATE
Mecca
ALMORAVID EMPIRE
YEMEN

Asia ca. 400

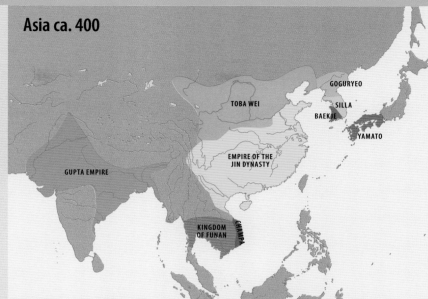

GOGURYEO
TOBA WEI
SILLA
BAEKJE
YAMATO
EMPIRE OF THE JIN DYNASTY
GUPTA EMPIRE
KINGDOM OF FUNAN
CHAMPA

through the Crusades to the Holy Land. European thought was shaped largely by the dominance of the Christian world-view and a social order based on stratification and relationships of fealty (loyalty, knight-hood and military vows). After 1200, the merchants of the cities of northern Italy, the Hanseatic League and other cities emerged as a new power.

Central and South America

The Zapotecs in southern Mexico and the Toltecs in central Mexico were at their zenith. The Maya formed large, powerful city-states on the Yuca-tán Peninsula—such as Palenque, Copan or Tikal—with impressive buildings. They used a glyphic writing system and possessed an

astonishingly accurate calendar. In South America, the Huari and Tiwanaku cultures arose. They reached their zenith in the 9th century only to disappear in the 10th. In their wake came the Chimú culture.

Africa

New empires arose all over the African conti-nent, not only in the north and the east, but also in the center and the west. The most important are Ghana, Songhai, Kanem, Mali and Great Zimbabwe, which prospered through trade with the north. Arab merchants quickly spread Islam along the northern and eastern coasts. By the end of the Middle Ages, the majority of the organized western and northern African states adhered to Islam.

Asia ca. 800

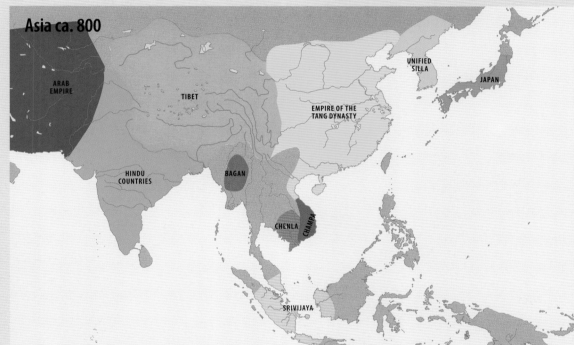

ARAB EMPIRE
TIBET
UNIFIED SILLA
JAPAN
EMPIRE OF THE TANG DYNASTY
HINDU COUNTRIES
BAGAN
CHENLA
CHAMPA
SRIVIJAYA

Central and South America ca. 1000

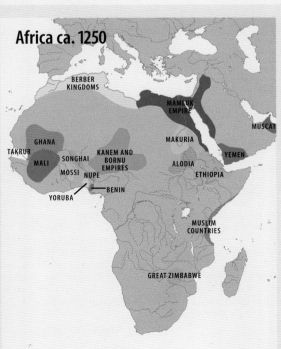

TOLTECS
MAYA
ZAPOTECS
CHIMOR
WARI CULTURE
TIWANAKU

Africa ca. 1250

BERBER KINGDOMS
MAMLUK EMPIRE
MUSCAT
MAKURIA
TAKRUR
GHANA
SONGHAI
KANEM AND BORNU EMPIRES
MALI
MOSSI
NUPE
YORUBA
BENIN
ALODIA
YEMEN
ETHIOPIA
MUSLIM COUNTRIES
GREAT ZIMBABWE

Muslim World

None of the other world religions spread as quickly as Islam: only eighty years after the death of the Prophet Muhammed, its founder, the Muslim conquerors ruled territory stretching from Spain in the west to northern India in the east. While initially mainly Arab in character, Islam opened itself to Persian influences after 750 and was dominated by Turkish military dynasties after 950, who used the religious authority of the caliph only to legitimize their rule. The years 800 to 1300 are considered the golden age of Muslim science and knowledge.

India and Southeast Asia

After the destruction of the Gupta empire

in India by the White Huns, several competing Hindu dynasties ruled the subcontinent ("Indian Middle Ages"). After the year 1000, northern India was Islamicized. In Southeast Asia, the culturally highly devel-oped Khmer kingdom became the preeminent power in Cambodia (Angkor Wat).

East Asia

The Song dynasty unified fragmented China and initiated a cultural flourishing. The Mongols took advantage of the political weakness of the empire in its later years and conquered China. In Japan, shoguns (military leaders) took control dur-ing the Kamakura period; the samurai (sword-wielding warriors) became the nobility of the country.

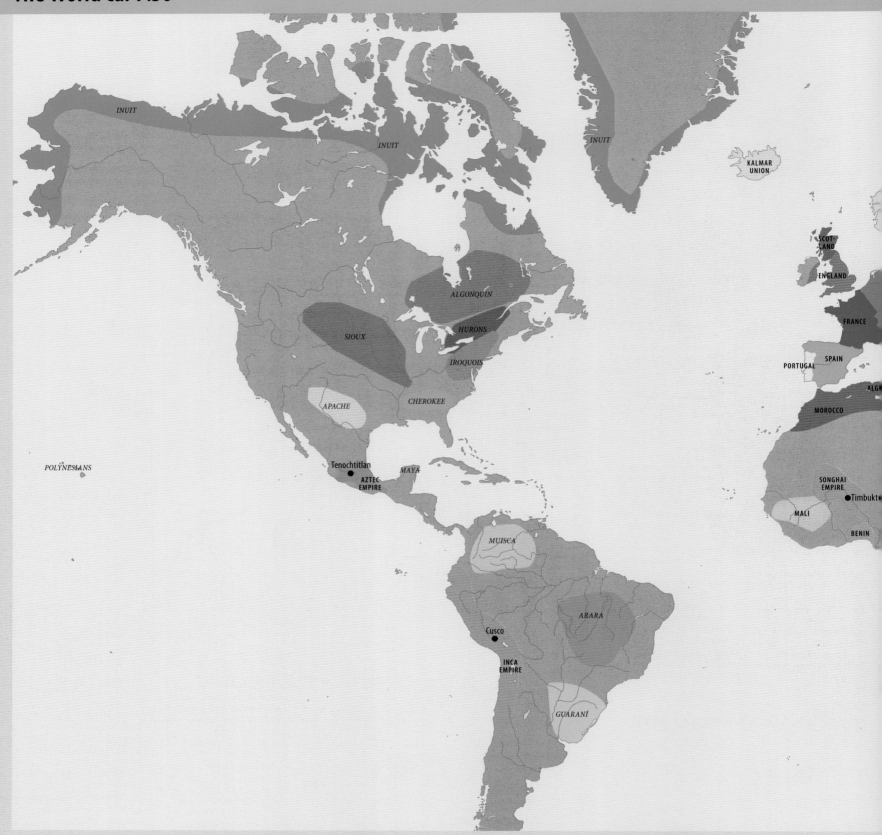

INUIT

INUIT

INUIT

KALMAR UNION

SCOT-LAND

ENGLAND

FRANCE

ALGONQUIN

HURONS

SIOUX

IROQUOIS

PORTUGAL

SPAIN

ALG

APACHE

CHEROKEE

MOROCCO

POLYNESIANS

Tenochtitlan
AZTEC EMPIRE

MAYA

SONGHAI EMPIRE

Timbukt

MALI

BENIN

MUISCA

ARARA

Cusco

INCA EMPIRE

GUARANÍ

The plague epidemic that raged in the mid-14th century claimed the lives of approximately a quarter of the population of the known world, which sank to the level of the 13th century: around 450 million people.

Europe

In the course of the Middle Ages, people in Europe grew increasingly discontent with some of the practices of the church (e.g., the sale of offices and indulgences), which ultimately led to attempts to reform. In Bohemia, the followers of Jan Hus took up

arms against the emperor and pope. Humanists spread their ideals from Italy throughout northern Europe. After the Ottomans conquered Constantinople, Western Europeans started looking for alternate sea routes to India and discovered the Americas in the process. The invention of the printing press around 1450 revolutionized the world and was a tremendous catalyst to education.

Muslim World

The Ottomans, a Turkic people, conquered the entire Balkan region and,

in 1453, finally also the Byzantine capital of Constantinople, thus becoming a player in European politics. During the same century, the Moors were ousted from Spain by local Christian rulers. In Asia, the great empire of the Timurid rulers crumbled quickly after 1447, while several peoples and dynasties vied for power in north Africa and Persia.

China

The era of the Ming dynasty began after the end of Mongol rule in 1368. Nanking lost its position as capital to

Beijing, where imperial palaces were built that form the "Forbidden City." Although Chinese mariners undertook lengthy expeditions to Southwest Asia during this time, the rest of "All under Heaven" sought cultural isolation from the rest of the world.

India

While the north of the subcontinent was ruled by the Afghan Lodi dynasty in the sultanate of Delhi, the Hindu-dominated center and south of India remained under the hegemony of the Vijayanagara empire, named after

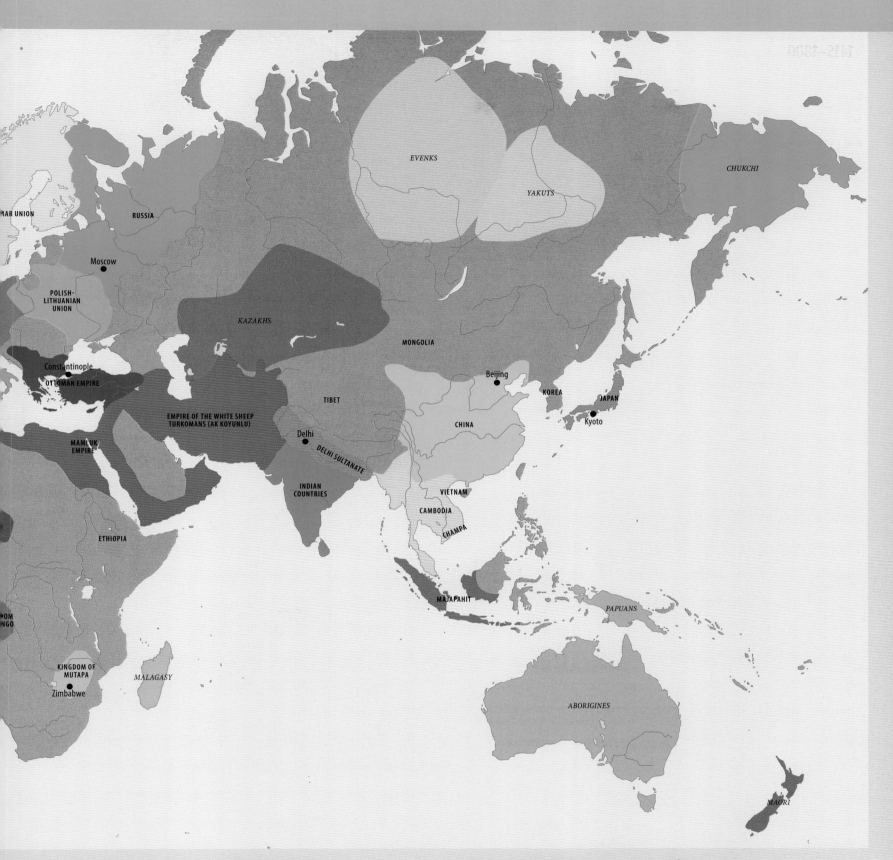

EVENKS

CHUKCHI

YAKUTS

MAR UNION

RUSSIA

Moscow

POLISH-
LITHUANIAN
UNION

KAZAKHS

MONGOLIA

Constantinople

OTTOMAN EMPIRE

Beijing

KOREA

JAPAN

TIBET

Kyoto

EMPIRE OF THE WHITE SHEEP
TURKOMANS (AK KOYUNLU)

Delhi

CHINA

MAMLUK
EMPIRE

DELHI SULTANATE

VIETNAM

INDIAN
COUNTRIES

CAMBODIA

ETHIOPIA

CHAMPA

MAJAPAHIT

PAPUANS

OM
NGO

KINGDOM OF
MUTAPA

MALAGASY

Zimbabwe

ABORIGINES

MAORI

its capital, whose impressive ruins
surround modern Hampi. Vijayanagara
proved to be a center of Indian
literature and learning.

Japan
In Japan, the military aristocracy, the
samurai caste, took over power. The
weakening of the central monarchy
and the empowerment of local military
dictators (daimyo) continued. The fall
of the Ashikaga shogunate led to a
period of continual civil wars that lasted
almost a hundred years.

North America
The Native American tribes of the
Wyandot (or Huron) Confederacy lived
on the shores of the Great Lakes; later,
it developed into the Iroquois League.
They held their own parliaments and
influenced the later development of
the United States democracy. In what
is now New Mexico, the Pueblo tribes
were heirs to the highly developed
Anasazi culture. Some North American
cultures, such as the Mississippian
culture, disappeared without a trace,
falling victim to epidemics introduced
by Spanish conquistadors.

Central and South America
After the decline of the civilization of
the Maya, a plethora of smaller states
came into existence that remained
politically weak due to their constant
warfare against each other. After 1427,
the empire of the Aztecs reached its
zenith after conquering large swaths
of new territories. In Peru, the Inca
started campaigning to gain more land.
Particularly after 1438, their empire
became the largest and most highly
organized empire in South America,
relying on a central government and
excellent administration.

Africa
In the northwest of the continent, the
Muslim Songhai empire established
itself around the centers of Timbuktu
and Gao. In Ethiopia, Muslims and
Christians fought each other. The ships
of the Portuguese explorers followed
the western coast of Africa southward,
while the Spanish began to settle parts
of the northern coasts. In the south,
the kingdom of Mutapa experienced
a short heyday before splitting up into
the northern state of Mutapa under
the control of the Shona tribes and the
empire of Changamire in Zimbabwe.

European Exploration of the World

1415–1800

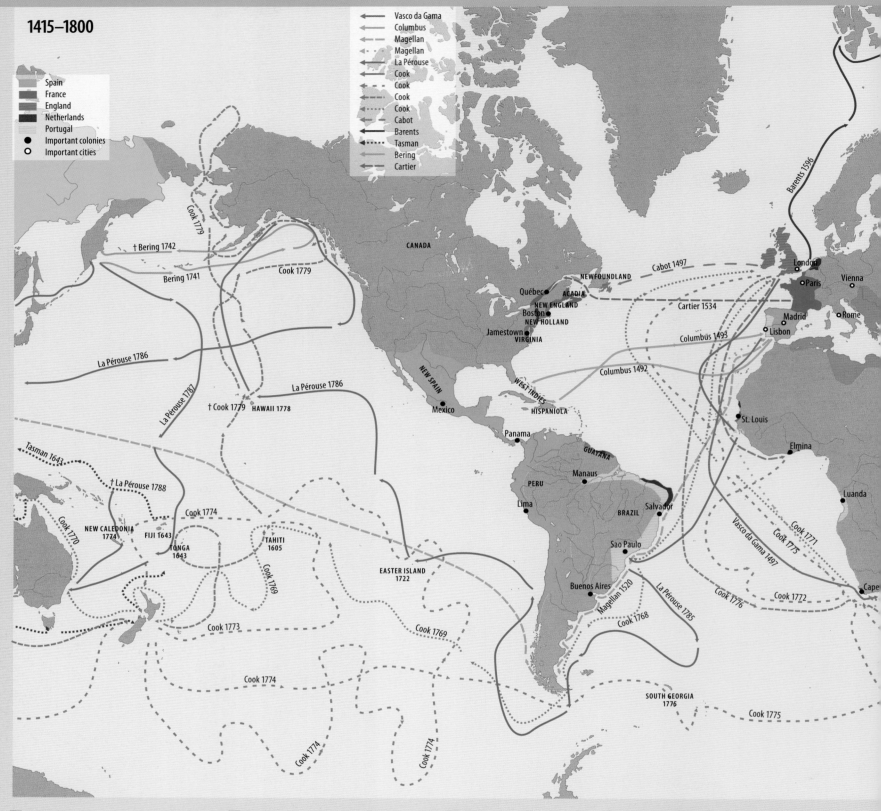

Legend (regions):
- Spain
- France
- England
- Netherlands
- Portugal
- ● Important colonies
- ○ Important cities

Legend (routes):
- Vasco da Gama
- Columbus
- Magellan
- Magellan
- La Pérouse
- Cook
- Cook
- Cook
- Cook
- Cabot
- Barents
- Tasman
- Bering
- Cartier

Map labels: Barents 1596, Cabot 1497, London, Paris, Vienna, Madrid, Rome, Lisbon, Columbus 1493, Columbus 1492, Cartier 1534, CANADA, NEWFOUNDLAND, Québec, ACADIA, NEW ENGLAND, Boston, NEW HOLLAND, Jamestown, VIRGINIA, NEW SPAIN, WEST INDIES, Mexico, HISPANIOLA, Panama, GUAYANA, St. Louis, Elmina, Manaus, PERU, Lima, BRAZIL, Salvador, Sao Paulo, Luanda, Buenos Aires, Magellan 1520, La Pérouse 1785, Cook 1776, Cook 1772, Cape, Vasco da Gama 1497, Cook 1771, Cook 1775, Cook 1768, SOUTH GEORGIA 1776, Cook 1775, † Bering 1742, Bering 1741, Cook 1779, Cook 1779, La Pérouse 1786, La Pérouse 1787, La Pérouse 1786, † Cook 1779, HAWAII 1778, Tasman 1643, † La Pérouse 1788, Cook 1774, NEW CALEDONIA 1774, FIJI 1643, TONGA 1643, TAHITI 1605, EASTER ISLAND 1722, Cook 1774, Cook 1769, Cook 1773, Cook 1769, Cook 1770, Cook 1774, Cook 1774, Cook 1774

Portuguese

1415–1488 Portuguese seafarers explore the coasts of western Africa.

1470 The Portuguese reach the equator.

1487–1488 Bartolomeu Dias circumnavigates the Cape of Good Hope.

1497–1499 Vasco da Gama sails around Africa and reaches India.

1500 Discovery of Brazil

1511 Conquest of Malacca, Malaysia on behalf of Portugal

1541 Portuguese arrive in Japan.

1555 Macau in China becomes a Portuguese colony.

Spanish

1492–1493 Columbus's first trip to America and founding of Hispaniola, the first Spanish colony

1494 Treaty of Tordesillas: the pope divides the New World between the Portuguese and the Spanish.

1513 Vasco Nunez de Balboa crosses the Isthmus of Panama.

1519–1521 Hernán Cortés takes Mexico.

1519–1522 First circumnavigation of the world by Ferdinand Magellan

1531–1534 Francisco Pizarro conquers Peru.

1564 Conquest of the Philippines

Dutch

1596–1597 Java and Maluku; Willem Barents discovers the Arctic island of Spitsbergen.

1598–1601 Olivier van Noort circumnavigates the globe.

1606 Willem Janszoon discovers Australia.

1609 Dutch East India Company founds Batavia (Jakarta).

1626 Peter Minuit purchases the island of Manhattan.

1630–1654 Attempt to conquer Brazil

1634 Conquest of some of the West Indies

1652 Founding of Cape Town

French

1524–1541 Seafarers explore the western coast of North America.

1604 Occupation of Guayana

1608 Founding of Québec; Canada emerges.

1626 French settle in Senegal.

1635 Martinique and Guadeloupe are colonized.

1668 The French arrive in India.

1763 As a consequence of the Treaty of Paris, the French withdraw from North America and India.

1785–1788 Jean-François de Galaup, Count of La Pérouse, explores the Pacific Ocean.

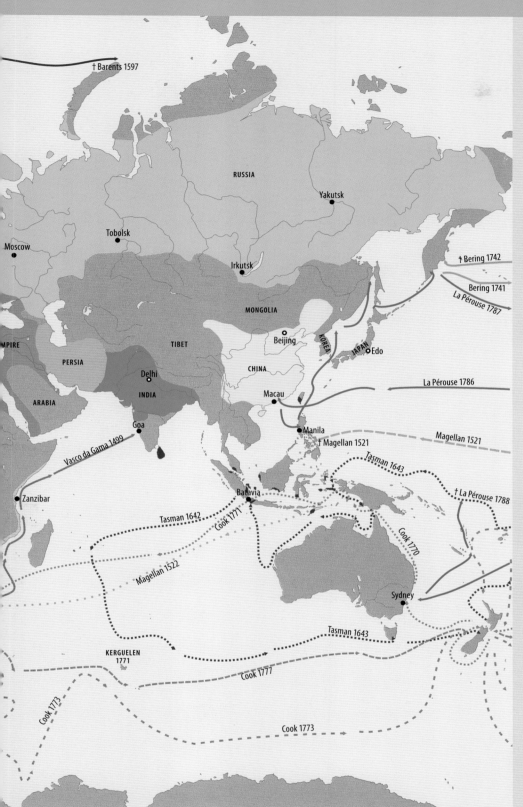

† Barents 1597

RUSSIA

Yakutsk

Tobolsk

Moscow

Irkutsk

† Bering 1742

Bering 1741

La Pérouse 1787

MONGOLIA

TIBET

Beijing

KOREA

JAPAN

Edo

...MPIRE

PERSIA

Delhi

CHINA

Macau

La Pérouse 1786

ARABIA

INDIA

Manila

† Magellan 1521

Magellan 1521

Goa

Vasco da Gama 1499

Tasman 1643

Zanzibar

Batavia

† La Pérouse 1788

Tasman 1642

Cook 1771

Cook 1770

Magellan 1522

Sydney

Cook 1773

Tasman 1643

KERGUELEN 1771

Cook 1777

Cook 1773

Cook 1773

The Known World ca. 1450

For a long time, Europeans concentrated on exploring the coastlines of the continents where they landed; the Vikings or Marco Polo were exceptions in this respect. Until the end of the Middle Ages, the world as it was known to the Europeans consisted only of Asia, North Africa and the islands closest to Europe.

The Known World ca. 1650

Once their navigational systems improved, the seafarers left the shorelines and set out into the open sea, thus enlarging their world. They discovered the Americas as they sought a sea route to India to enhance the spice trade.

The Known World ca. 1786

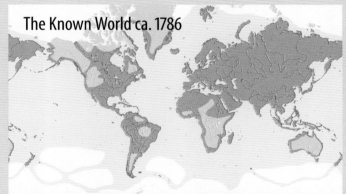

By the end of the 18th century, Europeans had established themselves on practically every continent. They were motivated not only by a spirit of inquiry and scientific curiosity, but also by trade and the establishment of monopolies. Wherever they went, they established trading colonies that quickly became large cities.

British

1497 Discovery of Newfoundland
1577–1580 Francis Drake circumnavigates the world.
1607 Founding of Jamestown, the first permanent English settlement in North America
1611–1612 The British arrive in India.
1620 The *Mayflower* reaches Plymouth, Massachusetts.
1655 The British forcibly evict the Spanish from Jamaica; British on the western coast of Africa
1765 Victory over the Bengals
1768–1779 Voyages of James Cook
1788 Founding of Sydney, Australia

Russian

1466–1472 Afanasy Nikitin travels in Asia.
1556 Russians at the Caspian Sea
1581–1587 Conquest of western Siberia
1643 Russians reach Lake Baikal.
1648 Discovery of the Bering Strait, unnamed at the time
1691 Discovery of the Kamchatka Peninsula
1741 Vitus Bering discovers Alaska and the Aleutian Islands.
1743 Russians reach the northernmost point of Asia on Taymyr Peninsula.
1799 Aleksandr Baranov founds Novo Arkhangelsk (near Sitka).

Those Who Gave the World Their Name

America	Amerigo Vespucci	Italian explorer, navigator and cartographer, 1451–1512
Tasmania	Abel Tasman	Dutch seafarer, 1603–1659
Columbia	Christopher Columbus	Italian seafarer, 1451–1506
Philippines	Philip II	King of Spain, Portugal, England, Sicily and the Netherlands, Duke of Milan and Count of Burgundy, 1527–1598
Mauritius	Maurice of Orange	Commander of the army of the United Netherlands, 1567–1625
Seychelles	Jean Moreau de Séchelles	French minister of finance, 1690–1761
Bermuda	Juan de Bermúdez	Spanish navigator, † 1570

Early Modern Times, ca. 1500–1776

The World ca. 1700

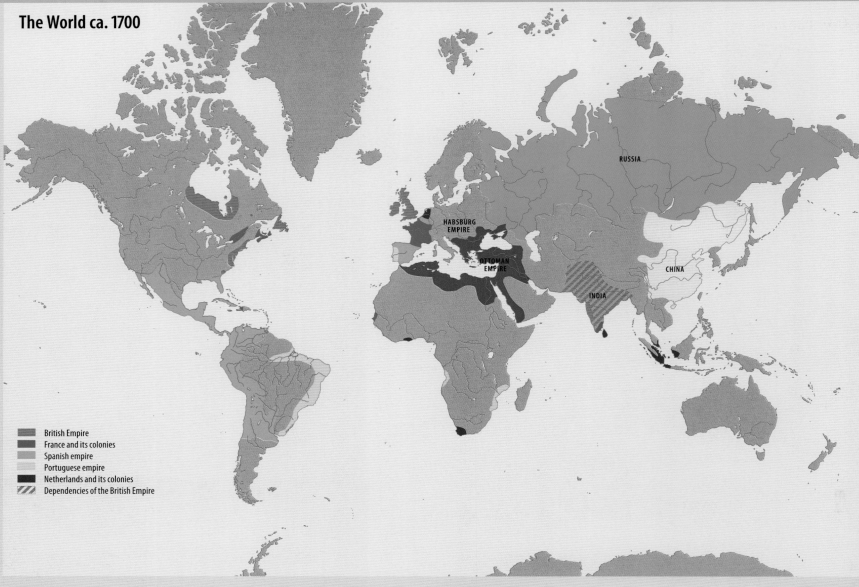

Legend:
- British Empire
- France and its colonies
- Spanish empire
- Portuguese empire
- Netherlands and its colonies
- Dependencies of the British Empire

Europe

From 1517 onward, Europe was shaped by the various currents of the Reformation, which led to the splitting of the church, the development of the Protestant churches (Lutheran, Reformer, Calvinist) and religious wars, culminating in the tragic Thirty Years' War (1618–1648). Spain, wealthy in part through exploitation of the resources of the New World, became the leading Catholic power in the 16th century. France dominated after 1620 (Richelieu, Louis XIV), but was held in check by the other powers through the wars of the 18th century. Absolutism, with its emphasis on the power of the central ruling force and prestigious building projects, became accepted by the states, while the concept of the separation of powers was already announcing itself through the Enlightenment; enlightened absolutism reduced the power of the church. The Netherlands as a trading republic, England as a sea power, Russia modernized by Peter the Great, and the firmly led Prussia became the leading powers.

Muslim World

The greatest gain in power was experienced by the Ottoman Empire from 1512 with the occupation of the Arab and northern African regions. In Europe, however, the Ottoman Empire was on the defensive after 1683 as a result of Prince Eugene of Savoy's wars with the Turks. In the east, the Ottomans' military competition was the Safavid shahs in Persia; both dynasties increasingly weakened themselves by raising their heir apparent in the "golden cage" of the harem.

India and Southeast Asia

The Muslim Mughal emperors displayed immeasurable wealth in India (Taj Mahal); their power, however, was substantially curtailed by the English East India Company after 1712. The European trade companies strategically built monopolies through mutual support of the various empires throughout Southeast Asia; colonialism made its presence felt.

East Asia

China intensified its cultural isolation even during the Manchu or Qing dynasty, which ruled from 1644. At the same time, however, China dominated the area up to and including Tibet, and experienced a last cultural zenith under the long rule of Emperor Qianlong (1735–1796). In Japan, the work of the great imperial unifier Toyotomi Hideyoshi (1574–1603) led to renewed rule of the shoguns, called the Edo or Tokugawa period (1600–1867).

Europe 1648

Legend:
- Border of the German Empire
- Disputed region (went to Russia)

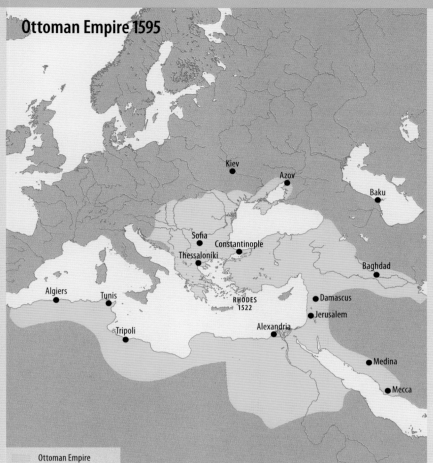

Ottoman Empire 1595

Kiev
Azov
Baku
Sofia
Constantinople
Thessaloníki
Baghdad
Algiers
Tunis
RHODES 1522
Damascus
Jerusalem
Tripoli
Alexandria
Medina
Mecca

Ottoman Empire

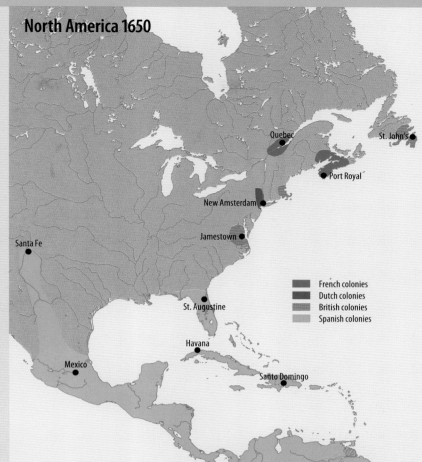

North America 1650

Quebec
St. John's
Port Royal
New Amsterdam
Santa Fe
Jamestown
St. Augustine
Havana
Mexico
Santo Domingo

French colonies
Dutch colonies
British colonies
Spanish colonies

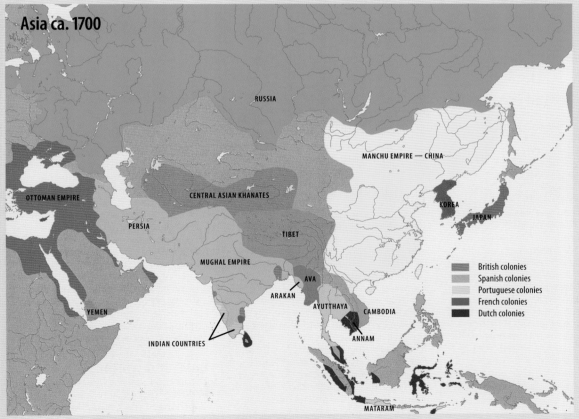

Asia ca. 1700

RUSSIA
MANCHU EMPIRE — CHINA
OTTOMAN EMPIRE
CENTRAL ASIAN KHANATES
KOREA
PERSIA
JAPAN
TIBET
MUGHAL EMPIRE
AVA
ARAKAN
AYUTTHAYA
YEMEN
CAMBODIA
INDIAN COUNTRIES
ANNAM
MATARAM

British colonies
Spanish colonies
Portuguese colonies
French colonies
Dutch colonies

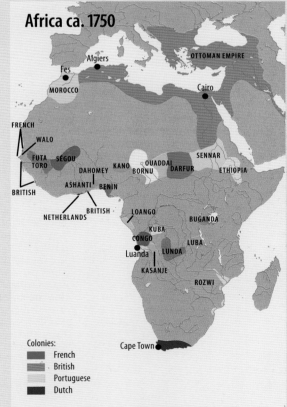

Africa ca. 1750

Fes
Algiers
OTTOMAN EMPIRE
MOROCCO
Cairo
FRENCH
WALO
FUTA TORO
SÉGOU
KANO
OUADDAI
SENNAR
BORNU
DARFUR
ETHIOPIA
DAHOMEY
BRITISH
ASHANTI
BENIN
NETHERLANDS
BRITISH
LOANGO
BUGANDA
KUBA
CONGO
LUBA
Luanda
LUNDA
KASANJE
ROZWI
Cape Town

Colonies:
French
British
Portuguese
Dutch

North America

The land was explored and colonized by Britain and France, among others, after they first squeezed out the Netherlands. Initially agreements were made between the first settlers (religious exiles) and the Native Americans, which led to those tribes' involvement in a British-French war in which the French lost most of their territory. The assertive New England states moved toward their own independence.

Middle and South America

After 1520, ancient American empires were conquered and largely annihilated at the hands of Spanish adventurers. South America was divided between Spain and Portugal, both of which forced Christianization, exploited native peoples as slave labor and eradicated native populations. Religious orders such as the Jesuits, who founded reductions (missions) in Paraguay during their self-government of natives from 1600 to 1767, tried to protect them.

Africa

In North Africa, Morocco remained independent and under the control of the Songhai empire, while other regions of Africa were under the suzerainty of the Ottomans. Portugal was the leading merchant power on the African coast, Christianizing as well as conducting the slave trade; later it also challenged the future colonial powers with trade companies and bases within these lands. A few regions built up powerful states.

The World in 1776

British colonies
French colonies
Dutch colonies
Spanish colonies
Portuguese colonies

United States 1789

Boston
New York
Philadelphia

UNITED STATES

United States 1840

Boston
New York
Washington D.C.

UNITED STATES

Charleston

New Orleans

United States 1864

Boston
St. Louis
New York
Washington D.C.
Richmond

San Francisco

New Orleans
Charleston

Confederacy
Slaveholding Union states
Union (north)

United States and Canada

The United States of America declared its independence from Great Britain in 1776 and underwent brisk economic development. Immediately it began to expand to the south and west, to the detriment of Spain and Mexico, as well as the Native Americans, who were displaced or settled on reservations. Conflict between the wealthy, industrialized North and the plantation economy predominant in the South, dependent on slave workers, resulted in the Civil War from 1861 to 1865. First and foremost, the victory of the Union (the northern states) resulted in the abolition of slavery. After Britain's successful war against the French (1761), all Canada became British territory. Nevertheless, the northern part of Canada remained Francophone and the area is still bilingual. Gradually, however, Canada began to win its independence from Great Britain.

Latin America

The nations in Central and South America followed the example of the United States. In several of the armed uprisings led by Simon Bolívar, those nations separated themselves from Spain and Portugal after 1810. The only nation to win its independence peacefully was Brazil, whose emperor, Pedro I, stood at the forefront of its independence movement. However, the majority of the Latin American nations have suffered from political instability, economic problems, ethnic crises, revolutions and military dictatorships into the 20th century. In Mexico, where these conflicts were especially strong, a revolution broke out in 1911.

Europe

For Europe, the late 18th century and the 19th century brought revolutions and national movements, beginning with the agitation of the French Revolution in 1789 and the formulation of universal human and civil rights. These ideas led to the wars of the French Revolution. Napoleon's expansionist policy collapsed under the weight of its own excess, but it did give rise to the civil code and disseminated the idea of equality before the law through Europe. The struggle against Napoleon awakened a national consciousness in many states. Although the Congress of Vienna in 1814–1815 and its mastermind, Austrian foreign minister Metternich, sought a return to the old status quo, national and democratic trends nonetheless resulted in the revolutions of 1830 and 1848–1849. Greece and Belgium earned their independence, while Germany and Italy unified themselves. The Habsburg monarchy felt greater stress in its various territories. The years following 1871 brought an economic boom, as well as an increasing power struggle between the Great Powers, which would explode in 1914.

Muslim World

The weakening Ottoman Empire made a series of attempts at internal political reform beginning in 1789, which culminated in the Tanzimat reforms of 1839. The autocratic regime of Abdulhamid II (1876–1909) gave rise to the Young Turks reform movement. From 1805, the extensive autonomy of both Egypt and Persia, ruled by the shahs of the Qajar dynasty, degraded in the course of the 19th century into financial and political dependence on European nations, especially Britain, which vied with Russia for influence in Persia and Afghanistan. Consequently, Russia annexed the khanate of Central Asia.

India and Southeast Asia

The British used the Indian Sepoy Mutiny of 1857–1858 to bring about the total control and occupation of India, which became the "Crown Jewel" of its colonial politics. The French and Dutch dominated the lands of Southeast Asia, parts of which were under direct colonial rule and parts of which were incorporated as protectorates.

East Asia

In the 19th century China was weakened by numerous local rebellions, which gave the European powers a pretext to intervene. As a result of the Opium Wars, Great Britain forcibly opened China to its goods. The Chinese Nationalist Boxer Rebellion in 1900 finally led to almost complete domination of its cities by the European powers. Also, in 1853, Japan was forcibly opened for trade by United States ships; with the establishment of the Meji era in 1868 came a national revival with aggressive imperialistic characteristics.

Africa

The abolition of the slave trade at the Congress of Vienna in 1814–1815 was an important milestone for Africa. In 1822, freed slaves from the United States founded a separate state in Africa: Liberia. The numerous expeditions of European explorers in the interior of Africa prepared the way for their countries' political influence. Beginning in the mid-19th century, in short order, nations such as Great Britain and France occupied the African lands as colonial territories. Other powers (Italy, Belgium, Germany and Spain) followed in the 1880s; Portugal retained its traditional colonies in Angola and Mozambique.

The Berlin Congress of 1884–1885 sought to loosen the tension between the European powers. It was decided there that the European states had the right to occupy and retain all the African territories that had not yet been colonized.

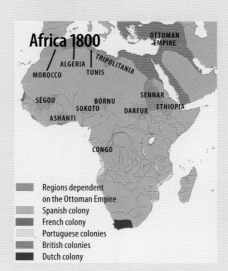

Africa 1800

Regions dependent on the Ottoman Empire
Spanish colony
French colony
Portuguese colonies
British colonies
Dutch colony

Colonial Powers at the Beginning of the 20th Century

Great Britain: ca. 22 million square miles (35 million km²), or one-fifth of the world

Population including its colonies: ca. 458 million
Dominions (territories with an independent administration): Canada, New Zealand, Newfoundland, Australia, South African Union (1910)
Colonies: Egypt, Sudan, Bechuanaland (Botswana), British East Africa, British Somalia, Gold Coast, Nigeria, Rhodesia, Southwest Africa, Zanzibar, India, Singapore, Burma, Bhutan, Ceylon, Nepal, Malacca, Hong Kong, Malaysia, Nauru, New Hebrides, Solomon Islands, Papua New Guinea, Bahamas, Barbados, Jamaica, Leeward Islands, Windward Islands

France: ca. 8 million square miles (12 million km²)

Colonies: French Indochina, Tunisia, Algeria, Central Africa, French Somalia, French Guinea, French Sudan, Morocco (1912), South Pacific Islands, New Caledonia, French Polynesia, Merkesen, Madagascar, New Hebrides (jointly with Great Britain), Comoros, Seychelles, Mauritius, Iles du Salut, French Guiana

Spain:

Spain lost Cuba, Puerto Rico, Guam and the Philippines to the USA in 1898.
Colonies: Spanish Sahara, Spanish Morocco (1912), Canary Islands, Ceuta and Melila

Germany: ca. 2.2 million square miles (3.5 million km²)

Colonies: German East Africa, German South West Africa, German West Africa (Cameroon, Togo), German New Guinea, Caroline Islands, German Samoa, Kaiser Wilhelm's Land, Marshall Islands, Nauru, Bismarck Archipelago, Northern Solomon Islands, Mariana Islands, Palau

Netherlands: ca. 1.7 million square miles (2.5 million km²)

Over time, most of the Dutch colonies came under the control of Great Britain
Colonies: Dutch East Indies, Suriname, Netherlands Antilles

Portugal:

Colonies: Angola, Mozambique, Macao, East Timor, Portuguese Guinea, São Tomé and Principe, Portuguese India (Goa)

Italy:

Colonies: Italian North Africa (1912), Italian Somalia

Belgium: ca. 1.7 million square miles (2.5 million km²)

Colonies: Belgian Congo

United States:

Colonies: Hawaiian Republic, the Philippines, Puerto Rico, American Samoa

Russia: empire spanning ca 13.5 million square miles (22 million km²)

In a sense, this was the most successful of the colonial empires. Its geographical position enabled Russia to add the territories colonialized as it expanded into the Far East and Central Asia to the motherland and successfully "Russianize" them.

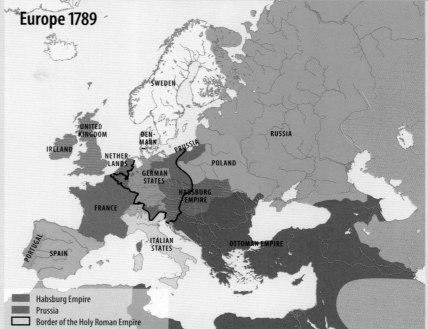

Europe 1789

Habsburg Empire
Prussia
Border of the Holy Roman Empire

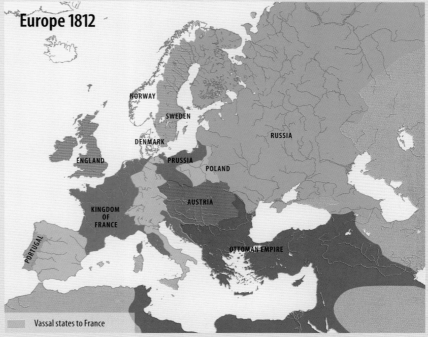

Europe 1812

Vassal states to France

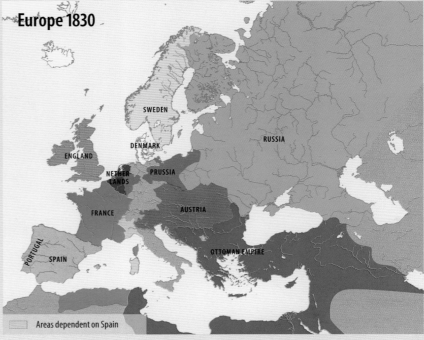

Europe 1830

Areas dependent on Spain

35

World War I and the Interwar Period, 1914–1933

The World 1914

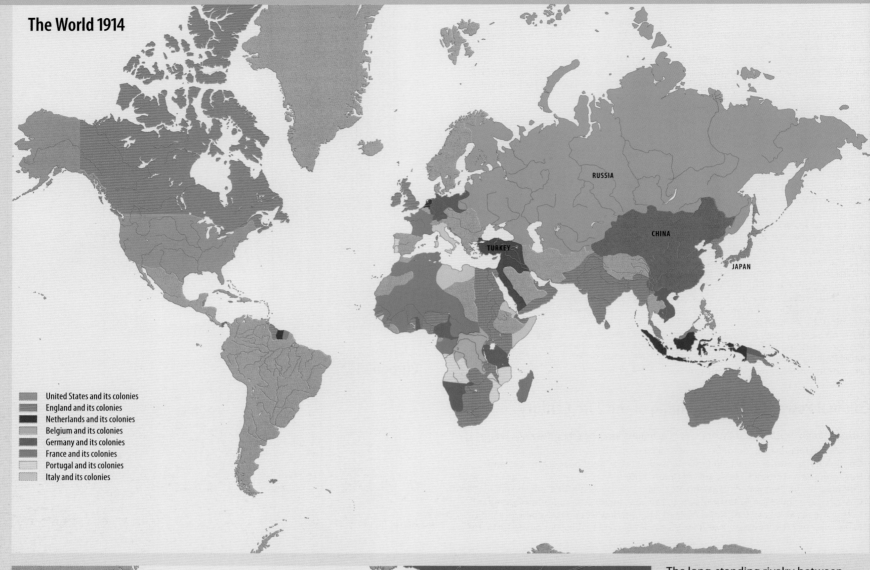

- United States and its colonies
- England and its colonies
- Netherlands and its colonies
- Belgium and its colonies
- Germany and its colonies
- France and its colonies
- Portugal and its colonies
- Italy and its colonies

Europe 1916

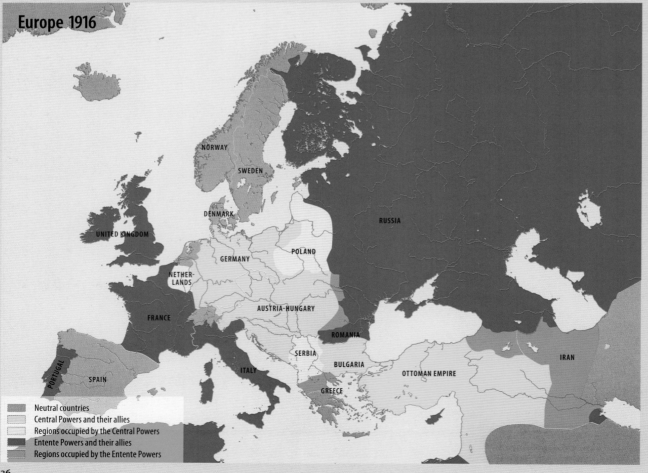

- Neutral countries
- Central Powers and their allies
- Regions occupied by the Central Powers
- Entente Powers and their allies
- Regions occupied by the Entente Powers

The long-standing rivalry between the various European nations and their division among two military alliances—the Entente Powers and the Central Powers—led to the outbreak of World War I, which resulted in material devastation and mass deaths on a scale previously unknown. The trigger was the assassination of the heir apparent to the Austro-Hungarian throne, Archduke Francis Ferdinand, in Sarajevo in June 1914. This led to Austria-Hungary's declaration of war on Serbia and the engagement of the full might of the military alliances. Germany immediately lost its overseas colonies to occupation, but initially won a victory against the Russians on the eastern front at Tannenberg. Following the German march through Belgium (the Schlieffen Plan), the German advance was halted at the Marne by September 1914. In the west there followed modern trench warfare and armed attacks on a massive scale, culminating in the Battle of Verdun in 1916. In 1915 Britain and its auxiliary forces suffered devastating casualties in their attempt to seize the Gallipoli Peninsula from Turkey. The superiority of the Entente Powers was demonstrated particularly following the entrance of the United States into the war in 1917, while the October Revolution of 1917 in Russia initially led to a favorable conclusion of the war in the east for the Central Powers (the Treaty of Brest-Litovsk, March 1918).

In November 1918 the Central Powers were forced to capitulate; immediately the German and Austrian-Hungarian monarchies collapsed, followed by brief rebellions. The Treaty of Versailles, which was dictated by the Entente Powers in 1919, imposed sole responsibility for the war, in addition to a high indemnity for reparations, on Germany. Germany's allies also had to accept great losses of territory. At the urging of United States President Woodrow Wilson, the League of Nations (forerunner of the United Nations) was founded in 1920.

Economic crises, dissatisfaction with postwar order, assasinations, political instability, undemocratic sentiment in the military, fragmentation of the democratic forces and the growing power of totalitarian movements strained the "unpopular" new democracies of central Europe, especially the Weimar Republic (1918/19–1933) in Germany. In many countries, this resulted in takeovers by right-leaning authoritarian or fascistic regimes. In 1922 the fascists took power in Italy under Benito Mussolini, while in the Soviet Union, totalitarian Stalinism established brutal policies of equalization. Earnest attempts to preserve peace, for example the efforts of politicians Aristide Briand and Gustav Stresemann between France and Germany, did not bring lasting success. In Germany as well, the presidential cabinet (from 1930) and the sway of popular sentiment prepared the way for an authoritarian turn. In 1933 the "surrogate kaiser," Reichspresident Paul von Hindenburg, named Adolf Hitler chancellor of the Third Reich.

Europe after the War (1918)

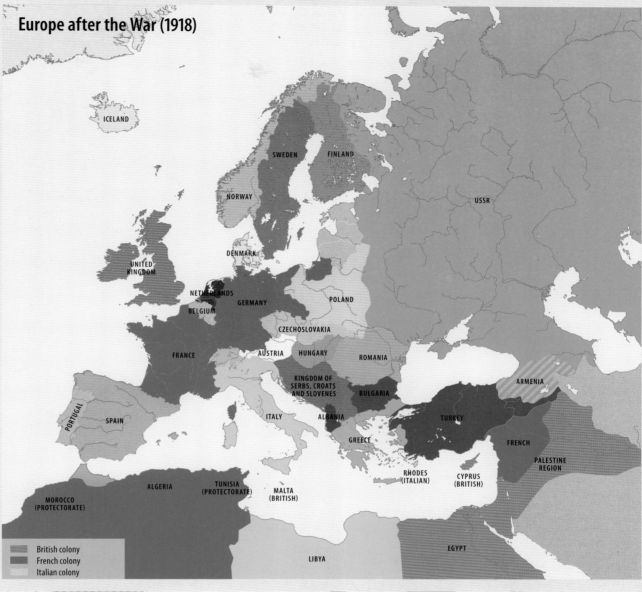

British colony
French colony
Italian colony

The World 1930

United States and dependencies
Other countries

British Empire and dependencies
Other European colonial powers and their colonies
Countries evolving from those defeated in World War I
USSR and dependencies
Japan and dependencies

The World in 1939

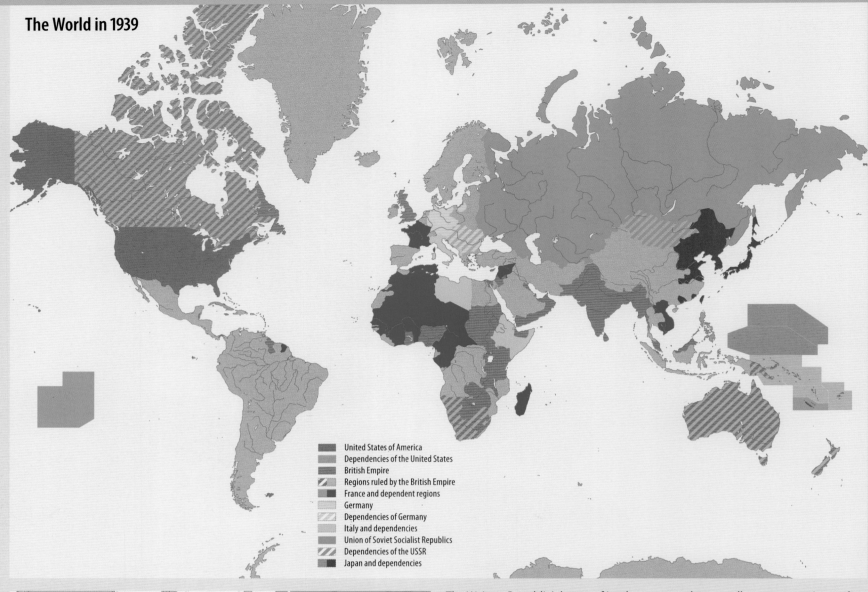

- United States of America
- Dependencies of the United States
- British Empire
- Regions ruled by the British Empire
- France and dependent regions
- Germany
- Dependencies of Germany
- Italy and dependencies
- Union of Soviet Socialist Republics
- Dependencies of the USSR
- Japan and dependencies

1942: World War II

- Western Allies and occupied countries
- Germany and occupied countries
- Allies of the Axis Powers
- USSR and occupied countries
- Italy and occupied countries
- Neutral countries

The Weimar Republic's hopes of implementing peaceful policy were quickly dashed by Germany's dissatisfaction with the conditions of the Treaty of Versailles and the racist expansionist plans of the National Socialists, who promulgated the ideas of Germans as *ein Volk ohne Lebensraum*, "a nation without living space," which needed to expand to the east. Right-wing ideologues knew how to denounce democratic politicians as *Vaterlandsverräter* (traitors of the fatherland) and democracy as utterly foreign. Accompanied by massive propaganda, the Nazis crushed all democratic institutions and propagated the "superiority of the Aryan master race." Their brutal anti-Semitism initially forced Jews out of public life, and from 1941 onward escalated into mass murder that was carried out by SS commandos, as well as concentration and extermination camps. The Nazis' goal was to wipe out European Jewry. In Europe alone, six million Jews fell victim to the Holocaust. The aggressive policies of the Axis Powers (Germany, Italy and Japan) and their dreams of imperial grandeur heightened political tensions. Great Britain and France tried to avoid war with Hitler through an indulgent policy of appeasement that led to the sacrifice of Czechoslovakia and Poland. A pact made in 1939 allowed Hitler and Stalin to divide Poland between themselves.

World War II began with the German attack on Poland on September 1, 1939. In a series of rapid strikes (blitzkrieg), German troops occupied Denmark, Norway, the Low Countries and most of France. Even the unoccupied portion of France (Vichy Regime) was effectively under German control. The Battle of Britain began in 1940, but encountered resistance. The war entered an even more brutal phase in June 1941: Germany attacked Russia and subsequently occupied Yugoslavia and Greece, openly committing acts of terror against the civilian populations. When Japan, Germany's ally, attacked Pearl Harbor in December 1941, the war in the Pacific commenced. At the end of 1942, the Battle of Stalingrad brought

Selection at Auschwitz, ca. 1944. Jewish people were required to wear yellow stars visible on their clothing.

The World in 1949

Legend:
- United States
- Members of NATO
- Colonies of NATO members
- Areas occupied by the United States and allies
- Dependencies of the USSR
- USSR
- Other allies of the United States
- Communist China

the Germans' initially successful eastward advance to a standstill and initiated a turning point in the war. The 1943 overthrow of Mussolini made it possible for American troops to land in southern Italy. The Red Army began to drive the Germans back westward in 1944, while the Western Allies launched the massive Normandy Invasion on D-Day

D-Day, Caen, France, 1944

(June 6, 1944) and pushed eastward toward Germany. Germany surrendered in May 1945. Japan capitulated in September 1945, after the United States dropped atomic bombs on Hiroshima and Nagasaki. World War II claimed 60 million lives and led to the destruction of entire cities. Beginning in 1945, hundreds of thousands were displaced and forced to resettle. The Holocaust had nearly extinguished Jewish life and culture in Europe. The Soviet Union bore the brunt of wartime destruction and in the end was allowed to bring half of Europe under its control.

Europe after World War II (1945)

Occupation zones in Germany and Austria
- British (United Kingdom)
- Soviet (USSR)
- French (France)
- American (USA)

- Countries under Soviet influence
- USSR

World War II

1944

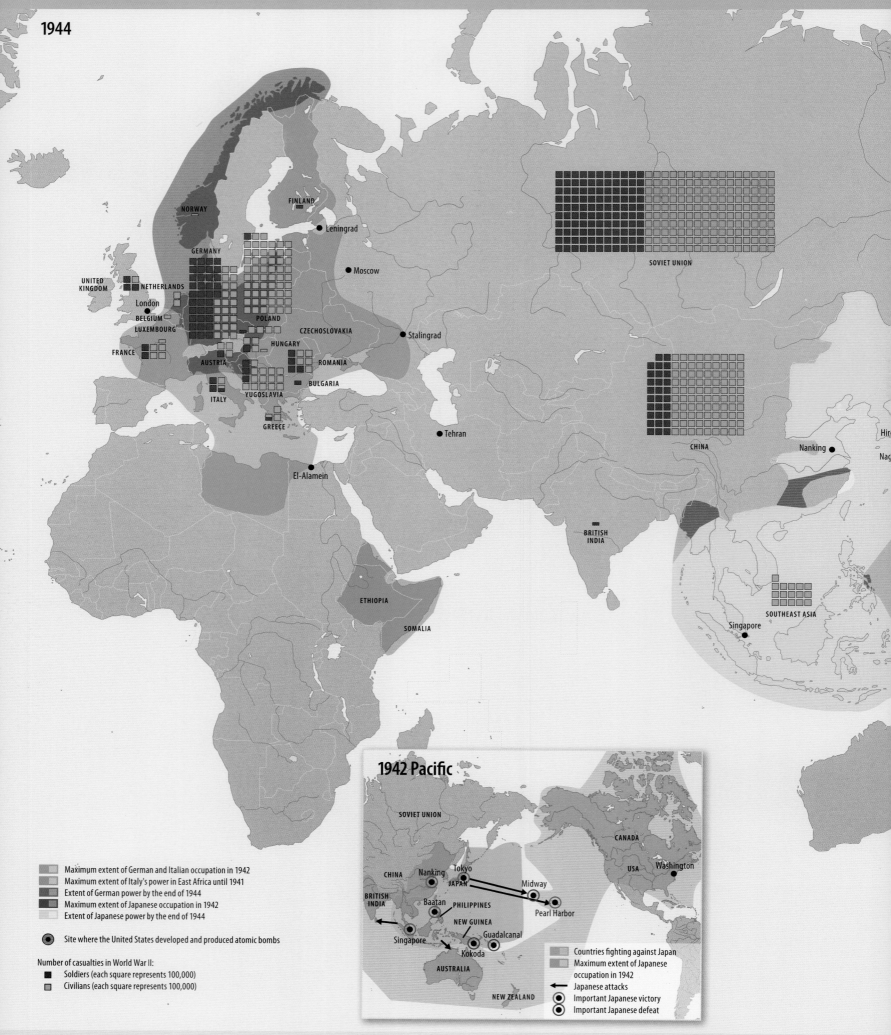

NORWAY · **FINLAND** · **GERMANY** · Leningrad · Moscow · **SOVIET UNION**

UNITED KINGDOM · **NETHERLANDS** · London · **BELGIUM** · **LUXEMBOURG** · **POLAND** · **CZECHOSLOVAKIA** · Stalingrad

FRANCE · **AUSTRIA** · **HUNGARY** · **ROMANIA** · **BULGARIA** · **ITALY** · **YUGOSLAVIA** · **GREECE** · Tehran

CHINA · Nanking

El-Alamein

ETHIOPIA · **SOMALIA** · **BRITISH INDIA** · **SOUTHEAST ASIA** · Singapore

Legend:

- Maximum extent of German and Italian occupation in 1942
- Maximum extent of Italy's power in East Africa until 1941
- Extent of German power by the end of 1944
- Maximum extent of Japanese occupation in 1942
- Extent of Japanese power by the end of 1944

- ◉ Site where the United States developed and produced atomic bombs

Number of casualties in World War II:
- ■ Soldiers (each square represents 100,000)
- ☐ Civilians (each square represents 100,000)

1942 Pacific

SOVIET UNION · **CANADA** · **USA** · Washington

CHINA · Nanking · Tokyo · **JAPAN** · Midway

BRITISH INDIA · Baatan · **PHILIPPINES** · **NEW GUINEA** · Pearl Harbor · Guadalcanal

Singapore · Kokoda

AUSTRALIA

NEW ZEALAND

- Countries fighting against Japan
- Maximum extent of Japanese occupation in 1942
- → Japanese attacks
- ◉ Important Japanese victory
- ◉ Important Japanese defeat

40

PAN

Tokyo

Midway

Pearl Harbor

CANADA

USA

Los Alamos

Washington

NEW GUINEA

Guadalcanal

1945 Pacific

SOVIET UNION

CHINA

CANADA

USA
Los Alamos

Washington

Hiroshima

JAPAN
Tokyo

Nagasaki

Kohima

Imphal

Okinawa

TINIAN

BRITISH
INDIA

Leyte

Singapore

NEW GUINEA

AUSTRALIA

NEW ZEALAND

NEW ZEALAND

Countries fighting against Japan in August 1945
Extent of Japanese dominance at the beginning of 1945
Extent of Japanese dominance in August 1945
Attacks on Japan
Important Japanese defeat
Site where the U.S. developed and produced atomic bombs
Transport of the atomic bombs
Site where atomic bomb was dropped

The World, 1949–1990

Wartime alliances between the Western powers and the USSR soon proved to be fragile and, beginning in 1947, devolved into the Cold War. This led to the de facto partitioning of the world—and in particular Europe—into two competing blocs in terms of politics, economics (the OEEC versus Comecon) and military might (NATO versus the Warsaw Pact). The most conspicuous symbol thereof was the partitioning of Germany and the city of Berlin. The Great Powers fought numerous proxy wars, especially significantly in Korea (1950–1953) and Vietnam (1964–1975), but also in numerous African and Latin American countries.

The Cuban missile crisis of 1962 brought the world to the brink of World War III. The Eastern and Western Blocs held themselves in check when it came to potential nuclear overkill, and many disarmament initiatives also started at this time.

In the shadow of these conflicts, the Asian and African continents freed themselves from colonial rule (from 1945 onward and 1957–1960, respectively), although this repeatedly led to new conflicts.

Intense economic imbalance between the Northern and Southern Hemispheres has led above all to the catastrophic impoverishment of Africa.

❶ Cuban Missile Crisis (1962)
Because of Cuba's strategic location, the conflict between the United States and the USSR escalated into the Cuban missile crisis of 1962. In the process, Cuba became a pawn in the match between two nuclear powers that subscribed to different ideologies. The Soviet Union placed troops and nuclear weapons systems in an area outside the Warsaw Pact countries for the first time, and was forced to retreat when the United States set up a naval blockade.

❷ War in Colombia (since 1948)
Civil war between various groups ended in a guerilla war directed against the government. Wars and acts of terrorism by the drug cartels followed and continue to threaten political stability.

❸ The Falkland Islands War (1982)
Argentina waged war against Great Britain over possession of the South Pacific islands it calls the **Islas Malvinas**. Though successful at first, the Argentineans eventually had to withdraw.

❹ Berlin Crisis (blockade 1948–1949, Berlin Wall built in 1961)
In 1945 Berlin was divided into four zones of occupation. Soviet-controlled East Germany erected a wall between East and West Berlin overnight in 1961.

❺ Hungarian Revolution (1956)
The Hungarian people's uprising against the communist government was initially successful, but was put down by the Soviet army.

❻ War in Yugoslavia (1991–2001)
Wars between the Serbs, Croats and other ethnic and religious groups caused the country to break apart,

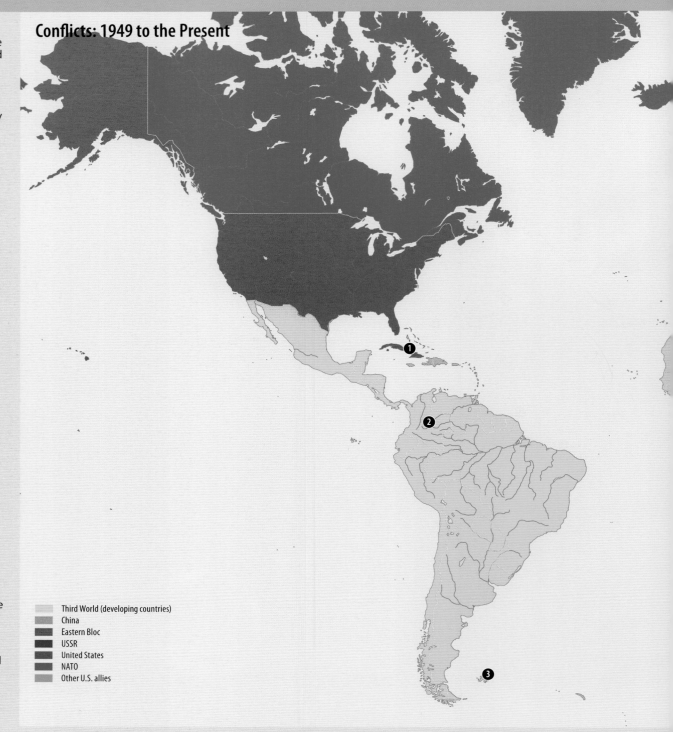

Conflicts: 1949 to the Present

Third World (developing countries)
China
Eastern Bloc
USSR
United States
NATO
Other U.S. allies

and led to ethnic cleansing and the formation of new states.

❼ Arab-Israeli Conflict (since 1948)
Conflict between Israel and its Arab neighbors has continued uninterrupted to the present day. The dispute is over parts of Israel and Palestine as well as the issue of an independent Palestinian state.

❽ Lebanon (1958–1990)
Civil war and internal crises over political alignment (Western or Arab) were followed by clashes between religious and ethnic militias as well as Palestinian groups. Israeli troops occupied southern Lebanon in 1982. The presence of the Syrian military ended civil war in 1990, but the situation remains unstable.

❾ Algeria (1954–1962, 1991–1999)
The struggle for liberation began in 1945, escalated into a bloody civil war (1954–1962) and sent shock waves through France, Algeria's colonial ruler from 1830 until 1962. When leaders elected in 1991 were banned, civil war broke out, involving terrorist acts against the government by the Islamic Salvation Front (FIS). One hundred twenty thousand people have died.

❿ War in Biafra (1967–1970)
A war in Nigeria in which the province of Biafra gained its independence; a catastrophic famine ensued.

⓫ War in the Sudan (since 1955)
From 1955 to 1972 and 1983 to 2005, wars broke out in the southern Sudan between the black, mainly Christian south, which claimed autonomy, and the Arab-Islamic north. Uprisings by the impoverished East Sudanese started in the 1990s. The present civil war between black African rebels and Arab mounted militias (Janjaweed) from western Sudan

has been going on since 2003. In the Darfur region, 400,000 people have died.

⓬ Civil War in Somalia (since 1988)
The civil war began with armed resistance to the rule of Mohamed Siad Barre (1969–1991) by various warlords and reached its zenith in 1991. No functioning central government has existed in Somalia since that time. The Somaliland and Puntland regions have formed in the northern part of the country and are relatively stable politically. The dissolution of governmental power led to terrible piracy along the Somali coastline, which the international community is trying to combat.

⓭ Congo (since 1960)
Civil war started over the secession of Katanga, a wealthy diamond province (1960–1963 and 1965), resulting in UN

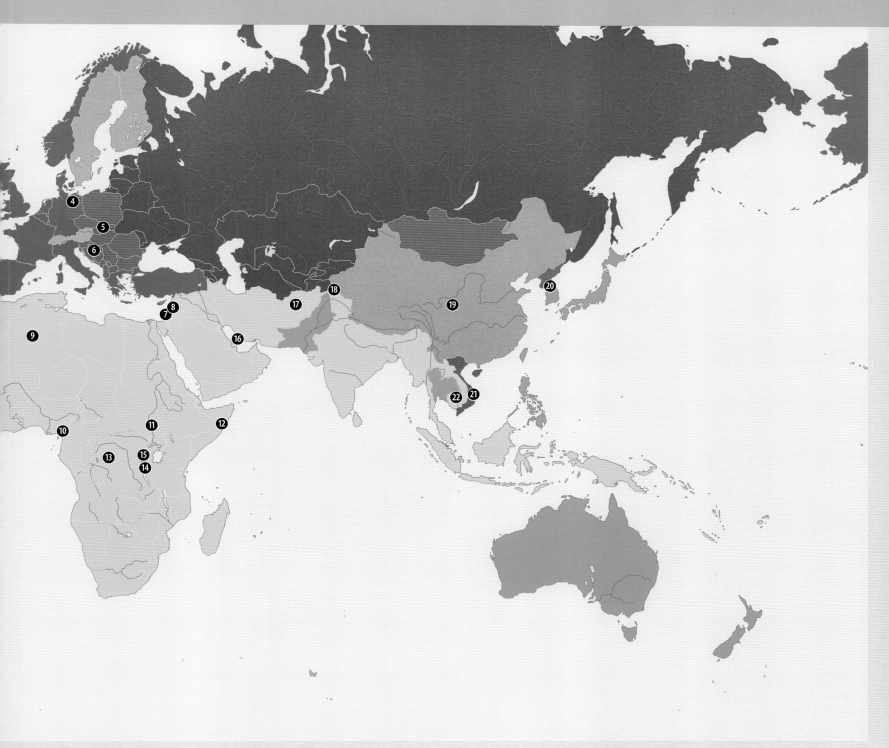

intervention. Angola invaded Katanga (Shaba 1971–1997) in 1977–1978. From 1996 to 2008 another civil war between ethnic factions led to the overthrow of Mobutu. The war in Kivu Province (1998–2003) flared up again in 2008, and UN peacekeepers are now in the region.

⑭ Genocide in Rwanda (1994)
Genocide in which members of the Hutu majority killed approximately 75 percent of the Tutsi minority.

⑮ Uganda (1971–1979)
The brutal dictator Idi Amin was known as "The African Butcher." Up to half a million people died during his reign of terror.

⑯ The Persian Gulf Wars (since 1980)
The first Gulf War (1980–1988) was between Iran and Iraq. The second Gulf War (1990–1991) pitted Iraq against a military coalition led by the United

States. The third Gulf War (2003), involving the same nations as the second conflict, ended the regime of Saddam Hussein.

⑰ Afghanistan (since 1979)
Communist takeover in 1978 led to Soviet invasion and occupation (1979–1989). The mujahideen fought the Soviets with Western support, but there was strife between mujahideen factions. The Islamic-extremist Taliban were victorious in 1996. A United States-led coalition invaded in 2001 and continues to fight the Taliban in southern Afghanistan and northwestern Pakistan.

⑱ Conflict in Kashmir (since 1949)
A series of long-standing disputes between India and Pakistan over Kashmir, an area in the northwestern region of the Indian subcontinent, including parts of the Himalayas.

⑲ "The Great Leap Forward" (1958–1962) and the Chinese Cultural Revolution
The goal of the political slogan "The Great Leap Forward" was to make the People's Republic of China into a great power. However, it left the country famine-stricken, and between 20 and 40 million people died. The Chinese Cultural Revolution was a political campaign waged by Mao Zedong to ensure his hold on power.

⑳ Korean War (1950–1953)
A war between North and South Korea that destroyed nearly all the country's industrial infrastructure and caused enormous loss of life among the civilian population.

㉑ Vietnam War (1946–1954 and 1960–1975)
Armed conflict broke out when the Vietnamese communists mounted

resistance to French colonial rule. This divided Vietnam into two states: the communist North and the anti-communist South. United States intervention began at a later time, and North Vietnam was repeatedly bombed. Heavy fighting ensued, and many civilians were massacred. The wars cost countless lives on both sides.

㉒ Genocide in Cambodia (1975–1979)
The Khmer Rouge under the leadership of Pol Pot launched a reign of terror. Around 2 million Cambodians were sacrificed to absurd "stone age communism."

The World Economy

Today

A comparison of gross national incomes (GNI) in 1970 and today makes it clear that in Southeast Asia alone, some 2.5 billion people have succeeded in climbing out of poverty within the past forty years.

The most important advances in terms of development have occurred in Asia, China, India and Indonesia, some of the most populous countries in the world. The average income of people in the countries of the former Soviet Union has also increased, although income differentials are glaring. The same is true of most countries in Latin America, where a few have even emerged as newly industrialized nations.

Along with higher standards of living, many countries in Central and South America have achieved political democratization and nationalization of revenues and resources by reducing or shutting down United States monopolies.

It is therefore all the more striking to see how little most African countries have been able to benefit economically from this upward trend. Africa is still "the world's poorhouse." Malnourishment as well as insufficient medical care and social programs continue to plague practically every country on the African continent. When it comes to looming scarcity of resources and global climate change, Africa also seems to be in a most difficult position.

1970

SPITSBERGEN (NORWAY)

SWEDEN
NORWAY
FINLAND
RUSSIA
ESTONIA
LATVIA
LITHUANIA
RUSSIA
UNITED KINGDOM
DENMARK
BELARUS
IRELAND
NETHER-LANDS
GERMANY
POLAND
LUXEMBOURG
CZECH REP.
UKRAINE
KAZAKHSTAN
MONGOLIA
FRANCE
SLOVAKIA
SWITZERL.
HUNGARY
MOLDOVA
ANDORRA
SLOVENIA
AUSTRIA
ROMANIA
ITALY
CROATIA
SERBIA
AZERBAIJAN
UZBEKISTAN
KYRGYSTAN
NORTH KOREA
PORTUGAL
SPAIN
BOSNIA HERZEGOVINA
BULGARIA
ARMENIA
GEORGIA
TURKMENISTAN
TAJIKISTAN
SOUTH KOREA
JAPAN
MONTENEGRO
GREECE
TURKEY
CHINA
ALBANIA
MACEDONIA
CYPRUS
SYRIA
IRAQ
IRAN
AFGHANISTAN
KASHMIR
LEBANON
MOROCCO
TUNISIA
ISRAEL
JORDAN
KUWAIT
NEPAL
BHUTAN
ALGERIA
LIBYA
EGYPT
SAUDI ARABIA
QATAR
PAKISTAN
BANGLADESH
TAIWAN
SAHARA
UNITED ARAB EMIRATES
MYANMAR
MAURITANIA
MALI
NIGER
CHAD
OMAN
INDIA
LAOS
ERITREA
YEMEN
THAILAND
VIETNAM
SUDAN
DJIBOUTI
SRI LANKA
CAMBODIA
PHILIPPINES
GUINEA
BURKINA FASO
NIGERIA
ETHIOPIA
SOMALIA
IVORY COAST
BENIN
CENTRAL AFRICAN REP.
CAMEROON
BRUNEI
LIBERIA
GHANA
TOGO
UGANDA
KENYA
MALAYSIA
EQUATORIAL GUINEA
GABON
CONGO
DEMOCRATIC REP. OF THE CONGO
RWANDA
SINGAPORE
BURUNDI
INDONESIA
PAPUA-NEW GUINEA
SOLOMON ISLANDS
CABINDA
TANZANIA
EAST TIMOR
ANGOLA
MALAWI
VANUATU
FIJI
ZAMBIA
MOZAMBIQUE
NEW CALEDONIA
NAMIBIA
ZIMBABWE
MADAGASCAR
BOTSWANA
AUSTRALIA
SWAZILAND
LESOTHO
SOUTH AFRICA
TASMANIA
NEW ZEALAND

Gross national income per inhabitant in US$:

- ≤ $999
- $1,000–2,999
- $3,000–4,999
- $5,000–9,999
- $10,000–19,999
- $20,000–29,999
- ≥ $30,000

45

Hunger and Poverty, Overpopulation, Terrorism, Climate Change and Natural Resources

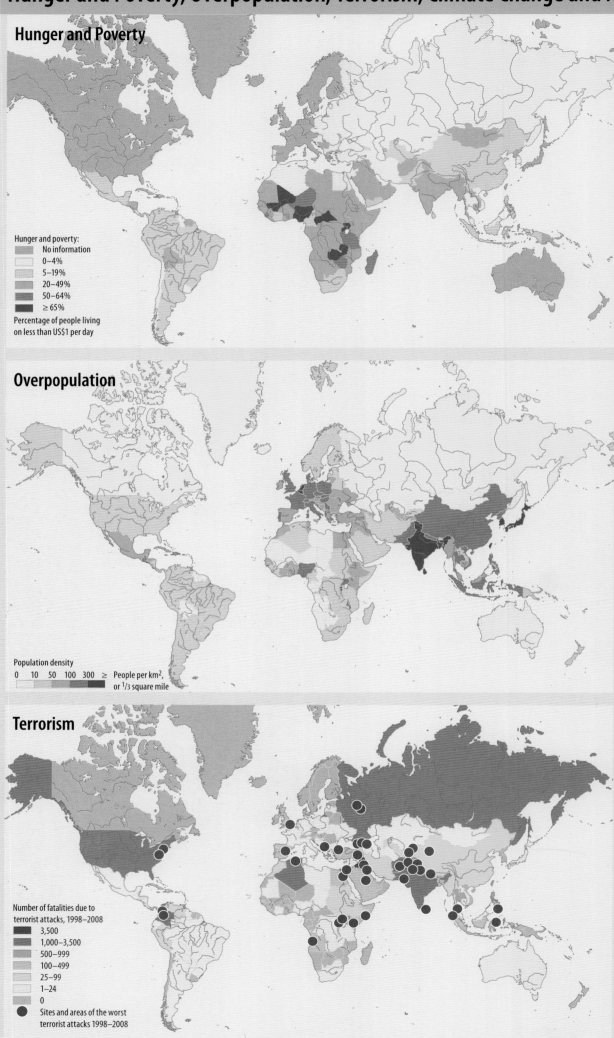

Hunger and Poverty

Hunger and poverty:
- No information
- 0–4%
- 5–19%
- 20–49%
- 50–64%
- ≥ 65%

Percentage of people living on less than US$1 per day

Overpopulation

Population density

0   10   50   100   300   ≥   People per km², or ¹/₃ square mile

Terrorism

Number of fatalities due to terrorist attacks, 1998–2008
- 3,500
- 1,000–3,500
- 500–999
- 100–499
- 25–99
- 1–24
- 0
- ● Sites and areas of the worst terrorist attacks 1998–2008

Hunger and Poverty
Even though thousands of tons of food are destroyed every year in the developed nations, 25,000 people die every day as a consequence of hunger, poverty and a lack of medical and hygienic services. Neither the repeated pledges of help by Western governments nor the aid provided by international organizations or global financial funds have thus far managed to remedy this drastic imbalance, or even get a grip on malnutrition.

Overpopulation
Since the turn of the 19th to the 20th century, the growth of the world population has increased dramatically. In the year 7000 BCE there were only approximately 10 million people on earth, and it took 2,500 years for their number to double. In 1960 there were already 3 billion people on the planet, and their number doubled to 6 billion by 1999—in less than forty years. Some estimates predict that there might be as many as 14 billion people on our planet by the end of the 21st century. This might well lead to severe competition for food, drinking water and living space.

Terrorism
Terrorism has developed into a global problem and is the domain of groups with a very tightly woven network of interrelations, even if their goals and their organizational structures might be different. Terrorism appears to some degree to have replaced international warfare in many parts of the world. And it rarely makes a difference whether attacks are directed toward governments, military institutions, or civilians with the goal of spreading anxiety and terror among the general population. In addition to guerilla tactics, the use of highly developed and modern weaponry and technology, and the media, suicide assassins instill a greater degree of fear than other tactics and often aim at targets with highly symbolic value.

Climate Change
In the course of the last decades, the average long-term temperatures have risen in many regions on Earth. There is a danger that vast areas of the planet might become desolate landscapes that are ultimately uninhabitable and that others will be permanently under water due to the rise of the level of the oceans. There is debate among scientists about whether these changes are solely a consequence of the noxious effects of greenhouse gases emitted as a result of human activity on the ozone layer in the atmosphere, or whether they might also have natural causes.

Natural Resources
Every year, 50 billion tons of natural resources are extracted from the depths of the Earth. If the developing countries reach the same living standard as most of the developed nations, the yearly mining of natural resources will have to be doubled. Even though most underdeveloped countries have access to a similar wealth of natural resources as the highly developed regions, they currently profit from only about 5 percent of these resources. An additional problem is the foreseeable depletion of many of these natural resources on our planet.

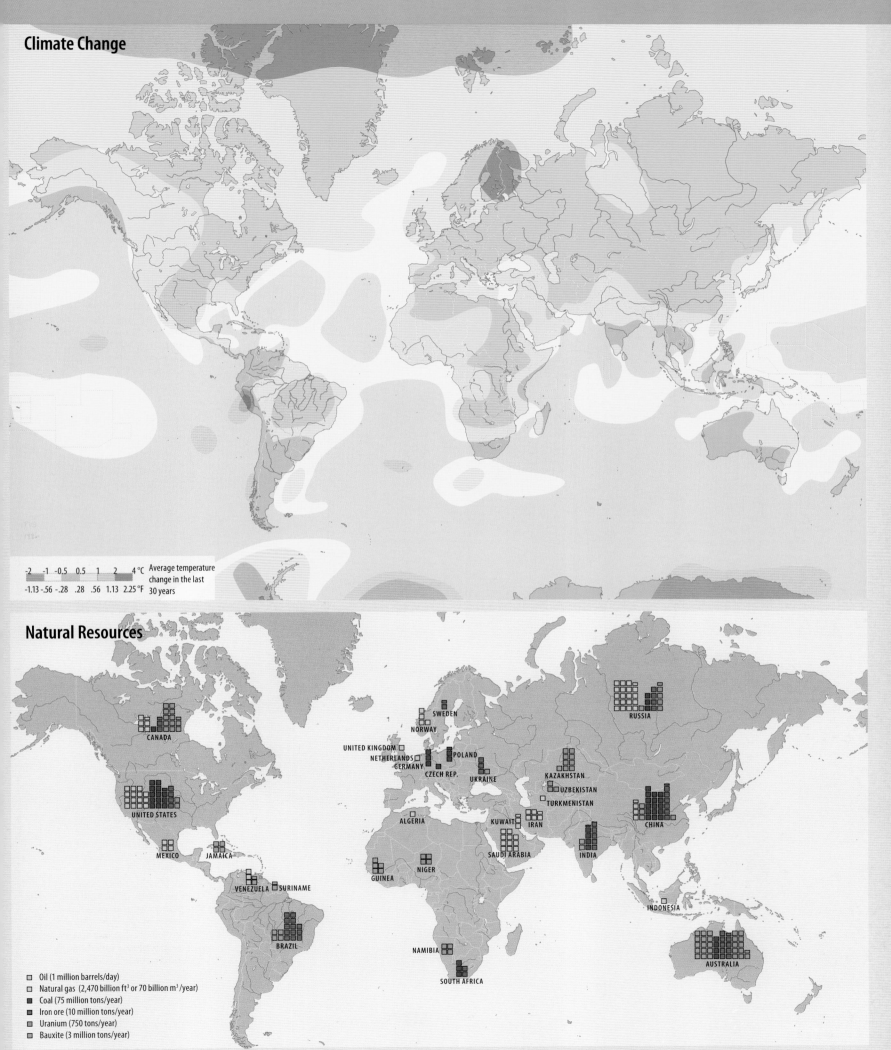

Climate Change

-2	-1	-0.5	0.5	1	2	4 °C
-1.13	-.56	-.28	.28	.56	1.13	2.25 °F

Average temperature change in the last 30 years

Natural Resources

SWEDEN

NORWAY

UNITED KINGDOM

NETHERLANDS

GERMANY

CZECH REP.

POLAND

UKRAINE

RUSSIA

KAZAKHSTAN

UZBEKISTAN

TURKMENISTAN

CANADA

UNITED STATES

MEXICO

JAMAICA

VENEZUELA

SURINAME

BRAZIL

ALGERIA

GUINEA

NIGER

NAMIBIA

SOUTH AFRICA

KUWAIT

IRAN

SAUDI ARABIA

INDIA

CHINA

INDONESIA

AUSTRALIA

- ▫ Oil (1 million barrels/day)
- ▫ Natural gas (2,470 billion ft³ or 70 billion m³/year)
- ◼ Coal (75 million tons/year)
- ◼ Iron ore (10 million tons/year)
- ◼ Uranium (750 tons/year)
- ◼ Bauxite (3 million tons/year)

World Religions

North American Protestantism

After 1620, the religions of the European immigrants formed the most prevalent Protestant communities in North America. Protestants now make up 51.3 percent, Mormons 1.7 percent and other evangelical groups 1.6 percent of the population.

European Christianity

Bloody religious wars broke out after Martin Luther (1483–1546) and other reformers sparked the Reformation in 1517. Western and central Europe were split between the supremacy of the Protestant churches (in Great Britain, Holland, northern Germany and Scandinavia) and Catholicism (southern Germany, Poland and southern Europe). Today most countries are multidenominational, and only in Northern Ireland does the potential for conflict between Christian denominations play a significant role.

Central and South American Catholicism

The Spanish and Portuguese conquerors proselytized to the native populations, yet elements of Indian religions have survived within Latin American Catholicism. Liberation theology, which arose in the mid-20th century, is a religious movement with political roots that understands itself as the "voice of the poor." More recently, evangelical revivalist movements have become enormously popular in Latin America.

Muslims in Africa

In 2000, Africa's population was ca. 45 percent Christian and 40.6 percent Muslim. What is remarkable is that 87.6 percent of Muslims and only ca. 9 percent of Christians lived in northern Africa, whereas in South Africa, Christians represented 82 percent and Muslims 2.2 percent of the population. In Africa both Christianity, and to an even greater extent Islam, have incorporated elements of traditional and folk religions.

Dominant religions:
- Catholic
- Protestant
- Orthodox
- Other Christian denominations
- Sunni Muslim
- Shi'ite Muslim
- Hindu
- Buddhist and East Asian religions (Tibetan Buddhism, Confucianism, Shinto)
- Other religions

Russian Orthodoxy
About 60 percent of the inhabitants belong to the Orthodox Church, which is the second-largest Christian community in the world after the Roman Catholic Church. After the collapse of state socialism, it experienced a revival in Eastern Europe.

Hinduism and Buddhism in Asia
The predominant religion in India and Nepal is Hinduism, whose adherents constitute 13 percent of the world population. In India, conflicts repeatedly arise between Hindus, Muslims and Sikhs. Buddhism represents 5.9 percent of the world population and is widespread in Bhutan, Cambodia, China, Japan, Tibet, Laos, Myanmar, North and South Korea, Singapore, Thailand and Vietnam.

Islam in the Middle East, Northern Africa, Central and Southeast Asia
With some 1.3 billion followers, Islam is the second-largest religion after Christianity. The two major groups within Islam are the Sunnis (90 percent) and the Shi'ites (particularly in Iran, Iraq, Azerbaijan, Bahrain and Lebanon), who are about 10 percent of all Muslims. The most densely populated Muslim country is Indonesia.

Australian Christianity
Census information gathered in 2001 showed that 26.6 percent of Australians consider themselves to be Roman Catholics, 20.7 percent belong to Anglican churches and another 20.7 percent to other Protestant denominations.

The United Nations (UN)

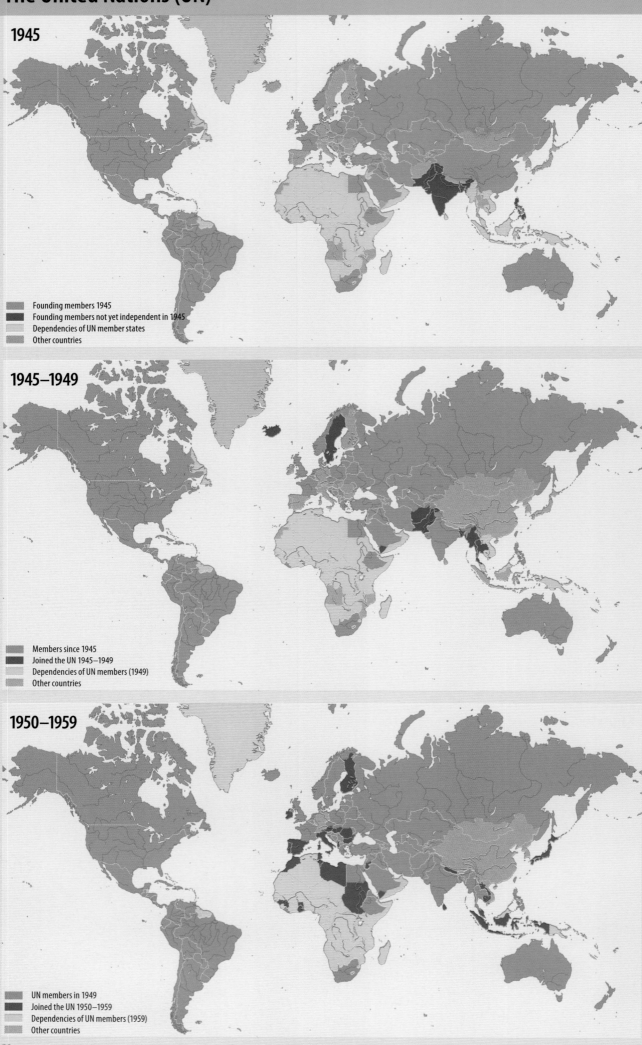

1945

- Founding members 1945
- Founding members not yet independent in 1945
- Dependencies of UN member states
- Other countries

1945–1949

- Members since 1945
- Joined the UN 1945–1949
- Dependencies of UN members (1949)
- Other countries

1950–1959

- UN members in 1949
- Joined the UN 1950–1959
- Dependencies of UN members (1959)
- Other countries

The United Nations, or UN for short, was founded in 1945 with the goal of preventing future wars.

Even while World War II was still raging, United States President F.D. Roosevelt was already undertaking efforts to replace the League of Nations with a new organization with a greater scope for action. The concrete form this organization would take was agreed upon during conferences held in Dumbarton Oaks and San Francisco. On June 26, 1945, representatives of fifty countries signed the United Nations Charter. In the following years, nations that had lost World War II and those that had declared their independence after the war also became members. In December 1947 the UN published the Universal Declaration of Human Rights.

Today the UN has 192 member states. In 2002 Switzerland, traditionally a neutral state, also joined. The structure of the UN adapts the principle of equality among nations (the UN General Assembly, in which every country has one vote) to actual power relations in the world, reflecting the dominant position of the major powers. The United States, Russia (formerly the USSR), the United Kingdom, France and China are therefore permanent members of the Security Council, the most important body of the UN, in which they also have veto power. In addition, ten other nonpermanent members sit on the Security Council, elected for a period of two years. The Security Council votes on and coordinates military intervention by the UN when conflicts break out. In recent years, there have been proposals to extend the number of the council's permanent members. Germany, Japan, Brazil and India have been mentioned as possible candidates. The General Assembly elects a secretary-general as head of the organization for a term of five years.

Organs of the UN:
- General Assembly
- Security Council
- Economic and Social Council
- Trusteeship Council
- International Court of Justice

1899 The first international peace conference devoted to finding peaceful solutions to international disputes and military conflicts is held in The Hague.

1902 The Permanent Court of Arbitration takes up its work.

1919 Founding of the League of Nations (forerunner of today's United Nations) with its headquarters in Geneva, established as part of the Treaty of Versailles to promote international cooperation and to achieve peace and security (especially in Europe)

1945 Founding of the United Nations (UN), with its headquarters in New York City

Secretaries-General of the United Nations

1946–1952   Trygve Lie (Norway)

1953–1961   Dag Hammarskjöld (Sweden)

1962–1971   U Thant (Myanmar)

1972–1981   Kurt Waldheim (Austria)

1982–1991   Javier Pérez de Cuéllar (Peru)

1992–1996   Boutros Boutros-Ghali (Egypt)

1997–2006   Kofi A. Annan (Ghana)

since 2007   Ban Ki-moon (Republic of Korea)

UNESCO The United Nations Educational, Scientific and Cultural Organization, dedicated to protecting the world's cultural heritage and monuments, and financed by the wealthier UN states

UNHCR The office of the United Nations High Commissioner for Refugees, whose task is to provide international protection and find solutions for the problems faced by refugees and displaced persons

UNICEF The United Nations Children's Fund raises funds in the industrialized countries to acquire aid for children in the Third World to help them live in accordance with the Convention on the Rights of the Child; among the organization's chief priorities are fighting illiteracy and child labor.

UNDP The United Nations Development Programme manages and distributes funds from voluntary contributions by the member states.

UNEP The United Nations Environment Programme takes steps to protect the environment and improve quality of life without placing undue burdens on future generations. It devotes special effort to preserving the world's reservoirs of clean drinking water.

IAEA The International Atomic Energy Agency monitors peaceful use of atomic energy around the world.

WHO The World Health Organization coordinates international cooperation in healthcare, trying to improve medical care and hygiene conditions in the developing countries, or so-called Third World.

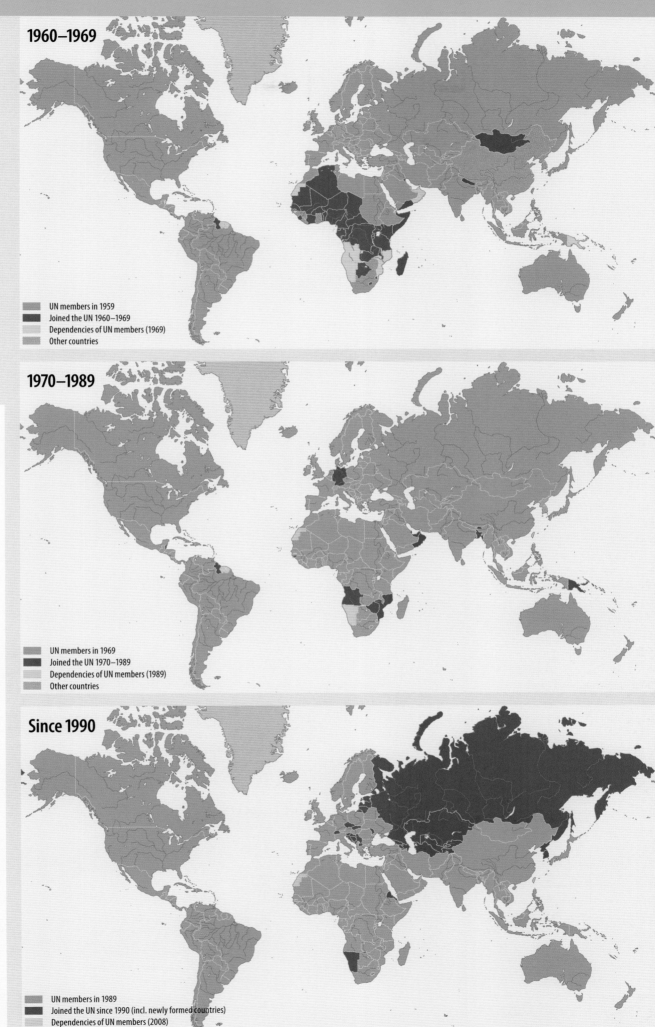

1960–1969

UN members in 1959
Joined the UN 1960–1969
Dependencies of UN members (1969)
Other countries

1970–1989

UN members in 1969
Joined the UN 1970–1989
Dependencies of UN members (1989)
Other countries

Since 1990

UN members in 1989
Joined the UN since 1990 (incl. newly formed countries)
Dependencies of UN members (2008)
Other countries

The Nobel Peace Prize Laureates

Year	Recipients	Nation
1901	Henri Dunant	Switzerland
	Frédéric Passy	France
1902	Élie Ducommun	Switzerland
	Charles-Albert Gobat	Switzerland
1903	Sir Randal Cremer	Great Britain
1904	Institute of International Law	Belgium
1905	Baroness Bertha von Suttner	Austria-Hungary
1906	Theodore Roosevelt	USA
1907	Ernesto Teodoro Moneta	Italy
	Louis Renault	France
1908	Klas Pontus Arnoldson	Sweden
	Fredrik Bajer	Denmark
1909	Auguste Beernaert	Belgium
	Paul Henri d'Estournelles de Constant	France
1910	Permanent International Peace Bureau	Switzerland
1911	Tobias Asser	Netherlands
	Alfred Hermann Fried	Austria-Hungary
1912	Elihu Root	USA
1913	Henri La Fontaine	Belgium
1917	International Committee of the Red Cross	Switzerland
1919	Woodrow Wilson	USA
1920	Léon Victor Bourgeois	France
1921	Hjalmar Branting	Sweden
	Christian Lange	Norway
1922	Fridtjof Nansen	Norway
1925	Sir Austen Chamberlain	Great Britain
	Charles Gates Dawes	USA
1926	Aristide Briand	France
	Gustav Stresemann	Germany
1927	Ferdinand Buisson	France
	Ludwig Quidde	Germany
1929	Frank Billings Kellogg	USA
1930	Nathan Söderblom	Sweden
1931	Jane Addams	USA
	Nicholas Murray Butler	USA
1933	Sir Norman Angell	Great Britain
1934	Arthur Henderson	Great Britain
1935	Carl von Ossietzky	Germany
1936	Carlos Saavedra Lamas	Argentina
1937	Lord Robert Cecil	Great Britain
1938	Nansen International Office for Refugees	Switzerland
1944	International Committee of the Red Cross	Switzerland
1945	Cordell Hull	USA
1946	Emily Greene Balch	USA
	John Raleigh Mott	USA
1947	Friends Service Council/Friends Service Committee	Great Britain/USA
1949	Lord Boyd Orr	Great Britain
1950	Ralph Bunche	USA
1951	Léon Jouhaux	France
1952	Albert Schweitzer	France
1953	George C. Marshall	USA
1954	United Nations High Commissioner for Refugees	UN
1957	Lester Bowles Pearson	Canada
1958	Georges Pire	Belgium
1959	Philip Noel-Baker	Great Britain
1960	Albert Lutuli	South Africa
1961	Dag Hammarskjöld	Sweden
1962	Linus Pauling	USA
1963	International Committee of the Red Cross	Switzerland
	League of Red Cross Societies	Switzerland

Year	Recipients	Nation
1964	Martin Luther King Jr.	USA
1965	United Nations Children's Fund (UNICEF)	UN
1968	René Cassin	France
1969	International Labour Organization (ILO)	Switzerland
1970	Norman E. Borlaug	USA
1971	Willy Brandt	Germany
1973	Henry Kissinger	USA
	Le Duc Tho (declined)	Vietnam
1974	Seán MacBride	Ireland
	Eisaku Satō	Japan
1975	Andrei Sakharov	Soviet Union
1976	Betty Williams	Northern Ireland
	Mairéad Corrigan-Maguire	Northern Ireland
1977	Amnesty International	Great Britain
1978	Anwar el-Sadat	Egypt
	Menachem Begin	Israel
1979	Mother Theresa	India
1980	Adolfo Pérez Esquivel	Argentina
1981	United Nations High Commissioner for Refugees	UN
1982	Alva Myrdal	Sweden
	Alfonso García Robles	Mexico
1983	Lech Walesa	Poland
1984	Desmond Tutu	South Africa

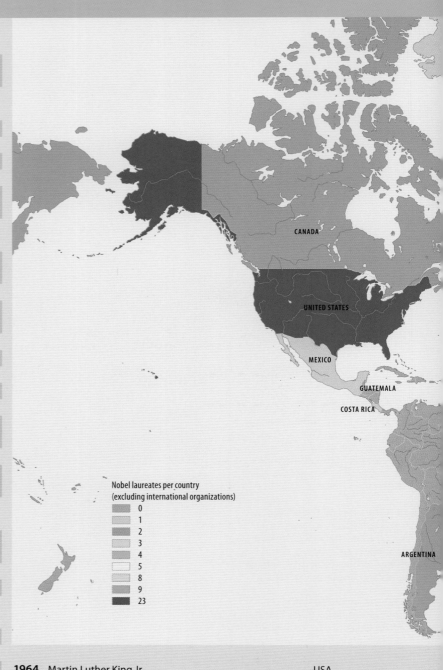

Nobel laureates per country
(excluding international organizations)

- 0
- 1
- 2
- 3
- 4
- 5
- 8
- 9
- 23

1985	International Physicians for the Prevention of Nuclear War	USA
1986	Elie Wiesel	USA
1987	Oscar Arias Sánchez	Costa Rica
1988	United Nations Peacekeeping Forces	UN
1989	Tenzin Gyatso, The 14th Dalai Lama	Tibet
1990	Mikhail Gorbachev	Soviet Union
1991	Aung San Suu Kyi	Myanmar
1992	Rigoberta Menchú Tum	Guatemala
1993	Nelson Mandela	South Africa
	Frederik Willem de Klerk	South Africa
1994	Yasir Arafat	Palestine
	Shimon Peres	Israel
	Yitzhak Rabin	Israel
1995	Sir Joseph Rotblat	Great Britain
	Pugwash Conferences on Science and World Affairs	Canada
1996	Carlos Filipe Ximenes Belo	East Timor
	José Ramos-Horta	East Timor
1997	International Campaign to Ban Landmines	USA
	Jody Williams	USA
1998	John Hume	Northern Ireland
	David Trimble	Northern Ireland
1999	Médecins Sans Frontières	Switzerland
2000	Kim Dae Jung	South Korea

2001	United Nations	UN
	Kofi Annan	Ghana
2002	Jimmy Carter	USA
2003	Shirin Ebadi	Iran
2004	Wangari Muta Maathai	Kenya
2005	International Atomic Energy Agency (IAEA)	UN
	Mohamed el-Baradei	Egypt
2006	Muhammad Yunus/Grameen Bank	Bangladesh
2007	Intergovernmental Panel on Climate Change (IPCC)	UN
	Al Gore	USA
2008	Martti Ahtisaari	Finland
2009	Barack H. Obama	USA

No Nobel Peace Prize was awarded in the years 1914–1916, 1918, 1923–1924, 1928, 1932, 1939–1943, 1948, 1955–1956, 1966–1967 and 1972.

The World Since 1990

Europe

Liberalization was made possible by the change of course initiated in the USSR in 1985 under Mikhail Gorbachev. It culminated in peaceful revolutions (except in Romania) in 1989 that ended the existing socialist systems in Eastern Europe and brought free elections and the reunification of Germany in 1990. In 1991 the USSR dissolved and regrouped into the Commonwealth of Independent States (CIS), of which Russia is still the most powerful. Despite nationalist tendencies, most Central and Eastern European countries adopted Western social models and prepared to become members of the EU, which many joined in 2004. In parallel with the dissolution of the Eastern Bloc, a bloody civil war broke out in 1990 in the former nation of Yugoslavia. Fought in many phases, the war led to the creation of several new states, accompanied by horrors such as massacres (the worst in Srebrenica in 1995), mass rape and ethnic cleansing. The war ended with all former sub-republics achieving independence, the last of which was Kosovo (2008).

Africa

The end of the Eastern Bloc also ushered in change in many African regimes that had been supported by the USSR. In some of these countries the ruling socialist parties now had to share power with other factions. In the ever-restless Congo, Mobutu's kleptocracy was put to an end in 1997. In Rwanda a wave of genocides erupted in 1994 as the Hutu majority attacked the Tutsi minority, resulting in a million deaths within just a few weeks. Conflicts between various ethnic groups continue today in the Sudan and in Somalia, where government authority collapsed after 1991. A positive development can be seen in South Africa, where the end of apartheid progressed relatively peacefully starting in 1990—in part thanks to the towering personality of Nelson Mandela. The southernmost African countries, in particular, are affected by an extremely high incidence of AIDS.

The Americas

After 1990 Latin American countries, with mounting self-confidence, began to free themselves from the political influence of the United States. Democratic or moderate left-wing systems now prevail in some of them. The United States tried to find its way as the sole remaining superpower. Its efforts at engagement in the Middle East and the Arab world, often perceived as heavy-handed, made it a target of Islamist criticism and accusations of global Western cultural imperialism. The utterly unexpected terrorist attacks of September 11, 2001, perpetrated by the Islamist group Al Qaeda, shook the United States to its very core, leading to major tightening of foreign and domestic policy (including Guantanamo, a maximum security prison in Cuba). As part of its "War on Terror," the United States removed the radical Islamist Taliban regime from power in Afghanistan in 2001 and toppled the heavily armed Iraqi dictator Saddam Hussein in 2003.

Asia

The sixty-year-old conflict between Israel and the Palestinians entered an especially bloody phase in late 2008/early 2009; a peaceful solution seems not to be in sight. In the Muslim countries, Islamist strivings are for now balanced by more secular or moderate Islamic state regimes. A kind of "cold war" continues between the emerging nations of India and Pakistan, both now heavily armed, in part due to disputes over the Kashmir region. While Japan and the four "Asian tigers" are participating in global economic developments, China is mobilizing its own prodigious economic resources; whether the Communist Party will be able to maintain its monopoly on political power as the country increasingly opens up economically remains to be seen.

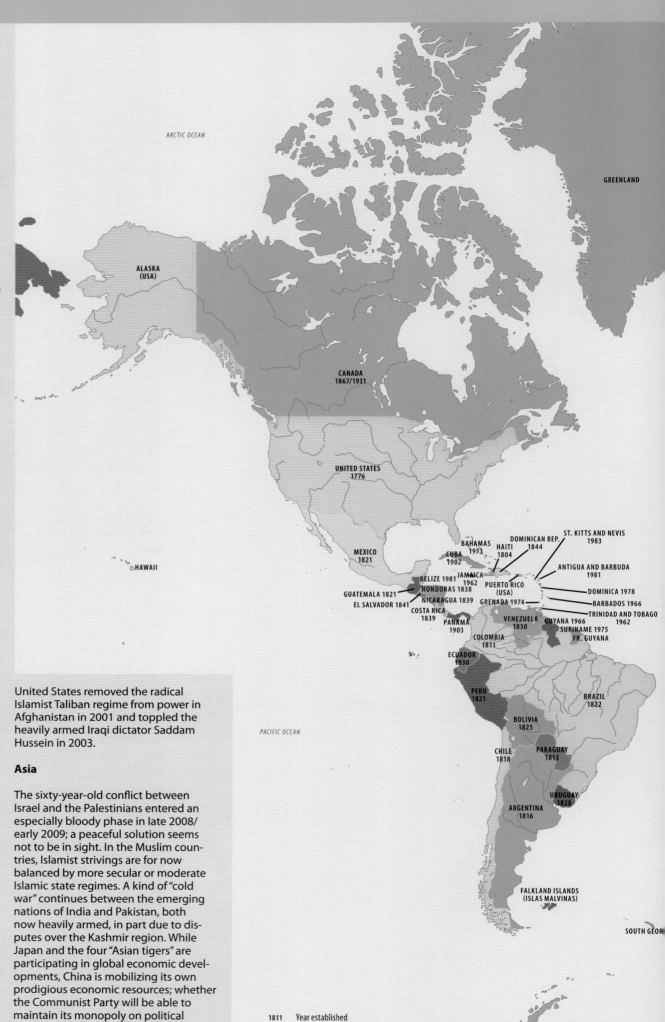

1811　Year established

SPITSBERGEN (NORWAY)

ARCTIC OCEAN

ICELAND
1944

SWEDEN
1523

NORWAY
1905

FINLAND
1917

ESTONIA 1991

LATVIA 1991

LITHUANIA 1991
RUSSIA

RUSSIA 1991

UNITED
KINGDOM
1707

DENMARK
987/1849

NETHER-
LANDS
1815

IRELAND
1921

GERMANY
1949

POLAND
1918

BELARUS
1991

LUXEMBOURG
1890

BELGIUM 1830

CZECH REP. 1993

UKRAINE 1991

KAZAKHSTAN 1991

MONGOLIA
1921

FRANCE
843/1789

SWITZERL.
1815

AUSTRIA

SLOVAKIA 1993

HUNGARY 1918

MOLDOVA 1991

ANDORRA
1993

SLOVENIA 1991

ITALY
1861

CROATIA 1991

ROMANIA 1878

AZERBAIJAN 1991

GEORGIA 1994

UZBEKISTAN 1991

KYRGYSTAN 1991

PORTUGAL
1640/1910

SPAIN
1479/
1975

BOSNIA &
HERZEGOVINA 1991

SERBIA 1992

ARMENIA
1991

TURKMENISTAN
1991

TAJIKISTAN 1991

NORTH KOREA 1948

MONTENEGRO 2006

BULGARIA
1908

GREECE
1822

TURKEY 1923

CHINA

SOUTH KOREA
1948

JAPAN
660 BCE/
1867 CE

ALBANIA 1912

MACEDONIA
1991

CYPRUS 1960

LEBANON 1946

SYRIA
1946

IRAQ
1932

IRAN
1979

AFGHANISTAN
1919

KASHMIR

PACIFIC OCEAN

MOROCCO
1956

TUNISIA
1956

ISRAEL 1948

JORDAN
1946

KUWAIT 1961

NEPAL
1923

BHUTAN 1910

TAIWAN 1949

WESTERN SAHARA

ALGERIA
1962

LIBYA
1951

EGYPT
1922

SAUDI ARABIA
1932

QATAR
1971

UNITED
ARAB EMIRATES 1971

PAKISTAN
1947

BANGLADESH
1971

MYANMAR
1947

LAOS 1954

MAURITANIA
1960

MALI
1960

NIGER
1960

CHAD
1960

SUDAN
1956

OMAN 1971

ERITREA
1993

YEMEN 1918

INDIA
1947

THAILAND
1238/1782

VIETNAM
1945/1954

SENEGAL 1960

A 1965

BURKINA FASO
1960

NIGERIA
1960

DJIBOUTI 1977

CAMBODIA
1954

PHILIPPINES
1946

A BISSAU
1974

GUINEA 1958

ETHIOPIA
1270

SRI LANKA
1948

BRUNEI 1984

SIERRA LEONE 1961

IVORY
COAST
1960

BENIN
1960

CENTRAL AFRICAN REP.
1960

MALAYSIA 1963

LIBERIA
1847

CAMEROON
1960

UGANDA
1962

KENYA
1963

SINGAPORE 1959

GHANA
1960

TOGO
1960

EQUATORIAL
GUINEA
1968

GABON
1960

CONGO 1960

DEMOCRATIC
REP. OF
THE CONGO
1960

RWANDA 1962

BURUNDI 1962

INDONESIA
1949

PAPUA-
NEW GUINEA
1975

CABINDA

TANZANIA
1961

SEYCHELLES
1976

EAST TIMOR
2002

SOLOMON ISLANDS
1978

ANGOLA
1975

ZAMBIA
1964

MALAWI 1946

COMOROS
1975

INDIAN OCEAN

VANUATU
1980

FIJI
1970

NAMIBIA
1990

ZIMBABWE
1980

MOZAMBIQUE
1975

MADAGASCAR
1960

MAURITIUS
1968

NEW CALEDONIA

BOTSWANA
1966

AUSTRALIA
1901/1931

SWAZILAND 1968

LESOTHO 1966

SOUTH AFRICA
1910/1931/1994

TASMANIA

NEW ZEALAND
1907/1931

OCEAN

SOUTHERN OCEAN

ANTARCTICA

GROENLANDIÆ PARS

OCEANVS SEP
TENTRIONALIS

Circulus
Arcticus

ISLANDIA

Fris:
land

OCEANVS

DEVCALEDONIVS

SVE
CIA

HIBERNIA

Noort
zee

OCEANVS

OCCIDENTALIS

MARE

ATLANTICVM

HISPANIA

BARBARIA

FESSA

MAROCHO

AFRICÆ

MARI

Angli

Galli

Belgi

Castiliani

Venetiani

Cautum est Illustr. DD. Ordinum
Hollandiæ et Westfrisiæ privilegio
ne quis Tabulas istas quatuor Orbis
terræ partium cibra voluntatem
Auctoris imitetur, sub pœna in
Diplomate expressa.

EUROPE

The term "Europe" comes from the Semitic word *ereb*, meaning "dark." But where exactly is Europe? Geographically speaking, it can be identified as being west of the Ural Mountains and north of the Bosporus. But looking back through history, the question becomes more complex. Dividing the ancient Roman, Greek and Egyptian epochs into a European, an African and an Asian history is not very helpful. In the following section, therefore, the history of North Africa, the Middle East and Mesopotamia have been included as part of European history until the emergence of Islam, and the history of North Africa from about 600 CE is addressed as both African history and Arabian history. Turkey remains part of Europe—where it would most likely place itself culturally, economically and politically.

Europe: An Overview	**58**
The Crusades	62
Europe in Detail	**74**
The Achievements of Antiquity	76
Roman Provinces and Trade Routes	82
Biblical Times Until 70 CE	84
Judaism	86
Christianity	88
The Legacy of Antiquity	94
The Most Important Royal Houses of Europe	98
Medieval Castles	102
Medieval Religious Orders and Monasteries	104
The Great European Universities of the 13th–15th Centuries	108
The Plague in the 14th Century	109
Significant Wars and Battles in European History	118
Scandinavia	**138**
United Kingdom and Ireland	**142**
The Low Countries	**156**
Germany and Switzerland	**162**
Central Eastern Europe	**186**
The Baltic Region and Russia	**212**
France	**230**
Spain and Portugal	**244**
Italy	**252**
The Popes	264
Southeast Europe	**266**

Caption: *Map of Europe by Willem Blaeu,* ca. 1630, on which the borders of Poland and Lithuania represent their largest historical extent.

Europe: An Overview

Archaic Period

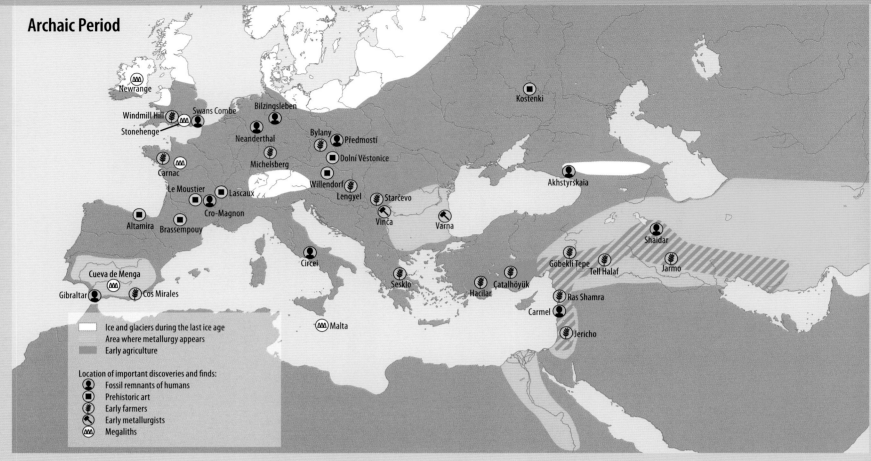

Ice and glaciers during the last ice age
Area where metallurgy appears
Early agriculture

Location of important discoveries and finds:
- Fossil remnants of humans
- Prehistoric art
- Early farmers
- Early metallurgists
- Megaliths

2.5 million–8000 BCE Paleolithic Period or Old Stone Age: The earliest humans are hunters and gatherers and make rudimentary tools out of stone.

~150,000–30,000 BCE Neanderthal man

~35,000–15,000 BCE Significant artistic activity takes place; humans create sculptures and cave paintings.

~30,000 BCE Cro-Magnon man

~8000–4500 BCE Mesolithic Period or Middle Stone Age: Glaciers melt following the most recent ice age, the Earth's temperature warms up and the

sea level rises by about 425 feet (130 m). People become more settled.

~6000–2000 BCE The Neolithic revolution, characterized by the spread of farming and animal husbandry, begins in different regions at various times; it starts much earlier in Anatolia and Mesopotamia than in northern Europe.

3000–1000 BCE Bronze Age: Humans learn to produce bronze from copper and tin.

~3000 BCE Sumer is settled in Mesopotamia (land of the two rivers, the Tigris and the Euphrates), and the Sumerian

culture flourishes in several city-states.

2707–2216 BCE Old Kingdom in Egypt, during which the great pyramids and the Great Sphinx are constructed

2350–2154 BCE The Akkadian empire supplants the Sumerians in Mesopotamia.

2010–1550 BCE The Middle Kingdom in Egypt

2000–1450 BCE Minoan civilization, noted for its accomplishments in building, trade and writing, reaches its zenith in Crete.

1950–1380 BCE The Old Assyrian empire dominates northern Mesopotamia.

1849–1595 BCE Old Babylonian empire: The Code of Hammurabi, an extensive collection of Babylonian laws with a long tradition, dates from this period.

1700–800 BCE The Iron Age, in which people learn to make tools out of iron, begins at different times in different regions: as early as ca. 1700 BCE in Mesopotamia, but not until ca. 1100 BCE in Greece.

1600–1000 BCE The Mycenaean civilization flourishes in Greece.

1550–1070 BCE The New Kingdom in Egypt

~1400 BCE The Middle Babylonian empire

1380–912 BCE The Middle Assyrian empire

1335–1200 BCE The Hittite empire rules an area in modern-day Turkey and Asia Minor.

1259 BCE The Hittites and Egyptians conclude what is perhaps the world's first peace treaty.

~1200 BCE The Phoenicians, a people known as traders and craftsmen, develop cities

in what is now Lebanon and spread their culture through colonization.

~1030–926 BCE The kingdom of Israel is ruled by the kings Saul, Ish-bosheth, David and Solomon. Following their reigns, the kingdom is divided.

912–610 BCE The Neo-Assyrian empire

814 BCE Founding of the Phoenician settlement of Carthage in North Africa

800 BCE The Etruscans' city-based culture flourishes in northern Italy.

Antiquity

776 BCE The first Olympic Games are held in Greece.

753 BCE Legendary founding of Rome

700–500 BCE The Greeks establish numerous colonies around the Mediterranean region

626–539 BCE Neo-Babylonian empire of the Chaldeans in lower Mesopotamia reaches its peak.

587 BCE The Neo-Babylonian ruler Nebuchadnezzar II plunders Jerusalem and the Jews are sent into exile (Babylonian Exile).

Bronze Age and First Empires

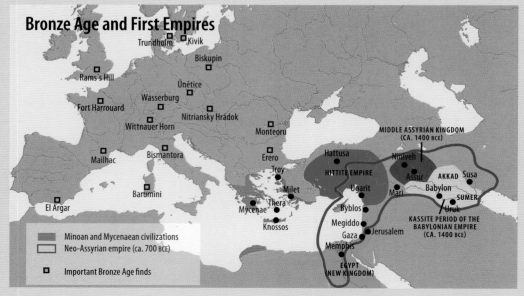

Minoan and Mycenaean civilizations
Neo-Assyrian empire (ca. 700 BCE)

- Important Bronze Age finds

Ancient Greece and Hellenism

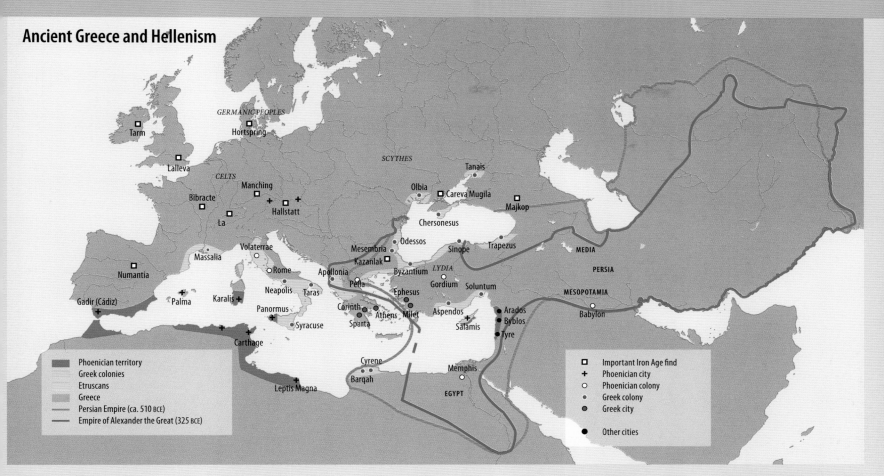

Map legend (left):
- Phoenician territory
- Greek colonies
- Etruscans
- Greece
- Persian Empire (ca. 510 BCE)
- Empire of Alexander the Great (325 BCE)

Map legend (right):
- □ Important Iron Age find
- + Phoenician city
- ○ Phoenician colony
- • Greek colony
- ● Greek city
- ● Other cities

Map labels: GERMANIC PEOPLES, Tarm, Hortspring, Lalleva, CELTS, Bibracte, Manching, Hallstatt, La, SCYTHES, Tanais, Olbia, Careva Mugila, Majkop, Chersonesus, MEDIA, Volaterrae, Massalia, Mesembria, Odessos, Sinope, Trapezus, Numantia, Rome, Apollonia, Kazanlak, Byzantium, LYDIA, PERSIA, Neapolis, Taras, Pella, Gordium, Soluntum, MESOPOTAMIA, Gadir (Cádiz), Palma, Karalis, Panormus, Corinth, Ephesus, Aspendos, Arados, Babylon, Syracuse, Athens, Milet, Byblos, Sparta, Salamis, Tyre, Carthage, Cyrene, Memphis, Barqah, EGYPT, Leptis Magna

Timeline

5th–4th centuries BCE Greek culture flourishes.

550–330 BCE The Persian Achaemenid empire

from 521 BCE Rise of the Persian Empire under Darius I. Persian soldiers invade the Balkans and Greece.

509–27 BCE Era of the Roman Republic, precursor to the Roman Empire

336–323 BCE Rule and military campaigns of the Macedonian King Alexander the Great

326 BCE Alexander the Great defeats King Porus of India.

Anatolia In addition to the sanctuary of Göbekli Tepe (ca. 9500 BCE), ancient Anatolia was also home to large settlements in the style of Çatalhöyük (ca. 6500 BCE) that represent the oldest form of organization yet discovered in the transition from small communities to large, village-like settlements (the beginnings of town planning). In the 2nd century BCE, the Indo-European Hittites moved southward from the steppes north of the Black Sea and settled the region that is now Turkey. Their empire vied with Egypt for hegemony in the Middle East. The massive influx of the Sea Peoples from the Aegean around 1200 BCE led to its destruction. In the first millennium BCE, the Greeks settled the coast of Anatolia.

321–30 BCE The Ptolemaic dynasty rules in Egypt.

320–64 BCE Seleucid empire rules Syria, Palestine and Iran.

44 BCE Julius Caesar, influential Roman ruler, is murdered.

27 BCE The imperial era in Rome begins.

98–117 CE The Roman Empire reaches its greatest extent under Emperor Trajan.

306–337 Reign of Emperor Constantine the Great, who converts to Christianity.

350 The Franks undertake raids into the Roman Empire.

375 The Huns expel the Goths from the Black Sea region.

378 The Goths defeat Rome near Adrianopolis; the great migration of European peoples begins (barbarian invasions).

392 Christianity becomes the Roman Empire's state religion.

395 Roman Empire is divided.

410 Visigoths conquer Rome.

418 The Visigoths settle in southern France.

429–439 The Vandals establish an empire in North Africa that lasts until 534.

5th–6th centuries Angles, Saxons and Jutes arrive in Britain.

453 Attila the Hun dies on the night of his wedding with the Germanic princess Ildico.

476 Romulus Augustulus, the last emperor of Rome, is deposed.

The Roman Empire at Its Greatest Extent

Map legend:
- Imperium Romanum (Roman Empire), 2nd century
- Parthian empire

Map labels: BRITANNIA, Londinium, GERMANIA, SARMATIA, Colonia Agrippina, Carnuntum, Lutetia-Parisiorum, GALLIA, PANNONIA, DACIA, ARMENIA, Mediolanum, ILLYRICUM, THRACIA, HISPANIA, ITALIA, Massalia, Roma, Neapolis, Pergamum, ASSYRIA (PERSIA), Pompeii, ACHAIA, ASIA, Antiochia, Gades (Cádiz), Corinthus, Ephesus, MESOPOTAMIA, SYRIA, MAURETANIA, Carthago, Caesarea, Hierosolyma, Alexandria, AFRICA, AEGYPTUS

Europe: An Overview

The Early Middle Ages began with the fall of Rome. Tribes that had taken part in the period of migration settled down. The Frankish empire arose, and in the 9th century divided to create France and the Holy Roman Empire of the German Nation.

486/487 The Merovingian king Clovis I defeats Syagrius, the last Roman ruler in Gaul, and lays the foundations for the Frankish kingdom (later empire).

498 Clovis I and the Frankish aristocracy are baptized as Christians.

493–526 Theodoric the Great, king of the Ostrogoths since 473, conquers Italy and rules as king of Italy.

~500–800 Small kingdoms emerge in England.

507–711 Visigoth kingdom of Toledo

511 Clovis I dies; the Frankish kingdom is divided among his four sons.

527–565 Emperor Justinian I rules the Byzantine Empire.

529 Symbolic beginning of the Middle Ages: Benedict of Nursia founds Monte Cassino monastery, and Emperor Justinian closes the Academy in Athens after nine centuries.

534 Decline of the Vandal kingdom in North Africa

552 Decline of the Ostrogoth kingdom in Italy

568 The Lombards conquer Italy; end of the migration period

597 The Anglo-Saxons are converted to Christianity by St. Augustine of Canterbury.

613–629 Unification of the Frankish kingdom under Chlotar II

751 With Pepin the Younger, the Carolingians succeed the Merovingians as Frankish rulers.

756 Founding of the Emirate (later Caliphate) of Córdoba; Muslims rule the Iberian Peninsula.

774 Charlemagne becomes ruler of the Lombard kingdom.

800 Charlemagne is crowned Holy Roman Emperor in Rome.

843 The Treaty of Verdun divides the Frankish empire into three parts.

870 The Treaty of Mersen (Meerssen) partitions the Frankish Empire into France and what will become the Holy Roman Empire of the German Nation.

882 Founding of the Kievan Rus state in eastern Europe

~900 Magyars enter the Carpathian Basin, leading to the fall of the Great Moravian Empire.

911 Normans (Vikings) settle in northern France (Normandy).

925 Rise of the kingdom of Croatia

955 The Magyars are defeated by Otto I, king of the Germans, at the Battle of Lechfeld.

962 Otto I the Great is crowned emperor, giving rise to the Holy Roman Empire.

987 Hugh Capet becomes king of France.

997 St. Stephen I assumes power (from 1000 as king of the Hungarians); the Magyars convert to Christianity.

1054 Strife between the Catholic (Roman) and Orthodox (Byzantine) churches leads to the East-West Schism.

1066 Battle of Hastings: The Normans, under the leadership of William the Conqueror, defeat the Anglo-Saxons and establish Norman rule of England.

1077 Height of the Investiture Controversy over secular versus religious power. Henry IV, Holy Roman emperor, does penance before the pope at Canossa ("Walk to Canossa").

507–534: Frankish Kingdoms

ca. 700–814: Arabs Penetrate Europe

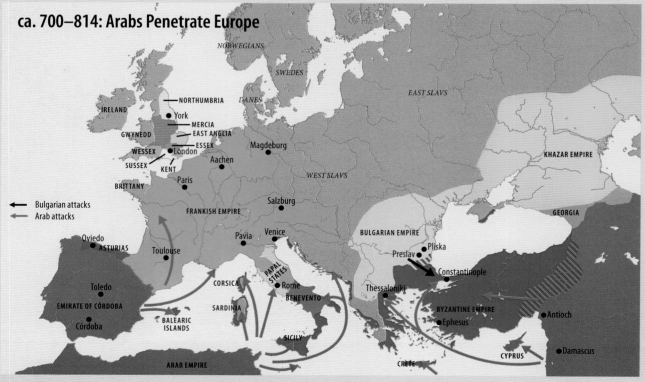

10th–11th Centuries: The Middle Ages

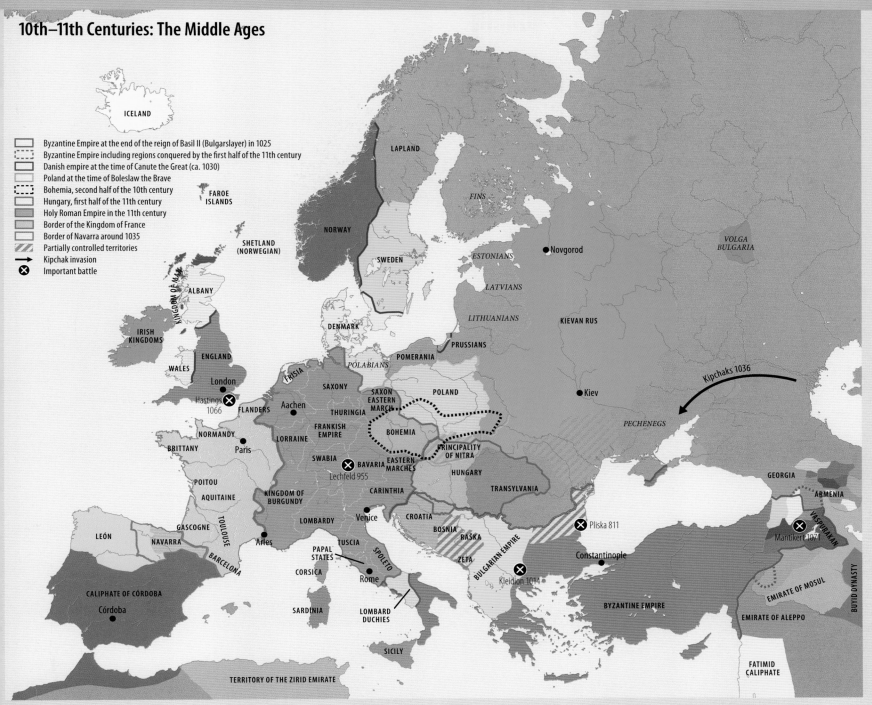

Byzantine Empire at the end of the reign of Basil II (Bulgarslayer) in 1025
Byzantine Empire including regions conquered by the first half of the 11th century
Danish empire at the time of Canute the Great (ca. 1030)
Poland at the time of Boleslaw the Brave
Bohemia, second half of the 10th century
Hungary, first half of the 11th century
Holy Roman Empire in the 11th century
Border of the Kingdom of France
Border of Navarra around 1035
Partially controlled territories
Kipchak invasion
Important battle

The Franks were a western Germanic tribal confederation that began to settle Gaul in the 3rd century. They originated in what is now the Netherlands (Salian Franks, Salii) and along the Rhine River (Rhine Franks, Ripuarian Franks). Starting in 482 they were united by Clovis, the first king of all Franks and founder of the Merovingian dynasty.

The Vandals were an eastern Germanic tribe. In the 5th century they crossed the Rhine and moved through Spain and into North Africa. In 429 they founded their kingdom there under the outstanding leader Gaiseric (Genseric), and in 455 plundered Rome. Their rule ended when the Byzantines conquered North Africa in 534.

The Burgundians left central Europe with the Vandals, but made it only as far as the Rhine region. Their first kingdom was destroyed by the Roman general Aetius in 436, and the second kingdom, on Lake Geneva, was conquered about a hundred years later by the Franks.

The Goths An east Germanic tribe from southern Sweden (Götaland), they settled along the Vistula River in the first century and later founded a kingdom in today's Ukraine. In the 3rd century they split into Visigoths and Ostrogoths. The Visigoths conquered Rome in 410 and later founded empires in southern France and northern Spain. In the early 6th century, the Ostrogoths formed an empire in Italy under Theodoric the Great, with its capital at Ravenna. In 552 the empire was broken up by the Byzantine Empire.

The Vikings Anglo-Saxon chronicles describe them as Danes, Frankish accounts as Normans ("men from the north"). The ancestors of today's Danes, Norwegians and Swedes undertook raids and campaigns of conquest during the 8th and 9th centuries, plundering many European cities. For a time they ruled Britain, and they also settled in Iceland, northern France (from 911) and later southern Italy (including Sicily) as well as in Russia. From their base in northern France the Normans conquered England in 1066.

The Slavs Sharing similar languages, this group came from the region between the upper Bug, middle Dnieper and Don rivers. In the 5th and 6th centuries they migrated northwest, southeast and westward as far as the Elbe, splitting up, partly as a result of Magyar expansion, into west, east and south Slavs.

The Magyars Originally a nomadic Finno-Ugric ethnic group, they came from the central Asian steppes in the 9th century led by Prince Árpád and made looting raids as far as Rome until their defeat at the Battle of Lechfeld (955). Thereafter they settled along the Danube in the former Roman province of Pannonia. They converted to Christianity after 997, founding the kingdom of Hungary.

The Lombards (Langobards) A west Germanic tribe from southern Scandinavia that settled in the Elbe region in the late first century BCE. In the 2nd century they joined other Germanic peoples in invading Pannonia. Traversing the territory of the modern-day Czech

Republic and Moravia, they penetrated the central Danube area. After 568 they settled in northern Italy, driving out the Byzantines. These lands were henceforth known as Lombardy; in 774 they became part of Charlemagne's Frankish empire.

The Saxons were a western Germanic tribe that occupied the region between the Harz mountains and the North Sea, or between the Rhine and Elbe rivers. Around 500 they ruled England jointly with the Angles, and the two tribes formed a federation. Forcefully incorporated into Charlemagne's realm in the Saxon wars of 772–804, they were compelled to convert to Christianity.

Avars A confederation of nomadic ethnic groups from western Siberia. In the 6th century they forced the eastern Turks westward and pushed into Pannonia, where they subjugated the Slavs. In the 7th century they successfully quelled a Slavic revolt. In the Avar wars (796–803) they were conquered by Charlemagne and the Bulgarians.

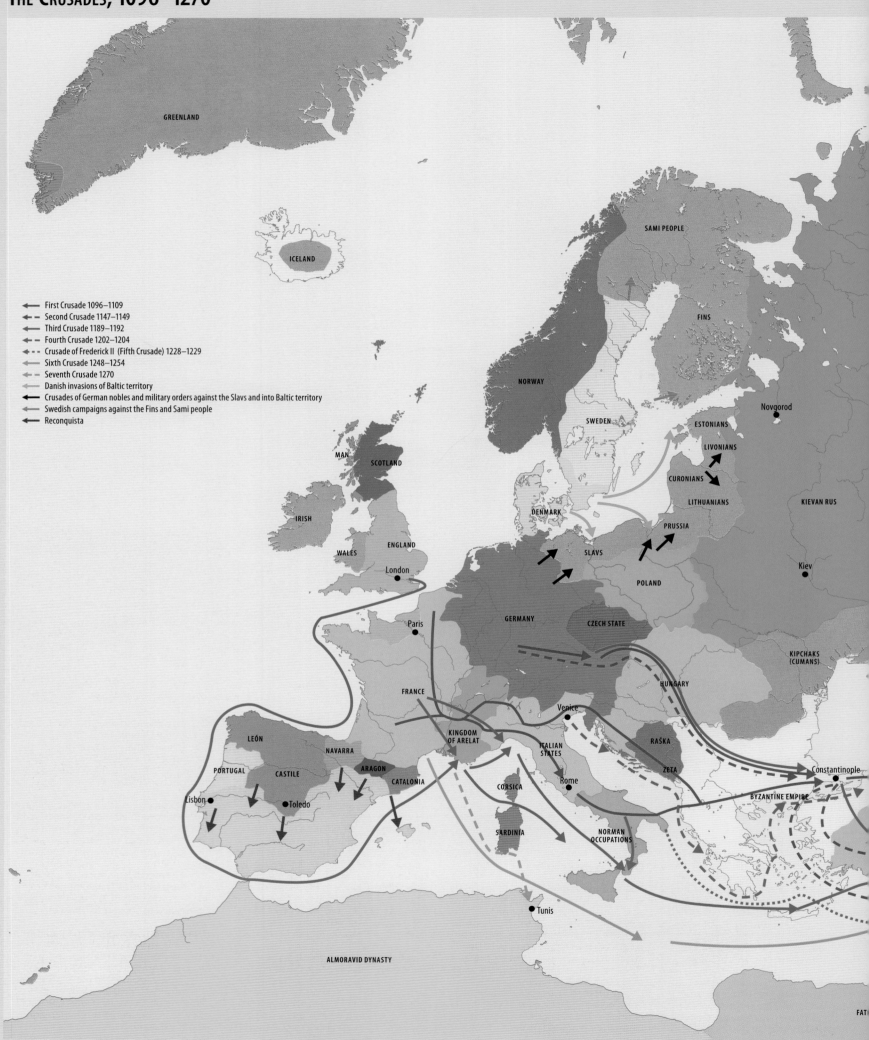

The Crusades, 1096–1270

← First Crusade 1096–1109
←- Second Crusade 1147–1149
← Third Crusade 1189–1192
← Fourth Crusade 1202–1204
←·- Crusade of Frederick II (Fifth Crusade) 1228–1229
← Sixth Crusade 1248–1254
←- Seventh Crusade 1270
← Danish invasions of Baltic territory
← Crusades of German nobles and military orders against the Slavs and into Baltic territory
← Swedish campaigns against the Fins and Sami people
← Reconquista

GREENLAND

ICELAND

SAMI PEOPLE

FINS

NORWAY

SWEDEN

ESTONIANS

LIVONIANS

CURONIANS

LITHUANIANS

Novgorod

KIEVAN RUS

MAN

SCOTLAND

IRISH

WALES

ENGLAND

London

DENMARK

PRUSSIA

SLAVS

POLAND

Kiev

Paris

FRANCE

GERMANY

CZECH STATE

KIPCHAKS
(CUMANS)

HUNGARY

Venice

RAŠKA

LEÓN

NAVARRA

KINGDOM
OF ARELAT

ITALIAN
STATES

ZETA

Constantinople

PORTUGAL

CASTILE

ARAGON

CATALONIA

CORSICA

Rome

BYZANTINE EMPIRE

Lisbon

Toledo

SARDINIA

NORMAN
OCCUPATIONS

Tunis

ALMORAVID DYNASTY

FAT

62

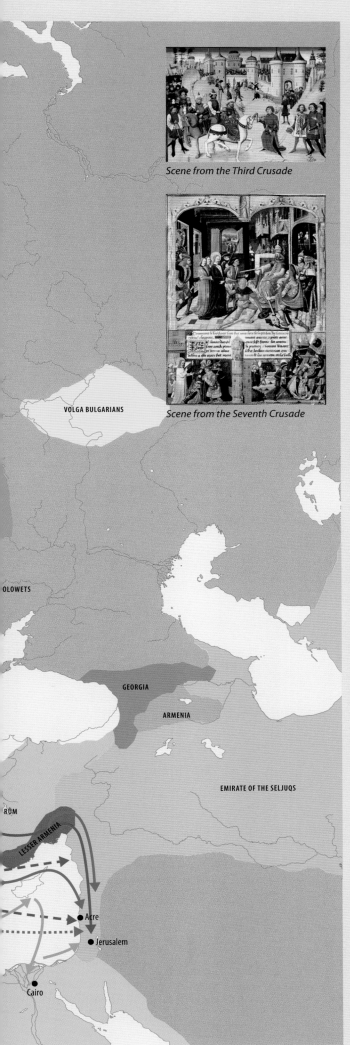

Scene from the Third Crusade

Scene from the Seventh Crusade

The Crusader States in the Near East ca. 1035 (between the First and Second Crusades)

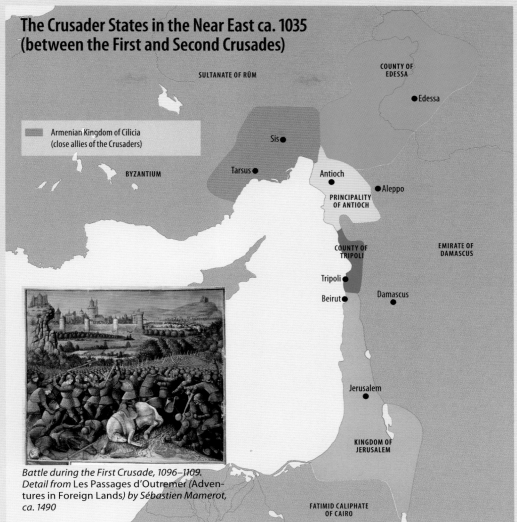

Armenian Kingdom of Cilicia
(close allies of the Crusaders)

Battle during the First Crusade, 1096–1109. Detail from Les Passages d'Outremer *(Adventures in Foreign Lands) by Sébastien Mamerot, ca. 1490*

The official objective of the Crusades was the conquest of Jerusalem and the liberation of the Holy Land from the hands of Muslims. But there also were political and economic motives.

1096–1109 First Crusade
After a difficult but successful conquest of Jerusalem, the Crusaders massacred the "infidels" in the year 1099 and founded the first Christian kingdom in the Holy Land (kingdom of Jerusalem) as well as several Christian principalities.

1147–1149 Second Crusade
When the county of Edessa was lost to Muslims in 1144, French and German kings, supported by St. Bernard of Clairvaux, called for a new crusade. It ended, however, in a disastrous defeat.

1189–1192 Third Crusade
In 1187, Sultan Saladin reconquered Jerusalem for Islam. The shock resulting from this event motivated the Third Crusade, initially under the leadership of Emperor Frederick I Barbarossa of the Holy Roman Empire. After he drowned in Asia Minor in 1190, King Philip II Augustus of France and King Richard Lion-heart of England competed for leadership. They managed to conquer several cities in the Holy Land, but were not able to maintain control over them. The Christians captured by Sultan Saladin were treated with great chivalry.

1202–1204 Fourth Crusade
Under the influence and leadership of the city of Venice, this Crusade deviated toward the Byzantine Empire, supposedly to help resolve internal disputes about succession to the throne. Constantinople was sacked in 1204 and a "Latin empire" was established (until 1261).

1212 Children's Crusade
This Crusade was fueled by popular piety; thousands of women and children set out on their own mission to free Jerusalem, spurred on by ecstatic preaching. This Crusade dissolved in southern France and in Italy, where many of the children were sold into slavery.

1217–1221 Fifth Crusade
The main proponents of the Fifth Crusade were the Hungarian king, Andrew II, and Duke Leopold VI of Austria. After failing to reclaim the Holy Land, the remaining Crusaders took Damietta, Egypt, after 1219 to gain a foothold near Jerusalem, but lost this city as well only two years later, in 1221.

1228–1229 Crusade of Frederick II
Emperor Frederick II managed to regain Jerusalem for the Christians by negotiating a truce with the sultan of Egypt. In 1244, however, Christians lost control of the city again and permanently.

1248–1254 Crusades of St. Louis
King Louis IX of France directed his first crusade not to the Holy Land, but to Damietta, Egypt. The Crusade failed: Louis IX was captured by the Muslims and had to be ransomed. He died in Tunis in 1270 during his second campaign (the Seventh Crusade). In the Holy Land, the last Crusader state of Acre in Palestine was conquered by the Mamluk dynasty of Egypt.

Europe: An Overview

ca. 1500: Dawn of the Modern Age

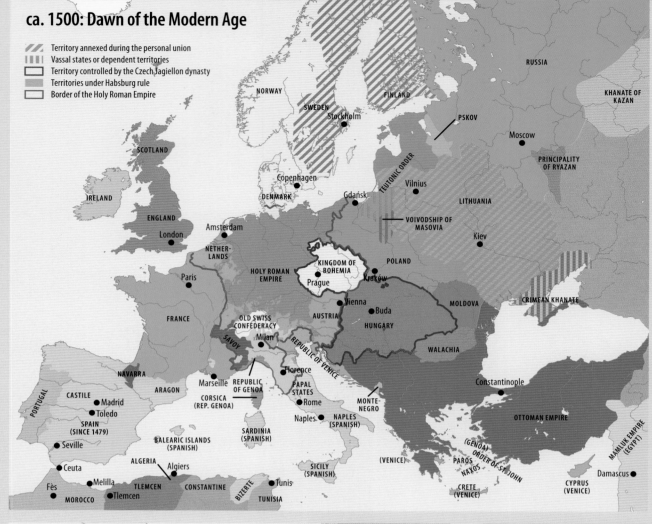

Territory annexed during the personal union
Vassal states or dependent territories
Territory controlled by the Czech Jagiellon dynasty
Territories under Habsburg rule
Border of the Holy Roman Empire

1337–1453 Hundred Years' War between England and France to determine who will rule France. The series of conflicts ends with the English expelled from most of France.

1347–1352 An epidemic of bubonic plague, also known as the Black Death, rages through Europe, killing as many as one of every three people in Europe.

1453 Ottomans conquer Constantinople, bringing about the downfall of the Byzantine Empire.

1492 Christians defeat the emirate of Granada, last stronghold of the Muslims (Reconquista), reestablishing a Christian Spain. Queen Isabella I supports voyages of exploration that led to European "discovery" of the New World and subsequent rapid colonization.

1517 German monk and theologian Martin Luther posts his *Ninety-Five Theses* protesting excesses of the Catholic Church, launching the Reformation.

1519–1556 Emperor Charles V rules Spain, the Netherlands, the German empire, northern Italy and the New World.

1523 The end of the Kalmar Union: Sweden declares its independence from Denmark.

1526 King Louis II of Hungary dies in the Battle of Mohács against the Ottomans; the Habsburgs ascend the Hungarian and Bohemian thrones.

ca. 1660–1700: Absolutism

Border of the Holy Roman Empire

1529 The Ottomans lay siege to Vienna for the first time.

1534 The Anglican Church breaks with the papacy in Rome after King Henry VIII of England comes into conflict with the pope.

1534 The Jesuit Order is founded and becomes the driving force behind the Catholic Counter-Reformation.

1555 Peace of Augsburg between Emperor Charles V and Protestant (Lutheran) princes seals the legal division of Christendom into Catholics and Protestants; Calvinists are excluded.

1572 St. Bartholomew's Day Massacre of Huguenots (Protestants) in France

Spain Thanks to its many discoveries overseas and a policy of large-scale colonial imperialism, Spain became the wealthiest world power in the 16th century. The Habsburg rulers supported the Counter-Reformation. The kingdom experienced economic and political decline in the 17th century.

France Following the Hundred Years' War with England, religious conflicts arose between the Calvinist Huguenots and the Catholics. Ongoing foreign policy conflicts with the Habsburgs and Louis XIV's wars of expansion led to an economic crisis and in 1789 to revolution. In the social and political upheaval that followed, Napoleon rose to power and conquered wide stretches of Europe.

1598 The Edict of Nantes ends the religious wars that have been raging in France since 1562, granting Protestants some measure of rights and protection.

1608 Founding of the Protestant Union, a military alliance between Protestant princes in the Holy Roman Empire

1609 Founding of the Catholic League

1618 Defenestration of Prague: Three imperial governors are literally thrown out of windows by representatives of the Protestant Estates, a defiant gesture that signals the start of the Thirty Years' War.

1624–1642 Leading statesman Cardinal Richelieu transforms France into a major power.

1642–1648 Conflicts with the king and parliament lead to civil war in England.

1643–1715 Louis XIV of France, the Sun King, greatly impacts the style of governance in Europe.

1648 The Peace of Westphalia ends the Thirty Years' War.

from 1648 Brandenburg-Prussia gradually becomes a major power.

from 1650 The medieval feudal system of princes gives way to absolutism.

1653–1658 Under Lord Protector Oliver Cromwell, England's status rises and the Puritans prevail.

1683 Ottomans again lay siege to Vienna, but are repelled.

1685 King Louis XIV revokes the Edict of Nantes and bans Protestantism in France.

1698 Peter the Great initiates modernization policies in Russia.

1700–1714 The Spanish Habsburg dynasty dies out. The ensuing War of the Spanish Succession between Austria and France ends with a compromise that favors France, and Bourbons take the Spanish throne.

1700–1721 In the Great (Second) Northern War, several powers fight with Sweden for control of the Baltic region.

After 1815: Restoration and the Pre-March Era

Border of the German Confederation

GRAND DUCHY OF FINLAND
KINGDOM OF NORWAY (PERSONAL UNION)
KINGDOM OF SWEDEN (PERSONAL UNION)
St. Petersburg
Bergen
Oslo
Stockholm
Moscow
Riga
COURLAND
Smolensk
RUSSIAN EMPIRE
Edinburgh
HELGOLAND (BRITISH)
Copenhagen
KINGDOM OF DENMARK
Gdańsk
Vilnius
Dublin
Hamburg
KINGDOM OF PRUSSIA
Kiev
UNITED KINGDOM OF GREAT BRITAIN AND IRELAND
Amsterdam
HANOVER
Berlin
Warsaw
London
NETHER-LANDS
KINGDOM OF SAXONY
POLAND
REPUBLIC OF KRAKÓW
Kraków
Paris
Prague
KINGDOM OF BAVARIA
Vienna
AUSTRIAN EMPIRE
MOLDOVA
CRIMEA
KINGDOM OF FRANCE
SWITZERLAND
PIEDMONT
Milan
Belgrade
WALACHIA
Turin
Venice
Genoa
Sarajevo
Sofia
Marseille
Florence
PAPAL STATES
Rome
MONTENEGRO (PARTLY AUTONOMOUS)
Thessaloníki
Constantinople
KINGDOM OF PORTUGAL
KINGDOM OF SARDINIA
CORSICA
GRAND DUCHY OF TUSCANY
Naples
Lisbon
Madrid
Barcelona
KINGDOM OF SPAIN
BALEARIC ISLANDS (SPANISH)
KINGDOM OF THE TWO SICILIES
OTTOMAN EMPIRE
Cádiz
Ceuta
Melilla
Oran
Algiers
Tunis
IONIAN ISLANDS (SINCE 1815 BRITISH PROTECTORATE)
MALTA (BRITISH)
CRETE
MOROCCO
ALGERIA
TUNISIA

In the end, Russia takes control of the Baltic region and part of Finland; Sweden loses its hegemony in the north.

1701 Prussia becomes a kingdom.

1740–1745 Prussia takes over Silesia in a war with Austria.

1756–1763 In the Seven Years' War, which involves most European powers and takes place both on the Continent and abroad in their colonized territories, Austria is unable to win back Silesia.

1770 Russia destroys the Ottoman fleet and conquers the northern Caucasus and the Crimea.

1772–1795 The Partition of Poland: Russia, led by Empress Catherine the

Great; Prussia under Frederick the Great; and Habsburg Austria divide Poland-Lithuania between themselves.

1789–1795 The French Revolution abolishes the feudal system and deposes the monarchy.

1795–1799 Creation of vassal states by the Netherlands, Switzerland and Italy.

1804 General Napoleon Bonaparte has himself crowned emperor of the French and undertakes several military campaigns, pushing eastward as far as Russia.

1809 Finland becomes part of Russia.

1814–1815 The Congress of Vienna, involving negotiations among Austria,

Russia, Prussia, Great Britain, France and other countries, restores order and reorganizes Europe following Napoleon's defeat and the end of the Holy Roman Empire.

1815 Napoleon's final defeat at Waterloo. The German Confederation is created as result of the Congress of Vienna: the German states are to remain independent, but connected in a confederation.

1829 Greece achieves independence from the Ottoman Empire.

1830 Belgium declares independence from the Netherlands.

1848 Revolutions in Germany, France, Austria, Hungary and Italy.

Netherlands The Protestant northern Netherlands fought for and achieved independence from the Spanish Habsburgs in 1648. In the 17th century the country became a considerable naval and trading power. Catholic southern Netherlands remained a Habsburg colony and became the Kingdom of Belgium in 1830.

England The Hundred Years' War, in which England lost almost all its territories on the Continent to France, was followed by the Wars of the Roses between the houses of Lancaster and York. Under the Tudors, Henry VIII broke ties with the papacy in Rome. Starting in the 17th century, England acquired large colonies overseas. Great Britain was created in the early 18th century through alliance with the Scottish crown.

Although the kingdom lost some of its North American colonies (the United States), it was still able to build the world's largest empire in the 19th century.

Austria Initially a Habsburg power base, the dynasty was divided in 1556 between a Spanish and an Austrian (imperial) line and then weakened by the Thirty Years' War and the War of Spanish Succession. Constant wars with the Ottoman Empire followed in the 16th and 17th centuries. In 1804 Austria became an independent empire; the Habsburgs lost the German imperial crown in 1806.

Hungary After losing the Battle of Mohács in 1526, two-thirds of the kingdom fell into the hands of the Ottomans, and the rest was

controlled by the Austrian Habsburg line. In the following century Hungary gradually began to recover its lost territories. At the same time, there were almost constant rebellions of the aristocracy against the Habsburgs.

Prussia Beginning in 1640, the Great Elector, Frederick William of Brandenburg, began to create a new, centralized state in northern Germany. His son Frederick I took advantage of the fact that the original territory of the Duchy of Prussia lay outside the imperial borders; he therefore did not require the emperor's consent to call himself the king of Prussia (1701). Prussia soon became Austria's chief rival in the ongoing struggle for hegemony over the German states.

Poland Poland had been embroiled in constant battles with its neighboring states since the late 16th century. The Polish nobles elected the king, which led to ongoing battles among them and prompted the European powers to back their own candidates. The weakened country became easy prey for Russia and Prussia at the end of the 18th century, which divided its lands between them.

Russia Peter the Great made great strides toward modernization from 1698 onward. In wars with Poland and Sweden, he reconquered the territories his predecessors had lost. His policies were continued, in particular by Catherine II. Russia claimed hegemony not only over Poland, but also over the ailing Ottoman Empire.

Europe: An Overview

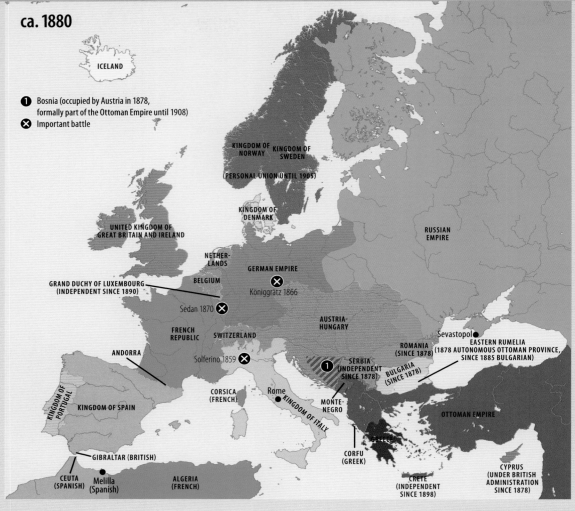

ca. 1880

ICELAND

❶ Bosnia (occupied by Austria in 1878, formally part of the Ottoman Empire until 1908)

❌ Important battle

KINGDOM OF NORWAY KINGDOM OF SWEDEN
(PERSONAL UNION UNTIL 1905)

KINGDOM OF DENMARK

UNITED KINGDOM OF GREAT BRITAIN AND IRELAND

NETHER-LANDS

GERMAN EMPIRE

BELGIUM

GRAND DUCHY OF LUXEMBOURG (INDEPENDENT SINCE 1890)

Königgrätz 1866 ❌

Sedan 1870 ❌

RUSSIAN EMPIRE

FRENCH REPUBLIC   SWITZERLAND

AUSTRIA-HUNGARY

ANDORRA

Solferino 1859 ❌

Sevastopol ●

ROMANIA (SINCE 1878) EASTERN RUMELIA (1878 AUTONOMOUS OTTOMAN PROVINCE, SINCE 1885 BULGARIAN)

SERBIA (INDEPENDENT SINCE 1878)

BULGARIA (SINCE 1878)

CORSICA (FRENCH)

Rome ● KINGDOM OF ITALY ❶

MONTE-NEGRO

KINGDOM OF PORTUGAL   KINGDOM OF SPAIN

OTTOMAN EMPIRE

GREECE

CORFU (GREEK)

GIBRALTAR (BRITISH)

CYPRUS (UNDER BRITISH ADMINISTRATION SINCE 1878)

CEUTA (SPANISH) Melilla (Spanish) ALGERIA (FRENCH)

CRETE (INDEPENDENT SINCE 1898)

1900–1917

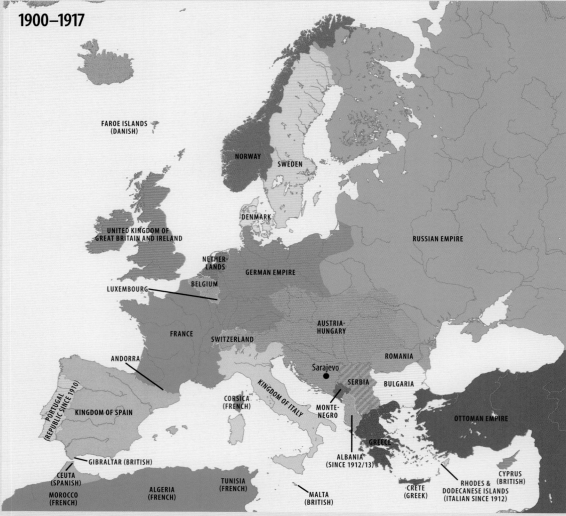

FAROE ISLANDS (DANISH)

NORWAY   SWEDEN

DENMARK

UNITED KINGDOM OF GREAT BRITAIN AND IRELAND

NETHER-LANDS

GERMAN EMPIRE

LUXEMBOURG   BELGIUM

RUSSIAN EMPIRE

FRANCE

SWITZERLAND

AUSTRIA-HUNGARY

ANDORRA

ROMANIA

Sarajevo

SERBIA   BULGARIA

CORSICA (FRENCH)

KINGDOM OF ITALY

MONTE-NEGRO

PORTUGAL (REPUBLIC SINCE 1910)   KINGDOM OF SPAIN

OTTOMAN EMPIRE

GREECE

GIBRALTAR (BRITISH)

ALBANIA (SINCE 1912/13)

CYPRUS (BRITISH)

CEUTA (SPANISH)

MOROCCO (FRENCH)   TUNISIA (FRENCH)

ALGERIA (FRENCH)

MALTA (BRITISH)

CRETE (GREEK)

RHODES & DODECANESE ISLANDS (ITALIAN SINCE 1912)

1853–1856 Crimean War: Russia fights against the Ottoman Empire, England and France over the balance of power in the Middle East.

1859 At the Battle of Solferino, at the end of the second Italian War of Independence, Italy and France defeat Austria.

1861 Proclamation of the Kingdom of Italy

1866 Prussia defeats Austria in the Austro-Prussian War (Königgrätz).

1870–1871 Franco-German War: Led by Prussia, German forces defeat France at Sedan.

1871 German unification and creation of the German Empire. Rome becomes capital of a united Italy.

1878 Bulgaria, Romania, Montenegro and Serbia declare independence from the Ottoman Empire.

1879 Austro-German Dual Alliance is formed: Germany and Austria-Hungary agree to defend each other in case of Russian aggression.

1894 Alliance between France and Russia

1907 Triple Entente between England, France and Russia

1912 First Balkan War: the Balkan League countries force the Ottoman Empire to relinquish almost all its European territories.

1913 Second Balkan War between former allied states in the Balkans (Serbia and Greece versus Bulgaria).

1914 Archduke Francis Ferdinand, heir to the Austrian throne, is assassinated in Sarajevo, resulting in the outbreak of World War I.

1915 Despite its alliance with Germany, Italy sides with the Triple Entente.

1917 Finland achieves independence from Russia. The October Revolution in Russia results in Bolshevik

Crimean War Conflict between Russia and the coalition of England, France and the Ottoman Empire under the pretext of protecting the rights of Orthodox Christians in the Ottoman Empire. Following initial Russian successes, England and France captured Sevastopol on the Crimean Peninsula. They feared increasing Russian influence in the Black Sea region and the possible division of the Ottoman Empire.

Austro-Prussian War War between Prussia and Austria for hegemony in Germany was precipitated by a dispute over the administration of Schleswig and Holstein, which had been annexed in 1864. Prussia and its allies defeated Austria and its thirteen German Confederation partners at Königgrätz. The German Confederation was dissolved, and the path was cleared for a united Germany under Prussian patronage and without Austria ("Lesser German Solution").

Franco-Prussian War Prussian Chancellor Otto von Bismarck wanted Prussian rule of Germany to be formally sealed. He therefore exploited French claims to the southern German states to provoke a war between the nations. After winning the Battle of Sedan, the Prussians traveled to Paris to proclaim the German Empire in January 1871. The Prussian king became the German emperor, and Germany annexed Alsace-Lorraine from France.

Balkan Wars After achieving independence from the Ottoman Empire in the 19th century, the small Balkan states of Serbia, Bulgaria, Greece and Montenegro formed an alliance, the Balkan League, in 1912. They fought the first Balkan War against the slowly dissolving Ottoman Empire, and then a second among themselves (Serbia and Greece against Bulgaria) to extend their territories.

victory. The Spanish flu pandemic claims tens of millions of lives, far more than died in World War I.

1918 Treaty of Brest-Litovsk between the Central Powers and Russia; the Bolsheviks end Russia's involvement in World War I. Germany, Austria-Hungary and their allies are defeated and the Polish monarchy overthrown. Czechoslovakia, Estonia, Latvia and Lithuania declare independence. The Yugoslavian kingdom is formed. World War I ends.

1922 Ireland achieves independence from England.

1922 Benito Mussolini seizes power in Italy.

1922–1923 The Ottoman sultan is deposed, and a period of modernization takes place in Turkey under the leadership of Kemal Atatürk.

1924–1928 In a power struggle in the USSR, Communist Party head Joseph Stalin prevails.

1933 National Socialists (Nazis) seize power in Germany.

1938 Austria is annexed to Nazi Germany. Munich agreement: the Great Powers force Czechoslovakia to cede the Sudetenland to Germany.

1939 Hitler makes a pact with Stalin concerning distribution of spheres of influence in eastern Europe. Germany invades Poland, beginning World War II, followed by occupation of the Netherlands, Belgium, France, Denmark, Norway, Yugoslavia and Greece.

1941 Beginning of the German offensive against and invasion of the USSR

1943 German forces are finally defeated at Stalingrad after a siege lasting almost seven months.

1944 Allied forces land on the beaches of Normandy (D-Day) and are able to establish a foothold in northern France; USSR annexes the Baltic republics.

May 8, 1945 World War II ends in German capitulation. War in the Pacific arena does not end until September.

World War I Long years of rivalry between the nations of Europe resulted in two hostile blocs. On one side, Germany was allied with Austria-Hungary, and opposing them was the Triple Entente, a coalition between England, France and Russia. The tense atmosphere led to the outbreak of World War I, with trench warfare and casualties on a magnitude never before seen. The United States entered the war in 1917 on the side of the Western allies.

Between the wars Germany was dissatisfied with the provisions of the Treaty of Versailles, which blamed it alone for the war and demanded immense reparations. Italy, where Mussolini's fascists had risen to power in 1922, did not want to submit to the Great Powers. Tensions grew, among other reasons due to authoritarian regimes in other countries (Hungary, Portugal, Spain). The situation was exacerbated by a world financial crisis. In Germany, the National Socialists established a fascist regime with widespread support among the populace and elevated anti-Semitism to a state doctrine.

World War II The expansive plans of the German leadership (Adolf Hitler and the Nazis) and the aggressive policies of Italy and Japan prepared the ground for renewed worldwide conflict. Lightning-quick invasions of the countries neighboring Germany and a failure on the part of England, the United States and the other major powers to take rapid action led to a "Total War" in which over 60 million people were killed, among them more than 6 million Jews who died in concentration camps in the Nazi-organized Holocaust.

After World War I

End of 1939: Beginning of World War II

Alliances of the fascist countries
Countries allied with or occupied by fascist powers after 1939
Poland
Territories annexed by the Soviets after 1939
Countries that remained neutral during the war
Countries that remained neutral, but cooperated with the fascist powers

Europe: An Overview

1945–1950: Postwar Period and Division of Europe

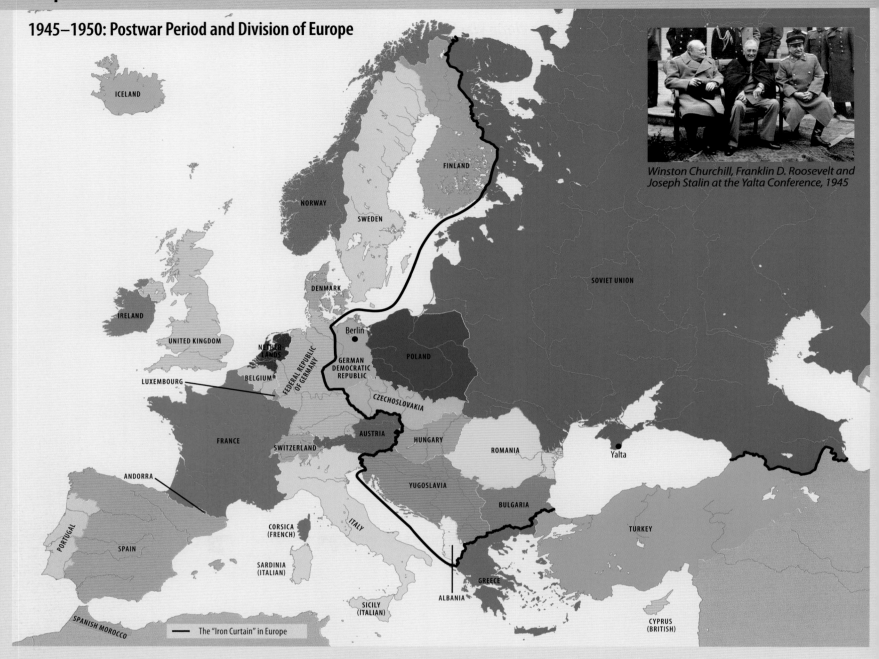

Winston Churchill, Franklin D. Roosevelt and Joseph Stalin at the Yalta Conference, 1945

— The "Iron Curtain" in Europe

1945 Allied leaders representing the victors of World War II hold the Yalta Conference to discuss the division of power following World War II; restoration of Poland, Czechoslovakia and Yugoslavia.

1945–1948 Gradual rise of communism and Soviet hegemony in the Eastern European states

1948–1949 Soviet blockade of West Berlin: for almost a year, West Berlin is supplied through the Berlin Airlift.

1949 Creation of two German states, the German Democratic Republic (GDR or DDR) in the east and the Federal Republic of Germany in the west (FRG or BRD). NATO is founded as a Western defensive alliance.

1951 The European Coal and Steel Community (ECSC) is founded by six western European countries; it is the core of what will later be the European Union.

1953 Strikes by workers in East Berlin ignite a two-

day uprising throughout East Germany (GDR) that is quelched by Soviet troops.

1955 The Warsaw Pact is formed as the defense alliance of the Eastern Bloc.

1956 Soviets crush a peaceful uprising in Hungary.

1961 The Berlin Wall is erected, the symbol of Europe's division by the Iron Curtain.

End of fascism The defeat of Germany and Italy sealed the downfall of the fascist regimes in both countries (the Spanish version of fascism, Falangism, would endure until 1975). Former members of the National Socialist Party in Germany were tried and sentenced at the Nuremberg trials (1945–1949) and other war crimes tribunals, or subjected to "denazification." In many of the countries formerly occupied by Germany there was a bloody settling of accounts with collaborators.

Cold War The alliance among the victors in World War II dissolved shortly after the end of the war. Western liberal systems (supported by the United States) confronted totalitarian "people's democracies" (under Soviet dominance). The Iron Curtain between East and West formed an ideological dividing line that was in fact also a fortified boundary. Despite—or because of—the nuclear arms race between the Soviet Union and the United States, the conflict never broke out into open warfare.

Warsaw Pact A military alliance of the Eastern European countries that was founded in 1955 in response to NATO. In practical terms, the Warsaw Pact defended the interests of the USSR, which was dissolved in 1991.

Comecon (Council for Mutual Economic Assistance) An organization of Eastern Bloc countries, based in Moscow, formed in 1949 and directed by the Soviet Union with the goal of collaborating on and coordinating five-year economic plans for the socialist countries as a counterpart to the Marshall Plan and the Organization for European Economic Co-operation (OEEC). Unlike the European Union, it never developed a functioning transnational economic mechanism. Its activities ended in 1990.

Helsinki Accords (Conference on Security and Co-operation in Europe, or CSCE) Meeting in Finland that resulted in recognition of the borders in Eastern Europe claimed by the USSR in return for Soviet assurance that

human rights would be respected and that people in the Eastern Bloc would have access to Western information. In August 1975, thirty-three European countries, the United States and Canada signed the final act on security and cooperation in Europe. This would become an important instrument for dissident movements in the East, the basis on which they demanded human rights and greater freedom.

Decline of the Eastern Bloc Mikhail Gorbachev came to the helm of the Communist Party in the USSR in 1985. With *glasnost* (openness) and *perestroika* (restructuring), he tried to salvage the economically and politically devastated Soviet Union, and at the same time hinted to Soviet satellite states that he would not hinder them in their own reform efforts. In 1989 the regimes in Poland and Hungary were the first to liberalize. Under their influence, peaceful revolutions took place at the end of the year in East Germany, Czechoslovakia and Bulgaria, along with a more violent revolution in Romania and the disintegration of the entire Eastern Bloc.

After the Fall of Communism in 1993

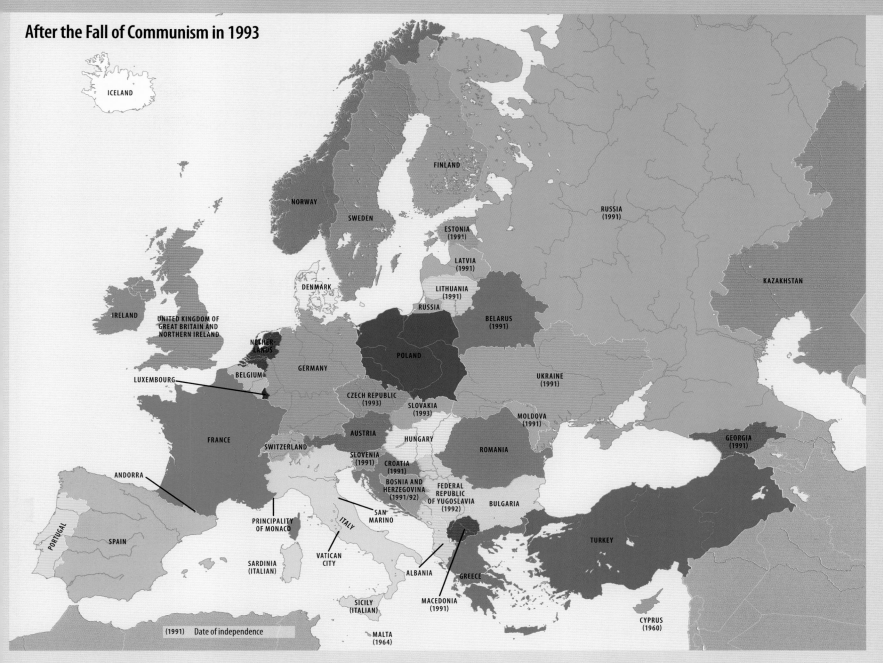

ICELAND

NORWAY
SWEDEN
FINLAND
ESTONIA (1991)
LATVIA (1991)
LITHUANIA (1991)
RUSSIA
RUSSIA (1991)
BELARUS (1991)
KAZAKHSTAN
DENMARK
IRELAND
UNITED KINGDOM OF GREAT BRITAIN AND NORTHERN IRELAND
NETHER-LANDS
GERMANY
POLAND
UKRAINE (1991)
BELGIUM
LUXEMBOURG
CZECH REPUBLIC (1993)
SLOVAKIA (1993)
MOLDOVA (1991)
AUSTRIA
HUNGARY
ROMANIA
GEORGIA (1991)
FRANCE
SWITZERLAND
SLOVENIA (1991)
CROATIA (1991)
ANDORRA
PRINCIPALITY OF MONACO
ITALY
SAN MARINO
BOSNIA AND HERZEGOVINA (1991/92)
FEDERAL REPUBLIC OF YUGOSLAVIA (1992)
BULGARIA
TURKEY
PORTUGAL
SPAIN
SARDINIA (ITALIAN)
VATICAN CITY
ALBANIA
GREECE
MACEDONIA (1991)
CYPRUS (1960)
SICILY (ITALIAN)
MALTA (1964)

(1991) Date of independence

1963 Franco-German Friendship Treaty

1968 Student unrest in Europe; protests and strikes by French workers lead to dissolution of the National Assembly. Warsaw Pact armies end the Prague Spring.

1970–1973 Federal Republic of Germany signs treaties on the normalization of relations with its Eastern European neighbors and the USSR.

1975 In Helsinki, the European countries as well as the United States and Canada sign the final act of the Conference on Security and Co-operation in Europe (CSCE).

1989 End of the communist regime in Eastern Europe; fall of the Berlin Wall

1990 Reunification of Germany

prior to 1980 President Josip Tito's authoritarian rule had suppressed all nationalist stirrings. The subrepublics achieved their independence only at the cost of many lives in bitter civil wars between the Orthodox Serbs, Catholic Croats and Muslim Bosnians in the 1990s and

1991 Beginning of the wars in Yugoslavia; conservative functionaries attempt a putsch in Moscow; dissolution of the Soviet Union and independence of the Soviet Republics (in Europe: Lithuania, Latvia, Estonia, Ukraine, Belarus and Russia)

1993 Czechoslovakia splits into the Czech Republic and Slovakia.

2004/2007 The EU expands by the addition of twelve former Eastern Bloc countries, for a total of twenty-seven member states.

the first decade of the 21st century. Ethnic cleansing campaigns and massacres of the civilian population are still being dealt with today before the war crimes tribunal in The Hague, while medical commissions are at work uncovering mass graves.

Unification of Europe European integration and economic cooperation were designed to prevent conflicts. In 1951 France, West Germany, Italy and the Low Countries (Netherlands, Belgium and Luxembourg) founded the European Coal and Steel Community. In 1957 the same countries signed the Treaties of Rome, the basis for the European Union. Today, the EU comprises twenty-seven member states with mostly open borders (Schengen Agreement), the majority of which have also shared a common currency, the euro, since 2002.

Brandenburg Gate shortly before the Berlin Wall was opened, December 1989

Disintegration of Yugoslavia The fall of the Iron Curtain in 1989 sparked nationalist movements in Eastern Europe. The bloodiest of these began in Yugoslavia in 1991, where

Sarajevo, Bosnia-Herzegovina, March 1996

Europe in Detail – Mesopotamia and the Near East Until 330 BCE

2375–1750 BCE: Akkad and Babylon

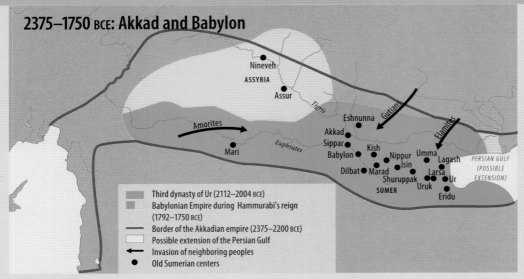

Third dynasty of Ur (2112–2004 BCE)
Babylonian Empire during Hammurabi's reign (1792–1750 BCE)
Border of the Akkadian empire (2375–2200 BCE)
Possible extension of the Persian Gulf
Invasion of neighboring peoples
Old Sumerian centers

15th–13th Centuries BCE: Babylon, Assyria and Mitanni

Land of Mitanni in the 15th century BCE
Middle Assyrian period empire and campaigns (14th–13th c. BCE)
Babylonian Empire–Kassite period
Possible expansion of the Persian Gulf

17th–13th Centuries BCE: The Hittite Empire

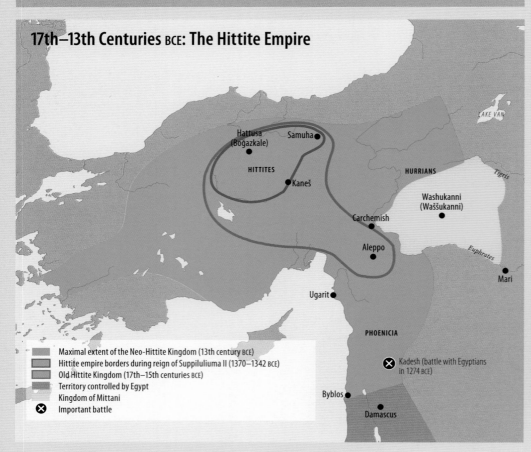

Maximal extent of the Neo-Hittite Kingdom (13th century BCE)
Hittite empire borders during reign of Suppiluliuma II (1370–1342 BCE)
Old Hittite Kingdom (17th–15th centuries BCE)
Territory controlled by Egypt
Kingdom of Mittani
⊗ Important battle

⊗ Kadesh (battle with Egyptians in 1274 BCE)

Mesopotamia, known as the "Fertile Crescent," lies between the Tigris and Euphrates rivers. It is the site of some of the world's most ancient civilizations, where the mighty empires of the Sumerians, Babylonians and Assyrians reigned supreme. The peoples who lived here played an important role in the development of European civilization.

~6000 BCE First fired ceramics and earliest known use of the potter's wheel

4000–2000 BCE Uruk becomes the most important Sumerian city.

~2650 BCE Gilgamesh, the hero of the *Epic of Gilgamesh*, becomes king of Uruk.

Gilgamesh in an Assyrian sculpture, 8th century BCE

2356–2300 BCE Sargon of Akkad rules the first great Near Eastern empire.

~2000 BCE The Hittites arrive in the Near East.

1950–1370 BCE The ancient Assyrian empire

1894–1595 BCE Old Babylonian period, including the reign of the lawgiver Hammurabi

~1570–1390 BCE Old Hittite period

1531–1155 BCE The Kassites seize power in Babylon during the Middle Babylonian period.

~1500–1300 BCE Hurrians, an Indo-European people from the kingdom of Mitanni, introduce the horse and chariot in the Near East before falling to the Hittites in 1355 BCE.

1380–912 BCE Middle Assyrian period, characterized by steady expansion

1335–1200 BCE Zenith of the Hittite Kingdom

1259 BCE The Hittites and the Egyptians make peace following the Battle of Kadesh (1274 BCE).

~1100 BCE The Israelites settle in Palestine.

~965–926 BCE Reign of Solomon as king of Israel

~926 BCE Israel is divided into the kingdoms of Judea (Judah) and Israel.

912–610 BCE Neo-Assyrian Empire

689 BCE Assyrian forces sack Babylon.

626–539 BCE The Neo-Babylonian period begins with the Chaldean dynasty.

614–612 BCE Medes and Babylonians conquer Assyria.

597/587 BCE The Babylonian king Nebuchadnezzar II sacks Jerusalem.

559–330 BCE The Achaemenid dynasty forms the first Persian empire.

~550 BCE The Persians conquer the Medes and become a world power.

539 BCE The Persians conquer the Babylonians.

490 BCE The Greeks defeat the Persians at the Battle of Marathon.

333–330 BCE Alexander the Great, Greek king of Macedonia, conquers Persia and continues to expand his empire as far east as India.

Detail of the Ishtar Gate in Babylon, 604–562 BCE

Palestine ca. 1000 BCE

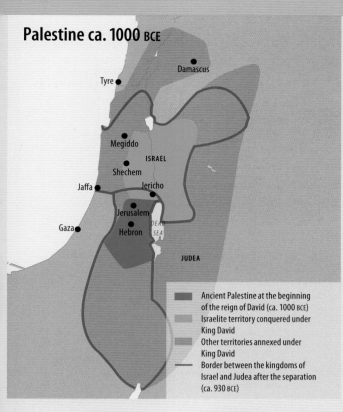

Ancient Palestine at the beginning of the reign of David (ca. 1000 BCE)

Israelite territory conquered under King David

Other territories annexed under King David

Border between the kingdoms of Israel and Judea after the separation (ca. 930 BCE)

The Neo-Assyrian Empire ca. 700 BCE

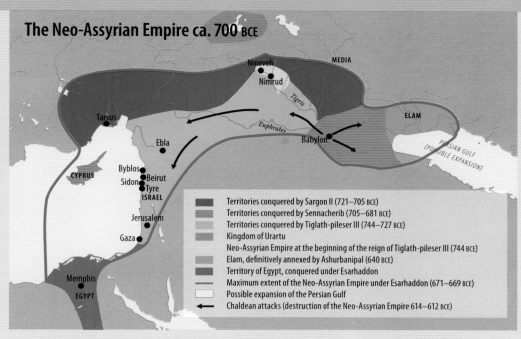

Territories conquered by Sargon II (721–705 BCE)

Territories conquered by Sennacherib (705–681 BCE)

Territories conquered by Tiglath-pileser III (744–727 BCE)

Kingdom of Urartu

Neo-Assyrian Empire at the beginning of the reign of Tiglath-pileser III (744 BCE)

Elam, definitively annexed by Ashurbanipal (640 BCE)

Territory of Egypt, conquered under Esarhaddon

Maximum extent of the Neo-Assyrian Empire under Esarhaddon (671–669 BCE)

Possible expansion of the Persian Gulf

Chaldean attacks (destruction of the Neo-Assyrian Empire 614–612 BCE)

The Neo-Babylonian Empire ca. 600 BCE

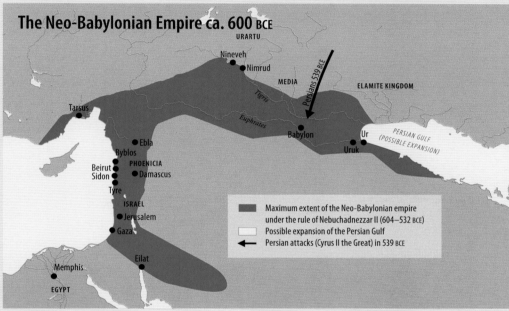

Maximum extent of the Neo-Babylonian empire under the rule of Nebuchadnezzar II (604–532 BCE)

Possible expansion of the Persian Gulf

Persian attacks (Cyrus II the Great) in 539 BCE

The origin of the **Sumerians** remains unknown. They settled the banks of the Euphrates River around 4000 BCE, founding the important city-states of Uruk, Eridu and Lagash, from where they ruled a small empire. The Sumerians invented the wheel, cuneiform writing, the plow and the dome. They devised the first school system, practiced advanced mathematics and astronomy, and perfected irrigation techniques. Sumerian religion served as the basis for all later religions in the Mesopotamian region.

The city of **Ur**, like Uruk (both located in what is now Iraq), is one of the most ancient Sumerian cities and a cradle of Mesopotamian culture. Ur was founded around 4000 BCE and is mentioned in the Bible. Abraham, the forefather of all Israelites, is said to have come from Ur. The city's most important building was its ziggurat, a temple tower. Among its ruins have been found a multitude of very early pictographic tablets listing deities, businesses, animals, workers and tools. Ur was destroyed around 2000 BCE by the Elamites, who came from what is today Iran.

Babylon was the capital city of Babylonia, situated on the banks of the Euphrates River in what is now Iraq. The city enjoyed its first golden age under the reign of King Hammurabi (1792–1750 BCE), whose name is associated with a famous code of laws. Over a thousand years later, Babylon enjoyed a second golden age as the center of the Neo-Babylonian empire under King Nebuchadnezzar II (604–562 BCE), who ruled over a vast territory stretching from Palestine to the Persian Gulf. Babylon is also mentioned in the Bible, where it is the site of the Tower of Babylon as

well as the Babylonian exile of the Jews following the Babylonians' plundering of Jerusalem.

The **Assyrians** were a Semitic people who first settled the banks of the upper Tigris River around 2000 BCE. In the 8th century BCE, the Neo-Assyrian Empire, an aggressive military power with well-trained soldiers, conquered and demanded tribute from nearly all of Mesopotamia, Egypt and parts of what are today the countries of Iran and Turkey. Tens of thousands of people were forced to leave their home territories to serve as laborers in Assyria.

Persia ca. 500 BCE: The Achaemenid Empire

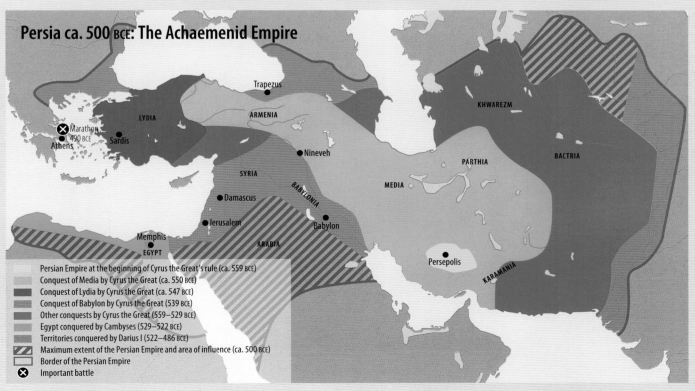

Persian Empire at the beginning of Cyrus the Great's rule (ca. 559 BCE)

Conquest of Media by Cyrus the Great (ca. 550 BCE)

Conquest of Lydia by Cyrus the Great (ca. 547 BCE)

Conquest of Babylon by Cyrus the Great (539 BCE)

Other conquests by Cyrus the Great (559–529 BCE)

Egypt conquered by Cambyses (529–522 BCE)

Territories conquered by Darius I (522–486 BCE)

Maximum extent of the Persian Empire and area of influence (ca. 500 BCE)

Border of the Persian Empire

⊗ Important battle

Europe in Detail – Ancient Greece

17th–12th Centuries BCE: Minoan and Mycenaean Cultures

Mycenaean civilization
Minoan civilization
Migration of the Achaeans (14th–12th c. BCE)
Migration of the Anatolians (ca. 3000 BCE)
Large palaces
Important centers

Of all ancient peoples, the Greeks had by far the greatest influence on the continued development of Western culture. They absorbed the knowledge of other peoples and transformed it into their own distinctive written language, science, philosophy, poetry and visual arts. Although they also made great strides in seafaring, engineering and government, the Greeks never achieved political unity. They lived in city-states on the Greek mainland and throughout the Mediterranean regions, where they founded agricultural and trading colonies. "Ancient Greece," therefore, does not refer to any one country, but to all the territories settled by Greeks. When threatened by outside forces, Greeks were capable of uniting in a variety of changing alliances to defend their lands. Philip II and Alexander the Great, both Macedonians, were the first to rule a larger Greek empire, which collapsed after Alexander's death.

2000–1450 BCE Minoan palace culture flourishes on Crete, with regional administration controlled by the palatial centers.

1600–1000 BCE The Mycenaean culture, characterized by fortified cities and chariot warfare, comes to power on the Greek mainland, with the city of Mycenae as its most important center. Its collapse is probably due to the invasion of the Sea Peoples.

~1250 BCE The Trojan War, the legendary conflict between the Greeks and the inhabitants of Troy, in Anatolia

~1200–900 BCE The Greek Dark Ages, characterized by the arrival of new ethnic groups. The "Dorian Invasion" resettles large parts of the Peloponnese, Asia Minor and Crete, displacing the Achaeans and northwestern tribes.

~900–600 BCE The Archaic period begins with the establishment of new Greek colonies in the Mediterranean and Black Sea coastal regions from Sicily to Asia Minor. City-states (*polis*, plural *poleis*) and their dependent territories form the core political unit. The most powerful of these are

The School of Athens, *fresco by Raphael (1483–1520) in the Vatican. From left to right:* **1.** *Zeno of Citium, founder of Stoic philosophy* **2.** *Epicurus, founder of Epicurean philosophy* **3.** *Anaximander, or possibly Boethius or Empedocles* **4.** *Pythagoras, mathematician* **5.** *Xenophon, historian, or possibly Antisthenes* **6.** *Aieschines or Xenophon* **7.** *Parmenides, founder of the Eleatic school* **8.** *Socrates, philosopher and teacher of Plato* **9.** *Heraclitus, pre-Socratic philosopher* **9.** *the philosopher Plato holding a text of Timaeus* **11.** *Aristotle, philosopher and student of Plato, with a copy of Nichomachean Ethics* **12.** *Diogenes, philosopher and cynic* **13.** *Plontinus, philosopher* **14.** *Euclid, mathematician* **15.** *Ptolemy, astronomer and geographer*

Sparta in the Peloponne and Athens in Attica.

776 BCE The first pan-Hellenic Olympic games take place in Olympia. This combined religious festival and athletic contest is so popular and held in such high esteem that wars are interrupted so that everyone can take part.

~650 BCE The code of Lycurgus defines Spartan government as having two kings (passed on through two family lines), the congress of the *gerousia* (council of elders), the *apella* (popular assembly) and five *ephors* (chief administrators). The Spartans dominate the peoples of the surrounding territories (*perioece*) and create a class of slaves of the state called *helots*. Male Spartans are raised in military societies with communal housing and meals.

594 BCE Athenian constitutional reform by Solon ends aristocratic rule and creates a citizen-based society that excludes women and slaves from most aspects of public life.

546–527 BCE The tyranny of Peisistratus is a period of construction of monumental buildings and economic advances in Athens. His sons rule after his death until the fall of the tyranny in 510 BCE.

508 BCE The constitutional reforms of Cleisthenes broaden the Athenian democracy to include a wider range of citizens. Isonomy (equality of all full citizens) and ostracism (exile of unpopular citizens by vote) are introduced, and Athens is subdivided

900–600 BCE: Greek Colonization

into ten administrative districts (*phyle*). The council of the five hundred, with fifty representatives from each district, controls the government.

500 BCE The Classical period begins.

499 BCE Ionian revolt marks the beginning of the Greco-Persian Wars, which will last more than forty years. The Greeks defeat the Persians at the Battle of Marathon in 490 BCE.

485–212 BCE Sicily under the Syracuse tyranny becomes the political and cultural center of western Greece, on par with Carthage and Rome. Its most famous tyrant is Dionysius I (405–367 BCE).

480 BCE The Persians begin a new military campaign against Greece. After defeating the Greeks led by Leonidas of Sparta at the Battle of Thermopylae, the Persians lose a decisive battle at sea near Salamis. They retreat from Greece following their defeat on land at the Battle of Plataea.

462 BCE The Athenian constitution is subject to further democratic reform. The Council of Elders (*Areopagus*) is weakened, and no longer functions as the highest court.

449 BCE The Persians officially recognize the sovereignty of Greek city-states in Asia Minor.

443–429 BCE Athenian democracy enters a golden age under the leadership of Pericles.

431–404 BCE Sparta wins the Peloponnesian War against Athens, a bloody confrontation in which nearly every Greek city-state as far west as Sicily is involved. Athenian democracy collapses with the defeat of its navy, and the walls of Athens are torn down.

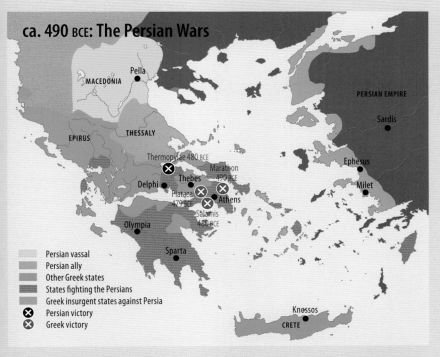

ca. 490 BCE: The Persian Wars

Persian vassal
Persian ally
Other Greek states
States fighting the Persians
Greek insurgent states against Persia
Persian victory
Greek victory

ca. 420 BCE: The Peloponnesian War

Sparta and its allies (Peloponnesian League)
Athens and its allies (Delian League)
Remaining Greek states

The **Minoan period** (ca. 2000–1450 BCE) was one in which a peaceful, palace-centered society flourished on the island of Crete. This bull-worshipping culture is named after the mythological King Minos.

The **Mycenaean period** (ca. 1650–1200 BCE) is named after the important city of Mycenae,

where Heinrich Schliemann discovered the golden mask of Agamemnon. Mycenaean Greek culture was characterized by power struggles between heavily fortified cities.

The **Archaic period** (ca. 700–500 BCE) served as the foundation for the Classical period with the development of the city-state as

a political unit and the emergence of the first tyrants (leaders who came to power illegitimately).

The **Classical period** (ca. 500–336/323 BCE) is the golden age of ancient Greek culture marked not only by the invention of democracy (Solon, Pericles) but also by

far-reaching advances in art, architecture (Pheidias), science (Hippocrates) and philosophy (Socrates, Plato, Aristotle).

The **Hellenistic period** (336/327–323 BCE) represents the spread of Greek culture to Europe, Asia and Africa in the wake of the conquests of Alexander the Great.

Europe in Detail – Ancient Greece

The Empire of Alexander the Great ca. 330 BCE

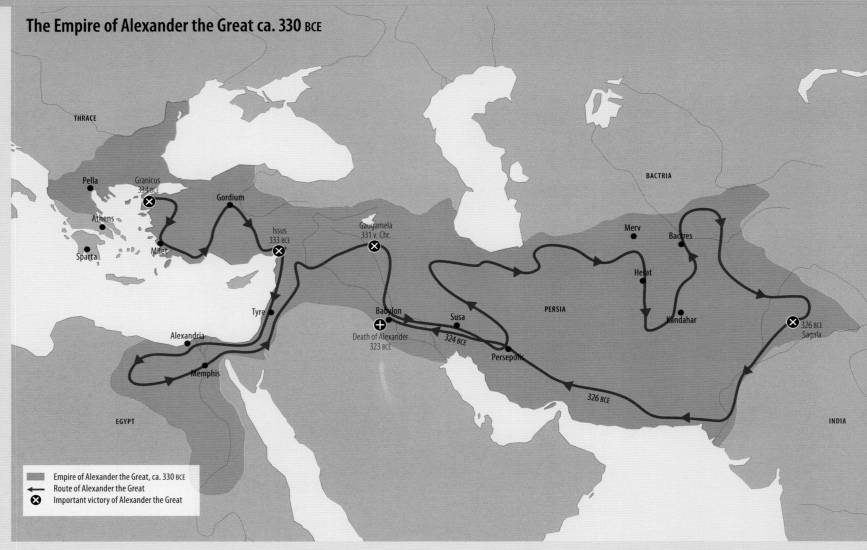

THRACE

Pella

Granicus
334 BCE ⊗

Gordium

Athens

Milet

Sparta

Issus
333 BCE ⊗

Gaugamela
331 v. Chr. ⊗

Merv

BACTRIA

Bactres

Herat

Tyre

PERSIA

Babylon ⊕
Death of Alexander
323 BCE

Susa

324 BCE

Kandahar

⊗ 326 BCE
Sagala

Alexandria

Persepolis

Memphis

326 BCE

EGYPT

INDIA

Empire of Alexander the Great, ca. 330 BCE
← Route of Alexander the Great
⊗ Important victory of Alexander the Great

The Battle of Issus, first century CE mosaic in the Museo Archeologica Nazionale, Naples

359–336 BCE Philip II of Macedon gradually gains control of the various territories of mainland Greece and part of Thrace, some by military force and others through diplomacy. He is the first to unite Greece and Macedonia under the banner of Pan-Hellenism.

338 BCE Philip II defeats the united armies of Athens and Thebes at the Battle of Chaeronea, making Macedonia the dominant power on the Greek mainland. His victory marks the end of the Classical Greek period.

336–323 BCE Alexander the Great, son of Philip II, rapidly conquers Mesopotamia, Egypt, Persia, Syria and Palestine, extending the boundaries of Greek-Macedonian power to the threshold of Afghanistan and India. In 326 BCE, a mutiny of his troops forces him to turn back.

324 BCE In a mass wedding in Babylon, Alexander and his generals marry Persian princesses as part of his plan (only partially successful) to create a new Greek-Macedonian-Asian nobility.

323 BCE Alexander dies in Babylon at age thirty-three, probably of malaria.

323–281 BCE A power struggle breaks out among Alexander's generals, the Diadochi, marking the beginning of the Hellenistic period. By 305/306 BCE, they establish themselves as dynastic rulers of several kingdoms carved out of Alexander's empire. The new dynasties include the Seleucids, ruling from southern Anatolia to Iran; the Ptolemids in Egypt; the Antigonids in Macedonia and Greece; and later (after 283 BCE) the Attalids in Asia Minor, ruling from Pergamum. In 281 BCE the death of Lysimachus, ruler of Macedonia and Thrace, ends the wars of succession.

319–297 BCE The last surviving members of Alexander the Great's family are executed on orders from the general

Athens and its surrounding territory were first settled as early as the Neolithic period. The owl-eyed goddess Athena was the city's protector. The 6th-century constitutional reforms of Solon and especially Cleisthenes made Athens the cradle of democracy. The city gained in importance during the Greco-Persian Wars, when it became the leader of the Greek city-states and a center of culture and learning.

Corinth was already an important location in 2000 BCE, when the original city was founded on a narrow isthmus joining mainland Greece with the Peloponnese peninsula. Tyrants ruled the city-state from the 7th century onward. During the Classical period, Corinth engaged in near-constant territorial and economic conflict with nearby Athens.

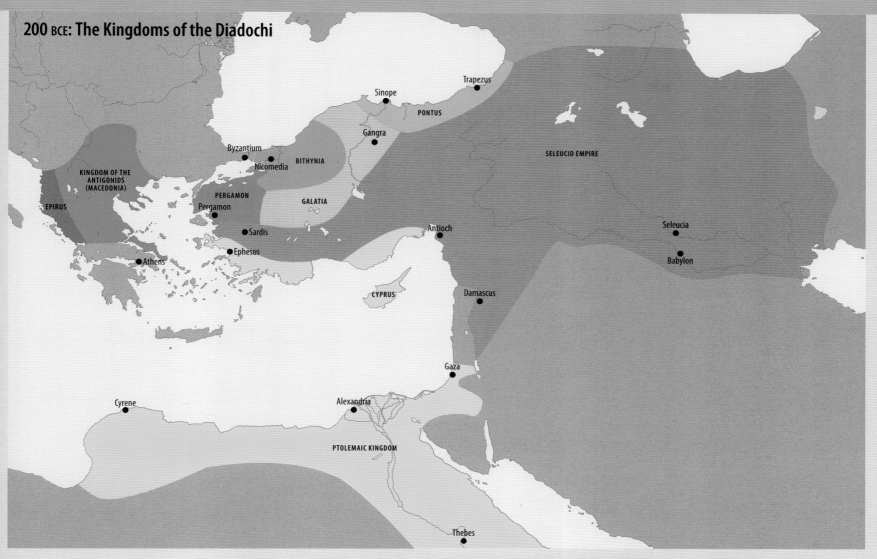

200 BCE: The Kingdoms of the Diadochi

(Map labels) Trapezus · Sinope · PONTUS · Gangra · BITHYNIA · Byzantium · Nicomedia · KINGDOM OF THE ANTIGONIDS (MACEDONIA) · PERGAMON · Pergamon · GALATIA · EPIRUS · SELEUCID EMPIRE · Sardis · Antioch · Seleucia · Ephesus · Athens · Babylon · CYPRUS · Damascus · Gaza · Cyrene · Alexandria · PTOLEMAIC KINGDOM · Thebes

Cassander during a war between competing generals from Macedonia and Greece.

283–133 BCE The Attalid dynasty of Pergamum in Asia Minor inherits the mantle of Classical Greek culture with great works of art and architecture, including the Pergamum Altar. The last Attalid king wills his kingdom to Rome upon his death in 133 BCE.

276–168 BCE The Antigonids, rulers on the Greek mainland since 306 BCE, establish themselves in Macedonia, giving the dynasty control over important Greek city-states, including Athens.

244–222 BCE Spartan kings Agis IV (244–241 BCE) and Cleomenes III (235–222 BCE) fail to revive Sparta's ancient glory despite reform attempts involving land redistribution, debt forgiveness and expanded citizenship.

The death of Alexander the Great in Babylon, 323 BCE, depicted in a relief sculpture by Bertel Thorvaldsen (1770–1844), Palazzo del Quirinale, Rome.

229–179 BCE Antigonus III Doson (229–221 BCE) and Philip V (221–179 BCE), kings of Macedonia, attempt to extend their control over the remaining Greek city-states. Rome's influence in the Greek world continues to grow after several cities request and receive military assistance, leading to Philip's retreat in 197 BCE.

212 BCE Rome occupies Sicily and the important Greek city-state of Syracuse, bringing the western Greek world under Roman control.

168 BCE Roman troops make Macedonia a Roman province after defeating Perseus, the last Macedonian king.

146 BCE Roman armies inflict a decisive defeat on their former allies, the Achaean League, utterly destroying the city of Corinth. All of Greece becomes a Roman province.

Delphi was the site of the most influential oracle of the ancient world as early as the 8th century BCE, when the first temple of Apollo was constructed. The oracle's prophecies, spoken in response to petitioners' questions, were believed to express the god's approval or displeasure.

Sparta was the most powerful city in the Peloponnese. Characterized by the strict "Spartan" military upbringing of its youth, the city's armed forces formed the basis of its power. During the Peloponnesian War (ca. 450–400 BCE), Sparta and its allies defeated Athens, making Sparta, for a time, the dominant city-state in Greece.

The **Delian League**, led by Athens, was formed in 478 BCE to defend the Greek mainland and islands against the Persians. It could not, however, defeat the Spartans.

Democracy enjoyed a golden age with the 5th-century BCE reign of Pericles, who called the Athenian assembly to vote more than forty times. Membership in the assembly was open to any male full citizen over the age of twenty. Assembly votes dealt with war, peace treaties, political alliances, religious questions, the city's infrastructure, maintenance issues and a wealth of other situations. The assembly functioned as both a legislative body and the high court.

THE ACHIEVEMENTS OF ANTIQUITY

1. The Pyramids of Giza in Egypt are the most ancient of the Seven Wonders. The pyramid of Khufu is the largest, with an original height of 479 feet (146 m); it is slightly shorter today. All three of the pyramids at Giza were built during the fourth dynasty (2620–2500 BCE) as funerary monuments for the Egyptian pharaohs Khufu (Cheops), Khafre (Chephren) and Menkaure (Mykerinos).

2. The Hanging Gardens of Babylon are the world's first recorded botanical gardens. They

were laid out on terraces built of fired bricks that were as much as 98 feet (30 m) high.

3. The Temple of Artemis in Ephesos was actually two

The Seven Wonders of the World

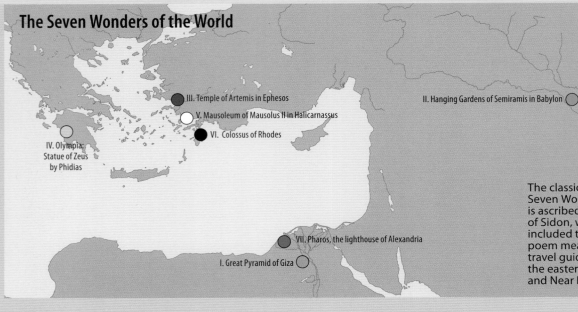

- III. Temple of Artemis in Ephesos
- II. Hanging Gardens of Semiramis in Babylon
- V. Mausoleum of Mausolus II in Halicarnassus
- IV. Olympia: Statue of Zeus by Phidias
- VI. Colossus of Rhodes
- VII. Pharos, the lighthouse of Alexandria
- I. Great Pyramid of Giza

The classic version of the Seven Wonders of the World is ascribed to Antipater of Sidon, who in 140 BCE included them in a long poem meant to serve as a travel guide for visitors to the eastern Mediterranean and Near East.

temples. The older of the two was built before 550 BCE and burned down in 356 BCE. Its replacement was built on the same site and destroyed by the invasion of the Goths in 262 CE.

4. The statue of Zeus at Olympia. The statue of an enthroned Zeus stood inside the temple dedicated to him at Olympia. It was 39 feet (12 m) tall, crafted from ivory and gold by the famous sculptor Phidias in 430 BCE. It was trans-

ported to Constantinople in the 4th century CE, where it was destroyed by fire in 475.

5. The Mausoleum of Halicarnassus was built sometime before 350 BCE to serve as a funerary monument for King Mausolus II of Caria, in what is now Anatolia, Turkey. Severely damaged by an earthquake during the medieval period, its ruins were

used as a quarry by the Knights of Malta to build the Castle of St. Peter in nearby Bodrum.

6. The Colossus of Rhodes was a monumental bronze statue, most likely depicting the sun god, that stood approximately 100–115 feet (30–35 m) high. It was erected around 300 BCE and was destroyed by an earthquake in

225 BCE. The majority of the debris was transported to Asia Minor, where it was sold.

7. The Lighthouse of Alexandria was constructed on the small island of Pharos in the harbor of Alexandria less than a mile from

the coast. At around 380–440 feet (115–135 m) high, it was the tallest structure on earth at the time. Constructed around 300–282/279 BCE, the lighthouse stood for over a millenium until it was destroyed by an earthquake in 1330. Its ruins were quarried to build the nearby fortress of Qaitbey.

Selected Egyptian Deities

Anubis: Jackal-headed guardian of the dead, oversaw mummification rituals and protected cemeteries

Apis: Sacred bull of the city of Memphis

Aton: A sun disk with rays that end in hands, he was the one and only god, worshipped as ruler of the universe under the renegade Pharaoh Akhenaton.

Geb and Nut: Gods of the earth and sky respectively, usually depicted together with Nut arching her body over Geb.

Hathor: A cow deity, the goddess of love, peace, dance and beauty.

Horus: Son of Isis and Osiris; has a falcon's head. The god of light and preserver of cosmic order, he serves as the pharaohs' protector, battling chaos in the form of the dark god Seth.

Isis: The mother goddess, sister and wife of Osiris. Isis put together the scattered pieces of his body after Seth murdered him.

Khnum: A ram-headed creation deity who formed the first humans and gods on his potter's wheel.

Maat: In charge of justice, she maintains balance in the universe by weighing hearts of the dead and deciding which should be allowed to proceed to the afterlife.

Osiris: Initially the king of the gods, he sits on a throne like a pharaoh. His brother Seth killed him and scattered the pieces of his body. Osiris is depicted with a green face.

Re: The sun god, father of all the gods. During the New Kingdom he was melded with the ancient god Amon to form Amon-Re, chief god of the Egyptian empire.

Seth: God of the desert, chaos, storms and violence, he has a beast's head. He murdered his brother Osiris, and battles Horus for control of the cosmic order.

Thoth: Usually depicted as an ibis or ape, he is god of science, magic and writing, scribe of the underworld, and author of the Book of the Dead.

Gods of the Greeks and Romans (selected)

Greek name	Roman	Description
Aphrodite	Venus	Goddess of love and beauty, daughter of Zeus
Apollo	Apollo	God of fine art, music and archery, son of Zeus
Ares	Mars	God of war, physical force and strength, son of Zeus and Hera, lover of Aphrodite
Athena	Minerva	Patron goddess of the city of Athens and goddess of wisdom and military strategy, daughter of Zeus
Demeter	Ceres	Goddess of the earth and fertility, sister of Zeus
Dionysus	Bacchus	God of wine and ecstasy, son of Zeus
Eros	Amor/Cupid	God of (sexual) love and desire
Hades	Pluto	God of death, ruler of the underworld, brother of Zeus
Helios	Sol	Sun god
Hephaistos	Vulcan	Lame god of the forge, fire and metalworking, son of Hera and husband of Aphrodite
Hera	Juno	Goddess of women, marriage and motherhood, older sister and wife of Zeus
Hermes	Mercury	Messenger of the gods, protector of travelers, businessmen and thieves, son of Zeus
Hestia	Vesta	Goddess of the hearth and housekeeping, sister of Zeus
The Muses	The Muses	Nine minor goddesses of the arts, daughters of Zeus
Persephone	Proserpina	Goddess of the growing season and later of the underworld, abducted by Hades and ransomed by her mother, Demeter (in later myths she's the daughter of Demeter and Zeus)
Poseidon	Neptune	God of the ocean seas, protector of sailors, brother of Zeus
Zeus	Jupiter	Ruler of Olympus and the gods, philandering husband of Hera

Early Writing

Cuneiform	𒀭𒈾𒇷𒄿... (cuneiform signs)
Hieroglyphs	(hieroglyphic signs)
Phoenician	(Phoenician letters)
Greek	Α Β Γ Δ Ε Ζ Η Θ Ι Κ Λ Μ Ν Ξ Ο Π Ρ Σ Τ Υ Φ Χ Ψ Ω
Latin	A B C D E F H I K L M N O P Q R S T V X Z

The Rosetta Stone bears the same text inscribed in three different scripts: hieroglyphic, demotic and Greek. Its discovery made it possible for J.F. Champollion to decipher Egyptian hieroglyphics in 1822.

Cuneiform is the world's oldest form of writing, invented by the Sumerians in its pictographic form around 4000 bce. The earliest script is logographic, with each sign standing for a word that could have a variety of meanings depending on what language was used. Later cuneiform is syllabic, with signs combined to form words.

Hieroglyphs are used in many cultures, but are best known from Egypt, where they are first used around 3200 bce. Hieroglyphs can be phonograms, indicating sounds, unvoiced determinatives (semagrams), which give other signs meaning, or pictograms, which are usually logographic signs for individual words. Phonograms are closest to what we think of as an alphabet, with signs corresponding directly to sounds. Determinatives clarify the meaning of the preceding word. A female figure might indicate that the speaker is a woman, or that the cattle listed in a funerary text were cows instead of bulls. Pictograms can be literal or associative. A throne and a building together is a "throne-house" (= palace), for example, and a flamingo hieroglyph can indicate the bird itself or its red color.

Phoenician is a true alphabetic script, with each sign corresponding to a sound. Like Egyptian hieroglyphs, however, there are no vowels. The first two letters in the Phoenician alphabet are *aleph* and *beth*, from which we derive the word "alphabet." The oldest version of the Phoenician alphabet from the city of Ugarit (Ras Shamra) uses signs similar to cuneiform and dates from 1400/1300 bce. Later versions that employ abstract symbols date from approximately 1300–900 bce and come primarily from Byblos.

Ancient Greek writing developed from Phoenician prototypes in the 9th century bce. Unlike Phoenician, which included only consonants, the Greek alphabet also had short and long vowels as well as diacritics used to indicate emphasis and pitch. Cyrillic script, used by many Slavic languages, is closely related.

Latin script, which developed from western Greek writing, is the most widely used alphabet in the world today. At first the Romans used only capital letters (*majuscule*); lower case letters (*miniscule*) were introduced later, during the late Classical and medieval periods.

Inventions of the Ancient World

~7500 bce	**Metalworking**
~5000 bce	**Millstone and loom** (Egypt, Mesopotamia)
~4000 bce	**The wheel** (Mesopotamia)
~3700 bce	**Stamp seals and counters** (Sumer)
~3500 bce	**The plow and potter's wheel** (Sumer)
~3250 bce	**Pictographic writing** (Sumer)
~3200 bce	**Winemaking** (Sumer)
~3000 bce	**Nails and the lathe** (Mesopotamia) and **Mold-made glass** (Egypt and Mesopotamia)
~2700 bce	**Cuneiform syllabic script** (Mesopotamia)
~2600 bce	**Carpenter's square** (Egypt)
~2500 bce	**Astronomy and medicine** (Egypt and Babylon)
~2300 bce	**Gears** (Mesopotamia)
~2100 bce	**Accurate measures, weights and scales** (Mesopotamia)
~2000 bce	**Sundial and large-scale canalization** (Egypt and Mesopotamia)
	and **Mathematics and star charts** (Babylon)
~1900 bce	**Iron smelting** (Mesopotamia)
~1750 bce	**Chariot** (Mesopotamia)
~1600 bce	**Enamel inlay** (Egypt)
~1400 bce	**Phoenician alphabet** (Ugarit) and **Parchment scrolls** (Egypt)
~1200 bce	**Compass** (China)
~1000 bce	**Spinning wheel** (India, China)
~750 bce	**Iron blades** (Assyria)
~700 bce	**Aqueducts** (Armenia, Urartu) and **Dentures** (Etruscans)
~600 bce	**Coins** (Lydia)
~550 bce	**Geographical maps** (Greece)
~400 bce	**Catapult** (Greece)
~85 bce	**Gristmill** (Greece)
~50 ce	**Horseshoes** (Romans)
~105 ce	**Paper** (China)
~250 ce	**Wheelbarrow** (China)

Ancient Intellectuals

Poets and Playwrights

Homer (8th century bce) marks the beginning of Western literature with his epic works *Iliad* and *Odyssey*, which tell of the Trojan War and wanderings of Odysseus.

Hesiod (ca. 700 bce) is best known for his epic poem *Theogony*, about the creation of the world and the gods. *Works and Days* focuses on the trials of daily life during the Greek Dark Ages.

Sappho (ca. 630–570 bce), born on the island of Lesbos, was one of the greatest lyric poets of Greek antiquity. Her work is best known for its intense emotional expression.

Aeschylus (525–456 bce) was the first to write stage plays for more than one actor. He authored eighteen plays including *Persians*, *Seven Against Thebes* and *Prometheus Bound*.

Pindar (ca. 522–445 bce), one of antiquity's most important lyric poets, is known through just seventeen surviving works, most of them short hymns and odes.

Sophocles (ca. 496–405 bce) won numerous competitions for tragedy, writing a total of 123 plays, including *Antigone*, *Oedipus Rex* and *Electra*.

Euripides (ca. 485–406 bce) wrote ninety plays, eighteen of which have survived, including *Bacchae*, *Electra*, *Trojan Women*, *Heracles* and *Cyclops*.

Aristophanes (ca. 448–385 bce) is the most important Greek comic playwright. His works include *Wasps*, *Birds*, *Frogs* and *Lysistrata*.

Philosophers

Thales of Miletus (ca. 640–550 bce) believed that water was the origin of all things. He was also an astronomer and mathematician.

Anaximander (ca. 610–545 bce) based his complex philosophy on the principle of *apeiron*, the "limitless origin" of all things.

Anaximenes (ca. 585–528 bce) viewed air as the original element and foundation of all life.

Pythagoras (ca. 570–510 bce), an important mathematician, devised the Pythagorean theorem. As a philosopher he focused on the relationship between changing and unchanging things.

Heraclitus (ca. 540–475 bce) came from Ephesus. He understood change as the principle guiding all life, summarized in his famous aphorism: "everything is in a state of flux" (*panta rhei*). He saw the universe as ruled by *logos*, an abstract concept related to reason.

Parmenides (ca. 540–475 bce), from Elea, described the unchanging state of "being" and its eternal relationship to a changeable state of "becoming."

Socrates (469–399 bce) taught his strictly ethical philosophy through dialogues with students in Athens, identifying himself more as a "midwife" (*maia*) of ideas than as an original thinker. Condemned for corrupting the youth of Athens, he was forced to commit suicide.

Plato (ca. 428–347 bce) saw himself as a teacher of ideas, a philosopher who strove to understand all things in their real and ideal forms, from which he hoped to derive the unchanging, truest essence of the universe. Plato's hierarchal ordering put the ideal of "the Good" at the center of all being. Christians later identified this concept with God.

Aristotle (384–322 bce) was a philosopher, scientist and tutor of Alexander the Great. His systematic descriptions make him the founder of natural science.

Historians

Herodotus (ca. 485–425 bce) is called "the father of history" based on his nine volumes covering the Greek and Persian war (*History*). He freely mixes folktale and myth with gripping narrative accounts of battles like the Spartan defeat by the Persians at Thermopylae.

Thucydides (ca. 460–396 bce) is the founder of critical historical investigation. His major work, which focused on the Peloponnesian War (431–404 bce), avoids mythological interpretations in favor of fact-based description and analysis.

Physicians

Hippocrates (ca. 460–370 bce) founded scientific medicine in his sixty-one-volume work *Corpus Hippocraticum*. In addition to describing treatments for a variety of diseases, he explained the human body in terms of the four "humors" (elements): blood, mucus, yellow bile and black bile.

Europe in Detail – Ancient Rome

6th–5th Centuries BCE: The Origins of Rome

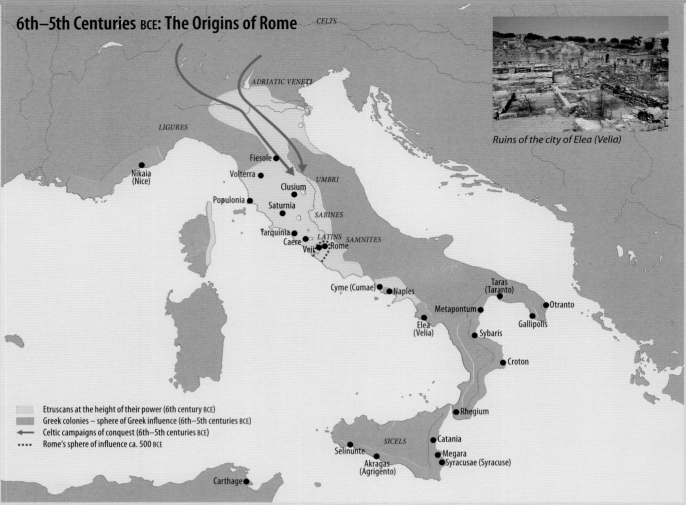

Ruins of the city of Elea (Velia)

Legend:
- Etruscans at the height of their power (6th century BCE)
- Greek colonies – sphere of Greek influence (6th–5th centuries BCE)
- Celtic campaigns of conquest (6th–5th centuries BCE)
- Rome's sphere of influence ca. 500 BCE

Map labels: CELTS, ADRIATIC VENETI, LIGURES, Nikaia (Nice), Fiesole, Volterra, Clusium, UMBRI, Populonia, Saturnia, SABINES, Tarquinia, Caere, Veji, LATINS, SAMNITES, Rome, Cyme (Cumae), Naples, Metapontum, Taras (Taranto), Otranto, Elea (Velia), Sybaris, Gallipolis, Croton, Rhegium, Catania, SICELS, Megara, Selinunte, Akragas (Agrigento), Syracusae (Syracuse), Carthage

282–264 BCE: Roman Expansion in Italy

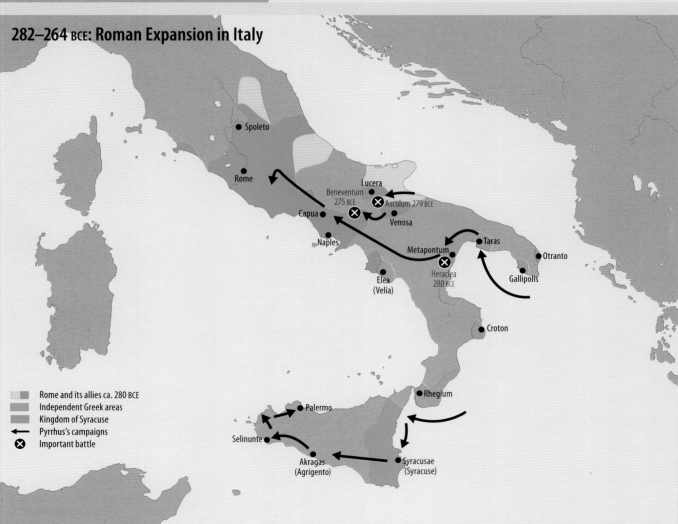

Legend:
- Rome and its allies ca. 280 BCE
- Independent Greek areas
- Kingdom of Syracuse
- Pyrrhus's campaigns
- Important battle

Map labels: Spoleto, Rome, Lucera, Beneventum 275 BCE, Asculum 279 BCE, Capua, Venosa, Naples, Taras, Metapontum, Otranto, Heraclea 280 BCE, Gallipolis, Elea (Velia), Croton, Rhegium, Palermo, Selinunte, Akragas (Agrigento), Syracusae (Syracuse)

Rome rose from modest beginnings to a position of military and political supremacy in the Mediterranean world and beyond. By the time of the Roman Republic (509–27 BCE), Rome's influence was already extending beyond the European continent into the Near East. During the period of the Roman Empire (27 BCE–476 CE), Roman culture became more refined, taking on the legacy of Hellenism and spreading it throughout its world empire. With the onset of the 3rd century CE the empire began to fall apart as barbarian tribes overran border defenses. In the end, its legacy would continue into the medieval period through the Byzantine Empire in the east, but also through the "barbarian" Germanic peoples who conquered the west.

from 800 BCE The Etruscan people settle in the Italian peninsula.

753 BCE Founding of Rome, according to legend, but the city was probably settled closer to 650 BCE.

~650 BCE Etruscan kings rule Rome.

510 BCE Rome deposes the last Etruscan king, Tarquinius Superbus.

509 BCE The Romans replace the monarchy with the Roman Republic.

494 BCE The first plebeian tribune with veto rights is established in Rome.

474 BCE Etruscans are defeated by the Greeks at sea in the Battle of Cumae, ending their dominance of central Italy.

~450 BCE The Law of the Twelve Tables, the oldest surviving Roman law code: it promotes equality under the law between patricians and plebeians.

393 BCE Rome conquers Veii, an important Etruscan city near Rome.

387 BCE Rome is sacked by a Celtic tribe from Gaul led by Brennus.

367 BCE Constitutional reform establishes the leadership of the republic under two consuls to be chosen by annual election.

343–290 BCE Victory in the Samnite and Latin Wars

consolidates Rome's position as the dominant power throughout central Italy.

~300 BCE Plebeians—citizens of Rome who are farmers, shopkeepers and artisans, rather than patricians—are granted access to higher offices previously open only to the noble patrician class.

from 300 BCE Rome begins to expand beyond Italy into the Mediterranean regions.

280–275 BCE Greek commander Pyrrhus retreats, ending Greek power in the western Mediterranean.

265 BCE Rome rules all of Italy.

264–241 BCE After victory in the First Punic War against Carthage, Rome controls Corsica, Sicily and most of the western Mediterranean.

218–201 BCE The Second Punic War begins with Hannibal's land campaign against Rome.

216 BCE Hannibal inflicts a crushing defeat on the Roman army at Cannae.

202 BCE Rome decisively defeats Carthage at Zama (in what is now Tunisia).

192–188 BCE Rome defeats the Seleucid king Antiochus the Great, taking control of large parts of Asia Minor.

168–146 BCE Rome defeats Macedonia, giving it control of most of Greece.

149–146 BCE The Third Punic War ends with Rome's complete destruction of Carthage.

133 BCE Rome begins rule in Spain, formerly a province of Carthage.

133–121 BCE The brothers Tiberius and Gaius Gracchus attempt but fail to pass land reform laws.

102–101 BCE General Gaius Marius drives the Germanic Cimbri and Teuton tribes out of Italy.

100–50 BCE Crisis grips the Roman Republic: expansion takes its toll on the people who labor and are taxed to support the widespread Roman armies, and rebellions erupt.

91–88 BCE The Social War: Rome's Italian allies demand full citizenship rights.

The Second Punic War, 218–201 BCE

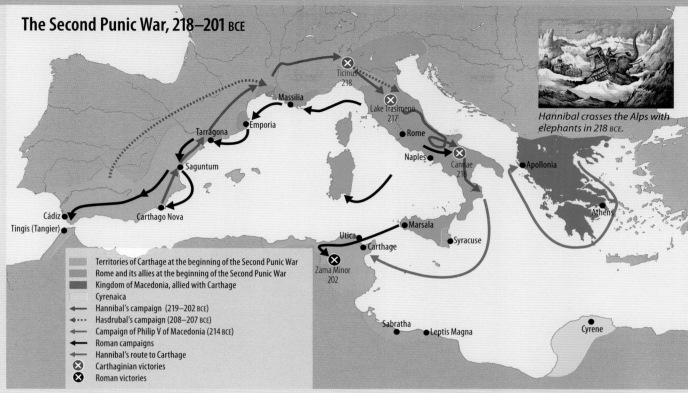

Hannibal crosses the Alps with elephants in 218 BCE.

Territories of Carthage at the beginning of the Second Punic War
Rome and its allies at the beginning of the Second Punic War
Kingdom of Macedonia, allied with Carthage
Cyrenaica
Hannibal's campaign (219–202 BCE)
Hasdrubal's campaign (208–207 BCE)
Campaign of Philip V of Macedonia (214 BCE)
Roman campaigns
Hannibal's route to Carthage
Carthaginian victories
Roman victories

Roman Expansion, 200–46 BCE

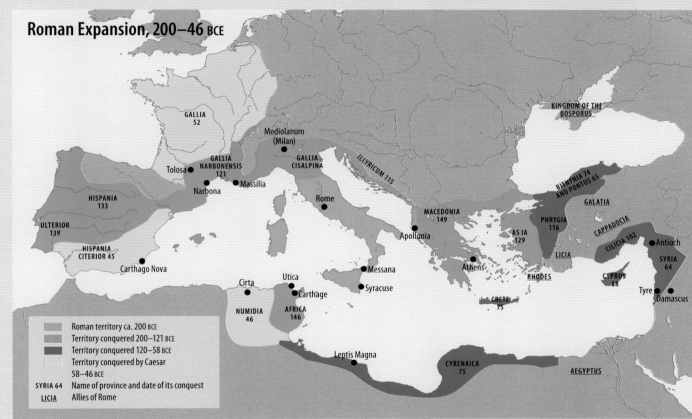

Roman territory ca. 200 BCE
Territory conquered 200–121 BCE
Territory conquered 120–58 BCE
Territory conquered by Caesar 58–46 BCE
SYRIA 64 Name of province and date of its conquest
LICIA Allies of Rome

88 BCE Civil war breaks out between supporters of Gaius Marius and Lucius Cornelius Sulla.

87–84 BCE Gaius Marius and Lucius Cornelius Cinna are the first to serve multiple terms as consuls.

87–63 BCE The Mithridatic Wars are fought between the Roman Empire and its last great enemy, Mithridates VI of Pontus (northern Anatolia).

Romulus and Remus were the twin brothers credited in legend with the founding of Rome. Children of the god Mars and the mother goddess Rhea Silvia, they were abandoned on the banks of the Tiber River after their birth, where a she-wolf rescued and raised them. Romulus struck down his brother during a dispute over who had the right to name and rule the new city.

Publius Cornelius Scipio Africanus the Elder (236–183 BCE) was the most renowned Roman general prior to Julius Caesar.

He defeated the Carthaginians in Spain in 210 BCE and invaded Africa to defeat Hannibal at the Battle of Zama in 202 BCE.

Tiberius Sempronius Gracchus (162–133 BCE) was an elected tribune who tried to pass land reform laws that would distribute public lands among landless plebeians, to the benefit of the republic as well as the commoners themselves. This plan failed due to opposition from the senate, which later had him clubbed to death in the Forum. His younger brother Gaius Sempronius Gracchus (153–121 BCE) continued

his work, only to meet with a similar fate during a skirmish between his followers and senate supporters.

Spartacus (? –71 BCE), slave and gladiator, probably came from Thrace. He led a slave revolt against Rome in 73–71 BCE before dying at the decisive Battle of Silarus. The victorious Roman general Crassus ordered the six thousand surviving slaves to be crucified along the Appian Way as a warning to others.

The Roman Empire at its Greatest Extent

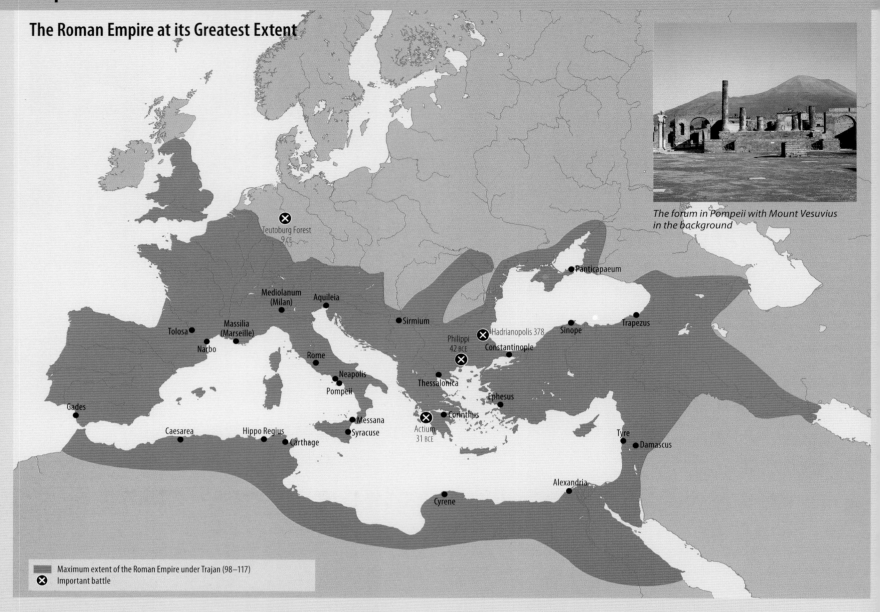

The forum in Pompeii with Mount Vesuvius in the background

Maximum extent of the Roman Empire under Trajan (98–117)

Important battle

82–79 BCE Sulla declares himself dictator; bloody persecution of supporters of Marius and Cinna follow.

by 63 BCE Syria, Palestine, Asia Minor and Armenia are all brought under Roman control.

60 BCE Julius Caesar, Pompey and Marcus Licinius Crassus form the First Triumvirate; the republican constitution is suspended.

58–51 BCE Caesar conquers Gaul.

49 BCE Civil war breaks out between Caesar and Pompey.

48 BCE Caesar defeats Pompey, who is murdered in Egypt. Caesar declares himself consul and later, in 45 BCE, dictator for life.

44 BCE Caesar is murdered in the senate by supporters of the republic.

42 BCE The Second Triumvirate of Mark Antony, Marcus Lepidus and Octavian (later Emperor Augustus) is in control. Lepidus and Octavian defeat Caesar's murderers at Philippi. Lepidus is excluded from the triumvirate in 36 CE.

31 BCE Octavian defeats the fleet of Mark Antony and Cleopatra at Actium.

27 BCE The Roman imperial period begins. The senate awards Octavian the honorary title of Augustus ("illustrious one").

9 CE Roman troops commanded by Publius Quinctilius Varus are defeated at the Teutoburg Forest by Germanic tribes led by Arminius.

14–68 The Julio-Claudian dynasty begins with the emperors Tiberius, Caligula, Claudius and Nero.

64 Rome is devastated by fire and Nero blames the Christians, beginning persecution.

69–96 The Flavian dynasty: Vespasian and in turn his sons, Titus and Domitian, are emperor.

70 Titus sacks Jerusalem.

79 Mount Vesuvius erupts, destroying Pompeii and Herculaneum.

96–180 The Antonine dynasty regulates imperial succession in that the ruling emperor officially adopts the most capable political successor as his son. The reigns of Trajan (98–117) and Hadrian (117–138) mark the high point of the Roman Empire.

166–180 Marcus Aurelius, the philosopher emperor, fights the Marcomannic Wars against Germans and Sarmatians.

193–211 Following a series of violent conflicts and oppressive measures, Emperor Septimus Severus consolidates the empire.

193–235 The Severan dynasty, which originated in North Africa, strengthens the military and imports oriental cults into Rome.

231–233 War against the Persian Sasanian (Sassanid) empire weakens Rome.

235–284 A series of soldier-emperors rule. Their short-lived reigns involve repeated violent overthrow of the throne, competing claims to succession, social and political instability, and the increased incursion of barbarian peoples.

257–258 Emperor Valerian begins executing Christians.

270–275 Emperor Aurelian builds the last great fortification around Rome: the Aurelian Wall. Roman armies destroy Palmyra in 273 and elevate one of its gods, Sol Invictus, the "undefeatable sun," to the highest rank of imperial deities.

285–305 Emperor Diocletian reorganizes the imperial government by establishing the Tetrarchy, which places Rome under the rule of two major emperors (*Augusti*) and two minor ones (*Caesares*). He also revives ancient Roman religious practices, giving himself the title of *Jovius* (Jupiter) and his co-emperor Maximian the title *Herculius* (Hercules).

286–287 Britain briefly frees itself from Roman imperial control.

303–305 The last great wave of Christian persecution takes place under Diocletian and Maximian.

306–337 Emperor Constantine the Great dissolves the Tetrarchy, declaring himself sole ruler in 324.

395–476 CE: The Collapse of the Roman Empire

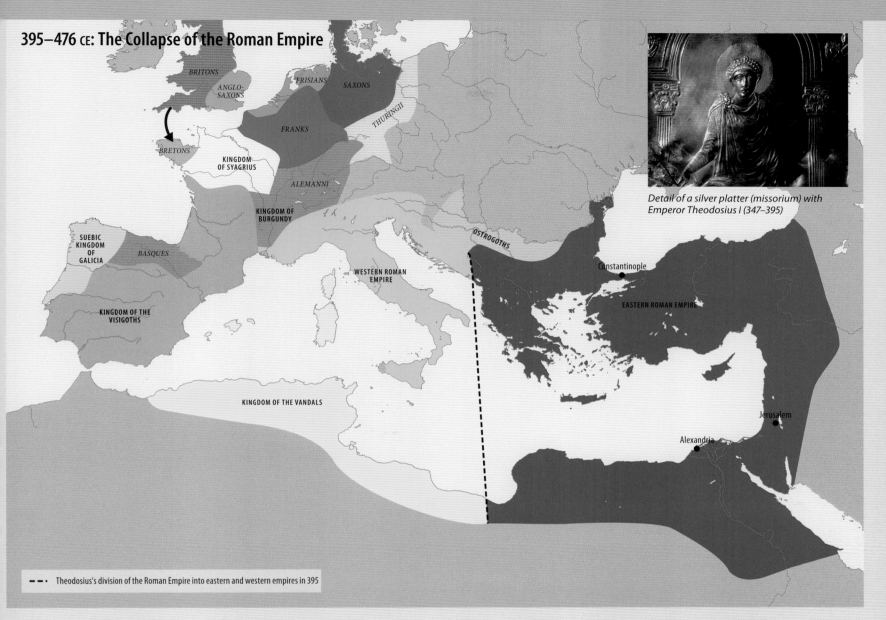

BRITONS

ANGLO-SAXONS

FRISIANS

SAXONS

FRANKS

THURINGII

BRETONS

KINGDOM OF SYAGRIUS

ALEMANNI

KINGDOM OF BURGUNDY

SUEBIC KINGDOM OF GALICIA

BASQUES

WESTERN ROMAN EMPIRE

OSTROGOTHS

Constantinople

EASTERN ROMAN EMPIRE

KINGDOM OF THE VISIGOTHS

Jerusalem

Alexandria

KINGDOM OF THE VANDALS

Detail of a silver platter (missorium) with Emperor Theodosius I (347–395)

- - - Theodosius's division of the Roman Empire into eastern and western empires in 395

313 The Edict of Milan grants Christians religious freedom.

330 Constantine makes Byzantium (later Constantinople) his imperial residence, declaring it capital of the Eastern Roman Empire.

337–363 Emperor Constantine is baptized a Christian on his deathbed in 337; Constantine's descendants rule the eastern empire.

361–363 Emperor Julian the Apostate, the last non-Christian emperor, attempts to revive pagan religion.

364–392 Valentinian I (364–375) seizes power, starting a new imperial dynasty.

378 Visigoths defeat the Romans at the Battle of Hadrianople (now Edirne).

379–395 Reign of Theodosius the Great, who reunites the empire a final time.

391–392 Theodosius declares Christianity the sole religion of the empire.

395 The Roman Empire is divided into eastern and western halves. Germanic armies rapidly overwhelm the western empire.

450–457 The rise of the eastern empire to become the Byzantine Empire begins with reign of Emperor Marcian.

451 General Aetius defeats invasion of Atilla the Hun and his hordes near Catalonia.

455 Valentinian III is murdered; the western empire falls to German chieftains and Byzantine emperors.

476 German chieftain Odoacer deposes Romulus Augustulus, the last western Roman emperor.

Marcus Tullius Cicero (106–43 BCE) was a politician, philosopher and magnificent orator who gave speeches defending republican principles. Opposed to the Second Triumvirate, he was murdered by followers of Mark Antony.

Julius Caesar (100–44 BCE) was a brilliant general and the conqueror of Gaul. After rejecting the title of king, he declared himself absolute dictator, accelerating the end of the Roman Republic.

Virgil (70–19 BCE) was a poet celebrated for verses including his epic *Aeneid*, which sang of the origins and glory of Rome.

Augustus (63 BCE–14 CE), the adoptive son of Julius Caesar, showed himself to be a gifted leader and politician in the wake of Caesar's murder. The first Roman emperor,

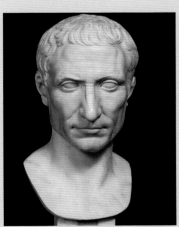

Julius Caesar (100–44 BCE)

he was given the name of Augustus by the Roman Senate in 27 BCE.

Livy (59 BCE–17 CE) was best known for his epic study *Ab urbe condita*, a work about the early history of Rome from its legendary origins to his own time.

Trajan (53–117), the first emperor to come from Spain, was crowned in 98 CE. He conquered the Parthians and Dacians, thus expanding the Roman Empire to its greatest extent, a legacy that his successors could not maintain.

Marcus Aurelius (121–180) was adopted by his predecessor, Antoninus Pius (121–180), and became emperor in 161. He fought defensive wars against the Marcomanni tribes, but was also the author of important philosophical works such as *Meditations*.

He broke with the successful practice of emperors adopting the most talented political successor and named his own son, Commodus (180–192), as his heir; Commodus proved unworthy.

Constantine I (285–337) seized the throne in 306 and abolished the Tetrarchy by eliminating all rivals for power. At the Battle of Milvian Bridge (312), where he fought his brother-in-law Maxentius for the throne, Constantine saw a cross in the sky. After his victory he recognized Christianity, which had previously been tolerated at best, alternating with periods of intense persecution. He ruled the young church with an iron hand, although he himself was baptized only on his deathbed.

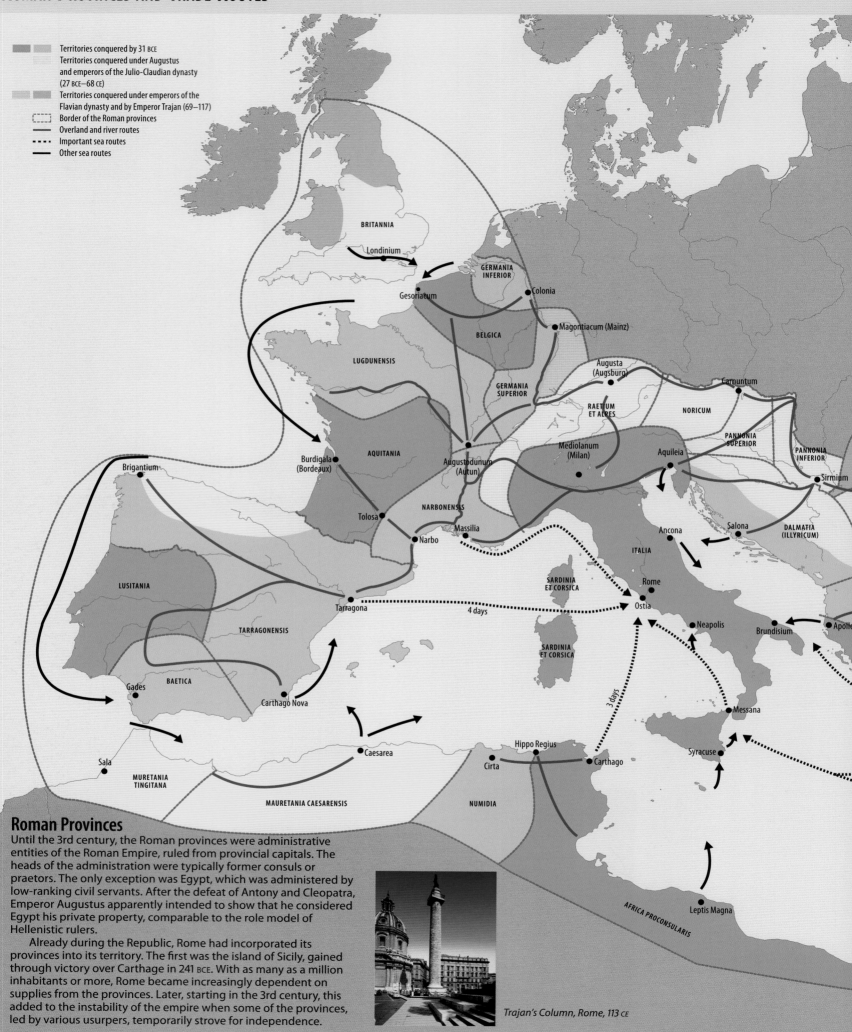

Roman Provinces and Trade Routes

BRITANNIA

Londinium

GERMANIA INFERIOR

Gesoriacum · Colonia

BELGICA

Magontiacum (Mainz)

LUGDUNENSIS

GERMANIA SUPERIOR

Augusta (Augsburg)

Carnuntum

RAETIUM ET ALPES

NORICUM

PANNONIA SUPERIOR

PANNONIA INFERIOR

Burdigala (Bordeaux)

AQUITANIA

Augustodunum (Autun)

Mediolanum (Milan)

Aquileia

Sirmium

Brigantium

Tolosa

NARBONENSIS

Massilia

Ancona

Salona

DALMATIA (ILLYRICUM)

Narbo

ITALIA

LUSITANIA

SARDINIA ET CORSICA

Rome

TARRAGONENSIS

Tarragona

4 days

Ostia

Neapolis

Brundisium

Apollon

SARDINIA ET CORSICA

Gades

BAETICA

Carthago Nova

3 days

Messana

Sala

Caesarea

Hippo Regius

Carthago

Syracuse

MURETANIA TINGITANA

Cirta

NUMIDIA

MAURETANIA CAESARENSIS

AFRICA PROCONSULARIS

Leptis Magna

Roman Provinces

Until the 3rd century, the Roman provinces were administrative entities of the Roman Empire, ruled from provincial capitals. The heads of the administration were typically former consuls or praetors. The only exception was Egypt, which was administered by low-ranking civil servants. After the defeat of Antony and Cleopatra, Emperor Augustus apparently intended to show that he considered Egypt his private property, comparable to the role model of Hellenistic rulers.

Already during the Republic, Rome had incorporated its provinces into its territory. The first was the island of Sicily, gained through victory over Carthage in 241 BCE. With as many as a million inhabitants or more, Rome became increasingly dependent on supplies from the provinces. Later, starting in the 3rd century, this added to the instability of the empire when some of the provinces, led by various usurpers, temporarily strove for independence.

Trajan's Column, Rome, 113 CE

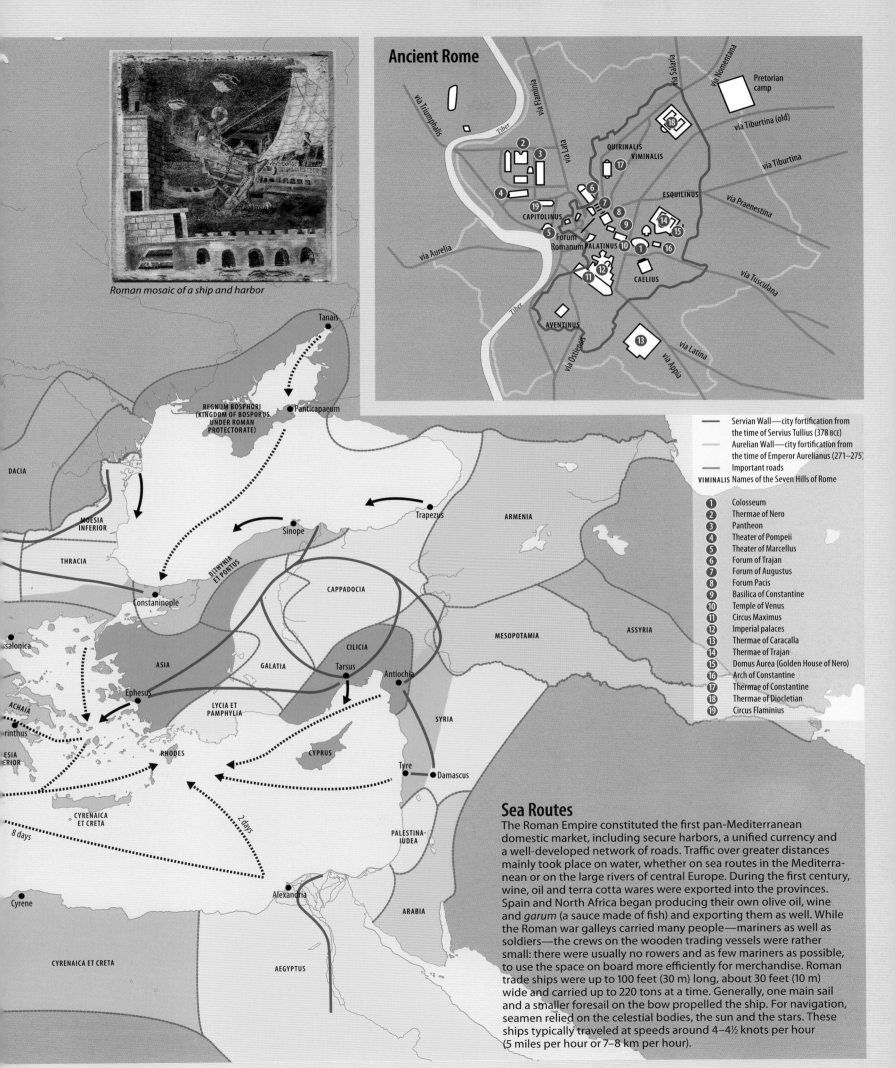

Roman mosaic of a ship and harbor

Ancient Rome

via Triumphalis
via Flaminia
via Salaria
via Nomentana
via Lata
Tiber
Pretorian camp
via Tiburtina (old)
via Tiburtina
QUIRINALIS
VIMINALIS
via Praenestina
ESQUILINUS
via Aurelia
CAPITOLINUS
Forum Romanum
PALATINUS
CAELIUS
via Tusculana
Tiber
AVENTINUS
via Ostiensis
via Latina
via Appia

① Colosseum
② Thermae of Nero
③ Pantheon
④ Theater of Pompeii
⑤ Theater of Marcellus
⑥ Forum of Trajan
⑦ Forum of Augustus
⑧ Forum Pacis
⑨ Basilica of Constantine
⑩ Temple of Venus
⑪ Circus Maximus
⑫ Imperial palaces
⑬ Thermae of Caracalla
⑭ Thermae of Trajan
⑮ Domus Aurea (Golden House of Nero)
⑯ Arch of Constantine
⑰ Thermae of Constantine
⑱ Thermae of Diocletian
⑲ Circus Flaminius

Servian Wall—city fortification from the time of Servius Tullius (378 BCE)
Aurelian Wall—city fortification from the time of Emperor Aurelianus (271–275)
Important roads
VIMINALIS Names of the Seven Hills of Rome

Tanais
REGNUM BOSPHORI (KINGDOM OF BOSPORUS UNDER ROMAN PROTECTORATE)
Panticapaeum
DACIA
MOESIA INFERIOR
THRACIA
Sinope
Trapezus
ARMENIA
BITHYNIA ET PONTUS
Constaninople
CAPPADOCIA
MESOPOTAMIA
ASSYRIA
...salonica
ASIA
GALATIA
CILICIA
Tarsus
Antiochia
ACHAIA
Ephesus
LYCIA ET PAMPHYLIA
SYRIA
...rinthus
RHODES
CYPRUS
Tyre
Damascus
...ESIA ...ERIOR
2 days
8 days
CYRENAICA ET CRETA
PALESTINA-IUDEA
Cyrene
Alexandria
ARABIA
CYRENAICA ET CRETA
AEGYPTUS

Sea Routes

The Roman Empire constituted the first pan-Mediterranean domestic market, including secure harbors, a unified currency and a well-developed network of roads. Traffic over greater distances mainly took place on water, whether on sea routes in the Mediterranean or on the large rivers of central Europe. During the first century, wine, oil and terra cotta wares were exported into the provinces. Spain and North Africa began producing their own olive oil, wine and *garum* (a sauce made of fish) and exporting them as well. While the Roman war galleys carried many people—mariners as well as soldiers—the crews on the wooden trading vessels were rather small: there were usually no rowers and as few mariners as possible, to use the space on board more efficiently for merchandise. Roman trade ships were up to 100 feet (30 m) long, about 30 feet (10 m) wide and carried up to 220 tons at a time. Generally, one main sail and a smaller foresail on the bow propelled the ship. For navigation, seamen relied on the celestial bodies, the sun and the stars. These ships typically traveled at speeds around 4–4½ knots per hour (5 miles per hour or 7–8 km per hour).

BIBLICAL TIMES UNTIL 70 CE

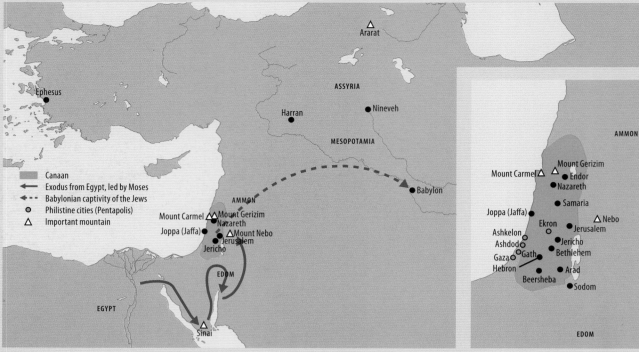

Canaan
→ Exodus from Egypt, led by Moses
⊷ Babylonian captivity of the Jews
○ Philistine cities (Pentapolis)
△ Important mountain

The Exodus of the Israelites from Egypt

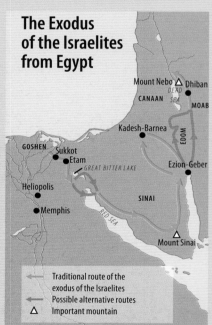

→ Traditional route of the exodus of the Israelites
→ Possible alternative routes
△ Important mountain

Palestine 10th Century BCE

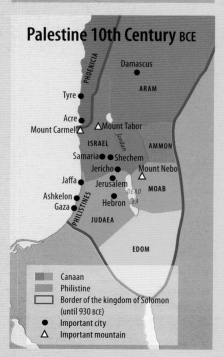

Canaan
Philistine
Border of the kingdom of Solomon (until 930 BCE)
● Important city
△ Important mountain

The Hebrew Bible

~2000 BCE The patriarchs of the Israelites—Abraham, his son Isaac and grandson Jacob—live in Mesopotamia. Jacob's twelve sons become the founding ancestors of the twelve tribes of Israel.

13th century BCE Moses leads the Israelites out of slavery in Egypt in the defining event known as the Exodus and then receives the Torah (religious law) from God on Mount Sinai. The Israelites arrive in Canaan, the "Promised Land."

1250–1100 BCE The Israelites settle in tribal groups in Canaan.

1250–1000 BCE The period of the Judges brings religious unity to the twelve tribes by regulating cultic duties and ritual behavior.

~1220–1210 BCE The Israelites are mentioned for the first time outside the Bible in the Israel Stele erected by the Egyptian pharaoh Merneptah. Its inscription may corroborate the biblical period of captivity in Egypt (15th–12th centuries BCE).

~1200 BCE The Sea Peoples, who may be the biblical Philistines, settle in the eastern Mediterranean region, entering into a nearly continual state of war with Israel.

11th century BCE Samuel, the final judge, anoints Saul as Israel's first king.

~1020 BCE Saul rules as Israel's first king.

~1004–965 BCE King David rules from his capital of Jerusalem, making the city an important religious center.

~965–926 BCE King Solomon builds the First Temple on the Temple Mount in Jerusalem, the seat of ancient Judaism.

926 BCE The kingdom of the Israelites is divided into two kingdoms, with Israel in the north and Judaea in the south. Revolts break out, resulting in religious strife and frequent changes of leadership.

722 BCE The Assyrians conquer Israel and make Judaea a subject nation.

626 BCE The Babylonians take control of the region.

597 BCE A revolt in Judaea leads the Babylonian ruler, Nebuchadnezzar II, to respond by destroying Israel and deporting its inhabitants.

587 BCE Babylonian soldiers sack Jerusalem, destroying the First Temple. Most of the Jewish population is deported (Babylonian Exile).

539 BCE Persian ruler Cyrus II occupies Babylon, freeing the Israelites to return to their homeland.

539–445 BCE The Israelites return to Jerusalem and Judaea.

539–332 BCE Palestine flourishes under Persian rule, gaining a high degree of autonomy and religious freedom.

536–519 BCE The Second Temple in Jerusalem is built. Herod the Great will enlarge it in the first century BCE.

332–200 BCE Palestine falls under the rule of Alexander the Great, and will be controlled by the Egyptian Ptolemaic dynasty after his death.

200–198 BCE The Seleucid king Antiochus III the Great occupies Israel and most of Palestine, promising religious freedom.

175–164 BCE Antiochus IV Epiphanes seizes the Temple treasures and bans Jewish worship in Jerusalem in an attempt to Hellenize Jewish culture, demanding Jews worship Zeus.

167 BCE The nationalist Maccabee movement revolts against Seleucid rule, forming an independent state in 165 BCE.

165/161–63 BCE The Hasmonean dynasty, led by high priests with kingly functions, rules the Maccabee state.

63 BCE The Roman general Pompey conquers all of Palestine.

37–4 BCE King Herod the Great rules as a client monarch under the protection of the Roman Empire, taking complete control of all religious matters.

The New Testament

~6 BCE Jesus and John the Baptist are born in Judaea.

4 BCE Roman King Herod the Great dies in Jericho.

5–6 CE Jesus preaches at the Temple in Jerusalem as a child of twelve.

~27 Herod Antipas, Herod the Great's successor, arrests John the Baptist.

28 Jesus begins his public life as an itinerant teacher.

~29 John the Baptist is executed by Herod Antipas.

~30 Jesus is crucified, and Christianity gradually emerges as a new religion. The apostles James and Simon Peter lead the new community.

~34 Paul (formerly Saul of Tarsus) converts to Christianity while traveling on the road to Damascus.

~38 Stephen, the first Christian martyr, is executed by stoning in Jerusalem.

44 The Romans arrest the apostle Peter.

44–48 The first Apostolic Council (or Council of Jerusalem) convenes in Jerusalem. Paul preaches Christianity to the non-Jewish population.

46–57 Paul makes his three major missionary journeys.

60–62 Paul is arrested in Jerusalem, imprisoned and eventually sent to Rome for trial.

62 The apostle James the Less is executed by stoning in Jerusalem.

64 The apostles Peter and Paul are martyred in Rome.

70 Titus sacks Jerusalem, destroying the Second Temple.

after ca. 70 The four gospel accounts attributed to the evangelists Matthew, Mark, Luke and John are composed.

Via Dolorosa

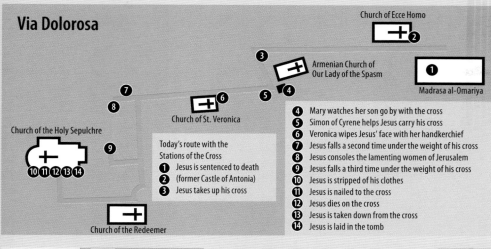

Church of Ecce Homo

Armenian Church of Our Lady of the Spasm

Madrasa al-Omariya

Church of St. Veronica

Church of the Holy Sepulchre

Church of the Redeemer

Today's route with the Stations of the Cross

1. Jesus is sentenced to death
2. (former Castle of Antonia)
3. Jesus takes up his cross
4. Mary watches her son go by with the cross
5. Simon of Cyrene helps Jesus carry his cross
6. Veronica wipes Jesus' face with her handkerchief
7. Jesus falls a second time under the weight of his cross
8. Jesus consoles the lamenting women of Jerusalem
9. Jesus falls a third time under the weight of his cross
10. Jesus is stripped of his clothes
11. Jesus is nailed to the cross
12. Jesus dies on the cross
13. Jesus is taken down from the cross
14. Jesus is laid in the tomb

Jerusalem

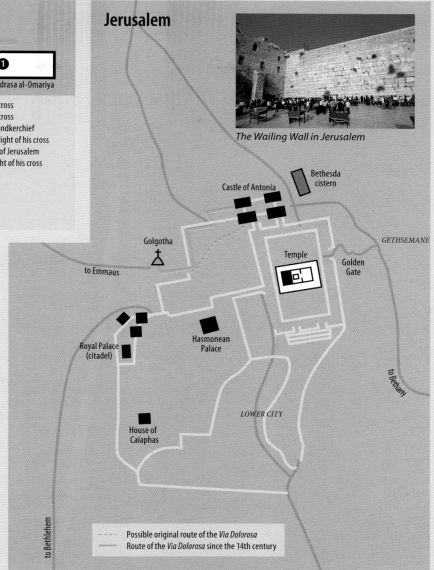

The Wailing Wall in Jerusalem

Bethesda cistern

Castle of Antonia

GETHSEMANE

Golgotha

to Emmaus

Temple

Golden Gate

Royal Palace (citadel)

Hasmonean Palace

to Bethany

LOWER CITY

House of Caiaphas

to Bethlehem

- - - - Possible original route of the *Via Dolorosa*
——— Route of the *Via Dolorosa* since the 14th century

Palestine at the Time of Jesus

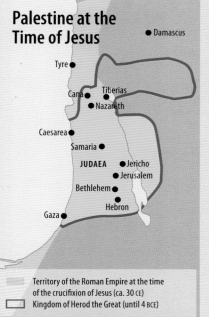

Damascus

Tyre

Cana · Tiberias
Nazareth

Caesarea

Samaria

JUDAEA · Jericho
· Jerusalem

Bethlehem

Hebron

Gaza

▨ Territory of the Roman Empire at the time of the crucifixion of Jesus (ca. 30 CE)
▢ Kingdom of Herod the Great (until 4 BCE)

The Hebrew Bible and New Testament have been printed in greater numbers than any other text. The Hebrew Bible (called the Old Testament by Christians) describes the revelation of God and documents the history and laws of the people of Israel. The New Testament is the Christian continuation of the Bible, which includes the four gospels about the life and teachings of Jesus and material about the early Christian church.

The Hebrew Bible describes the covenant between Yahweh and the people of Israel. The oldest version is a Greek translation of texts originally written in Hebrew. Variations between earlier and later versions led the Roman Catholic Church to accept forty-six Old Testament books, while the Jewish Bible, the *Tanakh*, contains just thirty-nine.

The New Testament focuses on the life and works of Jesus of Nazareth, from his teachings and miracles to his crucifixion and resurrection. In Christian tradition, the Via Dolorosa ("way of sorrows") in Jerusalem is the actual path along which Jesus carried the cross from Pontius Pilate's palace to the execution site at Golgotha.

The Journeys of Paul

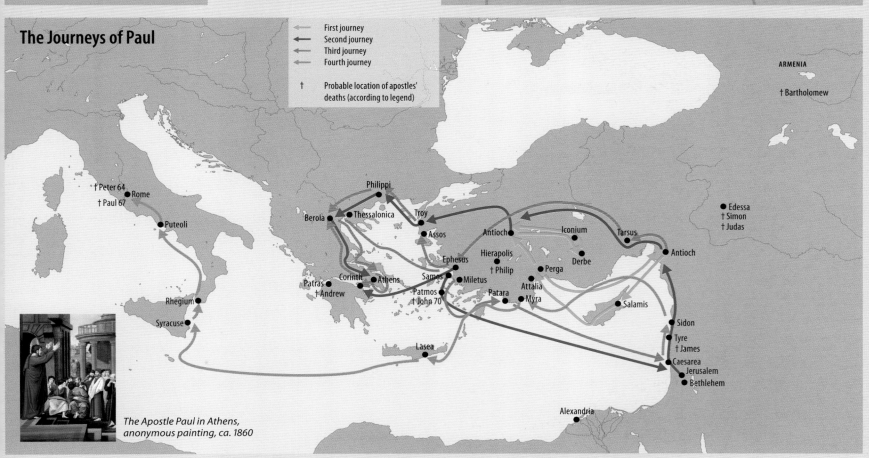

→ First journey
→ Second journey
→ Third journey
→ Fourth journey

† Probable location of apostles' deaths (according to legend)

ARMENIA

† Bartholomew

† Peter 64
Rome
† Paul 67

Puteoli

Philippi

Beroía · Thessalonica
Troy

Assos

Antioch

Iconium

Tarsus

Edessa
† Simon
† Judas

Antioch

Rhegium

Syracuse

Patras
† Andrew

Corinth

Athens

Ephesus

Hierapolis
† Philip

Samos

Miletus

Patmos
† John 70

Perga

Derbe

Patara

Attalia

Myra

Salamis

Sidon

Tyre
† James

Caesarea

Jerusalem

Bethlehem

Lasea

Alexandria

The Apostle Paul in Athens, anonymous painting, ca. 1860

JUDAISM

The origins of Judaism are ancient, beginning with the migration of the Israelite people to Palestine, where they founded a nation. Over time Jews evolved a strictly monotheistic religion based on the worship of Yahweh, who made a binding covenant with the Israelites, revealing himself as the one and only God and giving them the Torah ("law") so that all could comply with his laws and ethical precepts. After the unsuccessful Jewish Revolt of 70 CE, the Roman Empire forced Jews out of Palestine into the Diaspora ("dispersion"), which led to scattered Jewish communities settled throughout the known world. Jews were severely persecuted in medieval Europe because they refused to acknowledge Jesus Christ as the messiah. Violent attacks and pogroms continued into the 20th century, when Christian-motivated anti-Jewish sentiment evolved, in its most extreme form, into the political anti-Semitism of the German National Socialist (Nazi) Party. After forcing Jews out of public life in the period leading up to World War II, the Nazi government began the systematic extermination of European Jews in death camps such as Auschwitz. The Nazi Holocaust, supported by the pervasive anti-Semitism of much of German-occupied Europe, killed an estimated six million Jews. After 1945 a large proportion of the European Jews who had survived immigrated to Palestine, where the state of Israel was founded in 1948. The Palestinian Arabs living on the land that became Israel felt they had been robbed of their land. A long-term, workable solution to the Middle Eastern crisis that developed in the wake of what Palestinians perceive as Israel's wrongful appropriation of their land is not yet in sight.

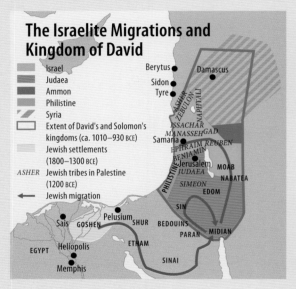

The Israelite Migrations and Kingdom of David

- Israel
- Judaea
- Ammon
- Philistine
- Syria
- Extent of David's and Solomon's kingdoms (ca. 1010–930 BCE)
- Jewish settlements (1800–1300 BCE)
- *ASHER* Jewish tribes in Palestine (1200 BCE)
- Jewish migration

The Assyrian Empire

- Edom
- Judaea
- Ammon
- Moab
- Greatest extent of the Assyrian empire in the first half of the 7th century
- The first Diaspora (722–586 BCE)

At the Birth of Christ

- Territory of the Roman Empire
- Vassals of the Roman Empire

13th century BCE The Israelites leave Egypt in the pivotal event called the Exodus, migrating to a new homeland in Canaan.

1020–926 BCE Israel becomes a monarchy ruled successively by the kings Saul, David and Solomon, after which the kingdom is divided.

722 BCE The Assyrian empire conquers Israel, and 33,000 Jews are deported from the northern kingdoms of Israel and Samaria.

587 BCE Nebuchadnezzar II sacks Jerusalem and destroys the Temple there, which had been built by King Solomon. Many Jews are forced into exile in Babylon.

from 539 BCE The Jews are allowed to return from Babylonian exile; the Second Temple is built in Jerusalem.

~500–200 BCE Prosperous Jewish enclaves develop within the multicultural societies of Damascus (Syria), Alexandria (Egypt) and Rome.

~250 BCE The Pentateuch (five books of Moses) is translated into Greek. Anti-Jewish polemics are written in Egypt.

from 200 BCE Palestine falls under the control of the Seleucid dynasty, inaugurating a short period of religious freedom.

175–164 BCE King Antiochus IV Epiphanes persecutes Jews in an effort to force them to Hellenize.

167 BCE The Maccabees revolt against the Seleucids.

38 BCE Pogroms in Alexandria destroy synagogues, and Jews are subjected to persecution.

70 The Romans respond to the First Jewish Revolt by destroying the Temple in Jerusalem.

Jewish Communities under the Roman Empire

- Significant Jewish population (Diaspora)
- Borders of the Roman Empire
- ⊗ Jewish revolts

Civil Rights for Jews 1789–1919

NORWAY 1851
SWEDEN 1865
DENMARK 1848
GREAT BRITAIN AND IRELAND 1890
NETHERLANDS 1796
BELGIUM 1830
GERMANY 1831
RUSSIAN EMPIRE 1917
FRANCE 1790
SWITZERLAND 1874
AUSTRIA-HUNGARY 1867
ROMANIA 1918
SERBIA 1878
BULGARIA 1878
PORTUGAL 1910
ITALY 1848
SPAIN 1919
OTTOMAN EMPIRE 1908
GREECE 1830

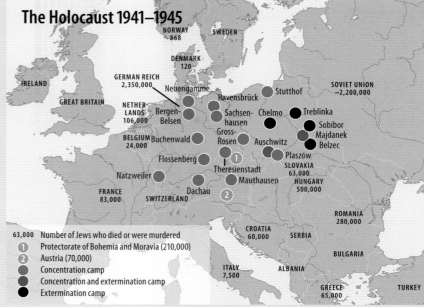

The Holocaust 1941–1945

NORWAY 868
SWEDEN
DENMARK 120
IRELAND
GREAT BRITAIN
GERMAN REICH 2,350,000
NETHERLANDS 106,000
BELGIUM 24,000
FRANCE 83,000
SWITZERLAND
SOVIET UNION ~2,200,000
Neuengamme
Ravensbrück
Stutthof
Bergen-Belsen
Sachsen-hausen
Chelmo
Treblinka
Buchenwald
Gross-Rosen
Auschwitz
Sobibor
Majdanek
Belzec
Flossenberg
Theresienstadt ①
Plaszów
Natzweiler
Dachau
Mauthausen ②
SLOVAKIA 63,000
HUNGARY 500,000
CROATIA 60,000
SERBIA
ROMANIA 280,000
ITALY 7,500
ALBANIA
BULGARIA
GREECE 65,000
TURKEY

63,000 Number of Jews who died or were murdered
① Protectorate of Bohemia and Moravia (210,000)
② Austria (70,000)
● Concentration camp
● Concentration and extermination camp
● Extermination camp

70–73 Following a failed rebellion against Roman rule, 973 Zealots (Jewish resistance fighters), fully aware of their impotence against 15,000 Roman soldiers, commit mass suicide at Masada, a fortified hill near the Dead Sea. Masada remains a symbol of Jewish resistance today.

132–135 The final Jewish uprising against the Romans takes place under the leadership of Simeon Bar-Kokhba ("son of a star"; the name refers to a prophecy). The victorious Romans ban all Jews from settling in Palestine, driving them into the Diaspora.

1st–4th centuries Jews continue to live in small communities throughout the Roman Empire.

5th–9th centuries The Early Middle Ages are marked by general tolerance of and respect toward Jews.

756–1100 The golden age of Jewish culture takes place in Spain during the period of the Muslim Caliphate (later Emirate) of Córdoba.

Jewish Holidays and Celebrations

Shabbat The last day of the Jewish week, the day of rest, begins at sundown Friday and ends at sundown on Saturday.

Rosh Hashanah New Year's celebration on the first day of the month of Tishri (in September or October in the Gregorian calender)

Yom Kippur Day of Atonement, the highest of holy days, marked by prohibition of any work and a strict fast

Pesach Seven-day celebration of Israel's freedom from bondage in Egypt, also known as Passover. In preparation, homes are cleaned of every breadcrumb, as leavened foods are prohibited. Instead Jews eat matzo, unleavened flatbread. Pesach begins on the full moon in March/April with a seder supper, a ritual meal in which four glasses of wine are drunk symbolizing God's promises: leading the Israelites out of Egypt, delivering them from slavery, redeeming them and claiming them as his chosen people.

Hanukkah Festival of lights in November or December, an eight-day celebration of the Jews' victory over Seleucid rulers. Special foods include doughnuts and latkes (potato pancakes), and children receive gifts.

Purim Joyous celebration of Queen Esther's foiling of a plot by the ancient Persian vizier Haman to exterminate the Jews. Costumes are worn, and lively retellings of the story in which the audience hisses and boos every time the villain's name is mentioned are favorite activities (February/March).

from 1000 Certain professions, such as money lending, are forbidden to Christians throughout Europe, creating primarily "Jewish" professions.

1103 Henry IV, German king and emperor, protects the Jews in the Holy Roman Empire

1290 King Edward I drives the Jews out of England.

until ~1400 Jews are driven out of the German states after being blamed for the plague known as the Black Death, among other things.

1516 Venice creates the first Jewish ghetto in Europe.

1567 The first Jewish university (*yeshiva*) is founded, in Poland.

1789 The French Revolution leads to full citizenship for Jews in France.

18th–20th centuries Jews are slowly granted civil rights throughout Europe, although racist anti-Semitism continues to characterize the German nationalist movement of the 19th century.

from 1880 The Zionist movement emerges as a reaction to pogroms against Jews in tsarist Russia. Jewish immigration to Palestine begins.

1939–1945 Nazi Germany systematically exterminates the Jews of Europe.

1948 The nation of Israel is founded.

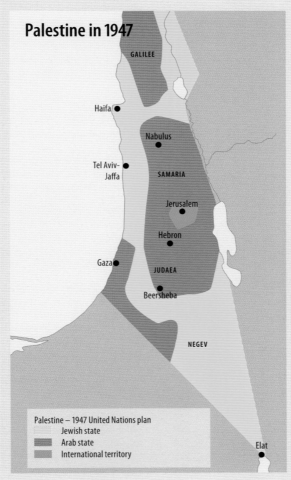

Palestine in 1947

GALILEE
Haifa
Nabulus
Tel Aviv-Jaffa
SAMARIA
Jerusalem
Hebron
Gaza
JUDAEA
Beersheba
NEGEV
Elat

Palestine – 1947 United Nations plan
Jewish state
Arab state
International territory

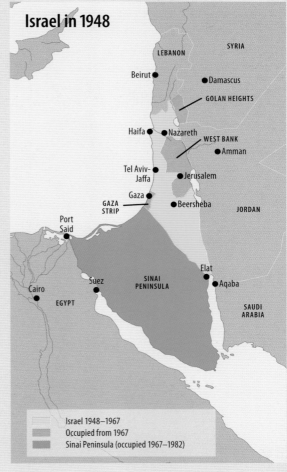

Israel in 1948

SYRIA
LEBANON
Beirut
Damascus
GOLAN HEIGHTS
Haifa
Nazareth
WEST BANK
Amman
Tel Aviv-Jaffa
Jerusalem
Gaza
Beersheba
JORDAN
GAZA STRIP
Port Said
Elat
Cairo
Suez
SINAI PENINSULA
Aqaba
EGYPT
SAUDI ARABIA

Israel 1948–1967
Occupied from 1967
Sinai Peninsula (occupied 1967–1982)

CHRISTIANITY

Until the Reign of Constantine I

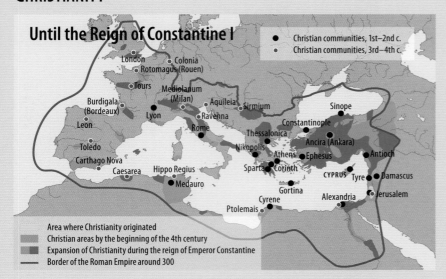

Christian communities, 1st–2nd c.
Christian communities, 3rd–4th c.

Area where Christianity originated
Christian areas by the beginning of the 4th century
Expansion of Christianity during the reign of Emperor Constantine
Border of the Roman Empire around 300

ca. 400

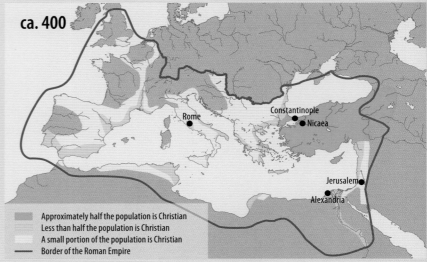

Approximately half the population is Christian
Less than half the population is Christian
A small portion of the population is Christian
Border of the Roman Empire

Followers of Jesus Christ spread Christianity throughout the eastern Mediterranean, Cyprus, North Africa, Greece and Rome. Persecution of Christians began during the reigns of the Roman emperors Claudius (41–54) and Nero (54–68).

By 800

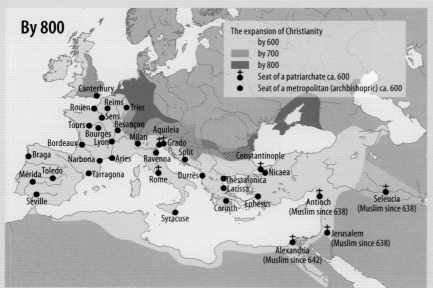

The expansion of Christianity
by 600
by 700
by 800
✠ Seat of a patriarchate ca. 600
● Seat of a metropolitan (archbishopric) ca. 600

By the 11th Century and Christian Missions

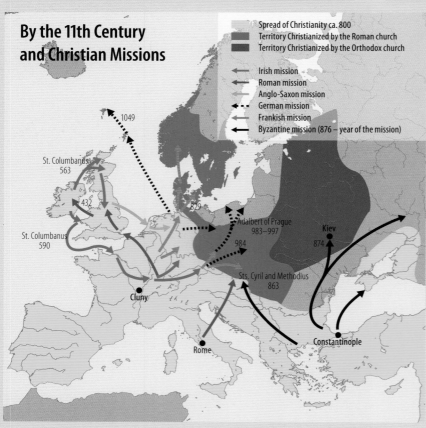

Spread of Christianity ca. 800
Territory Christianized by the Roman church
Territory Christianized by the Orthodox church

→ Irish mission
→ Roman mission
→ Anglo-Saxon mission
⇢ German mission
→ Frankish mission
→ Byzantine mission (876 – year of the mission)

~5 BCE–30 CE Lifetime of Jesus Christ

28–130 The early Christian church consolidates under the leadership of the apostles Peter and Paul and their successors.

64 Peter and Paul are martyred in Rome, where Peter was the first bishop of the Roman Catholic Church. His successors will use the title "pope."

66–70 The First Jewish Revolt against Roman rule ends with the destruction of Jerusalem, increasing the acrimony between Christians and Jews.

249 Emperor Decius orders a massive persecution of Christians throughout the Roman Empire.

303 Emperor Diocletian continues the program of systematic persecution.

313 Emperor Constantine I issues the Edict of Milan, which gives Christianity the same protected status granted to other religions in the Roman Empire.

Council, Synod Gathering of church authorities to make decisions about important theological or religious matters

Arianism Theological position formulated by Arius in the 4th century that says Christ does not have the same divine status as God the Father, but was created, and thus is not God. **Trinitarians** countered with the doctrine of the Trinity: Christ is of one substance with God the Father (homoousios), not only similar in substance (homoiousios). This conflict also had political consequences.

Schism Divisions within the church, but especially between the Eastern, Orthodox tradition and the Western, Roman Catholic church (East-West Schism of 1054). Political factors were key, especially the Roman pope's claim to secular authority.

Concordat A contract between the state and the church

Mendicant Orders Communities of monks who took vows of poverty, including Dominicans, Franciscans, Carmelites and Augustinians. They sustained themselves through work, donations and alms.

325 The First Ecumenical Council in Nicaea condemns Arianism as heresy.

354–430 St. Augustine, bishop of Hippo, lives and works in the Roman province of North Africa.

361–363 Emperor Julian the Apostate attempts to restore the ancient Roman pagan religion.

380 Emperor Theodosius II declares Christianity the state religion.

381 The Second Ecumenical Council (the First Council of Constantinople) reaffirms Trinitarian doctrine, condemning Arianism.

391 Emperor Theodosius bans all other religions from the Eastern and Western Roman Empires, making Christianity the only state-sanctioned religion.

440–461 Pope Leo the Great gives the office of the papacy both political and doctrinal leadership of the Roman Catholic Church.

Pietism Reaction of the German Protestants to the Thirty Years' War, emphasizing the personal aspects of faith and rejecting rigid dogma and superficial interpretations of the Bible. Home-based meetings at times had greater significance than worship services.

Monophysites Those who believe Christ has only one nature, which is divine; condemned in 451. The Coptic, Syrian and Ethiopian Orthodox churches are monophysite.

Methodism Protestant movement founded in England, now global but especially in the United States, that arose because of political, linguistic and cultural differences. With ca. 75 million adherents, it is one of the major Protestant denominations.

Nestorians Named after the patriarch Nestorius of Constantinople, they believe the two natures of Christ (divine and human) are entirely distinct and separate. Rejected in 451, this idea still has adherents in some Asian countries.

Anglicans State church of England, founded in 534 by Henry VIII, incorporating elements of Catholicism and Protestantism.

By 1517

Roman Catholic regions

After 1517: The Reformation

Roman Catholic regions
Growth of Protestantism

1560–1648: The Counter-Reformation

Roman Catholic regions
Protestant regions

451 Council of Chalcedon reaffirms the Holy Trinity as dogma: Christ is "God and man incarnate, two natures in one inseparable being." The Nestorians and Monophysites secede in protest.

5th century Ireland becomes Christian through the efforts of St. Patrick.

498 The Frankish king Clovis I is baptized, leading to the conversion of the Franks.

529 Benedict of Nursia founds the first Benedictine Abbey in Monte Cassino, Italy.

590–604 Pope Gregory the Great organizes the first Christian mission to convert pagan Europe.

from 563 Christian missionaries convert England and Scotland.

664 English clergy accept the rites of the Roman Catholic Church (as opposed to Celtic rites) at the Synod of Whitby.

7th–9th centuries Christian missionaries convert the Serbs.

8th–9th centuries Charlemagne converts the Saxons by force.

9th century The New Testament is translated into the Slavic languages, leading to the conversion of large parts of southeast Europe by Sts. Cyril and Methodius.

864 The Bulgarian king Boris is baptized, leading to the conversion of the Bulgars.

988 Kievan Rus (now the Ukraine) becomes Christian.

10th century Christianity spreads to Bohemia.

10th–11th centuries Poland and Hungary accept Christianity.

10th–13th centuries Prussia, Estonia and Latvia become Christian.

1054 The East-West Schism: the Eastern Orthodox Church splits from the Roman Catholic Church.

1073–1085 Pope Gregory VII introduces radical reforms and restores the power of the papacy.

1076–1122 The Concordat of Worms brings to an end a period of struggle between rulers and popes over which had the right to appoint bishops and other clergy.

1096–1254 The Crusades

early 13th century Founding of the Dominican and Franciscan orders

1294–1303 Pope Boniface VIII oversteps the boundaries of the papacy, leading

to his exile in Avignon (1305–1377) and to the Great Western Schism (1378–1417).

1387 Lithuania becomes Christian.

1517 Martin Luther posts his Ninety-five Theses, leading to the Reformation.

1534 St. Ignatius of Loyola founds the Jesuit Order. Henry VIII founds the Anglican Church.

1541 John Calvin, a radical Protestant reformer, becomes spiritual leader of the city of Geneva.

1545–1563 The Council of Trent marks the high point of the Counter-Reformation.

1555 The Peace of Augsburg brings peace between Catholics and Protestants according to the principle *cuius regio, eius religio* (whose realm, his

religion), which permits rulers to choose the religion of the territory they govern.

1562–1598 The French Wars of Religion break out between the Catholic French and the Protestant Huguenots.

1618–1648 Thirty Years' War involves most of Europe in bloody conflict over religious and territorial disputes.

late 17th century Pietism evolves out of Lutheranism.

18th century John Wesley founds the Methodist denomination.

1801 The French Republic signs an accord with the Catholic church.

1962–1965 Vatican II reforms encourage dialogue between the Catholic church and other faiths; mass is celebrated in vernacular languages rather than Latin.

Today

Predominantly:
Protestant
Roman Catholic
Orthodox
Armenian and Coptic

Europe in Detail – Northern Europe Before the Barbarian Invasions

500–200 BCE: Celtic and German Tribes

Legend:
- Celts in the 3rd century BCE
- Germanic tribes
- ○ Celtic oppida
- ← Celtic campaigns

Labels on map: IRISH, BRITANNIA, Colchester, Selsey, Titelberg, Stradonice, Alesia, Manching, Bratislava, GAULS, La Tène, PANNONIA, Numantia, CELTIBERIANS, 387 BCE, Rome, ITALY, 379 BCE, Delphi, TYLIS, GALATIA (INHABITED BY CELTS), 275–274 BCE

Europe at the Time of the Birth of Christ

Legend:
- Celts
- Germanic tribes
- Slavs
- Border of the Roman Empire
- ⊗ Important battle

Labels on map: IRISH, BRITONS, GOTHS, ANGLES, GOTHS, Battle of Teutoburg Forest, SUEBI, CHERUSCI, VANDALS, SLAVS, MARCOMANNI, QUADI, SARMATIANS, ROMANIZED CELTS, DACIANS

The forested regions northwest of the Alps were Celtic territory, and Germanic tribes controlled most of northern and northwestern Europe. The Celts were assimilated into the provincial Roman Empire. The Germans remained largely uninfluenced by classical Mediterranean civilization until the fall of Rome; then they took over much of the Roman Empire's organization and infrastructure. Around this time, the Slavic tribes began to form in eastern Europe.

500 BCE Ancient texts mention the Celts for the first time.

~400 BCE Celtic tribes march toward Greece, Italy and the Danube valley.

387 BCE Rome is sacked by Celtic tribes from Gaul.

279 BCE Celts plunder Delphi, advancing toward Anatolia.

275–274 BCE Antiochus I defeats the Celts, resettling some of them in Anatolia, where they will later become the Galatians.

~100 BCE A powerful Celtic state forms in Gaul.

58–51 BCE Julius Caesar conquers Gaul.

46 BCE Vercingetorix, king of the Gauls, is executed in Rome.

9 CE Germans led by the Cherusci tribe defeat the Romans at the Battle of Teutoburg Forest.

43 Rome conquers Britain.

166–182 The Roman Empire battles the Germanic tribes of the Danube in the Marcomannic Wars.

The Celts were a loose assemblage of clans and tribes that never formed a true state. From their homeland in what is now western France and southern Germany, the Celtic tribes advanced into large parts of western and southeastern Europe. In the 5th century, under pressure from the Germanic Anglo-Saxons, the Celtic tribes in Britain were forced to the north and west (Scotland, Wales and Ireland), where their culture and language still survive.

Vase from Saint-Pol-de-Léon, Finistère, 4th century CE, Musée de Morlaix

The Goths were an eastern Germanic tribe thought to have originated in what is today the island province of Gotland in southern Sweden. After an extensive migration that brought them into what is now the Ukraine, the Gothic tribes split up into western and eastern kingdoms. The Visigoths (western Goths) controlled most of Spain and France from 418–711. The Ostrogoths (eastern Goths) ruled in Italy from 493–552.

The Alemanni tribe formed on the upper Main River in what is now Germany. Roman

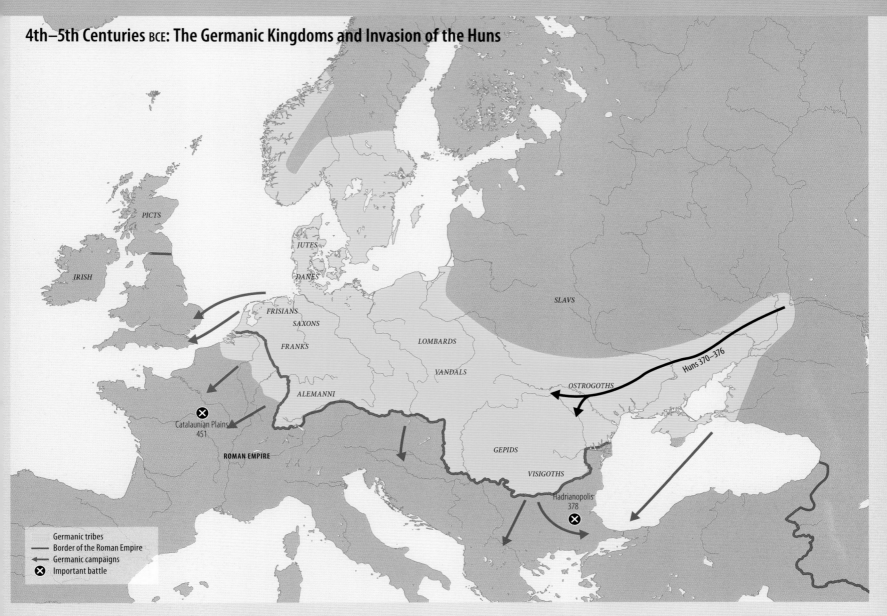

4th–5th Centuries BCE: The Germanic Kingdoms and Invasion of the Huns

Map labels: PICTS, IRISH, JUTES, DANES, FRISIANS, SAXONS, FRANKS, ALEMANNI, LOMBARDS, VANDALS, SLAVS, OSTROGOTHS, Huns 370–376, GEPIDS, VISIGOTHS, ROMAN EMPIRE, Catalaunian Plains 451, Hadrianopolis 378

Legend:
- Germanic tribes
- Border of the Roman Empire
- → Germanic campaigns
- ⊗ Important battle

historians describe them as fractious and easily provoked to battle. They regularly raided the Roman Empire from 496–506 before being overthrown by the Franks.

The Lombards were a western Germanic tribe originating in southern Scandinavia. In the first century BCE they migrated to the Elbe River. In the 2nd century they fell under the rule of the Roman province of Pannonia, as did many German tribes. They formed their own kingdom in Italy from 568–774.

The Frisians were an independent Germanic tribe never defeated by the Romans. They are the original inhabitants of the North Sea coastal territory between the mouths of the Rhine and Ems rivers in Germany and the Netherlands.

The Jutes were a Germanic tribe settled primarily in the northern part of today's Denmark, where the territory of Jutland is named after them.

The Quadi were a small Germanic tribe from north of the Main River. In the first century they migrated south to eastern Austria and the southwestern corner of Slovakia. Their king, Vannius (21–50 CE), was defeated by the Romans. In the 5th century they moved westward with the Vandals, occupying the Iberian Peninsula.

The Marcomanni were a Germanic tribe in what is today the Czech Republic. Their

name means "men of the border regions." In the 2nd century they joined the neighboring Quadi tribe in frequent attacks on Roman provincial territory. Emperor Marcus Aurelius marched against them in what became known as the Marcomannic Wars.

The Huns were the union of a number of Turkic and Mongol tribes originating in central Asia. In 370 they invaded Europe in massive numbers, setting off a wave of migration. The Huns ruled Europe from an empire centered in the lower Danube valley, whence they carried out raids as far west as the Rhine. After the death of their great leader Attila, the Huns fell into a steep decline. The Huns were overthrown by their former subjects in 454.

Attila (406–453), king of the Huns

The Cherusci were a Germanic tribe native to the Rhine valley in northwestern Germany. In the year 9 CE, under the leadership of Arminius (Hermann), they defeated three Roman legions in the Battle of Teutoburg Forest.

The Vandals were an eastern Germanic tribe settled on the lower Oder River. They

invaded the Iberian Peninsula after 400, founding their own kingdom in 429, one that eventually extended as far as North Africa. In 455 they sacked Rome. The Vandals were defeated by the Byzantine Empire in 534.

The Suebi were an eastern Germanic tribe. In 400 they joined the Vandals in the invasion of the Roman province of Gaul. They later established their own kingdom in what is now northern Spain and Portugal (411–585), which in turn was conquered by the Visigoths. Several Suebi tribes remained in the Visigoth kingdom, while others retreated eastward, where they eventually united with the Alemanni. The Suebi gave their name to Swabia in southwest Germany.

The Sarmatians were a union of nomadic Persian-speaking tribes occupying the vast territory between the Don River and the Aral Sea. Ancient sources describe them as traveling in wagon trains. As they moved west, they assimilated with other eastern European peoples.

The Angles were a western Germanic tribe from what is now Schleswig-Holstein and southern Denmark, ranging as far south as central Germany. The best-known group of Angles migrated with the Saxons to Britain, where they founded the first British (Anglo-Saxon) monarchy.

The Saxons were a western Germanic tribe from Holstein. In the 3rd century they

conquered most of northern Germany, from the North Sea to the Harz Mountains. Some migrated to Britain. The Saxons were not completely converted to Christianity until the 8th or 9th century.

The 6th-century Abbey of St. Augustus in Canterbury is the oldest monastery in southern England.

The Slavs have their original homeland somewhere in the northern Carpathians between the Oder, Vistula and Dnieper Rivers. From there, Slavic tribes spread out in successive waves of migration to the west and south. They make up the majority of the population of eastern and central Europe today.

The Dacians were a Thracian Indo-European group that moved into what is now Romania as early as the first millennium BCE. They founded the prosperous kingdom of Dacia, which was conquered by the Romans in 106. Over time the population was assimilated into Roman culture, sometimes by force. The present day Romanians are their descendants.

Europe in Detail – The Barbarian Invasions, 350–568

4th–7th Centuries

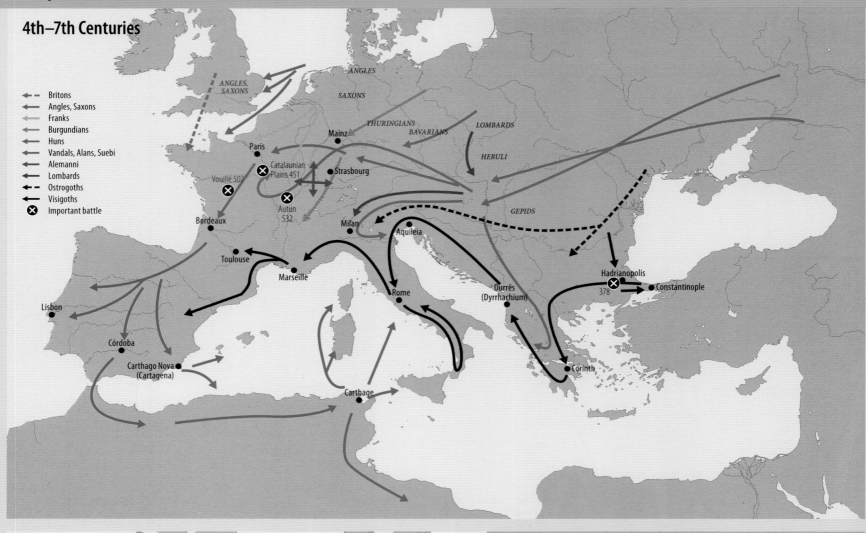

Britons
Angles, Saxons
Franks
Burgundians
Huns
Vandals, Alans, Suebi
Alemanni
Lombards
Ostrogoths
Visigoths
Important battle

ANGLES, SAXONS
ANGLES
SAXONS
THURINGIANS
BAVARIANS
LOMBARDS
HERULI
GEPIDS
Mainz
Paris
Vouillé 507
Catalaunian Plains 451
Strasbourg
Autun 532
Bordeaux
Milan
Aquileia
Toulouse
Marseille
Rome
Durrës (Dyrrhachium)
Hadrianopolis 378
Constantinople
Lisbon
Córdoba
Carthago Nova (Cartagena)
Carthage
Corinth

532: The Battle of Autun

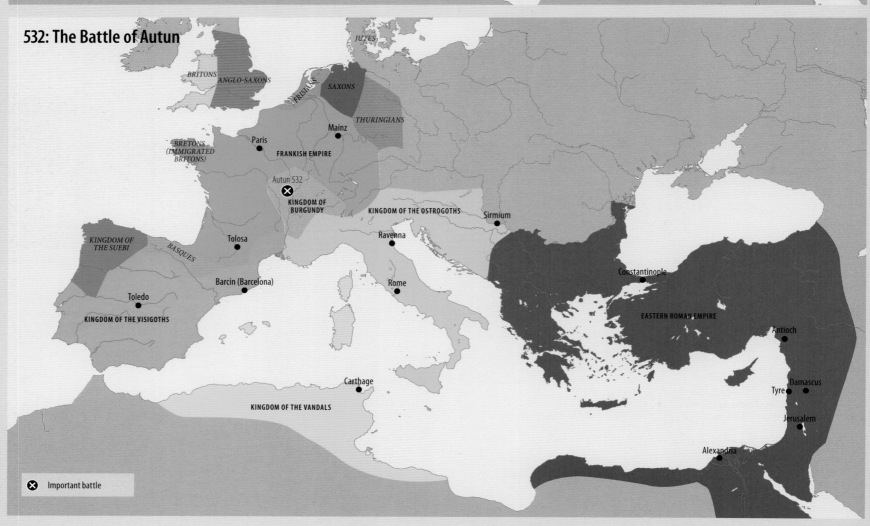

Important battle

JUTES
BRITONS
ANGLO-SAXONS
FRISIANS
SAXONS
THURINGIANS
BRETONS (IMMIGRATED BRITONS)
FRANKISH EMPIRE
Mainz
Paris
Autun 532
KINGDOM OF BURGUNDY
KINGDOM OF THE OSTROGOTHS
Sirmium
KINGDOM OF THE SUEBI
BASQUES
Tolosa
Ravenna
Barcin (Barcelona)
Rome
Constantinople
Toledo
EASTERN ROMAN EMPIRE
KINGDOM OF THE VISIGOTHS
Antioch
Carthage
Damascus
Tyre
KINGDOM OF THE VANDALS
Jerusalem
Alexandria

The barbarian invasions is the term some scholars use to describe the period between Late Antiquity and the beginning of the Medieval period. Massive migrations of tribal peoples transformed the urban, classical Roman Empire into the largely rural, locally governed principalities of medieval Europe.

370–376 The Huns invade Europe.

378 Visigoths fleeing the Huns defeat Byzantine armies at the Battle of Adrianople.

382 Emperor Theodosius I signs treaties that resettle large bands of Visigoths on the Lower Danube as *foederati* (non-citizen allies) of Rome.

395 Emperor Theodosius I divides the Roman Empire into western and eastern empires.

from 395 German military leaders rise steadily in the ranks of Roman provincial administration, ultimately ending up in control of the provinces themselves. In 471, Emperor Zeno bans them from the Eastern Roman Empire.

406–407 The Roman defenses along the Rhine collapse. Hordes of Vandals, Suebi and Alani invade the province of Gaul.

407–410 Roman forces retreat from Britain.

410 Visigoths led by Alaric I sack Rome.

from 418 The Visigoths settle in Aquitaine (southwestern France).

429 Approximately 80,000 Vandals move into North Africa from Spain.

436 The eastern Germanic kingdom of Burgundy is destroyed by the west Roman general Flavius Aëtius, who employs Huns as mercenaries. The region's inhabitants are forcibly resettled in Savoy and the Rhône valley.

451 The Huns are defeated by the combined forces of Flavius Aëtius and the Visigoth king Theodoric I at the Battle of Chalôns, effectively stopping the Huns from advancing further into Europe.

455 The Vandals invade and sack Rome.

476 German tribal leader Odoacer deposes the last western Roman emperor, Romulus Augustulus.

486–487 Clovis, king of the Franks, defeats Syagrius, the last Roman ruler in northern Gaul, and annexes the territory.

489–493 Theodoric the Great, leader of the Ostrogoths, conquers Italy and founds the Ostrogothic kingdom.

507 The Franks defeat the Visigoths at the Battle of Vouillé. After conquering Aquitaine, Frankish forces drive the last Visigoths into Spain.

532 The Franks defeat the Burgundians at the Battle of Autun.

533–534 Byzantine forces under Justinian I defeat the Vandal kingdom.

535–562 Byzantine Emperor Justinian I conquers the Ostrogothic kingdom.

568 The Lombards enter northern Italy from the Danube valley, founding the Lombard kingdom in 774.

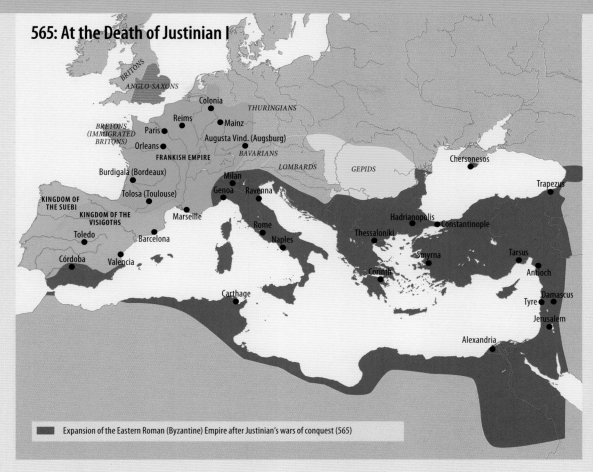

565: At the Death of Justinian I

■ Expansion of the Eastern Roman (Byzantine) Empire after Justinian's wars of conquest (565)

Das Nibelungenlied (*The Song of the Nibelungen*) is an anonymous verse composition based on German and Scandinavian tradition that dates from the beginning of the 13th century. The story takes place in the Rhine and Danube valleys of central Europe in what are now the countries of Germany, Austria and Hungary. Based on references within the tale to wars with the Huns and the fall of the Kingdom of Burgundy, the historical roots of the epic are thought to extend back to the 5th-century migrations of Germanic tribes.

The main characters of the epic all have magical powers. The hero, Siegfried, possesses the Niebelung Horde, a fantastic treasure. He has a wife, Kriemhild, and three brothers-in-law—Gunther, Gernot and Giselher—who are kings of Burgundy. Other characters include Brunhilde, an Icelandic princess, and Etzel (= Attila), the king of the Huns. The action follows Siegfried through a series of heroic deeds and the revenge taken by the Nibelungen for his murder, after which the Burgundian royal family takes possession of both the treasure and the Nibelungen name.

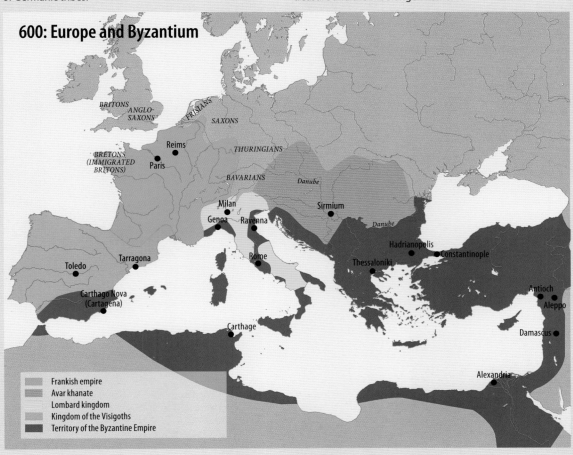

600: Europe and Byzantium

Frankish empire
Avar khanate
Lombard kingdom
Kingdom of the Visigoths
Territory of the Byzantine Empire

THE LEGACY OF ANTIQUITY (SELECTED EXAMPLES)

Great Britain
Bath Roman thermal baths
London Remains of the temple devoted to Mithras

Roman baths in Bath, England

France
Autun Roman city walls
Paris Arènes de Lutèce (amphitheater)
Toulouse Numerous traces in old Toulouse, Vieux-Toulouse
Narbonne The Via Domitia, a Roman road
Marseille Remains of a Greek harbor

Germany
Cologne Many sites, including the Dionysus mosaic
Trier Constantine Basilica, Roman city gate (Porta Nigra)
Mainz Remains of the Roman city and aqueduct
Augsburg Vestiges of Roman barracks

Austria
Bregenz Probably a Roman camp
Vienna Remains of a Roman camp and thermal baths
Petronell-Carnuntum Site of a Roman city

Italy
Milan Remains of an imperial palace and city wall
Aosta Vestiges of Roman fortifications
Padua Arena, parts of a cathedral
Verona Roman arena
Aquileia Ruins of a Roman city wall
Bologna Rectangular shape of a former Roman camp still recognizable
Ravenna Mausoleum of Empress Galla Placida
Pisa Roman amphitheater
Fiesole Roman theater and thermal baths
Ancona Trajan's Arch
Rome The Colosseum, Roman Forum, Pantheon and much more
Capua Roman amphitheater

Roman theater in Fiesole, Italy

Naples Mosaic from Pompeii in the National Archaeological Museum
Pompeii Roman city buried by ashes in the 79 CE eruption of Mount Vesuvius; excavated in the mid-18th century
Taranto Doric columns
Segesta Doric temple, left incomplete by the Elysians

Palermo Remains of Roman houses
Syracuse Greek theater, temple dedicated to Apollo

Croatia
Pula Roman amphitheater and temple
Split Palace of Emperor Diocletian

Narona (near Vid) Ruins of a Roman temple

Serbia
Belgrade Ruins of Roman baths
Sremska Mitrovica A hippodrome and imperial palace (Sirmium was one of the four capitals of the Roman Empire.)

Romania
Sarmizegetusa Remains of a Dacian fortress
Mangalia Archaeological museum devoted to the Hellenistic period, Scythian tomb

Hungary
Szombathely Ruins of a temple dedicated to Mithras

- Significant sites of the Roman Empire (temples, arches, bridges, aqueducts, forums, basilicas, baths, theaters, arenas, etc.)
- Roman Empire (extent in the 2nd century)

Aquae Sulis (Bath)
Londinium (London)
Luliobona (Lillebone)
Colonia Claudia Ara Agrippinensium (Cologne)
Mogontiacum (Mainz)
Augusta Treverorum (Trier)
Lutetia Parisiorum (Paris)
Augusta Vindelicorum (Augsburg)
Turonum Caesarodunum (Tours)
Brigantium (Bregenz)
Augustodunum (Autun)
Mediolanum Santonum (Saintes)
Augusta Praetoria (Aosta)
Patavium (Padua)
Lugdunum (Lyon)
Mediolanum
Aqu
Tolosa (Toulouse)
Nemausus (Nîmes)
Verona
Pul
Bononia (Bologna)
Ravenna
Arelate (Arles)
Pisa
Faesulae (Fiesole)
Ar
Massalia (Marseille)
Narbo Martius (Narbonne)
Roma (Rome)
Clunia
Tarragona
Naples
Olisipo Felicitas Julia (Lisbon)
Segobriga (Segóbriga)
Pollentia (Pollenza)
Augusta Emerita (Mérida)
Saguntum (Sagunto)
Corduba (Córdoba)
Gadir (Cádiz)
Carthago Nova (Cartagena)
Panormus (Palermo)
Segesta
Hippo Regius (Annaba)
Volubilis
Carthago (Carthage)
Cirta (Constantine)
Hadrumetum (Sousse)
Oea (Tripoli)
Sabratha

Roman city of Volubilis in Morocco

Triumphal arch of Marcus Aurelius, Tripoli, Libya

Head of Dionysus, fresco, Sremska Mitrovica, Serbia

The Parthenon in Athens, Greece

Mytilene Ruins of the Greek amphitheater
Chios Numerous excavation sites such as Agios Gala and Emborio
Kos Ruins of the Greek agora (central gathering place)
Gortyn (Crete) Code of law, Roman wall and aqueduct

Morocco
Volubilis Extensive remains of the Roman city

Algeria
Annaba Remains of the Roman city
Constantine Roman mosaic

Tunisia
Carthage Remains of the Roman city
Sousse Ruins of the Phoenician (Carthaginian) city

Libya
Tripoli Triumphal arch of Emperor Marcus Aurelius
Sabratha Roman theater, basilica from the time of Emperor Justinian
Lebda Remains of a Roman amphitheater, basilica and marketplace
Cyrene Apollo temple from the 7th century BCE

Egypt
Alexandria Roman amphitheater
Pelusium Ruins of the ancient city

Turkey
Istanbul Hagia Sophia, parts of the hippodrome of Constantinople
Bergama (Pergamum) Podium of the Pergamum Altar (partially reconstructed in the Pergamon Museum in Berlin)
Ephesus Hadrian's Temple, library of Celsus
Miletus Ancient amphitheater, Ionic temple
Iznik Ancient city fortifications
Antalya Hadrian's Gate
Tarsus Cleopatra Gate
Antakya Roman mosaics

Syria
Palmyra (Tadmur) Columns along the *decumanus* (main street)
Bosra Roman amphitheater

Lebanon
Baalbek Bacchus Temple
Tyre Ruins of the agora

Israel/Palastine
Jerusalem Ruins of Herod's Palace

Jordan
Jerash (Gerasa) Triumphal arch of Hadrian, temples dedicated to Artemis and Zeus, nymphaeum and colonnade

---

Portugal
Lisbon Field of ruins of the Teatro Romano de Lisboa in the museum of the same name

Spain
Clunia Roman amphitheater
Mérida Roman amphitheater
Segóbriga Ruins of a Roman amphitheater, basilica, arcades
Córdoba Remnants of the Roman city including a temple and mausoleum
Cartagena Roman amphitheater
Sagunto Remains of the Roman citadel and theater
Tarragona Roman aqueduct
Pollenzia Ruins of a Roman bridge

Macedonia
Stobi Remains of the Roman city

Greece
Epidaurus Ancient theater
Athens Acropolis, Parthenon
Corinth Apollo Temple
Thessaloníki Arch and tomb of Emperor Galerius

Colonnade in Jerash, Jordan

95

Europe in Detail – The Frankish Empires, 482–987

Under Clovis 482–511

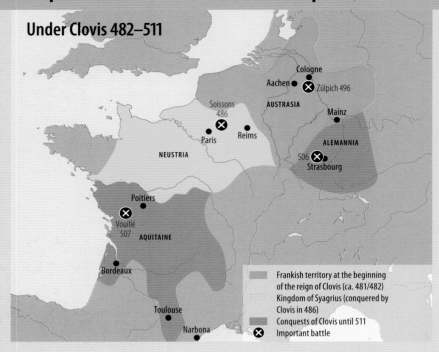

Frankish territory at the beginning of the reign of Clovis (ca. 481/482)
Kingdom of Syagrius (conquered by Clovis in 486)
Conquests of Clovis until 511
⊗ Important battle

After Clovis, from 511

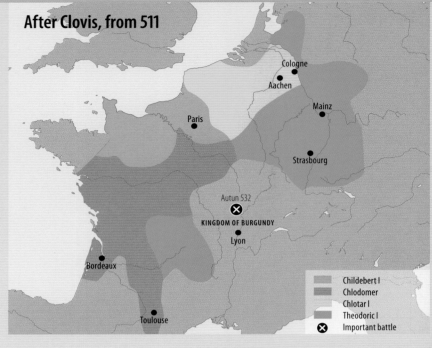

Childebert I
Chlodomer
Chlotar I
Theodoric I
⊗ Important battle

Germanic Franks settled in northeastern Gaul beginning in the 4th century CE and expanded their territories after the fall of the Roman Empire. When the Merovingian dynasty weakened, real power passed into the hands of their major-domos ("prime ministers") from the second half of the 7th century, when this office finally became hereditary. Under Charlemagne (768–814) their empire reached its largest extent, with its center in Aachen, Germany. Successor countries were East and West Francia, which in time evolved into France and the Holy Roman Empire.

482–511 Rule of the Frankish king Clovis I

486 Clovis I defeats Syagrius, the last Roman ruler in northern Gaul, at the Battle of Soissons.

496–506 Battles at Tolbiacum and Strasbourg result in Frankish victories over the Alemanni.

498 Clovis I is baptized a Christian.

507 Conquest of Aquitaine (Battle of Vouillé)

511 The Frankish empire is divided among Clovis's four sons

532–534 Conquest of the First Kingdom of Burgundy

558 King Chlotar I reunites the empire.

561 Division of the Frankish empire among the four sons of Chlotar I

613 Chlotar II reunites the empire.

639 Death of the last important Merovingian king, Dagobert I. The Carolingian major-domos take over power in the Frankish empire.

714–741 The Carolingian major-domo Charles Martel is the actual ruler.

732 Charles Martel defeats Arab forces near Tours and Poitiers.

751 The Carolingian Pippin the Short (Pippin III), father of Charlemagne, is elected king and crowned in the year 754. He formally deposes the Merovingians and tightly organizes the imperial church.

768–814 Rule of Charlemagne ("Charles the Great"); he unites much of Europe.

772–804 Campaigns against the Saxons

774 Charlemagne defeats the Lombards, adds Italy to his growing empire.

800 Charlemagne is crowned emperor in Rome.

814–840 Reign of Emperor Louis the Pious; civil wars between his sons

843 The Treaty of Verdun divides the empire among the sons of Emperor Louis the Pious: Lothar I (emperor), Louis the German and Charles the Bald.

855 Lothar I abdicates in Prüm and divides his empire among his own sons: Louis II (rules Italy as emperor), Lothar II (Lotharingia) and Charles (Burgundy and Provence)

870 Treaty of Mersen (Meerssen): Charles the Bald and Louis the German divide Lotharingia between themselves.

875 End of the Lothar family line (ruling Middle Francia, later only Italy)

880 With the Treaty of Ribémont, Middle Francia or Lotharingia (today Lorraine) becomes a part of East Francia.

911 End of the Carolingian line in Germany (East Francia)

978 End of the Carolingian line in France (West Francia)

Division after 561

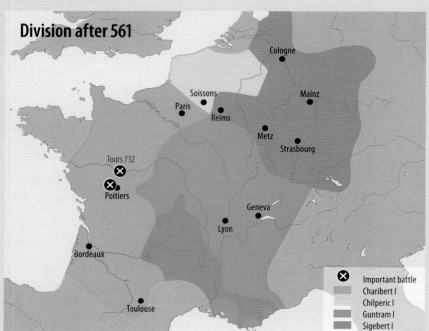

⊗ Important battle
Charibert I
Chilperic I
Guntram I
Sigebert I

Charlemagne 768–814

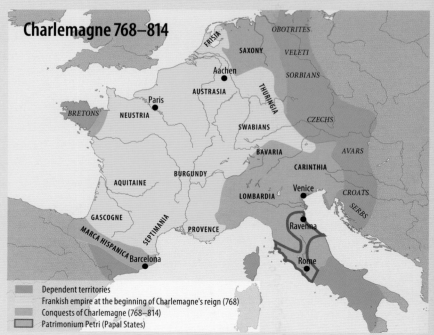

Dependent territories
Frankish empire at the beginning of Charlemagne's reign (768)
Conquests of Charlemagne (768–814)
Patrimonium Petri (Papal States)

843: Treaty of Verdun

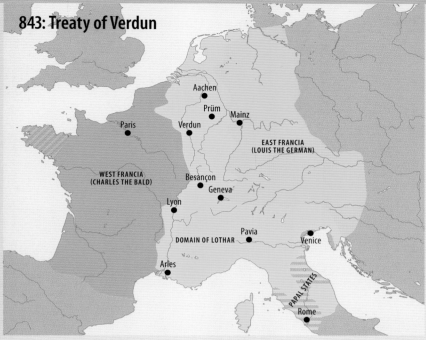

855: Treaty of Prüm

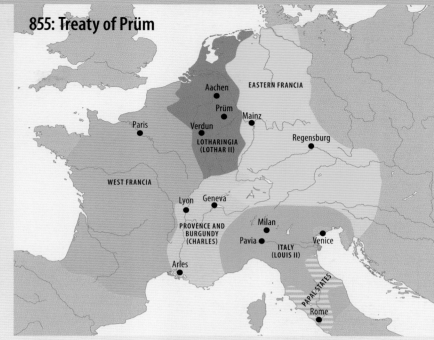

870: Treaty of Meerssen

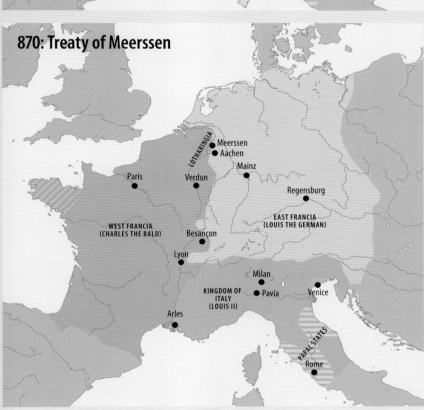

880: Treaty of Ribémont

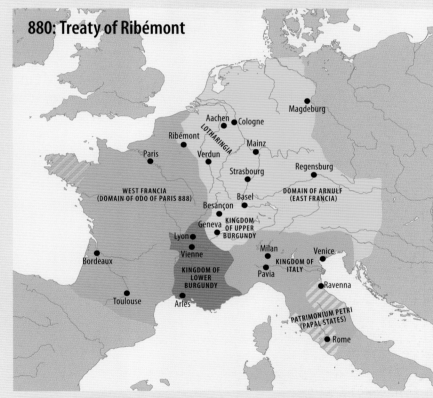

Merovingians and Carolingians Frankish royal dynasties in the early Middle Ages. The Merovingians traced their ancestry to the Salian Frank Merovech. They reached the zenith of their power under King Clovis I (482–511), then gradually lost control over their empire. In the year 751 they were displaced by the Carolingian dynasty.

Kingdom of Syagrius The Roman military commander in northern Gaul ruled independently after his father's death in 465. His empire outlived the Western Roman Empire, but he was ultimately defeated in 486 by Frankish King Clovis I in a battle near Syagrius's capital, Soissons. He fled to Toulouse, but was extradicted to the Merovingians and murdered in prison.

First Kingdom of Burgundy The First Kingdom was founded after 411 in the Rhine region around the city of Mainz

(Mogontiacum), but was destroyed again after only twenty years by Western Roman General Aetius in 436. After their defeat, the Burgundians settled in the region of modern-day eastern Switzerland, in Savoy and the Rhône valley, where they reestablished their country. They were defeated a final time in the Battle of Autun in 532 by the Franks, and their territory was occupied and incorporated into Francia.

Charlemagne (742–814) was the single most important ruler of the Franks (king since 768) and the Lombards (since 774). During annual military campaigns, he converted the Saxons to Christianity between 772 and 804. In 788 he defeated Tassilo III, duke of Bavaria, and pushed the Arab armies back to the Ebro River. In 796–803 he defeated the Avars east of his empire. His imperial coronation in Rome in 800 was intended to re-establish the Western Roman Empire.

Charlemagne, detail of painting by Albrecht Dürer, 1513

Lotharingia The empire of Lothar I, which evolved from the Treaty of Verdun in 843 (*Lotharii Regnum*), underwent several transformations and divisions (Treaties of Prüm and Meerssen) and became Lotharingia (named for Lothar's son, Lothar II), an empire that encompassed the regions of Frisia and today's Netherlands and Rhineland areas. The **Treaty of Ribémont** in 880 incorporated the western part of Lotharingia (or Lorraine) into East Francia. In the years that followed, the territories were divided into several medieval counties, duchies and bishoprics. The Duchy of Lorraine remained a part of the Holy Roman Empire until 1766, when it was incorporated into France according to a marriage treaty with Duke Francis Stephen, who became Mary Theresa's husband and Holy Roman emperor. The territory of the Duchy of Lorraine overlapped but was not identical to today's French region Lorraine.

THE MOST IMPORTANT ROYAL HOUSES OF EUROPE

The Merovingian Dynasty

Merovingian territory
- After 511 (death of Clovis I)
- After 561 (death of Chlotar I)

Merovingian Dynasty ca. 450–751 *Kings in the Frankish parts of the kingdom (Austrasia, West Francia, Aquitaine, Burgundy) as well as in the unified Frankish realm*

482–511	Clovis I
511–561	Chlotar I (sole king of the Franks 558–561)
584–629	Chlotar II (sole king of the Franks 613–629)
629–639	Dagobert I

Clovis I (466–511)

The Carolingian Dynasty

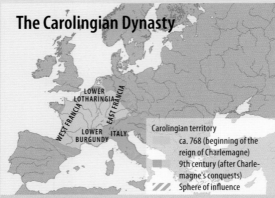

Carolingian territory
- ca. 768 (beginning of the reign of Charlemagne)
- 9th century (after Charlemagne's conquests)
- Sphere of influence

Carolingian Dynasty 751–987 *Kings and emperors of the unified realm of the Franks, then of the Frankish parts of the empire. They ruled until 911 in the kingdom of East Francia (Francia Orientalis), intermittently until 987 in West Francia (Francia Occidentalis), in Italy until 887, in Lower Burgundy until 963 and were dukes in Lower Lorraine until 1012.*

751–768	Pippin III (Pippin the Short, or Pippin the Younger)
768–814	Charlemagne, emperor from 800 onward
840–876	Louis (Ludwig) II the German (in East Francia)
840–877	Charles II the Bald (West Francia), emperor after 875

Saxon or Liudolfing Dynasty

Territory of the Liudolfings (Saxon dynasty)
- Under Henry I the Fowler
- Under Otto I the Great

Liudolfing or Saxon Dynasty 919–1024 *Kings of German and later Italian lands as well as emperors of the Holy Roman Empire*

919–936	Henry I
936–973	Otto I the Great, coronation as emperor in 962
973–983	Otto II
983–1002	Otto III
1002–1024	Henry II (the Holy)

Henry II (973–1024)

The Salian Dynasty

- ca. 1034 (greatest extent under Conrad II)

The Salian Dynasty 1024–1125 *Holy Roman Empire: Italian and German kings and emperors*

1024–1039	Conrad II
1056–1106	Henry IV
1106–1125	Henry V

The House of Luxembourg and The House of Wittelsbach

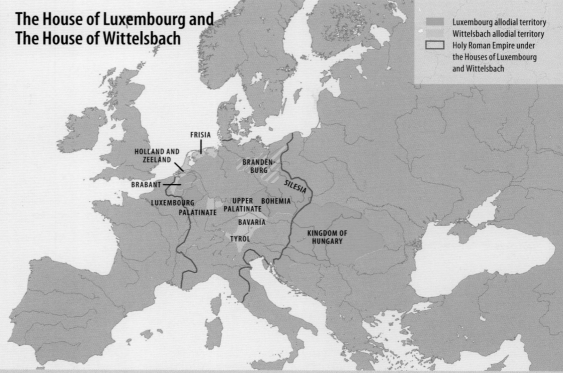

- Luxembourg allodial territory
- Wittelsbach allodial territory
- Holy Roman Empire under the Houses of Luxembourg and Wittelsbach

The House of Luxembourg 1214–1441 *Counts of Luxembourg*
1308–1313, 1347–1400 and 1410–1437 *Kings and emperors of the Holy Roman Empire*
1387–1437 *Kings of Hungary*
1311–1437 *Kings of Bohemia*
1373–1415 *Margraves of Brandenburg*

1308–1313	Henry VII
1347–1378	Carl IV
1410–1437	Sigismund

The House of Wittelsbach 1314–1328, 1400–1410, 1742–1745 *Kings and emperors of the Holy Roman Empire*
1214–1777 *Counts Palatine of the Rhine and electors palatine, succeeded in Bavaria in 1777*
1180–1918 *Dukes of the divided and (after 1508) unified Bavaria (electors from 1623, kings from 1806)*
1351–1425 *Counts of Holland, Zeeland and Hainaut*

1341–1363 *Counts of Tirol*
1322–1373 *Margraves of Brandenburg*

1314–1347	Ludwig IV the Bavarian
1400–1410	Rupert I, elector palatine
1742–1745	Carl VII

The Hohenstaufen Dynasty

Territory of the Hohenstaufens
- Until 1194
- After 1194
- Holy Roman Empire under the Hohenstaufens

The Hohenstaufen (or Staufer) Dynasty
1079–1266 *Dukes of Swabia*
1138–1254 *Holy Roman Empire: Italian and German kings and emperors*
1194–1266 *Kings of Sicily*

1138–1152	Conrad III
1152–1190	Frederick I Barbarossa
1190–1197	Henry VI
1212–1250	Frederick II

Louis IV (1282–1347) at the Battle of Mühldorf

Habsburg Dynasty

Allodial territory of the Habsburg dynasty in Austria ca. 1477

Holy Roman Empire under the Habsburgs ca. 1477

TYROL
AUSTRIA
STYRIA
CARNIOLA

Habsburg Dynasty

Habsburg Spain
Habsburg Austria
Border of the Holy Roman Empire

HABSBURG NETHERLANDS
KINGDOM OF BOHEMIA
SILESIA
BREISGAU
AUSTRIA
ROYAL HUNGARY
FREE COUNTY OF BURGUNDY
TYROL
DUCHY OF MILAN
HUNGARIAN TERRITORY OCCUPIED BY THE TURKS
KINGDOM OF PORTUGAL
KINGDOM OF SPAIN
SARDINIA
KINGDOM OF NAPLES
CEUTA
ORAN ALGIERS
BEJAIA
ANNABA BIZERTE
TUNIS

Capetian Dynasty

Paris

Capetian allodial territory (12th c.)
Kingdom of France under the House of Capet

Habsburg Dynasty

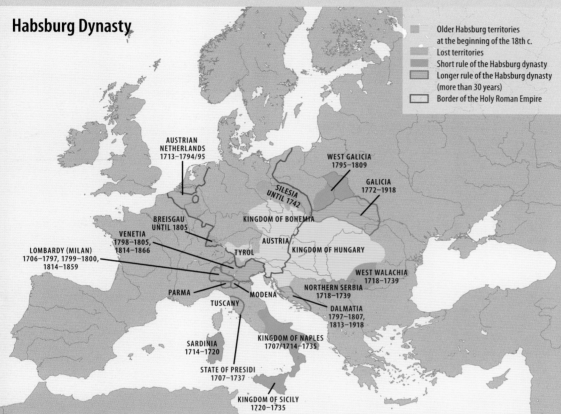

Older Habsburg territories at the beginning of the 18th c.
Lost territories
Short rule of the Habsburg dynasty
Longer rule of the Habsburg dynasty (more than 30 years)
Border of the Holy Roman Empire

AUSTRIAN NETHERLANDS 1713–1794/95
WEST GALICIA 1795–1809
SILESIA UNTIL 1742
GALICIA 1772–1918
BREISGAU UNTIL 1805
KINGDOM OF BOHEMIA
VENETIA 1798–1805, 1814–1866
AUSTRIA
LOMBARDY (MILAN) 1706–1797, 1799–1800, 1814–1859
TYROL
KINGDOM OF HUNGARY
WEST WALACHIA 1718–1739
PARMA
MODENA
NORTHERN SERBIA 1718–1739
TUSCANY
DALMATIA 1797–1807, 1813–1918
SARDINIA 1714–1720
KINGDOM OF NAPLES 1707/1714–1735
STATE OF PRESIDI 1707–1737
KINGDOM OF SICILY 1720–1735

Capetian Dynasty

Direct royal line 987–1328 in France
987–996 Hugh Capet
1180–1223 Philip II Augustus
1226–1270 Louis IX the Holy
1285–1314 Philip IV the Fair

Hugh Capet (941–996), painted by Charles Auguste Guillaume Steuben

Valois Dynasty

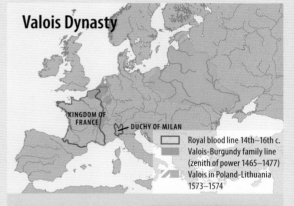

KINGDOM OF FRANCE
DUCHY OF MILAN

Royal blood line 14th–16th c.
Valois-Burgundy family line (zenith of power 1465–1477)
Valois in Poland-Lithuania 1573–1574

Habsburg and Habsburg-Lorraine – several lines

1273–1291, 1298–1308, 1438–1740 and 1745–1806 *Emperors of the Holy Roman Empire*
1282–1918 *Dukes (archdukes from 1457 onward) of Austria*
1438–1457 and 1527–1918 *Kings of Bohemia and Hungary*
1482–1794 *Sovereign princes and stadtholders of the Netherlands*
1504–1700 *Kings of Spain*
1535–1700, 1706–1797 and 1799–1800 *Dukes of Milan*
1580–1640 *Kings of Portugal*
1735–1748 and 1814–1847 *Dukes of Parma and Piacenza*
1737–1860 *Archdukes of Tuscany (intermittently)*
1804–1918 *Emperors of Austria*
1815–1866 *Kings of Lombardy-Venetia*

1814–1859 *Dukes of Modena and Reggio*
1273–1291 Rudolf I, king
1493–1519 Maximilian I, emperor
1519–1556 Charles V, emperor and king of Spain
1556–1598 Philip II, king of Spain (1580–1598 also king of Portugal)
1765–1790 Joseph II, emperor
1848–1916 Francis Joseph I, emperor of Austria

Francis Joseph I (1830–1916), by Wilhelm List

Valois

1328–1589 *Kings of France; 1499–1512 and 1515–1521 Dukes of Milan*
1573–1574 *Kings in Polish-Lithuanian commonweal*
1363–1482 *Valois-Burgundy branch in Burgundy and Netherlands*
1328–1350 Philip V
1422–1461 Charles VII the Conqueror
1461–1483 Louis XI
1515–1547 Francis I
1574–1589 Henry III (1573–1574)

Charles VII (1403–1461)

Hohenzollern Dynasty

MEDIEVAL MARGRAVIATE OF BRANDENBURG
DUCHY OF PRUSSIA

Under Hohenzollern rule until 1701 (ascension to the royal throne)
Under Hohenzollern rule until 1871
German empire under the Hohenzollerns 1871–1918

Hohenzollern – Brandenburg – Prussia Line

1415–1701 *Margrave and electors of Brandenburg*
1525–1701 *Dukes of Prussia*
1701–1871 *Kings in and of Prussia*
1871–1918 *German emperor*
1740–1786 Frederick II the Great, king of Prussia
1861–1888 William I, emperor from 1871
1888–1918 William II, emperor

Frederick II (1712–1786)

William II (1859–1941)

THE MOST IMPORTANT ROYAL HOUSES OF EUROPE

Bourbon Dynasty

French Bourbons
Spanish Bourbons and side lines
House of Bourbon-Parma

Bourbon 1589–1792 and 1814–1848 *Kings of France*
1700–1808, 1813–1868, 1874–1931 and 1975–present *Kings of Spain*
1700–1713 *Kings of Sardinia*
1734–1860 *Kings of Sicily and Naples (intermittently)*
1700–1706 *Dukes of Milan*
1748–1802 and 1847–1860 *Dukes of Parma and Piacenza (House of Bourbon-Parma)*
1801–1807 *Kings of Etruria (House of Bourbon-Parma)*
1589–1610 Henry IV, king of France
1643–1715 Louis XIV the Sun King
1774–1792 Louis XVI, king of France (executed)
1830–1848 Louis Philippe I, the "Citizen King"

Capetian House of Anjou

Main line
Side lines (Hungary and Poland)
Territories of vassals

Capetian House of Anjou
1246–1299 *Counts of Anjou*
1266–1282 *Kings of Sicily*
1266–1442 *Kings of Naples*
1278–1386 *Princes of Achaea (intermittently)*
1265–1382 *Counts of Provence*
Branch lines: *Kings in Hungary 1308–1386 and in Poland 1370–1386*
1266–1285 Charles I of Naples and Sicily
1309–1343 Robert the Wise of Naples
1342–1382 Louis the Great of Hungary (also king of Poland 1370–1382)

House of Normandy

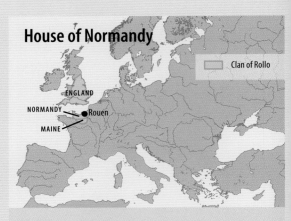

Clan of Rollo

Norman Dynasty
911–1135 *Counts of Rouen and dukes of Normandy*
1063–1126 *Counts of Maine*
1066–1137 *Kings of England*
911–927 Rollo, count of Rouen, duke of Normandy
1066–1087 William I the Conqueror, king of England
1100–1135 Henry I, king of England

William I (ca. 1027–1087)

House of Norman – Hauteville

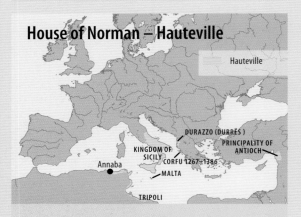

Hauteville

Norman – Hauteville (Altavilla in Latin)
1043–1130 *Counts and dukes of Apulia*
1088–1194 *Princes of Taranto*
1098–1163 *Princes of Antioch*
1130–1198 *Kings of Sicily*
1057–1085 Robert Guiscard
1127–1154 Roger II

House of Anjou-Plantagenet

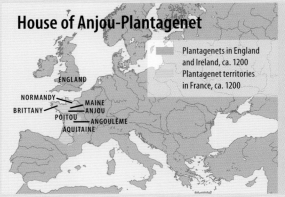

Plantagenets in England and Ireland, ca. 1200
Plantagenet territories in France, ca. 1200

House of Anjou-Plantagenet
1060/1129–1204 *Dukes of Anjou*
1110–1205 *Counts of Maine*
1144–1204 *Dukes of Normandy*
1152–1224 *Dukes of Aquitaine*
1154–1399 *Kings of England*
1169–1203 *Dukes of Brittany*
1169–1224 *Counts of Poitou*
1185–1399 *Lords of Ireland*
1154–1189 Henry II
1189–1199 Richard I Lion-heart
1272–1307 Edward I Longshanks
1327–1377 Edward III

House of Tudor

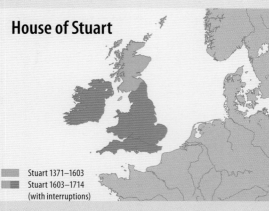

Tudor 1485–1603

Elizabeth I (1533–1603)

House of Stuart

Stuart 1371–1603
Stuart 1603–1714 (with interruptions)

Stuart 1371–1603 *Kings of Scotland* 1603–1649, 1660–1694 and 1702–1714 *Kings of Scotland, England and Ireland*
1707–1714 *Kings of Great Britain and Ireland*
1542–1567 Mary Stuart
1567–1625 Jacob I
1625–1649 Charles I (executed)

Tudor 1485–1603 *Kings of England and lords of Ireland, after 1542 also kings of Ireland*
1485–1509 Henry VII
1509–1547 Henry VIII
1553–1558 Mary Tudor ("Bloody Mary")
1558–1603 Elizabeth I

Piast Dynasty

- Various blood lines in the 10th–13th centuries
- Maximum extent in the early 11th century (under Boleslaw I the Brave)

Piast Dynasty 960–1290 and 1306–1320 *Several lines: dukes in Polish Duchy of Greater Poland, Lesser Poland, Masovia, Kuyavia, Silesia*
1002–1004 *Dukes of Bohemia*
1025–1032, 1076–1079 and 1320–1370 *Kings of Poland*
992–1025 Boleslaw I the Brave
1058–1079 Boleslaw II the Bold
1333–1370 Casimir III the Great

Jagiellon Dynasty

- Main line of the Jagiellon dynasty in Poland-Lithuania 1386–1572
- Bohemia (side line)
- Hungary (side line)
- Territories under Polish hegemony

Jagiellon Dynasty 1386–1572 *Kings in the joined Poland-Lithuania, branch line kings 1471–1526 in Bohemia and 1490–1526 in Hungary*
1386–1434 Władysław II (1377–1401 as Jogaila in Lithuania)
1447–1492 Casimir II (since 1440 as Casimir I in Lithuania)
1506–1548 Sigismund I the Old
1548–1572 Sigismund II Augustus (1545–1572 also as Sigismund III in Lithuania)

Přemyslid Dynasty

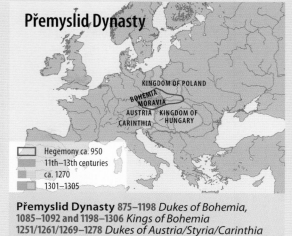

- Hegemony ca. 950
- 11th–13th centuries
- ca. 1270
- 1301–1305

Přemyslid Dynasty 875–1198 *Dukes of Bohemia*, 1085–1092 and 1198–1306 *Kings of Bohemia* 1251/1261/1269–1278 *Dukes of Austria/Styria/Carinthia and Carniola*
1300–1306 *Kings of Poland*
1301–1305 *Kings of Hungary*
921–935 Saint Wenceslas
1253–1278 Ottokar II Přemysl
1278–1305 Wenceslas II

Árpád Dynasty

- ca. 1038 (death of the king St. Stephen)
- 12th–13th centuries
- Dependent territories

Árpád Dynasty ca. 970–1000 *Princes of Hungary,*
1000–1301 *Kings of Hungary*
1102–1301 *Kings of Croatia (joined with Hungary)*
997–1038 Saint Stephen I
1077–1095 Saint Ladislas I
1205–1235 Andrew II
1235–1270 Béla IV

Stephen I (ca. 969–1038)

Nemanjić Dynasty

- End of 12th c.
- ca. 1320
- ca. 1350

Nemanjić Dynasty 1167–1217 *Grand chieftans*
1217–1371 *Kings of Raška (Serbia) and of the coastal lands (Montenegro, Herzegovina, South Dalmatia, North Albania)*
1167–1196 Stefan Nemanja
1243–1276 Stefan Uroš I
1282–1321 Stefan Uroš II Milutin
1331–1355 Stefan Uroš IV Dušan, 1346 Tsar of Serbia

Stefan Uroš IV (ca. 1308–1355)

House of Oldenburg

- Territory of the royal Danish line of the Oldenburgs, 15th–19th c.
- Temporary rule

Oldenburgs – Royal Danish Line
1448–1863 *Kings of Denmark (branch line 1863 to the present)*
1450–1814 *Kings of Norway (branch line 1814–1818 and 1905–present)*
1457–1464, 1497–1501, 1520–1523 *Kings of Sweden (branch line also 1751–1818)*
1460–1864 *Dukes of Schleswig-Holstein (after 1544 divided among the royal and branch lines)*
1440–1448, 1667–1773 *Counts of Oldenburg*

House of Vasa

- Sweden under the first king of the House of Vasa, Gustav I
- Territory gained by the Swedish Vasa by 1654
- The Vasa in Poland-Lithuania 1587–1668

House of Vasa 1521–1654 *Kings of Sweden, 1587–1668 Kings of Poland and grand dukes of Lithuania*
1521–1560 Gustav I Vasa
1592–1599 Sigismund (1587–1632 also Sigismund III of Poland-Lithuania)
1611–1632 Gustavus Adolphus

House of Savoy

- Territory of the House of Savoy before 1861
- Territory temporarily gained by the Savoys in the 17th century
- Kingdom of Italy 1870–1919
- Territory annexed after World War I

House of Savoy 1003–1861 *Counts of Savoy (dukes of Savoy after 1416)*
1713–1720 *Kings of Sicily*
1720–1798 and 1814–1861 *Kings of Sardinia-Piedmont*
1861–1946 *Kings of Italy*
1343–1383 Amedeus VI, the Green Count
1391–1440 Amedeus VIII the Peaceful, also Antipope Felix V 1439–1449
1849–1878 Victor Emmanuel II, after 1861 king of Italy

House of Trastámara

- Reign in the 14th century
- Gains and conquests in the 15th century

House of Trastámara 1369–1516 *Kings of Castile and León*
1412–1516 *Kings of Aragon, Sicily and Sardinia*
1425–1479 *Kings of Navarra*
1442–1516 *Kings of Naples*
1474–1504 Isabella I "the Catholic" of Castile and León
1479–1516 Ferdinand II "the Catholic" of Aragon (from 1506 also of Castile and León)

Medieval Castles

Castles

Castles were habitable fortresses built to protect kings and queens (royal castles), the nobility, orders of knights (*ordensburg*, a combination of cloister and military fortress), the population in times of danger (castles of refuge), but also to protect landowners from the masses during popular rebellions (strongholds). As a rule they were built on high ground (cliffs, hills)—at first of wood, later of massive stone—to give defenders a strategic advantage over attacking forces. Erecting a castle was a privilege reserved solely for the king or the lord of a territory (regalia). Those living in the region were often compelled to build the castle, and in exchange were allowed to seek protection inside the castle walls in case of danger. Cisterns (water reservoirs) and livestock within the fortress staved off starvation during times of siege. Most European castles date back to the High Middle Ages, including an estimated 20,000 in Germany alone; the greatest concentration of castles is found in Bohemia. As part of war negotiations, conquered castles often had to tear down their walls, or they were destroyed entirely in battle.

Knights

Heavily armed medieval soldiers ("riders": *Ritter* in German, *chevalier* in French, *caballero* in Spanish) were initially of noble birth, and emphasized their independence. In the Middle Ages, however, officers who served ruling lords also rose to knighthood. Once certain tests were passed, acceptance as a knight was a formal affair involving oaths of loyalty and ceremony. At first, knights were brutal, bloodthirsty warmongers who often acted as robber barons, but they came to understand themselves as obligated to uphold Christian ideals (nobleness, bravery, protection of the weak, the peace and truce of God). Even in the lifetime of Walther von der Vogelweide (ca. 1170–1230), knights were often noblemen well trained in military, religious and courtly-cultural matters, and dedicated to courtly love, the idealized adoration from afar of women to whom they dedicated their knightly deeds. The heavily armed but immobile knights on horseback fell from favor with the advent of archers in the 14th and 15th centuries, especially in England, and became obsolete with the arrival of firearms.

Feudalism

Feudalism is the economic and political system that prevailed in the Middle Ages. The feudal lord generally granted the vassal (a free person who agreed to serve a landowner) a piece of land (a fief), but also provided military protection. In exchange, the vassal vowed to fulfill certain obligations, in particular fealty and service as a soldier. Vassals were required to attend assemblies and pay certain taxes or dues. This hierarchical structure was held in place by mutual fealty and loyalty, made public by oaths.

Imperial Palaces

Imperial palaces were stations along the king's route as he traveled. The difficulty of communication and the splintering of power among individual feudal lords made central governments impossible. Rulers thus sought direct contact with their subjects, and into the 14th century the German kings and emperors, especially, were "wandering rulers." There was a dense network of imperial palaces throughout the land, no more than a day's journey apart (ca. 20 miles/30 km), ready to meet the needs of a mobile national administration (audiences, grants, adjudication, pronouncements).

Tower of London, England

Castillo de Loarre, Spain

Edinburgh
7th century

Richmond
1071

Caernarfon
1283

Tower of London
1078

Dover
11th century

Gravensteen
1180

Angers
ca. 1204

Beynac
12th century

Châteauneuf
15th century

Quéribus
13th century

Burgos
850

Loarre
11th–12th century

Cardona 886

Guimarães
958–968

Obidos
ca. 5th century

Albarracin

Elvas
13th century

Guadamur
1470

Almodovar del Rio
12th century

Alhambra
ca. 9th century

Royal castle
Castle of nobility
Ordensburg
Castle

Tre Kronor Stockholm
13th century

...entheim
...h century

Schwerin Castle
965

Malbork
1309

Wartburg
1067

Chojnik
1350

...Eltz
...h century

Wawel
ca. 9th century

Heidelberg
1225

Karlštejn
1348

Prague
ca. 870

Spiš
12th century

...igsbourg
...47

Trenčin
ca. 9th century

Diósgyőr
13th century

Bilhorod-Dnistrovskyi
15th century

Hohensalzburg
1077

Budapest
13th century

...century

Bran
1377

...Fénis
...1242

Beseno
10th century

Bled
1004

Sarzana
983

Kamerlengo
15th century

Golubac Fortress
13th century

Tsarevec
5th century

Baba Vida
10th century

Nvovo
1279

Castel del Monte
1240–1250

Malbork, Poland

Castello di Fénis, Italy

Castel del Monte, Italy

Medieval Religious Orders and Monasteries

Monasteries

A monastery is a complex of residential, sacred and other buildings in which monks or nuns live communally according to certain rules they have vowed to live in accordance with. European monasteries are primarily Christian and belong to the Catholic and Orthodox churches. There have been some Protestant religious communities as well, such as St. Peter's in Erfurt, Germany. Monasteries are not only places of spiritual life, but also centers of culture and education. They played an enormous role in the preservation and furtherance of knowledge passed down from antiquity. Monks copied old books, created artworks and conducted monastic and scribe schools. For a long time, reading and writing were maintained almost solely within monasteries. The monks developed practical techniques for farming and the cultivation of crops and shared them with the general population; the earliest cloisters, in particular, with their extensive lands, made entire regions of Europe arable. The rhythm of daily life in a monstery revolves around fixed times for prayer and work. The ideal of the earliest monasteries was to be an autonomous and self-sustaining universe; after 1200 the mendicant orders protested this life behind walls.

Monastic Hierarchy

Abbot The head of an abbey, freely elected by the monks. He exercises "fatherly" and judicious authority.
Prior Proxy for the abbot and named by him to head the monastic brothers. The mendicant orders have no abbot, and are led by priors.
Cellarmaster Administrator of the monastery and second only to the prior as a helpmate to the abbot
Monks Members of the orders whose main roles are prayer and work, living in accordance with the goals and rules of the order (in some orders this includes pastoral duties, teaching (schools), social or medical work, or tending to pilgrims)

The Most Important Orders

Benedictines

The Benedictine order, founded by Benedict of Nursia (ca. 480–547), is considered the seminal form of Western monasticism. Benedict wrote the Benedictine Rule for Monte Cassino, the monastery he founded in Italy in 529; the *Regula Benedicti* govern every aspect of communal life, both practical and spiritual, and are designed to encourage the monastic virtues of humility, self-discipline and obedience. The Benedictine's maxim is *ora et labora* – Pray and work! Idleness is understood to be the soul's greatest enemy. A correlation to common prayer are the diverse fields of activity in which Benedictine monks are active, including pastoral care, schools, agriculture and mission work. Benedictine cloisters, especially in central Europe, often managed enormous estates, the most important of which were independent principalities (abbey-principality).

Cistercians

This order was founded by Robert of Molesme in 1098 at Cîteaux, France as part of a move to reform the Benedictine order, but rose to prominence under the leadership of Bernhard of Clairvaux (1090–1153). Unlike the Benedictines, who had become prosperous, the Cistercians wanted to live entirely by the work of their own hands. They brought about enormous changes in society (farming, trade) as they spread rapidly through Europe. Later their order became just as wealthy and powerful as the Benedictines.

Premonstratensians

Also called Norbertines after Saint Norbert of Xanten, who founded the order in 1120 in Prémontré, France. This order was especially strong in Belgium and the Netherlands and from its very beginnings has combined cloistered life with pastoral work in parishes.

Dominicans

This highly democratic mendicant order was founded by St. Dominic in Prouille, France, in the early 13th century. All the superiors are elected for limited terms, and monks have great say in decisions. The Dominicans are a preaching order and gave rise to significant scholars (Albertus Magnus, Thomas Aquinas), which earned them the name *Canes Domini* ("Watchdogs of the Lord"); the church thus turned to this order to combat and persecute heretics. Dominicans also led the Inquisition and the persecution of witches. Heinrich Kraemer (Institoris), author of the infamous *Malleus Maleficarum* (*Hexenhammer*), was also a Dominican.

Franciscans

Founded by St. Francis of Assisi in the 13th century, Franciscan monks lived in strict poverty. Spiritual and physical care of the sick and poor played a greater role than in any other order. Conflict arose already around 1300, and the order divided over the issue of poverty: the radical sect insisted on renouncing all possessions and worldly power following Christ's example, and turned away from the pope. The Capuchins, devoted to missionary work, were also founded on Franciscan ideals.

Jesuits

Founded by Ignatius of Loyola in 1534, this order has high intellectual standards. The Jesuits were the driving force behind the Counter-Reformation and sumptuous decoration, especially of baroque church interiors. Jesuits have been involved in mission work around the world, particularly in Japan and China. Jesuits founded "reductions" (settlements) in South America to further and protect the native people there. Early on, Jesuits not only took over numerous universities, but also become political advisors of Catholic rulers. The sovereigns of Enlightened Absolutism protested vigorously in the 18th century and in 1773 forced the pope to dissolve the order, but it was reestablished in 1814.

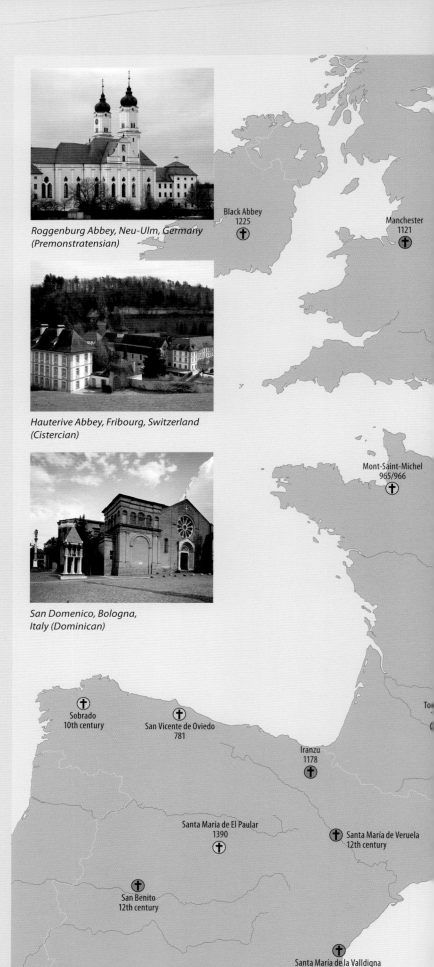

Roggenburg Abbey, Neu-Ulm, Germany (Premonstratensian)

Hauterive Abbey, Fribourg, Switzerland (Cistercian)

San Domenico, Bologna, Italy (Dominican)

Black Abbey 1225

Manchester 1121

Mont-Saint-Michel 965/966

Sobrado 10th century

San Vicente de Oviedo 781

Iranzu 1178

Santa María de El Paular 1390

Santa María de Veruela 12th century

San Benito 12th century

Santa María de la Valldigna 1298

Magdeburg
1129

Corvey
815/22

Hamborn
8th century
Cappenberg 1122

Fritzlar 1085

Grüssau
1242

Świętokrzyskie
1006

Hersfeld
769

Prémontré
1120

Trier
12th century

Fulda 744
Langheim 1133

Břevnov
993

Bildhausen 1158
Waldsassen 1142
Strahov 1140

Himmerod 1134

Ebrach 1127
Speinshart
1145
Plasy 1146

Teplá Abbey 1193

Spišský Štiavnik 1223

Heilsbronn
1132
Nepomuk 1145

Jasov 12th century

Dieu
1119

Pontigny
1114

Alpirsbach
1095

Amberg 1452

Metten 766

Zwettl Abbey 1138

Hronský Beňadik
1075

Morimond
1115

Aldersbach 1146

Melk Abbey 1089

Roggenburg
1126

Fontenay
1119

St. Gotthard 1183
Wilhering Abbey
1146

Reichenau
724

Clairvaux 1115

Heiligenkreuz Abbey
1133

Esztergom 1635

Oradea 12th century

Citeaux
1098

Wilten
1138

St. Peter
696

Rein Abbey 1129

Pannonhalma 10th century

Hauterive
1138

St. Gallen
719

Zirc 1182

Cluny
910

Cikádor
1142

Chiaravalle Milanese
1135

Bologna
1218

Montpellier
1365

Saint Trophime
12th century

Chiaravalle della Colomba
1132/36

Fontfroide
1093/1144

Chiaravalle d'Ancona 1147

Assisi
1208

Chiaravalle di Fiastra
1141

Mother house Il Gesù
1568

Monte Cassino
529

Casamari 1140

Monasteries
Benedictines
Premonstratensians
Cistercians
Dominicans
Franciscans
Jesuits

Il Gesù in Rome, Italy (Jesuit)

San Francesco Basilica in Assisi, Italy (Franciscan)

Melk Abbey in Austria (Benedictine)

105

Europe in Detail – The Late Middle Ages

1092

KINGDOM OF NORWAY
KINGDOM OF SWEDEN
KINGDOM OF SCOTLAND
IRELAND
KINGDOM OF ENGLAND
WALES
PRINCIPALITY OF POLOTSK
SUZDAL PRINCIPALITY
PRINCIPALITY OF NOVGOROD
PRINCIPALITY OF SMOLENSK
VOLGA BULGARIANS
DUCHY OF BRITTANY
DUCHY OF NORMANDY
POMERANIANS
KIEVAN RUS'
KINGDOM OF POLAND
HOLY ROMAN EMPIRE
VLADIMIR PRINCIPALITY
POLOVTSY (KIPCHAKS, CUMANS)
KINGDOM OF NAVARRA
KINGDOM OF FRANCE
KINGDOM OF HUNGARY
KINGDOM OF CROATIA
VENICE
KINGDOM OF ITALY
Pisa
PRINCIPALITY OF SERBIA
PECHENEGS
GEORGIA
KINGDOM OF LEON AND CASTILE
COUNTY OF BARCELONA
KINGDOM OF ZARAGOZA (MUSLIM)
CALIPHATE OF CORDOBA
KINGDOM OF SICILY (NORMANS)
BYZANTINE EMPIRE
SULTANATE OF THE RUM SELJUKS
EMIRATE OF BADAJOS (MUSLIM)

1200

NORWAY
KINGDOM OF SWEDEN
REPUBLIC OF NOVGOROD
KINGDOM OF SCOTLAND
IRELAND
KINGDOM OF ENGLAND
WALES
KINGDOM OF DENMARK
BALTIC TRIBES
RUSSIAN PRINCIPALITIES
DUCHY OF POMERANIA
MASOVIA
GREATER POLAND
MARGRAVATE OF BRANDENBURG
DUCHY OF SILESIA
LESSER POLAND
KINGDOM OF GALICIA-VOLHYNIA
HOLY ROMAN EMPIRE
KINGDOM OF BOHEMIA
POLOVTSY (KIPCHAKS, CUMANS)
KINGDOM OF FRANCE
DUCHY OF BAVARIA
KINGDOM OF HUNGARY
ENGLISH TERRITORIES IN FRANCE
VENICE
KINGDOM OF ITALY
BOSNIA
SERBIA
BULGARIAN EMPIRE
KINGDOM OF LEON
KINGDOM OF NAVARRE
PAPAL STATES
KINGDOM OF PORTUGAL
KINGDOM OF CASTILE
KINGDOM OF ARAGON
KINGDOM OF SICILY
BYZANTINE EMPIRE
ALMOHAD TERRITORY
Las Navas de Tolosa 1212
⊗ Important battle

1122 The Concordat of Worms ends the Investiture Controversy, a conflict between the pope and secular leaders over the authority to appoint bishops.

1204 An army of Crusaders sacks and plunders Constantinople.

1215 The Magna Carta, a charter of rights that bears similarities to a basic constitution, is signed in England.

1241 The Mongols raid Europe.

1283 The Teutonic Knights complete their Christianizing of the pagan Prussians.

1291 Acre (Akko), the last Crusader State in the Holy Land, falls. The Swiss Confederation is founded.

1309–1377 Avignon is the papal seat.

1328 With the death of the last ruler of the Capetian dynasty, the French crown passes to the related Valois dynasty. With a rival claim to the throne, the English monarchy initiates the Hundred Years' War (1337–1453).

1347–1352 The bubonic plague ("Black Death") ravages Europe.

1362 Ottoman Turks take Adrianople.

1363–1477 The dukes of Burgundy attempt to establish an independent state between France and the Holy Roman Empire. Flanders becomes the dominant region of Western Europe.

1378–1417 The Great Western Schism: Two rival popes, each with his own following, rule simultaneously in Rome and in Avignon, with a third appearing in Pisa in 1409.

1397 The Kalmar Union is established in Scandinavia.

1410 At the Battle of Tannenberg, a Polish-Lithuanian army defeats the Teutonic Knights.

1414–1418 The Council of Constance ends the Papal Schism and sentences reformer Jan Hus to death by burning (1415).

1419–1434 The Hussite Wars are fought in Bohemia, parts of Austria and eastern Germany.

1431 Joan of Arc is burned at the stake.

1438 The crown of the Holy Roman Empire passes to the Habsburgs, who will rule until 1806.

1453 Ottoman armies take Constantinople, thereby putting an end to the Byzantine Empire.

ca. 1360

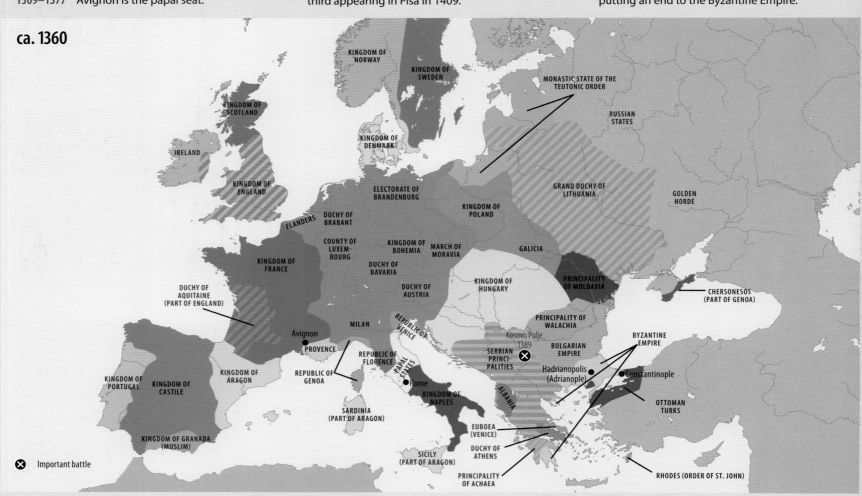

KINGDOM OF NORWAY
KINGDOM OF SWEDEN
MONASTIC STATE OF THE TEUTONIC ORDER
RUSSIAN STATES
KINGDOM OF SCOTLAND
IRELAND
KINGDOM OF ENGLAND
KINGDOM OF DENMARK
ELECTORATE OF BRANDENBURG
GRAND DUCHY OF LITHUANIA
GOLDEN HORDE
FLANDERS
DUCHY OF BRABANT
COUNTY OF LUXEMBOURG
KINGDOM OF POLAND
KINGDOM OF BOHEMIA
MARCH OF MORAVIA
GALICIA
KINGDOM OF FRANCE
DUCHY OF BAVARIA
DUCHY OF AUSTRIA
KINGDOM OF HUNGARY
PRINCIPALITY OF MOLDAVIA
CHERSONESOS (PART OF GENOA)
DUCHY OF AQUITAINE (PART OF ENGLAND)
PRINCIPALITY OF WALACHIA
Avignon
PROVENCE
MILAN
REPUBLIC OF VENICE
Kosovo Polje 1389
SERBIAN PRINCIPALITIES
BULGARIAN EMPIRE
BYZANTINE EMPIRE
REPUBLIC OF FLORENCE
REPUBLIC OF GENOA
PAPAL STATES
Rome
Hadrianopolis (Adrianople)
Constantinople
KINGDOM OF PORTUGAL
KINGDOM OF CASTILE
KINGDOM OF ARAGON
ALBANIA
OTTOMAN TURKS
KINGDOM OF NAPLES
SARDINIA (PART OF ARAGON)
EUBOEA (VENICE)
DUCHY OF ATHENS
RHODES (ORDER OF ST. JOHN)
KINGDOM OF GRANADA (MUSLIM)
SICILY (PART OF ARAGON)
PRINCIPALITY OF ACHAEA
⊗ Important battle

Venice

For over a thousand years, Venice was one of the world's great sea powers, with colonies stretching from the Crimea to the Maghreb.

828 Venetians steal the relics of St. Mark from Alexandria.

12th–14th centuries Venice repeatedly defies the German emperors and the popes by maintaining trade relations with Muslim states.

1378–1381 Venice defeats Genoa in the War of Chioggia.

from 1380 The Venetians conquer Verona, Vicenza, Padua, Brescia and Bergamo.

1416 At the naval battle of Gallipoli, Venetian ships defeat the Ottoman fleet.

1489 Venice conquers Cyprus.

Russia

1054 Kievan Rus, in existence since the 9th century, splits into smaller states.

1233 Mongol (Tatar) forces defeat the Rus army at the Battle of Kalka River.

1237–1242 Under Batu Khan, the Mongols sweep through Russia.

1240 At the Battle of the Neva, Alexander Nevsky halts the advance of the Swedish army.

1242 Alexander Nevsky defeats the Teutonic Knights at the Battle of Lake Peipus ("Battle of the Ice").

1328 Moscow's status is elevated from a metropolitan seat of the Russian Orthodox Church to a patriarchate.

1331 The Grand Duchy of Moscow

1380 The grand duke of Moscow, Dmitri Donskoy, defeats the Tatars.

1472 Grand Duke Ivan III assumes the title of tsar.

1480 Tatar domination ends.

Hanseatic League

~1150 A league of German merchants springs up along the coasts of the North and Baltic Seas, at first for mutual protection and then to improve trading conditions. These Hanseatic partners trade with the Swedish island of Gotland, gradually competing with the Scandinavian states.

~1240 The league of individual merchants begins to evolve into a league of primarily German cities and towns.

~1275 The city of Lübeck supplants Gotland as the leading power in the league.

1361–1370 The Hanseatic League successfully fights and wins a war with Denmark, thereby securing its trade monopoly in northern Europe.

~1425 Gradual decline of the influence of the Hanseatic League begins.

The Rise of Venice

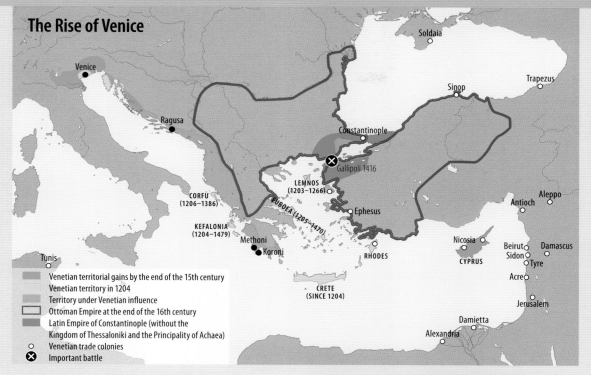

Venetian territorial gains by the end of the 15th century
Venetian territory in 1204
Territory under Venetian influence
Ottoman Empire at the end of the 16th century
Latin Empire of Constantinople (without the Kingdom of Thessaloniki and the Principality of Achaea)
○ Venetian trade colonies
⊗ Important battle

Joan of Arc (1412–1431) A farmer's daughter, she experienced visions and led the French to victory over the English at Orléans. She was captured by the English in 1430 and in the following year was burned at the stake for witchcraft and heresy.

Marco Polo (1254–1324) set off in 1271 on a trade mission to China, where he supposedly rose to favor at the court of Kublai Khan, becoming that ruler's confidant. The credibility of his accounts was doubted by his contemporaries.

Marco Polo

Rudolph I of Habsburg (1218–1291) was elected King of Germany in 1273 after a long interregnum. In 1278 he defeated Ottokar II Premysl, King of Bohemia, at the Battle on the Marchfeld. He invested his sons with the Duchy of Austria in 1283, leading to the ascent of the Habsburg dynasty.

Osman I Gazi (ca. 1258–1326) founded the Ottoman Empire (1299/1300), which was named after him. The symbol of this new dynasty was the sword of Osman, with which every Ottoman ruler was ritually coronated as sultan.

Russian Expansion

Under Daniel of Moscow until 1303
Conquests by Georgi III Danilovich (1303–1325)
Conquests by Ivan Kalita (1325–1340)
Conquests by Dmitri Donskoy (1359/1362–1389)
Conquests by Vasiliy I (1389–1425)
Conquests by Vasiliy II (1425–1462)
Conquests of Ivan III the Great (1462–1505)

The Hanseatic League

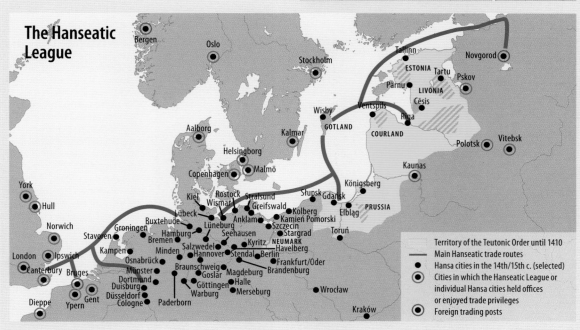

Territory of the Teutonic Order until 1410
Main Hanseatic trade routes
• Hansa cities in the 14th/15th c. (selected)
◉ Cities in which the Hanseatic League or individual Hansa cities held offices or enjoyed trade privileges
◉ Foreign trading posts

European Universities

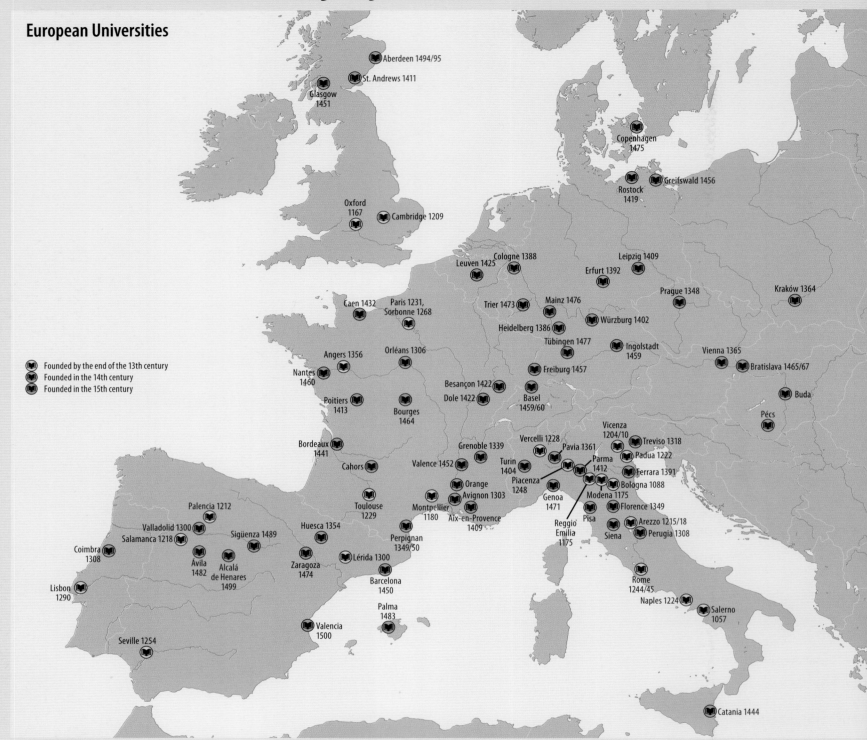

Aberdeen 1494/95

St. Andrews 1411

Glasgow 1451

Copenhagen 1475

Greifswald 1456

Rostock 1419

Oxford 1167

Cambridge 1209

Cologne 1388

Leuven 1425

Leipzig 1409

Erfurt 1392

Kraków 1364

Caen 1432

Paris 1231, Sorbonne 1268

Trier 1473

Mainz 1476

Prague 1348

Würzburg 1402

Heidelberg 1386

Tübingen 1477

Ingolstadt 1459

Vienna 1365

Angers 1356

Orléans 1306

Freiburg 1457

Bratislava 1465/67

Nantes 1460

Besançon 1422

Basel 1459/60

Buda

Poitiers 1413

Dole 1422

Bourges 1464

Pécs

Vicenza 1204/10

Bordeaux 1441

Grenoble 1339

Vercelli 1228

Treviso 1318

Pavia 1361

Padua 1222

Cahors

Valence 1452

Turin 1404

Parma 1412

Ferrara 1391

Orange

Piacenza 1248

Bologna 1088

Avignon 1303

Modena 1175

Genoa 1471

Florence 1349

Toulouse 1229

Montpellier 1180

Aix-en-Provence 1409

Reggio Emilia 1175

Pisa

Arezzo 1215/18

Palencia 1212

Huesca 1354

Siena

Perugia 1308

Valladolid 1300

Sigüenza 1489

Salamanca 1218

Coimbra 1308

Perpignan 1349/50

Rome 1244/45

Ávila 1482

Alcalá de Henares 1499

Zaragoza 1474

Lérida 1300

Naples 1224

Salerno 1057

Lisbon 1290

Barcelona 1450

Palma 1483

Valencia 1500

Seville 1254

Catania 1444

Founded by the end of the 13th century
Founded in the 14th century
Founded in the 15th century

Anatomy lecture hall at the university in Bologna, Italy

The first European universities originated in the 11th century through a process of emancipation from the educational monopoly of the Church and monasteries in Italy. While there are universities in Cairo, Egypt and Fes, Morocco, that predate it, the first such institution to be founded in Europe was the University of Bologna (1088), where administrative specialists were trained independently of the clergy. The University of Paris, on the other hand, was founded through a papal decree. It became the model for other Western universities, especially in England, where the University of Oxford (12th century) became significant because in 1167, King Henry II forbade Englishmen to study at the University of Paris. At first, the seven liberal arts formed a kind of core education: logic, Latin grammar, rhetoric, geometry, arithmetic, astronomy and music. Only after gaining a solid foundation in these areas did students choose between the subjects of theology, law or medicine. The organization of the universities resembled that of the nations: students from various countries resided together in certain quarters and houses which were usually provided and furnished by their sovereigns; students from smaller nations were included in the living quarters of the larger ones. In Paris, for example, the quarters were divided among four nations: the Gauls or Gallics (which also incorporated the Italians, Spanish and Greek), Picardians, Normans and British (to which the Germans and other central Europeans were assigned). The first university within the Holy Roman Empire was the University of Prague, founded in 1347/1348.

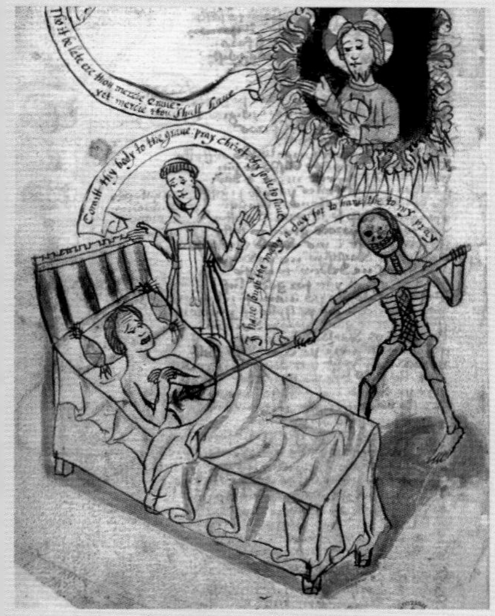

The Black Death

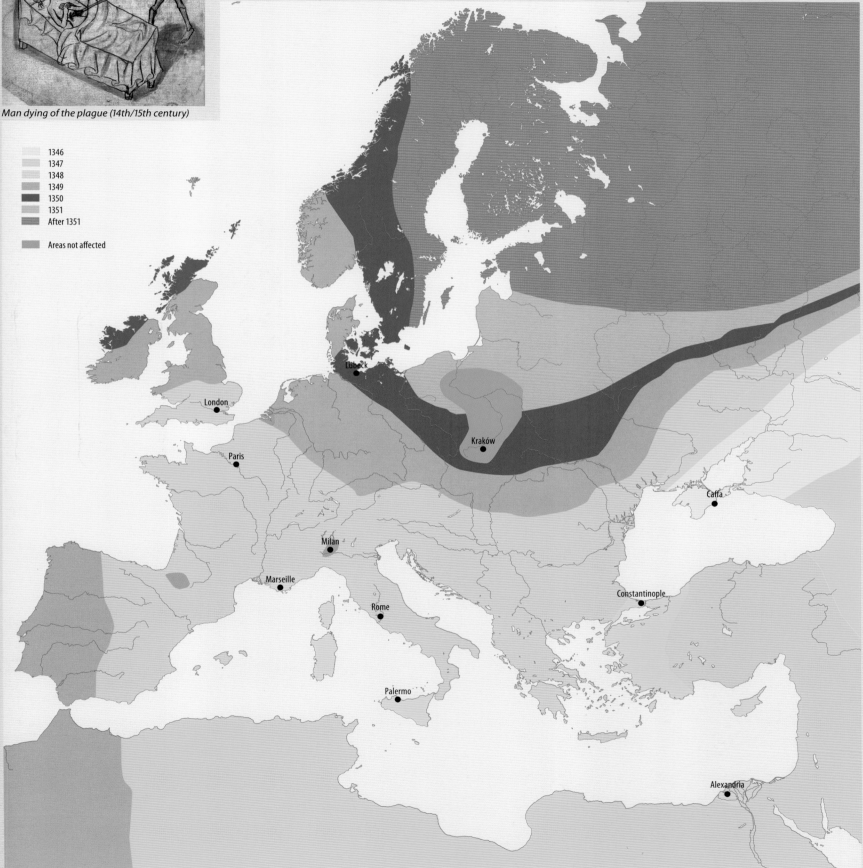

The plague, mentioned in the Bible as one of the seven plagues visited upon Egypt, was one of the worst catastrophes of the Middle Ages. Between 1347 and 1352, the outbreak of the Black Death—brought from Asia aboard trade ships and spread from the Crimean Peninsula through Europe—killed approximately 25 million people (one third of the European population at that time). Italy was especially hard hit. The plague is a highly contagious disease, usually transmitted through the bite of rat fleas, which jump onto people after the host animal dies; plague outbreaks are often preceded by a rash of rat deaths. Following exposure there is a brief incubation period, then symptoms appear including fever, headache and dark, swollen, pus-filled nodules called buboes. Other infectious diseases can also become deadly epidemics, for example cholera or typhus. In antiquity leprosy was often a problem, a disease that has its origins in eastern Africa and spread from there throughout the world. In the 20th century, the epidemic outbreak of flu in 1917/1918 known as the Spanish Flu also claimed more than 25 million lives.

Man dying of the plague (14th/15th century)

Legend:
- 1346
- 1347
- 1348
- 1349
- 1350
- 1351
- After 1351
- Areas not affected

Map labels: Lübeck, London, Paris, Kraków, Caffa, Milan, Marseille, Constantinople, Rome, Palermo, Alexandria

Europe in Detail – The Early Modern Era and Reformation

1492—the year in which the Moors were driven from their last stronghold in Spain, and when Columbus first sailed to the New World—is considered the symbolic beginning of the modern era. The monopoly of the Catholic Church's worldview was lost as a result of the Reformation, which originated in Germany and spread to many parts of Europe, shattering the unity of Western Christendom. The Renaissance, a cultural "rebirth" of the values and principles of antiquity, brought a new intellectual movement with it: humanism. Humanism encouraged humanity to make critical use of its own reason while drawing on the learning of all eras of human history. Science and experimental investigation, liberated from Christian taboos, experienced a phase of rapid growth. The invention of movable type made possible the lasting exchange of ideas and gave a much wider public access to knowledge, not least through the translation of the Bible into vernacular languages during the Reformation. Voyages of discovery expanded the known world to include whole new continents: the Americas.

~1450   Gutenberg invents movable type, revolutionizing the printing process and making books more widely accessible.

1453   The Ottoman Turks conquer Constantinople.

1526   The Ottomans defeat the army of Louis II, King of Hungary and Bohemia, at the Battle of Mohács. The Ottoman Empire expands into central Europe.

Johannes Gutenberg (1398–1468)

The Ottoman Empire 1400–1500

Legend:
- Ottoman vassals
- Ottoman Empire 1481
- Ottoman Empire, end of 14th c.
- *CRETE*   Venetian colonies
- (1461)   Date of conquest
- ⊗   Important battle

Spanish and Portuguese Explorations

Early 15th century   Portuguese explore the coasts of Africa.

1469   The marriage between Ferdinand of Aragon and Isabella of Castile (the "Catholic Monarchs") unites Spain.

1470   Portuguese sailors reach the equator.

1487–1488   Bartolomeu Dias sails around the Cape of Good Hope, the southernmost point of Africa.

1492   The Catholic Monarchs drive the last Muslim rulers from Granada after a lengthy war. Christopher Columbus makes his first journey to the New World.

1494   The Treaty of Torsedillas divides the New World into Portuguese and Spanish spheres of influence.

1497–1498   Vasco da Gama discovers a sea route to India.

1519–1522   Ferdinand Magellan and Juan Sebastián del Cano undertake the first circumnavigation of the globe. Magellan dies in 1521, and del Cano completes the journey the following year.

Voyages of Discovery 1487–1543

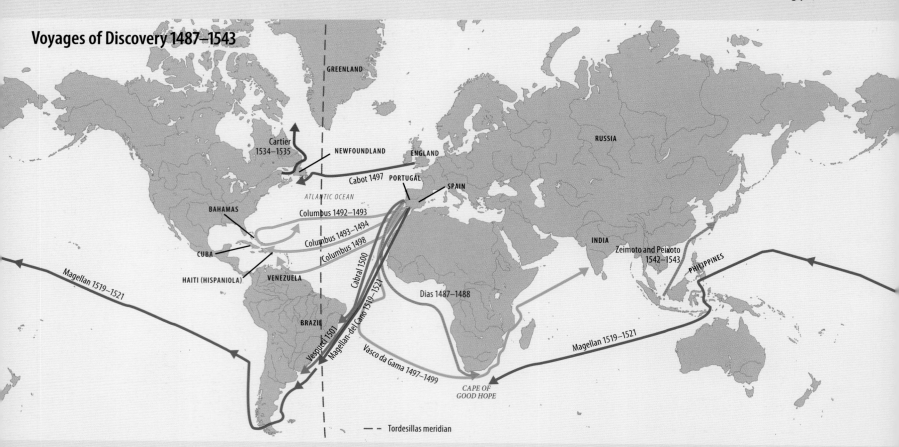

1500: Beginning of the Modern Era

Holy Roman Empire

KINGDOM OF SCOTLAND
Edinburgh
IRELAND
KINGDOM OF ENGLAND
London
Calais
Brussels
HABSBURG NETHERLANDS
Cologne
Paris
KINGDOM OF FRANCE
SWISS CONFEDERATION
DUCHY OF SAVOY
Marseille
DUCHY OF MILAN
Genoa
REPUBLIC OF GENOA
MODENA
DUCHY OF FLORENCE
REPUBLIC OF FLORENCE
Rome
PAPAL STATES
REPUBLIC OF VENICE
KINGDOM OF PORTUGAL
Lisbon
KINGDOM OF SPAIN
CASTILE
ARAGON
GRANADA UNTIL 1492
SARDINIA (SINCE 1326 PART OF THE KINGDOM OF ARAGON)
KINGDOM OF NAPLES (SPANISH)
KINGDOM OF SICILY (SPANISH)
KINGDOM OF NORWAY
KINGDOM OF SWEDEN
KALMAR UNION 1397–1523
KINGDOM OF DENMARK
Tallinn
TEUTONIC ORDER
Riga
Gdańsk
Minsk
GRAND DUCHY OF LITHUANIA
Kiev
Warsaw
KINGDOM OF POLAND
SILESIA
BOHEMIA
MORAVIA
BAVARIA
AUSTRIA
Buda
KINGOM OF HUNGARY
Zagreb
Belgrade
PRINCIPALITY OF MOLDAVIA
PRINCIPALITY OF WALACHIA
RUSSIA
GOLDEN HORDE, OR CRIMEAN KHANATE
OTTOMAN EMPIRE
Constantinople
CYPRUS (VENICE)

The Reformation

An ecclesiastical and spiritual movement beginning in the early 16th century, the original goal of the Reformation was to reform the Catholic Church and return to the Bible as the exclusive source of belief. The discrepancies between Biblical teaching and church practices such as the selling of indulgences were to be reconciled. The instigator of the Reformation was Martin Luther, an Augustinian theologian living in Wittenberg, Germany. His ideas spread quickly, especially in western and northern Europe.

1517   Luther writes and distributes Ninety-five Theses critical of the practices of the Catholic Church.

1520   Luther publicly burns the papal bull demanding that he recant his theses, along with scholarly writings on canon law.

1521   At the Diet of Worms, Luther refuses to recant his writings before Emperor Charles V. Elector Frederick III ("The Wise") of Saxony becomes Luther's protector.

1522/1523   Ulrich Zwingli begins his reformation efforts in Zurich, becoming the founder of the Reformed Church.

1525   The German Peasants' War—in part inspired by Luther's ideas, but from which Luther distanced himself—is defeated. Thomas Müntzer, a radical preacher of peasant liberation, faces death along with ca. 100,000 peasants, whose plight worsens. The last Grand Master of the Teutonic Knights converts to Lutheranism.

1534/1535   Radical Anabaptists establish a theocratic New Jerusalem in Münster, which comes to a bloody end.

1534   Ignatius of Loyola founds the Jesuit Order, the most important organization of the Counter-Reformation.

1541   French theologian John Calvin establishes a Puritan, Protestant theocracy in Geneva, Switzerland (Calvinists).

1545–1563   The Catholic Council of Trent challenges Protestant doctrine and calls for extensive reforms to be made within the Catholic Church.

1546–1547   The Schmalkaldic War between Holy Roman Emperor Charles V and princes of Protestant territories within the empire results in a temporary victory for the emperor.

1555   Charles V and the Lutheran leaders of the Schmalkaldic League sign the Peace of Augsburg, adopting the principle that the territorial princes of the Holy Roman Empire may choose between Catholicism and Lutheranism for themselves, and thus for their subjects (*cuius regio, eius religio*). The Calvinists are excluded.

The Reformation

Spread of the Reformation

NORWAY
SWEDEN
Stockholm
ESTONIA
SCOTLAND
Edinburgh
Riga
LIVONIA
COURLAND
IRELAND
Copenhagen
DENMARK
PRUSSIA
Gdańsk
LITHUANIA
BRANDENBURG
Warsaw
WALES
ENGLAND
London
NETHERLANDS
Münster
HOLY ROMAN EMPIRE
SILESIA
POLAND
Paris
Cologne
Prague
Worms
Munich
AUSTRIA
HUNGARY
TRANSYLVANIA
FRANCE
Zürich
SWISS CONFEDERATION
Geneva
Vienna
Buda

Europe in Detail – The 16th and 17th Centuries

1500–1600: The Reformation and Religious Wars

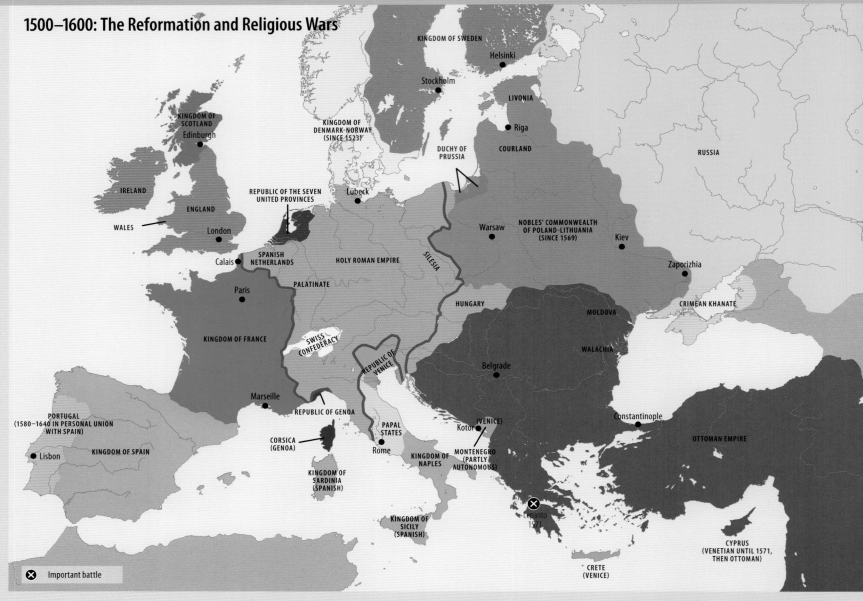

KINGDOM OF SWEDEN
Helsinki
Stockholm
LIVONIA
Riga
KINGDOM OF
DENMARK-NORWAY
(SINCE 1523)
COURLAND
DUCHY OF
PRUSSIA
RUSSIA
KINGDOM OF
SCOTLAND
Edinburgh
IRELAND
ENGLAND
REPUBLIC OF THE SEVEN
UNITED PROVINCES
Lübeck
WALES
London
Warsaw
NOBLES' COMMONWEALTH
OF POLAND-LITHUANIA
(SINCE 1569)
Kiev
Calais
SPANISH
NETHERLANDS
HOLY ROMAN EMPIRE
SILESIA
Zaporizhia
PALATINATE
Paris
HUNGARY
MOLDOVA
CRIMEAN KHANATE
KINGDOM OF FRANCE
SWISS
CONFEDERACY
WALACHIA
REPUBLIC OF
VENICE
Belgrade
Marseille
PORTUGAL
(1580–1640 IN PERSONAL UNION
WITH SPAIN)
REPUBLIC OF GENOA
(VENICE)
Kotor
Constantinople
CORSICA
(GENOA)
PAPAL
STATES
Rome
KINGDOM OF
NAPLES
MONTENEGRO
(PARTLY
AUTONOMOUS)
OTTOMAN EMPIRE
Lisbon
KINGDOM OF SPAIN
KINGDOM OF
SARDINIA
(SPANISH)
KINGDOM OF
SICILY
(SPANISH)
Lepanto
1571
CYPRUS
(VENETIAN UNTIL 1571,
THEN OTTOMAN)
CRETE
(VENICE)

⊗ Important battle

In Europe, the ideas of the Reformation with all their practical consequences began to spread, anchored mainly in the northern part of the continent. The Catholic church responded with its own, internal reforms and the Counter-Reformation, which was principally carried out by the Jesuits. Overseas discoveries extended the boundaries of the known world and promoted the emergence of world trade.

1517 Beginning of the Reformation in Germany

1519–1556 Emperor Charles V rules Spain, northern Italy, the Holy Roman Empire of the German Nations, Austria, the Netherlands and the New World.

1525 The Prussian territory of the Order of Teutonic Knights becomes the Duchy of Prussia.

1526/1540 After their victory over the Hungarians at the Battle of Mohács, the Ottomans dominate eastern and central Hungary until 1699.

1527 King Gustav I Vasa launches the Reformation in Sweden.

1534 King Henry VIII breaks with Rome to establish the state-sponsored Anglican Church of England.

1556–1598 Reign of King Philip II of Spain (also king of Portugal from 1580), son of Charles V. During this period, Spain attains the zenith of its influence and is Europe's leading Catholic power.

1558–1603 Rule of Elizabeth I of England: England becomes the leading mercantile power.

1562–1598 Religious wars in France end with the Edict of Nantes, opening the way to religious tolerance.

1567–1581 In their struggle for freedom, seven northern provinces of the Netherlands gain their independence from Spain.

1571 The fleet of the Holy League (an alliance of Christian forces) defeats the Ottomans at the Battle of Lepanto.

1572 The St. Bartholomew's Day massacre of the Huguenots in Paris

1582 Gregorian calendar reform is introduced, but accepted only in Catholic countries until the 18th century.

1588 The Spanish Armada is defeated by the English, ending Spanish dominion of the seas.

1608 Founding of the Protestant Union, a military alliance of German Protestant states

1609 Founding of the Catholic League

1618 The Protestant Diet of Bohemia deposes the Catholic Ferdinand II and elects Frederick V of Upper Palatinate ("The Winter King") king of Bohemia in his

stead. Defenestrations of Prague and the beginning of the Thirty Years' War between Catholic and Protestant forces.

1620 Troops of the Catholic League defeat the Bohemian Protestants and Frederick V at the Battle of White Mountain.

1622 The Catholic League occupies the Palatinate (German: *Pfalz*), deposes Frederick V and ends the status quo between Catholics and Protestants in the empire. Bavaria occupies the Electoral Palatinate.

1623–1629 Denmark enters the war on the side of the Protestants.

1624–1642 As chief minister to the French king, Cardinal Richelieu expands French power and draws Sweden into the war against the Habsburgs.

1629 The first phase of the Thirty Years' War ends with the Peace of Lübeck. Property that was confiscated during the Reformation is returned to the Roman Catholic Church.

1630 Sweden, threatened by the imperial troops in northern Germany, enters the war. King Gustav II Adolph marches through Germany toward Munich.

1631 Swedish victory over the imperial troops at Breitenfeld. Sweden occupies southern Germany and Bohemia.

1600–1700: The Thirty Years' War and Absolutism

KINGDOM OF SWEDEN

ESTONIA

LIVONIA

KINGDOM OF SCOTLAND (SINCE 1605 PERSONAL UNION WITH ENGLAND)

• Edinburgh

KINGDOM OF DENMARK-NORWAY

DUCHY OF PRUSSIA

COURLAND

RUSSIA

DUTCH REPUBLIC (SEVEN UNITED DUTCH PROVINCES)

GRAND DUCHY OF LITHUANIA

KINGDOM OF ENGLAND

• London

Münster

Lützen 1632 ⊗

Warsaw •

POLISH-LITHUANIAN COMMONWEALTH

Kiev •

⊗ Bílá hora 1620

KINGDOM OF POLAND

Calais • SPANISH NETHERLANDS

HOLY ROMAN EMPIRE

Zaporizhia •

Paris •

Vienna •

KINGDOM OF HUNGARY

Buda •

TERRITORY OF THE VASSALS OF THE OTTOMAN EMPIRE

KINGDOM OF FRANCE

SWISS CONFEDERACY

DUCHY OF MILAN

DUCHY OF SAVOY

PARMA MODENA

REPUBLIC OF VENICE

LUCCA

Marseille •

PAPAL STATES

Kotor •

Constantinople •

REPUBLIC OF GENOA

GRAND DUCHY OF TUSCANY

• Rom

MONTENEGRO (VENICE)

OTTOMAN EMPIRE

Lisbon •

KINGDOM OF SPAIN

KINGDOM OF NAPLES (SPANISH)

SARDINIA (SPANISH)

SICILY (SPANISH)

(VENICE)

CYPRUS (OTTOMAN)

• CRETE (VENITIAN UNTIL 1669, THEN OTTOMAN)

⊗ Important battle

1632 King Gustav II Adolph is killed at the Battle of Lützen; the Swedes' forward march is halted.

1634 The apostate captain of the imperial forces of the Holy Roman Empire, Albrecht von Wallenstein, is murdered in Eger with the emperor's knowledge.

1635 The Peace of Prague, an agreement between the Holy Roman emperor and the majority of Protestant princes, bridges divisions among Germans. France hinders Emperor Ferdinand's triumph by coming to the aid of the exhausted Swedes.

1642 First English Civil War between Royalists and Parliamentarians begins in England.

1643–1715 Louis XIV leads France to the height of its power.

1644 Peace negotiations begin in Münster and Osnabrück.

1648 The Thirty Years' War is ended with the Peace of Westphalia.

1649 Execution of King Charles I: England declares itself a republic.

from 1650 Absolutism

1653–1658 Puritan Oliver Cromwell becomes Lord Protector of England.

1660 Restoration of the British monarchy

1683 Vienna is besieged by the Ottomans.

1685 French King Louis XIV recalls the Edict of Nantes.

1688 King James II of England is deposed.

Protestant Union: A coalition of Protestant German states within the Holy Roman Empire formed in 1608 by Duke Maximilian I of Bavaria in response to the occupation of the free imperial city of Donauwörth. Its leader was the elector Palatine.

The Catholic League: An alliance of Catholic rulers in the Holy Roman Empire, founded in 1609 in response to the establishment of the Protestant Union.

Peace of Westphalia (1648): Treaty between the opposing parties in the Thirty Years' War, ending the Habsburg hegemony. The emperor's power was weakened by the fact that imperial princes were granted the right to pursue autonomous foreign policy, further increasing the fragmentation of Germany. Sweden's position strengthened substantially: formerly a marginal state, it became a major European power. France obtained sovereignty over a number of areas in the border region with Germany (eastern France). Another significant territorial provision was the recognition of the independence of Switzerland and The Netherlands. The monarchy of Brandenburg-Prussia was also among the victors.

Edict of Nantes: King Henry IV hereby recognized the rights of Protestants in 1598, ending the religious wars in France. Henry himself had converted to Catholicism in order to ascend the throne. His grandson, Louis XIV, revoked the edict in 1685 and banned Protestantism. Thousands of French Protestants fled, many to Calvinist Brandenburg.

Absolutism: The end of feudalism. Absolute power was now concentrated in the hands of monarchs and their state officials. Absolutism was characterized by state-building, centralized administration, state-controlled economic policy and iron *raison d'etat*. In many countries, absolutism replaced the previous feudal system of estates and monarchies with hereditary office-holders from among the high nobility. Many absolute rulers plunged their countries into debt with extravagant and prestigious buildings, the Palace of Versailles being a prime example.

The Palace of Versailles, residence of the French kings from around 1650 onward

Europe in Detail – The French Revolution and Congress of Vienna, 1789–1815

1789: Beginning of the French Revolution

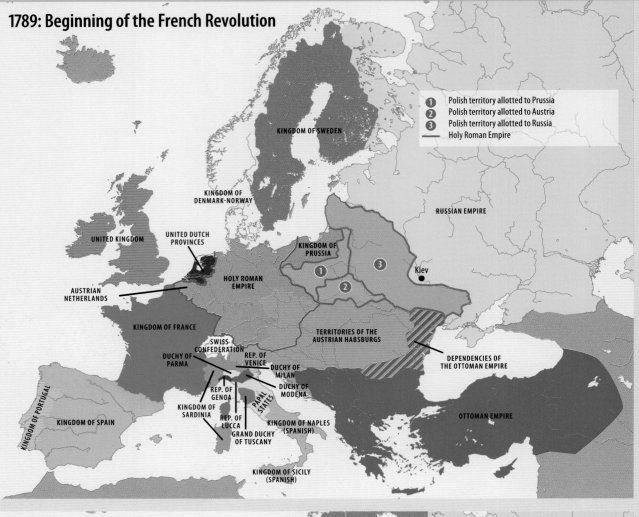

- ① Polish territory allotted to Prussia
- ② Polish territory allotted to Austria
- ③ Polish territory allotted to Russia
- — Holy Roman Empire

KINGDOM OF SWEDEN

KINGDOM OF DENMARK-NORWAY

RUSSIAN EMPIRE

UNITED KINGDOM

UNITED DUTCH PROVINCES

KINGDOM OF PRUSSIA

Kiev

AUSTRIAN NETHERLANDS

HOLY ROMAN EMPIRE

KINGDOM OF FRANCE

SWISS CONFEDERATION

TERRITORIES OF THE AUSTRIAN HABSBURGS

DEPENDENCIES OF THE OTTOMAN EMPIRE

DUCHY OF PARMA

REP. OF VENICE

DUCHY OF MILAN

DUCHY OF MODENA

REP. OF GENOA

PAPAL STATES

KINGDOM OF PORTUGAL

KINGDOM OF SPAIN

KINGDOM OF SARDINIA

REP. OF LUCCA

GRAND DUCHY OF TUSCANY

KINGDOM OF NAPLES (SPANISH)

OTTOMAN EMPIRE

KINGDOM OF SICILY (SPANISH)

1799–1800: The Rise of Napoleon

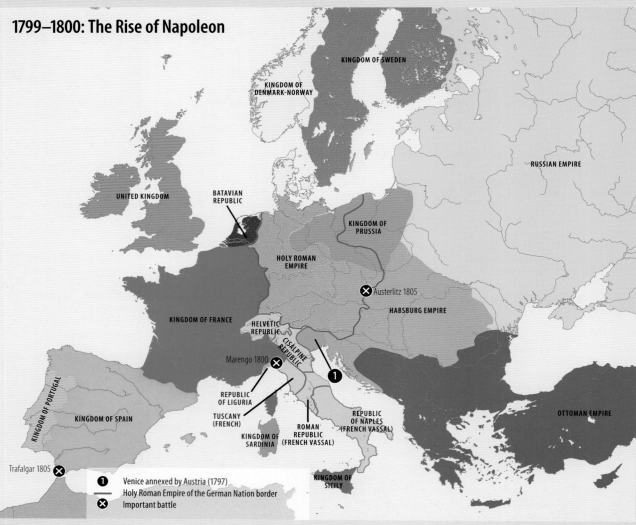

KINGDOM OF SWEDEN

KINGDOM OF DENMARK-NORWAY

RUSSIAN EMPIRE

UNITED KINGDOM

BATAVIAN REPUBLIC

KINGDOM OF PRUSSIA

HOLY ROMAN EMPIRE

⊗ Austerlitz 1805

HABSBURG EMPIRE

KINGDOM OF FRANCE

HELVETIC REPUBLIC

CISALPINE REPUBLIC

Marengo 1800 ⊗

❶

REPUBLIC OF LIGURIA

TUSCANY (FRENCH)

ROMAN REPUBLIC (FRENCH VASSAL)

REPUBLIC OF NAPLES (FRENCH VASSAL)

OTTOMAN EMPIRE

KINGDOM OF PORTUGAL

KINGDOM OF SPAIN

KINGDOM OF SARDINIA

Trafalgar 1805 ⊗

KINGDOM OF SICILY

- ❶ Venice annexed by Austria (1797)
- — Holy Roman Empire of the German Nation border
- ⊗ Important battle

The French Revolution was among the most important events in world history. It sought to establish the equality of all persons before the law, and to abolish the rule of the aristocracy. Napoleon Bonaparte, an officer in the French Revolutionary Army, posed an outside threat to the highest echelons of the French state.

1789 The storming of the Bastille marks the symbolic beginning of the French Revolution. The National Assembly issues a declaration of human and civil rights, as well as the freedom and equality of all persons under the law.

1791 King Louis XVI and his family try to escape from France but fail.

1792 Austria and Prussia form an alliance against France. The trial of Louis XVI begins: he stands accused of having foreign connections that are hostile to the revolution.

1792–1793 The power struggle between centrists (Girondists) and radicals (Jacobins) ends with the execution of the Girondists in 1793.

1793 Louis XVI is executed in January, as is his wife, Marie-Antoinette, in October. Jean-Paul Marat, a "friend of the people," is murdered. The Revolution intensifies.

1794 Georges Danton, a leading figure of the Revolution, is executed in April. Maximilien Robespierre launches a Reign of Terror as head of the Committee of Public Safety, imprisoning and killing thousands opposed to revolutionary ideas. Robespierre is overthrown by the Convention and guillotined, along with other members of the Jacobin Club.

1795–1799 The Directory (*Directoire*), a governing body of five men, rules France.

1795 The French Army occupies The Netherlands, founds the Batavian Republic, and crosses the Rhine River in September.

1797 Napoleon proclaims the Cisalpine Republic.

1799 French Consulate period: Napoleon becomes head of government with the title of first consul.

1800 Napoleon's victory over the Austrians at Marengo

1804 Napoleon proclaims himself emperor and is coronated in Notre Dame Cathedral by Pope Pius VII.

1805 The British defeat the French and Spanish naval fleets at the Battle of Trafalgar. Napoleon defeats the combined forces of Austria and Russia at the Battle of Austerlitz in Moravia (now Slavkov u Brno, Czech Rep.), also called the Battle of the Three Emperors.

1806 Napoleon presses ahead with the Rhine Confederation, an alliance of states in western and southern Germany. In October, Napoleon defeats the Prussian Army near Jena and Auerstädt.

1807 Napoleon signs a peace treaty with Russia at Tilsit.

1807–1808 Napoleon occupies Portugal and Spain. In Spain, there is a popular uprising against him.

1807–1813 The Illyrian Provinces are created in the Balkans under French administration.

1812 Napoleon's Russian campaign fails, and the Grande Armée collapses.

1813 Battle of Leipzig, or "Battle of the Nations": Napoleon is defeated by an Austrian-Russian-Swedish-Prussian alliance, and the Wars of Liberation begin in Germany.

1814–1815 At the Congress of Vienna, the Great Powers agree to return to the borders and states that existed prior to the Revolution. Napoleon is exiled to the island of Elba.

1815 Napoleon returns from exile. After one hundred days in power, he is defeated at Waterloo by the British and Prussian armies under the command of the Duke of Wellington and Field Marshal von Blücher. Napoleon is exiled to the island of St. Helena.

Maximilien de Robespierre (1758–1794) was a solicitor and leader of the Jacobin Club during the French Revolution. His intention to radically democratize France and his efforts to eliminate everyone who opposed the Revolution resulted in the bloody period known as the Reign of Terror. He finally ended up being guillotined himself.

Louis XVI (1754–1793) was the king of France leading up to and during the French Revolution. He was incapable of coming to grips with the sizable national debt. Unrest over the debt sparked the Revolution, and led to his subsequent flight, arrest and execution.

Napoleon Bonaparte (1769–1821) was originally an artillery commander of the Revolutionary Army. Due to his popularity among members of the army, he was able to establish the French Consulate. As first consul and later as emperor, he tried to make France the leading world power by waging war. France's failed invasion of Russia ushered in his demise.

Horatio Nelson (1758–1805) was a British admiral whose forces defeated the French and Spanish fleets at the Battle of Trafalgar, where he himself was killed.

Mikhail Kutuzov (1745–1813) was a Russian field marshal. His scorched-earth tactic led to the failure of Napoleon's Russian campaign.

1806–1819: First French Empire and Napoleon I of France

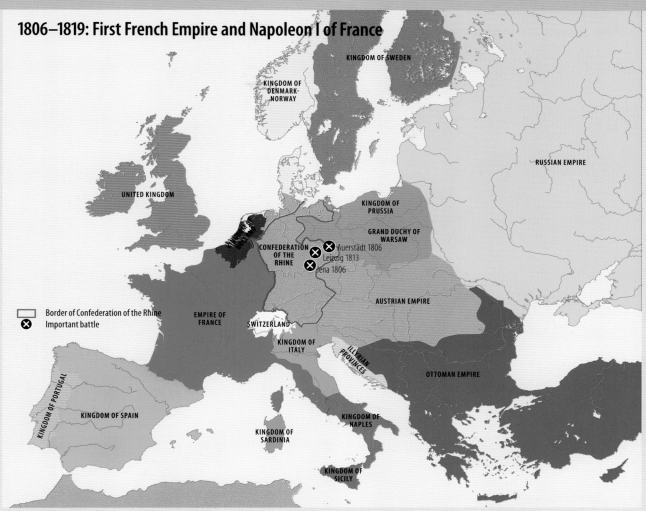

1815: Europe after the Congress of Vienna

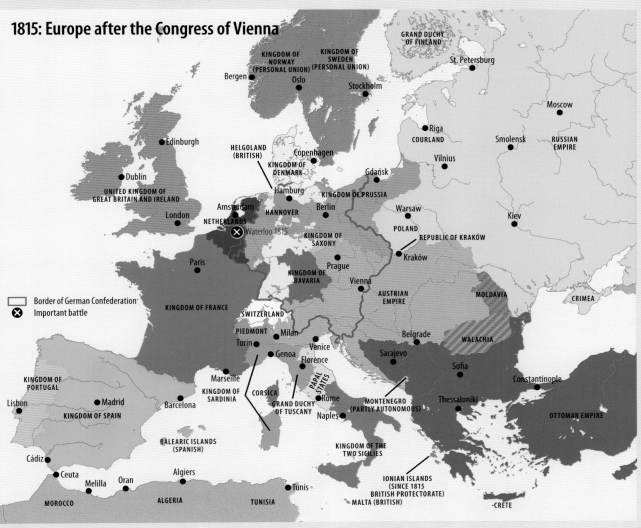

1848: Revolution in Europe

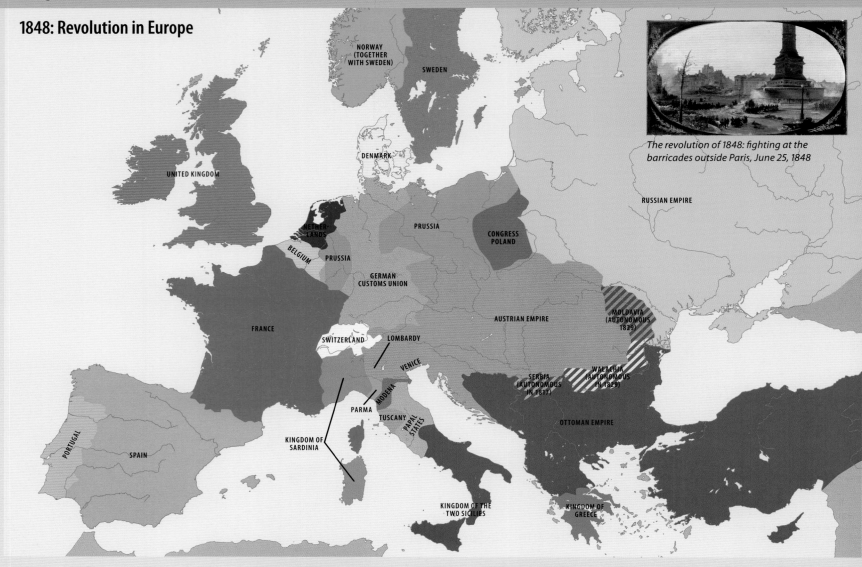

NORWAY (TOGETHER WITH SWEDEN)

SWEDEN

DENMARK

UNITED KINGDOM

NETHER-LANDS

BELGIUM

PRUSSIA

PRUSSIA

CONGRESS POLAND

RUSSIAN EMPIRE

GERMAN CUSTOMS UNION

FRANCE

SWITZERLAND

LOMBARDY

VENICE

AUSTRIAN EMPIRE

MOLDAVIA (AUTONOMOUS 1829)

MODENA

PARMA

TUSCANY

PAPAL STATES

KINGDOM OF SARDINIA

SERBIA (AUTONOMOUS IN 1817)

WALACHIA (AUTONOMOUS IN 1829)

OTTOMAN EMPIRE

PORTUGAL

SPAIN

KINGDOM OF THE TWO SICILIES

KINGDOM OF GREECE

The revolution of 1848: fighting at the barricades outside Paris, June 25, 1848

18th–19th Centuries: The Industrial Revolution

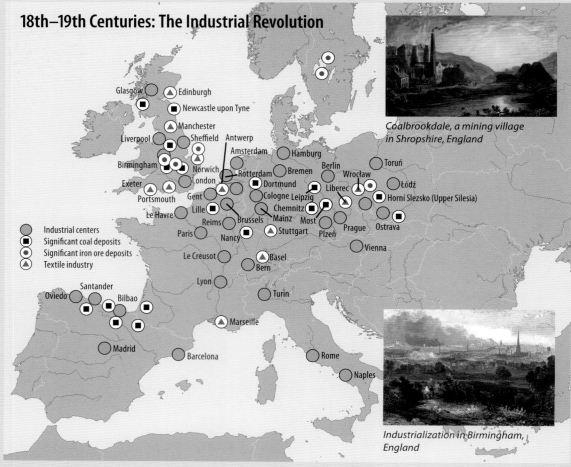

Glasgow
Edinburgh
Newcastle upon Tyne
Manchester
Liverpool
Sheffield
Antwerp
Amsterdam
Hamburg
Birmingham
Norwich
Rotterdam
Bremen
Berlin
Toruń
Wrocław
Exeter
London
Cologne
Leipzig
Liberec
Łódź
Portsmouth
Gent
Dortmund
Chemnitz
Horní Slezsko (Upper Silesia)
Le Havre
Lille
Mainz
Most
Brussels
Reims
Stuttgart
Plzeň
Prague
Ostrava
Paris
Nancy
Vienna
Le Creusot
Basel
Bern
Lyon
Santander
Turin
Oviedo
Bilbao
Marseille
Madrid
Barcelona
Rome
Naples

Legend:
- ● Industrial centers
- ■ Significant coal deposits
- ◉ Significant iron ore deposits
- ▲ Textile industry

Coalbrookdale, a mining village in Shropshire, England

Industrialization in Birmingham, England

1765 James Watt improves on previous designs and is credited with the invention of the steam engine, which leads to far-reaching developments that usher in the Industrial Revolution.

1786 The first steam-powered factory opens in Manchester, England.

1815 The Congress of Vienna consolidates the former German states of the Holy Roman Empire into a single confederation.

1817 Serbia gains autonomy within the Ottoman Empire.

1822 The mechanical steam-powered loom is invented in Lancashire, England.

1825 The first passenger train travels between Stockton and Darlington in England.

1829 Greece gains its independence. Walachia and Moldavia become autonomous territories within the Ottoman Empire.

1830 Belgium gains independence from the Netherlands.

1834 German Customs Union (*Zollverein*) is founded.

1848 Karl Marx and Friedrich Engels publish the *Communist Manifesto*.

1848–1849 Unsuccessful liberal and nationalistic revolutions break out across Europe.

1852 Louis-Napoléon Bonaparte, president of France, declares himself Emperor Napoleon III.

1853–1856 The Crimean War is fought between Russia and European countries allied with the Ottoman Empire.

1859–1861 Romania becomes a nation.

1861 Italian states unite into the kingdom of Italy.

1866 Prussian forces unite to defeat Austria at Hradec Králové (Königgrätz), prefiguring the unification of Germany.

1867 The Austro-Hungarian Compromise establishes the dual monarchy of Austria-Hungary.

1870 The Franco-Prussian war begins with the Prussian victory over France at the Battle of Sedan.

1871 Bismarck proclaims the German Empire at Versailles, with Prussian Wilhelm I crowned emperor (*Kaiser*) and Bismarck named chancellor. The unification of Italy is completed and Rome declared the capital of the new nation.

1878 Bulgaria, Serbia and Montenegro become nation states.

The German Customs Union (*Zollverein*, **1834–1919**) joined several German states in an economic union under Prussia's leadership. Trade restrictions within the German-speaking world were eased through the creation of a common tariff zone. Austria remained outside the union, accelerating its steady loss of influence within the German Confederation. The German Customs Union was an important step toward the eventual unification of Germany.

The German Confederation, formed during the Council of Vienna 1815–1816, was a loose association of what were originally thirty-nine German-speaking states, most of them former subjects of the Holy Roman Empire, which had been dissolved in 1806. In 1806–1813, Napoleon formed the Rhine Confederation as a buffer state between France and Germany.

The Communist Manifesto was an International League of Communists brochure written by Karl Marx and Frederic Engels, the fathers of socialism. Published in London, the *Manifesto* was based on Marx's theory of historical materialism as the "motor" driving world history, causing an endless struggle between the bourgeois and proletariat. The final result could only be revolution, with the workers of the world fighting for social change, a new world order and ultimately a classless society.

The Crimean War was fought between Russia and a coalition including Britain, France and the Ottoman Empire. After early successes against the Ottomans, Russia was driven back by British and French forces. The European allies feared Russia's increasing influence in the Black Sea region would end with Russia overrunning the weakened Ottoman Empire. British and French forces ended the war by taking Sevastopol on the Crimean Peninsula after eleven months of siege.

Otto von Bismarck (1815–1898) was a leading European statesman, Prussian prime minister, foreign minister and, in 1871, chancellor of the German Empire. He was instrumental in uniting Germany under Prussian military and political control.

Klemens von Metternich (1773–1859) was an Austrian minister of state and chancellor from 1809 to 1848. He was the main architect of the Holy Alliance to combat the wave of revolutionary movements sweeping Europe. He inaugurated the reactionary Congress of Vienna, censured the press and founded Austria's domestic spying agency. He fell from power in 1848.

Louis-Napoléon Bonaparte (1808–1873), nephew of Napoleon I, became president of the Second Republic in 1848. He declared himself emperor in 1852 in the wake of a national strike and took the name Napoleon III. He fell from power following Germany's victory in the Franco-Prussian War (1870–1871).

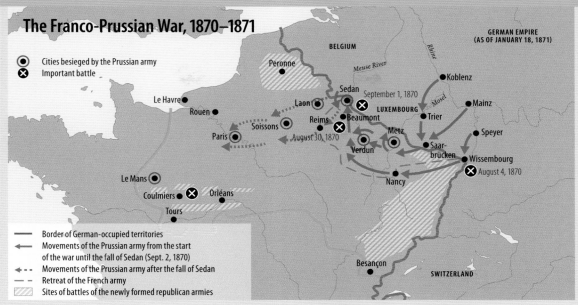

The Franco-Prussian War, 1870–1871

Nation States in 1871

The Eastern Balkans after 1878

SIGNIFICANT WARS AND BATTLES IN EUROPEAN HISTORY

War/Battle	Location	Victorious	Defeated
Persian Wars			
500–448 BCE		Greece	Persia
490 BCE	Marathon	Athens	Persia
480 BCE	Salamis	Greece	Persia
480 BCE	Thermopylae	Persia	Greece
Peloponnesian War			
431–404 BCE		Peloponnesian League	Delian League
405 BCE	Aigospotamai	Sparta	Athens
Macedonian Wars			
338 BCE	Chaeronea	Macedonia (Phillip II)	Athens & Thebes
333 BCE	Issos	Macedonia (Alexander the Great)	
Punic Wars			
217 BCE	Tyrrhenian Sea	Carthage	Rome
216 BCE	Cannae	Carthage	Rome
202 BCE	Zama	Rome	Carthage
Gallic Wars			
58–51 BCE		Rome	Gaul
52 BCE	Alesia	Rome	Gaul
Roman Civil Wars			
133–30 BCE		Monarchy	Republic
31 BCE	Actium	Octavian	Marc Antony & Cleopatra
Roman Imperial Wars			
9 CE	Teutoburg Forest	Germans	Rome
378 CE	Hadrianopolis	Visigoths	Rome
451 CE	Catalaunian Plains (Châlons)	Rome	Huns
Islamic Expansion			
732	Poitiers	Franks (Charles Martel)	Moors
Bulgarian Wars			
811	Pliska	Bulgars	Byzantine Empire
Civil War after the death of Charlemagne			
841	Fountenoy	Charles the Bald, Louis the German	Lothar I
Hungarian Wars			
907	Pressburg	Magyars	Bavaria
955	Lechfeld	East Francia (Otto the Great)	Magyars
Norman Expansion			
1066	Hastings	Normans (William the Conquerer)	Anglo-Saxons
Italian Wars			
1176	Legnano	Lombard League	Holy Roman Empire
The Crusades			
1204	Constantinople	Crusaders	Byzantine Empire
Battle of Bouvines			
1214	Bouvines	France (Philip II August)	England
Reconquista			
1212	Las Navas	Aragon, Castile (Peter II, Alfonso VIII)	Almohads
1492	Granada	Aragon, Castile (Ferdinand II & Isabella I)	Nasirids
Mongolian Expansion			
1223	Kalka	Mongols	Kievan Rus
1380	Kulikovo Pole	Kievan Rus	Mongols
German Baltic Expansion			
1242	Lake Peipus	Russians (Nevski)	Teutonic Knights
1410	Tannenberg	Poland-Lithuania (Wladyslaw II, Jagiello)	Teutonic Knights
Guelf and Ghibelline Wars			
1266	Benevento	Guelfs	Ghibellines
War of the Babenberg Succession			
1278	Marchfeld (Dürnkrut)	Holy Roman Empire (Rudolf I)	Bohemia
Hundred Years' War			
1346	Crécy	England (Edward III)	France
1415	Agincourt	England (Henry V)	France
Sempach War			
1386	Sempach	Switzerland (Swiss Confederation)	Austria
Ottoman Wars			
1389	Amselfeld	Ottomans (Murad I)	Serbia
1396	Nikopolis	Ottomans (Bayezit I)	France, Hungary, Walachia
1444	Varna	Ottomans (Murad II) / Ottomans (Mehmet II)	Poland, Hungary
1453	Constantinople	Ottomans (Suleyman II)	Byzantine Empire
1526	Mohács	Papal States, Spain, Venice	Hungary
1571	Lepanto	Holy Roman Empire,	Ottoman Empire
1683	Vienna	Poland-Lithuania, (Starhemberg, John III Sobieski)	Ottoman Empire
1687	Mohács	Holy Roman Empire, Austria (Charles IV Leopold)	Ottoman Empire
1697	Zenta	Holy Roman Empire (Eugene of Savoy)	Ottoman Empire
Hussite Wars			
1434	Lipany	Catholics, Ultraquists	Taborites
Burgundy Wars			
1477	Nancy	Switzerland, Lorraine	Burgundy
War of the Roses			
1485	Bosworth Field	House of Lancaster (Earl of Richmond)	House of York
War of the Holy League			
1509	Agnadello	League of Cambrai (Louis XII)	Venice
1515	Marignano	France (Francis I)	Switzerland
1525	Pavia	Habsburgs (de Avalos, Frundsberg)	France
Thirty Years' War			
1620	White Mountain	Catholic League (Charles of Bucquoy)	Bohemia
1626	Lutter	Holy Roman Empire (Tilly)	Denmark
1632	Lützen	Sweden (Gustav II Adolf, Bernhard von Sachsen-Weimar)	Holy Roman Empire
1643	Rocroi	France (Louis II)	Spain
1648	Lens	France (Louis II de Bourbon)	Spain
English Civil War			
1645	Nasby	Parliamentarians	Royalists
1648	Preston	Parliamentarians (Cromwell)	Royalists, Scotland
Great Northern War			
1700	Narva	Sweden (Charles XII)	Russia
1709	Poltawa	Russia (Peter the Great)	Sweden
Spanish War of Succession			
1704	Blenheim	Grand Alliance (England, House of Savoy)	France
Austrian War of Succession			
1745	Kesseldorf	Prussia (Leopold of Dessau)	Austria, Saxony
Seven Years' War			
1757	Rossbach	Prussia	France, Austria
Napoleonic Wars			
1792	Valmy	France (Kellermann)	Prussia
1800	Marengo	France (Napoleon)	Austria
1805	Trafalgar	England (Nelson)	France
1805	Austerlitz	France (Napoleon)	Austria, Russia
1807	Eylau (Prussia)	France (Napoleon)	Prussia, Russia
1809	Deutsch-Wagram	France (Napoleon)	Austria
1812	Borodino	France (Napoleon)	Russia
1813	Leipzig	Austria, Prussia, Russia (Schwarzenberg, Frederick III, Alexander I, Karl Johann)	France
1815	Waterloo	England, Prussia (Wellington, Blücher)	France
Italian War of Independence			
1859	Solferino	Sardinia-Piedmont, France (Napoleon III, Victor Emmanuel II)	Austria
Austro-Prussian (Seven Weeks') War			
1866	Königgrätz	Prussia (Moltke)	Austria, Saxony
Franco-Prussian War			
1870	Sedan	Prussia (Moltke)	France

Battles
- ⊗ Antiquity
- ▣ Middle Ages
- ⬡ Early modern era
- ⊙ Modern era (French Revolution to World War I)
- ✳ 20th century

Battle of Waterloo, June 18, 1815

Skagerrak (1916)

Siege of Leningrad (1941–44)
Narva (1700)
Lake Peipus (1242)

Borodino (1812)
Moscow (1941–42)

Smolensk (1943)

Kursk (1943)

Preston (1848)
Dunkirk (1940)
Minsk (Operation Bagration, 1944)

Stalingrad (1942–43)

Bosworth Field (1485)
Naseby (1645)
Battles of Ypres (1914, 1915, 1917)
Berlin (1945)
Teutoburg Forest (9)
Stębark (Gmina Grunwald, 1410)
Kharkiv (1942)

Hastings (1066)
Bouvines (1214)
Waterloo (1815)
Lütter (1626)
Lützen (1632)
Leipzig (1813)
Poltava (1709)
Kalka (1223)

Agincourt (1415)
Crécy (1346)
Rocroi (1643)
Ruhr Pocket (1945)
Kesseldorf (1745)
Rossbach (1757)
Hradec Králové (1866)

D-Day landing (1944)
Lens (1648)
Offensive of the Ardennes (1945)
Bílá hora (1620)
Lipan (1434)

Battle of the Somme (1916)
Battle on the Marne (1914)
Catalaunian Plains (Troyes, 451)
Sedan (1870)
Verdun (1916)
Nancy (1477)
Marchfeld (Dürnkrut, 1278)
Austerlitz (1805)
Jassy-Kishinev Offensive/Chișinău (1944)

Valmy (1792)
Höchstadt (1704)
Vienna (1683)
Bratislava (907)
Deutsch-Wagram (1809)

Fontenoy (841)
Alesia (52)

Poitiers (732)

Vittorio Veneto (1918)
Agnadello (1509)
Mohács (1526)
Zenta (1697)

Legnano (1176)
Pavia (1525)
Solferino (1859)
Marignano (1515)
Nikopolis (1396)
Pliska (811)
Varna (1444)

Marengo (1800)

Lake Trasimeno (217 BCE)
Kosovo Polje (1389)
Hadrianopolis (Edirne, 378)
Constantinople (1204 and 1453)

Benevento (1266)
Gallipoli (1915–16)
Aegospotami (405 BCE)
Issus (333 BCE)

Cannae (216 BCE)
Thermopylae (480 BCE)

Trafalgar (1805)
Actium (31 BCE)
Marathon (490 BCE)
Lepanto (1571)
Salamis (480 BCE)
Chaeronea (338 BCE)

War/Battle	Location	Victorious	Defeated
World War I			
1914	Marne	**France, Great Britain (Joffre, French)**	Germany
1914	West Flanders	**France, Great Britain (Foch, French)**	Germany
1915–1916	Gallipoli	**Ottoman Empire, Central Powers (Sanders)**	Triple Entente
1916	Verdun	**France, Great Britain (Joffre, Pétain, Nivelle)**	Germany
1916	Jutland (Skagerrak)	**Germany (Reinhard Scheer, Franz Hipper)**	Great Britain
1916	Somme	*undecided*	
1917	Ypres	**France, Great Britain (Haig)**	Germany
1918	Vittorio Veneto	**Italy (Diaz)**	Austria-Hungary
Spanish Civil War			
1936	Madrid	**Spanish Republic (Stern)**	Nationalists
1937	Guernica	**Germany (Richthofen)**	Republicans
1939	Madrid	**Nationalists (Franco)**	Republicans
World War II			
1940	Dunkirk	**Germany (Rundstedt)**	Great Britain, Belgium
1941–1944	Leningrad	**Soviet Union (Voroshilov, Zhukov)**	Germany
1941–1942	Moscow	**Soviet Union (Zhukov)**	Germany
1942	Kharkov	**Germany (Paulus)**	Soviet Union
1942–1943	Stalingrad	**Soviet Union (Timoshenko, Chuikov, Yeremenko)**	Germany
1943	Kharkov	**Germany (Manstein)**	Soviet Union
1943	Kursk	**Soviet Union (Rokossovsky, Rotmistrov, Konev)**	Germany
1943	Smolensk	**Soviet Union (Sokolovsky)**	Germany
1944	Normandy	**United States, Great Britain (Eisenhower, Montgomery)**	Germany
1944	Minsk	**Soviet Union (Zhukov, Chernyakhovsky, Rokossovsky)**	Germany
1944	Iași/Chișinău	**Soviet Union (Tolbukhin, Malinovsky)**	Germany, Romania
1944–1945	Ardenne	**United States, Great Britain (Eisenhower, Montgomery)**	Germany
1945	Ruhr area	**USA (Hodges, Simpson)**	Germany
1945	Berlin	**Soviet Union (Zhukov, Rokossovsky, Konev)**	Germany
Yugoslavian Wars			
1992–1995	Sarajevo	**NATO (Claes)**	Serbia

Europe in Detail – The Great Powers Around 1900

1878 Bulgaria, Romania, Serbia and Montenegro become independent from the Ottoman Empire.

1879 Dual Alliance between Germany and Austria-Hungary is formed in opposition to Russian westward expansion; this alliance lasts until the end of World War I.

1884–1885 The Congo Conference is held in Berlin and hosted by Chancellor Otto von Bismarck to discuss European countries' colonial claims in Africa; the fifteen countries fail to agree on a joint approach.

1890 Bismarck is dismissed and the "personal rule" of Emperor William II (Wilhelm II) begins; the kaiser makes frequent undiplomatic statements.

1896 The "Krüger telegram," in which Emperor William congratulates Ohm Krüger—the leader of the Boers and president of Transvaal—on repulsing a British raid, provokes Great Britain.

1898–1900 A German naval building program and a surge in construction of warships leads to an arms race with Great Britain, which aggressively asserts its supremacy on the seas.

1902 A non-aggression pact is formed between Italy and France; Italy leans toward the Western powers.

1904 Entente Cordiale is reached between France and Great Britain (originally intended to settle disputes over colonial interests in Africa).

1905–1906 First Morocco crisis: Germany attempts to prevent the de facto takeover of Morocco's markets by France.

1907 The Triple Entente, a military alliance between France, Great Britain and Russia, is formed; it lasts until World War I.

1908 Austria annexes Bosnia and Herzegovina, which it had occupied since 1878, and combats Serbia's pan-Slavic ambitions, which are supported by Russia; the Balkan crisis escalates ("Balkan powder keg").

1911 Second Morocco crisis: Emperor William sends the gunboat *Panther* to Agadir (called the "*Panther* leap") as a threatening gesture against France's occupation of Moroccan cities; some nationalist right-wingers in Germany demand preemptive war against France.

1911–1912 Italy battles the Ottoman Empire for control of Libya, which is occupied by the Italians.

1912 The Balkan League—a military alliance between Serbia, Bulgaria, Montenegro and Greece—is established in opposition to the Ottoman Empire and supported by Russia.

1912–1913 Two Balkan wars: The Balkan League fights against the Ottoman Empire; later the other Balkan states war against Bulgaria. The Ottoman Empire and Bulgaria suffer territorial losses.

1914 Rapprochement between the defeated parties in the Balkan wars and the German Reich and Austria-Hungary; alliances are formed with the Ottoman Empire (1914) and Bulgaria (1915). On June 28, 1914, Serbian nationalists assassinate Archduke Francis Ferdinand, heir to the Austrian-Hungarian throne, and his wife Sophie, in Sarajevo.

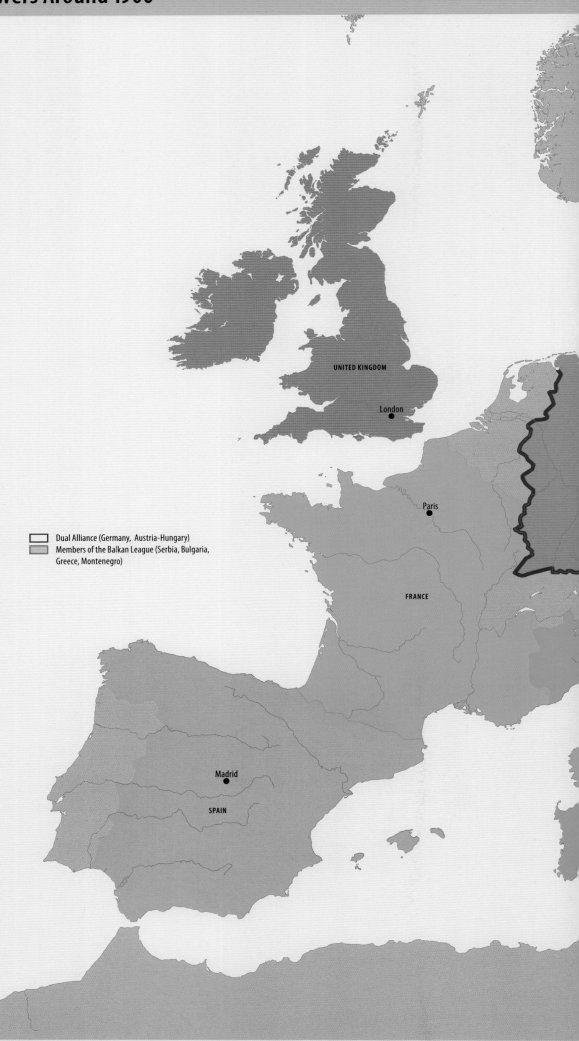

- Dual Alliance (Germany, Austria-Hungary)
- Members of the Balkan League (Serbia, Bulgaria, Greece, Montenegro)

St. Petersburg

Berlin

GERMANY

RUSSIAN EMPRIE

Vienna

AUSTRIA-HUNGARY

BOSNIA AND HERZEGOVINA
(ANNEXED BY AUSTRIA-HUNGARY
IN 1878)

SERBIA

MONTENEGRO

BULGARIA

ITALY

Rome

Constantinople

OTTOMAN EMPIRE

GREECE

*Queen Victoria
(1819–1901)*

*Emperor Francis Joseph I
(1839–1916)*

*Tsar Nicholas II
(1868–1918) with French
president Emile Loubet
(1836–1929)*

*King Alfonso XIII of
Spain (1886–1941)*

*Abdul Hamid II
(1842–1918), the last
sultan of Turkey*

Europe in Detail – World War I, 1914–1918

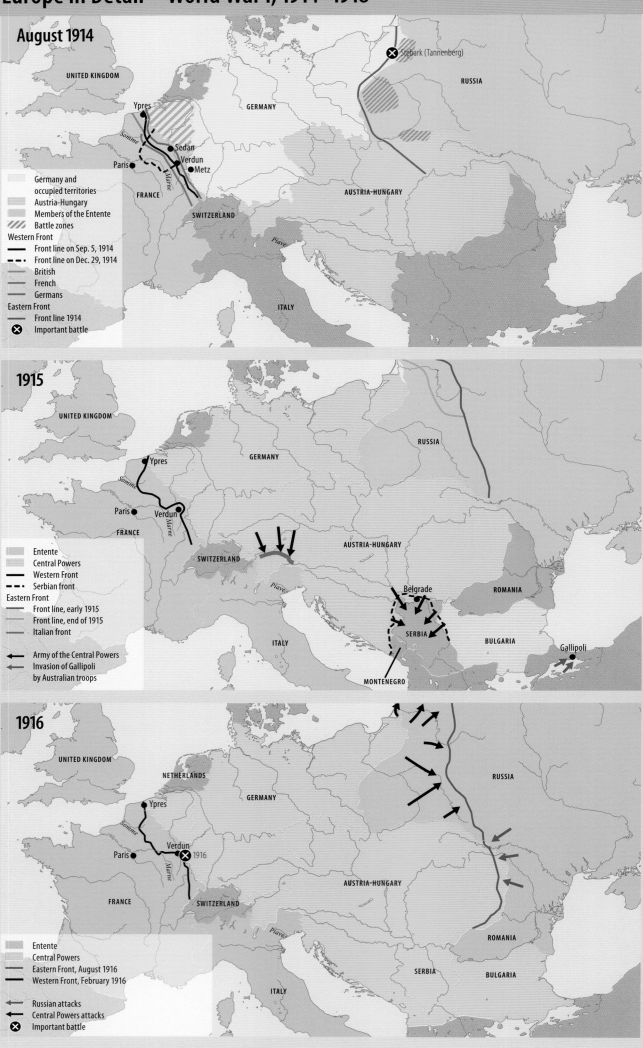

August 1914

UNITED KINGDOM

⊗ Stębark (Tannenberg)

RUSSIA

GERMANY

Ypres
Somme
Sedan
Verdun
Paris • Metz
Marne
FRANCE
SWITZERLAND

AUSTRIA-HUNGARY

Piave

ITALY

Legend:
- Germany and occupied territories
- Austria-Hungary
- Members of the Entente
- Battle zones

Western Front
- Front line on Sep. 5, 1914
- Front line on Dec. 29, 1914
- British
- French
- Germans

Eastern Front
- Front line 1914
- ⊗ Important battle

1915

UNITED KINGDOM

RUSSIA

GERMANY

Ypres
Somme
Paris • Verdun
Marne
FRANCE
SWITZERLAND

AUSTRIA-HUNGARY

Piave

Belgrade
ROMANIA
SERBIA
BULGARIA
Gallipoli

ITALY

MONTENEGRO

Legend:
- Entente
- Central Powers
- Western Front
- Serbian front

Eastern Front
- Front line, early 1915
- Front line, end of 1915
- Italian front

- ← Army of the Central Powers
- ← Invasion of Gallipoli by Australian troops

1916

UNITED KINGDOM

NETHERLANDS

GERMANY

Ypres
Somme
Verdun
Paris • ⊗ 1916
Marne
FRANCE
SWITZERLAND

RUSSIA

AUSTRIA-HUNGARY

Piave

ROMANIA
SERBIA
BULGARIA

ITALY

Legend:
- Entente
- Central Powers
- Eastern Front, August 1916
- Western Front, February 1916

- ← Russian attacks
- ← Central Powers attacks
- ⊗ Important battle

Conflicting imperialistic and economic interests of the European powers began to set the stage for World War I starting in the latter part of the 19th century. The event that unleashed war was the assassination of the heir to the Austro-Hungarian empire, Francis Ferdinand, in Sarajevo in 1914. The devastating war resulted in almost 10 million war dead and 13 million soldiers missing.

Arrest of the assassin of the archduke of Austria and his wife in Sarajevo, June 28, 1914

1914 June 28: Assassination in Sarajevo
July 28: Austria-Hungary declares war against Serbia.
early August: Germany declares war against Russia and France, and Great Britain enters the war.
August 26–30: Battle at Tannenberg (between Germany and Russia)
September 5–12: The German advance in France is halted at the Marne.
September: German counteroffensive in Galicia

1915 May 7: The British passenger ship *Lusitania* is sunk by a German torpedo.
May 23: Italy declares war against Austria-Hungary.
October: Serbia falls.

1916 The Central Powers occupy Romania and Montenegro.
February 21–July 21: Battles are fought around Verdun.

RMS Lusitania, *ca. 1915*

April 1917 The United States declares war against Germany.

1918 January: United States President Woodrow Wilson presents his Fourteen Point Program, which will serve as the basis for a peace treaty and a post-war order.
March 3: Peace of Brest-Litovsk between Germany and Bolshevik Russia
July: The German offensive is halted at the Marne; counteroffensive by the Entente
October: Austria-Hungary reaches a separate peace agreement with the Allies.
November 11: German capitulation at Compiègne

Entente An alliance between Great Britain and France, later joined by Russia

Central Powers During World War I, allied forces consisting of the German Reich, Austria-Hungary, the Ottoman Empire and Bulgaria

Paul von Hindenburg

Paul von Hindenburg (1847–1934) was a German field marshal, victor of the Battle at Tannenberg and president of the Weimar Republic between the World Wars (1925–1933).

Philippe Pétain (1856–1951) was a French general who repelled the German offensive near Verdun, but

Philippe Pétain

compromised himself during the last years of his life by leading the Vichy regime that collaborated with Nazi Germany between 1940 and 1944.

Georges Clemenceau (1841–1929), the French prime minister from 1917 to 1920, exacted severe terms for peace after the war and high reparation payments from Germany in the Treaty of Versailles.

Georges Clemenceau

World War I Casualties
(in representative countries)

Germany	2 million
Austria-Hungary	1.5 million
Russia	1.8 million
France	1.3 million
Great Britain	0.9 million
Italy	0.7 million
Serbia	0.1 million

1917

Entente
Central Powers
Western Front
Eastern Front (front at the time of Russian surrender)
Italian front
Direction of German-Austrian attacks

UNITED KINGDOM
NETHERLANDS
GERMANY
RUSSIA
Ypres
Somme
Reims
Verdun
Marne
FRANCE
SWITZERLAND
AUSTRIA-HUNGARY
Piave
ROMANIA
ITALY
SERBIA
BULGARIA
MONTENEGRO

1918

Entente
Central Powers
Russian-occupied territory
Italian front (Battel of the Piave River)
Western Front—front line of Entente forces during counteroffensive in July and August

UNITED KINGDOM
NETHERLANDS
GERMANY
RUSSIA
Brest-Litovsk
Ypres
Somme
Compiègne
Sedan
Paris
Verdun
Marne
FRANCE
SWITZERLAND
AUSTRIA-HUNGARY
Piave
ROMANIA
SERBIA
BULGARIA
MONTENEGRO
GREECE

Europe in Detail – Between the World Wars, 1919–1939

After 1920

ICELAND

NORWAY

SWEDEN

FINLAND

ESTONIA

LATVIA

SOVIET UNION

DENMARK AND THE PERSONAL UNION WITH ICELAND

MEMEL TERRITORY

LITHUANIA

FREE CITY OF DANZIG

NORTHERN SCHLESWIG

IRISH FREE STATE (SINCE 1922)

UNITED KINGDOM

NETHER-LANDS

GERMANY

WEST PRUSSIA

POZNAN

POLAND

BELGIUM

EAST UPPER SILESIA

LUXEM-BOURG

HLUČIN

ALSACE-LORRAINE

CZECHOSLOVAKIA

FRANCE

SWITZERLAND

AUSTRIA

HUNGARY

ROMANIA

KINGDOM OF SERBIA, CROATIA, SLOVENIA/YUGOSLAVIA

BULGARIA

PORTUGAL

SPAIN

ITALY

TURKEY

GREECE

ALBANIA

///// Territory forfeited in the Treaty of Versailles

The peace treaties that were signed at the close of World War I and the newly formed League of Nations were supposed to prevent a future catastrophic war. But the economies of the European countries had been so weakened by the staggering costs of war that even the victorious Entente powers accrued huge debts owed to the United States. The reparation payments that the young, fragile, democratic Weimar Republic was required to pay according to the Treaty of Versailles resulted in hyperinflation. Germany was economically devastated and politically isolated. At the same time, however, Berlin experienced a cultural resurgence in the 1920s ("the golden twenties").

1919/1920 Peace treaties are negotiated between the victorious powers and all the nations defeated in World War I.

1920 Formation of the League of Nations (headquartered in Geneva)

1921–1938 Little Entente in eastern Europe: Czechoslovakia, Yugoslavia and Romania reach a mutual defense agreement, supported by France, to ensure the status quo in the Danube River basin.

1922 Fascists march on Rome and oust the government, and Benito Mussolini takes over power as Italy's supreme leader (*Il Duce*).
Ireland gains independence from England.

1922/23 Modernization of Turkey: Under the leadership of Mustafa Kemal, the sultanate is abolished and Turkey becomes a republic.

1923 Germany experiences inflation and is unable to meet its reparation obligations. French (and later Belgian) forces occupy the Ruhr region, and the Germans mount resistance.

1924 American financier Charles Dawes advances a plan to revive the German economy, in part by renegotiating lower reparation payments

1924–1928 Joseph Stalin seizes power in the Soviet Union.

1925 France ends its occupation of the Ruhr Valley. The Locarno Pact is negotiated, in which Germany guarantees its western border, but not its eastern border.

beginning in 1929 Worldwide economic crisis

1932 Fascist dictatorship in Portugal (Antonio Salazar) 1932–1934; Chancellor Engelbert Dollfuss ushers in Austro-fascism in Austria.

1933 Hitler takes power in Germany, which withdraws from the Geneva

Disarmament Conference and from the League of Nations.

1935 Compulsory military draft introduced in Germany builds up German armed forces (*Reichswehr*). The Nuremberg Racial Laws prohibit marriages or sex between "Germans" and "Jews."

1936 German troops occupy the demilitarized Rhineland and the Ruhr region; the Spanish Civil War begins.

1936 The Berlin-Rome axis emerges.

1938 Germany annexes Austria; the Munich Agreement gives Germany control of the Sudetenland as well.

1939 The German-Soviet Nonaggression Pact is signed. The Republican government of Spain is defeated in the Spanish Civil War. Germany attacks Poland in September, and World War II begins.

Economic Crisis 1929–1933

Countries affected by the economic crisis

Alliances in the 1930s

- British-French coalition
- Neutral countries
- Axis powers (including Spain from 1939)
- Little Entente

Peace Treaty of Versailles As the war's main culprit, Germany was forced to give up 13 percent of its land, including Alsace-Lorraine to France and West Prussia and Poznan to Poland. Territories on the left bank of the Rhine were to be demilitarized and the German armed forces reduced to 100,000 soldiers. The treaty, signed only under strong pressure from the victors, required crushing reparation payments, especially to France. This placed a heavy burden on the young democracy from its very beginnings, as its politicians were villainized by militant right-wingers as "fulfillment politicians."

The spread of fascism in Europe

Mussolini's fascist movement took power in Italy in 1922. In 1933 Adolf Hitler, leader of the Nazi Party, became chancellor of the German Reich. Other dictatorships and authoritarian

Benito Mussolini and Adolf Hitler

regimes emerged in Europe in the 1930s, for example in Austria, Portugal, Spain and Greece.

Worldwide economic crisis After a period of prosperity, economies around the world experienced a precipitous fall. On Black Tuesday, October 29, 1929, five days after the initial stock market crash in the United States, huge numbers of panicked investors tried to sell their shares. During the Great Depression, production fell until 1932—in some countries even longer—as world trade volume sank to one-sixth of the pre-Depression level. Supply exceeded demand, and prices fell quickly. Layoffs triggered mass unemployment and social unrest.

Radical solutions voiced by fascist and communist parties gained in popularity. The economy only recovered in the late 1930s.

Alliances During the interwar years, Europe again split into two camps. Great Britain and France continued their coalition, though they took different stances on foreign policy: England opposed the hard line against Germany. France initiated the Little Entente of the newly created nation states in southeastern Europe against Hungary. It did not hold long, as Yugoslavia and Romania increasingly oriented themselves toward Hitler's Germany in the 1930s. In 1936, the fascist Rome-Berlin Axis was created, with Franco's Spain joining after the victory of the rebel forces in the Spanish Civil War. In 1938, France, Great Britain, Italy and the German Reich signed the Munich Agreement. The Sudetenland was taken from Czechoslovakia, which had not been represented at the conference ("About us without us"), and ceded to Germany. The destruction of what remained of Czechoslovakia was only a matter of time, and came about in 1939.

Appeasement policy The appeasement diplomacy of British Prime Minister Neville Chamberlain (1937–1940) was characterized by numerous concessions to Hitler, now viewed highly critically; Chamberlain believed in Hitler's peaceful intentions far too long.

Aristide Briand (1862–1932) French premier and minister. In 1928 he and US Secretary of State Frank B. Kellogg signed the Kellogg-Briand pact, renouncing war as a means of settling international disputes. Other European states and Japan signed the treaty, but it contained no sanctions for countries that violated its provisions.

Benito Mussolini (1883–1945) Originally a socialist politician, he came to power in 1922 as leader of the Fascists. He established a

dictatorship that was intended to recreate the glory of the Roman Empire and allied himself with Hitler's Germany in 1936.

Adolf Hitler (1889–1945) Originally from Austria, he led the Nazis (NSDAP, *Nationalsozialistische Deutsche Arbeiterpartei*, or National Socialist German Workers Party) to power in 1933 after a failed putsch in Munich in 1923. He established a racist, totalitarian regime with the goal of making Germany the leading world power and the Aryans, the "master race," the dominant race in Europe whom all other races would have to serve. He also intended to eradicate all the Jews in Europe.

Treaties of Paris: Reorganizing and Remapping Europe after World War I

Date	Treaty	Defeated power
June 28, 1919	Treaty of Versailles	Germany
September 10, 1919	Treaty of St. Germain	Austria
September 27, 1919	Treaty of Neuilly	Bulgaria
June 4, 1920	Treaty of Trianon	Hungary
August 10, 1920	Treaty of Sèvres	Turkey

Fascism 1922–1939

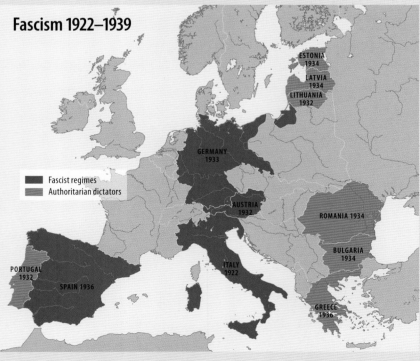

- Fascist regimes
- Authoritarian dictators

Europe in Detail – World War II, 1939–1945

1938/1939

1. Saar Protectorate, reincorporated into the German Empire after 1935 plebiscite
2. Sudetenland, occupied by Germany in October 1938
3. Protectorate of Bohemia and Moravia
4. Germany annexes Austria on March 13, 1938
5. Memel Territory (Klaipéda Region): Germany occupies Lithuania on March 23, 1939
6. Poland annexes the region around the city of Vilnius in 1920
7. Southern Slovakia and Carpatho-Ukraine are occupied by Hungary in November 1938 and March 1939 (the remainder of Carpatho-Ukraine)
8. Italy occupies Albania in April 1939

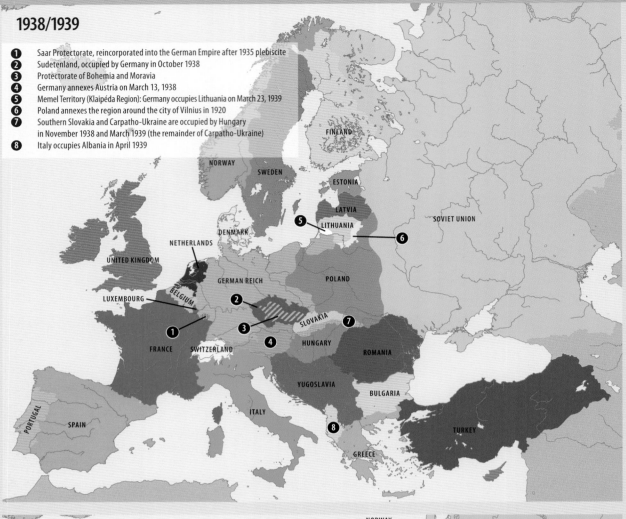

Shortly after the end of World War I, new oppositions emerged in Europe, with the Western democracies lining up against both the fascist Central Powers and the communist USSR.

Claiming nearly 60 million victims, World War II was the deadliest and the most devastating conflict in the history of humankind. The outbreak of World War II was prompted by Germany's attack on Poland on September 1, 1939, without a formal declaration of war being issued. Great Britain and France, who had guaranteed Poland's independence, declared war against Germany.

The German-Soviet Nonaggression Pact cleared the way for military expansion.

1939 September 1: German troops invade Poland, launching World War II
September 3: Great Britain and France declare war against Germany.
September 17: The Red Army of the Soviet Union marches into eastern Poland. By the end of September, Germany and the Soviet Union have divided Poland between them.
November 30: The Soviet Union attacks Finland, marking the beginning of the Winter War.
December 12: The Soviet Union is no longer part of the League of Nations. The Allies send troops to Norway to protect Finland.

1940 March 12: Finland and the Soviet Union sign a treaty in which Finland surrenders parts of Karelia to the Soviet Union.
April 9: Operation Weserübung begins – Germany occupies Denmark and Norway; Sweden allows German troops to pass through.
May 10–June 4: German troops invade and occupy the Netherlands, Belgium and Luxembourg.
May 15: The Netherlands capitulates to the Germans.

1940

1. Annexation of Luxembourg in 1940
2. Annexation of Eupen and Malmedy (now in Belgium) and Alsace-Lorraine to the German Reich in 1940
3. Protectorate of Bohemia and Moravia
4. Area around Varta annexed to the German Reich in 1939
5. General Government of Poland
6. Northern part of Transylvania, ceded by Romania to Hungary on Aug. 30, 1940
7. Area of Southern Dobruja that Romania acquired from Bulgaria on Sep. 7, 1940
8. Areas of Soviet Bukovina and Bessarabia acquired by the Soviet Union from Romania according to an agreement signed June 28, 1940
9. Areas of western Belarus and western Ukraine occupied by the Soviet Union following the defeat of Poland
10. Annexation of Estonia, Lithuania and Latvia by the Soviet Union in June 1940
11. Territory gained by the Soviet Union through a treaty with Finland in March 1940

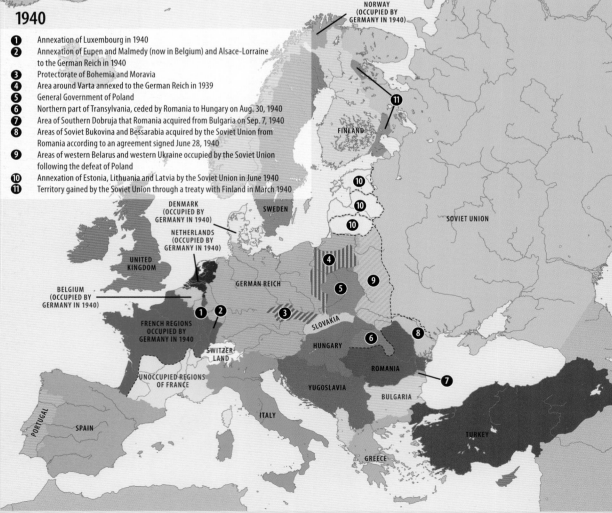

In 1940 the Belgians destroyed a bridge across the Meuse River to stop the German advance.

May 20–June 3: German troops trap French, British and Belgian forces at Dunkirk on the coast of France. Over several days, more than 300,000 Allied soldiers are successfully evacuated to England.

June 5: Germany launches the Battle of France (*Blitzkrieg*).

June 7: The Norwegian army capitulates.

June 14: German troops occupy Paris. By the end of June, Germany controls most of France and an armistice agreement has been signed.

July 10–October 31: The Battle of Britain: German and British air forces wage a massive campaign of destructive air raids.

September: Italian offensive against Egypt and Libya

October: Italy unsuccessfully invades Greece.

December: The British counteroffensive against Italy in Egypt is successful.

1941 January: The German Afrika Corps is established under the leadership of Erwin Rommel.

April 6: German bombardment of Belgrade marks the beginning of the war in the Balkans; German forces occupy Greece.

April 17: Yugoslavia surrenders to Germany.

April 27: German troops occupy Athens.

June 22: Germany attacks the Soviet Union in Operation Barbarossa, a confrontation on a massive scale involving around 6 million soldiers.

July 12: Great Britain and the Soviet Union join forces in an alliance against Germany (mutual assistance agreement).

August 25: Great Britain and the Soviet Union occupy Iran to secure Iranian oil resources.

December 5: The Nazis' advance on Moscow is stopped by the Red Army. German forces are weakened by severe cold, illness and exhaustion.

1942 January 1: The "United Nations," a cohort of twenty-six countries allied against the Axis Powers (Germany and its allies), sign a declaration according to which none of the countries may sign a separate peace agreement with the Axis Powers.

January 20: Nazis hold the Wannsee Conference in Berlin to plan the definitive annihilation of the European Jews ("the final solution to the Jewish problem").

June 20–25: A conference is held in Washington, D.C., to discuss opening a second front in Europe

August to November: Germany initiates the lengthy Battle of Stalingrad

November 22: German troops are surrounded at Stalingrad.

November 27: German troops occupy the port of Toulon, and the French sink their own fleet.

December 22–23: Hitler forbids the capitulation of the German troops near Stalingrad.

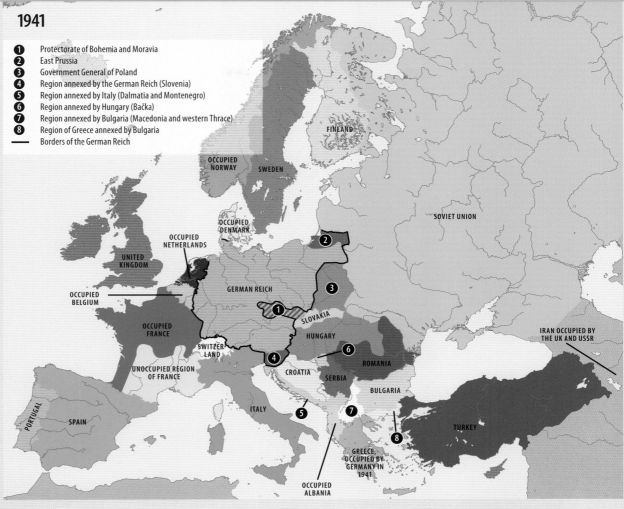

1941

1 Protectorate of Bohemia and Moravia
2 East Prussia
3 Government General of Poland
4 Region annexed by the German Reich (Slovenia)
5 Region annexed by Italy (Dalmatia and Montenegro)
6 Region annexed by Hungary (Bačka)
7 Region annexed by Bulgaria (Macedonia and western Thrace)
8 Region of Greece annexed by Bulgaria
— Borders of the German Reich

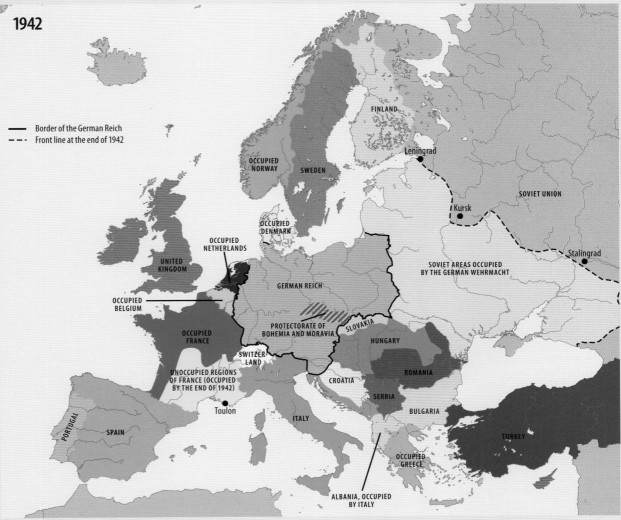

1942

— Border of the German Reich
--- Front line at the end of 1942

Europe in Detail – World War II, 1939–1945

1943–1944

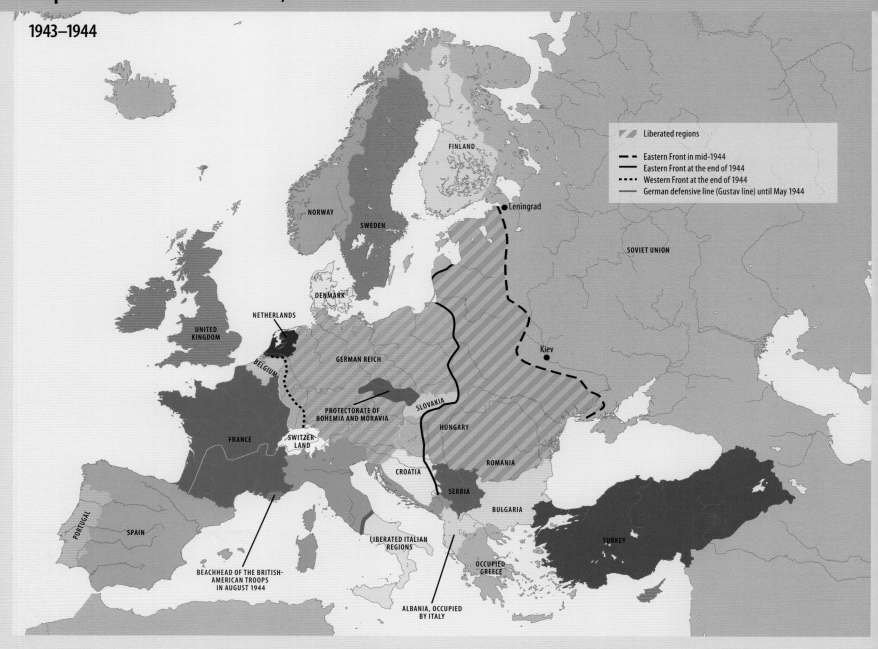

Liberated regions

- ▬▬ Eastern Front in mid-1944
- ——— Eastern Front at the end of 1944
- ▪▪▪▪ Western Front at the end of 1944
- ——— German defensive line (Gustav line) until May 1944

FINLAND

NORWAY

SWEDEN

Leningrad

SOVIET UNION

DENMARK

NETHERLANDS

UNITED KINGDOM

BELGIUM

GERMAN REICH

Kiev

FRANCE

SWITZER-LAND

PROTECTORATE OF BOHEMIA AND MORAVIA

SLOVAKIA

HUNGARY

CROATIA

ROMANIA

SERBIA

BULGARIA

PORTUGAL

SPAIN

LIBERATED ITALIAN REGIONS

TURKEY

OCCUPIED GREECE

BEACHHEAD OF THE BRITISH-AMERICAN TROOPS IN AUGUST 1944

ALBANIA, OCCUPIED BY ITALY

1943 January 14–24: At the Casablanca Conference, President Roosevelt and Prime Minister Churchill create a plan to systematically bomb German cities and agree the Germans must surrender unconditionally.

February 2: Germany's Sixth Army capitulates at Stalingrad and is taken captive.

February 18: Joseph Goebbels delivers a speech in Berlin announcing "total war"; women and men of all ages are now enlisted in the German war effort.

April 19–May 19: A Jewish uprising in the Warsaw ghetto is brutally suppressed by SS troops.

May 13: After weeks of fighting in Tunisia and elsewhere, Allied defeat of Italian and German forces ends the war in North Africa.

July 10–August 17: British and American forces fight for Sicily and in late July occupy it (Operation Husky).

July 25: Benito Mussolini is ousted by the Fascist Grand Council and arrested.

July 27/28: Air raids on Hamburg result in a devastating firestorm.

September 3: Following secret negotiations, Italy capitulates to the Allies.

September 8: German troops occupy Rome and several additional strategic points throughout Italy.

September 12: German commandos free Mussolini from captivity and Hitler names Mussolini head of the newly established fascist Republic of Saló in northern Italy.

October 13: Italy declares war against Germany.

November 28–December 1: First conference of the three major Allied leaders (Stalin, Roosevelt and Churchill) in Tehran to discuss strategy and the postwar reordering of Europe.

1944 January 27: Soviet troops are finally able to end the Siege of Leningrad after more than two years.

March 19: German forces occupy the territory of its former ally Hungary.

June 6: On D-Day, the Normandy Invasion involves Allied troops landing at five locations in Normandy, setting the stage for the liberation of northern France by August.

June 22: Beginning of the last major German offensive on the Eastern Front

July 20: Assassination attempt against Hitler by the conspirators around Colonel Claus von Stauffenberg

August: An uprising in Warsaw by the Polish Home Army against the Germans is unsuccessful; the Red Army, which is positioned near Warsaw, does not come to their aid.

August 15: Landing of the Allied forces in southern France (Operation Dragon)

August 23: Romania and the Soviet Union sign an armistice.

August 25: Paris is liberated by Allied troops.

September 5: The Soviet Union declares war against Bulgaria.

September 8: The Red Army occupies Bulgaria.

September 19: Finland and the Soviet Union sign an armistice.

December 28: Hungary declares war against Germany.

1945 January 12: Major Soviet offensive against Poland and Silesia

February 4–11: Stalin, Roosevelt and Churchill meet in Yalta about the postwar division of Germany.

February 13–14: Allied air forces firebomb Dresden, and the Red Army enters Budapest.

March 19: Hitler issues Nero Decree to liquidate all military production facilities, manufacturing plants, and all of Germany's infrastructure; orders are largely sabotaged.

April 25: The Red Army closes in on Berlin.

April 28: American troops liberate the Dachau concentration camp; Mussolini is executed.

April 30: Western Allies capture Munich, and Soviet troops storm the Reichstag in Berlin. Hitler commits suicide.

May 2: The Allies capture Berlin. German forces in Italy capitulate.

May 7–9: Capitulation of all German forces to the Allies; May 8 is designated V-E Day (Victory in Europe Day).

July 17–August 2: Conference in Potsdam on post war Germany and the ongoing war with Japan

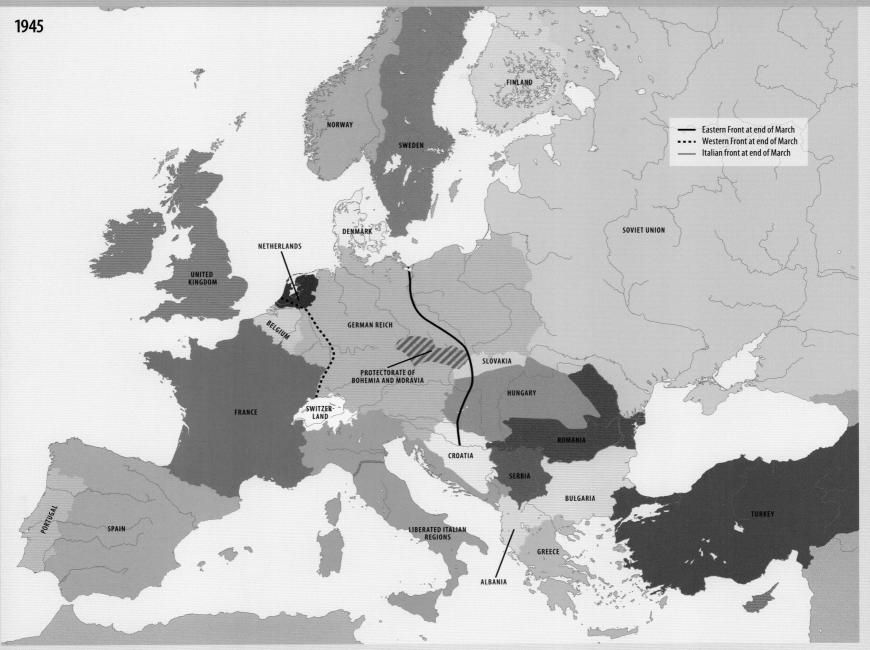

1945

FINLAND

NORWAY

SWEDEN

SOVIET UNION

DENMARK

NETHERLANDS

UNITED
KINGDOM

BELGIUM

GERMAN REICH

SLOVAKIA

PROTECTORATE OF
BOHEMIA AND MORAVIA

FRANCE

HUNGARY

SWITZER-
LAND

ROMANIA

CROATIA

SERBIA

PORTUGAL

SPAIN

BULGARIA

TURKEY

LIBERATED ITALIAN
REGIONS

GREECE

ALBANIA

Concentration and Extermination Camps

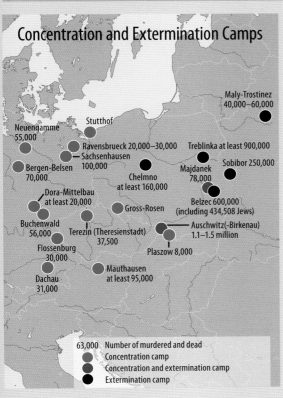

Maly-Trostinez
40,000–60,000

Stutthof

Neuengamme
55,000

Ravensbrueck 20,000–30,000   Treblinka at least 900,000

Sachsenhausen
100,000

Sobibor 250,000

Bergen-Belsen
70,000

Chelmno
at least 160,000

Majdanek
78,000

Dora-Mittelbau
at least 20,000

Gross-Rosen

Belzec 600,000
(including 434,508 Jews)

Buchenwald
56,000

Terezin (Theresienstadt)
37,500

Auschwitz(-Birkenau)
1.1–1.5 million

Flossenburg
30,000

Plaszow 8,000

Dachau
31,000

Mauthausen
at least 95,000

63,000   Number of murdered and dead
⬤   Concentration camp
⬤   Concentration and extermination camp
⬤   Extermination camp

The History of European Anti-Semitism

Anti-Semitism (hostility toward Jews) means prejudice and hatred toward Jews that goes as far as persecution. Jews have lived on the European continent since the days of ancient Greece and Rome, and they remained faithful to their religion that recognizes no God but Yahweh. As early as Roman times, Jews were treated with mistrust, as they refused to worship the statues of the deified emperors—as did Christians. The Christian religion justified discrimination against Jews using the reason that they did not recognize Jesus Christ as the Messiah; they even called them "Christ-murderers."

In the Middle Ages, the Church forbade Christians to lend money for interest, so this unpopular role fell to the Jews. Some rulers borrowed money to finance their court and employed so-called "court Jews" as their financiers. Jews were accused of absurd crimes (for example, poisoning wells, desecration of the host used in the sacrament of communion, or the ritual murder of children). This provoked violence against the Jews. As recently as the late 19th and early 20th centuries, campaigns called pogroms (Russian for havoc, destruction) against the Jews took place.

In the 19th and 20th centuries, malicious caricatures of successful Jewish bankers and industrialists were published. A number of socialists were of Jewish descent; nationalists saw them as enemies of the idea of a national state because they had no "fatherland." The nationalist endeavors toward unification in the 19th century often had aggressively anti-Semitic characteristics, and the theory of a Jewish conspiracy for world domination was popularized.

The Nazi race theory (which deemed race the most significant factor, rather than one's religion) made anti-Semitism a state program, and a political one. Race laws passed by Nazi Germany stripped Jewish people of their civil rights and aimed to marginalize them from public life. In the years prior to and during World War II, Jews were forbidden to hold public positions and were forced to wear visible identifying marks (yellow badges with the Star of David). During the November 1938 Kristallnacht pogrom ("Night of Broken Glass"), their synagogues were burned, shops were plundered, and many Jews were murdered or arrested and sent to concentration camps.

In 1941, systematic annihilation of the Jewish people began. In the Nazi concentration camps, especially in the extermination camps in eastern Europe, about 6 million Jews (but also Sinti and Roma) were murdered under barbaric conditions (gas chambers, arbitrary killings) or they were worked to death in German factories ("extermination through work"). Those who survived bore the marks of their ordeal for the rest of their lives.

Europe in Detail – War Damages and Postwar Order

War Damages and Casualties

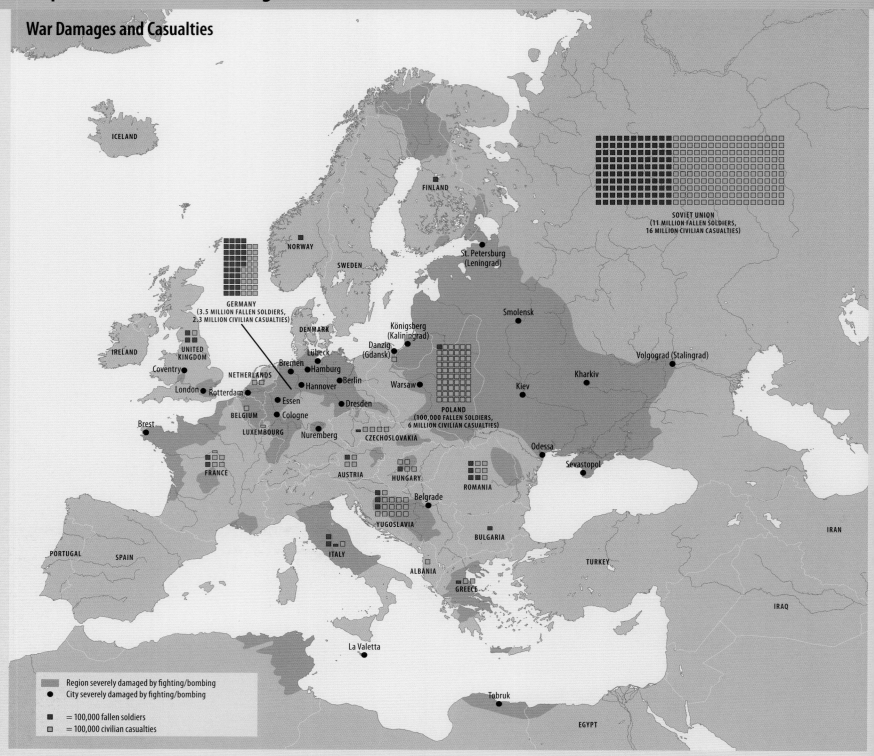

ICELAND

NORWAY

SWEDEN

FINLAND

St. Petersburg (Leningrad)

Smolensk

Königsberg (Kaliningrad)

Danzig (Gdansk)

Volgograd (Stalingrad)

GERMANY
(3.5 MILLION FALLEN SOLDIERS,
2.3 MILLION CIVILIAN CASUALTIES)

DENMARK

Warsaw

Kharkiv

Kiev

SOVIET UNION
(11 MILLION FALLEN SOLDIERS,
16 MILLION CIVILIAN CASUALTIES)

IRELAND

UNITED KINGDOM

Coventry

London

Lübeck

Bremen

Hamburg

Hannover

Berlin

NETHERLANDS

Rotterdam

Essen

Cologne

Dresden

POLAND
(100,000 FALLEN SOLDIERS,
6 MILLION CIVILIAN CASUALTIES)

Odessa

Sevastopol

Brest

BELGIUM

LUXEMBOURG

Nuremberg

CZECHOSLOVAKIA

FRANCE

AUSTRIA

HUNGARY

ROMANIA

Belgrade

YUGOSLAVIA

BULGARIA

IRAN

PORTUGAL

SPAIN

ITALY

ALBANIA

GREECE

TURKEY

IRAQ

La Valetta

Tobruk

EGYPT

Region severely damaged by fighting/bombing
City severely damaged by fighting/bombing

■ = 100,000 fallen soldiers
□ = 100,000 civilian casualties

After World War II

The consequences of World War II were unimaginably devastating: approximately 70 million people worldwide lost their lives, 60 million of them in Europe; another 20 million people became refugees or were displaced, and the destruction of cities and infrastructure was staggering. Following the war, Europe was split into two ideologically and economically hostile camps.

USSR

The Soviet Union suffered the greatest losses by far in the "Great Patriotic War." Entire cities and villages that had been occupied by the Germans were reduced to rubble and their population liquidated under the guise of "anti-partisan warfare"; SS units systematically wrought havoc behind the front lines of battle. After the war, the Soviet Union extended its territory to the detriment of Finland, Poland, Czechoslovakia, Germany and Romania and again annexed the Baltic States.

Germany

The war and its aftermath meant the loss of much territory, and the ethnic Germans living there were expelled or displaced. Many German cities and almost all historic city centers were destroyed. The country was occupied by the victorious Allies and divided into four zones. Surviving war criminals were tried and sentenced in the Nuremberg Trials. The majority of the population was "denazified." In 1949 the Federal Republic of Germany was created from the three Western zones, while the Russian zone became the German Democratic Republic. The Nazi trauma still casts its shadow over Germany's history today. Repeatedly, the Nazi past of high-ranking leaders in industry, politics, law and medicine has been exposed.

France

France had more than half a million dead and the northern part of the country was almost completely leveled. 400,000 people were found guilty of real or alleged collaboration with the Germans. The role of French collaborators and the Résistance between

1940 and 1945 has repeatedly been the topic of heated public debates.

Great Britain

Several British cities, but especially London and Coventry, were hard hit by German bombing. In 1945, the left-of-center Labour Party won the elections. After the war, the British Empire gradually broke up.

Italy

Destruction was less severe in Italy than in Germany, France or the Soviet Union. Mussolini sympathizers formed neo-fascist parties that have been gaining popularity since the 1980s.

Poland

Poland suffered 6 million war casualties, including approximately 2.5 million civilians and 3.5 million murdered Jews. It was forced to cede its eastern territories to the Soviet Union and was awarded Silesia in return. Germany did not recognize the new Oder-Neisse border until 1970.

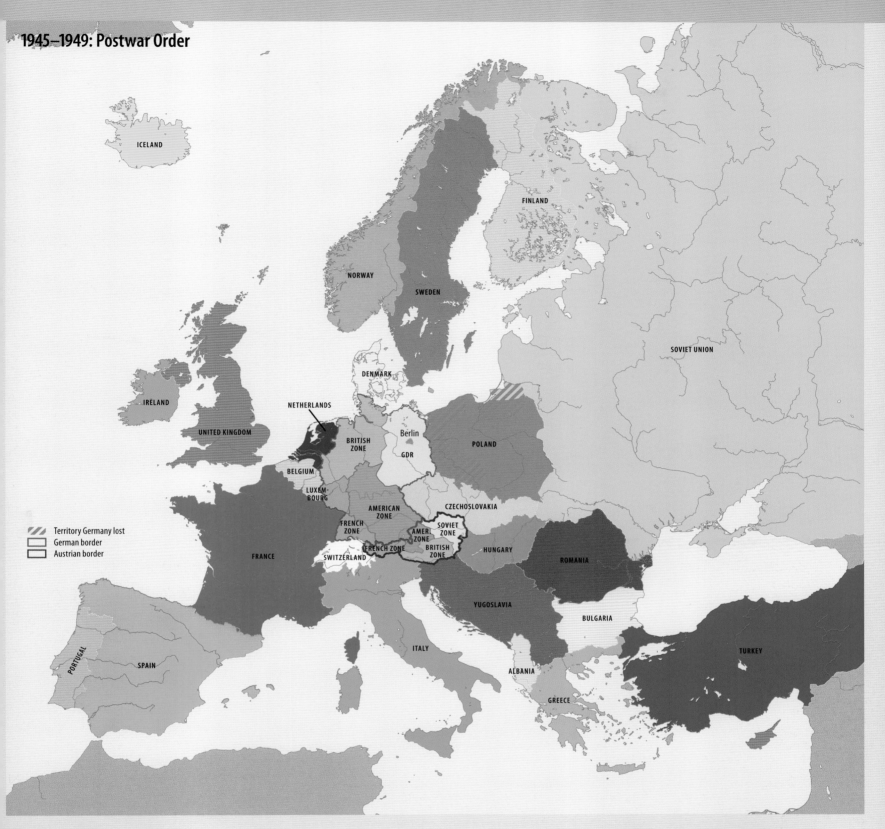

Territory Germany lost
German border
Austrian border

ICELAND

NORWAY

SWEDEN

FINLAND

DENMARK

SOVIET UNION

IRELAND

UNITED KINGDOM

NETHERLANDS

BRITISH ZONE

Berlin

GDR

POLAND

BELGIUM

LUXEM-BOURG

AMERICAN ZONE

CZECHOSLOVAKIA

FRENCH ZONE

AMER. ZONE

SOVIET ZONE

FRANCE

FRENCH ZONE

BRITISH ZONE

HUNGARY

ROMANIA

SWITZERLAND

YUGOSLAVIA

BULGARIA

PORTUGAL

SPAIN

ITALY

ALBANIA

GREECE

TURKEY

Defeated Allies of Germany after World War II

The Paris Peace Conference (involving twenty-one members of the United Nations) imposed certain reparation measures and losses of territory on the "smaller" vanquished nations, but guaranteed them full state sovereignty.

Austria

Like Germany, Austria was at first divided into four occupation zones. The Austrians were successful in persuading the world that they had been the first victims of Hitler's politics of aggression. They did not seriously confront their own Nazi past. Austria regained state sovereignty in 1955 by adopting a position of permanent neutrality.

Italy

In a 1946 referendum, the country transitioned from a constitutional monarchy to a parliamentary republic. It had to cede the Dodecanese Islands to Greece and the Dalmatian Islands and its part of Istria to Yugoslavia. The Italians lost their colonies and made reparation payments to Yugoslavia, Greece, the Soviet Union, Ethiopia and Albania.

Bulgaria

The country's 1941 borders were recognized, thus making Bulgaria one of the "winners" among the losers thanks to Soviet support.

Romania

Romania lost control of Bessarabia, the southern Dobruja region and the northern part of Bukovina

to the Soviet Union and was awarded Transylvania, which Hungary had regained in 1940; Romania made reparation payments to the Soviet Union.

Hungary

Hungary had to return territories it had occupied in Romania and Czechoslovakia. The border with Austria and Yugoslavia was drawn according to 1938 borders. Carpathian Ukraine, which had been occupied in 1939, went to the Soviet Union. Reparation payments were made to the USSR, Czechoslovakia and Yugoslavia.

Finland

Finland was forced to recognize the territorial losses of the Soviet-Finnish war (1939/40) and to make reparation payments to the Soviets. It lost the Karelian isthmus and the port of Petchenga.

Europe in Detail – NATO, the Warsaw Pact and the European Union

NATO and the Warsaw Pact

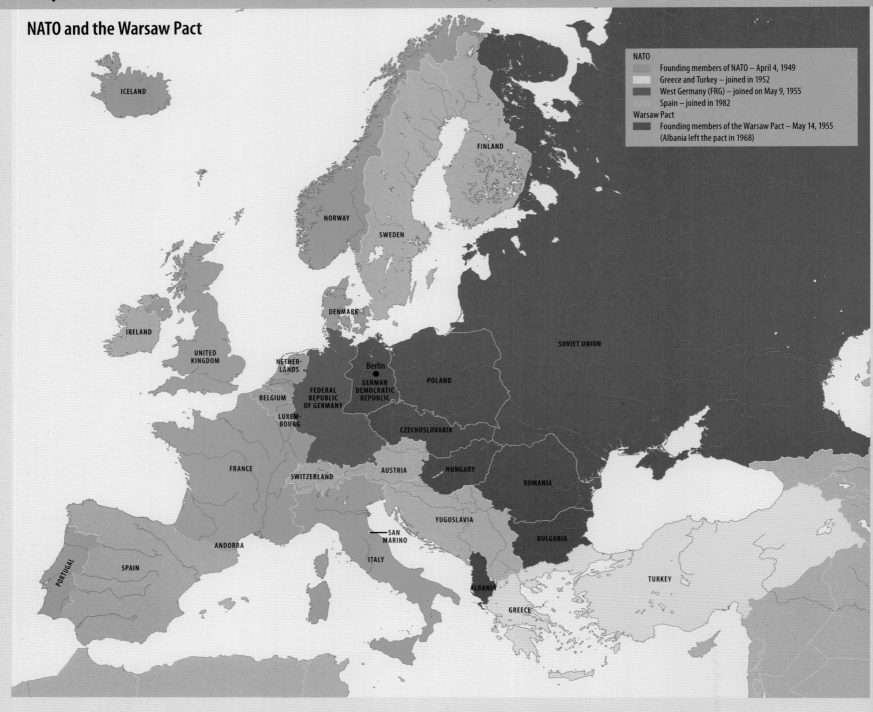

NATO
- Founding members of NATO – April 4, 1949
- Greece and Turkey – joined in 1952
- West Germany (FRG) – joined on May 9, 1955
- Spain – joined in 1982

Warsaw Pact
- Founding members of the Warsaw Pact – May 14, 1955
(Albania left the pact in 1968)

After World War II, Europe was divided into two enemy camps. In the West, liberal democracies with market economies predominated. These were militarily integrated under NATO, which was led by the United States. Eastern Europe came under the Soviet sphere of influence. Modeled on the USSR, socialist "people's democracies" with centrally planned economies were established, tightly bound to the USSR under the Warsaw Pact.

1948/49

1949 The North Atlantic Treaty Organization (NATO) is founded in Washington, D.C. Two German states are created: the Federal Republic (West Germany) and the German Democratic Republic (East Germany).

1953 Increased production quotas in East German factories lead to uprisings, brutally suppressed by Soviet tanks.

1955 West Germany joins NATO. The USSR's political response is the formation of the Warsaw Pact.

1956 Anticommunist revolt in Hungary. The Hungarian government announces its withdrawal from the Warsaw Pact. Soviet military units end the revolt with great bloodshed.

1960–1989 Stalinist East Germany orders guards to shoot any defectors attempting to cross the East German-West German border. Many fugitives are killed.

1961 Construction of the Berlin Wall

1968 A period of reform in Czechoslovakia ("Prague Spring") leads the Kremlin to accuse the reform movement of counterrevolution. In August, the Soviet Union and four other Warsaw Pact countries intervene militarily to suppress liberalization.

1980–1981 A critical economic situation in Poland causes a wave of strikes (*Solidarność* or "Solidarity" led by Lech Wałęsa). By the summer of 1981, the Soviet Union has threatened the Polish government with intervention. In reaction, the Polish government declares a state of emergency that remains in effect until July 1983.

1985 Mikhail Gorbachev becomes General Secretary of the Communist Party's Central Committee, initiating economic and political reform. Economically, the Soviet Union is in ruins. The other countries of the Eastern Bloc are given the hint that they may start their own reforms without fear of Soviet reprisal.

1989 Fall of the communist regimes of Eastern Europe ("Peaceful Revolution")

1991 Dissolution of the Soviet Union and the Warsaw Pact

The Berlin Wall

The European Union

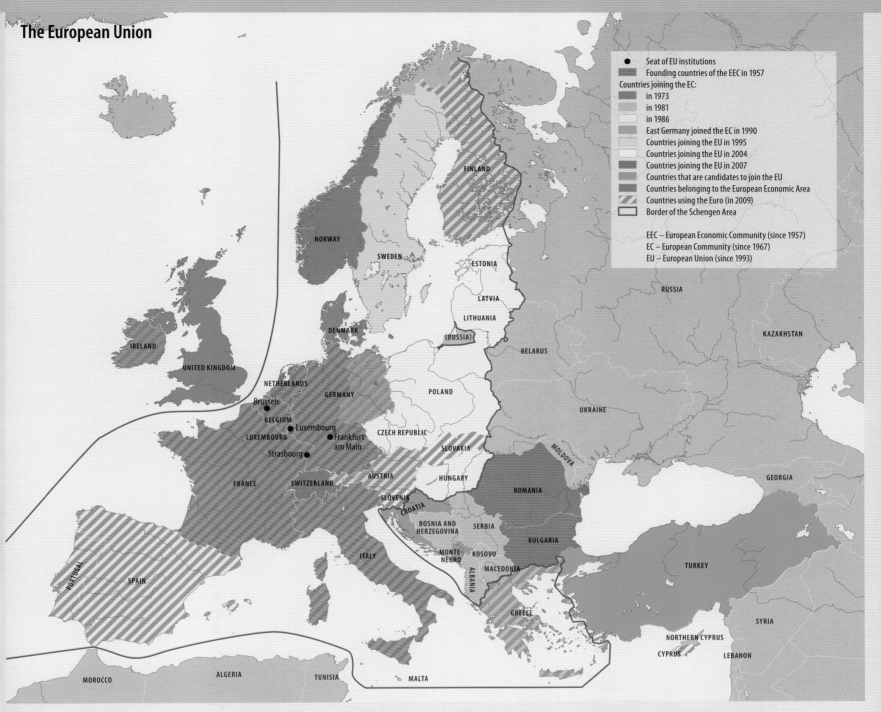

Legend:
- Seat of EU institutions
- Founding countries of the EEC in 1957
- Countries joining the EC:
  - in 1973
  - in 1981
  - in 1986
- East Germany joined the EC in 1990
- Countries joining the EU in 1995
- Countries joining the EU in 2004
- Countries joining the EU in 2007
- Countries that are candidates to join the EU
- Countries belonging to the European Economic Area
- Countries using the Euro (in 2009)
- Border of the Schengen Area

EEC – European Economic Community (since 1957)
EC – European Community (since 1967)
EU – European Union (since 1993)

The European Union (EU) is an international political and economic organization. It was created both to facilitate trade between the countries of Europe and to help prevent possible future military conflicts. More and more countries have joined the common market. This organization guarantees freedom of movement for people, goods, money and services between the member states, and encourages cultural exchange as well.

1951 Founding of the European Coal and Steel Community (ECSC) according to a plan devised by the French foreign minister, Robert Schuman. Members include Germany, France, Italy, Belgium, Luxembourg and the Netherlands. The UK is invited to participate but declines.

1954 The French National Assembly prevents the formation of a European Defense Community.

1957 Treaties of Rome. The member states of the ECSC found the European Economic Community (EEC) and the European Atomic Energy Community (Euratom).

1967 These organizations are unified in the European Community (EC).

1973 First major expansion: Denmark, Ireland and the United Kingdom are admitted to the EC.

1979 The European Monetary System goes into effect. Exchange rates may only fluctuate within a narrow range of +/– 2.25%. The ECU (European Currency Unit) is the precursor of the euro.

1981 Greece is admitted to the EC.

1984 The "UK rebate": Prime Minister Margaret Thatcher is able to negotiate a 40 percent reduction of Great Britain's compulsory contributions to the EC.

1985 An arrangement for unlimited and unhindered border transit is signed in Luxembourg.

1986 Spain and Portugal join the EU.

1990 With Germany's reunification, the addition of former East Germany marks the EC's first eastward expansion.

1992 The Maastricht Treaty (Treaty on European Union, or TEU) outlines unified citizenship, foreign and security policy, an enhanced legislative process and introduction of a common currency.

1993 The provisions of the Maastricht Treaty take effect and the EU is born.

1995 Austria, Sweden and Finland join the Union; Norway and Switzerland are the only remaining Western European countries that are not members.

2002 The euro becomes the common currency of twelve EU nations.

2004 Ten Eastern European nations are admitted as new member states.

2007 Bulgaria and Romania join the EU.

NATO (North Atlantic Treaty Organization) A military alliance of European and North American states, founded in 1949.

Turkey An associate member of the EEC since 1963, Turkey has unsuccessfully petitioned for admission to the EU. In 2005 the EU initiated accession talks, but made its definitive answer contingent on continued political and economic reforms (problems with Kurdish minority and maintaining a separation of religion and government). Some EU members have expressed doubt about Turkey's European orientation.

Warsaw Pact The military alliance of the Eastern Bloc, led by the Soviet Union, it was founded in 1955 and terminated in 1991.

The End of the Communist Regimes

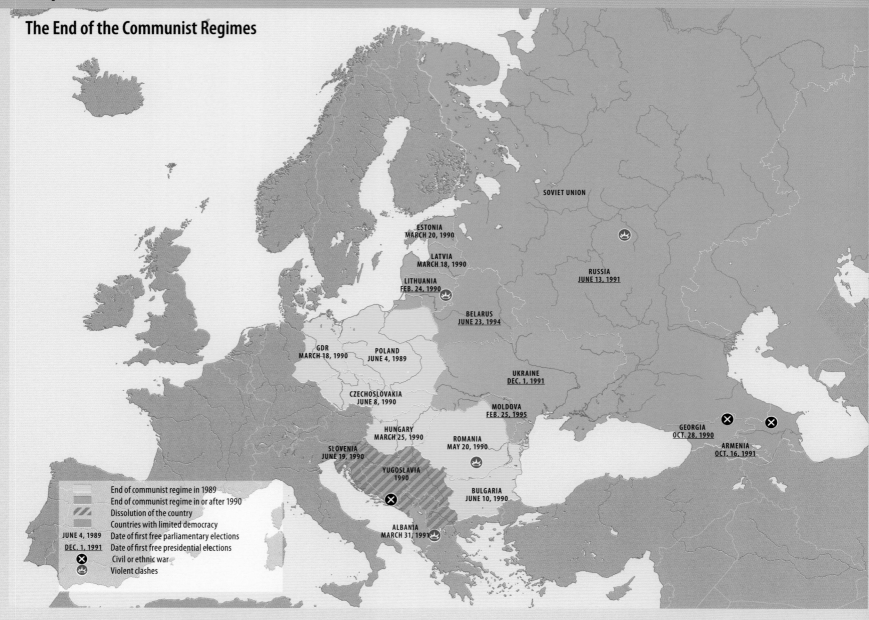

Map legend:
- End of communist regime in 1989
- End of communist regime in or after 1990
- Dissolution of the country
- Countries with limited democracy
- JUNE 4, 1989 — Date of first free parliamentary elections
- DEC. 1, 1991 — Date of first free presidential elections
- Civil or ethnic war
- Violent clashes

Map labels:
- SOVIET UNION
- ESTONIA MARCH 20, 1990
- LATVIA MARCH 18, 1990
- LITHUANIA FEB. 24, 1990
- RUSSIA JUNE 13, 1991
- BELARUS JUNE 23, 1994
- GDR MARCH 18, 1990
- POLAND JUNE 4, 1989
- CZECHOSLOVAKIA JUNE 8, 1990
- UKRAINE DEC. 1, 1991
- MOLDOVA FEB. 25, 1995
- HUNGARY MARCH 25, 1990
- ROMANIA MAY 20, 1990
- GEORGIA OCT. 28, 1990
- ARMENIA OCT. 16, 1991
- SLOVENIA JUNE 19, 1990
- YUGOSLAVIA 1990
- BULGARIA JUNE 10, 1990
- ALBANIA MARCH 31, 1991

In 1985, the new general secretary Mikhail Gorbachev was at the helm of a Soviet Union that, after an arms race with the United States and a catastrophic economic downturn, was facing ruin. The reforms known as Glasnost and Perestroika earned him praise abroad, but could not prevent the collapse of the system at home. The states of the Eastern Bloc quickly realized that Gorbachev would not interfere with their own plans for reform. Nothing more stood in the way of the fall of the Iron Curtain, which, with the exception of Romania, occurred without bloodshed. In 1991 the Warsaw Pact was officially dissolved.

Poland

1980 Quickly rising prices lead to a wave of strikes in Gdańsk. The independent union *Solidarność* ("Solidarity") is founded.

1981 December 13: In order to avoid Soviet military intervention, the Polish head of state Jaruzelski imposes martial law. The Solidarity movement is banned.

1988 After a series of strikes nationwide, the government initiates dialogue with *Solidarność* leaders.

1989 March 9: A bicameral legislature with freely elected representatives is signed into law.
June 4–18: Elections result in a landslide victory for *Solidarność*, but the party is only allowed to occupy 35 percent of the seats in the Sejm (lower house). *Solidarność* therefore gains 160 of 460 seats in the Sejm, and takes ninety-nine of the Senate's hundred seats.
September: First non-communist government takes office.

Hungary

1988 May: János Kádár resigns as general secretary of the Communist Party, and sweeping political and economic reforms are begun.

1989 February 11: Political parties are allowed.
August 19: At the Pan-European Picnic, a demonstration held near the Austrian-Hungarian border, a symbolic opening is made in the Iron Curtain between Austria and Hungary and several hundred East German citizens flee to the West.

September 18: A roundtable agreement paves the way for the transition to a pluralistic democracy.
October 23: The People's Republic of Hungary changes its constitution, thereby becoming the Republic of Hungary.

German Democratic Republic

1989 August–September: East German citizens occupy the West German embassies in Prague, Budapest and Warsaw.
September 11: Hungary finally opens its border with Austria to East German citizens.
September 30: East Germans who have taken refuge in the Prague embassy travel by special train into West Germany.
October 7: Agents of the East German Stasi (secret police) attack demonstrators on the fortieth anniversary of the founding of the East German state. Mikhail Gorbachev calls for acceptance and toleration of the protests.
October 18: Erich Honecker is dismissed as general secretary of the SED (Socialist Unity Party of Germany).

November 9: The fall of the Berlin Wall: the length of the border between East Germany and West Germany is unexpectedly opened, and Germans are allowed to pass through the Berlin Wall at will.

1990 October 3: Following several treaties between East and West Germany, German reunification becomes official—the five states of the former East Germany officially become part of the Federal Republic of Germany.

Czechoslovakia

1989 November 17: Police brutally attack a student demonstration in Prague.
November 20: Demonstrations against the government erupt throughout the country. Students and actors strike.
November 24: Resignation of General Secretary Gustáv Husák.
December 5: The border to Western Europe is opened.
December 10: "Government of national understanding" is convened. Husák is also removed from the office of president.

Romania

1989 December 16: The dictator Ceauşescu sends the army and the *Securitate* (secret police) to quash a demonstration of the Hungarian minority in Timişoara. Some protesters are killed.

December 17: News of the revolt spreads throughout Romania.

December 21: Uprising in Bucharest; on the following day, the army joins forces with the revolt.

December 24: Nicolae Ceauşescu and his wife Elena are charged with despotism, sentenced to death and shot. In total, approximately 1,100 people are killed during the revolution in Romania.

1990 January 3: The new president, Ion Iliescu, signs a decree permitting the return of political parties.

Bulgaria

1989 November 10: The Politburo forces Todor Zhivkov, head of state and head of the Communist Party, to resign.

November: Demonstrations are held throughout the country demanding political and economic reforms.

1990 The first free elections since 1931 are held in June.

War in Yugoslavia

In 1991, Serbian communists refused to recognize a federal government under the Croatian leader Stipe Mesić. Croatia and Slovenia declared independence shortly afterwards, at which point the largely Serb-controlled Yugoslavian army intervened. The conflict in Slovenia ended swiftly. In Croatia, however, the many ethnic Serbs living there proclaimed their own Republic of Serbian Krajina. Serbia seized large swathes of Croatia; supported by the West, the Croatian army was not able to reconquer all the lost territory until 1995/96. Many Serbs fled or were driven from their homes. In Bosnia and Herzegovina, three ethnic groups faced one another: Serbs, Croats and the Muslim Bosnians. In spite of the deployment of UN troops, many dreadful massacres occurred. In Srebrenica, Serbian units murdered about 8,000 Muslim men and boys. Acts of violence perpetrated on civilians and "ethnic cleansing," including expulsions and mass rape, were committed by other ethnicities as well. The fighting stopped at the end of 1995 with a peace settlement, and the country was divided into a Bosniac-Croat Federation and a Serbian Republic. Macedonia also gained its independence. In 2006 Montenegro split off from Serbia. Due to ethnic tension between Serbs and ethnic Albanians in Kosovo, this region was under international control after 1999. The Republic of Kosovo finally proclaimed its independence in 2008.

German Reunification

- Saarland, Jan. 1, 1957
- Five states of the former GDR, Oct. 3, 1990
- Federal Republic of Germany

SCHLESWIG-HOLSTEIN
MECKLENBURG-WEST POMERANIA
Hamburg
HAMBURG
BREMEN
LOWER SAXONY
Berlin
BERLIN
BRANDENBURG
SAXONY-ANHALT
NORTH RHINE-WESTPHALIA
Bonn
HESSE
THURINGIA
SAXONY
RHINELAND-PALATINATE
SAARLAND
Saarbrücken
BAVARIA
BADEN-WÜRTTEMBERG
Munich

German Reunification

The demise of the states of "real and existing socialism" meant the end of an independent German Democratic Republic. Around two thousand people were leaving the country daily, mainly the remaining elites, and the East German economy collapsed. Chancellor Helmut Kohl reacted to the fall of the Berlin Wall with a ten-point plan for reunification. He gathered the necessary international support at the "Two Plus Four" talks (East and West Germany with the United States, France, Great Britain and the USSR). The Soviet Union considered East Germany's continued existence to be a bulwark of its security and at first refused to condone admission of a unified Germany to NATO, but finally gave in after receiving international guarantees. The Final Settlement with Respect to Germany specified that the West German army had to be reduced in size, a reunified Germany was not permitted to station nuclear weapons or foreign troops on former East German territory, and the Oder-Neisse line had to be recognized as the permanent border with Poland.

From 1991: Civil War in Yugoslavia

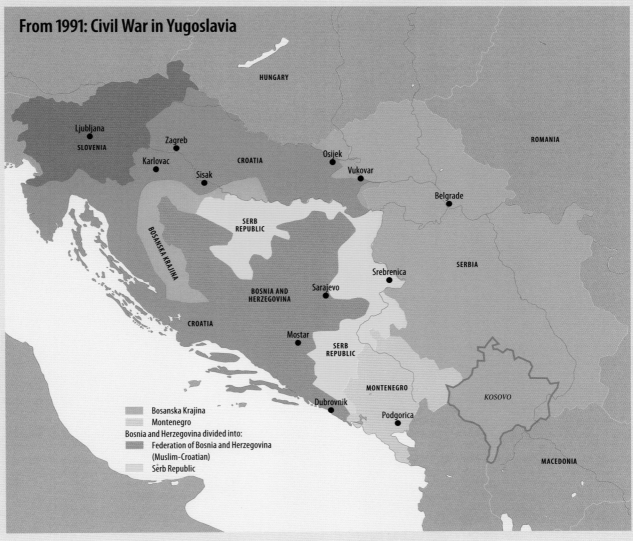

HUNGARY
Ljubljana
SLOVENIA
Zagreb
Karlovac
CROATIA
Osijek
Vukovar
Sisak
ROMANIA
Belgrade
BOSANSKA KRAJINA
SERB REPUBLIC
SERBIA
Srebrenica
BOSNIA AND HERZEGOVINA
Sarajevo
CROATIA
Mostar
SERB REPUBLIC
MONTENEGRO
KOSOVO
Dubrovnik
Podgorica
MACEDONIA

- Bosanska Krajina
- Montenegro
- Bosnia and Herzegovina divided into:
  - Federation of Bosnia and Herzegovina (Muslim-Croatian)
  - Serb Republic

Europe in Detail – Today

Europe Today

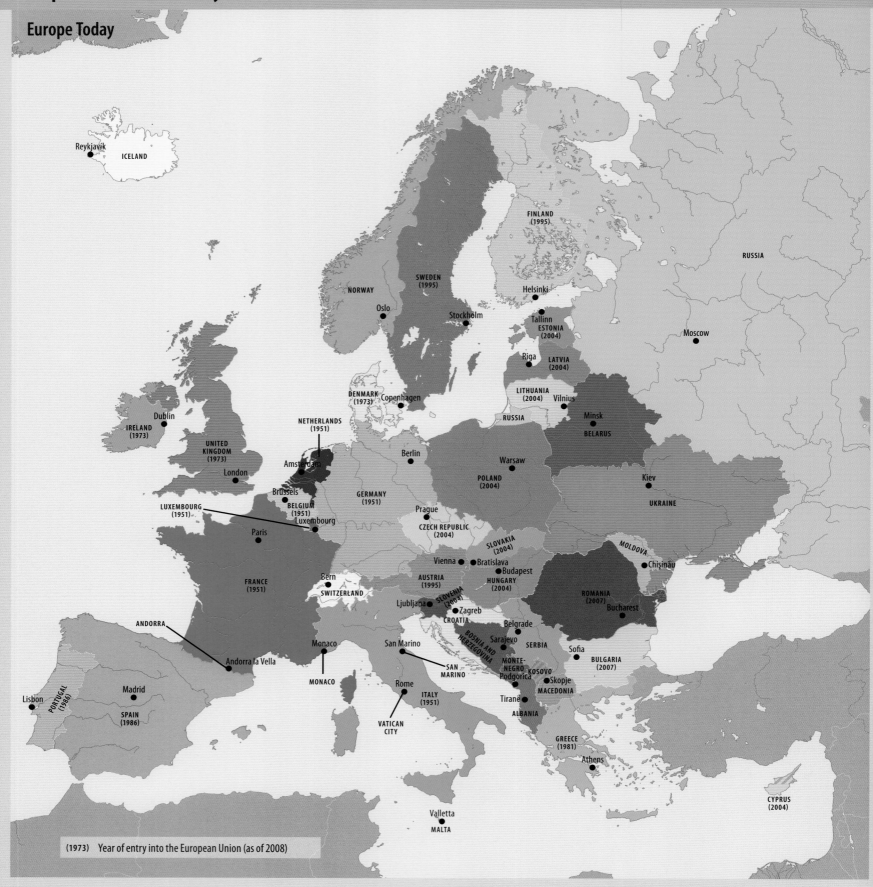

Reykjavík
ICELAND

FINLAND
(1995)

RUSSIA

NORWAY

SWEDEN
(1995)

Helsinki

Oslo

Stockholm

Tallinn
ESTONIA
(2004)

Moscow

Riga
LATVIA
(2004)

DENMARK
(1973)
Copenhagen

LITHUANIA
(2004)
Vilnius

Minsk
BELARUS

Dublin

IRELAND
(1973)

NETHERLANDS
(1951)

UNITED
KINGDOM
(1973)

Amsterdam

Berlin

Warsaw

London

Brussels
BELGIUM
(1951)

RUSSIA

Kiev

GERMANY
(1951)

POLAND
(2004)

UKRAINE

LUXEMBOURG
(1951)
Luxembourg

Prague

CZECH REPUBLIC
(2004)

SLOVAKIA
(2004)

MOLDOVA

Paris

Vienna
Bratislava
Budapest

Chișinău

AUSTRIA
(1995)
HUNGARY
(2004)

FRANCE
(1951)

Bern

SWITZERLAND

Ljubljana
SLOVENIA
(2004)
Zagreb
CROATIA

ROMANIA
(2007)

Bucharest

ANDORRA

Monaco

San Marino

Belgrade

Andorra la Vella

MONACO

SAN
MARINO

BOSNIA AND
HERZEGOVINA
Sarajevo
SERBIA

Sofia

BULGARIA
(2007)

Lisbon

Madrid

Rome

MONTE-
NEGRO
Podgorica
KOSOVO
Skopje
MACEDONIA

PORTUGAL
(1986)

SPAIN
(1986)

ITALY
(1951)

Tiranë

VATICAN
CITY

ALBANIA

GREECE
(1981)

Athens

Valletta

MALTA

CYPRUS
(2004)

(1973)   Year of entry into the European Union (as of 2008)

Until 1990, Europe was under the formative influence of rival economic and political power blocs. After the fall of real socialism, a vacuum emerged that brokered the illusion of eternal peace for many Europeans. That vacuum was quickly filled with new tensions, however, as nationalism and separatism flourished within it. While 19th- and early 20th-century Europeans sought to become superpowers, many regions all over Europe now pressed for independence.

Lack of assimilation by immigrants, many of the Muslim faith, posed an additional problem.

Europe had long denied these immigrants genuine integration. They had been recruited as inexpensive laborers (guest workers) or were economically disadvantaged holdovers from colonial policies, such as North Africans in France. Even when it became clear that many had stayed and were growing up as culturally uprooted second- and third-generation immigrants, they remained outsiders. These immigrants felt as if they could not relate to their ethnic origins, but were also not part of the mainstream in their new homelands.

One consequence has been increasing numbers of immigrants turning to conservative Islam, and inevitably isolating themselves further from the liberal, consumer-oriented European way of life.

Some Islamist groups have exploited much-misunderstood religious freedom, and a few have even prepared terrorists for their murderous trade on European soil. This has occurred to the chagrin of the majority of the Muslims, who have positively enriched Europe through their achievements and cultural contributions.

Current Conflicts in Europe

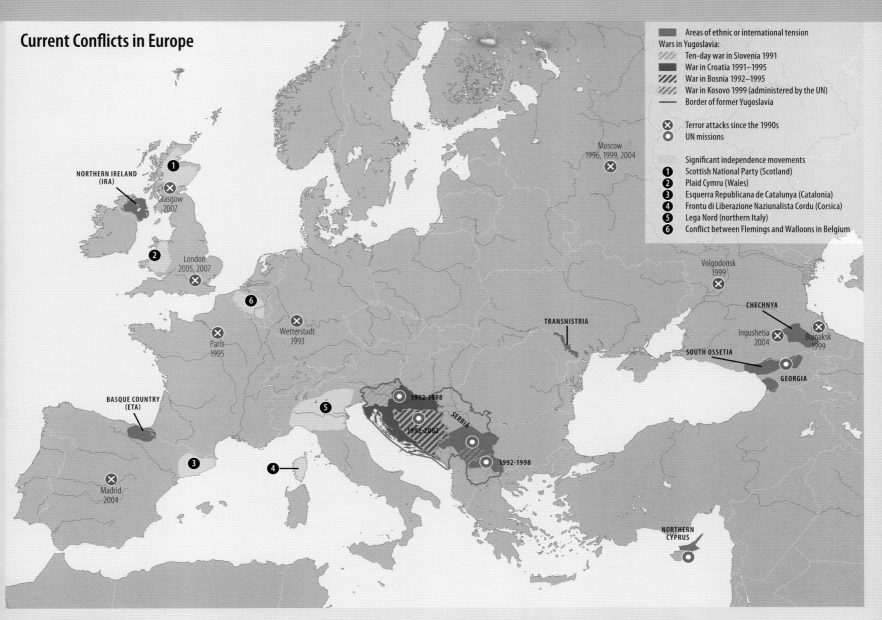

NORTHERN IRELAND (IRA)

Glasgow 2007

London 2005, 2007

Paris 1995

Wetterstadt 1993

BASQUE COUNTRY (ETA)

Madrid 2004

Moscow 1996, 1999, 2004

Volgodonsk 1999

CHECHNYA

Ingushetia 2004

Buinaksk 1999

TRANSNISTRIA

SOUTH OSSETIA

GEORGIA

SERBIA

1992-1998

1992-2002

1992-1998

NORTHERN CYPRUS

European Problems

Northern Ireland

From the time Ireland gained its independence in the 1920s, there was conflict between Catholics (Republic of Ireland) and Protestants loyal to the British Crown. Waves of violence came from both sides, and intensified in the 1970s. The officially banned Irish Republican Army (IRA) perpetrated a series of terrorist attacks. Genuine hope took root following the Friday Agreement of 1998. Political representatives from both camps began a dialogue and promised to renounce violence. The IRA declared an end to armed struggle in 2005.

The Basque Country

The ETA (*Euskadi Ta Askatasuna*, Basque Homeland and Freedom), an armed Basque separatist organization, wants to establish an independent state in the Basque Autonomous Community by force. Since 1968, more than 800 people have died in bomb attacks. Although they renounced the use of force in 2006, the moratorium only lasted until 2008.

Belgium

There is ongoing potential for conflict between the more industrialized, Dutch-speaking Flanders region in northwestern Belgium and the economically weaker, Francophone Wallonia. Complicated agreements between the various regions and official bilingual regulations often block the functioning of the central government for months. Flanders threatens to secede more often than the Walloon region.

Italy

Leading Italian politicians, particularly those who are members of the *Lega Nord*, have repeatedly advocated the north's separation from impoverished, structurally weak Sicily and southern Italy. Despite frantic reform efforts, southern Italy continues to sink deeper into the quagmire of communal corruption, garbage scandals and Mafia operations. The Mafia lost most of its public support after bomb attacks on examining magistrates in the 1970s and 1980s. The Roman Catholic Church has since also strongly opposed the Mafia.

Kosovo

In 1989 Slobodan Milosevic abolished the autonomy of the part of Serbia with a majority Albanian population. The initially non-violent situation escalated into a conflict between the Albanian UCK and the Serbian Army in 1996. The Dayton Agreement had not dealt with the issue of Kosovo's autonomy. NATO bombed Serbian targets in 1999 and Kosovo was occupied by UN troops. Further violence against the Serbs broke out in 2004. Kosovo unilaterally declared independence in 2008.

Georgia

After declaring independence on April 9, 1991, the former Soviet autonomous regions of Abkhazia and Ossetia rejected the sovereignty of Tbilisi. Wars of secession broke out. Moscow awarded Russian citizenship to many southern Ossetians and Abkhazians in 2008. Georgian President Saakashvili, believing that he had the support of the West, reacted with a bloody military attack to which Russia immediately responded with a counterstrike. Both sides also systematically destroyed each others' cultural facilities. Without failing to recognize Russia's hegemonic ambitions, critical voices have also blamed the West for its support of an independent, predominantly Albanian Kosovo while rejecting an independent, predominantly Russian Ossetia.

Cyprus

After numerous acts of repression by the Greek majority against the Turkish minority in the north, as well as armed conflict in 1974 that resulted in the Turkish occupation of Northern Cyprus, the resolution was a two-state solution for the island. The Turkish Republic of Northern Cyprus was founded in 1983, but only Turkey recognizes it as such. Although talks were held before the Republic of Cyprus (the southern Greek portion of the island) joined the European Union on May 1, 2004, they failed to achieve reunification. The status of Northern Cyprus remains unresolved.

Transnistria

Moldavia gained independence from the Soviet Union in 1990 and formed the Republic of Moldova. The part of Moldova that lies east of the Dniester River, called Transnistria, subsequently declared its independence from Moldova. An armed conflict in 1992 ended within a few months, but the region remains de facto an independent republic today. Transnistria has not yet been recognized by the international community, which still regards it as part of Moldova.

Scandinavia

The Vikings in the 8th–12th Centuries

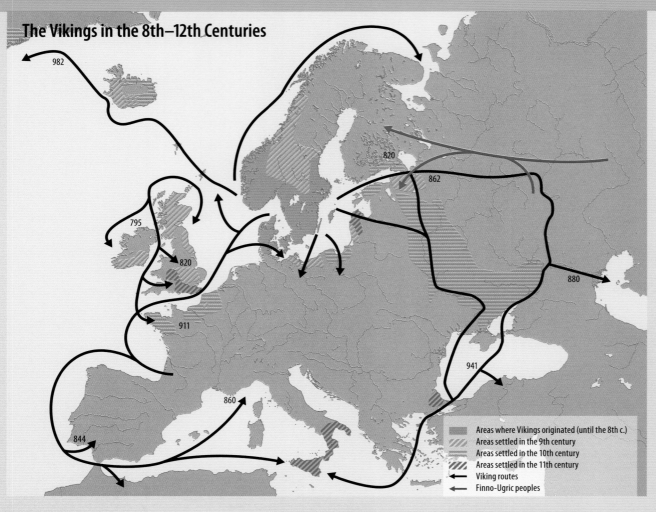

Areas where Vikings originated (until the 8th c.)
Areas settled in the 9th century
Areas settled in the 10th century
Areas settled in the 11th century
Viking routes
Finno-Ugric peoples

The Kingdom of Canute the Great

NORWAY (DANISH 1028–1035)

Helgeå (1026) ✕

DENMARK

ENGLAND (DANISH 1012/1014–1042)

Ashingdon (1016) ✕

✕ Important battle

1388 Queen Margaret of Denmark is recognized as the ruler of Sweden.

1397–1523 The Kalmar Union is founded, a personal union of Denmark, Norway and Sweden under one monarch; Iceland and Finland are also ruled by Margaret I.

1434–1436 Eric of Pomerania, king of the Kalmar Union, is deposed and driven out of Sweden.

1470–1523 Tension and conflict among the union kings increases; Sweden is ruled by regents.

1477 The first Swedish university is established in Uppsala; Swedish nationalist sentiment grows.

Back in the first century CE, Roman author Pliny the Elder mentioned the northern peninsula of *Scatinavia*, presumably a Latinization derived from a combination of *skadin* and *aujo* (Old Norse for "dangerous island"). The histories of Norway, Sweden, Denmark and Finland have been closely related for the past 1,500 years.

12,000–8000 BCE After the end of the last ice age, the first settlements in Norway and England appear.

4000–2000 BCE There is evidence of megalithic cultures in southern Scandinavia in this time period.

500 CE Danes from northern Scania (the southernmost part of the Scandinavian peninsula) settle in Jutland.

517 The first documented Viking raid of Gaul takes place: the Viking king Hygelac is killed and his fleet defeated.

800–1050 The Viking Age: Vikings attack Lindisfarne monastery on Holy Island off the coast of northeast England. The industrious but warfaring Danish, Norwegian and Swedish seafarers establish trading bases all over Europe and even reach North America, but also pillage and plunder numerous European cities, demanding tributes.

~870 Discovery of Iceland (Gardar Svavarsson), which is claimed by Norway.

~900 Danes conquer small English kingdoms in East Anglia and the Danelaw emerges: Danish law prevails in northern and eastern England. King Harald Hårfagre (Harald Fairhair) unites Norway.

911 The Viking leader Rollo establishes Normandy.

960 Poppo's miracle: Bishop Poppo of Schleswig is able to carry red-hot iron without being burned, convincing King Harald Bluetooth of Denmark to be baptized a Christian.

982 Erik the Red lands in southwest Greenland and the island is subsequently settled.

986–1014 King Sweyn I Forkbeard, son of Harald Bluetooth and the king of Denmark, conquers almost all of England by 1014.

1008 The Swedish king Olof Skötkonung (Olaf the Tax King) is baptized.

1028–1035 The kingdom of Canute the Great, son of Sweyn I, expands to include territory in Norway, in addition to England and Denmark.

1042–1047 Magnus I the Good is king of Norway and Denmark.

1066 The victory of William, duke of Normany, at the Battle of Hastings marks the end of Viking domination in England.

1154 King Erik IX of Sweden introduces Christianity to Finland.

1154–1809 The Swedish rule over Finland.

~1250 Norway emerges as a great power under Haakon IV Haakonsson.

1262 Icelandic chieftans sign a treaty subjecting Iceland to the rule of the king of Norway.

1323 The Treaty of Nöteborg establishes the boundaries between Sweden and the Novgorod republic (partition of Karelia).

1346 Denmark turns Estonia over to the Teutonic Order.

1350–1400 The rise of the German Hanseatic League in northern Europe, especially in the Baltic, leads to tensions with Denmark, particularly during the reign of Valdemar IV Atterdag (1340–1375).

1370 Following the second war between the Hanseatic League and Denmark, the league's power reaches its high point, even influencing Danish politics.

1380–1814 The marriage between Valdemar IV's daughter, Margaret, and Haakon VI of Norway (in 1363) leads to a Danish-Norwegian personal union (in fact, Denmark has primacy) that lasts for several centuries.

1520 Stockholm Bloodbath: Christian II of Denmark, the last king to head the Kalmar Union, quells a Swedish rebellion and is crowned king of Sweden, then commands the execution of eighty Swedish anti-unionists.

1521/23–1814 Personal union between Denmark and Norway continues.

1523 Gustav I Vasa is chosen as king of Sweden. Sweden secedes from Denmark, thus ending the Kalmar Union and marking the beginning of the Vasa Era (until 1611).

1536–1537 The Protestant Reformation reaches Denmark and Norway.

1561 After the state created by the Teutonic Order breaks down in the Livonian War, Estonia turns to Sweden for protection.

1593 Lutheranism becomes the state religion of Sweden.

1611–1632 Denmark and Sweden fight the Kalmar War over territory in northern Norway; Sweden becomes a major power.

1611–1632 Reign of Gustav II (Gustavus Adolphus) as king of Sweden, protector of the German Protestants

1630–1635 Sweden participates in the Thirty Years' War; Gustav II's troops fight brilliantly and secure territory as far south as Munich (1632).

The Kalmar Union

Contries of the Kalmar Union (1397–1523)
Areas temporarily part of the Kalmar Union

1635–1648 Franco-Swedish War against the Habsburgs

1645 Peace of Brömsebro: Denmark cedes control of the provinces of Jämtland, Härjedalen, Gotland and Saaremaa to Sweden.

1648 In the Peace of Westphalia, Sweden gains control of Bremen and Western Pomerania. Sweden's victories in the Thirty Years' War guarantee it hegemony in Scandinavia that lasts into the 18th century.

1658 Peace of Roskilde: Danish territories in Scania are lost to Sweden.

from 1660 Sweden—along with Finland, the Baltic and Karelia—is a Nordic great power.

1697–1718 Reign of Charles XII, King of Sweden, who in his youth was a European war hero

1700 Victory of Charles XII over the Russian troops of Peter the Great at Narva; Sweden, at the apogee of its power, drives the Saxons out of Poland.

1700–1721 Great Northern War: Russia, Denmark-Norway and Saxony-Poland fight Sweden for hegemony in the Baltic region.

1709 Sweden is defeated by Russia at Poltava (Ukraine) and loses Baltic territories to the victor; Sweden's power begins to diminish.

1721 The Peace of Nystad spells the end of Sweden's dominance. Finland, now partially occupied by Russia, is returned to Sweden, but the Baltic and parts of Karelia are lost to Russia.

1768–1772 Reforms by Count Johann Friedrich Struensee in Denmark (Enlightenment, freedom of the press, abolition of torture) end in 1772 with his downfall and execution.

1771–1792 Enlightened Absolutism in Sweden under King Gustav III; the king is shot at a masquerade ball and dies shortly thereafter.

1788 Peasant Wars in Denmark

1807 Destruction of Copenhagen's Old Town by an English expeditionary force

1808–1809 Russia wins the Finnish War. Sweden loses control of Finland in the Treaty of Fredrikshamn.

1809–1917 Finland becomes a Grand Duchy, part of the Russian Empire.

1810 French marshal Jean-Baptiste Bernadotte is elected Crown Prince of Sweden (becomes King Charles XIV John in 1818).

1814 Treaty of Kiel between Denmark and Sweden: due to its support of Napoleon, Denmark loses Norway to Sweden; Greenland, Iceland and the Faroe Islands (originally Norwegian territories) remain part of Denmark. Norway passes its constitution on May 17th, which is still a national holiday.

1814–1905 Personal union formed between Norway and Sweden.

1849 Denmark becomes a constitutional monarchy.

1863–1906 Reign of Christian IX, king of Denmark and called "father-in-law of Europe" due to the marriages of his many children with other royal houses

1864 Second Schleswig War; Denmark cedes Schleswig and Holstein to Prussia and Austria.

1905 Dissolution of the personal union between Norway and Sweden through a referendum; Haakon VII becomes king of Norway and rules for over fifty years.

16th–18th Century: Reformation and Absolutism

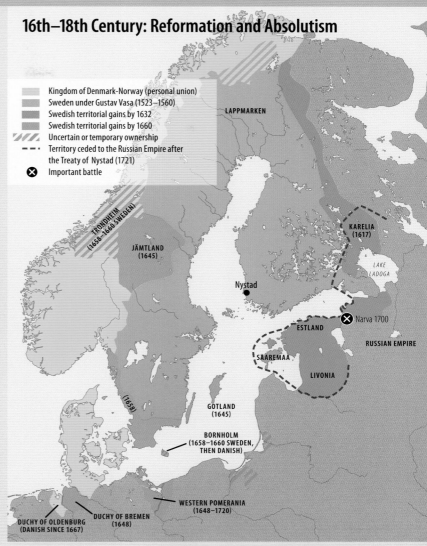

Kingdom of Denmark-Norway (personal union)
Sweden under Gustav Vasa (1523–1560)
Swedish territorial gains by 1632
Swedish territorial gains by 1660
Uncertain or temporary ownership
Territory ceded to the Russian Empire after the Treaty of Nystad (1721)
Important battle

After 1814

Sweden united with Norway by personal union (after 1814)
Finland as part of the Russian Empire (after 1809)

World War II

Norway

Finnish territories ceded to the Soviet Union after the Continuation War in 1944

Operations of the British fleet

Operations of the German fleet

Advance of German troops

PETSAMO

SALLA

Narvik

Namsos

Trondheim

Andalsnes

NORWAY

FINLAND

KARELIA

GULF OF FINLAND ISLANDS

GULF OF FINLAND

Bergen

HANGÖ

Stavanger

Oslo

SOVIET UNION

UNITED KINGDOM

Gdańsk

Hamburg

GERMANY

1907–1920 Introduction of democracy in the Scandinavian countries; universal suffrage in Sweden

1914–1918 In World War I, Sweden, Norway and Denmark remain neutral.

Dec. 6, 1917 Finland declares independence from Russia, prompted by the abdication of Tsar Nicholas II.

1920 The partition of Schleswig between Denmark and Germany is decided by referendum; Norway joins the League of Nations.

Nov. 30, 1939 The Soviet Union attacks Finland, launching the Winter War (Russo-Finnish War); Field

Marshal Carl Gustaf Mannerheim becomes Finland's leading politician.

1939–1945 In World War II, Sweden remains neutral, while Norway and Denmark are occupied by Germany in April 1940 (Operation Weserübung).

March 12, 1940 In the Moscow Peace Treaty, Finland cedes large parts of Karelia to the Soviet Union.

1941 Continuation War: Finland fights alongside Germany to retake Karelia, but must admit defeat in 1944 in a separate treaty and loses its claim on Karelia for good.

1943 German diplomat Georg Ferdinand Duckwitz arranges for almost all of the 7,500 Danish Jews to flee to Sweden, where they are given shelter.

1944 Iceland declares independence from Denmark (which is still Nazi-occupied).

1945 Denmark and Norway are freed from German occupiers.

1949 Norway and Denmark are among the founding members of NATO.

1960 The European Free Trade Association (EFTA) is founded by Denmark, Norway, Sweden, Austria,

Norway Today

Vadsø
FINNMARK
Tromsø
TROMS
Bodø
NORDLAND
NORD-TRØNDELAG
Steinkjer
Trondheim
SØR-TRØNDELAG
Molde
MØRE OG ROMSDAL
SOGN OG FJORDANE
Hermansverk
OPPLAND
Lillehammer
HEDMARK
Hamar
Bergen
HORDA-LAND
BUSKERUD
Drammen
Lillestrøm
AKERSHUS
Oslo
TELEMARK
Moss
OSLO
Skien
ØSTFOLD
VESTFOLD
Stavanger
AUST-AGDER
ROGALAND
VEST-AGDER
Arendal
Kristiansand

Sweden Today

NORRBOTTEN
Luleå
VÄSTERBOTTEN
Umeå
Östersund
VÄSTERNORRLAND
JÄMTLAND
Härnösand
GÄVLEBORG
KOPPARBERG
Falun
Gävle
VÄSTMANLAND
UPPSALA
VÄRMLAND
Västerås
Uppsala
Karlstad
ÖREBRO
STOCKHOLM
Örebro
Stockholm
SÖDERMANLAND
Nyköping
GÖTEBORG AND BOHUS
Linköping
ÖSTERGÖTLAND
Göteborg
Jönköping
JÖNKÖPING
KALMAR
Visby
GOTLAND
HALLAND
Växjö
Halmstad
KRONOBERG
Kalmar
BLEKINGE
MALMÖHUS
Karlskrona
Malmö

Iceland Today

GRIMSEY
Húsavík
Akureyri
NORTHEAST
NORTHWEST
Seydhisfjördhur
REYKJAVÍK NORTH
REYKJAVÍK SOUTH
SOUTH
Höfn
Keflavík
Reykjavík
Hafnarfjördhur
SOUTHWEST
Vík
SURTSEY

Portugal, Switzerland and the United Kingdom as an alternative to the European Economic Community (EEC), which evolves into the European Union (EU). Several member countries will later join the EU.

1969 Discovery of oil in the North Sea makes Norway a wealthy country.

1973 Denmark joins the European Community.

1979 Denmark grants Greenland home rule.

1986 Swedish Prime Minister Olof Palme is assassinated; the crime remains unsolved today.

1989 Denmark is the first country in the world to legalize same-sex marriage.

Finland Today

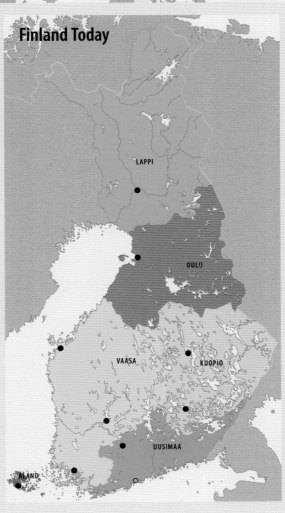

LAPPI
OULU
VAASA
KUOPIO
UUSIMAA
ÅLAND

Denmark Today

Ålborg
NORDJYLLAND
Viborg
MIDTJYLLAND
HOVEDSTADEN
Hillerød
Vejle
SJÆLLAND
Copenhagen
SYDDANMARK
Sorø

1994 The people of Norway decline to become part of the European Union in a referendum.

1995 Sweden and Finland join the European Union.

2000 Denmark decides against adopting the euro as its currency; except for Finland, the krone is still the valid currency in Scandinavia today.

2008 In the course of the international financial crisis, state bankruptcy looms for Iceland.

England Until 1066

4th Century: Under Roman Rule

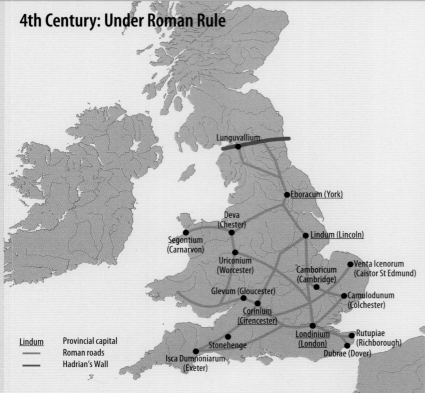

Lunguvallium

Eboracum (York)

Deva (Chester)

Segontium (Carnarvon)

Lindum (Lincoln)

Uriconium (Worcester)

Camboricum (Cambridge)

Venta Icenorum (Caistor St Edmund)

Glevum (Gloucester)

Camulodunum (Colchester)

Corinium (Cirencester)

Stonehenge

Londinium (London)

Rutupiae (Richborough)

Isca Dumnoniarum (Exeter)

Dubrae (Dover)

<u>Lindum</u>   Provincial capital
        Roman roads
        Hadrian's Wall

England, Scotland, Wales and Ireland all have their own Celtic-Anglo-Saxon traditions. For much of their early history they were divided into small kingdoms, and establishing a central authority was a slow process. Beginning in the days of the Normans, England attempted to rule Ireland, and it forced Wales into submission. Joint sovereignty of England and Scotland was established in 1603. The Act of Union followed in 1707, establishing parliamentary rights that prevented royal absolutism. From the 16th century onward, England rose to become the leading maritime and colonial power in Europe.

3100–1500 BCE   Stonehenge is built.

9th century–6th century BCE   Celtic settlement of the British Isles

55–54 BCE   Caesar's exploratory expeditions

5th–6th Century: Anglo-Saxon Land Claims

MIDDLE SAXONS

EAST SAXONS

WEST SAXONS

SOUTH SAXONS

Tribes
- Picts
- Britons
- Angles } Anglo-Saxons
- Saxons
- Jutes and Frisians

43 CE   Conquest of the British Isles by Emperor Claudius; the first Roman administrative center is Camulodunum (Colchester).

122–128   Construction of Hadrian's Wall as the northern border of the Roman Empire

287–296   Empire of Carausius (a Roman general and rebel emperor)

407–410   Withdrawal of Roman troops

5th century –6th century   Germanic Angle, Jute and Saxon tribes push into East and South Anglia and drive out part of the native Celtic population (Britons) toward the west.

5th century –7th century   Evangelization and Christianization of England spreading from the north English coast and the island of Jona and from the south (Roman mission in 597) leads to conflict between two Christian traditions.

7th–8th Century: The Early Kingdoms

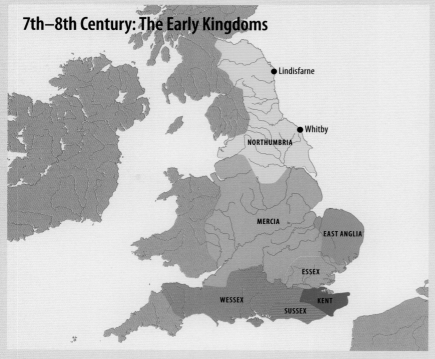

Lindisfarne

Whitby

NORTHUMBRIA

MERCIA

EAST ANGLIA

ESSEX

WESSEX

KENT

SUSSEX

After 878: Viking Conquests

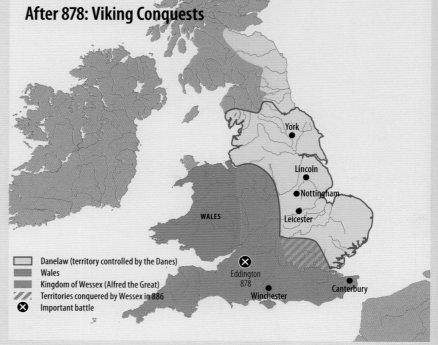

York

Lincoln

Nottingham

Leicester

WALES

Eddington 878

Winchester

Canterbury

- ▭ Danelaw (territory controlled by the Danes)
- ▨ Wales
- ▨ Kingdom of Wessex (Alfred the Great)
- ▧ Territories conquered by Wessex in 886
- ⊗ Important battle

Stonehenge (Old English, "hanging stones") A pilgrimage and burial site in southern England sacred to a sun-worshiping cult in the Neolithic and Bronze Ages. Rings of megaliths (transported from quarries hundreds of miles away) surround central ditches.

Hadrian's Wall Wall Emperor Hadrian built on the frontier between the Roman Empire and the Picts' territory (now Scotland). It is 64.5 miles (120 km) long, 10 feet (3 m) wide and 13–16½ feet (4–5 m) high with eighty paired gates and a tower between each pair.

Synod of Whitby A church council held in 664 at which it was decided that England would adhere to the Roman Catholic rites rather than the competing Celtic Irish-Scottish (Christian) rites.

Danelaw ("Danish law") The English regions conquered by the Danes 865–878 and held into the 10th century. After the Battle of Eddington in 878, the Danes were gradually driven out. With the death of King Erik I of Jorvik (=York) in 954, Scandinavian rule in

1016–1035: The Kingdom of Canute the Great

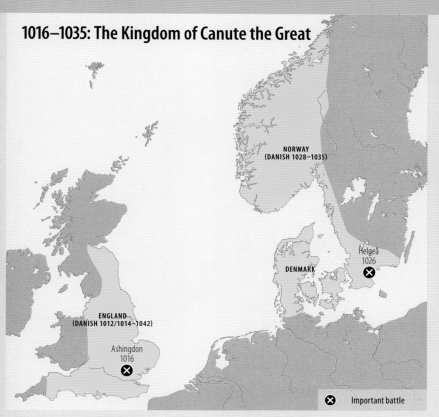

1066: The Battle of Hastings

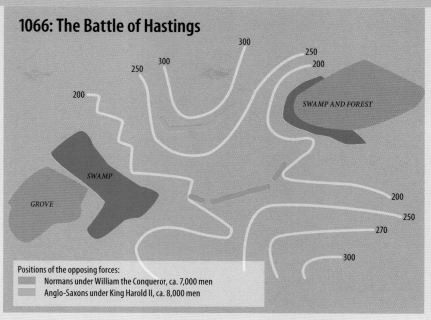

Positions of the opposing forces:
- Normans under William the Conqueror, ca. 7,000 men
- Anglo-Saxons under King Harold II, ca. 8,000 men

from the late 6th century Seven competing small Anglo-Saxon kingdoms form and gradually fuse.

664 Synod of Whitby is held to determine whether Christianity will adhere to Celtic or Roman precepts.

late 7th century Anglo-Saxon conquest of Cornwall

793 A Viking raid of the monastery of Lindisfarne in Northumberland

marks the beginning of the Viking Age (lasts until 1066).

after 865 The Danes press forward from East Anglia toward the south; the area they conquer is known as Danelaw.

878 Alfred the Great, king of Wessex, defeats the Danes at the Battle of Eddington.

886 Alfred conquers London.

899–924 Alfred's successor, Edward the Elder, reconquers the Danelaw and almost all of England.

911 Treaty between the Viking leader Rollo and Charles III, king of the West Franks; Rollo founds the Duchy of Normandy and is baptized.

1012–1014 Reconquest of England by the Danes

1016–1035 Canute the Great defeats

Edmund II in the Battle of Ashingdon and becomes king of England.

1042–1066 With Edward the Confessor, Anglo-Saxon rule is restored.

1066 Harold II (Godwinson) is the last Anglo-Saxon king.
Oct. 14: In the Battle of Hastings, William of Normandy (the Conqueror) defeats Anglo-Saxon King Harold II.
Dec. 25: William is crowned king of England.

11th Century: The Norman Conquests

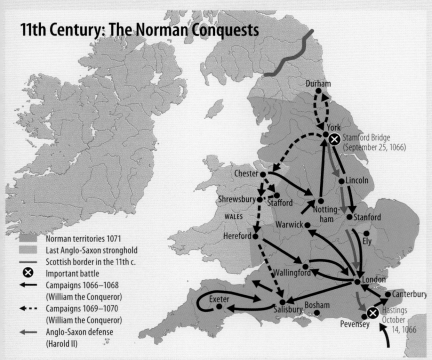

- Norman territories 1071
- Last Anglo-Saxon stronghold
- Scottish border in the 11th c.
- ⊗ Important battle
- → Campaigns 1066–1068 (William the Conqueror)
- ◄-- Campaigns 1069–1070 (William the Conqueror)
- → Anglo-Saxon defense (Harold II)

The Historic Counties from about the 11th Century

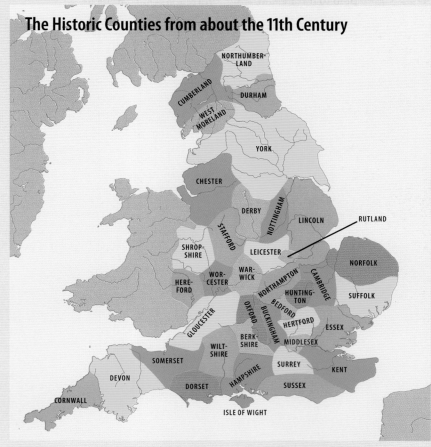

England ended until the reign of Canute the Great in the following century.

Alfred the Great (847/849–899) King of Wessex 871–899. After his victory over the Danes in 878 and conquest of London

in 886, he successfully united England under Wessex leadership and established administrative districts called shires. Another notable achievement of Alfred's was to codify the legal system in his territories.

William the Conqueror (1027/28–1087)
Duke of Normandy from 1035; after the death of the childless Edward the Confessor, William lay claim to the English throne against Edward's Anglo-Saxon successor, Harold II. After his victory at the Battle of

Hastings (the last successful invasion of England) and coronation in 1066, he established Norman rule in England, marking the end of Scandinavian influence, and laid the groundwork for an epic conflict with France that would last almost 900 years.

England in the 12th–17th Centuries

England and France in the 12th–16th Centuries

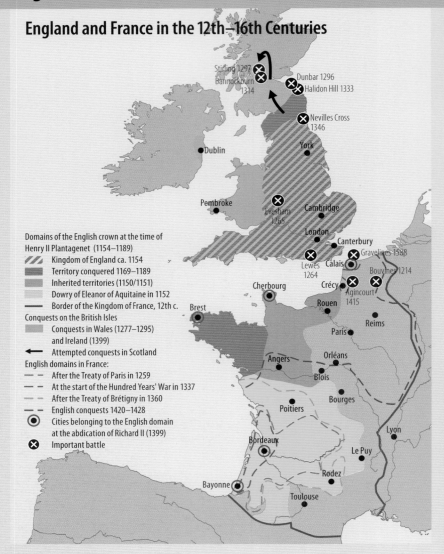

Domains of the English crown at the time of Henry II Plantagenet (1154–1189)
- Kingdom of England ca. 1154
- Territory conquered 1169–1189
- Inherited territories (1150/1151)
- Dowry of Eleanor of Aquitaine in 1152
- Border of the Kingdom of France, 12th c.

Conquests on the British Isles
- Conquests in Wales (1277–1295) and Ireland (1399)
- ← Attempted conquests in Scotland

English domains in France:
- – – – After the Treaty of Paris in 1259
- – – – At the start of the Hundred Years' War in 1337
- – – – After the Treaty of Brétigny in 1360
- – – – English conquests 1420–1428
- ⊙ Cities belonging to the English domain at the abdication of Richard II (1399)
- ⊗ Important battle

1455–1485: Wars of the Roses

- Area of influence of the House of York (White Rose)
- Area of influence of the House of Lancaster (Red Rose)
- Territories of Duke Clarence
- Crown domain controlled by the House of Lancaster
- ⊗ Victory of the House of York
- ⊗ Victory of the House of Lancaster
- ⊗ Bosworth Field 1485
- ← Campaign and victory of Henry VII Tudor

London ca. 1300

- Border of the city of London
- Built-up area

Under William the Conqueror (1027–1087), the Normans established a centralized feudal system in England, suppressing the native Anglo-Saxon nobility. All property was under the king's control, and the Domesday Book (1086) recorded all the feudal estates, taxes and dues. Important positions were held by Normans, whose language, along with Latin, was predominant over the Anglo-Saxon language of the general population.

1100 Death of William II; Henry I rules until 1135.

1106 Henry I defeats the Norman army and Normandy becomes a part of England.

1135–1154 Rival claims to the throne after Henry's death lead to civil war.

1154 Coronation of Henry Plantagenet (Henry II), launching the Plantagenet or Anjou dynasty, which rules until 1399. Their combined territories (England and French feudal lands) comprise the Angevin empire.

1170 Thomas Becket, archbishop of Canterbury and opponent of Henry II, is murdered.

1189–1199 Reign of King Richard I Lion-heart, son of Henry II. He is captured in 1192 in Austria on his way home from a Crusade; ransomed and released in 1194.

1214 Battle of Bouvines results in loss of English territory on the Continent under King John Lackland, Richard's brother.

1215 The Magna Carta, a charter of liberties, is signed by King John, making significant concessions to the nobility.

1259 Treaty of Paris regulating England's territories in France is signed.

1277–1307 Reign of Edward I, who conquers Wales by 1301.

1314 Battle of Bannockburn: Scottish victory against the English (Scotland remains independent until 1603)

1337–1453 Hundred Years' War begins as Edward III of England lays claim to the French throne.

1360 Treaty of Brétigny: France is forced to cede extensive territories to England.

1399 Richard II is forced to abdicate, and the House of Lancaster usurps the English throne.

1415 Henry V conquers Normandy in the Battle of Agincourt, and England forms an alliance with Burgundy against France.

1428 French resistance rallies under Joan of Arc.

1453 The French recapture Bordeaux; only Calais remains an English territory on French soil.

1455–1485 Wars of the Roses between the Houses of York (White Rose) and Lancaster (Red Rose), both of which claim the English throne

1461 Coronation of Edward IV: The House of York rules England.

1485 Battle of Bosworth Field marks the end of the Wars of the Roses. Henry Tudor is crowned Henry VII.

1534 Henry VIII breaks with the pope in Rome, creating the Anglican Church.

1558–1603 Reign of Elizabeth I

1587 Mary Stuart, Queen of Scots, who was supported by France, is beheaded; England's influence in Scotland grows.

1588 England defeats the Spanish Armada in the sea battle of Gravelines.

1603 James I (James Stuart), king of Scotland since 1567, ascends the English throne, resulting in a personal union of England and Scotland.

1642 Conflict between the monarchy and the Parliament lead to civil war (Great Rebellion).

1645 Charles I is defeated in the Battle of Naseby.

1648 The Battle of Preston ends the English Civil War.

1649 Charles I is beheaded in London, and England is proclaimed a republic.

1649 The Commonwealth of England is declared (from 1653 on, it includes Scotland and Ireland).

1653–1658 Oliver Cromwell rules as lord protector.

1660 Restoration of the English monarchy under Charles II

1666 Great Fire of London rages for days, leaving thousands homeless.

ca. 1500–1600: The Tudor Era

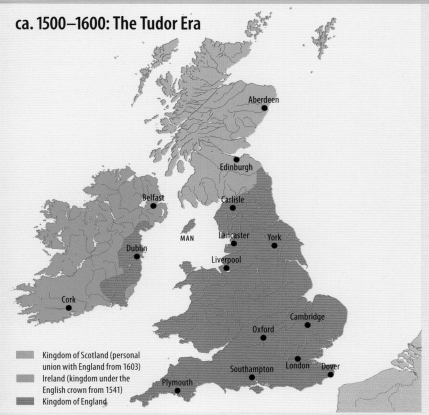

Kingdom of Scotland (personal union with England from 1603)

Ireland (kingdom under the English crown from 1541)

Kingdom of England

1642–1643: English Civil War

Royalist territory
Conquests of the Royalists
Parliamentarian territory
Conquests of the Parliamentarians
← Parliamentarian campaigns under O. Cromwell
← Campaigns of Charles I
⊗ Royalist victory
⊗ Parliamentarian victory
⊗ Undecided

1644–1649: English Civil War

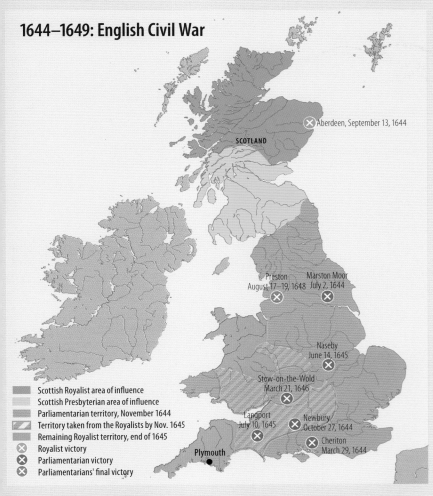

Scottish Royalist area of influence
Scottish Presbyterian area of influence
Parliamentarian territory, November 1644
Territory taken from the Royalists by Nov. 1645
Remaining Royalist territory, end of 1645
⊗ Royalist victory
⊗ Parliamentarian victory
⊗ Parliamentarians' final victory

1649–1660: Commonwealth

Commonwealth of England 1649–1653
Commonwealth of England, Scotland and Ireland 1653–1659

Thomas Becket (ca. 1118–1170) Archbishop of Canterbury, primate of all England, and lord chancellor of England who had many conflicts with King Henry II. As defender of the independence of ecclesiastical courts from the crown, he was forced to flee to France in 1164. Under a guarantee of safety he returned to England, but was murdered by four of the king's knights in Canterbury Cathedral on December 29, 1170. This led to a conflict with the pope and unrest in England.

Anglican Church The English state church was created as a result of the dispute between the pope and the crown to enable Henry VIII to divorce his first wife and remarry. It combines Catholic and Protestant elements of faith; the head of the Church of England is the British monarch.

The Elizabethan Age The long reign (forty-five years) of the final ruler of the Tudor dynasty, Elizabeth I, was the zenith of the English Renaissance, during which science and literature (William Shakespeare) blossomed. It saw the stabilization of the Anglican Church, a centralization of royal power and the beginning of British colonialism.

English Civil War (1642–1648/49) The conflict between Charles I and Parliament was also a religious war; it led to the declaration of a republic in 1649. Oliver Cromwell, who fought on the side of the Parliamentarians, ruled 1653–1658 as lord protector of England, Scotland and Ireland.

Wales, Ireland and Scotland

5th–8th Centuries: The Welsh Kingdoms

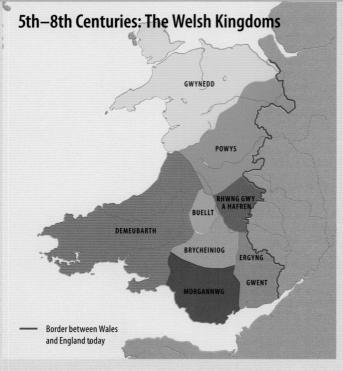

— Border between Wales and England today

1014: The Irish Kingdoms

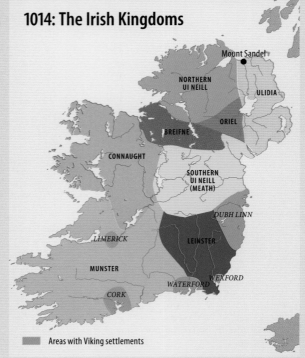

Areas with Viking settlements

1594–1603 Tyrone's Rebellion

1641 Rebellion of the (Catholic) Irish against the English (Protestant) settlers

1649–1653 Reconquest of Ireland by Oliver Cromwell

July 12, 1690 William of Orange defeats the former English king James II and his Irish supporters, the Jacobites, in the Battle of the Boyne.

Jan. 1, 1801 The Act of Union officially establishes the United Kingdom of Great Britain and Ireland and ensures Irish representation in Parliament.

19th century Great Potato Famine; massive emigration (primarily to the United States)

1919–1921 Anglo-Irish War: Twenty-six of thirty-two Irish counties become the Irish Free State, an independent member of the British Commonwealth. The remaining six counties become Northern Ireland.

1939–1945 World War II; Ireland remains neutral.

1949 Ireland, officially the Republic of Ireland, leaves the Commonwealth.

1973 Ireland joins the European Union.

1998 Belfast Agreement: Ireland revokes its claim on Northern Ireland.

Wales

48–410 CE Wales is under Roman rule.

ca. 500–700 "The Age of Saints": period of great missionary activity and founding of monasteries. Central organization breaks down into many small kingdoms.

9th century First unification of Welsh kingdoms under Rhodri Mawr

End of the 13th century England completes its conquest of Wales.

1412 Collapse of the last rebellion against England in Wales

1536 Act of Union: integration of Wales into the English legal system

Ireland

7000 BCE Mount Sandel in northern Ireland, a settlement dating from the Middle Stone Age

ca. 600 BCE Influx of Celtic tribes

5th century Christianization of Ireland; St. Patrick plays a leading role and becomes patron saint of Ireland.

6th–8th centuries Flowering of Irish monastic culture

9th–10th centuries Repeated Viking raids; they control Dublin after 823.

1005–1014 Unification of Ireland under King Brian Boru; that unity dissolves after his death.

11th–12th centuries English conquest of the east coast of Ireland; Anglo-Norman settlement gradually spreads westward from the east coast.

1185 Henry II establishes the Lordship of Ireland with his son John (Lackland), the first lord of Ireland.

1297 The Parliament of Ireland is established.

1541 Ireland enters a personal union with England: The king of England is recognized as king of Ireland. Beginning of the era of plantations, in which the English crown confiscates land and resettles it with English and Scottish immigrants.

Scotland

2000 BCE Callanish Circle of standing stones, monuments of the megalith culture, date from this time.

8th century BCE Settlement by Celts

122–128 CE Romans construct Hadrian's Wall to prevent invasion of barbarians.

6th century Christianization of Scotland by the Irish missionary St. Columba of Iona

843 The Celtic Scots and Picts are united under their first king, Kenneth MacAlpin.

1040–1057 Reign of King Macbeth

1058–1290 Kings of the House of Dunkeld

1296 Edward I of England annexes Scotland.

1297 Battle of Stirling Bridge: The Scots, led by William Wallace, defeat English forces.

1306 Robert the Bruce becomes king of Scotland (the House of Bruce reigns until 1371 in Scotland).

1314 The Battle of Bannockburn results in a Scottish victory over the English.

1300: Ireland

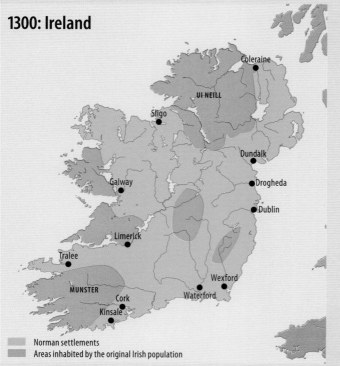

Norman settlements
Areas inhabited by the original Irish population

1690: Campaign of William of Orange (William III)

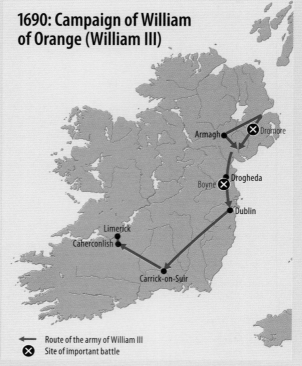

⟵ Route of the army of William III
⊗ Site of important battle

1320 Declaration of Arbroath asserts Scotland's independence from England.

1328 The Treaty of Edinburgh-Northampton recognizes Scottish independence.

1371 Stewart (Stuart) dynasty is established with King Robert II.

1542–1567 Reign of Mary Stuart, Queen of Scots; thereafter she is imprisoned in England for eighteen years.

Mary Stuart (1542–1587)

1587 Mary Stuart is beheaded in England.

1603 Personal union of the crowns of England and Scotland under James I

1651 Scotland is occupied by military forces led by Oliver Cromwell.

James I (1566–1625)

1692 Massacre of Glencoe: The Mac-Donald clan is violently attacked on orders of King William III.

1707 England and Scotland merge to become Great Britain.

1746 Battle of Culloden: The last Scottish rebellion of Jacobites, led by Charles Edward (Bonnie Prince Charlie), is overwhelmingly defeated.

1997–1999 Establishment of a Scottish Parliament with limited powers within the United Kingdom

Rhodri Mawr Roderick the Great in English (ca. 820–878, reigned 844–878), first Welsh ruler to be called "the Great." Originally he was king of Gwynedd (North Wales) and defeated the Danes in 856. In 855 Roderick inherited the Powys from his deceased uncle and later also the kingdom of Seisyllwg in southern Wales belonging to his brother-in-law, who had drowned. King Roderick was killed in 878 after fighting the English led by Alfred the Great.

St. Patrick of Ireland He was probably born before 400 in Wales and is believed to have been enslaved and brought to Ireland against his will. He fled to France, where he was ordained as a priest after years of study. He followed a vision to Christianize Ireland, and in 432 he was appointed the first bishop of Ireland. During his mission, he converted thousands of people to Christianity and founded numerous churches and monasteries. St. Patrick is considered the national saint of Ireland and Iceland, even though he was never formally canonized by the Catholic Church. The Irish-Scottish Church (or Celtic tradition) was not fully integrated into the Roman Catholic Church until the 12th century.

Plantations Widespread settlement by English and Scottish migrants to Ireland beginning in the second half of the 16th century triggered vehement resistance from the Irish population. A more serious uprising was Tyrone's Rebellion (or Nine Years' War), fought between 1594 and 1603 under the leadership of Hugh O'Neill, the second earl of Tyrone.

Macbeth (ca. 1005–1057) was a descendant of royalty and was thus eligible to be chosen king of Scotland. He became king after his cousin, Duncan I, was killed in a battle near Elgin in 1040. Contrary to Shakespeare's well-known literary portrayal, Macbeth's reign was characterized by stability and peace. He fell in battle in 1057 against Duncan's son, Malcolm III.

Declaration of Arbroath A letter submitted to Pope John XXII by Scottish nobles, it is considered the declaration of Scottish independence. It is the earliest formal declaration of independence by any nation.

Mary Stuart (1542–1587) was crowned as queen of Scotland before her first birthday, and reigned from 1542 to 1567. She was raised in France from 1548 on, and as the wife of King Francis II, Mary was queen of France in 1559–1560. After returning to Scotland, she met with vehement opposition from the Scottish nobility due to her strong Catholic faith and her quick remarriage after the death of her second husband. Mary fled to England, where she was imprisoned for many years because she also had a claim to the English throne. She was beheaded upon the orders of Queen Elizabeth I after a mock trial.

Massacre of Glencoe Traditionally, the MacDonald clan were supporters of the Stuart dynasty, which by 1692 had been deposed and exiled. On the pretense that they had been slow pledging their oath of allegiance to the new king, William of Orange, supporters of the king followed an elaborate plan in which they were taken in as guests by many of the MacDonalds in Glencoe, but then turned on their hosts and killed seventy-eight members of the clan.

13th Century: The Scottish Counties

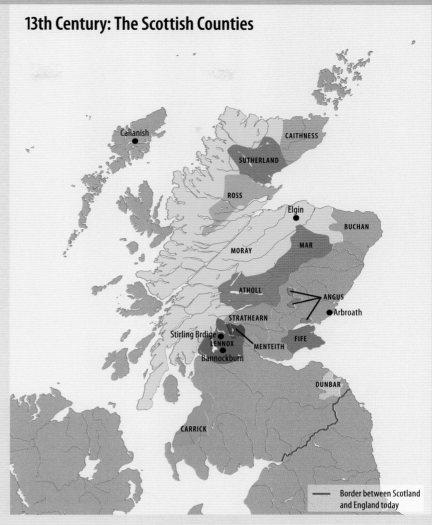

Border between Scotland and England today

1996: Scottish Unitary Authorities

Border between Scotland and England today

England and Great Britain in the 18th–20th Centuries

1707: Act of Union

United Kingdom of Great Britain after 1707

Edinburgh
Cardiff
London

1808–1814: Wellington's Campaign

September 8, 1813
Battle of the Nive
November 10, 1813
Orthez
February 27, 1814
Vitoria
San Sebastián
June 21, 1813
Nive
Pyrenees
July 25–30, 1813
Tarbes
April 10, 1814
March 20, 1814
Toulouse
Porto
May 12, 1809
First landing in Portugal in 1808
Second landing in 1809
Fuentes de Oñoro
May 3–5, 1811
July 22, 1812
Salamanca
Madrid
Buçaco
September 27, 1810
Talavera
July 27–28, 1809
Vimeiro
Roleja
Torres Vedras
Lisbon
Badajoz
May 6, 1812

1808   Landing at Lisbon on August 17, victory over the French near Roleja, on August 21 near Vimeiro
1809   2nd landing, May 12 victory near Porto, July 28 victory at Talavera
   Fort built near Torres Vedras, north of Lisbon, in 1808
– – – Wellington's campaign 1809–1811
– – – Wellington's campaign in 1811/1812
⦻ Battles in which the English defeated the French

18th–19th Century: The Industrial Revolution

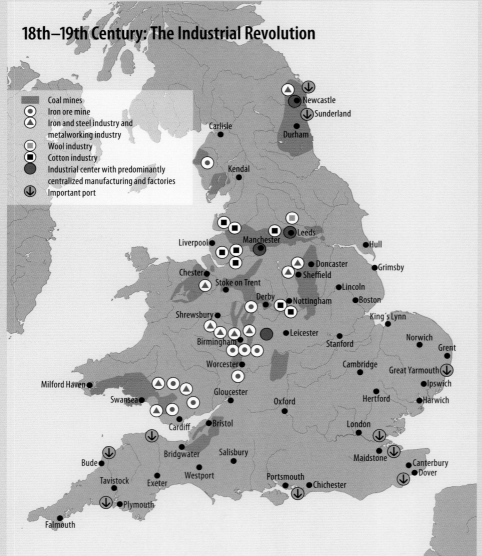

Coal mines
Iron ore mine
Iron and steel industry and metalworking industry
Wool industry
Cotton industry
Industrial center with predominantly centralized manufacturing and factories
Important port

Newcastle
Sunderland
Carlisle
Durham
Kendal
Liverpool
Manchester
Leeds
Hull
Chester
Doncaster
Sheffield
Grimsby
Stoke on Trent
Lincoln
Derby
Boston
Nottingham
Shrewsbury
King's Lynn
Birmingham
Leicester
Worcester
Stanford
Norwich
Grent
Cambridge
Great Yarmouth
Milford Haven
Ipswich
Gloucester
Hertford
Harwich
Swansea
Oxford
Cardiff
Bristol
London
Bridgwater
Salisbury
Maidstone
Bude
Westport
Canterbury
Dover
Tavistock
Exeter
Portsmouth
Chichester
Plymouth
Falmouth

1688–1689 The Glorious Revolution: End of royal absolutism, Bill of Rights

1701 Act of Settlement: Regulates the succession to the British throne

1707 Act of Union: Formation of the United Kingdom of Great Britain (England and Scotland)

1714–1760 Age of the Whigs, who dominate politics

Feb. 1, 1793 Revolutionary France declares war on Great Britain.

1801 Formation of the United Kingdom of Great Britain and Ireland

March 25–27, 1802 Treaty of Amiens with France (lasts until May 1803)

Oct. 21, 1805 Naval Battle of Trafalgar

1808–1814 Wellington campaigns against Napoleon in Portugal, Spain and France.

1837–1901 The Victorian Era of rapid change: Industrial Revolution, imperialism, two-party system and democratization through election reform

1907 Triple Entente: military alliance with France and Russia

Aug. 5, 1914 England declares war against the Germans. Between 1914 and 1918 there will be 850,000 British military casualties in World War I.

1921 The Anglo-Irish Treaty elaborates the formation of the United Kingdom of Great Britain and Northern Ireland (official name since 1927).

1938 Neville Chamberlain takes a stance of appeasement toward Germany.

Sept. 3, 1939 Great Britain declares war against Germany. Between 1939 and 1945, there will be 360,000 British military casualties in World War II.

1940–1945 Winston Churchill is British prime minister and an essential negotiator for the Allies.

1952 Elizabeth II ascends the English throne.

1973 Great Britain joins the European Community.

1979–1990 Margaret Thatcher, Conservative Prime Minister; Falkland War

from 1997 Era of Prime Ministers Tony Blair and Gordon Brown, both from the Labour Party

The Glorious Revolution This term was used to set this rebellion apart from the disorder of the English Civil War. William of Orange (son-in-law of the reigning King James II) was invited by Parliament to take over the throne. His campaign and victory led to establishment of the constitutional monarchy.

The Act of Settlement specified further the rules of inheritance of the crown. To this day, only Protestants may succeed to the English throne, and monarchs must join the Church of England. The crown went to the House of Hanover in 1714 after the Stuart dynasty died out upon the death of the childless Queen Anne.

The Act of Union This legislative agreement between England and Scotland, reached in 1707, merged the two countries and created the United Kingdom of Britain. The dissolution of the Scottish Parliament followed; sixteen Scottish peers (titled nobility) sat in the Upper House of the newly created British Parliament, and forty-five members of Parliament represented Scotland in the Lower House.

Two-party system: Tories and Whigs These two parties emerged in the English Parliament (the British Parliament after 1707) in the second half of the 17th century. The Tories (renamed the Conservative Party

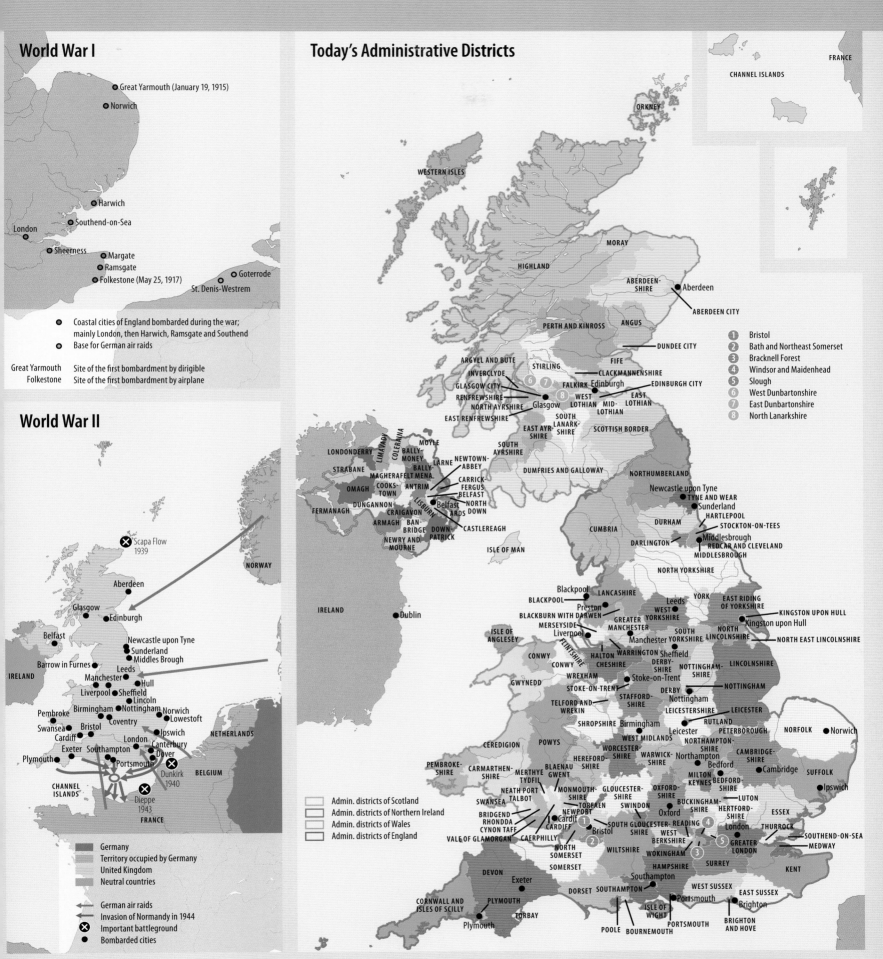

World War I

- Great Yarmouth (January 19, 1915)
- Norwich
- Harwich
- Southend-on-Sea
- London
- Sheerness
- Margate
- Ramsgate
- Folkestone (May 25, 1917)
- Goterrode
- St. Denis-Westrem

○ Coastal cities of England bombarded during the war; mainly London, then Harwich, Ramsgate and Southend

○ Base for German air raids

Great Yarmouth Site of the first bombardment by dirigible
Folkestone Site of the first bombardment by airplane

World War II

- Scapa Flow 1939
- NORWAY
- Aberdeen
- Glasgow
- Edinburgh
- Belfast
- Newcastle upon Tyne
- Sunderland
- Middles Brough
- Barrow in Furnes
- IRELAND
- Leeds
- Manchester
- Hull
- Liverpool
- Sheffield
- Lincoln
- Birmingham
- Nottingham
- Coventry
- Norwich
- Lowestoft
- Pembroke
- Swansea
- Bristol
- Cardiff
- Exeter
- Southampton
- London
- Ipswich
- Canterbury
- Dover
- Plymouth
- Portsmouth
- NETHERLANDS
- CHANNEL ISLANDS
- Dunkirk 1940
- BELGIUM
- Dieppe 1943
- FRANCE

Germany
Territory occupied by Germany
United Kingdom
Neutral countries

→ German air raids
→ Invasion of Normandy in 1944
⊗ Important battleground
● Bombarded cities

Today's Administrative Districts

FRANCE
CHANNEL ISLANDS
ORKNEY
WESTERN ISLES
MORAY
HIGHLAND
ABERDEEN-SHIRE — Aberdeen
ABERDEEN CITY
PERTH AND KINROSS
ANGUS
DUNDEE CITY
ARGYLL AND BUTE
STIRLING
FIFE
INVERCLYDE
CLACKMANNANSHIRE
GLASGOW CITY
FALKIRK — Edinburgh — EDINBURGH CITY
RENFREWSHIRE
WEST LOTHIAN
NORTH AYRSHIRE
Glasgow
MID-LOTHIAN
EAST RENFREWSHIRE
SOUTH LOTHIAN
EAST AYR-SHIRE
SOUTH LANARK-SHIRE
SCOTTISH BORDER

① Bristol
② Bath and Northeast Somerset
③ Bracknell Forest
④ Windsor and Maidenhead
⑤ Slough
⑥ West Dunbartonshire
⑦ East Dunbartonshire
⑧ North Lanarkshire

SOUTH AYRSHIRE
MOYLE
LONDONDERRY
LIMAVADY
COLERAINE
BALLY-MONEY
BALLY-MENA
STRABANE
MAGHERAFELT
NEWTOWN-ABBEY
LARNE
OMAGH
COOKS-TOWN
ANTRIM
CARRICK-FERGUS
DUNGANNON
BELFAST
FERMANAGH
CRAIGAVON
LISBURN
Belfast
NORTH DOWN
ARMAGH
BAN-BRIDGE
CASTLEREAGH
NEWRY AND MOURNE
DOWN-PATRICK
DUMFRIES AND GALLOWAY
ISLE OF MAN
NORTHUMBERLAND
Newcastle upon Tyne
TYNE AND WEAR — Sunderland
HARTLEPOOL
DURHAM
STOCKTON-ON-TEES
CUMBRIA
DARLINGTON
Middlesbrough
REDCAR AND CLEVELAND
MIDDLESBROUGH
IRELAND
Dublin
NORTH YORKSHIRE
Blackpool
LANCASHIRE
YORK
EAST RIDING OF YORKSHIRE
BLACKPOOL
Preston
Leeds
WEST YORKSHIRE
KINGSTON UPON HULL
BLACKBURN WITH DARWEN
GREATER MANCHESTER
Kingston upon Hull
MERSEYSIDE
Manchester
SOUTH YORKSHIRE
NORTH LINCOLNSHIRE
ISLE OF ANGLESEY
Liverpool
Sheffield
NORTH EAST LINCOLNSHIRE
CONWY
HALTON
CHESHIRE
DERBY-SHIRE
LINCOLNSHIRE
CONWY
WARRINGTON
NOTTINGHAM-SHIRE
GWYNEDD
WREXHAM
Stoke-on-Trent
DERBY
STOKE-ON-TRENT
STAFFORD-SHIRE
Nottingham
NOTTINGHAM
TELFORD AND WREKIN
LEICESTERSHIRE
LEICESTER
SHROPSHIRE
Birmingham
RUTLAND
WEST MIDLANDS
Leicester
PETERBOROUGH
NORFOLK — Norwich
CEREDIGION
POWYS
WORCESTER-SHIRE
WARWICK-SHIRE
NORTHAMPTON-SHIRE
Northampton
CAMBRIDGE-SHIRE
PEMBROKE-SHIRE
HEREFORD-SHIRE
Bedford
Cambridge
SUFFOLK
CARMARTHEN-SHIRE
MILTON KEYNES
BEDFORD-SHIRE
Ipswich
MERTHYR TYDFIL
BLAENAU GWENT
GLOUCESTER-SHIRE
OXFORD-SHIRE
LUTON
HERTFORD-SHIRE
ESSEX
NEATH PORT TALBOT
MONMOUTH-SHIRE
BUCKINGHAM-SHIRE
SWANSEA
TORFAEN
NEWPORT
SWINDON
Oxford
London
THURROCK
BRIDGEND
RHONDDA CYNON TAFF
Cardiff
SOUTH GLOUCESTER-SHIRE
READING ④
GREATER LONDON
SOUTHEND-ON-SEA
VALE OF GLAMORGAN
CARDIFF
① Bristol
WEST BERKSHIRE
⑤
MEDWAY
CAERPHILLY
② NORTH SOMERSET
WOKINGHAM ③
SURREY
KENT
WILTSHIRE
DEVON
SOMERSET
HAMPSHIRE
WEST SUSSEX
Exeter
Southampton
CORNWALL AND ISLES OF SCILLY
PLYMOUTH
DORSET
SOUTHAMPTON
Portsmouth
EAST SUSSEX
Brighton
ISLE OF WIGHT
PORTSMOUTH
BRIGHTON AND HOVE
Plymouth
TORBAY
POOLE
BOURNEMOUTH

Admin. districts of Scotland
Admin. districts of Northern Ireland
Admin. districts of Wales
Admin. districts of England

---

after 1830) were originally strong supporters of the monarchy and the Church of England, and later supported the policies of colonial imperialism, while the Whigs (after 1859, the Liberal Party) opposed absolutism and supported political and economic liberalism.

Appeasement policy Generally speaking, a policy of making concessions and placating gestures in the face of aggression. More specifically, the term refers to compliant Anglo-French policy toward the German Reich, which as a result of the Munich Treaty (September 30, 1938) led to the forcible relinquishment of the Czech border areas

and later to the annexation of Czech land and dissolution of Czechoslovakia.

Winston Churchill (1874–1965) was the most significant British politician of the 20th century. Churchill, who was unyielding in his stance toward Germany during World War II, succeeded the architect of

appeasement, Chamberlain, and was prime minister and minister of war from 1940 to 1945, heading an all-party government. An important strategist of the Allies, Churchill was elected to a second term as prime minister from 1951 to 1955. He received the Nobel Prize for Literature in 1953 for his historical writing and journalism.

The British Colonial Empire

1492–1763: Discoveries and Conquests

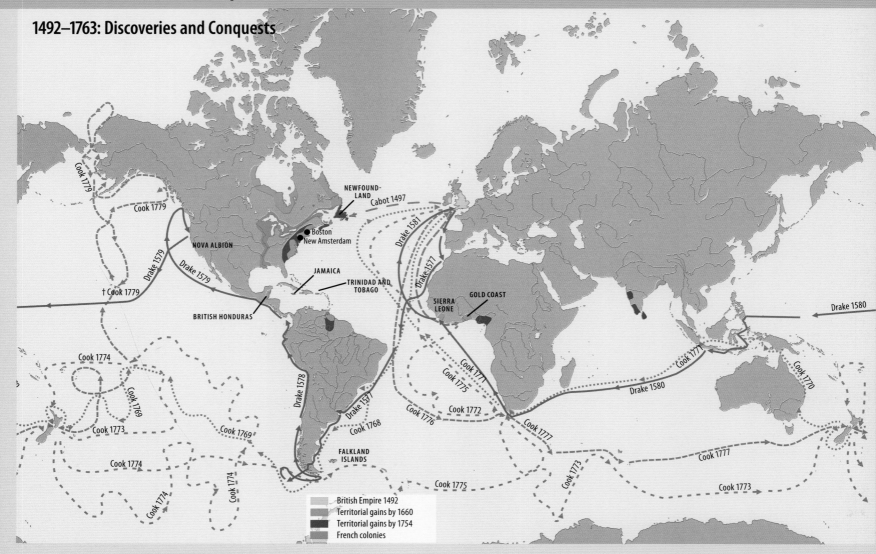

Cook 1779
Cook 1779
NEWFOUND-LAND
Cabot 1497
NOVA ALBION
Boston
New Amsterdam
Drake 1581
Drake 1579
Drake 1579
JAMAICA
TRINIDAD AND TOBAGO
† Cook 1779
Drake 1577
SIERRA LEONE
GOLD COAST
BRITISH HONDURAS
Drake 1580
Cook 1774
Cook 1771
Cook 1769
Drake 1578
Cook 1775
Cook 1772
Cook 1777
Cook 1770
Cook 1773
Drake 1577
Cook 1776
Cook 1777
Cook 1771
Cook 1774
Cook 1768
Cook 1777
Cook 1774
FALKLAND ISLANDS
Drake 1580
Cook 1775
Cook 1773
Cook 1773

British Empire 1492
Territorial gains by 1660
Territorial gains by 1754
French colonies

1822–1914: Establishment of Additional Colonies

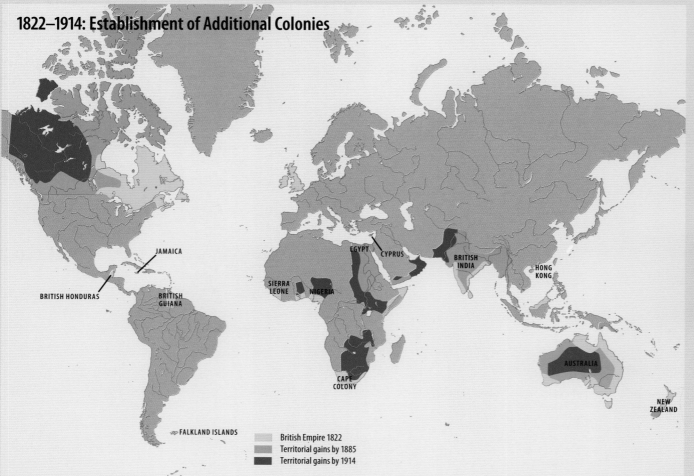

JAMAICA
EGYPT
CYPRUS
BRITISH INDIA
HONG KONG
SIERRA LEONE
NIGERIA
BRITISH HONDURAS
BRITISH GUIANA
CAPE COLONY
AUSTRALIA
NEW ZEALAND
FALKLAND ISLANDS

British Empire 1822
Territorial gains by 1885
Territorial gains by 1914

At its height, the British Empire was the largest colonial empire in history.

1485–1509 Rule of Henry VII, who founded a merchant navy and built dockyards.

1496–1497 John Cabot's voyages of exploration to North America

1577–1580 Sir Francis Drake circumnavigates the globe and lays claim to Nova Albion (now northern California).

Sir Francis Drake (1540–1595)

1583 Establishment of the first English settlement in the New World, St. John's in Newfoundland, Canada

1620 Plymouth Colony is founded in Massachusetts, soon followed by colonization of the eastern coast of North America.

1664 British seize the Dutch colony of New Amsterdam (now New York).

1756–1763 Colonial war with France results in conquest of French territories in India and North America (Ohio, Quebec, part of Louisiana).

from 1770 Australia is claimed for Britain by James Cook.

1776 Thirteen British colonies in North America sign the Declaration of Independence; the Revolutionary War ensues.

1783 The Treaty of Paris marks the official end of the war between Britain and its former American colonies.

1841 The British take control of Hong Kong.

1857 Territories of the East India Company come under direct control of the British Crown. The crown colony of British India is established (until 1947).

1877 Queen Victoria is proclaimed empress of India.

1882–1922 British rule in Egypt

1885–1914 Britain acquires significant colonial possessions in Africa (about one third of the continent).

1921 The Irish Free State (now Irish Republic) is declared.

After 1926 Imperial Conference in London and the Statute

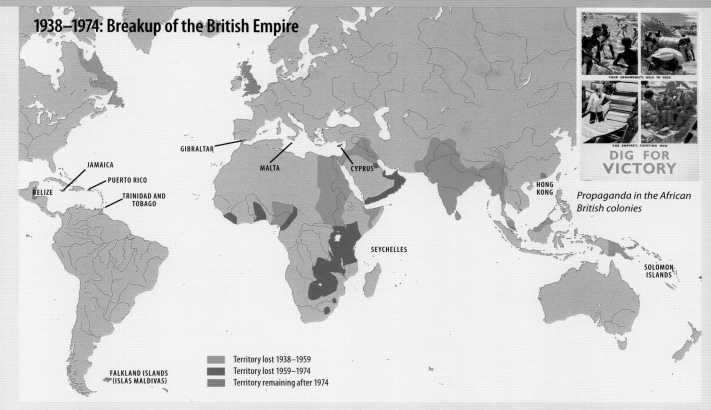

1938–1974: Breakup of the British Empire

- Territory lost 1938–1959
- Territory lost 1959–1974
- Territory remaining after 1974

Propaganda in the African British colonies

DIG FOR VICTORY

of Westminster (1931); Britain makes a transition from empire to commonwealth.

1947 India and Pakistan become independent nations (both remain members of the Commonwealth).

1948–1968 The British Empire comes to an end in Africa.

1997 End of Britain's ninety-nine-year lease on Hong Kong, which reverts to the People's Republic of China.

New Amsterdam – New York From 1624 to 1664, this settlement was the capital of the Dutch colony of New Netherlands in North America. Seized by the English on August 27, 1664, without a shot being fired, it was renamed New York in honor of James, Duke of York, who later became King James II.

The East India Company was a trading company established in England in 1600 that strictly controlled trade with India due to its trading monopoly. Later the company was granted the rights to build fortifications and

maintain armies, administer territories and mint coins. After 1773 the company was subject to the government's control in administrative matters. In 1857, following repeated Indian rebellions, the East India Company lost control of its territories, which came under direct rule of the Crown.

British Commonwealth of Nations A loose association of former British colonies that are all recognized as equal member states (called the Commonwealth of Nations after 1947)

Hong Kong Occupied in 1841 during the First Opium War with China, the British colony of Hong Kong was officially ceded by China to Great Britain on August 29, 1842. The ninety-nine-year lease signed on June 9, 1898, included the territories north of Hong Kong. In 1997 both territories controlled by the British reverted back to China, under the condition that their political and economic systems would be maintained.

Since 1974

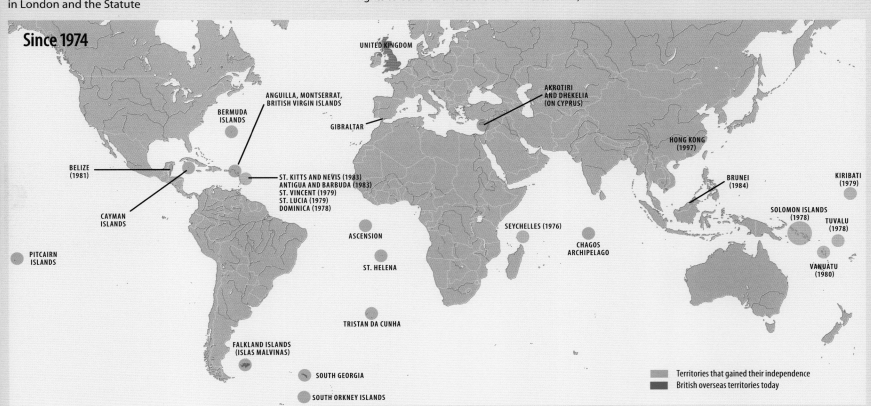

- Territories that gained their independence
- British overseas territories today

Ireland in the 20th Century

1922: Historic Counties

- Irish Free State
- Border between the Republic of Ireland and Northern Ireland
- Borders between the historic Irish provinces

1916 An anti-British uprising (Easter Rising) in Dublin is brutally suppressed.

1920 First "Bloody Sunday": Fourteen British police officers are murdered by the IRA.

1921 The Anglo-Irish Treaty between Great Britain and Ireland is signed, granting independence to twenty-six southern counties, which later become the Irish Free State. April: Civil War between supporters and opponents of partition from England.

1922 Creation of the Irish Free State (which becomes a British dominion); Northern Ireland (County of Ulster) remains part of Great Britain.

1932 Prime Minister de Valera refuses to swear allegiance to the British Crown.

1937 Ireland becomes a republic (Éire).

1939–1945 Ireland remains neutral during World War II.

1949 Ireland withdraws from the Commonwealth.

early 1960s A program of economic stimulus spearheaded by Prime Minister Lemass successfully raises the standard of living in Ireland.

1967 Northern Ireland Civil Rights Association is founded to pursue equality for Catholics in Northern Ireland.

1969 Militant Protestants attack a peaceful protest march of Northern Irish Catholics on the bridge in Burntollet, beginning a long and bloody civil war.

1972 Second "Bloody Sunday": Thirteen Northern Irish Catholics are shot by British troops at a protest march that had been banned.

1973 Ireland becomes a member of the EU. The IRA (Irish Republican Army) wages a terrorist campaign in Ulster and Great Britain.

1976 As revenge for the death of six Catholics, the IRA kills ten Protestants outside the village of Kingsmill.

1982 Two IRA bomb blasts in London result in ten casualties.

1985 The Anglo-Irish Agreement gives Ireland some say in the affairs of Northern Ireland.

1990s The Irish economy experiences a period of strong growth.

1993 Eight civilians are killed in an attack by pro-British loyalists at a bar in Greysteel (Derry).

1998 The Belfast (Good Friday) Agreement brings together the warring factions in Northern Ireland and creates structures for joint administration of Ireland and Northern Ireland; weapons are decommissioned. August: A republican splinter group calling itself the "Real IRA" plants a car bomb in the Northern Irish town of Omagh, killing twenty-nine people. Leaders of both parties condemn the attack.

2005 The IRA declares the end of armed conflict.

Eamon de Valera (1882–1975) was one of the leaders of the 1916 Easter Rising. He was sentenced to death as a terrorist, but the sentence was commuted to life imprisonment and he was granted amnesty a year later. In 1917 he was leader of Sinn Féin, from 1919–1921 president of the provisional government of the Republic of Ireland, and in 1922/23 a leader in the Irish Civil War. De Valera was prime minister of the Republic for most of the time between 1932 and 1959; he reached an agreement with Great Britain and from 1959 to 1973 was president of Ireland.

Counties Today

- Ireland – Northern Ireland border

Ireland

After decades of political and armed resistance, Ireland finally won its independence from Great Britain after World War I. This process was accelerated by the anti-British uprising in 1916 and by the bloody events of 1920. One year later, Ireland signed the Anglo-Irish Treaty with Great Britain, which granted independence to Southern Ireland; the treaty went into effect in 1922. The Irish Free State was created and formally became a British dominion (an independent nation with an allegiance to the Crown). Northern Ireland, however, remained part of Great Britain. During the next decade Ireland attempted to break off all formal ties with Great Britain. When he took office in 1932, Irish Prime Minister Eamon de Valera refused to swear allegiance to the British Crown. In 1937 Ireland became a republic and the British monarch was no longer its official sovereign. During World War II Ireland remained neutral, finally withdrawing from the Commonwealth after the war. Ireland became a member of the European Union in 1973. During the 1990s, thanks to its accession to the EU, its liberal tax legislation and prudent investments in infrastructure and education, Ireland experienced rapid economic growth. Ireland was the first European country to be pushed into recession by the financial crisis of 2008.

Conflict in Northern Ireland The northern counties remained part of Great Britain after the rest of the island became independent. Tensions between Catholics and Protestants in Northern Ireland were exacerbated by violence perpetrated by radicals who sought unification with the Republic of Ireland. After a peaceful period in the 1950s, the conflict was reignited in 1969. The paramilitary Protestant organizations responded to the IRA's terrorist attacks in kind. A breakthrough was finally achieved through the Belfast Agreement in 1998, which was negotiated between the governments of Great Britain and Ireland.

IRA The Irish Republican Army began its fight for independence from Great Britain in the 19th century. Terrorist attacks were its preferred method. After the creation of an independent Irish state, it continued to perpetrate violence against opponents of the unification of all Ireland. The group was officially declared illegal in 1936 by the Irish government. After a peaceful period in the 1950s, it returned to its tactics of bombing British targets in the 1970s and 1980s. After the Belfast Agreement of 1998, it agreed to disarm and use only peaceful means to further its cause. Various splinter groups of the IRA, however, continue to perpetrate violent acts from time to time.

Ulster Unionist Party (UUP) Protestant party in Northern Ireland founded in 1905. The UUP lost the leadership of the Protestants in 2005 to the more radical Democratic Unionist Party (DUP) led by Ian Paisley, a Presbyterian minister who took a hard line against the Catholics.

1969–1998: Civil War in Northern Ireland

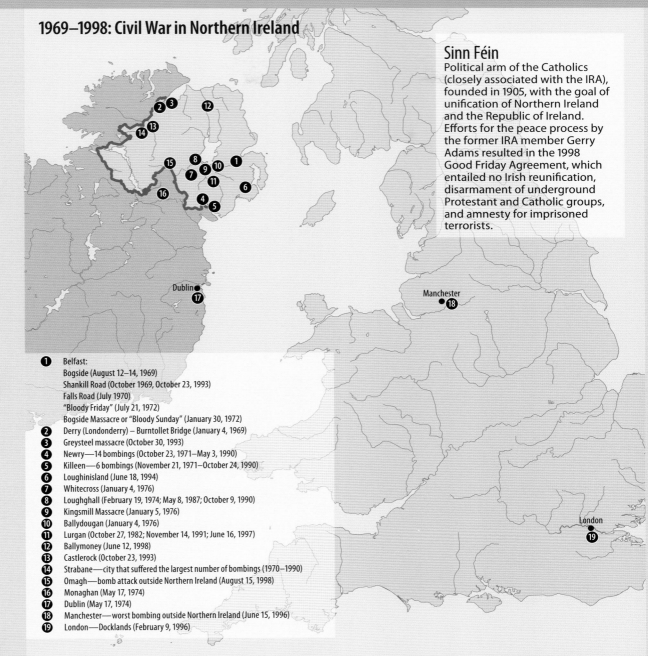

Sinn Féin

Political arm of the Catholics (closely associated with the IRA), founded in 1905, with the goal of unification of Northern Ireland and the Republic of Ireland. Efforts for the peace process by the former IRA member Gerry Adams resulted in the 1998 Good Friday Agreement, which entailed no Irish reunification, disarmament of underground Protestant and Catholic groups, and amnesty for imprisoned terrorists.

1. Belfast:
   Bogside (August 12–14, 1969)
   Shankill Road (October 1969, October 23, 1993)
   Falls Road (July 1970)
   "Bloody Friday" (July 21, 1972)
   Bogside Massacre or "Bloody Sunday" (January 30, 1972)
2. Derry (Londonderry) – Burntollet Bridge (January 4, 1969)
3. Greysteel massacre (October 30, 1993)
4. Newry—14 bombings (October 23, 1971–May 3, 1990)
5. Killeen—6 bombings (November 21, 1971–October 24, 1990)
6. Loughinisland (June 18, 1994)
7. Whitecross (January 4, 1976)
8. Loughghall (February 19, 1974; May 8, 1987; October 9, 1990)
9. Kingsmill Massacre (January 5, 1976)
10. Ballydougan (January 4, 1976)
11. Lurgan (October 27, 1982; November 14, 1991; June 16, 1997)
12. Ballymoney (June 12, 1998)
13. Castlerock (October 23, 1993)
14. Strabane—city that suffered the largest number of bombings (1970–1990)
15. Omagh—bomb attack outside Northern Ireland (August 15, 1998)
16. Monaghan (May 17, 1974)
17. Dublin (May 17, 1974)
18. Manchester—worst bombing outside Northern Ireland (June 15, 1996)
19. London—Docklands (February 9, 1996)

Denominations

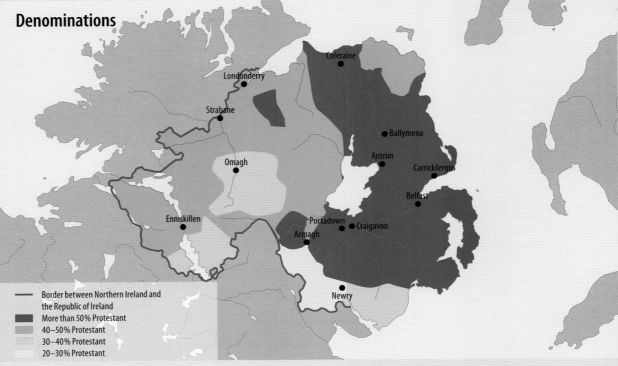

Border between Northern Ireland and the Republic of Ireland
More than 50% Protestant
40–50% Protestant
30–40% Protestant
20–30% Protestant

England and Great Britain – Kings, Rulers and Prime Ministers

Kings of England

Anglo-Saxons
886–899 Alfred the Great (king of Wessex from 871)

Alfred the Great (847–899)

899–924 Edward I the Elder
924 Alfweard (reign of 16 days)
924–939 Athelstan
939–946 Edmund I
946–955 Eadred
955–959 Eadwig (Eadwy)
959–975 Edgar
975–978 Edward II the Martyr
978–1013 Aethelred II the Unready; dethroned

Danish Jelling Dynasty – Personal Union with Denmark
1013–1014 Sweyn I Forkbeard (king of Denmark since 986, also of Norway since 1000)

Anglo-Saxons
1014–1016 Ethelred II (restored)
1016 Edmund II Ironside

Danish Jelling Dynasty – Personal Union with Denmark
1016–1035 Canute the Great (king of Denmark from 1019, also of Norway after 1028)
1035–1040 Harold I (king of England only)
1040–1042 Hardecanute or Canute II (king of Denmark since 1035)

Anglo-Saxons
1042–1066 Edward III the Confessor
1066 Harold II
1066 Edgar the Aetheling, uncrowned heir

Normans
1066–1087 William I the Conqueror (duke of Normandy since 1035)
1087–1100 William II Rufus
1100–1135 Henry I Beauclerc ("the good scholar")
1135–1154 Stephan of Blois, also duke of Normandy 1135–1137

House of Anjou-Plantagenet
1154–1189 Henry II, duke of Normandy since 1150, also count of Anjou and Maine
1189–1199 Richard I Lion-heart

Richard I Lion-heart (1157–1199)

1199–1216 John Lackland
1216–1272 Henry III

1272–1307 Edward I Longshanks
1307–1327 Edward II (deposed and killed)
1327–1377 Edward III
1377–1399 Richard II, deposed (killed in 1400)

House of Lancaster
1399–1413 Henry IV
1413–1422 Henry V
1422–1461 Henry VI, deposed

House of York
1461–1470 Edward IV, deposed

House of Lancaster
1470–1471 Henry VI, restored, deposed

House of York
1471–1483 Edward IV, restored
1483 Edward V (killed)
1483–1485 Richard III Plantagenet (died in battle)

House of Tudor
1485–1509 Henry VII
1509– Henry VIII (in 1542 becomes king of Ireland as well)

Henry VIII (1491–1547)

from 1542 Kings of England and Ireland
1542–1547 Henry VIII
1547–1553 Edward VI
1553 Lady Jane Grey, deposed and executed
1553–1558 Mary I ("Bloody Mary")
1558–1603 Elizabeth I

Kings of England, Scotland and Ireland

House of Stuart
1603–1625 James I (king of Scotland as James VI since 1567)
1625–1649 Charles I (executed)

Charles I (1600–1649)

The Commonwealth
1649–1653 Parliament with 40 members
1653–1658 Lord Protector Oliver Cromwell
1658–1659 Lord Protector Richard Cromwell

House of Stuart (restored)
1660–1685 Charles II
1685–1688 James II, deposed

House of Orange-Nassau
1689–1702 William III

House of Stuart (restored)
1702– Anne

from 1707 Queen of Great Britain (England and Scotland are fully united by the Act of Union) as well as Ireland
1707–1714 Anne

House of Hanover
1714–1727 George I
1727–1760 George II
1760– George III

from 1801 King of the United Kingdom of Great Britain and Ireland
1801–1820 George III (after 1811 under regency)
1820–1830 George IV (Prince Regent since 1811)
1830–1837 William IV
1837–1901 Victoria

Victoria (1819–1901)

House of Saxe-Coburg-Gotha (dynasty renamed due to Victoria's marriage with Albert of Saxe-Coburg-Gotha)
1901–1910 Edward VII
1910– George V

House of Windsor (dynasty renamed in 1917 due to hostilities with Germany)
1917– George V

from 1927 King of the United Kingdom of Great Britain and Northern Ireland
1927–1936 George V
1936 Edward VIII, abdicated
1936–1952 George VI
1952– Elizabeth II

Kings of Scotland

House of Alpin
843–858 Kenneth I
858–862 Donald I
862–877 Constantine I
877–878 Aed
878–889 Eochaid
889–900 Donald II
900–943 Constantine II
943–954 Malcolm I
954–962 Indulf
962–966 Dubh
966–971 Cuilean
971–995 Kenneth II
995–997 Constantine III
997–1005 Kenneth III
1005–1034 Malcolm II

House of Dunkeld
1034–1040 Duncan I

Various Houses
1040–1057 Macbeth
1057–1058 Lulach

House of Dunkeld (restored)
1058–1093 Malcolm III Canmore
1093–1094 Donald III
1094 Duncan II
1094–1097 Donald III (restored) and Edmund

1097–1107	Edgar
1107–1124	Alexander I
1124–1153	David I
1153–1165	Malcolm IV
1165–1214	William I the Lion
1214–1249	Alexander II
1249–1286	Alexander III
1286–1290	Margaret (the Maid of Norway)
1290–1292	*Interregnum – competition for the throne*

House of Balliol
1292–1296	John Balliol
1296–1306	*Interregnum – Scottish Wars of Independence against England*

House of Bruce
1306–1329	Robert I the Bruce
1329–1332	David II Bruce, expelled

House of Balliol
1332–1342	Edward Balliol, deposed

House of Bruce
1342–1371	David II Bruce (restored)

House of Stuart
1371–1390	Robert II
1390–1406	Robert III
1406–1437	James I
1437–1460	James II
1460–1488	James III
1488–1513	James IV
1513–1542	James V
1542–1567	Mary I
1567–1625	James VI
1603–1707	*Personal union with England*
Since 1707	*Union with England to form Great Britain*

Irish Rulers

High kings of Ireland (some dates are disputed) Ireland was divided into numerous small kingdoms; the high king was primarily an honorary title, with the single exception of Brian Boru.

846–860	Máel Sechnaill mac Máele Ruanaid
861–876	Aed Finnliath
877–914	Flann Sinna
915–917	Niall Glúndub
918–942	Donnchad Donn
943–954	Congalach Cnogba
955–978	Domnall O'Néill
979–1002	Máel Sechnaill mac Domnall
1002–1014	Brian Boru (from 1005 to 1014 he united Ireland under his sole rule)
1014–1022	Máel Sechnaill mac Domnaill (restored)
before 1064	Donnchad mac Briain
before 1072	Diarmait mac Maíl na mBó
before 1086	Toirdelbach Ua Briain
before 1121	Domnall Ua Lochlainn
before 1119	Muirchertach Ua Briain
before 1156	Turloch O'Connor
before 1166	Muirchertach O'Lochlainn
before 1185	Roderick O'Connor
1185	*Establishment of England's lordship over Ireland: English Prince John Lackland becomes lord of Ireland*
1199–1541	*Lordship of Ireland: personal union with England*
1541–1801	*Kingdom of Ireland: personal union with England/after 1707 Great Britain*
1801–1919	*United Kingdom of Great Britain and Ireland*
1919–1922	*Revolutionary Irish Republic*
1922–1937	*Irish Free State – constitutional monarchy under the umbrella of the British Empire*
1937–1949	*Ireland's status is in transition between a monarchy and a republic.*
1949–	*The Republic of Ireland*

British Prime Ministers

1721/30–1742	Robert Walpole (Whig)
1742–1743	Spencer Compton, 1st earl of Wilmington (Whig)
1743–1754	Henry Pelham (Whig)
1754–1756	Thomas Pelham-Holles, 1st duke of Newcastle (Whig)
1756–1757	William Cavendish, 4th duke of Devonshire (Whig)
1757–1762	Thomas Pelham-Holles, 1st duke of Newcastle (Whig), 2nd term
1762–1763	John Stuart, 3rd earl of Bute (Tory)
1763–1765	George Grenville (Whig)
1765–1766	Charles Watson-Wentworth, 2nd marquess of Rockingham (Whig)
1766–1768	William Pitt the Elder, 1st earl of Chatham

William Pitt the Elder (1708–1778)

	(Whig)
1768–1770	Augustus FitzRoy, 3rd duke of Grafton (Whig)
1770–1782	Frederick North, Lord North (Tory)
1782	Charles Watson-Wentworth, 2nd marquess of Rockingham (Whig)
1782–1783	William Petty, 2nd earl of Shelburne (Whig)
1783	William Henry Cavendish-Bentinck, 3rd duke of Portland (coalition)
1783–1801	William Pitt the Younger (Tory)
1801–1804	Henry Addington (Tory)
1804–1806	William Pitt the Younger (Tory), 2nd term
1806–1807	William Wyndham Grenville, 1st baron of Grenville (Whig)
1807–1809	William Henry Cavendish-Bentinck, 3rd duke of Portland (Tory), 2nd term
1809–1812	Spencer Perceval (Tory)
1812–1827	Robert Banks Jenkinson, 2nd earl of Liverpool (Tory)
1827	George Canning (Tory)
1827–1828	Frederick John Robinson, 1st earl of Ripon (Tory)
1828–1830	Arthur Wellesley, 1st duke of Wellington (Tory)
1830–1834	Charles Grey, 2nd Earl Grey (Whig)
1834	William Lamb, 2nd Viscount Melbourne (Whig)
1834	Arthur Wellesley, 1st duke of Wellington (Tory)
1834–1835	Sir Robert Peel (Conservative)
1835–1841	William Lamb, 2nd Viscount Melbourne (Whig), 2nd term
1841–1846	Sir Robert Peel (Conservative), 2nd term
1846–1852	Lord John Russell (Whig)
1852	Edward Smith-Stanley, 14th earl of Derby (Conservative)
1852–1855	George Hamilton-Gordon, 4th earl of Aberdeen (coalition)
1855–1858	Henry John Temple, 3rd Viscount Palmerston (Whig)
1858–1859	Edward Smith-Stanley, 14th earl of Derby (Conservative), 2nd term
1859–1865	Henry John Temple, 3rd Viscount Palmerston (Liberal), 2nd term
1865–1866	John Russell, 1st Earl Russell (Liberal)
1866–1868	Edward Smith-Stanley, 14th earl of Derby (Conservative), 3rd term
1868	Benjamin Disraeli (Conservative)
1868–1874	William Ewart Gladstone (Liberal)
1874–1880	Benjamin Disraeli (Conservative), 2nd term
1880–1885	William Ewart Gladstone (Liberal), 2nd term
1885–1886	Robert Cecil, 3rd marquess of Salisbury (Conservative)
1886	William Ewart Gladstone (Liberal), 3rd term
1886–1892	Robert Cecil, 3rd marquess of Salisbury (Conservative), 2nd term
1892–1894	William Ewart Gladstone (Liberal), 4th term
1894–1895	Archibald Primrose, 5th earl of Rosebery (Liberal)
1895–1902	Robert Cecil, 3rd marquess of Salisbury (Conservative/Unionist), 2nd term
1902–1905	Arthur Balfour (Conservative/Unionist)
1905–1908	Sir Henry Campbell-Bannerman (Liberal)
1908–1915	Herbert Henry Asquith (Liberal)
1915–1916	Herbert Henry Asquith (Liberal/coalition), 2nd term
1916–1922	David Lloyd George (National Liberal/coalition)
1922–1923	Andrew Bonar Law (Conservative)
1923–1924	Stanley Baldwin (Conservative)
1924	J. Ramsay MacDonald (Labour)
1924–1929	Stanley Baldwin (Conservative), 2nd term
1929–1931	J. Ramsay MacDonald (Labour), 2nd term
1931–1935	J. Ramsay MacDonald (National Labour/National Government), 3rd term
1935–1937	Stanley Baldwin (Conservative/National Government), 3rd term
1937–1940	Neville Chamberlain (Conservative/National Government)
1940–1945	Winston Churchill (Conservative/coalition)
1945	Winston Churchill (Conservative/transitional government), 2nd ministry
1945–1951	Clement Attlee (Labour)

Winston Churchill (1874–1965)

1951–1955	Sir Winston Churchill (Conservative), 3rd term
1955–1957	Sir Anthony Eden (Conservative)
1957–1963	Harold Macmillan (Conservative)
1963–1964	Sir Alec Douglas-Home (Conservative)
1964–1970	Harold Wilson (Labour)
1970–1974	Edward Heath (Conservative)
1974–1976	Harold Wilson (Labour), 2nd term
1976–1979	James Callaghan (Labour)

Margaret Thatcher (1925–)

1979–1990	Margaret Thatcher (Conservative)
1990–1997	John Major (Conservative)
1997–2007	Tony Blair (Labour)
2007–	Gordon Brown (Labour)

The Low Countries: The Netherlands, Belgium and Luxembourg

Prehistory until the 1st Century BCE

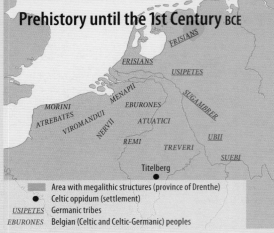

Area with megalithic structures (province of Drenthe)
● Celtic oppidum (settlement)
USIPETES Germanic tribes
EBURONES Belgian (Celtic and Celtic-Germanic) peoples

Early 2nd Century CE

Germania Inferior
Belgica

855: The Treaties of Verdun and Prüm

Lotharii Regnum: borders of the kingdom of Lothar I after the Treaty of Verdun in 843
Territory of Carolingian Lotharingia after the Treaty of Prüm in 855

880: The Treaty of Ribemont

West Francia (kingdom of Odo of France 888)
Kingdom of Arnulf (East Francia)
Kingdom of Upper Burgundy
Patrimonium Petri (Papal States)

482–814: The Frankish Empire

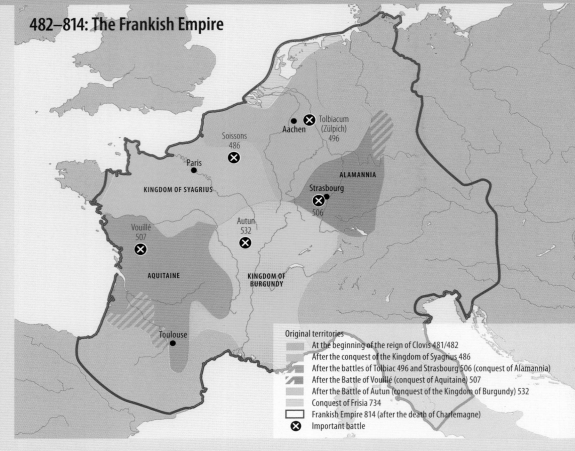

Original territories
At the beginning of the reign of Clovis 481/482
After the conquest of the Kingdom of Syagrius 486
After the battles of Tolbiac 496 and Strasbourg 506 (conquest of Alamannia)
After the Battle of Vouillé (conquest of Aquitaine) 507
After the Battle of Autun (conquest of the Kingdom of Burgundy) 532
Conquest of Frisia 734
Frankish Empire 814 (after the death of Charlemagne)
❌ Important battle

Over the course of an eventful history, the three states collectively known as the Low Countries first appeared in their current forms in the 19th century. The United Kingdom of the Netherlands was established in 1815 at the Congress of Vienna, while Belgium and Luxembourg became independent states in 1830.

3500–2800 BCE First evidence of human settlement dates from this time, for example the fifty-two megalithic structures in the Dutch province of Drenthe.

53–51 BCE Roman campaigns in the area result in the annihilation of the Belgic tribe of the Eburones.

27 BCE–14 CE The Roman province of *Belgica* is founded. What is now the southern Netherlands is gradually conquered under Caesar Augustus.

85–90 The Roman province of *Germania Inferior* is established.

355–358 The Franks are settled as Roman *foederati* south of the Rhine. Their heartland lies in today's Belgium and northern France.

734 The Franks conquer Frisia.

772–804 Charlemagne defeats and Christianizes the Saxons living in the northeastern Netherlands.

843 The Treaty of Verdun makes the Low Countries part of Lothar I's Middle Francia (*Lotharii Regnum*).

855 Lothar's domains are divided according to the Treaty of Prüm among his three sons: Louis II, Lothar II and Charles.

880 The Treaty of Ribemont: Lotharingia goes to East Francia. The territory subsequently splits into numerous medieval counties, duchies and bishoprics.

1302–1304 In Flanders' first struggle for independence, the wool weavers of Brugge stage a successful revolt against French rule.

1354 Luxembourg is elevated to the status of duchy.

1363/84–1477 The grand dukes of Burgundy establish a powerful state that stretches between France and the Holy Roman Empire. The Flemish cloth industry becomes Western Europe's driving economic force.

1382 At the Battle of Roosebeke, French forces defeat an uprising of Flemish burghers.

1384 The territories of Margaret, the heiress of the count of Flanders, become the property of her husband, Duke Philip the Bold of Burgundy.

1384–1556 The Burgundian Netherlands comprises the territories of today's Netherlands, Belgium and Luxembourg.

1421 Philip the Good, Duke of Burgundy, purchases the County of Namur.

1430 After the death of the childless Philip of Saint-Pol, Brabant and Limburg come under the control of Philip the Good.

1433 According to the Treaty of the Hague, Jacqueline of Bavaria cedes Holland, Zeeland and Hainaut to Philip the Good.

1441–1443 The last duchess of the House of Luxembourg sells her territory to Philip the Good.

1467–1477 Charles the Bold is duke of Burgundy. He attempts to elevate Burgundy to a kingdom and engages in bitter struggles with France.

1472–1473 Charles the Bold purchases the Duchy of Guelders, and Burgundy reaches the apex of its power.

1477 Charles the Bold is killed at the Battle of Nancy. His daughter, Mary of Burgundy, marries Maximilian of Austria against the wishes of the French crown.

959: Lotharingia

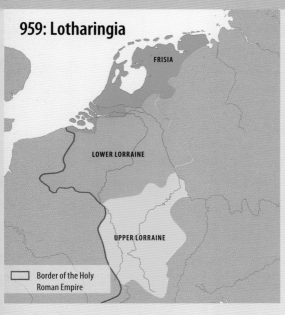

FRISIA

LOWER LORRAINE

UPPER LORRAINE

☐ Border of the Holy
  Roman Empire

Roman foederati Foreign tribes that were not granted Roman citizenship, but formed alliances with the Romans. The foederati supplied Rome's armies with soldiers in exchange for varying forms of support.

The Burgundian Netherlands The Burgundian Netherlands was a collection of territories acquired by the Burgundian branch of the Valois dynasty (1384–1477) through marriage, treaty and inheritance. The dukes of Burgundy held court in Brussels in the province of Brabant, while governors administered the remaining provinces. In some parts of Burgundy, the Valois dukes were followed by the Habsburgs (1477–1566), who owned territory along the Upper Rhine (Sundgau, Breisgau and the Austrian Forelands) and the Lower Rhine (Holland, Flanders, Zeeland, etc.).

1384–1477: The Burgundian Netherlands

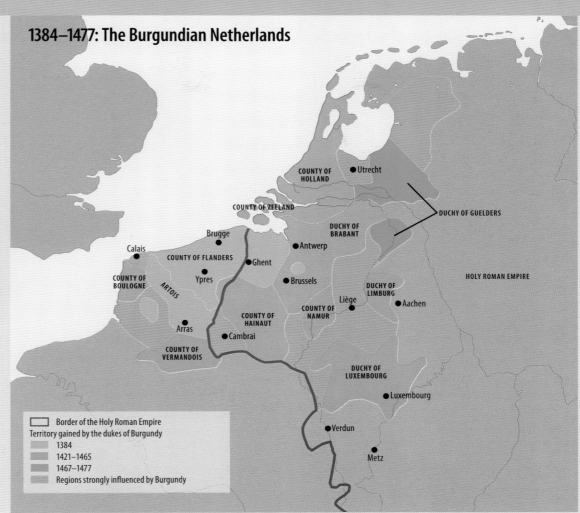

COUNTY OF HOLLAND · Utrecht
COUNTY OF ZEELAND
DUCHY OF GUELDERS
Brugge · DUCHY OF BRABANT
Calais · Antwerp
COUNTY OF FLANDERS · Ghent
COUNTY OF BOULOGNE · Ypres · Brussels
ARTOIS · Liège · DUCHY OF LIMBURG · Aachen
COUNTY OF NAMUR
HOLY ROMAN EMPIRE
Arras · COUNTY OF HAINAUT
Cambrai
COUNTY OF VERMANDOIS
DUCHY OF LUXEMBOURG
Luxembourg
Verdun
Metz

☐ Border of the Holy Roman Empire
Territory gained by the dukes of Burgundy
■ 1384
■ 1421–1465
■ 1467–1477
■ Regions strongly influenced by Burgundy

1467–1477: Burgundy under Charles the Bold

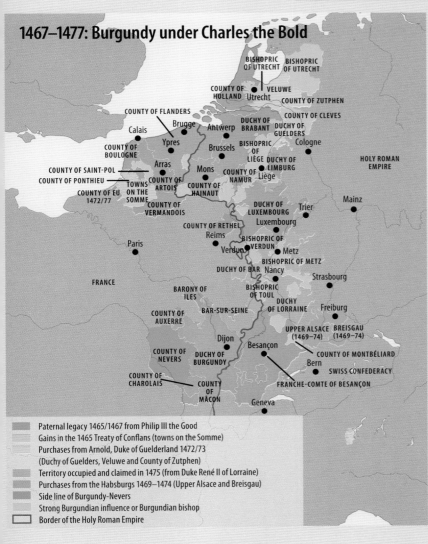

BISHOPRIC OF UTRECHT · BISHOPRIC OF UTRECHT
COUNTY OF HOLLAND · VELUWE
Utrecht · COUNTY OF ZUTPHEN
COUNTY OF FLANDERS · COUNTY OF CLEVES
Calais · Brugge · Antwerp · DUCHY OF BRABANT · DUCHY OF GUELDERS
Ypres · Brussels · Cologne
COUNTY OF BOULOGNE · BISHOPRIC OF LIÈGE
COUNTY OF SAINT-POL · Arras · Mons · DUCHY OF LIMBURG
COUNTY OF PONTHIEU · COUNTY OF NAMUR · HOLY ROMAN EMPIRE
COUNTY OF EU 1472/77 · TOWNS ON THE SOMME · COUNTY OF ARTOIS · COUNTY OF HAINAUT · Liège
COUNTY OF VERMANDOIS
DUCHY OF LUXEMBOURG · Trier · Mainz
COUNTY OF RETHEL · Luxembourg
Paris · Reims · BISHOPRIC OF VERDUN
Verdun · BISHOPRIC OF METZ · Metz
DUCHY OF BAR · Nancy
FRANCE · BARONY OF ILES · BISHOPRIC OF TOUL · Strasbourg
BAR-SUR-SEINE · DUCHY OF LORRAINE · Freiburg
COUNTY OF AUXERRE · UPPER ALSACE (1469–74) · BREISGAU (1469–74)
Dijon · Besançon · COUNTY OF MONTBÉLIARD
COUNTY OF NEVERS · DUCHY OF BURGUNDY · Bern · SWISS CONFEDERACY
COUNTY OF CHAROLAIS · COUNTY OF MÂCON · FRANCHE-COMTÉ OF BESANÇON
Geneva

■ Paternal legacy 1465/1467 from Philip III the Good
■ Gains in the 1465 Treaty of Conflans (towns on the Somme)
■ Purchases from Arnold, Duke of Guelderland 1472/73 (Duchy of Guelders, Veluwe and County of Zutphen)
■ Territory occupied and claimed in 1475 (from Duke René II of Lorraine)
■ Purchases from the Habsburgs 1469–1474 (Upper Alsace and Breisgau)
■ Side line of Burgundy-Nevers
■ Strong Burgundian influence or Burgundian bishop
☐ Border of the Holy Roman Empire

Burgundy after Charles the Bold

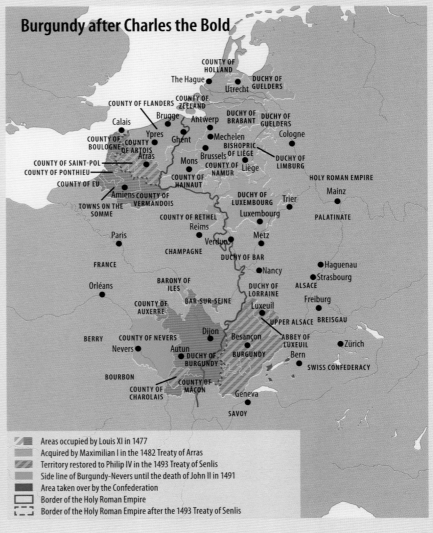

COUNTY OF HOLLAND
The Hague · Utrecht · DUCHY OF GUELDERS
COUNTY OF FLANDERS · COUNTY OF ZEELAND
Calais · Brugge · Antwerp · DUCHY OF BRABANT · DUCHY OF GUELDERS
Ypres · Ghent · Mechelen · Cologne
COUNTY OF BOULOGNE · COUNTY OF ARTOIS · BISHOPRIC OF LIÈGE
COUNTY OF SAINT-POL · Arras · Brussels · DUCHY OF LIMBURG
COUNTY OF PONTHIEU · Mons · COUNTY OF NAMUR · Liège
COUNTY OF EU · COUNTY OF HAINAUT · HOLY ROMAN EMPIRE
Amiens · COUNTY OF VERMANDOIS
TOWNS ON THE SOMME · DUCHY OF LUXEMBOURG · Trier · Mainz
COUNTY OF RETHEL · Luxembourg
Paris · Reims · PALATINATE
CHAMPAGNE · Verdun · Metz · DUCHY OF BAR
FRANCE · Nancy · Haguenau
Orléans · BARONY OF ILES · DUCHY OF LORRAINE · Strasbourg · ALSACE
COUNTY OF AUXERRE · BAR-SUR-SEINE · Luxeuil · Freiburg
BERRY · COUNTY OF NEVERS · UPPER ALSACE · BREISGAU
Nevers · Autun · Dijon · Besançon · ABBEY OF LUXEUIL · Zürich
BOURBON · DUCHY OF BURGUNDY · BURGUNDY · Bern
COUNTY OF CHAROLAIS · COUNTY OF MÂCON · Geneva · SWISS CONFEDERACY
SAVOY

▨ Areas occupied by Louis XI in 1477
■ Acquired by Maximilian I in the 1482 Treaty of Arras
▨ Territory restored to Philip IV in the 1493 Treaty of Senlis
■ Side line of Burgundy-Nevers until the death of John II in 1491
■ Area taken over by the Confederation
☐ Border of the Holy Roman Empire
┄ Border of the Holy Roman Empire after the 1493 Treaty of Senlis

The Low Countries: The Netherlands, Belgium and Luxembourg

1477–1648: The Habsburg Netherlands

Habsburg Netherlands under Charles V
Republic of the Seven United Netherlands in 1585
Spanish Netherlands after 1585
Border of the German Empire ca. 1547

1648–1795: The Netherlands

Republic of the Seven United Netherlands
Territory governed by the Republic of the Seven United Netherlands, called the "Generality Lands" after 1648
Spanish Netherlands 1679–1713, thereafter Austrian Netherlands until 1795
Territory of the Spanish Netherlands ceded to France 1659–1679
Border of the Holy Roman Empire after 1648

1795–1813: French Vassal States

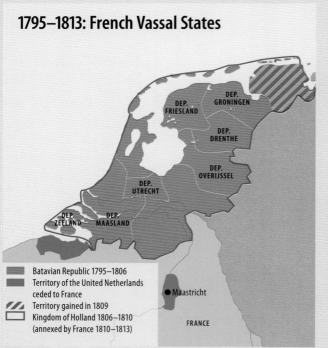

Batavian Republic 1795–1806
Territory of the United Netherlands ceded to France
Territory gained in 1809
Kingdom of Holland 1806–1810 (annexed by France 1810–1813)

1815–1890: The Kingdoms of the Netherlands and Belgium

Border of the Kingdom of the Netherlands 1815–1830
Independent Belgium since 1830
Personal union of Luxembourg and the Netherlands 1815–1890

The Seventeen Provinces The seventeen Dutch provinces were united under the Habsburg emperor Charles V, who had been born in Ghent and educated in Brussels. After his abdication in 1556, the provinces went to his son, King Philip II of Spain.

Republic of the Seven United Provinces (The United Netherlands) The seven Protestant Dutch provinces signed the Union of Utrecht in 1579, joining forces in opposition to their Catholic king, Philip II of Spain, and forming a republic that lasted from 1581 to 1795. The province of Drenthe was part of the union, but had no representation in the States-General. The remaining ten Dutch provinces made up the Spanish Netherlands (which became the Austrian Netherlands after 1713).

1672–1702 William III of Orange is stadtholder of the Netherlands. In the "Glorious Revolution" of 1689, he also becomes King of England.

1713–1714 The Treaties of Utrecht and Rastatt: At the conclusion of the War of Spanish Succession, the Spanish Netherlands becomes the Austrian Netherlands (until 1795).

1789–1790 The Brabant Revolution leads to the proclamation of the United States of Belgium.

1794–1797 France occupies and annexes the southern "Austrian" Netherlands.

1795–1806 The Batavian Republic in the northern Netherlands is a vassal state of France.

1806–1810 The Batavian Republic is replaced by another French vassal state, the Kingdom of Holland, which is ruled by Louis Bonaparte.

1810–1813/14 The Kingdom of Holland is absorbed into the French Empire.

1482 Mary of Burgundy dies. The Netherlands becomes the legacy of Philip the Fair, Mary's son through her marriage to the future king and emperor Maximilian I of Habsburg. Thus begins the rule of the Habsburg dynasty. France occupies southern Burgundy.

1493 Burgundy is divided between France and the House of Habsburg.

1506/15–1556 Charles V rules the Low Countries from 1506, then later becomes king of Spain and Holy Roman emperor. The Netherlands experiences a golden age under Habsburg rule.

1548 The Seventeen Provinces of the Low Countries become a political entity known as the Burgundian Circle under Charles V.

1556 With the abdication of Charles V, control of the Netherlands passes to the Spanish Habsburgs.

1567–1573 The duke of Alba, Spanish governor of the Netherlands, is sent by King Philip to quelch Protestant rebellion and initiates a reign of terror that leads to further tumult.

1568–1648 After the execution of the Dutch freedom fighters Egmont and Hoorn, mounting tension leads to the Eighty Years' War, in which the Dutch, led by William of Orange, fight for their independence from Spanish rule. The Netherlands are divided: the seven northern provinces renounce their ties to the Holy Roman Empire, while the ten in the south remain under Spanish overlordship (Treaty of Westphalia). The Generality Lands remain under the direct control of the States-General.

1579 The Union of Utrecht comprises the seven Protestant (Calvinist) northern provinces. The Catholic territories in the south join the Union of Arras.

July 24, 1581 The Republic of the Seven United Provinces is founded in the north.

1584 On orders of the Spanish, Stadtholder (Governor) William I of Orange is murdered. His sons succeed him as stadtholders.

1585 The Spanish take Antwerp. Flanders and Brabant come under the control of Spain.

1659 According to the terms of the Treaty of the Pyrenees, Spain cedes Artois, Flanders, Hainaut and parts of Luxembourg to France.

World War I

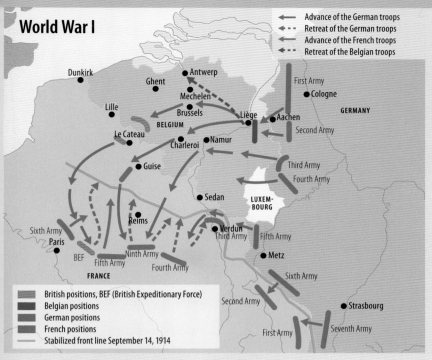

Advance of the German troops
Retreat of the German troops
Advance of the French troops
Retreat of the Belgian troops

British positions, BEF (British Expeditionary Force)
Belgian positions
German positions
French positions
Stabilized front line September 14, 1914

World War II

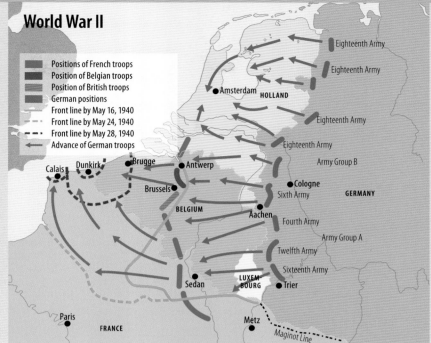

Positions of French troops
Position of Belgian troops
Position of British troops
German positions
Front line by May 16, 1940
Front line by May 24, 1940
Front line by May 28, 1940
Advance of German troops

Generality Lands The Generality Lands were territories conquered by the armies of the Seven United Provinces that were placed under direct control of the States-General (Dutch parliament), but which had no representatives in that body.

Brabant Revolution The Brabant Revolution was an uprising of the middle-class citizens in the Austrian Netherlands directed against their Habsburg rulers and provoked by Enlightenment-influenced reforms made by Emperor Joseph II. The rebellion led to the founding of the first Belgian state, the "United States of Belgium," which existed for only a short time.

Belgian Revolution The Belgian Revolution was a revolt by the Catholic population of the United Kingdom of the Netherlands' southern provinces against the hegemony of the Protestant north. The newly independent Flemish and Wallonian provinces united to become the Kingdom of Belgium under the German dynasty of Saxe-Coburg-Gotha.

Flemings and Walloons Flanders, the five northernmost regions of the Flemings, and Wallonia, the five southern regions of the francophone Walloons, have become increasingly alienated from each other. According to a poll taken in the fall of 2007, only 49.6 percent of Flemings support the continued existence of the Belgian state.

Today

Netherlands
Belgium
Luxembourg

1815 At the Vienna Congress, the United Kingdom of the Netherlands is established with William I of Orange-Nassau as its king. The Netherlands, Belgium and Luxembourg are united under the Dutch crown, yet tensions remain due to economic, religious and cultural/linguistic differences.

1815–1890 The Netherlands and Luxembourg are joined in a personal union.

1830–1831 The Belgian Revolution: Belgium becomes an independent kingdom; its rulers are members of the Saxe-Coburg-Gotha dynasty.

1831–1865 Leopold I is king of Belgium. As uncle to the British royal couple, he is an important shaper of European politics.

1839 The Kingdom of the Netherlands belatedly recognizes Belgian independence. Belgium and the Netherlands divide Limburg.

1867 The Luxembourg Crisis: France tries to purchase the duchy but Prussia and the other Great Powers object.

1890 Luxembourg becomes an independent grand duchy under the House of Nassau-Weillburg, a cadet branch of the Dutch dynasty.

1914–1918 During World War I, Germany occupies Belgium and Luxembourg. The Netherlands remains neutral.

May 10, 1940 The Low Countries' neutrality is violated. German troops attack and occupy the Netherlands, Belgium and Luxembourg.

Sept. 1944 The German *Wehrmacht* withdraws from Belgium and Luxembourg.

May 5, 1945 German forces in the Netherlands capitulate at Wageningen.

1950–1951 Controversy over the behavior of King Leopold III of Belgium during the German occupation leads to riots and a national crisis. In 1951 he abdicates in favor of his son Baudouin (reign from 1951 to 1993), who acts as a guarantor of national unity.

1953 Catastrophic flooding leaves many dead in Zeeland and southern Holland. The Netherlands reacts with

the implementation of the Delta Works, a massive dike-building project.

March 25, 1957 The Treaty of Rome is signed: Belgium, the Netherlands and Luxembourg are among the founding members of the European Economic Community.

Feb. 3, 1958 The Benelux Treaty of Economic Union, which goes into effect in 1960, strengthens economic cooperation between the Benelux countries. The European Economic Community's headquarters are in Brussels.

1960 The Netherlands adopts liberal policies regarding immigration and drugs.

1967 NATO headquarters are located in Brussels.

1980 Queen Beatrix succeeds Queen Juliana as the Dutch head of state.

1986 The new province of Flevoland is created from polders in the central Netherlands.

2002 The right-wing Dutch politician Pim Fortuyn is murdered just before elections.

2004 An Islamist murders Dutch filmmaker Theo van Gogh, whose work has been critical of Islam, thus opening an ongoing discussion about integration politics in the Netherlands.

Dutch and Belgian Colonies

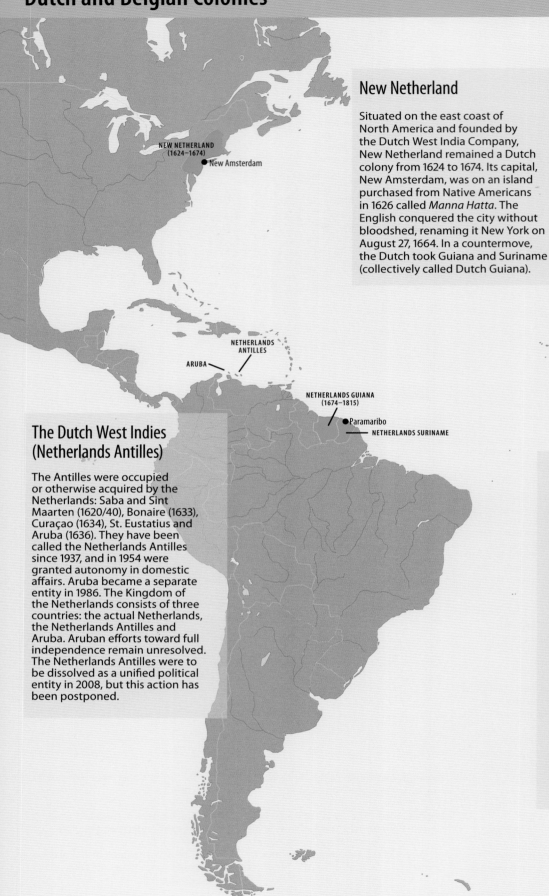

NEW NETHERLAND
(1624–1674)
● New Amsterdam

NETHERLANDS
ANTILLES

ARUBA

NETHERLANDS GUIANA
(1674–1815)
● Paramaribo
— NETHERLANDS SURINAME

BELGIAN
CONGO

Léopoldville ●

CAPE COLO
(1652–1796/
● Cape Town

New Netherland

Situated on the east coast of North America and founded by the Dutch West India Company, New Netherland remained a Dutch colony from 1624 to 1674. Its capital, New Amsterdam, was on an island purchased from Native Americans in 1626 called *Manna Hatta*. The English conquered the city without bloodshed, renaming it New York on August 27, 1664. In a countermove, the Dutch took Guiana and Suriname (collectively called Dutch Guiana).

Leopold II (1835-1909), king of the Belgians

The Dutch West Indies (Netherlands Antilles)

The Antilles were occupied or otherwise acquired by the Netherlands: Saba and Sint Maarten (1620/40), Bonaire (1633), Curaçao (1634), St. Eustatius and Aruba (1636). They have been called the Netherlands Antilles since 1937, and in 1954 were granted autonomy in domestic affairs. Aruba became a separate entity in 1986. The Kingdom of the Netherlands consists of three countries: the actual Netherlands, the Netherlands Antilles and Aruba. Aruban efforts toward full independence remain unresolved. The Netherlands Antilles were to be dissolved as a unified political entity in 2008, but this action has been postponed.

The Belgian Congo

Between 1879 and 1884, the British journalist and African explorer Henry M. Stanley was hired by King Leopold II of Belgium to research and revisit the Congo, where he negotiated hundreds of contracts with native chieftains over the sale of their lands to the Belgian king. Leopold established a private colony, which was named the Congo Free State at the Berlin Conference of 1884/85. Over the following decades, Belgian colonists systematically exploited the territory's inhabitants through forced labor on rubber plantations. Millions of Congolese died, and workers who did not collect enough rubber were punished by having their hands cut off. Only after international opprobrium did Leopold feel obliged to relinquish the colony, renamed the Belgian Congo, to the Belgian state in 1908.

1619 Jan Pieterszoon Coen founds Batavia (now Jakarta) in Indonesia for the United Dutch East India Company.

from 1620 The United Dutch East India Company establishes additional colonies in Indonesia (Dutch East Indies) and South Africa (Cape Colony).

1624–1667/1674 New Netherland is a Dutch colony on the east coast of North America.

1636 The island of Aruba becomes a Dutch colony.

1674 The Second Peace of Westminster:

New Netherland becomes an English colony, and in exchange the South American colony of Guiana becomes a Dutch possession.

1798 The United Dutch East India Company is dissolved.

1806 The Cape Colony in South Africa becomes a British possession.

1815 At the Congress of Vienna, Dutch Guiana is divided into British Guiana and Suriname, which remains a Dutch colony for more than 150 years.

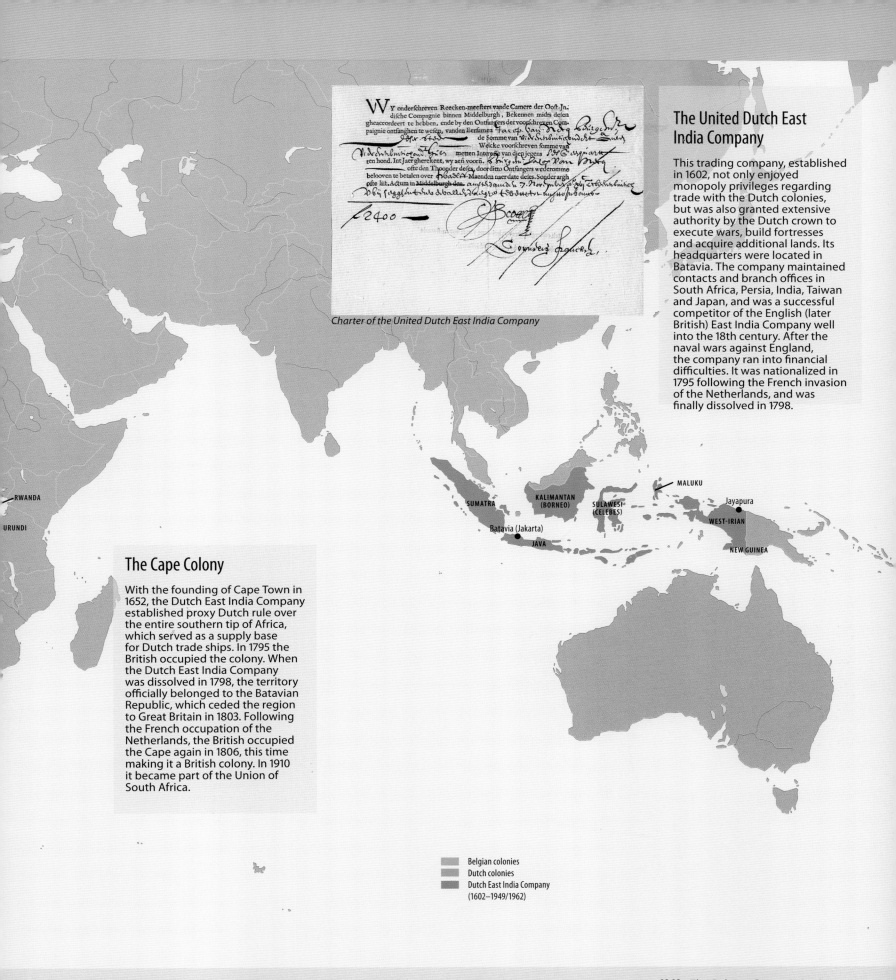

Charter of the United Dutch East India Company

The United Dutch East India Company

This trading company, established in 1602, not only enjoyed monopoly privileges regarding trade with the Dutch colonies, but was also granted extensive authority by the Dutch crown to execute wars, build fortresses and acquire additional lands. Its headquarters were located in Batavia. The company maintained contacts and branch offices in South Africa, Persia, India, Taiwan and Japan, and was a successful competitor of the English (later British) East India Company well into the 18th century. After the naval wars against England, the company ran into financial difficulties. It was nationalized in 1795 following the French invasion of the Netherlands, and was finally dissolved in 1798.

RWANDA

URUNDI

MALUKU

SUMATRA

KALIMANTAN (BORNEO)

SULAWESI (CELEBES)

Jayapura

WEST-IRIAN

Batavia (Jakarta)

JAVA

NEW GUINEA

The Cape Colony

With the founding of Cape Town in 1652, the Dutch East India Company established proxy Dutch rule over the entire southern tip of Africa, which served as a supply base for Dutch trade ships. In 1795 the British occupied the colony. When the Dutch East India Company was dissolved in 1798, the territory officially belonged to the Batavian Republic, which ceded the region to Great Britain in 1803. Following the French occupation of the Netherlands, the British occupied the Cape again in 1806, this time making it a British colony. In 1910 it became part of the Union of South Africa.

Belgian colonies
Dutch colonies
Dutch East India Company
(1602–1949/1962)

1824 An agreement is reached with Great Britain, dividing the Indian Ocean into spheres of influence.

1885–1960 The Congo Free State (private colony of King Leopold II and investors), after 1908 the Belgian Congo controlled by the Belgian government

1916 Belgian forces occupy the German colonies of Rwanda and Burundi, which are incorporated into the Belgian Congo.

1941–1945 Japanese forces occupy the Dutch East Indies.

1945–1949 The Indonesian War of Independence is followed by Dutch recognition of Indonesia.

1954 The Netherlands Antilles are granted complete autonomy.

1960 The Belgian Congo gains its independence.

1962 Burundi and Rwanda are independent, thus marking the end of Belgian colonialism.

Germany – Germania Until the End of the Frankish Empire

Until 200 BCE

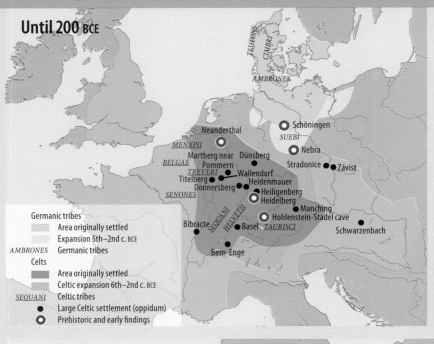

Germanic tribes
- Area originally settled
- Expansion 5th–2nd c. BCE
- *AMBRONES* Germanic tribes

Celts
- Area originally settled
- Celtic expansion 6th–2nd c. BCE
- *SEQUANI* Celtic tribes
- ● Large Celtic settlement (oppidum)
- ◎ Prehistoric and early findings

Roman Provinces in Germania

12 BCE–16 CE: Germania in Roman Times

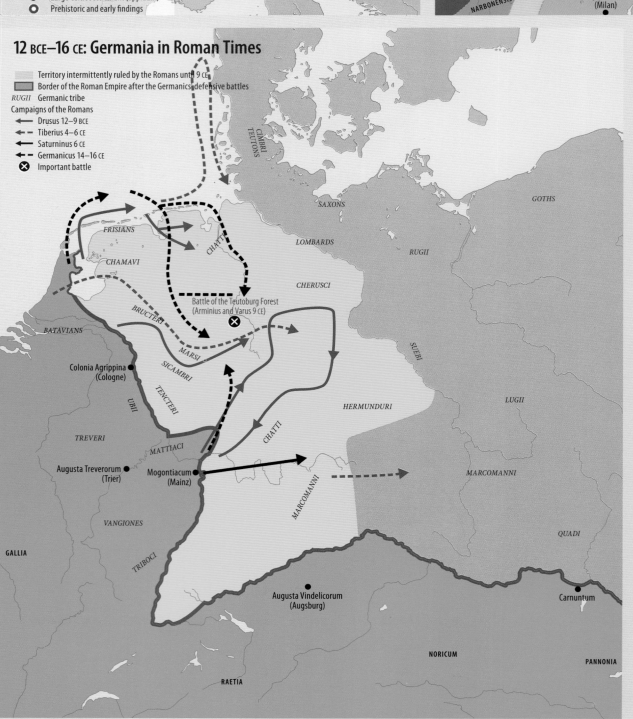

- Territory intermittently ruled by the Romans until 9 CE
- Border of the Roman Empire after the Germanics' defensive battles
- *RUGII* Germanic tribe

Campaigns of the Romans
- → Drusus 12–9 BCE
- ◄-- Tiberius 4–6 CE
- ← Saturninus 6 CE
- ◄-- Germanicus 14–16 CE
- ⊗ Important battle

Until the 3rd century BCE, the land that is now southern Germany was occupied by the Celtic peoples, while Germanic tribes had settled in northern Germany. After Roman Emperor Julius Caesar conquered Gaul in 58–51 BCE, the Roman Empire came into contact with the Germanic peoples. Until the 5th century, the territories on the west side of the Rhine as well as the land south of the Danube were part of the Roman Empire. Numerous cities, such as Trier, Cologne, Bonn, Worms and Augsburg, were founded by the Romans.

600,000–400,000 BCE *Homo heidelbergensis* leaves traces at Heidelberg and Schöningen.

130,000–30,000 BCE Dates of Neanderthal finds near Düsseldorf

~30,000 BCE Date of the ivory "lion man" figure found in a cave in the Swabian Alps

2100–1700 BCE The Nebra Sky Disk found in Saxony-Anhalt is the oldest known astronomical depiction of the night sky.

~500–100 BCE Celtic La Tène culture builds fortified settlements called *oppida*.

~200 BCE Germanic tribes penetrate into central and southern Germany.

9 CE The Cherusci people, led by Arminius, defeat the Romans under General Varus in the Teutoburg Forest.

from 90 The Rhine-Danube defensive wall (*Limes romanus*) is built and the provinces *Germania Superior* (Upper Germania) and *Germania Inferior* (Lower Germania) are established.

166–182 Marcomannic Wars between Germanic tribes and Romans under Marcus Aurelius and his son Commodus

406–407 Germanic peoples invade Gaul.

496–506 Battles of Tolbiac (Zülpich) and Strasbourg: The Franks are victorious over the Alamanni.

531–534 Triumph of the Franks over the Thuringians and Burgundians

751 The Carolingians replace the Merovingians as kings of the Frankish empire.

768–814 Reign of Charlemagne

772–804 Charlemagne's campaigns against the Saxons

788 Charlemagne defeats Bavarian Duke Tassilo III.

843 Treaty of Verdun gives control of East Francia to Louis the German.

855/870 The Treaty of Meerssen divides Middle Francia between the heirs of Lothar I.

880 Treaty of Ribemont: Lotharingia becomes part of East Francia.

899–955 Mounted Hungarian hordes lay waste to southern Germany.

911 End of the Carolingian line and formation of the German stem duchies

919 Henry I (Duke of Saxony) becomes king, beginning the Ottonian dynasty.

2nd–6th Centuries: Invasions by the Germanic Tribes

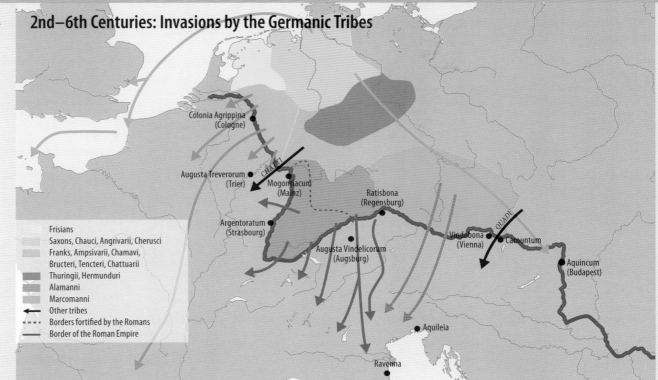

Frisians
Saxons, Chauci, Angrivarii, Cherusci
Franks, Ampsivarii, Chamavi, Bructeri, Tencteri, Chattuarii
Thuringii, Hermunduri
Alamanni
Marcomanni
→ Other tribes
--- Borders fortified by the Romans
— Border of the Roman Empire

Treaty of Verdun in 843 and Division of Frankish Realm in 855

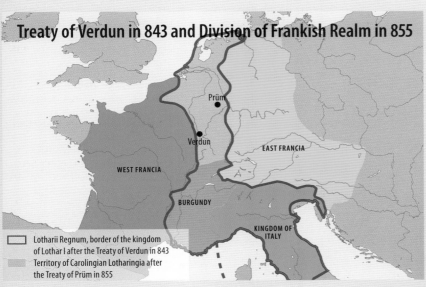

☐ Lotharii Regnum, border of the kingdom of Lothar I after the Treaty of Verdun in 843
▨ Territory of Carolingian Lotharingia after the Treaty of Prüm in 855

482–814: France

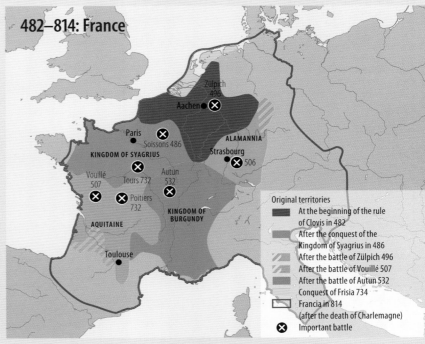

Original territories
■ At the beginning of the rule of Clovis in 482
■ After the conquest of the Kingdom of Syagrius in 486
▨ After the battle of Zülpich 496
▨ After the battle of Vouillé 507
■ After the battle of Autun 532
Conquest of Frisia 734
☐ Francia in 814 (after the death of Charlemagne)
⊗ Important battle

870: Treaty of Meerssen

▨ Dependent territories of West Francia

880: Treaty of Ribemont

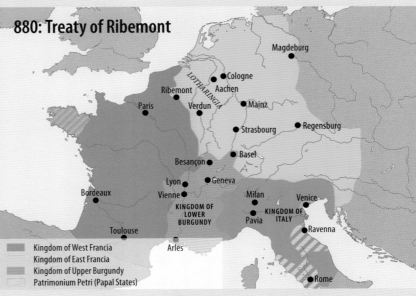

■ Kingdom of West Francia
■ Kingdom of East Francia
■ Kingdom of Upper Burgundy
▨ Patrimonium Petri (Papal States)

Germany – From the Founding of the Empire to Religious Schism

From 962: The Holy Roman Empire

FRISIA
DUCHY OF SAXONY
MARCH OF LUSATIA
THURINGIA
DUCHY OF LOWER LORRAINE
Cologne
DUCHY OF FRANCONIA
DUCHY OF BOHEMIA
Worms
MORAVIA
DUCHY OF UPPER LORRAINE
Regensburg
MARCH OF AUSTRIA
Lechfeld 955
Vienna
DUCHY OF SWABIA
DUCHY OF BAVARIA
DUCHY OF CARINTHIA
KINGDOM OF BURGUNDY (ARELAT)
MARGRAVATE OF VERONA
MARCH OF CARNIOLA
Verona
Venice
KINGDOM OF ITALY
Canossa
Rome

- Regnum Teutonicorum (Kingdom of the Germans)
- Regnum Italicum (Kingdom of Italy)
- Fiefdoms of the Roman-German emperor
- Marches of the empire
- Papal States
- Territory split off after the Slavs' rebellion in 983
- Border of the Holy Roman Empire
- Border of the Holy Roman Empire after 1032
- ⊗ Important battle

1180–1266: Hohenstaufens and Welfs

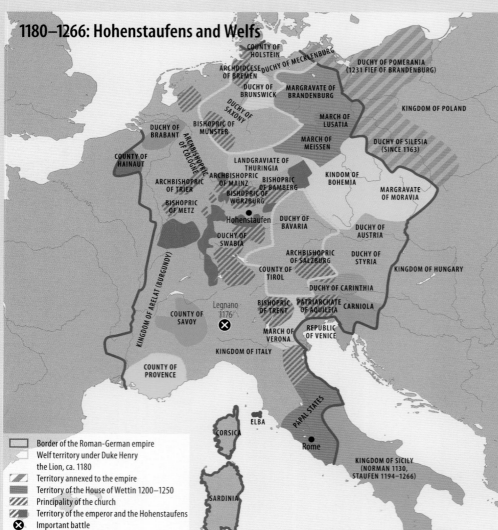

COUNTY OF HOLSTEIN
ARCHDIOCESE OF BREMEN
DUCHY OF MECKLENBURG
DUCHY OF POMERANIA (1231 FIEF OF BRANDENBURG)
DUCHY OF BRUNSWICK
MARGRAVATE OF BRANDENBURG
DUCHY OF SAXONY
DUCHY OF BRABANT
BISHOPRIC OF MÜNSTER
KINGDOM OF POLAND
ARCHBISHOPRIC OF COLOGNE
MARCH OF LUSATIA
COUNTY OF HAINAUT
MARCH OF MEISSEN
LANDGRAVIATE OF THURINGIA
DUCHY OF SILESIA (SINCE 1163)
ARCHBISHOPRIC OF TRIER
ARCHBISHOPRIC OF MAINZ
BISHOPRIC OF BAMBERG
KINDOM OF BOHEMIA
BISHOPRIC OF METZ
BISHOPRIC OF WÜRZBURG
MARGRAVATE OF MORAVIA
Hohenstaufen
DUCHY OF BAVARIA
DUCHY OF SWABIA
DUCHY OF AUSTRIA
ARCHBISHOPRIC OF SALZBURG
DUCHY OF STYRIA
KINGDOM OF ARELAT (BURGUNDY)
COUNTY OF TIROL
Legnano 1176
BISHOPRIC OF TRENT
PATRIARCHATE OF AQUILEIA
CARNIOLA
COUNTY OF SAVOY
MARCH OF VERONA
DUCHY OF CARINTHIA
KINGDOM OF HUNGARY
REPUBLIC OF VENICE
KINGDOM OF ITALY
COUNTY OF PROVENCE
PAPAL STATES
ELBA
CORSICA
Rome
KINGDOM OF SICILY (NORMAN 1130, STAUFEN 1194–1266)
SARDINIA

- Border of the Roman-German empire
- Welf territory under Duke Henry the Lion, ca. 1180
- Territory annexed to the empire
- Territory of the House of Wettin 1200–1250
- Principality of the church
- Territory of the emperor and the Hohenstaufens
- ⊗ Important battle

936–973 During the reign of Otto I the Great, central power is reinforced and the empire expands into northern and central Italy.

955 Battle of Lechfeld: Otto I defeats the Magyars.

962 Otto I is crowned emperor of the Holy Roman Empire.

982 At the Battle of Cape Colonna (southern Italy), Arabs are victorious over Otto II.

983 Slavic rebellion and loss of the territories east of the Elbe

1024 End of the Ottonian lineage. The Frankish Salian dynasty comes to power.

1032 Conrad II acquires Burgundy, and the Holy Roman Empire thus reaches its greatest extent.

1039–1056 Emperor Henry III puts German reform bishops on the papal throne.

1077 Climax of the Investiture Controversy, the ongoing battle between pope and emperor for control of clerical appointments, and Emperor Henry IV's penance before Pope Gregory VII at Canossa (Walk to Canossa)

1122 Concordat of Worms: compromise solution with the church under Henry V

1138 Conrad III becomes king, putting the House of Hohenstaufen on the throne.

1152–1190 Reign of Frederick I Barbarossa (crowned emperor in 1155), who struggles with Italian communes and the pope

1176 Battle of Legnano: An alliance of northern Italian cities (the Lombard League) defeats Frederick I Barbarossa.

1180 Barbarossa triumphs over Duke Henry the Lion of Bavaria and Saxony and acquires Bavaria for the Wittelsbachs.

1194 Frederick's son, Emperor Henry VI, conquers Sicily.

1212–1250 Reign of Frederick II (resides in Apulia and Sicily)

1254 With the end of the Hohenstaufen dynasty in Germany, the Great Interregnum begins and the empire is fragmented into numerous territorial lordships.

1268 Execution of the last member of the Hohenstaufen dynasty, Conradin, in Naples

1273 Rudolf of Habsburg becomes king.

1278 Rudolf is victorious over the Bohemian king Ottokar II, marking the beginning of Habsburg rule in Austria.

1308 The first German king from the House of Luxembourg, Henry VII, takes the throne.

1314–1347 The reign of Louis the Bavarian from the House of Wittelsbach is marked by power struggles with the Habsburgs.

1346–1378 The reign of Charles IV from the House of Luxembourg, the most important emperor of the late Middle Ages. He uses tactical and diplomatic means to expand the realm, with its capital and cultural center in Prague.

1356 Charles IV issues the Golden Bull, which determines certain political structures for the empire (including which seven prince-electors are eligible to be king).

1437–1438 End of the House of Luxembourg; the Habsburgs will occupy the German royal and imperial throne until 1806.

1495 The Diet of Worms: Maximilian I declares Perpetual Public Peace, outlines imperial reforms and abolishes the medieval right to wage feuds.

1517 Theologian Martin Luther posts his Ninety-Five Theses denouncing the granting of indulgences and other corrupt practices of the Catholic church. Although it was not Luther's intent, this leads to the Reformation.

1519–1556 Reign of Charles V, who through the varied lines of his ancestry holds sway over territories including not only the Holy Roman Empire, but also Spain, southern Italy and the Spanish colonies in the New World.

1525 The *Twelve Articles of the Peasants*, a formulation of the peasants' grievances and demands during the Peasants' War in Germany. It is perhaps the first declaration of human rights and, drawing on Luther, points to the Bible as justification for its claims.

1324–1437: Houses of Wittelsbach, Luxembourg and Habsburg

- Church territory
- Habsburg allodial territory, ca. 1375
- Wittelsbach allodial territory, ca. 1375
- Luxemburg allodial territory, ca. 1378
- Border of the Holy Roman Empire

COUNTY OF HOLSTEIN
ARCHBISHOPRIC OF BREMEN
DUCHY OF MECKLENBURG
DUCHY OF POMERANIA
TEUTONIC ORDER
BISHOPRIC OF UTRECHT
BISHOPRIC OF OSNABRÜCK
DUCHY OF BRUNSWICK-LÜNEBURG
ELECTORATE OF BRANDENBURG 1324–1373 WITTELSBACH 1373–1415 LUXEMBOURG
KINGDOM OF POLAND
COUNTY OF HOLLAND
DUCHY OF BRABANT
BISHOPRIC OF MÜNSTER
ARCHBISHOPRIC OF MAGDEBURG
ELECTORATE OF SAXONY
BISHOPRIC OF LIÈGE
ELECTORATE OF COLOGNE
COUNTY OF NASSAU
LANDGRAVIATE OF HESSE
LANDGRAVIATE OF THURINGIA
MARGRAVATE OF MEISSEN
COUNTY OF HAINAUT
COUNTY OF LUXEMBOURG
ELECTORATE OF TRIER
BISHOPRIC OF WÜRZBURG
ELECTORATE OF MAINZ
BISHOPRIC OF BAMBERG
KINGDOM OF BOHEMIA
MARGRAVATE OF MORAVIA
KINGDOM OF FRANCE
ELECTORAL PALATINATE
BISHOPRIC OF METZ
BISHOPRIC OF STRASBOURG
BISHOPRIC OF EICHSTÄTT
BISHOPRIC OF REGENSBURG
DUCHY OF BAVARIA
DUCHY OF AUSTRIA
Vienna
KINGDOM OF HUNGARY (1387–1437 LUXEMBOURG)
DUCHY OF LORRAINE
Habsburg
BISHOPRIC OF BASEL
BISHOPRIC OF AUGSBURG
ARCHBISHOPRIC OF SALZBURG
DUCHY OF CARINTHIA
DUCHY OF STYRIA
FREE COUNTY OF BURGUNDY
BISHOPRIC OF SION
BISHOPRIC OF CHUR
COUNTY OF TIROL
PATRIARCHATE OF AQUILEIA
COUNTY OF SAVOY

1547: Schmalkaldic War

- Spanish Habsburg line
- Austrian Habsburg line
- House of Wittelsbach
- Church territory
- Territory of free imperial cities
- House of Oldenburg
- House of Hohenzollern
- House of Wettin
- Border of the empire
- Theoretical border of the empire

DUCHY OF HOLSTEIN
DUCHY OF MECKLENBURG
POMERANIA
ARCHBISHOPRIC OF BREMEN
BISHOPRIC OF OSNABRÜCK
DUCHY OF BRUNSWICK
BISHOPRIC OF HILDESHEIM
ELECTORATE OF BRANDENBURG
NETHERLANDS
BISHOPRIC OF MÜNSTER
BISHOPRIC OF PADERBORN
ARCHBISHOPRIC OF MAGDEBURG
MARGRAVATE OF UPPER LUSATIA
BISHOPRIC OF LIÈGE
ARCHBISHOPRIC OF COLOGNE
LANDGRAVIATE OF HESSE
ELECTORATE OF SAXONY
DUCHY OF SILESIA
ARCHBISHOPRIC OF TRIER
DUCHY OF LUXEMBOURG
ARCHBISHOPRIC OF MAINZ
BISHOPRIC OF WÜRZBURG
BISHOPRIC OF BAMBERG
BAYREUTH
KINGDOM OF BOHEMIA
ELECTORAL PALATINATE
MARGRAVATE OF ANSBACH
UPPER PALATINATE
BISHOPRIC OF REGENSBURG
MARGRAVATE OF MORAVIA
BISHOPRIC OF METZ
MARGRAVATE OF BADEN
DUCHY OF WÜRTTEMBERG
BISHOPRIC OF AUGSBURG
DUCHY OF BAVARIA
BISHOPRIC OF PASSAU
ARCHDUCHY OF AUSTRIA
FREE COUNTY OF BURGUNDY
BISHOPRIC OF BASEL
SWISS CONFEDERACY
COUNTY OF TIROL
ARCHBISHOPRIC OF SALZBURG
DUCHY OF STYRIA
DUCHY OF CARINTHIA
DUCHY OF SAVOY
BISHOPRIC OF TRIENT
DUCHY OF CARNIOLA
DUCHY OF MILAN
DUCHY OF MANTUA
REPUBLIC OF VENICE
Genoa

1546–1547 Schmalkaldic War: the first war between different Christian confessions; the Catholic Charles V emerges triumphant.

Sept. 25, 1555 The Peace of Augsburg gives territorial lords the right to choose the confession practiced within their domains (reaffirming territorial independence from the empire).

1608–1609 The Protestant princes form a "Union," the Catholic princes a "League."

Walk to Canossa Emperor Henry IV walked from Speyer to Canossa (an Italian castle south of Reggio Emilia) and waited outside its gates for three days to demonstrate penance and convince the pope to lift his excommunication. The phrase is often used as synonym for an act of abasement and submission.

Henry IV kneels before the pope.

The Reformation in the Holy Roman Empire

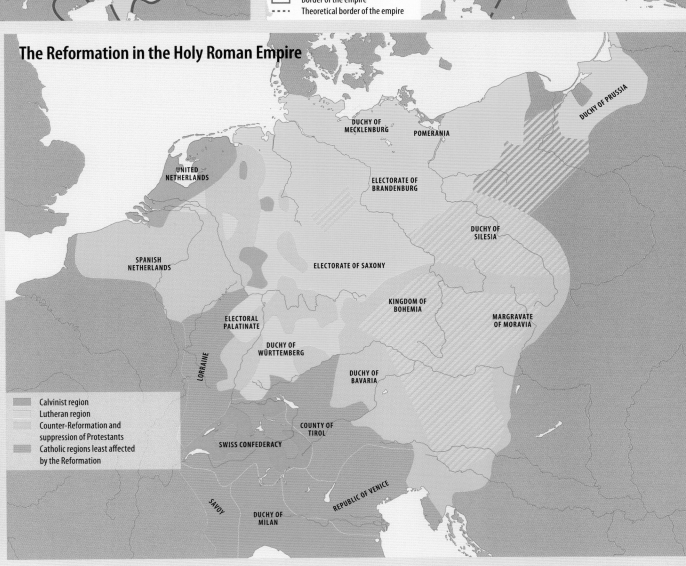

- Calvinist region
- Lutheran region
- Counter-Reformation and suppression of Protestants
- Catholic regions least affected by the Reformation

DUCHY OF MECKLENBURG
POMERANIA
DUCHY OF PRUSSIA
UNITED NETHERLANDS
ELECTORATE OF BRANDENBURG
DUCHY OF SILESIA
SPANISH NETHERLANDS
ELECTORATE OF SAXONY
KINGDOM OF BOHEMIA
MARGRAVATE OF MORAVIA
ELECTORAL PALATINATE
LORRAINE
DUCHY OF WÜRTTEMBERG
DUCHY OF BAVARIA
COUNTY OF TIROL
SWISS CONFEDERACY
SAVOY
DUCHY OF MILAN
REPUBLIC OF VENICE

Germany – The Thirty Years' War

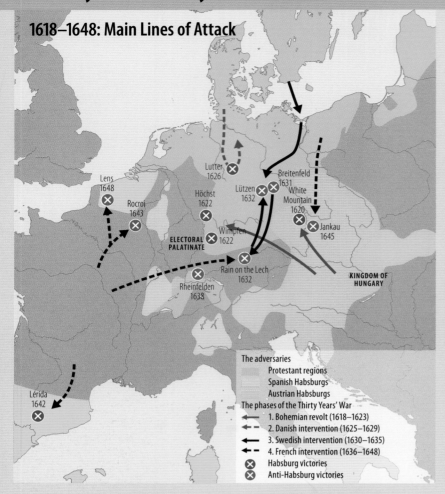

1618–1648: Main Lines of Attack

Lens 1648
Roctoi 1643
Lutter 1626
Höchst 1622
Lützen 1632
Breitenfeld 1631
White Mountain 1620
Wimpfen 1622
Jankau 1645
ELECTORAL PALATINATE
Rain on the Lech 1632
KINGDOM OF HUNGARY
Rheinfelden 1638
Lérida 1642

The adversaries
Protestant regions
Spanish Habsburgs
Austrian Habsburgs

The phases of the Thirty Years' War
1. Bohemian revolt (1618–1623)
2. Danish intervention (1625–1629)
3. Swedish intervention (1630–1635)
4. French intervention (1636–1648)
⊗ Habsburg victories
⊗ Anti-Habsburg victories

1618–1648: Depopulation

Loss of population
0–33%
33–66%
More than 66%
⊗ Important battle

Goldberg 1635
Wolfgast 1628
Bremen
Dömitz 1635
Wittstock 1636
Berlin
Kempen 1642
Lutter 1626
Magdeburg
Dessau 1626
Aschersleben 1645
Breitenfeld 1631
Glogau 1642
SPANISH NETHERLANDS
Lützen 1632
Steinau 1633
Höchst 1622
White Mountain 1620
Kösel 1627
Mergentheim
Mainz
Wimpfen 1622
Prague
Jankau 1645
Wiesloch 1622
Nuremberg 1632
Nördlingen 1634, 1645
Netolitz 1619
Wittenweier 1638
Zumarshausen 1648
Regensburg
Rain 1632
Augsburg
Wattweiler 1639
Tuttlingen 1643
Eferding 1626
Vienna
Sennheim 1638
Basel
Rheinfelden 1638

The Thirty Years' War was a hegemonial struggle between the Habsburgs and France as well as a religious conflict pitting the Protestant Union against the Catholic League that was played out out in Germany. France allied itself with the Protestant northern Netherlands, Denmark and Sweden together with the Protestant areas of Germany. They fought against Catholic Germany, under a Habsburg emperor and the leadership of Bavaria. After thirty years of battles, which ended with the Peace of Westphalia in 1648, large swaths of Germany were depopulated. The "Westphalian Order" formed the basis of the European system until the French Revolution. The conditions set out in that peace treaty included recognition of the independence of the United Provinces of the Netherlands and of the Swiss Confederation. Sweden was given control of Western Pomerania and the lands of the Archbishopric of Bremen; the prince-elector of Brandenburg gained control of Farther Pomerania and the bishoprics of Magdeburg, Halberstadt and Minden. The Protestant and Catholic confessions were set on equal footing.

Causes

1618 Bohemian Revolt: The Protestant aristocracy of Bohemia rebelled in protest of anti-Protestant acts (demolishing churches, for example) by Emperor Ferdinand II, leading to a dispute at Prague Castle. The Protestant leaders of the Bohemian estate literally threw two councilors sent by the emperor out the window; they survived with only slight injuries. This "Second Defenestration of Prague" set off the war. The House of Habsburg could not risk losing imperial Catholic power (the prevalence of Protestants in the electors' college made the election of a Protestant emperor likely) and so allied themselves with Duke Maximilian I of Bavaria, promising him the Upper Palatinate as reward for his military support.

1618–1623   The Bohemian-Palatinate Conflict

1619 The Bohemian army reaches the walls of Vienna. Frederick V, elector Palatine and a Protestant, becomes king of Bohemia for a short time, earning the name "Winter King."

1620 Frederick V is soundly defeated by the Catholic League at the Battle of White Mountain and flees. Ferdinand II, Holy Roman emperor and a staunch Catholic, resumes the throne as king of Bohemia.

June 21, 1621 The Bohemian nobility are executed.

1622 Duke Christian the Younger of Brunswick-Lüneburg ("Mad Christian") unites the Protestant commanders. After a few triumphs, the army loses against the Catholic League under General Tilly in Wimpfen and Höchst.

1623 Frederick V gives control of the Palatinate to Bavaria; the leader of Bavaria acquires the title of elector Palatine.

1623–1629   Danish intervention

1623 Ferdinand II appoints Albrecht von Wallenstein supreme commander of his army.

1623–1625 King Christian IV of Denmark, a Protestant, mobilizes troops against the triumphant imperial Catholic forces.

1626 Wallenstein and Tilly defeat Christian IV at Dessau and Lutter; Christian flees. The Catholic League is able to march onward as far as Denmark.

1628 Christian IV makes final, isolated and ineffective assaults against northern Germany.

1629 The Peace of Lübeck removes Denmark from the conflict, forbidding it to take part in the war any longer. The Imperial Edict of Restitution forces Protestant rulers to return all the ecclesiastical holdings taken from Catholics since 1555.

1630–1635   Swedish intervention

1630 King Gustav II Adolf (Gustavus Adolphus) of Sweden enters the fray, supported by France and the Netherlands, and conquers Pomerania, Mecklenburg, Brandenburg and Saxony.

1631 General Tilly lays siege to Protestant Magdeburg (Sack of Magdeburg). On Sept. 17, Swedish forces roundly defeat Tilly at Breitenfeld.

1632 Tilly dies, forcing the emperor to appeal again to Wallenstein, who had been pushed to the sidelines. The Swedes penetrate through to Munich and Austria.

Nov. 16, 1632 King Gustav II dies in the Battle of Lützen.

1633–1634 The Heilbronn League between Protestants and Sweden carries on fighting.

1634 Wallenstein, acting on his own authority, tries to negotiate peace. Ferdinand II responds by having him assassinated.

1635 In the Peace of Prague, the German Protestants distance themselves from Sweden and now ally with Ferdinand II against France.

1635–1648   French intervention

France mistrusts the peace agreement between the Habsburgs and Sweden and attacks Germany. The war continues in a horrific vein but without any decisive battles.

1645 Beginning of peace negotiations in Münster (Catholic) and Osnabrück (Protestant)

1648   Peace of Westphalia

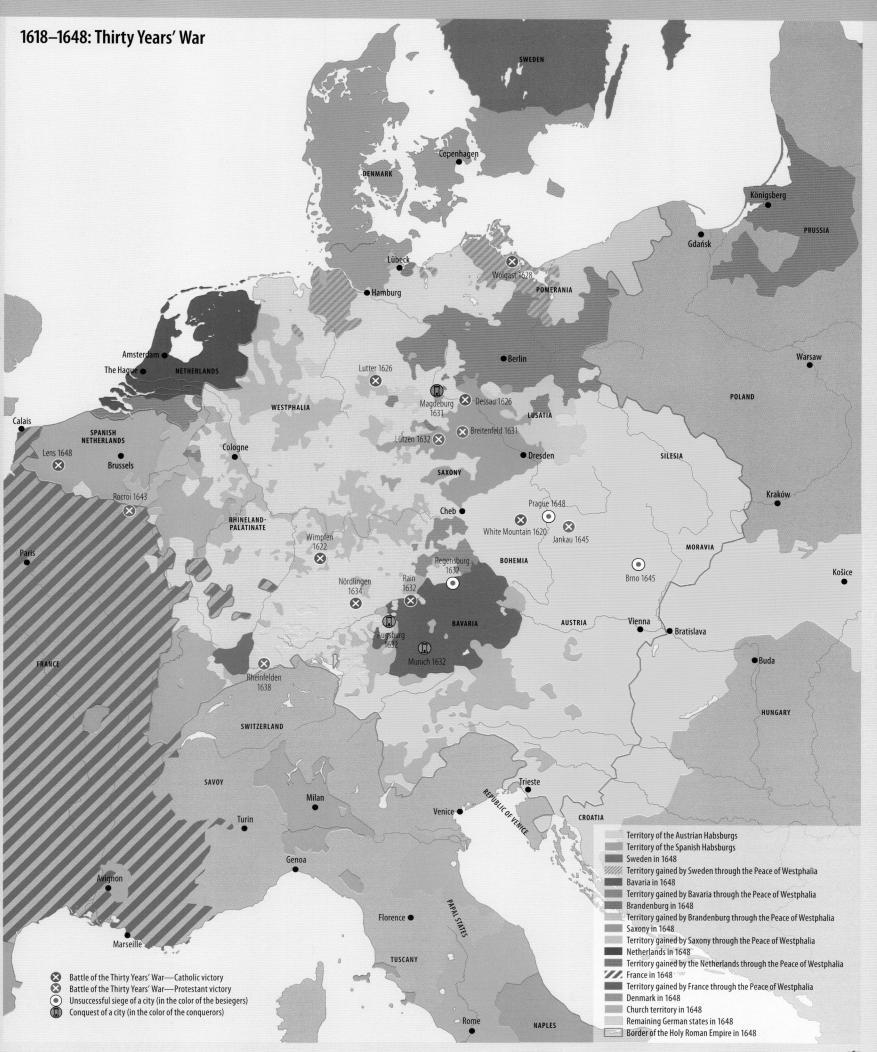

1618–1648: Thirty Years' War

SWEDEN

Copenhagen

DENMARK

Königsberg

PRUSSIA

Gdańsk

Lübeck

⊗ Wolgast 1628

POMERANIA

Hamburg

Berlin

Warsaw

Amsterdam

The Hague

NETHERLANDS

WESTPHALIA

POLAND

Lutter 1626 ⊗

⊡ Magdeburg 1631

⊗ Dessau 1626

LUSATIA

Calais

SPANISH
NETHERLANDS

Cologne

Lüttzen 1632 ⊗

⊗ Breitenfeld 1631

Lens 1648 ⊗

Brussels

Dresden

SILESIA

SAXONY

Kraków

Rocroi 1643 ⊗

RHINELAND-
PALATINATE

Cheb

Prague 1648 ⊙

Paris

Wimpfen
1622 ⊗

⊗ White Mountain 1620

⊗ Jankau 1645

MORAVIA

Košice

Regensburg
1632

BOHEMIA

Nördlingen
1634 ⊗

Rain
1632 ⊗

⊙

Brno 1645 ⊙

FRANCE

⊡ Augsburg
1632

BAVARIA

AUSTRIA

Vienna

Bratislava

⊡ Munich 1632

Buda

Rheinfelden
1638 ⊗

SWITZERLAND

HUNGARY

SAVOY

Trieste

Milan

REPUBLIC OF VENICE

CROATIA

Turin

Venice

Genoa

Avignon

PAPAL
STATES

Florence

Marseille

TUSCANY

NAPLES

Rome

⊗ Battle of the Thirty Years' War—Catholic victory
⊗ Battle of the Thirty Years' War—Protestant victory
⊙ Unsuccessful siege of a city (in the color of the besiegers)
⊡ Conquest of a city (in the color of the conquerors)

Territory of the Austrian Habsburgs
Territory of the Spanish Habsburgs
Sweden in 1648
Territory gained by Sweden through the Peace of Westphalia
Bavaria in 1648
Territory gained by Bavaria through the Peace of Westphalia
Brandenburg in 1648
Territory gained by Brandenburg through the Peace of Westphalia
Saxony in 1648
Territory gained by Saxony through the Peace of Westphalia
Netherlands in 1648
Territory gained by the Netherlands through the Peace of Westphalia
France in 1648
Territory gained by France through the Peace of Westphalia
Denmark in 1648
Church territory in 1648
Remaining German states in 1648
Border of the Holy Roman Empire in 1648

Prussia

1525–1618: Margravate of Brandenburg and Duchy of Prussia

Königsberg
Marienburg
POMERELIA
DUCHY OF PRUSSIA
KULMER-LAND
Thorn
NEW MARK
OLD MARK
Berlin
MIDDLE MARK

☐ Electorate of Brandenburg

1618–1701: Electorate of Brandenburg

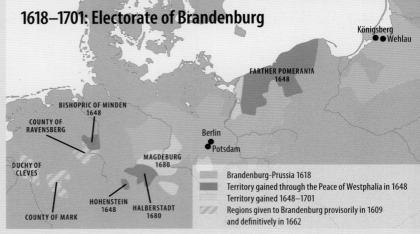

Königsberg
●● Wehlau
FARTHER POMERANIA 1648
BISHOPRIC OF MINDEN 1648
COUNTY OF RAVENSBERG
Berlin
● Potsdam
MAGDEBURG 1680
DUCHY OF CLEVES
HOHENSTEIN 1648
HALBERSTADT 1680
COUNTY OF MARK

■ Brandenburg-Prussia 1618
■ Territory gained through the Peace of Westphalia in 1648
■ Territory gained 1648–1701
▨ Regions given to Brandenburg provisorily in 1609 and definitively in 1662

The name "Prussia" originally referred to the territories in the later province of East Prussia, which is today northeast Poland, and the Russian city of Königsberg (Kaliningrad).

13th century Subjugation of Baltic Prussia by the Teutonic Order: founding of the State of the Teutonic Order

1415 Sigismund of Luxembourg (later emperor) invests Burgrave of Nuremberg Frederick VI of Hohenzollern with the feudal Margravate of Brandenburg.

1466 Second Peace of Thorn: Western Prussia (Pomerelia, Marienburg and Kulmerland) cedes to Poland. The rest of the State of the Teutonic Order (later the Duchy of Prussia) becomes a fiefdom of the Polish crown.

1525 The Reformation is introduced in the State of the Teutonic Order, and the secular Duchy of Prussia is founded.

1618 Emergence of Brandenburg-Prussia, a personal union between the Duchy of Prussia and the Electorate of Brandenburg under the rule of the House of Hohenzollern

1640–1688 Reign of the "Great Elector" Frederick William, elector of Brandenburg and duke of Prussia. A strong military leader, he also initiates economic reforms and develops an absolutist central administration.

1657 In the Treaty of Wehlau (today Znamensk in the Kaliningrad Oblast), Poland renounces its suzerainty over the Duchy of Prussia, which is officially ceded to the Margravate of Brandenburg.

1674–1675 The Swedish army attacks Brandenburg; occupation will end in 1679.

1685 The Edict of Potsdam: Prussia opens its doors to the Huguenots driven out of France due to religious persecution, boosting the economy.

1688–1713 The reign of Elector Frederick III (also King Frederick I of Prussia 1701–1713) is a period of cultural and artistic achievement in which academies for art and science are founded in Prussia and Berlin becomes known as "Athens on the Spree."

1701 Prussia becomes a kingdom and Prince-Elector Frederick III is crowned king in Königsberg.

1713–1740 Reign of the "Soldier King" Frederick William I, who builds a strong army and a lean, efficient and frugal bureaucracy.

1720 Treaty of Stockholm: Prussia receives Western Pomerania south of the Peene River.

1740–1786 The reign of Frederick II the Great is characterized by enlightened absolutism; Silesia is conquered.

1756–1763 Seven Years' War (or Third Silesian War): Although Prussia is defeated by the coalition of Austria, France and Russia, the kingdom is saved by the "Miracle of the House of Brandenburg," the timely death of Empress Elizabeth of Russia. Her

1701–1786: The Kingdom of Prussia

Königsberg
EAST FRISIA 1744
WEST PRUSSIA 1772
WESTERN POMERANIA 1720
NETZE DISTRICT 1772
LINGEN 1702
TECKLENBURG 1707
Berlin
GUELDERS 1713
MANSFELD 1780
SILESIA 1742

■ Kingdom of Prussia in 1701
■ Territory gained 1701–1720
■ Territory gained under Frederick II (1740–1786)

1772–1795: Partitioning of Poland

WEST PRUSSIA
NEW EAST PRUSSIA
Berlin
SOUTH PRUSSIA
MANSFELD (1780)
BAYREUTH
ANSBACH
—— NEW SILESIA

■ Prussia before 1772
■ Gains after the First Partition of Poland 1772
■ Territory gained by Prussia after 1793 (Second Partition of Poland and other territory)
□ Territory gained after the Third Partition in 1795
■ Lost territory

1815: The Congress of Vienna Strengthens Prussia

MECKLEN-BURG
HANOVER
Berlin
DUCHY OF BRUNSWICK
ELECTORATE OF HESSE-KASSEL
DUCHY OF NASSAU
THURINGIAN STATES
KINGDOM OF SAXONY
GRAND DUCHY OF LUXEMBOURG
GRAND DUCHY OF HESSE
DARMSTADT
BOHEMIA
PALATINATE
GRAND DUCHY OF BADEN
KINGDOM OF WÜRTTEM-BERG
BAVARIA
MORAVIA
PRINCIPALITY OF HOHENZOLLERN
AUSTRIA

■ Prussia after 1815
□ Border of the German Confederation

1850–1867

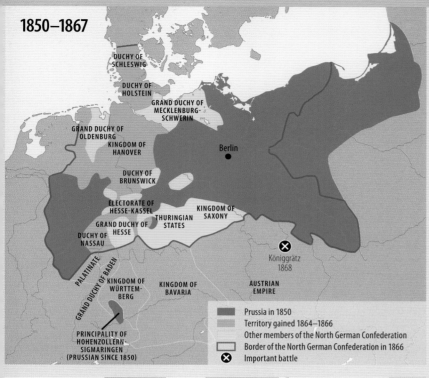

DUCHY OF SCHLESWIG
DUCHY OF HOLSTEIN
GRAND DUCHY OF MECKLENBURG-SCHWERIN
GRAND DUCHY OF OLDENBURG
KINGDOM OF HANOVER
Berlin
DUCHY OF BRUNSWICK
ELECTORATE OF HESSE-KASSEL
GRAND DUCHY OF HESSE
THURINGIAN STATES
KINGDOM OF SAXONY
DUCHY OF NASSAU
Königgrätz 1868
PALATINATE
GRAND DUCHY OF BADEN
KINGDOM OF WÜRTTEM-BERG
KINGDOM OF BAVARIA
AUSTRIAN EMPIRE
PRINCIPALITY OF HOHENZOLLERN-SIGMARINGEN (PRUSSIAN SINCE 1850)

- Prussia in 1850
- Territory gained 1864–1866
- Other members of the North German Confederation
- Border of the North German Confederation in 1866
- ⊗ Important battle

1871: The German Empire

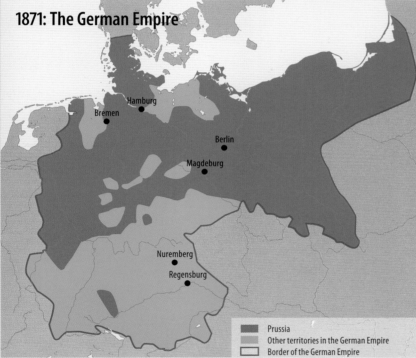

Hamburg
Bremen
Berlin
Magdeburg
Nuremberg
Regensburg

- Prussia
- Other territories in the German Empire
- Border of the German Empire

successor, Peter III, calls off the war with Prussia.

1772–1795 Austria, France and Russia partition Poland among themselves in three stages. The new provinces of South Prussia, New East Prussia and New Silesia are formed; the state of Poland ceases to exist in 1795.

1792–1815 Coalition wars and wars of liberation against revolutionary and then Napoleonic France

1806 Napoleon occupies Berlin.

1815 Congress of Vienna: Prussia receives the remainder of Western Pomerania, northern Saxony, Westphalia and the Rhineland province. Prussia enters the Holy Alliance with the

Russian tsar and Emperor Francis I of Austria.

1848 Liberal revolution and the Frankfurt Parliament; the romantic conservative King Frederick William IV refuses the offer of the German imperial crown.

1862 Otto von Bismarck becomes minister president of Prussia.

1866 Prussia defeats Austria in the Austro-Prussian War and annexes Schleswig-Holstein, Hanover, Hesse, Nassau and Frankfurt.

1870 Prussia defeats France in the Battle of Sedan.

1871 Proclamation of the German Empire

German Kings and Emperors

Carolingians
768–814 Charles the Great (emperor in 800)
814–840 Louis the Pious (emperor in 814)
840–876 Louis II the German
876–882 Louis III the Younger
882–887 Charles III the Fat (emperor in 881)
887–899 Arnulf of Carinthia (emperor in 896)
900–911 Louis IV the Child

Conradines
911–918 Conrad I

Ottonians (Saxon dynasty)
(962–1806 Holy Roman Empire of the German Nation)
919–936 Henry I
936–973 Otto I the Great (emperor in 962)
973–983 Otto II (co-emperor in 967)
983–1002 Otto III (emperor in 996)
1002–1024 St. Henry II (emperor in 1014)

Salians
1024–1039 Conrad II (emperor in 1027)
1039–1056 Henry III (emperor in 1046)
1056–1106 Henry IV (emperor in 1084)
1077–1080 *Rudolf of Rheinfelden (antiking)*
1081–1088 *Hermann of Salm (antiking)*
1087–1098 *Conrad (co-ruler, 1098–1101 antiking)*
1106–1125 Henry V (emperor in 1111)

Supplinburgs
1125–1137 Lothar III of Supplinburg (emperor in 1133)
1127–1135 *Conrad (III) of Hohenstaufen (antiking)*

Staufer (Hohenstaufen)
1138–1152 Conrad III
1147–1150 *Henry Berengar (co-king)*
1152–1190 Frederick I Barbarossa (emperor in 1155)
1190–1197 Henry VI (emperor in 1191)

Welfs (later Guelphs in Italy)
1198–1218 Otto IV of Braunschweig (emperor in 1209)

Staufer (Hohenstaufen)
1198–1208 Philip of Swabia
1212–1250 Frederick II (emperor in 1220)
1222–1235 *Henry VII (co-king)*
1246–1247 *Henry Raspe (antiking)*
1250–1254 Conrad IV

Interregnum
1247–1256 William of Holland
1257–1273 Alfonso of Castile (Alfonso X the Wise)
1257–1272 Richard of Cornwall

Various dynasties
1273–1291 Rudolf (I) of Habsburg
1292–1298 Adolf of Nassau
1298–1308 Albert I of Habsburg
1308–1313 Henry VII of Luxemburg (emperor in 1312)
1314–1347 Louis IV the Bavarian (Wittelsbach) (emperor in 1328)
1314–1330 *Frederick the Fair (Habsburg, first antiking, then co-king with Louis IV)*

Otto III (980–1002)

1347–1378 Charles IV (Luxembourg, emperor in 1355)
1349 *Günther of Schwarzburg (antiking)*
1378–1400 Wenceslas (Luxembourg)
1400–1410 Rupert (Wittelsbach)
1410–1411 Jobst of Moravia
1410–1437 Sigismund (Luxembourg, emperor in 1433)

Habsburgs
1438–1439 Albert II
1440–1493 Frederick III (emperor in 1452)
1493–1519 Maximilian I (emperor in 1508 but not crowned by pope, ending that ancient tradition)
1519–1556 Charles V
1531–1564 Ferdinand I (emperor in 1558)
1564–1576 Maximilian II
1576–1612 Rudolf II
1612–1619 Matthias

Ferdinand II (1578–1637)

1619–1637 Ferdinand II (emperor in 1619)
1637–1657 Ferdinand III
1653–1654 *Ferdinand IV (co-king)*
1658–1705 Leopold I
1705–1711 Joseph I
1711–1740 Charles VI
1742–1745 Charles VII Albert of Bavaria (Wittelsbach)

Habsburg-Lorraine
1745–1765 Francis I Stephan of Lorraine
1765–1790 Joseph II
1790–1792 Leopold II
1792–1806 Francis II
1806 *Holy Roman Empire abolished*

Hohenzollerns (German Empire)
1871–1888 William I
1888 Frederick III
1888–1918 William II

169

Germany – Principalities in the 17th and 18th Centuries

1648: Peace of Westphalia

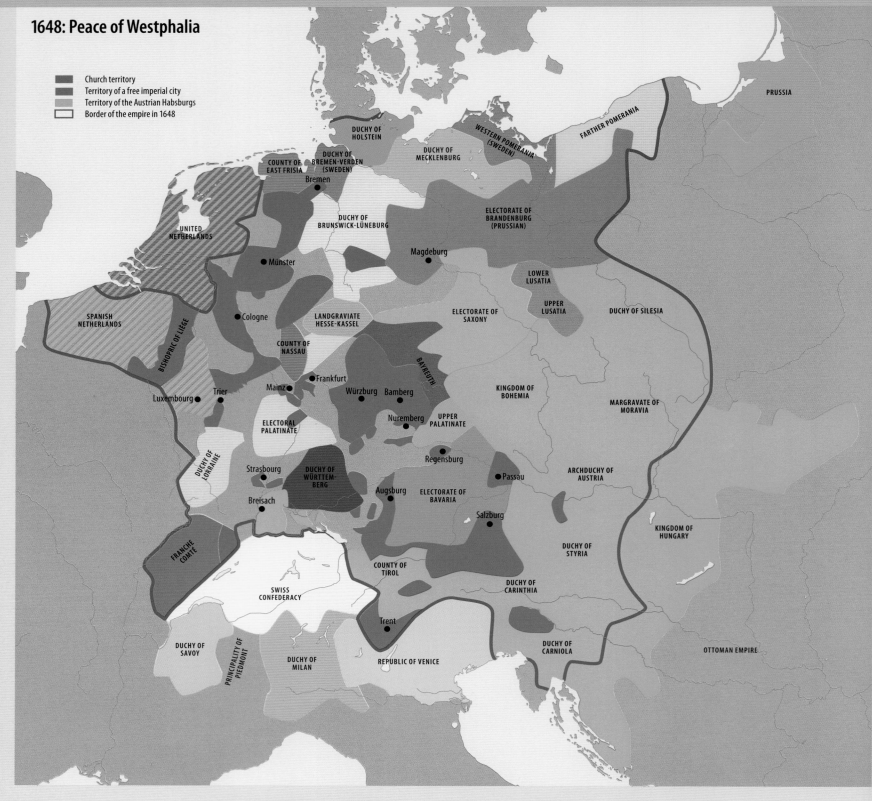

Church territory
Territory of a free imperial city
Territory of the Austrian Habsburgs
Border of the empire in 1648

PRUSSIA

DUCHY OF HOLSTEIN

DUCHY OF BREMEN-VERDEN (SWEDEN)

DUCHY OF MECKLENBURG

WESTERN POMERANIA (SWEDEN)

FARTHER POMERANIA

COUNTY OF EAST FRISIA

Bremen

UNITED NETHERLANDS

Münster

DUCHY OF BRUNSWICK-LÜNEBURG

ELECTORATE OF BRANDENBURG (PRUSSIAN)

Magdeburg

LOWER LUSATIA

SPANISH NETHERLANDS

Cologne

LANDGRAVIATE HESSE-KASSEL

ELECTORATE OF SAXONY

UPPER LUSATIA

DUCHY OF SILESIA

BISHOPRIC OF LIEGE

COUNTY OF NASSAU

Frankfurt

BAYREUTH

Luxembourg

Trier

Mainz

Würzburg

Bamberg

KINGDOM OF BOHEMIA

MARGRAVATE OF MORAVIA

ELECTORAL PALATINATE

Nuremberg

UPPER PALATINATE

DUCHY OF LORRAINE

Strasbourg

DUCHY OF WÜRTTEM-BERG

Regensburg

ARCHDUCHY OF AUSTRIA

Breisach

Augsburg

Passau

ELECTORATE OF BAVARIA

KINGDOM OF HUNGARY

Salzburg

FRANCHE COMTÉ

DUCHY OF STYRIA

KINGDOM OF HUNGARY

COUNTY OF TIROL

SWISS CONFEDERACY

DUCHY OF CARINTHIA

DUCHY OF SAVOY

PRINCIPALITY OF PIEDMONT

DUCHY OF MILAN

Trent

REPUBLIC OF VENICE

DUCHY OF CARNIOLA

OTTOMAN EMPIRE

After the Thirty Years' War, the numerous states in the German Empire adopted a brand of absolutism modeled on France. At first Bavaria and Saxony jostled for dominance within the empire, but beginning in 1740 Prussia and Austria came to the fore. The fierce, prolonged struggle between them is referred to as "German dualism."

1679–1726 Elector Maximilian II Emanuel of Bavaria; proliferation of baroque opulence

1688–1697 The Nine Years' War: Strasbourg and Alsace become French (until 1871).

1692 Hanover becomes an electorate; the Hanoverian Welfs dominate in the north and attain the British crown in 1714 (ruled as a personal union until 1837).

1694–1733 August the Strong (Frederick Augustus II), elector of Saxony and from 1697 king of Poland (personal union until 1763); grand architecture in Dresden gives it the title "Florence on the Elbe."

1700–1721 The Great Northern War: Sweden loses its territories in northern Germany to Hanover and Prussia.

1742–1745 With no male heirs to the Habsburg dynasty, Bavarian Elector Charles (VII) Albert becomes emperor; Bavaria has occupied Bohemia in the meantime.

1745 The House of Habsburg-Lorraine attains the imperial crown.

1756–1763 The Seven Years' War pits Prussia, Hanover and England versus France, Austria and Russia for

control of Silesia and colonial territories on several continents.

1766 Lorraine falls to France (until 1871).

1778–1779 War of the Bavarian Succession: The Inn region (part of Old Bavaria) is ceded to Austria.

The Miracle of the House of Brandenburg The sudden turnabout in Russian policy toward defeated Prussia following the death of Tsarena Elizabeth Petrovna in January 1762 came to be known as "the miracle of the House of Brandenburg." In the Treaty of St. Petersburg, signed on on May 5, 1762, Elizabeth's successor, Peter III, an admirer of Prussian King Frederick II, reversed Russia's military gains and returned the Prussian lands that had been occupied by the Russian army during the Seven Years' War to the Prussian king without any demand for compensation.

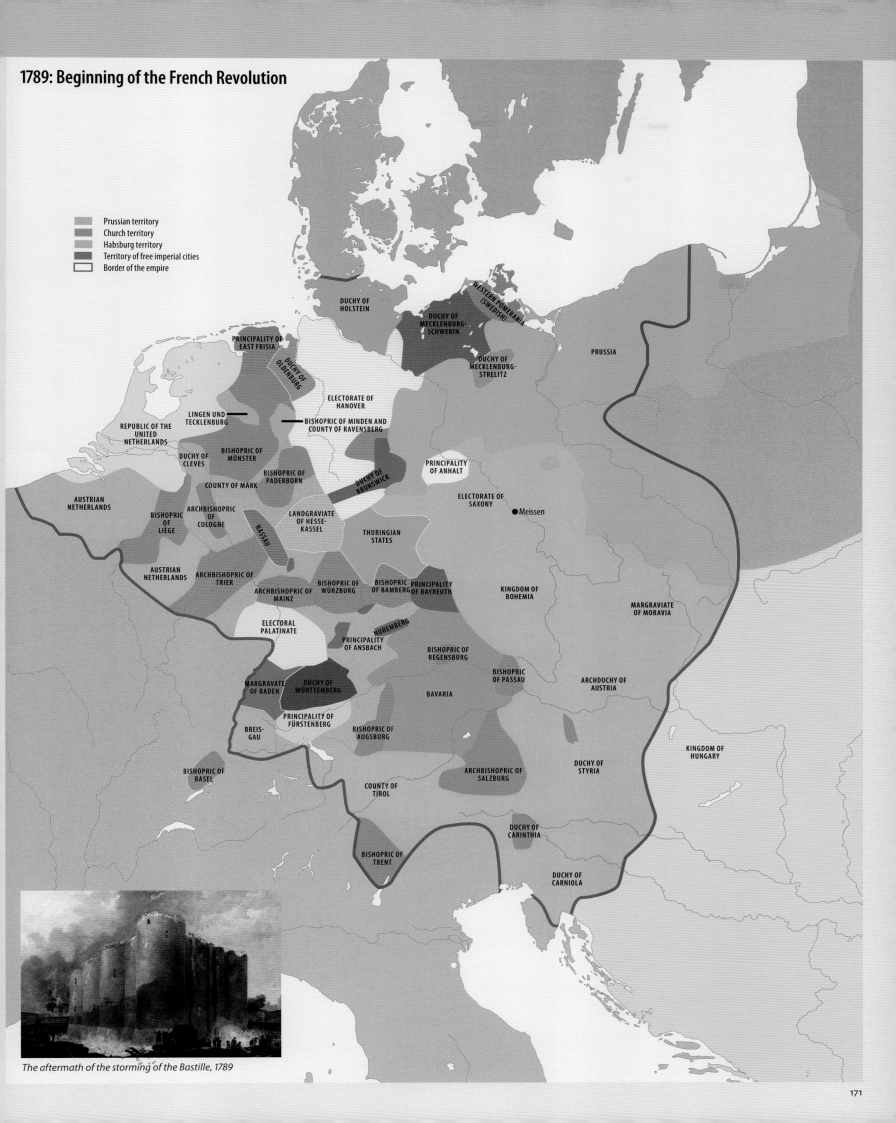

1789: Beginning of the French Revolution

Prussian territory
Church territory
Habsburg territory
Territory of free imperial cities
Border of the empire

DUCHY OF HOLSTEIN

WESTERN POMERANIA (SWEDISH)

DUCHY OF MECKLENBURG-SCHWERIN

DUCHY OF MECKLENBURG-STRELITZ

PRUSSIA

PRINCIPALITY OF EAST FRISIA

DUCHY OF OLDENBURG

ELECTORATE OF HANOVER

LINGEN UND TECKLENBURG

BISHOPRIC OF MINDEN AND COUNTY OF RAVENSBERG

REPUBLIC OF THE UNITED NETHERLANDS

DUCHY OF CLEVES

BISHOPRIC OF MÜNSTER

BISHOPRIC OF PADERBORN

DUCHY OF BRUNSWICK

PRINCIPALITY OF ANHALT

COUNTY OF MARK

ELECTORATE OF SAXONY

Meissen

AUSTRIAN NETHERLANDS

BISHOPRIC OF LIÈGE

ARCHBISHOPRIC OF COLOGNE

NASSAU

LANDGRAVIATE OF HESSE-KASSEL

THURINGIAN STATES

AUSTRIAN NETHERLANDS

ARCHBISHOPRIC OF TRIER

ARCHBISHOPRIC OF MAINZ

BISHOPRIC OF WÜRZBURG

BISHOPRIC OF BAMBERG

PRINCIPALITY OF BAYREUTH

KINGDOM OF BOHEMIA

MARGRAVIATE OF MORAVIA

ELECTORAL PALATINATE

NUREMBERG

PRINCIPALITY OF ANSBACH

BISHOPRIC OF REGENSBURG

MARGRAVATE OF BADEN

DUCHY OF WÜRTTEMBERG

BISHOPRIC OF PASSAU

ARCHDUCHY OF AUSTRIA

BAVARIA

PRINCIPALITY OF FÜRSTENBERG

BREIS-GAU

BISHOPRIC OF AUGSBURG

ARCHBISHOPRIC OF SALZBURG

DUCHY OF STYRIA

KINGDOM OF HUNGARY

BISHOPRIC OF BASEL

COUNTY OF TIROL

DUCHY OF CARINTHIA

BISHOPRIC OF TRENT

DUCHY OF CARNIOLA

The aftermath of the storming of the Bastille, 1789

171

Germany – Nationalism, Unification and Empire

1806–1808: Confederation of the Rhine

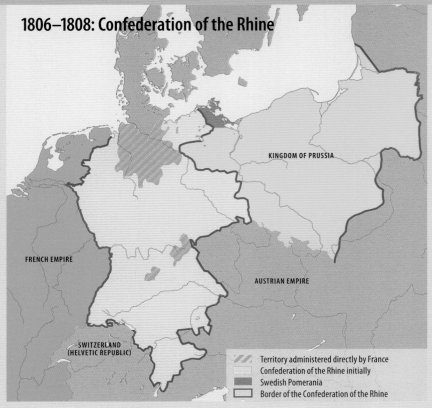

Territory administered directly by France
Confederation of the Rhine initially
Swedish Pomerania
Border of the Confederation of the Rhine

1812: Confederation of the Rhine

Confederation of the Rhine–federation of
4 kingdoms, 5 grand duchies, 13 duchies,
17 principalities and 3 free Hansa cities
Swedish Pomerania
Border of the Confederation of the Rhine

1815–1866: German Confederation

German territory of the German Confederation
Austrian territory of the German Confederation
Kingdom of Prussia
Border of the German Confederation
Changes in German Confederation borders in 1839
❶ Dutch city of Limburg, joined the German Confederation in 1839
❷ Territory of Luxembourg, ceded to Belgium in 1839
❸ Grand Duchy of Luxembourg, tied to the Netherlands through personal union
❹ Holstein, tied to Denmark until 1864 through personal union, then to Austrian in 1864–1866 and to Germany in 1866
❺ Kingdom of Hanover, tied to the United Kingdom through personal union
❻ Territory of Prussia, part of the German Confederation 1848–1851

For thousands of years, Germany was more of a geographic concept than a political entity. In the Middle Ages, dozens of territorial lordships emerged within the Holy Roman Empire, and the power of the German principalities and duchies was further strengthened after the Thirty Years' War. Following the Napoleonic Wars, however, the political map of Germany was consolidated into fewer, larger states. Resistance against French rule awakened a feeling of nationalism among the German people. The German Empire, established in 1871, then transformed power relations on the continent with the advent of a new, Prussian-dominated nation. Germany's injudicious foreign policy after 1890 nearly drove the country into isolation in the years leading up to 1914.

1806 Napoleon defeats the Holy Roman Empire in battle. Emperor Francis II abdicates; the Holy Roman Empire is dissolved. Napoleon initiates the Confederation of the Rhine, uniting sixteen German states. Bavaria, Württemberg and Saxony become kingdoms.

1813 Beginning of the Wars of Liberation, in which Europe frees itself from Napoleon.

1815 Founding of the German Confederation; Hanover becomes a kingdom.

1817 Wartburg Festival: founding of German nationalist student fraternities

1819 Efforts to suppress liberal and nationalist tendencies through censorship, restrictions on student organizations at the universities and a ban on assembly (Carlsbad Decrees)

1832 Hambach Festival: Democrats and patriots demand the unification of Germany; participants are prosecuted.

1834 Founding of the Zollverein, or German Customs Union (until 1919)

1848–1849 Revolution in German states: The Frankfurt National Assembly drafts a constitution, but Prussian King Frederick William IV refuses the imperial crown offered by the assembly. There is dispute about whether to adopt the

Confederation of the Rhine A free federation of the majority of German states, with the exception of Austria, that existed from 1806 to 1813. The confederation was initiated by Napoleon and was under his influence; it collapsed following his defeat.

The German Confederation A free federation of thirty-nine German states, created at the Congress of Vienna in 1815. The loose confederation was able to defend itself, but not to launch a concerted attack. Austria presided over a Federal Assembly that convened in Frankfurt am Main. At the Frankfurt Parliament in 1848/49, the members even wrote a German constitution

that included Austria. The aim of the German Confederation was to coordinate the German states' foreign policy, aligned against the growing influence of liberalism. It gradually became a tool for Austrian restoration policy.

Zollverein (German Customs Union) A coalition of German states formed in 1833 on Prussia's initiative in order to overcome customs barriers and thus stimulate trade. Austria was not a member.

Austro-German Alliance (Dual Alliance) A defensive military pact between Germany and Austria-Hungary created in 1879 in reaction to deteriorating German relations

with Russia. William I had refused to renew the Reinsurance Treaty of 1878 with Russia because it did not rule out Russian military aggression against Austria-Hungary. Germany and Austria-Hungary now pledged to come to each other's aid in case of an attack by Russia, but otherwise to remain neutral in international affairs.

German Navy League An organization formed in 1898 on the initiative of Admiral Alfred von Tirpitz with the goal of influencing public opinion in favor of a strong navy through propaganda. It was hoped that the expansion of the Imperial Navy would bolster Germany's status as major power.

Otto von Bismarck (1815–1898) Appointed Prussian prime minister in 1862, Bismarck was a leading architect of German unification and in 1871 became imperial chancellor of the German Empire. The empire's constitution, with its provision for a strong chancellor, was seemingly custom-made for him. He instituted the Anti-Socialist Laws to deter socialist parties, but at the same time introduced extensive social benefits for workers to sway citizens. In his foreign policy, he tried to hinder French-Russian relations and to maintain a balance between the Great Powers. In 1890 William II asked for his resignation.

1866–1871 North German Confederation

States of the North German Confederation
North German Confederation border
⊗ Important battle

1871: German Empire

Imperial Germany
Border of the German Empire

"Greater" or "Lesser" German Solution (with or without Austria). The National Assembly appoints Archduke John of Austria as regent (he resigns in 1849).

1861   William I becomes king of Prussia and appoints Otto von Bismarck prime minister in 1862.

1864   Prussia defeats Denmark and annexes Schleswig and Lauenburg; Holstein goes to Austria.

1864–1886   Louis II, the "Fairy-tale King" of Bavaria, plunges his kingdom into debt with grandiose building projects; by granting funding for them, Bismarck secures Bavaria's assent to Prussian rule until 1871.

1866   Prussia defeats Austria at Königgrätz; Prussia annexes Holstein and Hanover, and the German Confederation is disbanded. The "Lesser German Solution" triumphs under the leadership of Prussia (North German Confederation).

1870–1871   The Franco-Prussian War ends in Prussian victory at Sedan.

1871   Germany is unified with the assent of the imperial princes, and the German Empire is founded. Under the imperial constitution, William I of Prussia becomes the German emperor and Bismarck serves as the imperial chancellor.

1878–1890   Anti-Socialist Laws: A series of measures passed by the Reichstag fail to hinder the spread of socialist ideas.

1879   Austro-German Alliance (Dual Alliance): The German Empire and Austria-Hungary agree to defend each other against future Russian aggression.

1883–1889   Bismarck enacts social insurance programs (health and accident insurance, pensions) to stem the revolutionary tide.

April 1884   Adolf Lüderitz claims South West Africa (now Namibia) as a German colony.

July 1884   Togoland becomes a German "model colony"; Germany establishes a protectorate for Adolph Woermann's holdings in Cameroon.

February 1885   German East Africa becomes a colony.

April 1885   German Wituland in East Africa becomes a colony (ceded to Great Britain in 1890).

May 1885   Kaiser-Wilhelmsland and the Bismarck Archipelago become colonies.

1888   Year of the three emperors: William I dies, Frederick III rules for only 99 days and is succeeded by his son William II; occupation of Nauru and Tsingtao.

1890   Bismarck's political opponents win a majority in the Reichstag, and

"The pilot disembarks"

he resigns. William II tries his hand at foreign policy ("personal rule") and leads Germany into isolation.

1894   Dual Alliance between France and Russia (defensive alliance)

1898   Founding of the German Navy League, a private interest group, to further expansion of the Imperial Navy; competition with Great Britain for naval superiority

1899   Germany purchases the Caroline and Mariana Islands, Palau and Samoa.

1903   Construction of the Berlin–Baghdad railway begins.

1904   Entente Cordiale (cordial understanding) between France and England smooths tensions between those countries.

1904–1907   Herero rebellions in German South West Africa

1905–1906   Maji Maji uprising in German East Africa

1911   William II visits Morocco, where France has colonial ambitions, bringing confrontation with France to a head.

1914   World War I breaks out.

German Colonies in Africa

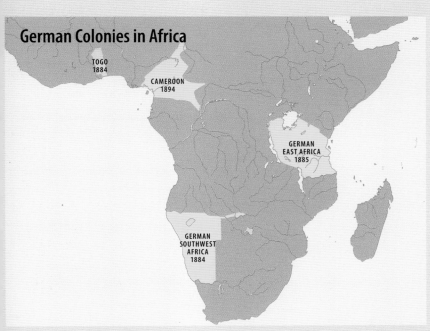

German Colonies in Oceania

German New Guinea

Germany in World War I, 1914–1918

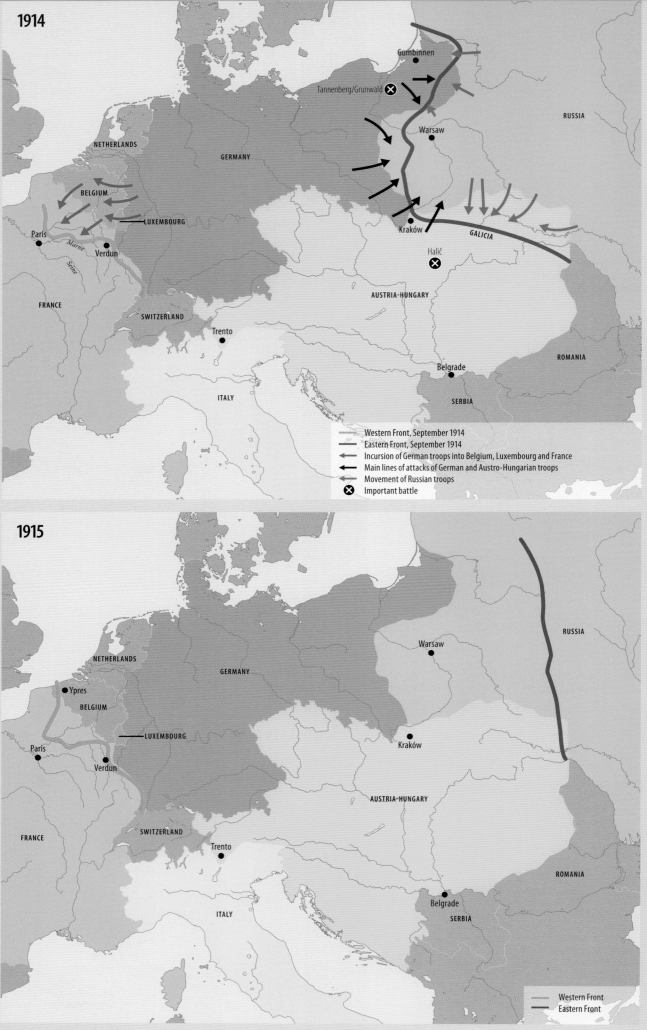

1914

1915

Western Front, September 1914
Eastern Front, September 1914
Incursion of German troops into Belgium, Luxembourg and France
Main lines of attacks of German and Austro-Hungarian troops
Movement of Russian troops
⊗ Important battle

Western Front
Eastern Front

World War I began auspiciously for Germany. In the west, its troops moved rapidly through Belgium and into France in accordance with the Schlieffen Plan, and the occupation of Paris seemed only a matter of time. After a month, however, the Germans' march was halted at the Marne River, and the conflict turned into a prolonged trench war; mechanized warfare and the Battle for Verdun ushered in an entirely new and utterly horrible kind of warfare.

June 28, 1914 Assassination of the heir to the Austro-Hungarian throne, Archduke Francis Ferdinand, in Sarajevo

August 1914 German troops advance rapidly through Belgium. Germany stops the Russian offensive in the east with a victory at Tannenberg; German counter-offensive in Galicia (Halič).

September 1914 German advance into France stopped at the Marne River

May 1915 Despite its membership in the Triple Alliance, Italy enters the war on the side of the Entente.

May 1915 The British passenger ship *Lusitania* is sunk by a German torpedo; the death of more than 120 US citizens aboard causes the mood in the United States to shift toward support for involvement in the war.

February 1916 The beginning of the protracted and bloody battle for the fortified city of Verdun, France

July–October 1916 Joint British-French offensive at the Somme River (the Western Front)

Triple Alliance A military alliance between Germany, Austria-Hungary and later Italy that lasted from 1879 to 1882. The coalition was directed against Russia and France. If one of the three members of the alliance were to be attacked, the others pledged to come to their aid.

Triple Entente A military alliance formed between France, Russia and Great Britain that was established in 1907. It grew out of the Franco-Russian alliance of 1894 and the 1904 Entente Cordiale between France and Great Britain.

Treaty of Brest-Litovsk Following the October (Bolshevik) Revolution in November 1917, Russia signed a separate peace treaty ending its involvement in World War I. Soviet Russia renounced its territorial claims in order to concentrate fully on securing power internally.

Alfred von Schlieffen (1833–1913) German field marshal and chief of the general staff from 1891–1905, von Schlieffen was the author of a secret strategy for conducting the war on two fronts. According to the Schlieffen Plan, Germany would launch a full-out attack on France (in violation of the neutrality of Belgium and the Netherlands) and achieve a quick victory there, so that it would be possible to deploy Germany's entire forces against the slowly mobilizing Russia.

May 1916 Battle of Jutland: The German and British fleets fight the biggest sea battle of the war in the Skagerrak off the coast of Denmark.

early 1917 Submarine warfare intensifies.

April 1917 The United States declares war on Germany.

Summer 1917 German troops break through the Italian front at Caporetto.

Canadian soldiers in a captured German trench, Battle of Crête de Vimy, France, 1917

March 1918 Treaty of Brest-Litovsk ends the war between Bolshevik Russia and the Central Powers (Germany and Austria-Hungary).

March–April 1918 German offensive at the Somme River, followed by an Allied counter-offensive

July 1918 The final German offensive at the Marne River fails.

November 1918 Germany surrenders in Compiègne.

June 1919 Germany signs the Treaty of Versailles, loses its colonies.

Paul von Hindenburg (1847–1934) German field marshal whose role in the victory at Tannenberg made him a national hero. Although initially reluctant, he was elected president of the Weimar Republic in 1925 by the national conservatives. His sway was such that he was called the "substitute emperor." Von Hindenburg appointed Hitler chancellor of the Reich in 1933 and died in 1934.

Erich Ludendorff (1865–1937) German general who rose to prominence by defeating the 1914 Russian offensive at Tannenberg at Hindenburg's side. In 1917 he helped Lenin return to Russia; Germany hoped to benefit from supporting the Russian revolution, a hope that was fulfilled at least in the short run. As an opponent of the Weimar Republic, Ludendorff participated in Adolf Hitler's failed coup attempt in 1923 (the Beer Hall Putsch).

Treaty of Versailles Germany, blamed for causing World War I, was forced to admit sole responsibility for the war, pay huge sums to France and Belgium in reparations, and cede land to France, Czechoslovakia and Poland. Germany's African colonies went to France, and those in China to Japan. The east side of the Rhine was demilitarized and administered by the victor states; the German army was reduced to 100,000 men without a general staff. The Treaty of Versailles has generally been viewed as unbalanced and as paving the way for World War II, though other scholars dissent.

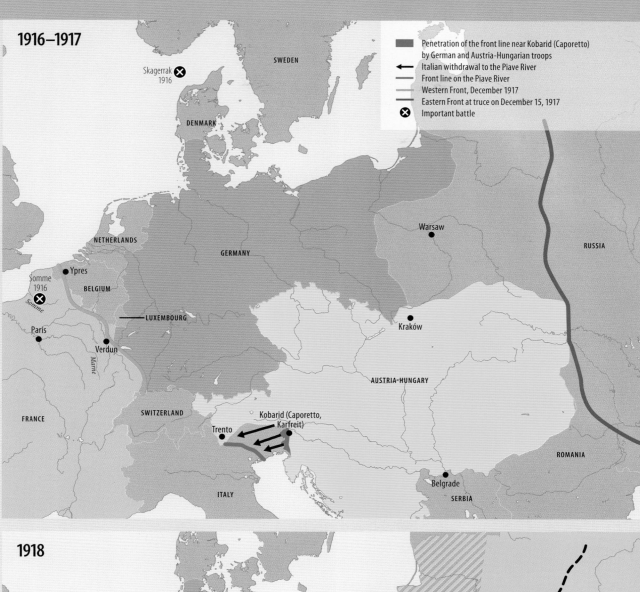

1916–1917

Penetration of the front line near Kobarid (Caporetto) by German and Austria-Hungarian troops
← Italian withdrawal to the Piave River
Front line on the Piave River
Western Front, December 1917
Eastern Front at truce on December 15, 1917
⊗ Important battle

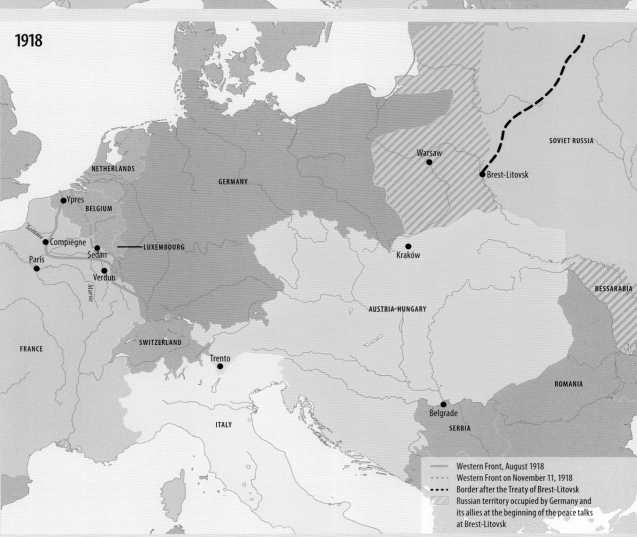

1918

Western Front, August 1918
Western Front on November 11, 1918
Border after the Treaty of Brest-Litovsk
Russian territory occupied by Germany and its allies at the beginning of the peace talks at Brest-Litovsk

Germany – The Weimar Republic and Third Reich, 1918–1933

After World War I, the democratic Weimar Republic was established in Germany. Rejected by both communists and right-wing nationalists, the new government was also unpopular with the overwhelming majority of German citizens. The public figures who founded the Republic and signed the Treaty of Versailles were regarded as traitors who were assisting the Allies to fulfill their goals. The highest levels of army command spread the legend that the German army had never actually been defeated in the Great War, but instead was sabotaged at home by "fellows without a fatherland" (Jews, communists, socialists, social democrats and others). The instability of the political system (with frequently changing regimes), exacerbated by the Great Depression, ultimately facilitated the rise of the National Socialists.

1918 Short-lived German Revolution and proclamation of the republic; Emperor William II abdicates; armistice is signed.

Jan. 15, 1919 The leaders of the communist Spartacus League, Karl Liebknecht and Rosa Luxembourg, are murdered. The Treaty of Versailles is signed; the National Assembly approves the Weimar Constitution in Weimar.

March 1920 Kapp Lüttwitz Putsch fails to restore the monarchy.

1922 Russian-German Treaty of Rapallo: both countries renounce claims to war reparations and agree to mutual supply of equipment and oil. Right-wing radicals assassinate Foreign Minister Walther Rathenau.

1923 France occupies the Ruhr Valley; Hitler attempts a coup in Munich (Beer Hall Putsch).

1925 Hindenburg, representing the old regime, is president. Treaty of Locarno: Germany accepts its western border.

1926 Friendship treaty with the Soviet Union

1930–1933 Ruling coalition falls apart; Hindenburg appoints a cabinet in an emergency decree.

1932 Unemployment reaches 30 percent. Conference in Lausanne ends reparations. NSDAP emerges as strongest party in the Reichstag in July elections and remains so despite some losses in November re-elections.

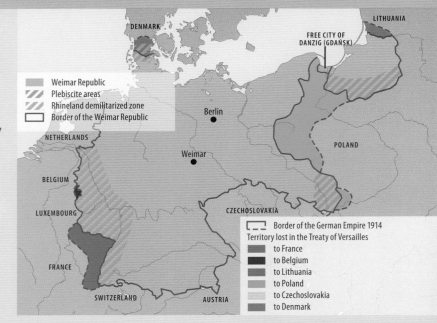

Weimar Republic
Plebiscite areas
Rhineland demilitarized zone
Border of the Weimar Republic

Border of the German Empire 1914
Territory lost in the Treaty of Versailles
to France
to Belgium
to Lithuania
to Poland
to Czechoslovakia
to Denmark

Kiel Naval Mutiny At the end of October 1918, the sailors on three battleships refused to set sail for a battle they had no chance of winning. In the ensuing **German Revolution**, workers' and soldiers' councils were formed in many cities, which proclaimed Council Republics in Munich and Bremen. After the Bavarian king abdicated, other German monarchs followed suit within days.

Weimar Republic A parliamentary republic, formed after the constitution was approved in 1919, and the first democratic system on German soil.

Kapp-Lüttwitz Putsch A militant right-wing, anti-government group tried to restore the monarchy. Its leaders were former East Prussian General Director Wolfgang Kapp and army commander Walther von Lüttwitz. General strikes and resistance by civil servants loyal to the government ended the putsch after four days.

Friedrich Ebert (1871–1925) Appointed SPD chairman in 1913, in February 1919 Ebert was elected the first president of the new republic. He tried to govern in an unbiased manner, but nevertheless had to deal with constant attacks from the right-wing opposition.

Gustav Stresemann (1878–1929) He changed in the 1920s from a resolute monarchist to a republican practitioner of *realpolitik*. Appointed foreign minister in 1923, he tried to normalize relations with France and to revise the Treaty of Versailles through diplomatic means; he helped Germany regain international esteem and was awarded the Nobel Peace Prize for his efforts in 1926.

Election Chaos

		KPD	USPD	SPD	Center	BVP	DDP/DStP	DVP	DNVP	NSDAP	Other
Jan. 19, 1919	%		7.6	**37.9**	19.7		18.6	4.4	10.3		1.5
	Seats		22	165	91		75	19	44		7
June 6, 1920	%	2.1	17.9	**21.6**	13.6	4.2	8.4	14.0	15.1		3.1
	Seats	4	84	102	64	21	39	65	71		9
May 4, 1924	%	12.6	0.8	**20.5**	13.4	3.2	5.7	9.2	19.5	6.6	8.5
	Seats	62		100	65	16	28	45	95	32	29
Dec. 7, 1924	%	9.0	0.3	**26.0**	13.7	3.7	6.3	10.1	20.5	3.0	7.5
	Seats	45		131	69	19	32	51	103	14	29
May 20, 1928	%	10.6	0.1	**29.8**	12.1	3.1	4.9	8.7	14.2	2.6	13.9
	Seats	54		153	62	16	25	45	73	12	51
Sept. 14, 1930	%	13.1	0.0	**24.5**	11.8	3.0	3.8	4.5	7.0	18.3	14.0
	Seats	77		143	68	19	20	30	41	107	72
July 31, 1932	%	14.6		21.6	12.5	3.2	1.0	1.2	5.9	**37.4**	2.6
	Seats	89		133	75	22	4	7	37	230	11
Nov. 6, 1932	%	16.9		20.4	11.9	3.1	1.0	1.9	8.8	**33.1**	2.9
	Seats	100		121	70	20	2	11	52	196	12
March 5, 1933	%	12.3		18.3	11.3	2.7	0.9	1.1	8.0	**43.9**	
	Seats	81		120	73	19	5	2	52	288	

Hyperinflation

Germany's poor economic situation was reflected not only in skyrocketing inflation, but its gold reserves also melted during the same period. Constant issuance of bank notes led to an uncontrollable surplus of currency. The dollar exchange rate developed as follows:

1914	4.20 marks
1919 (July)	14 marks
1922 (Jan.)	191.80 marks
1923 (Jan.)	17,972 marks
1923 (Aug.)	4,620,455 marks
1923 (Nov.)	4,200,000,000 marks

Party System

The Weimar Coalition included the three largest parties, the ones that carried the responsibility for governing: the **SPD** (Social Democratic Party of Germany), the **Center** and the **DDP** (German Democratic Party). In Bavaria, the **BVP** (Bavarian People's Party) held a position similar to the Center Party in Germany.
Left-wing opposition: **USPD** (Independent Social Democratic Party of Germany), **KPD** (Communist Party Germany).
Right-wing opposition: **DVP** (German People's Party—in the course of the 1920s this became the leading party under the influence of Chairman Gustav Stresemann), **DNVP** (German National People's Party) and the **NSDAP** (National Socialist German Workers' Party), which in 1918 was only a small party not represented in parliament by the name of German Workers' Party (DAP). It was renamed NSDAP after Hitler joined in September 1919.

Changes of Administration

1919	130 days	Scheidemann	SPD
1919–1920	277 days	Bauer	SPD
1920	72 days	Müller I	SPD
1920–1921	313 days	Fehrenbach	Center
1921	165 days	Wirth I	Center
1921–1922	384 days	Wirth II	Center
1922–1923	263 days	Cuno	–
1923	51 days	Stresemann I	DVP
1923	48 days	Stresemann II	DVP
1923–1924	177 days	Marx I	Center
1924	195 days	Marx II	Center
1925	223 days	Luther I	
1926	112 days	Luther II	
1926–1927	214 days	Marx III	Center
1927–1928	499 days	Marx IV	Center
1928–1930	636 days	Müller II	SPD
1930–1931	556 days	Brüning I	Center
1931–1932	233 days	Brüning II	Center
1932	170 days	von Papen	
1932–1933	57 days	von Schleicher	

Jan. 30, 1933 Against his better judgment and without the consent of the Reichstag, Hindenburg appoints Hitler chancellor on the advice of former chancellor Franz von Papen (Center Party), who hopes to be able to control Hitler. Industrialists and certain national conservatives finance the Nazis.

Feb. 27, 1933 The Reichstag burns; Hitler blames opponents, paving the way for his takeover.

Feb. 28, 1933 The Reichstag Fire Decree bans the Communist Party.

March 23, 1933 The Enabling Act gives the government legislative powers, effectively abolishing the separation of powers enshrined in the constitution.

April 1933 Boycott of Jewish businesses

June 27, 1933 Reich Motorway Act: Rapid building of an extensive highway network provides full employment.

1934 Justice system brought into line with Nazi strategy (*Gleichschaltung*)

July 1934 Night of the Long Knives; Hitler has the SA leaders including their chief of staff, Ernst Röhm, executed, also purging other political opponents.

August 1934 Hindenburg dies; Hitler names himself Führer and Reichskanzler.

Jan. 13, 1935 A plebiscite in Saarland decides in favor of incorporation into the German Reich (rather than France).

Sept. 15, 1935 Nuremberg Race Laws: Non-Jews are forbidden to marry Jews.

March 1936 German military units occupy the demilitarized Rhineland and Ruhr Valley.

Reichstag Elections, November 6, 1932

Legend:
- National Socialists
- Center Party
- Communist Party
- Social Democrats

Of the 35 voting districts, the Nazis won the highest percentage of votes in these 10:

District	Percentage
Schleswig-Holstein	45.7%
Chemnitz-Zwickau	43.4%
Pomerania	43.1%
East Hanover	42.9%
Frankfurt/Oder	42.6%
Palatinate	42.5%
Hesse-Nassau	41.2%
South Hanover-Brunswick	40.6%
Breslau	40.4%
Hesse-Darmstadt	40.2%

August 1936 Olympic Games in Berlin; the Nazi regime uses the opportunity for clever cultivation of their image.

March 12, 1938 Anschluss (annexation) of Austria

Sept. 30, 1938 Annexation of the Sudetenland (Munich Agreement)

Nov. 9, 1938 *Kristallnacht* (Night of Broken Glass): Throughout Germany and Austria, Jews are attacked, arrested and murdered, synagogues set on fire, and Jewish businesses and homes ransacked.

March 1939 German forces occupy the rest of Czechia.

Adolf Hitler (1889–1945) A failed artist, he served as a corporal in World War I and from 1921 was a leader of the National Socialist German Workers' Party (NSDAP). After a putsch attempt in Munich in 1923 he served a short prison term during which he recorded his basic tenets in *Mein Kampf*, including a racist emphasis on the "Aryan super race," social Darwinism, conquering of "living space in the east," the revision of the Treaty of Versailles ("Versailles dictates") and a bitter war against "international Judaism." Apart from the brutal war, his greatest crime was the industrialized mass murder of millions of Jews, Sinti and Roma as well as the mentally ill, homosexuals and opponents of his regime. Already during the Weimar Republic, Hitler surrounded himself with the **Sturmabteilung** (**SA** – Storm Troopers) as personal bodyguards and paramilitary thugs who fought off any opposition. After Hitler came to power, some members of the SA under Chief of Staff **Ernst Röhm** (1887–1934) felt robbed of the "fruits of the revolution" and wanted to take the place of the regular army. Hitler put an end to such plans on the Night of the Long Knives in 1934. The SA was purged and replaced by the **Schutzstaffel** (**SS** – Shield Squadron) under Heinrich Himmler (1900–1945). Himmler saw his "Black Corps" as a Nazi elite troop; as the chief of German police (1936) he intermingled the SS with the regular police and the feared **Geheime Staatspolizei** (**Gestapo** – Secret State Police), in charge of eliminating actual and alleged opponents of the regime, and created the **Sicherheitsdienst** (**SD** – Security Service) and the **Reichssicherheitshauptamt** (**RSHA** – Reich Main Security Office) under the control of the SS. The SS organized the concentration and extermination camps; SS and SD task forces systematically liquidated Jews and "partisans" behind the Eastern Front; as **Waffen-SS** (Armed SS), SS divisions also fought alongside the army and were noted for their ruthlessness.

The Reich Ministry of Public Enlightenment and Propaganda, founded in 1933 and led by **Joseph Goebbels** (1897–1945), proved to be a versatile tool for brainwashing the public with Nazi ideology. Goebbels unscrupulously took advantage of modern mass media—the press, radio, film—to spread the Führer cult. Propagandistic high points were the party rallies, staged as spectacular shows for the masses.

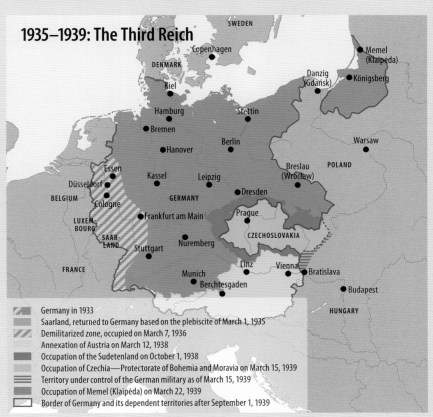

Joseph Goebbels, 1933

1935–1939: The Third Reich

Legend:
- Germany in 1933
- Saarland, returned to Germany based on the plebiscite of March 1, 1935
- Demilitarized zone, occupied on March 7, 1936
- Annexation of Austria on March 12, 1938
- Occupation of the Sudetenland on October 1, 1938
- Occupation of Czechia—Protectorate of Bohemia and Moravia on March 15, 1939
- Territory under control of the German military as of March 15, 1939
- Occupation of Memel (Klaipėda) on March 22, 1939
- Border of Germany and its dependent territories after September 1, 1939

Germany in World War II, 1939–1945

Encouraged by the appeasement policies, ignorance and accommodation of the Western powers, and playing on old resentments that the Germans as a people had historically gotten a raw deal ("a people without living space"), Nazi Germany was able to build a formidable military machine. In 1939 Germany invaded Poland and then wide swaths of Western Europe, attacked England from the air, and finally subjected the Soviet Union to an unparalleled war of annihilation. A ruthless mixture of racism, ignorance and megalomania escalated into "Total War," Holocaust and genocide of the Jews. Strikingly, a parallel development was taking place in Japan under quite different historical circumstances.

1939 Attack on Poland

EAST PRUSSIA

TERRITORIES DIRECTLY ANNEXED TO THE GERMAN REICH

GENERAL GOVERNMENT

PROTECTORATE OF BOHEMIA AND MORAVIA

☐ Border of the German Reich

March 1939 German occupation of the rest of Czechoslovakia, creation of a protectorate in Bohemia and Moravia

September 1939 The German invasion of Poland begins World War II.

April 1940 German units invade Denmark and Norway (Operation Weserübung).

May–June 1940 Attack on the Benelux countries and France; Paris is occupied.

June 1940 France is divided into an occupied zone in the north and the Vichy regime under Marshal Pétain in the south, which is willing to collaborate with the Germans.

August 1940 Beginning of the air war for England; Germany does not succeed in gaining sovereignty in the skies.

March–April 1941 German units force the British to withdraw from Libya.

April 1941 The German army carries out a concerted campaign in the Balkans, defeating Greece and Yugoslavia.

June 22, 1941 Beginning of the Russian campaign; after initial victories, the German advance is halted before the gates of Moscow.

July–September 1941 German troops encircle Soviet forces near Smolensk.

1940

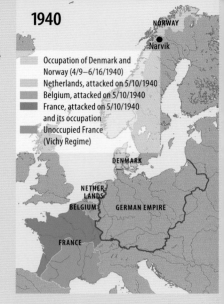

NORWAY

Narvik

Occupation of Denmark and Norway (4/9–6/16/1940)
Netherlands, attacked on 5/10/1940
Belgium, attacked on 5/10/1940
France, attacked on 5/10/1940 and its occupation
Unoccupied France (Vichy Regime)

DENMARK

NETHER-LANDS

BELGIUM

GERMAN EMPIRE

FRANCE

1941–1944 German blockade of Leningrad

January 1942 Wannsee Conference: Nazis resolve that a programmatic "final solution to the Jewish question" will be implemented under the leadership of the SS.

May–October 1942 The German campaign in North Africa ends in failure.

August 1942 Attack of the German Sixth Army begins the Battle of Stalingrad.

November 1942 US troops land in Morocco and Algeria; Germany occupies southern France and Algeria.

December 1942 Failed attempt by Army Group D to free the Sixth Army in Stalingrad ("Operation Winter Storm")

February 1943 Battle of Stalingrad ends with encirclement of German troops. Propaganda Minister Goebbels declares "Total War."

April/May 1943 An uprising in the Jewish Warsaw Ghetto fails.

July 1943 Americans and British invade Sicily ("Operation Husky")
Allied air attacks on Hamburg, firestorm ("Operation Gomorrah")
Mussolini is deposed and arrested; Germans free and reinstate him two months later.

Nov. 28–Dec. 1, 1943 Roosevelt, Churchill and Stalin negotiate postwar world order in Tehran.

February 1944 Battle of Monte Cassino

June 1944 Thousands of Allied troops land in Normandy (D-Day).
Beginning of a major Soviet offensive in the east.

July 20, 1944 The German resistance founders when Claus Schenk Graf von Stauffenberg's attempt to assassinate Hitler miscarries. The July 20th conspirators were the most spectacular

1941

Germany until 1941
Territories dependent on Germany
Territory occupied by Germany by 1941
Territory annexed by Germany by 1941
Territory occupied by Germany by 1941
Allies of Germany and its occupied territories in 1941
Territory in collaboration with Germany
Countries fighting against Germany in 1941

Murmansk

ICELAND

Arkhangelsk

FINLAND

FAROE ISLANDS (DENMARK)

SWEDEN

SOVIET UNION

NORWAY

Oslo

Stockholm

Helsinki

Leningrad (St. Petersburg)

Tallinn

Riga

Moscow

DENMARK

Copenhagen

Vilnius

Smolensk

IRELAND

UNITED KINGDOM

Hamburg

Königsberg

Minsk

Stalingrad (Volgograd)

London

NETHER-LANDS

Essen

Berlin

Warsaw

Kharkiv

BELGIUM

GERMANY

Prague

Kraków

Kiev

Rostov

Paris

Munich

Vienna

Lemberg (L'viv)

FRANCE

SLOVAKIA

Budapest

Odessa

Novorossiysk

Vichy

SWITZERLAND

Bordeaux

Zagreb

ROMANIA

Sevastopol

Belgrade

Bucharest

ITALY

BULGARIA

Marseille

Rome

Sofia

Madrid

Barcelona

TURKEY

PORTUGAL

ALBANIA (ITALIAN)

SPAIN

GREECE

SYRIA (FRENCH)

Gibraltar (British)

Athens

DODECANESE (ITALIAN)

CYPRUS

LEBANON (FRENCH)

Algiers

Tunis

TRANSJORDAN (BRITISH)

Casablanca

MALTA (BRITISH)

PALESTINE (BRITISH)

MOROCCO (FRENCH)

ALGERIA (FRENCH)

TUNISIA (FRENCH)

Tobruk

Alexandria

Cairo

SAUDI ARABIA

Tripoli

Benghazi

EGYPT

LIBYA (ITALIAN)

El Agheila

→ German attacks in 1941
→ UK counterattacks in 1941
→ Soviet counterattacks end of 1941
⊗ Important battle

German resistance group to fight against the Nazis, but not the only one.

August 1944 Warsaw Uprising by the Polish Home Army; Battle of Paris

December 1944 Beginning of the last major German offensive on the Western Front at Ardennes, the "Battle of the Bulge."

February 1945 Churchill, Roosevelt and Stalin meet at the Yalta Conference to discuss postwar order.

April 30, 1945 Hitler commits suicide in Soviet-occupied Berlin.

May 8, 1945 Germany signs an unconditional surrender.

May 23, 1945 Dissolution of the last Reich government, Dönitz in Flensburg

German Army's Africa campaign

In December 1940, the British routed the Italian troops in North Africa in a series of devastating defeats. To support his allies, Hitler ordered the creation of an Afrika Korps under General Field Marshal Erwin Rommel (1891–1944, "The Desert Fox"), which advanced to Tripoli in February 1941. Following initial triumphs, a lack of reinforcements and weapons forced Rommel to retreat and surrender. In 1944, having been implicated in the July 20th attempt to assassinate Hitler, Rommel committed suicide.

Wannsee Conference

Hitler's plans to eradicate the Jews had been no secret since the contents of his programmatic book *Mein Kampf* became well known. In January 1942, Reinhard Heydrich (born 1904, assassinated in 1942), head of the Reich Main Security Office, drafted a plan for a "final solution to the Jewish question" and presented it to the state bureaucracy and party functionaries in Wannsee.

1942–1943

Germany until 1942
Dependencies of Germany
Territory occupied by Germany by 1942
Territory occupied by Germany at the end of 1943
Germany's allies and territory they occupied in 1943
Territory freed by the Allies 1942–1943
Countries fighting against Germany in 1943
→ Allied offensives 1942–1943
→ German counterattacks 1942–1943
Important battle
Bombardment

1945 Yalta Conference

A conference of the Allied heads of state—Winston Churchill, Franklin D. Roosevelt and Joseph Stalin—in the resort town of Yalta on the Crimean Sea. The "Big Three" agreed on their respective spheres of influence after the war and the division of Germany into four occupation zones, along with its demilitarization and denazification.

July Plot

July Plot was an attempted assassination of Hitler in July 1944. Various German resistance groups and some military leaders had reached the conclusion that a lasting change of course would only be possible if Hitler were assassinated. Claus Schenk Graf von Stauffenberg (1907–1944), a lieutenant colonel in the general staff, carried a bomb in his briefcase to a consultation at the Führer's Wolfsschanze headquarters in East Prussia on July 20, 1944. After Hitler's death the insurgents planned to form a new government. Stauffenberg returned to Berlin after the deed, convinced that the assassination had succeeded, and began to execute the next steps of the plan (Operation Valkyrie). But Hitler had survived with only slight injuries. More than 200 members of the resistance movement were sentenced to death by the People's Court and executed by April 1945; a further 7,000 were imprisoned.

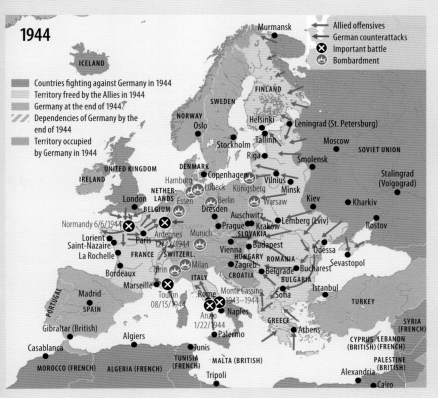

1944

→ Allied offensives
→ German counterattacks
Important battle
Bombardment

Countries fighting against Germany in 1944
Territory freed by the Allies in 1944
Germany at the end of 1944
Dependencies of Germany by the end of 1944
Territory occupied by Germany in 1944

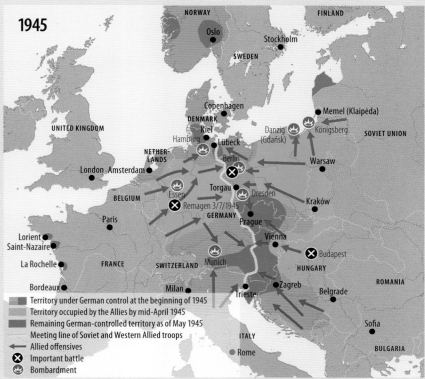

1945

Territory under German control at the beginning of 1945
Territory occupied by the Allies by mid-April 1945
Remaining German-controlled territory as of May 1945
Meeting line of Soviet and Western Allied troops
→ Allied offensives
Important battle
Bombardment

Germany After 1945

1945/46: Occupation Zones

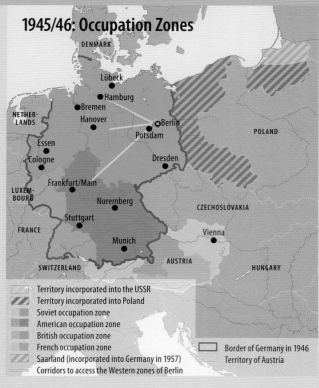

DENMARK

Lübeck
Hamburg
Bremen
Hanover
NETHER-
LANDS
Berlin
Potsdam
POLAND
Essen
Cologne
Dresden
LUXEM-
BOURG
Frankfurt/Main
Nuremberg
FRANCE
Stuttgart
Munich
Vienna
SWITZERLAND
AUSTRIA
HUNGARY
CZECHOSLOVAKIA

Territory incorporated into the USSR
Territory incorporated into Poland
Soviet occupation zone
American occupation zone
British occupation zone
French occupation zone
Saarland (incorporated into Germany in 1957)
Corridors to access the Western zones of Berlin
Border of Germany in 1946
Territory of Austria

Division in 1949

Berlin
GERMAN DEMOCRATIC REPUBLIC
(GDR)
FEDERAL REPUBLIC OF GERMANY
(FRG)
Bonn

In the years following World War II, occupied Germany became the first arena of the Cold War. Deteriorating relations between the Western powers and the USSR led to the division of Germany into two states with differing ideologies. The divided city of Berlin became symbolic of the Cold War.

July 1945 Political parties are allowed to resume their activities.

August 1945 The Allied Control Council oversees four German occupation zones.

November 1945 Nuremberg Trials against major war criminals begin.

1946 In the Soviet Zone, the KPD and SPD parties unite to form what later becomes the state SED party (Socialist Unity Party Germany).

January 1947 American and British zones are joined (bi-zone).

June 1947 The Marshall Plan (named for George Marshall, US foreign minister) for the reconstruction of Europe is unveiled (realized 1948–1952).

March 1948 The USSR withdraws from the Allied Control Council.

June 1948 Currency reform, conducted separately in the Western zones and the Soviet zone

1948–1949 Berlin Blockade by the USSR; Berlin is supplied through Allied airlift ("raisin bombers").

1949 Creation of two German states, the Federal Republic of Germany (FRG) in the west and the German Democratic Republic (GDR) in the east

1952 Reparations Agreement between Israel and West Germany: The Federal Republic of Germany compensates Israel for Jewish property stolen by the Nazis by delivering goods worth three billion marks.

June 17, 1953 Popular revolt against the communist regime in the GDR

1954 "Miracle of Bern": West Germany wins the championship World Cup soccer match against Hungary.

1955 West Germany joins NATO. The Warsaw Pact is established with East Germany. Hallstein (CDU) doctrine on German foreign policy: West Germany represents all Germans and will have no further diplomatic relations with states that recognize East Germany.

May 1955 With the founding of the Bundeswehr, the German Federal Defense Force, Germany rearms.

October 1955 The last prisoners of war return from the USSR to Germany after Konrad Adenauer's visit to Moscow.

The Destruction of Germany

Bombs (force in tons)
(97 %) Extent of destruction

Kiel 29,000 t
Lübeck (30%)
Szczecin (70%)
Hamburg 38,000 t
Emden (80%)
Bremen 4,000 t
Berlin 68,000 t
Hanover 23,000 t
Hildesheim (90%)
Magdeburg (90%)
Osnabrück (65%)
Emmerich (97%)
Paderborn (85%)
Zerbst (80%)
Dessau (80%)
Essen 36,000 t
Gelsenkirchen 22,000 t
Duisburg 30,000 t
Bochum 11,000 t
Kassel (80%) 8,000 t
Nordhausen (85%)
Leipzig 11,000 t
Jülich (97%)
Düsseldorf 18,000 t
Dresden 7,000 t
Düren (99%) 2,700 t
Cologne 48,000 t
Remscheid (82%)
Chemnitz (75%)
Koblenz (87%)
Plauen (75%) 2,000 t
Frankfurt 29,000 t
Bingen (96%)
Offenbach (60%) 3,000 t
Mainz (80%)
Darmstadt (78%)
Würzburg (82%)
Mannheim 25,000 t
Heilbronn (62%)
Nuremberg 20,000 t
Bruchsal (96%)
Pforzheim (98%) 1,500 t
Stuttgart (68%) 24,000 t
Karlsruhe 10,000 t
Ulm (81%)
Munich 27,000 t
Friedrichshafen (75%)

Cologne after the Allied bombardment on April 24, 1945.

1957 Berlin Crisis: West Germany signs the Treaty of Rome, laying the foundation for European integration.

1958 Soviet Premier Khrushchev delivers an ultimatum that the Western powers must leave Berlin.

1961 Erection of the Berlin Wall; prior to this date around 2.5 million East German citizens fled to the West.

1963 Élysée Treaty reestablishes extensive cooperation between France and Germany; President Kennedy gives "Ich bin ein Berliner" speech.

1967 At a demonstration in West Berlin against the shah of Iran, the police shoot and kill student Benno Ohnesorg.

1968 Student unrest in West Germany

1970 Federal Chancellor Willy Brandt's genuflection before the Warsaw Ghetto memorial is seen by many as a sign that Germany is addressing its Nazi past.

1970–1973 West Germany signs agreements that normalize relations with its Eastern European neighbors and the USSR, mainly due to the instigation of Chancellor Willy Brandt.

1972 Munich Massacre: At the summer Olympic Games in Munich, the militant Palestinian group "Black September" takes Israeli athletes hostage. The attempt to free the hostages fails, and seventeen people die.

1973 Both the Federal Republic of Germany and the German Democratic Republic join the United Nations.

1977 German Autumn: Red Army Faction (RAF) terrorists kidnap Hans Martin Schleyer, head of the Confederation of German Employers' Associations. A hijacked Lufthansa plane is stormed after landing in Mogadishu, Somalia. Three of the four hijackers are killed; the hostages escape uninjured. Imprisoned

terrorists commit suicide in reaction to the rescue, and Schleyer is found shot dead in Mulhouse, France.

1982–1998 Helmut Kohl is chancellor of West Germany for eight years and of reunited Germany for another eight.

1983 West Germany extends a billion marks in credit to East Germany.

1985 Mikhail Gorbachev becomes general secretary of the Central Committee of the Communist Party of the Soviet Union.

Sept. 30, 1989 Thousands of East German citizens wanting to leave the country gather at the German embassy in Prague, where Foreign Minister Genscher famously announces that they may depart. The undemocratic system of the German Democratic Republic is over.

November 1989 Fall of the Berlin Wall: East and West Germans can move freely from one country to the other.

Oct. 3, 1990 Reunification of Germany: The five East German states become part of the Federal Republic of Germany.

1991 Berlin is named capital of reunified Germany (the government moves from Bonn in 1998).

since 2005 Angela Merkel is chancellor.

Berlin in 1945

FRENCH ZONE
BRITISH ZONE
SOVIET ZONE
AMERICAN ZONE

West and East Berlin

WEST BERLIN   EAST BERLIN

Berlin from 1990

Federal States and Administrative Regions Today

Kiel
SCHLESWIG-HOLSTEIN
MECKLENBURG-WEST POMERANIA
Schwerin
Hamburg
HAMBURG
Bremerhaven
BREMEN   LÜNEBURG
Bremen
WESER-EMS
LOWER SAXONY
MAGDEBURG
Berlin
HANOVER
BERLIN
Hanover
Magdeburg
Potsdam
SAXONY-ANHALT
BRANDENBURG
MÜNSTER
DESSAU
DETMOLD
NORTH RHINE-WESTPHALIA
HALLE   LEIPZIG
DÜSSELDORF
BRAUNSCHWEIG
DRESDEN
Düsseldorf
ARNSBERG
SAXONY
KASSEL
Erfurt
Dresden
COLOGNE
THURINGIA
CHEMNITZ
GIESSEN
HESSE
KOBLENZ
Wiesbaden
UPPER FRANCONIA
TRIER
DARMSTADT
LOWER FRANCONIA
Mainz
RHINELAND-PALATINATE
SAARLAND   RHINE-HESSE-PALATINATE
MIDDLE FRANCONIA
UPPER PALATINATE
Saarbrücken
KARLSRUHE
STUTTGART
LOWER BAVARIA
Stuttgart
BAVARIA
BADEN-WÜRTTEMBERG
SWABIA
UPPER BAVARIA
FREIBURG   TÜBINGEN
Munich

Nuremberg Trials and denazification Series of court proceedings to punish the main perpetrators of Nazi war crimes. Less severe criminals were classified as candidates for denazification and punished accordingly (although former Nazis still occupied several official posts until the 1980s). The trials began in November 1945 and continued until 1949, and the case against the twenty-one major war criminals was heard until October 1946. Hitler, Goebbels and Himmler committed suicide before the trials, and Hermann Göring afterward. Allied trials against hundreds of concentration camp guards also took place from 1945 to 1949.

Konrad Adenauer (1876–1967) He served as lord mayor of Cologne from 1917 until he was unseated by the Nazis in 1933. As chairman of the newly formed Christian Democratic Union (CDU), from 1949 to 1963 he was the first chancellor of the Federal Republic of Germany. He pushed for West Germany's

alignment with the Western powers and reconciliation with France.

Walter Ulbricht (1893–1973) A Communist Party politician in the Weimar Republic, he lived in exile in Paris and Prague after 1933, and in Moscow from 1938. In 1945 he became Moscow's man for East Germany. Ulbricht was general secretary of the SED (Socialist Party) 1950 to 1971, president of East Germany 1960 to 1973, and supported East Germany's alignment with the Eastern Bloc. When he tried to surpass the USSR in technology, he was divested of power.

Ludwig Erhard (1897–1977) He was federal economics minister from 1949 to 1963 (for the CDU) and is generally recognized as the mastermind of West Germany's postwar "economic miracle"; his stint as chancellor from 1963 to 1966 was less successful.

Erich Honecker (1912–1994) Imprisoned as a communist during the Third Reich, after

1949 Honecker was leader of the party-run Free German Youth in East Germany and head of the SED (Socialist Party) 1971–1989. As leader of East Germany 1976–1989, he allowed some relations with West Germany but under tight control and only reluctantly took part in Gorbachev's reforms after 1985. He was imprisoned 1992/93 and emigrated to Chile after his release.

Willy Brandt (1913–1992) A socialist, he fled to Norway and Sweden during the Third Reich. He was mayor of Berlin 1957 to 1966, SPD chairman 1964 to 1987, foreign minister 1966 to 1969, and from 1969 to 1974 the first SPD chancellor and architect of Eastern Bloc policy. Brandt was dedicated to world policy issues (north-south conflict) and won the 1971 Nobel Peace Prize.

Willy Brandt with United States President John F. Kennedy in the White House, March 1961

Helmut Kohl (born 1930) was minister president of Rhineland-Palatinate 1966 to 1976, CDU chairman 1973 to 1998 and chancellor of West and then united Germany from 1982 to 1998. Kohl was instrumental in German reunification in 1989/90 and deeply committed to the process of European unification.

Switzerland Until the 16th Century

Prehistoric Times

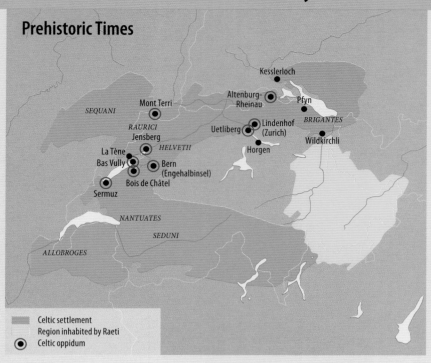

Legend:
- Celtic settlement
- Region inhabited by Raeti
- ⊙ Celtic oppidum

58 BCE–400 CE: Under the Romans

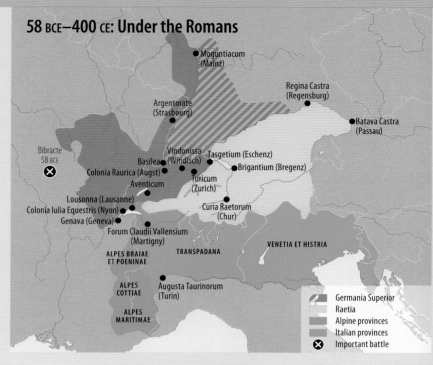

Legend:
- Germania Superior
- Raetia
- Alpine provinces
- Italian provinces
- ⊗ Important battle

50,000–30,000 BCE Neanderthal remains dating from this period have been found in the Wildkirchli caves.

3900–2800 BCE Dates of the stilt houses of the Horgen and Pfyn cultures.

~800 BCE Raetians and Celts settle the western Alps.

6th–1st centuries BCE Age of the La-Tène culture, characterized by fortified Celtic settlements known as oppida.

58 BCE The Battle of Bibracte: Julius Caesar defeats the Helveticans as they attempt to migrate to Gaul. This leads to the subsequent founding of the Roman colonies Colonia Raurica (Augst) and Colonia Iulia Equestris (Nyon).

25–15 BCE Roman subjugation of the Helveticans and the founding of the province of Raetia.

68–69 CE Rebellion of the Helveticans and their repression by the Roman general Caecina.

~90 Settling of the province Germania Superior.

after 401 Fallback of the Roman troops and the end of Roman domination.

443 The Burgundians settle the Rhône Valley as a foederatus of the Romans.

532 Battle of Autun: The Franks' victory over the Burgundians leads to the Frankish conquest of the Burgundian kingdom.

843 Treaty of Verdun: Western Switzerland is incorporated into Lotharingia, while eastern Switzerland becomes part of the East Frankish realm.

880 Treaty of Ribemont: Western Switzerland is made part of Upper Burgundy, while eastern Switzerland is given to the East Frankish realm (from 911, Swabian tribal duchy).

951 Upper Burgundy and Lower Burgundy are unified and become the kingdom of Arles (or Arelat).

1032 Arles reverts to the Holy Roman Empire.

11th century Habsburg Castle is built in Aargau.

12th–13th centuries Habsburgs contend to establish Habsburg sovereignty of Switzerland

1291 The free communities of Uri, Schwyz and Unterwalden band together to create the Old Swiss Confederacy, the traditional charter of the Swiss Confederation (the Old Confederation).

1315 Battle of Morgarten: fighters from Schwyz and others of the confederation are victorious in this confrontation with the Habsburgs, the first of many.

1332 Lucerne is admitted to the confederation.

1351–1353 Admission of Zurich, Zug, Glarus and Bern to the confederation, called the *Acht Alte Orte* in German ("eight old places").

1386 The Battle of Sempach ends in victory for the Swiss Confederation over the Habsburgs. Duke Leopold III of Austria also falls in this battle.

1415 The confederation captures Aargau, strategically located in between Zurich and Lucerne and Bern.

443–532

Legend:
- → Burgundian relocation after 436
- Burgundian territory as Roman "foederati" (allies)
- Kingdom of Burgundy ca. 476

Stilt houses In the Neolithic period, settlers on the soggy lands in areas along the sea, on islands or swampy lands built elevated houses of this type.

The Burgundian Kingdom
The first Burgundian kingdom was established in Mainz (Mogonaticum) after 411 and was annihilated by the Roman general Aetius in 436. After this defeat, the Burgundians moved to the region of present-day western Switzerland and Savoie. They also settled in the Rhône Valley, where they established the Burgundian kingdom anew. At the Battle of Autun in 532 they were decisively defeated by the Franks, and their territory was annexed to the Frankish Kingdom.

482–814: The Franks

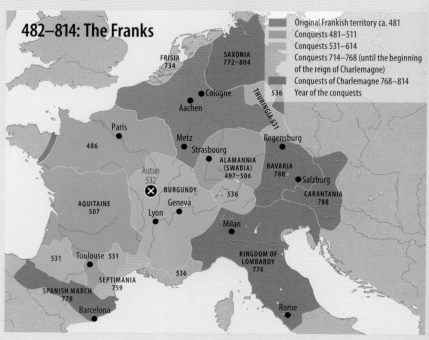

Legend:
- Original Frankish territory ca. 481
- Conquests 481–511
- Conquests 531–614
- Conquests 714–768 (until the beginning of the reign of Charlemagne)
- Conquests of Charlemagne 768–814
- 536 Year of the conquests

After the Treaty of Verdun

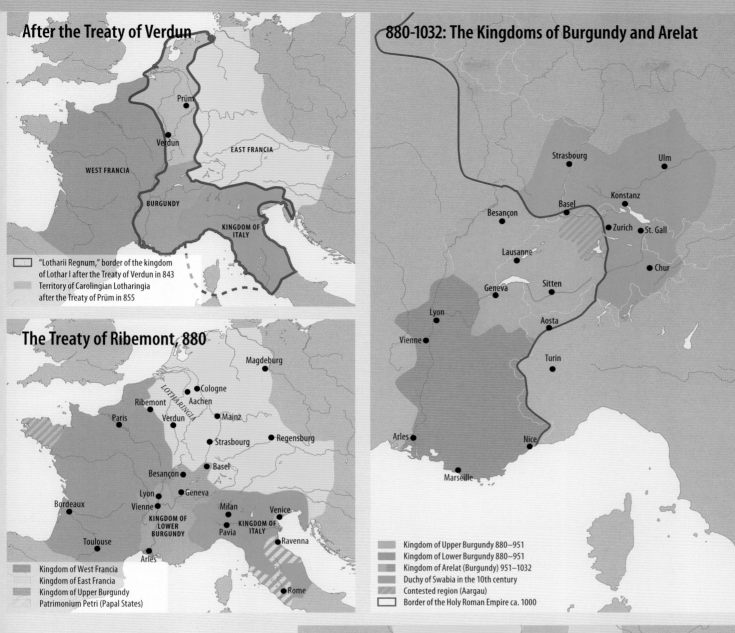

Prüm

Verdun

EAST FRANCIA

WEST FRANCIA

BURGUNDY

KINGDOM OF ITALY

☐ "Lotharii Regnum," border of the kingdom of Lothar I after the Treaty of Verdun in 843

▨ Territory of Carolingian Lotharingia after the Treaty of Prüm in 855

The Treaty of Ribemont, 880

Magdeburg

Cologne

LOTHARINGIA

Ribemont
Aachen

Paris
Verdun
Mainz

Strasbourg
Regensburg

Besançon
Basel

Lyon
Geneva

Bordeaux
Vienne

Milan
Venice

KINGDOM OF LOWER BURGUNDY
Pavia
KINGDOM OF ITALY

Toulouse
Ravenna

Arles

Rome

▨ Kingdom of West Francia
▨ Kingdom of East Francia
▨ Kingdom of Upper Burgundy
▨ Patrimonium Petri (Papal States)

880–1032: The Kingdoms of Burgundy and Arelat

Strasbourg
Ulm

Konstanz
Besançon
Basel
Zurich
St. Gall

Lausanne

Geneva
Sitten
Chur

Lyon
Aosta

Vienne
Turin

Arles
Nice

Marseille

Venice

Rome

▨ Kingdom of Upper Burgundy 880–951
▨ Kingdom of Lower Burgundy 880–951
▨ Kingdom of Arelat (Burgundy) 951–1032
▨ Duchy of Swabia in the 10th century
▨ Contested region (Aargau)
☐ Border of the Holy Roman Empire ca. 1000

1440–1450   The Old Zurich War: Zurich, acting in league with the German Habsburg king Frederick III against the rest of the confederation, is defeated.

1474   The *Ewige Richtung* ("eternal course"), a treaty of peace and alliance with the Habsburg duke Sigismund of Tirol, which reaffirms the status quo, is signed. The Habsburg emperor does not recognize this treaty.

1477   The Battle of Nancy: The victory of the Swiss Confederation over Charles the Bold, Duke of Burgundy, contributes to the excellent reputation of Swiss soldiers. As a result, these soldiers begin to work in the service of the European powers.

1481   Admission of Solothurn and Freiburg (Fribourg) to the confederation.

1499   Swabian War: The Swiss Confederation's victory over Habsburg Emperor Maximilian I and the Swabian League allied with him leads to virtual acceptance of the confederation's autonomy (although it formally still belongs to the Holy Roman Empire).

1501   Admission of Schaffhausen and Basel to the confederation.

1506   Pope Julius II establishes the Swiss Guard, the personal guard that still protects the pope today.

ca. 1300: Autonomy

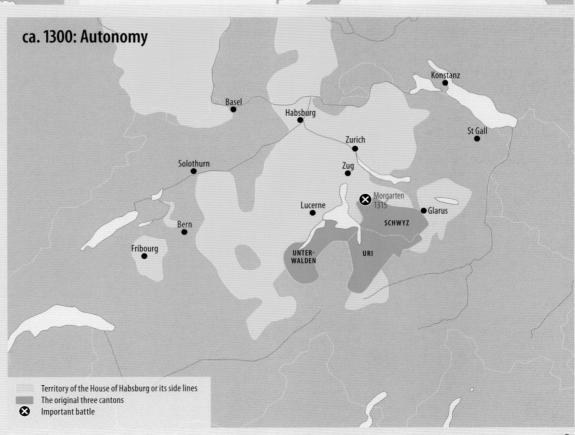

Konstanz

Basel
Habsburg
St Gall

Zurich

Solothurn
Zug

Lucerne
Morgarten 1315
Glarus

Bern
SCHWYZ

Fribourg
UNTER-
WALDEN
URI

▨ Territory of the House of Habsburg or its side lines
▨ The original three cantons
⊗ Important battle

Switzerland and Liechtenstein

1291–1531: The Swiss Confederation

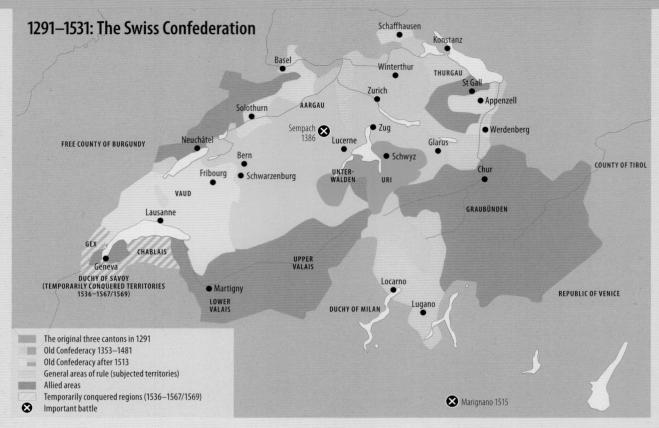

Legend:
- The original three cantons in 1291
- Old Confederacy 1353–1481
- Old Confederacy after 1513
- General areas of rule (subjected territories)
- Allied areas
- Temporarily conquered regions (1536–1567/1569)
- ⊗ Important battle

1531

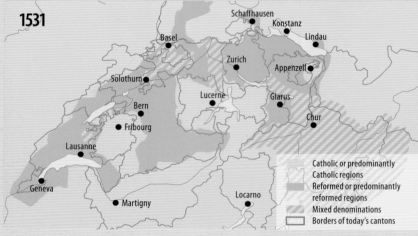

Legend:
- Catholic or predominantly Catholic regions
- Reformed or predominantly reformed regions
- Mixed denominations
- Borders of today's cantons

1798–1813: The Helvetican Republic

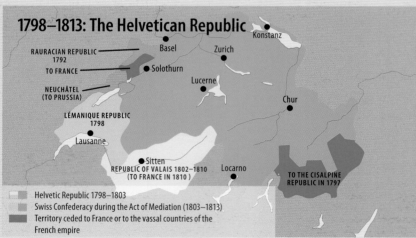

Legend:
- Helvetic Republic 1798–1803
- Swiss Confederacy during the Act of Mediation (1803–1813)
- Territory ceded to France or to the vassal countries of the French empire

---

1511 The *Erbeinung*, a binding and hereditary non-aggression treaty with the Habsburgs, is signed and remains in effect until 1798.

1513 Appenzel is admitted to the confederation, bringing its membership to thirteen (until 1798).

1515 Battle of Marignano: France's victory over the confederation establishes a stable southern border until 1798.

1522–1528 Beginning of the Reformation in Zurich, led by Ulrich Zwingli

1527 The Swiss Guard defending the pope is defeated during the Sack of Rome by troops of Emperor Charles V.

1529–1531 The Kappel Wars between the Protestant and Catholic cantons leads to a compromise: each canton is allowed to determine its religion.

1541 Beginning of the Reformation in Ghent ("the City of God"), the domain of John Calvin (1509–1564), founder of Calvinism, who insists on a strict interpretation of the Bible.

1586 The Golden League, a confessional alliance of the seven Catholic territories in the Old Confederation, is established.

1618–1648 The Old Confederation remains neutral in the Thirty Years' War.

1648 The Peace of Westphalia formally separates Switzerland from the Holy Roman Empire, guaranteeing its full sovereignty.

1653 Swiss Peasants' War

1792–1793 The French Revolution spreads to Switzerland, and a republic is briefly established in the Basel region.

1798 The French Revolution again impacts Switzerland; pro-French Swiss establish the Lemanic Republic in what is now the canton of Vaud.

1798–1803 Napoleon occupies Switzerland and establishes the Helvetic Republic in place of the Swiss Confederation. The cantons are reduced from virtually self-sufficient states to administrative units.

1802–1810 Valais becomes the Rhodanic Republic; joined to France in 1810.

1803 Acts of Mediation are enacted to curb the disorder that results when French troops withdraw; the Swiss Confederation of nineteen cantons is reinstated with a federalist government.

1815 Congress of Vienna: Following Napoleon's defeat, international agreements recognize the independence and neutrality of the Swiss Confederation; three additional cantons are added.

Nov. 3–29, 1847 Sonderbund War, the last armed dispute fought on Swiss territory

Sept. 12, 1848 A federal constitution is enacted: Switzerland is a federal state.

1859 The export of mercenary soldiers is forbidden by law.

1864 The Red Cross is founded. The first Geneva Convention concerning treatment of prisoners of war, expanded and renewed in 1906, 1929 and 1949.

1873–1878 The *Kulturkampf* ("cultural struggle") of the Swiss states against the Catholic Church, leading to the abolishment of dioceses

1874 The federal constitution is revised and includes direct democracy, marked by obligatory referenda on legislation.

1914–1918 World War I: Switzerland remains neutral.

The Swiss Habsburg Wars and the Old Confederation The Habsburg Wars were a series of conflicts that took place between 1291 and 1474 and in 1511. Numerous battles were waged between the gradually awakening Swiss Confederation and the absolute monarchy of the Habsburgs, which continually sought to assert its claim to power through armed force, in vain. The three original rural communities—Uri, Schwyz and Unterwalden—formed a union in 1291, and additional regions and cities joined over time. There were eight members ("eight old places") until 1353 and thirteen ("thirteen old places") until 1513. Other territories were allied with the confederation through a system of treaties (without voting rights) or were administered after their conquest as "common dominions." The Habsburgs were finally ousted from Switzerland in the *Erbeinung* of 1511, which was a result of their final attempt at takeover during the Swabian War of 1499.

Sonderbund War The Sonderbund, an alliance of the seven Catholic cantons—Lucerne, Freiburg, Schwyz, Unterwalden, Uri, Valais and Zug—tried to withdraw from the confederation after being provoked by anti-Catholic measures taken by the liberal majority. This attempted secession led to a brief civil war in November 1847. The confederate army, in strict compliance with the principles of humanitarianism, defeated the Sonderbund cantons within three weeks with fewer than 150 casualties.

1847: The Sonderbund War

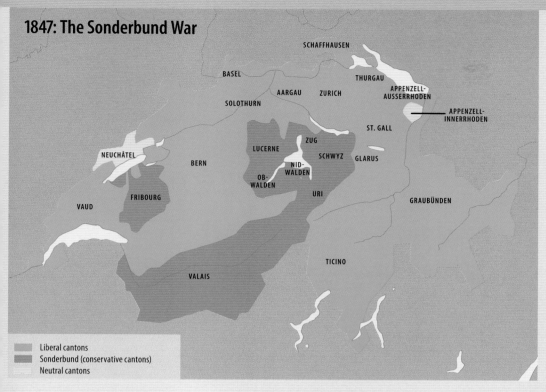

Liberal cantons
Sonderbund (conservative cantons)
Neutral cantons

EFTA: European Free Trade Association

Former members of the EFTA
Current members of the EFTA (2010)

Nov. 11–18, 1918 Political confrontation between the conservative alliance and the labor movement culminates in a national strike, which is quelled by the army; resentment against the working class lingers.

1939–1945 World War II: Switzerland remains neutral and grants refuge to over 300,000 displaced people seeking asylum.

after 1945 Switzerland remains neutral in the Cold War.

1960 Switzerland becomes a charter member of the European Free Trade Association (EFTA).

1971 A national referendum gives Swiss women the right to vote and hold office at the federal level.

1990 The Swiss government forces the canton Appenzell-Innerrhoden to grant suffrage and enfranchisment to women, the last canton to do so.

2001 Switzerland declines entry into the European Union following a referendum.

2002 Switzerland joins the UN.

Switzerland Today

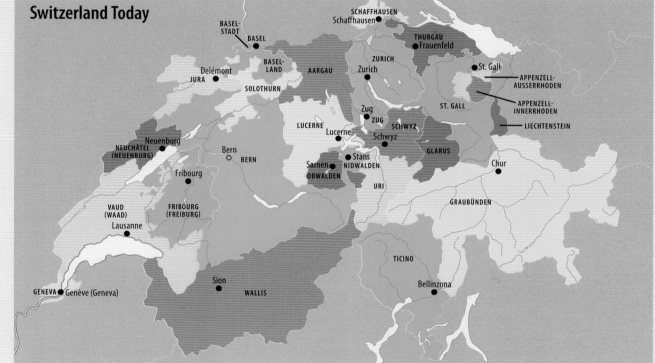

Liechtenstein

1699–1712 Prince Hans Adam von Liechtenstein purchases the lordships Schellenberg and Vaduz.

1719 Charles VI grants the territories the status Principality of Liechtenstein, part of the Holy Roman Empire.

1805 Liechtenstein introduces compulsory universal education.

1806 Liechtenstein is a sovereign state in the Confederation of the Rhine.

1815 Liechtenstein is part of the German Confederation.

1842 A sovereign prince visits the principality for the first time.

1852–1919 Trade agreement with the Austro-Hungarian Empire is enacted.

1861 Foundation of the federal state bank

1862 A constitutional monarchy is established.

1921 Liechtenstein adopts a democratic constitution.

1923 A trade union with Switzerland is established.

1938 Prince Francis Joseph II ascends the throne and makes his home in Vaduz.

1939–1945 Liechtenstein declares its neutrality in World War II.

ca. 1965 Liechtenstein begins to promote itself as a tax haven and headquarters for offshore holding companies.

1984 Women gain suffrage.

1990–1995 Liechtenstein joins the UN, EFTA, European Economic Association and World Trade Organization.

2003 Constitutional reforms: The prince is given the right of veto.

Liechtenstein

Central Europe: An Overview

Before 450 BCE: Prehistory

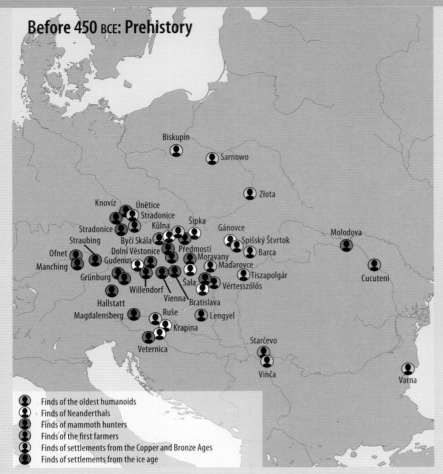

Finds of the oldest humanoids
Finds of Neanderthals
Finds of mammoth hunters
Finds of the first farmers
Finds of settlements from the Copper and Bronze Ages
Finds of settlements from the ice age

1st–4th Centuries: The Roman Period

Region settled by Germanic tribes, 1st–2nd centuries
Region settled by Slavs in the 2nd century
Roman Empire, 1st–4th centuries
Region under Roman dominance 106–270
Amber Road
Celtic oppidum

6th–8th Centuries: Tribes of Southeastern Europe

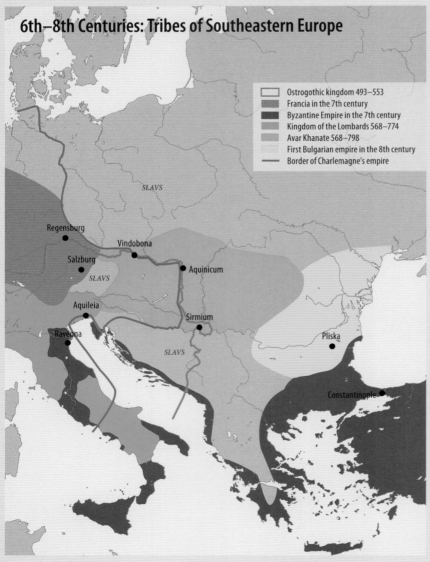

Ostrogothic kingdom 493–553
Francia in the 7th century
Byzantine Empire in the 7th century
Kingdom of the Lombards 568–774
Avar Khanate 568–798
First Bulgarian empire in the 8th century
Border of Charlemagne's empire

100,000 BCE Skeletal remains of Neanderthals in Gánovce, Slovakia dated to this period

29,000–22,000 BCE Paleolithic Venus figures carved in Dolní Věstonice (Czech Republic), Morvany (Slovakia) and Willendorf (Austria).

4900–3900 BCE Height of the Neolithic Lengyel culture (archaeological site in Lengyel, Hungary); painted ceramics dated to this period.

1200–500 BCE Lusatian culture (extensive burial sites) of the Bronze and Iron Ages (archaeological site in Biskupin, Poland)

750–450 BCE Hallstatt culture of the Iron Age: cemetery and artifacts created in Hallstatt (Austria), a center of trade and salt mining

450 BCE–1 CE Celtic oppida are built in what is now the Czech Republic.

8 BCE The Roman province of Dalmatia is established.

9 CE The Roman province of Pannonia is established; after 100 CE it was divided into Pannonia Superior (western part) and Pannonia Inferior (eastern part).

41–54 Kingdom of Noricum becomes a Roman province.

1st–2nd centuries Construction of the Rhein-Danube border defense (*Limes Romanus*) between the Roman Empire and "barbarians"; Aquincum (Budapest)

and Vindobona (Vienna) are founded.

166–182 Marcomannic Wars: Emperor Marcus Aurelius dies, presumably in Vienna, on March 17, 180; the war is concluded by his son, Commodus.

5th–6th centuries The Slavic peoples settle the region.

568–798/803 The Avars build an empire in Pannonia, subjugating and mingling with the Slavs.

796–803 Charlemagne's campaigns against and victory over the Avars; he establishes the Avar March on the eastern frontier of his empire.

895 Bohemia submits to the East Frankish empire.

907 Pannonia is occupied by Magyars.

after 960 Emergence of the Polish states under the Piast dynasty

976–1156 The margravate of Austria under the House of Bamberg is an administrative part of the duchy of Bavaria.

1000 Hungary becomes a kingdom (including Slovakia).

1102 Hungary and Croatia enter a personal union (one king rules two distinct kingdoms).

1308–1386 Reign of the Anjou dynasty in the Kingdom of Hungary

1310–1437 The reign of the House of

The First Empire

German states
Border of the Holy Roman Empire
Russian duchies
Italian states
Croatia (Hungarian from 1102)
Dependencies of Hungary (from the 12th century)
Republic of Venice
Dependencies of the Byzantine Empire

ca. 1410

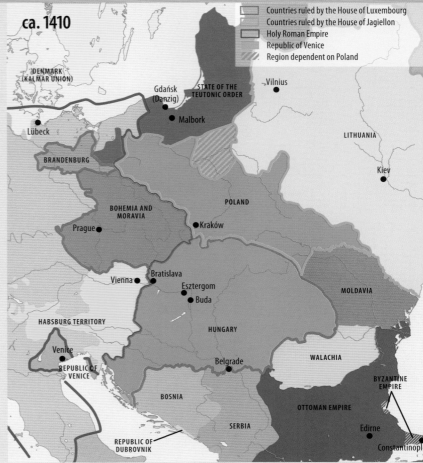

Countries ruled by the House of Luxembourg
Countries ruled by the House of Jagiellon
Holy Roman Empire
Republic of Venice
Region dependent on Poland

Luxembourg in Bohemia begins with John I; after 1386 the Luxembourg dynasty rules Hungary as well (King Sigismund, later emperor).

1386 Personal union of Poland with Lithuania under the Latvian Jagiellons

1490–1526 Personal union of Hungary and Bohemia under the line of the Polish-Lithuanian Jagiellon dynasty

1515 Double wedding of the heirs of the Jagiellon and Habsburg dynasties

1526 Battle of Mohács results in an Ottoman victory over the Kingdom of Hungary; beginning of the Habsburg reign in Bohemia and Hungary (Habsburg kingdom until 1918).

1529 The first Ottoman siege of Vienna

1541 Ottoman occupation of the Hungarian capital, Ofen (Buda). Transylvania comes under Ottoman suzerainty.

1569–1791/1795 Union of Lublin: Poland and Lithuania become a federated commonwealth in which "golden liberty" or nobles' democracy gives noblemen power and freedom unknown in other European countries.

Marcomannic Wars 166–182 A series of conflicts between the Roman Empire and the Germanic tribes of the Marcomanni, Quadi and Vandals peoples who settled along the central regions of the Danube. With their offensives, the Roman troops advanced deep into German territory. The northernmost

presence of the Roman army in central Europe (outside of Germany) is indicated by a Roman inscription on a rock in Trenčín (Latin *Laugaritio*, Slovakia) dating from 179.

Regnum Noricum – Celtic Kingdom
The first formal state that existed in the eastern part of central Europe had an important center at the site of Magdalensberg (Latin *Virunum*, Austria) in the 2nd to 1st centuries BCE. During the reign of Emperor Augustus, in 15 BCE, it was captured by the Romans.

The Amber Road in Antiquity This was the trade route along which precious amber was transported from the Baltic Sea through what are now Poland, the Czech Republic, Austria and Slovakia all the way to Italy and possibly even Egypt. Its peak was in the 2nd century CE.

The Avars These nomadic natives of central Asia fled under the pressure of the eastern Turks first into the area around the Black Sea, and then to Pannonia, where they joined forces with the Lombards to destroy the Gepid Kingdom in 567.

Battle of Mohács On August 29, 1526, the young King Louis II of Hungary and Bohemia fell in battle, and the Turks conquered the kingdom in eastern central Europe. The Kingdom of Hungary was divided into three parts:
—Royal Hungary (Slovakia, Burgenland and part of Croatia) fell to the Habsburgs (through the marriage of Archduke Ferdinand I with its heiress, Anna, a sister of Louis II).
—The Turkish Dominion (central Hungary)
—Transylvania, initially ruled by the rival King John (János Zápolya), became a vassal state of the Ottoman Empire; possession of this region would be fiercely contested over and over again during the following centuries.

From ca. 1526: Ottoman Wars

Holy Roman Empire
Vassal states of the Ottoman Empire
⊗ Important battle

Central Europe: An Overview

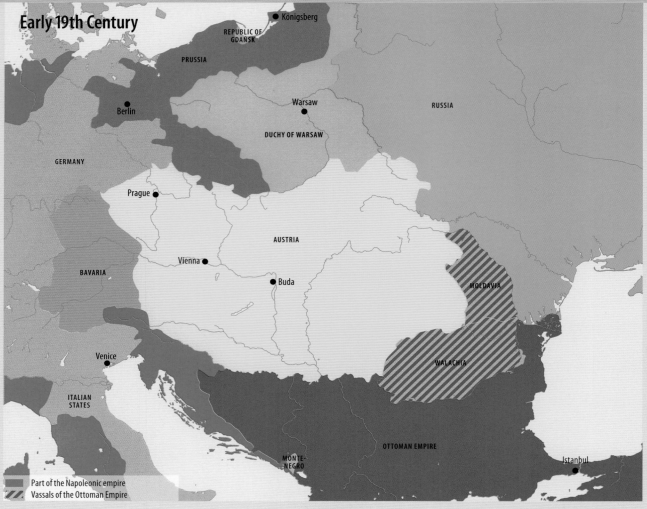

Early 19th Century

Königsberg

REPUBLIC OF GDAŃSK

PRUSSIA

Berlin

Warsaw

DUCHY OF WARSAW

RUSSIA

GERMANY

Prague

AUSTRIA

Vienna

BAVARIA

Buda

MOLDAVIA

Venice

WALACHIA

ITALIAN STATES

OTTOMAN EMPIRE

MONTE-NEGRO

Istanbul

Part of the Napoleonic empire
Vassals of the Ottoman Empire

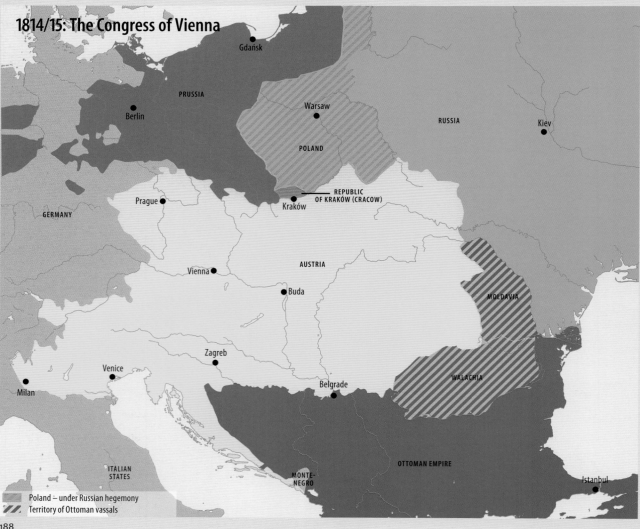

1814/15: The Congress of Vienna

Gdańsk

PRUSSIA

Berlin

Warsaw

RUSSIA

Kiev

POLAND

REPUBLIC OF KRAKÓW (CRACOW)

Prague

Kraków

GERMANY

Vienna

AUSTRIA

Buda

MOLDAVIA

Zagreb

Venice

Milan

Belgrade

WALACHIA

ITALIAN STATES

OTTOMAN EMPIRE

MONTE-NEGRO

Istanbul

Poland – under Russian hegemony
Territory of Ottoman vassals

1604–1711 Anti-Habsburg nobles' rebellions in Hungary

1683–1699 Great Turkish War: The Ottomans are expelled from central Europe.

1740–1780 Reign of Empress Maria Theresa, called "the most human of the Habsburgs."

1765–1790 Enlightened Absolutism ("Josephinism") in the Habsburg Empire

1772, 1793, 1795 The Partitions of Poland among Prussia, Austria and Russia

1807–1813 Napoleon controls the French vassal states, the Duchy of Warsaw and the Illyrian provinces.

1815 After the Congress of Vienna, Congress Poland is established, a Russian vassal state.

1815–1846 The Republic of Kraków exists under the protection of Russia, Prussia and Austria.

1815–1848 Era of Klemens von Metternich, whose reactionary policies shape central Europe.

1848/49 Revolutions in the Habsburg territories lead to the ascension of Francis Joseph I to the throne.

1852–1867 Age of Neo-Absolutism

1867 Austro-Hungarian *Ausgleich* (compromise) regulates relations between Austria and Hungary and establishes the Dual (k. u. k.) Monarchy.

1879 Dual Alliance: A political-military coalition between the German Empire and Austria-Hungary. Italy joins in 1882 to form the Triple Alliance.

1889 Suicide of Crown Prince Rudolf, who wanted to achieve more rights for the Slavs.

1896 Archduke Francis Ferdinand becomes the heir apparent.

1908 Austria-Hungary annexes Bosnia and Herzegovina.

1912/13 Balkan Wars

June 28, 1914 Assassination of heir to the throne Archduke Francis Ferdinand in Sarajevo. Uproar over this immediately leads to World War I.

1914–1918 World War I: Austria-Hungary is an ally of Germany.

1918 Austria-Hungary collapses.

June 4, 1920 Peace Treaty of Trianon: the multinational Kingdom of Hungary loses two-thirds of its territory and population and is divided among successor states and other nations.

1908: Danubian Monarchy

GERMANY

Lublin

RUSSIA

Częstochowa

Liberec

Lviv

Przemysl

Tarnopal

SILESIA

Kraków

GALICIA

Hradec Králové

Opava

Český Těšín

Prague

Ostrava

Kamianets-Podilskyi

Plzeň

Olomouc

Černovice

BOHEMIA

Žilina

Prešov

BUKOWINA

MORAVIA

Turčiansky sv. Martin

Uzhhorod

Brno

Mukachevo

Suceava

České Budějovice

Banská Bystrica

Košice

LOWER AUSTRIA

Trnava

Nitra

Miskolc

Satu Mare

Passau

Vienna

Bistriţa

Linz

Bratislava

Budapest

UPPER AUSTRIA

Győr

Komárno

Debrecen

Munich

HUNGARY

Cluj

Salzburg

Oradea

Bregenz

SALZBURG

STYRIA

Békescsaba

Blaj

VORARL- BERG

Innsbruck

Graz

Arad

Sibiu

Brasov

TIROL

Szeged

CARINTHIA

Timisoara

Klagenfurt

Pécs

Ljubljana

GORICA

CARNIOLA

Osjek

Novi Sad

ROMANIA

Bucharest

Triest

Zagreb

CROATIA-SLAVONIA

Venice

Rijeka (Fiume)

Pożoga

Belgrade

ISTRIA

BOSNIA AND HERZEGOVINA

SERBIA

Zadar

Sarajevo

DALMATIA

ITALY

Split

Mostar

MONTE- NEGRO

OTTOMAN EMPIRE

Dubrovnik

Kotor

Cetinje

Part of the Austrian Empire
Part of the Kingdom of Hungary
Bosnia and Herzegovina, annexed in 1908
Austro-Hungarian border in 1908
O Important capital

Habsburg Empire (also called the Habsburg Monarchy or Austrian Monarchy) Through successful marriages and inheritances, a complex network of lands developed under the reign of the Habsburgs, who at the same time were the emperors of the Holy Roman Empire. The dynasty was ruled by the male line until 1740, and through union with Lorraine by the female line until 1918 under the name of Habsburg-Lorraine. Historically, the core of the empire was the Austrian hereditary lands that had been acquired since the 13th and 14th centuries. Ferdinand I married Anna, sister of Louis II (who died at the battle of Mohács); thus the kingdoms of Bohemia and Hungary fell to the Habsburgs.

Enlightened Absolutism Under Empress Maria Theresa (1740–1780) and primarily under her son Joseph II (1765/80–1790), numerous reforms were implemented. These included land reform (the Urbarium of Maria Theresa for the regulation of devilries and obligations of the farmers, 1767); uniform criminal law in Bohemia and Austria (1768); compulsory education for children (1774); the Subject Law abolishing serfdom (1781 in Austria, 1785 in Hungary) and the Tolerance Law allowing free religious practice and gaving Jews full citizenship (1781). Other measures included more efficient bureaucratization, the installation of a central and effective state administration, and abolishment of contemplative monasteries in favor of schools, orphanages and hospitals.

Neo-Absolutism A reactionary period between 1852 and 1867 after the accomplishments of the Revolution of 1848/49 had been abolished. It was characterized by reintroduction of censorship and strengthening of church influence in the school system. The most important advocates of neo-absolutism were Minister President Prince Felix zu Schwarzenberg and Minister of the Interior Baron Alexander von Bach (author of the "Bach System").

Austro-Hungarian *Ausgleich* (German for "compromise") *Cisleithania* and *Transleithania* are Latin for the countries on this side of and beyond the river Leitha, which were the Austrian and Hungarian dominions. In the the 1867 *Ausgleich*, the Austrian and Hungarian parts of the Habsburg Empire united in the Dual Monarchy of Austria-Hungary, frequently abbreviated as *k.u.k.* (*kaiserlich und königlich*, or "imperial and royal"). This was a personal union of two distinct states that nonetheless shared a common ruler, foreign policy, economic policy, army and navy.

Treaty of Trianon A portion of the Versailles Treaty that concerned the reorganization of Europe in the aftermath of World War I. The treaty specified the division of the multinational Kingdom of Hungary into the successor states Hungary, Czechoslovakia and the Kingdom of the Serbs, Croats and Slovenes as well as sections of Austria, Romania, Poland and Italy.

Central Europe: An Overview

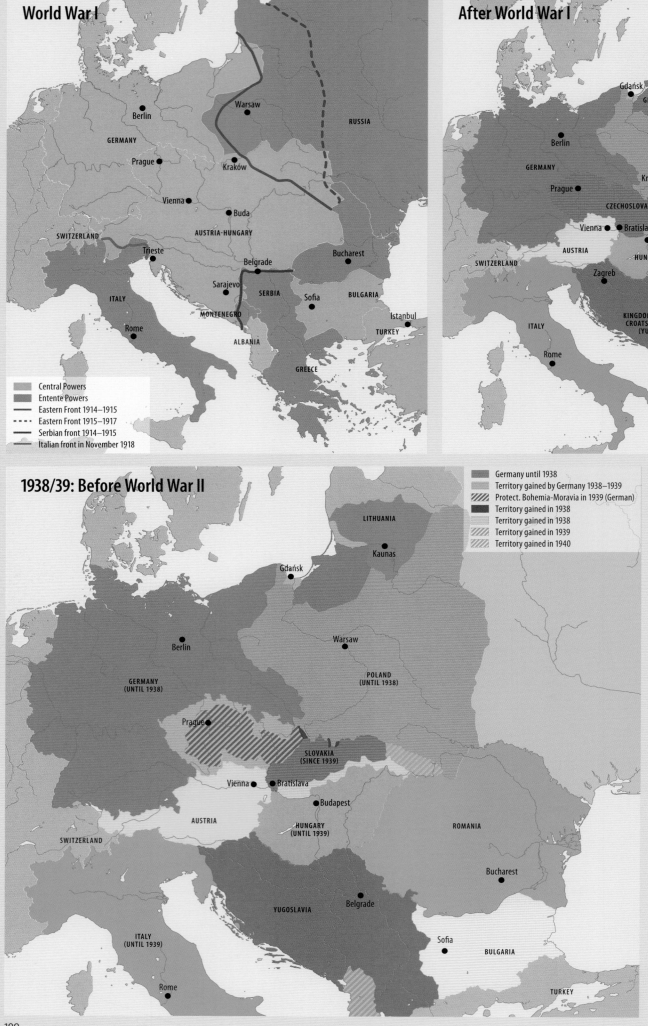

World War I

Berlin
Warsaw
GERMANY
Prague
Kraków
RUSSIA
Vienna
Buda
AUSTRIA-HUNGARY
SWITZERLAND
Trieste
Belgrade
Bucharest
ITALY
Sarajevo
SERBIA
Sofia
BULGARIA
Rome
MONTENEGRO
Istanbul
ALBANIA
TURKEY
GREECE

	Central Powers
	Entente Powers
———	Eastern Front 1914–1915
– – –	Eastern Front 1915–1917
———	Serbian front 1914–1915
———	Italian front in November 1918

After World War I

LITHUANIA
Kaunas
Vilnius
Gdańsk
GERMANY
Warsaw
Berlin
SOVIET UNION
POLAND
GERMANY
Kraków
Prague
CZECHOSLOVAKIA
Vienna
Bratislava
Budapest
AUSTRIA
HUNGARY
ROMANIA
SWITZERLAND
Zagreb
Belgrade
Bucharest
ITALY
KINGDOM OF THE SERBS,
CROATS AND SLOVENES
(YUGOSLAVIA)
Sofia
BULGARIA
Rome
Istanbul
TURKEY

1938/39: Before World War II

	Germany until 1938
	Territory gained by Germany 1938–1939
▨	Protect. Bohemia-Moravia in 1939 (German)
	Territory gained in 1938
	Territory gained in 1938
▨	Territory gained in 1939
▨	Territory gained in 1940

LITHUANIA
Kaunas
Gdańsk
Berlin
Warsaw
GERMANY
(UNTIL 1938)
POLAND
(UNTIL 1938)
Prague
SLOVAKIA
(SINCE 1939)
Vienna
Bratislava
Budapest
AUSTRIA
HUNGARY
(UNTIL 1939)
ROMANIA
SWITZERLAND
Bucharest
YUGOSLAVIA
Belgrade
ITALY
(UNTIL 1939)
Sofia
BULGARIA
Rome
TURKEY

March 2–13, 1938 The German Reich annexes Austria (*Anschluss*).

Sept. 30, 1938 Munich Agreement: France, Great Britain and Italy negotiate with Germany over the fate of the Sudetenland.

Nov. 2, 1938 First Vienna Award: Renegotiation of territory between Hungary and Czechoslovakia

March 14–15, 1939 Emergence of the Slovak Republic, a dependency of Germany; German troops occupy what remains of Czechoslovakia.

Sept. 1, 1939 Germany invades Poland: Outbreak of World War II; the entire eastern part of Central Europe is under the influence of the German Reich.

Aug. 30, 1940 Second Vienna Award cedes northern Transylvania to Hungary.

1945–1948 In the aftermath of World War II, the Communist Party gradually seizes power in the region.

1956 The Hungarian Revolution, at first successful, is suppressed by Soviet troops.

1968 Prague Spring: Communist reforms inspire a mass movement for change in Czechoslovakia, but are crushed by a Soviet invasion.

1988–1989 Fall of communism in the countries of the Warsaw Pact (founded in 1955)

During World War II

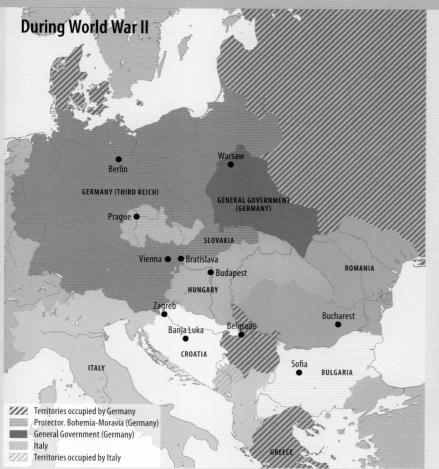

Legend (During World War II):
- Territories occupied by Germany
- Protector. Bohemia-Moravia (Germany)
- General Government (Germany)
- Italy
- Territories occupied by Italy

The Warsaw Pact

Legend (The Warsaw Pact):
- Neutral countries
- NATO members
- Socialist countries with year the Communist Party came to power
- Other socialist countries
- Opposition, rebellion, attempts to reform the communist regime
- ···· Iron Curtain in 1949
- — Iron Curtain in 1955

Central Europe Today

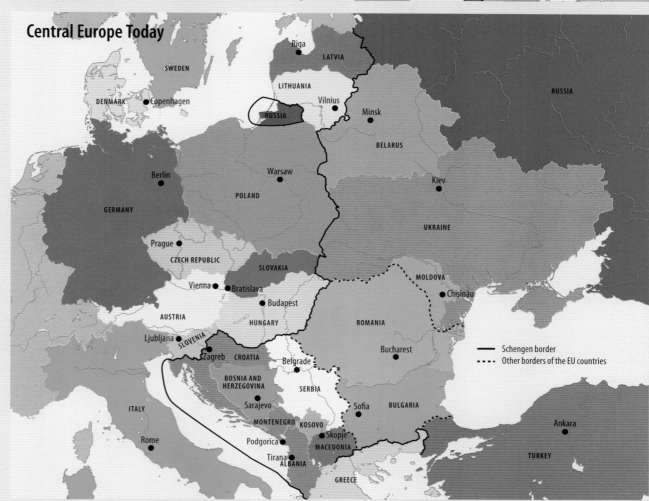

Legend (Central Europe Today):
- — Schengen border
- ···· Other borders of the EU countries

June 25, 1991 Slovenia and Croatia declare independence from Yugoslavia.

1993 Czechoslovakia divides peacefully into two independent states, the Czech Republic and Slovakia.

1999 Hungary, the Czech Republic and Poland join NATO.

2004 Slovenia, Slovakia, the Czech Republic, Poland and Hungary join the European Union; Slovenia and Slovakia join NATO.

2007 Opening of borders between Slovenia, Slovakia, the Czech Republic, Poland and Hungary (Schengen Area); Slovenia adopts the euro as its currency.

Munich Agreement A treaty among representatives of Germany, Italy, Great Britain and France at the expense of a third state, Czechoslovakia, that forced cession of Czech border regions (the Sudetenland, where millions of people of German ancestry lived) to the German Reich, presumably averting an impending German invasion and war. Regarded as a betrayal, the Munich Agreement is one of the most important causes of the later suspicion of the Czechoslovakian government and people toward the Western democracies. In a 1973 treaty between Germany and Czechoslovakia, the Munich Agreement was officially annulled.

Second Vienna Award Under the leadership of National Socialist Germany and fascist Italy, areas in Slovakia, Ukraine and Romania were awarded to an allied Hungary.

Fall of Communism Peaceful revolutions in Eastern Europe were allowed through the détente and policies of reform in the Soviet Union. The undemocratic socialist state system was abolished without bloodshed, with the exception of Romania.

Austria

9th Century

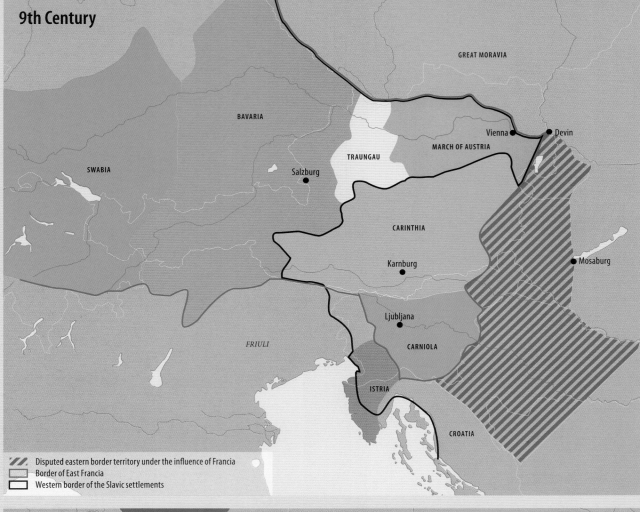

1180

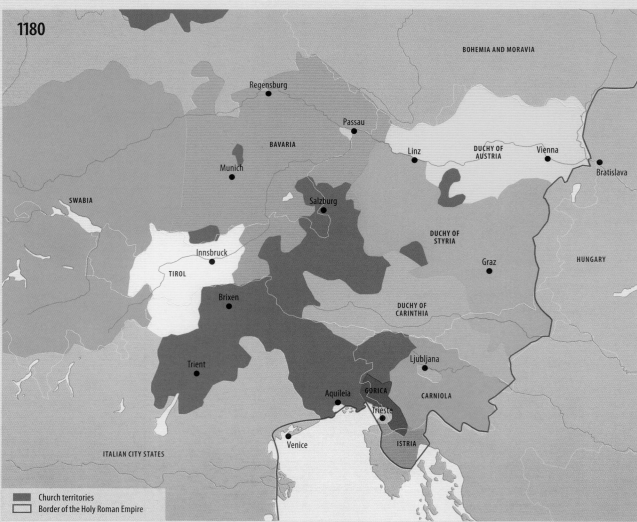

■ Church territories
☐ Border of the Holy Roman Empire

6th–7th centuries Settlement by Germanic Bavarian (Bavarii) tribes; Roman power breaks down.

788–803 Charlemagne defeats Bavaria and assimilates its land as well as Karantania and Krain (Carinthia and Carniola) into the Frankish kingdom.

856 The Bavarian Eastern March, or frontier province, is established as a buffer zone between the Frankish empire and other tribes; it is the nucleus of what will later become Austria.

976 Carinthia is divided from the Duchy of Bavaria by Emperor Otto II, establishing the Duchy of Carinthia.

976–1156 The Ostmark, or Eastern March, becomes the Margraviate of Austria under the Babenberg dynasty as part of the Duchy of Bavaria; it is soon known as *Ostarrichi*.

1139–1156 The Babenbergs are also dukes of Bavaria.

1156 *Privilegium minus*: Austria is elevated to a duchy (as compensation for renouncing Bavaria), and Vienna becomes the ducal residence.

1180 Styria becomes a duchy.

1192 The Babenbergs inherit Styria.

1246 The male Babenberg line dies out; there are clashes between competing claims to the Babenberg inheritance.

1278 Battle on the Marchfeld: Rudolf of Habsburg defeats the king of Bohemia, Ottokar II.

1282 With Rudolf's sons, the Habsburgs take over the duchies of Austria and Styria.

1335–1369 The Habsburgs acquire Carinthia (Kärnten), Carniola (Krain) and Tirol.

1379–1490 Division of territories between the Albertine and Leopoldine Habsburg lines

1438 Albrecht II is elected king of the Romans and Germans; from this time until 1806, Habsburgs rule as emperors of the Holy Roman Empire (with the exception of 1742–1745).

1453 Austria is elevated to an arch-duchy (*Privilegium maius*).

1526 Turkish victory and occupation of all but northwestern Hungary; Habsburgs ascend the thrones of Bohemia and unoccupied Hungary (the Habsburg Empire lasts until 1918).

1529 First Turkish siege of Vienna

16th century Protestantism spreads among large portions of the Austrian nobility; conflicts arise between the monarchs and the estates.

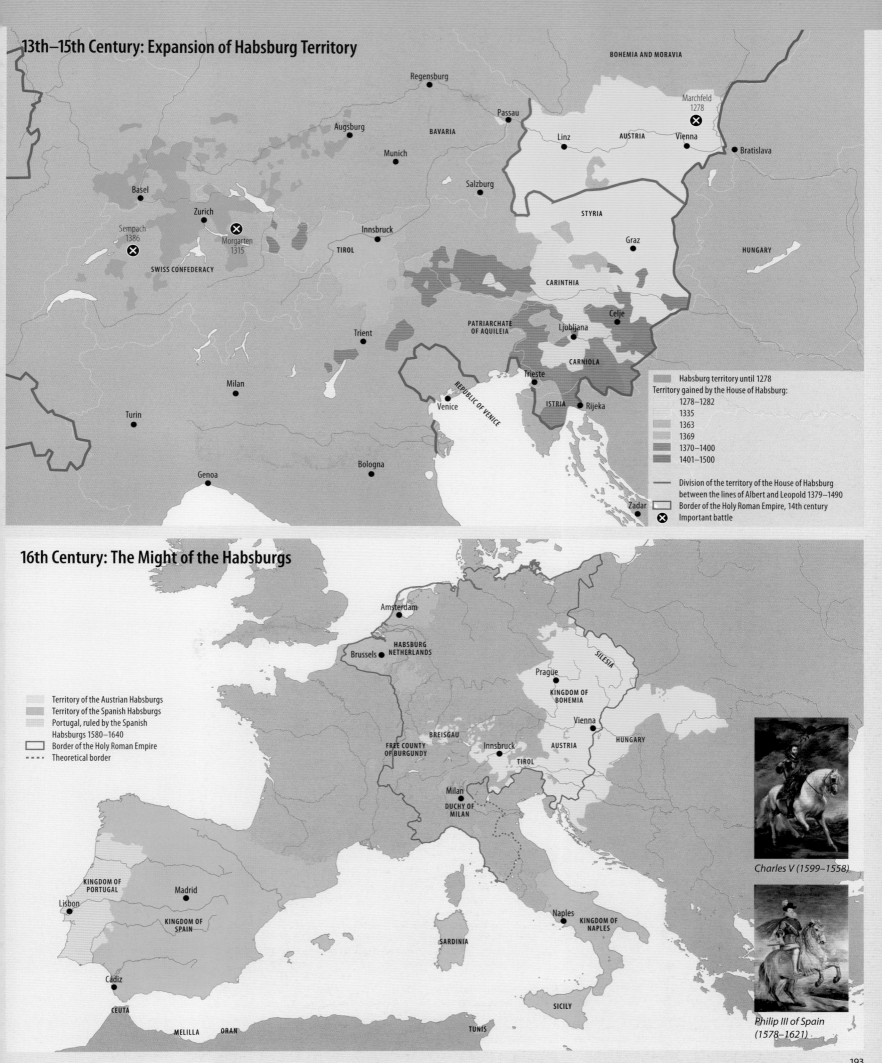

13th–15th Century: Expansion of Habsburg Territory

BOHEMIA AND MORAVIA

Regensburg

Passau

Augsburg

BAVARIA

Munich

Marchfeld
1278

Linz

AUSTRIA

Vienna

Bratislava

Salzburg

Basel

Zurich

Sempach
1386

Morgarten
1315

STYRIA

Graz

HUNGARY

SWISS CONFEDERACY

Innsbruck

TIROL

CARINTHIA

Trient

PATRIARCHATE
OF AQUILEIA

Ljubljana

Celje

CARNIOLA

Milan

Trieste

REPUBLIC
OF VENICE

Venice

ISTRIA

Rijeka

Turin

Bologna

Genoa

Zadar

	Habsburg territory until 1278

Territory gained by the House of Habsburg:

	1278–1282
	1335
	1363
	1369
	1370–1400
	1401–1500

Division of the territory of the House of Habsburg
between the lines of Albert and Leopold 1379–1490

Border of the Holy Roman Empire, 14th century

Important battle

16th Century: The Might of the Habsburgs

Amsterdam

HABSBURG
NETHERLANDS

Brussels

SILESIA

Prague

KINGDOM OF
BOHEMIA

Vienna

BREISGAU

FREE COUNTY
OF BURGUNDY

Innsbruck

AUSTRIA

HUNGARY

TIROL

Milan

DUCHY OF
MILAN

	Territory of the Austrian Habsburgs
	Territory of the Spanish Habsburgs
	Portugal, ruled by the Spanish Habsburgs 1580–1640
	Border of the Holy Roman Empire
----	Theoretical border

KINGDOM OF
PORTUGAL

Madrid

Lisbon

KINGDOM OF
SPAIN

Naples

KINGDOM OF
NAPLES

SARDINIA

Cádiz

CEUTA

MELILLA

ORAN

TUNIS

SICILY

Charles V (1599–1558)

*Philip III of Spain
(1578–1621)*

193

Austria

1526–1800: The Austrian Habsburgs

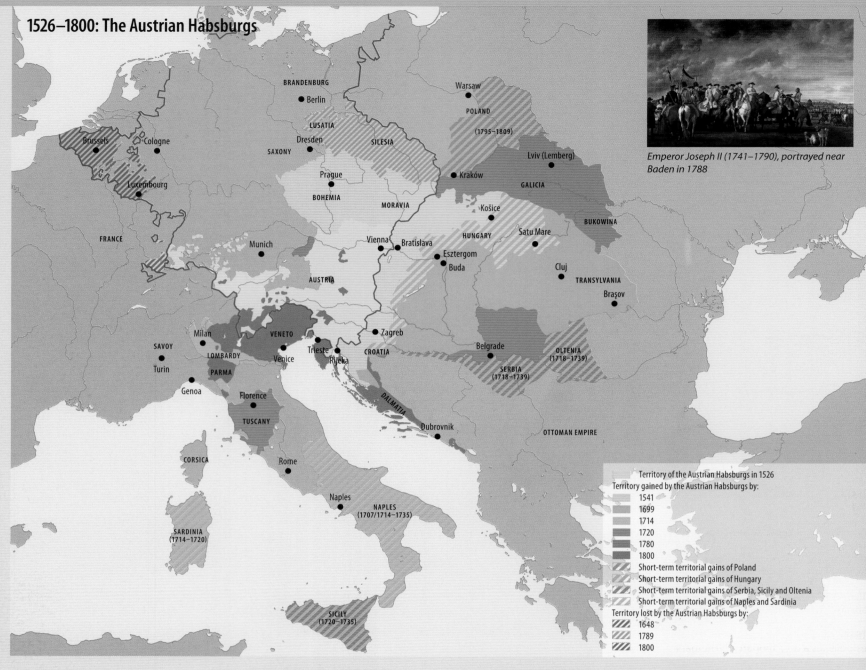

Emperor Joseph II (1741–1790), portrayed near Baden in 1788

Territory of the Austrian Habsburgs in 1526
Territory gained by the Austrian Habsburgs by:
1541
1699
1714
1720
1780
1800
Short-term territorial gains of Poland
Short-term territorial gains of Hungary
Short-term territorial gains of Serbia, Sicily and Oltenia
Short-term territorial gains of Naples and Sardinia
Territory lost by the Austrian Habsburgs by:
1648
1789
1800

1556 Division of the House of Habsburg into the Spanish line (continues until 1700) and the Austrian line (the imperial line, until 1918; Habsburg-Lorraine after 1740)

1564 Habsburg branches split between rulers in Tirol (until 1665) and of Inner Austria (becomes the main line in 1619).

1608–1612 *Fraternal Strife in the House of Habsburg:* The later emperor Matthias gradually forces his brother, Emperor Rudolf II, to yield sovereignty over Austria, Hungary and Bohemia to him.

1657–1705 Long reign of Emperor Leopold I, a period of absolutism and Austria's rise as an economic power. Austria joins a European alliance against France in order to maintain a balance of power.

July–September 1683 The second Turkish siege of Vienna is repelled in September by joint Austrian-Polish-German forces.

1699 Reconquest of Hungary and Transylvania: Expulsion of the Ottomans from central Europe

1706–1859 Spanish-ruled Lombardy becomes Austrian (Austrian rule is interrupted 1797–1814).

1707–1735 Spanish-ruled Naples is ceded to Austria.

1713 Charles VI issues the Pragmatic Sanction of 1713 to establish the hereditary claim of his daughters (should he die with no male heir); princes of the empire (the Imperial Diet) officially acknowledge the abrogation of the Salic Law of (male) Succession.

1714–1720 Spanish-ruled Sardinia is ceded to Austria.

1714–1795 Spanish-ruled Netherlands pass to Austria ("Austrian Netherlands").

1720–1735 Spanish-ruled Sicily comes under Austrian rule.

1737–1860 The Grand Duchy of Tuscany is ruled by the House of Habsburg-Lorraine (Austrian rule is interrupted 1801–1814).

1740–1748 The War of the Austrian Succession: Prussia makes its acceptance of the Pragmatic Sanction contingent on cession of Silesia. It occupies Silesia, initiating the war; Bavaria temporarily occupies Bohemia.

1740–1780 Reign of Maria Theresa, daughter of Charles VI; her husband, Francis Stephen of Lorraine, becomes Holy Roman Emperor Francis I in 1745.

1765/80–1790 Zenith of enlightened absolutism under Emperor Joseph I ("Josephinism")

1772–1795 Austria acquires Galicia (a region now in Poland and Ukraine) as a result of the Partition of Poland.

1778–1779 War of the Bavarian Succession: Joseph II attempts to gain

Bavaria; acquires only the Innviertel (border region on the Inn River between Austria and Bavaria).

1792–1814 Wars with revolutionary and Napoleonic France

1798–1866 Venetia and Dalmatia come under Austrian rule.

1804 Francis I creates the hereditary Austrian Empire; he abdicates as holy Roman emperor in 1806.

1815 Congress of Vienna: Following Napoleon's defeat, Salzburg and the Innviertel pass to Austria.

1815–1848 Metternich era: Conservative policies including censorship of the press and suppression of democratic movements

1848 Popular revolutions in March and October: People insist on a greater role in government, and tension between several nationalist groups runs high.

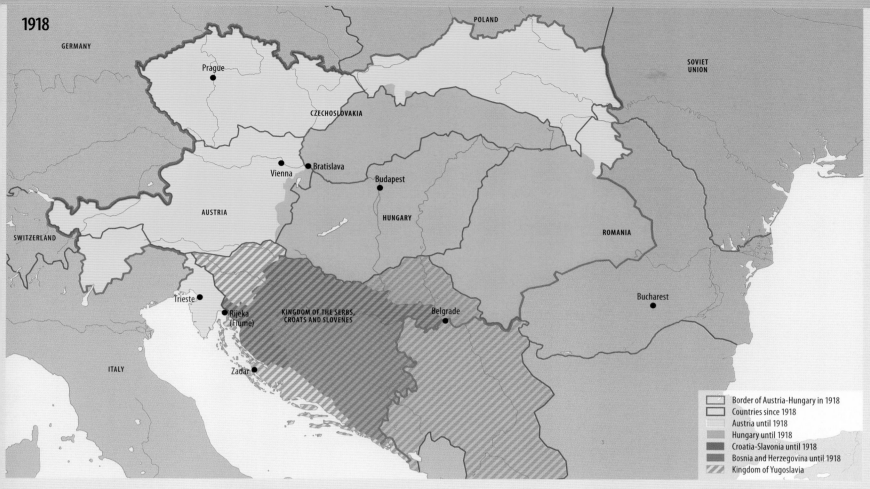

1918

GERMANY · POLAND · SOVIET UNION · Prague · CZECHOSLOVAKIA · Bratislava · Vienna · Budapest · AUSTRIA · HUNGARY · SWITZERLAND · ROMANIA · Trieste · Rijeka (Fiume) · KINGDOM OF THE SERBS, CROATS AND SLOVENES · Belgrade · Bucharest · ITALY · Zadar

Border of Austria-Hungary in 1918
Countries since 1918
Austria until 1918
Hungary until 1918
Croatia-Slavonia until 1918
Bosnia and Herzegovina until 1918
Kingdom of Yugoslavia

1848–1916 Reign of Emperor Francis Joseph I

Dec. 31, 1851 New Year's Eve Patent: The emperor rescinds the constitution, revoking popular representation and a free press, among other things.

1852–1867 Era of conservative neo-absolutism

1867 Austro-Hungarian Compromise establishes a dual monarchy (Hungary and the remaining Habsburg lands).

1897–1910 Modernization of Vienna under the Christian Socialist and anti-Semitic mayor Karl Lueger; around 1900, Vienna is the center of modern European culture.

1908 Austria-Hungary's annexation of Bosnia and Herzegovina leads to heightened tension in the Balkan region and the Balkan Wars of 1912–1913.

June 1914 Archduke Francis Ferdinand, heir apparent of Francis Joseph I, is murdered in Sarajevo.

1914–1918 World War I: Austria-Hungary is allied with Germany (the Central Powers).

Nov. 11–12, 1918 End of the Habsburg Empire. The Republic of German-Austria is proclaimed, a republic of Austrian German-speaking territories. In addition to Austrian territories, it also lays claim to the Sudetenland, German Bohemia, South Tirol and southern Carinthia.

April 3, 1919 The Habsburg Law is passed, stripping nobility of their titles.

Sept. 10, 1919 Treaty of St. Germain: Dissolution of the Republic of German-Austria

1932/33–1934 Austrofascist regime under Engelbert Dollfuss

July 25, 1934 Dollfuss is assassinated and Austrian National Socialists unsuccessfully attempt to seize power.

1934–1938 Authoritarian government of Kurt von Schuschnigg, under increasing pressure from Germany

March 12–13, 1938 *Anschluss* of Austria: The country is annexed by the German Reich.

April 13, 1945 Battle of Vienna: Soviet troops defeat the German army and liberate the city from the Nazis.

1945–1955 After World War II, Austria and its capital, Vienna, are divided into four occupation zones.

May 15, 1955 State Treaty: Austria and the occupation forces (the Soviet Union, the United States, France and Great Britain) reestablish an independent Austrian republic; Austria joins the UN.

Oct. 26, 1955 Constitutional law passed declaring Austria's permanent neutrality

1995 Austria joins the European Union.

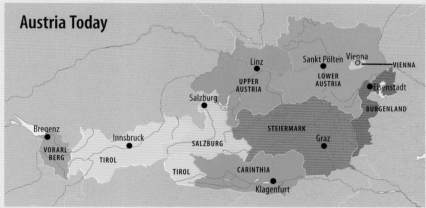

Austria Today

Linz · Sankt Pölten · Vienna · VIENNA · UPPER AUSTRIA · LOWER AUSTRIA · Eisenstadt · Salzburg · BURGENLAND · Bregenz · Innsbruck · STEIERMARK · Graz · VORARL-BERG · SALZBURG · TIROL · CARINTHIA · TIROL · Klagenfurt

March Revolution of 1848 After the rebellion of citizens fighting for greater liberties, the symbolic figure of the "old order," Chancellor Prince Metternich, had to resign. The first Austrian constitution was drafted, but it never went into effect and was revoked by the New Year's Eve Patent of 1851.

October Revolution of 1848 Rioting by Viennese workers and students was suppressed by Field Marshal Prince Windischgrätz and the Croatian general Joseph Jelačič.

Habsburg Law Enacted on April 3, 1919, this legislation banished the last Habsburg emperor (Charles I) from Austria. The other members of the House of Habsburg-Lorraine had the choice between renouncing their titles and claims to their hereditary rights and positions to become common citizens of the new government, or living in exile. Their property was expropriated.

Austrofascism An authoritarian regime in Austria modeled after fascist Italy. The Christian Socialist chancellor, Engelbert

Dollfuss, suspended Parliament, and many political parties were prohibited. The uprising of the socialists in February 1934 was suppressed, as was an attempted coup by the National Socialists on July 25, 1934, during which Dollfuss was assassinated.

Anschluss of Austria German troops marched into Austria, and Austria was annexed by the German Reich. The Austrian NSDAP (National Socialist Party) was prohibited in Austria in 1933, but Hitler provided the Austrian Nazis with political support in opposition to the Austrofascists who were in power. Through blackmail, agents in the Austrian government and ever greater demands for concessions, Hitler increasingly restricted Austria's independence. When a plebiscite was announced to decide on Austria's future independence, Hitler ordered his troops to occupy Austria. The plebiscite finally did take place on March 10, 1938, after Austria was already occupied, and following a campaign of propaganda and threats. It confirmed Austria's annexation with very nearly 100 percent of the vote.

Hungary

Avar Kingdom, 7th–8th Centuries

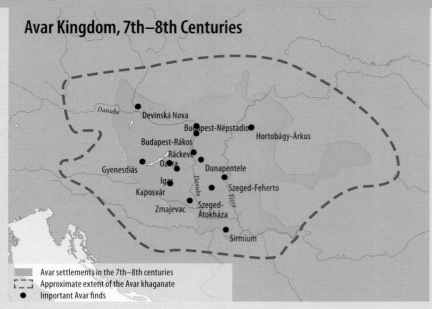

Avar settlements in the 7th–8th centuries
- - - Approximate extent of the Avar khaganate
● Important Avar finds

Magyars The Magyars were a Finno-Ugric tribe of horse-riders originally from the Ural Mountain region. At the end of the 9th century they began settling in the territory of modern-day Hungary, dominating the Slav peoples there. For many decades, they conducted raids on unsuspecting people in western Europe, roaming as far as northern Germany and western France. This first phase of the Magyar presence in Europe came to an end with their devastating defeat at the hands of the German king Otto the Great in 955 at the Battle of Lechfeld (near Augsburg). The nomadic Magyars then intermingled with the Slavic tribes living in the Carpathian valley and settled there.

The term "Magyar" originally referred to the most powerful of the seven-tribe association that brought the other tribes in the region under their control. The first Hungarian ruling house, the Árpád dynasty, is named for the leader who emerged from that tribe in the late 9th century, Árpád. The word "Hungary" derives from Bulgaro-Turkish *on-ogur*, which means "ten tribes."

568–798 Period of the Avar empire (also known as the Avar khaganate) in Pannonia

839–876/884 Slavs create a principality (called the Balaton or Pannonian principality) that is a dependency of the East Frankish empire.

884–894 The Slavic principality becomes a part of Great Moravia; later it is a feudal territory belonging to the East Frankish empire.

899–955 Tribes of Magyar riders on horseback raid southern Germany (known as the "Hungarian misery").

901 The Magyars conquer the Slavic principality and occupy its territories.

907 Battle of Brezalauspurc (Bratislava): The Magyars' victory over Bavarian forces results in the settlement of the Magyars in Pannonia.

955 Battle of Lechfeld (near Augsburg): The Magyars are driven back by German King Otto I.

1000 Stephen I is crowned king of Hungary; the pagan Magyars are subsequently Christianized.

1102–1918 Coloman, king of Hungary, establishes a personal union with the Kingdom of Croatia.

1241 Mongol invasions destroy the Hungarian kingdom. Depopulation of the region in the wake of catastrophic losses at the Battle of Mohi (April 11, 1241) leads to a massive emigration of Germans into the united kingdoms. Many new cities are founded and trade begins to flourish, especially in the region of present-day Slovakia and the Romanian Carpathians.

1301 The Árpád dynasty dies out.

1308–1386 Rule of the Angevin kings, Charles I and Louis I

from 1312 Central authority under a monarch is reestablished. During the reigns of Charles Robert and Louis I of Anjou, business and trade flourish.

1370–1382/1386 (and 1440–1444) Personal union of the Kingdom of Hungary with the Kingdom of Poland.

1396 Battle of Nicopolis: The Ottomans win a decisive victory against a coalition of European forces including France and Hungary.

Arrival of the Magyars

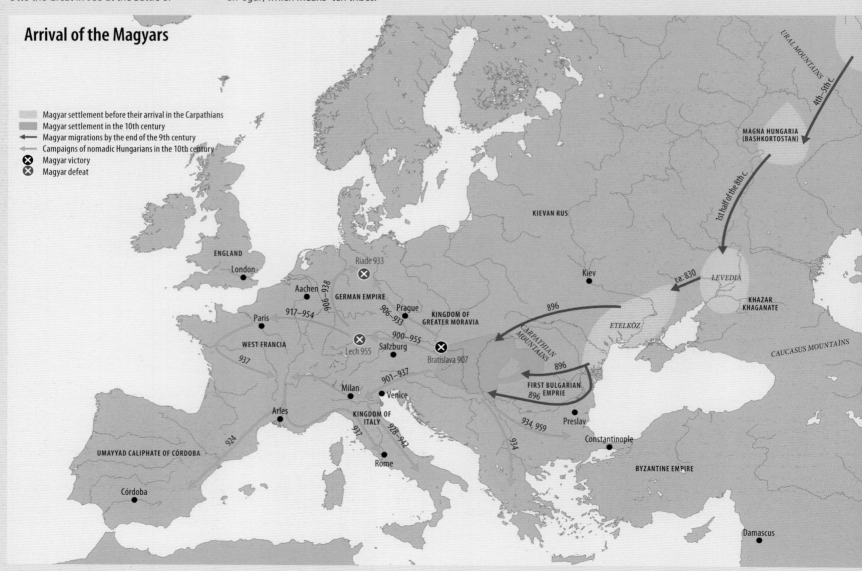

Magyar settlement before their arrival in the Carpathians
Magyar settlement in the 10th century
← Magyar migrations by the end of the 9th century
← Campaigns of nomadic Hungarians in the 10th century
⊗ Magyar victory
⊗ Magyar defeat

11th–13th Centuries: The Kingdom of Hungary

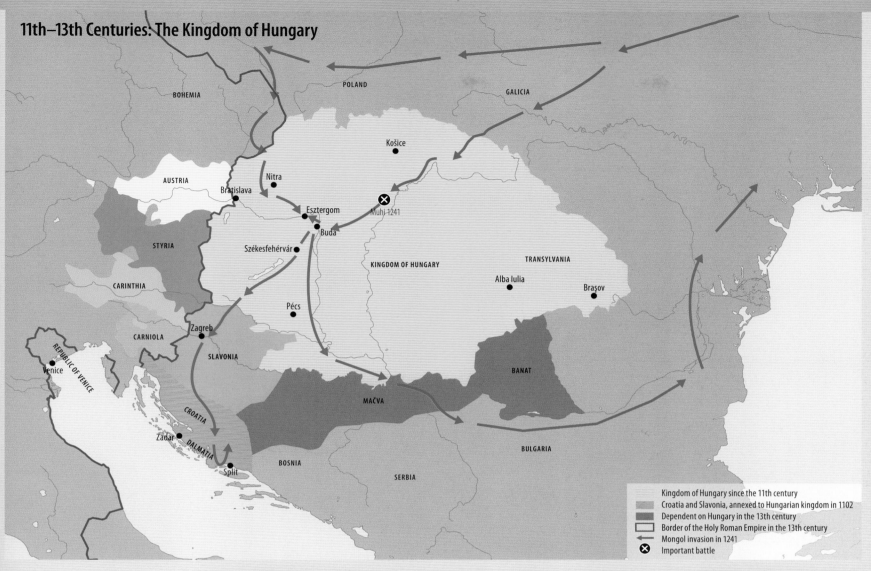

BOHEMIA

POLAND

GALICIA

Košice

AUSTRIA

Nitra

Bratislava

Esztergom

Muhi 1241

Buda

STYRIA

Székesfehérvár

KINGDOM OF HUNGARY

TRANSYLVANIA

Alba Iulia

Braşov

CARINTHIA

Pécs

Zagreb

CARNIOLA

REPUBLIC OF VENICE

Venice

SLAVONIA

CROATIA

BANAT

MAČVA

Zadar

DALMATIA

Split

BOSNIA

SERBIA

BULGARIA

	Kingdom of Hungary since the 11th century
	Croatia and Slavonia, annexed to Hungarian kingdom in 1102
	Dependent on Hungary in the 13th century
	Border of the Holy Roman Empire in the 13th century
→	Mongol invasion in 1241
⊗	Important battle

1456 The Hungarians win a great victory, defeating the Ottoman siege of Belgrade.

1458–1490 The reign of Matthias Corvinus, an era of cultural flourishing (called the Hungarian Renaissance), also marked by the establishment of a standing army as the Hungarian Kingdom went to war with Bohemia and Austria.

1490–1526 Personal union with Bohemia under a side branch of the Polish-Lithuanian Jagellon dynasty

1515 Negotiation of a double marriage between the Jagellon and Habsburg dynasties assures shared hereditary titles.

Aug. 29, 1526 Battle of Mohács: The victory of the Ottomans effectively destroys the kingdom and leads to their conquest of present-day Hungary. Lands not conquered pass into the hands of the Habsburgs.

1527–1538 Civil war between Ferdinand I of Habsburg and his rival, John Zápolya of Transylvania. The war ends with the Peace of Oradea.

1541–1686 Period of 145 years of Ottoman attacks on Buda.

15th Century: The Kingdom of Hungary under Matthias Corvinus

BRANDENBURG

LUSATIA

SILESIA

POLAND

Prague

Olomouc

Kraków

BOHEMIA

MORAVIA

Košice

AUSTRIA

Vienna

Bratislava

MOLDAVIA

STYRIA

Buda

HUNGARY

TRANSYLVANIA

CARINTHIA

Graz

Alba Iulia

Braşov

CARNIOLA

Zagreb

REPUBLIC OF VENICE

Venice

SLAVONIA

WALACHIA

CROATIA

Jajce

Belgrade
1456

Nicopolis
1392

Varna
1444

BOSNIA

OTTOMAN EMPIRE

Kosovo Polje
1389, 1448

	Hungary in the 15th century
	Territory temporarily gained by Matthias Corvinus 1458–1490
	Border of the Holy Roman Empire
⊗	Important battle

197

Hungary

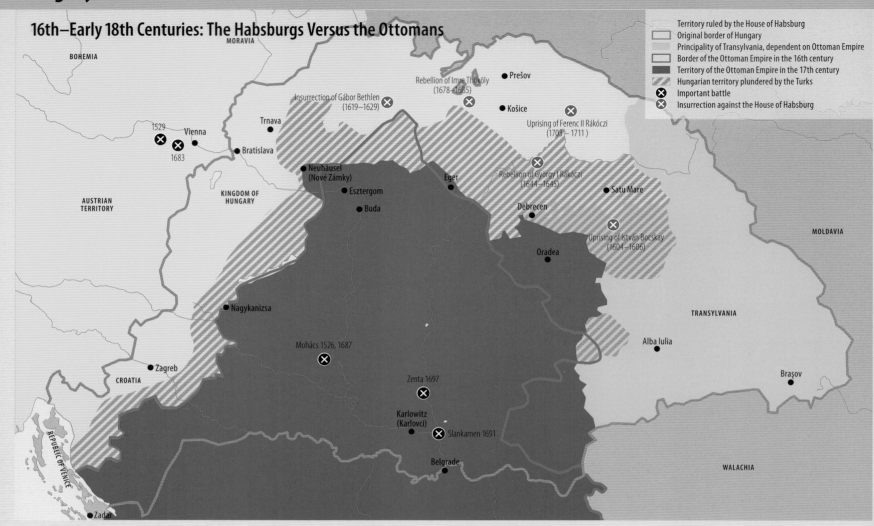

16th–Early 18th Centuries: The Habsburgs Versus the Ottomans

Legend:
- Territory ruled by the House of Habsburg
- Original border of Hungary
- Principality of Transylvania, dependent on Ottoman Empire
- Border of the Ottoman Empire in the 16th century
- Territory of the Ottoman Empire in the 17th century
- Hungarian territory plundered by the Turks
- Important battle
- Insurrection against the House of Habsburg

Map labels: MORAVIA, BOHEMIA, Rebellion of Imre Thököly (1678–1685), Prešov, Insurrection of Gábor Bethlen (1619–1629), Košice, Uprising of Ferenc II Rákóczi (1703–1711), 1529, Vienna, Trnava, 1683, Bratislava, Neuhäusel (Nové Zámky), Eger, Rebellion of György I Rákóczi (1644–1645), Satu Mare, Esztergom, Buda, Debrecen, AUSTRIAN TERRITORY, KINGDOM OF HUNGARY, Oradea, Uprising of István Bocskay (1604–1606), MOLDAVIA, Nagykanizsa, TRANSYLVANIA, Alba Iulia, Mohács 1526, 1687, Zenta 1697, Brașov, Zagreb, CROATIA, Karlowitz (Karlovci), Slankamen 1691, Belgrade, REPUBLIC OF VENICE, Zadar, WALACHIA

1604–1645 Era of anti-Habsburg revolts by the nobility led by István Bocskay (1604–1606), Gábor Bethlen (1619–1629) and György Ráckóczi (1644–1645)

1663 Ottoman conquest of the fortress at Neuhäusel (Nové Zámky, Slovakia)

1678–1685 A rebellion of the anti-Habsburg Kurucs is led by Imre Thököly, who is allied with the Ottomans.

1687 Second Battle of Mohács: The troops of the Habsburg emperor defeat the Ottomans.

1691 Battle of Slankamen: the troops of the Habsburg emperor defeat the Ottomans.

1697 Battle of Zenta on the Theiss: Ottoman forces are annihilated by Prince Eugene of Savoy.

1699 The Treaty of Karlowitz is signed: The Habsburgs again take control of Hungary and Transylvania.

1703–1711 An anti-Habsburg rebellion is led by Ferenc II Rákóczi.

1711 A peace treaty is negoatiated and signed in Szatmár (present-day Satu Mare, Romania), ending Rákóczki's rebellion.

1740–1790 An era of enlightened reform in the Habsburg Empire during the reign of Empress Maria Theresa and Emperor Joseph II.

1848/49 Anti-Habsburg revolts erupt, led by Lajos Kossuth. These rebellions are bloodily suppressed.

1867 Austro-Hungarian *Ausgleich* leads to the establishment of the Dual Monarchy.

1914–1918 World War I: As a part of the Austro-Hungarian Empire, Hungary fights as an ally of Germany.

Oct. 31, 1918 Hungary ends its political union with Austria, declaring itself a republic.

March–August 1919 Establishment of a Hungarian Soviet republic led by Béla Kun. It is a Soviet-style republic based on the Russian model.

March 1, 1920 The monarchy is reestablished under the regency of Admiral Miklós Horthy. His rule is authoritarian, but a stable Hungary is established under his leadership.

June 4, 1920 Treaty of Trianon: The Kingdom of Hungary is partitioned.

1932–1936 Premier Gyula Gömbös brings Hungary over to the side of the fascist nations.

Nov. 2, 1938 First Vienna Award: As a result of the Munich Agreement, territory in southern Slovakia and Subcarpathian Ukraine is ceded to Hungary.

Aug. 30, 1940 Second Vienna Award: Hungary receives the territory located in Romanian Transylvania.

June 27, 1941 Hungary enters the war against the Soviet Union as an ally of Germany.

1944 Germany occupies Hungary. Miklós Horthy is forced out of power and a brutal Hungarian fascist regime is established, known as the "Arrow Cross Party." The new regime is led by Ferenc Szálasi until his execution in 1946.

April 4, 1945 End of World War II: The fighting in Hungary comes to an end, and the nation is freed. As a result of the terms of the Gotha Agreement, the country falls under the influence of the Soviet Union.

1946 According to the terms of the Paris Peace Conference, Hungary is forced to cede all the territory it has acquired since 1938.

1946–1956 Brutal rule of Mátyás Rákosi, known as "Stalin's best pupil."

1949 Show trial of László Rajk and other functionaries of the Communist Party; the Minister of the Interior, János Kádár, is imprisoned and tortured.

Oct. 23–Nov. 4, 1956 Revolt of the Hungarian populace against the Soviets. This revolt is suppressed following an invasion by the Red Army.

1956–1988 János Kádár, head of the Communist Party and a very powerful man during the Hungarian revolt, serves as the leader of Hungary. Beginning in 1962, he pursues a policy of gradual and careful liberalization that is known as "Goulash Communism."

1988–1989 The fall of communism results in a peaceful transition of government and much reform.

Oct. 23, 1989 A democratic and parliamentarian Hungarian republic is proclaimed.

1999 Hungary joins NATO.

2004 Hungary joins the European Union.

2007 Hungary signs the Schengen Agreement.

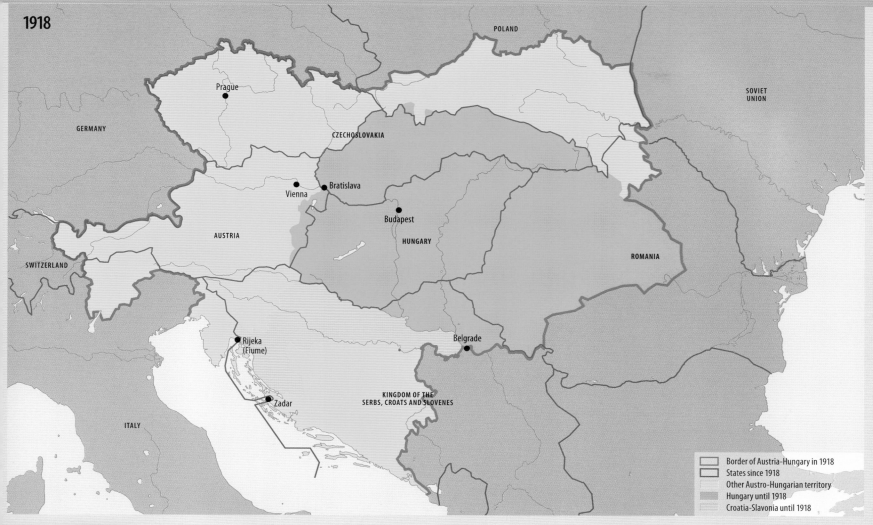

1918

GERMANY

POLAND

SOVIET UNION

Prague

CZECHOSLOVAKIA

Vienna • Bratislava

AUSTRIA

Budapest

HUNGARY

SWITZERLAND

ROMANIA

Rijeka (Fiume)

Zadar

ITALY

Belgrade

KINGDOM OF THE SERBS, CROATS AND SLOVENES

Border of Austria-Hungary in 1918
States since 1918
Other Austro-Hungarian territory
Hungary until 1918
Croatia-Slavonia until 1918

King Ludwig II (1506–1526)

Kingdom of Hungary
The Hungarian kingdom formally arose with the coronation of Stephen I in 1000. The core area of the kingdom was formed from present-day Hungary, Transylvania (northwest Romania), Slovakia, the Sub-carpathian region of present-day Ukraine and Vojvodina (today Serbia).

The Ottomans and the Kingdom of Hungary The first military encounters between the Kingdom of Hungary and the Ottomans occurred outside of Hungarian territory: Hungary's defeat at the Battle of Nicopolis in 1396, its victory at Varna in 1444 and the Second Battle of Kosovo in 1448. No serious territorial losses occurred as a result of these battles. In 1456 the Ottomans were foiled in their attempt to conquer the fortress at Belgrade, on the Hungarian border. At Hungary's defeat at the Battle of Mohács in 1526, the king of Hungary, Louis II Jagiello, was killed, and the Ottomans conquered more than two-thirds of the Hungarian empire as a result. This territory remained under Ottoman control for over 150 years. The rest of the Hungarian kingdom (Slovakia, Burgenland and portions of Croatia) came under the rule of the Habsburgs, who continued the continual warfare with the Ottomans. The Ottomans' failed attempt to conquer Vienna in 1683 was a turning point, and the Turks gradually

lost control of their territory in Europe. After their defeat at the Battles of Mohács and Zenta during the period of the Great Turkish Wars (1683–1699), the Ottomans were expelled from Hungary.

Anti-Habsburg Rebellions, 1604–1711
These rebellions, called kuruc in Hungarian, were a series of armed conflicts between the Habsburg kings and Hungarians under the leadership of either Transylvanian princes or Hungarian magnates. The skirmishes took place chiefly in the regions of Slovakia that had not been conquered by the Ottomans. Some of the factors that led to these revolts were the restrictions placed on local privi-

Siege of Buda, 1598

leges, the absolutism of the Habsburg monarchy, and the immense Counter-Reformation movement (a large portion of the Hungarian nobility had converted to Protestantism). Several times, the rebels allied themselves with the Ottomans. With the Peace of Szatmár (now Satu Mare, Romania) in 1711, the Hungarian nobles achieved far-reaching powers of self-government, and in exchange vowed to definitively recognize the hereditary rights of the Habsburgs in the Kingdom of Hungary.

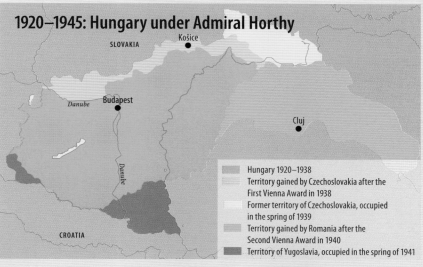

1920–1945: Hungary under Admiral Horthy

SLOVAKIA

Košice

Danube

Budapest

Cluj

Danube

CROATIA

Hungary 1920–1938
Territory gained by Czechoslovakia after the First Vienna Award in 1938
Former territory of Czechoslovakia, occupied in the spring of 1939
Territory gained by Romania after the Second Vienna Award in 1940
Territory of Yugoslavia, occupied in the spring of 1941

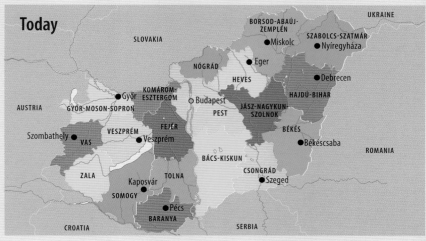

Today

UKRAINE

SLOVAKIA

BORSOD-ABAÚJ-ZEMPLÉN

SZABOLCS-SZATMÁR

Miskolc

Nyíregyháza

NÓGRÁD

Eger

HEVES

Debrecen

KOMÁROM-ESZTERGOM

Győr

Budapest

HAJDÚ-BIHAR

AUSTRIA

GYŐR-MOSON-SOPRON

PEST

JÁSZ-NAGYKUN-SZOLNOK

VESZPRÉM

FEJÉR

BÉKÉS

Szombathely

VAS

Veszprém

Békéscsaba

ZALA

BÁCS-KISKUN

ROMANIA

TOLNA

CSONGRÁD

Kaposvár

Szeged

SOMOGY

Pécs

BARANYA

CROATIA

SERBIA

Czech Republic and Slovakia

The Great Moravian Empire

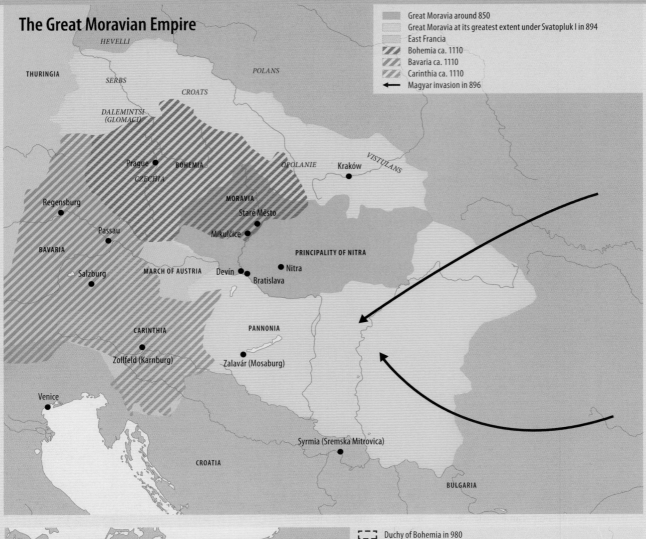

Great Moravia around 850
Great Moravia at its greatest extent under Svatopluk I in 894
East Francia
Bohemia ca. 1110
Bavaria ca. 1110
Carinthia ca. 1110
← Magyar invasion in 896

10th–11th Centuries: Bohemia and Moravia

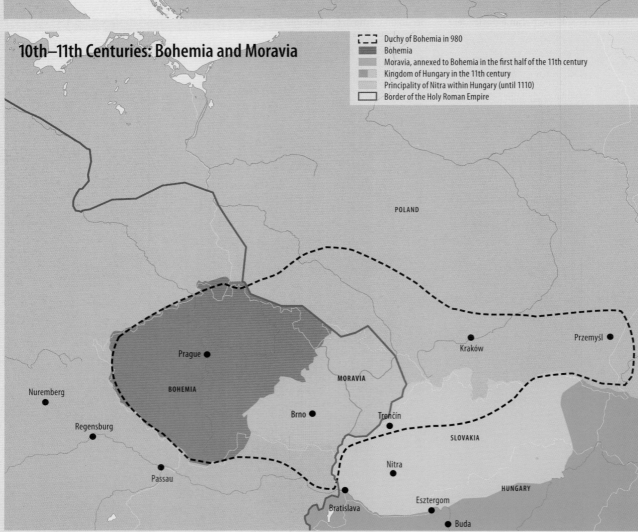

Duchy of Bohemia in 980
Bohemia
Moravia, annexed to Bohemia in the first half of the 11th century
Kingdom of Hungary in the 11th century
Principality of Nitra within Hungary (until 1110)
Border of the Holy Roman Empire

5th–6th centuries CE Slavs settle the Czechoslovakian region.

568–798/803 Period of the Avar kingdom (khanate) in Pannonia.

623–658 The kingdom of Samo unites the Slavic peoples for the first time.

end of the 8th century The principalities of Moravia and Nitra form in what are now Moravia and Slovakia.

833 The kingdom of Great Moravia unites the principalities of Moravia and Nitra under Prince Mojmír I.

863 Great Moravia is Christianized.

871–894 During the long reign of Svatopluk I, the kingdom of Great Moravia is solidified and reaches its greatest extent, including temporary conquest of Bohemia.

882–885 The first historically attested Přemyslid princes (or dukes) are baptized in Bohemia.

895 Bohemia secedes from Great Moravia and freely submits itself to the rule of the East Frankish king, Arnulf of Carinthia.

907 The Magyars defeat Great Moravia in the Battle of Brezalauspurc (Bratislava), bringing the kingdom to a decisive end.

929/935–972 A centralized Bohemian state forms under the rule of Prince Boleslav I.

955 The Duchy of Bohemia occupies the territory of Silesia and Little Poland as far north as Kraków.

1001–1108 Slovakia is absorbed into the Hungarian kingdom.

1019 Moravia becomes a vassal state to the duchy of Bohemia.

1085–1086 The Holy Roman emperor makes Vratislav II the king of Bohemia.

after 1198 The Přesmyldian princes become hereditary rulers of the kingdom of Bohemia. Bohemia becomes a member of the college of electors, participating in the selection of the Holy Roman emperor.

1241 Mongol invasion and the Battle of Mohi

1251/56–1276/78 The Bohemian king Ottokar II rules over Austria, Styria, Carinthia and Carinola.

1260 Ottokar II defeats the king of Hungary at the Battle of Kressenbrunn.

1278 Rudolf of Habsburg defeats Ottokar II at Marchfeld.

1296–1306 Bohemia and Poland enter a personal union under one ruler.

after 1302 Hungarian baron Matthew Csák (Máté Csák) takes independent control of most of western Slovakia.

1306 The Přemysliden dynasty dies out in Bohemia.

1308–1386 The Angevin dynasty takes the throne in Hungary, reestablishing centralized rule. Slovakia becomes the most important urbanized region in Hungary due to the flourishing of the mining industry in cities such as Kremnica and Banská Štiavnica.

1310–1437 The House of Luxembourg rules Bohemia.

1312 Charles I defeats the baron Matthew Csák in battle at Rozgony (now Rozhanovce).

1335–1526 Silesia falls under the control of the Bohemian crown.

1347–1378 Charles IV reigns as king of Bohemia (after 1355 as Holy Roman emperor). Bohemia as a whole, and especially the city of Prague, becomes the political, economic and cultural center of central Europe.

1415 Bohemian Christian reformer Jan Hus is burned at the stake in Konstanz. His followers, the Hussites, demand social, political and religious reforms.

1419 The first defenestration of Prague: Hussites storm the town hall of Prague and literally throw the Catholic councilmen out the windows. They die from the fall or are murdered by the angry mob below.

1420–1434 The Hussite War spreads from Prague to eastern Germany. Pope Martin V pronounces the Hussites heretics and declares the war against them a holy crusade.

14th–15th Centuries: The Kingdoms of Bohemia and Hungary

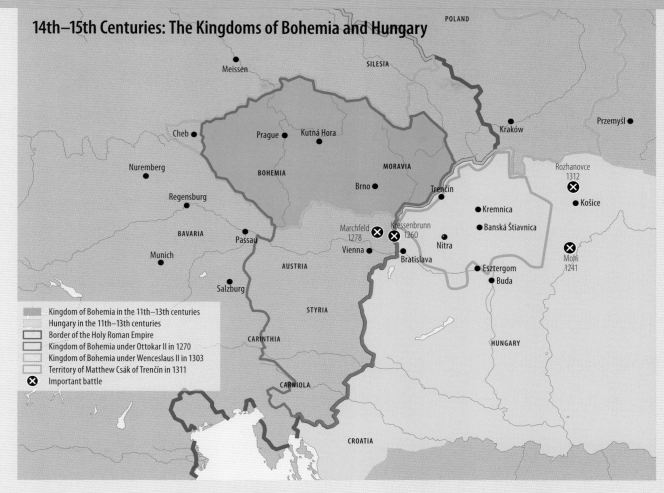

Legend:
- Kingdom of Bohemia in the 11th–13th centuries
- Hungary in the 11th–13th centuries
- Border of the Holy Roman Empire
- Kingdom of Bohemia under Ottokar II in 1270
- Kingdom of Bohemia under Wenceslaus II in 1303
- Territory of Matthew Csák of Trenčín in 1311
- ⊗ Important battle

Kingdom of Samo The kingdom of Samo was established in 623/624 by Samo, a Frankish merchant who became the leader of the Slavs after leading them to victory against the Avars. In 631 the Frankish king Dagobert failed in his attempt to take over Samo's kingdom.

Great Moravia (833–ca. 907) Great Moravia was a unified western Slavic state established through the union of the principalities of Moravia and Nitra. The kingdom is regarded as a forerunner of the later union of the Czechs and Slovakians into Czechoslovakia.

Bohemia and Moravia Bohemia, Moravia and Silesia are historical regions presently occupied by the Czech Republic and once ruled by the Bohemian crown. The kingdom of Bohemia annexed Moravia in 1019 and Silesia in 1335.

Hussite Wars The Hussite Wars broke out after Jan Hus, a reformist theologian and rector at the University of Prague (a forerunner of Martin Luther) was burned at the stake for heresy in Konstanz. In 1415 his followers, the Hussites, began a series of violent protests. The pope invoked five crusades against them, none of which succeeded. The Bohemian Hussite rebellion spread to Bavaria, Silesia, Austria, Slovakia, Brandenburg and even as far north as the Baltic region. In 1434 the more moderate Hussite Ultraquists defeated the radical Hussite Taborites, leading to negotiated peace with the Holy See.

1350: Bohemia under Charles IV

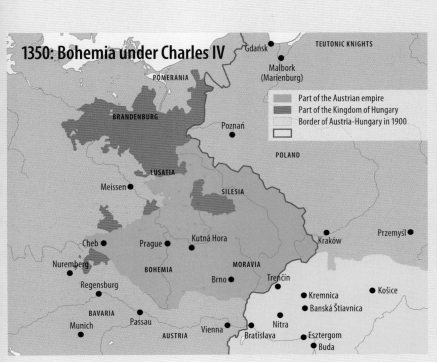

Legend:
- Part of the Austrian empire
- Part of the Kingdom of Hungary
- Border of Austria-Hungary in 1900

1420–1434: Hussite Wars

Legend:
- Kingdom of Bohemia
- Hungary
- Border of the Holy Roman Empire
- Region of the Hussite movement
- Attacks of the Hussites
- ⊗ Important battle

Czech Republic and Slovakia

17th Century

Habsburg Empire 1620
Territory ceded to Saxony in 1635
Ottoman Empire in 1600
Territory occupied by the Ottoman Empire in 1663
Transylvania, vassal of the Ottoman Empire
Border of the Holy Roman Empire

⊗ Important battle
⊗ Rebellions against Habsburg rule

19th Century

Part of the Austrian empire
Part of the Kingdom of Hungary
Border of Austria-Hungary in 1900

1930: Czechoslovakia

Bohemia
Moravia and Silesia
Slovakia
Carpathian Ruthenia

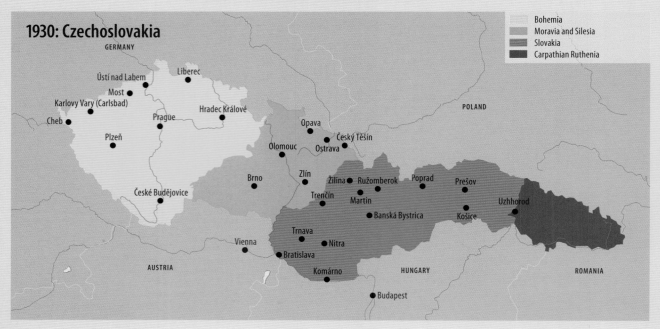

1471–1526 Rule of the Jagiellon dynasty in Bohemia.

1526 Ferdinand I of the House of Habsburg becomes king of Bohemia and Hungary.

1526–1699 Slovakia becomes the economic center of Habsburg Hungary following the Battle of Mohács.

1536–1784 Pressburg (Bratislava) becomes the capital and crown city of the Hungarian kingdom.

1604–1711 Ethnic Hungarian nobility stage revolts against Habsburg rule in Slovakia.

May 23, 1618 The Second Defenestration of Prague leads to the beginning of the Thirty Years' War.

1618–1648 More than half the population of Bohemia is killed in the Thirty Years' War.

Nov. 8, 1620 The Battle of White Mountain in Prague: The defeat of the (Protestant) Bohemian nobility leads to renewed Catholicization of Bohemia and the establishment of absolute rule by the Habsburgs.

1663 Ottoman Turks seize the border fortress of Nové Zámky and occupy southern Slovakia.

1740–1790 Maria Theresa and Joseph II introduce reforms; the populace resists the centralizing policies of Joseph II.

1805 The Battle of Austerlitz (Slavkov, Czech Republic) results in a great victory for Napoleon. The Treaty of Pressburg (Bratislava) forces Austria to cede land to its neighboring countries and ends the Holy Roman Empire.

June 1848 The Slavic Congress in Prague establishes the doctrine of Austroslavism, which demands an equal role for Slavs under Habsburg rule.

Habsburg prince Alfred von Windisch-Graetz surpresses a Slavic uprising in Prague.

1848–1849 Slovakian revolt against Magyar domination.

1867 The Austro-Hungarian Compromise (*Ausgleich*) establishes the dual monarchy of Austria-Hungary. Bohemia is allotted to the Austrian (Cisleithanian) half, and Slovakia to the Hungarian (Transleithanian) half.

1867–1914 Peak of Magyarization in Slovakia

1914–1918 World War I: Czechoslovakia fights in France, Italy and Russia.

May 30, 1918 The Pittsburgh Agreement is signed by Czech and Slovak exiles, paving the way for a united state.

Oct. 28, 1918 The state of Czechoslovakia is proclaimed in Prague; it exists until its dissolution in 1992.

1918–1935 Philosopher Tomás Garrigue Masaryk, the founder of Czechoslovakia, is its first president and enjoys worldwide esteem.

Sept. 30, 1938 The Munich Agreement results in a forced surrender of Czech borderlands (the Sudetenland) to the German Reich.

Nov. 2, 1938 The first Vienna Awards force the transfer of the southern Slovakian borderlands to Hungary.

March 14–15, 1939 Nazi Germany declares Slovakia a dependent republic. It later occupies the rest of Czechoslovakia, renaming it the Reich Protectorate of Bohemia and Moravia.

Aug. 29–October 1944 The Slovakian national rebellion at Banska Bystrica leads to the direct occupation of Slovakia by German troops.

May 8–9, 1945 Czechoslovakia is reestablished following the liberation of Prague by the Russians.

February 1948 A communist government is instituted in Prague.

1948–1953 Czechoslovakia is led by the Stalinist Klement Gottwald.

1952 The last Eastern Bloc show trials are held against Czech Communist party head Rudolf Slansky, foreign minister Vladimir Celmentis and other important Czech government functionaries.

1953–1968 Communist Party chief and head of state Anatonian Novotny leads Czechoslovakia on a neo-Stalinist course.

Jan. 5, 1968 Reformer Alexander Dubček becomes leader of the Communist Party, marking the beginning of the Prague Spring. Reformist policies

1938–1945: German Occupation (Reich Protectorate)

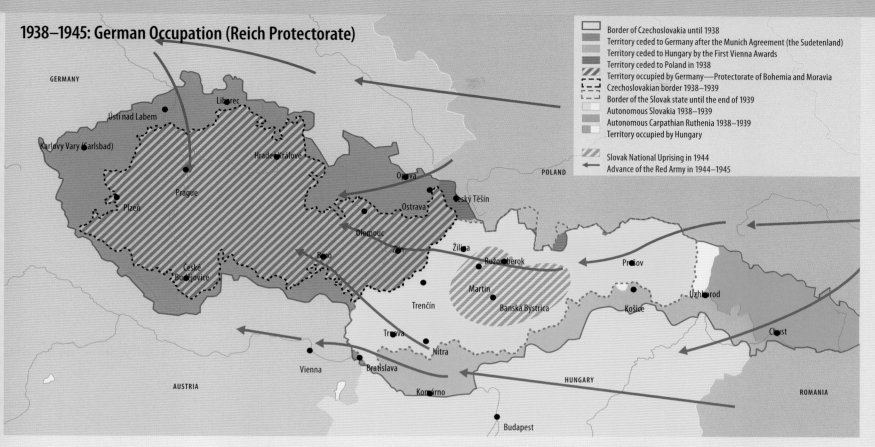

Legend:
- Border of Czechoslovakia until 1938
- Territory ceded to Germany after the Munich Agreement (the Sudetenland)
- Territory ceded to Hungary by the First Vienna Awards
- Territory ceded to Poland in 1938
- Territory occupied by Germany—Protectorate of Bohemia and Moravia
- Czechoslovakian border 1938–1939
- Border of the Slovak state until the end of 1939
- Autonomous Slovakia 1938–1939
- Autonomous Carpathian Ruthenia 1938–1939
- Territory occupied by Hungary
- Slovak National Uprising in 1944
- Advance of the Red Army in 1944–1945

win the support of both workers and intellectuals.

Aug. 21, 1968 Soviet troops supress the Prague Spring reform movement, marking the beginning of a period of normalization of relations with the USSR.

1969–1989 Gustave Husak becomes leader of an increasingly petrified Czechoslovakian Communist party.

November 1989 The Velvet Revolution brings the fall of communism and beginning of democracy. Václav Havel is elected president of Czechoslovakia, and later of the Czech Republic (from 1992 to 2003).

Jan. 1, 1993 Czechoslovakia is split into the independent states of the Czech Republic and the Slovak Republic.

1993–1998 Government of authoritarian premier Mečiar in Slovakia leads to stagnation of reforms compared to more democratic Czech Republic.

1999 Czech Republic joins NATO.

2004 Slovakia joins NATO; Czech Republic and Slovakia join the EU.

The Prague Spring began as an experiment in "socialism with a human face" led by Czechoslovakian Communist Party head Alexander Dubček, attempting to establish a politically pluralistic system permitting "humane economic democracy." Factories owned by workers would be encouraged to compete against each other, forging a "third path" between communism and capitalism. Instead, it was violently suppressed by Warsaw Pact forces acting under Soviet orders. The rapid overthrow of the Prague Spring movement demonstrated the USSR's reaction to any deviation from the Moscow party line. Soviet troops remained in Czechoslovakia until 1991.

1946–1992

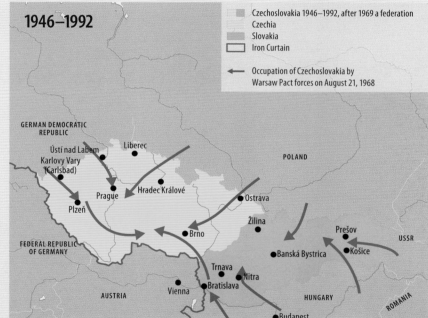

Legend:
- Czechoslovakia 1946–1992, after 1969 a federation
- Czechia
- Slovakia
- Iron Curtain
- Occupation of Czechoslovakia by Warsaw Pact forces on August 21, 1968

Czech Republic Today

Slovakia Today

Slovenia and Croatia

Antiquity

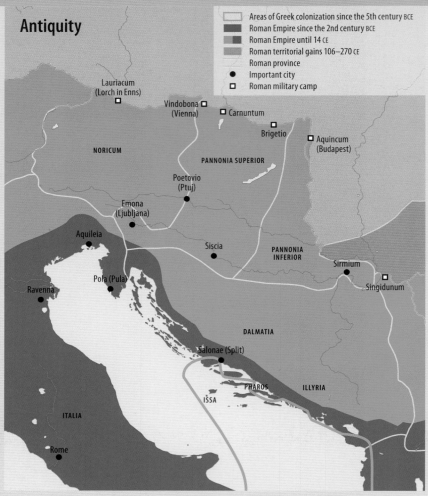

	Areas of Greek colonization since the 5th century BCE
	Roman Empire since the 2nd century BCE
	Roman Empire until 14 CE
	Roman territorial gains 106–270 CE
	Roman province
●	Important city
□	Roman military camp

840: Rise of the Franks

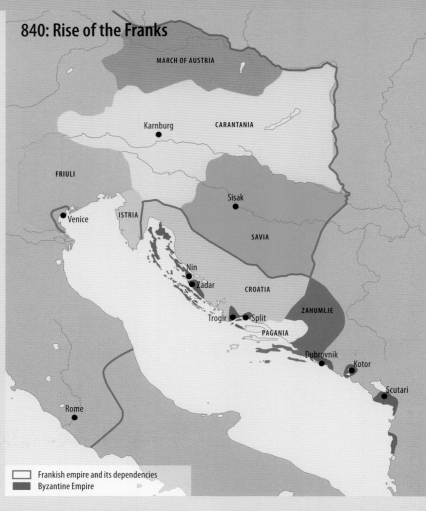

	Frankish empire and its dependencies
	Byzantine Empire

11th–13th Centuries: High Middle Ages

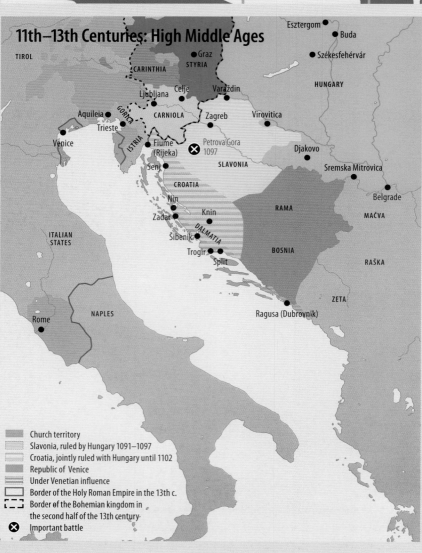

	Church territory
	Slavonia, ruled by Hungary 1091–1097
	Croatia, jointly ruled with Hungary until 1102
	Republic of Venice
	Under Venetian influence
	Border of the Holy Roman Empire in the 13th c.
	Border of the Bohemian kingdom in the second half of the 13th century
⊗	Important battle

8th century BCE–54 CE Founding of the first settlements in the regions, which in the 2nd century BCE will become the Roman provinces of Dalmatia, Pannonia and Nordicum (until 54 CE).

4th century BCE The Greek colonies Pharos (Stari Grad on the island Hvar), Issa (on the island Vis) and Aspalathos (Split, Croatia) are established.

229–219 BCE Rome takes control of the coastal regions following victory in the Illyrian Wars.

295–305 CE The Palace of Diocletian is built in the Roman town of Salona (Split).

6th–7th centuries Slavs settle Slovenia and Croatia.

788 The Slavic principality of Carantania is incorporated into the Frankish empire.

9th century Croatian principalities established in northern and central Dalmatia are loosely associated with both the Byzantine and Frankish empires. They are frequently in conflict with the Venetians.

925 Tomislav I is recognized as the king of Croatia by the pope.

976 Duchy of Carinthia is established

1000 The Dalmatian islands and coastline are conquered by the Venetians.

1040 The margravate of Carniola (much of present-day Slovenia) is established.

1097 Hungary takes control of Croatia following the Battle of Gvozd (Petrova Gora).

1102 The Pacta Conventa unites Croatia and Hungary under a single ruler.

12th–15th centuries Conflicts rage between the Republic of Venice and the kingdom of Hungary along the Dalmatian coast, which is predominantly Venetian.

1202 The Venetians conquer Zadar during the Fourth Crusade.

1335 Carniola and Carinthia (Slovenia) fall to the Habsburgs.

1358–1420 Period of Hungarian control of Dalmatia

1420–1797 The Venetians take control of Dalmatia: only the Republic of Ragusa (Durbrovnik) maintains some autonomy.

1493 Battle of Krbava Field: Croatians' attempts to resist the Ottoman Empire are futile.

1527 Ferdinand of Habsburg becomes King of Croatia.

1664 Habsburg armies defeat Ottoman forces in the primarily defensive battle at St. Gotthard.

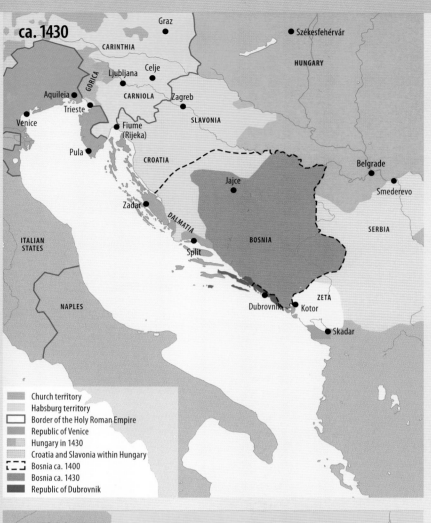

ca. 1430

- Church territory
- Habsburg territory
- Border of the Holy Roman Empire
- Republic of Venice
- Hungary in 1430
- Croatia and Slavonia within Hungary
- Bosnia ca. 1400
- Bosnia ca. 1430
- Republic of Dubrovnik

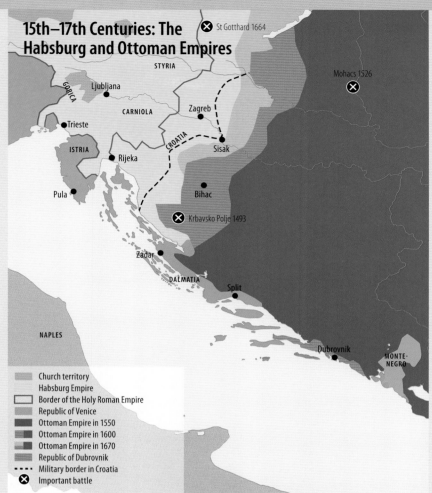

15th–17th Centuries: The Habsburg and Ottoman Empires

- Church territory
- Habsburg Empire
- Border of the Holy Roman Empire
- Republic of Venice
- Ottoman Empire in 1550
- Ottoman Empire in 1600
- Ottoman Empire in 1670
- Republic of Dubrovnik
- Military border in Croatia
- ⊗ Important battle

St Gotthard 1664
Mohacs 1526
Krbavsko Polje 1493

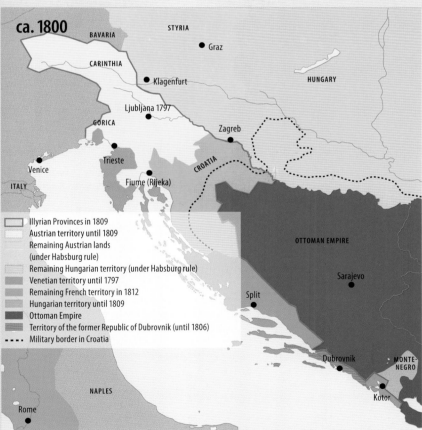

ca. 1800

- Illyrian Provinces in 1809
- Austrian territory until 1809
- Remaining Austrian lands (under Habsburg rule)
- Remaining Hungarian territory (under Habsburg rule)
- Venetian territory until 1797
- Remaining French territory in 1812
- Hungarian territory until 1809
- Ottoman Empire
- Territory of the former Republic of Dubrovnik (until 1806)
- Military border in Croatia

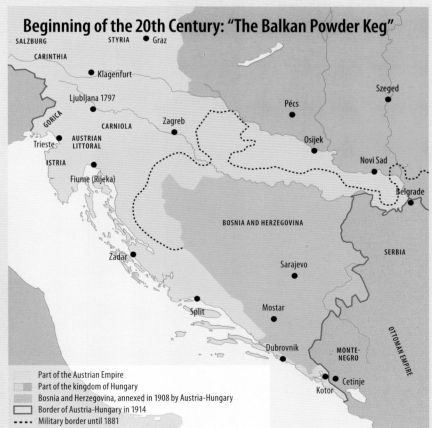

Beginning of the 20th Century: "The Balkan Powder Keg"

- Part of the Austrian Empire
- Part of the kingdom of Hungary
- Bosnia and Herzegovina, annexed in 1908 by Austria-Hungary
- Border of Austria-Hungary in 1914
- Military border until 1881

1683 Ottoman authority declines as the region comes under Habsburg control.

1745 The triune kingdom of Croatia-Slovenia-Dalmatia is established as a Habsburg monarchy; Venetian Dalmatia is only nominally under its control.

1797 Napoleonic invasion leads to the end of Venetian influence in Dalmatia; Dalmatia is ceded to Austria.

1807–1813 The Napoleonic Illyrian Province, an independent province of the French Empire, brings Slovenia and

Croatia under a single administration for the first time.

1848 End of the union between Croatia and the kingdom of Hungary through the efforts of Croatian lord (dignitary) Joseph Jelačič.

1868 The Hungarian-Croatian Compromise (the Nagodba) gives Croatia independence in local affairs, control of education and limited cultural autonomy.

Slovenia and Croatia

1914–1918: World War I

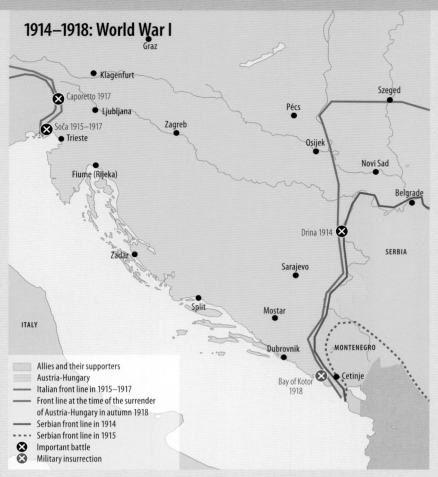

Graz
Klagenfurt
Caporetto 1917
Ljubljana
Soča 1915–1917
Trieste
Zagreb
Fiume (Rijeka)
Szeged
Pécs
Osijek
Novi Sad
Belgrade
Zadar
Drina 1914
SERBIA
Sarajevo
Split
Mostar
ITALY
Dubrovnik
MONTENEGRO
Bay of Kotor 1918
Cetinje

Legend:
- Allies and their supporters
- Austria-Hungary
- Italian front line in 1915–1917
- Front line at the time of the surrender of Austria-Hungary in autumn 1918
- Serbian front line in 1914
- Serbian front line in 1915
- ⊗ Important battle
- ⊗ Military insurrection

1914 World War I begins: fierce fighting rages between Austro-Hungarian and Serbian forces.

1915–1917 Bitter conflict takes place between Italy and Austria-Hungary (Battles of the Isonzo).

Dec. 1, 1919 Proclamation of the Kingdom of Serbs, Croats and Slovenes; Trieste, Istria, Zadar and coastal territories are ceded to Italy.

1920 Treaty of Rapallo with Italy settles the border between Italy and the Kingdom of Serbs, Croats and Slovenes.

1920–1924 Era of the independent Free State of Fiume (today the Croatian city of Rijeka).

1929 After a coup, the kingdom's parliament is dissolved and constitution suspended, to be replaced by a royal dictatorship. The nation is renamed the Kingdom of Yugoslavia.

1934 King Alexander I is murdered by the Ustasha, a terrorist organization.

1939 The constitution is amended to give Croatia partial autonomy under the leadership of a Croatian *ban* (lord).

April 6–17, 1941 Germany invades Yugoslavia. Slovenia is partitioned between Italy, Hungary and Germany. A Nazi-supported Croatian independence movement is established under the leadership of the fascist Ustasha, initiating a reign of terror.

1944–1945 Yugoslavia is liberated as a result of the partisan movement led by Josip Broz Tito.

1945–1963 Croatia and Slovenia become republics of the democratic Federated People's Republic of Yugoslavia (renamed the Socialist Federated People's Republic of Yugoslavia in 1963).

1948 Yugoslavia breaks with the Soviet Union following Tito's attempt to establish an independent Balkan Federation with Albania and Bulgaria.

1948–1980 Titoism, the policy of Yugoslav president Josip Broz Tito, provides both authoritarian control and internal self-government. Supported by the West, Tito minimizes the role of ethnic conflict by emphasizing the shared struggle of all Yugoslavians against Nazism and Soviet hegemony.

1918–1941: The Kingdom of Yugoslavia

AUSTRIA
HUNGARY
Ljubljana
Trieste
Zagreb
Venice
Fiume (Rijeka)
ROMANIA
Bucharest
Belgrade
Zadar (Italy)
Sarajevo
Split
Rome
ITALY
Sofia
BULGARIA
Tirana
Naples
ALBANIA
GREECE

Legend:
- Kingdom of the Serbs, Croats and Slovenes (Yugoslavia after 1929)
- Border of the autonomous Banovina of Croatia in 1939

Josip Broz Tito (1892–1980)

1954 The Free Territory of Trieste is divided between Italy and Yugoslavia.

1974 A new constitution strengthens the autonomy of the Yugoslavian republics, leading to the Croatian Spring reformist independence movement.

June 25, 1991 Slovenia and Croatia declare their independence, leading to the start of the Yugoslav War.

Dec. 14, 1995 Dayton Peace Accords are signed, ending the Croatian and Bosnian Wars.

2004 Slovenia joins NATO and the European Union.

Illyrians were an Indo-European tribe that inhabited the northwestern regions of the Balkan Peninsula.

Pacta Conventa These are a controversial series of agreements between the Croatian nobility and the Hungarian king concerning the sovereignty of Hungary. In practice, the Pacta Conventa united Croatia and the kingdom of Hungary under a single ruler (personal union).

The Kingdom of Serbs, Croats and Slovenes This kingdom existed from 1918 until 1941 under the Karadjordjevic dynasty, whose members had previously been Serbian princes and kings. Pressure for the establishment of a single state was driven by the fear of Italian imperialism. The dominant position in the kingdom was controlled by the Serbs.

Ustasha Founded in 1929, the Ustasha was a Croatian fascist movement based on the Italian model and focused on reducing Serb hegemony in the region. Its founder, Ante Pavelić, immigrated to Italy to advance his cause. In 1934 the Utasha assassinated King Alexander I during a state visit to

1941–1945: World War II

AUSTRIA
Budapest
HUNGARY
Ljubljana
Trieste
Zagreb
ROMANIA
Rijeka
Jasenovac
Belgrade
CROATIA
Zadar (Italy)
Banja Luka
SERBIA
Sarajevo
Split
MONTENEGRO
ITALY
ALBANIA

Legend:
- Hungary
- Territory occupied by Germany
- Territory occupied by Italy
- Croatian nation
- Main areas of partisan opposition
- Border of Yugoslavia in 1945
- □ Concentration camp

1945–1991: Federal People's Republic of Yugoslavia

AUSTRIA
HUNGARY
Ljubljana
Zagreb
ROMANIA
Trieste
Rijeka
CROATIA
Belgrade
BOSNIA AND HERZEGOVINA
SERBIA
Sarajevo
BULGARIA
Split
Sofia
ITALY
MONTENEGRO
Titograd
Rome
Skopje
ALBANIA
MACEDONIA
Tirana
Naples
GREECE

Legend:
- Yugoslavia since 1945
- Territory gained from Italy in 1945
- Free Territory of Trieste 1945–1953
- Territory of Trieste, annexed by Yugoslavia in 1954
- Territory of Trieste, annexed by Italy in 1954
- Border of the Yugoslav republics

1991–1998: Yugoslavian Wars

AUSTRIA
Maribor
HUNGARY
Ljubljana 1991
Trieste
SLOVENIA
Zagreb 1991
Daruvar 1991
Karlovac
CROATIA
Osijek
Rijeka
Bljesak 1995
SLAVONIA
ISTRIA
Bihać
Vukovar 1991
Oluja 1995
Banja Luka
Brčko
Maslenica 1993
BOSNIA AND HERZEGOVINA
Tuzla
SERBIA
Zadar 1991
Travik
Zadar 1993
Knin 1995
Zenica
1992
Gornji Vakuf
Sarajevo
Zagreb
DALMATIA
Mostar 1993
ITALY
MONTENEGRO
Podgorica
Dubrovnik 1992

Legend:
- Croatian territory occupied by Serbs in 1991
- Croatian territory occupied by Serbs 1992–1994 (Republic of Serbian Krajina)
- Croatian territory occupied by Serbs until early 1998 (Eastern Slavonia)
- Territory in Bosnia and Herzegovina controlled by Croats 1992–1995 (Croatian Republic of Herzeg-Bosnia)
- ⊗ Locations of heaviest fighting

Today

SPODNJEPOSAVSKA
OSREDNJESLOVENSKA
ZASAVSKA
Maribor
KOROŠKA
POMURSKA
GORENJSKA
PODRAVSKA
SAVINJSKA
MEĐIMURJE
GORIŠKA
VARAŽDIN
KRAPINA-ZAGORJE
KOPRIVNICA-KRIŽEVCI
Ljubljana
NOTRANJSKO-KRAŠKA
JUGOVZHODNA SLOVENIJA
Zagreb
ZAGREB-GRAD
VIROVITICA-PODRAVINA
Trieste
OBALNO-KRAŠKA
ZAGREB
BJELOVAR-BILOGORA
OSIJEK-BARANJA
Rijeka
PRIMORJE-GORSKI KOTAR
Karlovac
Daruvar
Osijek
ISTRIA
SISAK-MOSLAVINA
KARLOVAC
POŽEGA-SLAVONIJA
Vukovar
BROD-POSAVINA
VUKOVAR-SRIJEM
Brčko
LIKA-SENJ
Zadar
ZADAR
Knin
ŠIBENIK-KNIN
Zagreb
SPLIT-DALMATIJA
DUBROVNIK-NERETVA
Dubrovnik

Legend:
- Slovenia
- Croatia

France. During World War II, when Germany controlled Yugoslavia, with Nazi support, the Ustasha established established a reign of terror that pitted the Catholic Croats against the Orthodox Serbs as well as Jews. Ustasha also established concentration camps that matched the Nazi camps in brutality.

Josip Broz Tito (1892–1980) Tito, the son of a Croat and a Slovene, arrived in Russia during World War I as a prisoner of war. He stayed on after his release and participated in the October Revolution. In 1937 he became General Secretary of the banned Yugoslav Communist Party. As a partisan leader during World War II, he liberated the Yugoslavian republics—without Soviet aid, he claimed—an achievement he would later use to promote national unity. He became president of Yugoslavia in 1945 and served as head of state from 1953 to 1980, taking the title "marshal." His policy of "Titoism" tolerated private industry and promoted artistic and cultural freedom within a political system that remained profoundly authoritarian and committed to socialist ideals. Tito's stand against Soviet intervention in the Balkan states brought him increased support from Western nations throughout the period of the Cold War.

Poland

ca. 1025: The Polish Monarchy

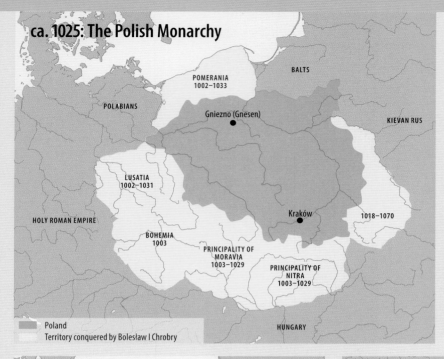

Legend:
- Poland
- Territory conquered by Bolesław I Chrobry

Poland's history is one of the most complex in all of Europe. The borders of the Polish state changed frequently, often through the machinations of its neighbors, Russia and Germany. Poland even disappeared altogether for a time, consumed by the Great Powers' hunger for land. Polish nationalism, the expression of the people's desire for freedom, has always played a strong role. Despite a chaotic past filled with political turmoil, war and defeat, Polish culture is one of the richest in Europe. Even during the worst periods, the Roman Catholic Church was a source of support for the people, which has contributed to the deep religious faith of Poles today.

Prince Mieszko I (935–992)

922–1025 Bolesław I Chrobry (the Brave) expands and consolidates Polish territory.

966 Prince Mieszko I, duke of Polans of the Piast dynasty, converts to Christianity and consolidates the Polish state.

1000 The Archdiocese of Gniezno is founded, an important step toward Poland's independence from foreign interference.

1025 Bolesław Chrobry is crowned king of Poland, now completely independent.

11th century Poland weakens under attacks from the Holy Roman Empire and Kievan Rus.

1138 Poland is subdivided into duchies, six of which are controlled by descendants of the various lines of the Piast dynasty.

1241: Mongol Invasion of Europe

Legend:
- Polish duchies
- Other small duchies
- Teutonic Knights
- → Mongol (Tatar) invasion in 1241
- ⊗ Important battle

ca. 1386: Poland under the Jagiellon Dynasty

Legend:
- Teutonic Knights
- Kingdom of Poland
- Polish fief
- Hungarian-Polish union 1370–1382

12th–13th centuries The duchies engage in nearly constant civil war as the nation collapses under border incursions and German settlement in Silesia and Pomerania. Polish cities rapidly become Germanized.

1226 The Order of the Teutonic Knights founds a state on Poland's northern borders, ostensibly to defend Poles from attacks by pagan Prussians.

1241 The Mongol invasion in the form of invading hordes of Tatars plunders Polish cities, including Kraków. The Mongols retreat toward Hungary after the Battle of Legnica (also known as the Battle of Liegnitz).

1300–1305 Wacław II founds the Přemyslid dynasty, ruling from both Poland and Bohemia.

1320 The Polish monarchy revives with the return of the Piast dynasty under Władysław Lokietek (the Short). Most of Poland is reunited, with the exception of Pomerania, Silesia and Masovia. Kraków becomes the capital.

1333–1370 Kazimir III the Great, the last Piast king, expands Polish territory to the east.

1335 Silesia becomes part of Bohemia and the Holy Roman Empire.

1370–1382 Hungarian King Ludwig I of Anjou rules Poland.

1386 The Jagiellons seize the throne, uniting Poland with Lithuania. Lithuania becomes Christian.

1410 The Polish-Lithuanian army defeats the Order of Teutonic Knights at the Battle of Tannenberg.

1466 After another victory over the Order of Teutonic Knights, Poland regains its access to the sea by taking control of the city of Gdańsk (Danzig).

ca. 1490: The Polish-Lithuanian Union

Legend:
- Teutonic Knights
- Kingdom of Poland
- Polish vassals
- Polish-Lithuanian Union after 1386
- ⊗ Important battle

1569 The Union of Lublin creates the Polish-Lithuanian Commonwealth, a closer bond than the preceding union, in which Poland and Lithuania become a single state.

1587–1668 The Swedish Vasa dynasty takes control after Poland is drawn into the Russo-Swedish Wars.

16th–17th centuries Polish nobles form a republic (*rzeczpospolita*), electing both a king and a parliament. The monarchy continues to weaken as anarchy reigns among the nobility. The Roman Catholic Church defends itself against inroads by the Reformation and the Russian Orthodox Church, leading to a revolt by Orthodox Cossacks living on the Ukraine border. Polish power declines rapidly in the wake of a series of devastating wars with Sweden, Russia and the Ottoman Empire.

1648–1668 Sweden occupies Poland despite heavy resistance during a low point in Polish history referred to as "the deluge." Poland loses the eastern Ukraine to Russia after an uprising on the eastern border.

1674–1696 Jan Sobieski III becomes king of Poland. In 1683 he leads the Christian army against the Turks, becoming the "Savior of Vienna."

1697–1763 August II and August III, electors of Saxony and kings of Poland, introduce an era of great cultural achievement.

18th century Poland serves as a buffer zone between Russia and western Europe. Russian interference in Polish internal politics includes choosing the monarch and dictating to parliament. The anarchic Polish nobility does nothing in response.

1764–1795 Stanislaus Poniatowski, the last Polish king, rules under Russian protection.

1772 Prussia, Austria and Russia partition Poland, each annexing Polish territory.

1791 Calls for reform within Poland lead to the Constitution of the 3rd of May, creating a constitutional monarchy to govern territories still under direct Polish control.

1792 Catherine the Great invades Poland. Tadeusz Kościuszko, a colonel in the American Revolutionary army, returns and wins support of the Polish people for resistance to Russia.

1793 The reforms are banned as Russia and Prussia partition Poland again.

1794 Prussian and Russian forces crush Kościuszko's uprising against the partition.

1795 The third and final partition erases Poland from the map.

The Polish-Lithuanian Commonwealth

- Poland-Lithuania
- Polish fief
- Lithuania after 1569

Until 1772: Poland

First Partition of Poland, 1772

- Territory to Prussia
- Territory to Russia
- Territory to Austria

Second Partition of Poland, 1793

- Territory to Prussia
- Territory to Russia
- Territory to Austria

Third Partition of Poland, 1795

- Territory to Prussia
- Territory to Russia
- Territory to Austria

Poland

1807: The Duchy of Warsaw

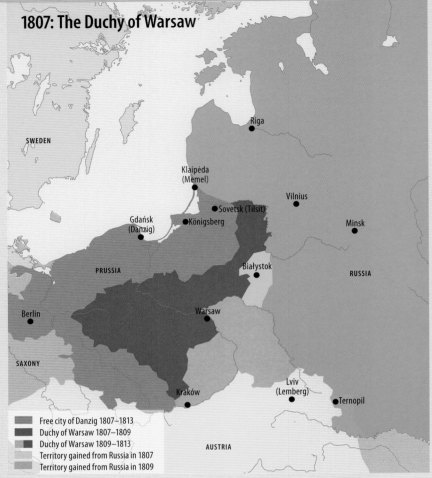

Free city of Danzig 1807–1813
Duchy of Warsaw 1807–1809
Duchy of Warsaw 1809–1813
Territory gained from Russia in 1807
Territory gained from Russia in 1809

1807–1914: Poland under Foreign Rule

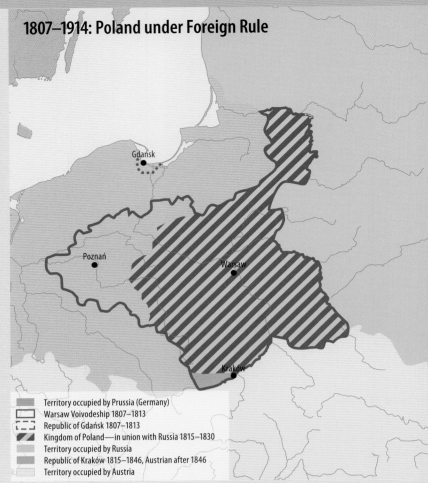

Territory occupied by Prussia (Germany)
Warsaw Voivodeship 1807–1813
Republic of Gdańsk 1807–1813
Kingdom of Poland—in union with Russia 1815–1830
Territory occupied by Russia
Republic of Kraków 1815–1846, Austrian after 1846
Territory occupied by Austria

1815: Poland after the Congress of Vienna

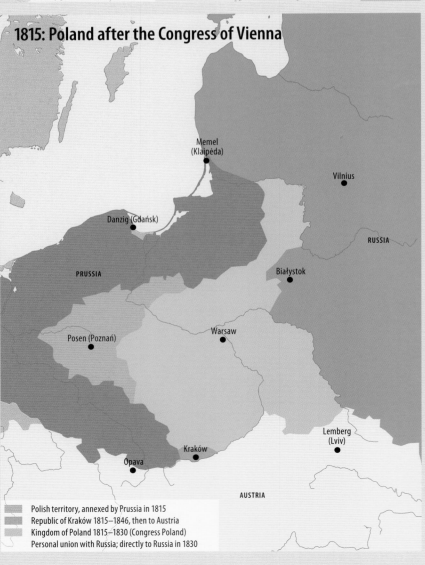

Polish territory, annexed by Prussia in 1815
Republic of Kraków 1815–1846, then to Austria
Kingdom of Poland 1815–1830 (Congress Poland)
Personal union with Russia; directly to Russia in 1830

1807 The Napoleonic Wars revive Polish statehood, creating the duchy of Warsaw, a French client state.

1815 The Congress of Vienna repartitions Poland, creating the Kingdom of Poland as a dependant protectorate of the Russian tsar. Remaining territories are allotted to Russia, Prussia and Austria.

1830 After a failed revolt, the kingdom of Poland is dissolved by the tsar and annexed to Russia.

1863 As uprising after uprising fails, Poland is stripped of all independence and "Poland" becomes little more than a geographic description, with no national or political autonomy.

1918–1921 The Treaty of Versailles restores Polish sovereignty in the aftermath of World War I. Territorial conflicts with Czechoslovakia, Ukraine, Lithuania and Soviet Russia quickly arise. Polish troops occupy Belarus (White Russia).

1920 Marshall Pilsudski turns back the invading Bolsheviks at the Battle of Warsaw.

1926–1935 Authoritarian Marshall Pilsudski takes control of the government in the wake of a national strike, putting down uprisings by ethnic minorities.

1934 Poland signs the German-Polish Non-Aggression Pact.

Sept. 1, 1939 Germany invades Poland, a move that leads to the start of World War II. The Soviet Red Army crosses into Poland a month later, bringing down the Polish government. Poland is divided between Russian and German occupying forces during a period marked by civilian unrest, terror and persecution of Polish intellectuals.

1940 The Massacre at Katyn Forest: some 20,000 Polish military and police officers are murdered on orders from Stalin.

1942 The Nazi extermination of European Jews begins in Polish death camps including Auschwitz, Treblinka and Sobibor.

1944 The Warsaw Uprising led by the Polish resistance is brutally suppressed by the Nazis, with nearly all of Warsaw destroyed in its aftermath. Nearby Soviet troops, on which the resistance was counting for help, chose not to enter the city and come to its aid.

1944–1956 Stalinist Boleslaw Bierut rules under the protection of the USSR.

1945 Stalin creates the People's Republic of Poland, placing the Polish Communist Party in control of the government.

World War I

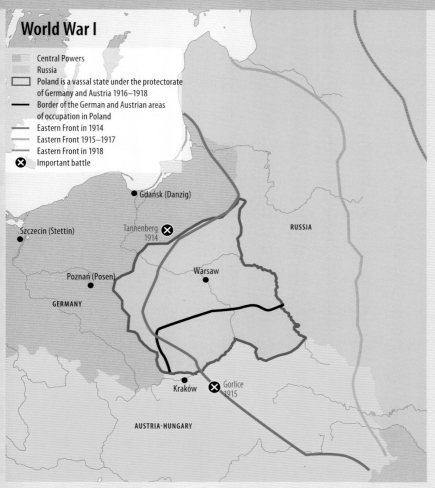

Legend:
- Central Powers
- Russia
- Poland is a vassal state under the protectorate of Germany and Austria 1916–1918
- Border of the German and Austrian areas of occupation in Poland
- Eastern Front in 1914
- Eastern Front 1915–1917
- Eastern Front in 1918
- ⊗ Important battle

Szczecin (Stettin), Gdańsk (Danzig), Tannenberg 1914, Poznań (Posen), Warsaw, GERMANY, RUSSIA, Kraków, Gorlice 1915, AUSTRIA-HUNGARY

1920–1938: Between the Wars

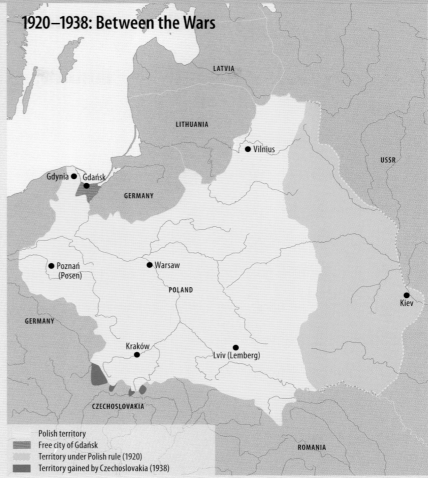

LATVIA, LITHUANIA, Vilnius, USSR, Gdynia, Gdańsk, GERMANY, Poznań (Posen), Warsaw, POLAND, Kiev, GERMANY, Kraków, Lviv (Lemberg), CZECHOSLOVAKIA, ROMANIA

Legend:
- Polish territory
- Free city of Gdańsk
- Territory under Polish rule (1920)
- Territory gained by Czechoslovakia (1938)

1956 Worker unrest brings Władysław Gomułka to power. De-Stalinization begins.

1970–1980 After Gomulka falls from power, the new party leader Edward Gierek introduces a policy of "socialist normality."

1978–2005 Karol Wojtyla, archbishop of Kraków, becomes Pope John Paul II. His election revitalizes Catholicism in Poland.

1980–1981 Social unrest and protests against communist rule bring about the formation of *Solidarność* (Solidarity), a trade union led by Lech Wałęsa. In response, General Wojciech Jaruzelski declares martial law, which will remain in place until 1983, in part to stave off Soviet intervention.

1989 Communist government ends in Poland. A democratic government is elected and the parliament ends the term of president Jaruzelski, paving the way for constitutional reform.

1990–1995 Solidarity's leader, Lech Wałęsa, is president of Poland.

1999 Poland joins the NATO.

2004 Poland becomes a member of the European Union. Poland's economy rapidly becomes one of the most dynamic in eastern Europe.

1939

Legend:
- German attack on Sept. 1, 1939
- Soviet attack on Sept. 17, 1939
- ⊗ Important battle

SWEDEN, Klaipėda (Memel), LITHUANIA, Westerplatte September 7, 1939, Kaunas, Vilnius, Königsberg, Gdańsk (Danzig), SOVIET UNION, Białystok, Poznań (Posen), Warsaw September 29, 1939, Brest-Litovsk, POLAND, GERMANY, Gliwice, Kraków, Lviv (Lemberg), PROTECTORATE OF BOHEMIA AND MORAVIA, SLOVAKIA, HUNGARY

— Line of contact between Soviet and German troops

1939–1944

Katyn, Gdańsk, Treblinka, Białystok, Poznań, Warsaw, Chelmno (Kulmhof), Majdanek, Sobibór, Belzec, Gliwice, Kraków, Lviv (Lemberg), Auschwitz

Legend:
- Territory annexed by Germany
- General Government (German)
- Territory annexed by Slovakia
- — Border of the USSR 1939–1941
- ● Concentration and extermination camps
- ● Massacre of Polish soldiers by the Soviets (Katyn)

Poland Today

POMORSKIE, Gdańsk, WARMIŃSKO-MAZURSKIE, Olsztyn, PODLASKIE, Białystok, ZACHODNIO-POMORSKIE, Szczecin, Bydgoszcz, KUJAWSKO-POMORSKIE, MAZOWIECKIE, Warsaw, Poznań, WIELKOPOLSKIE, Łódź, Lublin, LUBUSKIE, Zielona Góra, ŁÓDZKIE, LUBELSKIE, Wrocław, Kielce, ŚWIĘTOKRZYSKIE, DOLNOŚLĄSKIE, Opole, ŚLĄSKIE, OPOLSKIE, Katowice, Kraków, PODKARPACKIE, Rzeszów, MAŁOPOLSKIE

Estonia, Latvia and Lithuania

The Baltic Region in the Dark Ages

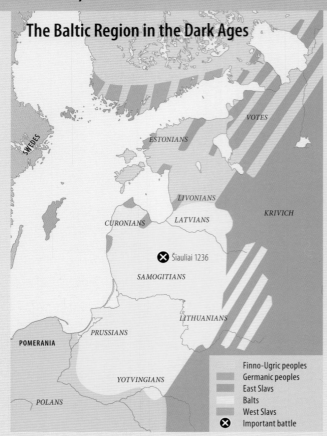

	Finno-Ugric peoples
	Germanic peoples
	East Slavs
	Balts
	West Slavs
⊗	Important battle

14th and 15th Centuries: The Polish-Lithuanian Union

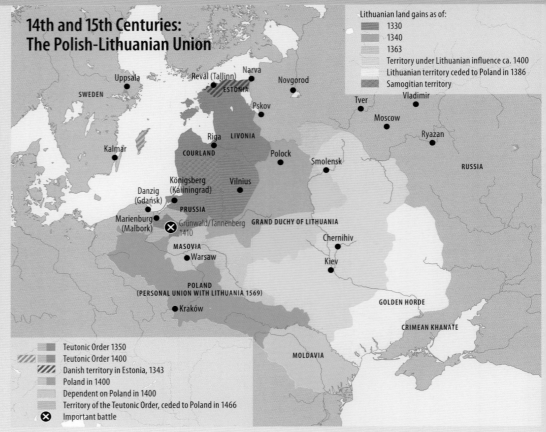

Lithuanian land gains as of:
- 1330
- 1340
- 1363
- Territory under Lithuanian influence ca. 1400
- Lithuanian territory ceded to Poland in 1386
- Samogitian territory

	Teutonic Order 1350
	Teutonic Order 1400
	Danish territory in Estonia, 1343
	Poland in 1400
	Dependent on Poland in 1400
	Territory of the Teutonic Order, ceded to Poland in 1466
⊗	Important battle

9th–10th centuries Viking invasions of the Baltic states

after 1202 The historical boundaries of Livonia and Courland (present-day Latvia and southern Estonia) are established by the Livonian Brothers of the Sword as they dominate and Christianize the land under their control. Northern Estonia is under Danish suzerainty.

1236 Samogitian and Semigallian Lithuanians annihilate the Livonian Brothers of the Sword at the Battle of Saule.

1237 The Livonian Brothers of the Sword are incorporated as a Teutonic Order. As a result, Livonia and Courland are incorporated as territories belonging to the Teutonic Knights.

1253 The Lithuanian prince Mindaugas obtains sanction from the pope to unify the Lithuanian principality with his royal lands. Despite this religious sanction, the prince abandons Christianity after a few years and Lithuania descends into internal conflict that lasts until the end of the 13th century.

1261–1271 The Baltic Prussians (Pruzzen) are subjugated by the Teutonic Knights.

until ca. 1300 The Baltic region is besieged by Baltic tribes, leading to the expulsion of the Finno-Ugric tribes toward the north.

1316–1341 Rule of Lithuanian Grand Duke Gediminas, who turns Lithuania into one of the great powers of Europe. Lithuania expands its territory, primarily to the south and the east.

1320/65 Kiev is under the control of Lithuania.

1323 The Lithuanian capital, Vilnius, is established.

1356 The Teutonic Knights wrest control of northern Estonia from Denmark.

1385 The Act of Kreva is signed: the Lithuanian grand duke Jogiello becomes the king of Poland, taking the name Wladyslaw II, thus establishing a personal union of the kingdom of Poland with the Jagiellons.

1401–1430 Vytautas the Great, grand duke of Lithuania, rules Poland following his nephew Wladyslaw II, stabilizing the union between Poland and Lithuania.

1410 The Battle of Tannenberg. The Teutonic Knights are annihilated by a joint Polish-Lithuanian army. As a result, the Samogitian and Semigallian lands are assigned to what is now Lithuania.

1418 Vytaustas the Great forces the Mongols of the Golden Horde to sign a peace treaty.

1558–1583 Livonian War. Control of the old lands belonging to knightly orders is parceled out. Sweden takes control of present-day Estonia, Poland-Lithuania receives Livonia and Courland, and Denmark receives the smaller territories in the region.

1569 The Union of Lublin: The Polish-Lithuanian Commonwealth is established, replacing the prior personal union with an actual union of the states under an elective monarchy. This will be dissolved with the Polish constitution of 1791 and in 1795 with the final partition of Poland.

1629 The Truce of Altmark is signed. Livonia (northwestern Latvia) is ceded to Sweden.

1700–1721 The Great Northern War and the Peace of Nystad: Sweden is forced to forfeit its territories in the Baltic. Estonia and Latvia come under Russian control.

1707 Livonian statesman Johann Reinhold von Patkul, whose alliance with Russia and Saxony against Sweden triggered the Great Northern War, is executed by being broken on the wheel and then drawn and quartered.

1795 The Third Partition of Poland: Courland and Lithuania come under Russian suzerainty. Throughout the 18th century these lands are subjected to a policy of Russification.

1863 Revolts in Poland and Lithuania are surpressed by the Russians.

1915 Lithuania is occupied by German troops.

16th–18th Centuries

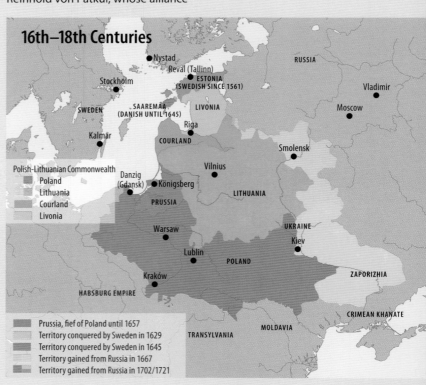

Polish-Lithuanian Commonwealth
- Poland
- Lithuania
- Courland
- Livonia

	Prussia, fief of Poland until 1657
	Territory conquered by Sweden in 1629
	Territory conquered by Sweden in 1645
	Territory gained from Russia in 1667
	Territory gained from Russia in 1702/1721

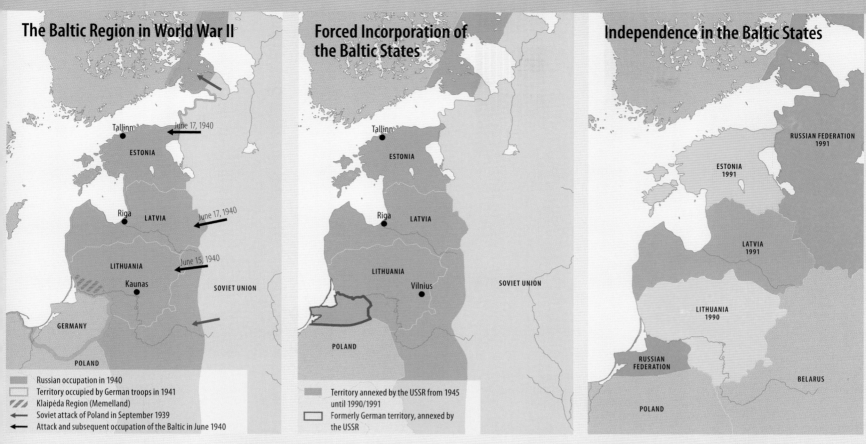

The Baltic Region in World War II

Tallinn — June 17, 1940
ESTONIA
Riga — June 17, 1940
LATVIA
LITHUANIA — June 15, 1940
Kaunas
SOVIET UNION
GERMANY
POLAND

- Russian occupation in 1940
- Territory occupied by German troops in 1941
- Klaipėda Region (Memelland)
- Soviet attack of Poland in September 1939
- Attack and subsequent occupation of the Baltic in June 1940

Forced Incorporation of the Baltic States

Tallinn
ESTONIA
Riga
LATVIA
LITHUANIA
Vilnius
SOVIET UNION
POLAND

- Territory annexed by the USSR from 1945 until 1990/1991
- Formerly German territory, annexed by the USSR

Independence in the Baltic States

RUSSIAN FEDERATION 1991
ESTONIA 1991
LATVIA 1991
LITHUANIA 1990
RUSSIAN FEDERATION
BELARUS
POLAND

1918 The Lithuanian Republic is proclaimed on February 16th, the Estonian Republic on February 24th and the Latvian Republic on November 18th.

Feb. 2, 1920 The Treaty of Tartu (Dorpat): The Soviet Union recognizes Estonia as an independent state.

Aug. 11, 1920 The Treaty of Riga: The Soviets recognize Latvia as an independent state.

October 1920 The Polish-Lithuanian War ends with Poland's annexation of the territory of Vilnius. Kaunas becomes the capital of Lithuania until 1940.

January 1923 The Klaipėda Revolt: Lithuania annexes the Memel Territory (Klaipėda), which formerly belonged to Prussia. The annexation was formally recognized internationally in 1924.

1926–1940 Antanas Smetona stages a military coup in Lithuania and establishes an authoritarian regime.

1934–1940 Authoritarian governments control the states of Estonia (under Konstantin Päts) and Latvia (under Karlis Ulmanis).

March 22, 1939 The Memel Territory is ceded to the German Third Reich.

June 15–17, 1940 The Soviet Union attacks the Baltic states.

Aug. 3–6, 1940 Estonia, Latvia and Lithuania are forcibly incorporated into the Soviet Union.

1941 Germany occupies the Baltic states. The Nazi policies against the Jews are readily adopted, leading to the extermination of most of the Jewish population.

1944/1945 The Soviets again occupy the Baltic states and reincorporate them into the Soviet Union. Deportations, political persecutions, the immigration of primarily Russian-speaking people and Russification are all hallmarks of the reoccupation by the Soviets.

1987–1992 The "Singing Revolution" represents a national awakening among the populations of the Baltic states.

1990–1991 A gradual transfer of power and sovereignty takes place as the Baltic republics gain their full independence. Democracies emerge in the three Baltic states following their emancipation.

Jan. 13, 1991 Bloody Sunday in Vilnius: fourteen people are killed and 1,000 are injured in an attempt to overthrow the pro-Soviet government in Lithuania.

from 1995 An economic boom occurs in the three Baltic republics ("The Baltic Tiger").

2003/04 Accusations of perjury by President Rolandas Paksas lead to a political crisis in Lithuania that results in the impeachment of Paksas, known as "Paksagate."

2004 The Baltic states join NATO and the European Union.

The Teutonic Knights were a Christian spiritual order of knights in the 12th century. They originated in Bremen and Lübeck, and were founded with the purpose of recapturing Jerusalem. Around 1230 the knights turned their attention to northwestern Europe. In 1237 they acquired the territory of the Livonian Brothers of the Sword, launching German colonization of the Baltic region.

Estonia Today

Tallinn, Rakvere, Jõhvi, HARJUMAA, LÄÄNE-VIRUMAA, IDA-VIRUMAA, Kärdla, Haapsalu, Rapla, Paide, HIIUMAA, LÄÄNEMAA, RAPLAMAA, JÄRVAMAA, Jõgeva, JÕGEVAMAA, SAAREMAA, PÄRNUMAA, Viljandi, Tartu, Pärnu, VILJANDIMAA, TARTUMAA, Kuressaare, PÕLVAMAA, Põlva, VALKAMA, Võru, VÕRUMAA, Valka, LITHUANIA

Lithuania Today

LATVIA, Telšiai, Šiauliai, PANEVĖŽYS, Klaipėda, TELŠIAI, Panevėžys, KLAIPĖDA, ŠIAULIAI, Utena, UTENA, TAURAGĖ, Jurbarkas, KAUNAS, Kaunas, RUSSIA, MARIJAMPOLĖ, Marijampolė, Vilnius, ALYTUS, Alytus, VILNIUS, BELARUS

Latvia Today

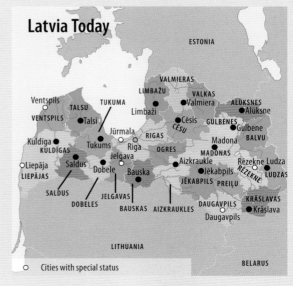

ESTONIA, VALMIERAS, LIMBAŽU, VALKAS, Ventspils, TALSU, TUKUMA, Limbaži, Valmiera, ALŪKSNES, Alūksne, VENTSPILS, Talsi, CĒSU, Cēsis, GULBENES, Jūrmala, RIGAS, Gulbene, BALVU, Kuldīga, Tukums, Riga, OGRES, Madona, KULDĪGAS, Jelgava, MADONAS, Liepāja, Saldus, Dobele, Aizkraukle, Rēzekne, Ludza, LIEPĀJAS, Bauska, JĒKABPILS, RĒZEKNE, Jēkabpils, PREIĻU, LUDZAS, SALDUS, JELGAVAS, KRĀSLAVAS, DOBELES, BAUSKAS, AIZKRAUKLES, DAUGAVPILS, Krāslava, Daugavpils, LITHUANIA, BELARUS

○ Cities with special status

Russia Until 1600

Early Russia

- Finds of the oldest hominoids
- Neanderthal finds
- Mammoth hunter finds
- Finds of the first farmers
- Finds of Bronze Age settlements
- Finds of Iron Age settlements

9th Century: Kievan Rus and the Khazars

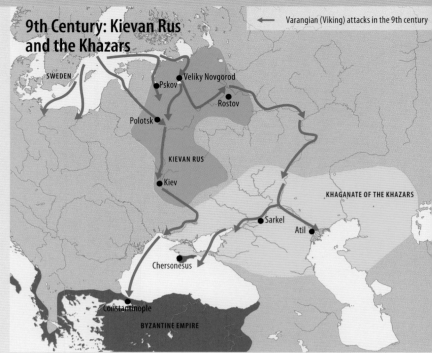

← Varangian (Viking) attacks in the 9th century

12th Century: Russian Principalities

☐ Russian principalities

Until the first century of the Common Era, the steppes of southern Russia were inhabited by nomadic peoples such as the Scythians and the Sarmatians. Western Russia, along with White Russia (now Belarus) and the northern Ukraine, is considered the original home of the Slavic peoples. The word "Rus" presumably derives from the Finnish *Ruotsi* ("Swedes"), which points to Viking (Varangian) settlement.

859 The legendary Varangian leader Rurik founds Veliky Novgorod.

end of the 9th century The Varangian dominions unite around Novgorod and Prince Oleg's Kiev; Kievan Rus comes into existence.

965–969 The Khazar empire (khaganate) is conquered, as are portions of the Bulgarian empire.

988 The Byzantines Christianize the Kievan Rus.

1019–1054 Yaroslav the Wise presides over a cultural golden age in Kievan Rus.

11th–12th centuries Kievan Rus splits into smaller states.

1113–1125 The last unification and reinvigoration of centralized power

after 1125 Following the death of Vladimir II Monomachus, Kievan Rus disintegrates. Many small successor states (principalities) arise on Russian soil.

1147 Moscow is founded.

12th–15th centuries The Republic of Novgorod, situated on Lake Ilmen, becomes a prosperous city-state that maintains strong trade relations with the Hanseatic League.

1223 The Mongols defeat Polovstian and Ruthenian forces at the Battle of the Kalka River.

1237–1242 The great Mongol invasion of Rus results in the destruction of forty-nine of seventy-two major cities. The Turkic-Mongol Empire, commonly known as the Golden Horde, stretches from western Siberia to eastern Europe until 1480.

1240–1242 Forces of the Republic of Novgorod defeat the Swedish army on the Neva River and the Teutonic Knights on Lake Peipus (Battle of the Ice).

1241 The Mongols take control of Kiev.

1380 Moscow defeats the Mongols at the Battle of Kulikovo.

14th century The principality of Moscow gains power and influence under Ivan I Kalita, becoming a grand duchy. The Muscovite grand dukes now refer to themselves as "rulers of all Rus."

14th–18th centuries Belarus and Ukraine are territories of the grand duchy of Lithuania (and the Polish-Lithuanian Commonwealth from 1569).

1424–1783 The southern Ukraine falls to the Crimean Khanate, a vassal state of the Ottoman Empire.

1462–1505 Under Ivan III the Great, the land area controlled by the grand duchy of Moscow quadruples.

1480 The Great Stand on the Ugra: After weeks of facing off on the banks of the Ugra River, the Russian and Mongol armies withdraw without fighting. Mongol rule of Russia is over.

1547 Ivan IV the Terrible is crowned grand prince. Introducing reforms designed to consolidate his own power, he exercises his rule with severity, even in his dealings with the church.

1552–1556 Ivan the Terrible conquers the Golden Horde's successor states. The khanates of Kazan and Astrakhan become Russian, and the road to colonization of Siberia is opened.

1558–1583 War with the Polish-Lithuanian Commonwealth and Sweden

1572–1582 The Cossack leader Yermak conquers Siberia.

1598–1612 The extinction of the Rurik dynasty leads to chaos and the era of the False Dmytris, impostors who pretend to be sons of Ivan the Terrible. Polish troops occupy Moscow.

Kievan Rus This major power of the Middle Ages was based in the city of Kiev. Between 882 and 1125 it occupied territories that are now part of present-day Russia, Ukraine and Belarus.

Ivan the Terrible (1530–1584) Grand duke of Moscow from 1533, he was the tsar of Russia from 1547 to 1584. His Russian epithet "Grozny" is perhaps better translated as "the Severe" than "the Terrible." He consolidated and centralized the state's power through bureaucratic, military and juristic reforms, thereby supporting the lesser nobility. He was considered pious, intelligent and well-educated, but also cruel and unpredictable. Thousands of people were executed on his orders, and in 1581 he even killed his own son in a quarrel.

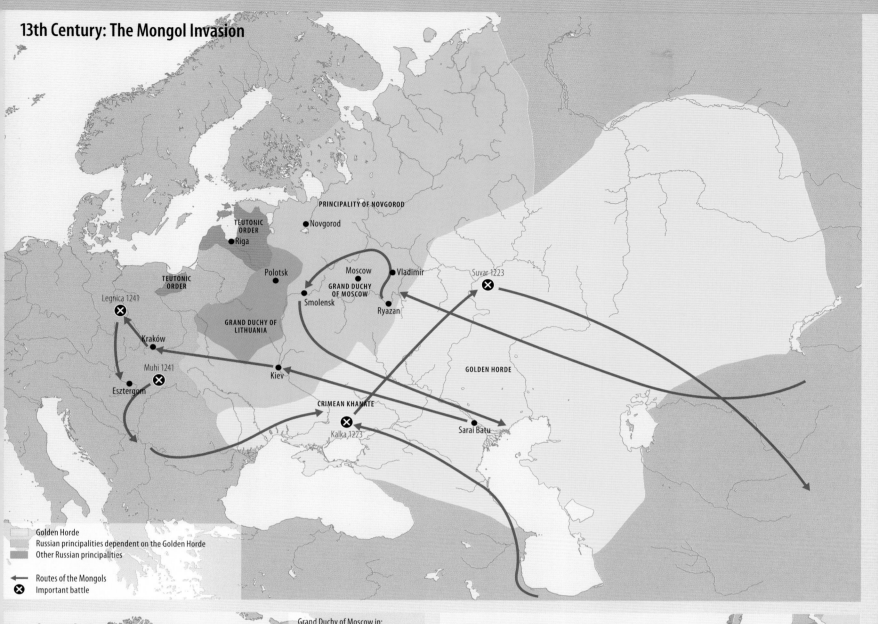

13th Century: The Mongol Invasion

PRINCIPALITY OF NOVGOROD

Novgorod

TEUTONIC ORDER
Riga

TEUTONIC ORDER

Polotsk

Moscow • Vladimir
GRAND DUCHY OF MOSCOW
Smolensk
Ryazan

Suvar 1223 ⊗

Legnica 1241 ⊗

Kraków

GRAND DUCHY OF LITHUANIA

GOLDEN HORDE

Muhi 1241 ⊗

Esztergom

Kiev

CRIMEAN KHANATE

Kalka 1223 ⊗

Sarai Batu •

Golden Horde
Russian principalities dependent on the Golden Horde
Other Russian principalities

→ Routes of the Mongols
⊗ Important battle

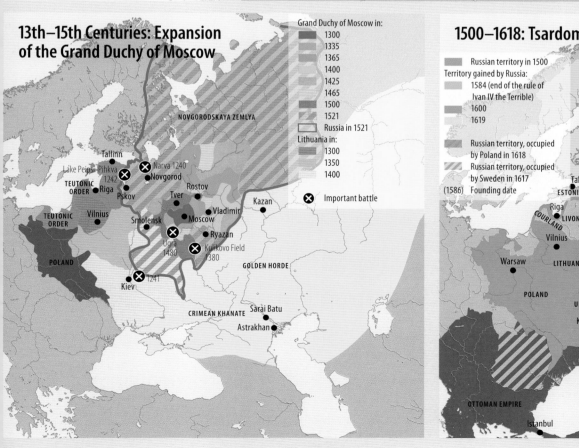

13th–15th Centuries: Expansion of the Grand Duchy of Moscow

Grand Duchy of Moscow in:
1300
1335
1365
1400
1425
1465
1500
1521
Russia in 1521
Lithuania in:
1300
1350
1400
⊗ Important battle

NOVGORODSKAYA ZEMLYA

Tallinn
Lake Peipsi-Pihkva 1242
Narva 1240
Novgorod
TEUTONIC ORDER
Riga
Pskov
Tver
Rostov
Vilnius
Smolensk
Moscow
Vladimir
Kazan
Ugra 1480
Kulikovo Field 1380
Ryazan

POLAND

Kiev 1241

GOLDEN HORDE

CRIMEAN KHANATE

Sarai Batu

Astrakhan

1500–1618: Tsardom

Russian territory in 1500
Territory gained by Russia:
1584 (end of the rule of Ivan IV the Terrible)
1600
1619
Russian territory, occupied by Poland in 1618
Russian territory, occupied by Sweden in 1617
(1586) Founding date

SWEDEN

Pustozyorsk (1499)
Obdorsk (1595)

FINLAND

Ust-Tsylma (1555)
Arkhangelsk (1584)

Obskiy Gorodok (1585)

Tallinn
Narva
ESTONIA
Riga
Pskov
Novgorod
COURLAND
LIVONIA
Vilnius

RUSSIA

Soly-Kamskaya
Kankor (1560)
Verkhoturye (1598)
STROGANOV REGION
Tyumen (1586)

Nizhny Novgorod
Kazan
Ufa (1612)
KAZAN KHANATE

Warsaw
LITHUANIA
Smolensk
Moscow
Ryazan
Tula

SIBERIA (1572–1582)

POLAND
UKRAINE
Voronezh (1586)
Kiev
Belgorod (1596)

Samara (1586)
Saratow (1590)
Jayik Gorodok (Uralsk, 1612)

LITTLE KAZAKH HORDE

ZAPORIZHZHYA
Tsaritsyn (Volgograd, 1589)

Azov
CRIMEAN KHANATE
ASTRAKHAN KHANATE
Astrakhan

OTTOMAN EMPIRE
Sunzhensky (1567)

Istanbul
PERSIA

Russia Until the Death of Peter the Great (1725)

1619–1800: Russia Becomes a Great Power

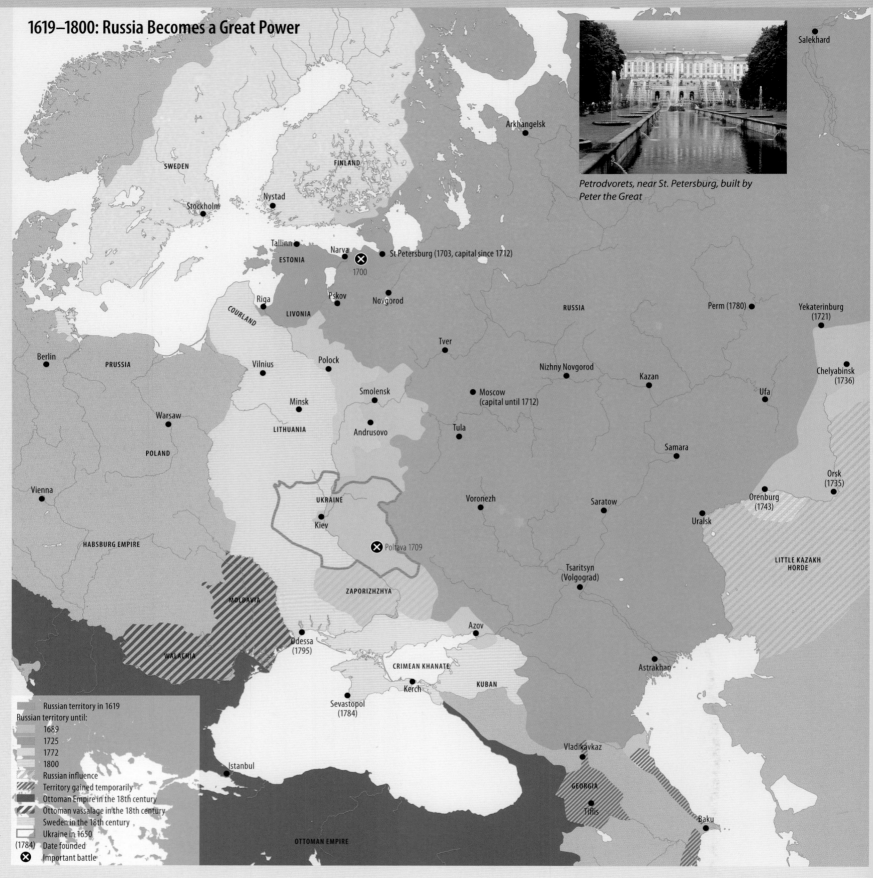

Petrodvorets, near St. Petersburg, built by Peter the Great

Salekhard

Arkhangelsk

SWEDEN

FINLAND

Stockholm

Nystad

Tallinn

Narva

St Petersburg (1703, capital since 1712)

1700

ESTONIA

Riga

Pskov

Novgorod

RUSSIA

Perm (1780)

Yekaterinburg (1721)

COURLAND

LIVONIA

Tver

Berlin

PRUSSIA

Vilnius

Polock

Nizhny Novgorod

Kazan

Chelyabinsk (1736)

Smolensk

Moscow (capital until 1712)

Ufa

Minsk

Warsaw

LITHUANIA

Andrusovo

Tula

Samara

POLAND

Vienna

HABSBURG EMPIRE

UKRAINE

Kiev

Voronezh

Saratow

Orsk (1735)

Orenburg (1743)

Uralsk

LITTLE KAZAKH HORDE

Poltava 1709

ZAPORIZHZHYA

Tsaritsyn (Volgograd)

MOLDAVIA

Azov

Odessa (1795)

CRIMEAN KHANATE

Astrakhan

WALACHIA

Kerch

KUBAN

Sevastopol (1784)

Vladikavkaz

Istanbul

GEORGIA

Tiflis

Baku

OTTOMAN EMPIRE

Legend

Russian territory in 1619
Russian territory until:
1689
1725
1772
1800
Russian influence
Territory gained temporarily
Ottoman Empire in the 18th century
Ottoman vassalage in the 18th century
Sweden in the 18th century
Ukraine in 1650
(1784) Date founded
❌ Important battle

1613 Mikhail Fyodorovich Romanov is elected tsar, thus founding the Romanov dynasty, which will rule Russia until 1917.

1648–1654 Bogdan Khmelnytsky leads a Cossack revolt in the steppes of the southern Ukraine. Pogroms against the Jewish population follow.

1654–1667 In the Russo-Polish War, all territories east of the Dnieper River fall under Russian control.

1670–1671 A revolt led by Stenka Razin leads to intervention by the tsar's armies.

1682/1689–1725 Peter I the Great begins a program of modernization modeled on Western examples, making Russia a great European power.

1703 The newly planned Russian capital of St. Petersburg is founded.

1709 The Russian army wins a decisive victory over the Swedes at the Battle of Poltava.

1721 The Treaty of Nystad leads to Russian territorial expansion in the Baltic and the creation of the Russian Empire (the tsar becomes emperor).

1725 Death of Peter the Great

Stenka Razin (1630–1671) An ataman of the Cossacks (semi-autonomous groups of horsemen), Razin conquered large portions of southern Russia including Astrakhan and Samara. Farmers and religious minorities joined his revolt, which was eventually put down by the tsar's armies. Razin was sentenced to death, and drawn and quartered in Red Square.

Russian Rulers and Heads of State

Due to the principle of agnatic seniority (after a ruler's death, the crown passes to the oldest living member of the dynasty), there were many controversies over succession and territorial divisions in the Middle Ages, as well as simultaneously ruling governments with multiple heads of state.

Grand Princes of the Kievan Rus of the Rurik Dynasty

862–879	Rurik
879–912	Oleg of Kiev
912–945	Igor I
945–972	Svyatoslav I
972–980	Iaropolk I
980–1015	Vladimir I the Great
1015–1019	Svyatopolk I, dethroned
1019–1054	Yaroslav I the Wise
1054–1068	Izyaslav I, dethroned
1068–1069	Vseslav Briatshislav o Polotsk, dethroned
1069–1073	Izyaslav I (renewed)
1073–1076	Svyatoslav II
1076	Vsevolod I Jaroslavitch
1076–1078	Izyaslav I (renewed)
1078–1093	Vsevolod I (renewed)
1093–1113	Svyatopolk II (son of Izyaslav I)
1113–1125	Vladimir II Monomachus
1125–1132	Mstislav I the Great
1132–1139	Yaropolk II
1139	Vyacheslav, dethroned after 12 days
1139–1146	Vsevolod II
1146	Igor II, dethroned
1146–1149	Vyacheslav II, dethroned
1149–1150	Yury Dolgoruky
1150	Vyacheslav II (renewed)
1150–1151	Yury Dolgoruky (renewed)
1151–1154	Vyacheslav II (renewed)
1154–1155	Rostislav, dethroned
1154–1157	Yury Dolgoruky (renewed)
1157–1158	Vyacheslav III Davidovich, dethroned
1158–1167	Rostislav (renewed)
1162	Vyacheslav III Davidovich (renewed)
1167–1169	Mstislav II

Grand Princes of Vladimir-Susdal of the Rurik Dynasty

1157/1168–1174	Andrew Bogolyubsky
1174	Yaropolk and Mstislav
1174–1176	Michael I
1176–1212	Vsevolod III
1212–1216	Yury II, dethroned
1212–1218	Konstantin
1218–1238	Yury II (renewed)
1238–1246	Yaroslav II Fyodor (son of Vsevolod III)
1246–1248	Svyatoslav III (son of Vsevolod III), dethroned
1248–?	Michael (son of Yaroslav II)
1248–1249	Svyatoslav III (renewed), dethroned
1249–1252	Andrew I (son of Yaroslav II), dethroned
1252–1263	St. Alexander I Nevsky (son of Yaroslav II)
1264–1272	Yaroslav III
1272–1277	Vassilii
1277–1281	Dmitry I, banished
1281–1283	Andrew II, abdicated
1283–1293	Dmitry I (renewed)
1293–1304	Andrew II (renewed)
1304–1318	St. Michael of Tver
1318–1322	Yury III Danilovich of Moscow
1322–1325	Dmitry II
1326–1327	Alexander
after 1328	united with Moscow

Dukes of Moscow of the Rurik Dynasty

1277–1303	Daniel (son of Alexander I Nevsky)
1303–1325	Yury III, 1318–1322 also grand prince of Vladimir-Suzdal
1325–	Ivan I Kalita ("Moneybag"), after 1328 grand duke

Grand Dukes of Moscow of the Rurik Dynasty

1328–1340	Ivan I Kalita ("Moneybag")
1340–1353	Semyon the Proud
1353–1359	Ivan II the Red
1359–1389	Dmitry Donskoy
1389–1425	Vasily I
1425–1462	Vasily II the Blind
1462–1505	Ivan III the Great
1505–1533	Vasily III
1533–	Ivan IV the Terrible, after 1547 tsar of all of Russia

Tsars of Russia from the Rurik Dynasty

1547–1584	Ivan IV the Terrible
1584–1598	Fyodor I, the last ruler of the Rurik dynasty

Tsars of Russia from various dynasties

1598–1605	Boris Godunov
1605	Fyodor II
1605–1606	Dmitry II, the first False Dmitry
1606–1610	Vassily IV Shuysky, dethroned
1608–1610	The second False Dmitry
1610–1613	Polish ruler: Wladyslaw IV Vasa (son of the Polish king, Sigismund III Vasa), Polish king from 1632–1648

Tsars of Russia from the House of Romanov

1613–1645	Michael I
1645–1676	Alexis I
1676–1682	Fyodor III
1682–1696	Ivan V (son of Alexis I by his first marriage; feeble-minded), co-ruler with Peter I, 1682–1689 Regency of Sophia Alexeyevna (daughter of Alexis I by his first marriage)
1682–1721	Peter I the Great (son of Alexis I by his second marriage), until 1696 co-ruler with Ivan V
1721–	Imperator: Peter I is declared emperor

Tsars and Emperors of Russia from the House of Romanov

1721–1725	Peter I the Great
1725–1727	Catherine I (wife of Peter I)
1727–1730	Peter II
1730–1740	Anna
1740–1741	Ivan VI
1741–1762	Elizabeth
1762	Peter III
1762–1796	Catherine II the Great (wife of Peter III)
1796–1801	Paul
1801–1825	Alexander I
1825–1855	Nicholas I
1855–1881	Alexander II
1881–1894	Alexander III
1894–1917	Nicholas II

General Secretaries of the Russian Communist Party (after 1925 the All-Union Communist Party, after 1952 the Communist Party of the Soviet Union)

1917–1922/24	Vladimir Ilich Lenin (party head from 1912)
1922/24–1953	Joseph Vissarionovich Stalin (Dzhugashvili)
1953	Georgy Maksimilianovich Malenkov
1953–1964	Nikita Sergeyevich Khrushchev
1964–1982	Leonid Ilich Brezhnev
1982–1984	Yury Vladimirovich Andropov
1984–1985	Konstantin Ustinovich Chernenko
1985–1991	Mikhail Sergeyevich Gorbachev

Presidents of the Russian Federation

1991–1999	Boris Nikolayevich Yeltsin
2000–2008	Vladimir Vladimirovich Putin
2008–	Dmitry Anatolyevich Medvedev

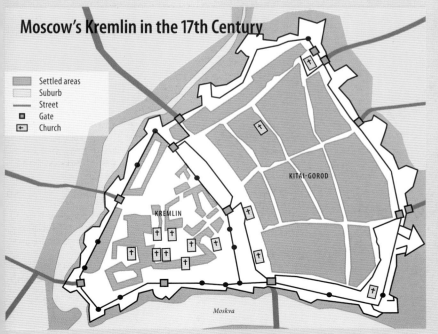

Moscow's Kremlin in the 17th Century

Legend:
- Settled areas
- Suburb
- Street
- Gate
- Church

KITAI-GOROD

KREMLIN

Moskva

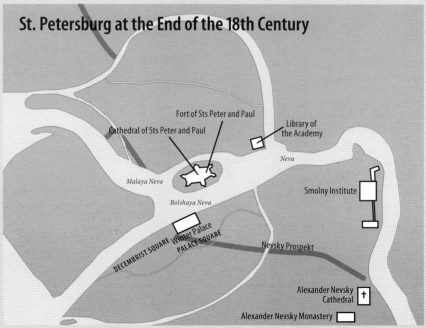

St. Petersburg at the End of the 18th Century

Fort of Sts Peter and Paul
Cathedral of Sts Peter and Paul
Library of the Academy
Neva
Malaya Neva
Bolshaya Neva
Smolny Institute
DECEMBRIST SQUARE
Winter Palace
PALACE SQUARE
Nevsky Prospekt
Alexander Nevsky Cathedral
Alexander Nevsky Monastery

Russia Until the End of the 19th Century

Napoleon's Russian Campaigns

Legend:
- Russian territory in 1800
- Territory dependent on Russia in 1800
- Territory conquered by Russia in 1807 and 1809
- Finland, conquered by Russia in 1809
- Bessarabia, conquered by Russia in 1812
- Ottoman Empire in 1812
- Ottoman vassal territory in the 18th century
- → Napoleon's 1807 campaign
- ⇢ Napoleon's 1812 campaign
- ⊗ Important battle
- Area of opposition to Napoleon

1725–1741 Following the death of Peter the Great, centralized power is weakened, and foreign dignitaries (especially Germans) gain influence in the Russian state. Peter the Great's reforms are over.

1741–1762 Under Tsarina Elizabeth Petrovna, Peter's reforms are taken up again, and Russia experiences an economic and cultural boom.

1755 The University of Moscow is founded.

1756–1763 In the Seven Years' War, Russia sides with Austria and France against Prussia.

May 5, 1762 The "Miracle of the House of Brandenburg": Tsar Peter III comes to the throne and ceases hostilities, preventing the defeat of Russia's opponent, Prussia.

July 1762 Peter III is deposed and murdered.

Sept. 12, 1762 Catherine II the Great, who rules Russia until 1796, is crowned.

after 1763 German immigrants settle along the Volga.

1768–1774 and 1787–1792 Russo-Turkish Wars: The annihilation of the Turkish fleet at Chesma in 1770 leads to the Russian conquest of the Crimea (southern Ukraine).

1772–1795 Russia gains much territory through the Partitions of Poland.

1773–1775 The army bloodily puts down Pugachev's Rebellion (the Cossack Rebellion).

1783 Catherine the Great conquers the Khanate of Crimea, ending Cossack rule.

1799–1815 Russia participates in wars of coalition and liberation against Napoleon's France.

1801 Tsar Paul I is murdered. Alexander I accedes to the throne, beginning a period of friendly relations with France that will last until 1804.

September 1809 In the Treaty of Hamina, Sweden cedes control of Finland to Russia (until 1917).

May 1812 In the Treaty of Bucharest, the Ottoman Empire cedes control of Bessarabia to Russia.

June–December 1812 Napoleon's disastrous Russian campaign.

Sept. 7, 1812 France wins a Pyrrhic victory at the Battle of Borodino. Moscow falls to the French.

1813 The forces of the Sixth Coalition (Austria, Prussia, Russia) defeat Napoleon at the Battle of Leipzig (Battle of the Nations). The French are driven from Russia.

March 31, 1814 The coalition armies, led by Tsar Alexander I, enter Paris.

September 1814–June 1815 The realignment of Europe is engineered at the Congress of Vienna with heavy Russian influence. Most of Poland is ceded to Russia.

Sept. 26, 1815 Tsar Alexander forms the conservative "Holy Alliance" with Austria and Prussia against revolutionary and liberal tendencies. France joins in 1818.

December 1825 The Decembrists launch their revolt in St. Petersburg.

1825–1855 Rule of conservative-autocratic Tsar Nicholas I, "the gendarme of Europe"

1830–1831 The November Uprising in Poland is defeated.

1852–1888 Russian expansion in Asia marks the era of Russian imperialism.

1853–1856 In the Crimean War, Russia is defeated by the allied armies of Great Britain, France and the Ottoman Empire (after 1855 also Piedmont-Sardinia), and must cede southern Bessarabia to Moldavia.

1855–1881 Tsar Alexander II "the Liberator" attempts to implement necessary reforms, most of which are unsuccessful. Expansionist policies are accelerated.

1858/1860 As required by the Treaty of Aigun and the Peking Treaty of 1860, large sections of Manchuria are ceded to Russia.

Russia Versus Napoleon

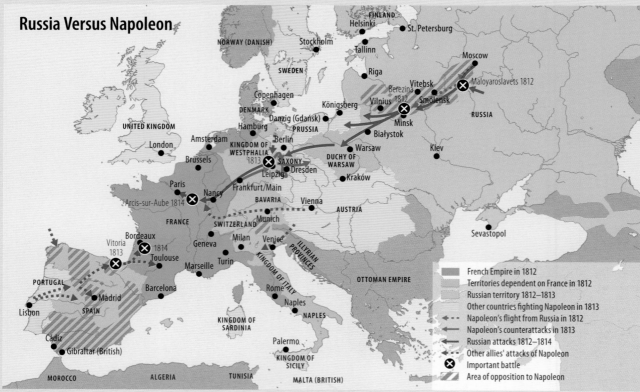

Legend:
- French Empire in 1812
- Territories dependent on France in 1812
- Russian territory 1812–1813
- Other countries fighting Napoleon in 1813
- ⇢ Napoleon's flight from Russia in 1812
- → Napoleon's counterattacks in 1813
- → Russian attacks 1812–1814
- ⇢ Other allies' attacks of Napoleon
- ⊗ Important battle
- Area of opposition to Napoleon

16th–19th Centuries: Russia's Influence in Asia

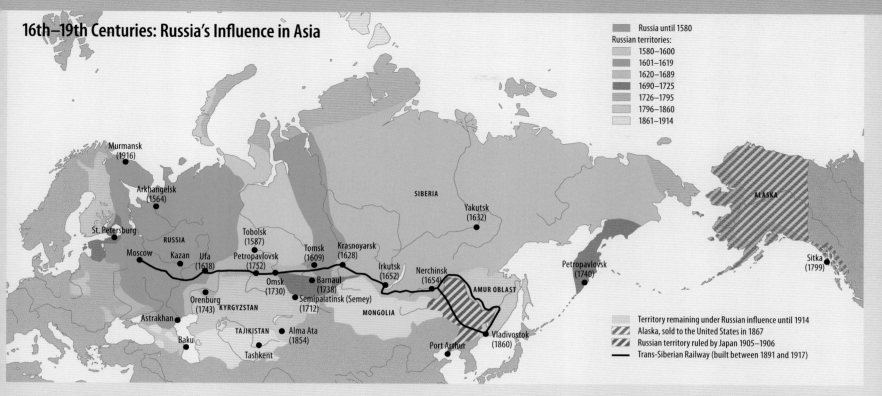

Russia until 1580

Russian territories:
1580–1600
1601–1619
1620–1689
1690–1725
1726–1795
1796–1860
1861–1914

Territory remaining under Russian influence until 1914
Alaska, sold to the United States in 1867
Russian territory ruled by Japan 1905–1906
Trans-Siberian Railway (built between 1891 and 1917)

Murmansk (1916)
Arkhangelsk (1564)
St. Petersburg
RUSSIA
Moscow
Kazan
Ufa (1618)
Petropavlovsk (1752)
Orenburg (1743)
KYRGYZSTAN
Astrakhan
Baku
TAJIKISTAN
Alma Ata (1854)
Tashkent
Omsk (1730)
Tobolsk (1587)
Semipalatinsk (Semey) (1712)
Barnaul (1738)
Tomsk (1609)
Krasnoyarsk (1628)
MONGOLIA
Irkutsk (1652)
Nerchinsk (1654)
SIBERIA
Yakutsk (1632)
Port Arthur
Vladivostok (1860)
AMUR OBLAST
Petropavlovsk (1740)
ALASKA
Sitka (1799)

1860 Vladivostok, the Russian Empire's primary base of operations in the Far East, is founded.

1861 Tsar Alexander II abolishes serfdom.

1867 Alaska is sold to the United States.

1868/1873 The Muslim emirates of Bukhara and Khiva (present-day Uzbekistan) acknowledge Russian sovereignty.

1877–1878 The Ottoman Empire's defeat in the Russo-Turkish War leads to the founding of Bulgaria.

March 11, 1881 Anarchists murder the liberal Alexander II. He is succeeded by the reactionary, anti-reform Alexander III, who rules until 1894.

1881–1918 The revolutionary-anarchistic Narodniks ("friends of the people") make spectacular assassination attempts on members of the tsar's family, government leaders, ministers, high-ranking bureaucrats and finally Lenin in 1918.

1884 The Turkmen are conquered.

1891–1916 The Trans-Siberian Railway is built, reaching from Vladivostok on the Sea of Japan to Chelyabinsk in the Ural Mountains.

1894–1917 The reign of Nicholas II, the last Russian tsar, is marked by indecisive governance. In 1906 he falls under the influence of the dubious "Mad Monk" Grigory Rasputin, who is murdered in 1916.

1898 The Russian Social Democratic Workers' Party (renamed the Communist Party in 1918) is founded in Minsk.

Catherine II the Great (1729–1796) was the tsarina of Russia for over thirty years, from 1762 until 1796. Born in Stettin (Szczecin), she married the Russian heir apparent Peter Fyodorovich when she was fifteen years old. Arriving in Russia in 1744, she converted to the Russian Orthodox faith and assumed the name Yekaterina. With the help of Russian officers, she had her husband Peter III deposed and murdered half a year after his accession to the throne in 1762. Her reign was characterized by centralized administrative reforms, religious tolerance and a marked policy of intervention. She maintained regular correspondence with Voltaire and Montesquieu, and was heavily influenced by the Enlightenment. Among her many lovers was Prince Grigory Potemkin (1739–1791).

Grigory Aleksandrovich Potemkin (1739–1791) was Catherine the Great's lover for two years and remained her friend—and the most powerful man in Russia—for seventeen. He helped bring Catherine to power as empress and distinguished himself in the Turkish war of 1768–1774. Catherine appointed him governor general of New Russia (southern Ukraine), and he was instrumental in planning and carrying out the conquest of Crimea. His extravagant habits made him the subject of many anecdotes.

Decembrists (Dekabristy) In December (*dekabr* in Russian) 1825, a group of "noble revolutionaries," most of whom had a military background or came from the upper classes, attempted to take advantage of the uncertain situation following the death of the childless Alexander I. Their revolt was quickly defeated, and the new tsar, Nicholas I, had the leaders executed, imprisoned or exiled.

Russia in the 19th Century

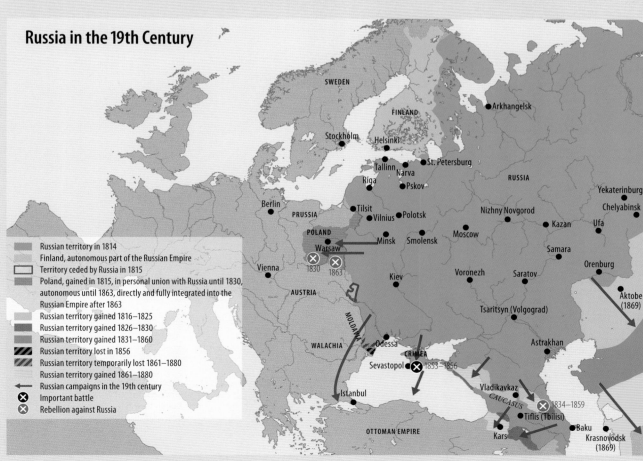

Russian territory in 1814
Finland, autonomous part of the Russian Empire
Territory ceded by Russia in 1815
Poland, gained in 1815, in personal union with Russia until 1830, autonomous until 1863, directly and fully integrated into the Russian Empire after 1863
Russian territory gained 1816–1825
Russian territory gained 1826–1830
Russian territory gained 1831–1860
Russian territory lost in 1856
Russian territory temporarily lost 1861–1880
Russian territory gained 1861–1880
Russian campaigns in the 19th century
Important battle
Rebellion against Russia

SWEDEN
FINLAND
Arkhangelsk
Stockholm
Helsinki
St. Petersburg
Tallinn
Narva
Riga
Pskov
Berlin
PRUSSIA
Tilsit
Vilnius
Polotsk
POLAND
Warsaw
Minsk
Smolensk
Moscow
Nizhny Novgorod
Kazan
Ufa
Yekaterinburg
Chelyabinsk
Vienna
1830
1863
Kiev
Voronezh
Saratov
Samara
Orenburg
AUSTRIA
MOLDAVIA
WALACHIA
Odessa
CRIMEA
Sevastopol
1853–1856
Istanbul
OTTOMAN EMPIRE
Tsaritsyn (Volgograd)
Astrakhan
Aktobe (1869)
Vladikavkaz
CAUCASUS
1834–1859
Tiflis (Tbilisi)
Kars
Baku
Krasnovodsk (1869)

219

Russia: From the Revolution to the Soviet Union

Paradoxically, in the wake of the Revolution of 1917, and economically and politically still rudimentary, Russia became the leading nation of the socialist society of the future. In the 1930s the state became a totalitarian dictatorship with a semi-religious cult of personality centered on Joseph Stalin, the "father of all workers," in which not only real and alleged political opponents, but also rivals within the party, were suppressed and liquidated. On the eve of World War II, Russia entered a non-aggression pact with Hitler, from which Stalin hoped to profit through westward expansion of the USSR (Union of Soviet Socialist Republics). Two years later, Nazi Germany invaded its erstwhile ally.

1900 Russia occupies the remainder of Manchuria.

1903 The Bolshevik faction under Vladimir Ilich Lenin takes control of the Social Democratic Workers' Party.

1905–1907: Revolution

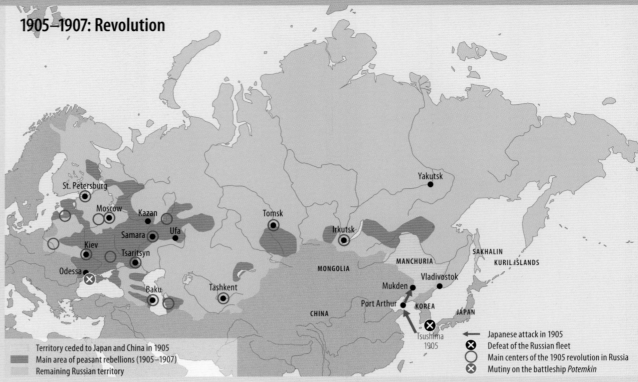

Territory ceded to Japan and China in 1905
Main area of peasant rebellions (1905–1907)
Remaining Russian territory

→ Japanese attack in 1905
⊗ Defeat of the Russian fleet
○ Main centers of the 1905 revolution in Russia
⊗ Mutiny on the battleship *Potemkin*

World War I

Russia in 1914
Russian territory occupied by the Central Powers in 1918
⊗ Important battle
Front lines
—— Autumn of 1914
---- End of 1915
—— End of 1916
—— End of 1917
—— Summer of 1918

1904–1905 Following its defeat in the Russo-Japanese War, Russia cedes Liaoyang, Port Arthur and the southern part of Sakhalin to Japan. Manchuria reverts to Chinese sovereignty.

January 1905 Bloody Sunday in St. Petersburg: The Soviet army fires on a peaceful workers' demonstration, killing hundreds. This brutal action inspires the revolutionary strike and protest of the 1905 Russian revolution.

June 1905 The uprising of sailors on the battleship *Potemkin*, anchored in the harbor of Odessa, is violently put down.

1905–1917 Tsar Nicholas attempts to transform Russia's government into a constitutional monarchy. A pseudo-parliamentary system of governance is introduced with the *Duma* (People's Assembly), a body whose every action must be approved by the tsar.

July 1914 The Austro-Hungarian Empire declares war on Serbia, and Russia begins general mobilization in support of its Balkan ally.

Aug. 1, 1914 Germany declares war on Russia. Within weeks, German forces halt an attempted Russian invasion at Tannenberg and the Masurian Lakes.

December 1914 Russian armies advance into Hungary.

August 1915 German armies oust the Russians from Warsaw and Brest-Litovsk.

1917 The Bolshevik Revolution

March 1917 Military units support striking workers in St. Petersburg, forcing Tsar Nicholas II to abdicate (called the February Revolution after the Julian calendar). Aleksander Kerensky is at the head of the bourgeois revolution.

April 1917 Aided by Germany, Bolshevik leader Lenin returns to Russia from Swiss exile.

November 1917 Lenin's Bolsheviks overthrow Kerensky's government (October Revolution).

March 3, 1918 The Treaty of Brest-Litovsk: The Bolsheviks end Russia's involvement in World War I.

March 25, 1918 The Belarusian People's Republic declares independence under German protection.

November 1918–July 1919 The Polish-Ukrainian War: East Galicia is ceded to Poland.

1918–1922 The Russian Civil War ends with the victory of the Bolshevik Red Army over the combined forces of conservatives, monarchists and non-socialists (called the White Army).

August 1918–July 1920 Poland occupies Belarus.

1918–1921 Lenin's policy of War Communism, which nationalizes all production and abolishes the use of money, brings the Russian economy to the brink of collapse.

1919 Lenin founds the Comintern (or Third International), an association of national communist parties. Nominally designed to promote worldwide revolution, its main function is to maintain Soviet control over the international communist movement. In September, Czechoslovakia incorporates Carpathian Ukraine.

1920 The Polish-Soviet War ends, and the Peace of Riga is signed in 1921. Poland and the Soviet Union divide Belarus and the Ukraine between them.

1921–1928 With the Russian economy in ruins, the Bolsheviks institute the New Economic Policy, reintroducing money and returning to some decentralized trade and private ownership.

1922 The Belarusian and Ukrainian Soviet Socialist Republics are founding members of the Soviet Union.

April 1922 The Soviet Union and Germany sign the Treaty of Rapallo. The Russian Soviet Federative Socialist Republic joins the Ukrainian and Belarusian Soviet Socialist Republics to form the Union of Soviet Socialist Republics. Stalin becomes General Secretary of the Communist Party.

1924 The major European nations recognize the Soviet Union.

1924–1928 A power struggle follows Lenin's death. Step by step, Stalin disempowers all his rivals in the party, especially the left wing and its leader, Leon Trotsky.

1917: The October Revolution

Vladimir Ilich Ulyanov Lenin

February Revolution of 1917
October Revolution (November 7, 1917)
Main areas of Bolshevik power at the end of 1917:
Russian territory occupied by the Central Powers
Bolshevik takeover by mid-November 1917
Bolshevik takeover by March 1918
Territory controlled by the White Army in March 1918
Central Powers offensives in spring 1918

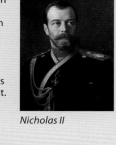

Nicholas II

Nicholas II (1868–1918) The last Russian tsar acceded to the throne in 1894. From the beginning, he reacted helplessly to the growing dissatisfaction surrounding Russia's lack of development. After the February Revolution of 1917, he was forced to abdicate. One year later, the Bolsheviks killed Nicholas and his entire family in Yekaterinburg. The Russian Orthodox Church canonized him as a martyr in 2000.

Vladimir Ilich Lenin (1870–1924) was the leader of the Russian Bolsheviks. Following the October Revolution of 1917, he became chairman of the Council of People's Commissars, the first Soviet government. Beginning in 1922, a series of strokes made it increasingly difficult for him to carry out his duties, and he retreated from public life. Millions visit his mummified remains every year in the Lenin Mausoleum on Moscow's Red Square.

Leon Trotsky (1879–1940) One of Lenin's closest colleagues, Trotsky was a brilliant writer and orator of Jewish heritage. He founded the Red Army and was at its helm during the October Revolution. After Lenin's death, Trotsky was one of Stalin's main rivals and a leftist proponent of the theory of "permanent revolution." He lost the struggle for power in 1927, and was relieved of all duties and forced into exile. In 1940 Trotsky was murdered in Mexico by an agent of Stalin's secret police.

Bolsheviks Originally Lenin's faction of the Social Democratic Workers' Party of Russia, the Bolsheviks (meaning "members of the majority" in Russian) began in 1903 to advocate for an imminent overthrow of the government. They finally split from the Social Democrats (the Mensheviks, or "members of the minority") in 1912. The Bolsheviks believed they could bring about a socialist revolution in Russia by organizing an alliance of workers and farmers, without having to wait for the preliminary capitalist revolution postulated by Marx.

Treaty of Brest-Litovsk This treaty, signed on March 3, 1918, ended hostilities between Russia, Germany and Austria-Hungary. Although the terms involved heavy loss of territory for Russia, the Bolsheviks wanted to withdraw from World War I to solidify their uncertain power, and to instigate land reforms.

1918–1922: The Russian Civil War

Front lines:
Summer 1918
Summer 1919
End of 1919
Trans-Siberian Railway controlled by the Czechoslovak Legion 1918–1919
Attacks by the White Army and intervening foreign powers 1918–1922
Murder of the tsar's family on July 16, 1918

Territory under continuous Boshevik control until:
Summer 1918
Summer 1919
Spring 1920
Summer 1921
Territory occupied by Japan, Bolshevik after 1922
Territory occupied by Japan, Bolshevik after 1925

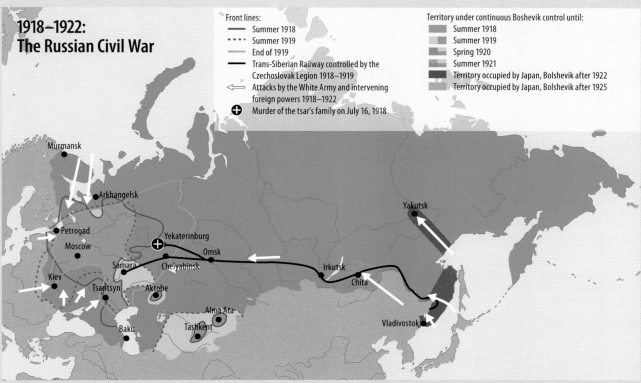

The Soviet Union from 1928 Through World War II

1936: The Great Purge

Legend:
- Area of labor camps (Gulags)
- Main area affected by famine 1932–1933
- Border of the Soviet Union
- (1929) Year of founding

Map labels: Murmansk, Leningrad, Moscow, Minsk, BELARUS, Kiev, UKRAINE, Samara, Yekaterinburg (Sverdlovsk 1723), Magnitogorsk (1929), RUSSIA, Tomsk, Novosibirsk, Krasnoyarsk, Karaganda, KAZAKHSTAN, TUVA REPUBLIC (UNDER SOVIET CONTROL), Irkutsk, MONGOLIA (UNDER SOVIET CONTROL), Yakutsk, Komsomolsk (1932), Magadan (1929), Petropavlovsk, Vladivostok, GEORGIA, Baku, ARMENIA, AZERBAIJAN, TURKMENISTAN, USBEKISTAN, Tashkent, KYRGYZSTAN, TAJIKISTAN

1928 Stalin abandons Lenin's New Economic Policy and institutes the disastrous practice of five-year plans in industry and the forcible collectivization of agriculture.

1932–1933 Due to Stalin's policies of collectivization, an estimated 4 to 6 million people die of famine and epidemics in Ukraine and parts of Russia.

1934 The USSR joins the League of Nations. The murder of Leningrad party leader Sergei Kirov signals the beginning of the purges, which last until about 1940.

1936–1938 In Moscow, members of the Bolshevik "old guard" are given show trials, and Red Army Chief Marshal Tukhachevsky is liquidated along with most of the military leadership. The terror reaches its climax under People's Commissar Nikolai Yezhov, head of the NKVD (secret police).

Sept. 17, 1939 The Red Army invades eastern Poland (Western Belarus).

1939–1940 The Winter War against Finland ends with the Moscow Peace Treaty. Finland cedes Karelia to the Soviet Union.

1940 The Soviet Union annexes the Baltic States and Bessarabia.

June 1941 Germany invades the USSR.

December 1941 The Red Army halts the advance of Nazi Germany's armed forces at the gates of Moscow.

The Battle of Stalingrad, 1942

1941–1944 Germany occupies Belarus (General Commissariat of White Ruthenia) and the Ukraine (Reich Commissariat). Ukraine and Belarus witness the heaviest fighting.

1943 German forces are encircled at Stalingrad, marking the war's turning point.

February 1945 At the Yalta Conference, Stalin negotiates with the other Allied leaders to divide Europe into spheres of influence.

May 1945 Berlin falls to the Red Army, and Nazi Germany surrenders. The Czechoslovakian district Carpatho-Ukraine is ceded to the USSR as part of the Ukrainian SSR.

1939–1940: Expansion

Legend:
- Germany and dependent territory until summer 1939
- Territory occupied by Germany during autumn 1939
- Soviet Union until 1939
- Territory occupied by the Soviet Union in autumn 1939
- Polish territory ceded by the Soviet Union to Lithuania in autumn 1939
- Finland until 1939
- Finnish territory taken by the Soviet Union during the Winter War of 1939–1940
- Lithuanian, Latvian and Estonian territory annexed by the Soviet Union in 1940
- Romanian territory annexed by the Soviet Union in 1940

- → German attacks 1939
- → Soviet attacks 1939–1940
- ⊗ Important battle
- ♔ Soviet bombardment

Map labels: Petsamo (Pechengsky district), NORWAY, Murmansk, SWEDEN, Arkhangelsk, Jan. 1940, FINLAND, Jan.–Feb. 1940, KARELIA, Vyborg March 8, 1940, Mannerheim Line Dec. 1939–Feb. 1940, Turku, Helsinki, Leningrad (St. Petersburg), Stockholm, Hanko (Soviet 1940–1941), Tallinn, ESTONIA, Pskov, Moscow, Riga, LATVIA, LITHUANIA, Memel (Klaipėda), Kaunas, Vilnius, Königsberg (Kaliningrad), Minsk, SOVIET UNION, Danzig (Gdańsk), Białystok, Brest-Litovsk, Kiev, Poznan, Warsaw, GERMANY, POLAND, Lemberg (Lviv), Prague, Gliwice, Kraków, PROTECTORATE OF BOHEMIA AND MORAVIA, SLOVAKIA, Chişinău, Odessa, Vienna, Bratislava, Budapest, HUNGARY, ROMANIA, Sevastopol

Joseph Vissarionovich Stalin

Joseph Vissarionovich Stalin (1878–1953)
In contrast to Trotsky, Stalin, a native of Georgia, was a proponent of establishing "socialism in one country" taking precedence over world revolution, thereby giving Bolshevism a nationalist orientation. By 1928 he had consolidated his power and established a dictatorship based on a cult of personality and supported by terror. In 1939 he entered an alliance with Nazi Germany, only to face devastating losses at the Nazis' hands in 1941. He nevertheless knew how to use the "Great Patriotic War" not only to his personal advantage, but also to the advantage of his regime, promulgating the spread of the Soviet system throughout Eastern Europe.

Forced collectivization Starting in 1928, Stalin forced the Soviet Union's peasants to form agricultural cooperatives. Landowners were denounced as enemies of the state,

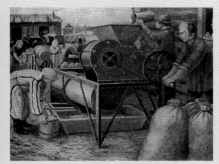

Sorting seeds in a kolkhoz, Mordvinia, 1933

their property was seized, and many of them were interned in Siberian labor camps. Ineffective cooperatives were one cause of the devastating famines (*Holodomor*) that followed within a few years.

The Great Purge During the Great Purge (1935–1939), Stalin eliminated all of his actual, potential and imagined opponents. Millions of people were tried as spies or enemies of the state and liquidated or sent to work camps called Gulags (an acronym for their Russian designation). One particularly horrible scenario was the show trial during which Bolsheviks of the old guard, having been tortured, were forced to confess to ridiculous crimes and were subsequently executed. Two-thirds of those who were members of the Communist Party's Central Committee in 1934 were dead by 1938. This period also witnessed the forced resettlement of entire peoples.

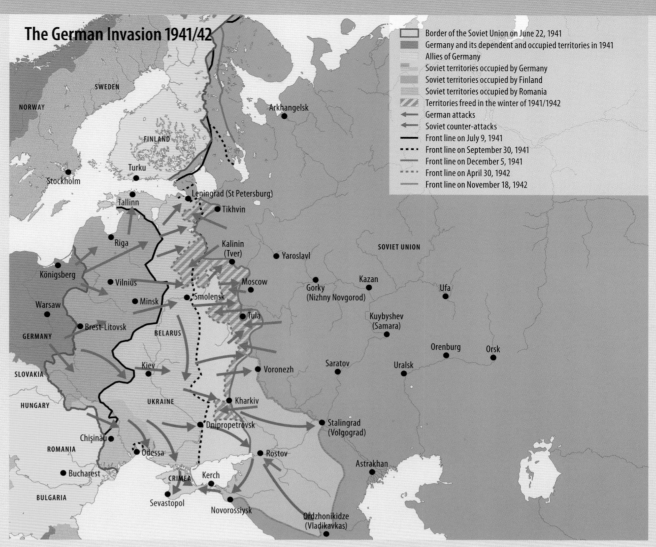

The German Invasion 1941/42

	Border of the Soviet Union on June 22, 1941
	Germany and its dependent and occupied territories in 1941
	Allies of Germany
	Soviet territories occupied by Germany
	Soviet territories occupied by Finland
	Soviet territories occupied by Romania
	Territories freed in the winter of 1941/1942
←	German attacks
←	Soviet counter-attacks
—	Front line on July 9, 1941
····	Front line on September 30, 1941
--	Front line on December 5, 1941
····	Front line on April 30, 1942
—	Front line on November 18, 1942

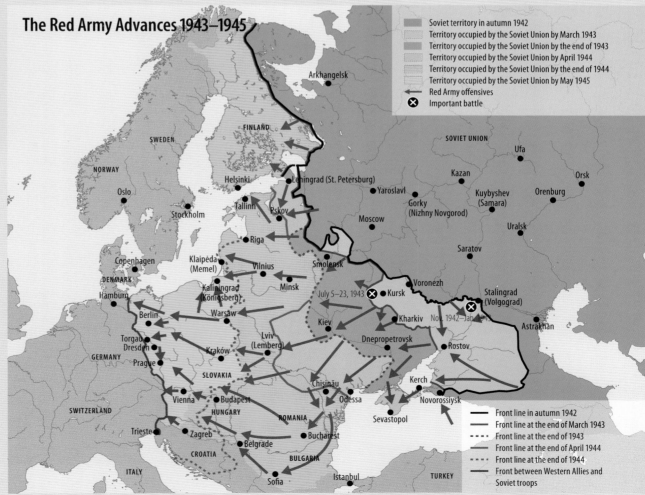

The Red Army Advances 1943–1945

	Soviet territory in autumn 1942
	Territory occupied by the Soviet Union by March 1943
	Territory occupied by the Soviet Union by the end of 1943
	Territory occupied by the Soviet Union by April 1944
	Territory occupied by the Soviet Union by the end of 1944
	Territory occupied by the Soviet Union by May 1945
←	Red Army offensives
⊗	Important battle

—	Front line in autumn 1942
—	Front line at the end of March 1943
····	Front line at the end of 1943
—	Front line at the end of April 1944
····	Front line at the end of 1944
—	Front between Western Allies and Soviet troops

The Soviet Union After World War II (1945–1991)

Soviet Domination of Eastern Europe

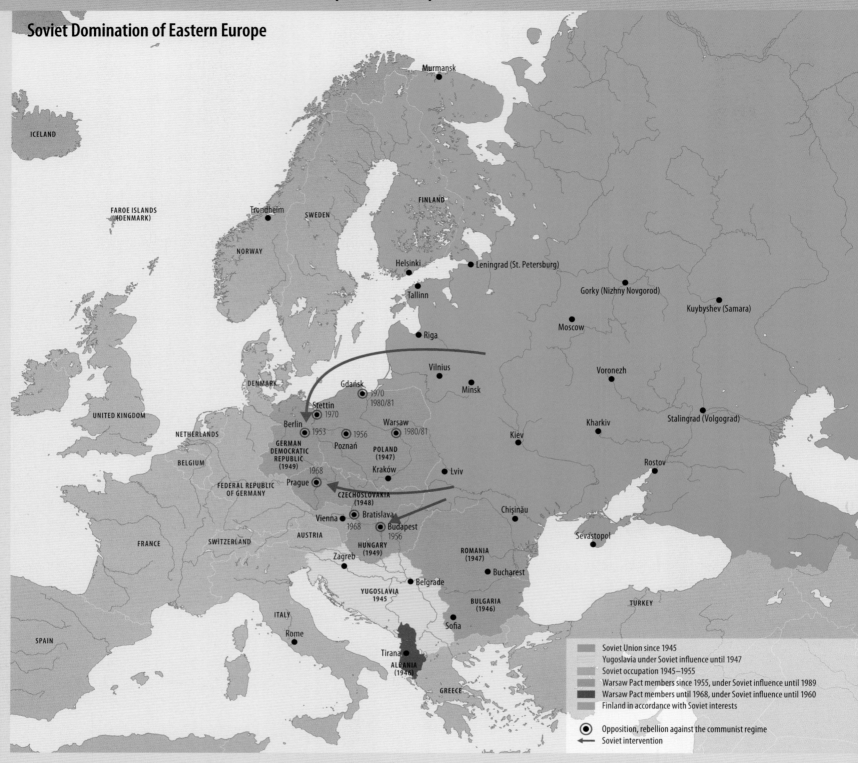

Legend:
- Soviet Union since 1945
- Yugoslavia under Soviet influence until 1947
- Soviet occupation 1945–1955
- Warsaw Pact members since 1955, under Soviet influence until 1989
- Warsaw Pact members until 1968, under Soviet influence until 1960
- Finland in accordance with Soviet interests
- ⊙ Opposition, rebellion against the communist regime
- ← Soviet intervention

After the Allied victory in World War II, the USSR gained control of half of Europe and became one of two superpowers in a divided world. In the 1980s, weakening caused by the arms race and economic trouble led Mikhail Gorbachev to undertake groundbreaking reforms that ended with the disintegration of the Eastern Bloc and the fall of the USSR, but also resulted in an economically and politically strong Russia.

1945 Stalin is actively involved in negotiating the division of the Europe after World War II.

1945–1948 Pro-Soviet regimes are formed across Eastern Europe.

1947 The USSR declines to participate in the Marshall Plan and demands the same of the Eastern European countries.

1948 Stalin breaks off relations with Tito's Yugoslavia, which has extracted itself from Soviet domination.

1948–1949 Soviet units blockade Berlin. The Cold War, a conflict between two economically and ideologically opposed camps, begins.

1952 In the "Stalin Note," the Soviet leader suggests a reunification of Germany in which the superpowers withdraw and Germany is kept politically neutral and disarmed (similar to the Austrian model). The Western powers mistrust this initiative.

1953 Stalin's death leads to a power struggle between Khrushchev and Malenkov. Beria, the head of the secret service, is eliminated. Soviet tanks end the workers' uprising in East Germany on June 17.

1954 The Crimea is Nikita Khrushchev's "gift" to the Ukraine.

1955 The Warsaw Pact is founded. Malenkov is removed from power.

1956 Khrushchev, the new general secretary of the Communist Party, gives a speech at the twentieth party congress in which he acknowledges Stalin's crimes; a cultural thaw follows. The Soviet Army represses a revolution in Hungary.

1957 The satellite Sputnik I is launched successfully, leading to "Sputnik shock" in the West and the beginning of the "space race" between the United States and the USSR.

1960–1962 Diplomatic tensions arise between the USSR and China.

April 12, 1961 Yuri Gagarin is the first man in space.

1962 The Cuban Missile Crisis: Khrushchev begins to install nuclear-armed missiles in Cuba that are capable of reaching the United States in minutes. US President John F. Kennedy responds by instituting a naval block of Cuba. For several days the two superpowers hover on the brink of nuclear war until Khrushchev backs down and withdraws the missiles.

1964 Khrushchev is removed by the Politburo. Party head Brezhnev becomes the new strong man, beginning policies of "socialist normalization" and bureaucratization.

1968 The Soviet invasion of Czechoslovakia ends the Prague Spring period of liberalization.

1974–1979 Treaties regarding deceleration of US and Soviet strategic missile programs are signed at the Strategic Arms Limitations Talks (SALT I and II).

1979 The Soviet invasion and occupation of Afghanistan leads to a de-escalation of the civil war there.

after 1981 The arms race between the USSR and the United States leads US President Ronald Reagan to advocate the "Star Wars" missile defense program.

1982–1984 Following Brezhnev's death, Yury Andropov becomes the head of state and party chief. The first internal reforms are begun.

1984–1985 Andropov dies and is succeeded by his former rival, Konstantin Chernenko, who returns to the policies of Brezhnev.

1985 Mikhail Gorbachev is elected general secretary of the Central Committee of the USSR. He initiates the policies of glasnost and perestroika, and reopens disarmament talks with the United States.

April 26, 1986 An explosion occurs in the nuclear power plant at Chernobyl (Ukraine), the worst in the history of nuclear power generation.

1987–1989 Soviet units withdraw from Afghanistan.

1989 The fall of the Berlin Wall. East and West Germany prepare to unify, and the Eastern Bloc disintegrates.

1991 The August Coup: Communist hardliners unsuccessfully attempt to reverse the reform process. The USSR ceases to exist and is replaced by the Commonwealth of Independent States (CIS).

Rift with China China condemned Khrushchev's theory of peaceful coexistence between the Eastern and Western Blocs. Chairman Mao Zedong felt called upon to preserve the idea of world revolution in opposition to the "revisionist USSR." China developed its own nuclear weapons in 1964, thus attempting to become an equal partner of the United States and the USSR.

Glasnost and perestroika were reforms introduced by Mikhail Gorbachev. *Glasnost*, or "openness," refers to greater transparency in government and cultural liberalization. *Perestroika* was the "restructuring" or modernization of the state and the economy.

Georgy Maksimilianovich Malenkov (1902–1988) Joining the Politburo in 1946, by 1950 Malenkov was Stalin's heir apparent. Serving as the Soviet premier from 1953 to 1955, he at first had the upper hand in the power struggle that followed Stalin's death. Malenkov set a new course, emphasizing agriculture and the production of consumer goods, but lost his base in the party. Khrushchev weakened his power in 1955, finally forcing his resignation in 1957.

Nikita Sergeyevich Khrushchev (1894–1971) As the general secretary of the Communist Party from 1953 to 1964, Khrushchev publicized Stalin's crimes, moderated the party's cultural control and released many prisoners from the Gulags. In his foreign policy he moved between open conflict with the United States and his belief in peaceful coexistence. Khrushchev's unpredictability and increasing self-aggrandizement led to his fall in 1964.

Leonid Ilich Brezhnev (1906–1982) General secretary from 1964 to 1982, Brezhnev's hallmarks were "socialist normality," a cumbersome government bureaucratization, but also initiatives to end the arms race that had brought his country to the verge of economic collapse. Critics of the regime, the most famous of whom were the intellectuals Andrey Sakharov and Aleksander Solzhenitsyn, were persecuted but not liquidated, being sent instead to psychiatric institutes.

Mikhail Sergeyevich Gorbachev (1931–) General secretary of the Communist Party from 1985 to 1991, Gorbachev was also the first and last Soviet President (1990/91). Aware of his country's economic weakness, he considered an end to the endless confrontations with the United States to be the only way out of the crisis. He signaled far-reaching freedoms to the Soviet satellite states of Eastern Europe, thus preparing the way for the mostly peaceful revolutions of 1989. His reforms set into motion the ensuing collapse of the USSR.

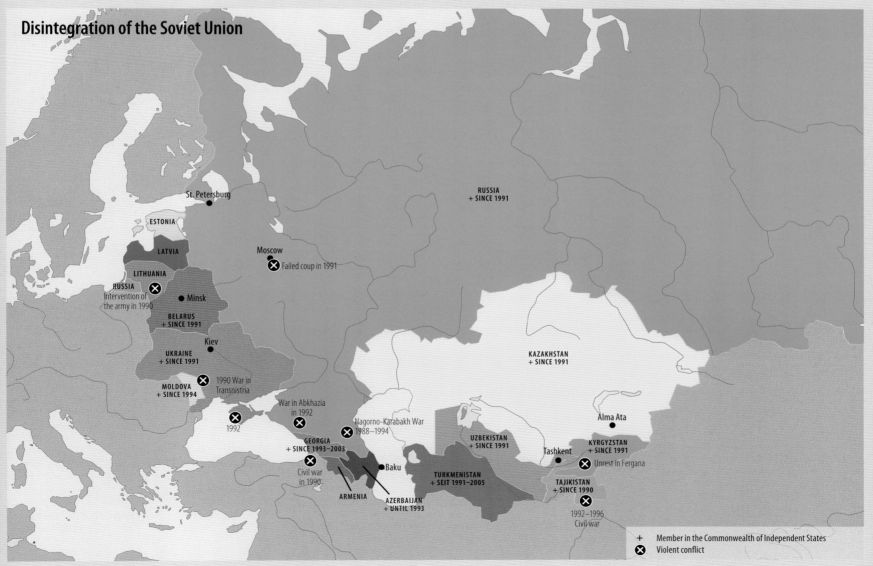

Disintegration of the Soviet Union

St. Petersburg

ESTONIA

LATVIA

LITHUANIA

RUSSIA
Intervention of
the army in 1990

Minsk

BELARUS
+ SINCE 1991

UKRAINE
+ SINCE 1991

Kiev

MOLDOVA
+ SINCE 1994

1990 War in
Transnistria

War in Abkhazia
in 1992

1992

GEORGIA
+ SINCE 1993–2003

Civil war
in 1990

ARMENIA

AZERBAIJAN
+ UNTIL 1993

Baku

Nagorno-Karabakh War
1988–1994

Moscow
Failed coup in 1991

RUSSIA
+ SINCE 1991

KAZAKHSTAN
+ SINCE 1991

Alma Ata

UZBEKISTAN
+ SINCE 1991

Tashkent

TURKMENISTAN
+ SEIT 1991–2005

KYRGYZSTAN
+ SINCE 1991

Unrest in Fergana

TAJIKISTAN
+ SINCE 1990

1992–1996
Civil war

+   Member in the Commonwealth of Independent States
⊗   Violent conflict

Russia, Ukraine and Belarus from 1991 to the Present

Russia Today

After the fall of the USSR, Russia became a federation of independent states. With international support, President Yeltsin was able both to hinder conservative forces' attempts to overthrow the new regime and to establish a democracy with a president in a strong position of power. But economically, the country was facing a catastrophe, a state of affairs that did not change until Vladimir Putin took office in 2000. Thanks to rising oil prices and Putin's resolve in fighting corruption, Russia experienced rapid economic growth. Russia was also determined to show the world its renewed strength. It protested the eastward expansion of NATO and the EU into its former sphere of influence, demonstrating its determination to maintain and increase its power in Eastern Europe.

1991 Russia becomes an independent state, cofounding with Ukraine and Belarus the Commonwealth of Independent States (CIS), whose members include all the former Soviet Republics with the exception of the Baltic States.

November 1991 Chechen President Dzhokhar Dudayev declares his country's independence from Russia.

Dec. 1, 1991 A referendum results in the Ukraine leaving the Soviet Union.

1991–1999 Boris Yeltsin is president of Russia.

September 1993 President Yeltsin relieves parliament of all its functions; the army occupies the parliament building in October.

June 1994 Russia joins NATO's Partnership for Peace program.

July 20, 1994 Alexander Lukashenko is elected president of Belarus, initiating an authoritarian regime often referred to as "Europe's last dictatorship."

December 1994 Russian occupation of Chechnya begins; more than 500,000 Chechens are killed or displaced in the 1990s.

1994–2005 Leonid Kuchma is president of Ukraine; his administration is surrounded by controversy.

May 1997 President Yeltsin and Chechen President Maskhadov sign a peace treaty, but Chechnya's status remains unresolved.

1998 Russian currency rapidly loses its value while Russia's international debts mount.

1999–2002 Second Chechen War

March 2000 Vladimir Putin is elected president. He adopts an increasingly strict "sovereign democracy," which

exercises control of the press and manipulation of cultural politics.

October 2002 Chechen rebels occupy Dubrovka Theater in Moscow, taking hundreds of people hostage. When a Soviet special task force retakes the building, 120 people die.

2003 The political ambitions of oligarch Mikhail Khodorkovsky are destroyed when he is arrested for tax evasion.

2004 Putin is reelected president.

Sept. 1–4, 2004 Terrorist groups of Chechen separatists occupy a school in the North Ossetian town of Beslan.

When Russian security forces retake the school, 330 people—at least half of them children—are killed.

November–December 2004 The "Orange Revolution" in Ukraine begins with peaceful protests against election fraud. During the presidential campaign, candidate Viktor

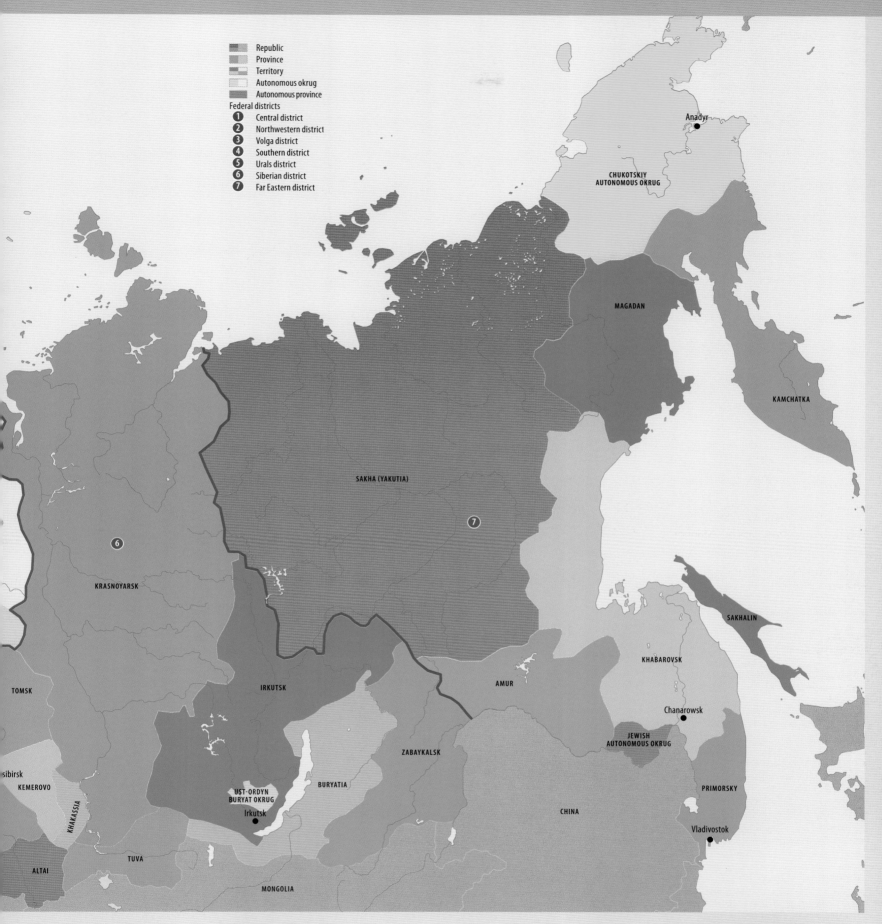

Republic
Province
Territory
Autonomous okrug
Autonomous province
Federal districts
1 Central district
2 Northwestern district
3 Volga district
4 Southern district
5 Urals district
6 Siberian district
7 Far Eastern district

Anadyr

CHUKOTSKIY
AUTONOMOUS OKRUG

MAGADAN

KAMCHATKA

SAKHA (YAKUTIA)

7

6

KRASNOYARSK

SAKHALIN

KHABAROVSK

AMUR

TOMSK

IRKUTSK

Chanarowsk

JEWISH
AUTONOMOUS OKRUG

ZABAYKALSK

KHAKASSIA

PRIMORSKY

sibirsk
KEMEROVO

UST-ORDYN
BURYAT OKRUG

BURYATIA

CHINA

Irkutsk

Vladivostok

TUVA

ALTAI

MONGOLIA

Yushchenko is almost fatally poisoned with dioxin. He later accuses Russia of this attempt on his life.

since 2005 Viktor Yushchenko is president of Ukraine. His term is marked by conflicts with the (former) prime ministers Yulia Tymoshenko and Viktor Yanukovych.

2005/06 and 2009 Disputes about natural gas delivery arise between Russia and Ukraine.

2006 The regime-critical journalist Anna Politovskaya is murdered, and Putin critic Alexander Litvinenko is fatally poisoned with radioactive polonium. Members of the opposition

level accusations against the government in association with both cases.

March 2008 Dmitry Medvedev is elected president of Russia but Putin, who becomes prime minister, remains the strong man in the background.

August 2008 An armed conflict with Georgia begins after Moscow recognizes two separatist republics within Georgia's borders.

Former Soviet Republics from 1989 to the Present

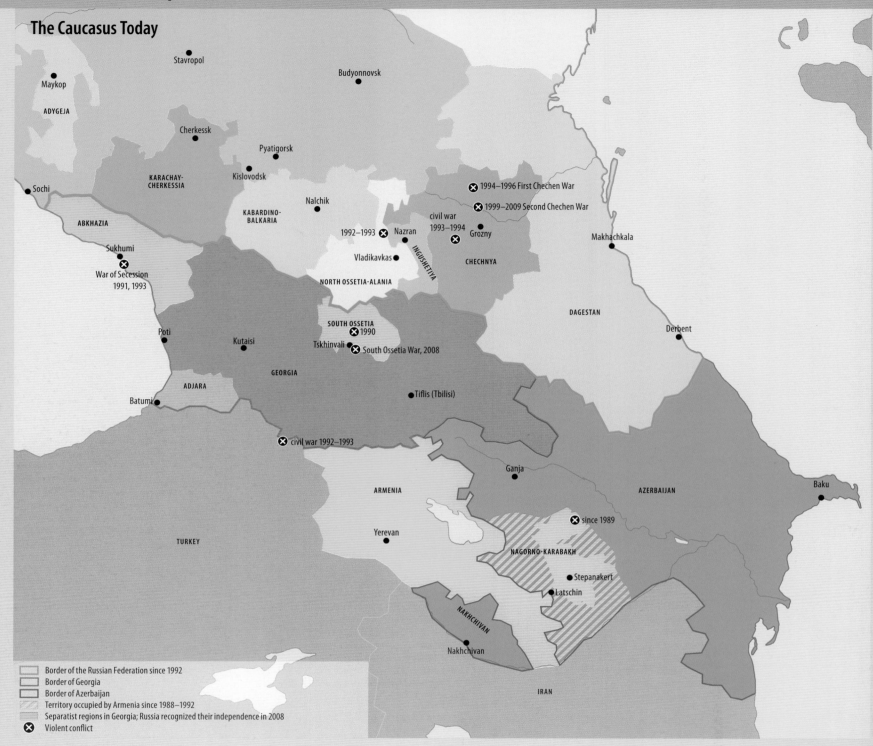

The Caucasus Today

Stavropol

Budyonnovsk

Maykop

ADYGEJA

Cherkessk

Pyatigorsk

KARACHAY-CHERKESSIA

Kislovodsk

Sochi

Nalchik

⊗ 1994–1996 First Chechen War

KABARDINO-BALKARIA

⊗ 1999–2009 Second Chechen War

ABKHAZIA

civil war 1993–1994

⊗ 1992–1993 Nazran

Sukhumi

Grozny

Makhachkala

⊗ War of Secession 1991, 1993

Vladikavkas

CHECHNYA

NORTH OSSETIA-ALANIA

INGUSHETIYA

DAGESTAN

Derbent

Poti

SOUTH OSSETIA

⊗ 1990

Kutaisi

Tskhinvali ⊗

⊗ South Ossetia War, 2008

GEORGIA

ADJARA

Batumi

Tiflis (Tbilisi)

⊗ civil war 1992–1993

Ganja

AZERBAIJAN

Baku

ARMENIA

⊗ since 1989

NAGORNO-KARABAKH

TURKEY

Yerevan

Stepanakert

Latschin

NAKHCHIVAN

Nakhchivan

IRAN

☐ Border of the Russian Federation since 1992
☐ Border of Georgia
☐ Border of Azerbaijan
▨ Territory occupied by Armenia since 1988–1992
▨ Separatist regions in Georgia; Russia recognized their independence in 2008
⊗ Violent conflict

Conflict in the Caucasus

Following the kidnapping of Russian soldiers by Chechen separatists, the Russian army occupied the Chechen capital of Grozny in March 1995. Moscow refused to recognize the elected president of Chechnya, Aslan Maskhadov, who subsequently joined the illegal resistance. The Second Chechen War broke out in 1999 after a series of separatist strikes on targets in Russia. Declining in intensity, the armed conflict lasted until 2005. The Chechen rebels retaliated with terrorist attacks, of which the most tragic—the Dubrovka Theater in Moscow and a school in the North Ossetian town of Beslan—ended with great loss of life when the buildings were retaken by antiterrorism units.

Economic growth
GDP per person in US dollars:

1992:	4,500
1999:	2,000
2004:	6,000
2007:	14,000

Georgia

1992   After fighting with Georgian troops, the separatist regions of Abkhazia and South Ossetia declare independence. They receive no recognition from the West. Civil war follows, and nationalist President Zviad Gamsakhurdia is replaced by former Soviet foreign minister Eduard Shevardnadze.

2003   Demonstrations protesting manipulated election results force Shevardnadze to resign in what is known as the Rose Revolution.

2004   The pro-Western Mikheil Saakashvili is elected president.

2006   Denouncing Georgia's pro-Western development, Russia begins to boycott Georgian wine and mineral water.

2007   At a NATO summit, long-term plans for the admission of Georgia and Ukraine are discussed. Russia views this as provocation.

2008   Russia uses a brutal attack by Georgian units on South Ossetian separatists as an excuse for military intervention. Many Georgians are driven from South Ossetia. Shortly thereafter, Russia recognizes South Ossetian and Abkhazian independence. The European Union insists that the regions belong to Georgia.

Mikheil Saakashvili, 2005

Ukraine Today

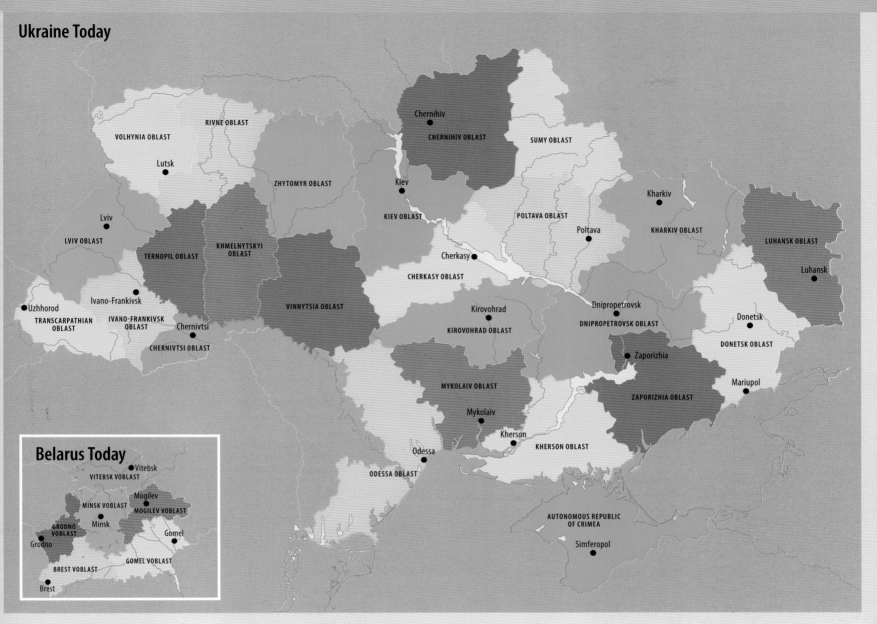

Belarus Today

Armenia and Azerbaijan

1989 A bloody war erupts in the Azeri region of Nagorno-Karabakh, which is primarily inhabited by Armenians.

1991 Nagorno-Karabakh declares its independence from Azerbaijan but is not recognized by the international community.

1993 After reaching an agreement with the leaders of Nagorno-Karabakh, Armenian soldiers attack Azerbaijan.

1994 A ceasefire is signed in Nagorno-Karabakh.

2001 Armenia and Azerbaijan become members of the Council of Europe.

2008 Armenia and Azerbaijan sign a pact in which both parties agree to seek a political solution to the conflict, which has claimed at least 30,000 lives.

Oil and natural gas Much of Europe is dependent on Russia as a source for acquiring natural resources. Rising oil and gas prices since 2000 can largely be attributed to the unprecedented economic growth of the late 1990s. Moscow has used the demand for oil and gas as a weapon against obstinate neighbors. In January 2009, for example, natural gas deliveries to Ukraine were temporarily stopped. While the Russians insisted that the reason for the shut-off was

a disagreement over the price, the opinion in Ukraine was that they were being blackmailed into abandoning their aspirations of European integration and admission to NATO.

The Soviet Invasion of Afghanistan

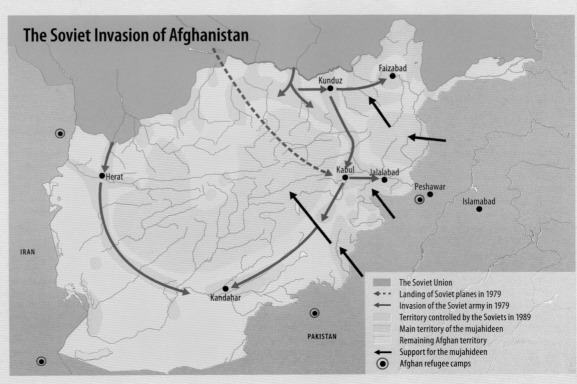

The Soviet Union
Landing of Soviet planes in 1979
Invasion of the Soviet army in 1979
Territory controlled by the Soviets in 1989
Main territory of the mujahideen
Remaining Afghan territory
Support for the mujahideen
Afghan refugee camps

France Until the 10th Century

Celtic Cultures

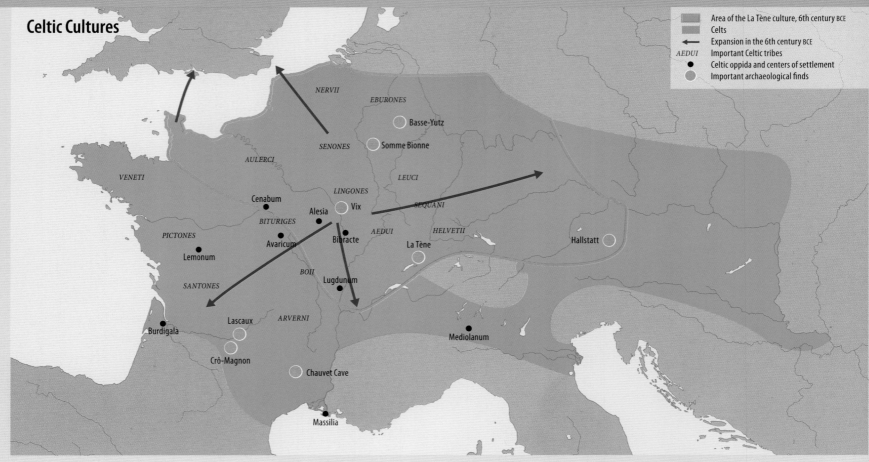

NERVII

EBURONES

Basse-Yutz

SENONES

Somme Bionne

AULERCI

VENETI

LEUCI

LINGONES

Cenabum

Vix

SEQUANI

Alesia

BITURIGES

PICTONES

Avaricum

Bibracte

AEDUI

HELVETII

Hallstatt

Lemonum

La Tène

BOII

SANTONES

Lugdunum

ARVERNI

Burdigala

Lascaux

Mediolanum

Crô-Magnon

Chauvet Cave

Massilia

The Gallic Wars

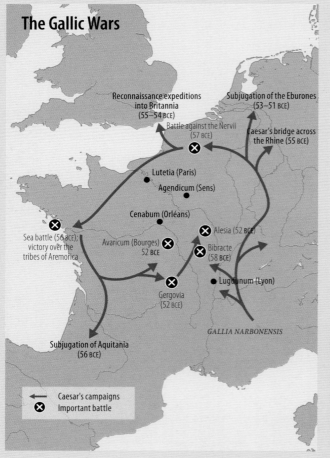

Reconnaissance expeditions into Britannia (55–54 BCE)

Subjugation of the Eburones (53–51 BCE)

Battle against the Nervii (57 BCE)

Caesar's bridge across the Rhine (55 BCE)

Lutetia (Paris)

Agendicum (Sens)

Cenabum (Orléans)

Alesia (52 BCE)

Sea battle (56 BCE); victory over the tribes of Aremorica

Avaricum (Bourges) 52 BCE

Bibracte (58 BCE)

Gergovia (52 BCE)

Lugdunum (Lyon)

GALLIA NARBONENSIS

Subjugation of Aquitania (56 BCE)

Caesar's campaigns
Important battle

200 CE: Roman Provinces in Gaul

GERMANIA INFERIOR

BELGICA

Lutetia

Mogontiacum

LUGDUNENSIS

GERMANIA SUPERIOR

AQUITANIA

Lugdunum

Burdigala

GALLIA CISALPINA

NARBONENSIS

Narbo Martius

Massilia

33,000–30,000 BCE Important cave paintings in Chauvet are dated to this period.

17,000–15,000 BCE Creation of the Lascaux cave paintings

~ 700 BCE France is settled by the Celts.

~ 600 BCE The Greeks found Massilia (Marseille).

~ 480–50 BCE The La Tène period, named after important Celtic finds in western Switzerland

121 BCE The Romans establish the province of *Gallia Narbonensis* (Narbonnese Gaul), located in the areas known today as Provence and Languedoc-Roussillon.

~ 58–51 BCE The conquest of Gaul by Gaius Julius Caesar, as described in his report, *De bello Gallico*.

52 BCE The Romans suppress the Gallic uprising led by Vercingetorix, who is executed in Rome in 46 BCE.

50–69 CE Celts are granted Roman citizenship. In the period that follows,

The Merovingian and Carolingian Dynasties were Frankish dynasties of the Early Middle Ages. The Merovingians were descended from Merovech, ruler of the Salian Franks. They reached their height of power under Clovis I (482–511 CE), and a period of gradual decline followed. They were displaced in 751 by the Carolingians, who were originally stewards of royal domains or "mayors of the palace" in charge of administration and running the court.

Gaul, an ancient region roughly equivalent to today's France and Belgium, was settled by Celtic tribes beginning in the 7th century BCE. The Romans first established themselves in Provincia along the Mediterranean coast before Caesar conquered the rest of Gaul in the same century. After the collapse of the Roman Empire in the 6th century, Teutonic tribes penetrated into the region, and it was soon conquered by the Franks. In 843 the vast Frankish kingdom was divided among the three grandsons of Charlemagne.

Vercingetorix (ca. 82–46 BCE) was the chieftain of the Gallo-Celtic tribes of the Arverni. He united the Gauls in an uprising against the Romans and was taken prisoner after their defeat at Alesia, which is modern-day Alise-Sainte-Reine, in 52 BCE. In 46 BCE he was led through Rome in Caesar's triumphal procession and subsequently executed by strangulation.

Gallic and Roman cultures merge to become the Gallo-Roman culture, and the French language develops from Vulgar Latin. Impressive buildings from the Roman period still adorn southern France. Gaul experiences a period of economic prosperity.

~200 The beginning of Christianization

~ 400 Beginning of the barbarian migrations: Franks, Visigoths and Burgundians found their own kingdoms.

486–487 Battle of Soissons: The Frankish king Clovis defeats Syagrius, the former Roman governor of northern Gaul, whose realm is incorporated into the Frankish empire.

498 Baptism of Clovis I: The Franks convert to Christianity.

507 Battle of Vouille between the Franks and Visigoths: The Franks conquer Aquitaine.

532–534 Battle of Autun: Frankish conquest of Burgundy

639 Death of Dagobert I, the last great Merovingian ruler

732 The Carolingian majordomo Charles Martel (Charles the Hammer) pushes back the Arab invaders as far as France near Tours and Poitiers.

751 The election of Carolingian King Pippin III the Younger: His coronation takes place in Saint-Denis in 754.

768–814 Charlemagne is ruler of the Frankish kingdom.

800 The pope crowns Charlemagne Holy Roman emperor in Rome.

843 The Treaty of Verdun divides the Frankish kingdom among Lothar I, Louis the German and Charles the Bald, the three surviving sons of Emperor Louis the Pious.

855 The Treaty of Prüm: Lothar I divides his realm among his three sons, Louis II, Lothar II and Charles.

870 Treaty of Meerssen: After the death of Lothar II, Charles the Bald and Louis the German divide Lotharingia.

880 The Treaty of Ribemont: Lorraine is ceded to East Francia.

987 Hugh Capet, son of a Frankish duke, is elected king. He is the first king of the Capetian dynasty, which lasts over 300 years.

"Kingdom" of Syagrius The Roman governor of northern Gaul established independent rule in 465 CE. After the collapse of central rule in the Western Roman Empire, he continued to rule until he was defeated by Clovis I in a battle near the capital of Soissons in 486 CE. He fled to Toulouse, where he was handed over to the Franks and executed.

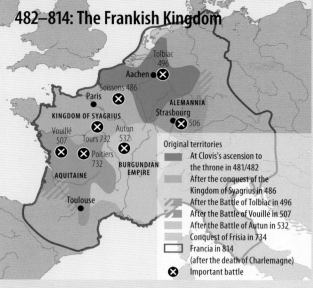

482–814: The Frankish Kingdom

Original territories
- At Clovis's ascension to the throne in 481/482
- After the conquest of the Kingdom of Syagrius in 486
- After the Battle of Tolbiac in 496
- After the Battle of Vouillé in 507
- After the Battle of Autun in 532
- Conquest of Frisia in 734
- Francia in 814 (after the death of Charlemagne)
- ⊗ Important battle

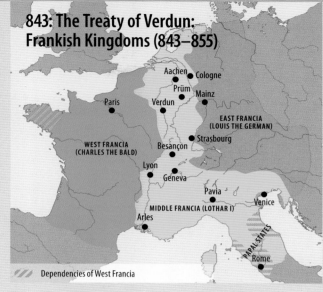

843: The Treaty of Verdun: Frankish Kingdoms (843–855)

Dependencies of West Francia

855: Treaty of Prüm

870: Treaty of Meerssen

Dependencies of West Francia

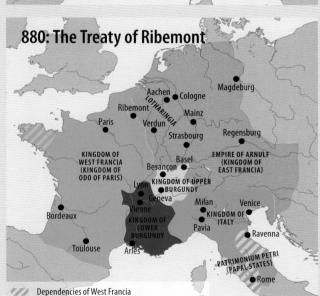

880: The Treaty of Ribemont

Dependencies of West Francia

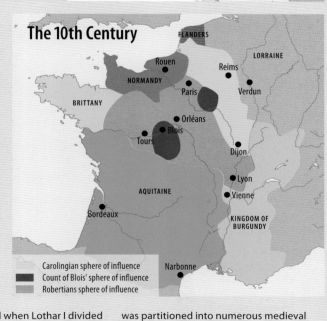

The 10th Century

- Carolingian sphere of influence
- Count of Blois' sphere of influence
- Robertians sphere of influence

Burgundy The first kingdom of Burgundy was founded in 411 in the Rhine region near Mainz (Latin: *Mogontiacum*) and was destroyed by the Roman general Aetius in 436. After their defeat the Burgundians moved to what is currently western Switzerland and Savoy, as well as the Rhone Valley, where they established a new kingdom. They were decisively defeated by the Franks at the Battle of Autun in 532, and their land became part of the Frankish empire.

Lorraine was created when Lothar I divided his kingdom (*Lotharii Regnum*) by means of the Treaty of Verdun in 843. It was further divided by the Treaty of Prüm and became Lotharingia, which comprised the regions of Frisia and the Netherlands up to the Rhineland. Lotharingia (Lorraine) was named for his son, Lothar II. Lorraine was given to East Francia in the Treaty of Ribemont (880 CE). In the period that followed, the region

was partitioned into numerous medieval counties, duchies and bishoprics. The Duchy of Lorraine was part of the Holy Roman Empire until 1766, at which point it fell into French hands. The present-day region of Lorraine in France is not identical to the territory of the former duchy.

France in the 12th–18th Centuries

ca. 1180

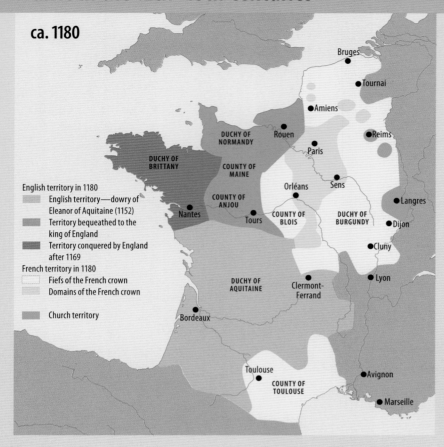

English territory in 1180
- English territory—dowry of Eleanor of Aquitaine (1152)
- Territory bequeathed to the king of England
- Territory conquered by England after 1169

French territory in 1180
- Fiefs of the French crown
- Domains of the French crown
- Church territory

1337–1415: Hundred Years' War, Phase I

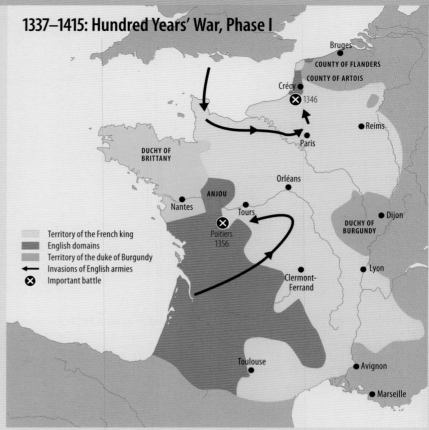

- Territory of the French king
- English domains
- Territory of the duke of Burgundy
- ← Invasions of English armies
- ⊗ Important battle

1415–1453: Hundred Years' War, Phase II

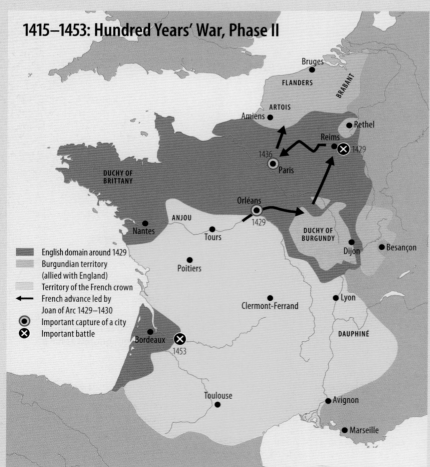

- English domain around 1429
- Burgundian territory (allied with England)
- Territory of the French crown
- ← French advance led by Joan of Arc 1429–1430
- ◉ Important capture of a city
- ⊗ Important battle

1106–1137 Louis VI the Great: rise of the Capetians

1144 The Basilica of Saint-Denis, one of the structures that establishes the style of the Gothic period, is dedicated.

1152 After her marriage to Louis VII of France, a Capetian, is annulled,

Eleanor of Aquitaine marries Henry Plantagenet, King Henry II of England, Duke of Normandy and Earl of Anjou, Maine and Touraine.

1209–1229 Albigensian crusades against the heretical Cathars in southern France

1214 Battle of Bouvines: Philip Augustus of France expels the British from French territory.

1226 Louis VIII establishes a hereditary monarchy.

1259 England recognizes French King Louis IX as its liege lord.

1285 Philip IV the Fair: the French nation state is established through strict power politics. Conquest of Champagne

1309–1377 The papacy is forcibly moved to Avignon, and Philip the Fair takes the pope hostage.

1328 The Capetian dynasty dies out and the Valois dynasty ascends the throne.

1337 Philip VI of France seizes Gascony and triggers the Hundred Years' War. King Edward III of England claims the French throne.

1346 English conquest of Crécy by longbowmen

1347 The English conquer Calais.

1356 The English are victorious in the Battle of Poitiers, and the French king, John II, is taken captive.

1415 The Battle of Agincourt is a victory for the English, and many prominent Frenchmen are killed.

1429 French troops led by Joan of Arc lift the English siege of Orléans. Joan's army is also victorious at Patay.

1431 Joan of Arc is burned at the stake.

1435 Reconciliation of France and Burgundy

1436 The French retake Paris.

1453 The French recapture Bordeaux and Normandy. The Hundred Years' War comes to an end.

1461–1483 The reign of King Louis XI, known as the Spider King, marks the beginning of French hegemony. Louis strongly supports the merchant class, increasing France's wealth and influence throughout Europe.

1467–1477 Reign of Charles the Bold, Duke of Burgundy. Tensions with the French crown intensify.

1477 Charles the Bold is defeated and killed at the Battle of Nancy.

1493 The Treaty of Senlis settles the troubles over Burgundy. The former Burgundian territories are divided: Flanders and Artois fall to the Habsburgs, and France retains control of Burgundy, Nevers and Picardy.

1515–1547 François I reigns during the Renaissance. The Loire Valley castles are constructed.

1562–1598 The Catholics and Huguenots fight the French Wars of Religion.

Aug. 23–24, 1572 Many Huguenots are slaughtered in the St. Bartholomew's Day Massacre.

1589 The Valois dynasty ends. Henry IV of Navarre, of the House of Bourbon,

Burgundy until 1477

Burgundian territory until 1477
Royal domains of the Capetian line (Valois, Dunois, Bourbon)
Domains of other families and houses
Church domain (Avignon-Venaissin)
Border of France

1598: Edict of Nantes

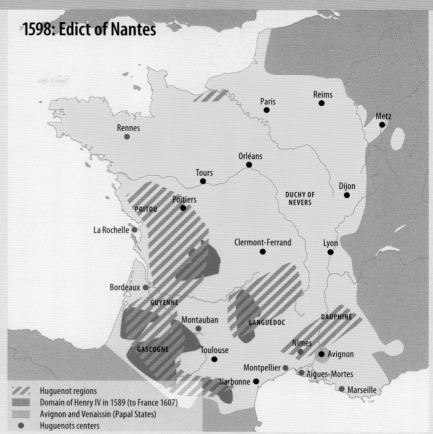

///// Huguenot regions
Domain of Henry IV in 1589 (to France 1607)
Avignon and Venaissin (Papal States)
● Huguenots centers

1552–1798

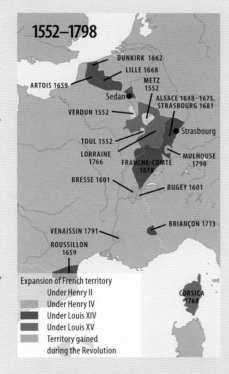

Expansion of French territory
Under Henry II
Under Henry IV
Under Louis XIV
Under Louis XV
Territory gained during the Revolution

1643–1715: Louis XIV

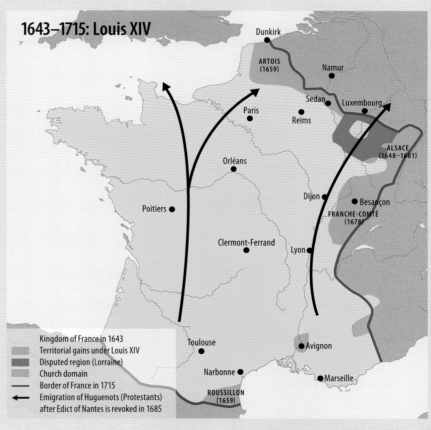

Kingdom of France in 1643
Territorial gains under Louis XIV
Disputed region (Lorraine)
Church domain
Border of France in 1715
◄— Emigration of Huguenots (Protestants) after Edict of Nantes is revoked in 1685

ascends the throne and converts to Catholicism in 1593: "Paris is worth a mass."

1598 Edict of Nantes: Henry IV grants tolerance to Protestants (Huguenots).

1624–1642 Richelieu becomes cardinal and later chief minister to Louis XIII. The "Red Eminence" pulls many strings in the Thirty Years' War, helping prepare the way for absolutism, and campaigns against the Huguenots.

1643–1715 The reign of Louis XIV, the Sun King, represents the pinnacle of French absolutism.

1667–1668 War of Devolution: France and Spain fight for control of the Spanish Netherlands. Initially dominant, Louis XIV was ultimately forced to yield to the Triple Alliance of Spain, England and the Dutch Republic.

1672–1678 Franco-Dutch War: France regains control of Franche-Comté and part of Flanders.

1685 The Edict of Fontainebleu abolishes the Edict of Nantes: the Huguenots are driven out of France.

1688–1697 War with the League of Augsburg/Grand Alliance

1701–1713 France wins the War of the Spanish Succession, curtailing Habsburg power in Europe.

The Hundred Years' War (1337–1453) was a prolonged conflict, fought in multiple stages, between England and France over supremacy in western Europe. More specifically, it had to do with the succession to the throne of France and

the feudal rights of the English kings to the kingdom of France in their capacity as dukes of Aquitaine. The war ended with a French victory.

Joan of Arc, also called the Virgin of Orléans (1412–1431) Joan was a peasant girl who felt called by God to free her country of English rule in the Hundred Years' War. She successfully convinced the dauphin, who later became Charles VII, of her divine mission. He therefore trusted her to lead the French army against the British. After several military victories, she guided the dauphin to his coronation in Reims in 1429. She was betrayed and captured. The Burgundians turned her over to the British, who burned her at the stake in 1431. She was rehabilitated in 1456 and canonized in 1920.

The Huguenots This is the appellation for French followers of Calvinism. The term is presumably derived from the French word *aignos*, meaning confederates, who were responsible for the connection to Switzerland as the center of Calvinism. With the exception of the early decades of the 16th century, the Huguenots were vigorously repressed and persecuted in their homeland until the time of the French Revolution .

The Sun King The apt sobriquet of King Louis XIV (1638–1715) of France, who is famously, but falsely, quoted as having said, "I am the state." An exponent of absolutism and aggressive foreign policy, he distinguished himself as the longest reigning European head of state (1643–1715). He ordered the renovation of the Palace of Versailles into a magnificent baroque residence beginning in 1661, and Versailles became the paragon of 18th-century European architecture that all other royal houses emulated.

France: The End of Absolutism, and Revolution

1789–1794

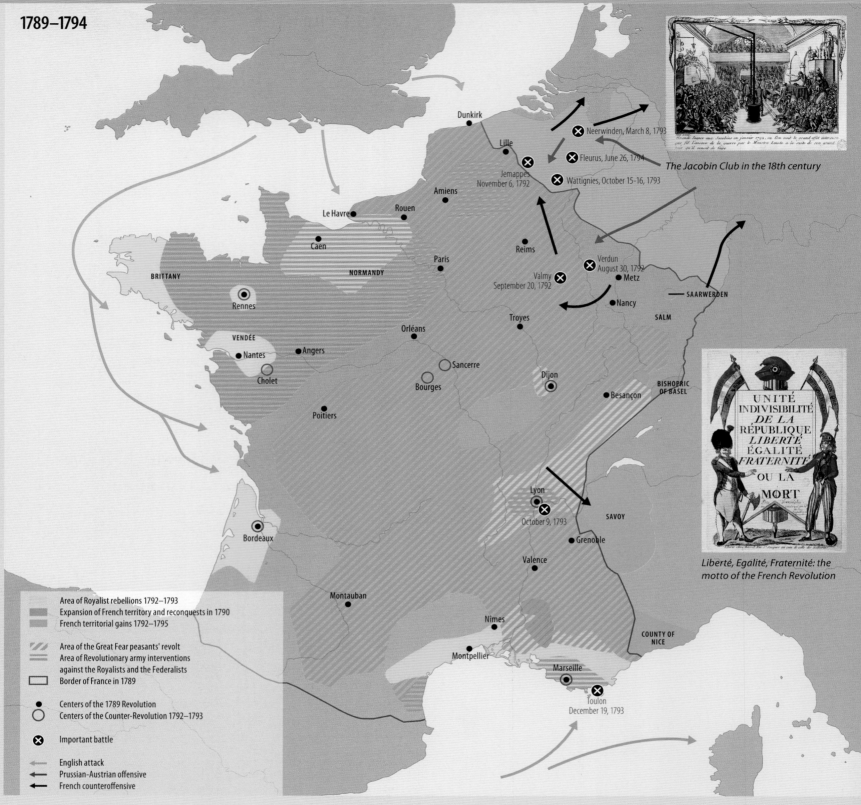

Dunkirk

Neerwinden, March 8, 1793

Lille

Fleurus, June 26, 1794

Jemappes
November 6, 1792

Wattignies, October 15–16, 1793

Amiens

Le Havre

Rouen

Caen

NORMANDY

Reims

Verdun
August 30, 1792

Paris

Metz

Valmy
September 20, 1792

SAARWERDEN

Nancy

BRITTANY

SALM

Rennes

Troyes

Orléans

VENDÉE

Angers

Sancerre

Dijon

BISHOPRIC
OF BASEL

Nantes

Cholet

Bourges

Besançon

Poitiers

Montauban

Lyon
October 9, 1793

SAVOY

Grenoble

Bordeaux

Valence

Nimes

COUNTY OF
NICE

Montpellier

Marseille

Toulon
December 19, 1793

The Jacobin Club in the 18th century

Liberté, Egalité, Fraternité: the motto of the French Revolution

Legend:
- Area of Royalist rebellions 1792–1793
- Expansion of French territory and reconquests in 1790
- French territorial gains 1792–1795
- Area of the Great Fear peasants' revolt
- Area of Revolutionary army interventions against the Royalists and the Federalists
- Border of France in 1789
- ● Centers of the 1789 Revolution
- ○ Centers of the Counter-Revolution 1792–1793
- ⊗ Important battle
- ← English attack
- ← Prussian-Austrian offensive
- ← French counteroffensive

Estates-General of 1789 Meeting of representatives of the three estates, or classes, within the kingdom of France: the clergy, the nobility and the Third Estate, comprised of free farmers and the bourgeoisie. Ever since 1302, the king had summoned this body in times of crisis to give their approval for important decisions. This took place most frequently in the 14th century. The penultimate assembly of the Estates-General was in 1614, and the last was in 1789.

The Bastille was a fortress in the eastern part of Paris that had served as a jail since the beginning of the 17th century. Although there were no important prisoners there at the time, the storming of the Bastille on July 14, 1789, is considered the symbolic

date on which the French Revolution began. Understood as a symbol of kingship, the Bastille was demolished, though the outlines of the former fortress walls are still visible at ground level today.

The Guillotine This device used to behead those who were condemned to death was named after its inventor, Dr. J. I. Guillotin (1736–1814). The guillotine was introduced for "humanitarian" reasons and was intended to reduce or eliminate the suffering of the condemned, who had previously been executed by a variety of cruel and undignified means. On March 20, 1792, the National Assembly decreed that guillotining was to be the sole method of execution in France.

Sans-Culottes Literally meaning "without shorts," it became a term for those who did not wear the knickerbockers of the nobility and clergy. Sans-culottes included workers, the petit bourgeois, Jacobin supporters and, particularly in Paris, radicalized crowds.

The Jacobins Led by Robespierre, they were members of the most radical political faction during the French Revolution. In mid-1793 the Jacobins took control of the Committee of Public Safety, the executive organ of the National Convention, which gave them unlimited authority. They then carried out a Reign of Terror that lasted more than four years, until July 1794.

The French Directory After the Jacobins were overthrown, the actual French govern-

ment consisted of a five-man Directory selected by the Convention. There were a total of seven Directory regimes between 1795 and 1799.

The French Consulate The period from November 10, 1799 to December 1, 1804 is called the French Consulate. Napoleon Bonaparte installed his dictatorship during this time. He was under pressure from the military, but was nevertheless named first consul by parliamentary authority, a title later approved by referendum. The Consulate actually consisted of three consuls, but the first consul (Napoleon) was granted extensive powers and became for all intents and purposes the sole ruler. The other two consuls served merely in an advisory capacity.

Paris 1789–1794

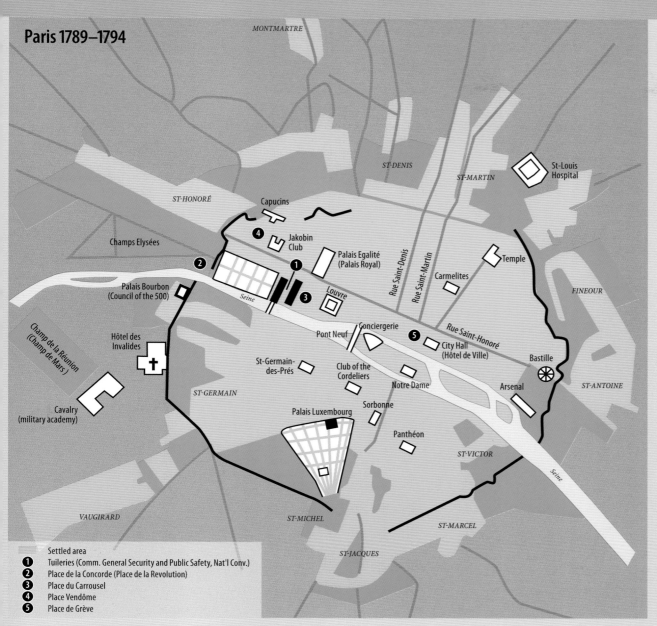

MONTMARTRE

ST-DENIS   ST-MARTIN

St-Louis Hospital

ST-HONORÉ

Capucins

Champs Elysées

Jakobin Club

④

Palais Egalité (Palais Royal)

Temple

Rue Saint-Denis

Rue Saint-Martin

Carmelites

FINEOUR

②

Palais Bourbon (Council of the 500)

Seine

①

③

Louvre

Hôtel des Invalides

Champ de la Réunion (Champ de Mars)

Pont Neuf

Conciergerie

⑤

Rue Saint-Honoré

City Hall (Hôtel de Ville)

Bastille

ST-ANTOINE

St-Germain-des-Prés

Club of the Cordeliers

Notre Dame

Arsenal

Cavalry (military academy)

ST-GERMAIN

Sorbonne

Palais Luxembourg

Panthéon

ST-VICTOR

Seine

VAUGIRARD

ST-MICHEL

ST-MARCEL

ST-JACQUES

Settled area
① Tuileries (Comm. General Security and Public Safety, Nat'l Conv.)
② Place de la Concorde (Place de la Revolution)
③ Place du Carrousel
④ Place Vendôme
⑤ Place de Grève

1715–1774 The reign of Louis XV, characterized by an economic boom and inordinate influence of a royal mistress. The history of his romantic affairs (Madame de Pompadour and others) and illegitimate children fills volumes.

1756–1763 France is embroiled in the Seven Years' War against Prussia and Great Britain.

1763 Treaty of Paris: France loses all its overseas territories in North America, as well as parts of India.

1774 Louis XVI ascends the throne. France's participation in the American War of Independence increases the already large national debt, and Louis XVI is unpopular. In addition, thoughts of revolution and Enlightenment ideas circulate, even among the nobility. The Affair of the Diamond Necklace, a scandal involving the king's wife, Marie-Antoinette, puts an additional strain on the monarchy. The queen is completely innocent in the matter.

May 5, 1789 The French Estates-General are summoned.

June 17, 1789 The Third Estate declares itself the National Assembly.

July 14, 1789 Storming of the Bastille

Aug. 26, 1789 With the Declaration of the Rights of Man and the Citizen, democracy is adopted in France.

April 2, 1791 Death of Count de Mirabeau, leader of the moderate phase of the Revolution

June 20–25, 1791 The king attempts to flee the country, but fails.

Sept. 3, 1791 With the passage of the Constitution in the National Assembly, France becomes a constitutional monarchy.

Aug. 10, 1792 Storming of the Tuileries and end of the monarchy

Sept. 22, 1792 Proclamation of the First Republic: The power struggle between moderate Girondists and radical Jacobins leads to the execution of Girondists in 1793.

Jan. 21, 1793 Louis XVI is executed by guillotine, as is Marie-Antoinette nine months later.

1793–1794 Jacobin Reign of Terror: The Committee of Public Safety under Maximilien de Robespierre, Antoine de Saint-Just and George Couthon. Jean-Paul Marat, a radical "friend of the people," is murdered in July 1793. In an attempt to dechristianize France, the Committee closes churches and introduces the revolutionary calendar.

March–April 1794 Jacques Hébert and his left-wing radical associates, as well as George Danton and his more moderate group, are executed. Robespierre is overthrown and executed in July 1794.

1795–1799 Rule by the Directory

1797 Suppression of an early communist conspiracy led by François Neol "Gracchus" Babeuf; Babeuf is executed.

Nov. 9, 1799 Napoleon's coup d'état: autocracy of the First Consul, Napoleon Bonaparte

Dec. 24, 1799 A public referendum on the Consulate ends the French Revolution and leads to the founding of the First Republic.

Rulers of France

The Carolingian Dynasty
843–877	Charles II the Bald (emperor from 875)
877–879	Louis II the Stammerer
879–882	Louis III
879–884	Carloman II
884–888	Charles III the Fat (emperor from 881)
888–898	Eudes (Robertian family)
893–923	Charles III the Simple
922–923	Robert I (Robertian)
923–936	Rudolph of Burgundy
936–954	Louis IV the Transmarinus
954–986	Lothar I
986–987	Louis V the Indolent

The Capetian Dynasty (descended from the Robertians)
987–996	Hugh Capet
996–1031	Robert II the Wise
1017–1025	Hugh Magnus
1031–1060	Henry I
1060–1108	Philip I
1108–1137	Louis VI the Fat
1130–1131	Philip of France (co–king)
1137–1180	Louis VII the Young
1180–1223	Philip II Augustus
1223–1226	Louis VIII the Lion
1226–1270	Louis IX the Saint
1270–1285	Philip III the Bold
1285–1314	Philip IV the Fair
1314–1316	Louis X the Quarreler
1316	John I
1316–1322	Philip V the Tall
1322–1328	Charles IV the Fair

The Valois Dynasty
1328–1350	Philip VI of Valois
1350–1364	John II the Good
1364–1380	Charles V the Wise
1380–1422	Charles VI the Mad
1422–1461	Charles VII the Victorious
1461–1483	Louis XI
1483–1498	Charles VIII
1498–1515	Louis XII
1515–1547	Francis I
1547–1559	Henry II
1559–1560	Francis II
1560–1574	Charles IX
1574–1589	Henry III

The Bourbon Dynasty
1589–1610	Henry IV
1610–1643	Louis XIII
1643–1715	Louis XIV the Sun King
1715–1774	Louis XV the Well-Beloved
1774–1792	Louis XVI
1814–1815	Louis XVIII
1815–1824	Louis XVIII
1824–1830	Charles X

The First Republic
1792–1793	Georges Danton
1793–1794	Maximilien de Robespierre
1794–1797	Lazare Carnot
1797–1799	Paul de Barras
1799	Emmanuel Joseph Sieyès
1799–1804	Napoleon Bonaparte

First Empire
1804–1814	Napoleon I
1815	Napoleon I

House of Orléans
1830–1848	Louis–Philippe (Citizen King)

Second Republic
1848	Louis–Eugène Cavaignac
1848–1852	President Charles–Louis–Napoleon Bonaparte

Second Empire
1852–1870	Napoleon III

France and Europe in the Napoleonic Era

Thanks to his military and strategic genius, Napoleon brought the greater part of Europe under his direct or indirect control through conquests and alliances beginning around 1800. His main opponents were England, Prussia, Austria and Russia; these nations formed a total of seven coalitions against France.

August 1792 Prussian and Austrian troops take Longwy and Verdun.

Sept. 20, 1792 The French cannonade Valmy and are victorious. The first militia is subsequently established.

June 26, 1794 French victory over Austria near Fleurus leads to annexation of the Austrian Netherlands; the Batavian Republic is founded in Holland.

1799 Napoleon marries Joséphine de Beauharnais, the former mistress of several leading politicians.

1796–1797 Napoleon's Italian campaign

Oct. 17, 1797 Treaty of Campo Formio: Austria accepts the formation of the independent Cisalpine Republic.

1797–1799 French-controlled vassal republics are established, including the Helvetic (Switzerland), and the Roman and Parthenopaean Republics in southern Italy.

May 19, 1798 Start of Napoleon's Egyptian expedition

Aug. 1–2, 1798 The Battle of Abukir in Egypt results in an English victory over the French fleet.

Aug. 23–Oct. 9, 1799 Napoleon withdraws from Egypt.

June 14, 1800 Battle of Marengo, in which Napoleon defeats Austria.

1802–1804 Haitian Revolution: After Napoleon reinstates slavery in France's American colonies, he sends an army to St-Dominigue to quell slave revolts. His army is defeated by disease as well as the Haitian generals. Struggling financially due to impending war with Britain, Napoleon sells France's possessions on the North American mainland to the United States: the Louisiana Purchase.

Aug. 2, 1802 By means of a plebiscite, Napoleon becomes First Consul for Life.

Dec. 2, 1804 Napoleon is crowned emperor of France.

Oct. 21, 1805 The English defeat France in the Battle of Trafalgar.

Nov. 13, 1805 The French take Vienna for the first time.

Dec. 2, 1805 Napoleon is victorious against Austria and Russia in the Battle of the Three Emperors at Austerlitz.

Oct. 27, 1806 The French occupy Berlin, and the Confederation of the Rhine is founded, unifying all the German states except for Austria and Prussia under Napoleon.

1806–1814 Napoleon's embargo cuts England off from trade with continental Europe.

1808 Conquest of Spain and Portugal: Joseph Bonaparte, Napoleon's brother, is named king of Spain.

May 1809 Napoleon is defeated for the first time by Austrian troops at Aspern near Vienna. The Battle of Wagram is also fought, in which the French capture Vienna for a second time.

1810 Napoleon divorces Joséphine and marries Marie-Louise von Habsburg.

June–December 1812 Napoleon's Russian campaign fails.

Oct. 16–19, 1813 France loses the Battle of Leipzig.

April 6, 1814 Napoleon is forced to abdicate and is exiled to Elba.

September 1814–June 1815 Congress of Vienna and the realignment of Europe: France must relinquish conquered territories, but is allowed to retain its former territory, including Alsace-Lorraine.

Feb. 26–June 22, 1815 The Hundred Days of Napoleon's short-lived revival

June 18, 1815 The Battle of Waterloo: Napoleon is defeated once and for all.

Napoleon Bonaparte (1769–1821)
A native of Corsica, he was a French general, statesman and emperor. Beginning in 1785, he was on active duty as an artillery lieutenant. The events surrounding the French Revolution made Napoleon's career possible. After taking Toulon in 1793, he was appointed to the rank of brigadier general. French influence expanded as a result of his

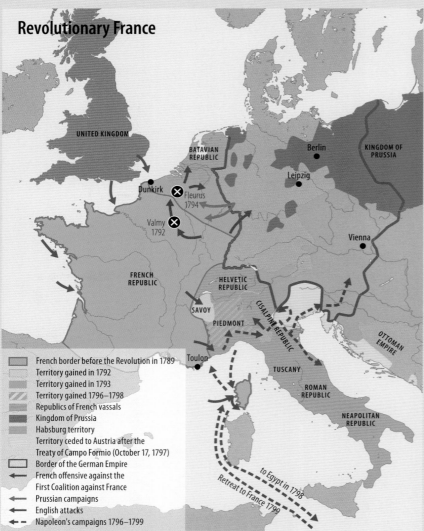

Revolutionary France

UNITED KINGDOM
BATAVIAN REPUBLIC
Berlin
KINGDOM OF PRUSSIA
Leipzig
Dunkirk
Fleurus 1794
Valmy 1792
Vienna
FRENCH REPUBLIC
HELVETIC REPUBLIC
SAVOY
CISALPINE REPUBLIC
PIEDMONT
OTTOMAN EMPIRE
Toulon
TUSCANY
ROMAN REPUBLIC
NEAPOLITAN REPUBLIC
Retreat to France 1799
to Egypt in 1798

- French border before the Revolution in 1789
- Territory gained in 1792
- Territory gained in 1793
- Territory gained 1796–1798
- Republics of French vassals
- Kingdom of Prussia
- Habsburg territory
- Territory ceded to Austria after the Treaty of Campo Formio (October 17, 1797)
- Border of the German Empire
- French offensive against the First Coalition against France
- Prussian campaigns
- English attacks
- Napoleon's campaigns 1796–1799

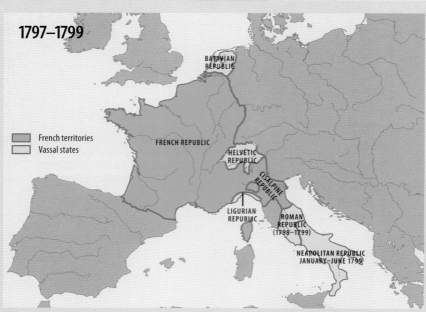

1797–1799

BATAVIAN REPUBLIC
FRENCH REPUBLIC
HELVETIC REPUBLIC
CISALPINE REPUBLIC
LIGURIAN REPUBLIC
ROMAN REPUBLIC (1798–1799)
NEAPOLITAN REPUBLIC JANUARY–JUNE 1799

- French territories
- Vassal states

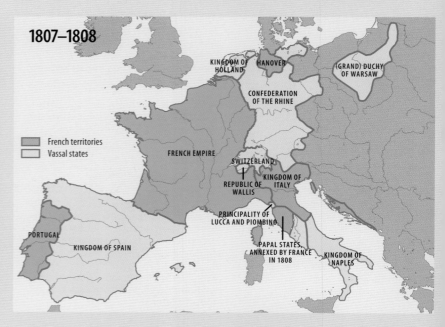

1807–1808

KINGDOM OF HOLLAND
HANOVER
(GRAND) DUCHY OF WARSAW
CONFEDERATION OF THE RHINE
FRENCH EMPIRE
SWITZERLAND
REPUBLIC OF WALLIS
KINGDOM OF ITALY
PRINCIPALITY OF LUCCA AND PIOMBINO
PORTUGAL
KINGDOM OF SPAIN
PAPAL STATES ANNEXED BY FRANCE IN 1808
KINGDOM OF NAPLES

- French territories
- Vassal states

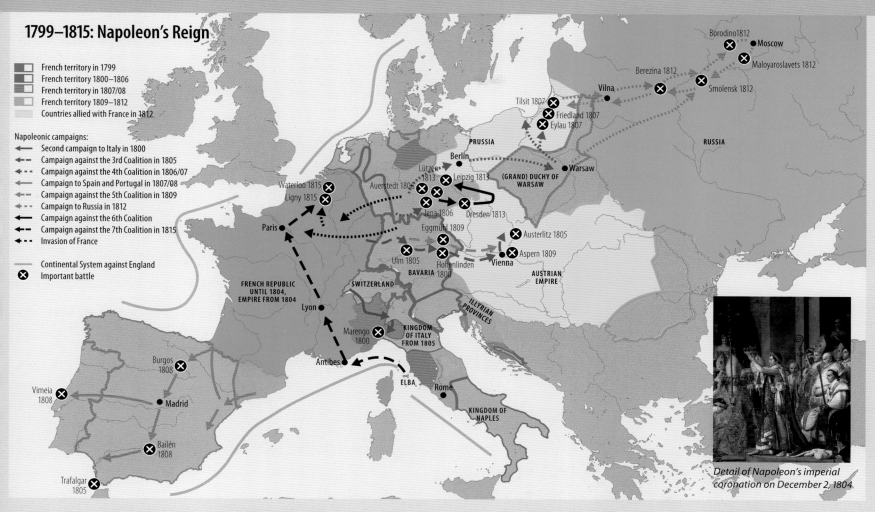

1799–1815: Napoleon's Reign

French territory in 1799
French territory 1800–1806
French territory in 1807/08
French territory 1809–1812
Countries allied with France in 1812

Napoleonic campaigns:

Second campaign to Italy in 1800
Campaign against the 3rd Coalition in 1805
Campaign against the 4th Coalition in 1806/07
Campaign to Spain and Portugal in 1807/08
Campaign against the 5th Coalition in 1809
Campaign to Russia in 1812
Campaign against the 6th Coalition
Campaign against the 7th Coalition in 1815
Invasion of France

Continental System against England
Important battle

Borodino 1812
Moscow
Maloyaroslavets 1812
Berezina 1812
Vilna
Smolensk 1812
RUSSIA
Tilsit 1807
Friedland 1807
Eylau 1807
PRUSSIA
Berlin
Warsaw
(GRAND) DUCHY OF WARSAW
Lützen 1813
Leipzig 1813
Auerstedt 1806
Waterloo 1815
Ligny 1815
Jena 1806
Dresden 1813
Paris
Eggmühl 1809
Austerlitz 1805
Ulm 1805
Hohenlinden
Aspern 1809
Vienna
BAVARIA
1800
AUSTRIAN EMPIRE
FRENCH REPUBLIC UNTIL 1804, EMPIRE FROM 1804
ILLYRIAN PROVINCES
SWITZERLAND
Lyon
Marengo 1800
KINGDOM OF ITALY FROM 1805
Burgos 1808
Antibes
ELBA
Rome
Vimeia 1808
Madrid
KINGDOM OF NAPLES
Bailén 1808
Trafalgar 1805

Detail of Napoleon's imperial coronation on December 2, 1804.

military successes in the Italian campaign. He reached the height of his power when he was crowned emperor in 1804. In 1806 he put an end to the Holy Roman Empire, which had existed for centuries. That same year, he achieved decisive victories over Prussia at Jena and Auerstädt. This meant that practically all of continental Europe was under his control.

Only his failed Russian campaign and subsequent defeat at Leipzig by the forces of the sixth coalition ended Napoleon's career. He was first exiled to the island of Elba. After the collapse of his Hundred Day return to power in 1815, he was banished to the island of St. Helena in the South Atlantic, where he died on May 5, 1821.

The vassal states After the success of the French Revolution and the intervention of the French Revolutionary Army on foreign soil, the so-called "export of the Revolution" began. Nearly all of Italy, Holland and Switzerland were affected. Sister republics were formed, including the Batavian, Cisalpine, Ligurian, Piedmontese, Parthenopaean and Roman Republics. The same is true of vassal monarchies, such as the kingdoms of Italy, Etruria, Naples and Westphalia.

The Egyptian expedition (1798–1799) In order to cut off England's access to India, Napoleon recommended that the French government conquer Egypt, which was officially part of the Ottoman Empire.

Despite several victories on the Egyptian mainland, the French were defeated by the English fleet under Admiral Nelson in the Battle of Abukir (August 1–2, 1798). The complicated military and political situation at home ultimately forced Napoleon to withdraw and return to France. Napoleon's Egyptian expedition admittedly failed to achieve its goal, but the participation of numerous scholars and Napoleon's interest in Egyptology led to important discoveries—including that of the Rosetta Stone—and contributed significantly to historical research.

The Hundred Days of Napoleon After the victorious Allied forces conquered Paris, Napoleon was exiled to Elba, an island off the coast of Tuscany, in May 1814. Thanks to a vote of confidence by the French people, he was able to land in Antibes with a thousand soldiers as early as February 1815. He then marched to Paris, and the imperial troops defected to his side. Despite his efforts to safeguard peace within the national borders of 1792, Austria, Russia, England and Prussia decided to intervene against him militarily. His one hundred day rule ended in defeat at Waterloo on June 18, 1815.

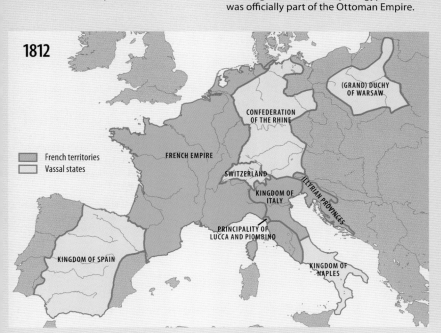

1812

French territories
Vassal states

CONFEDERATION OF THE RHINE
(GRAND) DUCHY OF WARSAW
FRENCH EMPIRE
SWITZERLAND
ILLYRIAN PROVINCES
KINGDOM OF ITALY
PRINCIPALITY OF LUCCA AND PIOMBINO
KINGDOM OF SPAIN
KINGDOM OF NAPLES

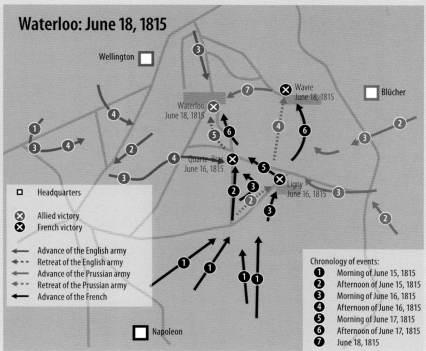

Waterloo: June 18, 1815

Wellington
Blücher
Wavre June 18, 1815
Waterloo June 18, 1815
Quatre-Bras June 16, 1815
Ligny June 16, 1815

Headquarters
Allied victory
French victory

Advance of the English army
Retreat of the English army
Advance of the Prussian army
Retreat of the Prussian army
Advance of the French

Napoleon

Chronology of events:
1. Morning of June 15, 1815
2. Afternoon of June 15, 1815
3. Morning of June 16, 1815
4. Afternoon of June 16, 1815
5. Morning of June 17, 1815
6. Afternoon of June 17, 1815
7. June 18, 1815

France from the Congress of Vienna to the End of World War I

France continued to be the scene of stormy political upheavals throughout the 19th century. There were two brief revivals of the monarchy. After Napoleon's defeat at the hands of the Prussians, the republican form of government was finally able to prevail.

1814 The return of the House of Bourbon: Louis XVIII, younger brother of Louis XVI, is restored to the throne.

1824–1830 Reactionary regime of Charles X

1830 France conquers Algeria and begins colonization. King Charles X is deposed in the July Revolution. His successor is Louis-Philippe of Orléans, who calls himself king of the French rather than king of France. The bourgeois monarchy lasts until 1848.

1848 The February Revolution: the Second Republic is proclaimed. Louis Napoleon, nephew of Napoleon I, is elected president.

1852 The Second French Empire: In a coup d'état, Louis Napoleon declares himself Emperor Napoleon III.

1870 Prussia defeats France, which loses Alsace-Lorraine. Napoleon III is deposed.

1871 The Third Republic is proclaimed. The socialist Paris Commune falls in May.

1875 The Constitutional Laws of 1875 establish a regime based on parliamentary supremacy.

1894 Franco–Russian Alliance

1904 France forms the Entente Cordiale with Great Britain; Russia joins in 1907 to form the Triple Entente.

1905 Separation of church and state. The Dreyfus Affair takes place.

August 1914 Germany declares war on France.

September 1914 The advance of the German Army is stopped in the Battle of the Marne.

February–July 1916 The Battle of Verdun

February–March 1917 French offensive on the Western Front fails.

April 1917 The United States enters the war on the side of the Allied Powers.

July 1918 The last German offensive is stopped at the Marne.

November 1918 Germany surrenders and signs the Versailles Treaty at Compiègne.

Europe after the Congress of Vienna in 1815

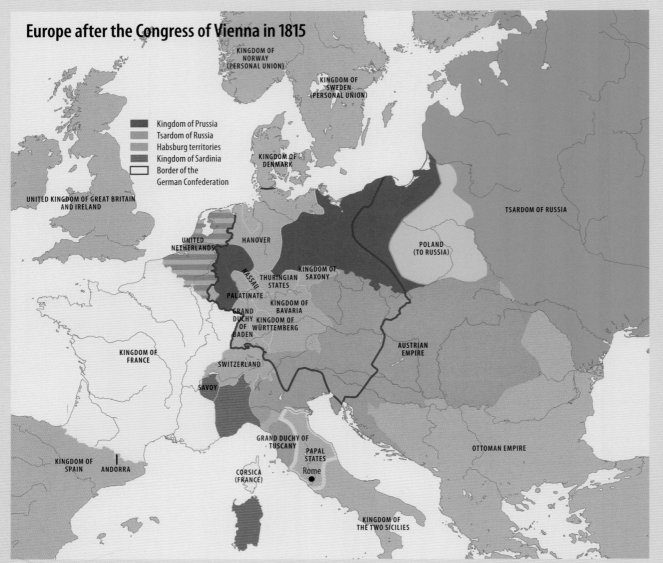

Legend:
- Kingdom of Prussia
- Tsardom of Russia
- Habsburg territories
- Kingdom of Sardinia
- Border of the German Confederation

The February Revolution of 1848

- Non-urban revolutionary movements
- Centers of the revolution

1870–1871: Franco-Prussian War

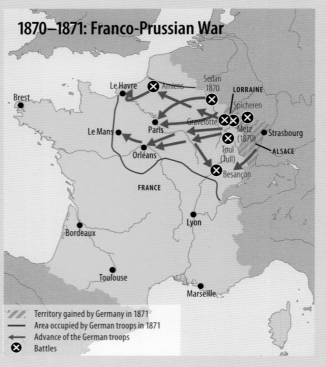

- Territory gained by Germany in 1871
- Area occupied by German troops in 1871
- Advance of the German troops
- Battles

The Conquest of Algeria During the reign of Charles X, France conquered Algeria, which had been part of the Ottoman Empire until that time. For over 130 years, Algeria was one of France's most important colonies and provided a market for French industrial products. Thousands of French settlers, called *pieds-noirs* ("black feet"), lived there.

The Paris Commune is the Paris City Council that formally ruled the city from March 18–May 28, 1871. The Commune was the result of an insurrection that took place in the capital in the wake of France's catastrophic defeat by Prussia. Following a referendum, it was comprised of twenty-five workers, eight officials and more than thirty artists and intellectuals. Socialists considered it the first government of the working class in French history. The Commune's troops were finally put down by the army in street fighting. More than 30,000 Communards died, and thousands were executed or exiled.

The Third Republic Of the five French Republics, the Third Republic lasted the longest. Established at the end of the Franco-Prussian War in 1871, it was a period of social stability and industrial progress.

1914–1915: World War I

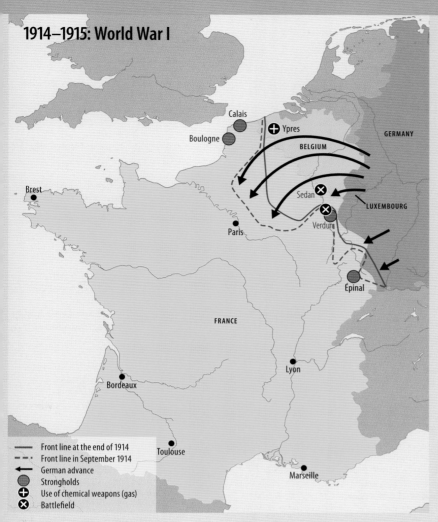

Front line at the end of 1914
Front line in September 1914
German advance
Strongholds
Use of chemical weapons (gas)
Battlefield

The Third Republic existed until 1940, when the Nazis defeated France.

Verdun The Battle of Verdun was fought over a bulwark that symbolized French national pride. The German strategy was to decisively weaken the French Army. One of the bloodiest battles of World War I, it remains a metaphor for trench warfare to this day. Approximately 377,000 French and 337,000 German soldiers had lost their lives by war's end.

Entente A coalition initially formed between France, Russia and Great Britain that led to the Allied forces in World War I. The first step in the formation of the alliance was the Franco-Russian political and military pact of 1894. The Entente Cordiale, frequently translated as "cordial understanding," between the British and the French was signed in 1904, and the Anglo-Russian Entente followed in 1907. These pacts were originally intended to solve points of contention regarding colonial territories outside of Europe. Later on, however, they led to broad political and military cooperation.

Charles X (1757–1836) was the leader of strong opposition against supporters of the Revolution and Napoleon. As heir to the throne, he headed up the archconservative faction of the nobility. After ascending the throne in 1824, he instituted reactionary policies that targeted liberals. In the wake of the July Revolution, Charles X was forced to abdicate and lived in exile in England.

Adolphe Thiers (1797–1877) A French liberal politician and historian who served as prime minister at several different times. During the Third Republic he also served as France's head of state from 1871 to 1873.

Louis-Napoleon (1808–1873) was elected president of the Second Republic in 1848. He put the restoration of the empire to a vote in a public referendum in December 1851, and proclaimed himself Emperor Napoleon III in 1852. He was open to modern technology, but overextended himself in foreign policy issues. After Prussia's defeat in the Battle of Sedan on September 1, 1870, he was captured by the forces of the Third Republic in Paris.

Alfred Dreyfus (1859–1935) was a French officer of Jewish descent and a member of the French general staff. He was convicted in 1894 of spying for the Germans. Following a trial that was marred by the fabrication of false evidence against Dreyfus, he was sentenced to lifelong imprisonment at Devil's Island in French Guiana. The Dreyfus Affair enflamed anti-Semitic sentiment and led to a sharp division in French society. Dreyfus was completely exonerated in 1906.

Dreyfus is demoted, 1895

Raymond Poincaré (1860–1934) served five times as prime minister of France. His first term as prime minister was in 1912–1913. On the basis of his strong anti-German position, he was elected president of the Republic in 1913 and served in that capacity until 1920. Due to Prime Minister Aristide Briand's policy of rapprochement with Germany, Poincaré defeated him in the election held in 1922. From 1922 to 1924 and 1926 to 1929 Poincaré served two additional terms as prime minister.

1916–1917: World War I

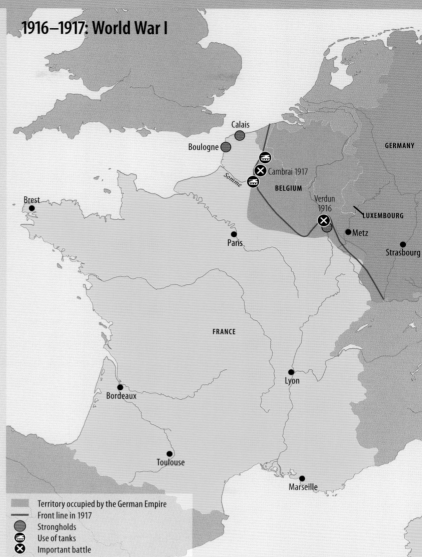

Territory occupied by the German Empire
Front line in 1917
Strongholds
Use of tanks
Important battle

1918: End of World War I

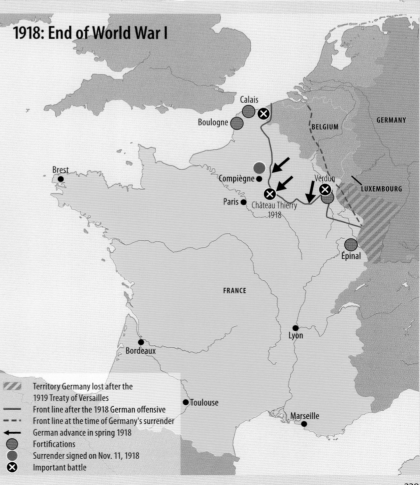

Territory Germany lost after the 1919 Treaty of Versailles
Front line after the 1918 German offensive
Front line at the time of Germany's surrender
German advance in spring 1918
Fortifications
Surrender signed on Nov. 11, 1918
Important battle

France – Between the Wars and World War II

France ignored Germany's breaches of the Treaty of Versailles, an attitude that further encouraged Hitler's desire to unleash a new conflict. France was ultimately conquered and occupied by German troops in 1940.

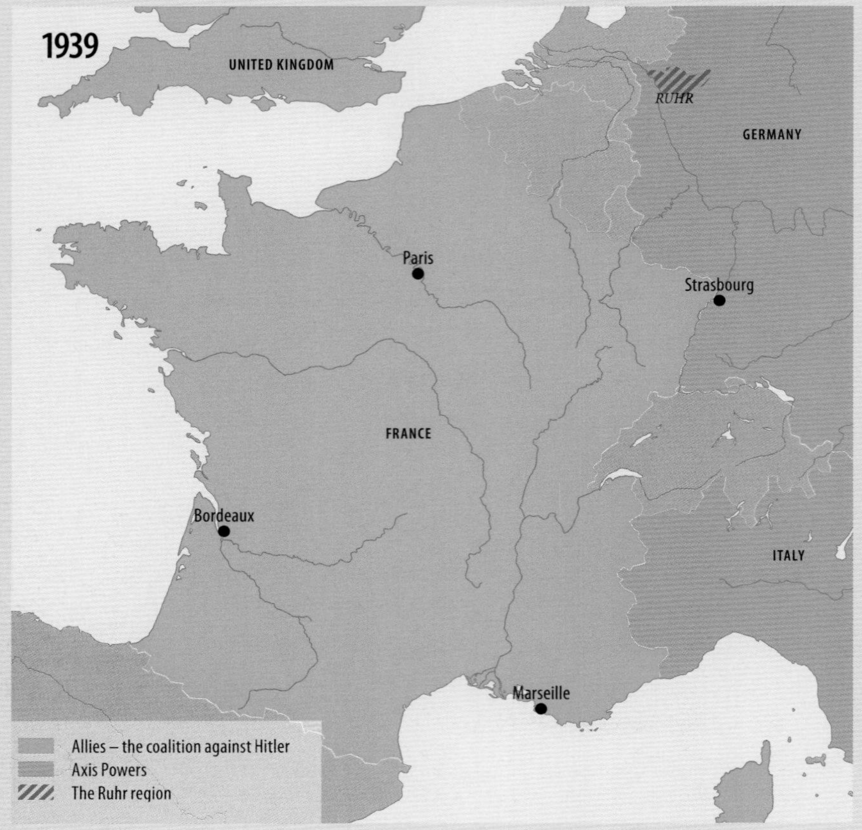
1939
UNITED KINGDOM
RUHR
GERMANY
Paris
Strasbourg
FRANCE
Bordeaux
ITALY
Marseille
Allies – the coalition against Hitler
Axis Powers
The Ruhr region

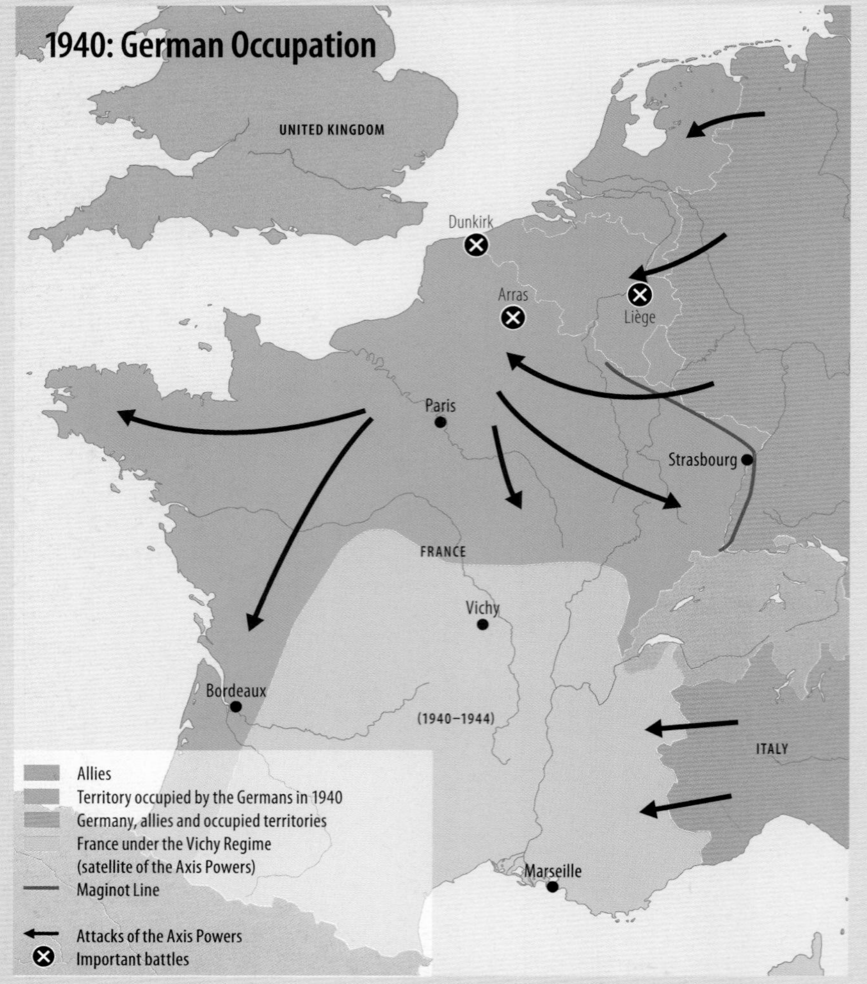
1940: German Occupation
UNITED KINGDOM
Dunkirk
Arras
Liège
Paris
Strasbourg
FRANCE
Vichy
Bordeaux
(1940–1944)
ITALY
Marseille
Allies
Territory occupied by the Germans in 1940
Germany, allies and occupied territories
France under the Vichy Regime
(satellite of the Axis Powers)
Maginot Line
Attacks of the Axis Powers
Important battles

1919 Signing of the Treaty of Versailles: Germany loses Alsace-Lorraine to the French, as well as a number of its African colonies.

1923–1925 When the Germans fail to pay the heavy reparations demanded by the Treaty of Versailles, the French occupy the Ruhr region.

1925 Treaty of Locarno: Germany guarantees the inviolability of the French border.

1926 Gustav Stresemann, foreign minister of Germany, and Aristide Briand, foreign minister of France, are joint recipients of the Nobel Peace Prize.

1926–1936 Building of the Maginot Line, a series of fortifications and other defenses along the French border with Germany

1927 End of military control over Germany

1930 Withdrawal of the last occupying forces

1933 Geneva Disarmament Conference: The French-led conference on disarmament ends in failure after the Germans withdraw from the talks.

February 1934 The February 6 crisis: Several far-right groups unsuccessfully try to organize an anti-parliamentary coup d'état. The incident results in formation of new organizations to block the rise of facism in France.

1935 Franco-Soviet Treaty of Mutual Assistance and a military accord with Great Britain

1936 In violation of the Treaty of Versailles, German troops occupy the Rhineland demilitarized zone. Great Britain and France remain passive.

1938 France signs the Munich Agreement that forces Czechoslovakia to cede control of the Sudetenland to Germany.

1939 Following Germany's attack on Poland, Great Britain and France declare war on Germany.

1940 Defeat at the hands of the Germans: occupation of northern France and installation of a puppet regime in Vichy in the south of France under Marshal Pétain and Pierre Laval. A ceasefire is declared in June.

1942 The deportation of French Jews begins, and the French police cooperate. Following the Allied invasion of French colonies in North Africa, the Germans occupy all of France. The French resistance goes into action.

1943 The French Committee of National Liberation is founded under the leadership of Charles de Gaulle.

June 6–30, 1944 Operation Overlord: the massive Allied landing at Normandy and the liberation of Paris. The French resistance plays a key role, providing valuable intelligence and assisting the Allied advance.

1945 Germany surrenders: Laval is executed, Marshal Pétain goes on trial, and collaborators face bloody retribution.

Occupation of the Ruhr According to the peace treaty ending World War I, a defeated Germany was to pay high war reparations. Due to economic and currency crises, however, this became impossible. When the quotas of wood and coal were not delivered, French Premier Poincaré ordered the occupation of the Ruhr in January 1923. From an economic perspective, this was a mistake that served to further weaken the German economy. The German government appealed for passive resistance to the occupiers. The occupation ended in 1925.

The Vichy Regime Following the defeat in 1940, the Germans divided France into two zones. The northern part, which included Paris and the Atlantic Coast, fell under direct occupation. The French authorities were to govern two-thirds of the southern portion. In the spa town of Vichy, an authoritarian, fascist regime sprang up and collaborated with the Germans. The head of state was Marshal Pétain and the prime minister was Pierre Laval.

The French Committee of National Liberation was an organization that, beginning in 1943, united all French forces that were opposed to the Nazi occupation. As of November 1943, General Charles de Gaulle was its chairman. After the liberation of Paris, the Allies recognized it as the provisional government of France.

Operation Torch In November 1942, British and American troops—along with de Gaulle's Free French Forces—occupied French territories in Algeria and Morocco. Admiral Jean Darlan, who had been ordered by Pétain to resist the Allies, switched over to their side. This move provoked Hitler into occupying Vichy France.

Léon Blum (1872–1950) A French socialist politician who was prime minister of the left-wing Popular Front government in 1936–1937 and 1938. He served yet again in 1946–1947. He was imprisoned in the Buchenwald concentration camp from 1943 until war's end, and his brother René died in Auschwitz.

Edouard Daladier (1884–1970) A radical French socialist, he served as prime minister from 1933 to 1934 and 1938 to 1940, and signed the Munich Agreement in 1938. He was deported to Germany and interned from November 1942 until the end of World War II. After the war he was a member of parliament and mayor of Avignon. He was also among the opponents of de Gaulle's policies.

Albert Lebrun (1871–1950) was a moderate, right-wing French politician. He served as the last president of the Third Republic from 1932 to 1940. Along with Daladier, he was interned in Germany from 1943 to 1945. He was not active in politics after the war.

Henri-Philippe Pétain (1856–1951) French marshal who became known as the "Hero of Verdun" through his service in World

1944: The Allied Landing at Normandy

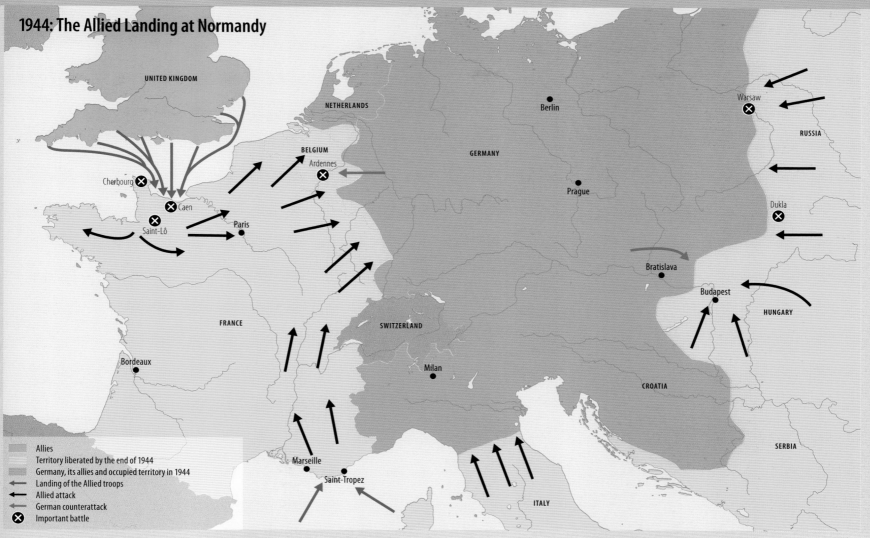

UNITED KINGDOM

NETHERLANDS

Berlin

GERMANY

Warsaw

RUSSIA

BELGIUM

Ardennes

Prague

Cherbourg

Caen

Saint-Lô

Paris

Dukla

FRANCE

SWITZERLAND

Bratislava

Budapest

HUNGARY

Bordeaux

Milan

CROATIA

Marseille

SERBIA

Saint-Tropez

ITALY

Legend:
- Allies
- Territory liberated by the end of 1944
- Germany, its allies and occupied territory in 1944
- Landing of the Allied troops
- Allied attack
- German counterattack
- ⊗ Important battle

War I. As head of the Vichy Regime that collaborated with Germany, he brought shame upon himself in World War II, and was sentenced to death after the war. Due to his advanced age, however, de Gaulle commuted his sentence to life in prison.

Pierre Laval (1883–1945) was prime minister in 1931–32 and 1935–36. Beginning in 1940, he pursued a policy of collaboration with Germany. In 1940 and 1942 to 1944, he was prime minister, foreign minister and Pétain's deputy in the Vichy Regime. Unlike Pétain, who was pardoned, Laval was executed by firing squad after the war.

Charles de Gaulle (1890–1970) French general and leader of the French resistance against German occupation from 1943 on. Along with exiled French officers in England, he organized the Free French Forces. After the war, he was prime minister of the French Provisional Government, and from 1959 to 1969 served as the first president of the Fifth Republic. As president, he worked to reach greater understanding with the Federal Republic of Germany.

Charles de Gaulle

1945: End of World War II

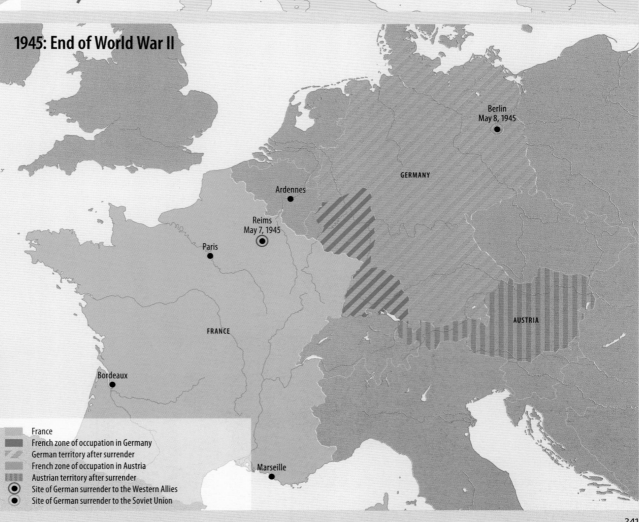

Berlin
May 8, 1945

GERMANY

Ardennes

Reims
May 7, 1945

Paris

AUSTRIA

FRANCE

Bordeaux

Marseille

Legend:
- France
- French zone of occupation in Germany
- German territory after surrender
- French zone of occupation in Austria
- Austrian territory after surrender
- ◉ Site of German surrender to the Western Allies
- ○ Site of German surrender to the Soviet Union

France Since World War II

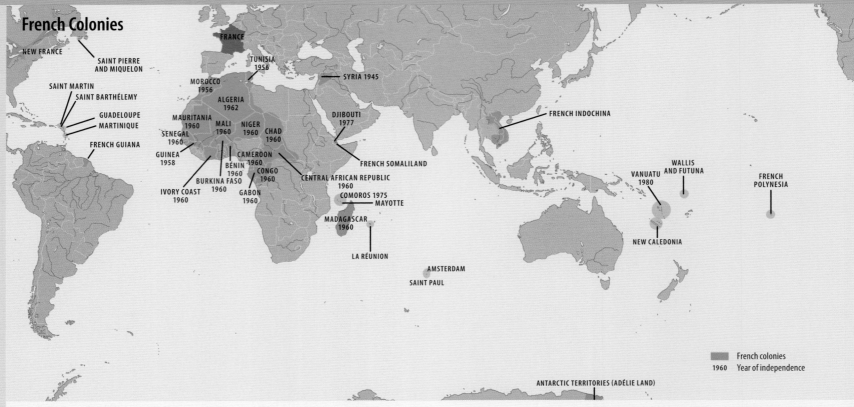

French Colonies

FRANCE
NEW FRANCE
SAINT PIERRE AND MIQUELON
SAINT MARTIN
SAINT BARTHÉLEMY
GUADELOUPE
MARTINIQUE
FRENCH GUIANA
TUNISIA 1956
MOROCCO 1956
ALGERIA 1962
MAURITANIA 1960
MALI 1960
NIGER 1960
CHAD 1960
SENEGAL 1960
GUINEA 1958
BÉNIN 1960
BURKINA FASO 1960
IVORY COAST 1960
CAMEROON 1960
CONGO 1960
GABON 1960
SYRIA 1945
DJIBOUTI 1977
FRENCH SOMALILAND
CENTRAL AFRICAN REPUBLIC 1960
COMOROS 1975
MAYOTTE
MADAGASCAR 1960
LA RÉUNION
AMSTERDAM
SAINT PAUL
FRENCH INDOCHINA
WALLIS AND FUTUNA
VANUATU 1980
NEW CALEDONIA
FRENCH POLYNESIA
ANTARCTIC TERRITORIES (ADÉLIE LAND)

French colonies
1960 Year of independence

Saint Pierre and Miquelon: This archipelago has been settled by the French since the 17th century. From 1689, France and England contended over its rich fishing grounds; it has been part of France since 1815. It became a French overseas territory in 1976, a territorial collectivity in 1985, and an overseas collectivity in 2003.

Saint Martin: The French part of this island was coded as GP, Guadeloupe, until 2007, and has been an overseas collectivity since that time.

Guadeloupe: Annexed in 1674, Guadeloupe was a French DOM (overseas department) from

1946 until 1982; it then became a French territorial collectivity and part of the EU.

French Guiana: French settlement of this department of France began in 1643. After disputes with Portugal and England, it became part of France in 1763, and a penal colony as of 1794. Since 1944 it has been a DOM and part of the EU.

Martinique: The French navigator Pierre Belain d'Esnambuc landed here in 1635. It has been an overseas department of France since 1946, a region of France since 1974, and is part of the EU.

Saint Barthélemy: Annexed by

France in 1648, it was given to Sweden in exchange for trade rights in 1784. The French bought it back in 1877. Since 2007 it has been an overseas collectivity of France. Prior to that, it was part of the overseas department of Guadaloupe.

French Polynesia: The French annexed it in 1842. The remaining islands were conquered in 1881. It became an overseas territory in 1946, and has been an overseas collectivity since 2004.

Wallis and Futuna Islands: French missionaries arrived here in 1837. A French overseas collectivity since 2003, it became

a French protectorate at the end of 1887. Beginning in 1888, they were put under the authority of French New Caledonia. The islands voted to become a French overseas territory in 1959, effective as of 1961.

New Caledonia: A French territory since 1853, it became a penal colony in 1864 and a French overseas territory in 1946. Since 2003, it has been a *sui generis* collectivity of France. Its future status will be determined by a referendum in or after 2014.

French Southern and Arctic Lands: The French occupied Amsterdam Island and Saint Paul

in 1892. These lands have been French overseas territories since 1955. French claims to Adélie Land are not internationally recognized, however.

La Réunion: annexed by Jacques Pronis on behalf of Louis XIII in 1642. Réunion has been a French overseas department since 1946 and a region of France since 1982. It is also part of the EU.

Departmental Collectivity of Mayotte: A French territory since 1843, Mayotte voted in 1974 and 1976 to forgo independence and retain its link to France. But the Comoros, an island nation in the Indian Ocean, also claims Mayotte.

With the United States and USSR dominant after World War II, France lost its status as a world power. The country no longer controlled most of its colonies, and the bloody Algerian War of Independence led to a governmental crisis that ushered in the Fifth Republic.

1946 The constitution of the Fourth Republic is adopted.

1954–1962 Bloody fight for independence in Algeria: Many rival movements were involved, including the FLN, the MNA and the OAS, as was the French government.

1957 France is a founding member of the EEC (European Economic Community), a precursor of the European Union.

1958 The new constitution of the Fifth French Republic establishes a semi-presidential democracy. The Algerian Statute: In order to defend his Algerian policy, de Gaulle thwarts numerous attempted coups by the right-wing military until 1961.

1963 The Élysée Treaty promotes Franco-German friendship and cooperation.

1966–1971 France withdraws its troops from NATO (but remains part of the organization) and orders the removal of U.S. military bases from French soil.

1968 Student unrest and the nationwide general strike of May 1968 lead de Gaulle to announce early legislative elections. The Gaullist Union wins an absolute majority.

1969 After his changes to the constitution are rejected in a nationwide referendum, President Charles de Gaulle resigns.

1969–1974 Georges Pompidou, a Gaullist, becomes president. He pursues an agenda including liberalization of the economy and rapprochement with the United States.

1972 Founding of the extreme-right National Front, led by Jean-Marie Le Pen, which is successful in the 1990s and in the 2002 presidential election.

1974–1981 Valéry Giscard d'Estaing, a liberal, becomes president: close cooperation with the former West Germany and Chancellor Helmut Schmidt.

1978 Nationalization of French oil companies

1981–1995 François Mitterrand is the first socialist president of the Fifth Republic.

1981 The death penalty is abolished in France.

1986 After the Conservative victory in parliamentary elections, "cohabitation" occurs for the first time: the president and prime minister represent different political camps.

1995–2007 Jacques Chirac, a neo-Gaullist, becomes president.

2005 There is widespread unrest among descendants of Algerian and Maghreb immigrants living on the outskirts of major cities.

2006 President Chirac threatens to deploy nuclear weapons against terrorists in the event of an attack on France.

2007 Nicolas Sarkozy, a neo-Gaullist, becomes president.

François Mitterrand (1916–1996) The first socialist president of France in the period of the Fifth Republic. During his period in office from 1981 to 1995, he modernized French cities—and Paris in particular—with the construction of prestigious buildings.

Jacques Chirac (1932–) A neo–Gaullist centrist for many years, as well as Mitterrand's rival. He was mayor of Paris from 1977 to 1995 and prime minister from 1974 to 1976 and 1986 to 1988 ("cohabitation"). From 1995 to 2007 he served as president, succeeding Mitterrand in that position.

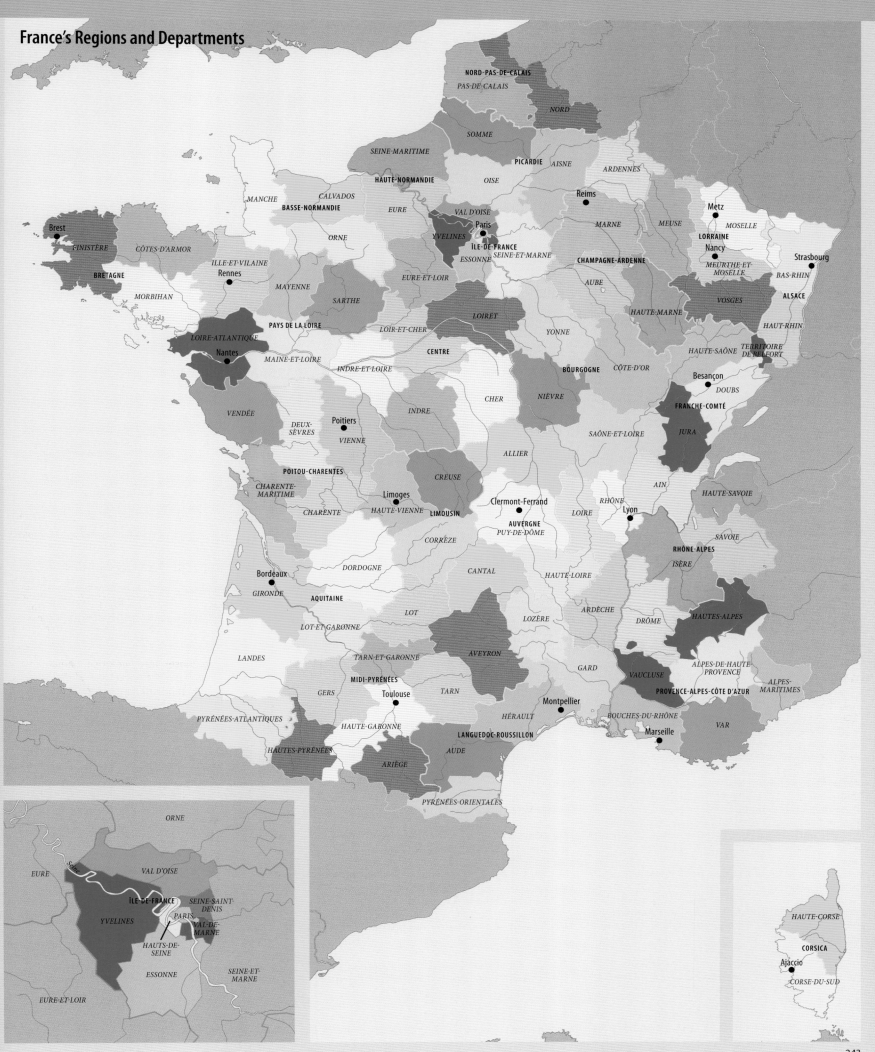

France's Regions and Departments

NORD-PAS-DE-CALAIS
PAS-DE-CALAIS
NORD
SOMME
SEINE-MARITIME
PICARDIE
AISNE
ARDENNES
HAUTE-NORMANDIE
OISE
Reims
MANCHE
CALVADOS
EURE
MARNE
MEUSE
Metz
MOSELLE
BASSE-NORMANDIE
VAL D'OISE
Paris
LORRAINE
Nancy
Strasbourg
Brest
ORNE
YVELINES
ÎLE-DE-FRANCE
CHAMPAGNE-ARDENNE
MEURTHE-ET-MOSELLE
BAS-RHIN
FINISTÈRE
CÔTES-D'ARMOR
ESSONNE
SEINE-ET-MARNE
AUBE
VOSGES
ALSACE
ILLE-ET-VILAINE
Rennes
MAYENNE
SARTHE
LOIRET
HAUTE-MARNE
HAUT-RHIN
BRETAGNE
MORBIHAN
PAYS DE LA LOIRE
LOIR-ET-CHER
YONNE
HAUTE-SAÔNE
TERRITOIRE DE BELFORT
LOIRE-ATLANTIQUE
Nantes
MAINE-ET-LOIRE
CENTRE
Besançon
DOUBS
INDRE-ET-LOIRE
BOURGOGNE
CÔTE-D'OR
FRANCHE-COMTÉ
VENDÉE
CHER
NIÈVRE
JURA
DEUX-SÈVRES
Poitiers
INDRE
VIENNE
SAÔNE-ET-LOIRE
POITOU-CHARENTES
CREUSE
ALLIER
AIN
HAUTE-SAVOIE
CHARENTE-MARITIME
Limoges
Clermont-Ferrand
RHÔNE
Lyon
CHARENTE
HAUTE-VIENNE
LIMOUSIN
AUVERGNE
PUY-DE-DÔME
LOIRE
SAVOIE
CORRÈZE
RHÔNE-ALPES
ISÈRE
Bordeaux
DORDOGNE
CANTAL
HAUTE-LOIRE
GIRONDE
AQUITAINE
LOT
ARDÈCHE
DRÔME
HAUTES-ALPES
LOT-ET-GARONNE
LOZÈRE
LANDES
TARN-ET-GARONNE
AVEYRON
GARD
VAUCLUSE
ALPES-DE-HAUTE-PROVENCE
ALPES-MARITIMES
MIDI-PYRÉNÉES
GERS
Toulouse
TARN
PROVENCE-ALPES-CÔTE D'AZUR
Montpellier
HÉRAULT
BOUCHES-DU-RHÔNE
VAR
PYRÉNÉES-ATLANTIQUES
HAUTE-GARONNE
LANGUEDOC-ROUSSILLON
Marseille
HAUTES-PYRÉNÉES
AUDE
ARIÈGE
PYRÉNÉES-ORIENTALES

ORNE
EURE
VAL D'OISE
ÎLE-DE-FRANCE
SEINE-SAINT-DENIS
YVELINES
Paris
VAL-DE-MARNE
HAUTS-DE-SEINE
EURE-ET-LOIR
ESSONNE
SEINE-ET-MARNE

HAUTE-CORSE
CORSICA
Ajaccio
CORSE-DU-SUD

Spain and Portugal Until the 15th Century

200 BCE: Spread of Various Ethnic Groups

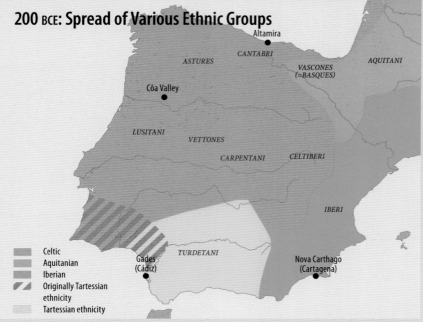

Celtic
Aquitanian
Iberian
Originally Tartessian ethnicity
Tartessian ethnicity

From 201 CE: Spain under the Romans

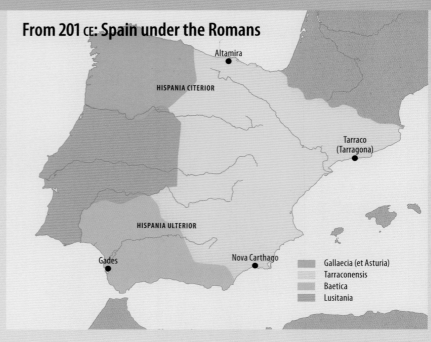

Gallaecia (et Asturia)
Tarraconensis
Baetica
Lusitania

418–711: Spain under the Visigoths

Kingdom of Toulouse 418–507
Kingdom of Toledo (Visigoth kingdom) during the 6th century
⊗ Important battle

711–722: Arab Expansion in Al-Andalus

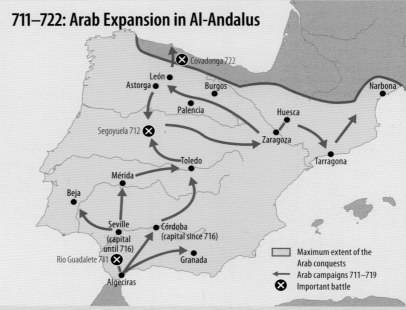

Maximum extent of the Arab conquests
Arab campaigns 711–719
⊗ Important battle

In the wake of the First Punic War, the original inhabitants of the Iberian Peninsula and Celtic tribes from Gaul were conquered by Carthage. Their territory was then successively occupied by Rome, overrun by Germanic Vandals and ruled by Visigoths. Beginning in 711, North African Berbers began the conquest of what they called "Al-Andalus." Christians and Muslims would live side by side under a variety of circumstances for 780 years: there were Muslim kingdoms in Spain until 1492, when the Reconquista came to an end with the defeat of the Nasrid Kingdom of Granada. That same year, the Iberians began their colonial conquest of the New World.

~15,000 BCE   The Altamira cave paintings date from this time.

8th century BCE   The first city-states are founded by the Phoenicians, and Gades (today Cádiz) is their most important colony.

from 400 BCE   Carthaginian conquest: Cartagena is founded, and Spain becomes a base for Carthaginian military expeditions against Rome.

201 BCE   The Second Punic War: The Carthaginians are forced to cede control of Hispania to the Romans.

19 BCE   Cantabrian Wars: The Romans finally end Cantabrian resistance under Caesar Augustus and control the entire peninsula.

406–429 CE   With the onset of the decline of the Roman Empire, the Romans' hold on power decreases, and the Vandals and Suebi invade. The Vandals march through Spain and onward into Africa.

411–585   Suebi kingdom of Germanic peoples in northwestern Hispania

418   Advance of the Visigoths, who establish the kingdom of Toulouse. Under the command of Alaric II, the Visigoths in Gaul are defeated by the Franks, led by Clovis, in the Battle of Vouillé. The Visigoths retreat toward Spain, and Toledo becomes the capital of what is called the Catholic "kingdom" of Toledo.

July 711   Berbers and Arabs triumph over the Christian Visigoths in the Battle of Guadalete.

711–725   Conquest of the Visigothic kingdom by Muslim Arabs and Berbers from North Africa. They call the Iberian Peninsula "Al-Andalus."

718–722   The Visigothic nobleman Pelagius rebels against Arab rule. He defeats the Moors in the Battle of Covadonga and founds the kingdom of Asturias. Pelagus is credited with initiating the Reconquista.

732   The Arabs carry out raids as far afield as southern France. They are defeated by the Franks near Tours and Poitiers.

756   Founding of the Emirate of Córdoba under the Spanish Umayyads. In the 9th century it will become the leading cultural power in western Europe.

778   Charlemagne's campaign over the Pyrenees: seizure and sacking of Pamplona, which becomes part of the *Marca Hispanica*.

Aug. 15, 778   The epic ballad *Song of Roland* relates the story of the crushing defeat of the Frankish army by the Basques at Roncesvalles during Charlemagne's retreat over the Pyrenees.

905–1164   Christian kingdoms in the north: León becomes the successor kingdom of Asturias. The kingdom of Navarre emerges in the Basque-speaking region, the kingdom of Aragon out of the *Marca Hispanica*, and the kingdom of Portugal from the *Condado de Portucale*.

722–929: The Reconquista

Poitiers 732
Oviedo
GALICIA
León
Porto
CASTILE
Pamplona
Roncesvalles 778
Coimbra
Barcelona
Zaragoza
Toledo
Tarragona
Mérida
Valencia
Seville
Córdoba
ANDALUSIA
Granada
Málaga

Kingdom of Asturias, first half of the 8th century (core)
Kingdom of Asturias, end of the 9th century
Conquests of Charlemagne (Marca Hispanica)
Emirate of Córdoba (Caliphate of Córdoba from 929)
⊗ Important battle

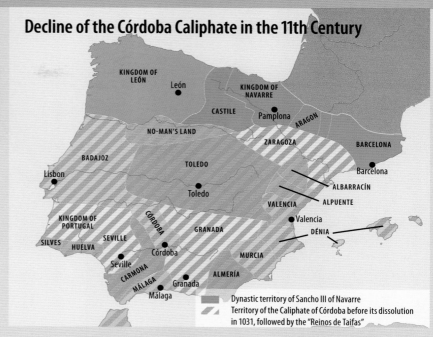

Decline of the Córdoba Caliphate in the 11th Century

KINGDOM OF LEÓN
León
KINGDOM OF NAVARRE
CASTILE
Pamplona
ARAGON
NO-MAN'S LAND
ZARAGOZA
BARCELONA
BADAJOZ
TOLEDO
Barcelona
Lisbon
Toledo
ALBARRACÍN
ALPUENTE
VALENCIA
CÓRDOBA
Valencia
KINGDOM OF PORTUGAL
GRANADA
DÉNIA
SILVES
SEVILLE
HUELVA
Seville
Córdoba
MURCIA
CARMONA
ALMERÍA
MÁLAGA
Granada
Málaga

Dynastic territory of Sancho III of Navarre
Territory of the Caliphate of Córdoba before its dissolution in 1031, followed by the "Reinos de Taifas"

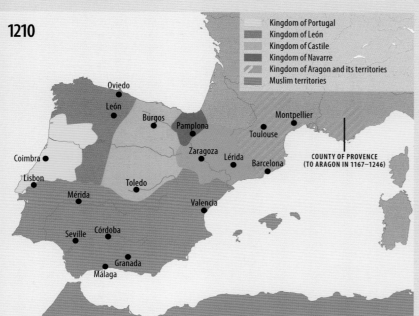

1210

Kingdom of Portugal
Kingdom of León
Kingdom of Castile
Kingdom of Navarre
Kingdom of Aragon and its territories
Muslim territories

Oviedo
León
Burgos
Pamplona
Montpellier
Zaragoza
Toulouse
Lérida
Barcelona
Coimbra
COUNTY OF PROVENCE (TO ARAGON IN 1167–1246)
Lisbon
Toledo
Mérida
Valencia
Seville
Córdoba
Granada
Málaga

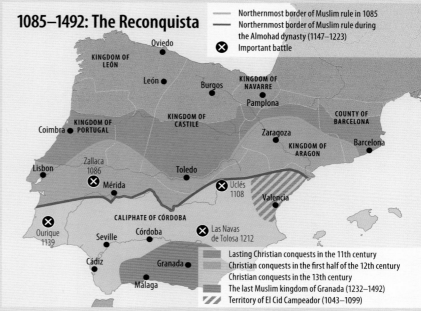

1085–1492: The Reconquista

Northernmost border of Muslim rule in 1085
Northernmost border of Muslim rule during the Almohad dynasty (1147–1223)
⊗ Important battle

KINGDOM OF LEÓN
Oviedo
León
Burgos
KINGDOM OF NAVARRE
Pamplona
KINGDOM OF PORTUGAL
Coimbra
KINGDOM OF CASTILE
Zaragoza
COUNTY OF BARCELONA
Barcelona
KINGDOM OF ARAGON
Lisbon
Zallaca 1086
Mérida
Toledo
Uclés 1108
Valencia
CALIPHATE OF CÓRDOBA
Ourique 1139
Seville
Córdoba
Las Navas de Tolosa 1212
Cádiz
Granada
Málaga

Lasting Christian conquests in the 11th century
Christian conquests in the first half of the 12th century
Christian conquests in the 13th century
The last Muslim kingdom of Granada (1232–1492)
Territory of El Cid Campeador (1043–1099)

912–961 The reign of Emir 'Abd ar-Rahman III, who rules nearly all of what is now Spain, marks the pinnacle of power in Córdoba.

929 The Caliphate of Córdoba is founded by 'Abd ar-Rahman III. Islamic culture flourishes.

1066 Jewish pogrom

1085 Following the Christian conquest, Toledo becomes the capital of the kingdom of Castile.

1094 Conquest of Valencia by the Castilian knight and national hero, El Cid Campeador (1043–1099)

1147 The Berber Almohad dynasty drives the Almoravids from Spain; they are defeated in Africa as well.

July 16, 1212 The Battle of Las Navas de Tolosa is a decisive victory of the Christians over the Almohads and a turning point in the Reconquista.

1213–1276 Jaime I of Aragon captures the *Baleares* (Balearic Islands) from the Moors.

1217–1252 Saint Ferdinand III of Castile and León conquers Córdoba (1236), Seville (1248) and Cádiz (1250): moderate Christianization policies

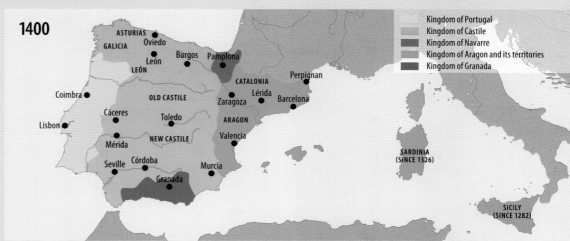

1400

Kingdom of Portugal
Kingdom of Castile
Kingdom of Navarre
Kingdom of Aragon and its territories
Kingdom of Granada

ASTURIAS
GALICIA
Oviedo
Burgos
León
Pamplona
CATALONIA
Perpignan
Coimbra
OLD CASTILE
Zaragoza
Lérida
Barcelona
Cáceres
Toledo
ARAGON
Lisbon
NEW CASTILE
Valencia
Mérida
Córdoba
Murcia
Seville
Granada
SARDINIA (SINCE 1326)
SICILY (SINCE 1282)

from 1237 The Nasrids in Granada are the last Arab and Muslim dynasty in western Europe; they gradually pay tribute to Castile.

1232–1492 The Alhambra is built in Granada.

1252–1284 Alfonso X the Wise of Castile and León unites Arab and Christian scholarship.

1282 Sicilian Vespers massacre: Rebellion against Charles I of Anjou. Peter III the Great of Aragon conquers Sicily.

Al-Andalus is the Arabic name for the region of the Iberian Peninsula that was ruled by Muslims from 711 to 1492. It was a period of cultural and intellectual blossoming in science, culture and irrigation technology, and was accompanied by great religious tolerance and asylum for oppressed Jews from other countries.

Spain in the 15th–18th Centuries

The Voyages of Columbus

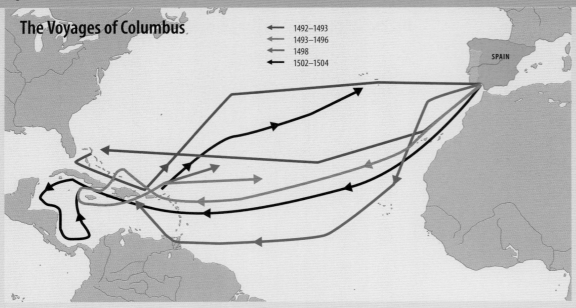

←	1492–1493
←	1493–1496
←	1498
←	1502–1504

SPAIN

16th–17th Centuries: Spain and the Habsburgs

- ░ Territory ruled by the Spanish branch of the Habsburg dynasty 1477–1581
- ▓ Spain under the rule of the Habsburg dynasty 1516–1700
- ░ Portugal as part of the kingdom of Spain 1580–1640

SPANISH NETHERLANDS (1482–1713)

LUXEMBOURG (1482–1684)

FREE COUNTY OF BURGUNDY (FRANCHE-COMTÉ, 1493–1678)

COUNTY OF CHAROLAIS

MILAN (1535–1706)

NAPLES (1516–1707)

KINGDOM OF PORTUGAL

KINGDOM OF SPAIN

SARDINIA (1516–1708)

BALEARIC ISLANDS

KINGDOM OF SICILY (1516–1713)

MELILLA (1497 UNTIL TODAY)

ORAN (1509–1708)

Burning of heretics convicted by the Spanish Inquisition

The Spanish Inquisition, a continuation of the medieval Papal Inquisition, was a period of brutal repression of "heretics" and people of other religions directly supervised by the Spanish kings (1478–1834). At first almost all of the accused were Jews (later Muslims) who had converted to Catholicism.

Auto-da-fé means "act of faith" and refers to elaborate public religious rituals involving sentencing and acts of penance performed while processing through the city; the burning at the stake sometimes associated with the *auto-da-fé* could only be carried out by secular authorities.

The Spanish Netherlands comprised the area of today's Low Countries (Belgium, Netherlands and Luxembourg). Beginning in 1482 it was ruled by the Habsburgs as heirs to the duchy of Burgundy, and from 1516 onward the area was under Spanish control. The growing tax burden and above all the lack of religious freedom in the northern, Protestant provinces led to conflict and the break with Spain. The southern Catholic provinces (today's Belgium) remained Spanish until 1713–1714.

The Battle of Lepanto The united fleets of the Holy League—comprised of Spain, Venice, Genoa, the papacy, the duchy of Savoy and the Knights Hospitaller (Maltese)—defeated the Ottomans in a naval battle in the Gulf of Patras on the west coast of Greece. They were led by Don Juan de Austria (John of Austria), an illegitimate son of Holy Roman Emperor Charles V. The victory prevented the Ottomans from gaining control of the Mediterranean, and protected Rome and large parts of Europe from further Ottoman incursions.

Spain Becomes a Great Power

In the 15th and 16th centuries, following the union of the kingdoms of Castile and Aragon, as well as Navarre at a later point in time, a new Catholic world power emerged. Spain and Portugal built empires in which the "sun never set." Under the Habsburgs, they appropriated gold and other valuable raw materials from the Americas, and evangelized the Philippines. Economic decline and state bankruptcy led to the loss of their position as a world power to the French and English.

1469 Union of Castile and Aragon through the marriage of Isabella I of Castile and Ferdinand II of Aragon (who are known as the Catholic Monarchs)

1478 Advent of the Spanish Inquisition and expulsion of the Jews from Spanish territory

Jan. 2, 1492 The Reconquista is complete with the conquest of the last Muslim emirate in Granada.

Oct. 12, 1492 Christopher Columbus reaches the Bahamas.

1494 Treaty of Tordesillas: The newly discovered lands overseas are divided between Spain and Portugal with the approval of Pope Alexander VI.

1506 Philip I the Fair of the House of Habsburg ascends the throne of Castile.

1512 Union of Castile and Navarre

1516 The kingdoms of Castile and Aragon are united after the death of King Ferdinand II. Charles I becomes king of Spain, and in 1519 is crowned Holy Roman Emperor Charles V.

1519–1522 In the service of Spain, Portuguese maritime explorer Ferdinand Magellan undertakes the first circumnavigation of the globe.

1521 Spanish conquistadors subjugate the Aztec Empire in Mexico and found Mexico City on the site of its capital.

1533–1539 Conquest of the Inca Empire in Peru

1556 Charles V abdicates: The Habsburg empire is divided between Austria (imperial line) and Spain.

1556–1598 Philip II is king of Spain. Spain becomes the leading Catholic world power.

1561 The Spanish royal court moves from Toledo to Madrid (the El Escorial complex).

1565 Spain conquers the Philippines, which are named after Philip II.

1571 The Battle of Lepanto: The Spanish achieve their first victory on the seas against the Ottomans.

The Battle of Lepanto in 1571

1588: Defeat of the Spanish Armada

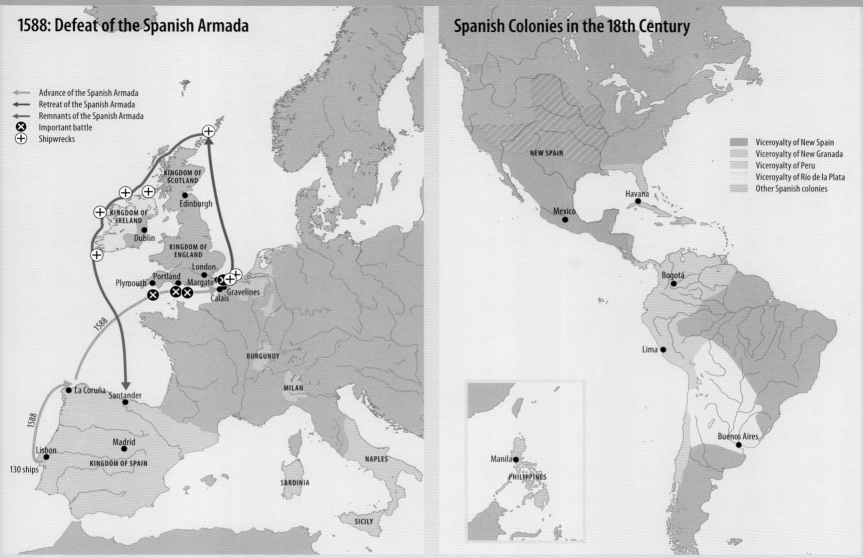

← Advance of the Spanish Armada
← Retreat of the Spanish Armada
← Remnants of the Spanish Armada
⊗ Important battle
⊕ Shipwrecks

KINGDOM OF SCOTLAND
Edinburgh
KINGDOM OF IRELAND
Dublin
KINGDOM OF ENGLAND
London
Plymouth
Portland
Margate
Gravelines
Calais
1588
BURGUNDY
MILAN
La Coruña
Santander
1588
Lisbon
Madrid
KINGDOM OF SPAIN
130 ships
NAPLES
SARDINIA
SICILY

Spanish Colonies in the 18th Century

NEW SPAIN
Mexico
Havana
Bogotá
Lima
Buenos Aires

Manila
PHILIPPINES

Viceroyalty of New Spain
Viceroyalty of New Granada
Viceroyalty of Peru
Viceroyalty of Río de la Plata
Other Spanish colonies

1580–1640 A personal union of the Spanish and Portuguese crowns follows the Portuguese dynastic crisis that left the Avis dynasty without an heir.

1581 The northern provinces of the Netherlands break with Spain and become the Republic of the Seven United Netherlands.

1588 An attempt to bring England back into the Roman Catholic sphere of influence ends with the destruction of the Spanish Armada. Spain loses its naval supremacy.

until 1627 Spain experiences several state bankruptcies and economic decline.

1648 End of the Thirty Years' War: The Peace of Westphalia recognizes Protestant equality and the United Netherlands.

1659 The Treaty of the Pyrenees ends further wars between Spain and France. Spain loses part of the southern Netherlands to France and cedes Jamaica to England.

1665–1700 The Spanish population is decimated (reduced to less than 6 million) under Charles II, and economic conditions are disastrous. The French king Louis XIV marries Philip's daughter, Maria Theresa, and thereby lays claim to the throne. With the death of Charles II in 1700, Habsburg rule in Spain comes to an end. The War of Spanish Succession begins.

1648: The Peace of Westphalia

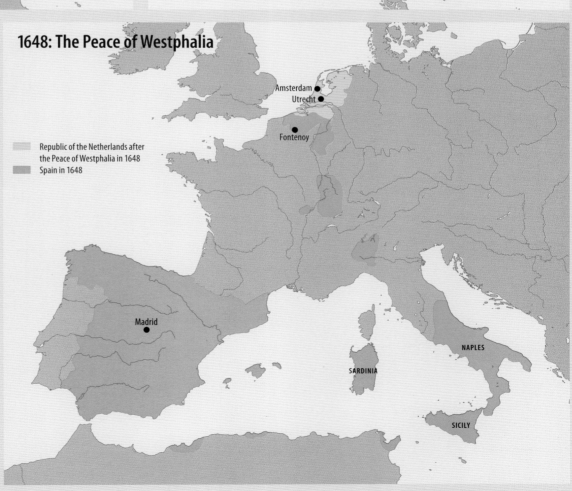

Amsterdam
Utrecht
Fontenoy

Republic of the Netherlands after the Peace of Westphalia in 1648
Spain in 1648

Madrid

NAPLES
SARDINIA
SICILY

Spain from the 18th Century to the Present

1713: Treaty of Utrecht

Territory belonging to the Habsburg Empire
Territory of the Savoys
Spanish territory (recognized as Bourbon)

NETHERLANDS
AUSTRIA
HUNGARY
SAVOY
PIEDMONT
MILAN
SPAIN
NAPLES (REVERTED TO SPAIN 1734)
SARDINIA (1713–1720 TO AUSTRIA, 1720 TO SAVOY)
SICILY (1713–1720 TO SAVOY, 1720–1734 TO AUSTRIA, 1734 BACK TO SPAIN)

1715: Spain and the House of Bourbon

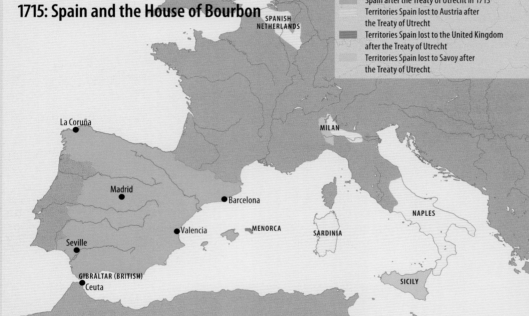

Spain after the Treaty of Utrecht in 1713
Territories Spain lost to Austria after the Treaty of Utrecht
Territories Spain lost to the United Kingdom after the Treaty of Utrecht
Territories Spain lost to Savoy after the Treaty of Utrecht

SPANISH NETHERLANDS
La Coruña
Madrid
Barcelona
MILAN
Seville
Valencia
MENORCA
SARDINIA
NAPLES
GIBRALTAR (BRITISH)
Ceuta
SICILY

1806–1814: The Napoleonic Wars

Spanish guerilla
British troops
French troops
Continental System since 1806
Important battle

UNITED KINGDOM OF GREAT BRITAIN AND IRELAND
Brest
Paris
FRANCE
Bordeaux
Lyon
La Coruña
San Sebastián
Bayonne
Toulouse
Vitoria 1813
Burgos
1814
Salamanca
PORTUGAL
Madrid
Zaragoza
Barcelona
Genoa
KINGDOM OF ITALY
CORSICA
KINGDOM OF NAPLES
Lisbon
SPAIN
Valencia
SARDINIA
Seville
Bailén
Trafalgar 1805
Cádiz
Granada
SICILY

After the Spanish War of Succession, the French House of Bourbon laid claim to the Spanish throne. Spain flourished, but was forced into costly wars with England. The Napoleonic and the Carlist Wars, the latter involving followers of the Infante Carlos, took place in the 19th century. The colonies in the Americas fought for their independence. Spain remained neutral in both World Wars and suffered from 1939–1975 under the fascist Franco regime. Juan Carlos I ascended the throne in 1975 and made possible the transition to a democratic system. Within the young constitutional monarchy, various regions fought for independence—and continue to do so—including the Basque country and Catalonia.

1700–1713 Spanish War of Succession over Austrian and French claims. The House of Bourbon is awarded the throne in the Treaty of Utrecht (1713). The southern Netherlands and parts of Italy go to the Habsburg Empire. Economic recovery ensues, but Spain has to wage two wars against England in 1761–1762 and 1780–1783.

1700–1746 Philip V, grandson of the Sun King, becomes the first Bourbon king of Spain.

1759–1788 *Despotismo ilustrado* ("enlightened despotism") under Charles III: His reign is a period of major achievements in modernization and settlement policy.

1767 Charles III orders the expulsion of the Jesuits from Spain and from the Spanish colonies in the Americas.

1792–1808 María Luisa, wife of Charles IV, who reigned as king from 1788–1808, procures the position of prime minister for her lover, Manuel de Godoy. His policies lead Spain into war with France and then, allied with France, against England.

1796 Second Treaty of San Ildefonso: Spain and France enter into an alliance against Great Britain.

1805 Battle of Trafalgar: The Spanish-French fleet is defeated by the British.

Battle of Trafalgar on October 21, 1805

1808–1812 The Spanish War of Independence. Aided by the British, the Spanish fight to oust the French from their territory.

1808–1813 Period of the Napoleonic Wars. As a special favor, Napoleon names his brother, Joseph Bonaparte, king of Spain. The Spaniards fight a bloody guerilla war "to the finish." The British Duke of Wellington decisively defeats the French in Vitoria, and Spain becomes an independent nation.

from 1810 The Spanish colonies in the Americas fight for their independence.

The Carlist Wars were a series of civil wars between absolutist-Catholic traditionalists, who supported Don Carlos, the pretender to the throne following the death of Ferdinand VII, and supporters of liberalism (and later republicanism). Don Carlos was the brother of Ferdinand VII. While progressive forces revolted against conservative governments throughout Europe around 1850, conservatives and clerics in support of Don Carlos fought against the liberal government of his niece, Isabella II.

1814 The Bourbons return to the Spanish throne when Ferdinand VII is crowned king after Napoleon's defeat.

1814–1833 Reactionary, clerical regime of Ferdinand VII

1833–1873 The Carlist Wars between traditionalists and modernists

1873–1874 The First Republic: coup and restoration of the monarchy

1898 The Spanish-American War: Spain loses Cuba, Puerto Rico, Guam and the Philippines to the United States, retaining only small settlements in Africa.

1912 Morocco is divided into French and Spanish protectorates.

1914–1918 Spain remains neutral in World War I.

1923–1930 King Alfonso XIII tolerates the dictatorship of General Primo de Rivera.

1926 Suppression of the Moroccan nationalist movement

1931 The Second Republic emerges under President Alcala-Zamora. Catalonia, Galicia and the Basque country are granted autonomy.

1936 Start of the Spanish Civil War: A socialist coalition of the PSOE, the Republican left and others wins elections. The radical right and part of the military revolt under the leadership of General Francisco Franco (1892–1975).

1937 The German Condor Legion bombs Guernica, a harbinger of the coming air war.

1939 With the support of Italy and Germany, Franco conquers Barcelona and Madrid. The Republic is defeated, and Franco establishes a Falangist (fascist) dictatorship with himself as *caudillo* (leader).

1940 Despite its alliances with Germany and Italy, Spain remains neutral in World War II.

1956 The Spanish protectorate in Morocco attains independence.

1958 The Ifni War: Moroccan rebels threaten to take over Spanish West Africa.

1975 Death of Franco: Juan Carlos I, a Bourbon and the grandson of King Alfonso XIII, ascends the throne, ushering in a gradual return to democracy.

1978 Parliamentary monarchy

1979 The Basque country and Catalonia are granted limited autonomy.

1981 Colonel Antonio Tejero and others in the military attempt a coup. They occupy parliament but the coup fails, especially because Juan Carlos opposes it.

1982 Spain becomes a member of NATO.

1986 Spain becomes a member of the European Union.

Spanish Civil War When military leaders, conservative nationalists and fascist (Falangist) circles rebelled against the young Republic in 1936, this marked the beginning of a long and bloody civil war. Volunteers from many countries were the only ones to fight on the side of the Republic, whereas Italy and Germany supplied the rebels with weapons and regularly dispatched military units on their behalf. After the Republicans were defeated, Franco established his dictatorship. The Franco regime settled accounts with Republicans and Socialists in a bloody manner, leading to the deaths of over 100,000 people.

1936–1939: Civil War

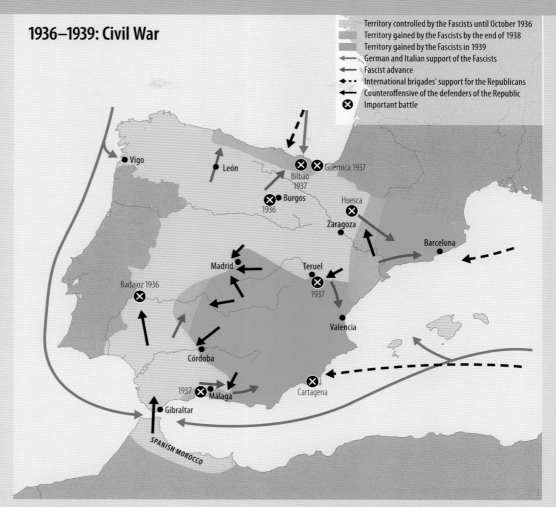

Territory controlled by the Fascists until October 1936
Territory gained by the Fascists by the end of 1938
Territory gained by the Fascists in 1939
German and Italian support of the Fascists
Fascist advance
International brigades' support for the Republicans
Counteroffensive of the defenders of the Republic
Important battle

Spain Today

Portugal

1147–1300: Autonomy

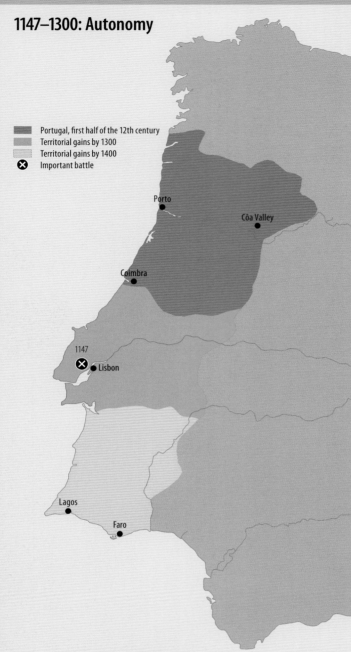

Portugal, first half of the 12th century
Territorial gains by 1300
Territorial gains by 1400
⊗ Important battle

Porto

Côa Valley

Coimbra

1147
⊗ Lisbon

Lagos

Faro

During the Reconquista, the autonomous kingdom of Portugal took shape in the western part of the Iberian Peninsula. Thanks to its discoveries in the 15th and 16th centuries, it became a great colonial power; in fact, Portugal was a worldwide naval power prior to Spanish dominion of the seas. In the following centuries, a lack of economic development caused Portugal and Spain to lose their powerful positions. This was especially true of Portugal, since a large portion of the upper class and finally even the king himself left the country to make their fortunes in Brazil. In the 20th century, the country was shaped by decades of dictatorship. When dictatorship ended, Portugal quickly became a democracy and a member state of the European Union.

1071–1095 During the course of the Reconquista, the duchy of Portugal secedes from Galicia.

1143 The kingdom of Portugal becomes an independent state. Alfonso I assumes the title of king.

1250 The Algarves, also known as the district of Faro, become the southernmost part of the kingdom. As of 1256, Lisbon is its capital.

1427 The Portuguese discover the Amazon.

1487–1488 Bartolomeu Diaz sails around the Cape of Good Hope at the southern tip of Africa.

1495–1521 Portugal is at the zenith of her trading and maritime power under King Manuel I the Fortunate.

1498 Vasco da Gama reaches the coast of India.

1500 Pedro Álvares Cabral discovers Brazil.

1578 King Sebastian I dies, along with the majority of his army, in an attempt to conquer Morocco for Christendom. He becomes a mythical figure for the nation, and many legends about him arise.

1580–1640 Personal union of the Spanish and Portuguese crowns after the Avis dynasty, which had ruled since 1383, fails to produce an heir.

1640 Renewal of Portuguese independence: With the support of England, John IV of the

Braganca dynasty ascends the throne. The Brangancas rule until 1853.

1658–1663 The Netherlands occupies the Portuguese Moluccas and Ceylon.

1750 King Joseph I and his minister, the Marquis of Pombal: period of enlightened despotism, urban construction projects and the reduction of ecclesiastical power.

1755 A great earthquake destroys Lisbon, and Pombal has it built anew in modern style.

1759 Expulsion of the Jesuit order from Portugal and Brazil

1807 Napoleon's army conquers Portugal, and the royal family escapes to Brazil.

The Marquis of Pombal (1699-1782)

1500–1600: Portuguese Colonies

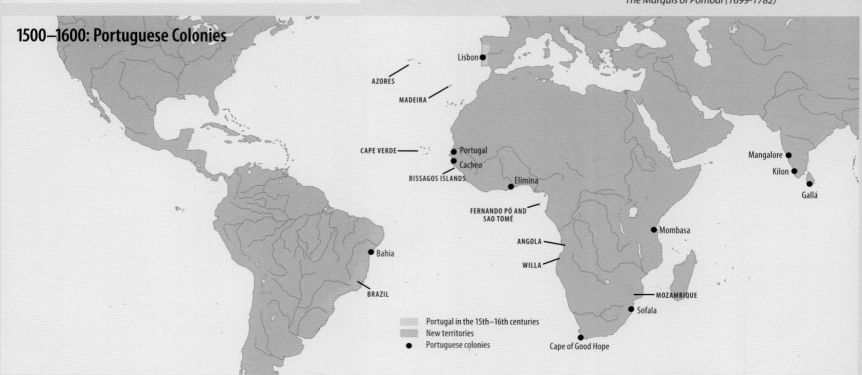

Lisbon

AZORES

MADEIRA

CAPE VERDE

Portugal
Cacheo

BISSAGOS ISLANDS

Elimina

Mangalore

Kilon

Gallá

FERNANDO PÓ AND
SAO TOMÉ

Mombasa

ANGOLA

WILLA

Bahia

BRAZIL

MOZAMBIQUE

Sofala

Cape of Good Hope

Portugal in the 15th–16th centuries
New territories
● Portuguese colonies

1808–1811 The country is liberated from the French with the assistance of England.

1821 King John VI returns from exile in Brazil, but his son, Pedro, remains there and is at the vanguard of the movement for Brazilian independence.

1822 Portugal officially recognizes Brazilian independence.

1846–1847 An uprising against the dictatorship of Prime Minister Costa Cabral fails.

1853–1910 The royal House of Saxe-Coburg-Gotha rules Portugal.

1910 The monarchy is overthrown and the First Republic declared.

1916 Portugal enters World War I on the side of the Triple Entente.

1926 The republic is overthrown in a coup and a military dictatorship is established.

1928 Antonio de Oliveira Salazar is minister of finance. A new constitution in 1933 initiates the *Estado Novo*, or New State. Salazar is prime minister and establishes a dictatorship.

1939 The country remains neutral during World War II.

1968 Salazar suffers a serious stroke that ends his rule. Marcelo Caetano carries on the dictatorship.

1974–1976 A military coup and the subsequent Carnation Revolution end Caetano's dictatorship; Portugal transitions to democracy.

1975 All Portuguese colonies, with the exception of Macao, win hard-fought independence.

1986 Portugal joins the European Union.

The Carnation Revolution After the death of Antonio de Oliveira Salazar in 1970, the dictatorship did not last long. The country was worn out from long-standing wars with its overseas colonies. In April 1974 a group of officers carried out a military coup d'état, and over the next two years a peaceful transition to democracy took place. Known as the Carnation Revolution, it was named after the flowers on the soldiers' weapons. It ended with the adoption of a new constitution and democratic elections.

Angola and Mozambique The Carnation Revolution made it possible for the African colonies of Mozambique and Angola to gain their independence. In response to independence movements, Portugal had for decades perpetrated terrible massacres through the use of mercenaries. While Mozambique became independent in June 1975, an intermittent civil war broke out in Angola that lasted from 1975–2002. It began immediately after Angola's independence from Portugal and quickly expanded into a proxy war between the Eastern Bloc and NATO. Later on, it would turn into an internal Angolan conflict.

Portugal Today

1700–1800: Portuguese Colonies

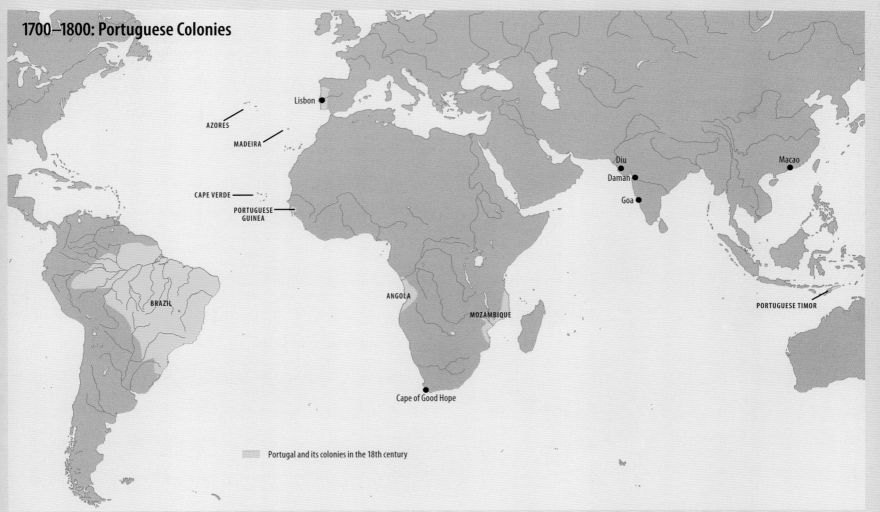

Portugal and its colonies in the 18th century

Italy Until the 14th Century

800–500 BCE: Pre-Roman Italy

CELTS

Hauslabjoch, Ötztal Alps

CELTS

RAETI

Val Camonica

VENETI

Mantua

LIGURIAN TRIBES

Placentia (Piacenza)

Massalia (Marseille)

Nicaea (Nice)

Faesulae (Fiesole)

Arretium

PICENER

Cortona

Volterra

Perugia

UMBRI

VESTINI

Populonia

Vetulonia

FRENTANI

Saturnia

Vulci

SABINES

Tarquinia

Veie

Caere

Roma

LATINS

VOLSCI

AUSONES

AURUNCI

SAMNITES

IAPYGES

Taras (Taranto)

Aleria

Neapolis

LUCANI

Metapontum

Gallipolis

SARDINIANS

Krothon

Caralis

Nora

Messina

Palermo

Tyndaris

Mozia

SICANI

Imera

SICELS

Akragas (Agrigento)

Syracusae

Utica

Carthago

← Celtic conquests (6th–4th centuries BCE)
Location of Ötzi the Iceman mummy

- Area of Greek influence
- Area of Etruscan influence
- Territory of the ancient Italic peoples
- Area of Carthaginian influence
- Villanovan culture (900 BCE)

7th Century: The Lombards and Byzantines

BAVARIA

Mediolanum (Milan)

Opitergium

FRANCIA

Padova

Pavia

Mantua

Pula

Ravenna

Pisa

Perugia

Spoleto

Rome

Barium (Bari)

Beneventum

Naples

Tarentum (Taranto)

Brundisium (Brindisi)

Amalfi

Caralis

Regium (Reggio)

Palermo

Syracuse

- Byzantine territory in 603
- Lombard territory in 603
- Lombard territory conquered during reign of King Agilulf (590–616)
- Lombard territory conquered during reign of King Rothari (636–652)

27 BCE–14 CE: Roman Provinces in the Age of Augustus

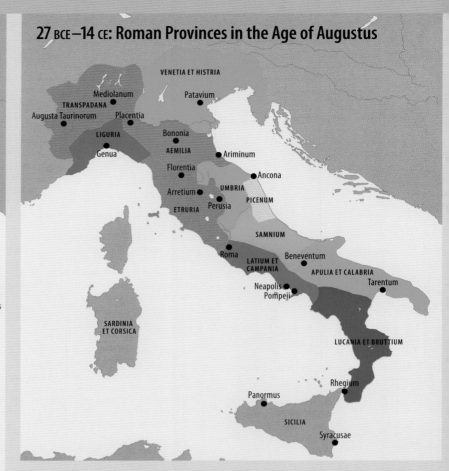

VENETIA ET HISTRIA

Mediolanum

Patavium

TRANSPADANA

Augusta Taurinorum

Placentia

LIGURIA

Bononia

Genua

AEMILIA

Ariminum

Florentia

Ancona

Arretium

UMBRIA

PICENUM

Perusia

ETRURIA

SAMNIUM

Roma

LATIUM ET CAMPANIA

Beneventum

APULIA ET CALABRIA

Neapolis

Pompeji

Tarentum

SARDINIA ET CORSICA

LUCANIA ET BRUTTIUM

Panormus

Rhegium

SICILIA

Syracusae

In pre-Roman times (753 BCE), northern Italy was under Etruscan influence, while southern Italy and Sicily were controlled by the Greeks. Italic tribes lived in central Italy, but nowhere else. In the wake of subjugation by Rome, Italy extended from the foothills of the Alps all the way to Istria. After the fall of the Roman Empire, Ostrogoths and Byzantines expanded into the country. Under the successors of Charlemagne, a separate kingdom developed in northern and central Italy that, with the exception of Venice, belonged to the Holy Roman Empire from the tenth century onward. As trade and transportation expanded in the 11th century, northern Italian cities became increasingly independent; their affiliation with the Holy Roman Empire was more of a formality than a political reality.

~8000 BCE Petroglyphs in Valcamonica are dated to this period.

~3400 BCE Age of Ötzi the Iceman, rediscovered in a glacier in 1991.

~1000–500 BCE Time of the Villanova (Iron Age) culture in Tuscany; they are predecessors of the Etruscans.

753 BCE The legendary founding of Rome: beginning of the Roman Empire under the Etruscan monarchs, Romulus and Remus

509 BCE Fall of the Etruscans: The last king, Tarquinius Superbus, is driven out of Rome. This marks the beginning of the Roman Republic.

387 BCE The Gauls invade Italy. The ancient Italic people are subject to Rome.

343–275 BCE Roman expansion throughout Italy

202 BCE With their victory over Carthage in the Second Punic War, the Romans establish their supremacy in the western Mediterranean.

49 BCE Julius Caesar crosses the Rubicon at Arminium in defiance of the Roman senate. This act marks the start of Caesar's unrivaled leadership in the Roman world.

45–44 BCE Caesar's dictatorship: Rome controls the Mediterranean.

27 BCE–14 CE Beginning of the Principate: Octavianus Augustus is the first Roman emperor.

64 CE Rome burns under Emperor Nero.

79 Mount Vesuvius erupts, destroying Pompeii.

138–161 The reign of Antoninus Pius; commerce and culture flourish.

270–275 Emperor Aurelian has a new wall built around Rome.

313 Constantine issues the Edict of Milan: Christians are given the same rights as those of other religions within the Roman Empire.

379–395 Emperor Theodosius: Christianity becomes the state religion.

410 The Visigoths, led by Alaric I, conquer Rome.

455 Vandals conquer and plunder Rome.

ca. 1000: Italy in the Middle Ages

Border of the territory theoretically belonging to the Papal States

Border of the Holy Roman Empire around 1034

Territory of the Italian kingdom
March of Verona
Territory dependent on the Byzantine Empire
Papal States
Byzantine territory
Lombard duchies
Arabs (in Sicily since 827)

12th–13th Centuries: Italy under Hohenstaufen Rule

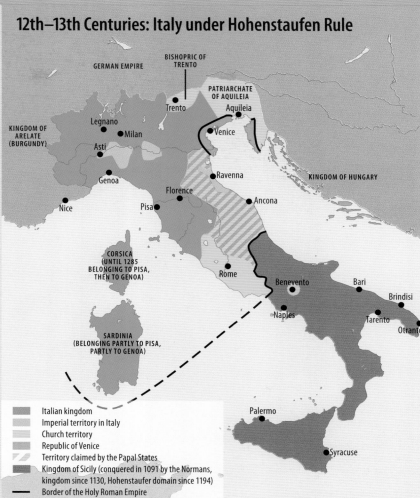

Italian kingdom
Imperial territory in Italy
Church territory
Republic of Venice
Territory claimed by the Papal States
Kingdom of Sicily (conquered in 1091 by the Normans, kingdom since 1130, Hohenstaufer domain since 1194)
Border of the Holy Roman Empire

476 Romulus Augustulus, the last Western Roman emperor, is deposed by the Germanic military commander Odoacer.

489–493 Theoderic the Great, leader of the Ostrogoths, conquers Italy and briefly establishes the Ostrogothic empire.

535–562 Italy is partially controlled by the Byzantines.

568 The Lombards invade from Pannonia. Italy breaks up into several small duchies.

754–756 In return for making his coronation possible, the Frankish king Pippin III gives territories in northern Italy to the pope; these are the origin of the Papal States.

774 Charlemagne conquers the Lombards; the Franks conquer northern Italy.

827 Islamic conquest of Sicily

1030–1091 The Normans conquer southern Italy and Sicily.

1130 The Kingdom of Sicily is founded by the Norman king Roger II. It exists until 1860.

1176 Battle of Legnano: The Lombard League is victorious over Emperor Frederick I Barbarossa.

1194–1266 Hohenstaufen rule in the Kingdom of Sicily

~1200–1400 Ongoing war between the Guelfs and the Ghibellines, supporters of the pope and the Holy Roman emperor respectively, creates a state of chronic unrest in northern Italy for almost two centuries.

1266 Battle of Benevento: The French Angevin dynasty seizes power in the Kingdom of Sicily.

1282 Sicilian Vespers: The Angevins are massacred and expelled from Sicily, and southern Italy is partitioned. King Peter III of Aragon is crowned Peter I of Sicily. The Angevins rule the Kingdom of Naples until 1442.

1324–1326 Aragon conquers Sardinia.

14th Century: Italian City-States and Signorias

Church domains
Territory claimed by the Papal States
Border of the Holy Roman Empire

The Roman Republic (509–27 BCE) Power was held by state officials who were elected annually by popular assembly. Later on, the Senate had the greatest influence. All senior officials of the Roman state were given a seat in the Senate at the end of their term in office. Early on there were around 300 members, and in Caesar's time, up to 900.

Dictator In the period of the Roman Republic, political appointments were only made in times of crisis, such as war, or political turmoil, and came with extensive powers that were limited to a maximum of

six months. Toward the end of the Republic, Sulla and Caesar were able to extend their dictatorial tenure.

The Principate was the name of the first post-Republic Roman state, which comes from the Latin word *princeps*, meaning "first" or "principal." The Princeps was a de facto autocratic ruler, although much effort was expended to create the public impression that he was "first among equals." The Republic still formally existed.

253

Italy in the 15th–18th Centuries

After 1454: Creation of Italian Regional States

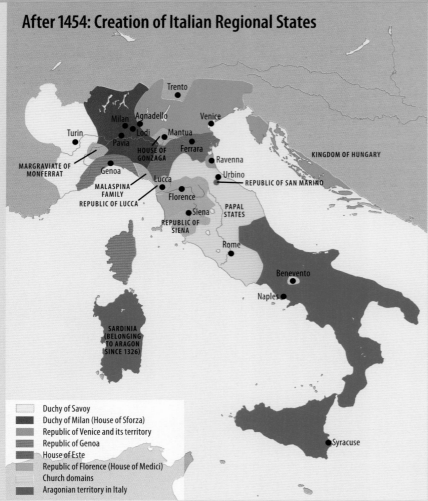

Legend:
- Duchy of Savoy
- Duchy of Milan (House of Sforza)
- Republic of Venice and its territory
- Republic of Genoa
- House of Este
- Republic of Florence (House of Medici)
- Church domains
- Aragonian territory in Italy

After 1559: Spanish Dominance in Italy

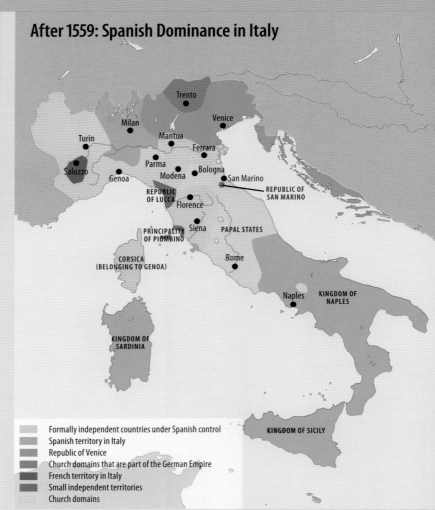

Legend:
- Formally independent countries under Spanish control
- Spanish territory in Italy
- Republic of Venice
- Church domains that are part of the German Empire
- French territory in Italy
- Small independent territories
- Church domains

After 1637: Increasing Influence of the French

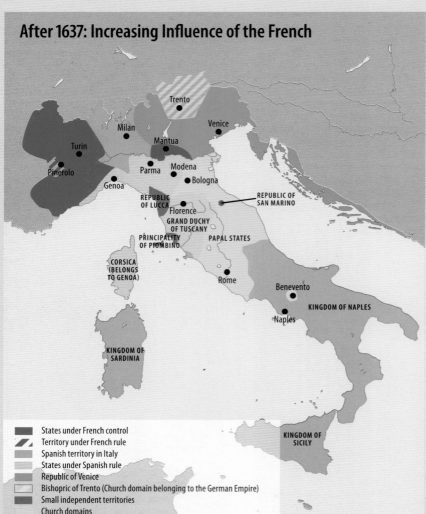

Legend:
- States under French control
- Territory under French rule
- Spanish territory in Italy
- States under Spanish rule
- Republic of Venice
- Bishopric of Trento (Church domain belonging to the German Empire)
- Small independent territories
- Church domains

After 1494, Italy became a pawn in the games played by the larger powers surrounding it, namely Spain, France and the Austrian Empire.

1442 Aragon conquers the Kingdom of Naples.

1454 The Peace of Lodi spells the end of longstanding clashes between the regional states, leading to equilibrium in Italy and several decades of peace.

1469–1492 Lorenzo de' Medici is ruler of the Florentine Republic. His reign is a period of cultural flowering, even as the economic situation in Florence deteriorates.

1494 French King Charles VIII launches a military campaign against Italy, beginning a phase in which the great powers meddle in Italian politics. The next half-century is marked by violent conflicts between foreign powers and great suffering for the people of Italy.

1509 Battle of Agnadello: The League of Cambrai is victorious over Venice, ending its supremacy among the Italian regional states.

1525 Battle of Pavia: Milan falls under Spanish control.

1527 The Spanish plunder Rome.

1559 The Peace of Cateau-Cambrésis: Italy ends the long struggle between France and Spain for dominance of Italy; the Spanish Habsburgs control most of Italy for the next 150 years.

1627 Mantua comes under the control of the French Gonzaga-Nevers family.

1631–1696 Pinerolo is occupied by France.

1713–1714 End of the War of the Spanish Succession, Treaties of Utrecht and Rastatt: Spain cedes Lombardy, Naples and Sardinia to Austria.

1720 In an agreement with Austria, the duke of Savoy exchanges Sicily for Sardinia.

1735 and 1738 Austria cedes Naples and Sicily to Spain.

1768 The Republic of Genoa sells the island of Corsica to France.

1796–1799 Napoleon subjugates Italy, and the vassal states are formed.

Signorias and regional states in Italy

During the 14th and 15th centuries, regional states arose through the expansion of the strongest city-states or out of dominions ruled by powerful families. The term *signoria* comes from the Italian word *signore*, meaning "lord." The Republic of Florence, the Duchy of Milan, the Duchy of Savoy, the Papal States and the Republic of Venice shared political power through varying coalitions. Since regional states were self-

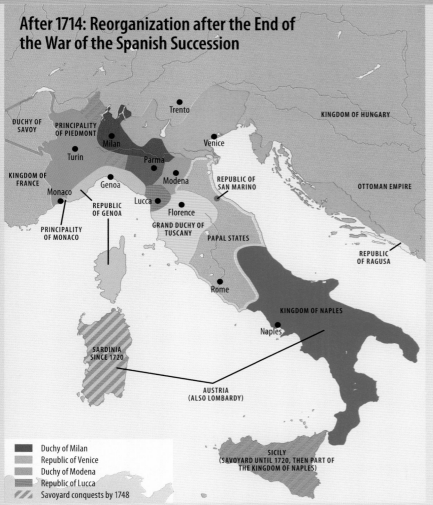

After 1714: Reorganization after the End of the War of the Spanish Succession

DUCHY OF SAVOY
PRINCIPALITY OF PIEDMONT
Trento
Milan
Turin
Parma
KINGDOM OF FRANCE
Monaco
Genoa
Modena
Lucca
Venice
KINGDOM OF HUNGARY
REPUBLIC OF SAN MARINO
OTTOMAN EMPIRE
PRINCIPALITY OF MONACO
REPUBLIC OF GENOA
Florence
GRAND DUCHY OF TUSCANY
PAPAL STATES
REPUBLIC OF RAGUSA
Rome
KINGDOM OF NAPLES
Naples
SARDINIA SINCE 1720
AUSTRIA (ALSO LOMBARDY)
SICILY (SAVOYARD UNTIL 1720, THEN PART OF THE KINGDOM OF NAPLES)

- Duchy of Milan
- Republic of Venice
- Duchy of Modena
- Republic of Lucca
- Savoyard conquests by 1748

1796: Incursion by the French

FRENCH REPUBLIC
KINGDOM OF SARDINIA
Milan
Turin
VENETO
Venice
KINGDOM OF HUNGARY
CISALPINE REPUBLIC
Parma
Genoa
DUCHY OF PARMA
Lucca
REPUBLIC OF SAN MARINO
DALMATIA (BELONGING TO AUSTRIA)
OTTOMAN EMPIRE
REPUBLIC OF GENOA
Florenz
REPUBLIC OF LUCCA
GRAND DUCHY OF TUSCANY
CORSICA (FRENCH SINCE 1768)
PAPAL STATES
Rome
REPUBLIC OF RAGUSA
KINGDOM OF SARDINIA
Naples
KINGDOM OF NAPLES

- Territory of the Kingdom of Sardinia
- States dependent on or allied with France

governing, Savoy, Milan and Florence were only nominal members of the Holy Roman Empire.

Lorenzo de' Medici (1449–1492), called *il Magnifico* (the Magnificent), was probably the most famous ruler of the Italian Renaissance. After the conclusion of the Peace of Lodi in 1454, his political skills made long-term peace in Italy possible. As signore of Florence, he promoted the greatest artists

Battle of Malplaquet during the War of the Spanish Succession (1701–1714)

Lorenzo de 'Medici (Agnolo Bronzino School)

and humanists of his time, including Sandro Botticelli, Michelangelo and the philosopher Marsilio Ficino.

Spanish domination After the death of King Ferdinand of Naples in 1494, the

major European powers—in particular France, the Spanish Habsburg states and the Holy Roman Empire of the German Nation—began to intervene in Italian affairs. Italy became the scene of numerous battles and wars in which the Italian regional states gradually lost their independence to Spain. Only the Republic of Venice remained free of Spanish control.

The vassal states The so-called "export of revolution" in the wake of the French Revolution affected almost all of Italy. Thus, the first daughter republics were formed by Napoleon, including the Cisalpine, Ligurian, Parthenopean and Roman republics. The French vassal monarchies of Etruria, Naples and the Kingdom of Italy emerged subsequently.

The League of Cambrai was a military alliance formed in 1508 by the Holy Roman emperor and the French king. The pope, Spain, Hungary and the smaller Italian states (Mantua, Ferrara, Urbino), among others, concluded the pact in order to prevent the Republic of Venice from dominating the Apennine Peninsula.

1799: The French Vassal States

REPUBLIC OF PIEDMONT
CISALPINE REPUBLIC
Milan
VENETO (TO AUSTRIA)
Venice
KINGDOM OF HUNGARY
FRENCH REPUBLIC
Turin
DUCHY OF PARMA
Parma
Genoa
LIGURIAN REPUBLIC
Lucca
Florence
REPUBLIC OF SAN MARINO
OTTOMAN EMPIRE
DALMATIA
TUSCANY (TO FRANCE)
ELBA (FRENCH)
ROMAN REPUBLIC
CORSICA (FRENCH)
Rome
NEAPOLITAN REPUBLIC (JANUARY–JUNE 1799)
KINGDOM OF SARDINIA
Naples
KINGDOM OF SICILY

- States dependent on or allied with France

Italy Until Unification in 1861

1805: Italian States under French Rule

HELVETIC REPUBLIC

RHODANIC REPUBLIC 1802

PIEDMONT

FRENCH REPUBLIC

Turin
Milan
Marengo
Genoa
LIGURIAN REPUBLIC

DUCHY OF PARMA
Parma

CISALPINE REPUBLIC

VENETO (TO AUSTRIA)
Venice

KINGDOM OF HUNGARY

REPUBLIC OF SAN MARINO

DALMATIA

Florence

KINGDOM OF ETRURIA (SINCE 1801)

ELBA (FRENCH)

PAPAL STATES

Rome

CORSICA (FRENCH)

KINGDOM OF SARDINIA

Naples

KINGDOM OF THE TWO SICILIES

States dependent on or allied with France

1806: All of Italy under French Influence

SWITZERLAND

RHODANIC REPUBLIC 1803–1810

FRENCH EMPIRE

KINGDOM OF BAVARIA

AUSTRIAN EMPIRE

KINGDOM OF ITALY

KINGDOM OF HUNGARY

Lucca

PRINCIPALITY OF LUCCA AND PIOMBINO

REPUBLIC OF SAN MARINO

OTTOMAN EMPIRE

DALMATIA (TO THE KINGDOM OF ITALY)

Florence
KINGDOM OF ETRURIA

ELBA (FRENCH)

PAPAL STATES

Rome

CORSICA (FRENCH)

KINGDOM OF SARDINIA

Naples

KINGDOM OF NAPLES

KINGDOM OF SICILY

States dependent on or allied with France

1810: The Napoleonic Division of Italy

KINGDOM OF BAVARIA

AUSTRIAN EMPIRE

KINGDOM OF HUNGARY

KINGDOM OF ITALY

ILLYRIAN PROVINCES

FRENCH EMPIRE

OTTOMAN EMPIRE

PRINCIPALITY OF LUCCA

Florence

REPUBLIC OF SAN MARINO

CORSICA (FRENCH)

PRINCIPALITY OF PIOMBINO

Rome

KINGDOM OF SARDINIA

Naples

KINGDOM OF NAPLES

KINGDOM OF SICILY

■ French territory

1815: After the Congress of Vienna

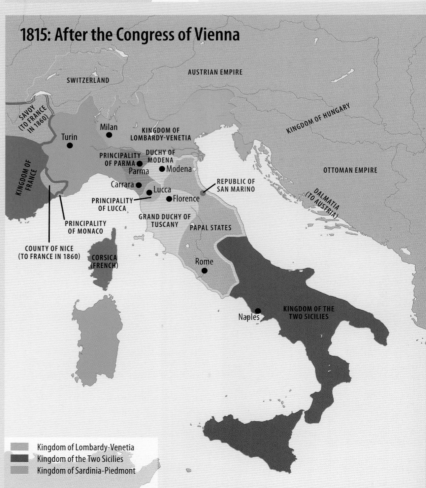

SWITZERLAND

AUSTRIAN EMPIRE

SAVOY (TO FRANCE IN 1860)

Turin
Milan

KINGDOM OF LOMBARDY-VENETIA

KINGDOM OF HUNGARY

KINGDOM OF FRANCE

PRINCIPALITY OF PARMA
Parma

DUCHY OF MODENA
Modena

Carrara

REPUBLIC OF SAN MARINO

OTTOMAN EMPIRE

DALMATIA (TO AUSTRIA)

Lucca
Florence

PRINCIPALITY OF LUCCA

PRINCIPALITY OF MONACO

GRAND DUCHY OF TUSCANY

PAPAL STATES

COUNTY OF NICE (TO FRANCE IN 1860)

CORSICA (FRENCH)

Rome

Naples

KINGDOM OF THE TWO SICILIES

☐ Kingdom of Lombardy-Venetia
■ Kingdom of the Two Sicilies
■ Kingdom of Sardinia-Piedmont

After the Congress of Vienna, as always, the princes of Italy strove for power, whereas revolutionary forces no longer saw Napoleon as a despot, but as an anti-absolutist ruler. The *Risorgimento* ("resurgence") that followed led to the unification of Italy.

1800 Battle of Marengo (Piedmont): France is victorious over Austria.

1801 The grand duchy of Tuscany becomes the Kingdom of Etruria.

1805 Emergence of the "French" Kingdom of Italy, which includes Venice

1806 Napoleon's brother Joseph becomes king of Naples.

1808 The French annex the Papal States and Etruria (Tuscany).

1814–1815 Collapse of Napoleonic rule in Italy

1815 The Congress of Vienna and the reorganization of Italy: Austria receives Veneto and Lombardy. The Papal States and the grand duchy of Tuscany are reestablished. Genoa goes to the Kingdom of Sardinia-Piedmont.

1834 In Marseilles, Guiseppe Mazzini founds the *Giovine Italia* ("Young Italy") political movement.

1848–1849 First War of Italian Independence

1859 Second War of Italian Independence

after 1861 The Kingdom of Italy

1848–1849 Sardinia-Piedmont is defeated by Austrian field marshal J.W. Radetzky in the first War of Italian Independence.

February–July 1849 Revolution in Rome; the Roman Republic under Giuseppe Mazzini is proclaimed. The pope calls on Catholic countries for help, and the republic is quickly crushed by the French army.

May–June 1859 The Second War of Italian Independence, also called the Sardinian War: Lombardy falls to Sardinia-Piedmont after Piedmontese prime minister Cavour's victory over Austria.

March 1860 The Habsburg territories of Emilia and Tuscany pass referenda on union with the Kingdom of Sardinia-Piedmont. Savoy is ceded to France in return for its support.

May–October 1860 Expedition of the Thousand and conquest of southern Italy on October 21st. Plebiscite on the annexation of the Kingdom of the Two Sicilies to the Kingdom of Italy.

March 17, 1861 The Kingdom of Italy is proclaimed.

After 1861: The Kingdom of Italy

1848–1849: The First Italian War of Independence

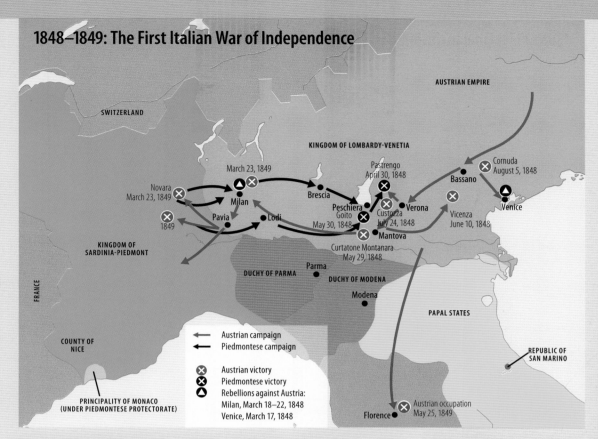

1859: The Second Italian War of Independence

Giuseppe Mazzini (1805–1872) was an Italian freedom fighter, philosopher and politician. He became politically active in the 1830s while living in exile. As a democrat, he opposed the unification of Italy under the Piedmontese monarchy that was pushed through between 1859 and 1861, and was persecuted. While he did not participate in Garibaldi's expedition to Sicily in 1860, that action has been called "Mazzini's gift,"

as it was based in part on plans Mazzini had devised years earlier. He was arrested and imprisoned in 1870 for his participation in an attempt to free Sicily. His last years were spent under a false name in Pisa.

Giuseppe Garibaldi (1807–1882) was an Italian freedom fighter, charismatic revolutionary and national hero. In 1849 he distinguished himself as a leader by defending the

short-lived Roman Republic. After it was defeated, he fled abroad. In 1860 he made his greatest contribution to the unification of Italy during the "Expedition of the Thousand." In 1862 and 1867, against the will of his own government, he attempted to free the Papal States in central Italy and to make Rome the capital of the Kingdom of Italy. However, the Italian and French governments prevented him from doing so.

Expedition of the Thousand On May 6, 1860, more than a thousand "Red Shirt" volunteers embarked from Genoa under the command of Giuseppe Garibaldi. They landed in Sicily on May 11 and finally brought down the Bourbon monarchy (the Kingdom of the Two Sicilies). On October 26, Garibaldi handed over the conquered territories to King Victor Emmanuel II at a meeting that took place in Naples .

The Risorgimento (1815–1870) is the term given to the political unification of historically and politically different regions on the Italian peninsula. The term also represents an epoch in Italian cultural history.

Carbonari ("charcoal burners") were secret societies of Italian patriots founded after 1815. The name and some of their practices (obedience, secrecy, hierarchical structure) were adopted from the charcoal selling trade.

Italy 1866 to the Present

1866–1870: Final Inclusion of Veneto and the Papal States

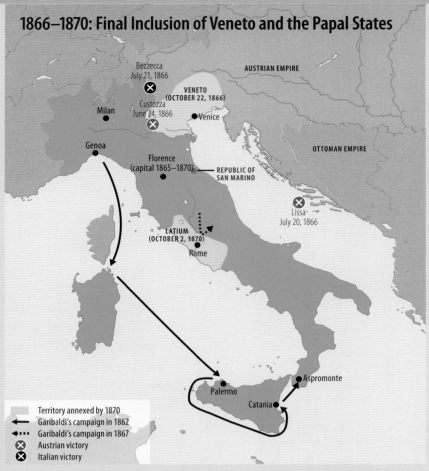

Legend:
- Territory annexed by 1870
- ← Garibaldi's campaign in 1862
- ◄···· Garibaldi's campaign in 1867
- ⊗ Austrian victory
- ⊗ Italian victory

After World War I

Legend:
- Italy before World War I
- Territory annexed after World War I
- —— Italian front on October 24, 1917
- —— Italian front at the end of 1917
- —— Italian front on November 4, 1918

During World War II

Legend:
- Resistance (partisans)
- German-occupied territory at the end of 1944
- —— German defensive lines
- —— Front line January–April 1945
- ← Advance of the Allied troops with dates of battles, landings and occupation of cities

Italy has continued to develop under difficult conditions, having to survive fascism and two World Wars. For the past sixty years, it has experienced more frequent changes of government than any European country and suffered from the effects of organized crime (the Mafia).

1865–1870 Florence is the capital of Italy.

1866 Italy gains the Austrian Veneto.

1870 The Kingdom of Italy annexes the Papal States.

1871 Rome becomes the capital of Italy.

1881–1890 Italy becomes a colonial power with its African conquests in Eritrea and Somalia.

1882 Italy joins the Triple Alliance with Germany and Austria-Hungary.

1914 Italy is initially neutral in World War I.

April 26, 1915 Treaty of London: Allied promises of land in the Adriatic region convince Italy to renounce its alliance with Austria-Hungary.

May 23, 1915 Italy declares war on Austria-Hungary.

1915–1917 Battles of the Isonzo: Italy suffers heavy casualties in twelve battles on the Italian-Austrian border in the area that is now Slovenia.

1919 Treaty of St. Germain: Trentino, southern Tirol, and the coastal areas are ceded to Italy.

Oct. 27–31, 1922 The March on Rome and Mussolini's rise to power

Feb. 11, 1929 The Lateran Accords and resolution of the "Roman question"

1935–1936 Italian-Ethiopian War: Ethiopia is subjected to Italian rule.

1936 Rome-Berlin Axis, an alliance with Germany, is formalized by the Pact of Steel, which is signed by Hitler and Mussolini in 1939.

April 1939 Italy occupies Albania.

June 10, 1940 Italy declares war on Great Britain and France.

July 10, 1943 Allied troops land in Sicily.

The Roman question In the years after the incorporation of Rome and the Papal States into the Italian kingdom (1870–1929), the pope had diplomatic conflicts with the Roman Catholic Church, on the one hand, and the Italian government on the other. In the Lateran Accords concluded with the fascist government in 1929, the Church finally officially recognized Rome as Italy's capital. The accords also guaranteed the sovereignty of the Vatican throughout Italy.

The March on Rome Following Mussolini's appeal, his fascist supporters began to occupy administration buildings, especially in northern Italy. Around 50,000 *Il Duce* followers from the provinces gathered near the capital. Under pressure from conservative politicians and due to the threat of civil war, King Victor Emmanuel III refused to sign an emergency decree that would have mobilized the army against the fascists. In the end, he felt he had no other choice than to appoint Mussolini the new premier.

Benito Mussolini (1883–1945) After starting out in the Italian Socialist Party, Mussolini shifted to the right politically. In 1919 he brought together the local Milanese political organizations *(fasci di combattimento)* that would become the Fascist Party. Their nationalist manifesto was anticapitalist, antimonarchist and anti-

1943: Italy Occupied by the Germans and the Allies

Territory controlled by the Italian king
Italian territory annexed to Germany
Territory occupied by the Allies
Italian Social Republic (Repubblica Sociale Italiana)

19th–20th Centuries: In Africa

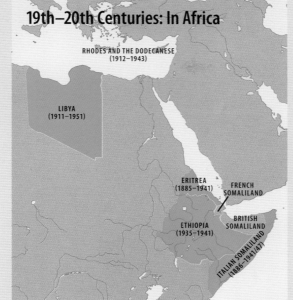

RHODES AND THE DODECANESE (1912–1943)

LIBYA (1911–1951)

ERITREA (1885–1941)

FRENCH SOMALILAND

ETHIOPIA (1935–1941)

BRITISH SOMALILAND

ITALIAN SOMALILAND (1886–1941/47)

1935–1936: The Italian-Ethiopian War

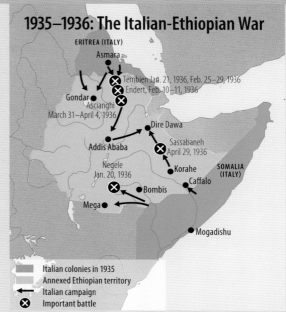

ERITREA (ITALY)
Asmara
Tembien Jan. 21, 1936, Feb. 25–29, 1936
Endert, Feb. 10–11, 1936
Gondar
Ascianghi March 31–April 4, 1936
Dire Dawa
Addis Ababa
Sassabaneh April 29, 1936
Negele Jan. 20, 1936
Korahe
Caffalo
SOMALIA (ITALY)
Mega
Bombis
Mogadishu

Italian colonies in 1935
Annexed Ethiopian territory
Italian campaign
⊗ Important battle

July 25, 1943 The fascist government is overthrown and Mussolini is imprisoned.

September 1943 German troops occupy northern Italy: A fascist puppet government, the Italian Social Republic, is established under German control.

April 29, 1945 Surrender of German Wehrmacht units in Italy

July 2, 1946 A referendum votes to end the monarchy and establishes the Republic of Italy.

1940s–1960s Rapid modernization and economic growth postwar

1947 Paris Conference: Italy loses its colonies in Africa.

1949 Italy joins NATO.

March 25, 1957 Treaties of Rome: Italy is a founding member of the European Union.

late 1960s–1970s Economic slump and the rise of neo-fascist terrorist movements

1978 Assassination of prime minister Aldo Moro

1993 Media tycoon Silvio Berlusconi founds the Forza Italia Party. Prime minister 1994–1996; despite charges of corruption and fraud he is re-elected to the office 2001–2006 and 2008 to the present.

Aldo Moro (1916–1978)

Benito Mussolini (1883–1945)

clerical. In 1922 he became the head of state. He installed his own dictatorship in 1925 by dissolving all other political parties. After siding with Adolf Hitler in a strategically flawed war, Mussolini was deposed by his own supporters, arrested, and then reappointed by the Germans in September 1943. After the defeat of Hitler's Germany he attempted to flee the country, but was captured and shot at the Swiss border.

The Italian Colonies Compared with colonial powers such as Great Britain and France, Italy was a late starter in building its colonial empire. Despite major problems at home, it joined the scramble for Africa toward the end of the 19th century. After Mussolini's troops conquered Ethiopia in 1936, Italian East Africa spanned an area from Eritrea to Somalia. The colony was dissolved after Italy's 1941 defeat in World War II.

1947: Northern Italy

Territory ceded after the Paris Peace Conference (February 10, 1947)
Territory ceded to France
Free Territory of Trieste (1947–1954)
Territory ceded to Yugoslavia

SWITZERLAND
COL DU PETIT ST. BERNARD
Aosta
COL DU MONT CENIS
Milan
Verona
Venice
Trieste
Piran
Rijeka
Umag
ISTRIA
Susa
Turin
Rovinj
Pula
Cres
ITALY
REPUBLIC OF SAN MARINO

Today

Bolzano
TRENTINO-ALTO ADIGE
FRIULI-VENEZIA GIULIA
Udine
VALLE D'AOSTA
LOMBARDY
Verona
VENETO
Trieste
Turin
Milan
Venice
PIEDMONT
EMILIA-ROMAGNA
LIGURIA
Genova (Genoa)
Bologna
Ravenna
SAN MARINO
Pisa
Florence
Ancona
MARCHE
TUSCANY
UMBRIA
ELBA
Terni
Pescara
Rome
ABRUZZI
MOLISE
LAZIO
Isernia
Foggia
Bari
VATICAN CITY
Benevento
CAMPANIA
PUGLIA
Naples
BASILICATA
Taranto
Salerno
SARDINIA
CALABRIA
Cagliari
Catanzaro
Palermo
Messina
SICILY
Catania
Siracusa

Venice and the Major City-States

Venice until 1500

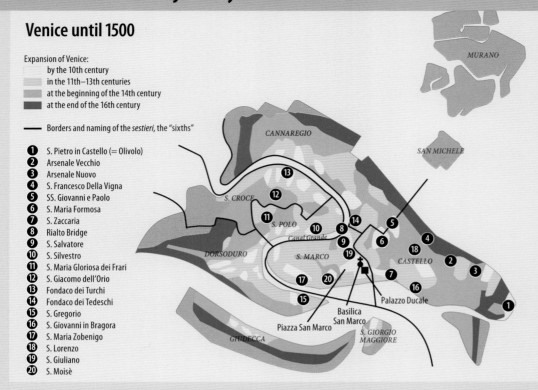

Expansion of Venice:
- by the 10th century
- in the 11th–13th centuries
- at the beginning of the 14th century
- at the end of the 16th century

— Borders and naming of the *sestieri*, the "sixths"

1. S. Pietro in Castello (= Olivolo)
2. Arsenale Vecchio
3. Arsenale Nuovo
4. S. Francesco Della Vigna
5. SS. Giovanni e Paolo
6. S. Maria Formosa
7. S. Zaccaria
8. Rialto Bridge
9. S. Salvatore
10. S. Silvestro
11. S. Maria Gloriosa dei Frari
12. S. Giacomo dell'Orio
13. Fondaco dei Turchi
14. Fondaco dei Tedeschi
15. S. Gregorio
16. S. Giovanni in Bragora
17. S. Maria Zobenigo
18. S. Lorenzo
19. S. Giuliano
20. S. Moisè

The Rise of Venice

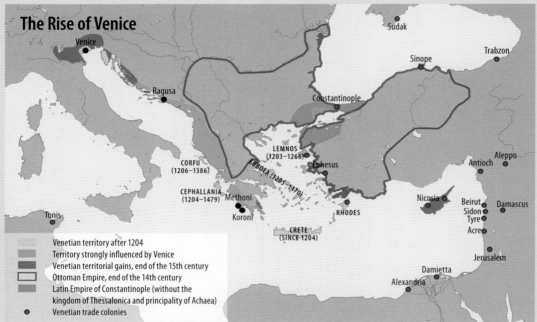

- Venetian territory after 1204
- Territory strongly influenced by Venice
- Venetian territorial gains, end of the 15th century
- Ottoman Empire, end of the 14th century
- Latin Empire of Constantinople (without the kingdom of Thessalonica and principality of Achaea)
- ● Venetian trade colonies

CORFU (1206–1386)
LEMNOS (1203–1266)
EUBOEA (1205–1470)
CEPHALLANIA (1204–1479)
CRETE (SINCE 1204)

Venice in the 16th–18th Centuries

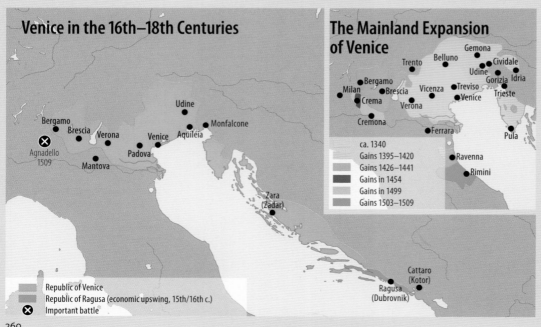

- Republic of Venice
- Republic of Ragusa (economic upswing, 15th/16th c.)
- ⊗ Important battle

The Mainland Expansion of Venice

- ca. 1340
- Gains 1395–1420
- Gains 1426–1441
- Gains in 1454
- Gains in 1499
- Gains 1503–1509

Venice

The Republic of Venice was and still is known as *La Serenissima* ("The Most Serene"). Her history spanning eleven centuries places Venice second only to Byzantium as the longest continuously enduring European state of the past two millennia. Venice was a typical example of an aristocratic republic. Unlike the Signorias, in which a single family had control of the government, many Venetian families had access to power.

March 25, 421 The legendary founding of Venice: Refugees from the mainland reach a group of islands in the Venetian lagoon (laguna).

697 First mention of the election of a doge

828 The relics of St. Mark arrive in Venice. He is the city's patron saint.

~1000 Venetian conquest of Dalmatia

1082 The Venetians are exempted from all taxes by Emperor Alexius I Comnenus, opening up trade between Byzantium and Venice.

1104 Creation of the Arsenal shipyard district

1202–1204 The Fourth Crusade: Venice establishes a colonial empire in the Mediterranean.

1271–1295 Marco Polo's journeys to Asia and China

1297 From this point on, eligibility to serve on the Great Council is limited to those who have already served and/or their descendants.

1339–1454 Expansion of Venice's mainland territories

1378–1381 War of Chioggia: The Genoese are defeated at Chioggia in the Venetian lagoon.

May 14, 1509 Battle of Agnadello: The League of Cambrai is victorious over Venice. By 1517, Venice wins back most of its mainland holdings.

1571 Venice loses Cyprus to the Ottomans.

~1600–1800 Venice is the only Italian state to remain entirely free of Spanish control during this period.

1669 Crete falls to the Ottomans.

1684–1699 Venice temporarily controls the Peloponnese.

May 14, 1797 Napoleon conquers Venice.

Oct. 17, 1797 Treaty of Campo Formio: Former Venetian territories are ceded to Austria.

The Arsenal is the renowned shipyard and naval base of the Venetian Republic. It was the largest production facility in Europe before the era of industrialization. Today it encompasses seventy-nine acres, the equivalent of one-tenth of Venice's historic center.

Doge The title of Venice's official head of state. Unlike other officials, the doge was elected for life. Beginning in the 13th century, the doge's powers were gradually reduced in order to eliminate the autocratic tendencies of some who held the office.

Marco Polo (1254–1324) was a Venetian merchant and adventurer. At the age of seventeen, he accompanied his father and uncle on a trading and diplomatic voyage to China. He then spent seventeen years at the court of Kublai Khan, the great ruler of the Mongols. The travelers did not return to Venice until 1295. When he was imprisoned in Genoa following a naval battle, he described his experiences in the Far East in his book *Il Milione* ("The Million"), better known in English as *The Travels of Marco Polo*.

Florence

The population of medieval Florence was divided among the nobility and guilds. Beginning in the 12th century, power fell into the hands of fewer and fewer great families who competed with one another, even as the election process became increasingly complex. These included the various overlapping power brokers of the time: Guelfs and Ghibellines, democrats and aristocrats.

1293 *Ordinamenti della giustizia*: Government positions are limited to guild members.

~1400–1500 Florentine hegemony in Tuscany: Regional states are formed.

1406 Conquest of Pisa

1434 Cosimo de' Medici is victorious over the Albizzi family.

1469–1492 Lorenzo the Magnificent rules Florence, and cultural development reaches its zenith.

1478 The Pazzi conspiracy against the Medici family: Giuliano de' Medici is murdered.

1494 and 1527: The Medici are driven out of Florence.

1530 Imperial and Spanish troops return the Medici to power.

1555 Conquest of Siena

1737 The Medici line dies out, and Florence passes to the House of Lorraine.

Florence

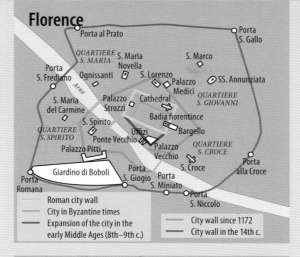

- Roman city wall
- City in Byzantine times
- Expansion of the city in the early Middle Ages (8th–9th c.)
- City wall since 1172
- City wall in the 14th c.

By 1494: The Expansion of Florence

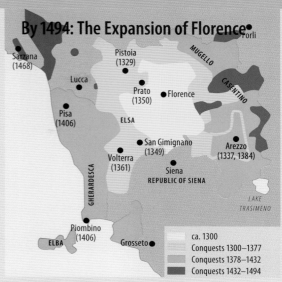

- ca. 1300
- Conquests 1300–1377
- Conquests 1378–1432
- Conquests 1432–1494

Regional State of Milan

- 1339 (at the death of Azzo Visconti)
- Territory of Gian Galeazzo Visconti in 1402

Milan

During the early Middle Ages, Milan was subjected to rule by the archbishop. In the midst of power struggles between the nobility and the people, the *Signoria* was formed, in which the city was ruled by a single family.

1241–1277 Rule of the Della Torre family

1277–1447 Rule of the Visconti family

1395 Gian Galeazzo Visconti receives the title of duke of Milan.

1423–1433 War with Venice: Brescia and Bergamo are handed over to the Venetians.

1450 The Sforza family ascends to power.

1525 Milan passes into Spanish control.

Della Scala Rule

- Zenith of the power of the della Scala family of Verona in 1336
- Domains of other important families in northern Italy

Scaligeri

The Della Scala family, also known as the Scaligeris, ruled the city of Verona and the surrounding region for 125 years, from 1262 to 1387. They reached the height of their power under Cangrande I (1311–1329) and his nephew Mastino II (1329–1351).

By 1503: The Expansion of Savoy

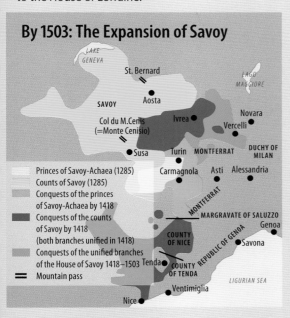

- Princes of Savoy-Achaea (1285)
- Counts of Savoy (1285)
- Conquests of the princes of Savoy-Achaea by 1418
- Conquests of the counts of Savoy by 1418 (both branches unified in 1418)
- Conquests of the unified branches of the House of Savoy 1418–1503
- Mountain pass

The House of Savoy

Ever since the 11th and 12th centuries, the lords of the region south of Lake Geneva in the Aosta Valley and Northern Piedmont called themselves the counts of Savoy. The Savoy-Achaia branch controlled territories in southern Piedmont, including Turin. They split off from the House of Savoy after 1289.

1416 The counts of Savoy are elevated to the status of dukes.

1418 The branches of the Savoy dynasty reunite.

1536–1559 France occupies Savoy.

1713 The duke of Savoy receives the title of king.

1720 Sicily is exchanged for Sardinia; the Kingdom of Sardinia-Piedmont comes into existence.

1861 Unification of Italy under the leadership of the Sardinia-Piedmont monarchy: Savoy is ceded to the French Empire.

By 1020: Formation of the Papal States

- Patrimonium Petri (= Ducatus Romanus)
- Donation of Pepin in the year 756
- Desiderius after 757
- Charlemagne
- ca. 1020

The Papal States

The Papal States had expanded to approximately their current size already in the early Middle Ages.

756 Pippin III gives the northern Italian territories to the pope in return for making his coronation possible.

1503–1513 The largest expansion of the Papal States occurs under Pope Julius II.

1798–1799 The Roman Republic becomes a Napoleonic vassal state.

1801–1808 Treaty with Napoleon: The Papal States are reestablished.

1808–1814 The French Empire annexes the Papal States.

1815 The Congress of Vienna reestablishes the Papal States.

1870 Annexation by Italy

Feb. 11, 1929 The Lateran Accords are signed.

Rulers of Italy

Lombard (Langobard) Kings

(Lombardy, Italy)

568–572	Alboin
572–574	Cleph
574–584	Interregnum
584–590	Authari
590–616	Agilulf
616–626	Adaloald
626–636	Arioald
636–652	Rothari
652–653	Rodoald
653–661	Aripert I
661–662	Godepert und Perctarit
662–671	Grimoald
671	Garibald
671–688	Perctarit (restored)
688–700	Cunipert
700	Liutprand
701	Ragimpert
701–712	Aripert II
712	Ansprand
712–744	Luitprand the Lombard
744	Hildeprand
744–749	Ratchis
749–756	Aistulf
756–757	Ratchis (restored)
757–774	Desiderius
774	*Lombard kingdom is conquered by the Franks*

Kings of Italy

The Lombard crown (at the time the most powerful kingdom in Italy) was assumed by Charlemagne. The Italian kingdom became part of the Frankish empire.

Carolingians

774–781	Charlemagne
781–810	Pippin
810–818	Bernard
818–822	Louis I the Pious, emperor
822–855	Lothar I, emperor
844/855	Louis II, from 855
–875	emperor
875–877	Charles II the Bald, emperor in personal union
877–879	Charlesman
879–888	Charles III the Fat, emperor

Various Houses

(Kingship of Italy is distinct from the title of emperor; multiple kings and challengers)

888–891	Berengar I
891–894	Guy of Spoleto
894–896	Lambert of Spoleto
896–899	Arnulf of Carinthia, emperor
899–905	Louis III the Blind
905–924	Berengar I (restored)
924–926	Rudolf II of Burgundy
926–945	Hugh of Arles (Provence)
945–950	Lothar
950–961	Berengar II
951/963	*Sovereignty of Italy is transferred to the Holy Roman emperor.*
1530–1648	*The Holy Roman emperor is no longer crowned the king of Italy; formally Italy remains part of the Holy Roman Empire.*
1805–1814	*Napoleon Bonaparte establishes the Kingdom of Italy and declares himself its king.*

House of Savoy: *United Italy*

1861–1878	Victor Emmanuel II
1878–1900	Umberto I
1900–1946	Victor Emmanuel III
1946	Umberto II

End of the Italian monarchy; Italy becomes a republic.

Doges of Venice

697–717	Paolo Lucio Anafesto
717–726	Marcello Tegalliano
726–737	Orso Ipato
742–755	Teodato Ipato
755–756	Galla Gaulo
756–764	Domenico Monegario
764–787	Maurizio Galbaio
787–804	Giovanni Galbaio
804–809	Obelerio Antenoreo
809–827	Angelo Participazio
827–829	Giustiniano Participazio
829–837	Giovanni I Participazio
837–864	Pietro Tradonico
864–881	Orso I Participazio
881–887	Giovanni II Participazio
887	Pietro I Candiano
887–912	Pietro Tribuno
912–932	Orso II Participazio
932–939	Pietro II Candiano
939–942	Pietro Participazio (Badoer)
942–959	Pietro III Candiano
959–976	Pietro IV Candiano
976–978	Pietro I Orseolo
978–979	Vitale Candiano
979–991	Tribuno Memmo
991–1009	Pietro II Orseolo
1009–1026	Otto Orseolo
1026–1032	Pietro Barbolano (Centranigo)
1032–1043	Domenico Flabanico
1043–1071	Domenico Contarini
1071–1084	Domenico Selvo
1084–1096	Vitale Faliero
1096–1102	Vitale I Michiel
1102–1117	Ordelafo Faliero
1117–1130	Domenico Michele
1130–1148	Pietro Polani
1148–1156	Domenico Morosini
1156–1172	Vitale II Michele
1172–1178	Sebastiano Ziani
1178–1192	Orio Mastropiero
1192–1205	Enrico Dandolo
1205–1229	Pietro Ziani
1229–1249	Jacopo Tiepolo
1249–1252	Marino Morosini
1252–1268	Reniero Zeno
1268–1275	Lorenzo Tiepolo
1275–1280	Jacopo Contarini
1280–1289	Giovanni Dandolo
1289–1311	Pietro Gradenigo
1311–1312	Marino Zorzi
1312–1328	Giovanni Soranzo
1328–1339	Francesco Dandolo
1339–1342	Bartolomeo Gradenigo
1343–1354	Andrea Dandolo
1354–1355	Marino Faliero
1355–1356	Giovanni Gradenigo
1356–1361	Giovanni Dolfin
1361–1365	Lorenzo Celsi
1365–1367	Marco Cornaro
1367–1382	Andrea Contarini
1382	Michele Morosini
1382–1400	Antonio Venier
1400–1413	Michele Steno
1413–1423	Tommaso Mocenigo
1423–1457	Francesco Foscari
1457–1462	Pasquale Malipiero
1462–1471	Cristoforo Moro
1471–1473	Nicolo Tron
1473–1474	Nicolo Marcello
1474–1476	Pietro Mocenigo
1476–1478	Andrea Vendramin
1478–1485	Giovanni Mocenigo
1485–1486	Marco Barbarigo
1486–1501	Agostino Barbarigo
1501–1521	Leonardo Loredan
1521–1523	Antonio Grimani
1523–1538	Andrea Gritti
1538–1545	Pietro Lando
1545–1553	Francesco Donato
1553–1554	Marcantonio Trivisan
1554–1556	Francesco Venier
1556–1559	Lorenzo Priuli
1559–1567	Girolamo Priuli
1567–1570	Pietro Loredan
1570–1577	Alvise I Mocenigo
1577–1578	Sebastiano Venier
1578–1585	Nicolò da Ponte
1585–1595	Pasquale Cicogna
1595–1606	Marino Grimani
1606–1612	Leonardo Donato
1612–1615	Marcantonio Memmo
1615–1618	Giovanni Bembo
1618	Nicolò Donato
1618–1623	Antonio Priuli
1623–1624	Francesco Contarini
1624–1630	Giovanni I Cornaro
1630–1631	Nicolò Contarini
1631–1646	Francesco Erizzo
1646–1655	Francesco Molin
1655–1656	Charles Contarini
1656	Francesco Cornaro
1656–1658	Bertuccio Valiero
1658–1659	Giovanni Pesaro
1659–1674	Domenico II Contarini
1674–1676	Nicolò Sagredo
1676–1684	Alvise Contarini
1684–1688	Marcantonio Giustinian
1688–1694	Francesco Morosini
1694–1700	Silvestro Valiero
1700–1709	Alvise II Mocenigo
1709–1722	Giovanni II Cornaro
1722–1732	Alvise III Sebastiano Mocenigo
1732–1735	Charles Ruzzini
1735–1741	Alvise Pisani
1741–1752	Pietro Grimani
1752–1762	Francesco Loredan
1762–1763	Marco Foscarini
1763–1779	Alvise IV Mocenigo
1779–1789	Paolo Renier
1789–1797	Ludovico Manin
V–X 1797	*French occupation*
1798–1805	*Venice falls to Austria*
1805–1814	*Venice is a French vassal state, part of the Kingdom of Italy (Napoleon Bonaparte)*
1814–1866	*Kingdom of Lombardy-Venetia falls to Austria*
XI 1866	*Venice becomes part of the Kingdom of Italy*

Savoy

Counts of Savoy

1003–1047	Humbert I the Whitehanded
1048–1056	Amadeus I Coda
1057–1060	Otto
1060–1078	Peter I
1060–1080	Amadeus II
1080–1103	Humbert II the Fat
1103–1148	Amadeus III the Crusader
1148–1188	Humbert III the Blessed
1189–1233	Thomas I
1233–1253	Amadeus IV
1253–1263	Boniface
1263–1268	Peter II
1268–1285	Philip I
1285–1323	Amadeus V the Great
1323–1329	Edward the Liberal
1329–1343	Aimone the Peaceful
1343–1383	Amadeus VI, the Green Count (il Conte Verde)
1383–1391	Amadeus VII, the Red Count (il Conte Rosso)
1391–1416	Amadeus VIII the Peaceful (il Pacifico)

Dukes of Savoy

1416–1440	Amadeus VIII the Peaceful (il Pacifico)
1440–1465	Louis
1465–1472	Amadeus IX the Blessed (il Beato)
1472–1482	Philibert I the Hunter (il Cacciatore)
1482–1490	Charles I the Warrior
1490–1496	Charles II (Charles John Amadeus)
1496–1497	Philip II the Landless (Senza Terra)
1497–1504	Philibert II the Good or the Handsome
1504–1536	Charles III (Charles the Good)
1536–1559	*French occupation of Savoy*
1559–1580	Emmanuel Philibert Ironhead (Testa di ferro)
1580–1630	Charles Emmanuel I the Great
1630–1637	Victor Amadeus I (Lion of Susa)
1638–1675	Charles Emmanuel II
1675–1730	Victor Amadeus II (from 1713 also king of Sicily)
from 1720	*the dukes of Savoy are also the kings of Sardinia:*
until 1730	*Victor Amadeus II (I)*
1730–1773	*Charles Emmanuel III (I)*
1773–1796	*Victor Amadeus III (II)*
1796–1798	*Charles Emmanuel IV (II)*
1798–1814	*French occupation (interrupted 1799–1800)*
1814–1821	Victor Emmanuel I
1821–1831	Charles Felix
1831–1849	Charles Albert
1849–1878	Victor Emmanuel II
from 1861	*The kings of Sardinia become the kings of united Italy; Savoy becomes part of France.*

Kings of Sicily

Normans

1130–1154	Roger II
1154–1166	William I
1166–1189	William II
1189–1194	Tancred
1194	William III

Hohenstaufens

1194–1197	Henry I (VI)
1198–1250	Frederick I (II)
1250–1254	Conrad I (IV)
1254–1258	Conradin (Conrad II)
1258–1266	Manfred

House of Anjou (Angevin)

1266–1282	Charles I

Aragons

1282–1285	Peter I (III) the Great
1285–1296	James I
1296–1337	Frederick II
1337–1342	Peter II
1342–1355	Louis (the Child)
1355–1377	Frederick III the Simple
1377–1402	Mary
1395–1409	Martin I the Younger
1409–1410	Martin II the Elder
1410–1713	*The Kingdom of Sicily falls directly to the Crown of Aragon, after 1512 to the Spanish Crown.*
1713–1720	*The Kingdom of Sicily falls to the House of Savoy.*
1720–1735	*The Kingdom of Sicily falls to Austria.*
1735–1825	*The kingdoms of Sicily and Naples are united under Spanish Bourbons.*
1735–1759	*Charles VII (1759–1788 Charles III of Spain)*
1759–1825	Ferdinand I
1799 & 1806–1815	*Sicily is separate from Naples.*
from 1815	*House of Bourbon, Kingdom of the Two Sicilies: Naples and Sicily are reunited.*
1825–1830	Francis I
1830–1859	*Ferdinand II*
1859–1860	*Francis II*
XII 1860	*Becomes part of unified Italy*

Monarchs of Naples

Naples is united with Sicily under the Normans, Hohenstaufens and under Charles I of Anjou until 1282.

House of Anjou

1266–1285	Charles I
1285–1309	Charles II
1309–1343	Robert the Wise
1343–1381	Joan I
1382–1386	Charles III the Short
1386 (nominal)/1400–1414	Ladislas
1389–1399	Louis II (rival king)
1414–1435	Joan II
1435–1442	René

House of Aragon

1442–1458	Alfonso I
1458–1494	Ferdinand I
1494–1495	Alfonso II
1495–1496	Ferdinand II (Ferrandino)
1496–1501	Frederick
1501–1707	*Naples falls to the Aragonese/Spanish crown.*
1707–1734	*Naples falls to Austria.*
1735–1799	*Kingdom of Naples is united with Sicily under the Spanish Bourbons.*
1735–1759	*Charles VII (1759–1788 Charles III of Spain)*
1759–1799	Ferdinand IV
1799	*January 23–June 23 Parthenopean Republic (French vassal state)*
1799–1806	Ferdinand IV (restored)

House of Bonaparte *(Naples; separate from Sicily)*

1806–1808	Joseph Bonaparte
1808–1815	Joachim Murat (Napoleon's brother-in-law)

House of Bourbon *(Kingdom of the Two Sicilies)*

1815–1825	Ferdinand I
1825–1830	Francis I
1830–1859	Ferdinand II
1859–1860	Francis II
XII 1860	*Becomes part of unified Italy*

House of Este

(Ferrara, Modena, Reggio)

Lords of Ferrara *(originally from Este in the Veneto)*

262

1209–1212 Azzo VI
1212–1215 Aldobrandino I
1215–1222 Azzo VII Novello
1222–1236 Salinguerra Torelli
1240–1264 Azzo VII Novello
(restored)

Lords of Ferrara, Modena and Reggio (from 1288/1289)
1264–1293 Obizzo II
1293–1308 Azzo VIII
1308 Aldobrandino II
1308–1309 Venetian occupation of Ferrara
1309–1317 Ferrara falls to the Papal States.

Lords of Ferrara (1317) **and Modena** (from 1336)
1317–1335 Rinaldo
1344 Nicolò I
1352 Obizzo III
1352–1361 Aldobrandino III
1361–1388 Nicolò II
1388–1393 Alberto I

Lords of Ferrara, Modena and Reggio (from 1419)
1393–1441 Nicolò III
1441–1450 Leonello

Dukes of Ferrara, Modena and Reggio
1450–1471 Borso
1471–1505 Ercole I
1505–1534 Alfonso I
1534–1559 Ercole II
1559–1597 Alfonso II
1598 Cesare: Ferrara is lost to direct papal rule.

Dukes of Modena and Reggio
1597–1628 Cesare
1628–1629 Alfonso III
1629–1658 Francesco I
1658–1662 Alfonso IV
1662–1694 Francesco II
1694–1737 Rinaldo I
1737–1780 Francesco III
1780–1796 Ercole III

French vassal states
1796/97–1802/05 Cispadane/ Cisalpine/Italian Republic
1805–1814 Kingdom of Italy (Napoleon Bonaparte)

Dukes of Modena and Reggio from the Habsburg Dynasty (Austria-Este)
1814–1846 Francesco IV
1846–1859 Francesco V
March 1860 Becomes part of unified Italy

Urbino

Counts of Urbino (House of Montefeltro)
1213–1241 Bonconte I da Montefeltro
1241–1255 Montefeltrano II da Montefeltro
1255–1286 Guido I da Montefeltro
1285–1304 Papal rule (with interruptions)
1296–1322 Federico I da Montefeltro
1323–1359 Nolfo da Montefeltro
1359–1377 Papal rule
1377–1404 Antonio da Montefeltro
1404–1443 Guidantonio da Montefeltro

Dukes of Urbino (House of Montefeltro)
1443–1444 Oddantonio da Montefeltro

1444–1482 Federico III da Montefeltro
1482–1502 Guidobaldo da Montefeltro

Borgia
1502–1504 Cesare Borgia

House of Della Rovere
1508–1516 Francesco Maria I della Rovere
1516–1519 Lorenzo II de' Medici
1521–1538 Francesco Maria I della Rovere (restored)
1538–1574 Guidobaldo II della Rovere
1574–1621 Francesco Maria II della Rovere
1621–1623 Federico Ubaldo della Rovere
1623–1631 Francesco Maria II della Rovere (restored)
1631–1796 Urbino falls to the Papal States.

Milan

Lords of Milan
House of della Torre
1240–1247 Pagano della Torre
1257–1259 Martino della Torre
1263–1265 Filippo della Torre
1265–1277 Napoleone della Torre

House of Visconti
1277–1294 Ottone Visconti, Archbishop of Milan
1287–1302 Matteo I Visconti
1302–1311 Guido della Torre
1311–1322 Matteo I Visconti (restored)
1322–1327 Galeazzo I Visconti
1328–1339 Azzo Visconti
1339–1349 Luchino Visconti
1349–1354/1378/1385
Brothers Matteo II/ Galeazzo II/Bernabò Visconti
1378/85–1395 Gian Galeazzo Visconti (becomes Duke of Milan)

Dukes of Milan (House of Visconti)
1395–1402 Gian Galeazzo Visconti
1402–1412 Giovanni Maria Visconti
1412–1447 Filippo Maria Visconti
1447–1450 Ambrosian Republic

Dukes of Milan (House of Sforza)
1450–1466 Francesco I Sforza
1466–1476 Galeazzo Maria Sforza
1476–1494 Gian Galeazzo Sforza
1494–1499 Lodovico Sforza the Moor (il Moro)
1499–1512 First French occupation: Louis XII of France
1512–1515 Massimiliano Sforza
1515–1521 Second French occupation: Francis I of France
1521–1535 Francesco II Sforza
1535–1706 Milan ruled by Spain
1706–1797 Milan ruled by Austria

French vassal states
1797–1802/05 Cisalpine/Italian Republic
1805–1814 Kingdom of Italy (Napoleon Bonaparte)
1814–1859 Milan falls under Austrian rule as part of the Kingdom of Lombardy-Venetia.
XI 1859 Lombardy becomes part of unified Italy.

Verona

Della Scala family
Lords of Verona
1260/1262–77 Mastino I della Scala
1277–1301 Alberto I della Scala
1301–1304 Bartolomeo I della Scala
1304–1311 Alboino I della Scala
1311–1329/52 Cangrande I
1329–1351 Brothers Mastino II / Alberto II della Scala
1352–1359 Cangrande II della Scala
1359–1365 Alboino II della Scala
1365–1375 Cansignorio della Scala
1375–1381 Bartolomeo II della Scala
1381–1387 Antonio I della Scala
1387–1404 Verona is ruled by Milan.
1405–1797 Verona is ruled by Venice.

Mantua

Lords of Mantua
House of Bonacolsi
1272–1291 Pinamonte Bonacolsi
1291–1299 Bardellone Bonacolsi
1299–1309 Guido Bonacolsi
1309–1328 Rinaldo Bonacolsi (Passerino)

House of Gonzaga
1328–1360 Luigi I (Ludovico)
1360–1369 Guido
1369–1382 Luigi II (Ludovico II)
1382–1407 Giovan Francesco I (Francesco I)

Marquesses of Mantua from 1433
1407–1444 Giovan Francesco II (Gianfrancesco)
1444–1478 Luigi III (Ludovico) the Turk (il Turco)
1478–1484 Federico I
1484–1519 Giovan Francesco III (Francesco II)

Dukes of Mantua from 1530, **Monferrato** 1536–1708
1519–1540 Federico II
1540–1550 Francesco III
1550–1587 Guglielmo
1587–1612 Vincenzo I
1612 Francesco IV
1612–1626 Ferdinando
1626–1627 Vincenzo II

Junior branch of Gonzaga-Nevers
1627–1637 Charles I
1637–1665 Charles II
1665–1708 Ferdinand Charles (Charles III)
1708–1797 Mantua falls to Austria.

French vassal states
1797–1802/05 Cisalpine/Italian Republic
1805–1814 Kingdom of Italy (Napoleon Bonaparte)
1814–1866 Mantua falls under Austrian rule as part of the Kingdom of Lombardy-Venetia.
XI 1866 Venetia becomes part of unified Italy.

Ravenna

House of da Polenta
Lords of Ravenna
1275–1297 Guido I da Polenta (Guido the Old)
1297–1316 Lamberto I da Polenta
1316–1322 Guido II Novello da Polenta
1322–1329 Ostasio da Polenta
1329–1333 Ravenna falls to the Papal States.

1333–1346 Ostasio da Polenta (restored)
1346–1359 Bernardino da Polenta
1359–1389 Guido III da Polenta
1390–1396/1404/1406/1431
Brothers Ostasio II/ Pietro/Aldobrandino/ Obizzo da Polenta
1431–1441 Ostasio III da Polenta
1441–1509 Ravenna is ruled by Venice.
1509–1796 Ravenna is ruled by the Papal States.

Rimini

House of Malatesta
Lords of Rimini
1295–1312 Malatesta I da Verruchio
1312–1317 Malatestino dell'Occhio
1317–1326 Pandolfo I Malatesta
1326–1335 Ferrantino Malatesta
1335–1363 Malatesta II Guastafamiglia
1363–1372 Malatesta III Ungaro
1372–1385 Galeotto I Malatesta
1385–1429 Carlo I Malatesta
1429–1432 Galeotto II Roberto Malatesta
1432–1468 Sigismondo Pandolfo Malatesta
1468–1482 Roberto Malatesta
1482–1500 Pandolfo IV Malatesta
1500–1503 Cesare Borgia
1503–1509 Rimini is ruled by Venice.
1509–1522 and 1523–1527 Rimini falls to the Papal States.
1522–1523 and 1527–1528 Pandolfo IV Malatesta (restored)
1528–1797 Rimini is ruled by the Papal States.

Dukes of Parma and Piacenza

House of Farnese
1545–1547 Pier Luigi Farnese
1547–1586 Ottavio Farnese
1586–1592 Alessandro Farnese
1592–1622 Ranuccio I Farnese
1622–1646 Odoardo I Farnese
1646–1694 Ranuccio II Farnese
1694–1727 Francesco Farnese
1727–1731 Antonio Farnese

House of Bourbon
1731–1735 Charles I (Charles VII of Naples 1735–1759, Charles III of Spain 1759–1788)

House of Habsburg
1735–1740 Charles II Habsburg (Emperor Charles VI 1711–1740)
1740–1748 Maria Theresa of Habsburg

House of Bourbon-Parma
1748–1765 Philip I
1765–1802 Ferdinand I
1802–1814 French occupation (Napoleon Bonaparte)
1806–1808 Pauline Bonaparte Duchess of Parma
1808–1814 Jean Jacques Régis de Cambacérès titular Duke of Parma, Charles-François Lebrun titular Duke of Piacenza

House of Habsburg
1814–1847 Marie Louise of Austria

House of Bourbon-Parma
1847–1849 Charles Louis (had been king of Etruria 1803–1807)
1849–1854 Charles III
1854–1860 Robert I
III 1860 The duchy is incorporated into unified Italy.

Florence and Tuscany

Lords of Florence (Florence was a republic from 1115, ruled de facto by the House of Medici after 1434, even though the republic officially continues to exist.)
1434–1464 Cosimo de' Medici
1464–1469 Piero I de' Medici
1469–1492 Lorenzo I the Magnificent (joint rule with his brother Giuliano until 1478)
1492–1494 Piero II the Unfortunate
1494–1512 Republic
1512–1513 Cardinal Giovanni de' Medici (Pope Leo X 1513–1521)
1513–1516 Giuliano II de' Medici (Duke of Nemours)
1513–1519 Lorenzo II de' Medici (Duke of Urbino)
1519–1523 Cardinal Giulio de' Medici (Pope Clement VII 1523–1534)
1523–1527 Cardinal Ippolito de' Medici
1523–1527 Alessandro de' Medici
1527–1530 Republic
1530–1531 Alessandro de' Medici (becomes Duke of Florence)

Dukes of Florence (House of Medici)
1531–1537 Alessandro de' Medici
1537–1569 Cosimo I de' Medici (becomes Grand Duke of Florence)

Grand Dukes of Tuscany (House of Medici)
1569–1574 Cosimo I de' Medici
1574–1587 Francis I de' Medici
1587–1609 Ferdinand I de' Medici
1609–1621 Cosimo II de' Medici
1621–1670 Ferdinand II de' Medici
1670–1723 Cosimo III de' Medici
1723–1737 Gian Gastone de' Medici

Grand Dukes of Tuscany (House of Habsburg-Lorraine)
1737–1765 Francis (II) Stephan (Emperor Francis I 1745–1765)
1765–1790 Peter Leopold (Emperor Leopold I 1790–1792)
1790–1801 Ferdinand III

Kings of Etruria (House of Bourbon-Parma)
1801–1803 Louis I
1803–1807 Charles Louis (Louis II)
Tuscany is occupied by the French.
1807–1814 Elisa Bonaparte titular Grand Duchess of Tuscany

Grand Dukes of Tuscany (House of Habsburg-Lorraine)
1814–1824 Ferdinand III (restored)
1824–1848 Leopold II
1849 Tuscan Republic
1849–1859 Leopold II
1859–1860 Ferdinand IV
II–III 1860 Tuscany becomes part of unified Italy.

THE POPES

33–67(?) Peter	(Simon)
67(?)–79(?) Linus	
79(?)–88(?) Anacletus	
88(?)–97(?) Clement I	
97(?)–105(?) Evaristus	
105(?)–115(?) Alexander I	
115(?)–125(?) Sixtus I	
125(?)–136(?) Telesphorus	
136(?)–140(?) Hyginus	
140(?)–155(?) Pius I	
155(?)–166(?) Anicetus	
166(?)–175(?) Soter	
175(?)–189(?) Eleutherius	
189(?)–199(?) Victor I	
199(?)–217(?) Zephyrinus	
217(?)–222(?) Callistus I	
217(?)–235(?) Hyppolytus (antipope)	
222–230 Urban I	
230–235 Pontain	
235–236 Anterus	
236–250 Fabian	
251–258 Novatian (antipope)	
251–253 Cornelius	
253–254 Lucius I	
254–257 Stephen I	
257–258 Sixtus II	
259–268 Dionysius	
269–274 Felix I	
275–283 Eutychian	
283–296 Caius	
296–304 Marcellinus	
304–308 **Sede vacans** (Holy See unoccupied)	
308–309 Marcellus I	
309–310 Eusebius	
311–314 Miltiades	
314–335 Sylvester I	
336 Marcus	
337–352 Julius I	
352–366 Liberius	
355–365 Felix II (antipope)	
366–384 Damasus I	
366–367 Ursicinus (antipope)	
384–399 Siricius	
399–401 Anastasius I	
401–417 Innocent I	
417–418 Zosimus	
418–422 Boniface I	
418–419 Eulalius (antipope)	
422–432 Celestine I	
432–440 Sixtus III	
440–461 Leo I (the Great)	
461–468 Hilarius	
468–483 Simplicius	
483–492 Felix II	
492–496 Gelasius I	
496–498 Anastasius II	
498–514 Symmachus	
498–506 Laurentius (antipope)	

514–523 Hormisdas	
523–526 John I	
526–530 Felix III	
530 Dioscurus (antipope)	
530–532 Boniface II	
533–535 John II	(Mercurius)
535–536 Agapetus I	
536–537 Silverius	
537–555 Vigilius	
556–561 Pelagius I	
561–574 John III	
575–579 Benedict I	
579–590 Pelagius II	
590–604 Gregory Magnus (the Great)	
604–606 Sabinian	
607 Boniface III	
608–615 Boniface IV	
615–618 Adeodatus I	
619–625 Boniface V	
625–638 Honorius I	
640 Severinus	
640–642 John IV	
642–649 Theodore I	
649–653 Martin I	
654–657 Eugene I	
657–672 Vitalian	
672–676 Adeodatus II	
676–678 Donus	
678–681 Agatho	
682–683 Leo II	
684–685 Benedict II	
685–686 John V	
686–687 Conon	
687 Theodorus (antipope)	
687–692 Paschal (antipope)	
687–701 Sergius I	
701–705 John VI	
705–707 John VII	
708 Sisinnius	
708–715 Constantine I	
715–731 Gregory II	
731–741 Gregory III	
741–752 Zachary	
752 Stephen II died before being consecrated (three-day pontificate)	
752–757 Stephen III	
757–767 Paul I	
767–768 Constantine II (antipope)	
768 Philip (antipope)	
768–772 Stephen IV	
772–795 Adrian I	
795–816 Leo III	
816–817 Stephen V	
817–824 Paschal I	
824–827 Eugene II	
827 Valentine	
827–844 Gregory IV	
844–847 Sergius II	
844 John VIII (antipope)	

847–855 Leo IV	
855–858 Benedict III	
855 Anastasius III (antipope)	
858–867 Nicholas I (the Great)	
867–872 Adrian II	
872–882 John VIII	
882–884 Marinus I	
884–885 Adrian III	
885–891 Stephen VI	
891–896 Formosus	
896 Boniface VI	
896–897 Stephen VII	
897 Romanus	
897 Theodore II	
898–900 John IX	
900–903 Benedict IV	
903 Leo V	
903–904 Christopher (antipope)	
904–911 Sergius III	
911–913 Anastasius III	
913–914 Lando	
914–928 John X	
928 Leo VI	
928–931 Stephen VIII	
931–935 John XI	
936–939 Leo VII	
939–942 Stephen IX	
942–946 Marinus I	
946–955 Agapetus II	
955–964 John XII	Octavian of Spoleto
963–965 Leo VIII	
965–972 John XIII	
973–974 Benedict VI	
974 Boniface VII (antipope)	Franco Ferruci
974–983 Benedict VII	
983–984 John XIV	Pietro Canepanova
984–985 Boniface VII (antipope) restored	Franco Ferruci
985–996 John XV	
996–999 Gregory V	Bruno of Carinthia
997–998 John XVI (antipope)	Johannes Philagathos
999–1003 Sylvester II	Gerbert d'Aurillac
1003 John XVII	Giovanni Siccone
1004–1009 John XVIII	John Fasano
1009–1012 Sergius IV	Pietro da Albano
1012–1024 Benedict VIII	Theophylactus II of Tusculum
1012 Gregory VI (antipope)	
1024–1032 John XIX	Romanus of Tusculum
1032–1045 Benedict IX	Theophylactus III of Tusculum
1045 Sylvester III	Giovanni di Sabina
1045 Benedict IX (2nd term)	Theophylactus III of Tusculum
1045–1046 Gregory VI	Giovanni Gratiano Pierleoni
1046–1047 Clement II	Suidger of Morsleben and Hornburg
1047–1048 Benedict IX (3rd term)	Theophylactus III of Tusculum

Dates	Name	Birth name
1048	Damasus II	Poppo of Brixen
1049–1054	Leo IX	Bruno, Count of Egisheim-Dagsburg
1055–1057	Victor II	Gebhard of Dollnstein-Hirschberg
1057–1058	Stephen IX (X)	Frederick of Lorraine
1058–1061	Nicholas II	Gerard of Burgundy
1058–1059	Benedict X (antipope)	Giovanni Mincio of Tusculum
1061–1073	Alexander II	Anselm of Baggio
1061–1064	Honorius II (antipope)	Peter Cadelo
1073–1085	Gregory VII	Hildebrand
1084–1100	Clement III (antipope)	Guibert of Ravenna
1086–1087	Victor III	Daufer (Desiderius) of Benevento
1088–1099	Urban II	Odo de Lagery
1099–1118	Paschal II	Raniero di Bieda
1100–1102	Theodoric (antipope)	
1102	Albert (Adalbert) (antipope)	Albert of Sabina
1105–1111	Sylvester IV (antipope)	Maginulfo
1118–1119	Gelasius II	John of Gaeta (Giovanni Da Gaeta)
1118–1121	Gregory VIII (antipope)	Mauritius Burdinus (Maurice Bourdin)
1119–1124	Calixtus II	Guy de Bourgogne
1124–1130	Honorius II	Lamberto Scannabecchi
1124	Celestine II (antipope)	Teobaldo Buccapeco
1130–1143	Innocent II	Gregorio Papareschi
1130–1138	Anacletus II (antipope)	Pietro Pierleoni
1138	Victor IV (antipope)	Gregory Conti
1143–1144	Celestine II	Guido de Castellis
1144–1145	Lucius II	Gherardo Caccianemici
1145–1153	Eugene III	Bernardo Paganelli di Montemagno
1153–1154	Anastasius IV	Corrado della Suburra
1154–1159	Adrian IV	Nicholas Breakspear
1159–1181	Alexander III	Rolando Bandinelli
1159–1164	Victor IV (antipope)	Octavian (Ottaviano de Monticelli)
1164–1168	Paschal III (antipope)	Guido di Crema
1168–1178	Calixtus III (antipope)	Giovanni di Struma
1179–1180	Innocent III (antipope)	Lando Di Sezze
1181–1185	Lucius III	Ubaldo Allucingoli
1185–1187	Urban III	Umberto Crivelli
1187	Gregory VIII	Alberto de Morra
1187–1191	Clement III	Paolo Scolari
1191–1198	Celestine III	Giacinto Bobone
1198–1216	Innocent III	Lotario (Lothar) di Segni
1216–1227	Honorius III	Cencio Savelli
1227–1241	Gregory IX	Ugolino di Segni
1241	Celestine IV	Goffredo Castiglioni
1241–1243	**Sede vacans** (Holy See unoccupied)	
1243–1254	Innocent IV	Sinibaldo Fieschi
1254–1261	Alexander IV	Rinaldo Conte, Count of Segni
1261–1264	Urban IV	Jacques Pantaléon
1265–1268	Clement IV	Guido Fulcodi (Guy Foulques)
1268–1271	**Sede vacans** (Holy See unoccupied)	
1271–1276	Gregory X	Tebaldo Visconti
1276	Innocent V	Pierre de Tarantaise
1276	Adrian V	Ottobono Fieschi
1276–1277	John XXI	Pedro Julião
1277–1280	Nicholas III	Giovanni Gaetano Orsini
1281–1285	Martin IV	Simon de Brion
1285–1287	Honorius IV	Giacomo Savelli
1288–1292	Nicholas IV	Girolamo Masci
1292–1294	**Sede vacans** (Holy See unoccupied)	
1294	Celestine V	Pietro da Morrone
1294–1303	Boniface VIII	Benedetto Caetani
1303–1304	Benedict XI	Niccolò Boccasini
1305–1314	Clement V	Bertrand de Got
1314–1316	**Sede vacans** (Holy See unoccupied)	
1316–1334	John XXII	Jacques Duèse
1328–1330	Nicholas V (antipope)	Pietro Rainalducci
1334–1342	Benedict XII	Jacques Fournier
1342–1352	Clement VI	Pierre Roger
1352–1362	Innocent VI	Étienne Aubert
1362–1370	Urban V	Guillaume de Grimoard
1370–1378	Gregory XI	Pierre Roger de Beaufort
1378–1389	Urban VI	Bartolomeo Prignano
1378–1394	Clement VII (antipope)	Robert de Genève
1389–1404	Boniface IX	Pietro Tomacelli
1394–1423	Benedict XIII (antipope)	Pedro de Luna
1404–1406	Innocent VII	Cosimo Migliorati
1406–1415	Gregory XII	Angelo Correr
1409–1410	Alexander V (antipope)	Peter of Candia (Petros Philargos)
1410–1415	John XXIII (antipope)	Baldassare Cossa
1417–1431	Martin V	Oddo Colonna
1423–1429	Clement VIII (antipope)	Gil Sánchez Muñoz
1425–1430	Benedict XIV (antipope)	Bernard Garnier
1431–1447	Eugene IV	Gabriele Condulmer
1439–1449	Felix V (antipope)	Amadeus VIII, Duke of Savoy
1447–1455	Nicholas V	Tommaso Parentucelli
1455–1458	Calixtus III	Alfonso de Borgia (Alfonso de Borja)
1458–1464	Pius II	Enea Silvio Piccolomini
1464–1471	Paul II	Pietro Barbo
1471–1484	Sixtus IV	Francesco della Rovere
1484–1492	Innocent VIII	Giovanni Battista Cibo
1492–1503	Alexander VI	Rodrigo Borgia (Rodrigo de Borja)
1503	Pius III	Francesco Todeschini Piccolomini
1503–1513	Julius II	Giuliano della Rovere
1513–1521	Leo X	Giovanni de' Medici
1522–1523	Adrian VI	Adrian Florenszoon Boeyens
1523–1534	Clement VII	Giulio de' Medici
1534–1549	Paul III	Alessandro Farnese
1550–1555	Julius III	Giovanni Maria Ciocchi del Monte
1555	Marcellus II	Marcello Cervini
1555–1559	Paul IV	Gian Pietro Carafa
1559–1565	Pius IV	Giovanni Angelo de' Medici
1566–1572	Pius V	Antonio Michele Ghislieri
1572–1585	Gregory XIII	Ugo Boncompagni
1585–1590	Sixtus V	Felice Peretti di Montalto
1590	Urban VII	Giovanni Battista Castagna
1590–1591	Gregory XIV	Niccolò Sfondrati
1591	Innocent IX	Giovanni Antonio Facchinetti
1592–1605	Clement VIII	Ippolito Aldobrandini
1605	Leo XI	Alessandro Ottaviano de' Medici
1605–1621	Paul V	Camillo Borghese
1621–1623	Gregory XV	Alessandro Ludovisi
1623–1644	Urban VIII	Maffeo Barberini
1644–1655	Innocent X	Giovanni Battista Pamfili
1655–1667	Alexander VII	Fabio Chigi
1667–1669	Clement IX	Giulio Rospigliosi
1670–1676	Clement X	Emilio Altieri
1676–1689	Innocent XI	Benedetto Odescalchi
1689–1691	Alexander VIII	Pietro Vito Ottoboni
1691–1700	Innocent XII	Antonio Pignatelli
1700–1721	Clement XI	Giovanni Francesco Albani
1721–1724	Innocent XIII	Michelangelo dei Conti
1724–1730	Benedict XIII	Pietro Francesco Orsini
1730–1740	Clement XII	Lorenzo Corsini
1740–1758	Benedict XIV	Prospero Lambertini
1758–1769	Clement XIII	Charles Rezzonico
1769–1774	Clement XIV	Giovanni Vincenzo Antonio Ganganelli
1775–1799	Pius VI	Giannangelo Braschi
1800–1823	Pius VII	Barnaba Chiaramonti
1823–1829	Leo XII	Annibale Sermattei della Genga
1829–1830	Pius VIII	Francesco Saverio Castiglioni
1831–1846	Gregory XVI	Bartolomeo Mauro Cappellari
1846–1878	Pius IX	Giovanni Maria Mastai-Ferretti
1878–1903	Leo XIII	Gioacchino Pecci
1903–1914	Pius X	Giuseppe Sarto
1914–1922	Benedict XV	Giacomo della Chiesa
1922–1939	Pius XI	Achille Ratti
1939–1958	Pius XII	Eugenio Pacelli
1958–1963	John XXIII	Angelo Giuseppe Roncalli
1963–1978	Paul VI	Giovanni Battista Montini
1978	John Paul I	Albino Luciani
1978–2005	John Paul II	Karol Józef Wojtyła
2005–	Benedict XVI	Joseph Alois Ratzinger

An antipope is someone who claims to be the rightful pope of the Roman Catholic Church in opposition to a lawfully elected bishop of Rome and whose claim has some measure of support.

Southeast Europe – Byzantium: An Overview

6th Century: The Empire under Justinian I

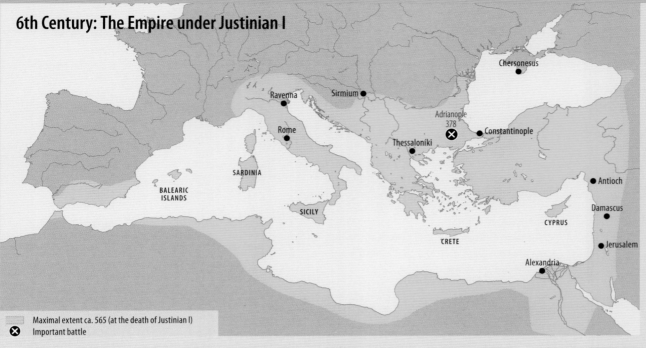

Maximal extent ca. 565 (at the death of Justinian I)
⊗ Important battle

7th Century

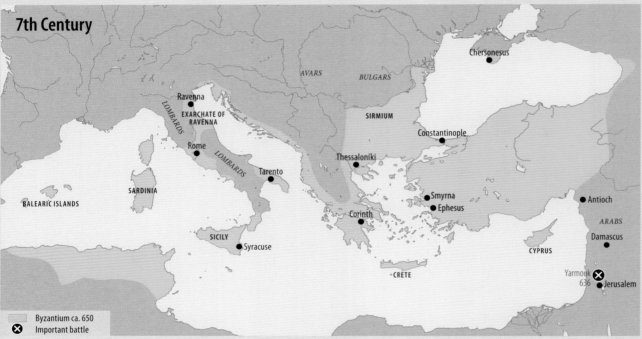

Byzantium ca. 650
⊗ Important battle

717: The Empire under Leon III

Byzantine territories 717
Territories dependent on the Byzantine Empire

The Byzantine Empire came into being in 395 as part of an administrative division of the Roman Empire into western and eastern halves. The Byzantine Empire, the eastern division, outlived the western half of the Roman Empire by nearly a millennium, extending its cultural and political influence throughout southeastern Europe. The Ottoman Empire brought the Byzantine Empire to an end with its conquest of Constantinople in 1453.

330 The Greek colonial city of Byzantium becomes "New Rome," the new capital of the Roman Empire. It will be renamed Constantinople, and later Istanbul.

378 Visigoths fleeing the Huns defeat Byzantine armies at Adrianople.

379–395 Emperor Theodosius I divides the Roman Empire into western and eastern halves, marking the beginning of the Byzantine Empire.

382 Emperor Theodosius I resettles large bands of Visigoths on the Lower Danube as foederati (non-citizen allies) of Rome.

from 395 Emperor Zeno bans Germanic tribes from the eastern Roman Empire, ending the influence of powerful German military leaders.

527–565 Emperor Justinian I reigns during the early high point of Byzantine culture.

532–537 Justinian I builds Hagia Sophia in Constantinople. For the next thousand years, it will be the largest cathedral in the world.

533/34 Byzantine forces under Justinian I defeat the Vandal kingdom, taking possession of Vandal territories in North Africa.

535–552/562 The Byzantine Empire under Justinian I conquers the Ostrogothic kingdom.

541 The Justinian plague, a pandemic originating in Egypt, ravages the Byzantine Empire.

553–555 Justinian I defeats the Visigoths in the southern Iberian Peninsula, completing the Byzantine recovery of the western Roman Empire.

568 The Lombards occupy large parts of Italy.

584 Justinian founds the Exarchate of Ravenna.

611–619 The Byzantine war with Persia results in the loss of Syria and Egypt.

626 The Byzantine navy beats back the Slavic siege of Constantinople.

627 Byzantine armies defeat Persia at Nineveh.

636 Arabs defeat the Byzantine Empire at the Battle of Yarmouk, gaining control of nearly all Byzantine eastern territories.

674–678 The Arab siege of Constantinople fails after the Byzantine defenders respond with Greek fire. Arabs will besiege the city again in 717–718.

688 Thessaloniki successfully defends against siege by the Bulgarians.

698 Most of the Byzantine Empire's North African territories are lost to the Arabs. The Arab Umayyad dynasty threatens Byzantine shipping in the Mediterranean.

726–842 Byzantine iconoclasm brings the empire to the brink of social and political collapse.

754 The iconoclastic Council of Hiereia bans all sacred images (icons).

787 The ecumenical Council of Nicaea lifts the ban on images. Periods of renewed Byzantine iconoclasm will continue on a smaller scale for the next 200 years.

797–802 Empress Irene rules as the first woman on the throne. Her attempt to prevent Charlemagne from crowning himself Holy Roman Emperor fails.

811 Bulgarian forces led by Khan Krum annihilate the Byzantine army at Pliska.

827 Arabs conquer Crete and Sicily.

913 Bulgarian forces besiege Constantinople, halting only when the Byzantine patriarch crowns Simeon tsar of Bulgaria.

961 Byzantine forces retake Crete.

971–972 Byzantine forces conquer eastern Bulgaria.

976–1025 Basileios II, known as Bulgaroktonos ("Bulgarian killer"), inaugurates the golden age of the Macedonian dynasty.

1014–1018 The Byzantine Empire defeats the Bulgarians at the Battle of Kleidon, ending the first Bulgarian empire. Historical sources say that the Bulgarian tsar Samuel died on the spot after seeing 14,000 Byzantine soldiers lined up against him.

The Code of Justinian is the collection of laws complied by Emperor Justinian I in 528–534. During the medieval period, this code would serve as the basis of civil law throughout Europe. The French and Prussian legal systems followed Justinian precepts well into the 19th century.

The Exarchate of Ravenna was the center of Byzantine administration in the Italian Peninsula from 584 to 751. As the residence of the exarch (governor), the city of Ravenna was adorned with magnificent architecture

9th–10th Centuries: Under the Macedonian Dynasty, Part I

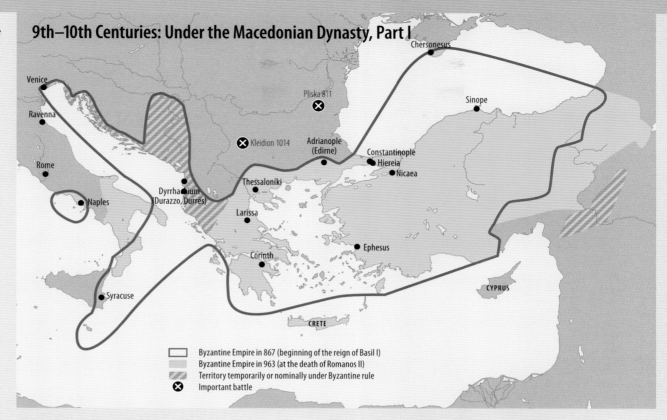

	Byzantine Empire in 867 (beginning of the reign of Basil I)
	Byzantine Empire in 963 (at the death of Romanos II)
	Territory temporarily or nominally under Byzantine rule
⊗	Important battle

and mosaics, including some of the most important examples of Byzantine art to survive the empire's collapse.

Themas were the Byzantine descendants of Roman provinces. These imperially administered territories were originally set up to defend Byzantine possessions in Asia Minor. Local government, including civil law and military recruitment, was under the command of the *strategos* (general). By the 8th to 10th centuries, most themas had developed into military colonies manned by peasant armies.

Greek fire was the 677 invention of the Greek architect Kallinikos. This powerful weapon consisted of an easily ignited liquid that could be shot across water at enemy

Greek fire

ships, or filled into pots and dropped on the heads of attackers besieging a city wall. The exact formula for Greek fire was a state secret that even today is only partially known. The base of the incendiary liquid was probably a petroleum product, either tar or crude oil, mixed with naphtha, quicklime or sulfur.

The Eastern Orthodox Church formed out of centuries of doctrinal struggle between the Greek and Roman Christian churches. Disagreements included the nature of the Holy Spirit, celibacy for priests, the primacy of the papacy, and whether the Eucharist bread should be leavened or unleavened. In 1054 these differences led to a final break with the Roman Catholic Church. After the collapse of the Byzantine Empire and the fall of Constantinople, the patriarch in Moscow became the head of the Eastern Orthodox Church.

ca. 1045: Under the Macedonian Dynasty, Part II

	Borders of the Byzantine area of influence after the conquests of Basil II (976–1025) and Constantine IX Monomachos (1042–1055)
	The "theme"—Byzantine provinces, ca. 1045
	Territories nominally under Byzantine rule

Southeast Europe – Byzantium: An Overview

11th–12th Centuries: The Empire under the Comnenian Dynasty

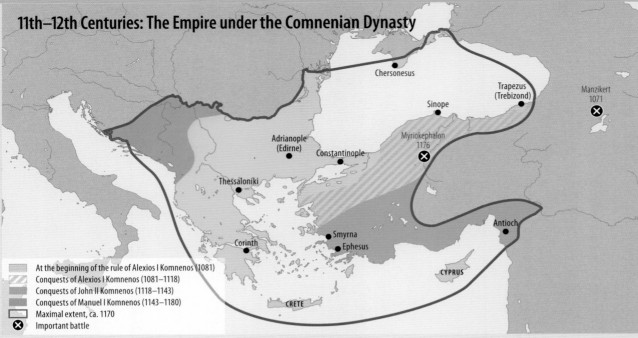

Chersonesus
Trapezus (Trebizond)
Sinope
Manzikert 1071
Adrianople (Edirne)
Myriokephalon 1176
Constantinople
Thessaloníki
Antioch
Smyrna
Corinth
Ephesus
CYPRUS
CRETE

At the beginning of the rule of Alexios I Komnenos (1081)
Conquests of Alexios I Komnenos (1081–1118)
Conquests of John II Komnenos (1118–1143)
Conquests of Manuel I Komnenos (1143–1180)
Maximal extent, ca. 1170
Important battle

1204: The Crusader Conquest of Constantinople

Kaffa
Chersonesus
Trapezus (Trebizond)
Sinope
KIPCHAK (CUMAN) KHANATE
BULGARIAN KHANATE
Adrianople (Edirne)
Constantinople
KINGDOM OF THESSALONÍKI
Nicaea
Thessaloníki
LEMNOS
DESPOTATE OF EPIRUS
SELJUQ SULTANATE OF RUM
EUBOEA
DUCHY OF ATHENS
Smyrna
PRINCIPALITY OF ACHAEA
Athens
Ephesus
RHODES
KARPATHOS
CRETE

Latin Empire (1204–1261)
Venetian domains
Empire of Trebizond (1204–1262)
Empire of Nicaea (1204–1261)
Despotate of Epirus

13th–14th Centuries: Ottoman Invasion

Adrianople (Edirne)
Constantinople
Ankara 1402
Nicaea
Pelekanon 1329
Thessaloníki
LEMNOS
LESBOS
EUBOEA (VENETIAN)
Smyrna
DUCHY OF ATHENS
Ephesus
Athens
DUCHY OF THE ARCHIPELAGO
Mystras
RHODES
CYPRUS
CRETE (VENETIAN)

Contested by Byzantium and Italian sea republics
Byzantine Empire, ca. 1270
Byzantine Empire, ca. 1350
Important battle

July 1054 The Great Schism: the (Eastern) Orthodox Church breaks with Rome.

1071 The Seljuqs defeat Byzantine armies at the battle of Manzikert.

1171 The Byzantine emperor arrests all the Venetians in the empire and seizes their property and goods.

1176 The Seljuqs defeat Byzantine armies at the battle of Myriokephalon (Ankara).

1186 Byzantium loses Bulgaria. The second Bulgarian empire is formed.

1204 The Fourth Crusade, led by Venetians, conquers Constantinople. The Byzantine Empire is divided, and a series of successor states form.

1261 Byzantine forces reconquer Constantinople, leading to a revival of the Byzantine Empire.

1274 The Council of Lyon agrees to reunite the Eastern Orthodox and Roman Catholic churches, but the agreement falls apart in practice.

1329 Ottoman armies defeat Byzantine forces in the battle of Pelekanon (Maltepe) leading to rapid Ottoman expansion in Asia Minor.

1331 Ottoman victory at Nicaea

1361 Ottoman victory at Adrianople (Edirne)

1379 The Byzantine Empire is made a vassal of the Ottoman sultans.

1402 Ottoman armies besiege Constantinople but are defeated by Timur Lenk (Tamerlane) near Ankara, leading to a temporary weakening of the Ottoman Empire. Timur Lenk imprisons Bayezid I and forces Ottoman armies to retreat to the Balkans.

1413 Ottoman expansion begins again; the Byzantine Empire loses all territory except for Constantinople and its immediate surroundings. Ottoman sultans build castles and other military installations along the Bosporus in preparation for a final assault on the city.

1439 The Councils of Ferrara and Florence force a union between the Eastern Orthodox and Roman Catholic churches in hopes of increasing military resources to fight the Ottoman Empire. Opposition from the religious hierarchy forces the Byzantine emperor back to the Eastern Orthodox rite ("Better a sultan's turban than a cardinal's hat.")

May 29, 1453 Ottoman forces conquer Constantinople, bringing down Constantine XI, the last Byzantine emperor. Mehmed II (the Conqueror) declares Constantinople the new capital of the Ottoman Empire.

1450: Before the Fall of Constantinople

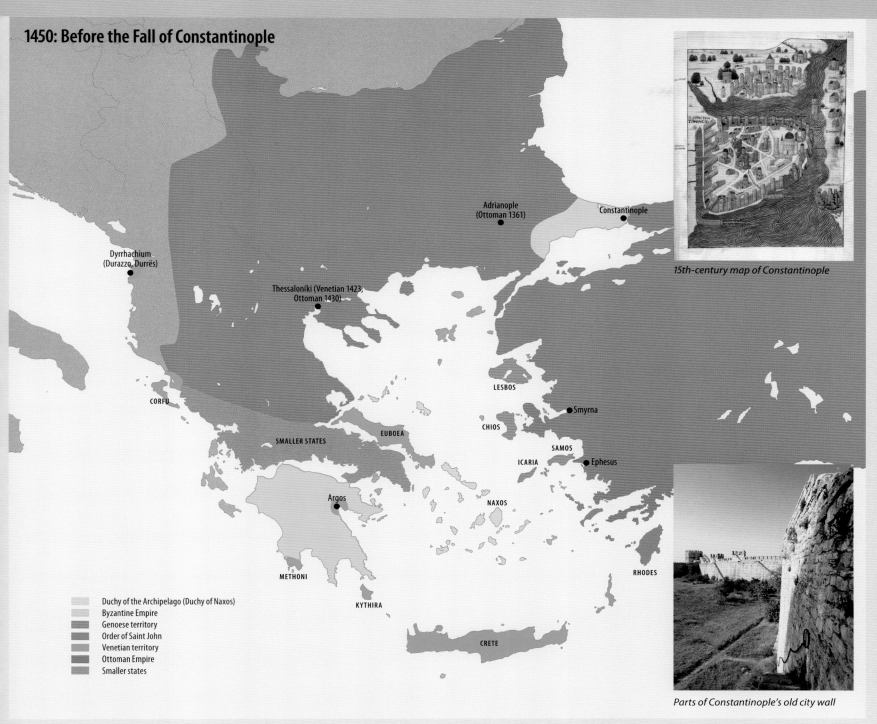

Adrianople
(Ottoman 1361)

Constantinople

Dyrrhachium
(Durazzo, Durrës)

Thessaloníki (Venetian 1423,
Ottoman 1430)

CORFU

LESBOS

Smyrna

CHIOS

SMALLER STATES

EUBOEA

SAMOS

ICARIA

Ephesus

Argos

NAXOS

METHONI

RHODES

KYTHIRA

CRETE

CHALCEDON

Duchy of the Archipelago (Duchy of Naxos)
Byzantine Empire
Genoese territory
Order of Saint John
Venetian territory
Ottoman Empire
Smaller states

15th-century map of Constantinople

Parts of Constantinople's old city wall

4th–15th Centuries:
City of Constantinople

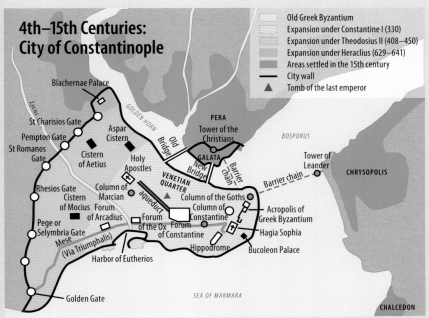

Old Greek Byzantium
Expansion under Constantine I (330)
Expansion under Theodosius II (408–450)
Expansion under Heraclius (629–641)
Areas settled in the 15th century
City wall
Tomb of the last emperor

Blachernae Palace

Lychos

GOLDEN HORN

PERA

BOSPORUS

St Charisios Gate

Aspar
Cistern

Old
Bridge

Tower of the
Christians

GALATA

Pempton Gate

St Romanos
Gate

Cistern
of Aetius

Holy
Apostles

New
Bridge

Barrier
Chain

Tower of
Leander

CHRYSOPOLIS

VENETIAN
QUARTER

Barrier chain

Rhesios Gate

Cistern
of Mocius

Column of
Marcian

aqueduct

Column of the Goths

Forum
of Arcadius

Column of
Constantine

Acropolis of
Greek Byzantium

Pege or
Selymbria Gate

Mese
(Via Triumphalis)

Forum
of the Ox

Forum
of Constantine

Hagia Sophia

Bucoleon Palace

Hippodrome

Harbor of Eutherios

Golden Gate

SEA OF MARMARA

CHALCEDON

Constantinople

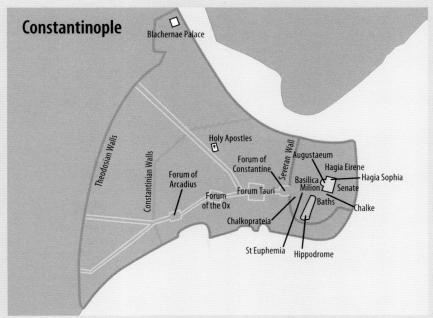

Blachernae Palace

Theodosian Walls

Constantinian Walls

Holy Apostles

Forum of
Constantine

Severan Wall

Augustaeum

Hagia Eirene

Hagia Sophia

Forum of
Arcadius

Forum
of the Ox

Forum Tauri

Basilica
Milion

Senate

Chalke

Baths

Chalkoprateia

St Euphemia

Hippodrome

Southeastern Europe – The Ottoman Empire: An Overview

1299–1402: Early Conquests

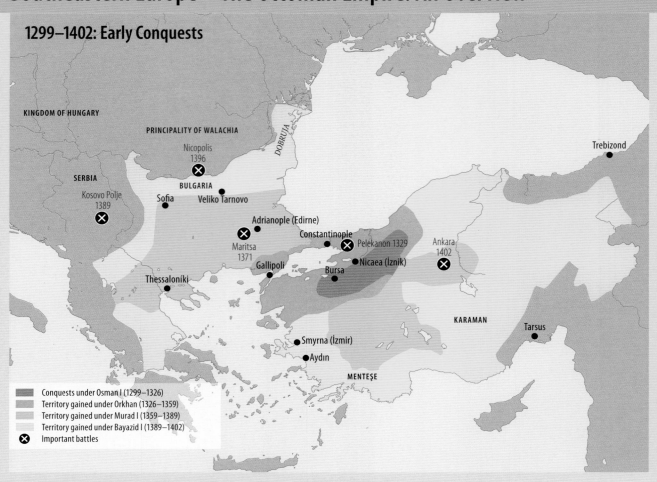

Legend (map 1):
- Conquests under Osman I (1299–1326)
- Territory gained under Orkhan (1326–1359)
- Territory gained under Murad I (1359–1389)
- Territory gained under Bayazid I (1389–1402)
- ✕ Important battles

Map labels: KINGDOM OF HUNGARY; PRINCIPALITY OF WALACHIA; DOBRUJA; Trebizond; SERBIA; BULGARIA; Nicopolis 1396; Kosovo Polje 1389; Sofia; Veliko Tarnovo; Adrianople (Edirne); Constantinople; Maritsa 1371; Pelekanon 1329; Ankara 1402; Gallipoli; Nicaea (Iznik); Bursa; Thessaloníki; KARAMAN; Tarsus; Smyrna (Izmir); Aydın; MENTEŞE

Beginning in 1299, the Ottoman Empire rapidly conquered southeastern Europe, becoming a great European empire. Ottoman sultans would go on to conquer most of the Near East and North Africa. By 1595 the empire encompassed almost 8 million square miles (20 million km²), more than twice the size of the United States.

1299 Osman I founds the Ottoman Empire by declaring his independence from the collapsing Sultanate of Rum.

1326 Ottoman armies capture Bursa, which will be capital of the empire until 1368. Osman I dies shortly after his most important victory.

1331 Conquest of Iznik (Nicaea)

1354 Conquest of Gallipoli (Gelibolu) and in 1361 Adrianople

1368–1453 Adrianople (Edirne) is the Ottoman capital.

Sept. 29, 1371 Sultan Murad I claims victory over Serbo-Bulagrian forces at the Battle of Maritza, forcing the Bulgarian empire to become a vassal of the Ottoman Empire.

1383 Conquest of Serdica (Sofia)

1413–1481: Ottoman Expansion Resumes

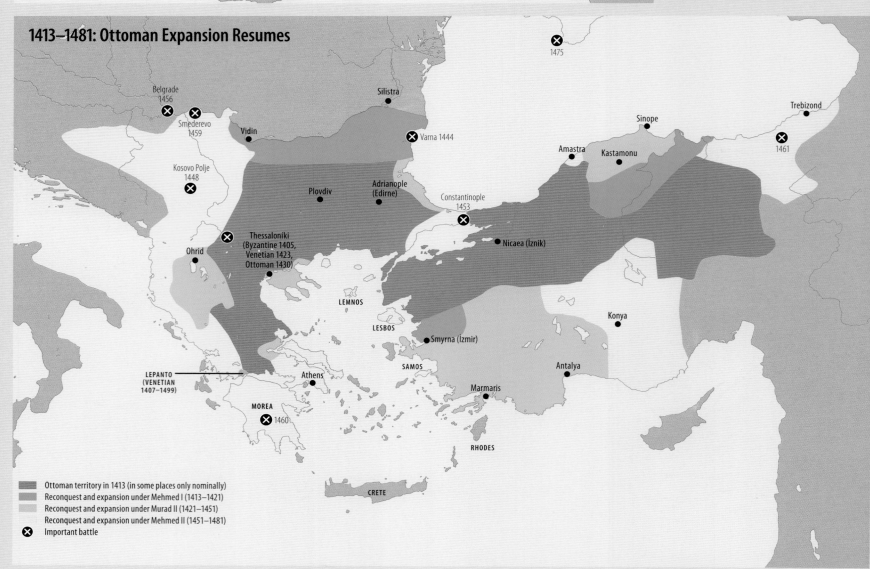

Legend (map 2):
- Ottoman territory in 1413 (in some places only nominally)
- Reconquest and expansion under Mehmed I (1413–1421)
- Reconquest and expansion under Murad II (1421–1451)
- Reconquest and expansion under Mehmed II (1451–1481)
- ✕ Important battle

Map labels: 1475; Belgrade 1456; Silistra; Trebizond; Smederevo 1459; Vidin; Sinope; Varna 1444; Amastra; Kastamonu; 1461; Kosovo Polje 1448; Plovdiv; Adrianople (Edirne); Constantinople 1453; Thessaloníki (Byzantine 1405, Venetian 1423, Ottoman 1430); Ohrid; Nicaea (Iznik); LEMNOS; Konya; LESBOS; Smyrna (Izmir); LEPANTO (VENETIAN 1407–1499); SAMOS; Athens; Antalya; Marmaris; MOREA 1460; RHODES; CRETE

1481–1683: Flourishing of the Ottoman Empire

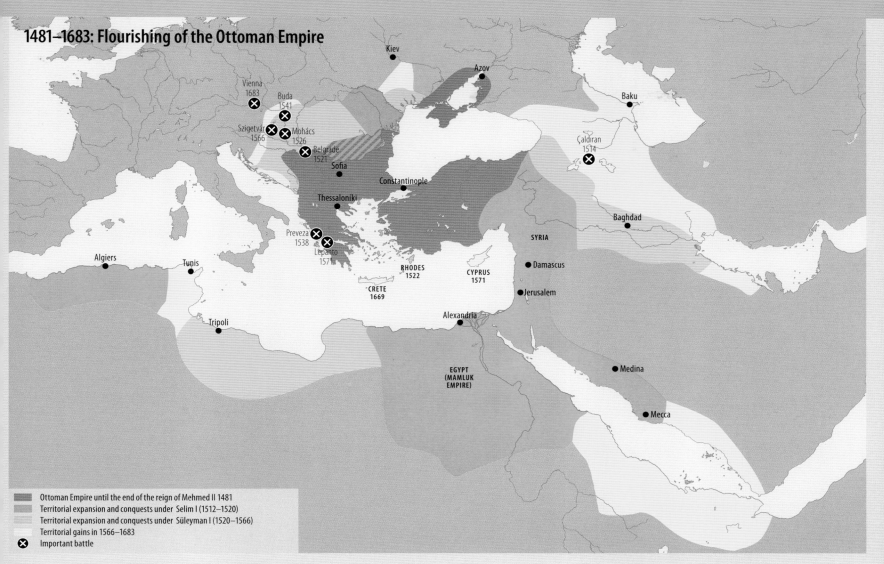

- Ottoman Empire until the end of the reign of Mehmed II 1481
- Territorial expansion and conquests under Selim I (1512–1520)
- Territorial expansion and conquests under Süleyman I (1520–1566)
- Territorial gains in 1566–1683
- ⊗ Important battle

1389 Battle of the Field of the Black-birds (Kosovo Polje): The Ottomans defeat the allied Christian princes, making them imperial subjects under Ottoman rule administered by the province of Serbia.

1390 Conquest of Aydin and the Emirate of Menteşe in Anatolia.

1393–1396 Ottoman complete their takeover of the Bulgarian kingdoms of Tarnovo, Vidin and Dorbudja.

1396 Battle of Nicopolis: Ottoman victory over a united French-Hungarian-Wallachaian army.

1402 Timur Lenk (Tamerlane) defeats Ottoman forces at Ankara, capturing Bayezid I and forcing the surrender of all Ottoman territory in Anatolia.

1402–1413 Ottoman succession crisis: Bayezid's sons struggle for power.

1413 Unification of the Ottoman Empire under Mehmed I leads to a renewed period of Ottoman expansion.

1424 Conquest of Smyrna (Izmir)

1430 Conquest of Thessaloniki

1444 Ottoman forces defeat a united Polish-Hungarian army at Varna.

1448 Hungarian forces are annihilated at the second battle of Kosovo Polje.

1449 A Janissary rebellion leads to better pay and conditions for the elite Janissary corps.

May 29, 1453 Mehmed II captures Constantinople. The city will be called Istanbul ("the city"), but retains Constantinople as its official name until 1920.

1456 Hungarian success in holding off the siege of Belgrade leads to a period of relative peace between Hungary and the Ottoman Empire.

1459 Smederevo becomes a tax-paying dependency of the Ottomans. Serbia comes completely under Ottoman control.

1460 Conquest of the principality of Morea (Peloponnesus)

1461 Mehmed II conquers Trebizond, the last remaining Byzantine successor state.

1466 Ottoman conquest of Konya,

1475 the Crimean Peninsula

1478 and Albania.

Selim the Grim and Süleyman the Magnificent

1512–1520 The reign of Sultan Selim I ("the Grim") doubles the size of the Ottoman Empire. In 1517 he declares himself caliph.

Selim I (ca. 1465–1520)

1514 Selim I defeats Shah Ismail at Chaldiran, taking control of large parts of formerly Persian territory.

1516 Selim I conquers Syria.

1517 Selim I conquers Egypt and becomes guardian of the holy cities of Mecca and Medina.

1520–1566 Selim's son, Süleyman I the Magnificent, rules during the golden age of Ottoman culture.

Süleyman I (ca. 1494–1566)

1521 Süleyman captures Belgrade.

1522 Süleyman conquers Rhodes.

1526 Süleyman defeats the kingdom of Hungary at Mohács.

Battle of Mohács

1529 First Ottoman Siege of Vienna

1534 Süleyman conquers Mesopotamia and Azerbaijan.

1538 Ottoman admiral Barbarossa defeats the fleet of the Holy League at Preveza.

1540 Süleyman conquers Yemen.

1541 Süleyman captures the Hungarian capital of Buda, part of today's Budapest. Ottoman armies rapidly occupy all but the northwestern corner of the kingdom of Hungary.

Southeastern Europe – The Ottoman Empire: An Overview

1683–1923: Stagnation and Decline

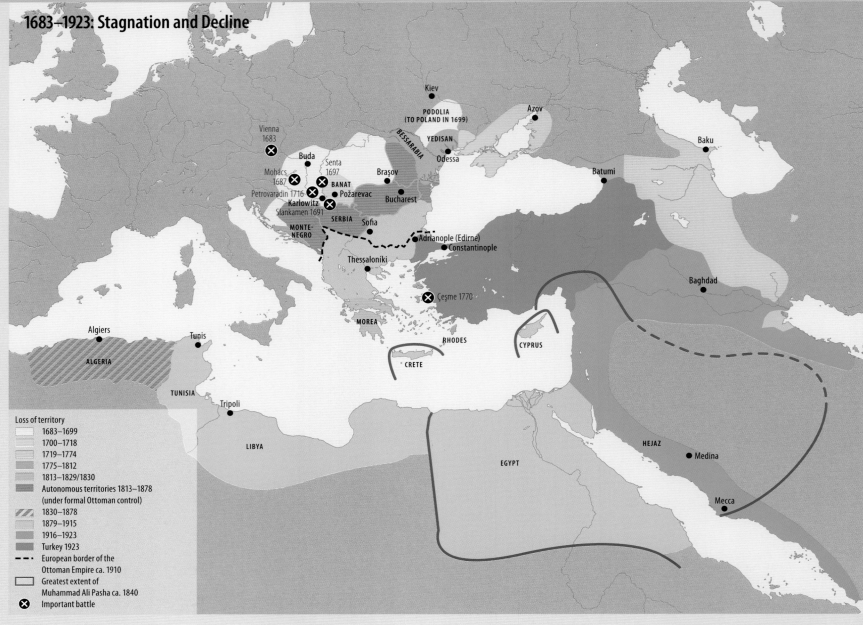

Loss of territory
- 1683–1699
- 1700–1718
- 1719–1774
- 1775–1812
- 1813–1829/1830
- Autonomous territories 1813–1878 (under formal Ottoman control)
- 1830–1878
- 1879–1915
- 1916–1923
- Turkey 1923
- European border of the Ottoman Empire ca. 1910
- Greatest extent of Muhammad Ali Pasha ca. 1840
- ⊗ Important battle

1566 Siege and capture of the Hungarian fortress at Szigetvár

August 1571 Annexation of Cyprus

Oct. 7, 1571 Spain and Venice defeat the Ottoman fleet in the Battle of Lepanto.

~1595 The Ottoman Empire reaches its greatest extent.

1623–1640 Murad IV, the last powerful Ottoman sultan, rules with exceptional harshness.

1669 Conquest of Crete

1683 The Ottomans are repelled at the second Siege of Vienna, initiating a long period of gradual decline.

1687 Imperial armies led by Austria defeat Ottoman forces at the second Battle of Mohács.

1691 Imperial forces led by Louis of Baden defeat Ottoman armies at Slankamen.

1696–1711 Sultan Ibrahim surrenders Azov to Russia. The Ottoman Empire regains control in 1642, only to lose Azov to Russia again in 1739.

1697 Eugene of Savoy annihilates Ottoman forces at the Battle of Senta.

1699 The Habsburgs regain control of Hungary and Transylvania through the Peace of Karlowitz, effectively ending Ottoman influence in central Europe.

1716 Austria defeats Ottoman forces at Petrovaradin.

1718 The Ottoman sultan signs the Treaty of Passarowitz, ceding the Banat of Temesvar, the last remaining Ottoman Hungarian territory, to Austria.

1768–1774 In the first Russo-Turkish War the Ottoman fleet is destroyed at Cesme, leading to the loss of Crimea.

1789–1807 Sultan Selim III fails in his attempt to reform the Ottoman Empire according to European models.

1804–1813 (and 1815–1817) Two Serbian revolts lead to autonomy from the Ottoman Empire.

1805 Egypt becomes largely independent under Muhammad Ali.

1808–1839 Sultan Mahmud II "the Reformer" disbands the Janissaries.

1812 The Treaty of Bucharest cedes the Ottoman province of Bessarabia to Russia. Bessarabia becomes part of the principality of Moldavia, now part of the Republic of Moldova.

1821–1829 Greece wins independence with European support.

1829 War with Russia ends with the Treaty of Adrianople, giving Russia control of the lower Danube Valley. Moldova and Wallachia remain part of the Ottoman Empire, but with increased autonomy.

1830 French occupation of Algeria

1839–1876 Tanzimat (Turkish for "reorganization") reforms begin under sultans Abdülmecid I and Abdülaziz. The reforms standardize civil rights throughout the empire for all subjects, including non-Muslims.

1853–1856 The Crimean War against Russia ends with Moldova and Wallachia under the administration of Ottoman allies Britain and France.

1876–1909 The despotic sultan Abdulhamid II abolishes the Tanzimat reforms and enters into an alliance with Germany.

1877–1878 The final Russo-Turkish War ends with Ottoman defeat.

1878 The Congress of Berlin grants independence to Serbia and Montenegro, and autonomy to Bulgaria. Austria-Hungary occupies Bosnia.

1881 France annexes Tunisia.

1882 Britain occupies Egypt.

1908 Bulgaria gains full independence; Bosnia is annexed by Austria-Hungary.

1908–1918 The Young Turk movement attempts to set a new direction for national reform.

1910 Revolt in Kosovo against Ottoman rule

1918–1923: Founding of the Turkish Republic

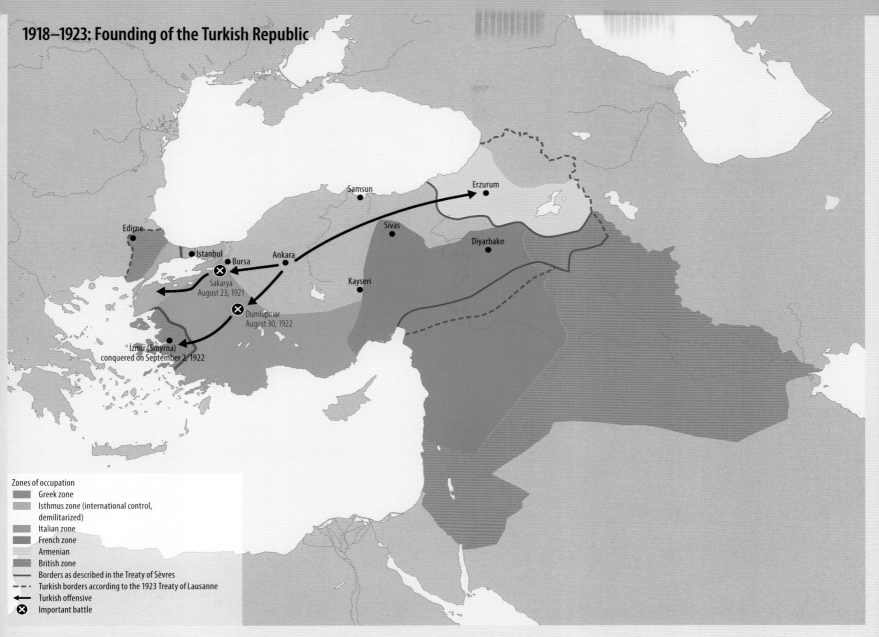

Zones of occupation
- Greek zone
- Isthmus zone (international control, demilitarized)
- Italian zone
- French zone
- Armenian
- British zone
- Borders as described in the Treaty of Sèvres
- Turkish borders according to the 1923 Treaty of Lausanne
- Turkish offensive
- ⊗ Important battle

Samsun
Erzurum
Edirne
Sivas
Istanbul
Bursa
Ankara
Diyarbakır
⊗ Sakarya August 23, 1921
Kayseri
⊗ Dumlupınar August 30, 1922
İzmir (Smyrna) conquered on September 2, 1922

1911 Surrender of Tripolitania (Libya) to Italy

October 1912–May 1913 An alliance of Serbia, Bulgaria, Montenegro and Greece defeat the Ottoman Empire in the First Balkan War. Nearly all remaining Ottoman European possessions are lost.

June–August 1913 The Ottoman Empire regains Eastern Thrace from Bulgaria in the Second Balkan War.

Aug. 2, 1914 William II, the German emperor, signs a secret treaty with the Ottoman Empire.

Nov. 3–5, 1914 Russia, France and Great Britain declare war on the Ottoman Empire, which enters World War I as an ally of Germany.

1915 Armenian genocide

1916 The British occupy Iraq, which becomes a British protectorate in 1920.

1916–1918 The Arab Revolt expels Ottoman troops from the Hejaz, the northwestern portion of the Arabian Peninsula (including the holy sites of Mecca and Medina).

Oct. 30, 1918 The Ottoman Empire signs the Armistice with the victorious powers Great Britain, France, Italy and Greece, ending World War I.

May 19, 1919 Mustafa Kemal Pasha (Ataturk) arrives in Samsun to lead the Turkish War of Independence.

July–September 1919 Congresses are held in Erzurum and Sivas. They provide for Turkish independence within the parameters of the World War I peace agreements. Turkey agrees to abandon imperial policies.

March–April 1920 Ataturk convenes a national assembly in Ankara after the British occupy Istanbul (Constantinople).

August 1920 Ataturk refuses to abide by the Treaty of Sèvres, which called for the partition of Turkey. Greek troops invade Asia Minor, where they will remain as an occupying force until 1922.

November 1922 Ataturk abolishes the sultanate, formally establishing the Republic of Turkey. Ataturk will become the republic's first president, an office he will hold until his death in 1938.

July 24, 1923 The Treaty of Lausanne, a revision of the Treaty of Sèvres, retracts the provisions for partition. To stabilize Asia Minor, Greece and Turkey exchange populations, creating refugee populations in both countries numbering over 1 million.

Janissaries were elite special military forces first established in 1330 by Ottoman sultan Murad I. The corps was composed of young boys from Ottoman Christian territories. Functioning like an elite version of forced adoption (devshirme), the most promising Balkan Christian youths were "collected," like a tax, once a year. The boys were raised on Ottoman agricultural estates, where they learned the Turkish language and Ottoman customs. Most were then enrolled in military units, where they were subject to strict discipline and intense training. Their enforced social isolation (including a ban on marriage), ability to adapt to harsh physical conditions, and daily life devoted almost exclusively to military drilling made the Janissaries ideal soldiers. At its greatest strength, the Janissary corps numbered 200,000, most specializing in light and heavy artillery. By the late 17th century the Janissaries had become more powerful than the weakened Ottoman sultanate, becoming a state within a state. In 1826 Sultan Mahmud II disbanded the Janissaries, killing most of them and driving the rest into exile.

The Sick Man of Europe was a term coined by Russian Czar Nicholas I to describe the weakened state of the Ottoman Empire in the 19th century. At the onset of World War I, the Ottoman sultan was little more than a pawn in the hands of the Great Powers of Europe.

The Young Turks was a nationalist political movement that developed within the Ottoman Empire in the last decade of the 19th century. Coming to power as part of a 1913 military revolt, the Young Turks attempted an ambitious program of Western-influenced reform. At the onset of World War I, the Young Turk triumvirate of Enver, Talat and Cemal Pashas, though officially ministers of war, the navy and interior, ruled Turkey as virtual dictators.

Ismail Enver Pasha (1881–1922), a leader of the Young Turks

Serbia and Montenegro Until the 15th Century

Antiquity

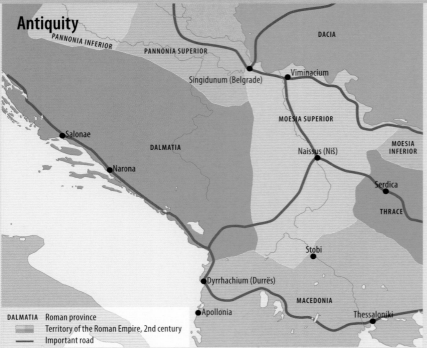

DALMATIA — Roman province
— Territory of the Roman Empire, 2nd century
— Important road

6th–7th Centuries: Migration of the Slavs and Avars

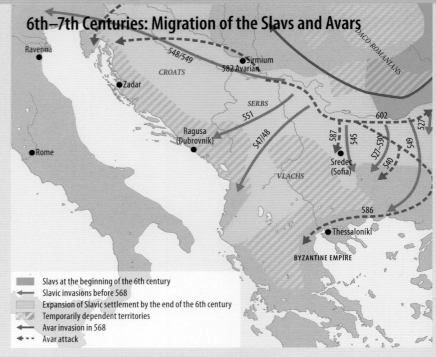

Slavs at the beginning of the 6th century
Slavic invasions before 568
Expansion of Slavic settlement by the end of the 6th century
Temporarily dependent territories
Avar invasion in 568
Avar attack

10th–11th Centuries: The Bulgarian Empire

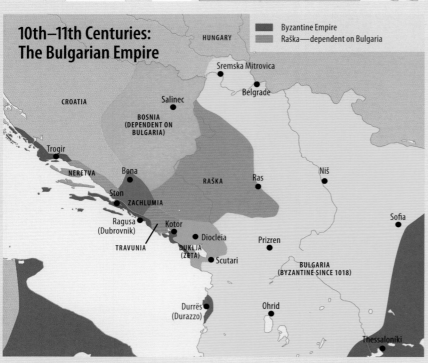

Byzantine Empire
Raška—dependent on Bulgaria

The medieval principalities of Serbia and Montenegro withstood attacks from the Byzantine, Bulgarian and Ottoman empires. Although Serbia lost its autonomy, the smaller, more isolated Montenegro was able to remain largely independent due to its remote location.

2nd century BCE The Thracians, an Indo-European tribe, settle the eastern and central Balkan regions.

1200–1100 BCE The Illyrians settle the western Balkan Peninsula.

4th–3rd centuries BCE The city of Navissos is founded (Roman Nassius, today Niš).

148/146 BCE–**106** CE The Romans found the Balkan provinces of Illyricum, Macedonia, Moesia and Dacia.

395 The Roman Empire is divided in two. Serbia becomes part of the Eastern Roman (Byzantine) Empire.

568–803 The Avars north of the Danube move south and establish the Serbian principalities of Zeta and Raška.

~600 The territory of present-day Serbia comes under the control of the Albanian Župans.

6th–7th centuries Arrival of the Slavs

~825 Prince Vlastimir becomes Grand Župan of Raška. The Vlastirmirić dynasty rules Raška until 950.

~871–875 Raška is Christianized.

924–927 Raška becomes a province of the Bulgarian Empire.

927–950 Časlav Klonimirović rules as Grand Župan of Raška.

950–1050 A large portion of the region falls under the control of the Byzantine Empire.

1196–1227: The Nemanjidan Regime

Raška at the end of the reign of Stefan I Nemanja in 1196
Raška at the end of the reign of Stefan II Nemanjić Prvovenčani in 1228
✝ Important monastery

1291–1321: Raška and Dragutin and Milutin

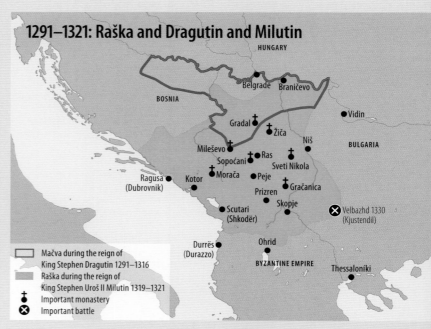

Mačva during the reign of King Stephen Dragutin 1291–1316
Raška during the reign of King Stephen Uroš II Milutin 1319–1321
✝ Important monastery
⊗ Important battle

1355: The Golden Age of Serbia

Serbia at the end of the rule of Stephen Uroš IV Dušan in 1355
✝ Important monastery

The Second Half of the 14th Century

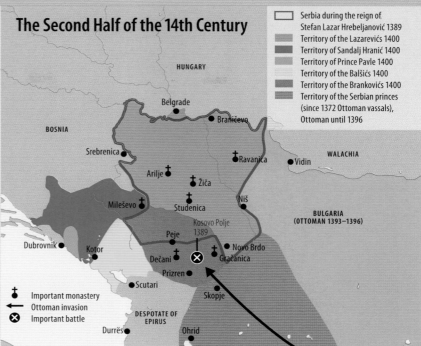

Serbia during the reign of Stefan Lazar Hrebeljanović 1389
Territory of the Lazarevićs 1400
Territory of Sandalj Hranić 1400
Territory of Prince Pavle 1400
Territory of the Balšićs 1400
Territory of the Brankovićs 1400
Territory of the Serbian princes (since 1372 Ottoman vassals), Ottoman until 1396

✝ Important monastery
← Ottoman invasion
⊗ Important battle

1427–1459

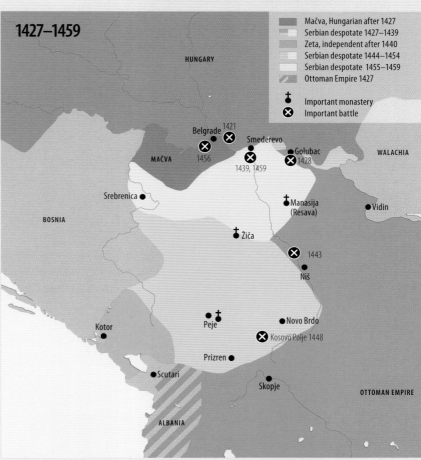

Mačva, Hungarian after 1427
Serbian despotate 1427–1439
Zeta, independent after 1440
Serbian despotate 1444–1454
Serbian despotate 1455–1459
Ottoman Empire 1427

✝ Important monastery
⊗ Important battle

1077 Prince and Grand Župan Mihailo of Zeta is proclaimed king of Serbia by the pope.

after 1101 Duklja (Zeta) gradually declines. The Urošević dynasty assumes control of Raška.

1130 Zeta comes under the direct control of Raška until 1360.

1167–1196 Grand Župan Stefan I Nemanja rules Raška. The Nermanjidan dynasty will remain in power for two centuries, until 1371.

1219 Saint Sava of Serbia, the brother of King Stefan II, establishes the Serbian archbishopric. He is also the author of the first Slavic law code, the Nomocanon.

1243–1276 The reign of Stefan Uroš I brings economic prosperity to Serbia through the establishment of a mining industry and improved trade connections through the port city of Dubrovnik (Ragusa).

1282–1321 During the reign of Stefan Uroš II Milutin, Serbia becomes the leading power in the Balkans, and numerous churches and monastaries are established throughout the kingdom.

1330 The Battle of Velbazdh (Kyustendil, now in Bulgaria) brings Bulgaria under Serbian influence.

1331–1355 The reign of Stefan Uroš IV Dušan inaugurates Serbia's golden age. With the subjugation of Albania and Macedonia, the Serbian empire is established.

Stefan Uroš IV Dušan (ca. 1308–1335)

1346 Stefan Uroš IV Dušan declares himself emperor. The Serbian national church is established.

1355–1371 Independent principalities are established as Serbian central authority disintigrates during the reign of Stefan Uroš V ("the Weak")

1356–1421 Zeta (Montenegro) falls under the control of local princes.

1371 The Ottoman Empire defeats combined Serbian and Bulgarian forces at the Battle of Maritza.

1386 The capture of Niš marks the beginning of Ottoman aggression in Serbia.

1389 Serbia is defeated at Kosovo Polje (the Battle of Blackbird's Field), giving the Ottoman Empire suzerainty over Serbia.

1420–1797 The Venetians take control of Kotor (Montenegro).

1421–1451 Zeta is absorbed into the Serbian Despotate.

after 1427 Belgrade is ceded to the Kingdom of Hungary.

1448 The Ottomans defeat Hungary at the second battle of Kosovo Polje.

Stefan Uroš II Milutin (ca. 1253–1321)

1456 Ottoman forces besiege Belgrade. Hungarian national hero John Hunyadi leads a valiant defense against Mehmed II, overrunning Turkish lines and wounding the sultan to force his retreat. It will be seventy years before the Ottoman Empire attacks Belgrade again.

1459 Ottoman armies seize the capital, Smederevo, marking the end of the Serbian Despotate and beginning of the Ottoman province of Serbia (the Sandžak of Smederevo).

The Grand Župan was the clan chief acknowledged as supreme by other local tribal leaders (župan) throughout Greater Serbia.

Raška was a medieval state located in what is now southwest Serbia, northern Montenegro and western Bosnia. Its capital was Stari Ras (near Novi Pazar), a city that was settled by Serbs shortly after their arrival in the Balkans, and the source of the principality's name. Raška was one of the most important regions under the control of Serbia throughout the medieval period.

Serbia and Montenegro 16th Century–1945

1683–1691: Advance of the Habsburg Army

Attacks of Habsburg troops
Northward escape of the Serbs 1689–1690
⊗ Important battle

Szeged
Arad ⊗
Zenta 1697 ⊗
Petrovaradin
⊗ Slankamen 1691
Belgrade
⊗ 1688
⊗ 1690
Sarajevo
Kruševac
Novi Pazar
Niš
Pirot
Cetinje
Peć
Prizren
Skopje

Habsburg Empire and Transylvania until 1685
Ottoman Empire until 1683
Territory occupied by the Habsburg Empire until 1687
Border of territory controlled by Habsburg troops in 1689
Territory of the Serbian rebels
Montenegro

18th Century: The Habsburg and Ottoman Empires

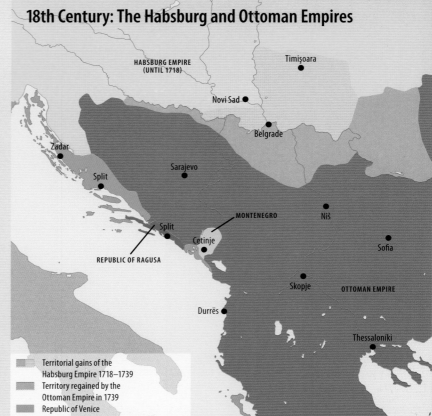

HABSBURG EMPIRE (UNTIL 1718)
Timişoara
Novi Sad
Belgrade
Zadar
Sarajevo
Split
Split
MONTENEGRO
Niš
Cetinje
REPUBLIC OF RAGUSA
Sofia
Skopje
Durrës
OTTOMAN EMPIRE
Thessaloníki

Territorial gains of the Habsburg Empire 1718–1739
Territory regained by the Ottoman Empire in 1739
Republic of Venice

19th Century

HUNGARY
BOSNIA AND HERZEGOVINA
Belgrade
Sarajevo
Niš
Cetinje
Sofia
Scutari
Skopje
Durrës
MACEDONIA
ITALY
Thessaloniki
GREECE

Ottoman Empire and its vassals in 1830
Serbia 1817–1833 (Sanjak of Smederevo)
Serbia 1833–1878
Serbia since 1878
Montenegro ca. 1800
Montenegro in 1860
Montenegro in 1878
Ottoman territory, occupied by Austria-Hungary from 1878
Remaining Ottoman territory, lost 1878–1883
Ottoman Empire in 1908
Military border in Austria until 1881
Autonomous Province of Vojvodina in Austria 1844–1860

1521 The Ottomans capture Belgrade.

1593–1607 Serbian rebellion in the Vojvodina is bloodily suppressed.

1688–1690 The defeat of the Serbian rebellion following the Habsburg victory over the Ottomans leads to massive emigration to the north (to the Kingdom of Hungary).

1697 Danilo I founds the Petrović-Njegoš dynasty in Montenegro.

1718–1739 Northern Serbia is under Austrian control.

1797–1805 and 1814–1918 Austria controls Kotor.

1804–1813 The first Serbian rebellion led by Djordje Petrović, "Karadjordje", is violently suppressed.

1815–1817 The second Serbian rebellion leads to the establishment of a Serbian principality under Ottoman rule.

June–July 1878 The Congress of Berlin recognizes the full independence of Serbia and Montenegro.

March 6, 1882 Proclamation of the Kingdom of Serbia

1910 Montenegro becomes a kingdom.

October 1912–May 1913 First Balkan War

May 30, 1913 The Treaty of London divides Ottoman Macedonia among the members of the Balkan League.

June–August 1913 The Second Balkan War: Serbia acquires northern Macedonia.

Aug. 10/Sep. 29, 1913 The Treaty of Bucharest/Constantinople establishes new borders between Serbia, Greece and the Ottoman Empire.

June 28, 1914 Archduke Francis Ferdinand, heir to the Austro-Hungarian throne, is assassinated in Sarajevo. The secret society known as the Black Hand is suspected of supporting the Serbian assassin, Gavrilo Princep. He was also a member of Young Bosnia, a Serbian nationalist group.

July 28, 1914 Austria-Hungary declares war on Serbia, setting in motion the events of World War I.

Serbia (and Yugoslavia) since 1914

August–November 1914 Serbia withstands two offensives by the Austro-Hungarians.

October 1915–February 1916 Austro-Hungarian, German and Bulgarian forces attack Serbia and occupy Belgrade. The Serbian government retreats, and the king goes into exile. Serbia refuses to sign the surrender.

July 1917 The Corfu Declaration calls for the establishment of a nation state composed of Serbs, Croats and Slovenes.

1918 Austria-Hungary surrenders in October; the Kingdom of Serbs, Croats and Slovenes is founded as the first united Yugoslav state on December 1st.

1921 The Little Entente is signed, forming an alliance between Czechoslovakia, Rumania and Yugoslavia against Germany and Hungarian aggression in the Danube River basin.

1928 The internal political struggle between the Serbs and Croats ends with the death of nationalistic Croatian politician Stjepan Radić at the hands of Serbian radical Puniš Račić.

January 1929 Alexander I of Serbia dismisses the regency council and declares a "royal dictatorship."

1934 King Alexander I is shot and killed in Marseilles by Croatian and Bulgarian fascists.

1937 Josip Broz Tito rises to the leadership of the Communist Party.

1939 Croatia wins its autonomy.

March 1941 A coup in Belgrade leads to establishment of a pro-British government.

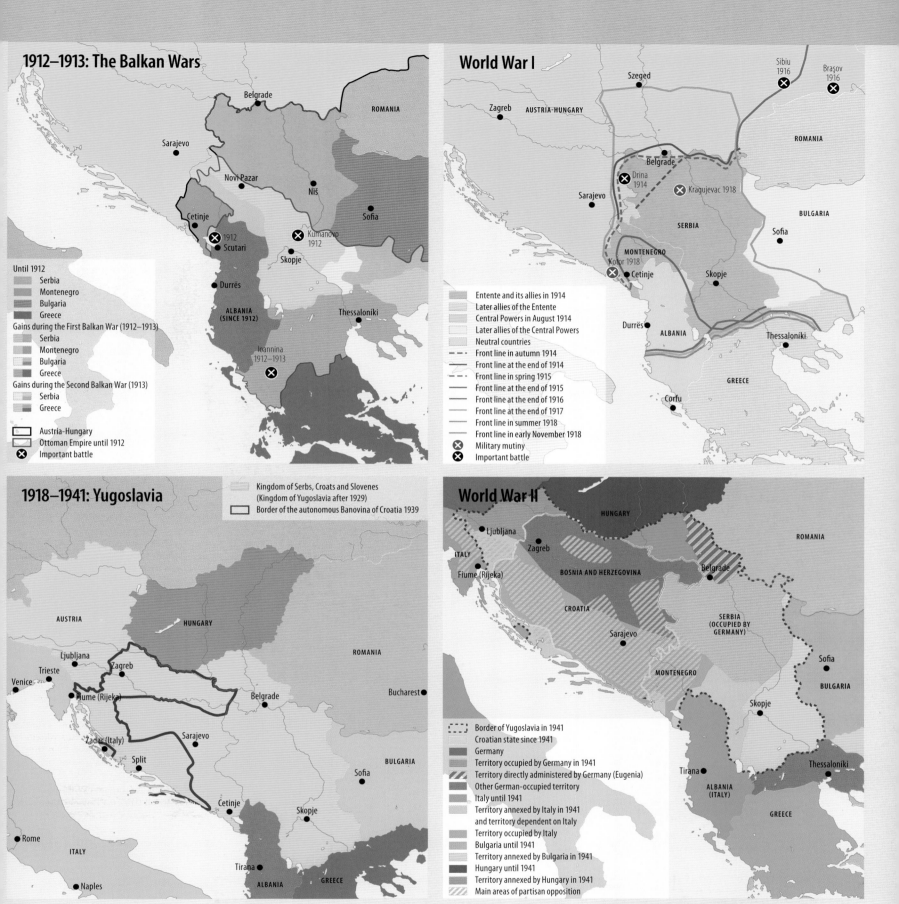

1912–1913: The Balkan Wars

Until 1912
- Serbia
- Montenegro
- Bulgaria
- Greece

Gains during the First Balkan War (1912–1913)
- Serbia
- Montenegro
- Bulgaria
- Greece

Gains during the Second Balkan War (1913)
- Serbia
- Greece

- Austria-Hungary
- Ottoman Empire until 1912
- ⊗ Important battle

Belgrade · Sarajevo · Novi Pazar · Niš · Sofia · Cetinje · ⊗ 1912 Scutari · Kumanovo 1912 ⊗ · Skopje · Durrës · ALBANIA (SINCE 1912) · Thessaloníki · Ioannina 1912–1913 ⊗ · ROMANIA

World War I

- Entente and its allies in 1914
- Later allies of the Entente
- Central Powers in August 1914
- Later allies of the Central Powers
- Neutral countries
- Front line in autumn 1914
- Front line at the end of 1914
- Front line in spring 1915
- Front line at the end of 1915
- Front line at the end of 1916
- Front line at the end of 1917
- Front line in summer 1918
- Front line in early November 1918
- ⊗ Military mutiny
- ⊗ Important battle

Sibiu 1916 ⊗ · Brașov 1916 ⊗ · Szeged · Zagreb · AUSTRIA-HUNGARY · ROMANIA · Belgrade · ⊗ Drina 1914 · Kragujevac 1918 ⊗ · Sarajevo · SERBIA · BULGARIA · Sofia · MONTENEGRO · Kotor 1918 ⊗ · Cetinje · Skopje · Durrës · ALBANIA · Thessaloníki · GREECE · Corfu

1918–1941: Yugoslavia

- Kingdom of Serbs, Croats and Slovenes (Kingdom of Yugoslavia after 1929)
- Border of the autonomous Banovina of Croatia 1939

AUSTRIA · HUNGARY · Ljubljana · Zagreb · Trieste · Venice · Fiume (Rijeka) · Zadar (Italy) · Sarajevo · Split · Cetinje · Skopje · Belgrade · ROMANIA · Bucharest · BULGARIA · Sofia · Rome · ITALY · Naples · Tirana · ALBANIA · GREECE

World War II

- ⊏⊐ Border of Yugoslavia in 1941
- Croatian state since 1941
- Germany
- Territory occupied by Germany in 1941
- Territory directly administered by Germany (Eugenia)
- Other German-occupied territory
- Italy until 1941
- Territory annexed by Italy in 1941 and territory dependent on Italy
- Territory occupied by Italy
- Bulgaria until 1941
- Territory annexed by Bulgaria in 1941
- Hungary until 1941
- Territory annexed by Hungary in 1941
- Main areas of partisan opposition

HUNGARY · Ljubljana · Zagreb · ITALY · Fiume (Rijeka) · BOSNIA AND HERZEGOVINA · Belgrade · ROMANIA · CROATIA · Sarajevo · SERBIA (OCCUPIED BY GERMANY) · Sofia · MONTENEGRO · BULGARIA · Skopje · Tirana · ALBANIA (ITALY) · Thessaloníki · GREECE

April 1941 Yugoslavia capitulates. Serbia is conquered by German troops, and portions of its territory are given to Bulgaria and Hungary. An independent Croatian state is established that includes Bosnia and Herzegovina. Jews and Serbs in the new Croatian state are persecuted, deported (to the concentration camp Jasenovac) and killed. The partisan struggle led by Tito begins.

1943 Allied leaders meet at the Tehran Conference; they support the resistance movement led by Tito.

May 1945 Partisans led by Tito together with Soviet troops liberate Yugoslavia. Formerly occupied territories are returned to Yugoslavia. Tito takes the title of Marshal of Yugoslavia; he will lead the nation until his death in 1980.

Balkan Wars, 1912–1913 The Balkan League (a military alliance of Serbia, Bulgaria, Montenegro and Greece) fought the first war against the Ottoman Empire. After the victory of the Balkan League, the conquered territory was divided according to the London Treaty of 1913.

The Second Balkan War began when Bulgaria, unhappy with that distribution, attacked Serbia and Greece. A coalition of Serbia, Greece, Romania, Montenegro and Turkey defeated Bulgaria. Although Serbia received Macedonian territory in compensation, it failed to gain access to the Adriatic due to the Great Powers' desire to support the establishment of Albania.

Balkan War, 1912

Serbia and Yugoslavia 1945 to the Present

1945: Yugoslavia

Legend:
- Border of Yugoslavia
- MACEDONIA Federal republic
- KOSOVO Autonomous territory within Serbia
- Serbia

1991: The Collapse of Yugoslavia

Legend:
- Republics declaring independence in 1991
- Croatian territory controlled by the Serbs in 1991
- Border of the separatist Republic of Serbian Krajina in Croatia 1992–1995
- Bosnia and Herzegovina, declared independence in 1992
- Republic of Serbia in Bosnia and Herzegovina since 1993 (status as of 1995)
- Kosovo, under UN control since 1999, unilaterally declared independence in 2008
- Montenegro, independent since 2006

1999: War in Kosovo

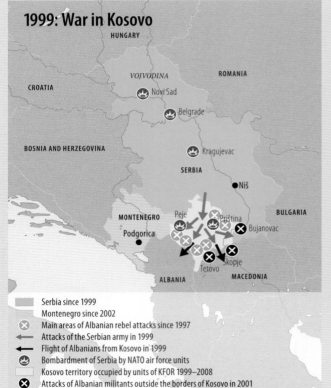

Legend:
- Serbia since 1999
- Montenegro since 2002
- Main areas of Albanian rebel attacks since 1997
- Attacks of the Serbian army in 1999
- Flight of Albanians from Kosovo in 1999
- Bombardment of Serbia by NATO air force units
- Kosovo territory occupied by units of KFOR 1999–2008
- Attacks of Albanian militants outside the borders of Kosovo in 2001

Serbia Today

Legend:
- Serbia
- Autonomous Vojvodina
- Kosovo, unilaterally declared independence in 2008

Serbian forces in the southern part of the province, leading to a subsequent attack by Serbian troops. Thousands of civilians are evacuated from Kosovo.

1999 The crisis in Kosovo escalates. Milošević refuses to negotiate a peace settlement with the international community. As a result, NATO attacks Yugoslavia, and Kosovo is placed under the protection of the UN.

2000 After accusations of voting fraud, mass demonstrations force Milošević to resign.

2001 Premier Zoran Djindić hands Milošević over to the High Court at the International Court of Justice (The Hague) because of his antagonism.

2002 The euro becomes the official currency of Montenegro. Yugoslavia is renamed Serbia and Montenegro.

2003 Djindić is assassinated in Belgrade. Djindić had been a frequent target of Serbian radicals due to his pro-Western stance, and had survived several earlier assassination attempts.

2005 Serbia and Montenegro begin talks to join the EU.

March 2006 Milošević commits suicide in prison. Montenegro declares its independence.

February 2008 Kosovo declares its independence, which Serbia refuses to recognize.

July 2008 The Bosnian Serb politician Radovan Karadžić is arrested on charges of war crimes.

1945 The monarchy is abolished and the Yugoslavian Federal People's Republic is established. Montenegro becomes a Yugoslav republic.

1948 Tito breaks with the USSR. Titoism develops as an independent socialist system.

1955 Tito reconciles with the USSR.

1961 Yugoslavia becomes one of the founding members of the Non-Aligned Movement.

1974 A new constitution is proclaimed granting greater rights to the members of the republic.

1980 Tito dies.

1987 Nationalist Slobodan Milošević, the leader of the Serbian Communist Party, provokes a conflict with the Croats and Slovenes.

1989 Milošević sends troops into the Albanian minority provinces of Vojvodina and Kosovo, effectively ending their autonomy.

June 1991 Slovenia and Croatia become independent.

December 1991 The Republic of Serbian Krajina is proclaimed on the Croatian frontier.

1991–1995 The Croatian and Bosnian War

1992 Bosnia and Herzegovina declares independence.

1998 The Albanian Kosovo Liberation Army begins armed resistance against

1991–1995: Croatian and Bosnian War

- Federal Republic of Yugoslavia
- Bosnia and Herzegovina before the beginning of the civil war
- Croatian territories occupied by the Serbs in 1991
- Remaining Croatian territory
- Republic of Serbian Krajina in Croatia in 1992–1995
- Eastern Slavonia under Serbian control until 1998
- ⊗ Locations of heaviest fighting

1992/1993: Croatian War

- Federal Republic of Yugoslavia
- Remaining territory of Croatia in 1993
- Republic of Serbian Krajina in Croatia in 1993
- Republika Srpska in Bosnia in 1993
- Territory under Bosnian control in Bosnia and Herzegovina in 1993
- Territory occupied by Croats in Bosnia and Herzegovina in 1993
- ⊗ Locations of heaviest fighting

1994: Croatian War

- Federal Republic of Yugoslavia
- Remaining territory of Croatia in 1994
- Republic of Serbian Krajina in Croatia in 1994
- Separatist Muslim territory in western Bosnia
- Territory in Bosnia and Herzegovina under Bosnian control in 1994
- Republika Srpska in Bosnia in 1994
- Territory in Bosnia and Herzegovina under Croatian occupation in 1994
- ⊗ Location of heaviest fighting

1995: Croatian War

- Federal Republic of Yugoslavia
- Remaining territory of Croatia at the end of 1995
- Republic of Serbian Krajina in Croatia at the end of 1995
- Republika Srpska in Bosnia at the end of 1995 (after the Dayton Agreement)
- Federation of Bosnia and Herzegovina in Bosnia and Herzegovina since 1995
- ⊗ Locations of heaviest fighting

Young Bosnia was an organization whose membership included primarily nationalist Bosnian Serbs, but also included Croats and Bosnian Muslims. It opposed the incorporation of Bosnia into the Yugoslav state, often resorting to violent means of protest.

Conflict with the USSR Yugoslav conflict with the USSR dates back to 1948. Tito and Stalin disagreed over the role of Moscow, and Stalin opposed Yugoslavia's attempts to form a Balkan federation with Albania and Bulgaria. Reconciliation first came after the death of Stalin, with Nikita Khrushchev's visit to Belgrade in 1955. Despite the efforts of the USSR, Yugoslavia never became a member of the Warsaw Pact.

Non-Aligned Movement was an organization of states that chose to remain neutral during the Cold War, seeking closer economic ties with each other instead of with the United States or the USSR. Yugoslavia, Egypt and India were the most prominent founding members.

Kosovo Liberation Army (KLA) is a guerilla army known by the abbreviation UÇK. It was created in 1994 with the purpose of separating Kosovo from Yugoslavia. Its former political leader Hashim Thaçi became the premier of Kosovo in January 2008.

The International Criminal Tribunal for the Former Yugoslavia was established by the UN Security Council in 1993 to prosecute and sentence war criminals, specifically those responsible for atrocities in the former Yugoslavia.

Kosovo Today

- Serbian enclaves

Montenegro Today

Bosnia and Herzegovina, Macedonia

12th Century: Bosnia

Dependencies of Hungary in the 12th century
Territory under the influence of Venice
Territory of the Byzantine Empire in the first half of the 12th century
Maximum expansion of the Byzantine Empire in the second half of the 12th century
Territory of Bosnia during the 12th century, under alternating Byzantine and Hungarian influence

14th–15th Centuries: Bosnia

Maximum territorial expansion of Bosnia 1389–1394
Bosnia, first half of the 15th century
Territory gained from Hungary in 1408/1427
⊗ Important battle

15th–16th Centuries: Ottoman Conquest of Bosnia

Ottoman territorial gains
1460
1463
1482
1516
1526
1538
1543

17th–19th Centuries: Defeat of the Ottoman Empire

Territory lost
by 1688
by 1699
by 1718
by 1791
by 1878
in 1878

Territory under the administration of Austria-Hungary 1878–1908
Bosnia and Herzegovina, annexed by Austria-Hungary in 1908
Regions of rebellion in Bosnia 1875–1878
Ottoman Empire in 1908

Bosnia and Herzegovina Today

Republika Srpska
Federation of Bosnia and Herzegovina (10 cantons)
Brčko district

After the loss of its independence in the 15th and 16th centuries, Bosnia and Herzegovina became a part of the Ottoman Empire for several centuries. In 1918 it was incorporated into Yugoslavia. The present independent state is a federation of two distinct entities: Republika Serpska (Serb Republic) and the Federation of Bosnia and Herzegovina.

1200–1100 BCE The Illyrians settle the western half of the Balkan Peninsula.

4th–3rd centuries BCE Celts colonize the Balkan Peninsula.

229–219 BCE Wars between Rome and Illyria lead to Roman control of the Adriatic coast.

376–401 BCE During the great migrations, the Visigoths cross the Danube and enter the Balkans.

395 CE After the division of the Roman Empire, what is now Bosnia and Herzegovina becomes part of the Western Roman Empire.

441–447 The invasion of the Huns

490–530 Bosnia and Herzegovina become part of the Ostrogothic kingdom, and later part of the Byzantine Empire.

after 558 The northern part of Bosnia becomes part of the Avar kingdom.

6th–7th centuries Slavs settle throughout the region, but the coast retains its Latin-Roman character.

7th–9th centuries Small principalities begin to form under the nominal control of the Byzantine Empire. Christianization of the region begins.

10th century Croatian, Serbian and Bulgarian influences alternate and converge in Bosnia.

~950–1050 Bosnia falls under direct Byzantine rule for the first time.

after 1080 The Serbian kings of Zeta rule Bosnia from what is now Montenegro.

after 1102 The union of Hungary and Croatia under a single monarch leads to claims on Bosnian territory by Hungary, Serbia and the Byzantine Empire. The Bosnian Ban ("lord") becomes a vassal of the king of Hungary.

after 1137/1138 Hungary claims northern Bosnia.

1180–1204 Bosnian ruler Ban Kulin's skilled political negotiations with Hungary, Serbia and the Byzantine Empire lead to the first Bosnian golden age, a period of lucrative trade agreements with Venice and Dubrovnik.

1232–1250 The reign of Matej Ninoslav is a period of fierce conflict with Hungary.

1314/1322–1353 Ban Stefan II Kotromanić reigns during an economic boom that includes the development of a mining industry, renewed trade contacts and the first Bosnian coinage.

1326 Zahumlje (Herzogovina) is incorporated into Bosnia, marking the first union of Bosnia and Herzegovina.

1377 Ban Tvrtko I is crowned king of Bosnia (and nominal King of Serbia), ruling until 1391.

1388 First Ottoman attacks on Bosnia and Herzogovina territory

1389 The Battle of Kosovo Polje (Field of the Black-birds) gives the Ottoman Empire victory over the united Christian princes, which includes a force of Bosnians.

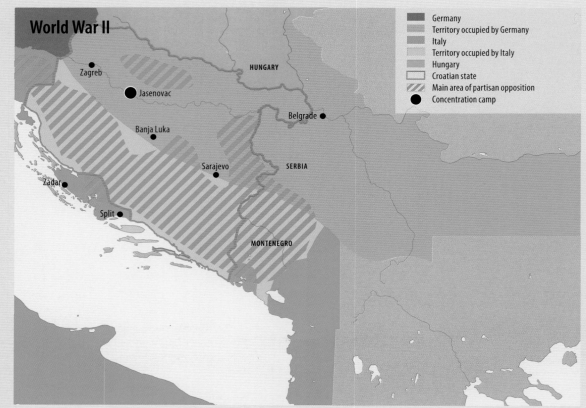

World War II

Germany
Territory occupied by Germany
Italy
Territory occupied by Italy
Hungary
Croatian state
Main area of partisan opposition
● Concentration camp

Bosnian War

Federal Republic of Yugoslavia
Serbian-occupied territories in Croatia in 1995
Border of Bosnia and Herzegovina
Serbian-ruled territories in Bosnia and Herzegovina 1992–1994
Croatian-ruled territories in Bosnia and Herzegovina since 1992
Territory administered by the Bosnian government 1992–1994
Separatist province of Western Bosnia 1993–1994
Dayton Line under United Nations control since 1995—border between the Republika Srpska and the Federation of Bosnia and Herzegovina
Republika Srpska in Bosnia and Herzegovina since 1995
⊗ Important battle

Macedonia Today

▨ Region settled by Albanians
⊗ Violent conflicts in 2001

1390   Bosnia claims territory in Dalmatia.

1391   The death of Tvrtko I is followed by a period of weak central governments and internal conflict. Ottoman influence in Bosnia increases.

1440   The Ottomans capture Srebrenica, the main mining region of Bosnia.

1463   Sultan Mehmed II leads the Ottoman invasion of Bosnia. He executes the last Bosnian king, Stephen Tomašević, and takes over large parts of the country.

1464–1527   The Banat of Jajce in northern Bosnia becomes a part of Hungary and later of the Ottoman Empire.

1483   The Ottoman Empire conquers Herzegovina.

1556–1566   The Old Bridge (Stari Most) is built in Mostar (Herzegovina).

Old Bridge, Mostar

1831–1832   Husein Kapetan Gradaščević, the "Dragon of Bosnia," leads a rebellion against the Ottoman Empire that is ultimately crushed.

1876–1878   The Bosnian Serbs revolt.

1878   The Congress of Berlin places Bosnia under the administration of Austria-Hungary, although it is still nominally part of the Ottoman Emire.

1908   Bosnia and Herzegovina are annexed by Austria-Hungary.

June 28, 1914   The heir to the Austrian throne, Archduke Francis Ferdinand, is assassinated in Sarajevo, triggering World War I.

1918   Austria-Hungary collapses after World War I. Bosnia and Herzegovina become part of the newly established Kingdom of Serbs, Croats, and Slovenes (Yugoslavia).

1941   Yugoslavia collapses after Germany invades. Hitler establishes an independent fascist Croatian state, which annexes Bosnia and Herzegovina.

1945   Bosnia and Herzegovina become part of the new Yugoslavia.

1990   Despite their widely varying goals, anti-Communist nationalists unite to win the national elections. Bosnian Muslims want independence, Bosnian Croats want a union with Croatia and Bosnian Serbs want to remain part of Yugoslavia.

March–April 1992   Bosnia and Herzegovina declares independence. In April, a bloody conflict begins, marked by violence directed against the civilian population and ethnic cleansing. Bosnians, Croats and Serbs fight each other in shifting alliances.

1994   The Bosnian Croats agree to become part of a Bosnian federal state.

July 1995   Massacre in Srebrenica.

September 1995   Bosnian Croats and Muslims, with support from NATO bombing, carry out a successful offensive against the Bosnian Serbs.

October 1995   A cease-fire is declared.

November 1995   The Dayton Peace Accords are signed in the United States. Bosnia is divided into a Croat-Muslim federation and a Serbian republic.

2005   Bosnia–Herzegovina begins negotiations to join the EU.

2006   Bosnia and Herzegovina join the NATO-sponsored Partnership for Peace.

Massacre in Srebrenica   In July 1995, soldiers from the Serbian Republic under the command of Ratko Mladic killed approximately 8,000 Bosnian Muslims, many of whom were children. Shortly before that, the United Nations had declared Srebrenica a "Safe Area." Around 400 Dutch United Nations Peacekeepers stationed in the region did not intervene in the worst massacre in Europe since the end of World War II. In February 2007, the International Court in The Hague recognized the events that took place in Srebrenica in 1995 as genocide.

Greek–Macedonian Conflict: The government in Athens feared that the creation of a Macedonian state could inflame separatist tendencies among the approximately 200,000 Slavs in northern Greece. Recognition of the Republic of Macedonia by Greece first occurred in 1995, after Macedonia modified the ancient symbol of the Macedonian dynasty on its flag and officially recognized the inviolability of its border with Greece. Nevertheless, this did not end their conflict. Athens does not permit Macedonian airplanes to enter its airspace and, in 2008, vetoed the admittance of the Republic of Macedonia into NATO.

Macedonia since 1913

1913   After the Second Balkan War, the historical region of Macedonia is divided into territories ceded to the neighboring countries. The southern coast including Thessaloniki (about 51% of Macedonia) is absorbed by Greece, Serbia obtains the northwestern portion of Macedonia (about 39%, the present-day state of Macedonia), and the southwest part goes to Bulgaria (9%). The remainder (about 1%) is incorporated into the newly formed Albania.

1914   During World War I, Bulgaria occupies the Serbian portion of Macedonia.

1918   Serbian Macedonia is incorporated into the Kingdom of Serbs, Croats and Slovenes.

1941   After the collapse of Yugoslavia, parts of Serbian and Greek Macedonia become part of Bulgaria. The Albanian section is seized by Italian occupying forces.

1944   After Bulgaria surrenders, German occupying forces declare an independent Macedonian state. It lasts just two months.

1945   Serbian Macedonia becomes an independent republic within Yugoslavia. The rest of Macedonia remains divided according to the 1913 agreement.

1991   Serbian Macedonia gains its independence, although its formal recognition by the international community is delayed by Greece. Because of Greece's objections, the Republic of Macedonia joins the United Nations under the name Former Yugoslav Republic of Macedonia (FYROM).

1994   Greece imposes economic sanctions against the Republic of Macedonia.

1995   Greece recognizes the independence of the Republic of Macedonia.

1999   Thousands of ethnic Albanians flee from Kosovo to the Republic of Macedonia after oppression by Milošević's troops. The refugees increase the number of ethnic Albanians in the Republic of Macedonia to 30% of the total population.

2001   Protests by ethnic Albanians seeking equal rights with Macedonians are defused by the rapid response of NATO peacekeeping forces. Negotiations between insurgents and the Macedonian government begin.

June 2002   The Albanian language is recognized as the second official language of the Republic of Macedonia.

March 2004   The Republic of Macedonia applies to join the EU.

Albania

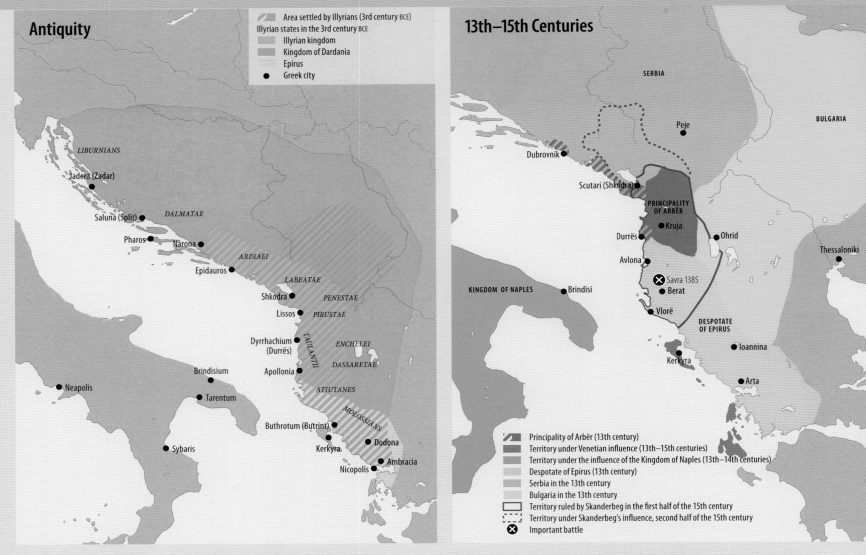

Antiquity

Area settled by Illyrians (3rd century BCE)
Illyrian states in the 3rd century BCE
- Illyrian kingdom
- Kingdom of Dardania
- Epirus
- Greek city

LIBURNIANS
Jadera (Zadar)
Saluna (Split) DALMATAE
Pharos
Narona
ARDIAEI
Epidauros
LABEATAE
Shkodra PENESTAE
Lissos PIRUSTAE
Dyrrhachium ENCHELEI
(Durrës) DASSARETAE
Brindisium
Apollonia TAULANTII
ATIUTANES
Neapolis MOLOSSIANS
Tarentum
Buthrotum (Butrint)
Kerkyra Dodona
Sybaris Ambracia
Nicopolis

13th–15th Centuries

SERBIA
BULGARIA
Peje
Dubrovnik
Scutari (Shkodra)
PRINCIPALITY OF ARBËR
Durrës Kruja Ohrid
Avlona Thessaloniki
KINGDOM OF NAPLES Brindisi Savra 1385 Berat
Vlorë DESPOTATE OF EPIRUS
Kerkyra Ioannina
Arta

- Principality of Arbër (13th century)
- Territory under Venetian influence (13th–15th centuries)
- Territory under the influence of the Kingdom of Naples (13th–14th centuries)
- Despotate of Epirus (13th century)
- Serbia in the 13th century
- Bulgaria in the 13th century
- Territory ruled by Skanderbeg in the first half of the 15th century
- Territory under Skanderbeg's influence, second half of the 15th century
- Important battle

For centuries, Albania was involved in an ongoing power struggle among Greece, Macedonia, the Romans, the Byzantines, Slavs, Normans, Crusaders and Venetians in southern Europe. After the 15th century, Albania successfully resisted invasion by the Ottoman Empire on multiple occasions. Following years under isolationist communist rule (1945–1990), Albania now seeks to rejoin the rest of Europe.

7th–6th centuries BCE Greek colonies are established along the coast.

5th–3rd centuries BCE Multiple Illyrian kingdoms and principalities compete for power.

317–303 BCE The reign of King Glaucias is marked by conflict with Macedonia.

280–275 BCE The Pyrrhic wars fought between Pyrrhus of Epirus (southern Albania) and Rome give rise to the term "Pyrrhic victory" after Pyrrhus wins on the battlefield, but at a disproportionately high cost.

229–219 BCE Rome takes control of the strategically important coastline after victory in the Illyrian wars.

148/146 BCE Establishment of the Roman province of Macedonia.

395 CE The Roman Empire is divided: most of the territory of what is now Albania becomes part of the Eastern Roman (Byzantine) Empire.

6th–7th centuries Slavic peoples colonize large parts of Albania.

~880–~1014 Central and southern Albania, formerly the Byzantine thema (province) of Dyrrhachium, become part of the Bulgarian empire. The Byzantine Empire gradually reconquers all of this territory beginning in 980.

1081 Battle of Durrës: The Normans defeat the Byzantines and take control of the Albanian coast.

after 1190 Northern Albania comes under Serbian control and remains under Serbian rule for more than six centuries, until 1839.

1190–1216 Central Albania is ruled by the independent principality of Arbanon.

1204–1285 The Despotate of Epirus takes control of southern Albania.

1257–1266 The House of Swabia rules over the Albanian coast from its kingdom in Sicily.

1272–1367 The House of Anjou rules the kingdom of Albania from Naples, controlling the strategic Albanian coast.

1343/47–1355 All of Albania falls under the control of the Greater Serbia empire, led by Tsar Stefan Uroš IV Dušan.

1359–1388 Tribal chief Charles Thopia declares himself king of Albania.

1385 Charles Thopia defeats his Serbian rival, Balša II of Montenegro, at the Battle of Savra.

1392 Charles Thopia's son, George, surrenders Durazzo (Durrës) to the Venetians.

1392–1501 Venetian rule in Durazzo is followed by Ottoman control of the region.

1396–1479 The Venetians rule Shkodër.

1417 Ottoman armies conquer the southern Albanian regions of Vlorë and Berat.

1443–1468 Skanderbeg, the national hero of Albania, leads successful resistance of the Ottoman siege of Kruja Castle.

1479 Venetian Shkodër falls to Ottoman forces, beginning over 400 years of Ottoman domination.

19th century Emergence of an Albanian national consciousness

1878–1881 The Albanian nationalist movement led by the League of Prizren (Albanian League) reestablishes Albanian autonomy.

1910–1912 Revolt against Ottoman control in Kosovo spreads into northern Albania.

Nov. 28, 1912 The sovereign state of Albania is declared in Vlorë.

October 1912–May 1913 The First Balkan War: Serbian, Montenegrin and Greek forces occupy Albania.

May 30, 1913 The Great Powers recognize Albanian sovereignty in the Treaty of London.

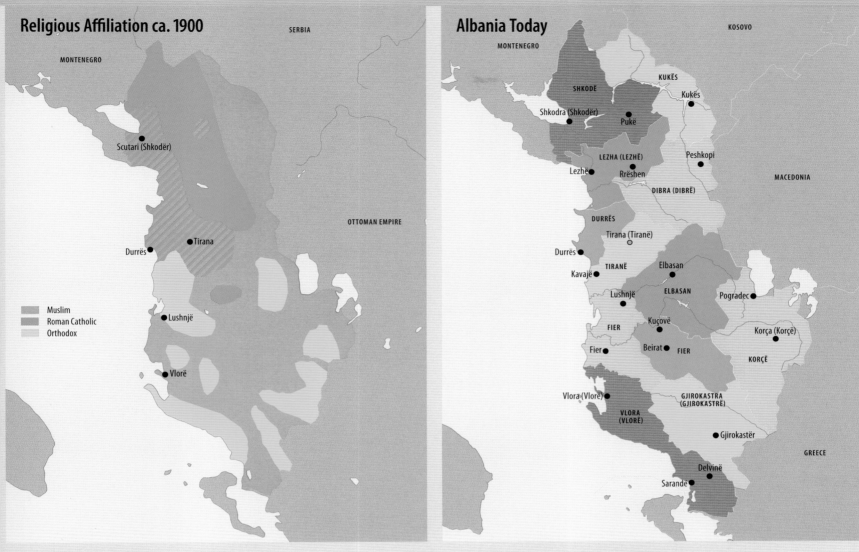

Religious Affiliation ca. 1900

SERBIA

MONTENEGRO

Scutari (Shkodër)

Durrës • Tirana

OTTOMAN EMPIRE

■ Muslim
■ Roman Catholic
■ Orthodox

• Lushnjë

• Vlorë

Albania Today

KOSOVO

MONTENEGRO

KUKËS

SHKODË

Shkodra (Shkodër) • Pukë • Kukës

LEZHA (LEZHË) • Peshkopi

Lezhë • Rrëshen

DIBRA (DIBRË)

MACEDONIA

DURRËS

Tirana (Tiranë)

Durrës •

Kavajë • TIRANË • Elbasan

Lushnjë • ELBASAN • Pogradec

FIER • Kuçovë

Fier • Beirat • Korça (Korçë)

FIER • KORÇË

Vlora (Vlorë) • GJIROKASTRA
(GJIROKASTRË)

VLORA
(VLORË) • Gjirokastër

GREECE

Delvinë

Sarandë

1914–1918 Albania is occupied by Austria, Italy and France during World War I.

1919–1920 The Paris Peace Conference rejects a proposal to divide Albania between Italy, Greece and Yugoslavia.

1920 The Congress of Lushnjë recognizes the national borders of 1912 and relocates the Albanian capital to Tirana.

1928 Ahmed Bey Zogu, president of the Albanian republic since 1925, takes the title King Zog I.

1939 Italy invades and annexes Albania, forcing King Zog into exile in Greece.

1941 Emergence of the outlawed Albanian Communist Party led by Enver Hoxha.

1943 Albania is occupied by Nazi Germany.

Palace of King Zog I in Tirana

1944 The communist resistance movement expels Germany from Albania. Hoxha governs Albania from Tirana.

1945 Yugoslavia is the first nation to recognize the communist government led by Hoxha.

January 1946 The monarchy is dissolved, and the People's Republic of Albania is proclaimed.

June 1948 After the falling out between Stalin and Tito (resulting in Yugoslavia's expulsion from the association of socialist states), Albanian communists side with Moscow.

May 1949 Following the execution of his adversary Koci Xoxe as part of a show trial, Hoxha rules as an absolute dictator.

1960 Albania breaks from the USSR, leading to increasing international isolation.

1961 Albania signs a pact with China.

1967 All religious organizations are banned.

1968 After the invasion of Czechoslovakia by the Eastern Bloc, Albania leaves the Warsaw Pact.

1978 Albania's international isolation becomes absolute after a split with China.

1985 Hoxha dies and is succeeded by Ramiz Alia.

1990 Mass demonstrations against the communist regime take place. Religious freedom is restored.

1991 The first democratic elections are held.

1992 Sali Berisha becomes the first democratically elected president of Albania.

1996 Bankruptcies linked to a pyramid scheme cause hundreds of thousands of Albanians to lose their savings.

1997 A referendum to reestablish the monarchy is defeated.

2006 Albania signs a treaty of association with the European Union (EU).

2008 Albania is invited to join the EU.

Skanderbeg (George Kastrioti, 1405–1468) was an Albanian prince and national hero. After his father's defeat, George Kastrioti was sent to be educated at the Ottoman court, where he converted to Islam and was given the Turkish name Iskander Bey from which Skanderbeg is derived. In 1443, after defecting from the Ottoman army during a battle with the Hungarians, he reconverted to Christianity and started an anti-Ottoman resistance movement of ethnic Albanians and Montenegrin nobles (the League of Lezha). He received support from Hungary, Venice and Naples, enabling his army of 10,000 to successfully battle much larger Ottoman forces and win concessions for Albanian autonomy. After his death of natural causes in 1468, Pope Pius II gave Skanderberg the honorary title of *Athleta Christi*, or "Champion of Christ."

Skanderbeg (1405–1468)

Bulgaria Until the 19th Century

Antiquity

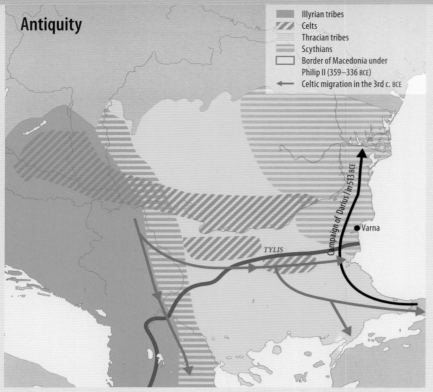

Illyrian tribes
Celts
Thracian tribes
Scythians
Border of Macedonia under Philip II (359–336 BCE)
→ Celtic migration in the 3rd c. BCE

Roman Era

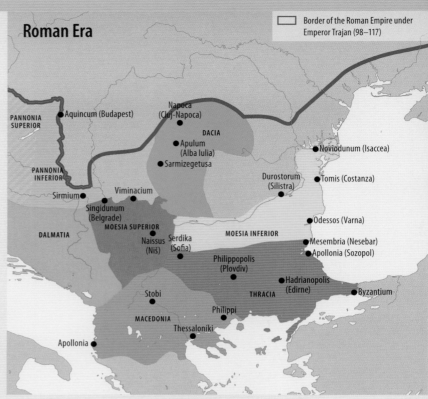

☐ Border of the Roman Empire under Emperor Trajan (98–117)

7th Century: Invasion of the Bulgar Tribes

680–888: Khanate (Old Bulgarian Kingdom)

ca. 681 (Khan Asparukh)
Conquests and territorial expansions under Khan Tervel (700–718/721)
Conquests and territorial expansions under Krum (803–814) and Omurtag (814–831)
Conquests and territorial expansions under Malamir (831–836)
Conquests and territorial expansions under Presian I (836–852) and Boris I (852–888)
⊗ Important battle

4600–4200 BCE Date of the Varna burial ground, containing the world's oldest known gold treasure.

2nd century BCE The Indo-European Thracians settle the Balkan Peninsula.

513 BCE Persian King Darius I conquers the Thracians.

341 BCE Philip II of Macedonia conquers the southwestern part of Thrace.

278–212 BCE Period of the Celtic kingdom at Tylis

29 BCE Rome conquers the Thracians.

44/46 CE Founding of the Roman province of Thrace (Thracia)

106/107 Rome conquers territory north of Thrace and establishes the province of Dacia.

after 395 Thrace becomes part of the Eastern Roman Empire.

6th–7th centuries The Slavs migrate to the Balkan Peninsula.

~620 The state of Great Bulgaria is established by the Bulgar leader Kubrat.

~650–670 Death of Khan Kubrat: The Proto-Bulgarians (semi-nomadic Turkic peoples) disperse and migrate to the north, west and south.

~680 The Proto-Bulgarians, led by Kubrat's son Asparukh, cross the Danube River and defeat Byzantine forces at Mount Ongal.

681 Peace with Byzantium leads to recognition of the first Bulgarian empire.

700–721 Bulgaria becomes a great power during the reign of Tervel.

803–814 Khan Krum expands his empire, effectively doubling it through a decisive defeat of the Avars.

893–1014: First Bulgarian Empire

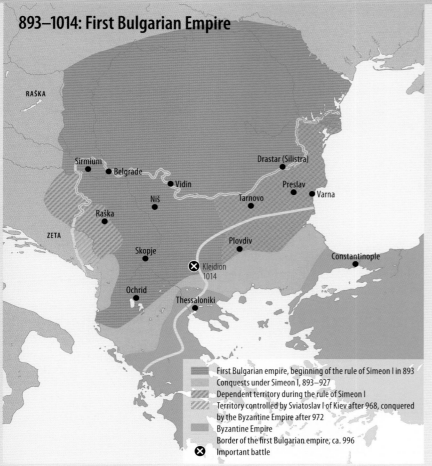

First Bulgarian empire, beginning of the rule of Simeon I in 893
Conquests under Simeon I, 893–927
Dependent territory during the rule of Simeon I
Territory controlled by Sviatoslav I of Kiev after 968, conquered by the Byzantine Empire after 972
Byzantine Empire
Border of the first Bulgarian empire, ca. 996
⊗ Important battle

From 1186: Second Bulgarian Empire

Under Ivan Asen I (1187–1196)
Conquests under Kalojan (1196–1207)
Territory lost under Boril (1207–1218)
Border of the Byzantine Empire ca. 1205
Conquests under Ivan Asen II (1218–1241)
Territory under the influence of Ivan Asen II
⊗ Important battle

811   Khan Krum annihilates the Byzantine army at Pliska, inflicting enormous casualties.

831   Malamir becomes the first khan of Slavic origin.

864–865   The concept of Bulgarian nationality becomes established with the arrival of Christianity, which erases many of the cultural differences between the pagan Bulgars and Christian Slavs.

870   The primacy of the papacy is rejected. As a result, the Bulgarian church falls under the control of the patriarch of Constantinople.

913   Simeon I takes the title of tsar of all Bulgarians and Romanians.

927   The Golden Centruy of Slavic culture begins. An independent Bulgarian patriarchal church is established.

968–976   Eastern Bulgaria is conquered by the Russian prince Sviatoslav, who takes over this region after he is banished from the Byzantine Empire.

976–1014   Rule of Tsar Samuel, who reconquers eastern Bulgaria.

1014–1018   The Byzantine Empire conquers Bulgaria following their overwhelming victory at Kleidion, marking the end of the first Bulgarian empire.

1018–1186   Bulgaria is ruled by the Byzantine Empire.

1186   Revolt of the Boyars leads to the founding of the second Bulgarian empire.

1205   Battle of Adrianople: Bulgarian Tsar Kaloyan defeats the army of Crusaders led by Baldwin I.

1230   Bulgaria defeats the Despotate of Epirus at the battle of Klokotnitsa.

after 1256   Internal conflicts lead to the weakening of central authority as Bulgaria confronts threats from Serbia and the Mongols.

1292–1299   Mongol rule in Bulgaria

1330   Following defeat at the Battle of Velbuzhd, Bulgaria falls under Serbian influence.

14th century   Bulgaria is restored.

1364   Ottoman armies take the strategically important city of Plovdiv.

1371   Bulgaria is divided into the kingdoms of Vidin, Tarnovo and Dobruja.

Sept. 29, 1371   Ottoman troops defeat the kingdom of Tarnovo at Maritza. Bulgaria becomes a vassal of the Ottoman Empire.

1393   The Ottoman Empire conquers Tarnovo, bringing the second Bulgarian empire to an end.

1395–1396   As local resistance falls apart, the Ottoman army occupies Dobruja and the important Romanian city of Vidin.

end of the 14th century–1878   Bulgaria remains under Ottoman rule. Any revolts by the Bulgarian people are violently suppressed.

14th Century: Reestablishment of Bulgaria

Bulgaria under Ivan Alexander (1331–1371)
Venetian territories
⊗ Important battle

Bulgaria, 19th Century Until Today

1878: Recognition by the Ottomans

- Mangalia
- Vidin
- Pleven
- Varna
- **BULGARIAN PRINCIPALITY**
- Sofia
- Burgas
- **EASTERN RUMELIA (1885 TO BULGARIA)**
- Plovdiv
- Istanbul
- Skopje
- Ohrid
- Thessaloniki
- Korçë
- Kastoria

Legend:
- ☐ Bulgarian border after the Treaty of San Stefano in March 1878
- ☐ Bulgarian border determined at the Congress of Berlin in July 1878

After the First Balkan War

Territory occupied by the Ottoman Empire:
- in Montenegro
- in Serbia
- in Greece
- in Bulgaria
- ■ Ottoman Empire after the First Balkan War
- ☐ Ottoman Empire border before the First Balkan War
- ☐ Demarcation line according to the Treaty of London
- ⊗ Important battle

Labels on map:
- Bucharest
- Belgrade
- **ROMANIA**
- **AUSTRIA-HUNGARY**
- Sofia
- **BULGARIA**
- Priština
- Cetinje
- ⊗ Kumanovo October 24, 1912
- Skopje
- Plovdiv
- Adrianople (Edirne)
- ⊗ Kırklareli October 23–24, 1912
- ⊗ Lüleburgaz October 31–November 3, 1912
- Istanbul
- **ALBANIA**
- Thessaloniki

After the Second Balkan War

Labels on map:
- Bucharest
- Belgrade
- Silistra
- **ROMANIA**
- Bazargic (Dobrich)
- **AUSTRIA-HUNGARY**
- Varna
- Sofia
- **BULGARIA**
- Burgas
- Priština
- Cetinje
- Plovdiv
- Skopje
- Strumica
- Adrianople (Edirne)
- Dimotika (Didymóteicho)
- Istanbul (Constantinople)
- **OTTOMAN EMPIRE**
- **WESTERN THRACE**
- **EAST THRACE**
- **ALBANIA**
- Xanthi
- Durrës
- Alexandroupoli
- Thessaloniki

Legend:
- Newly founded country (Albania)
- Territory gained by Montenegro
- Territory gained by Serbia
- Territory gained by Greece
- Territory gained by Bulgaria
- Territory lost by Bulgaria (southern Dobruja)
- ☐ Original border of the Ottoman Empire until October 1912 (before the First Balkan War)
- ☐ Demarcation lines in the Treaties of Bucharest/Constantinople

April 1876 The Ottoman Empire suppresses a Bulgarian popular revolt.

Ferdinand I (1861–1948)

March 3, 1878 Treaty of San Stefano: Ottoman territory in the Balkans is partitioned, forcing the recognition of Romania, Serbia, Montenegro and Bulgaria.

June–July, 1878 The Congress of Berlin establishes the borders of the principality of Bulgaria.

September 1885 A revolt against Ottoman control in eastern Rumelia leads to Ottoman acceptance of a union between Rumelia and Bulgaria.

1908 Bulgaria gains its independence from the Ottoman Empire; Ferdinand I is crowned tsar.

October 1912–May 1913 First Balkan War: The Balkan League nations successfully wage war against the Ottoman Empire.

June–August 1913 Second Balkan War among the nations of the Balkan League revises borders in the Balkans.

Sept. 16, 1915 Bulgaria forms an alliance with the German empire.

Oct. 14, 1915 Bulgaria enters World War I on the side of the Central Powers.

October–November 1915 German and Austro-Hungarian forces occupy Serbia.

September–October 1916 Romanian Dobruja is occupied.

May 7, 1918 Dobruja is formally ceded to Bulgaria.

Sept. 29, 1918 Bulgaria's surrender leads to the abdication of Ferdinand I in favor of his son, Boris III.

Nov. 27, 1919 The Treaty of Neuilly assigns the ethnic Bulgarian Western Outlands to Yugoslavia. Western Thrace is ceded to Greece in 1920. Bulgaria is forced to pay heavy reparations.

1923 The September Uprising, led by communists, is suppressed by the army. The Communist Party is outlawed.

1930s The Bulgarian tsar establishes a ruthlessly authoritarian regime.

Sept. 15, 1939 Bulgaria declares its neutrality in World War II and attempts to remain neutral throughout the war.

Sept. 7, 1940 Treaty of Craiova: Bulgaria reacquires the southeastern part of Dobruja (lost in 1913 after the Second Balkan War) and begins establishing closer ties to the German Reich.

February 1941 German forces invade Bulgaria.

March 1, 1941 Bulgaria agrees to sign the Tripartite Pact (Germany, Italy and Japan) and occupies Western Thrace and Vardar-Macedonia.

December 1941 Bulgaria declares war on Great Britain and the United States, leading to air raids on Sofia from 1943 to 1944.

September 1944 The Soviet Red Amy occupies Bulgaria and supports a communist coup. The monarchy is formally maintained with Simeon II, a minor, on the throne.

1946 A fraudulent referendum abolishing the monarchy forces the young tsar and his family to flee. A communist government is formed under party leader Georgi Dimitrov.

1949 Show trial takes places against Dimitrov's subordinate Traycho Kostov and other top-ranking members of the Communist Party. Kostov is condemned and executed in December.

1954–1989 Tenure of Communist Party leader and head of state Todor Zhivkov, the longest of any communist leader in Europe. Bulgaria is one of the Soviet Union's most reliable Balkan allies.

1981–1984 Forced assimilation of Bulgaria's ethnic Turkish minority

Nov. 10, 1989 Communist rule comes to an end in Bulgaria as opposition groups force Zhikov to "voluntarily" hand over power. Multiparty elections follow, and a democratic constitution is adopted in 1991.

2001–2005 Simeon II (Simeon Saxeco-burggotski) returns to Bulgaria as democratically elected president supported by the National Movement for Simeon II party. He begins a program of liberal economic reform.

2004 Bulgaria is admitted to NATO.

2007 Bulgaria is admitted to the EU.

Russo-Turkish War and the establishment of Bulgaria in 1878 After brutal suppression of the Bulgarian revolt of April 1876, European powers convened in Constanti-nople to force the Ottomans to recognize Balkan autonomy. Russia's domination of the conference led the Great Powers to reject Bulgarian independence as favorable to Russian interests. In the name of pan-Slavism, Russia attacked the Ottoman Empire in 1877, starting the Russo-Turkish War of 1877–1878. Russia was declared the victor in the Treaty of San Stefano. The threat of Russian hegemony in the Balkans worried the Great Powers, which met at the 1878 Congress of Berlin to revise the Treaty of San Stefano and try to reach a compromise. The result was increased autonomy for Bulgaria as a dependent principality of the Ottoman Empire, ruled by the House of Battenberg (later Saxe-Coburg), but not full independence. Another newly created autonomous province, Eastern Rumelia, formed a union with Bulgaria in 1885.

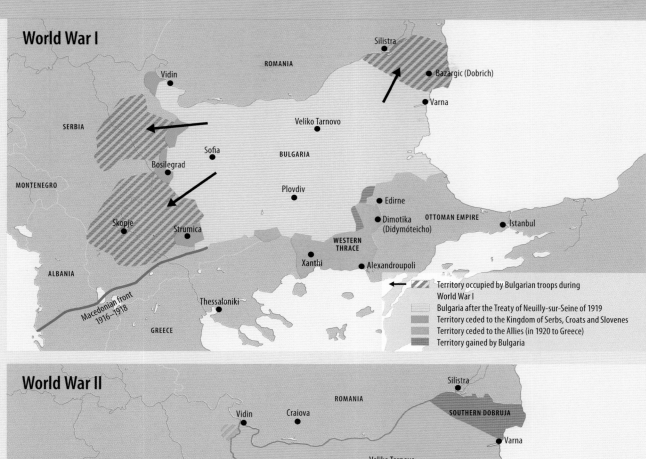

World War I

Territory occupied by Bulgarian troops during World War I
Bulgaria after the Treaty of Neuilly-sur-Seine of 1919
Territory ceded to the Kingdom of Serbs, Croats and Slovenes
Territory ceded to the Allies (in 1920 to Greece)
Territory gained by Bulgaria

World War II

Bulgaria 1919–1940
Territory gained through the 1940 Treaty of Craiova
Bulgarian border today (after World War II)
Territory occupied by Bulgaria

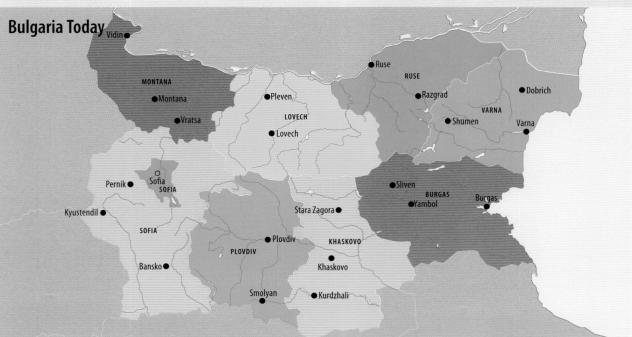

Bulgaria Today

Romania and Moldova Until the 18th Century

Antiquity

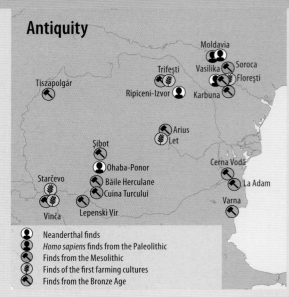

What is now Romania emerged from the historical territories of Walachia in the south, Moldavia (Bukovina and Bessarabia) in the northeast and Transylvania in the northwest.

4800–3500 BCE The Cucuteni culture occupies northern Romania, Bessarabia and Moldavia, living in two-story houses and creating distinctive polychrome pottery.

6th century BCE The Dacians and the Getans (Thracian tribes) settle in the eastern Balkans.

4th century BCE Conflicts erupt between the Getans and the Macedonians.

~70 BCE The Dacian kingdom, a union of the Dacian and Getan tribes, falls apart after King Burebista is murdered.

85–106 CE Dacians and Getans under the leadership of King Decebalus fight against Roman incursions.

106/107 Emperor Trajan conquers the Dacians and Getans and establishes the Roman province of Dacia, leading to rapid Romanization of the population.

after 270–275 During the reign of Emperor Marcus Aurelius, the Romans abandon all territory north of the Danube.

376 The Goths cross the Danube and migrate further south.

end of the 4th century–567 The Germanic Gepids settle in this region until they are wiped out by the Lombards in 567.

5th–8th centuries Nomadic tribes (first the Huns, after 567 the Avars) incorporate parts of Romania into their territories.

7th century Slavs settle the southern Romanian lowlands.

9th–10th centuries The majority of the territory of present-day Romania and Moldova becomes part of the first Bulgarian empire.

896 Magyars from the Black Sea region (Bessarabia, including present-day Moldova) move westward after suffering a series of devastating defeats at the hands of the Bulgarians (under Simeon I) and Pechenegs.

896–934 The Magyars settle Transylvania.

~971–1186 The Dobruja region (the Danube delta) falls under the control of the Byzantine Empire

1000 Founding of the Kingdom of Hungary, which includes present-day northern and western Romania.

11th century The Turkic Pechenegs, a nomadic tribal people, settle Walachia and rule over a loosely organized federation of tribute-paying villages.

1122 The Byzantine emperor John II Comnenus defeats the Pechenegs at Beroia.

1186–1371 Dobruja falls under the control of the second Balkan empire.

13th century After the region is depopulated in the wake of Mongol invasions in 1241, Germans colonize Transylvania.

1290 Radu Negra becomes the traditional founder of Walachia after migrating to the region from southern Transylvania.

1349 The Voivodes (generals, dukes) Dragos and Bogdan found the principality of Moldavia.

1359 The principality of Moldavia becomes independent from the Kingdom of Hungary.

1380 The principality of Walachia becomes independent from the Kingdom of Hungary.

1386–1418 The reign of Mircea the Old in Walachia sees the expansion of the principality to its greatest extent, although it is formally a vassal of the Ottoman Empire.

1387 The principality of Moldavia becomes a vassal of Poland.

1396 The Ottomans conquer the Dobruja region.

Antiquity (map legend)

- Neanderthal finds
- *Homo sapiens* finds from the Paleolithic
- Finds from the Mesolithic
- Finds of the first farming cultures
- Finds from the Bronze Age

During the Roman Empire

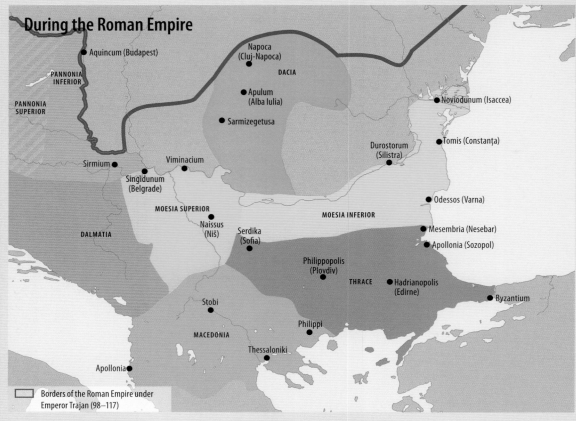

Borders of the Roman Empire under Emperor Trajan (98–117)

14th Century: Principalities of Moldavia and Walachia

Principality of Walachia ca. 1330
Principality of Moldavia ca. 1365
Banat of Severin

1446–1456 Transylvanian nobleman and Turk fighter John Hunyadi becomes regent of Hungary.

1448, 1456–1462 and 1476 Prince Vlad III Dracul's reign of terror in Walachia

1457–1503 Prince Stephen the Great ends Polish domination of Moldavia.

1459–1462 Vlad III Dracul refuses to pay tribute to the Ottoman Empire, successfully fighting off Ottoman attempts at retribution. Ottoman forces abandon Walachia without collecting the tax.

1462 Vlad III is deposed by his brother Radu, who is pro-Ottoman. Vlad flees to Hungary.

1476 Vlad III briefly returns to power, but is imprisoned and beheaded by the Turks.

1484 The Ottomans conquer Budjak (now southern Moldova).

after 1512 Moldavia preserves local autonomy by becoming a vassal of the Ottoman Empire.

after 1526 Transylvania becomes an Ottoman vassal after the Battle of Mohács, maintaining local autonomy.

1593/1599/1600 Michael the Brave becomes the first to unite the three Romanian historical territories under one rule, becoming prince of Walachia, Transylvania and Moldavia.

1604–1711 Transylvanian nobles revolt against the Kingdom of Hungary.

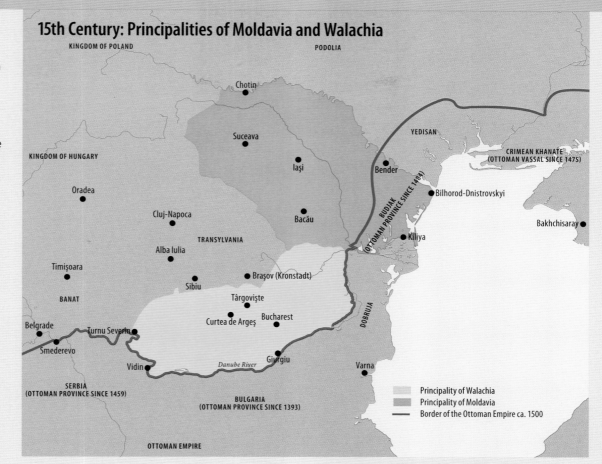

15th Century: Principalities of Moldavia and Walachia

Legend:
- Principality of Walachia
- Principality of Moldavia
- Border of the Ottoman Empire ca. 1500

Vlad III Dracul, called Tepes, "the Impaler" (1431–1476)
As a young man, Vlad III Dracul spent several years within the intensely despised Ottoman Empire as a hostage for his father, who was the ruler of Walachia. After his father's murder in 1448, Vlad became head of what was little more than a pro-Turkish puppet state. Driven from the throne, he returned in 1556 with Hungarian support. He was infamous for impaling condemned prisoners on long stakes—usually Turks, rebellious nobles or Saxons, but also criminals and any other opponents. His harsh regime brought order to the land by attacking corruption, an achievement for which he is revered in Romania to this day. Vlad II is the inspiration for the title character in Bram Stoker's famous novel *Dracula*.

16th–17th Centuries: Moldavia, Walachia and Transylvania

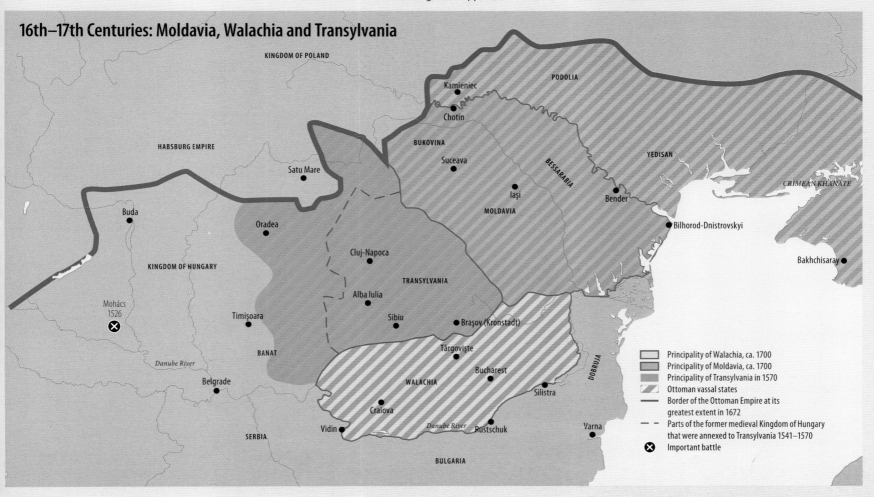

Legend:
- Principality of Walachia, ca. 1700
- Principality of Moldavia, ca. 1700
- Principality of Transylvania in 1570
- Ottoman vassal states
- Border of the Ottoman Empire at its greatest extent in 1672
- Parts of the former medieval Kingdom of Hungary that were annexed to Transylvania 1541–1570
- ⊗ Important battle

Romania and Moldova, 18th Century to the Present

1775–1861

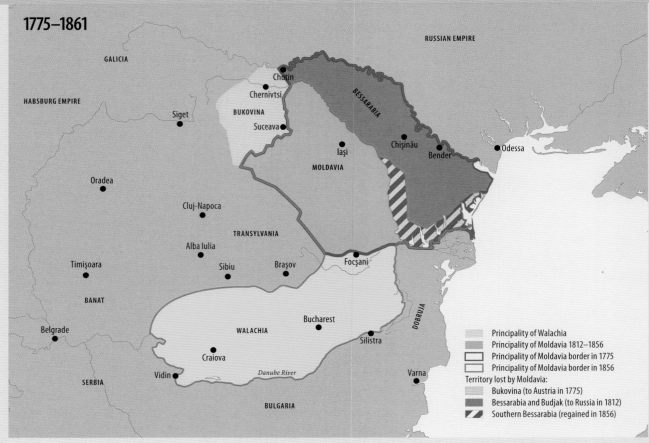

1859 The principality of Walachia is united with the remnants of the principality of Moldavia to form the new state of Romania. Moldavian prince Alexandru Ioan Cuza leads the new nation. The capital is Iași.

December 1861 Romania officially names Bucharest its new capital.

1866 Alexandru Ioan Cuza is forced to abdicate. He is replaced by Prince Karl of Hohenzollern-Sigmaringen, who takes the name Carol I. His dynasty rules Romania until 1947.

1877–1878 Russo-Turkish War: Romania fights on the side of Russia.

1878 The Congress of Berlin. The Great Powers recognize the borders of Romania and give the new nation control of Dobruja. Russia is ceded the territory of southern Bessarabia.

1881 Carol I is crowned king of Romania.

1912/1913 Romania remains neutral during the First Balkan War. In the Second Balkan War, Romania fights against Bulgaria.

Aug. 10, 1913 The Treaty of Bucharest gives Romania the formerly Bulgarian territory of southern Dobruja.

1914 Romania declares its neutrality in World War I.

1916 Romania enters World War I on the side of the Allied Powers.

1917 Romania agrees to a ceasefire with Germany and Austria-Hungary.

October 1918 Austria-Hungary surrenders and is partitioned. Transylvania votes to unite with Romania.

November 1918 Political union of Bukovina and Bessarabia with Romania.

1919 Romanian troops resist intervention by Soviet forces.

1921 Romania joins the Little Entente, which is directed against the revisionist policies of Hungary.

1938 King Carol II establishes himself as dictator.

June 1940 Romania surrenders Bessarabia and the northern Bukovina to the Soviet Union; this territory becomes the Moldavian Soviet Socialist Republic.

August 1940 Romania is forced to cede northern Transylvania to Hungary and the southern Dobruja region to Bulgaria.

1941–1944 As an ally of Germany against the Soviet Union, Romania regains Bessarabia and the eastern bank of the Dniester River.

Map legend (1775–1861)

Principality of Walachia
Principality of Moldavia 1812–1856
Principality of Moldavia border in 1775
Principality of Moldavia border in 1856
Territory lost by Moldavia:
Bukovina (to Austria in 1775)
Bessarabia and Budjak (to Russia in 1812)
Southern Bessarabia (regained in 1856)

1861–1920: Kingdom of Romania

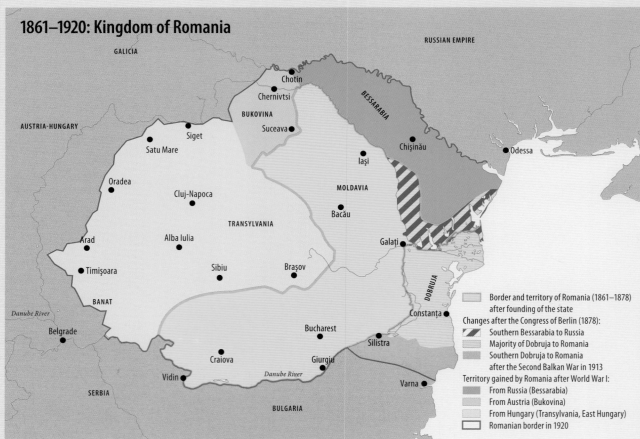

Map legend (1861–1920)

Border and territory of Romania (1861–1878) after founding of the state
Changes after the Congress of Berlin (1878):
Southern Bessarabia to Russia
Majority of Dobruja to Romania
Southern Dobruja to Romania after the Second Balkan War in 1913
Territory gained by Romania after World War I:
From Russia (Bessarabia)
From Austria (Bukovina)
From Hungary (Transylvania, East Hungary)
Romanian border in 1920

1699 Expulsion of the Ottomans: Transylvania becomes a part of the Hungarian empire under the Habsburgs.

1711–1821 Walachia and Moldavia decline in importance within the Ottoman Empire during the Phanariote period.

1718–1739 The Treaty of Passarowitz temporarily cedes western Walachia to Austria.

1775 Bukovina, the northwestern part of what is now Moldova, goes to Austria.

1812 The Treaty of Bucharest gives Russia control of Bessarabia (now Moldova) and Budjak.

1829 The Treaty of Adrianople gives Russia the Danube delta and a protectorate over Moldavia and Walachia.

1856 The Treaty of Paris ends the Crimean War. Russia cedes southern Bessarabia to the principality of Moldavia.

1942 Thousands of Romanian soldiers perish in the Battle of Stalingrad.

1945 Communist-led government is established with the support of the Soviet Union; Bessarabia and the northern Bukovina are lost once again.

1945–1965 The head of the Communist Party, Gheorghe Gheorghiu-Dej, places Romania on the path toward communism beginning in 1958.

1947 Romania becomes a people's republic, controlled by the Communist Party.

1955 Romania becomes a charter member of the Warsaw Pact.

1965 Nicolae Ceaușescu becomes the new head of the Communist Party. After 1975, he establishes a bizarre cult of personality and a brutal nationalistic communist regime.

1968 Romania condemns the invasion of Czechoslovakia (Prague Spring), refusing to participate in Warsaw Pact military action.

1969 United States President Richard Nixon visits Bucharest. Cold War politics cause the Western international community to turn a blind eye to the abuses of the the Ceaușescu government.

1984 Romania participates in the Eastern Bloc boycott of the Olympic Games in Los Angeles.

Dec. 16, 1989 A revolt by the ethnic Hungarian minority in Timișoara is violently suppressed. Five days later, revolutionary protest marches spread to Bucharest.

Dec. 25, 1989 Nicolae Ceaușescu and his wife Elena are imprisoned and executed without trial. Revelation of Romania's poverty under the dictatorship, particularly the plight of the mentally ill, aged and orphans, shocks the world.

1990 The first free Parliamentary elections are held in Romania.

1991 The Republic of Moldova declares independence from the Soviet Union. Economic reforms bring stability and international support.

1992 Russian-speaking inhabitants residing on the eastern bank of the Dniester proclaim the Transdniestrian Republic. This state in not recognized internationally.

1994 The majority of the inhabitants of Moldova vote against union with Romania in a national referendum.

2001 Communist Vladimir Voronin becomes president of Moldova.

January 2007 Romania becomes a member of the EU.

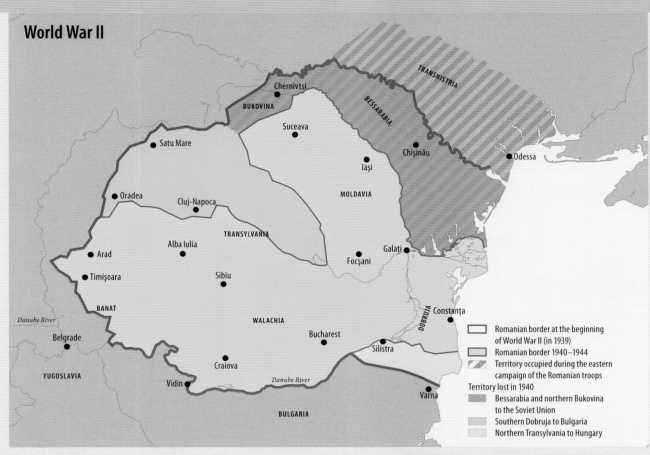

World War II

Romanian border at the beginning of World War II (in 1939)
Romanian border 1940–1944
Territory occupied during the eastern campaign of the Romanian troops
Territory lost in 1940
Bessarabia and northern Bukovina to the Soviet Union
Southern Dobruja to Bulgaria
Northern Transylvania to Hungary

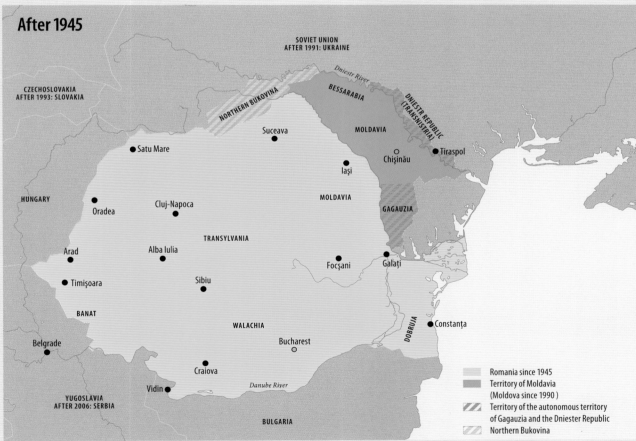

After 1945

Romania since 1945
Territory of Moldavia (Moldova since 1990)
Territory of the autonomous territory of Gagauzia and the Dniester Republic
Northern Bukovina

Nicolae Ceaușescu (1918–1989)

The Phanariotes were high-ranking Greeks from Constantinople who were regarded by the Ottoman Empire as especially loyal subjects. During the Phanariote period in the 18th and 19th centuries, they held important posts in the military as well as administrative positions in Moldavia and Walachia.

Bessarabia Historical territory bordered by the Dniester and Prut Rivers and the Black Sea. Between 1918 and 1940 it belonged to Romania. Today it is divided between Moldova and the Ukraine.

Bukovina Historical terriorty in the northeastern Carpathians on the border between Romania and Ukraine. After 1918, it became a part of Romania. Since World War II the northern portion has belonged to the USSR (now Ukraine) and the southern part to Romania.

Greece Until the 15th Century

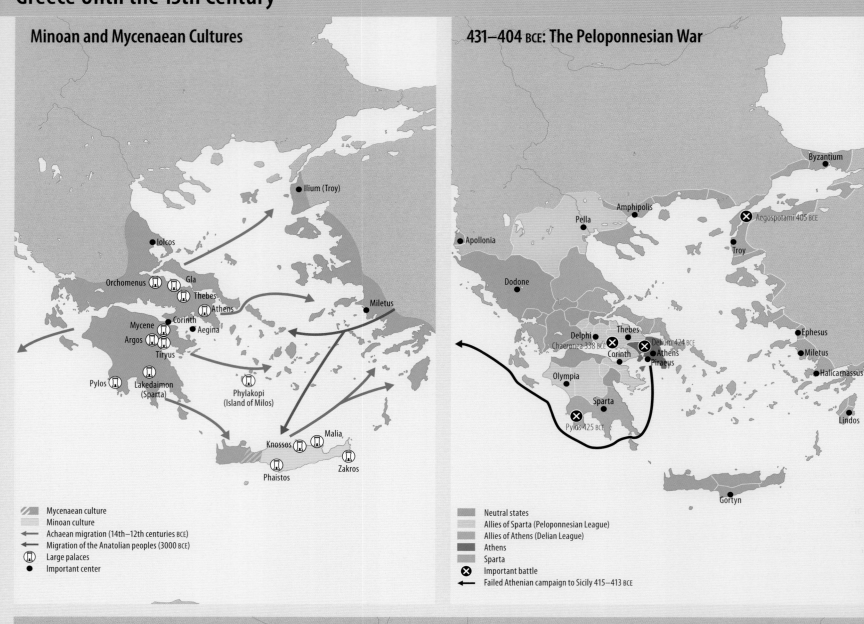

Minoan and Mycenaean Cultures

- Ilium (Troy)
- Iolcos
- Orchomenus
- Gla
- Thebes
- Athens
- Mycene
- Corinth
- Aegina
- Argos
- Tiryus
- Pylos
- Lakedaimon (Sparta)
- Phylakopi (Island of Milos)
- Miletus
- Knossos
- Malia
- Phaistos
- Zakros

Legend:
- Mycenaean culture
- Minoan culture
- Achaean migration (14th–12th centuries BCE)
- Migration of the Anatolian peoples (3000 BCE)
- Large palaces
- Important center

431–404 BCE: The Peloponnesian War

- Byzantium
- Amphipolis
- Pella
- Apollonia
- Aegospotami 405 BCE
- Troy
- Dodone
- Delphi
- Thebes
- Ephesus
- Chaeronea 338 BCE
- Corinth
- Delium 424 BCE
- Athens
- Piraeus
- Miletus
- Olympia
- Halicarnassus
- Sparta
- Pylos 425 BCE
- Lindos
- Gortyn

Legend:
- Neutral states
- Allies of Sparta (Peloponnesian League)
- Allies of Athens (Delian League)
- Athens
- Sparta
- Important battle
- Failed Athenian campaign to Sicily 415–413 BCE

Empire of Alexander the Great

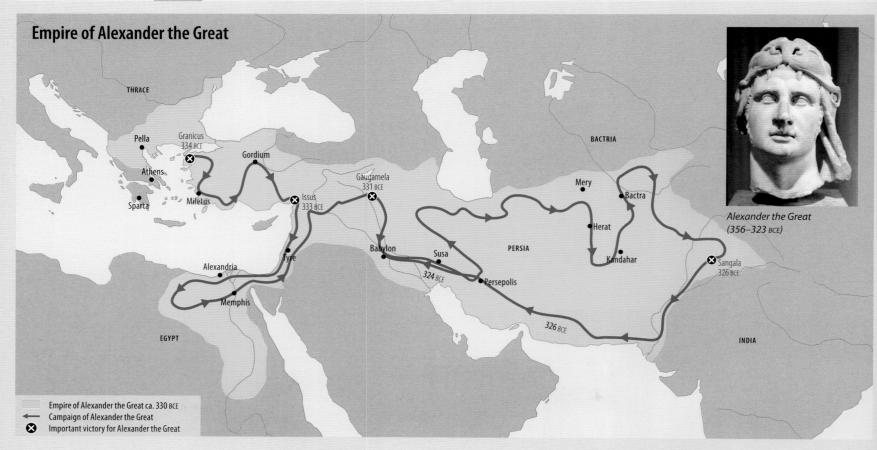

- THRACE
- Pella
- Granicus 334 BCE
- Gordium
- BACTRIA
- Athens
- Mery
- Bactra
- Sparta
- Miletus
- Issus 333 BCE
- Gaugamela 331 BCE
- Herat
- Tyre
- Babylon
- Susa
- PERSIA
- Kandahar
- Sangala 326 BCE
- Alexandria
- 324 BCE
- Persepolis
- Memphis
- 326 BCE
- EGYPT
- INDIA

Alexander the Great (356–323 BCE)

Legend:
- Empire of Alexander the Great ca. 330 BCE
- Campaign of Alexander the Great
- Important victory for Alexander the Great

Roman Provinces ca. 120

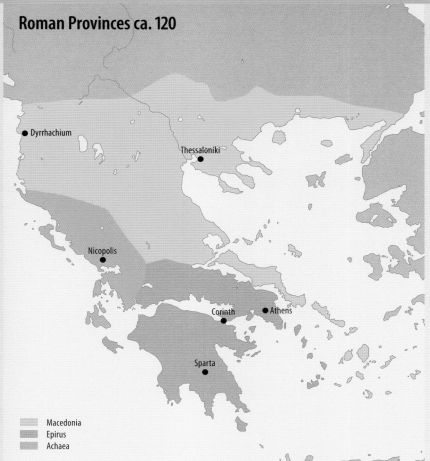

- Dyrrhachium
- Thessaloníki
- Nicopolis
- Corinth
- Athens
- Sparta

Macedonia
Epirus
Achaea

1204: The Latin Empire of Constantinople

KINGDOM OF THESSALONÍKA
- Thessaloníki

DESPOTATE OF EPIRUS
- Arta

DUCHY OF ATHENS
- Athens

PRINCIPALITY OF ACHAEA
- Mystras

- Candia (Iráklion)

Territory ruled by Venice
Territory ruled by the Nicaean empire

Greece, the cradle of Western civilization, was a world power for a brief period under Alexander the Great. Within two hundred years of his death, however, most Greeks were ruled by Rome. Greece would go on to form the core of the Byzantine Empire. In the wake of the Ottoman conquest, Greece's struggle to regain its independence lasted into the 19th century.

~2000–1450 BCE Minoan culture flourishes on the island of Crete.

~1600–1000 BCE Mycenaean culture, made up of independent and rival city-states, expands from the Greek mainland to the islands and the coast of Asia Minor.

~1450–1400 BCE The palaces on Crete are destroyed.

~1250 BCE The conquest of Troy and end of the Trojan War

after 1190 BCE The Mycenaean culture comes to an end after the invasion of the Sea Peoples, who probably came from the western Mediterranean region.

12th–9th centuries BCE The Greek Dark Age begins a period of uncertainty characterized by migrations of new peoples from the north into central Greece and the Peloponnese.

10th–9th centuries BCE Greeks settle the Asia Minor coast and islands.

700–500 BCE The Archaic period is characterized by development of the Greek city-state (*polis*) and by Greek colonization of the Mediterranean area.

~550 BCE The Peloponnesian League is formed under the leadership of Sparta.

499–448 BCE Allied Greek forces defeat a much larger invading Persian army.

478/477 BCE The Delian League forms under the leadership of Athens.

443–429 BCE Pericles is *strategos* (elected general) of Athens, inaugurating the golden age of Greek democracy.

431–404 BCE The Peloponnesian War between the Peloponnesian League and the Athenian empire ends with Sparta's victory over Athens.

338 BCE A decisive victory for Philip II of Macedon over an alliance of Greek city-states at Chaeronea makes him ruler of most of Greece.

336–323 BCE Philip's son, Alexander III the Great, sets out to conquer the world. His death marks the beginning of the Hellenistic period.

306–168 BCE Macedon and parts of Greece fall under the rule of the Antigonids, descendants of General Antigonus who served Alexander the Great.

215–205, 200–196 and 171–168 BCE Three successive wars are fought between Macedon and Rome.

168 BCE Rome defeats Macedon, bringing to an end the period of political independence on the Greek mainland.

148/146 BCE Macedon becomes the Roman province of Macedonia.

27 BCE Achaia becomes a Roman province.

67 CE Epirus becomes a Roman province.

from 395 Greece is a core territory of the Eastern Roman Empire; Greek language and traditions are passed on and define the culture of the Byzantine Empire.

527–565 Justinian I reigns during the first golden age of the Byzantine Empire.

688 The Greeks successfully defend Thessaloníki during a siege by the Bulgarians.

7th century Slavic peoples migrate into Greece as far as the Peloponnese.

726–842 The Byzantine Iconoclastic Controversy divides society between those who reject all religious images and wish to destroy them, and those who continue to revere them. Icons are banned from 737 to 787 and again from 814 until 842.

867–1057 The Macedonian dynasty rules the Byzantine Empire.

Justinian I in a mosaic at San Vitale, Ravenna

976–1025 Basileios II, known as *Bulgaroctonos* (the Bulgarian killer), inaugurates the golden age of the Macedonian dynasty.

978 and 995 Bulgarian armies invade Thessaly.

1054 The Eastern Orthodox Church, based in Constantinople, splits from the Western Catholic Church with its base in Rome.

11th–12th centuries Greece becomes the most Westernized and prosperous province of the Byzantine Empire.

1204 Division of the Byzantine Empire due to the depredations of the Fourth Crusade leads to the formation of the Latin Empire.

1261 The rulers of Nicaea revive Byzantine power in northern Greece.

1430 Ottoman armies conquer Thessaloníki.

Greece from the 15th Century to Today

1500: Greece under Ottoman Rule

- ■ Territory ruled by the Ottoman Empire
- ■ Territory of the Republic of Venice
- ■ Territory of the Order of St. John
- ⊗ Important battle

1821–1829: The Greek War of Independence

- ■ Greek territory after the War of Independence 1821–1829
- ⊗ Important battle

1432–1460 The principality of Achaea thrives under Byzantine and Ottoman rule.

1453 Ottoman Sultan Mehmed II conquers Constantinople.

1456 The duchy of Athens falls under Ottoman control.

1460–1540 Ottoman-Venetian conflict leads to Ottoman settlement of the Greek islands.

Oct. 7, 1571 The Ottoman navy is defeated by Spain and Venice at the Battle of Lepanto.

1687 The Parthenon on the Acropolis is badly damaged during the Venetian siege of Athens.

1669 Crete, a Venetian possession, is taken by Ottoman forces.

1684–1699 and 1715–1718 Venice temporarily regains control of Morea (Peloponnese).

1770 Ottoman forces successfully defend the Greek islands from a Russian invasion.

1821 The Greek Revolution begins; Athens is reconquered in 1822.

Oct. 20, 1827 At the Battle of Navarino, the allied naval forces of England, France and Russia defeat the Ottomans.

1828 Ioánnis Kapodístrias is elected the first president of modern Greece. He is murdered in 1831.

1830 The London Protocol calls for international recognition of the nation of Greece.

1832 The London Convention establishes a Greek monarchy, and Otto of Bavaria is named king.

1864 The Ionian Islands are returned to Greece.

1881 Thessaly is returned to Greece.

October 1912–May 1913 The First Balkan War between the Balkan League and the Ottoman Empire over Macedonia.

May 30, 1913 The Treaty of London divides the former Ottoman province of Macedonia among the Balkan countries.

June–August 1913 The Second Balkan War breaks out among the Balkan League countries over the division of Macedonia.

1916 British and French troops land at the request of the Greek government, which is in exile in Thessaloníki.

Greece During World War I

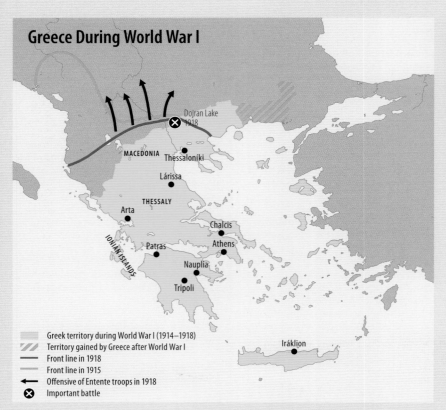

- ■ Greek territory during World War I (1914–1918)
- ▨ Territory gained by Greece after World War I
- —— Front line in 1918
- —— Front line in 1915
- → Offensive of Entente troops in 1918
- ⊗ Important battle

Greece During World War II

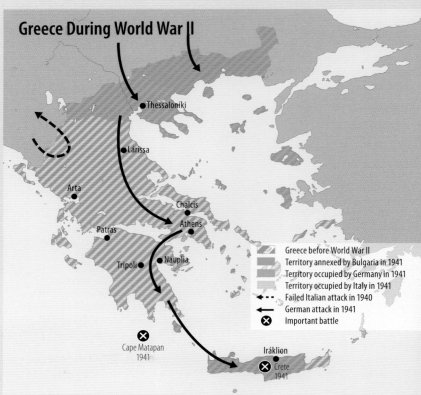

- ▨ Greece before World War II
- ■ Territory annexed by Bulgaria in 1941
- ■ Territory occupied by Germany in 1941
- ■ Territory occupied by Italy in 1941
- ⇠ Failed Italian attack in 1940
- ← German attack in 1941
- ⊗ Important battle

1917 King Constantine I promotes Greek neutrality in World War I, leading to his self-imposed exile after elected prime minister Eleuthérios Venizélos provides Greek support to Allied forces.

1918 The Allied offensive in Thessaloníki ends with the surrender of Bulgarian forces fighting on the German side.

1920 Royalist victories in national elections return Constantine I to the throne.

1920–1922 Mass emigration of Greek inhabitants of Turkish territories follows in the wake of the Greek-Turkish War.

autumn 1922 Following a military coup, Constantine I abdicates the throne in favor of George II.

1923 Mussolini tries to take Corfu, without success.

1924 The Greek Republic is formed.

1925–1926 General Theodoros Pangalos comes to power as dictator.

1930 Relations between Greece and Turkey are normalized.

1935 Royalists manipulate a referendum in favor of a return to monarchy. George II returns to the throne.

1936 General Ionannis Metaxas leads a military dictatorship with fascist leanings.

November 1940 Greek troops halt an Italian invasion, and in their counter-attack Greece advances into Albania.

January 1941 Metaxas dies.

April 1941 Germany invades Greece, which is divided into German, Italian and Bulgarian zones of occupation.

1942–1944 Royalists join with communists to resist occupation forces.

1944 Germany withdraws from Greek territory.

1944–1945 Rightists supported by Britain battle communists in a bloody civil war.

1946 Rightists win national elections.

1947 The Paris Peace Conference returns the Dodecanese islands to Greece. The United States provides military and economic support for rightists in opposition to the Greek Communist Party, which is supported by Soviet Russia.

1949 Communist Party forces are defeated, bringing an end to the Greek Civil War.

1952 Greece joins NATO.

1961 Greece joins the Organization for Economic Co-operation and Development (OECD).

1963 The government changes hands twenty times within a single year, followed by a Center Union Party victory by Georgios Papandreou.

1967 Rightist military junta led by a group of colonels seizes power. A retaliatory coup led by Constantine II fails.

1973 The military junta abolishes the monarchy in favor of rule by an authoritarian presidium of colonels.

1974 The military junta's attempt to annex Cyprus by overthrowing Cypriot President Makarios fails, contributing to the fall of the rightist colonels. Turkey occupies northern Cyprus. In November, a government led by Konstantinos Karamanlis restores democracy in Greece.

1981 Greece becomes a member of the European Union (EU). In October, Andreas Papandreou leads the leftist party PASOK to victory in national elections.

1991–1994 Greece refuses to recognize the Republic of Macedonia.

1995 Greece recognizes Macedonia.

1997 Greece and Turkey pledge to resolve all territorial disputes peacefully.

2002 The euro replaces the Greek drachma as Greece's currency.

The Greek War of Independence and the Philhellene Movement were intimately intertwined. The term "philhellenism" means "the love of Greek culture." In the early 18th century, aristocratic European sympathizers with neohumanistic leanings called on their governments to support Greeks in their struggle against Ottoman rule. One of the most famous Philhellenes was the British poet George Gordon, better known as Lord Byron (1788–1824).

The **Megali Idea** ("Great Idea") refers to the concept formulated in the mid-19th century of Greater Greece, a state that would include large parts of the Balkans, Thrace, islands, coastal Asia Minor and cities such as Istanbul (formerly Constantinople) that are not currently under Greek control. The Megali Idea held sway into the 20th century and affects Greek foreign and domestic policy to this day.

The Colonels were the military junta led by Giorgios Papadopoulos that ruled Greece from 1967–1973. The junta abolished civil rights, political parties and freedom of expression, and introduced martial law, military justice and torture. Papadopoulos was elected president in 1973.

Greece Today

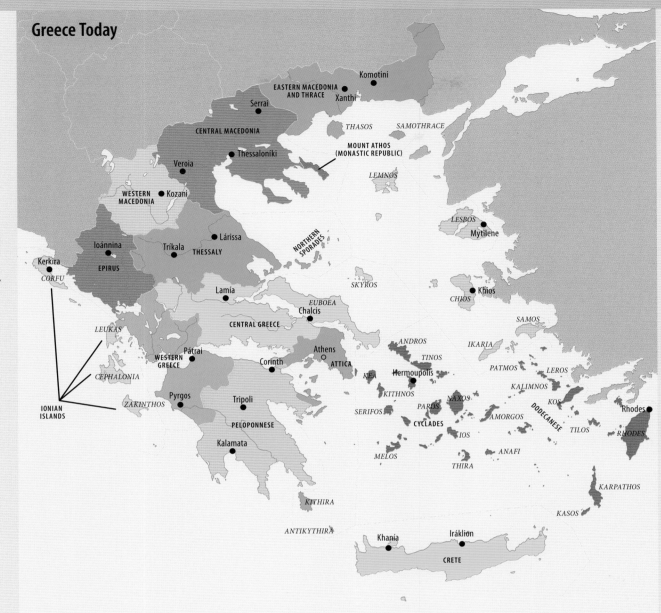

Giorgios Papadopoulos

Turkey Until the Founding of the Republic

ca. 1600–1300 BCE: The Hittite Empire

Legend:
- Territory of the Hittite Empire in 1300 BCE
- Territory of the Hittite Empire in 1590 BCE
- ⊙ Capital
- ⊗ Important battle

The first highly developed cultures were followed by centuries of Persian, Greek and Roman occupation in what is now the Republic of Turkey. Constantinople was the center of the great Byzantine imperial culture and later (as Instanbul) of the Turkish Ottoman Empire. After the fall of the Ottoman sultans in the wake of World War I, Kemal Atatürk founded a modern Turkish republic that is oriented toward the West.

~9500 BCE The world's oldest known sanctuary is built at Göbekli Tepe.

7300–6200 BCE The oldest known pottery is produced at the Neolithic site of Çatalhöyük.

1650 BCE The Hittite empire flourishes in central Anatolia.

1370–1330 BCE Hittite kings correspond with Egyptian pharaohs during the peak of the Anatolian Bronze Age.

1274 BCE The Egyptians defeat the Hittites in the Battle of Kadesh.

1200 BCE The Hittite empire comes to an end with the invasion of the Sea Peoples.

10th–9th centuries BCE Greeks settle the Asia Minor coast and islands.

8th–7th centuries BCE The Phrygian empire controls western Anatolia; the kingdom of Urartu controls the east.

680–546 BCE The kingdom of Lydia, with its capital in Sardis, rises from the ashes of the Phrygian collapse.

560 BCE Croesus, the legendarily wealthy king of Lydia, invents coinage.

546–333 BCE The Persian Achaemenian Empire dominates Anatolia.

333–323/281 BCE Asia Minor becomes part of the vast empire of Alexander the Great. General Lysimachus rules after Alexander's death.

281–133 BCE The kingdom of Pergamum enters into an alliance with Rome. It becomes the center of Hellenistic art and culture.

133 BCE The childless King Attalus III leaves Pergamum to Rome in his will. Anatolia becomes part of the Roman province of Asia.

102 BCE Cilicia, located in what is today south-central Turkey, becomes a Roman province.

95–55 BCE Tigranes II (the Great) rules the kingdom of Armenia in what is now eastern Turkey.

74/64 BCE The Romans found the province of Bithynia-Pontus on the Black Sea.

25 BCE Galatia becomes a Roman province.

18 CE Cappadocia in central Turkey becomes a Roman province.

43 Lycia in southwest Turkey becomes a Roman province.

1st century The first Christians arrive in Asia Minor.

after 395 Anatolia becomes part of the Byzantine and Ottoman Empires.

1071 The Battle of Manzikert brings the Seljuq Turks, led by Alp-Arslan, into direct conflict with the Byzantine Empire.

1075 The Seljuq sultanate of Rum (after the Arabic word for "Rome") is formed when Süleyman Kutalmish takes the title of sultan; Nicaea is its first capital.

~1086–1176 The Danishmend kingdom rules northeast Anatolia.

1097 The armies of the First Crusade defeat the Rum-Seljuq at Nicaea.

1101 The Rum-Seljuq Turks conquer the city of Iconium (Ikónian, modern Konya), making it their new capital in 1116.

1147 The Battle of Dorylaeum (modern Eskişehir) brings the Rum-Seljuq troops a decisive victory over the armies of the Second Crusade.

1176 The Rum-Seljuq army defeats Byzantine forces at the Battle of Myriocephalon. They go on to conquer the Danishmend territories.

1204 Constantinople is sacked by Venetian soldiers in the Fourth Crusade. The Byzantine Empire is divided into numerous small, independent states.

1243 The Battle of Köse Dag (modern Sivas) gives Mongol invaders victory over the Rum-Seljuq. The sultanate begins to fall apart.

1299 Osman I declares independence from the collapsing Rum-Seljuq sultanate.

1307 The Rum-Seljuq territories are absorbed by the Karaman sultanate of central Anatolia. Konya remains the capital.

from 1326 Ottoman forces begin their attack on the Byzantine Empire.

May 29, 1453 After years of siege, Ottoman armies led by Mehmed II take Constantinople.

1459–1571 The Ottoman Empire conquers a large part of the Balkans, advancing as far as Hungary.

Oct. 7, 1571 The Battle of Lepanto is a decisive victory for Spain and Venice over the Ottoman navy.

1669 The Ottoman Empire expands its territory to the Greek islands, including Crete.

from 1683 The Turks' unsuccessful siege of Vienna marks the begin of the long decline of the Ottoman Empire.

200 BCE: Hellenistic Kingdoms

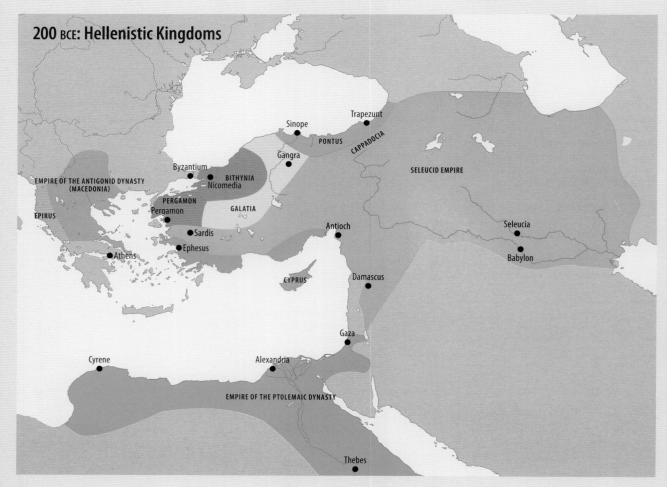

ca. 1025: The Byzantine Empire

Sirmium
Split
Skopje 1004 ⊗
Preslav 971 ⊗
Varna
Sinope
Trebizond
Constantinople
Ankara
Nicaea (Iznik) ⊗ 1097
Myriocephalon 1176
Doryiaeum 1147 (Eskişehir) ⊗
Iconium (Konya)
Smyrna
Antioch

▨ Byzantine Empire at the end of the rule of Basil II in the year 1025
⊗ Important battle

ca. 1355: Ottoman Territories

EMPIRE OF TREBIZOND
BYZANTINE EMPIRE
OTTOMAN TURKS
SELJUQ TURKS
Köse Dağ 1243 ⊗
Iconium (Konya)
ARMENIAN KINGDOM OF CILICIA

⊗ Important battle

1839–1876 Tanzimat ("reorganization") reforms give equality to all Ottoman subjects, including non-Muslims.

1876–1909 Sultan Abdülhamid II abolishes the Tanzimat and increases the Ottoman Empire's dependency on Germany.

1877–1878 The Ottoman Empire is defeated in the Russo-Turkish War.

1878 At the Congress of Berlin, the European Great Powers call for the independence of most Ottoman territories in the Balkans.

1908–1918 The Young Turk nationalist movement calls for reform.

October 1912–May 1913 As a result of the First Balkan War, the Ottoman Empire loses nearly all of its European territories.

1913 The Second Balkan War is fought against Bulgaria; the Ottoman Empire regains control of Eastern Thrace.

1914 The Ottoman government makes a secret pact with Germany.

1914 Russia, France and Great Britain declare war on the Ottoman Empire at the start of World War I.

1915 Armenian genocide: Turkish soldiers under Sultan Abdühmahid II deport and massacre as many as a million Turkish Armenians.

Oct. 30, 1918 Armistice brings the victorious powers to the table to discuss the division of what remains of the Ottoman Empire. Greece is allotted large parts of Asia Minor.

May 19, 1919 The Turkish War of Independence, under the leadership of Mustafa Kemal (later known as Kemal Atatürk), begins.

1919 National Congress in Erzurum and Sivas calls for Turkish independence within the boundaries set by the peace treaty, rejecting all imperial claims and policies.

1920 The British occupy Constantinople in March. The Turkish National Assembly meets for the first time under Atatürk in Ankara. The Treaty of Sèvres, which divided Turkish territory among the victorious Allies, is annulled. Greek troops are expelled from Asia Minor.

November 1922 The Ottoman sultanate is abolished. Atatürk declares the Republic of Turkey.

July 24, 1923 The Treaty of Lausanne revises the Treaty of Sèvres in favor of Turkey. Population exchange between Greece and Turkey begins.

Turkic peoples form the largest ethno-linguistic group in Central Asia. Nomadic Turks were led by tribal leaders such as Osman, the founder of the Ottoman Empire (which bears his name) and Seljuq, who gave his name to the Seljuq Turks. There have been many Turkish states, including the Gökturk empire, which ruled central Mongolia in the 6th through 8th centuries, and its successor, the Uighur empire, which collapsed in the 9th century. The Khasarids

ruled in what is now Kazakhistan in the 7th through 11th centuries, and the Ghaznavids ruled in Iran and Afghanistan in the 11th through 12th centuries. In addition to the Rum-Seljuq in Anatolia and Asia Minor, other Seljuq groups controlled vast amounts of territory in central Asia and the Middle East. The Ottoman Empire was by far the largest and most important Turkish state.

The Seljuq Turks founded the Great Seljuq empire that marked the beginning of Turkish dominance of the Islamic world. The Rum-Seljuq ruled over conquered Byzantine territory in western Anatolia. The name "Rum" means "Rome." The Byzantine Empire was considered Roman territory because it began as the Eastern Roman Empire.

The Ottoman Turks were originally followers of Osman, a nomadic tribal chieftain. In 1299 Osman created an independent *beylik* (principality) in northwest Turkey, which over time expanded into the Ottoman Empire. By the 14th century, his namesake Ottoman Turks had driven Byzantine forces out of Asia Minor. The Ottoman Turks went on to conquer the largest empire the world had known, one that would play an important role in European history into the 20th century. Most Turks today consider themselves descendants of the Ottomans.

Atatürk (1881–1938), born Mustafa Kemal, was a highly successful military commander during World War I. In 1915 he led Turkey's successful defense of Gallipoli against invading British and Australian troops. His authority was so great that he was able to muster organized resistance to the Treaty of Sèvres that deposed the weak sultan who had signed it. As first president of the Republic of Turkey, Atatürk governed with

Kemal Atatürk (1881–1938)

a firm hand, rapidly introducing programs that promoted the Turkish language, secularization, calendar reform, compulsory education and women's rights. To encourage Turks to take Western-style surnames, he adopted one himself: Atatürk, which means "father of the Turks."

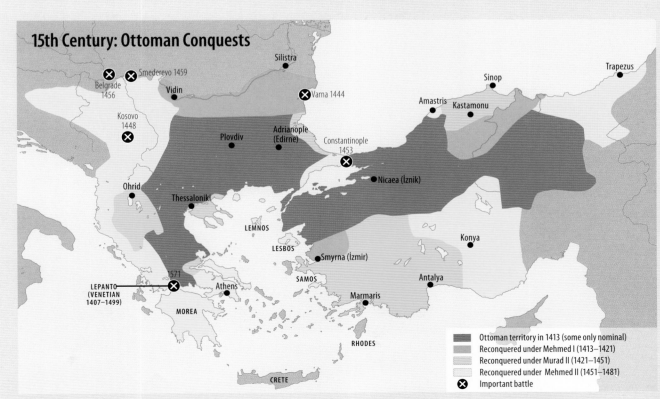

15th Century: Ottoman Conquests

Belgrade 1456 ⊗
Smederevo 1459 ⊗
Silistra
Vidin
Varna 1444 ⊗
Sinop
Trapezus
Kosovo 1448 ⊗
Plovdiv
Adrianople (Edirne)
Amastris
Kastamonu
Constantinople 1453 ⊗
Nicaea (Iznik)
Ohrid
Thessaloniki
LEMNOS
LESBOS
Konya
Smyrna (İzmir)
SAMOS
Antalya
LEPANTO (VENETIAN 1407–1499)
1571 ⊗
Athens
Marmaris
MOREA
RHODES
CRETE

▨ Ottoman territory in 1413 (some only nominal)
▨ Reconquered under Mehmed I (1413–1421)
▨ Reconquered under Murad II (1421–1451)
▨ Reconquered under Mehmed II (1451–1481)
⊗ Important battle

The Republic of Turkey / Cyprus and Malta

1925 Clothing reform discourages religious garb and makes wearing a fez illegal. The Gregorian calendar and metric system are introduced.

1928 The Latin alphabet replaces Arabic script.

1934 Women gain the right to vote. Turkey signs the Balkan Pact with Greece, Romania and Yugoslavia.

1938 Kemal Atatürk dies in Istanbul.

1939 Turkey declares neutrality during World War II.

1945 Turkey becomes a founding member of the United Nations. The Soviet Union's attempts to control the Bosporus and Dardanelles lead Turkey to ally itself with the United States.

1950 The Democratic Party led by Adnan Menderes wins national elections. Religious elements start to return to politics.

1952 Turkey becomes a full member of NATO.

1960 A military coup led by General Cemal Gürsel ousts Menderes.

1961 Menderes is executed by the military.

1965 The Justice Party led by Süleyman Demirel wins national elections.

1971 The military topples Demirel and forms a government known for its human rights violations.

1973 The Social Democratic Party led by Bülent Ecevit wins national elections.

1980 Turkey's third military coup, led by General Kenan Evren, dissolves the parliament and bans the formation of new political parties. Thousands of people are imprisoned.

1982 Turkey's new constitution is approved by popular referendum. The military voluntarily gives up power.

1983 The liberal-conservative Motherland Party led by Turgut Özal promotes closer relationships with the West.

1993 Tansu Çiller, Turkey's first female prime minister, takes office.

1995 The Islamic Welfare Party wins local and national elections. Within three years, however, it will be banned.

2002 The Islamic Justice and Development Party led by Recep Tayyip Erdogan wins national elections.

2005 Turkey applies for admission to the European Union.

2007 Turkish-Armenian author Hrant Dink, an important critic of Turkey's denial of the Armenian genocide, is murdered in Istanbul.

2008 With Erdogan's support, the Turkish Parliament votes to lift the ban of headscarves from universities. The decision is overturned by the highest Turkish court four months later.

The Turkish military views itself as the defender of secularism and as protector of the legacy of Kemal Atatürk. This has led to three military coups since 1945, each time after the military leadership determined that Islamic elements were posing a threat to the Turkish republic. The influence of the military on Turkish politics has been a major stumbling block for Turkey's admission to the European Union.

The Armenian Genocide took place during World War I after the Turkish military accused the minority Christian Armenians of collaborating with Russian aggressors.

While the first pogroms against Armenians occurred as early as the 19th century, approximately 1.5 million Armenians died in 1915 alone. Many starved on a death march through the desert. Although most Western nations accept the Armenian genocide as a well-proven fact, the Turkish government continues to deny it took place.

The "Kurdish problem" refers to the situation of the millions of Kurds who live inside the borders of Turkey, Iran and Iraq. In Turkey, Kurds make up 20 percent of the population. Officially recognized in 1991, Turkish Kurds continue to strive for increased autonomy. The Kurdish Workers Party (PKK), led by Abdullah Öcalan, has repeatedly challenged Turkish authority, leading to the death of tens of thousands of people per year in clashes with the Turkish military. The PKK, which had frequently resorted to terrorist methods, was weakened by the 1999 imprisonment of Abdullah Öcalan.

Kurdish demonstration by followers of Abdullah Öcalan

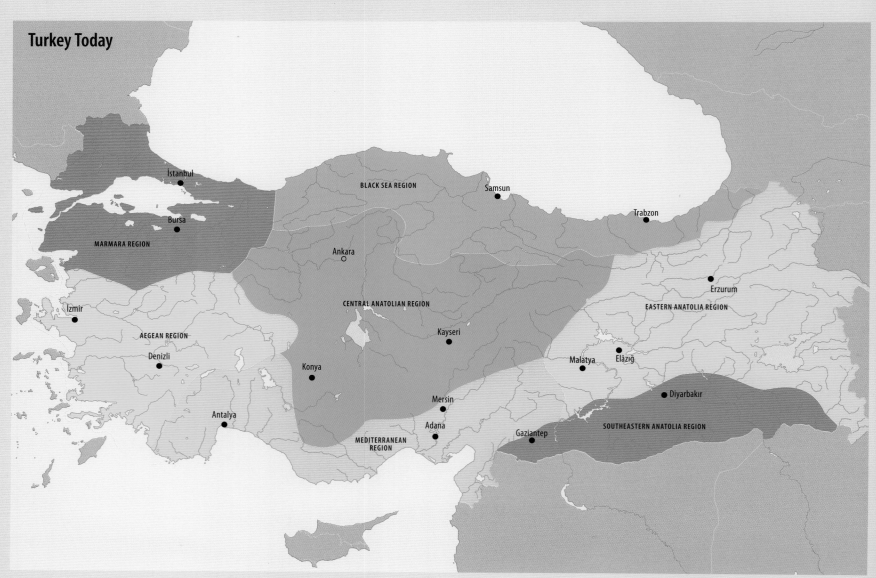

Turkey Today

İstanbul
Bursa
MARMARA REGION
İzmir
AEGEAN REGION
Denizli
Antalya
BLACK SEA REGION
Samsun
Trabzon
Ankara
CENTRAL ANATOLIAN REGION
Kayseri
Konya
Mersin
Adana
MEDITERRANEAN REGION
Gaziantep
Erzurum
EASTERN ANATOLIA REGION
Malatya
Elâzığ
Diyarbakır
SOUTHEASTERN ANATOLIA REGION

Cyprus: Second Half of the 20th Century

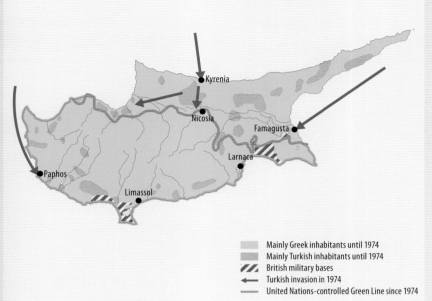

Mainly Greek inhabitants until 1974
Mainly Turkish inhabitants until 1974
British military bases
Turkish invasion in 1974
United Nations-controlled Green Line since 1974

Cyprus Today

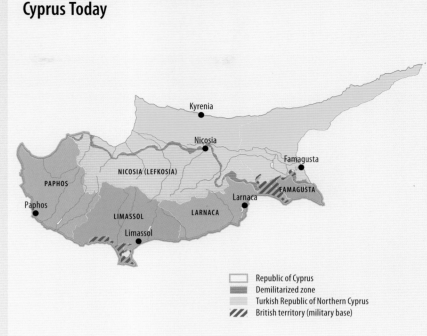

Republic of Cyprus
Demilitarized zone
Turkish Republic of Northern Cyprus
British territory (military base)

Cyprus

from 8200 BCE First permanent settlements are established at Khirokitia.

1200 BCE Mycenaean culture arrives.

from 800 BCE Cyprus falls under the control of the Phoenicians, Assyrians, Persians, Greeks and Romans.

395 CE Cyprus becomes part of the Eastern Roman Empire.

from 649 Cyprus is divided between the Byzantine Empire and Arabs.

1192–1489 The Crusader Lusignan dynasty purchases the island from the Knights Templar.

1489–1571 Cyprus falls under the control of Venice.

1571 Ottoman forces invade.

1878 Cyprus becomes an administrative protectorate of Great Britain.

1914 Great Britain annexes Cyprus in the wake of World War I. It will become a crown colony in 1925.

1955 Guerilla war begins with Greek and Turkish Cypriots allied against Great Britain. Rebels call for annexation by Greece.

1960 Greek and Turkish Cypriots agree to a common constitution. Cyprus becomes an independent nation with Makarios III (born Mikhail Mouskos) as its president.

1963 Tensions increase between Greeks and Turks. Makarios amends the constitution to limit the rights of Turkish Cypriots.

1964 United Nations peacekeeping forces arrive.

1974 The Greek military junta supports an unsuccessful coup against Makarios. Turkish troops occupy the northern part of the island; Greek refugees flee to the south.

1975 Cyprus is divided into Turkish and Greek sectors. Turkish Cypriots in the north demand an independent state.

1980 Peace talks brokered by the United Nations begin.

1983 Cypriot Turks led by Rauf Denktash break off negotiations, forming the Turkish Republic of Northern Cyprus.

2002–2003 Reunification talks fail.

2004 The European Union extends membership only to the southern Greek Republic of Cyprus.

Malta

from 11,000–4000 BCE First permanent settlement

from 3600 BCE Monumental temple building begins, followed by megalithic fortifications and tombs.

800–217 BCE Phoenicia and Carthage rule Malta.

217 BCE–395 CE Malta is part of the Roman Empire.

455–870 Vandals, Ostrogoths (494) and Byzantine imperial forces successively occupy Malta.

870–1090 The Umayyad Arabs conquer the island.

1090–1530 The southern half of the island becomes a Norman kingdom, later controlled by France and Spain.

1530–1798 The Knights of Malta take control.

1798–1800 Napoleon leads the French invasion of the island.

from 1800 Malta becomes part of the British Empire, becoming a crown colony in 1814.

1947 Malta gains the right to self-administration, which is suspended from 1959–1962.

1964 Malta becomes an independent state and member of the British Commonwealth.

1964–1971 The National Party controls the government.

1971 The Social Democrats under Dom (Dominic) Mintoff win national elections. Malta initiates diplomatic relations with Libya and maintains strong ties to Eastern Bloc nations.

1974 Malta becomes a republic.

1984 Mintoff steps down as prime minister.

1987 The National Party improves relationships with the West and applies for membership in the European Union.

2004 Malta becomes a member of the EU.

2008 The euro replaces the Maltese lira as the official currency.

Malta Today

AFRICA

AFRICA

Africa is the cradle of humankind, home to the oldest documented cultures, and yet its history remained largely unexplored until quite recently. This is where the first hominids evolved. Just about two million years ago, *Homo erectus* made its way from the southern regions of Africa to more northerly climes. The first traces of our own ancestors, *Homo sapiens*, are also to be found here. The oldest remains discovered thus far date from 150,000 years ago. It was this *Homo sapiens* who some 100,000 years ago began to conquer the world, beginning with Europe, then moving on to Asia and North America and further into the Amazon region, where *Homo sapiens* settled about 15,000 years ago. The descendants of the earliest Africans settled throughout the entire world.

Nowhere has history been so precisely documented for more than 5,000 years than in North Africa, and almost nowhere is there such a paucity of information as in the southern part of the continent.

No other region of the world has been so exploited—economically and in terms of human flesh—over such an extended period of time. The majority of Africa was dominated by European colonial interests in the 19th century, and released into a chaotic freedom late in the 20th century. At the threshold of the third millenium, Africa continues to suffer a significant development deficit in comparison to other areas of the world, and faces very complex challenges.

Africa: An Overview	**302**
European Exploration of Africa and the Slave Trade	304
Africa: An Overview	**306**
Ancient Egypt Until 395 CE	**308**
The Maghreb	**310**
Libya and Egypt	**312**
Western and Central Africa	**314**
Eastern Africa	**316**
Southern Africa	**318**
Current Issues on the African Continent	320

Africa

Palazzo Farnese, Caprarola

Africa: An Overview

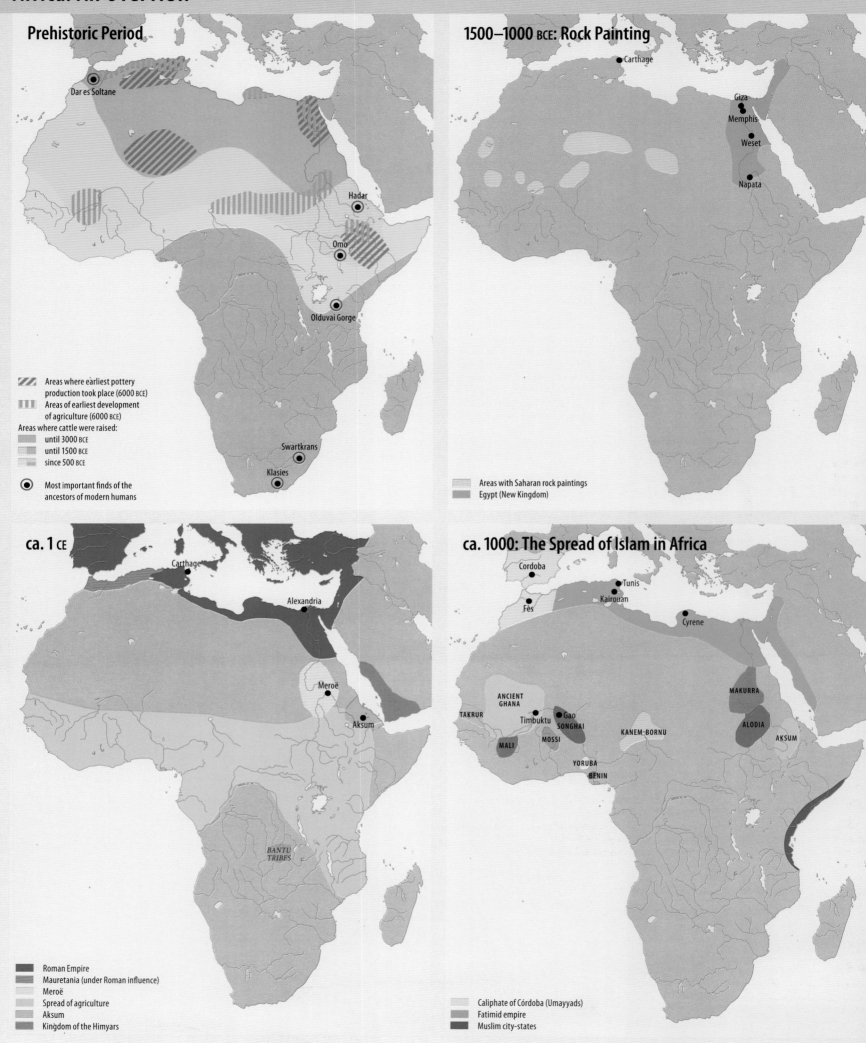

Prehistoric Period

Dar es Soltane

Hadar

Omo

Olduvai Gorge

Swartkrans

Klasies

▨ Areas where earliest pottery production took place (6000 BCE)
▥ Areas of earliest development of agriculture (6000 BCE)

Areas where cattle were raised:
  until 3000 BCE
  until 1500 BCE
  since 500 BCE

◉ Most important finds of the ancestors of modern humans

1500–1000 BCE: Rock Painting

Carthage

Giza
Memphis
Weset

Napata

Areas with Saharan rock paintings
Egypt (New Kingdom)

ca. 1 CE

Carthage

Alexandria

Meroë

Aksum

BANTU TRIBES

Roman Empire
Mauretania (under Roman influence)
Meroë
Spread of agriculture
Aksum
Kingdom of the Himyars

ca. 1000: The Spread of Islam in Africa

Cordoba

Tunis
Kairouan

Fès

Cyrene

TAKRUR

ANCIENT GHANA
Timbuktu
MALI
MOSSI
Gao
SONGHAI
YORUBA
BENIN
KANEM-BORNU

MAKURRA

ALODIA

AKSUM

Caliphate of Córdoba (Umayyads)
Fatimid empire
Muslim city-states

Islam in Africa

Islam came to Africa via the Arabian Peninsula not long after the revelations of the Prophet Muhammad in the second half of the 7th century. In the north, it met with a generally positive response. Beginning in the 8th century, Islam played an important role in eastern Africa and subsequently spread to the west coast. To the extent that it weakened tribal bonds and strengthened the role of centralized power, Islam was a modernizing force in the history of Africa. Unlike Christianity, Islam did not directly contradict local traditions, and it did endorse polygamy. Today Islam is among the most widespread religions in Africa.

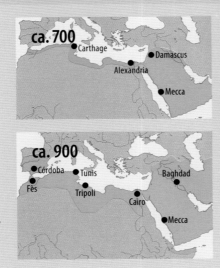

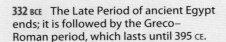

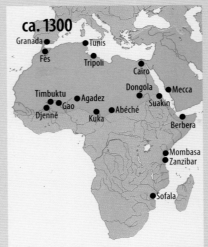

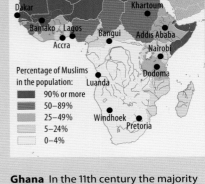

Percentage of Muslims in the population:
- 90% or more
- 50–89%
- 25–49%
- 5–24%
- 0–4%

Morocco Thanks to Uqba ibn Nafi, an Umayyad general and a Sunni, Islam reached Morocco in 670 CE.

Egypt Islam was introduced to Egypt in the 7th century. Cairo became a center of Islam, and to this day the majority of Egypt's population are Sunni.

Algeria Uqba ibn Nafi brought Islam to Algeria. In 1991, after the anticipated victory of the Islamic Salvation Front (FIS) in preliminary rounds of voting, elections were cancelled, leading to a bloody civil war.

Libya Islam spread to Libya as early as the 7th century. Following the 1969 coup led by Muammar al-Qaddafi, the role of Islam in society was strengthened.

Tunisia Some 98 percent of the population profess the Islamic faith, most of which is Sunni.

Ethiopia The first Muslims in Ethiopia were refugees who had fled from Mecca. In contrast to neighboring Somalia, the majority of the population here does not profess the Islamic faith. About one-third of Ethiopians are Muslim.

Nigeria Islam reached Nigeria in the 9th century. In the 16th century it was recognized as the state religion by the ruling dynasty of the Kanem-Bornu empire.

Ghana In the 11th century the majority of court officials in the historical Ghana empire professed the Islamic faith. Today Muslims comprise 11 percent of the population.

Mali Islam was brought to Mali and nearly all of western Africa in the 9th century by Berber and Tuareg traders. Today, 90 percent of the population is Muslim, and the majority belongs to the Sunni sect.

---

7 million BCE The first ancestors of later australopithecines and hominids walk upright. "Lucy," an *Australopithecus afarensis*, lived near Hadar, Ethiopia some three million years ago.

2 million BCE *Homo erectus* learns to use tools and leaves Africa.

144,000 BCE The first fossil evidence of *Homo sapiens* in East Africa

100,000–60,000 BCE *Homo sapiens* populate the earth.

10,500–4000 BCE The fertile region, known today as the Sahara, dries up at the end of the Stone Age. People settle in the Nile Valley, in areas south of the Sahara and in eastern Africa.

3100 BCE Menes, the first Egyptian pharaoh, unites Upper and Lower Egypt: thirty dynasties follow.

3000 BCE The first advanced cultures develop in Ethiopia.

2000 BCE Egypt conquers Lower Nubia, called Kush (Sudan). Kush later regains its independence.

1000 BCE The Phoenicians colonize wide stretches of the North African Mediterranean coastline.

631 BCE The Greeks found Cyrene in North Africa.

400–300 BCE Meroë, the capital of Kush and long the center of a flourishing kingdom, declines and is finally sacked by Aksumites.

332 BCE The Late Period of ancient Egypt ends; it is followed by the Greco–Roman period, which lasts until 395 CE.

200 BCE Founding of the kingdom of Mauretania

~1 CE The Bantu colonize Uganda and repress the Pygmies.

~1 CE–7th century The Aksumite empire in Ethiopia. At the height of its power, Aksum is the main trade market of northeastern Africa.

500–1000 The ancient Ghana empire, one of the first great medieval trading empires of western Africa, flourishes on the edge of the southwestern Sahara. It is not identical to the modern-day Republic of Ghana.

~600 Founding of the Benin (or Edo) empire, which reaches the apex of its power in the 15th century

~800 Arab merchants reach Zanzibar.

1300 The kingdom of Mutapa is wealthy due to rich gold deposits. The famous walls of Great Zimbabwe date from this time.

~1350 Mali reaches its greatest expansion after the decline of the Ghana empire.

1370 Lukeni lua Nimi founds the kingdom of Kongo.

1415 The sultanate of Adal originates in the area that is now Somalia.

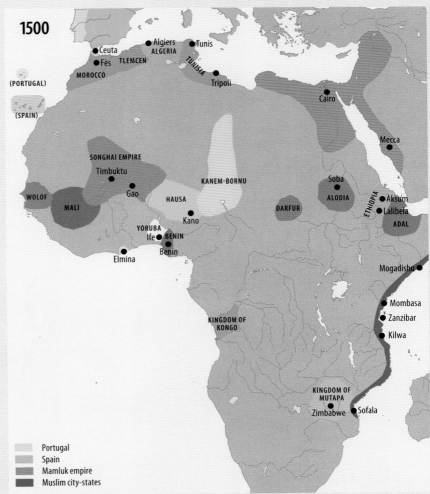

Portugal
Spain
Mamluk empire
Muslim city-states

1464 The Songhai empire conquers large parts of the Sahel region.

~1500 European colonization of Africa begins.

~1680–1896 The Asante empire exists in what is now Ghana and is active in the slave trade in the 18th and 19th centuries.

European Exploration of Africa and the Slave Trade

Areas of Africa Known to Europeans in 1800

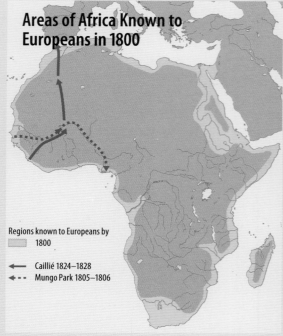

Regions known to Europeans by 1800

→ Caillié 1824–1828
⇢ Mungo Park 1805–1806

Areas of Africa Known to Europeans in 1850

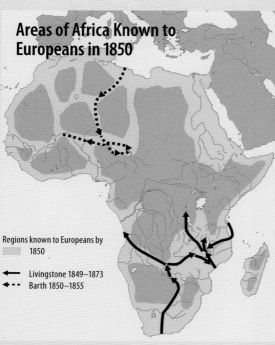

Regions known to Europeans by 1850

→ Livingstone 1849–1873
⇢ Barth 1850–1855

Areas of Africa Known to Europeans in 1880

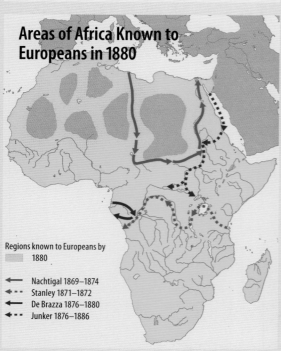

Regions known to Europeans by 1880

→ Nachtigal 1869–1874
⇢ Stanley 1871–1872
→ De Brazza 1876–1880
⇢ Junker 1876–1886

The Slave Trade

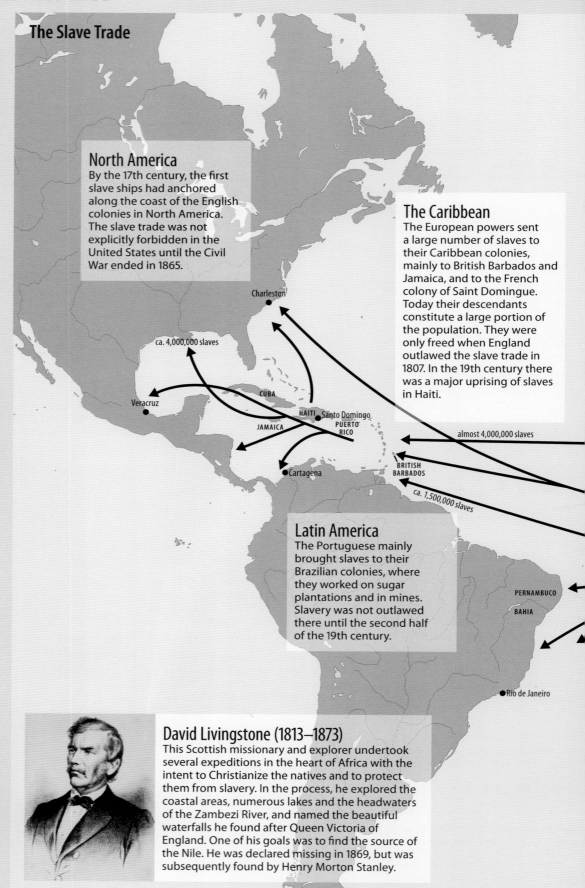

North America
By the 17th century, the first slave ships had anchored along the coast of the English colonies in North America. The slave trade was not explicitly forbidden in the United States until the Civil War ended in 1865.

The Caribbean
The European powers sent a large number of slaves to their Caribbean colonies, mainly to British Barbados and Jamaica, and to the French colony of Saint Domingue. Today their descendants constitute a large portion of the population. They were only freed when England outlawed the slave trade in 1807. In the 19th century there was a major uprising of slaves in Haiti.

Latin America
The Portuguese mainly brought slaves to their Brazilian colonies, where they worked on sugar plantations and in mines. Slavery was not outlawed there until the second half of the 19th century.

ca. 4,000,000 slaves

almost 4,000,000 slaves

ca. 1,500,000 slaves

Charleston

Veracruz

CUBA

HAITI · Santo Domingo
PUERTO RICO

JAMAICA

Cartagena

BRITISH BARBADOS

PERNAMBUCO

BAHIA

Río de Janeiro

David Livingstone (1813–1873)
This Scottish missionary and explorer undertook several expeditions in the heart of Africa with the intent to Christianize the natives and to protect them from slavery. In the process, he explored the coastal areas, numerous lakes and the headwaters of the Zambezi River, and named the beautiful waterfalls he found after Queen Victoria of England. One of his goals was to find the source of the Nile. He was declared missing in 1869, but was subsequently found by Henry Morton Stanley.

European Exploration of Africa

With the exception of North Africa, for centuries most Europeans were only familiar with the coastal regions of African, where European ships docked to trade for Africans to be used as slaves. The great majority of the African continent remained unknown during a period when North and South America as well as most of Asia (except for the central mountainous regions) were thoroughly explored and mapped. This situation changed dramatically in the early 19th century, when Europe expanded its horizons with a series of African expeditions.

The European discovery of Africa created momentum for colonization, but the explorers first had to face many challenges in central Africa. The climate was uncongenial, and they found that most African rivers were not navigable along their entire length. These problems could overwhelm even the most adventurous pioneers, many of whom initially went to Africa as missionaries.

Europe

Only a small fraction of the African slaves reached Europe because, unlike in the United States, there was no shortage of manpower there. Most blacks were placed in the courts of the nobility as servants and novelties.

The Abolition of Slavery

Country	Year	Country	Year	Country	Year
Upper Canada	1793	Portugal	1836	Somalia	1920
Haiti	1794	Spain	1837	The Sudan	1924
Lower Canada	1803	Denmark	1848	Ethiopia	1923
Wales	1807	France	1848	Iraq	1924
Chile	1823	Peru	1869	Iran	1928
Argentina	1813	The Netherlands	1863	Morocco	1930s
Ecuador	1821	United States	1865	Northern Nigeria	1936
Colombia	1821	Puerto Rico	1873	Qatar	1952
Panama	1821	Ottoman Empire	1876	Saudi Arabia	1962
Venezuela	1821	Cuba	1886	Yemen	1962
Guatemala	1824	Brazil	1888	United Arab Emirates	1963
Nicaragua	1824	Madagascar	1896	Oman	1970
Costa Rica	1824	Zanzibar	1897	Mauritania	1980
Mexico	1829			Niger	2003

Arabia

Even before the Europeans, Arab sailors brought slaves from the east coast of Africa to Arabia and Persia. Some slaves left Africa via the caravan routes. Their numbers were small compared with those taken by Europeans.

India

Most of the slaves that Arab traders brought to India in the 11th to 19th centuries came from eastern Africa. Their modern descendants are the Siddi, who live in western India and Pakistan.

Prisoners on a slave ship, West Africa, ca. 1880

Slavery

For centuries, Africa was a source of cheap labor for Europe and the Americas. The slave trade flourished until it was gradually outlawed in the 19th century. The main reason for slavery was the lack of manpower on the continuously expanding plantations in America. Slaves were highly profitable for their traders. It is estimated that at least 10 million human beings were forcibly abducted from Africa and transported to America between the 16th and 19th centuries.

more than 3,500,000 slaves

- ▪ Main areas of slave export in the 15th–17th centuries
- ▪ Main areas of slave export in the 18th century
- ▪ Main areas of slave export in the 19th century
- ← Main directions of the export of slaves
- ● Most important slave markets and cities

The Most Famous European Expeditions

Mungo Park (1771–1806) A Scot who explored the Niger River over the course of nearly 1,000 miles (1,600 km).

René Caillié (1799–1838) This Frenchman traveled through the western Sahara and crossed the Niger River.

Heinrich Barth (1821–1865) A German explorer who crossed the Sahara and explored territories south of Lake Chad.

Gustav Nachtigal (1834–1885) A German explorer who traveled through the central Sahara from Tripoli to Khartoum.

Henry Morton Stanley (1841–1904) A Welshman who went in search of the missing explorer

Henry Morton Stanley

David Livingstone. He explored the Lualaba River and the lower course of the Congo.

Pierre Savorgnan de Brazza (1852–1905) Born in Italy, this naturalized Frenchman reached the Congo River and established the first French settlement in the area.

Wilhelm Junker (1840–1892) A Russian who undertook several expeditions through eastern and sub-Saharan Africa between the Nile and Congo rivers, and traveled all the way to Uganda.

Africa: An Overview

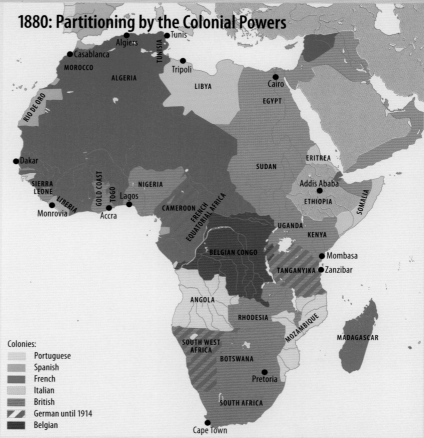

1750: Early Colonization

OTTOMAN EMPIRE

Algiers
Fès
MOROCCO
Cairo

(FR.) WALO
FOUTA-TORO
SEGU
(PORTUGAL)
DAHOMEY
(BRITAIN)
ASANTE
BENIN
(NETHERLANDS) (BRITAIN)

KANO BORNU WADAI DARFUR SENNAR
ETHIOPIA

LOANGO
KUBA
CONGO
BUGANDA
LUBA
Luanda
LUNDA
KASANJE
ROZWI

Cape Town

Colonies:
- French
- British
- Portuguese
- Dutch

1880: Partitioning by the Colonial Powers

Tunis
Algiers
TUNISIA
Casablanca
MOROCCO
Tripoli
ALGERIA
LIBYA
Cairo
EGYPT

RIO DE ORO
SUDAN
ERITREA
Dakar
SIERRA LEONE
GOLD COAST
TOGO
NIGERIA
Addis Ababa
LIBERIA
Lagos
CAMEROON
ETHIOPIA
SOMALIA
Monrovia
Accra
FRENCH EQUATORIAL AFRICA
UGANDA
KENYA
BELGIAN CONGO
Mombasa
TANGANYIKA Zanzibar
ANGOLA
RHODESIA
MOZAMBIQUE
MADAGASCAR
SOUTH WEST AFRICA
BOTSWANA
Pretoria
SOUTH AFRICA
Cape Town

Colonies:
- Portuguese
- Spanish
- French
- Italian
- British
- German until 1914
- Belgian

Decolonization

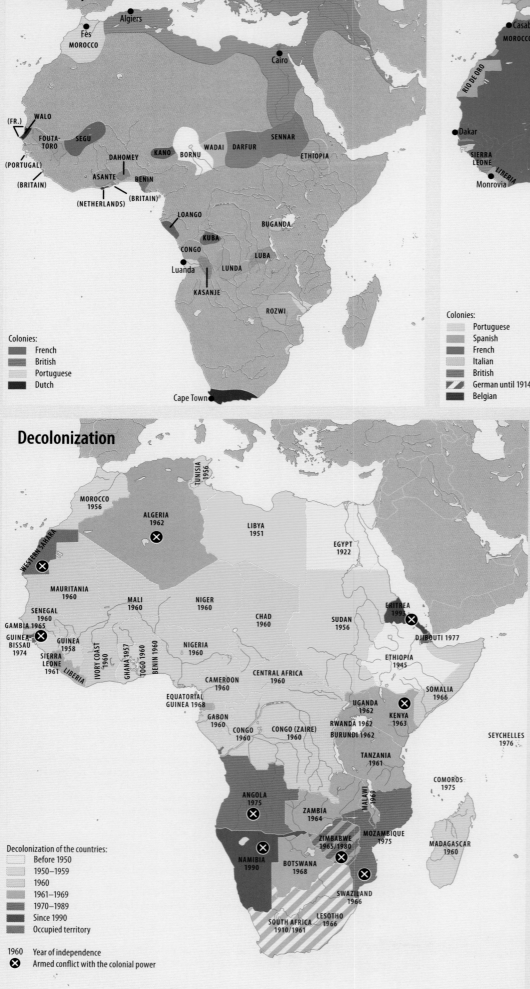

TUNISIA 1956
MOROCCO 1956
ALGERIA 1962
LIBYA 1951
EGYPT 1922
WESTERN SAHARA
MAURITANIA 1960
MALI 1960
NIGER 1960
CHAD 1960
SUDAN 1956
ERITREA 1993
SENEGAL 1960
GAMBIA 1965
GUINEA BISSAU 1974
GUINEA 1958
DJIBOUTI 1977
SIERRA LEONE 1961
IVORY COAST 1960
GHANA 1957
TOGO 1960
BENIN 1960
NIGERIA 1960
LIBERIA
ETHIOPIA 1945
CENTRAL AFRICA 1960
CAMEROON 1960
SOMALIA 1966
EQUATORIAL GUINEA 1968
UGANDA 1962
KENYA 1963
GABON 1960
CONGO 1960
CONGO (ZAIRE) 1960
RWANDA 1962
BURUNDI 1962
TANZANIA 1961
SEYCHELLES 1976
ANGOLA 1975
MALAWI 1969
COMOROS 1975
ZAMBIA 1964
MOZAMBIQUE 1975
MADAGASCAR 1960
NAMIBIA 1990
ZIMBABWE 1965/1980
BOTSWANA 1968
SWAZILAND 1966
SOUTH AFRICA 1910/1961
LESOTHO 1966

Decolonization of the countries:
- Before 1950
- 1950–1959
- 1960
- 1961–1969
- 1970–1989
- Since 1990
- Occupied territory

1960 Year of independence
⊗ Armed conflict with the colonial power

The Portuguese were the first Europeans to establish colonies on the African continent, as early as the 15th century. Beginning in the 18th century Great Britain and France also competed there. Other European powers vied for African colonies at the end of the 19th century. Colonial rule ended only after World War II.

1481 Founding of the first Portuguese trading post on the coast of Ghana

1491 The Portuguese Christianize the Kongo kingdom.

after 1530 British expedition to Benin

1652 A Dutch fort is established on the Cape of Good Hope.

18th century The British control Gambia, Sierra Leone and Ghana; the French control Senegal, French Guinea and the Cote d'Ivoire (Ivory Coast).

1830 France conquers Algeria.

1878 Founding of the Belgian Congo

1881 France annexes Tunisia.

1884 The Berlin Conference (also "Congo Conference"): The major European countries meet to resolve competing claims regarding African territories, especially the Congo River basin.

1891 Germany colonizes Togo and Cameroon.

1899–1902 Great Britain wins the Second Boer War.

1912 Turkey cedes Libya to Italy.

1914 Egypt becomes a British protectorate.

1936 Italy annexes Ethiopia.

1951 Following passage of a UN resolution, Libya becomes an independent kingdom.

1960 Year of African Independence: Nearly all African colonies gain their independence.

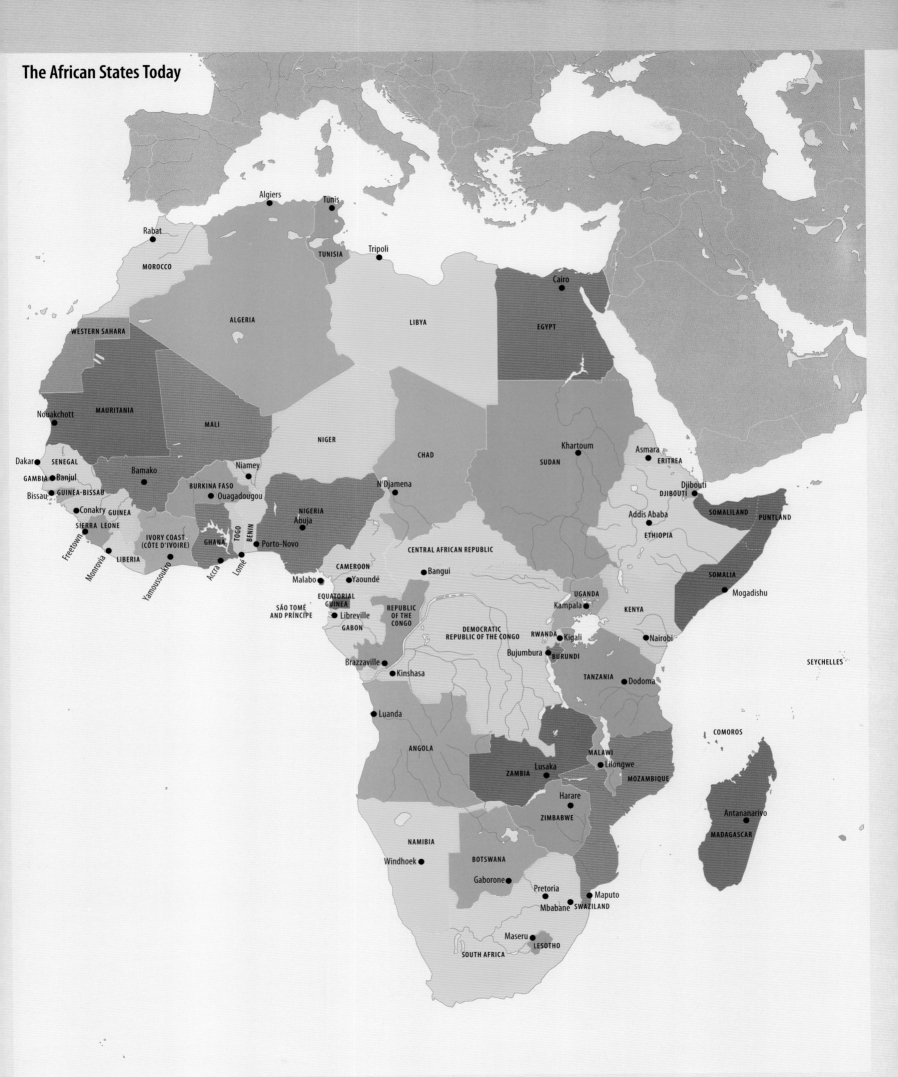

The African States Today

ALGIERS
TUNIS
Rabat
MOROCCO
TUNISIA
Tripoli
Cairo
ALGERIA
LIBYA
EGYPT
WESTERN SAHARA
Nouakchott
MAURITANIA
MALI
NIGER
Khartoum
Asmara
Dakar
SENEGAL
Bamako
Niamey
CHAD
SUDAN
ERITREA
GAMBIA
Banjul
BURKINA FASO
N'Djamena
Djibouti
Bissau
GUINEA-BISSAU
Ouagadougou
DJIBOUTI
Conakry
GUINEA
NIGERIA
Addis Ababa
SOMALILAND
PUNTLAND
SIERRA LEONE
Abuja
Freetown
IVORY COAST
(CÔTE D'IVOIRE)
GHANA
TOGO
BENIN
Porto-Novo
ETHIOPIA
Monrovia
LIBERIA
Accra
Lome
Malabo
CAMEROON
Bangui
SOMALIA
Yamoussoukro
Yaoundé
CENTRAL AFRICAN REPUBLIC
Mogadishu
SÃO TOMÉ
AND PRÍNCIPE
EQUATORIAL
GUINEA
Libreville
UGANDA
Kampala
KENYA
GABON
REPUBLIC
OF THE
CONGO
DEMOCRATIC
REPUBLIC OF THE CONGO
RWANDA
Kigali
Nairobi
SEYCHELLES
Brazzaville
Bujumbura
BURUNDI
Kinshasa
TANZANIA
Dodoma
Luanda
COMOROS
ANGOLA
MALAWI
Lusaka
Lilongwe
Antananarivo
ZAMBIA
MOZAMBIQUE
Harare
MADAGASCAR
ZIMBABWE
NAMIBIA
BOTSWANA
Windhoek
Maputo
Gaborone
Pretoria
SWAZILAND
Mbabane
Maseru
LESOTHO
SOUTH AFRICA

Ancient Egypt Until 395 CE

2707–1550 BCE: From Unification to the Middle Kingdom

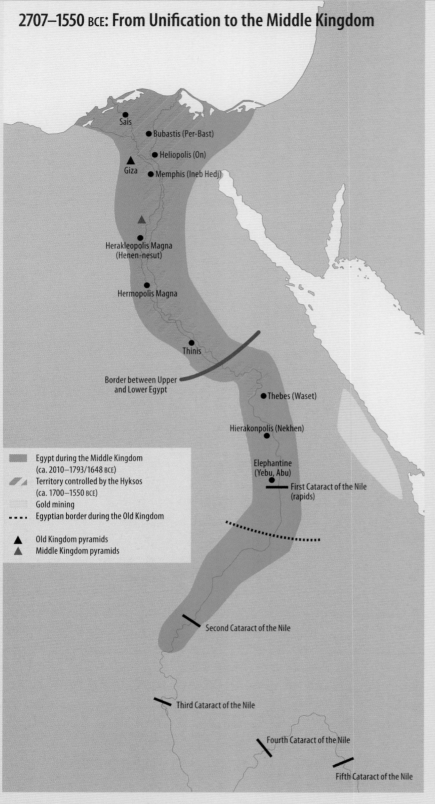

Sais
Bubastis (Per-Bast)
Heliopolis (On)
Giza ▲
Memphis (Ineb Hedj)
Herakleopolis Magna (Henen-nesut)
Hermopolis Magna
Thinis
Border between Upper and Lower Egypt
Thebes (Waset)
Hierakonpolis (Nekhen)
Elephantine (Yebu, Abu)
First Cataract of the Nile (rapids)
Second Cataract of the Nile
Third Cataract of the Nile
Fourth Cataract of the Nile
Fifth Cataract of the Nile

Egypt during the Middle Kingdom (ca. 2010–1793/1648 BCE)
Territory controlled by the Hyksos (ca. 1700–1550 BCE)
Gold mining
Egyptian border during the Old Kingdom
▲ Old Kingdom pyramids
▲ Middle Kingdom pyramids

1550–1085 BCE: The New Kingdom

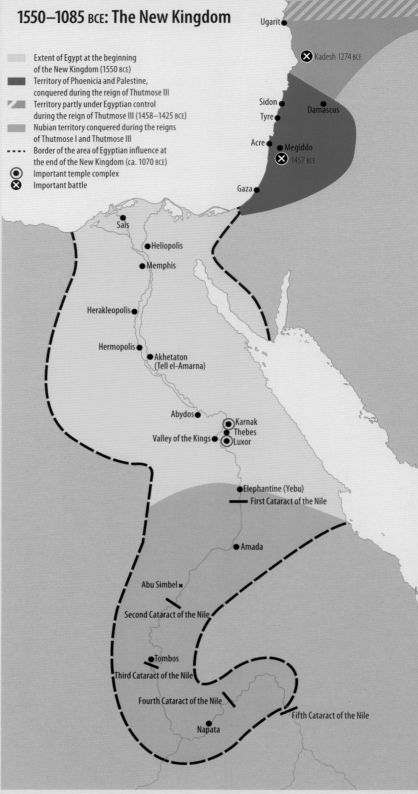

Extent of Egypt at the beginning of the New Kingdom (1550 BCE)
Territory of Phoenicia and Palestine, conquered during the reign of Thutmose III
Territory partly under Egyptian control during the reign of Thutmose III (1458–1425 BCE)
Nubian territory conquered during the reigns of Thutmose I and Thutmose III
Border of the area of Egyptian influence at the end of the New Kingdom (ca. 1070 BCE)
⊙ Important temple complex
⊗ Important battle

Ugarit
⊗ Kadesh 1274 BCE
Sidon
Tyre
Damascus
Acre
⊙⊗ Megiddo 1457 BCE
Gaza
Sais
Heliopolis
Memphis
Herakleopolis
Hermopolis
Akhetaton (Tell el-Amarna)
Abydos
Karnak
Thebes
Valley of the Kings
Luxor
Elephantine (Yebu)
First Cataract of the Nile
Amada
Abu Simbel ×
Second Cataract of the Nile
Tombos
Third Cataract of the Nile
Fourth Cataract of the Nile
Fifth Cataract of the Nile
Napata

The history of Egypt is divided into five great epochs: the Old Kingdom, the Middle Kingdom, the New Kingdom, the Late Period and the Ptolemaic empire. Each phase has distinct characteristics, yet they maintain a cultural unity expressed in an elaborate cult of the dead and deity worship. Pyramids are most strongly associated with the the Old and Middle Kingdoms, and some of the most beautiful Egyptian temples stem from the New Kingdom. The Late Period is characterized by the reign of pharaohs from Nubia, while the Ptolemaic dynasty is defined by a synthesis of Egyptian and Greek culture. Egypt lost its autonomy when the Ptolemaic dynasty came to an end.

~5000–2702 BCE Predynastic period and first and second dynasties

~5000 BCE Oldest Neolithic cultures produce stone tools, ceramic vessels, textiles and the first permanent settlements.

~3100 BCE The pharaoh Menes unites Upper and Lower Egypt.

~3000 BCE The first hieroglyphs appear; Memphis becomes the capital.

~2780 BCE The Egyptian state is stabilized by the third dynasty pharaohs.

2702–2025 BCE The Old Kingdom and first intermediate period

~2600 BCE The Great Pyramid of Khufu (Cheops) is built.

~2500 BCE The Great Sphinx, a portrait statue of King Khafre, is built.

2216 BCE Egypt collapses; political decay, famine and violence ensue.

2047 BCE Egypt is reunited under the reign of Mentuhotep II.

2025 BCE Mentuhotep II reconquers Nubia.

2010–1550 BCE The Middle Kingdom and the second intermediate period

1950–1550 BCE The magnificent Middle Kingdom papyri are produced.

~1700 BCE The Hyksos, Semitic immigrants, rule Egypt and introduce the chariot. Their capital is the Nile delta city of Avaris.

~1550 BCE Ahmose conquers the Hyksos territory, reuniting Egypt.

1550–664 BCE The New Kingdom and the third intermediate period. Memphis

950–332 BCE: Third Intermediate Period and Late Period

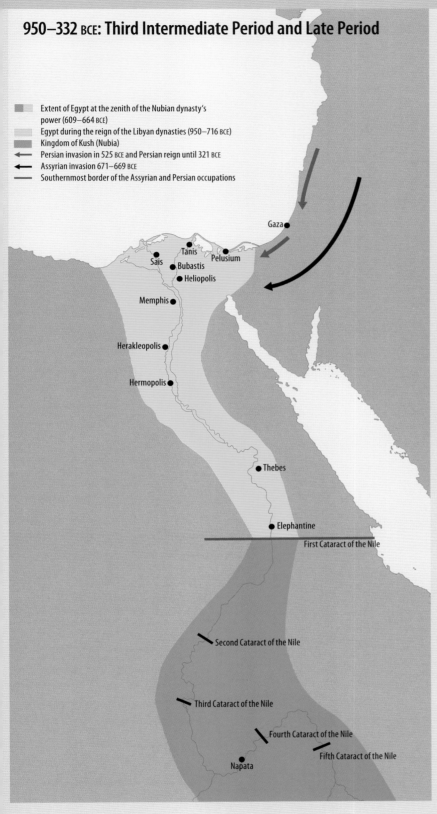

Extent of Egypt at the zenith of the Nubian dynasty's power (609–664 BCE)

Egypt during the reign of the Libyan dynasties (950–716 BCE)

Kingdom of Kush (Nubia)

Persian invasion in 525 BCE and Persian reign until 321 BCE

Assyrian invasion 671–669 BCE

Southernmost border of the Assyrian and Persian occupations

Gaza

Tanis
Sais
Bubastis Pelusium
Heliopolis

Memphis

Herakleopolis

Hermopolis

Thebes

Elephantine

First Cataract of the Nile

Second Cataract of the Nile

Third Cataract of the Nile

Fourth Cataract of the Nile

Fifth Cataract of the Nile

Napata

321–30 BCE: The Ptolemaic Empire

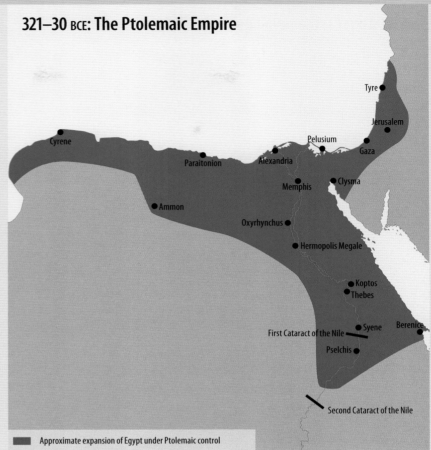

Tyre

Jerusalem

Cyrene
Pelusium
Paraitonion
Gaza
Alexandria
Clysma
Memphis

Ammon

Oxyrhynchus

Hermopolis Megale

Koptos
Thebes

First Cataract of the Nile
Syene
Berenice

Pselchis

Second Cataract of the Nile

Approximate expansion of Egypt under Ptolemaic control

Pyramids are the final resting place of the pharaohs. The oldest is the third dynasty Step Pyramid of the Old Kingdom pharaoh Djoser. The most important are the three fourth dynasty pyramids at Giza. The largest is the Great Pyramid of the pharaoh Khufu (Cheops), which is 479 feet (146 m) high and one of the Seven Wonders of the World.

Temples are monumental buildings for the worship of the gods. Among the best-preserved are the New Kingdom temples at Karnak and Luxor.

Mummification is a process that preserves a corpse by drying it out, soaking it in special oils, and wrapping it in linen bindings before it is placed in a sarcophagus. The inner organs are removed

beforehand and stored in special containers called canopic jars. Egypt's extremely dry climate helped preserve the corpse for life after death.

Hieroglyphs are the symbols used in Egyptian pictorial writing of sacred texts and monumental inscriptions. There were originally more than 700 signs—and no vowels.

The Rosetta Stone is an inscription dating to 196 BCE. It records the same prayer of thanksgiving by Ptolemy V in hieroglyphic, demotic and Greek scripts. Discovered during Napoleon's 1799 invasion of Egypt, it enabled Jean-François Champollion to decipher Egyptian hieroglyphs for the first time in 1822.

~1279–1213 BCE Seti's son, Rameses II, revives the Egyptian empire.

~1274 BCE The Battle of Kadesh is fought between the Egyptians and Hittites.

~1259 BCE A peace treaty is made between Rameses II and Hattusilis III, king of the Hittites.

~950–716 BCE A Libyan dynasty rules Egypt.

~716–671 BCE Pharaohs from the Nubian kingdom of Kush rule Egypt.

671 BCE The Assyrians occupy Egypt.

664–332 BCE The Late Period: Assyrian leaders decline in power. Demotic script is developed, and religious animal worship gains in popularity.

525 BCE The Persian king Cambyses II conquers Egypt.

332 BCE Alexander the Great conquers Egypt and founds the city of Alexandria, marking the beginning of Hellenistic rule.

321 BCE Ptolemy I founds the Ptolemaic dynasty, a long era of great prosperity, taking the title of pharaoh in 305 BCE.

47 BCE Julius Caesar arrives in Egypt, where he becomes involved with the pharaoh, Cleopatra VII. Their union results in a son, Ptolemy Caesar, called Caesarion.

31 BCE Octavian (later Emperor Augustus) defeats Mark Antony and Cleopatra at the battle of Actium.

30 BCE Cleopatra, the last ruler of the Ptolemaic dynasty, commits suicide. Egypt falls under Roman control.

395 Egypt becomes part of the Byzantine Empire.

becomes a military city, and Thebes serves as the religious capital.

from 1504 BCE New temples are constructed throughout Egypt under Thutmose I, the first pharaoh whose tomb is located in the Valley of the Kings.

1479–1458 BCE Queen Hatshepsut reigns. Her mortuary temple is one of the most important monuments in Egypt.

1457 BCE The defeat of local rulers in the Battle of Megiddo makes Pharaoh Thutmose III the ruler of what are today Syria and Palestine.

1458–1425 BCE The Egyptian empire reaches its greatest extent under Thutmose III.

~1353–1334 BCE The reign of Akhenaton brings religious reform and a new capital at El-Amarna, but foreign policy is weakened and the empire collapses soon thereafter.

1290–1279 BCE Seti I, a successful military leader, reasserts Egypt's authority in the Middle East.

1333–1323 BCE Reign of Tutankhamon; the discovery of his intact tomb in 1922 is a sensation.

The Maghreb

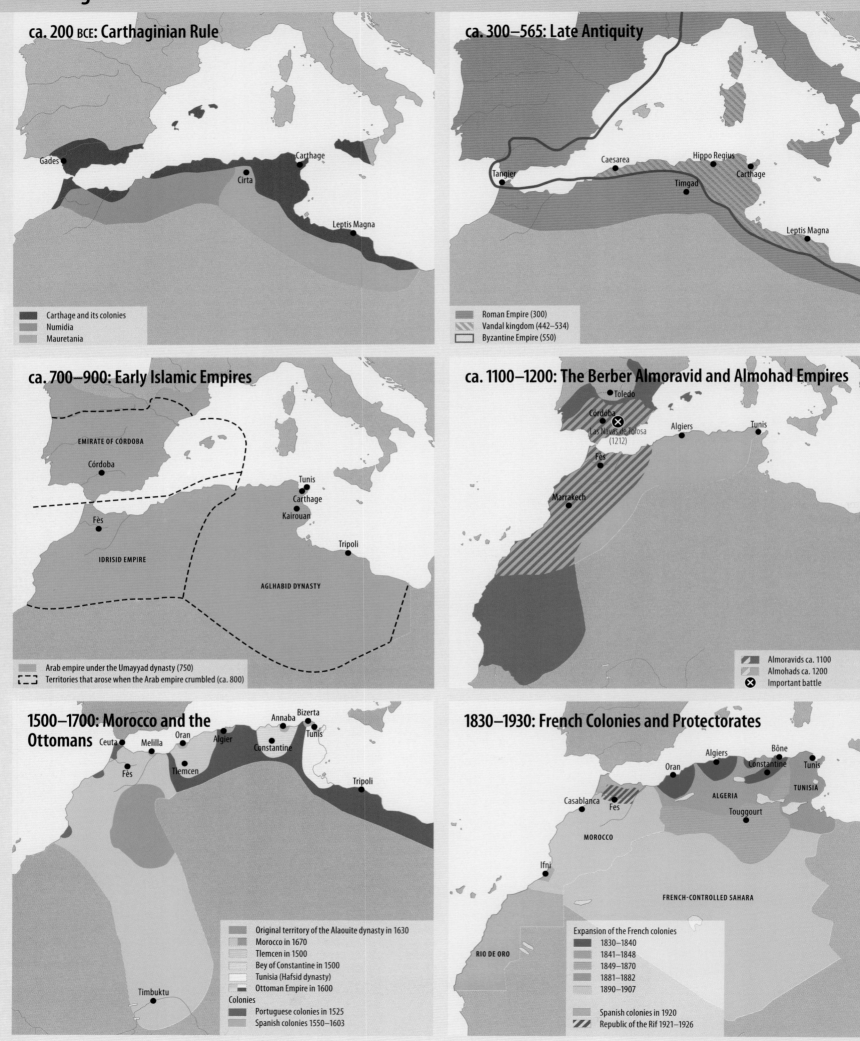

ca. 200 BCE: Carthaginian Rule

Gades
Carthage
Cirta
Leptis Magna

- Carthage and its colonies
- Numidia
- Mauretania

ca. 300–565: Late Antiquity

Tangier
Caesarea
Hippo Regius
Timgad
Carthage
Leptis Magna

- Roman Empire (300)
- Vandal kingdom (442–534)
- Byzantine Empire (550)

ca. 700–900: Early Islamic Empires

EMIRATE OF CÓRDOBA
Córdoba
Fès
IDRISID EMPIRE
Tunis
Carthage
Kairouan
Tripoli
AGLHABID DYNASTY

- Arab empire under the Umayyad dynasty (750)
- Territories that arose when the Arab empire crumbled (ca. 800)

ca. 1100–1200: The Berber Almoravid and Almohad Empires

Toledo
Córdoba
Las Navas de Tolosa (1212)
Algiers
Tunis
Fès
Marrakech

- Almoravids ca. 1100
- Almohads ca. 1200
- Important battle

1500–1700: Morocco and the Ottomans

Ceuta
Melilla
Oran
Algier
Annaba
Bizerta
Tunis
Fès
Tlemcen
Constantine
Tripoli
Timbuktu

- Original territory of the Alaouite dynasty in 1630
- Morocco in 1670
- Tlemcen in 1500
- Bey of Constantine in 1500
- Tunisia (Hafsid dynasty)
- Ottoman Empire in 1600

Colonies
- Portuguese colonies in 1525
- Spanish colonies 1550–1603

1830–1930: French Colonies and Protectorates

Oran
Algiers
Bône
Constantine
Tunis
Casablanca
Fes
ALGERIA
TUNISIA
Touggourt
MOROCCO
Ifni
FRENCH-CONTROLLED SAHARA
RIO DE ORO

Expansion of the French colonies
- 1830–1840
- 1841–1848
- 1849–1870
- 1881–1882
- 1890–1907

- Spanish colonies in 1920
- Republic of the Rif 1921–1926

The Maghreb Today

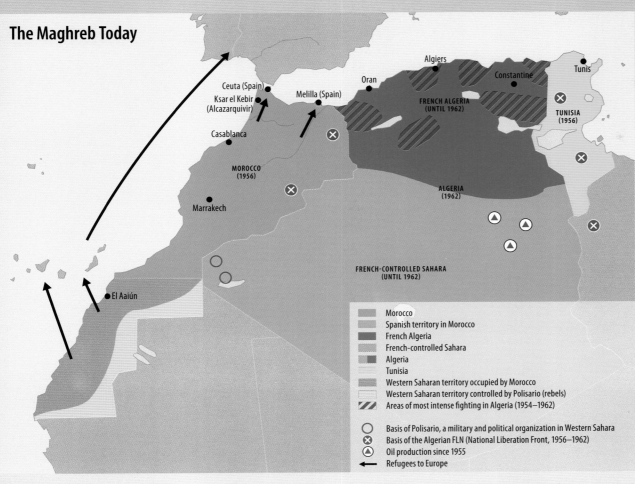

1954 Tunisia, Morocco and Sudan begin their march toward independence. The Suez Canal is nationalized.

1956 France recognizes Algerian independence.

1957 Tunisia gains independence from France.

1962 The Algerian War of Independence ends.

1972 A military coup against King Hassan II of Morocco is brutally suppressed.

1979 Morocco occupies the former Spanish colony of Western Sahara.

1992–1999 Civil war rages in Algeria.

1999 Mohammed VI becomes king of Morocco.

Mohammed VI of Morocco meets with U.S. President George W. Bush in 2002.

Legend:

- Morocco
- Spanish territory in Morocco
- French Algeria
- French-controlled Sahara
- Algeria
- Tunisia
- Western Saharan territory occupied by Morocco
- Western Saharan territory controlled by Polisario (rebels)
- Areas of most intense fighting in Algeria (1954–1962)

○ Basis of Polisario, a military and political organization in Western Sahara
⊗ Basis of the Algerian FLN (National Liberation Front, 1956–1962)
△ Oil production since 1955
← Refugees to Europe

The Phoenicians settled the Maghreb region as early as the second millennium BCE. Later, the Berber tribes would successfully defend their territory from Roman rule, but eventually Arab invaders conquered and spread Islam throughout North Africa. In the 16th century, the northern coast of Africa attracted the attention of European colonial powers such as Spain and Portugal. In the 19th century the French ruled much of what is today Tunisia and Algeria. Morocco and Tunisia achieved independence from France in 1956–1957, inaugurating a period of relative peace in the region. In neighboring Algeria, which was home to many immigrants from France, a bloody war of independence broke out in 1954; it would last until 1962. The Algerian Civil War of 1992–1999 also claimed many thousands of lives.

814 BCE Phoenicians of Tyre found the city of Carthage.

3rd–2nd centuries BCE Punic Wars between Carthage and Rome

146 BCE Rome destroys Carthage.

429 CE The Vandals invade Roman North Africa and rule for nearly a century.

550 Justinian I reconquers North Africa as part of the Byzantine Empire.

7th century Arabs conquer North Africa.

697/698 CE Arabs found the city of Tunis on the rubble of Carthage.

740 Berbers revolt against Umayyad rule in Morocco.

10th century The Córdoba Caliphate rules the Maghreb.

after 1160 Algeria and Morocco are parts of the Islamic empire of the Almoravids, which will be brought down by the Almohad dynasty a century later.

1269–1465 The Berber Marinid dynasty rules Morocco and parts of Spain.

1479–1516 The Spanish conquer the harbor cities of Algiers and Oran.

16th century Spanish and Ottoman forces battle for control of the region.

after 1524 The Saadi dynasty rules in southern Morocco.

1556–1574 The Ottoman Empire rules Algeria and Tunisia.

1578 The Portuguese are defeated at the Battle of Alcazarquivir in Morocco.

1666 The Alaouite Dynasty comes to power; it still rules Morocco today.

1671 The Janissaries, elite Ottoman troops, take control of Algeria.

1830 French forces occupy Algeria.

1831 Tunisia becomes a French protectorate.

1912 Morocco becomes a French protectorate.

The Sahara

Legend:

- Desert
- Important trade route
- ● Important city/oasis

Western Sahara

The territory of Western Sahara is primarily uninhabited desert. Morocco and Mauritania divided the former Spanish colony in 1979. Morocco annexed the region in the same year, and the Algerian-supported Polisario Front has been fighting for Western Sahara's independence ever since. The surrounding desert is rich in phosphate and oil.

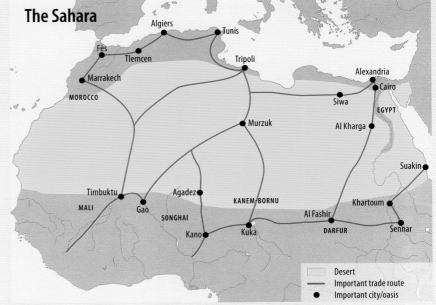

The Sahel zone, Africa

Libya and Egypt

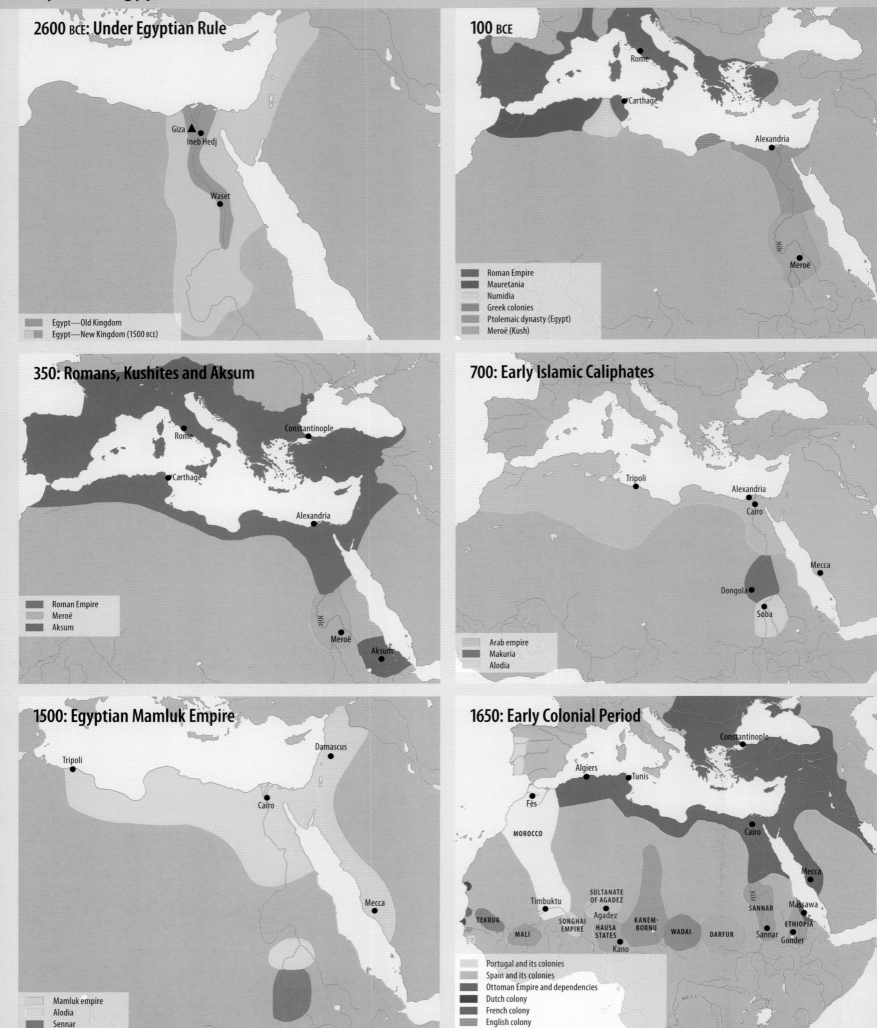

2600 BCE: Under Egyptian Rule

Giza
Ineb Hedj
Waset

Egypt—Old Kingdom
Egypt—New Kingdom (1500 BCE)

100 BCE

Rome
Carthage
Alexandria
Nile
Meroë

Roman Empire
Mauretania
Numidia
Greek colonies
Ptolemaic dynasty (Egypt)
Meroë (Kush)

350: Romans, Kushites and Aksum

Rome
Constantinople
Carthage
Alexandria
Nile
Meroë
Aksum

Roman Empire
Meroë
Aksum

700: Early Islamic Caliphates

Tripoli
Alexandria
Cairo
Mecca
Dongola
Soba

Arab empire
Makuria
Alodia

1500: Egyptian Mamluk Empire

Tripoli
Damascus
Cairo
Mecca

Mamluk empire
Alodia
Sennar

1650: Early Colonial Period

Constantinople
Algiers
Tunis
Fès
MOROCCO
Cairo
Mecca
Timbuktu
SULTANATE OF AGADEZ
Nile
Massawa
TEKRUR
Agadez
SANNAR
ETHIOPIA
MALI
SONGHAI EMPIRE
HAUSA STATES
KANEM-BORNU
WADAI
DARFUR
Sannar
Gonder
Kano

Portugal and its colonies
Spain and its colonies
Ottoman Empire and dependencies
Dutch colony
French colony
English colony

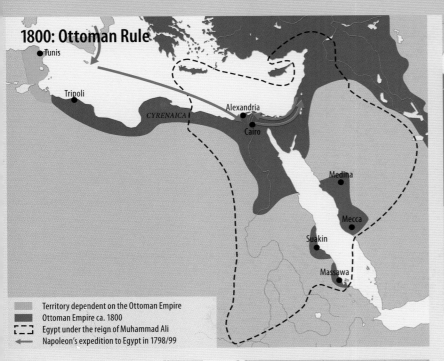

1800: Ottoman Rule

CYRENAICA

Tunis
Tripoli
Alexandria
Cairo
Medina
Mecca
Suakin
Massawa

Territory dependent on the Ottoman Empire
Ottoman Empire ca. 1800
Egypt under the reign of Muhammad Ali
Napoleon's expedition to Egypt in 1798/99

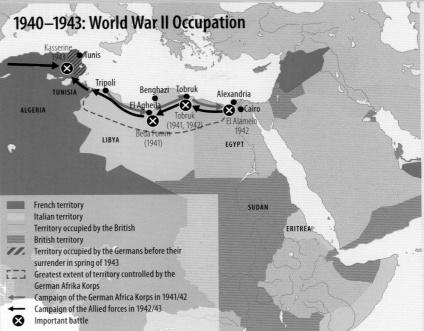

1940–1943: World War II Occupation

Kasserine 1943
Tunis
TUNISIA
ALGERIA
Tripoli
Benghazi
Tobruk
El Agheila
Tobruk (1941, 1942)
Beda Fomm (1941)
LIBYA
Alexandria
Cairo
El Alamein 1942
EGYPT
SUDAN
ERITREA

French territory
Italian territory
Territory occupied by the British
British territory
Territory occupied by the Germans before their surrender in spring of 1943
Greatest extent of territory controlled by the German Afrika Korps
Campaign of the German Africa Korps in 1941/42
Campaign of the Allied forces in 1942/43
Important battle

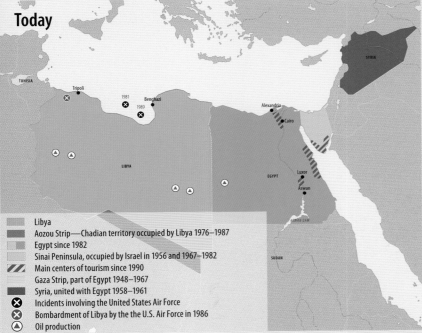

Today

TUNISIA
Tripoli
1981
Benghazi
1989
SYRIA
Alexandria
Cairo
LIBYA
EGYPT
Luxor
Aswan
SUDAN
ASWAN DAM

Libya
Aozou Strip—Chadian territory occupied by Libya 1976–1987
Egypt since 1982
Sinai Peninsula, occupied by Israel in 1956 and 1967–1982
Main centers of tourism since 1990
Gaza Strip, part of Egypt 1948–1967
Syria, united with Egypt 1958–1961
Incidents involving the United States Air Force
Bombardment of Libya by the the U.S. Air Force in 1986
Oil production

The area that is Libya became part of the Roman Empire in the first century BCE, and later fell under Byzantine and Islamic control. Libya became part of the Ottoman Empire in the mid-16th century, and remained so until its collapse in 1911. Thereafter Libya became an Italian protectorate, gaining its independence in 1951. Libya's strategic location and long Mediterranean coastline has made it the focal point of French and British interests in Northern Africa at various times in history.

~500 BCE Egypt and other parts of North Africa fall under Persian rule.

~400 BCE The Kushite empire rules from the capital city of Meroë.

30 BCE Egypt becomes part of the Roman Empire.

~1 CE–7th century The Aksum empire flourishes.

~300 The Meroë culture collapses.

640 Islamic conquest of Egypt.

969 The Fatimids found the city of Cairo.

1171 The Ayyubids take control of Egypt.

1250 The Mamluk Turks, originally military slaves, come to power, ruling Egypt and Syria for 250 years.

1510 The Spanish occupy the coast of Libya.

1517 Libya becomes part of the Ottoman Empire.

1798–1801 France occupies Egypt.

1805 Mehmet Ali (Muhammad Ali) becomes viceroy (pasha) of Egypt, bringing an end to Mamluk power in the region.

1832–1839 Mehmet Ali wages war against the Ottoman sultan.

1854 Construction of the Suez Canal begins, led by Ferdinand de Lesseps.

1882 Egypt is occupied by Great Britain.

1889–1902 The first Aswan Dam is completed.

1911 Fall of the Ottoman Empire. Libya becomes an Italian protectorate.

1922 Egypt gains its independence.

1934 The region of Cyrenaica is annexed by the Italian colony of Libya.

1941 Africa campaign of World War II

1951 Libya gains its independence.

1952 Military coup ends with the founding of the Egyptian republic.

late 1950s The discovery of oil there makes Libya a wealthy nation.

1958–1961 Egypt and Syria unite to form the United Arab Republic (UAR); Syria withdraws in 1961.

1967 The Six-Day War between Israel and the neighboring Arab states, Egypt, Syria and Jordan

1969 Muammar al-Qaddafi's military coup in Libya leads to the founding of the Libyan Arab Republic.

1979 Egypt and Israel sign a peace treaty

Oct. 6, 1981 Egyptian president Anwar Sadat is murdered.

1980s Relations between Libya and the United States are tense due to Qaddafi's support of Arab Palestinian militants. Skirmishes culminate in the US bombing of Libya in 1986.

Nov. 17, 1999 More than sixty tourists are killed in a terrorist attack at Luxor.

Empires

2707–2216 BCE	Old Kingdom Egypt
2010–1550 BCE	Middle Kingdom Egypt
1550–1070 BCE	New Kingdom Egypt
1070–350 BCE	The Kushite empire (Nubia) rules northeast Africa from its capital of Napata, later Meroë.
814–146 BCE	Carthage, a Phoenician empire
712–332 BCE	Late Period Egypt
304–30 BCE	Ptolemaic dynasty rules Egypt.
100–940	The kingdom of Aksum
910	The Shiite Fatimid dynasty rules Egypt and Libya.
1046–1147	The Berber Almoravid dynasty
1250–1517	The Mamluk Turks rule Egypt and the Levant.
1550–1911	The Ottoman Empire
1882–1922	British occupation (Egypt)
1912–1934	Italian protectorate (Libya)

Lockerbie

In 1988, the Libyan secret service exploded a bomb on a Pan Am flight from New York to London. It crashed to the ground near the Scottish city of Lockerbie, killing all 259 passengers and a further eleven people on the ground. Most of the victims were Americans, including four agents of the CIA. The attack was seen as Muammar al-Qaddafi's revenge for the American bombing of Libya in 1986. In 1999 Libya handed over two members of its secret service to the Scottish courts to be prosecuted.

313

Western and Central Africa

1350: The Empire of Mali

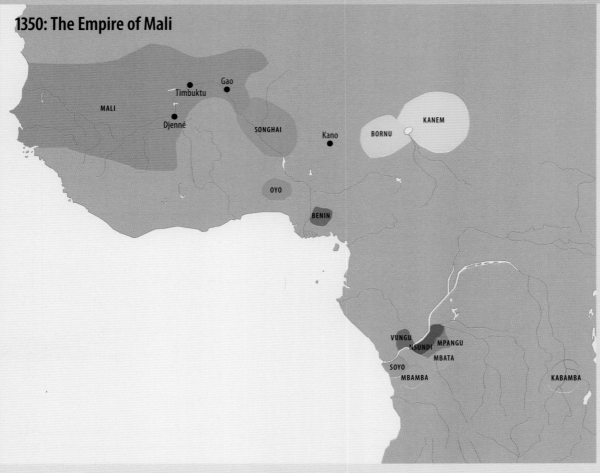

MALI

Timbuktu
Gao

Djenné

SONGHAI

Kano

OYO

BENIN

BORNU

KANEM

VUNGU
NSUNDI   MPANGU
MBATA
SOYO
MBAMBA

KABAMBA

5th century   The Ghana empire is founded in western Africa (not identical to today's Ghana).

11th century   Ghana is destroyed by the northern African Almoravid dynasty. Rulers of the Kanem-Bornu empire convert to Islam.

13th century   The two kingdoms of Kongo and Baluba form in central Africa. The kingdom of Mali rules western Africa

~1400   Mali collapses and is replaced by the Muslim Songhai empire, which controls western Africa.

1491   Nzinga, the *manikongo* (second-in-command) of the kingdom of Kongo, converts to Christianity through contact with Portuguese traders.

~1500   The Benin empire (Yoruba) allows the Portuguese to establish trading colonies in western Africa.

1637   The Portuguese are driven out by Dutch settlers from Elmina, a town on the Gold Coast.

1668   The kingdom of Kongo collapses under pressure from neighboring non-Christian tribes.

1822   Freed slaves from the United States found the colony of Liberia.

1847   The colony of Liberia gains its independence from the United States.

1750: Early Colonial Period

St Louis

Gorée

KAARIA

Timbuktu

FUTA TOORO

SÉGOU

Fort James

KAABU

Cachev

KONG

FOUTA DJALLON

Bunce Island

GOBIR   Kano

KABI   KANO

BORGU   KATSINABENIN

ZARIA

DZUKUN

BORNU

OUADDAI

DARFUR

ASANTE

DAHOMEY

OYO

Accra

Axim   Cape Coast Castle
Elmina

BENIN

French colony
British colony
Portuguese colony
Dutch colony
Danish colony
Exportation of slaves

LOANGO

KUBA

CONGO

WANDU   YAKA

Luanda   MATAMBA

LUNDA

LUBA

URUNDI

KASANZE

Benguela

MBAILUNDU

J.M.W. Turner, Slave Ship, *1840*

1874–1877 An expedition led by Welsh-born American journalist Henry Morgan Stanley opens the African interior to Europeans.

1878 The colony of the Belgian Congo is founded in Central Africa.

1891 Cameroon and Togo are colonized by Germany.

end of the 19th century The French establish a colony in the Congo with Brazzaville as its capital.

1960 The French Congo and Belgian Congo win their independence, forming the Republic of the Congo-Brazzaville and the Democratic Republic of the Congo (later Zaire), respectively.

1970 The People's Republic of Congo, a communist state, forms with Brazzaville as its capital.

1992 Multi-party elections resume in the Republic of Congo-Brazzaville, but political unrest is ongoing.

1997 A military coup deposes Mobutu, president of Zaire. Zaire restores its former name, the Democratic Republic of the Congo.

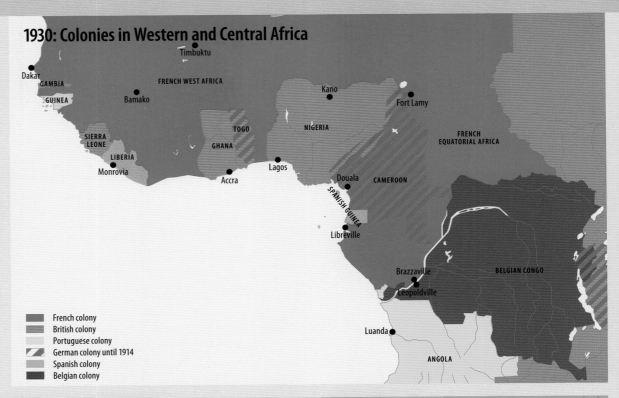

1930: Colonies in Western and Central Africa

- French colony
- British colony
- Portuguese colony
- German colony until 1914
- Spanish colony
- Belgian colony

Today

Human Zoos

Human zoos were a common manifestation of racist European and American attitudes toward Africans and other indigenous peoples. Hundreds of Africans were put on display in exhibitions designed to conform to and perpetuate the clichéd ideas of whites about how "primitive" people lived. Most of these exhibits took place in zoos, often alongside the great apes. "Cannibals" eating raw flesh was a popular dramatization. It was Adolf Hitler who banned human zoos in Germany and all Nazi-occupied territories, less for humanitarian reasons than to protect European racial purity.

Human zoos continued into the late 20th century with the exhibition of a "Congo village" at the Belgian World's Fair. As late as 2006 there was still an African village at the zoo in Augsburg, Germany, and a display of living Australian Aborigines opened in Adelaide in 2007.

Ota Benga was a Congolese pygmy. After his village was destroyed by the troops of Belgian King Leopold II, Ota Benga was sold into slavery, and was eventually purchased by American businessman Samuel Phillips Verner.

In 1906, he was put on display in the monkey house at the Bronx Zoo. The sign hung on his "cage" read as follows:

The African Pygmy, "Ota Benga." Age: 23 years. Height: 4 feet 11 inches. Weight: 103 pounds. Brought from the Kasai River, Congo Free State, South Central Africa, by Dr. Samuel P. Verner. Exhibited each afternoon during September.

Protests by African American clergy led to Ota Benga's release into their custody. He committed suicide in 1916.

315

Eastern Africa

Prehistoric Times

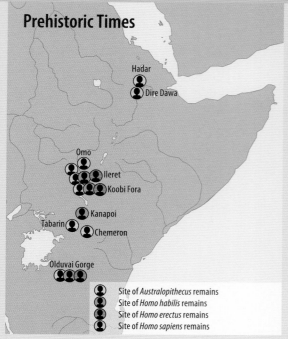

Hadar
Dire Dawa

Omo
Ileret
Koobi Fora
Kanapoi
Tabarin
Chemeron

Olduvai Gorge

- ☻ Site of *Australopithecus* remains
- ☻ Site of *Homo habilis* remains
- ☻ Site of *Homo erectus* remains
- ☻ Site of *Homo sapiens* remains

ca. 500: Empire of Aksum

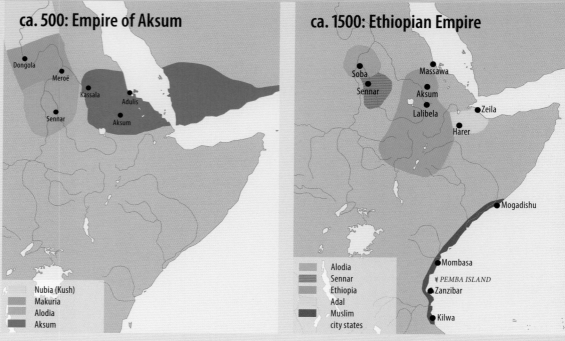

Dongola
Meroë
Kassala
Adulis
Sennar
Aksum

- Nubia (Kush)
- Makuria
- Alodia
- Aksum

ca. 1500: Ethiopian Empire

Soba
Sennar
Massawa
Aksum
Lalibela
Zeila
Harer

Mogadishu

Mombasa
PEMBA ISLAND
Zanzibar

Kilwa

- Alodia
- Sennar
- Ethiopia
- Adal
- Muslim city states

ca. 1750

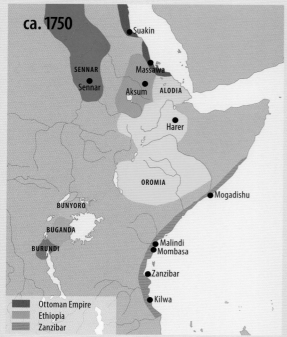

Suakin
SENNAR
Massawa
Sennar
Aksum
ALODIA
Harer

OROMIA
BUNYORO
Mogadishu
BUGANDA
Malindi
Mombasa
BURUNDI
Zanzibar
Kilwa

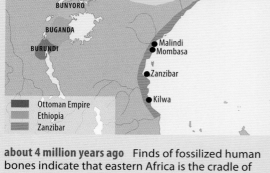

- Ottoman Empire
- Ethiopia
- Zanzibar

about 4 million years ago Finds of fossilized human bones indicate that eastern Africa is the cradle of humankind. *Australopithecus*, *Homo habilis*, *Homo erectus* and *Homo sapiens* (modern humans) all evolved here.

~4500 BCE First evidence of ceramic production

800 BCE–300 CE The kingdom of Kush in Nubia enters a golden age, with capital cities at Napata and Meroë.

~0 The Aksum empire emerges in what is now Ethiopia, controlling trade on the Red Sea from its port city of Adulis.

~400 Ezana, king of Aksum, converts to Christianity and expands his empire to include the coast of Yemen.

500–1365 The Christian empire of Makuria flourishes in Nubia. It will be conquered by the Muslim Mamluk Turks.

500–1500 The Christian kingdom of Alwa rules in southern Nubia. It was probably conquered by the Muslim Funj.

1935–1946: The Italian–Ethiopian War

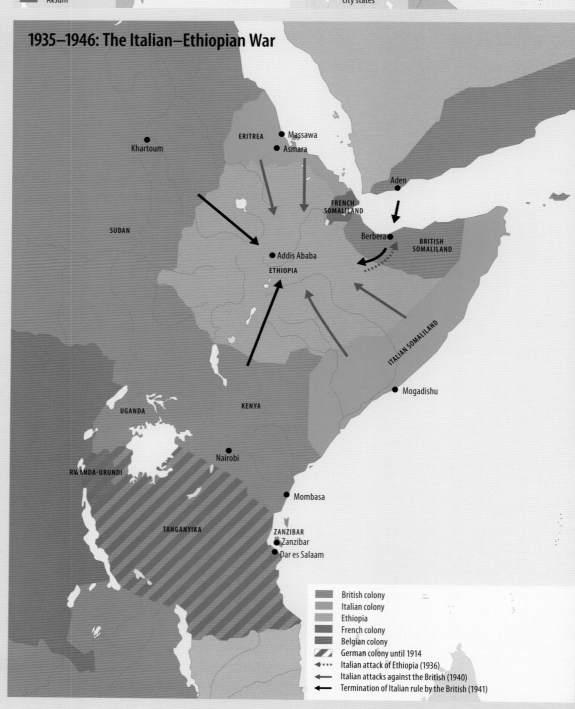

Khartoum
ERITREA
Massawa
Asmara
Aden
FRENCH SOMALILAND
Berbera
BRITISH SOMALILAND
SUDAN
Addis Ababa
ETHIOPIA
ITALIAN SOMALILAND
Mogadishu
UGANDA
KENYA
Nairobi
RWANDA-URUNDI
Mombasa
TANGANYIKA
ZANZIBAR
Zanzibar
Dar es Salaam

- British colony
- Italian colony
- Ethiopia
- French colony
- Belgian colony
- German colony until 1914
- → Italian attack of Ethiopia (1936)
- → Italian attacks against the British (1940)
- → Termination of Italian rule by the British (1941)

25–570 Aksum intervenes in Yemen as an ally of the Byzantine Empire to secure trade routes and to protect Christians threatened with persecution.

700 Islam spreads from North Africa and the Arabian Peninsula into Ethiopia, and Aksum declines. Muslim domination of the region virtually cuts off trade with Europe until the 15th century.

960 The Zagwe dynasty rules in Ethiopia; Christianity flourishes during this period.

After 1000 The cities of the Swahili eastern coast trade with Arabia, India and China.

268 The Solomonian dynasty comes to power in Ethiopia, where it engages in near-constant warfare with neighboring Muslim states. Its last ruler will be Haile Selassie.

From 1200 The Adal Sultanate rules in Somalia.

543 Portuguese merchant ships dominate trade along the eastern African coast. Cristóvão da Gama, son of explorer Vasco da Gama, defeats the Ethiopian and Somali navies and controls vital ports.

839 The British occupy the port city of Aden. Extensive European exploration of eastern Africa begins.

853 The Abyssinian empire rules Ethiopia.

885 Rwanda, Burundi and Tanzania (as Tanganyika) become part of German East Africa. After 1918 they fall under British control.

896 Italian troops are defeated in Abyssinia.

916 Tafari Makonnen (Haile Selassie) assumes regentship of Ethiopia. He is crowned emperor in 1930.

920 Kenya, a British protectorate since 1888, is a crown colony.

935–1936 The Italian-Ethiopian War begins. Mussolini attacks the capital of Addis Ababa with poison gas, causing heavy casualties.

941 Ethiopia is liberated with help from the British.

960 The northern part of British Somaliland, administered by the Crown since the late 19th century, unites with Italian Somaliland to the south to form the independent nation of Somalia.

961 The colony of Tanganyika joins with Zanzibar to form the independent nation of Tanzania.

962 and 1963 Uganda and Kenya gain independence.

971 Idi Amin forms a military dictatorship in Uganda. Hundreds of thousands of people die opposing him.

974 Ethiopian rebels depose Emperor Haile Selassi in the wake of economic crisis and devastating drought. The Soviet-backed Derg, led by Mengistu Haile Mariam, hold power until 1991.

977 German elite troops storm a highjacked Lufthansa aircraft in Somalia, freeing all the hostages.

991 As the Mengistu government falls, within thirty-six hours Operation Solomon flies the approximately 14,000 Jews remaining in Ethiopia to Israel for their own protection.

993 Years of bloody civil war with Ethiopia give birth to the independent nation of Eritrea.

994 The Hutu majority commits genocide against the Tutsi minority in Rwanda, killing more than 1 million.

008 November 6, Election Day in the United States, is declared a national holiday in Kenya to celebrate the election of Barack Obama, son of a Kenyan father, as US president.

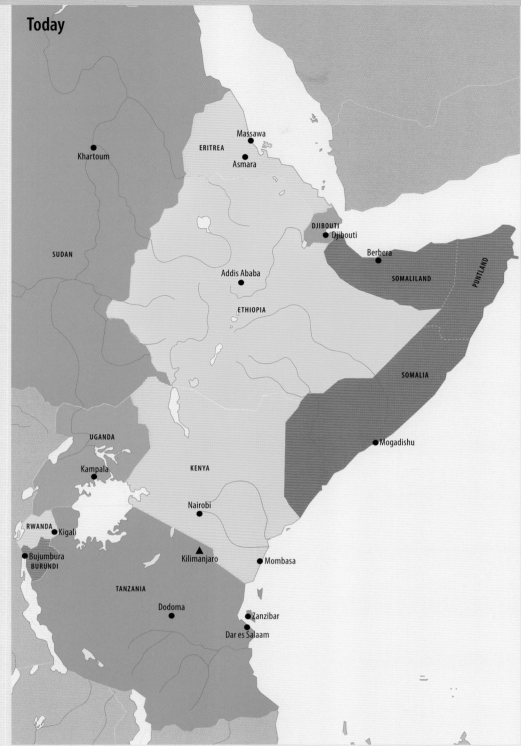

Today

Emperor Haile Selassie (1892–1975), born Tafari Makonnen, introduced general elections to Ethiopia, bringing the nation into the modern age. Head of state during the wars with Mussolini's fascist Italy, he greatly improved living conditions for many Ethiopians and encouraged his many followers in the Caribbean to return to Africa. The Rastafari movement, which developed primarily in Jamaica, believed that Selassie was God incarnate. Haile Selassie was deposed by a military coup in 1974.

Ethiopian religion has long followed a different path from the rest of Africa. Jews settled in Ethiopia as early as the 5th century BCE, arriving from Egypt, Sudan and the Arabian Peninsula. The legendary King Menelik was identified as the offspring of King Solomon and the Queen of Sheba. In the beginning of the first century, Coptic Christianity was already widespread, but by the 7th century most Christians had been forced into the Ethiopian interior by Muslim expansionism. The ruling Ethiopian dynasty remained Christian, in part due to assistance from the Portuguese.

Haile Selassie

Southern Africa

Prehistoric Times

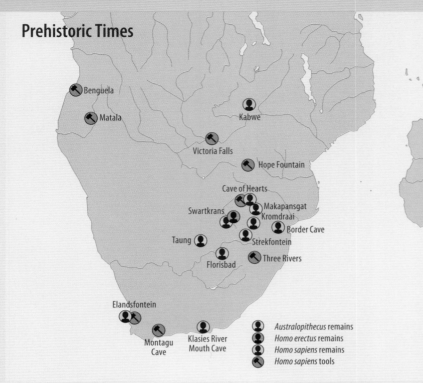

1500: The Mutapa Empire

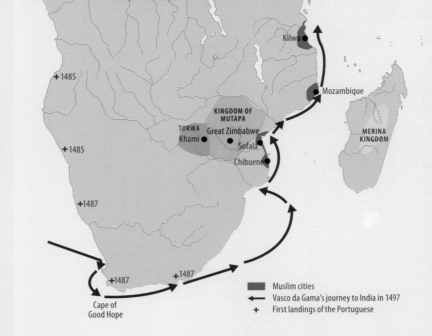

Muslim cities

⟵ Vasco da Gama's journey to India in 1497

+ First landings of the Portuguese

~35,000 BCE 20th-century finds at the Mesolithic site in Border Cave (Swaziland) include a baboon fibula with incised tally marks dating from this period.

~34,000 BCE Hunters and gatherers live in what is now Lesotho.

~24,000 BCE The oldest rock paintings in Namibia are created.

~330 CE The Bantu tribes begin to herd cattle.

12th century The Bantu-speaking Shona people form a state in what is today Mozambique and Zimbabwe.

Their trade relationships extend as far as China.

15th century The Mutapa empire conquers much of what had been Shona territory.

later 15th century The Portuguese arrive on the west coast of Africa, including Angola.

1488 Portuguese explorer Bartolomeo Diaz successfully sails around the Cape of Good Hope.

1497 Vasco da Gama explores the west coast of southern Africa.

1575 The Portuguese begin to colonize Angola.

1595 Dutch colonists, the Boers, arrive in South Africa.

1652 Eighty Boer colonists found the city of Cape Town.

~1655 The Boers import slaves from Asia and other parts of Africa to work on their farms.

1795 The British take control of Cape Colony and the city of Cape Town.

1800–1801 The First Boer War breaks out between displaced Boer farmers and the British.

1829 Shaka Zulu, king of the Zulu nation, is murdered.

1839 The Boers, who have abandoned the Cape Colony for the interior, defeat the Zulu and found the Republic of Natal. It is annexed four years later by the British.

second half of the 19th century The colony of German South-West Africa is founded in what is now Namibia.

1867 Diamonds are discovered at Kimberley Mine.

1879 The British defeat the Zulu in Natal.

1700–1850: The Boers

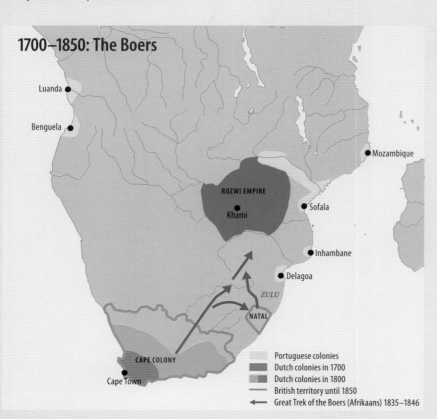

Portuguese colonies

Dutch colonies in 1700

Dutch colonies in 1800

British territory until 1850

⟶ Great Trek of the Boers (Afrikaans) 1835–1846

1900: Colonies in Southern Africa

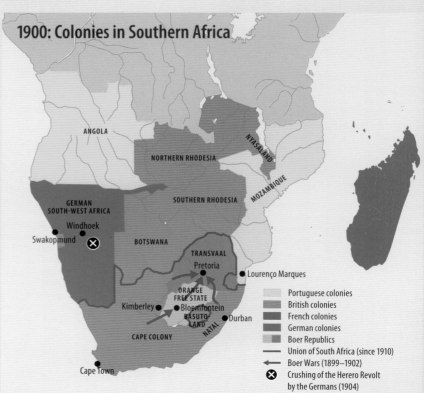

Portuguese colonies

British colonies

French colonies

German colonies

Boer Republics

Union of South Africa (since 1910)

⟶ Boer Wars (1899–1902)

⊗ Crushing of the Herero Revolt by the Germans (1904)

1899 The Second Boer War between Great Britain and the Boer states of Transvaal and Orange Free State

1910 The Union of South Africa is formed.

1961 The Portuguese colonies Angola and Mozambique begin their fight for independence.

1965 Rhodesia declares independence from Britain; economic sanctions follow.

1975 Angola becomes independent.

1990 Apartheid ends in South Africa. In the country's first free elections, Nelson Mandela is elected as South Africa's first black president.

Cecil Rhodes (1853–1902) was a British colonialist, prime minister of the Cape Colony, diamond trader and founder of Rhodesia (modern-day Zambia and Zimbabwe). He is credited with provoking the Boers into war with England in 1899. Today Rhodes, who wanted to create a string of colonies stretching from Cape Town to Cairo, serves as a symbol of British colonial policies.

Cecil Rhodes

Nelson Mandela (1918–) was sentenced to hard labor for life in 1964 after the South African government accused him of plotting the violent overthrow of the state. Offered clemency in the 1980s, he rejected it, becoming a symbol of the fight against apartheid. After his release in 1990 he

Nelson Mandela

became president of the African National Congress (ANC) and worked to lift South Africa's racist segregation laws. In 1994 he became South Africa's first democratically elected president. He was awarded the Nobel Peace Prize in 1993.

Apartheid was the ideology of racial segregation imposed on South Africa after the 1948 victory of the African Nationalist Party. Segregation, which had always existed to some extent between whites and Africans, was made enforceable national policy. More than sixty racial laws fell under the heading, including the segregation of schools and government offices. Only whites and mixed-race citizens were given the right to vote, and sexual relations between whites and "colored" (the term included South Africans of Indian descent as well as native Africans) were expressly forbidden.

The Boers were Afrikaans-speaking inhabitants of South Africa and Namibia. They arrived as colonists in the 17th century, primarily from the Netherlands. The term *boer* comes from the Dutch word for "farmer." After the British annexed the Cape Colony, Boer farmers trekked inland to colonize Transvaal, Orange Free State and Natal.

1970: Apartheid

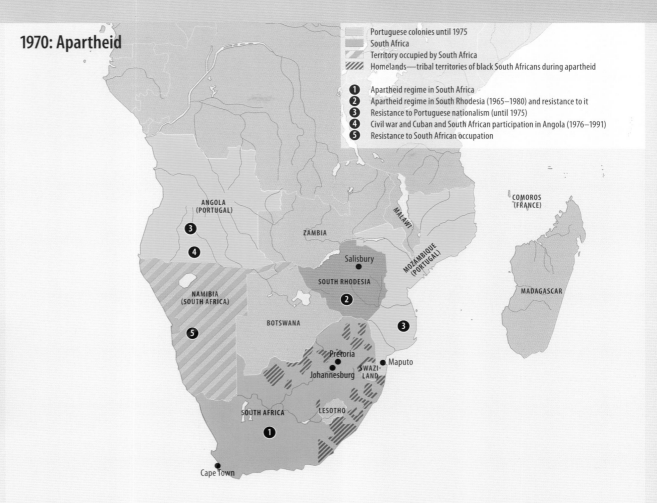

Portuguese colonies until 1975
South Africa
Territory occupied by South Africa
Homelands—tribal territories of black South Africans during apartheid

❶ Apartheid regime in South Africa
❷ Apartheid regime in South Rhodesia (1965–1980) and resistance to it
❸ Resistance to Portuguese nationalism (until 1975)
❹ Civil war and Cuban and South African participation in Angola (1976–1991)
❺ Resistance to South African occupation

Southern Africa Today

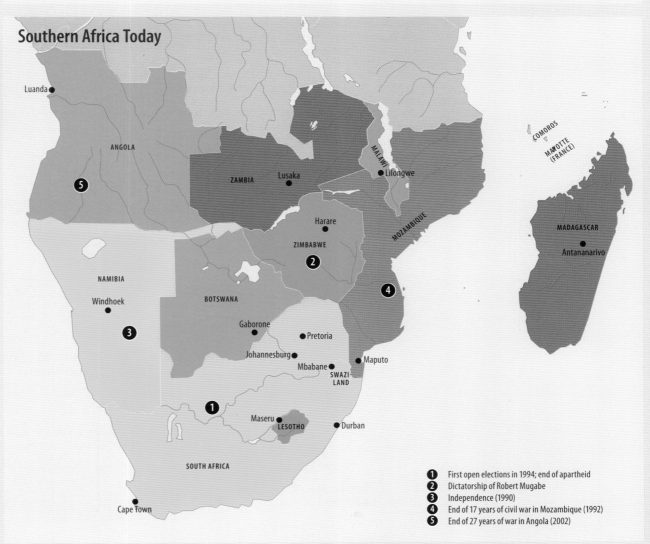

❶ First open elections in 1994; end of apartheid
❷ Dictatorship of Robert Mugabe
❸ Independence (1990)
❹ End of 17 years of civil war in Mozambique (1992)
❺ End of 27 years of war in Angola (2002)

CURRENT ISSUES ON THE AFRICAN CONTINENT

Africa's Poorest Nations

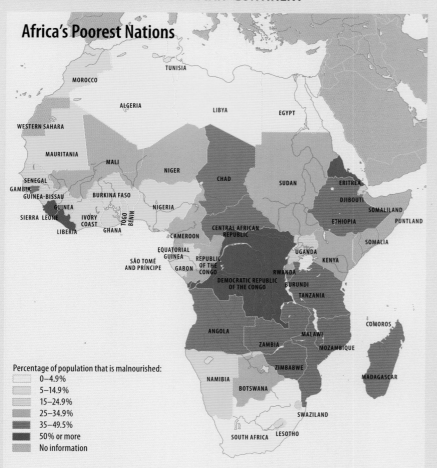

Percentage of population that is malnourished:
- 0–4.9%
- 5–14.9%
- 15–24.9%
- 25–34.9%
- 35–49.5%
- 50% or more
- No information

The Health Crisis in Africa

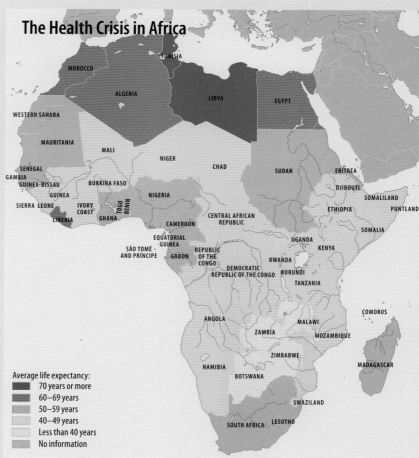

Average life expectancy:
- 70 years or more
- 60–69 years
- 50–59 years
- 40–49 years
- Less than 40 years
- No information

Natural Resources

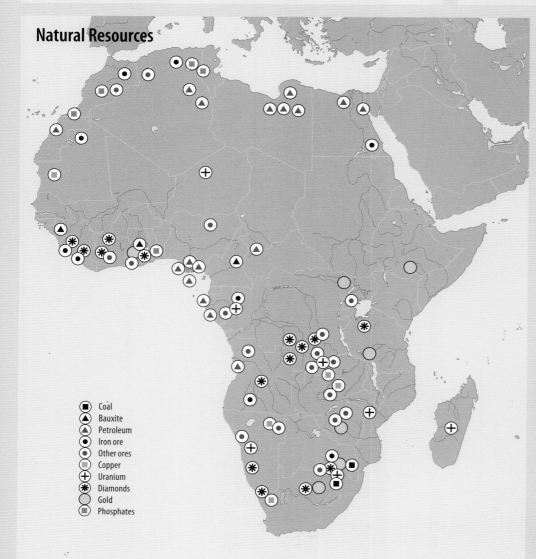

- ■ Coal
- ▲ Bauxite
- ▲ Petroleum
- ◉ Iron ore
- ◉ Other ores
- ◉ Copper
- ⊕ Uranium
- ✳ Diamonds
- ○ Gold
- ▣ Phosphates

Africa's natural resources

Africa is rich in natural resources, yet despite its mineral wealth, it remains one of the poorest regions in the world. Europeans have been coming to Africa to exploit its immense resources for over four centuries. Independence has not benefited most Africans, as corrupt leaders kept profits, leaving their nations impoverished. African dictators amassed fantastic fortunes exploiting resources much as the colonial powers had before them.

Africa's poorest nations

In the poorest countries in Africa, 300 million people have a combined annual net income less than that of a single major city in the United States.

Country	GDP per inhabitant
Somalia	US$ 200
Democratic Republic of the Congo	US$ 300
Zimbabwe	US$ 500
Ethiopia	US$ 600
Malawi	US$ 600
Niger	US$ 600
Burundi	US$ 700
Mozambique	US$ 700
Central African Republic	US$ 700
Tanzania	US$ 800
Rwanda	US$ 800

Africa's most widespread diseases

Sleeping sickness is caused by the bite of the tsetse fly, and it affects the central nervous system and heart. More than six million Africans are affected by sleeping sickness, which kills 150,000 people a year.

Malaria is spread by mosquitoes. Between one and three million Africans die of malaria every year, including many children.

AIDS (acquired immune deficiency syndrome) is a viral disease of the immune system. As of 2007, more than 22 million Africans were infected with AIDS. Two-thirds of all the AIDS cases in the world are in Africa, and more than two million Africans have died of the disease.

1. Illegal immigrants and refugees from Africa attempt to enter Europe via Morocco.

2. Islamic fundamentalists supporting the Islamic Salvation Front (ISF) battle the government in Algeria. Al-Qaeda attacks began there in 1990.

3. Libyan dictator Muammar al-Qaddafi supported terrorist attacks against the West throughout the 1980s and 1990s. In recent years he has taken on a more conciliatory role.

4. Al-Jama'a al-islamiyya, a splinter group of the Muslim Brotherhood, led terrorist actions in the 1990s in an attempt to topple the Egyptian government and replace it with an Islamic republic.

5. Ethnic cleansing and genocide by the Muslim Janjaweed killed 400,000 black Africans in Sudan between 2001 and 2007.

6. Civil war over the autonomy of the southern tribes raged between Sudan and non-Muslim native groups from 1983 to 2005.

7. War between the Ethiopian government and the province of Eritrea ended with Eritrea's independence in 1991. New conflicts arose between the two countries in the late 1990s, and continue to this day.

8. Somalia is beset by anarchy, civil war and piracy.

9. In 1979 Morocco occupied the sovereign nation of Western Sahara. Despite a 1991 cease-fire, conflicts between Morocco and the separatist Polisario front continue, and Western Sahara's political status remains unresolved.

10. The humanitarian crisis brought on by the brutal civil war (until 2002) between competing warlords in Sierra Leone continues today.

11. The unemployment rate reached 85 percent during the Liberian civil war, which lasted from 1989 to 2003.

12. Piracy and terrorist attacks against oil refineries in Nigeria have damaged the economy. Illegally tapped pipelines siphon off the nation's riches.

13. Northern Nigeria became a hotbed of Islamic fundamentalism in the late 1990s and 2000s.

14. Inter-tribal conflicts beset the Democratic Republic of the Congo.

15. Rwanda's mountain gorilla population is threatened by local poverty and social unrest. American zoologist Dian Fossey was murdered in 1985, presumably by poachers.

16. In the 1990s, the Hutu majority murdered some 75 percent of the Tutsi minority in Rwanda, leaving a million people dead.

17. The dictatorship of Robert Mugabe has brought economic collapse to once-prosperous Zimbabwe.

18. The AIDS pandemic threatens Botswana.

19. Two decades of civil war have led to economic collapse in Angola.

20. Decades of civil war have mired Mozambique in extreme poverty.

21. South Africa suffers from one of the highest crime rates and highest AIDS infection rates in the world.

Recent or Ongoing Conflicts in Africa

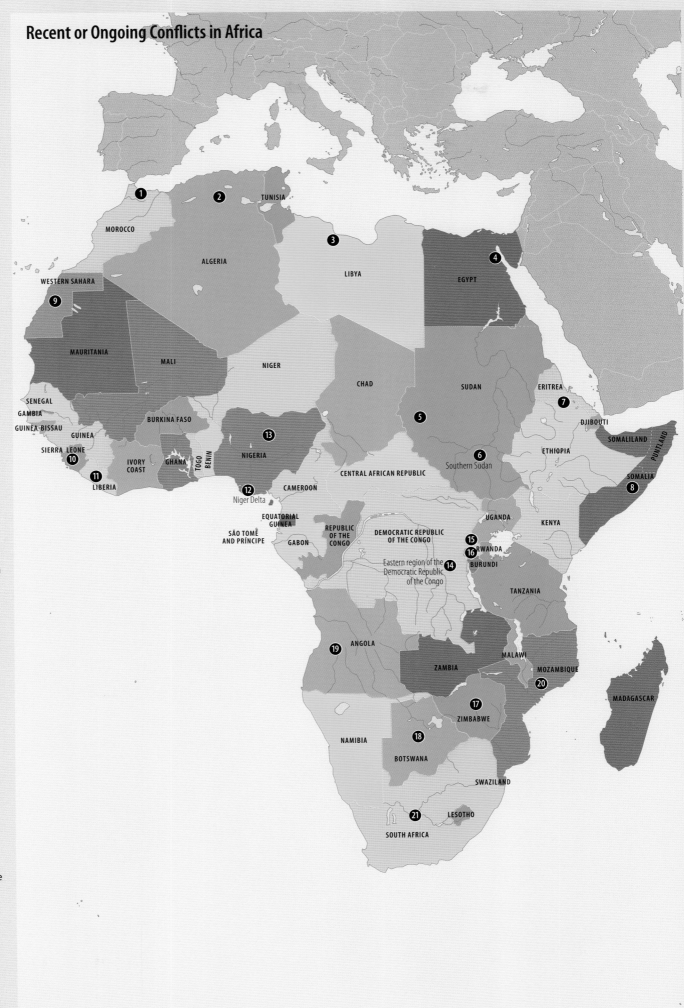

ASIAE NOVA DESCRIPTIO.

ASIA

The earliest permanent settlements in Asia, the Middle East and the valleys of the Indus, Ganges, Yangtze and Huang He rivers were formed as early as 10,000 years ago. Our ancestors transitioned from hunter-gatherers to sedentary farmers raising cattle and cultivating grain, primarily wheat and barley. Preparing land for cultivation, and especially constructing irrigation systems to provide fields with water, required coordinated labor. The earliest settled Asian populations lived in villages, which were followed by highly developed, sophisticated states. Trade routes brought merchants to the West, bringing western Asiatic culture into the Mediterranean regions. Further east, the Karakoram and Himalaya mountain chains separated western Asia from the Far East, where the cultures of India, China, Japan and other nations flourished independent of western influence. Asia is also the cradle of the great world religions: Judaism, Christianity and Islam all developed in western Asia (the Middle East, or Near East), and the great oriental religions of Hinduism, Buddhism and Shinto originated in the Far East.

Asia: An Overview	324
The Arab World: An Overview	332
THE HISTORY AND EXPANSION OF ISLAM	336
Israel and Palestine	338
The Levant – Syria, Lebanon, Jordan	342
The Arabian Peninsula	346
OIL AND ENERGY	348
Iraq and Kuwait	350
Persia / Iran	354
Transcaucasia	356
Central Asia	358
Siberia and Mongolia	360
India, Pakistan and Bangladesh	362
Tibet and Bhutan / Buddhism and Hinduism	366
China	368
Korea	376
Japan	378
Vietnam, Laos, Cambodia, Thailand and Myanmar	382
Malaysia, Brunei, Singapore	386
Philippines	388
Indonesia	390

Asiae Nova Descriptio,
published 1575–1612 by Abraham Ortelius

Asia: An Overview

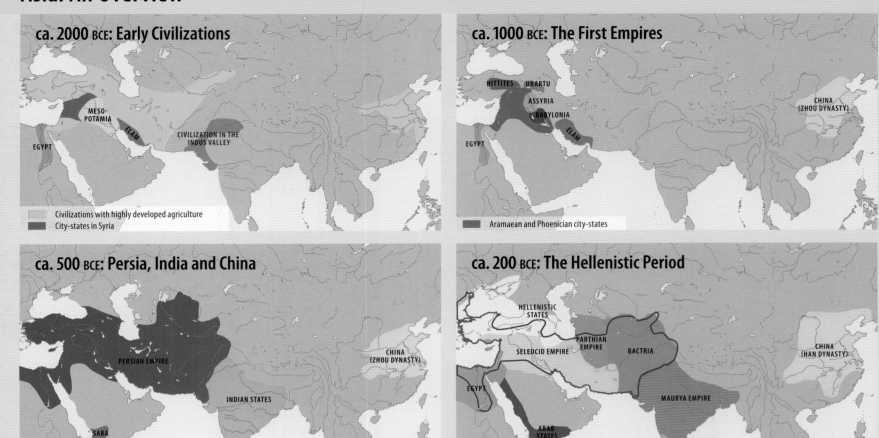

ca. 2000 BCE: Early Civilizations

- EGYPT
- MESO-POTAMIA
- ELAM
- CIVILIZATION IN THE INDUS VALLEY

Civilizations with highly developed agriculture
City-states in Syria

ca. 1000 BCE: The First Empires

- HITTITES
- URARTU
- ASSYRIA
- BABYLONIA
- EGYPT
- ELAM
- CHINA (ZHOU DYNASTY)

Aramaean and Phoenician city-states

ca. 500 BCE: Persia, India and China

- PERSIAN EMPIRE
- INDIAN STATES
- SABA
- CHINA (ZHOU DYNASTY)

ca. 200 BCE: The Hellenistic Period

- HELLENISTIC STATES
- SELEUCID EMPIRE
- PARTHIAN EMPIRE
- BACTRIA
- EGYPT
- ARAB STATES
- MAURYA EMPIRE
- HINDU STATES
- CHINA (HAN DYNASTY)

Empire of Alexander the Great in 323 BCE

ca. 400 CE: Empires Along the Silk Road

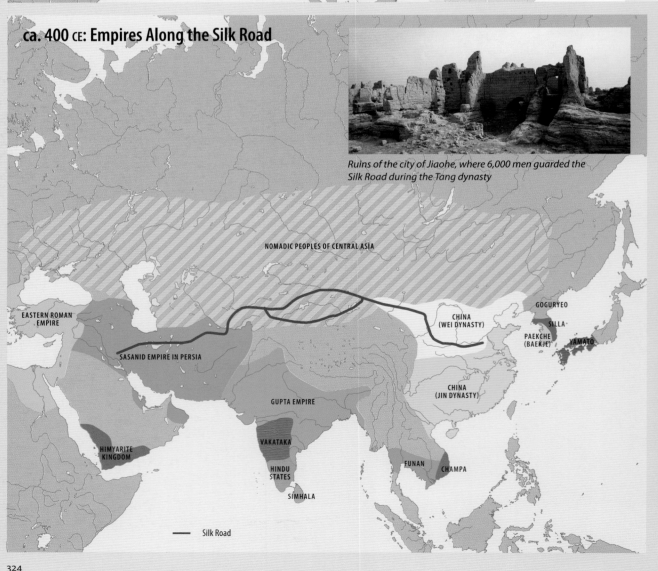

Ruins of the city of Jiaohe, where 6,000 men guarded the Silk Road during the Tang dynasty

- NOMADIC PEOPLES OF CENTRAL ASIA
- EASTERN ROMAN EMPIRE
- SASANID EMPIRE IN PERSIA
- HIMYARITE KINGDOM
- GUPTA EMPIRE
- VAKATAKA
- HINDU STATES
- SIMHALA
- FUNAN
- CHAMPA
- CHINA (JIN DYNASTY)
- CHINA (WEI DYNASTY)
- GOGURYEO
- SILLA
- PAEKCHE (BAEKJE)
- YAMATO

— Silk Road

The Ancient Orient and Central Asia

3500 BCE The first great civilization develops in Sumer, in southern Mesopotamia. Other peoples immigrate into the "fertile crescent," the part of western Asia that receives the most rainfall and is most suited to agriculture.

3000–2700 BCE The first states emerge in Mesopotamia, including the Biblical city-states of Ur and Uruk.

2700 BCE Cuneiform, the world's oldest script, is developed in Sumer.

2500–639 BCE Elam, the ancestral city of the Persians, is founded in what is today Iran.

2300–2193 BCE Sargon I of Akkad conquers Mesopotamia. The Akkadian empire becomes history's first great empire.

2000 BCE Indo-European tribes move south, becoming the Hittites in central Anatolia and the Achaeans in what is today Greece.

1800–609 BCE The Assyrian empire begins to expand.

1728–1686 BCE The Old Babylonian period begins, with the reign of Hammurabi marking its golden age.

722 BCE Assyria conquers Israel.

550–330 BCE The Persian Empire dominates the Near East and Egypt during the Achaemenid dynasty.

539 BCE The Persians conquer Babylon.

334–330 BCE Alexander the Great conquers Persia and most of the Near East.

247/38 BCE–224 CE The Parthian empire reclaims Achaemenid Persian territory until its defeat by Rome.

4 BCE–31 CE Lifetime of Jesus Christ

224–651 The Persian Empire expands in the Near East during the Sassanid dynasty.

350 The White Huns (Hephthalites) invade Persia.

570–632 Lifetime of the Prophet Muhammad

630–800 Islam rapidly expands throughout the Middle East and northern Africa.

India and the Himalayas

2800–1800 BCE The advanced civilizations of Harappa and Mohenjo-daro cultivate the fertile Indus Valley.

1500 BCE Aryan (Vedic) immigrants enter Punjab and the Ganges valley, introducing an early form of Hinduism.

563–483 BCE Siddhartha Gautama takes the name Buddha and founds the Buddhist religion.

320–185 BCE The Maurya dynasty rules over most of the Indian subcontinent.

320–510 CE The Gupta dynasty forms an empire in northern India.

427 The White Huns (Hephthalites) invade India.

600–1000 India is divided into principalities.

from 1001 Northwest India comes under the control of the Muslim ruler Mahmud of Ghazni.

China and the Far East

7000–2000 BCE Chinese cultures make great technical strides in firing ceramics.

1570–1066 BCE The Shang (Yin) dynasty provides the first textual evidence of advanced civilization in China. Bronzes, coins and chariots have also been found.

1045–221 BCE The great philosophers Confucius and Laozi (Lao-tse) complete their masterworks during the Zhou dynasty.

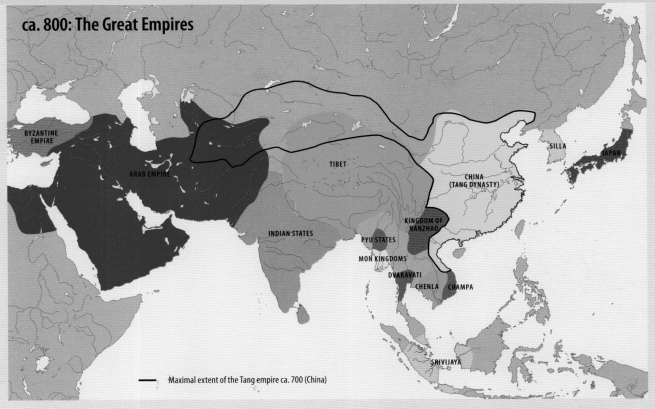

ca. 800: The Great Empires

— Maximal extent of the Tang empire ca. 700 (China)

221 BCE Qin Shihuangdi becomes the first Chinese emperor.

100 BCE The Silk Road, a trade route already in existence for more than a thousand years, provides a connection between China and Europe.

~400 CE The Japanese empire forms as an alliance between competing princes.

618–907 The Tang dynasty brings great economic prosperity to China.

650 The golden age of Tibet

660 The "three kingdoms" (Silla, Goguryeo and Baekje) period of Korea comes to an end.

702 Japan develops a strong centralized state.

802–1431 The Khmer empire, ruled from what is now Cambodia, reaches the height of its power in the 10th century.

960 The Song dynasty brings centralized government to China.

1123–1150 The Mongol tribes are united under the leadership of Khabul Khan, great-grandfather of Genghis Khan.

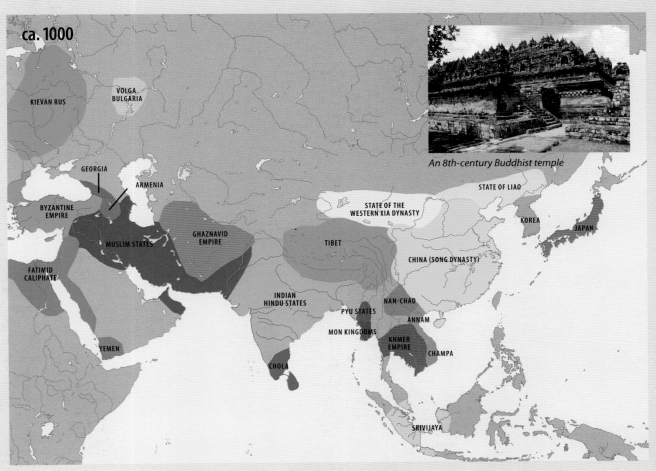

ca. 1000

An 8th-century Buddhist temple

325

Asia: An Overview

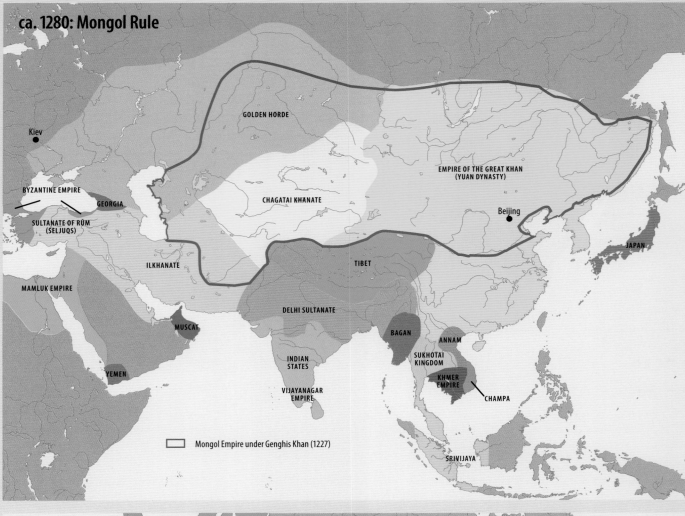

ca. 1280: Mongol Rule

Kiev

GOLDEN HORDE

EMPIRE OF THE GREAT KHAN
(YUAN DYNASTY)

BYZANTINE EMPIRE

GEORGIA

CHAGATAI KHANATE

Beijing

SULTANATE OF RÛM
(SELJUQS)

ILKHANATE

TIBET

JAPAN

MAMLUK EMPIRE

DELHI SULTANATE

MUSCAT

BAGAN

ANNAM

YEMEN

INDIAN
STATES

SUKHOTAI
KINGDOM

KHMER
EMPIRE

CHAMPA

VIJAYANAGAR
EMPIRE

☐ Mongol Empire under Genghis Khan (1227)

SRIVIJAYA

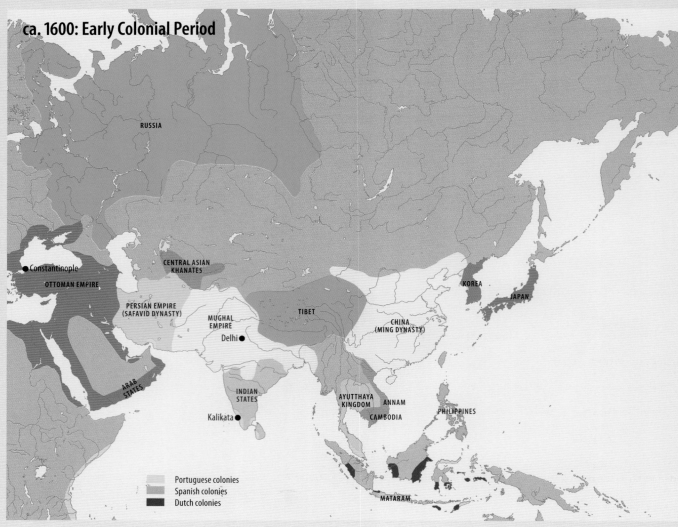

ca. 1600: Early Colonial Period

RUSSIA

Constantinople

CENTRAL ASIAN
KHANATES

OTTOMAN EMPIRE

KOREA

PERSIAN EMPIRE
(SAFAVID DYNASTY)

MUGHAL
EMPIRE

TIBET

JAPAN

Delhi

CHINA
(MING DYNASTY)

ARAB
STATES

INDIAN
STATES

AYUTTHAYA
KINGDOM

ANNAM

PHILIPPINES

Kalikata

CAMBODIA

☐ Portuguese colonies
☐ Spanish colonies
■ Dutch colonies

MATARAM

1206 Founding of the Muslim Sultanate of Delhi. The Mongolian leader Temüjin (who later adopted the name Genghis Khan) unites the nomadic people and tribes of central Asia.

1215 Genghis Khan conquers Beijing.

1240 The Mongols conquer Kiev, beginning their expansion into Europe.

1274 and 1281 Typhoons (*kamikaze*, meaning "divine wind") spare Japan from Mongol incursions.

1279 The Mongol Yuan dynasty led by Kublai Khan, grandson of Genghis Khan, comes to power in China.

1300 Founding of the Ottoman Empire. It will endure until 1922.

1336 The Hindu kingdom of Vijayanagar is founded in southern India.

1350 The Ayutthaya kingdom originates in Siam (present-day Thailand).

1368 The Mongol Yuan dynasty is driven out of China and the Ming dynasty takes over rule.

1370–1405 The Turkoman-Mongol ruler Timur (also known as Timur Lenk or in English as Tamerlane) founds an empire in central Asia.

1380 Russian forces defeat the Mongols in the Battle of Kulikovo.

1389 Ottomans defeat an alliance of Balkan tribes.

1398 Timur conquers Delhi.

1402 Timur defeats the Ottomans near Ankara.

1414 Islam spreads to the Malay Peninsula and nearby islands.

1453 Constantinople, the last remnant of the Byzantine Empire, is conquered by Ottoman forces led by Sultan Mehmed II.

1498 Portuguese explorer Vasco da Gama arrives in the Indian city of Calicut.

after 1512 The Ottoman Empire rules all of the Near East and most of the Islamic world.

1549 Missionaries of the newly founded Jesuit order, led by Spaniard St. Francis Xavier, bring Christianity to Japan.

1556–1605 Akbar the Great rules the Mughal Empire in India, greatly expanding its territories.

1565 Spain stakes its claim to the Philippines.

1580 Tsar Ivan IV begins the Russian conquest of Siberia.

1587–1629 Shah Abbas I the Great of the Safavid dynasty rules the Persian Empire during a period of military victories and great cultural achievements.

1600 The Dutch found colonies in Indonesia.

1603 The Tokugawa shogunate rules Japan.

1616/44 The Qing dynasty rules in China (until 1911).

1639 Japan begins a period of self-imposed isolation in which all contact with foreigners, but Europeans in particular, is shunned.

1648 The Taj Mahal in Agra, India, is completed.

1696 China annexes Mongolia.

1736–1747 Nāder Shāh, ruler of Persia, conquers Kabul in 1738/39 and later Delhi as well.

1751 China rules Tibet.

1759–1779 Kurdish ruler Karīm Khān Zand rules Persia.

1765 The Bengals fall under British colonial rule.

1796 China's long period of decline begins.

1796–1925 The shahs of the Qājār dynasty rule Persia.

1802 The short-lived Tay-Son dynasty comes to an end in Vietnam, and French influence in the land increases.

1839–1842 The First Opium War is fought between Great Britain and China over the (illegal) flow of opium to British India.

1841 Great Britain occupies Hong Kong.

1849 Great Britain annexes the Sikh principality of Punjab.

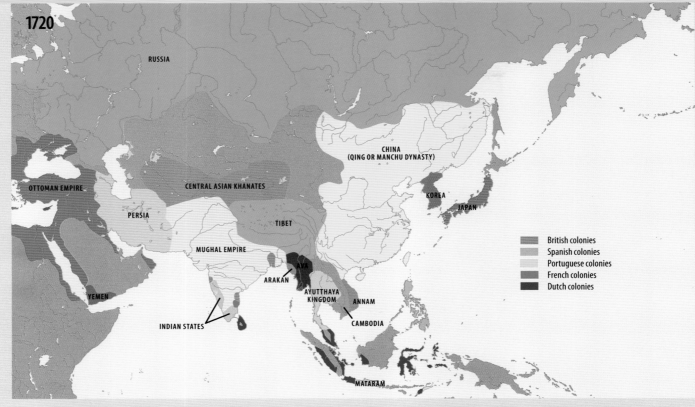

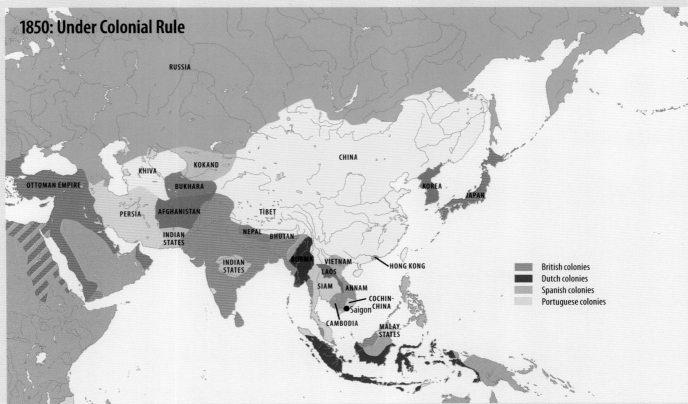

1853 Great Britain controls Myanmar (Burma). American warships open the harbors of Japan to trade and other exchange.

1856–1860 Second Opium War; China is defeated and cedes Hong Kong to Britain.

1858 Mughal rule comes to an end in India as the British take control.

1859 Saigon is conquered by the French.

1867 Shogun rule collapses in Japan. The Meiji period begins (until 1912).

1875 Economic collapse of the Ottoman Empire

1885 Founding of the Indian National Congress

1898 The Philippine Islands declare their independence.

1900 The Boxer Rebellion in China, an uprising of Chinese against foreign (especially Western) and Christian influences

1912 Puyi, the last emperor of China, abdicates as China becomes a republic.

1914 Tibet declares its independence after 300 years of Chinese rule.

Asia: An Overview

1920

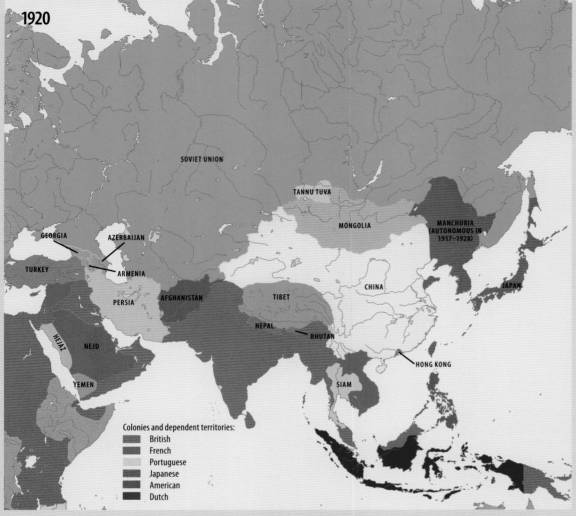

Colonies and dependent territories:
- British
- French
- Portuguese
- Japanese
- American
- Dutch

1942: World War II in the Pacific

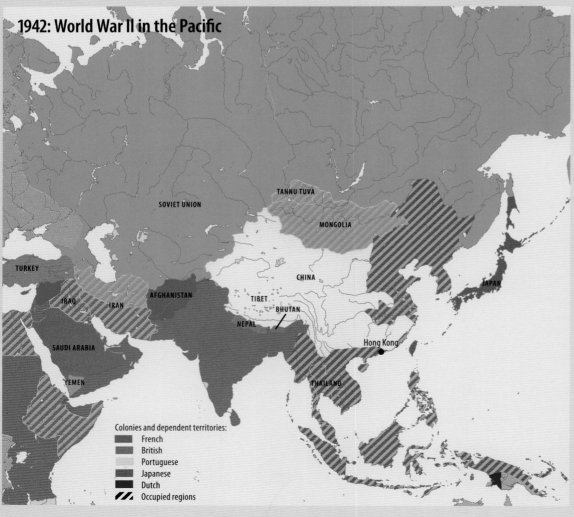

Colonies and dependent territories:
- French
- British
- Portuguese
- Japanese
- Dutch
- Occupied regions

1921 Both the Kingdom of Iraq and the Emirate of Transjordania are founded. Beginning of Ghandi's nonviolent resistance to British rule in India

1925 General Chiang Kai-shek comes to power in China. After seizing power in a military coup, Reza Shah rules Iran, starting the Pahlavi dynasty.

1931 Manchuria is occupied by Japan.

1932 Iraq declares its independence from Great Britain. The Kingdom of Saudi Arabia is founded under the leadership of the Al-Saud family.

1935 Persia is officially renamed Iran.

1941 Japan occupies Hong Kong. In Iran, Russian and British forces depose Reza Shah and secure critical supplies for the Allies.

1942 Japan occupies Manila; most Asian countries are involved in the Asian-Pacific War (until 1945).

1945 Indonesia and Vietnam declare independence. the Netherlands only accepts Indonesia's claim following international pressure; the First Indochina War ensues in Vietnam (until 1954).

1947 India gains its independence from Great Britain. Pakistan divides from India following the 1947/48 civil war.

1948 In the wake of World War II, the state of Israel is declared.

1949 Mao Tse-tung forms the People's Republic of China.

1950 The Korean War breaks out. Communist China occupies Tibet.

1951 The king of Jordan, Abdallah I, is murdered in Jerusalem.

1953 Shah Mohammad Reza Pahlavi is removed from power in Iran but with support from the United States is reinstated.

1954 The French are defeated in Vietnam. Cambodia gains its independence from Laos. Gamal Abdel Nasser becomes president of Egypt and leader of the Pan-Arabism movement (until 1970).

1957 Malaysia gains its independence from Great Britain.

1958 Founding of the United Arab Republic (UAR), a union of Egypt and Syria, which lasts until 1961. The monarchy in Iraq is overthown in a bloody coup. Civil war breaks out in Lebanon. Brought under control by Syria in 1990, religious conflict continues to flare up even today.

1960 OPEC (Organization of Petroleum Exporting Countries) is founded by Iran, Iraq, Kuwait, Saudi Arabia and Venezuela to coordinate policies and represent their interests.

1961 Kurds demand their own state.

1964 The Vietnam War begins: Communist-leaning North Vietnam fights against South Vietnam, which is supported by the United States.

1965 Singapore wins its independence from Malaysia.

1966 Mao Tse-tung instigates the Cultural Revolution in China, a period of social, political and economic turmoil. Indira Gandhi becomes the prime minister of India.

1967 ASEAN (Association of Southeast Asian Nations) is founded by ten countries to jointly further their development. Yemen is divided into two states, North Yemen and South Yemen. The Six-Day War rages between Arab states and Israel.

1970 Civil war in Jordan ("Black September") breaks out briefly; the power of the Palestinian Liberation Organization in Jordan is broken. Hafiz al-Assad begins a period of authoritarian rule in Syria that will last until 2000.

1971 Bangladesh becomes independent from Pakistan.

1973 Paris Peace Accords are signed between the United States and Vietnam, ending the Vietnam War. Egypt and Israel fight the Yom Kippur War.

1975 The Lebanese Civil War begins; it will last until 1990. Saigon falls to North Vietnam. India declares a state of emergency that lasts twenty-one months, including martial law. King Faisal of Saudi Arabia is shot by his nephew. Pol Pot begins his reign of terror in Cambodia (until 1979), leaving two million dead.

1976 Founding of the Socialist Republic of Vietnam

1978 A military coup in Afghanistan leads to invasion by Soviet troops.

1979 The shah of Iran flees the country as Ayatollah Khomeini forms the Islamic Republic of Iran. The Vietnamese topple the regime of Pol Pot in Cambodia in the Cambodian-Vietnamese War. Saddam Hussein comes to power in Iraq. Fundamentalists occupy the Great Mosque in Mecca and are brutally suppressed by the Saudi military.

1980–1988 The Iran-Iraq War

1982 Syrian air forces bloodily quelch a revolt by the Muslim Brotherhood in Hama. In September, Christian militants massacre Muslims in the Palestinian refugee camps Sabra and Shatila in southern Lebanon.

1984 Indira Gandhi is assassinated in New Delhi.

1985 Iraq bombs Iranian cities.

1986 A coup in the Philippines deposes dictator Ferdinand Marcos.

1987 Unrest in Tibet

1988 Founding of the terrorist group al-Qaeda

1989 The Soviet army retreats from Afghanistan. Ayatollah Khomeini dies. The Chinese military violently suppresses peaceful demonstrations in Tiananmen Square in Beijing.

1990 Yemen is reunited. Iraq invades Kuwait. One-party rule ends in Mongolia.

1991 The USSR collapses. Civil war ends in Cambodia. The Iraq War ends.

1993 Israel agrees to limited autonomy for Palestinians living in Gaza.

1997 Hong Kong is returned to China. Reformer Mohammad Khatami wins election in Iran.

1998 Peace talks begin between North Korea and South Korea.

1999 King Hussein of Jordan, who has ruled since 1952, dies.

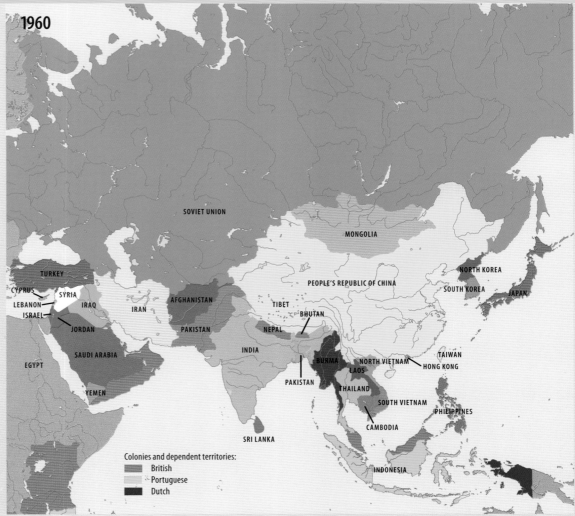

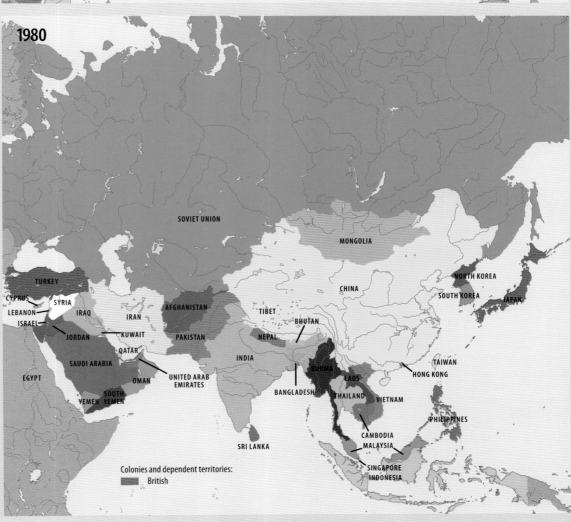

Asia: An Overview – 2000 to Today

2000 The relationship between Israel and the Palestinians worsens. Bashar al-Assad succeeds his father as president of Syria.

Sept. 11, 2001 Al-Qaeda terrorist attack on the World Trade Center in New York and other targets (9/11). The United States retaliates against the Taliban in Afghanistan, occupying the northern part of the country.

2002 The former Portuguese colony of East Timor gains its independence.

2003 The United States invades Iraq and removes Saddam Hussein from power.

2004 A disastrous tsunami devastates the coasts of Southeast Asia.

2005 Islamic parties win elections in Iran.

2008–2009 Israeli military offensives in Gaza

Areas of Conflict in Asia
The beginning of the third millennium finds Asia in the grip of longstanding, unresolved economic, ethnic and religious disputes. In some countries, increasing Islamic radicalism has led to near-constant armed conflict.

The Afghanistan War (1979–1989)
Leftist militias came to power in Afghanistan following the fall of Premier Mohammed Daoud Khan. Muslim resistance fighters (mujahideen) fought the leftists with assistance from the United States. The Afghanistan government was propped up by the USSR, which wanted to preserve and extend its political influence in the region. The lengthy war ended with the retreat of Soviet forces, and the mujahideen dissolved into several smaller groups, some of them radical extremists. Soviet withdrawal did not end the conflict between the Islamists and ruling Afghan military government. In 1996 the Taliban, the most radical of all the mujahideen, seized power.

The American War on the Afghani Taliban
In 1996 the Taliban effectively ruled Afghanistan, transforming the country into a base for international terrorism. After the 9/11 terrorist attacks in the United States, American and allied forces bombed Taliban military bases, forcing them to flee. By the end of the year, the Taliban had fallen from power in northern Afghanistan, but still maintained control of the high mountain ranges on the Afghan-Pakistani border.

The Second Gulf War (1990–1991)
Iraq, financially ruined after the Iran-Iraq War, occupied Kuwait in 1990. After Iraq ignored a United Nations resolution calling for its immediate withdrawal, an international alliance under the leadership of the United States invaded Iraq, launching Operation Desert Storm. The Iraqi army was defeated by March 1991. The UN declared international security zones: a Kurdish zone in the north and a Shi'ite zone in the south. Economic sanctions were imposed on the government of Saddam Hussein.

The Third Gulf War (2003)
In March 2003 American and British forces invaded Iraq, toppling the military dictatorship of Saddam Hussein. One of the justifications for the invasion was the supposed presence of weapons of mass destruction in Iraq, as well as Saddam Hussein's support of international terrorism. A connection between Iraq and al-Qaeda was never conclusively proven.

The Middle East Conflict
The Middle East Conflict began with the Jewish settlement of Palestinian territories in the late 19th century, which the Arab population protested. In 1947 the UN attempted to ameliorate the situation by dividing Palestine into Jewish and Arab sectors. After Israel declared its statehood in 1948, within hours, its Arab neighbors launched an attack. Israel successfully defended itself and, in a counterattack, occupied the Gaza Strip, the West Bank of the Jordan River, West Jerusalem and Galilee.

Israel occupied the rest of Jerusalem and additional territories in the Six-Day War in 1967, including the Golan Heights in Syria. In the ensuing years a near-permanent state of tension has reigned,

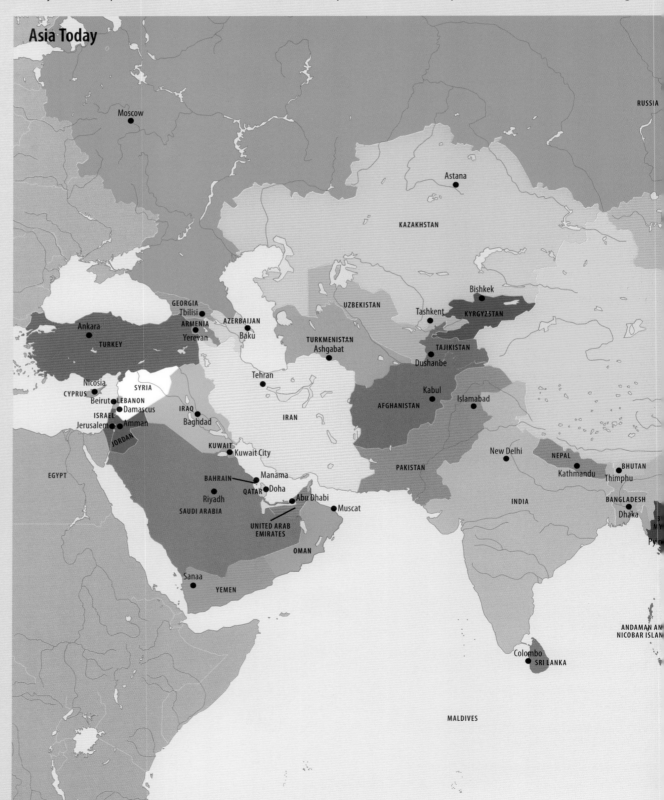

Asia Today

despite a host of international efforts to bring peace to the region. At the beginning of the third millennium, an internationally recognized independent Palestinian state has yet to become a reality.

Russian-Chechnya Conflict

Chechnya is an autonomous republic of the Russian Federation. In 1991 it declared its independence from the federation, which Russia refused to recognize, and Russian troops invaded Chechnya in 1994 and again in 1999.

Chechnya remains under Russian control today.

Russian-Georgia Conflict

Georgia gained its independence from Russia in 1990, a development that was rejected by separatist movements in the majority-Russian provinces of Abkhazia and South Ossetia. Since 1992 both regions have been trying to secede from Georgia and rejoin the Russian Federation. In August 2008 the dispute led to armed conflict between Russian and Georgian troops.

Chinese-Tibet Conflict

Tibet is a region of central Asia with an independent national identity. China has long had aspirations to control Tibetan territory. After a short period of Tibetan independence in the first half of the 20th century, the People's Republic of China invaded Tibet in 1950 and initiated a military occupation. The Dalai Lama, the religious leader and traditional head of government of Tibet, fled to India in 1959, and settlement in Tibet by ethnic Han Chinese increased. Despite an

economic revival, Tibetans considered themselves an oppressed minority in their own country.

Tibet has revolted against Chinese control several times, and international opinion has been marshaled against the Chinese occupation. Were Tibet to gain its independence, ethnic conflict would likely continue, as the majority of its population now consists of Chinese settlers.

The Arab World: An Overview

600–800: The Early Expansion of Islam

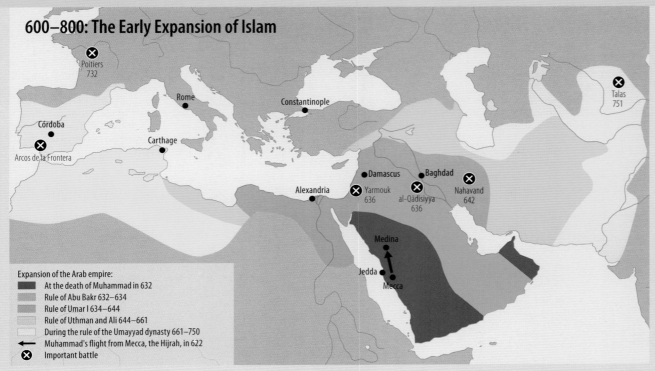

Expansion of the Arab empire:
- At the death of Muhammad in 632
- Rule of Abu Bakr 632–634
- Rule of Umar I 634–644
- Rule of Uthman and Ali 644–661
- During the rule of the Umayyad dynasty 661–750
- ← Muhammad's flight from Mecca, the Hijrah, in 622
- ⊗ Important battle

800–1100: The Formation of Regional Dynasties

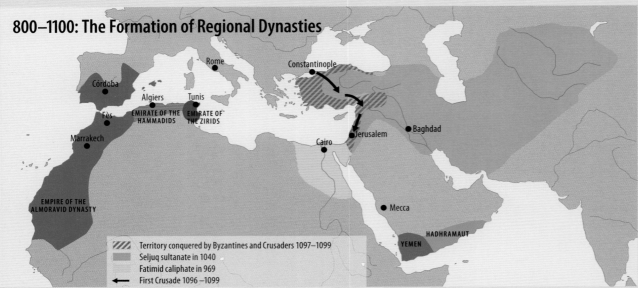

- ▨ Territory conquered by Byzantines and Crusaders 1097–1099
- Seljuq sultanate in 1040
- Fatimid caliphate in 969
- ← First Crusade 1096 –1099

Like European or African history, the history of the Arab world is geographically complex, involving territories currently occupied by Arab peoples as well as lands that were involved in the period of rapid expansion of Islam following the death of the Prophet Muhammad in 632. Limiting a historical survey to current members of the Arab League would be analogous to limiting the study of European history to the continent of Europe.

642–700 Arabs spread to the north, and in Africa as far west as Morocco.

661–750 The first dynastic caliphate of the Ummayads rules from its capital in Damascus and from desert palaces in Jordan.

673 Arabs conquer Rhodes.

674–678 + 717/718 Arabs twice besiege Constantinople, both times without success.

680 The defeat and murder of Imam al-Husayn ibn Ali and his family at Karbala by an overwhelming Sunni (Umayyad) army leads to the Shi'ite schism and civil war that persists until 692.

711–719 Arabs conquer most of the Iberian Peninsula.

732 Defeat in the battles of Tours and Poitiers in France bring a halt to further Arab expansion into Europe.

750–1258 The Abbasid dynastic caliphate is founded, with its new capital at Baghdad after 762.

756–1031 The Umayyads form the emirate of Córdoba, which after 929 becomes the caliphate of Córdoba, ruling North Africa and Spain.

786–809 Caliph Harun al-Rashid rules; Baghdad is one of the most important cities in the world.

after 800 The Abbasid Caliphate dissolves into smaller kingdoms.

813–833 The reign of Caliph al-Ma'mun is the period when Islamic scholarship begins to flourish.

909–1171 The Shi'ite Fatimid C aliphate comes to power.

969 The Fatimids conquer Egypt.

977–1186 The Turkish Ghaznavid empire rules from Ghazni, Afghanistan.

998–1030 Mahmud of Ghazni, great conqueror of early Islam, occupies northern India from 1001 onward.

10th century Collapse of the first Arab empire

3000 BCE Semitic tribes from the Arabian Peninsula settle in Sumerian Mesopotamia.

2300 BCE The Magan culture in what will become Oman supplies Mesopotamia with copper and diorite (a hard black stone).

1000–300 BCE The kingdom of 'Ād flourishes in what will later be known as Yemen and Oman.

900–275 BCE The kingdom of Saba' rules Yemen.

700–525 BCE The empires of Ma'in, Qatabān, Hadramaut and Himyar control Yemen.

550 BCE The Nabateans, based in the Jordan Valley, rule the surrounding territory.

100 BCE The Thamud found Mada'in Salih, building more than a hundred monumental rock-cut graves.

100 BCE–106 CE The city of Petra, carved out of rock, is founded and inhabited by the Nabateans.

50 BCE Palmyra in Syria becomes a flourishing city along the major caravan route between Persia and the Mediterranean.

106 CE Romans occupy the Nabatean city of Petra.

273 Emperor Aurelian conquers and destroys the Palmyran kingdom.

570–630 The Persian Sassanids rule Yemen and other parts of the Arabian Peninsula. Arab territories along the Mediterranean coast are made part of the Byzantine Empire.

570–632 Lifetime of the Prophet Muhammad

~600 Numerous Bedouin tribes cross the Arabian Peninsula.

622 Persecuted in Mecca, Muhammad and his followers flee to Medina in what is known as the Hijrah.

~600 Numerous Bedouin tribes cross the Arabian Peninsula.

630 The Prophet Muhammad reenters Mecca victoriously with a much larger following.

634–644 Caliph Umar ibn al-Khattab expands the Arab empire.

636 The Battle at Yarmouk River is a decisive defeat for the Byzantine Empire and allows Arab expansion into Syria and Palestine. A further battle against the Sassanids near al–Qādisiyya results in further victory for the Arabs and their conquest of Mesopotamia.

638 Arab conquest of Jerusalem

642 Persia is conquered by Arabs after decisive battles against the Sassanid empire (Battle of Nahāvand).

1038–1194 The Seljuq dynasty, a Turkish (Sunni) sultanate, declares itself protector of the Abbasid caliph.

1046–1147 The Almoravid (Berber) dynasty rules northwest Africa and Spain.

1096–1099 The Christian armies of the First Crusade conquer Jerusalem.

1171–1193 The empire of Saladin (Kurdish Ayyubid dynasty)

1187 Saladin retakes Jerusalem from the Crusaders.

1250–1517 The Mamluks (originally military slaves) rule Egypt.

1258 The Mongol invasion: Mongols conquer Baghdad, destroying the Abbasid Caliphate and founding the Persian-Mongolian Ilkhanate, which will rule until 1335.

1260–1277 Mamluk Sultan Barbar I retakes most of Palestine from the Crusaders.

1299–1922 Period of the Ottoman Empire, extending to the Balkans at its peak, lasting more than six centuries.

1370–1405 The empire of Timur (Tamerlane) dominates central Asia. The Timurids will reign until 1506.

1459 The Ottoman Empire controls the Balkan region.

1501–1722 The Safavids rule in Iran, making Shi'ism the state religion.

1512–1520 Sultan Selim I conquers the Middle East for the Ottomans.

1516/17 Azerbaijan, Syria and Egypt become part of the Ottoman Empire.

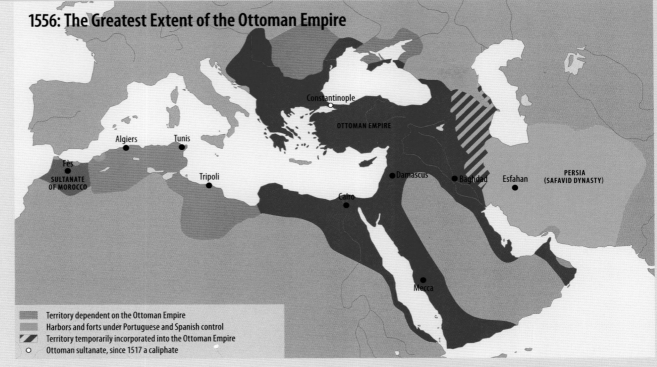

1556: The Greatest Extent of the Ottoman Empire

■ Territory dependent on the Ottoman Empire
■ Harbors and forts under Portuguese and Spanish control
▨ Territory temporarily incorporated into the Ottoman Empire
○ Ottoman sultanate, since 1517 a caliphate

1520–1566 Sultan Süleyman the Magnificent brings the Ottoman Empire to its cultural highpoint during his long reign of more than four decades.

1539–1551 Algeria, Tunisia and Libya gain their independence from the Ottoman Empire.

1566 Süleyman I dies while the Ottoman Empire is at its most expansive.

1587–1629 Shah Abbas the Great inaugurates a Safavid golden age.

16th–17th centuries Morocco increasingly falls under European influence.

1638 The Ottomans conquer Iraq.

1683 Ottoman armies besiege Vienna;

their defeat begins a period of declining Ottoman influence in Europe.

1699 The Treaty of Carlowitz: Ottoman Empire gives up Hungary and Dalmatia.

1705–1957 Tunisia is ruled by the Husainid dynasty (beys).

1736–1747 Nadir Shah of Persia conquers Kabul and Delhi in 1738/39.

1794/96–1925 The Qajar Dynasty rules Iran.

1798 Napoleon ends Ottoman rule in Egypt.

1830 Greece wins its independence. Serbia becomes an independent principality. France annexes Algeria.

1853–1856 The Crimean War breaks out between Russia and the Ottoman Empire.

1878 The Congress of Berlin addresses the balance of power in the Balkans; the Ottoman Empire is weakened.

1881 Algeria becomes part of France.

1881–1885 The Mahdi Revolt breaks out in Sudan and southern Egypt, leading to the 1885 conquest of Khartoum by the British.

1883 Tunisia is made a protectorate of France.

1899 Sudan becomes a protectorate of Great Britain.

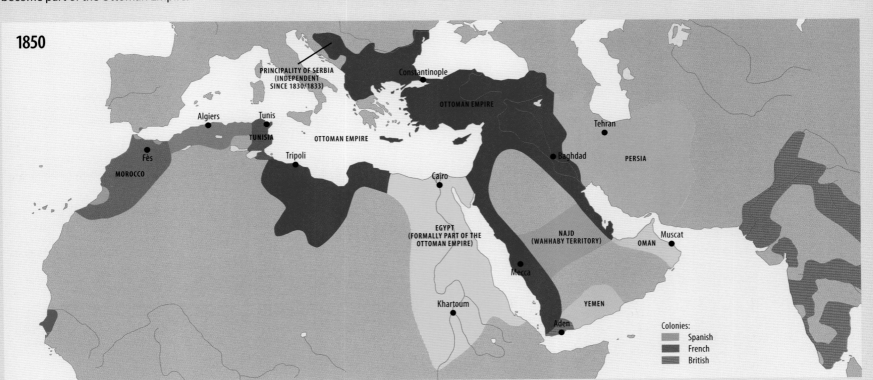

1850

Colonies:
■ Spanish
■ French
■ British

The Arab World: An Overview

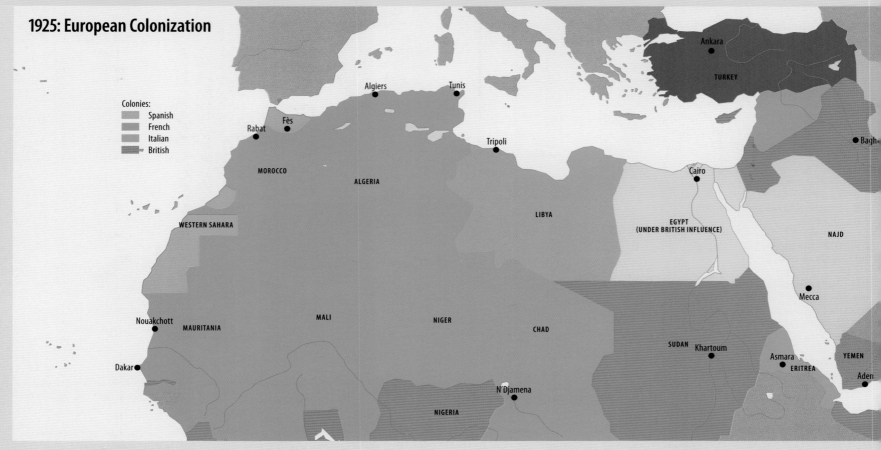

1925: European Colonization

Colonies:
Spanish
French
Italian
British

(Map labels: TURKEY — Ankara, Tunis, Algiers, Rabat, Fès, Tripoli, Bagh[dad], Cairo, MOROCCO, ALGERIA, LIBYA, EGYPT (UNDER BRITISH INFLUENCE), NAJD, WESTERN SAHARA, MALI, NIGER, CHAD, Mecca, Nouakchott, MAURITANIA, SUDAN, Khartoum, Asmara, ERITREA, YEMEN, Dakar, N'Djamena, NIGERIA, Aden)

The Arab League

(Map labels: LEBANON (1945), SYRIA (1945), IRAQ (1945), TUNISIA (1958), MOROCCO (1958), PALESTINE (1976), JORDAN (1945), KUWAIT (1961), BAHRAIN (1971), UNITED ARAB EMIRATES (1971), ALGERIA (1962), LIBYA (1945), EGYPT (1945), SAUDI ARABIA (1945), QATAR (1971), WESTERN SAHARA (OCCUPIED BY MOROCCO), OMAN (1971), MAURITANIA (1973), YEMEN (NORTH YEMEN 1945, SOUTH YEMEN 1967), SUDAN (1956), DJIBOUTI (1977), SOMALIA (1974), COMOROS (1993))

Countries in the Arab League
(1973) Year of joining the Arab League

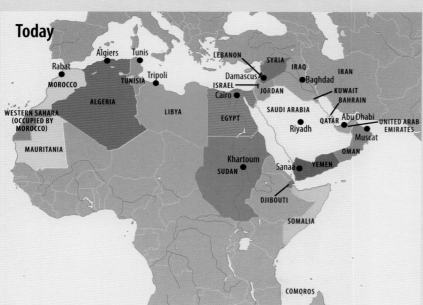

Today

(Map labels: Algiers, Tunis, Rabat, LEBANON, SYRIA, IRAQ, IRAN, MOROCCO, TUNISIA, Tripoli, Damascus, ISRAEL, Baghdad, JORDAN, KUWAIT, BAHRAIN, Cairo, ALGERIA, LIBYA, EGYPT, SAUDI ARABIA, QATAR, Abu Dhabi, UNITED ARAB EMIRATES, Riyadh, Muscat, WESTERN SAHARA (OCCUPIED BY MOROCCO), MAURITANIA, Khartoum, OMAN, Sanaa, YEMEN, SUDAN, DJIBOUTI, SOMALIA, COMOROS)

1911 Libya becomes a protectorate of Italy.

1912 Morocco becomes a protectorate of France while Spanish and German influence in the area increases.

1914–1918 The Ottoman Empire fights on the side of Germany during World War I.

1914 Egypt becomes a protectorate of Great Britain.

1920 In the course of World War I the Ottoman Empire loses all its territories except the Anatolian peninsula.

1921 Founding of the kingdom of Iraq

1922 The kingdom of Egypt gains its independence from Great Britain. The Ottoman sultan is deposed.

1923 Founding of the emirate of Transjordan

1925–1979 The Pahlavi shahs rule Iran.

1932 Saudi Arabia is united and the Saudi Arabian kingdom is founded, ruled by Ibn Sa'ūd.

1938 Petroleum is discovered in al-Dammam, Saudi Arabia.

1943 Lebanon gains its independence.

1945 Egypt, Iraq, Transjordan (Jordan after 1946), Lebanon, Saudi Arabia and Syria agree to form the Arab League; Yemen joins the following year.

1945 Libya falls under British and French administration.

1946 Syria becomes an independent Arab republic. Jordan gains its independence under the Hāshemite royal dynasty.

May 14, 1948 The founding of the state of Israel leads immediately to the first Arab-Israeli war.

1951 Libya gains its independence from Italy. King Abdullāh I of Jordan is murdered in Jerusalem.

1952 Hussein II becomes king of Jordan. In July, Egypt forms a republic.

1954 The Algerian war for independence breaks out against France.

1954–1970 Gamal Abdel Nasser becomes president of Egypt and leader of the Pan-Arab movement.

1956 Morocco, Tunisia and Sudan gain their independence. Civil war breaks out between northern and southern Sudan.

1958 Egypt and Syria unite to form the United Arab Republic (UAR) until 1961. The Lebanon crisis ends after United States intervention. The Iraq monarchy falls after a bloody coup.

1960 OPEC (Organization of Petroleum Exporting Countries) is founded in Baghdad.

1962 Algeria wins its independence.

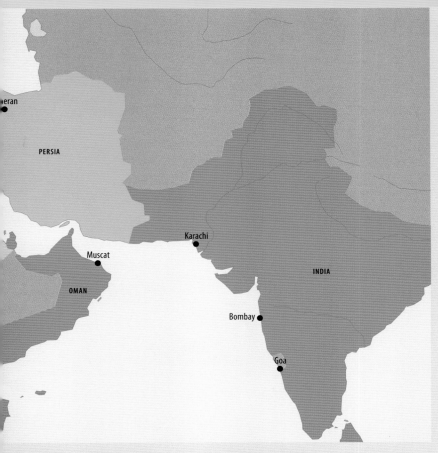

1967 The Six-Day War in Israel and partition of Yemen

September 1969 Muammar al-Qaddafi overthrows the previous government and takes control of Libya.

1971 Founding of the United Arab Emirates and independence of Oman

1972 Civil war ends in Sudan.

1973 The Yom Kippur War, also called the Fourth Arab-Israeli War

1979 Peace between Egypt and Israel. Saddam Hussein comes to power in Iraq.

1979 Ayatollah Khomeini proclaims the Islamic Republic of Iran on April 1st as the shah flees the country. The occupation of the Great Mosque in Mecca is ended forcibly by Saudi troops.

1979–1981 The occupation of the American embassy in Tehran

1980–1988 The Iran-Iraq War (also called the First Gulf War) breaks out between Iran and Iraq.

1982 The Lebanon war breaks out. Israel occupies southern Lebanon (until 2000).

1983 Civil war breaks out again in the Sudan.

1985 A bomb blast explodes an airplane over the Scottish town of Lockerbie. Libya is accused of supporting international terrorism.

1987 The first intifada: Palestinian frustration with Israeli policies, especially concerning Gaza and the West Bank, lead to open rebellion.

1990–1991 Iraqi troops invade Kuwait, setting off the Persian Gulf War (Second Gulf War). They are driven out by Western coalition forces in 1991.

1991 Algeria moves toward becoming an Islamic state, leading to a bloody civil war. The Sudan becomes a base camp for al-Qaeda.

1992 Economic sanctions are imposed on Libya.

1996 The Taliban occupy Kabul, Afghanistan.

2000 The second intifada

Sept. 11, 2001 The September 11 terrorist attacks on the World Trade Center Towers in New York City, the Pentagon in Washington, D.C., and a fourth target that was not reached leave 3,000 people dead. Western troops march against the Taliban in Afghanistan.

2003 The Iraq War topples Saddam Hussein.

2005 Civil war ends in Sudan.

since 2005 Mahmud Ahmadinejad has been president of Iran.

The Most Important Islamic Dynasties

661–750	**Umayyads (Arabs)** First dynastic caliphate; rule the Islamic realm from Damascus.
749/50–1258	**Abbasids (Arabs, Persian culture)** A dynastic caliphate that is united as a great empire only until around 800, after which it dissolves into smaller kingdoms. Its capital is Bagdad.
756–1031	**Spanish Umayyads** rule Spain (al-Andalus, caliphate after 929).
788–974	**Idrisids (Arabs)** rule Morocco.
800–909	**Aghlabids (Arabs)** control Algeria, Tunisia, Libya, Sicily and southern Italy.
819/74–999/1005	**Samanids (Iranian)** rule Transoxania and parts of Persia and Afghanistan.
840–1212	**Karakanids (Turks)** rule Transoxania.
868–905	**Tulunids (Arabs-Turks)** rule Egypt, Syria and Palestine.
909–1171	**Fatimids (Arabs)** The Shi'ite caliphate rules Tunisia, Egypt, northern Africa, and Syria.
932/45–1056/62	**Buyids (Iranians)** control western Persia and Mesopotamia and protect the Abbasid caliph.
977–1150/86	**Ghaznavids (Turks)** The dynasty of Mahmud of Ghazni rules Afghanistan, Khorasan and northern India.
1038–1157/94	**Seljuqs (Great Seljuqs – Turks)** rule Afghanistan, Iran, Iraq, eastern Anatolia, Syria and the Arabian Peninsula.
1042/56–1147	**Almoravids (Berbers)** control western and northern Africa as well as Spain.
1077–1220/31	**Khwarazm-Shahs / Khwarazmids (Turks)** rule Khwarazm (Transoxania), Turkestan, Afghanistan, Iran and parts of Persia
1077–1308	**Anatolian Seljuqs / Rum Seljuqs (Turks)** control Anatolia.
1127–1174/1262	**Zangids (Turks)** rule northern Syria and Iraq, in later years from Mosul.
1130–1267	**Almohads (Berbers)** control northern Africa and Spain.
1150–1206/12	**Ghurids (Afghani)** rule Afghanistan and northern India.
1171–1250/60	**Ayyubids (Kurdish)** The dynasty of Saladin rules Egypt, Syria and Iraq.
1206–1526	**Delhi Sultanate (Turkish-Indian)** rule the Punjab and northern India through several dynasties.
1224/1378–1502	**The Golden Horde (Mongols)** rules Russia Sibiria and finally the Crimea.
1229/36–1574	**Hafzids (Berbers)** rule Tunisia, eastern Algeria and Libya.
1232/38–1492	**Nasrids (Hispano-Arabs)** rule southern Spain (Granada).
1244–1465	**Merinids (Berbers)** rule Morocco.
1250–1517	**Mamluks (Turks-Caucasians)** Originally military slaves, they rule Egypt, Syria and Iraq.
1252/56–1335	**Ilkhane (Mongol-Turkomans)** rule Persia, Iraq, Syria, Anatolia the Caucasus.
1300–1922	**Ottomans (Turks)** rule from the Balkans to Anatolia, northern Africa, and the Arabian Peninsula (Ottoman Empire)
1363/70–1506	**Timurids (Turkomans)** The dynasty of Tamerlane: Transoxania, Afghanistan, northern India, Persia, Iraq, Syria, eastern Anatolia and parts of the Caucasus.
1380/90–1469	**Kara Koyunlu (Turkomans)** rule eastern Anatolia, Azerbaijan, the Caucasus and parts of Iran and Iraq.
1467–1502	**Ak Koyunlu (Turkomans)** control eastern Anatolia, Azerbaijan, Iran, Iraq and Afghanistan.
1472–1554	**Wattasids (Berbers)** rule Morocco.
1500–1599	**Sheibani (Uzbekis)** rule Transoxania and Afghanistan.
1501–1722/36	**Safavids (Turkomans)** rule as shahs of Iran.
1526–1857	**Mughals (Turkomans-Indians)** rule India.
1554–1659	**Saadi / Saadites (Arabs)** rule Morocco.
1599–1785	**Astrakhanids / Janids (Mongols)** are the khans of Bukhara in Central Asia.
from 1666	**Alaouites (Arabs)** rule Morocco.
1705–1957	**Husainids (Turks)** are the beys of Tunisia.
since 1735	**Sauds (Arabs)** rule Saudi Arabia, since 1932 as kings.
1736–1796	**Afsharids (Afghani)** The dynasty of Nadir Shah controls Persia and Afghanistan.
1747–1826	**Durrani (Afghans)** rule Afghanistan.
since 1756	**Al-Sabah (Arabs)** rule Kuwait.
1779/96–1925	**Qajar (Turkomans)** rule as shahs of Iran.
1826–1973	**Barakzai (Afghanis)** control Afghanistan.
from 1916	**Hashemites (Arabs)** are the sharifs of Mecca,
1916–1925	kings of the Hejaz,
1921–1958	kings of Iraq,
since 1921	and the emirs and kings of Jordan.
1925–1979	**Pahlavis (Iranians)** rule Iran.

The History and Expansion of Islam

Until 720: Early Expansion

Expansion of Islam

Until 900: Regional Dynasties

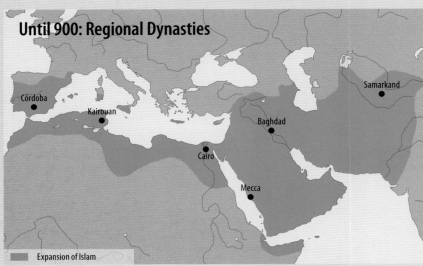

Expansion of Islam

Until 1100: Islam in North Africa

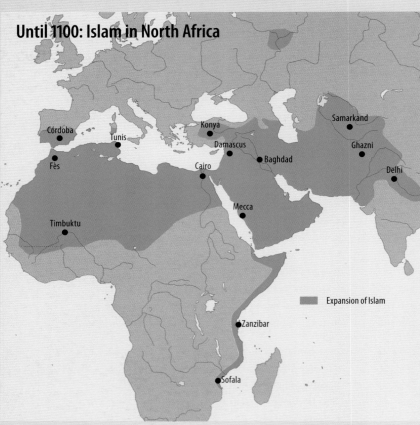

Expansion of Islam

1500: Expansion into Asia

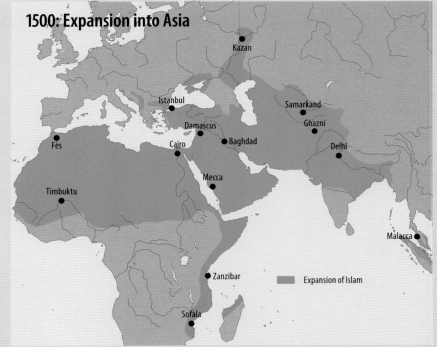

Expansion of Islam

570 Birth of the Prophet Muhammad in Mecca

622 The Hijrah: Muhammad leaves Mecca with a small group of followers and goes to Medina.

623–628 Muhammad leads campaigns against Mecca.

629 The first Islamic hajj (pilgrimage) to Mecca, where the Kaaba has been a pilgrimage site since pre-Islamic times.

630 Mecca opens its gates to Muhammad.

632 Muhammad dies, leaving behind one daughter, Fatima.

632–661 Rapid expansion of Islam under the first four caliphs (successors): Abu Bakr, 632–644; Umar ibn al-Khattab, 634–644; Uthman ibn Affan, 644–656; and Ali ibn Abi Talib, 656–661, who is murdered. Ali's followers, the Shi'ites, lead a schismatic movement in which Ali is the first imam. The Alevi (the name derives from Ali) are also Shi'ites.

~653 The Koran is compiled for the first time.

661–750 The Sunni dynastic caliphate of the Umayyads rises to power.

680 Shi'ite Imam Husayn ibn Ali is murdered at Karbala, deepening the schism between Sunnis and Shi'ites.

708 Arab conquest of Morocco

711–1492 Muslim rule in Spain, *conquista* and *reconquista*

749–1258 The Abbasid dynasty rules from its capital in Baghdad during a golden age of scholarship. The Bayt al Hikma (House of Wisdom) academy is founded in 825–830.

751 Arab forces defeat the Chinese at the Battle of Talas in central Asia, allowing Islam to spread farther east.

786–809 Caliph Harun al-Rashid transforms Baghdad into a magnificent city, the setting of the tales of *1001 Nights*.

813–833 The reign of Caliph al-Ma'mun; Islamic science begins to flourish.

909–1171 The Ismaili Shi'ite Fatimids declare a caliphate in the Mahgreb and Egypt. They name their capital city al-Qahira ("the strong"), or Cairo.

929 The third caliphate is proclaimed in Córdoba.

1096 Beginning of the Crusades.

1206–1526 The Delhi sultanate rules northern India.

after 1250 Synthesis of Mongol and Islamic cultures.

1299–1922 The Sunni Ottoman Turks bring Islam into southeastern Europe.

after 1414 Arab traders spread Islam to the Malay Peninsula and Indonesia.

1453 The Ottoman Empire conquers Constantinople, bringing the Byzantine Empire to an end.

1460 The Ottoman Empire conquers Greece.

after 1501 The Safavids make Twelver Shi'ism the state religion of Persia.

1894 The first wave of massacres of Christian Armenians by Turks

1906 The Muslim League is founded in India.

1923 Founding of the secular Turkish Republic; end of Islamic Ottoman rule

1945 Indonesia gains its independence. Moderate Islam predominates.

1947 Founding of Pakistan as an Islamic state

1957 Malaysia gains its independence and declares Islam its state religion.

1971 Bangladesh gains independence from Pakistan; Islam is the state religion.

1979 The Islamic Republic of Iran is founded.

1989 After author Salman Rushdie publishes *The Satanic Verses*, Ayatollah Khomeini issues a *fatwa* calling for his murder.

1991–1999 Civil war breaks out between Islamist groups in Algeria.

1996 The Taliban come to power in Afghanistan.

2001 Al-Qaeda unleashes terrorist attacks on the United States.

2005 Sunni clerics in England issue *fatwas* against terrorism and against female circumcision in Somalia.

2008 The majority Sunni region of Kosovo calls for independence.

The Five Pillars of Islam:
1. *Shahada* (profession of faith) Belief in one and only one God—Allah—and in his prophet, Muhammad
2. *Salat* (obligatory prayer) Regular prayer five times a day in the direction of Mecca
3. *Zakat* (alms, or poor tax) Obligatory sharing of profits and the value of goods and other products
4. *Sawm* (fasting) Obligatory fasting and abstention from other pleasures from sunrise to sunset during the month of Ramadan
5. *Hajj* (pilgrimage) Pilgrimage to Mecca at least once during one's lifetime

An imam reads from the Koran.

Islam means submission (to the will of God). Believers are called Muslims, and their one God is Allah. Islam began with the Prophet Muhammad, the "seal (last) of the prophets." Islam also recognizes Abraham, Moses and Jesus as prophets. The Prophet Muhammad is understood by Muslims not as the founder of a new religion, but as the restorer of the original, true monotheistic religion that was first revealed to Abraham. Islam's holy book is the Koran, which contains the revelations received by the prophet Muhammad from the archangel Gabriel. Islam's holiest site is Mecca, with the cubical Kaaba shrine at its center. Medina is the second holiest city, and Jerusalem the third holiest. Islam's scriptures also include the Hadith, which are collected reports of the life of the Prophet and his inner circle, and how they dealt with day-to-day situations.

The Sunni "Sunna" refers to the "tradition" of the Prophet Muhammad. Approximately 90 percent of all Muslims worldwide are Sunni. Historically, they have based religious practice on the sunna, and supported the Islamic caliphates (theocratic rule).

The Shi'ites About 10 percent of Muslims are Shi'ite, for whom spiritual leadership of the community exists solely in the person of imams in the direct family line of the Prophet and his cousin and son-in-law Ali ibn Abi Talib. Some Shi'ite sects accept twelve imams (the Imami, or Twelvers) while others accept seven (the Ismaili, or Seveners) and some accept only five (the Zaidi, or Fivers). "Imam" can also be used as an honorary title, as with Imam Ayatollah Ruhollah Musavi Khomeini. Both the Imami and Ismaili believe in the imminent return of the "last imam" as the "mahdi" (rightly guided one), who will rule over the end of time.

Sharia and fatwa are aspects of Islamic law, parts of which have been heavily criticized, including corporal punishment (*hadd*). In practice most sharia refers to family law and legal matters such as inheritance rights. Fatwas are legal opinions requested by the faithful, and issued by specialists in Islamic law. There are four schools of Sunni law, and one Shi'ite school.

Jihad, often translated as "holy war," in reality refers to the general struggle for Islam, which is not necessarily a military one. Most Islamic legal scholars dispute the fundamentalist use of the term *jihad* to justify terrorist attacks.

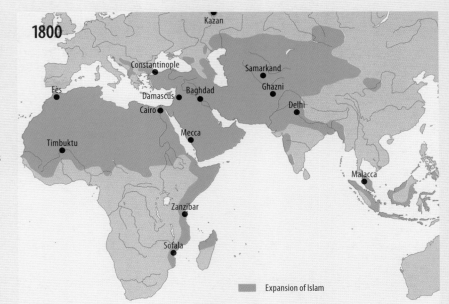

1800

Kazan · Constantinople · Samarkand · Fès · Damascus · Baghdad · Ghazni · Cairo · Delhi · Timbuktu · Mecca · Malacca · Zanzibar · Sofala

Expansion of Islam

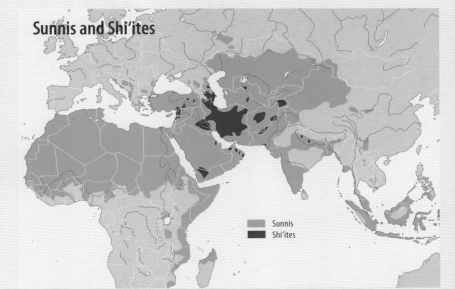

Sunnis and Shi'ites

Sunnis
Shi'ites

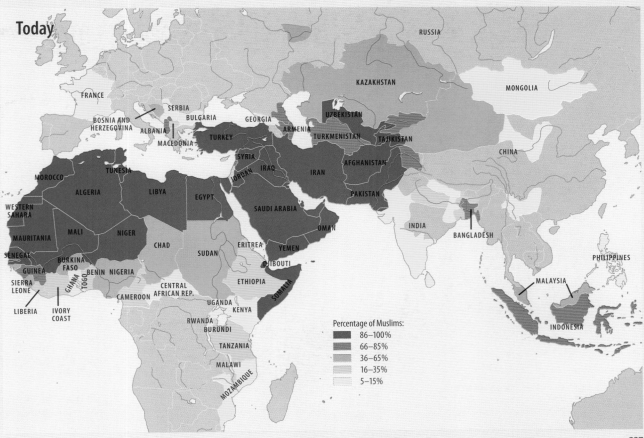

Today

RUSSIA · FRANCE · SERBIA · BULGARIA · GEORGIA · KAZAKHSTAN · MONGOLIA · BOSNIA AND HERZEGOVINA · ALBANIA · MACEDONIA · TURKEY · ARMENIA · UZBEKISTAN · TURKMENISTAN · TAJIKISTAN · CHINA · SYRIA · IRAQ · IRAN · AFGHANISTAN · MOROCCO · TUNISIA · JORDAN · PAKISTAN · WESTERN SAHARA · ALGERIA · LIBYA · EGYPT · SAUDI ARABIA · OMAN · INDIA · BANGLADESH · MAURITANIA · MALI · NIGER · CHAD · SUDAN · ERITREA · YEMEN · SENEGAL · GUINEA · BURKINA FASO · BENIN · NIGERIA · DJIBOUTI · PHILIPPINES · SIERRA LEONE · GHANA · TOGO · CENTRAL AFRICAN REP. · ETHIOPIA · SOMALIA · MALAYSIA · LIBERIA · IVORY COAST · CAMEROON · UGANDA · KENYA · RWANDA · BURUNDI · INDONESIA · TANZANIA · MALAWI · MOZAMBIQUE

Percentage of Muslims:
86–100%
66–85%
36–65%
16–35%
5–15%

337

Israel and Palestine Until 1947

ca. 1200 BCE

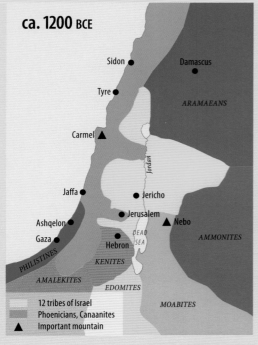

12 tribes of Israel
Phoenicians, Canaanites
▲ Important mountain

ca. 1000–900 BCE: The Kingdoms of David and Solomon

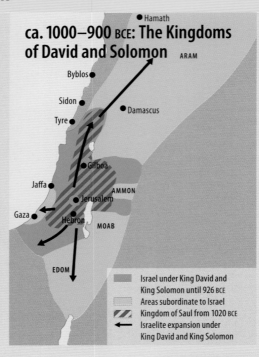

Israel under King David and King Solomon until 926 BCE
Areas subordinate to Israel
Kingdom of Saul from 1020 BCE
← Israelite expansion under King David and King Solomon

ca. 926–587 BCE: Divided Monarchy

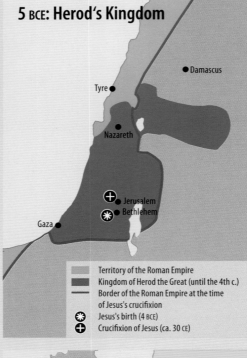

Judah 900 BCE
Israel 900 BCE
Northern Kingdom until 722/721 BCE
⊗ Samaria and Israel conquered by the Assyrians 722/721 BCE
⊗ Jerusalem and Judah conquered by the Babylonians in 587 BCE

5 BCE: Herod's Kingdom

Territory of the Roman Empire
Kingdom of Herod the Great (until the 4th c.)
Border of the Roman Empire at the time of Jesus's crucifixion
✳ Jesus's birth (4 BCE)
✛ Crucifixion of Jesus (ca. 30 CE)

ca. 70 CE: Roman Occupation

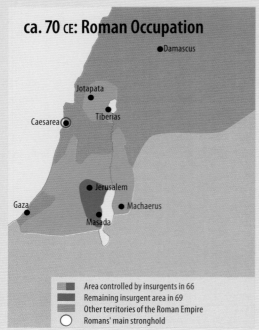

Area controlled by insurgents in 66
Remaining insurgent area in 69
Other territories of the Roman Empire
○ Romans' main stronghold

ca. 900–1100: Islamic Rule

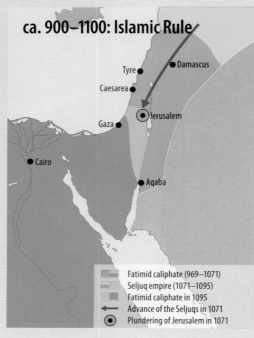

Fatimid caliphate (969–1071)
Seljuq empire (1071–1095)
Fatimid caliphate in 1095
→ Advance of the Seljuqs in 1071
⊙ Plundering of Jerusalem in 1071

Palestine, originally the name of a Roman province in the Near East, now refers to what was at one time the biblical region of Canaan.

2500 BCE Semitic tribes settle the region known as Palestine.

~1250 BCE The first Hebrew tribes arrive in the area.

~1200 BCE The Philistines, descendants of the Sea Peoples and militarily superior to the Hebrews, settle the coastal areas of Palestine. The Hebrew tribes form a monarchy.

1200–1025 BCE The period of the Judges unites the Hebrew tribes. The "judges" were more akin to military leaders than to jurists.

~1020 BCE Saul becomes the first king of Israel.

1004 –965 BCE The reign of King David brings the defeat of the Philistines. Jerusalem becomes the capital of Israel.

965–926 BCE King Solomon further strengthens the kingdom during his reign.

926 BCE Following Solomon's death, the kingdom is divided into two: Israel in the north, and Judah in the south.

722–721 BCE Assyrians conquer the northern kingdom of Israel, leaving the kingdom of Judah extant but weakened.

587–586 BCE Babylon under the rule of King Nebuchadnezzar conquers Jerusalem and Judah, destroying the First Temple (built by Solomon) and sending the Jewish priestly and upper classes into exile (the Babylonian Exile).

539 BCE The Persians, led by Cyrus II, conquer Babylon. Cyrus permits Jews to return to Jerusalem if they wish, ending the Jews' period of exile in Babylon.

520–515 BCE Parts of the Hebrew scripture (Torah) are written down in the form that will later be copied into the Dead Sea Scrolls found in Qumran (West Bank) in the 1950s and 1960s.

332 BCE Alexander the Great conquers Palestine, ending Persian rule.

321–200 BCE The Ptolemaic dynasty rules Israel from its seat in Egypt.

Israel served as the name of both the people and the religion of the Jews until approximately 135. It has been the name of a state since 1948.

300–100 BCE The Second Temple is built and consecrated in Jerusalem.

250 BCE Parts of the Hebrew scriptures are translated into Greek for the first time (the Septuagint).

200/198 BCE The Seleucid dynasty occupies Palestine.

167–161 BCE Jews fight for independence during the successful Maccabean Revolt against the Seleucids (celebrated at Hannukah).

135–37 BCE The Hasmoneans, rulers who are also high priests, rule over an independent Jewish state.

63 BCE Palestine falls under Roman rule.

37–4 BCE King Herod the Great reigns as a client of the Roman Empire. During his reign, the Second Temple in Jerusalem is renewed and expanded.

4 BCE–39 CE Herod's three sons divide the kingdom between them, ruling as tetrarchs.

4 BCE Jesus is born in Nazareth.

26 CE Pontius Pilate becomes prefect of Judaea.

30/33 Jesus Christ is crucified in Jerusalem.

41–70 Herod Agrippa I and II inherit the throne.

70 Conquering of Jerusalem and near-complete destruction of the Second (Herodian) Temple by the Romans under the leadership of Titus.

70–73 Nine hundred seventy-three Jewish zealots (resistance fighters) defend the mountain fortress of Masada against 15,000 Roman legionnaires. After the Romans build earthen ramps against the outer walls, the zealots, led by Elazar ben Ya'ir, choose death instead of captivity. Drawing lots, several men are chosen to kill the others before committing suicide. The Romans enter the fortress to find just seven women and children alive to tell the story. Today, Masada is a Jewish national monument.

Ca. 1100: The Early Crusades

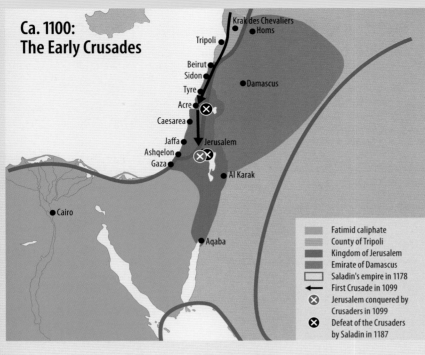

Legend:
- Fatimid caliphate
- County of Tripoli
- Kingdom of Jerusalem
- Emirate of Damascus
- Saladin's empire in 1178
- First Crusade in 1099
- Jerusalem conquered by Crusaders in 1099
- Defeat of the Crusaders by Saladin in 1187

ca. 1200–1300: End of the Crusader States

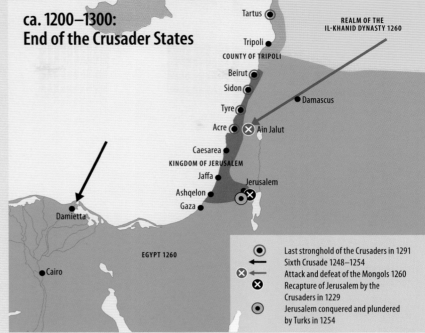

Legend:
- Last stronghold of the Crusaders in 1291
- Sixth Crusade 1248–1254
- Attack and defeat of the Mongols 1260
- Recapture of Jerusalem by the Crusaders in 1229
- Jerusalem conquered and plundered by Turks in 1254

115–117 Jews revolt against the Roman emperor Trajan in Mesopotamia, Judaea and North Africa.

132–135 Jews under the leadership of Simon Bar Kochba revolt against Rome and are brutally suppressed. Jews are forbidden to settle in Palestine, marking the beginning of the Jewish diaspora (i.e., living outside the land of Canaan). Jewish people spread out and form communities throughout the world.

636–638 Muslims rule in Palestine following the conquest of Jerusalem.

691 Muslim rulers build the Dome of the Rock on the Temple Mount in Jerusalem, the same hill where the two sacred Jewish Temples were located.

1099 Christian Crusaders retake Jerusalem, slaughtering many of its inhabitants.

1187 Saladin, the sultan of Egypt and Syria, retakes Jerusalem, placing it once again under Muslim rule.

1260 Palestine becomes part of the Mamluk Empire.

1517 Palestine becomes part of the Ottoman Empire.

1881 The first wave of Jewish immigrants from Russia arrives in Palestine. At this point in time, more than 400,000 Muslims, 13,000 Jews and 40,000 Greek Orthodox Christians live in Palestine.

1897 Theodor Herzl convenes the first Zionist Conference promoting the idea of a Jewish state.

1917 In the Balfour Declaration, Britain promises the Jews a nation-state.

1918 The Ottoman Empire collapses.

1919 With the Faisal–Weizmann Agreement, Arabs agree to cooperate in the development of a Jewish state.

1920 Arabs protest Jewish settlement in Palestine.

1922 The British Mandate on Palestine, approved by the League of Nations, recognizes the right to a Jewish state.

1936–1939 Arabs demand an Arab state in Palestine.

1939 Britain sets quotas on Jewish immigration.

1945–1948 The British mandate attempts to block Jewish access to Palestine. Zionist terrorist organizations unleash a series of bloody attacks.

1947 The United Nations Partition Plan divides Palestine into Arab and Jewish sectors.

Theodor Herzl (1860–1904) was an Austrian Jewish journalist and the father of modern Zionism. Author of the book *The Jewish State* (published in 1896), Herzl presented the founding of a Jewish national homeland as a necessary response to the violent pogroms against Jews in Russia.

From 1517: Ottoman Empire

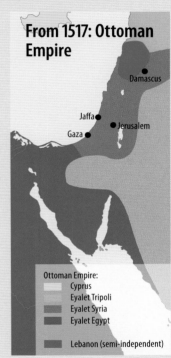

Ottoman Empire:
- Cyprus
- Eyalet Tripoli
- Eyalet Syria
- Eyalet Egypt
- Lebanon (semi-independent)

After 1900: Jewish Settlements

Ottoman Empire:
- Independent sanjak of Jerusalem
- Damascus vilayet
- Beirut vilayet
- Egypt (occupied by Great Britain)
- Jewish settlements prior to 1914

1925: British and French Mandates

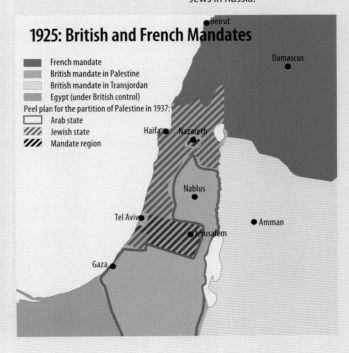

- French mandate
- British mandate in Palestine
- British mandate in Transjordan
- Egypt (under British control)

Peel plan for the partition of Palestine in 1937:
- Arab state
- Jewish state
- Mandate region

1947–1949: Founding of Israel

- Area occupied by Jordan
- Israel since 1949
- Area occupied by Egypt
- Jewish settlement in 1947
- Borders of Palestine in 1947

UN plan to partition Palestine in 1947
- Jewish state
- Arab state
- Jerusalem

Israel and Palestine 1948 Until Today

1956–1957: Suez Crisis

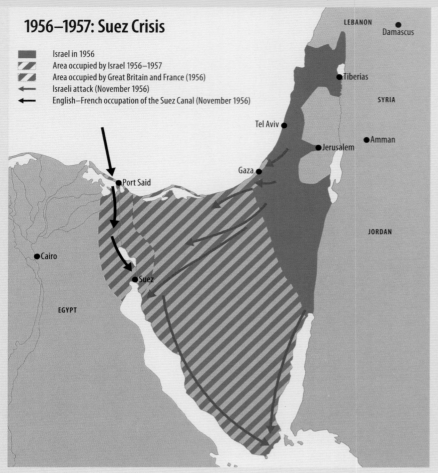

- Israel in 1956
- Area occupied by Israel 1956–1957
- Area occupied by Great Britain and France (1956)
- Israeli attack (November 1956)
- English–French occupation of the Suez Canal (November 1956)

1967: Six-Day War

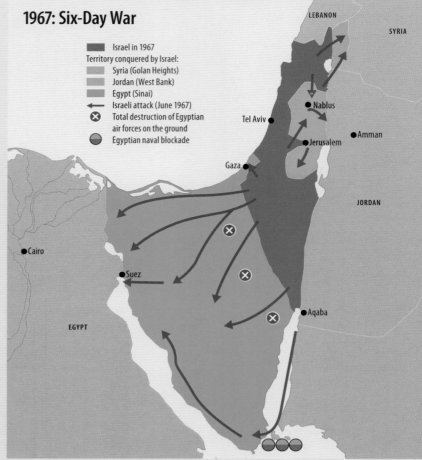

- Israel in 1967
- Territory conquered by Israel:
  - Syria (Golan Heights)
  - Jordan (West Bank)
  - Egypt (Sinai)
- Israeli attack (June 1967)
- ⊗ Total destruction of Egyptian air forces on the ground
- Egyptian naval blockade

1973: Yom Kippur War

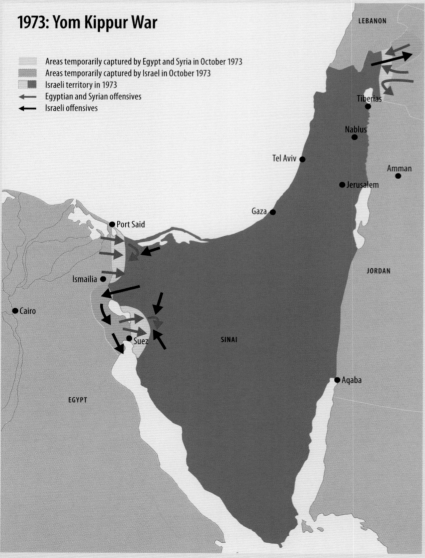

- Areas temporarily captured by Egypt and Syria in October 1973
- Areas temporarily captured by Israel in October 1973
- Israeli territory in 1973
- Egyptian and Syrian offensives
- Israeli offensives

Israel and Palestine occupy a narrow strip of land. The Gaza Strip is between 4 and 12.5 miles (6–12 km) wide, and only 25 miles (41 km) long along its border with the Mediterranean Sea. Small though it is, the region has both high mountains and deep depressions, including the Jordan Valley, which lies 1,240 feet (378 m) below sea level at its lowest point. In the north, the Golan Heights, which are partially controlled by Syria, serve as an important strategic plateau overlooking the low-lying city of Tiberius on the Sea of Galilee. In Israel, military service often means national defense.

May 14, 1948 The state of Israel is founded, and British troops withdraw. Overnight, the surrounding Arab countries declare war on Israel.

1948–1949 The Arab-Israeli War ends with a victory and territorial gains for Israel; many Palestinian Arabs become refugees.

1949–1953 David Ben-Gurion serves as the first prime minister of Israel; he will also hold the post from 1955–1963.

1950 The Knesset (Israeli parliament) passes the Law of Return, granting all Jews and people of Jewish descent anywhere in the world the right to immigrate to Israel.

1952–1954 The Lavon Affair scandal breaks, revealing that the Israeli secret service planned and carried out bomb attacks on American targets in Egypt to undermine improving political relations between Egypt and the West.

1956 The Suez Crisis develops after Egypt bars Israeli ships from passing through the strategically crucial Suez Canal. With covert aid from France and Great Britain, Israel occupies the Gaza Strip and Sinai Peninsula in retaliation.

1960 Adolf Eichmann, one of the chief architects of the Holocaust, is kidnapped in Argentina and brought to Israel to stand trial.

1964 The Palestinian Liberation Organization (PLO) is founded.

1967 The Six-Day War in June involving Israel, Syria, Jordan and Egypt results in Israel's occupation of East Jerusalem and the Golan Heights.

1969–1974 Golda Meir serves as prime minister of Israel.

1972 Israel attacks southern Lebanon. Palestinian terrorists hold hostage and murder eleven Israeli athletes at the Summer Olympics held in Munich, Germany.

1973 Israel loses territory for the first time in the Yom Kippur War, but regains it three weeks later.

1979 Israel's Prime Minister Menachem Begin and President Anwar El-Sadat of Egypt sign a peace agreement at Camp David.

1982 Israel invades southern Lebanon to destroy PLO bases used in terrorist attacks against Israel.

1987 The first intifada, a Palestinian uprising against Israel, begins with the founding of the group called Hamas.

1975–1984: Israel's Settlement Policies

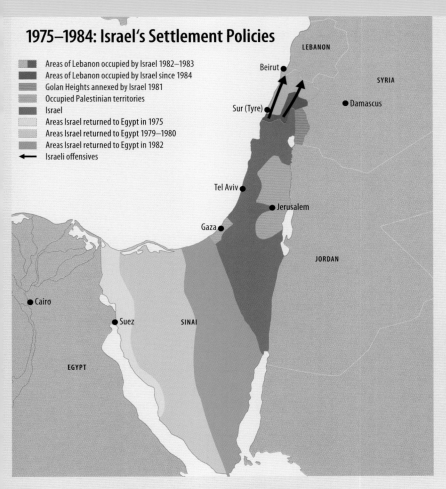

- Areas of Lebanon occupied by Israel 1982–1983
- Areas of Lebanon occupied by Israel since 1984
- Golan Heights annexed by Israel 1981
- Occupied Palestinian territories
- Israel
- Areas Israel returned to Egypt in 1975
- Areas Israel returned to Egypt 1979–1980
- Areas Israel returned to Egypt in 1982
- → Israeli offensives

1995

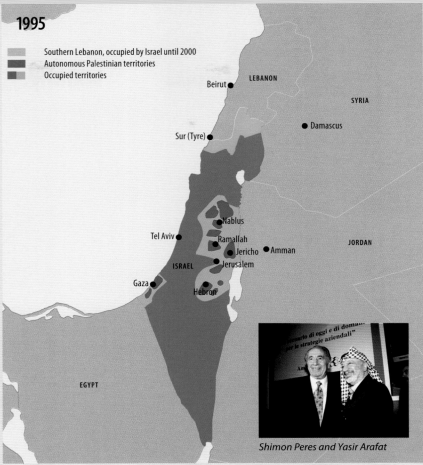

- Southern Lebanon, occupied by Israel until 2000
- Autonomous Palestinian territories
- Occupied territories

Shimon Peres and Yasir Arafat

1988 Palestinians call for an independent Arab state.

1990 Saddam Hussein, president of Iraq, fires thirty Scud rockets at Israel. Yasir Arafat, leader of the PLO, declares his support for Saddam Hussein.

1991 The Madrid Conference, involving both the United States and the USSR, convenes in Spain to discuss the Middle East situation.

1992 Negotiations between Israel and the PLO are initiated.

1993 The Oslo Accords (Declaration of Principles), negotiated in Norway and signed in Washington, D.C., lay a framework for the future, including Israeli support for Palestinian autonomy.

1994 Shimon Peres, Yasir Arafat and Yitzhak Rabin jointly receive the Nobel Peace Prize for their involvement in the Oslo Accords. The Palestinian National Authority (PNA or PA) comes into being.

Nov. 4, 1995 Israeli Prime Minister Rabin is murdered during a peace rally in Tel Aviv.

1997 Palestine gains limited autonomy in the Gaza Strip and West Bank.

2000 Peace talks between Bill Clinton (president of the United States), Ehud Barak (prime minister of Israel) and Yasir Arafat (president of the PNA) take place at Camp David. In September, the second intifada breaks out.

2001 Israel bombs terrorist targets in the Palestinian autonomous area.

2003 Plans are made for Israel to recognize a Palestinian state. Israel builds a wall stretching 436 miles (703 km) along its border with the West Bank.

2004 The Israeli parliament calls for the removal of Jewish settlements from the Gaza Strip. Yasir Arafat dies. Mahmoud Abbas is elected Palestinian president.

2006 Hezbollah, an Iranian political organization active in Lebanon, attacks Israel. Responsible for terrorist attacks since the 1980s, Hezbollah has a strong presence in the Lebanese parliament.

2007 The Israeli air force bombs a Syrian nuclear reactor. The relationship between Hamas and Fatah deteriorates further into "two Palestinian states": radical Gaza (led by Hamas and the Muslim Brotherhood) and the moderate West Bank (governed by Fatah).

2008/2009 Israel responds to rocket attacks by bombing the Gaza Strip.

The term "Palestinians" once meant all the inhabitants of Palestine, but today refers to the Arab population of the West Bank and Gaza Strip. Palestinians who fled the Six-Day War live in refugee camps in desperate conditions. Yasir Arafat founded the Palestinian Liberation Organization (PLO) in 1964, beginning a cycle of military and terrorist activity directed against Israel. More recently, the hope of reconciliation through a two-state solution, while still possible, has been weakened by uneven support of the PLO (Fatah) by Palestinians, and by increasing popular support for Hamas-led militants in Gaza.

Today

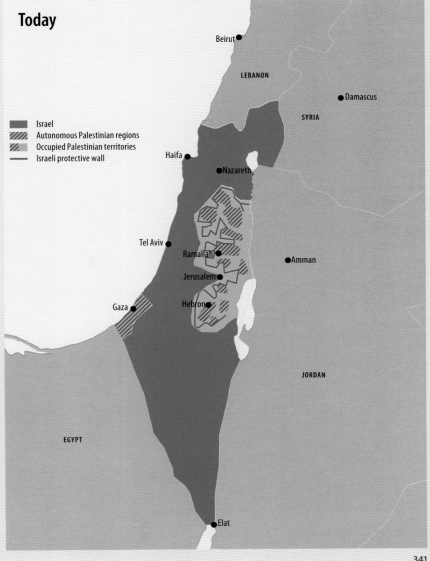

- Israel
- Autonomous Palestinian regions
- Occupied Palestinian territories
- — Israeli protective wall

The Levant – Syria, Lebanon and Jordan Until 1918

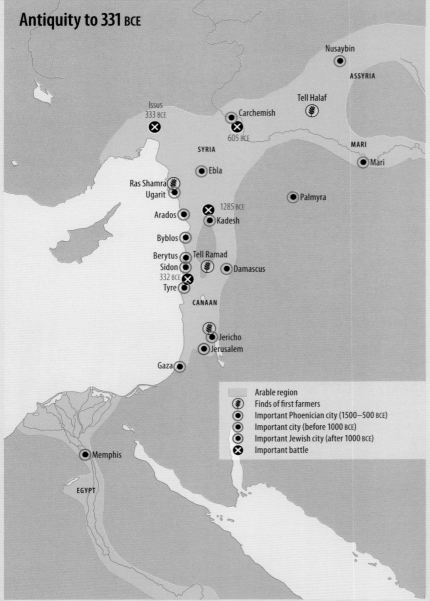

Antiquity to 331 BCE

Nusaybin

ASSYRIA

Issus
333 BCE

Carchemish
605 BCE

Tell Halaf

SYRIA

MARI

Mari

Ebla

Palmyra

Ras Shamra
Ugarit

Arados

1285 BCE
Kadesh

Byblos

Berytus   Tell Ramad
Sidon
332 BCE

Damascus

Tyre

CANAAN

Jericho
Jerusalem

Gaza

Memphis

EGYPT

Arable region
Finds of first farmers
Important Phoenician city (1500–500 BCE)
Important city (before 1000 BCE)
Important Jewish city (after 1000 BCE)
Important battle

331 BCE – 634: From Alexander the Great to Late Antiquity

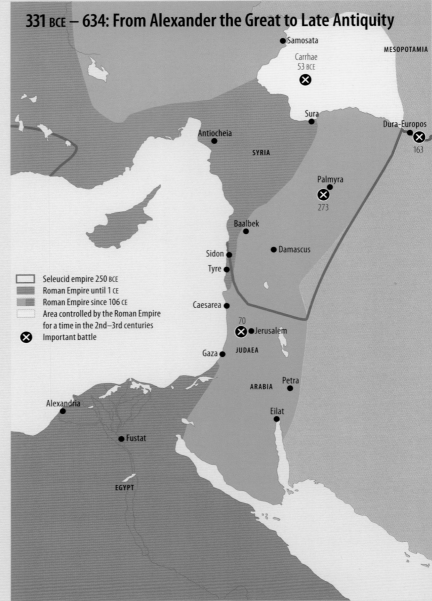

Samosata

MESOPOTAMIA

Carrhae
53 BCE

Sura

Dura-Europos
163

Antiocheia

SYRIA

Palmyra
273

Baalbek

Sidon   Damascus

Tyre

Caesarea

70
Jerusalem

Gaza   JUDAEA

Alexandria

ARABIA   Petra

Eilat

Fustat

EGYPT

Seleucid empire 250 BCE
Roman Empire until 1 CE
Roman Empire since 106 CE
Area controlled by the Roman Empire
for a time in the 2nd–3rd centuries
Important battle

634–945: The Umayyad and Abbasid Caliphates

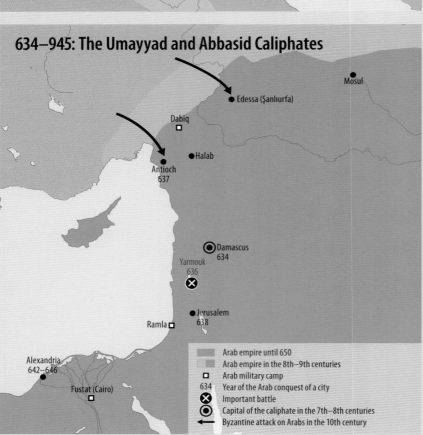

Mosul

Edessa (Şanlıurfa)

Dabiq

Halab

Antioch
637

Damascus
634

Yarmouk
636

Jerusalem
638

Ramla

Alexandria
642–646

Fustat (Cairo)

Arab empire until 650
Arab empire in the 8th–9th centuries
Arab military camp
634   Year of the Arab conquest of a city
Important battle
Capital of the caliphate in the 7th–8th centuries
Byzantine attack on Arabs in the 10th century

ca. 2250 BCE The Levant becomes part of the Akkadian empire.

ca. 1500 BCE Phoenician city-states thrive, bringing about a golden age of culture and trade.

800 BCE The Levant is incorporated into the Assyrian empire.

ca. 500 BCE The Levant becomes part of the Persian Empire.

333–331 BCE Alexander the Great takes control of the Levant following the Battle of Issus.

321 BCE Following the death of Alexander the Great in 323 BCE, the empire is divided, and the Seleucid dynasty takes control of its eastern lands.

168 BCE The Nabateans rule the Levant from Petra, introducing a new golden age.

87–62 BCE Petra reaches the height of its power under King Aretas III, ruling territories as far away as Jerusalem.

64 BCE Syria and Palestine become part of the Roman Empire.

106 CE Rome occupies Nabatean territories.

273 Rome dominates the Syrian desert kingdom of Palmyra.

395 The Levant is absorbed into the Byzantine Empire.

634 Muslims invade and quickly dominate the Levant.

661 Damascus becomes the capital of the Umayyad Caliphate.

750 The Abbasids wrest power from the Umayyads; their dynasty will rule until the 13th century.

1063 The Seljuq Turks invade Syria.

from 1098 Large parts of the Levant are conquered by Crusaders.

1099/1100 Crusaders found the kingdom of Jerusalem.

12th–13th Centuries: Crusader States and the Mamluk Empire

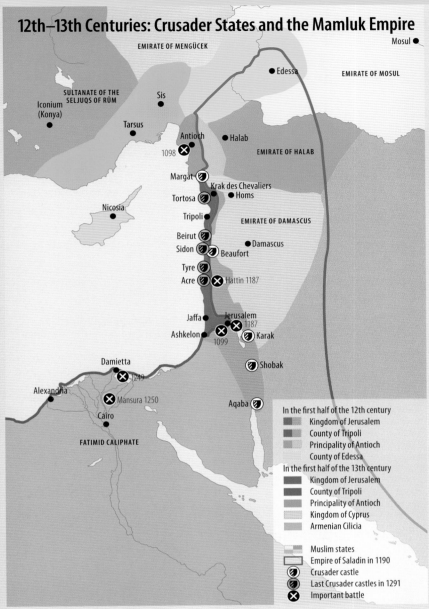

EMIRATE OF MENGÜCEK

Mosul

Edessa

EMIRATE OF MOSUL

SULTANATE OF THE SELJUQS OF RÛM

Iconium (Konya)

Sis

Tarsus

Antioch
1098

Halab

EMIRATE OF HALAB

Margat

Krak des Chevaliers

Tortosa

Homs

Tripoli

EMIRATE OF DAMASCUS

Beirut

Sidon

Beaufort

Damascus

Tyre

Acre

Hattin 1187

Jaffa

Jerusalem
1187

Ashkelon
1099

Karak

Damietta
1249

Shobak

Alexandria

Mansura 1250

Cairo

Aqaba

FATIMID CALIPHATE

Nicosia

In the first half of the 12th century
- Kingdom of Jerusalem
- County of Tripoli
- Principality of Antioch
- County of Edessa

In the first half of the 13th century
- Kingdom of Jerusalem
- County of Tripoli
- Principality of Antioch
- Kingdom of Cyprus
- Armenian Cilicia

- Muslim states
- Empire of Saladin in 1190
- Crusader castle
- Last Crusader castles in 1291
- Important battle

1350–1517: Under Egyptian Rule

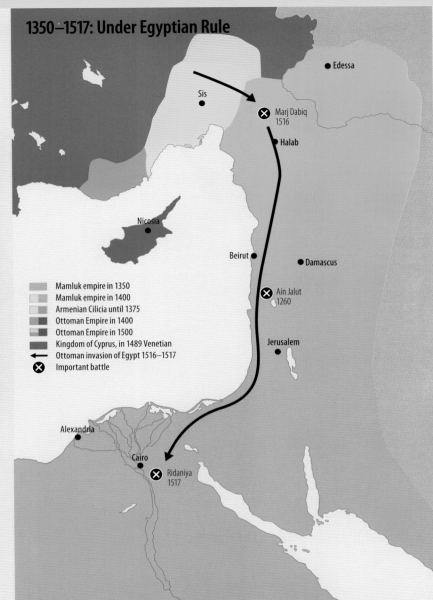

Edessa

Sis

Marj Dabiq
1516

Halab

Nicosia

Beirut

Damascus

Ain Jalut
1260

Jerusalem

- Mamluk empire in 1350
- Mamluk empire in 1400
- Armenian Cilicia until 1375
- Ottoman Empire in 1400
- Ottoman Empire in 1500
- Kingdom of Cyprus, in 1489 Venetian
- Ottoman invasion of Egypt 1516–1517
- Important battle

Alexandria

Cairo

Ridaniya
1517

1104 The duchy of Tripoli is founded in northern Palestine.

1174 Sultan Saladin conquers Damascus.

1187 Sultan Saladin defeats the Crusaders at the Battle of Hattin, returning Jerusalem to Muslim control.

1260 Syria is ruled by the Mamluk empire.

1517 Ottoman Sultan Selim I takes control of Syria and Palestine. The Levantine harbors become the primary departure point for the Ottoman navy.

1820 Egyptian governor Muhammad Ali takes advantage of the decline of the Ottoman Empire to advance his own interests in the Levant.

1841 The Egyptian army withdraws as national liberation movements in Lebanon and Syria gain force.

1861 Lebanon gains its autonomy.

The Levant is an imprecise geographic/historic term that can apply to the entire Near East, or to the part of it presently controlled by Lebanon, Jordan, Syria and Israel. The region attracted the interest of all the great civilizations of the ancient world. Its absorption into the Ottoman Empire brought a deceptive stability. During the colonial period, England and France competed for control of the volatile region.

The Phoenicians were a Semitic group settled on the Syrian coast. Bold craftsmen, merchants and sailors, they controlled trade throughout the Mediterranean, establishing monopolies on the supply of purple dye and lumber from the famous cedars of Lebanon. During the 10th century, Phoenicians founded trade colonies throughout the Mediterranean, including the famous city of Carthage.

Petra, a city hewn out of rock, was the capital of the kingdom of the Nabateans in what is today Jordan. Most of the city was cut into sandstone cliffs. At its greatest extent in 62 BCE, Petra had as many as 30,000 inhabitants. The city was abandoned after a catastrophic earthquake in the 6th century. It is now considered one of the wonders of the world.

1517–1918: Under Ottoman Rule

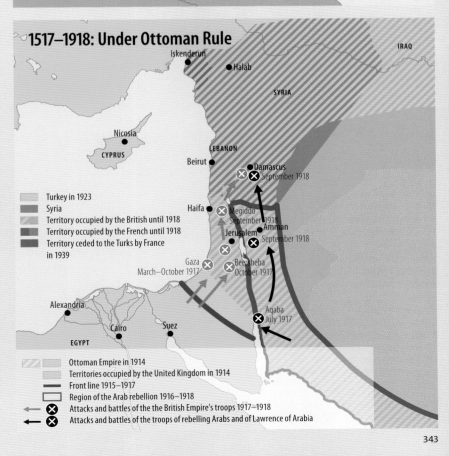

İskenderun

Halab

IRAQ

SYRIA

Nicosia

CYPRUS

LEBANON

Beirut

Damascus
September 1918

Haifa

Megiddo
September 1918

Jerusalem

Amman
September 1918

Gaza
March–October 1917

Beersheba
October 1917

Alexandria

Cairo

Suez

Aqaba
July 1917

EGYPT

- Turkey in 1923
- Syria
- Territory occupied by the British until 1918
- Territory occupied by the French until 1918
- Territory ceded to the Turks by France in 1939

- Ottoman Empire in 1914
- Territories occupied by the United Kingdom in 1914
- Front line 1915–1917
- Region of the Arab rebellion 1916–1918
- Attacks and battles of the the British Empire's troops 1917–1918
- Attacks and battles of the troops of rebelling Arabs and of Lawrence of Arabia

The Levant – Syria, Lebanon and Jordan from 1918 to the Present

Today

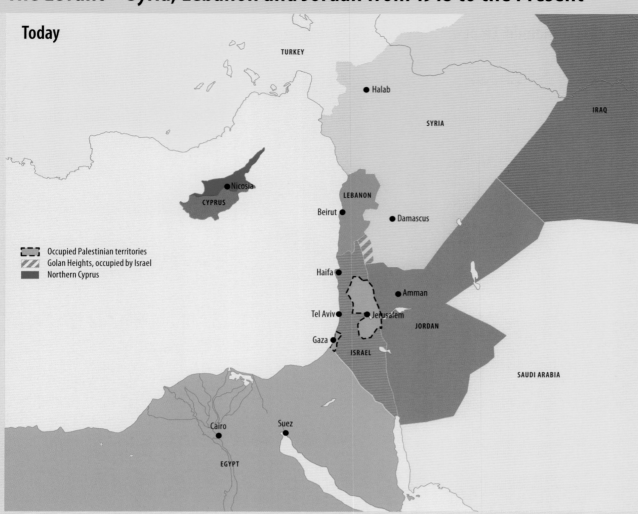

Occupied Palestinian territories
Golan Heights, occupied by Israel
Northern Cyprus

TURKEY

CYPRUS
· Nicosia

· Halab

SYRIA

IRAQ

LEBANON
Beirut ·
· Damascus

Haifa ·

· Amman

Tel Aviv ·
Jerusalem
JORDAN
Gaza ·
ISRAEL
SAUDI ARABIA

· Cairo
· Suez

EGYPT

1918 Syria and Lebanon fall under French administration.

1923 Transjordan is founded as a nation-state under British administration.

1925 Lebanon gains its independence from Syria.

1944 Lebanon gains its independence from France.

May 1946 The independent kingdom of Jordan is formed under the rule of Abdullah I.

April 1946 Syria gains its independence.

from 1948 Jordan takes in thousands of Palestinian refugees.

1951 King Abdallah of Jordan is murdered in Jerusalem by Palestinian nationalists.

1952–1999 King Hussein II ascends to the throne of Jordan, eventually promoting peaceful relations with Israel.

1958 The Lebanon crisis disrupts the Middle East.

1958–1961 Syria briefly becomes part of the United Arab Republic (UAR) with Egypt.

Civil War in Lebanon and the Conflict with Israel (1975–2006)

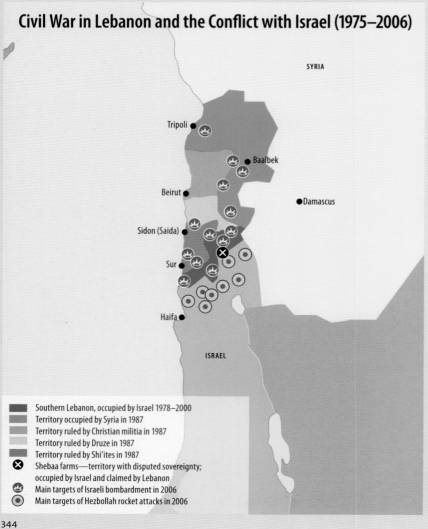

SYRIA

Tripoli ·
Baalbek
Beirut ·
· Damascus
Sidon (Saida) ·
Sur ·
Haifa ·
ISRAEL

Southern Lebanon, occupied by Israel 1978–2000
Territory occupied by Syria in 1987
Territory ruled by Christian militia in 1987
Territory ruled by Druze in 1987
Territory ruled by Shi'ites in 1987
⊗ Shebaa farms—territory with disputed sovereignty; occupied by Israel and claimed by Lebanon
⊕ Main targets of Israeli bombardment in 2006
◎ Main targets of Hezbollah rocket attacks in 2006

Lebanon Today: Religions

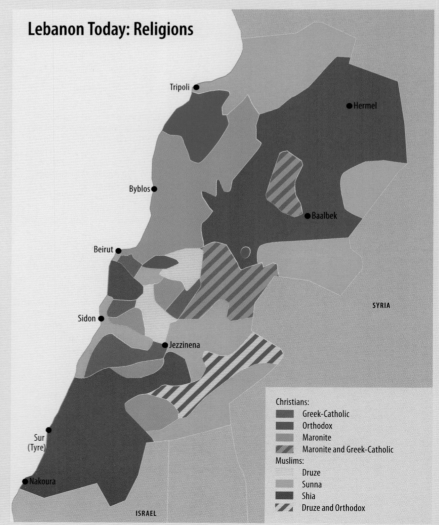

Tripoli ·
· Hermel
Byblos ·
· Baalbek
Beirut ·
Sidon ·
· Jezzinena
SYRIA
Sur (Tyre) ·
· Nakoura
ISRAEL

Christians:
Greek-Catholic
Orthodox
Maronite
Maronite and Greek-Catholic
Muslims:
Druze
Sunna
Shia
Druze and Orthodox

1970 During "Black September," King Hussein disarms Palestinian terrorist groups in Jordan.

1970–2000 The Ba'th Party, led by Hafiz al-Assad, institutes authoritarian rule in Syria.

1973 Syria declares war on Israel.

1975–1990 The Lebanese Civil War breaks out.

1976 Syria occupies part of southern Lebanon.

1982 Israel occupies part of southern Lebanon until 2000. Maronite Christian militias massacre Palestinian refugees in the Sabra and Shatila camps. The Syrian air force bombs Islamic separatists in the city of Hama.

1991 Syrian recognizes Lebanese independence.

1994 Israel enters peace talks with Jordan.

1999 Abdullah II becomes king of Jordan.

2000 Bashar al-Assad succeeds his father as president of Syria.

2005 Lebanese Prime Minister Rafiq al-Hariri is murdered in Lebanon. The Syrian army withdraws.

2006 Conflict continues along the Lebanese-Israeli border, with Israel bombing Lebanese targets.

Lebanon

Lebanon is one of the youngest nations in the Middle East, having gained its independence only in 1944. The multicultural nation is made up of Maronite Christians and Muslims. The once prosperous country known as the "Switzerland of the Middle East" has been under near-permanent military attack since the 1970s due to the Lebanese Civil War, terrorist actions, attacks by Israel and ongoing conflict between Maronite Christian and Druze militias. Many Lebanese are Druze, a Muslim sect with secret teachings and a belief system revolving around reincarnation.

King Hussein II of Jordan (1935–1999)

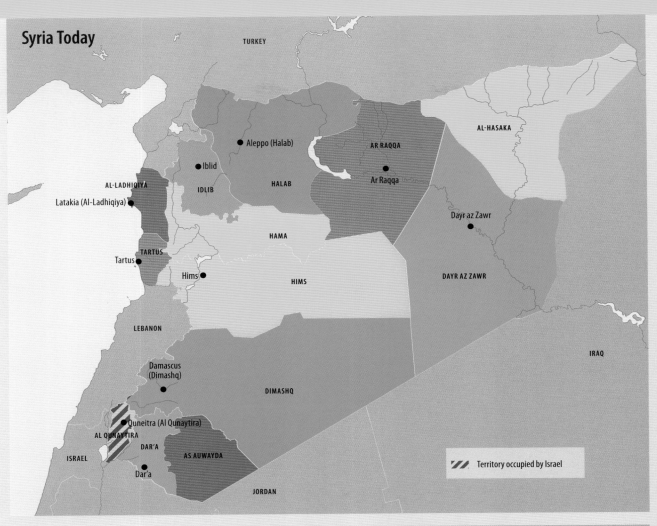

Syria Today

TURKEY

AL-HASAKA

Aleppo (Halab)

AR RAQQA

Iblid

HALAB

Ar Raqqa

AL-LADHIQIYA

IDLIB

Latakia (Al-Ladhiqiya)

Dayr az Zawr

HAMA

DAYR AZ ZAWR

Tartus

TARTUS

Hims

HIMS

LEBANON

IRAQ

Damascus (Dimashq)

DIMASHQ

Quneitra (Al Qunaytira)

AL QUNAYTIRA

DAR'A

AS AUWAYDA

ISRAEL

Dar'a

JORDAN

▨ Territory occupied by Israel

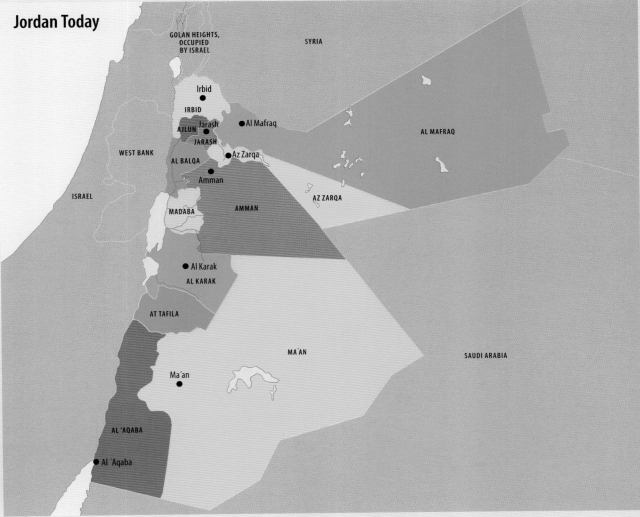

Jordan Today

GOLAN HEIGHTS, OCCUPIED BY ISRAEL

SYRIA

Irbid

IRBID

AJLUN

Jarash

Al Mafraq

AL MAFRAQ

JARASH

WEST BANK

Az Zarqa

AL BALQA

Amman

AZ ZARQA

ISRAEL

MADABA

AMMAN

Al Karak

AL KARAK

AT TAFILA

MA'AN

SAUDI ARABIA

Ma'an

AL 'AQABA

Al 'Aqaba

345

The Arabian Peninsula

ca. 600: Pre-Islamic Arabia

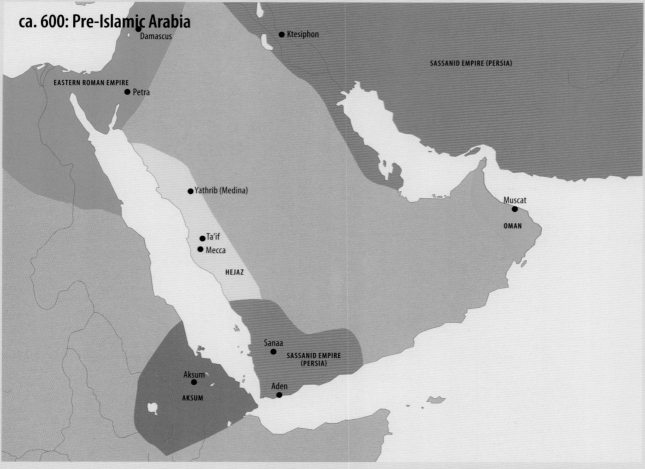

Caravan and trade routes have crossed the Arabian Peninsula for millennia, providing a link between Asia and Africa. Southern Arabia has long been the site of powerful empires.

1500 BCE Domestication of the camel increases the trade in frankincense along some of the oldest caravan routes in the world.

900 BCE–525 CE The ancient Arabian kingdoms of Saba, Qataban, Ma'in, Hadhramaut and Himyar flourish in the south.

~0 The Roman Empire names the fertile region of Yemen *Arabia Felix* ("fortunate Arabia").

525 The Ethiopian kingdom of Aksum conquers part of Yemen.

622–632 The Prophet Muhammad unites the Arabian tribes under Islam.

from 632 The caliphs, successors of Muhammad, spread Islamic culture from Spain to India from their capital cities of Damascus and (later) Baghdad.

901–1962 The Zaidi Imams (Fiver Shi'ites) rule in Yemen.

1154 The royal dynasty of Oman is founded.

15th century Portuguese traders arrive in Arabian ports.

1517 Ottoman forces under Selim I occupy what are today Saudi Arabia and Yemen.

1538–1635 Aden becomes an important naval base for the Ottoman fleet.

1602 Portuguese traders in Bahrain are driven out by Persia, leading to an increase in Persian influence in the Gulf.

1650 Oman regains its autonomy.

1735 The Saud dynasty, led by Muhammad Al-Saud, rises to power. Wahhabism, a conservative form of Islam, becomes the state religion.

1744–1818 The first Saudi state is founded.

1744–1861 Oman becomes a sultanate.

1747–1780 Bedouin pirates sailing out of Qawasim in what is today the United Arab Emirates rule large parts of the Gulf.

1756 The Al-Sabah dynasty comes to power, and has continued to rule Kuwait to the present day.

1761 Dubai is founded.

1783 Bahrain gains its independence under the Al-Khalifa dynasty.

1000: Islamic Empires

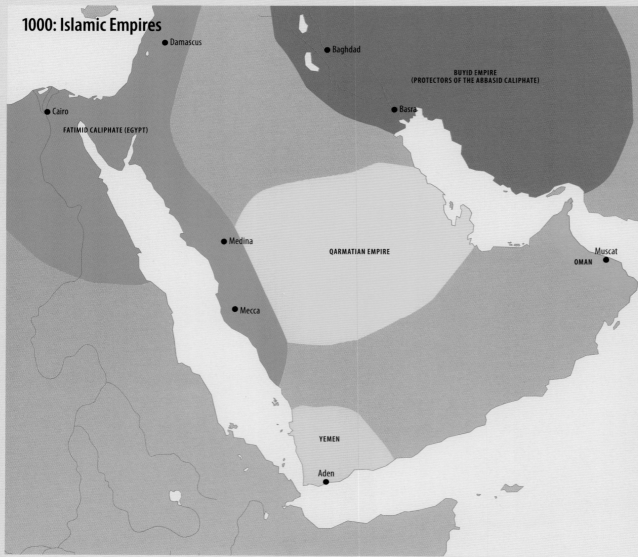

1805/06 Bedouin tribes united by the Saudis liberate Mecca and Medina from Ottoman rule.

1811–1818 The Ottoman-Saudi War breaks out, ending with the total defeat of Saudi forces.

1824–1884 The second Saudi state forms and lasts sixty years.

1834–1839 British influence over Yemen increases. South Yemen remains a British colony until 1967, while North Yemen becomes independent of the Ottoman Empire during World War I.

1861 Bahrain falls under the influence of Great Britain.

1867 Qatar becomes an autonomous emirate within the British sphere of influence.

1883 Abu Dhabi is founded.

1884 The Bedouin Shammar tribe drives the Saud family to Kuwait, where they will live in exile for twenty years.

1899 Kuwait falls under British influence.

1902 Abdulaziz Al-Saud besieges the fortress at Riyadh to reclaim his family seat and founds the third Saudi state.

1904–1948 Imam Yahya drives Ottoman forces out of North Yemen, adopting the royal title in 1926.

1914–1962 Northwest Yemen continues to be ruled by the Zaidi imams.

1932 Saudi Arabia becomes a monarchy under Abdulaziz Al-Saud.

1939–1945 Saudi Arabia declares its neutrality in World War II.

1945 The Arab League is founded.

1951 The British protectorate of Oman is abolished.

1962 Northern Yemen is renamed the Yemen Arab Republic.

1963 Saudi Arabia abolishes slavery.

1964–1975 Faisal, son of King Abdulaziz, becomes the monarch of Saudia Arabia and advocates a program of controlled reform.

1967 Southern Yemen falls under Communist rule.

1971 Oman, Qatar, Bahrain and the United Arab Emirates gain independence.

1979 War breaks out between northern and southern Yemen.

1982–2005 Fahd, a younger son of King Abdulaziz, becomes king of Saudi Arabia, taking the title "Protector of the Holy Cities (of Mecca and Medina)."

1990 Yemen is reunited. Iraqi forces occupy Kuwait.

1991 Kuwait is freed with support from a coalition led by American troops.

from 1992 Fundamentalist trends gather force in Saudi Arabia. Islamic law (sharia) is introduced. Saudi funds support Palestinian refugees and possibly Palestinian suicide bombers.

2000 The Treaty of Jeddah settles a longstanding border dispute between Saudi Arabia and Yemen.

2005 Abdullah bin Abdulaziz becomes king of Saudi Arabia.

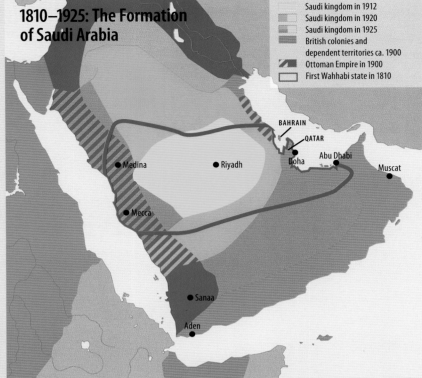

1810–1925: The Formation of Saudi Arabia

Saudi kingdom in 1912
Saudi kingdom in 1920
Saudi kingdom in 1925
British colonies and dependent territories ca. 1900
Ottoman Empire in 1900
First Wahhabi state in 1810

BAHRAIN
QATAR
Doha Abu Dhabi
Muscat
Medina • Riyadh
• Mecca
• Sanaa
Aden

Abdullah ibn Abdulaziz (1924–)

Osama bin Laden (1957–) was born in Riyadh, Saudi Arabia, into a prosperous family of businessmen. As leader of the terrorist organization al-Qaeda, he directed the terrorist attacks on the United States that took place on September 11, 2001. Prior to that he had financially supported the Afghani mujahideen (Islamic resistance fighters) following the Soviet invasion of Afghanistan.

After 1967: Petroleum Resources in the Arabian Peninsula

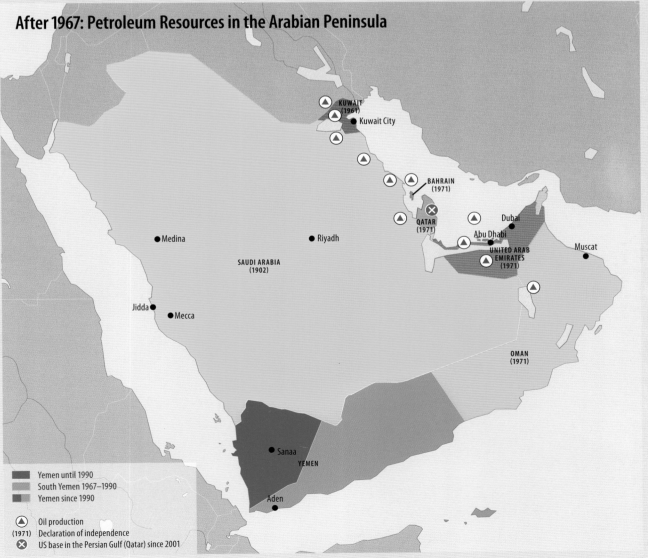

KUWAIT (1961)
Kuwait City
BAHRAIN (1971)
QATAR (1971)
Dubai
Abu Dhabi
UNITED ARAB EMIRATES (1971)
Muscat
Medina • Riyadh
SAUDI ARABIA (1902)
Jidda • Mecca
OMAN (1971)
• Sanaa
YEMEN
Aden

Yemen until 1990
South Yemen 1967–1990
Yemen since 1990

Oil production
(1971) Declaration of independence
US base in the Persian Gulf (Qatar) since 2001

OIL AND ENERGY

Petroleum Production in 1970

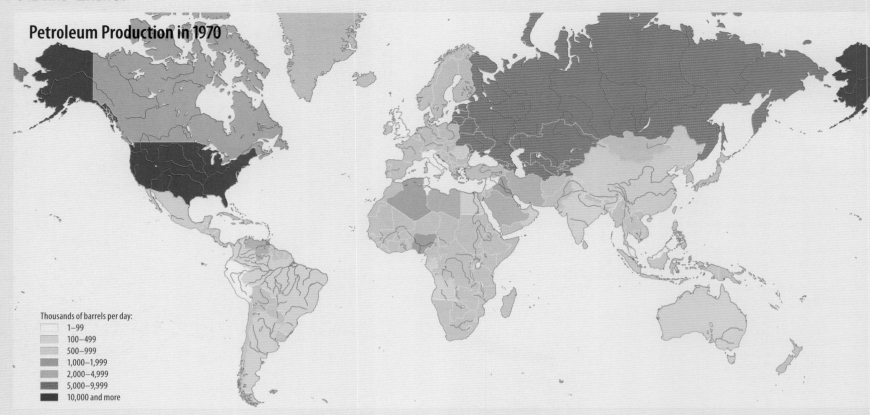

Thousands of barrels per day:
- 1–99
- 100–499
- 500–999
- 1,000–1,999
- 2,000–4,999
- 5,000–9,999
- 10,000 and more

The world's petroleum reserves are estimated at between 1.25 and 3 billion barrels (1 barrel is equal to 42 US gallons, or 159 liters). All the oil on Earth would fill a lake 43 miles (70 km) in diameter and 330 feet (100 m) deep. That is equivalent to 10 billion people each filling a 13-gallon (50-liter) tank at the gas station a thousand times. If gasoline cost roughly US$8 a gallon (€2 per liter) over the next century, the bill at the gas pump would be nearly 1.4 quadrillion dollars (that's 15 zeros), or 1 quadrillion euros. To pay for all that fossil fuel, every individual on the planet would have to pay US$140,000 (€100,000).

The total revenues from petroleum production amount to about 200 times the cost of the recent worldwide financial crisis of 2008. Approximately half of that revenue flowed into the Middle East. The three other regions that are large-scale petroleum producers are Russia, Latin America and Africa. Oil has brought unimaginable wealth to the Arab world, and it also provides parts of Africa and South America with an opportunity to break the cycle of poverty.

4000 BCE Petroleum products, primarily in the form of tar and pitch, are used to waterproof ship planks in Mesopotamia.

1852 Petroleum refining is invented.

1857 Drilling for oil begins in Germany, near Celle.

1859 Edwin Drake drills the first productive oil well in Titusville, Pennsylvania.

1870 John D. Rockefeller founds Standard Oil company.

1904 John Paul Getty begins drilling in Oklahoma.

1907 Royal Dutch Shell is founded.

1911 The United States Supreme Court calls for Standard Oil to be broken up into smaller companies. Mobil Oil and Standard Oil of New Jersey (ESSO) are formed. They will reunite in 1999 as Exxon Mobil.

Petroleum Production in 2008

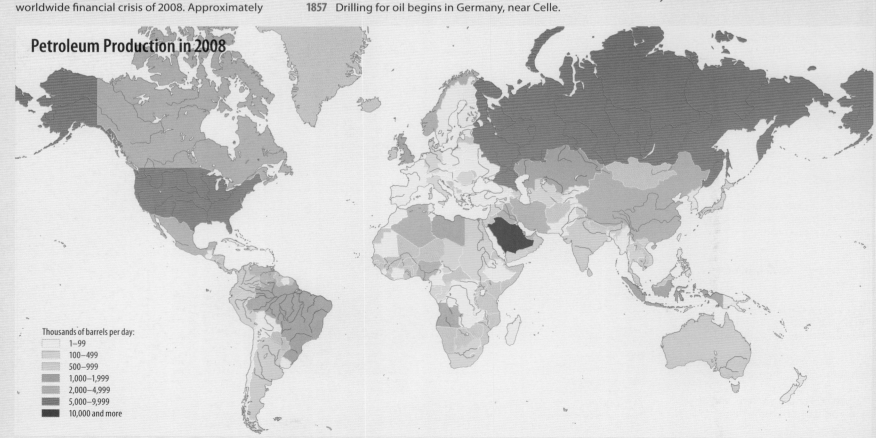

Thousands of barrels per day:
- 1–99
- 100–499
- 500–999
- 1,000–1,999
- 2,000–4,999
- 5,000–9,999
- 10,000 and more

Petroleum Reserves in 2008

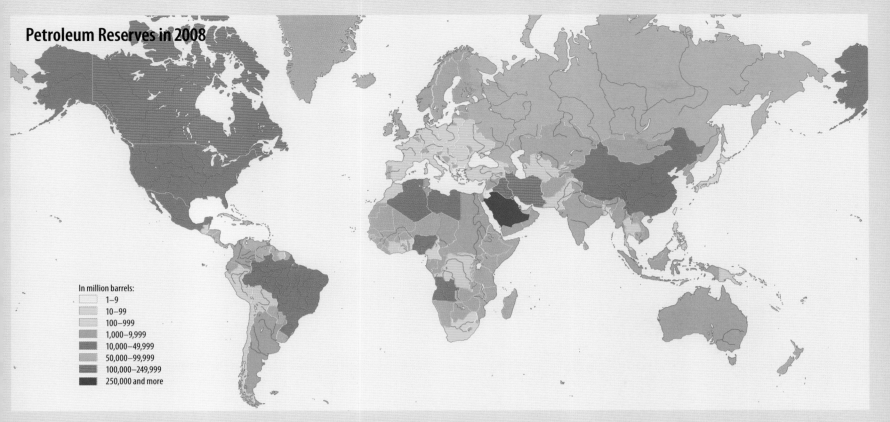

In million barrels:
- 1–9
- 10–99
- 100–999
- 1,000–9,999
- 10,000–49,999
- 50,000–99,999
- 100,000–249,999
- 250,000 and more

1913 Just 5.2 percent of the world's energy needs are met by petroleum and natural gas.

1917 British Petroleum is founded.

1930 Petroleum is discovered in the Arabian Peninsula.

1938 24.4 percent of the energy consumed in the world is provided by petroleum.

1960 Petroleum accounts for 69.2 percent of the energy consumed in the world. The Organization of Petroleum Exporting Countries (OPEC) is formed.

1973/1979–1980 The first and second oil crises: OPEC dramatically raises the price of oil and at times stops exporting to Western countries, causing dramatic shortages and price increases in Europe and America.

2003–2006 Giant pipelines running from Russia to Baku, Azerbaijan, increase Russia's role in petroleum production.

2004 Critics accuse US President George W. Bush of invading Iraq in order to control Iraq's oil fields.

2060–2120 Estimated period in which current petroleum reserves will be depleted

Development of Price per Barrel

1865: US $105
1900: US $33
1940: US $27
1980: US $90
2008: US $150
end of 2008:
  ca. US $50

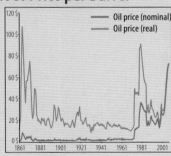

Oil price (nominal)
Oil price (real)

Nuclear Power Plants 2000–2008

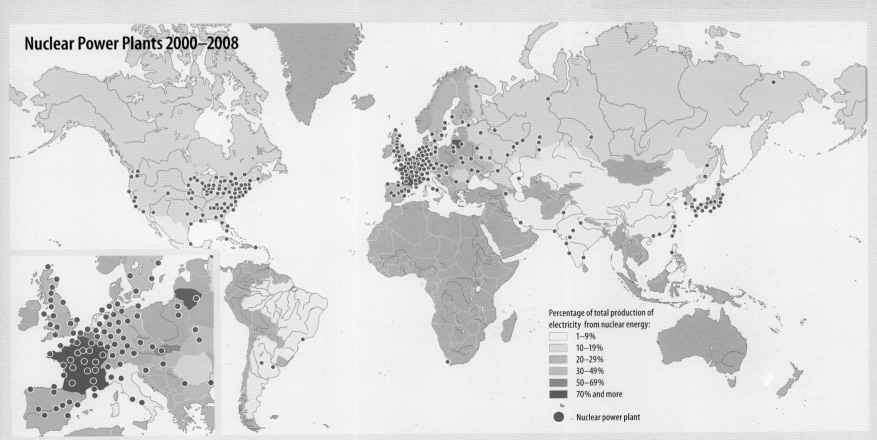

Percentage of total production of electricity from nuclear energy:
- 1–9%
- 10–19%
- 20–29%
- 30–49%
- 50–69%
- 70% and more

● Nuclear power plant

Iraq and Kuwait Until the 17th Century

3rd Millennium BCE: Sumer, Akkad and Elam

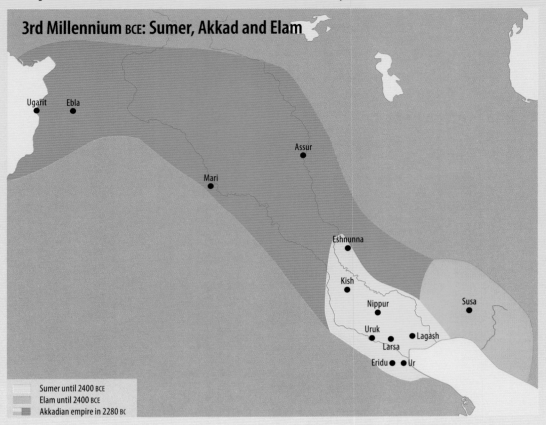

Sumer until 2400 BCE
Elam until 2400 BCE
Akkadian empire in 2280 BC

2nd Millennium BCE: Babylonian Empire

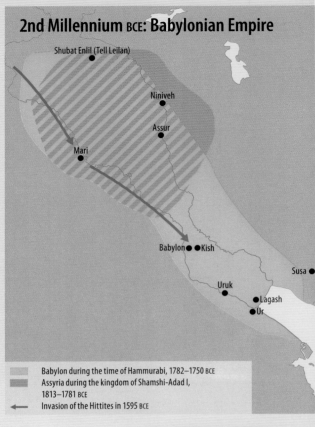

Babylon during the time of Hammurabi, 1782–1750 BCE
Assyria during the kingdom of Shamshi-Adad I, 1813–1781 BCE
Invasion of the Hittites in 1595 BCE

7th–6th Centuries BCE: Assyrian and Neo-Babylonian Empires

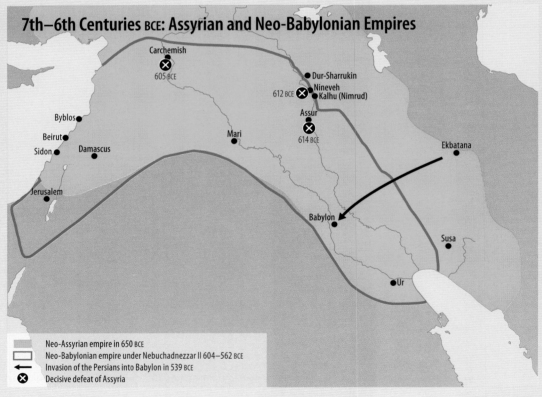

Neo-Assyrian empire in 650 BCE
Neo-Babylonian empire under Nebuchadnezzar II 604–562 BCE
Invasion of the Persians into Babylon in 539 BCE
Decisive defeat of Assyria

4th–1st Centuries BCE: Greeks and Persians

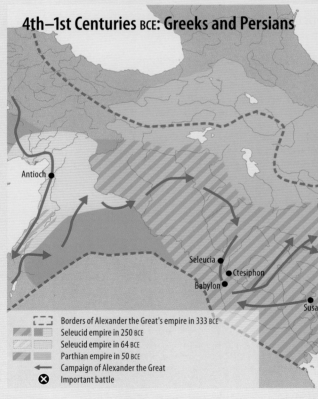

Borders of Alexander the Great's empire in 333 BCE
Seleucid empire in 250 BCE
Seleucid empire in 64 BCE
Parthian empire in 50 BCE
Campaign of Alexander the Great
Important battle

Iraq is where the most ancient human cultures in the world developed. Medieval Baghdad became a flourishing center of science and other scholarly disciplines during the Abbasid Caliphate, between 750 and the mid-13th century.

~3400 BCE The first city-states form. Uruk emerges as the largest and most powerful of them.

~3000 BCE The Sumerians settle in Mesopotamia.

2334–2154 BCE The Akkadian empire arises, based in the city of Akkad.

1894–1595 BCE The Old Babylonian empire

1782–1750 BCE Hammurabi, author of the famous Code of Hammurabi, one of the first code of laws, rules in Babylon and extends his empire.

1595 BCE The Hittites invade Mesopotamia from Anatolia, ousting the Babylonian rulers.

626–539 BCE Neo-Babylonian Empire

604–562 BCE The Babylonian Empire reaches its greatest extent during the reign of King Nebuchadnezzar II.

605 BCE Nebuchadnezzar II defeats the Egyptians in the Battle of Carchemish.

539 BCE Persian armies invade Mesopotamia.

539–330 BCE The Achaemenid Persian Empire rules Mesopotamia.

from 490 BCE The Persians invade Greece.

333 BCE Alexander defeats the Persians at the Battle of Issus.

331 BCE Alexander defeats the Persians in the decisive Battle of Gaugamela.

330–312 BCE Persia, including what is now Iraq, becomes part of Alexander's empire.

312–250 BCE The Seleucid empire rules Mesopotamia.

247 BCE The Parthian empire is founded.

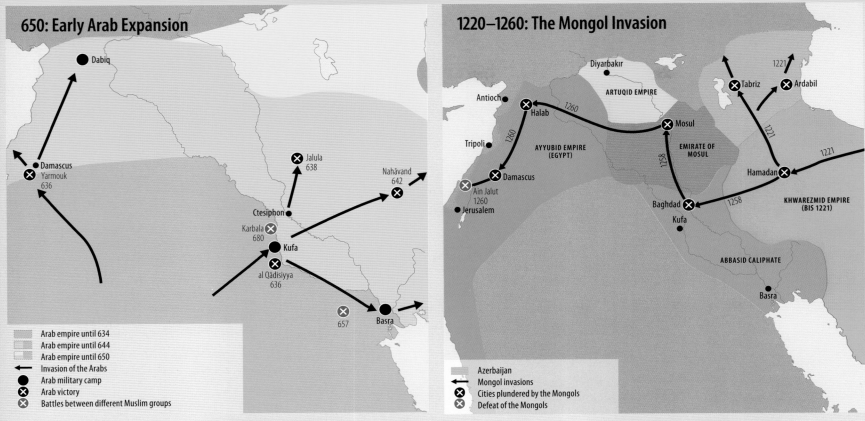

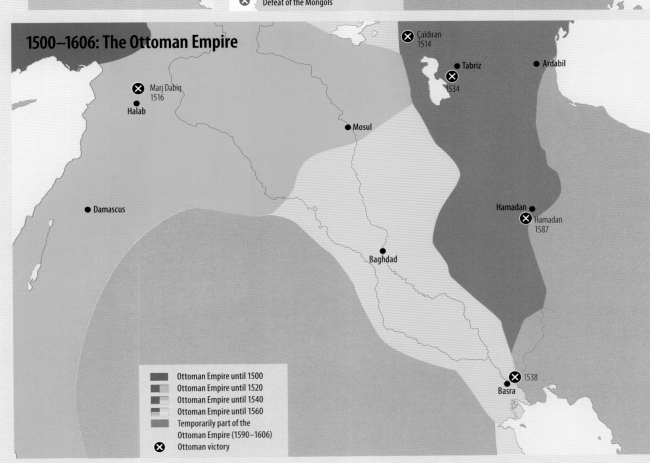

115 CE Roman forces conquer some parts of Mesopotamia.

224–627 The Sassanid empire rules Mesopotamia.

637 The Battle of Kadesh gives Arabs their first victory against the Sassanids.

642 An Arab victory in the Battle of Nahavand marks the end of the Sassanid empire.

680 The Battle of Karbala ends with the murder of the Shi'ite leadership.

762–1055 The city of Baghdad is founded by Caliph al-Mansur, leading to an Abbasid golden age.

945–1055 The Buyids, a Shi'ite military dynasty, become the real power in the region.

from 1055 Baghdad is conquered by the Seljuq Togrul Beg. The Seljuqs and succeeding Turkish dynasties become protectors of the Baghdad caliphs.

1258 Mongols led by Hulegu Khan invade Baghdad, ruling as the Il-Khanid dynasty.

1401 Baghdad is destroyed by Timur (Tamerlane).

1534 Mesopotamia is annexed by the Ottoman Empire.

Ruling Dynasties of Iraq (Islamic period)

661–750	Umayyad Caliphate	1258–1335	Il-Khanid dynasty (Mongols)	1831–1918	Ottoman occupation
749/50–1258	Abbasid Caliphate (after 932/45 in name only)	1336–1432	Jalayirids (only part of the region in late years)	1918–1921	British Mandate Territory
932/45–1055	Buyid dynasty (protectors of the caliphate)	1411–1467	Kara Koyunlu (Black Sheep Turkomans)	1921–1958	Hashemite dynasty
950–980/1121	Hasanwayhid principality	1467–1501	Ak Koyunlu (White Sheep Turkomans)	1958–1979	Military dictatorships
1055–1187	The great Seljuq dynasty (protectors of the caliphate)	1501–1534	Safavid dynasty	1979–2003	Saddam Hussein
1187–1220	Khwarezm-Shahs (protectors of the caliphate)	1534–1704	Ottoman occupation	2003–2005	Transitional government
		1704–1831	Iraqi Mamluks	since 2005	Democratically elected government

Iraq and Kuwait: 18th Century to the Present

1896–1932: British and French Mandate Territories

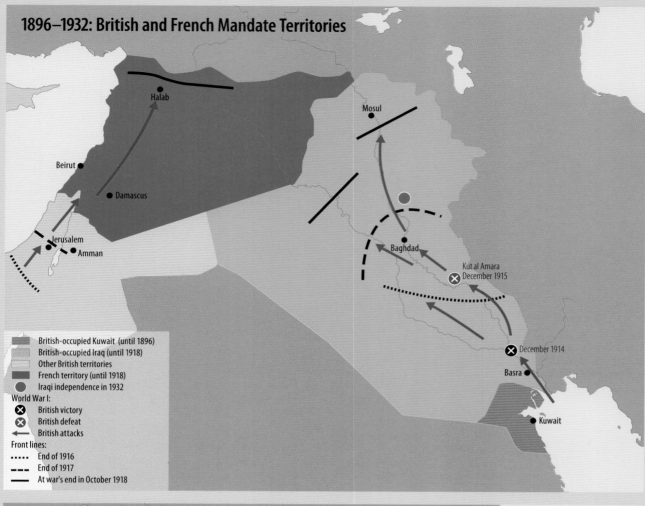

Legend:

- British-occupied Kuwait (until 1896)
- British-occupied Iraq (until 1918)
- Other British territories
- French territory (until 1918)
- ● Iraqi independence in 1932

World War I:
- ⊗ British victory
- ⊗ British defeat
- ← British attacks

Front lines:
- ⋯⋯ End of 1916
- --- End of 1917
- — At war's end in October 1918

1980–1988: The Iran-Iraq War

Legend:

- Iraq 1980
- Furthest incursion of Iraqi troops into Iran until 1982
- Furthest incursion of Iranian troops into Iraq 1984–1986
- Kuwait
- ⊙ Bombed city
- ⊗ Iraqi use of poison gas in Kurdish regions
- ← Iranian attacks against tankers in the Persian Gulf

1756 The al-Sabah family comes to power in Kuwait; they continue to rule today.

end of the 19th century European influence continues.

1899 Sheikh Mubarak Al Sabah signs a territorial agreement between Kuwait and Iraq and perpetuates British control of Kuwait affairs.

1914 World War I begins. The British occupy Baghdad and the Persian oilfields.

1920 The British unite the provinces of Basra, Mosul and Baghdad to form the new nation of Iraq.

1921 Hashemite Prince Faisal becomes the king of Iraq under British protection.

1930 Large reserves of oil are discovered in Iraq.

1932 Iraq gains its formal independence as a constitutional monarchy.

1939–1945 Iraq sympathizes with Germany during World War II.

1945 Iraq becomes a member of the United Nations and the Arab League.

1958 The Iraqi monarchy collapses after the murder of King Faisal II and his family. A military dictatorship with ties to Soviet Russia comes to power.

1960 OPEC is founded in Baghdad.

1961 Kuwait gains its independence from Great Britain. Iraq declares its right to Kuwaiti territory.

1963 Iraq is forced to recognize Kuwait's sovereignty. The Ba'th Party launches a coup.

1968–2003 The Ba'th Party takes control of the government in Iraq after a second coup.

1972 Iraq signs a friendship agreement with Soviet Russia.

1975 Iraq-Kuwait relations worsen.

1979 Saddam Hussein becomes president of Iraq.

1980–1988 The Iran-Iraq War (or First Persian Gulf War)

1981 Israeli air strikes destroy an Iraqi nuclear reactor under construction.

1988 Saddam Hussein unleashes poison gas attacks in the Kurdish territories of northern Iraq, killing approximately 10,000 people.

Aug. 1, 1990 Iraq occupies Kuwait.

January–February 1991 The (Second) Persian Gulf War: U.S. forces liberate

Kuwait, and Iraqis fire nearly forty Scud missiles at Israel and Saudi Arabia. The UN creates a no-fly zone above Kurdish territories in the north and Shi'ite territories in the south, and imposes international economic sanctions.

1996 Saddam Hussein's son-in-law, who had fled the country, is executed.

1998 British and American forces bombard Iraqi military targets in Operation Desert Fox.

2000–2003 Hans Blix, UN weapons inspector in Iraq, finds no evidence that Iraq possessed weapons of mass destruction, and accuses the United States and Great Britain of human rights violations based on the lack of justification for the invasion.

March 20, 2003 American forces invade Iraq, toppling Saddam Hussein in May. Since then, extremist terrorist groups in Iraq have claimed thousands of victims. US troops are still stationed in Iraq as the country rebuilds.

2005 Parliamentary elections in January are marred by battles between radical Sunni and Shi'ite terrorist organizations.

2005/07 The trial of Saddam Hussein and his top functionaries ends with executions.

The Third Persian Gulf War, also called the War on Iraq or simply the Iraq War, began with an American invasion, supported by troops from forty other countries, legitimized by unsubstantiated claims that Iraq had ties with al-Qaeda and possessed weapons of mass destruction. By May 2003 the fighting had all but ended, and Saddam Hussein was ousted from power. It is estimated that some 400,000 people have lost their lives in the war so far. Many nations did not share President George W. Bush's assessment of the necessity of the war, making Bush one of the more internationally unpopular U.S. presidents in history.

The Ba'th Party (Arab Socialist Renaissance Party) was founded in 1943 by Syrian Christian Arab Michel Aflaq. Its principles include unity, freedom, socialism, pan-Arabism and moderate secularism. It is the dominant political party in Syria, and was the ruling party in Iraq until 2003. In both countries, Ba'th leaders opposed and persecuted Islamic fundamentalists. The Ba'th Party is now banned in Iraq.

Saddam Hussein (1937–2006) ruled Iraq as a brutal dictator. Saddam Hussein became president of Iraq in 1979, and his regime had long enjoyed the support of the United States and other Western countries, which supplied him with arms during the Iran-Iraq War. He instigated both the Iran-Iraq War and the invasion of Kuwait. A hero in the eyes of many Arabs, his politics nonetheless revealed him to be an unscrupulous, ruthless and brutal enforcer of his policies with a tendency toward a cult of personality. After the United States' invasion of Iraq in 2003, he fled Baghdad, only to be captured and condemned to death.

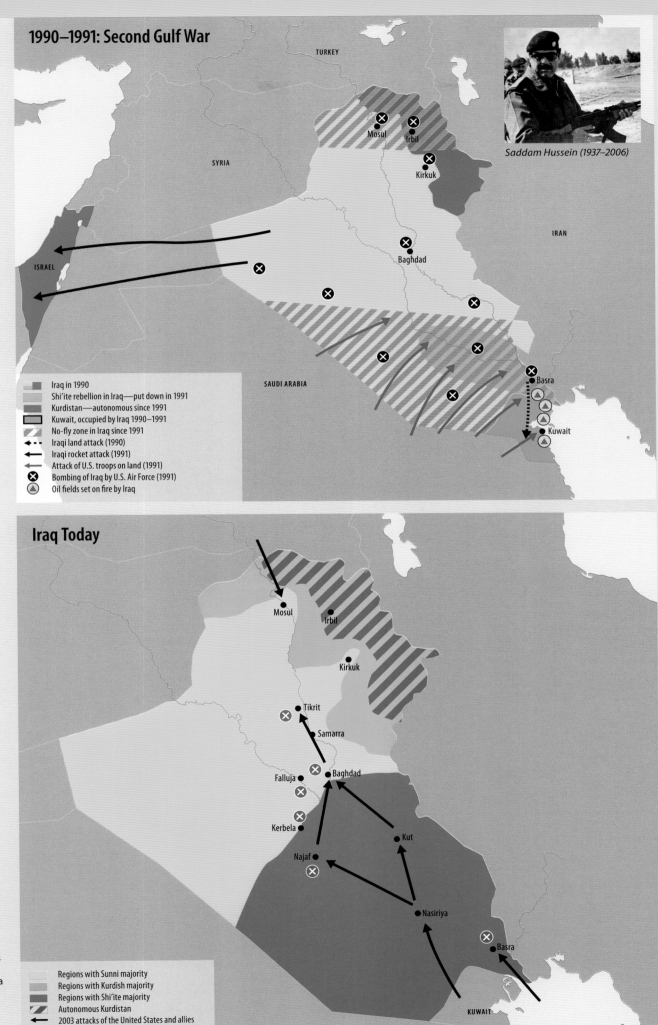

1990–1991: Second Gulf War

Saddam Hussein (1937–2006)

	Iraq in 1990
	Shi'ite rebellion in Iraq—put down in 1991
	Kurdistan—autonomous since 1991
	Kuwait, occupied by Iraq 1990–1991
	No-fly zone in Iraq since 1991
◄┈┈	Iraqi land attack (1990)
◄—	Iraqi rocket attack (1991)
◄—	Attack of U.S. troops on land (1991)
⊗	Bombing of Iraq by U.S. Air Force (1991)
▲	Oil fields set on fire by Iraq

Iraq Today

	Regions with Sunni majority
	Regions with Kurdish majority
	Regions with Shi'ite majority
	Autonomous Kurdistan
—	2003 attacks of the United States and allies
⊗	Main areas of conflict since 2003

Persia / Iran

560–449 BCE: Achaemenid Empire

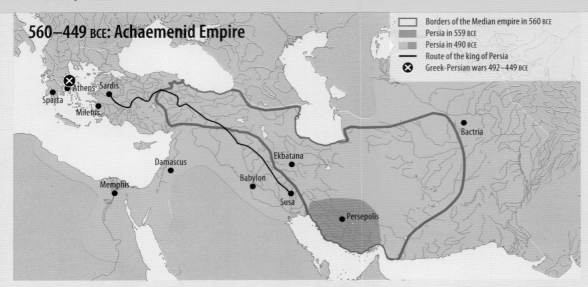

☐	Borders of the Median empire in 560 BCE
	Persia in 559 BCE
	Persia in 490 BCE
⎯	Route of the king of Persia
⊗	Greek-Persian wars 492–449 BCE

Persian/Iranian Ruling Dynasties

ca. 3500–639 BCE	Elamite Empire (kingdom as of 2500 BCE)
728–550 BCE	Median Empire
559–330 BCE	Achaemenid Empire
330–312 BCE	Empire of Alexander the Great
312–141 BCE	Seleucid Empire
247 BCE–224 CE	Parthian Empire (Arsacid Dynasty)
224–638	Sassanid Empire
Islamic Dynasties	
661–750	Umayyad Caliphate
750–819	Abbasid Caliphate
819–1005	Samanid dynasty
945–1038	Buyid dynasty
1040–1187	Great Seljuq Empire
1187–1220/31	Khwarezm-Shah
1252/56–1336	Ilkhans (Mongols)
1244–1383	Kartid dynasty (Khorasan)
1314–1393	Muzaffar dynasty (in the south)
1358–1393/1401	Jalayirid dynasty
1393/1401–1495	Timur Lenk (Tamerlane) and Timurids
1380–1469	Kara Koyunlu ("Black Sheep" Turkomans)
1467–1501	Ak Koyunlu ("White Sheep" Turkomans)
1501–1722/36	Safavid dynasty (shahs)
1736–1796	Nādir Shah and the Afsharid dynasty (after 1747 only in the north)
1750–1779/96	Karim Khan Zand and family (in the south)
1796–1925	Qajar dynasty (shahs)
1925–1979	Pahlavi dynasty (shahs)
1978/79	Iranian Revolution (Islamic Revolution)

Khorasan is the historical name for the expansive region that encompassed parts of Persia, Afghanistan, Tajikistan, Turkmenistan and Uzbekistan from ancient times, but was consolidated under the Sassanids.

Ruhollah Musavi Khomeini (1900 or 1902–1989) is the legal scholar who, in 1961, became a leading Ayatollah (esteemed Twelver Shi'ite cleric) in Iran. He opposed liberal reforms and rejected "Western culture," but was also a sharp opponent of the corrupt regime of the shahs. Forced into exile in 1964 (first in Iraq and after 1978 in France), he returned in triumph in 1979. Although Khomeini served as leader of the Iranian Revolution and spiritual leader for life (*rahbar*) of Iran, he never held an official government title or office.

3500–639 BCE Elamite empire

~1500 BCE Indoeuropean tribes, primarily Scythian, enter Persia.

~728–550 BCE Median empire

559–330 BCE Cyrus the Great, the first "great king" of Persia (559–529 BCE), founds the Achaemenid empire.

522–486 BCE Darius I the Great expands the Achaemenid empire to its greatest extent.

492–449 BCE War erupts between Persia and Greece.

331 BCE Alexander the Great defeats Darius III at the Battle of Gaugamela.

330–312 BCE Alexander's empire extends to Khorasan.

312–141 BCE The Seleucid empire rules Persia.

247 BCE–224 The Arsacid dynasty founds the Parthian empire.

224–638 CE The Sassanid dynasty rules Persia.

260 Shapur I inflicts a crushing defeat on the Romans, taking Emperor Valerian prisoner.

531–579 Khosrau I leads the Sassanid empire into a golden age as an enemy of the Byzantine Empire and victor over the invading Hephthalites (White Huns).

642 Islamic armies defeat Sassanid forces at Nahavand.

661–750 The Umayyad Caliphate rules Persia.

~700 Muslim forces conquer Khorasan.

750–1258 The Abbasid Caliphate rules Persia, but does so in name only after 945.

977–1186 The Ghaznavid dynasty rules Persia, primarily the eastern half after 1045.

1040 Togrul Beg, founder of the Seljuq dynasty, defeats the Ghaznavids in the Battle of Dandanaqan.

1040–1187/94 The Seljuq Turks rule Persia.

1256–1336 Persia is laid waste by the Mongols. It will flourish again under the Mongol Il-Khanid dynasty.

1380 Rival tribal federations, the Ak Koyunlu and Kara Koyunlu ("White Sheep" and "Black Sheep" Turkomans), control most of Persia.

1393–1495 The Timurids rule Persia.

1501–1722 The Safavid dynasty makes Twelver Shi'ism the state religion.

1587–1629 Shah Abbas the Great reigns during the golden age of Safavid rule. The holy city of Esfahān becomes "the pearl of the world."

1736–1747 Nādir Shah conquers Kabul in 1738/1739, and Delhi thereafter.

323–64 BCE: Seleucid Empire

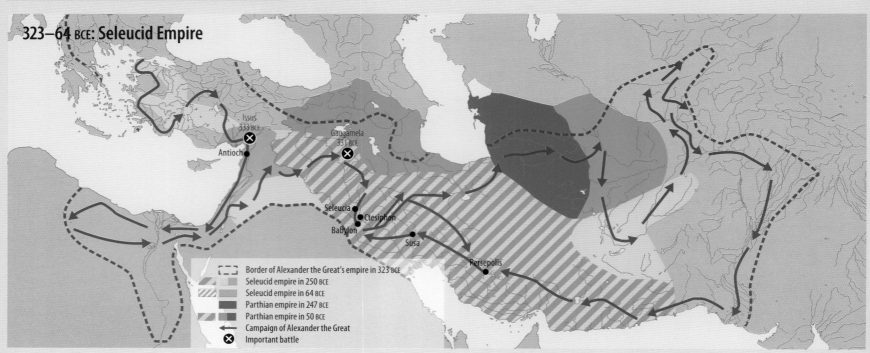

⊏⎓⊐	Border of Alexander the Great's empire in 323 BCE
	Seleucid empire in 250 BCE
	Seleucid empire in 64 BCE
	Parthian empire in 247 BCE
	Parthian empire in 50 BCE
⟵	Campaign of Alexander the Great
⊗	Important battle

600–737: Muslim Conquest

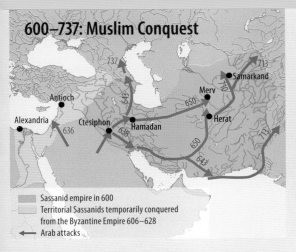

Sassanid empire in 600
Territorial Sassanids temporarily conquered from the Byzantine Empire 606–628
→ Arab attacks

1000–1220: Empire of the Khwarezm-Shahs

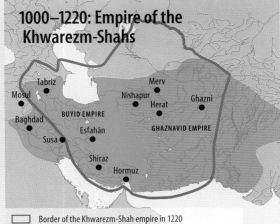

Border of the Khwarezm-Shah empire in 1220

1500–1622: Empire of the Safavid Shahs

Stabilized border between the Ottoman Empire and Persia in the 17th century
Uzbek attacks
⊗ Important defeat of the Safavids

Original territory of the Safavids 1500
Empire of the Safavid dynasty in 1512
Territory conquered by the Ottoman Empire 1514–1606
Disputed territory with the Uzbeks
Portuguese territory 1507–1622

1720–1785: Empire of Nādir Shah

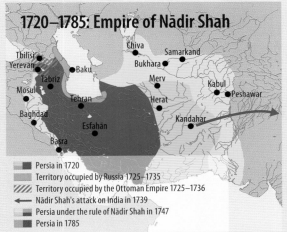

Persia in 1720
Territory occupied by Russia 1725–1735
Territory occupied by the Ottoman Empire 1725–1736
← Nādir Shah's attack on India in 1739
Persia under the rule of Nādir Shah in 1747
Persia in 1785

1800–1946: The Qajar and Pahlavi

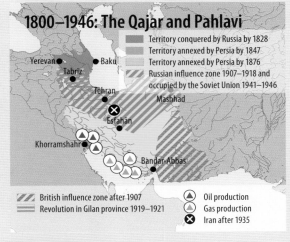

Territory conquered by Russia by 1828
Territory annexed by Persia by 1847
Territory annexed by Persia by 1876
Russian influence zone 1907–1918 and occupied by the Soviet Union 1941–1946

British influence zone after 1907
Revolution in Gilan province 1919–1921
▲ Oil production
▲ Gas production
⊗ Iran after 1935

Today

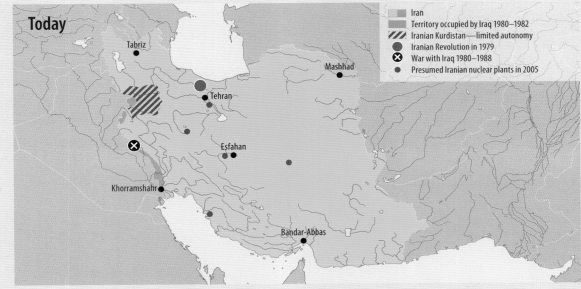

Iran
Territory occupied by Iraq 1980–1982
Iranian Kurdistan—limited autonomy
● Iranian Revolution in 1979
⊗ War with Iraq 1980–1988
● Presumed Iranian nuclear plants in 2005

1750–1779 Karim Khan Zand rules over southern Persia.

1794/96–1925 The Qajar dynasty becomes economically dependent on European nations.

19th century Russian and British influence increases.

1848–1896 Shah Naser od-Din begins a period of liberal, pro-Western reform.

1890 The British monopoly on tobacco leads to unrest, including opposition by Shi'ite clerics.

1906 The Persian parliament is convened for the first time.

1908 Crude oil is discovered in southern Persia.

1914–1918 Persia is occupied by British, Russian and Turkish troops during World War I.

1919 Persia continues to be occupied by Great Britain.

1921 Reza Pahlavi comes to power as Reza Shah Pahlavi.

1925–1979 The Pahlavi dynasty—pro-Western modernizers following the model of President Kemal Atatürk of Turkey—rules Persia.

1935 Iran ("land of the Aryans") replaces Persia as the official name of the country.

1939–1941 Iran collaborates with Hitler's Germany during World War II.

1941 Iran is occupied by Russian and British troops. Mohammad Reza Pahlavi succeeds his father on the throne after Reza Shah Pahlavi is forced to abdicate due to his support for Nazi Germany.

1943 The Tehran Conference to end World War II convenes with heads of state Stalin, Roosevelt and Churchill in attendance.

1951–1953 Mohammad Mosaddeg is elected prime minister. He is later overthrown by the shah with the assistance of the United States CIA.

from 1963 Mohammad Reza Shah Pahlavi begins the White Revolution, including land reform and granting women the right to vote. The shah becomes a puppet of American interests and directs SAVAK, a brutal secret police organization.

1964 Ayatollah Ruhollah Khomeini, a prominent Shi'ite religious leader and fierce opponent of the shah who called for strict adherence to Islamic law in Iran, is forced into exile.

1978 The Iranian Islamic Revolution begins.

1979 The Pahlavi dynasty tumbles, and the shah flees the country. Ayatollah Khomeini returns from exile and declares the Islamic Republic of Iran.

1979–1981 Islamic revolutionaries occupy the American embassy in Tehran, holding more than fifty U.S. citizens hostage for over a year. An American attempt to free the hostages (Operation Eagle Claw) fails miserably in the desert.

1980–1988 The Iran-Iraq War rages.

1981–1989 Ali Khamenei is elected and serves as president of Iraq.

1989 Ayatollah Khamenei takes over spiritual leadership of the country following the death of Ayatollah Khomeini.

1989–1997 Ali Akbar Hashemi Rafsanjani serves as president, steering a more pragmatic course and renewing some economic ties with Western countries.

1997–2005 President Mohammad Khatami attempts to liberalize Iran.

2005 Mahmud Ahmadinejad is elected president, promising Islamic and social welfare reform. Iran's nuclear program and vow to eradicate Israel lead to conflict with the West.

Transcausia

100–70 BCE: Greater Armenian Empire

KOLKHIS
Phasis
Mtskheta
IBERIA
Trapezus
CAUCASIAN ALBANIA
Armavir
LESSER ARMENIA
GREATER ARMENIA
SOPHENE
Van
Tigranakert (Amid)
ATROPATENE

Kingdom of Armenia in 70 BCE

300–387 BCE: Between Rome and Persia

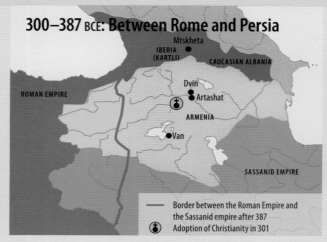

Mtskheta
IBERIA (KARTLI)
CAUCASIAN ALBANIA
ROMAN EMPIRE
Dvin
Artashat
ARMENIA
Van
SASSANID EMPIRE

— Border between the Roman Empire and the Sassanid empire after 387
☩ Adoption of Christianity in 301

1000–1025: Various Kingdoms

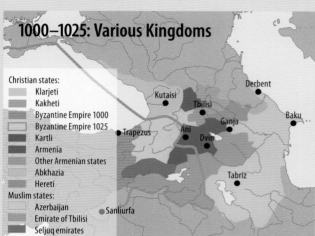

Derbent
Kutaisi
Tbilisi
Baku
Ganja
Trapezus
Ani
Dvin
Tabriz
Sanliurfa

Christian states:
Klarjeti
Kakheti
Byzantine Empire 1000
Byzantine Empire 1025
Kartli
Armenia
Other Armenian states
Abkhazia
Hereti
Muslim states:
Azerbaijan
Emirate of Tbilisi
Seljuq emirates

1200–1450: Georgia

Georgia in 1200
Muslim states

EMPIRE OF TREBIZOND
Kutaisi
Tbilisi
Baku
Trebizond (Trapezus)
Erzurum
Ani
Ganja
Kars
KARABAKH
OTTOMAN EMPIRE
Dvin
Tabriz
Diyarbakir
Urfa
Mosul
EMPIRE OF THE KARA KOYUNLU (BLACK SHEEP TURKMEN)

Georgian states:
Imereti
Samtskhe
Kartli
Kakheti

1780–1878: Under Russian Rule

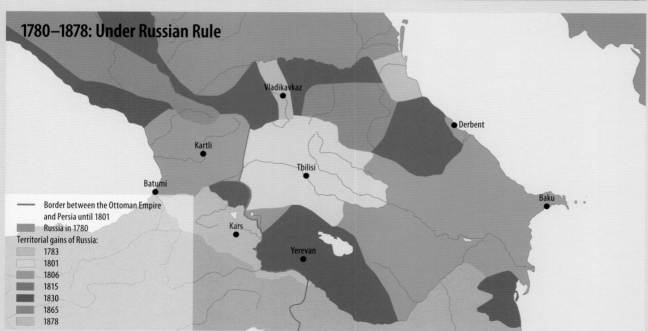

Vladikavkaz
Derbent
Kartli
Tbilisi
Batumi
Baku
Kars
Yerevan

— Border between the Ottoman Empire and Persia until 1801
Russia in 1780
Territorial gains of Russia:
1783
1801
1806
1815
1830
1865
1878

More than thirty nationalities share the oft-disputed territory of the Transcaucasian states of Armenia, Azerbaijan and Georgia. This relatively small area has long been characterized by a wide variety of cultural traditions and religious beliefs.

13th–8th centuries BCE Kingdom of the Diadochi rules in Georgia.

860–547 BCE The kingdom of Urartu controls a large part of what will later be Armenia.

6th century BCE Greater Armenia begins to emerge.

4th century BCE Greater Armenia is an independent nation.

3rd century BCE Georgia is an independent entity.

95–55 BCE Tigranes II the Great, ruler of Armenia, conquers Mesopotamia and Syria, breaking the Seleucids' hold on power in the region and solidifying Armenian unity.

66 BCE Rome conquers Georgia. In the same year, Tiridates I, a Parthian puppet ruler, is crowned by Emperor Nero to reign over Armenia.

301 or 313/14 Christianity becomes the state religion of Armenia.

387 Armenia is divided between the Eastern Roman Empire and the Sassanid empire of Persia.

8th century Arabs take control of southern Transcaucasia, large parts of which remain Christian.

885/86–1071 The kingdom of the Bagratids rises in Armenia.

1068 Multiple Georgian principalities unite to form a single kingdom under Bagrat III.

1080–1342 The independent Armenian kingdom of the Rubenids forms in Cilicia.

1375 Mamluk Turks from Egypt depose the Rubenid ruler.

1385 Timur (Tamerlane), a Turkic Mongol warrior, conquers Georgia.

from the 13th century Transcaucasia falls under the control of the Seljuq Turks, Mongols and later of Persians of the Safavid dynasty.

from 1512 Ottoman armies conquer Georgia, meeting heavy resistance.

1515 The Ottoman Empire conquers western Armenia. Eastern Armenia remains under Persian control.

1770 Russian armies invade Transcaucasia.

1801 Russia absorbs Georgia into the Russian Empire.

1804–1813 Russia battles Persia for control of Transcaucasia. Persia loses most of its territory.

1828–1829 The Russo-Turkish War comes to an end with the Treaty of Adrianople, which grants Russia additional territory in the Caucasus.

1853–1856 The Crimean War rages between Russia and the Ottoman Empire over disputed Caucasus territory.

1875 The Azerbaijan port city of Baku becomes a center of petroleum production.

from 1895/96 Turkish pogroms against Armenians begin.

1911 The Musavat (Muslim Democratic Party) forms in Azerbaijan.

1915 The Young Turk government in Turkey orders genocide against Armenians. As many as 1.5 million Armenians are murdered.

1918 Anti-Soviet revolts begin in Baku, resulting in the formation of the Transcaucasian Democratic Federative Republic in April. In May the federation dissolves into the republics of Azerbaijan, Armenia and Georgia.

1920/21 The Soviet Union invades, creating the Soviet Socialist Republics of Azerbaijan and Armenia, followed by Georgia in 1921.

1922–1936 The Transcaucasian Socialist Federative Soviet Republic forms.

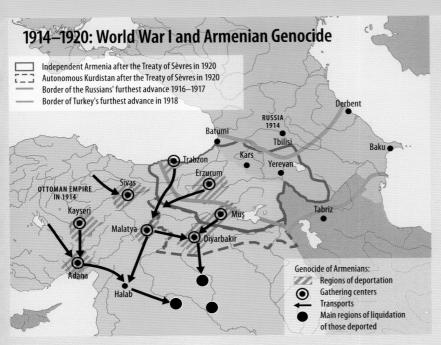

1914–1920: World War I and Armenian Genocide

- Independent Armenia after the Treaty of Sèvres in 1920
- Autonomous Kurdistan after the Treaty of Sèvres in 1920
- Border of the Russians' furthest advance 1916–1917
- Border of Turkey's furthest advance in 1918

RUSSIA 1914

Derbent
Batumi
Tbilisi
Baku
Trabzon
Kars
Yerevan
Erzurum
Sivas
OTTOMAN EMPIRE IN 1914
Kayseri
Muş
Tabriz
Malatya
Diyarbakır
Adana
Halab

Genocide of Armenians:
- Regions of deportation
- ⊙ Gathering centers
- → Transports
- ● Main regions of liquidation of those deported

1914–1956: Soviet Republics

- Russia in 1914
- Territory ceded to Turkey in 1921
- Borders of the Soviet Union after 1922
- Transcaucasian Socialist Federative Soviet Republic 1922–1936
- Georgian Soviet Socialist Republic (after 1936)
- Abkhazia Autonomous Soviet Socialist Republic
- Adjara Autonomous Soviet Socialist Republic
- South Ossetian autonomous oblast
- Armenian Soviet Socialist Republic (after 1936)

Vladikavkaz
Batumi
⊛ Gori (Stalin's birthplace)
Tbilisi
Baku

- Azerbaijan Soviet Socialist Republic (after 1936)
- Autonomous region of Nagorno-Karabakh
- Nakhichevan Autonomous Soviet Socialist Republic
- Deportation of Chechens 1944–1956
- ← Furthest advance of German troops in 1942

1936–1991 Georgia, Armenia and Azerbaijan become independent republics within the Union of Soviet Socialist Republics (USSR).

1987 Armenia demands that Azerbaijan return the territory of Nagorno-Karabakh to Armenian control.

1991 The Transcaucasian republics gain their independence from the USSR.

The Kurds are the largest stateless ethnic group in the world. Kurdish tribes first settled the Iranian highlands in the 2nd century BCE. After World War I, the Treaty of Sèvres promised Kurds their own state, but the parties to the treaty did not follow through. Today, some 28 million Kurds live in Kurdistan, a region that includes parts of Turkey, Syria, Iraq and Iran. Their situation is difficult in each country, but particularly so in Turkey, which has attacked the banned the Kurdistan Workers' Party (PKK) with military force.

1991–1994 War breaks out between Azerbaijan and Armenia over the disputed territory of Nagorno-Karabakh.

1992–1994 The Georgian Civil War erupts over the disputed territories of Abkhazia and South Ossetia.

1992–2003 Eduard Shevardnadze becomes president of Georgia. He is deposed in November 2003.

2003/04 Protests rage in Georgia over disputed election results.

2008 Separatist movements by Abkhazia and South Ossetia destabilize Georgia. Russian-Georgian conflict breaks out in August.

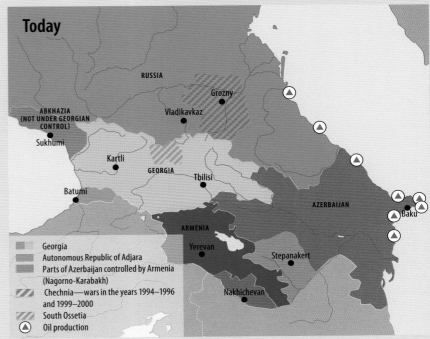

Today

RUSSIA
Grozny
Vladikavkaz
ABKHAZIA (NOT UNDER GEORGIAN CONTROL)
Sukhumi
Kartli
GEORGIA
Tbilisi
Batumi
AZERBAIJAN
Baku
ARMENIA
Yerevan
Stepanakert
Nakhichevan

- Georgia
- Autonomous Republic of Adjara
- Parts of Azerbaijan controlled by Armenia (Nagorno-Karabakh)
- Chechnia—wars in the years 1994–1996 and 1999–2000
- South Ossetia
- ▲ Oil production

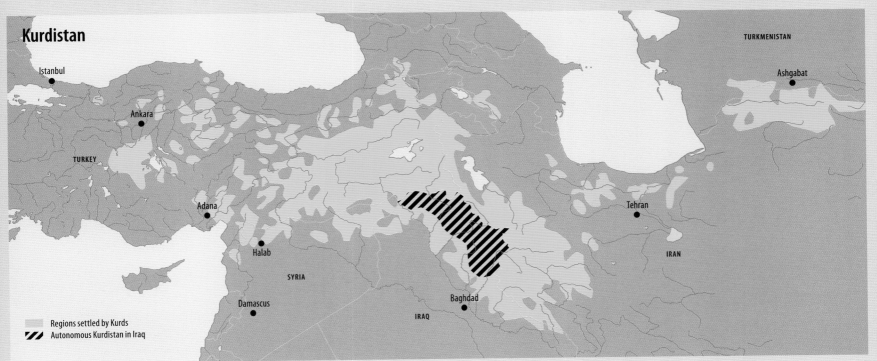

Kurdistan

Istanbul
Ankara
TURKEY
Adana
Halab
SYRIA
Damascus
Baghdad
IRAQ
TURKMENISTAN
Ashgabat
Tehran
IRAN

- Regions settled by Kurds
- Autonomous Kurdistan in Iraq

Central Asia

10th–11th Centuries: Turkish Dynasties

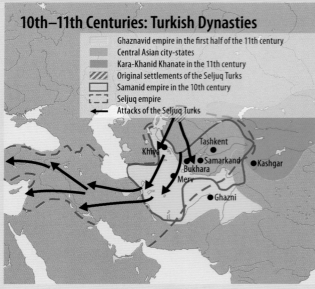

- Ghaznavid empire in the first half of the 11th century
- Central Asian city-states
- Kara-Khanid Khanate in the 11th century
- Original settlements of the Seljuq Turks
- Samanid empire in the 10th century
- Seljuq empire
- ← Attacks of the Seljuq Turks

1400–1700: Khanates

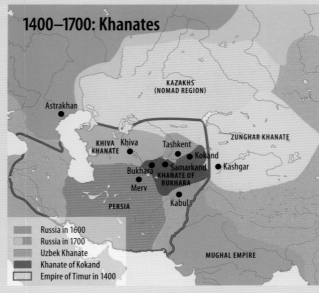

- Russia in 1600
- Russia in 1700
- Uzbek Khanate
- Khanate of Kokand
- Empire of Timur in 1400

6th century Turkic Tatar tribes invade central Asia.

7th–9th centuries The Arab Empire takes control of most of central Asia.

819–1005 The region experiences a golden age under the Muslim Samanid dynasty, who rule from their capital of Bukhara.

1077–1220 The Ghaznavid and Khwarazm-Shahs lead central Asia to new cultural heights.

from 1220 Mongol tribes led by Genghis Khan lay waste to most of central Asia.

1370–1405 Timur (also known as Tamerlane) makes Samarkand his capital city and cosmopolitan center of his empire.

1405–1506 Rulers of the Timurid dynasty, descendants of Timur, divide his empire into smaller holdings.

1506–1598 The Uzbek Shaybanids control most of central Asia.

1511–1696 The Uzbek Khiva khanate takes over from the Shaybanids. The ethnic groups of contemporary central Asia consolidate from the 16th century onward.

1764 Modern Afghanistan forms under the influence of the British Empire.

19th century The khanates are dissolved, making Kyrgyzstan, Tajikistan, Uzbekistan, Turkmenistan and Kazakhstan part of Russia. They will become Soviet republics under the USSR.

1919 Afghanistan gains independence from Great Britain.

1933–1973 King Zahir Shah rules in Afghanistan.

1964 Afghanistan becomes a constitutional monarchy.

1800–1907: Russian Conquests

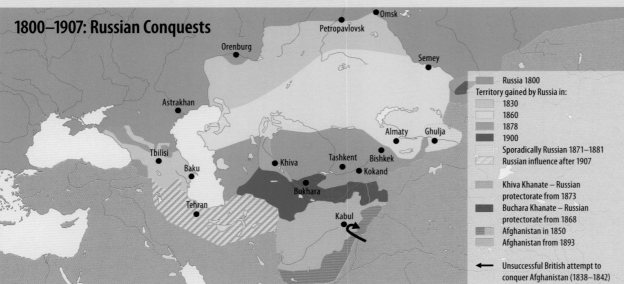

- Russia 1800
- Territory gained by Russia in:
  - 1830
  - 1860
  - 1878
  - 1900
- Sporadically Russian 1871–1881
- Russian influence after 1907
- Khiva Khanate – Russian protectorate from 1873
- Buchara Khanate – Russian protectorate from 1868
- Afghanistan in 1850
- Afghanistan from 1893
- ← Unsuccessful British attempt to conquer Afghanistan (1838–1842)

Central Asia, with its harsh climate of extreme variations in temperature and difficult terrain, has never been amenable to classical agriculture-based civilization. Instead, its vast, grass-covered steppes became home to tribes of nomadic herdsmen.

7th–6th centuries BCE The Mede people rule most of central Asia.

549–330 BCE Central Asia is part of the Persian Empire.

330–312 BCE Alexander the Great's armies conquer central Asia.

312–280 BCE The Seleucids rule Alexander's former possessions.

280–220 BCE The Parthian empire rules from northern Iran.

250–125 BCE The Grecian kingdom of Bactria: synthesis of Greek culture with Asiatic-Indian culture

135 BCE–ca. 100 CE The Kushan (Kusana) empire, based in what is now Tajikistan, controls central Asia.

224–651 CE The Persian Empire administers central Asia under the name Khorasan.

1926

- Other regions of the Soviet Union
- Khorezm People's Rep. (until 1926)
- Bukharan People's Rep. (until 1924)
- Border of the Soviet Union

1929

- Other regions of the Soviet Union
- Uzbekistan (1924–1929)
- Uzbekistan (1929)
- Tajikistan (1929)
- Autonomous Republic of Kyrgyzstan (within Russia)
- Border of the Soviet Union

1936

- Additional Soviet Union regions
- Areas of famine 1932–1933
- Border of the Soviet Union
- ○ Regions of Stalinist Gulags

1973 Mohammed Daoud Khan topples the monarchy in Afghanistan; a Communist coup follows.

1979 The United States government supports the mujahideen, who are armed fundamentalist Muslims opposed to the Communist government. Soviet-friendly Babrak Karmal becomes president after the murder of President Hafizullah Amin.

1979–1989 Soviet troops battle the mujahideen.

1991 Kyrgyzstan, Tajikistan, Uzbekistan, Turkmenistan and Kazakhstan become independent, majority Islamic, states. Turkmenbashi (born Saparmurat Niyazov) becomes president of Turkmenistan.

1996 The ultra-Islamic Taliban faction takes power in Afghanistan, instituting a rigid form of *sharia* (Islamic law). The Northern Alliance forms in opposition.

March 2001 The Taliban blow up the 1,500-year-old statues of Buddha in Bamiyan. Following the terrorist attacks of September 11th, attributed to Afghan-based al-Qaeda, US-led forces topple the Taliban government in Kabul, driving the Taliban toward the Afghan-Pakistani border.

2004–today Pro-American Hamid Karzai is president of Afghanistan; his re-election in 2009 is surrounded by controversy. Violent attacks against the Afghani government continue; US and NATO troops are still engaged.

The war in Afghanistan between the United States and its allies and the Taliban began in the wake of the September 11, 2001, terrorist attacks as a military response to the Taliban's protection of al-Qaeda leader Osama bin Laden. The war has since liberated large parts of the northern regions of Afghanistan from Taliban control. Operations in the south and on the Pakistani border continue.

1979–1989: Afghanistan War

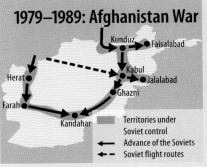

Territories under Soviet control
→ Advance of the Soviets
⇠ Soviet flight routes

1996: The Taliban and Northern Alliance

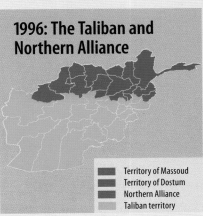

■ Territory of Massoud
■ Territory of Dostum
■ Northern Alliance
□ Taliban territory

Saparmurat Niyazov Turkmenbashi (1940–2006), president of Turkmenistan, constructed a cult of personality, adopting a name that means "father of all Turkomans." Once an estranged minor functionary in the Communist Party, he became president after Turkmenistan's 1991 independence, declaring himself "president for life" in 1999. He devoted his time in office to toppling Turkoman and Islamic traditions in favor of those that worshipped his person and his family. The often bizarre manifestations of his personality cult were abolished upon his death.

Al-Qaeda is a jihadist terrorist network that is based in Afghanistan and/or Pakistan.

Hamid Karzai, president of Afghanistan

Central Asia Today

▨ Russian settlement
△ Oil production
◍ Gas production

Ethnic Diversity in Afghanistan

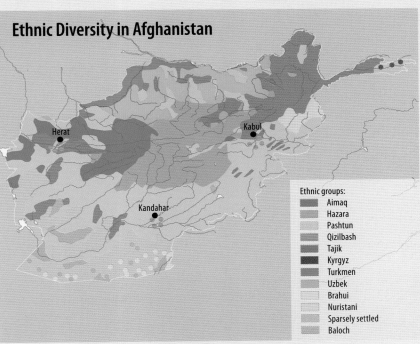

Ethnic groups:
■ Aimaq
■ Hazara
■ Pashtun
■ Qizilbash
■ Tajik
■ Kyrgyz
■ Turkmen
■ Uzbek
■ Brahui
■ Nuristani
□ Sparsely settled
■ Baloch

Attacks by al-Qaeda

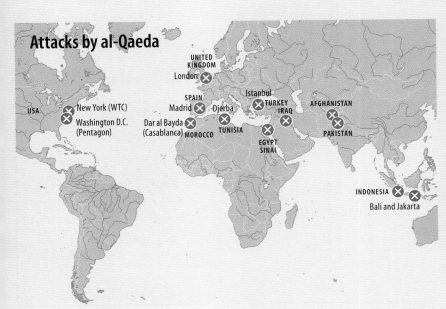

2001: International Security Assistance Force (ISAF)

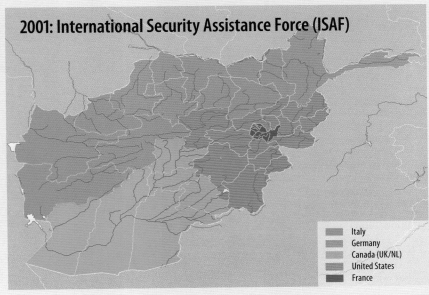

■ Italy
■ Germany
■ Canada (UK/NL)
■ United States
■ France

Siberia and Mongolia

260 BCE–600 CE: Xiongnu and Turkic Khanates

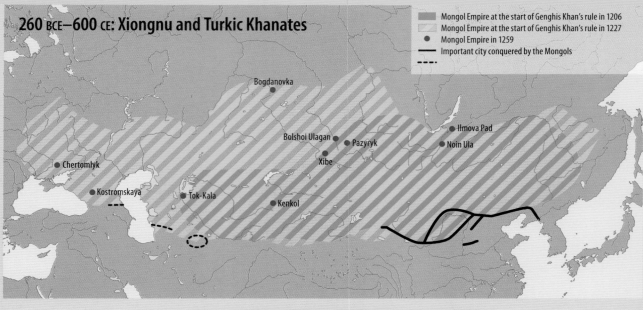

Mongol Empire at the start of Genghis Khan's rule in 1206
Mongol Empire at the start of Genghis Khan's rule in 1227
Mongol Empire in 1259
Important city conquered by the Mongols

1500–1917: Russian Conquest

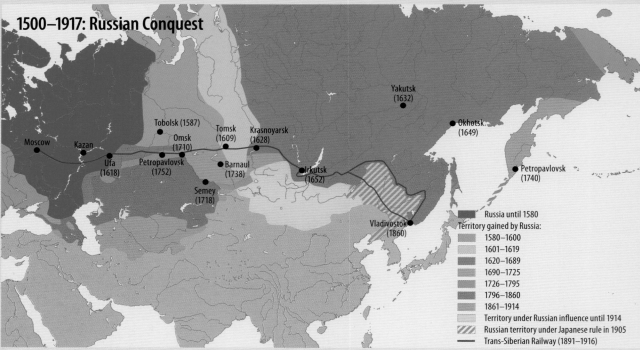

Russia until 1580
Territory gained by Russia:
1580–1600
1601–1619
1620–1689
1690–1725
1726–1795
1796–1860
1861–1914
Territory under Russian influence until 1914
Russian territory under Japanese rule in 1905
Trans-Siberian Railway (1891–1916)

1932–1996: Natural Resources and Railroads

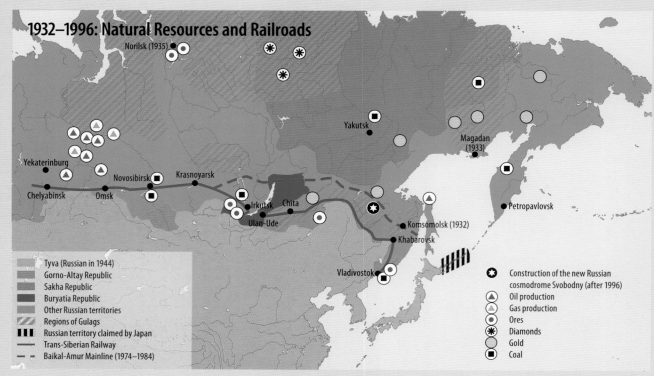

Tyva (Russian in 1944)
Gorno-Altay Republic
Sakha Republic
Buryatia Republic
Other Russian territories
Regions of Gulags
Russian territory claimed by Japan
Trans-Siberian Railway
Baikal-Amur Mainline (1974–1984)

Construction of the new Russian cosmodrome Svobodny (after 1996)
Oil production
Gas production
Ores
Diamonds
Gold
Coal

Siberia

2nd century BCE–1st century CE Siberia is part of the Xiongnu empire, forerunner of the Huns.

6th century Siberia becomes a Turkic khanate.

middle of the 8th century The Uyghur empire controls Siberia from what is now western China.

13th century The Mongols conquer most of Siberia.

1206 Siberia is mentioned in writing for the first time.

1227–1428/1502 The Mongol Orda Horde khanate rules.

1378–1395 The Siberian khan Toqtamish becomes leader of the Mongols in Russia (the Golden Horde).

from the 16th century Siberia is systematically developed and its resources exploited in the service of the Russian tsars.

17th century Russia rules northern Siberia.

18th century Russia occupies southern Siberia, where it settles exiles who have been banned from Russia.

1891 Construction of the Trans–Siberian Railroad begins.

1920 Siberia becomes part of the USSR, leading to industrialization and exploitation of its vast mineral wealth. The Soviet government builds the first *Gulags* (prison camps).

1994 Election of the first governor of Siberia weakens central government's control of the region.

The Trans-Siberian Railroad, which traverses approximately 5,770 miles (9,288 km), is the longest railway line in the world, stretching from Moscow to Vladivostok. It was begun at the end of the 19th century and was completed in 1916. It connects to the Baikal-Amur Railroad (1974–1984), which joins central Russia to eastern Siberia.

The Gulags were Soviet labor camps built primarily by Communist leaders Lenin and Stalin to house political prisoners. The word "Gulag" is an acronym for the Russian words for "Chief Administration of Corrective Labor Camps and Colonies," a division administered by the national secret police. The concentration camps were populated with enemies of the state crammed into housing in inhuman conditions. Many had once worked on important Soviet projects. At the time of Stalin's death, some 200 Gulags were in existence and imprisoned an estimated total of 13 million people.

Mongolia

The harsh steppes of Mongolia lie nearly a mile (1,500 meters) above sea level, and they have long been the homeland of nomadic herders. The first historical mention of Mongol tribes comes from ancient Chinese chronicles. By the 13th century, the Mongols had conquered the largest empire the world has ever known.

4th–3rd centuries BCE The first Mongol tribes cross the steppes.

3rd century BCE–1st century CE The Xiongnu empire, a forerunner of the Huns, successfully invades China multiple times.

10th–12th centuries Mongolia becomes part of the Khitan empire.

1123–1150 Khabul Khan unites the Mongol tribes.

1206 Genghis Khan, who had united the many nomadic tribes of the region, becomes emperor, thus founding the powerful, long-lasting Mongol Empire.

13th century Mongols expand their realm through Asia and the Middle East.

1229–1241 Strife over the succession of the great khan Ogodel, who had established the Mongol imperial administration system, brings Mongol expansion in Europe to an end.

1251–1259 Great khan Mongke reigns.

1260 Kublai Khan becomes great khan.

1279 Kublai Khan conquers China and founds the Yuan dynasty.

after 1335 The Mongol Empire begins its slow and gradual decline.

17th century Mongolia becomes part of China under the Qing dynasty.

1911 Mongolia declares independence from China.

by 1921 Chinese forces are driven out of Mongolia with Soviet support.

1924 The Mongolian People's Republic is formed under the influence and protection of the USSR.

1946 China officially recognizes Mongolia.

1961 Mongolia joins the UN.

1992 Mongolia's first free elections result in a communist victory.

Genghis Khan (1155–1227), born with the name Temujin, was the founder of the Mongol Empire. Following his escape from enemy tribes who had captured him as a child, he became involved in a series of bloody intertribal wars. As a warrior he was famed for his diplomacy, military tactics and brutality. In 1206 an assembly of Mongol chiefs declared him great khan, or "ruler of the world." Following his election, Genghis Khan went on to conquer vast territories, creating the most expansive empire in the history of the world.

Mongke Khan (1208–1259), a grandson of Genghis Khan, became great khan in 1251, with the Karakoram region in what is now Pakistan as his administrative center. Under his command, his younger brothers Hulegu and Kublai conquered China and Persia. His cousins Batu and Orda marched into Russia and Siberia. An astute politician, Mongke promoted religious tolerance, and went so far as to send ambassadors to the pope. Mongke died during a military campaign in China.

Kublai Khan (1215–1294) was the founder of the Chinese Mongol Empire, the Yuan dynasty. In 1260 he succeeded his brother Mongke as the great khan, continuing the Mongol policy of endless conquest. His capital was located near what is today Beijing. By 1280 he controlled all of China, taking over the Chinese administrative system and adopting Chinese political traditions to ensure the security of his empire. The writings of the explorer Marco Polo brought the name of Kublai Khan to Europe.

Marco Polo (1154–1324) was a Venetian merchant and world traveler who brought news of the Far East to Europeans for the first time. In 1264 he journeyed to Beijing, where he gained the favor of the Mongol Kublai Khan, who appointed him to several administrative positions. After twelve years in China, Marco Polo returned to Europe, where he described his travels in the book *Il milione* ("The Million"), better known in English as *The Travels of Marco Polo*.

1206–1259: Empire of Genghis Khan until Mongke's Death

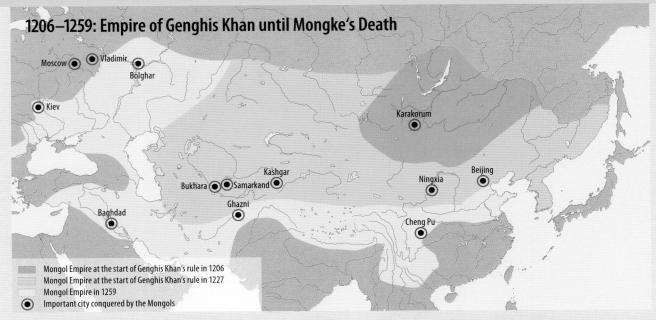

- ▨ Mongol Empire at the start of Genghis Khan's rule in 1206
- ▨ Mongol Empire at the start of Genghis Khan's rule in 1227
- ▢ Mongol Empire in 1259
- ◉ Important city conquered by the Mongols

1260–1368: Mongol Khanate and Yuan Dynasty

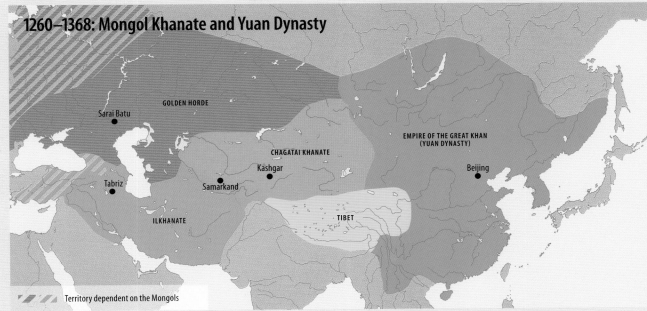

▨▨ Territory dependent on the Mongols

1911–1988: Independence and Soviet Domination

- ▨ Mongolia, autonomous in 1911, independent in 1924
- ▨ Inner Mongolia, autonomous region in China (after 1947)
- ▨ Tannu Tuva, independent 1921–1944, Russian after 1944
- ⊗ Soviet occupation of Mongolia 1922–1988
- ⊗ Defeat of Japanese troops by Soviet troops in 1939

India Until the Early 18th Century

The Indian subcontinent has been moving northward into Asia for millions of years, creating the world's most towering mountain range: the Himalayas. This most heterogeneous of lands has been home to millennia of ancient civilizations. Its venerable trade routes cross tropical rainforests, deserts and snowy mountain peaks. The religions and philosophical systems developed here influence the spiritual life of the entire world. Many different peoples have conquered India, most of them coming from the north through the region known as the Hindu Kush. More than a billion people, speaking a thousand different languages and practicing a broad range of religions, live here in a uniquely hierarchal society characterized by stark poverty and pervasive inequality.

~3000 BCE The cities of Mohenjo-daro and Harappa, the oldest civilizations in India, are established in the Indus Valley.

1500–600 BCE Waves of Indo-European Aryan tribes arrive from the north, merging with the local cultures. Indian identity forms with the introduction of the Vedas, the holy texts from which Hinduism will develop.

900 BCE The Aryans arrive in the Ganges River valley.

600 BCE As many as sixteen different kingdoms rule India. The caste system begins.

563–483 BCE Life of Gautama Buddha

530 BCE The Persians control the east bank of the Indus River.

327/26 BCE The Vedic period comes to an end. Alexander the Great's troops arrive in India.

320–185 BCE The Maurya dynasty rules India's first empire.

268–232 BCE Reign of Ashoka, the greatest Maurya ruler and most influential supporter of Buddhism

185 BCE–319 CE The Maurya empire dissolves into several smaller states. Large parts of India are ruled by foreigners.

141–94 BCE The Scythians (Saka) invade from the northwest.

320–500 CE Northern India is united under the Gupta empire. Mathematics, astronomy and philosophy flourish during India's first golden age. Gupta emperors found Nalanda University, the largest in the ancient world.

~500 The White Huns (Hephtalites) invade from Central Asia, sacking cities and plundering the countryside.

from 711 Muslims invade northern and central India.

8th–13th centuries Regional dynasties rule during India's medieval period, temporarily halting Muslim incursion. These include the kingdoms of Rashtrakua (752–973), Pala (750–1151) and Pratihara (730–1036).

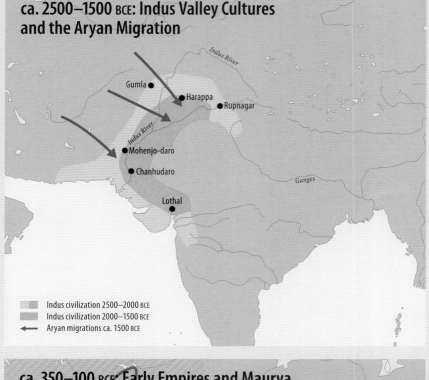

ca. 2500–1500 BCE: Indus Valley Cultures and the Aryan Migration

Indus civilization 2500–2000 BCE
Indus civilization 2000–1500 BCE
← Aryan migrations ca. 1500 BCE

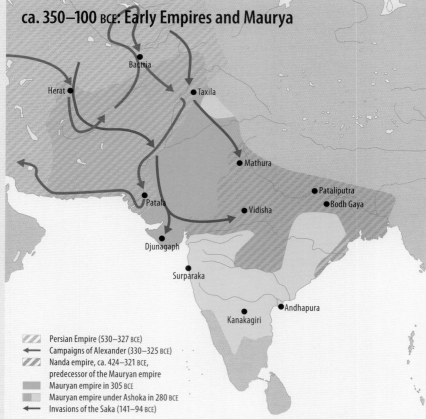

ca. 350–100 BCE: Early Empires and Maurya

Persian Empire (530–327 BCE)
← Campaigns of Alexander (330–325 BCE)
Nanda empire, ca. 424–321 BCE, predecessor of the Mauryan empire
Mauryan empire in 305 BCE
Mauryan empire under Ashoka in 280 BCE
← Invasions of the Saka (141–94 BCE)

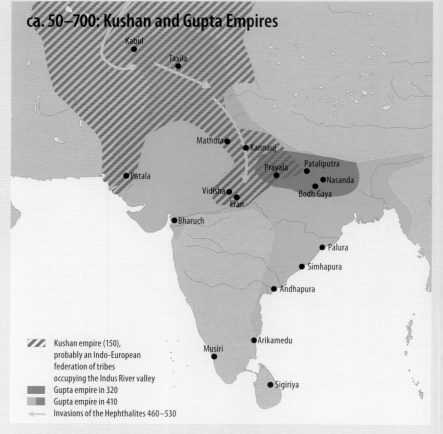

ca. 50–700: Kushan and Gupta Empires

Kushan empire (150), probably an Indo-European federation of tribes occupying the Indus River valley
Gupta empire in 320
Gupta empire in 410
← Invasions of the Hephtalites 460–530

The Vedas ("knowledge") are four sacred texts of Indian Hindus, testaments to a long Indian spiritual and intellectual tradition. They are considered the oldest source stemming from an Indo-European culture (1500 BCE). Originally passed on orally by the scholar caste (Brahmins), the Vedas were first written down in Sanskrit around 800 BCE.

Ashoka (304–232 BCE) is the most famous ruler of ancient India. After victory in the Kalinga War, Ashoka converted to Buddhism. Instead of ruling as a despot, he spread the teachings of Buddha throughout the land. During his long reign of more than thirty years, the Mauryan empire expanded to include nearly all of present-day India and Pakistan as well as parts of Afghanistan, Kashmir and Nepal.

The Ghaznavid Turk dynasty ruled in Afghanistan, eastern Iran and Pakistan from 962/77–1186. The golden age of the dynasty took place under the rule of Mahmud of Ghazna (998–1030).

Chola temples are temples that were constructed during the Tamil Chola dynasty, which ruled southern India and nearby islands from the 9th through the 13th centuries. Three Chola temples—Thanjavur, Gangakondacholisvaram and Darasuram—have been named to the UNESCO World Heritage Site list.

850–1279 The Chola dynasty rules in southern India, a center of Hinduism and Dravidian culture.

1001 Mahmud of Ghazna (998–1030) conquers northern India.

1206 Muslims found the Delhi sultanate, conquering much of northern and central India.

1398 Timur Lenk (Tamerlane) invades from Central Asia in an attempt to revive the Mongol Empire. His attacks weaken the Delhi sultanate, leading to a revival of Hinduism.

1498 Portuguese sailors led by Vasco da Gama discover a sea route from Europe to India.

1526–1858 The Mughal Empire, ruled by descendants of Tamerlane, controls most of India. Muslim culture in India enters a golden age. Akbar the Great (reigns 1556–1605) tries to find common ground between the Hindu and Muslim religions.

1558 England governs the ports on the western coast of India through the British East India Company, tightly controlling trade privileges and territorial rights.

1609 The first diplomatic exchange between a Mughal ruler and British ambassador takes place in Agra.

1648 The Taj Mahal in Agra is completed by Mughal emperor Shah Jahān to memorialize his wife, Mumtāz Mahal, who had died in childbirth.

1658–1707 The reign of Aurangzeb, the last important Mughal ruler, is followed by a steep decline throughout the empire.

1756–1763 The Seven Years' War between England, France and their allies determines which colonial power will control India. Land and sea battles between rival colonial outposts bring local provincial governors (nawabs) into the conflict as allies of the European powers.

1757 The Battle of Plassey: A small British East India Company force soundly defeats the armies of the nawab of Bengal despite being outnumbered five to one. In London, parliament votes to annex Bengal, marking the beginning of British colonial India.

1763 Bengalis revolt after the Treaty of Paris grants Britain territorial rights in India.

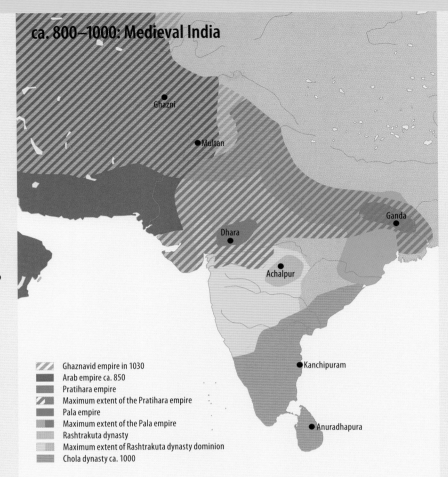

ca. 800–1000: Medieval India

Ghazni
Multan
Ganda
Dhara
Achalpur
Kanchipuram
Anuradhapura

- Ghaznavid empire in 1030
- Arab empire ca. 850
- Pratihara empire
- Maximum extent of the Pratihara empire
- Pala empire
- Maximum extent of the Pala empire
- Rashtrakuta dynasty
- Maximum extent of Rashtrakuta dynasty dominion
- Chola dynasty ca. 1000

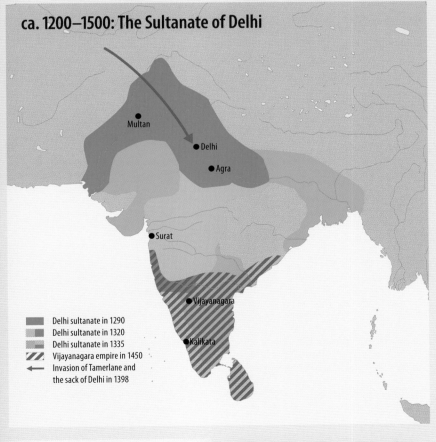

ca. 1200–1500: The Sultanate of Delhi

Multan
Delhi
Agra
Surat
Vijayanagara
Kalikata

- Delhi sultanate in 1290
- Delhi sultanate in 1320
- Delhi sultanate in 1335
- Vijayanagara empire in 1450
- Invasion of Tamerlane and the sack of Delhi in 1398

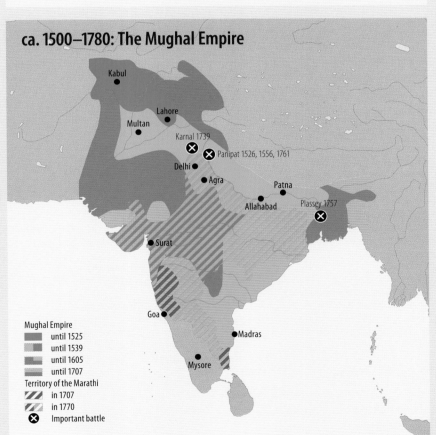

ca. 1500–1780: The Mughal Empire

Kabul
Lahore
Multan
Karnal 1739
Panipat 1526, 1556, 1761
Delhi
Agra
Patna
Allahabad
Plassey 1757
Surat
Goa
Madras
Mysore

Mughal Empire
- until 1525
- until 1539
- until 1605
- until 1707

Territory of the Marathi
- in 1707
- in 1770
- Important battle

Brihadisvara Temple, Thanjavur, Tamil Nadu, India

Akbar the Great (1542–1605) was the first important Mughal emperor. Although he began his reign with extreme violence against Hindus, he later promoted religious tolerance, and let Hindu nobles to retain their estates. This led to an extended period of economic and political stability, one in which Akbar invited members of all religions to his court for conversation. His attempt at creating Muslim-Hindu doctrinal syncretism failed, although his efforts inspired the founding of the Sikh religion.

Maharajas (*mahaa* = great, *raja* = king) were Hindu rulers who controlled large territories with more than one *raja* (= king or ruler of a territory).

India, Pakistan and Bangladesh from British Colonization to Today

British Influence until 1798

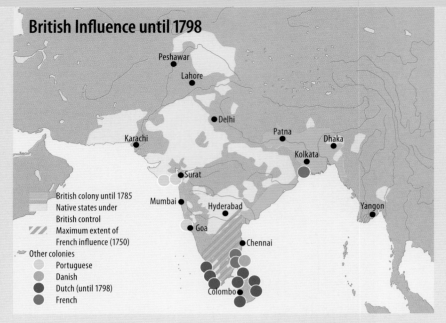

British colony until 1785
Native states under British control
Maximum extent of French influence (1750)
Other colonies
Portuguese
Danish
Dutch (until 1798)
French

British Influence 1798–1805

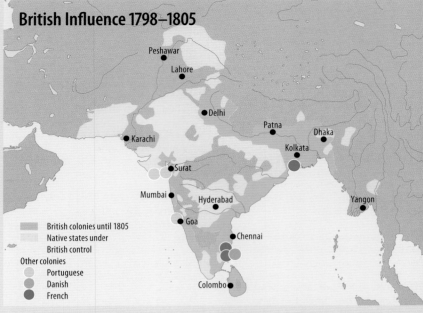

British colonies until 1805
Native states under British control
Other colonies
Portuguese
Danish
French

British Influence to 1858: The Sepoy Mutiny

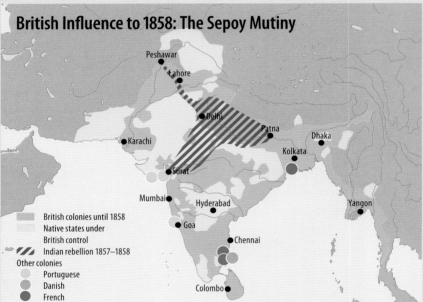

British colonies until 1858
Native states under British control
Indian rebellion 1857–1858
Other colonies
Portuguese
Danish
French

British Colonial Period 1858–1914

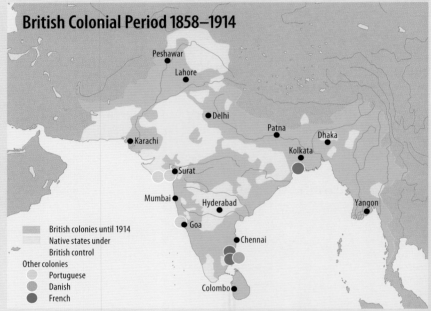

British colonies until 1914
Native states under British control
Other colonies
Portuguese
Danish
French

1848 The British Empire annexes Punjab.

1857 The Sepoy Mutiny breaks out when native soldiers revolt against both their English officers and British rule in general.

1858 Bahadur Shah II, the last Mughal emperor, is deposed by the British. Parliament votes to make India an imperial colony, declaring all holdings of the British East India Company property of the crown.

1858–1947 British colonial rule in India

1878 Queen Victoria is crowned empress of India.

1885 An alliance of Hindus and Muslims founds the Indian National Congress as part of a joint effort for India's independence.

1905 The British partition Bengal into Muslim and Hindu zones.

1906 The Muslim League is formed in Dhaka.

1914–1918 Over a million Indian soldiers fight on the side of England in World War I.

1919 The British brutally suppress anti-British demonstrations at Amritsar.

1920–1922 Gandhi begins his non-violent campaign for independence.

1930 The Salt Satyagraha (salt march), a non-violent march of Ghandi's followers to the Dandi salt works, becomes the independence movement's first important act of civil disobedience.

1930–1932 The Round Table Conference meets in three sessions in London to discuss the future of India.

1937 Britain grants India the right to local self-government.

1939 India fights on the side of England in World War II. The Indian National Congress begins a new campaign of non-violent civil disobedience.

1940 The Muslim League calls for a separate Muslim state.

1942 The Indian National Congress asks Britain to leave India.

1947 Louis Mountbatten is the last viceroy of India. Mahatma Gandhi and Jawaharlal Nehru (prime minister 1947–1964) achieve their goal of independence for India with a heavy Hindu majority. Within months, Muslim Pakistan splits from Hindu India. Several million people are displaced as Muslims leave India for Pakistan, and Hindus and Sikhs leave Pakistan for India, leading to a bloody civil war. Fundamentalist Islamic and secular interests battle for control in the new states of West Pakistan and East Pakistan (now Bangladesh).

1947–1965 Tensions between India and Pakistan increase in part due to territorial claims in Kashmir.

1948 Gandhi is murdered by a Hindu extremist.

1949/1950 The Republic of India forms.

1961 India occupies the last remaining Portuguese colonies, ending the period of colonial rule.

1962 The Indian-Chinese war ends in India's defeat on its northwest border.

1964 Nehru dies. His daughter Indira Gandhi becomes prime minister in 1966 (until 1977) and serves again from 1980–1984.

1971 East Pakistan's secession from West Pakistan brings bloody civil war. Indian support leads to victory for the new nation of Bangladesh.

1972 Zulfikar Ali Bhutto becomes president of Pakistan in the wake of the loss of Bangladesh.

1975 Unrest in India leads an increasingly authoritarian Indira Gandhi to impose martial law.

1977 A military coup by Zia ul-Haq overthrows Bhutto's democratically elected government and leads to an increase in Islamic fundamentalism in Pakistan. Zia dies in a plane crash in 1988.

1979 Arrested by the military on false charges, Zulfikar Ali Bhutto is sentenced to death and executed. His politically active daughter, Benazir, is placed under house arrest. In 1984, she goes into voluntary exile in England.

1982–1984 Sikhs demand an independent state in Punjab. Sikh extremists occupy the Golden Temple of Amritsar, the most important Sikh religious site. Indira Gandhi orders soldiers to storm the temple, leaving many dead. She is murdered by a Sikh in 1984.

1988 Pakistan's Benazir Bhutto becomes the first female Prime Minister of an Islamic nation.

1991 Tamil separatists from Sri Lanka assassinate former Indian Prime Minister Rajiv Gandhi (1984–1989).

1998 India and Pakistan both have atomic weapons, increasing tensions in a highly volatile area.

1999 General Pervez Musharraf leads a military coup in Pakistan. He steps down in 2008.

2001 Pakistan is accused of harboring radical Islamic terrorists, including Osama bin Laden, in the wake of the September 11 attacks on the USA.

2007 Benazir Bhutto is assassinated.

Mohandas Karamchand Gandhi (Mahatma = great spirit; 1869–1948) was born into an important merchant family. After legal studies in England, he fought for the rights of Indians in South Africa. In 1914, he returned to India,

Mahatma Gandhi

where he developed a philosophy of active, non-violent civil disobedience as a means to gain India's independence from Britain. After Indian independence in 1947, Gandhi worked to ease tensions between Muslims and Hindus. He was assassinated by a Hindu extremist in 1948.

The Kashmir conflict is rooted in the 1947 decision of Hari Singh, prince of Kashmir, to stay on the Indian side of the border rather than letting Kashmir, which was 65 percent Muslim, become part of Pakistan. Pakistan objected, and the Indian-Pakistan War began. A peace treaty divided Kashmir between the two countries but did little to prevent two further wars over disputed territory. In 1962, China became involved when it claimed the northern Kashmir territory of Ladakh. Presently, Kashmir is divided into the Indian states Jammu and Kashmir, and the Pakistani Northern Territories and Asad Kashmir. China claims the Akasi Chin region. The conflict continues today.

Louis Mountbatten (1900–1979), the last viceroy of India, in 1952

Indira Gandhi (1917–1984)

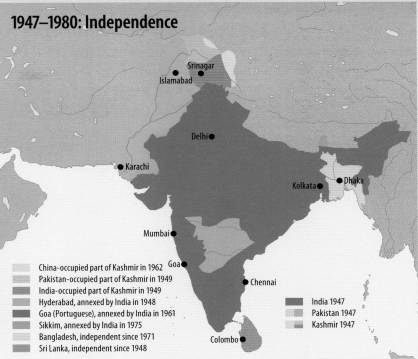

1947–1980: Independence

- China-occupied part of Kashmir in 1962
- Pakistan-occupied part of Kashmir in 1949
- India-occupied part of Kashmir in 1949
- Hyderabad, annexed by India in 1948
- Goa (Portuguese), annexed by India in 1961
- Sikkim, annexed by India in 1975
- Bangladesh, independent since 1971
- Sri Lanka, independent since 1948
- India 1947
- Pakistan 1947
- Kashmir 1947

Srinagar • Islamabad • Karachi • Delhi • Mumbai • Goa • Chennai • Colombo • Kolkata • Dhaka

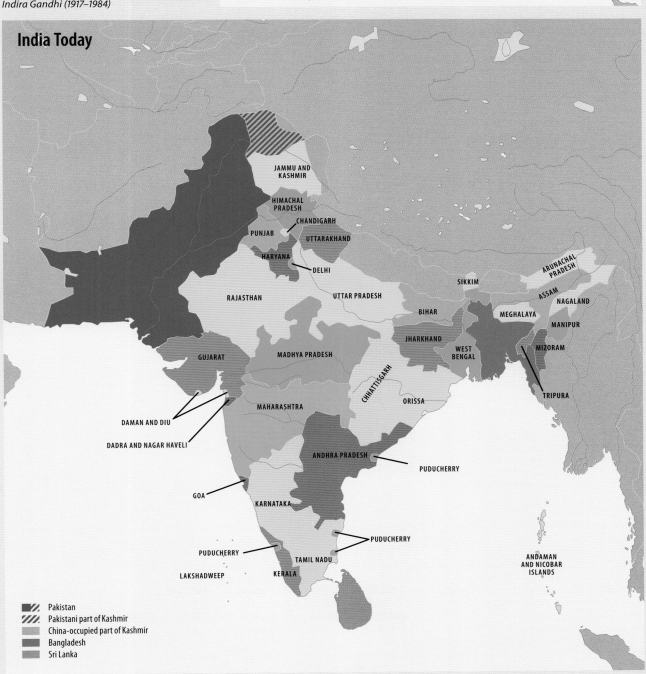

India Today

JAMMU AND KASHMIR, HIMACHAL PRADESH, CHANDIGARH, PUNJAB, UTTARAKHAND, HARYANA, DELHI, RAJASTHAN, UTTAR PRADESH, SIKKIM, ARUNACHAL PRADESH, ASSAM, NAGALAND, BIHAR, MEGHALAYA, MANIPUR, JHARKHAND, WEST BENGAL, MIZORAM, GUJARAT, MADHYA PRADESH, CHHATTISGARH, ORISSA, TRIPURA, DAMAN AND DIU, DADRA AND NAGAR HAVELI, MAHARASHTRA, ANDHRA PRADESH, PUDUCHERRY, GOA, KARNATAKA, PUDUCHERRY, PUDUCHERRY, TAMIL NADU, LAKSHADWEEP, KERALA, ANDAMAN AND NICOBAR ISLANDS

- Pakistan
- Pakistani part of Kashmir
- China-occupied part of Kashmir
- Bangladesh
- Sri Lanka

Tibet and Bhutan / Buddhism and Hinduism

Buddhism ca. 200 BCE

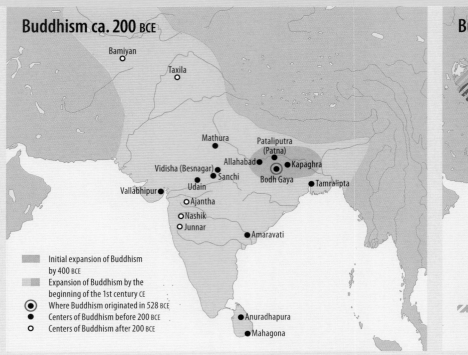

Initial expansion of Buddhism by 400 BCE

Expansion of Buddhism by the beginning of the 1st century CE

◉ Where Buddhism originated in 528 BCE

● Centers of Buddhism before 200 BCE

○ Centers of Buddhism after 200 BCE

Buddhism ca. 1000

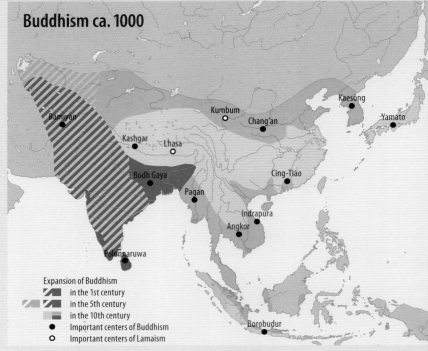

Expansion of Buddhism

in the 1st century

in the 5th century

in the 10th century

● Important centers of Buddhism

○ Important centers of Lamaism

Buddhism Today

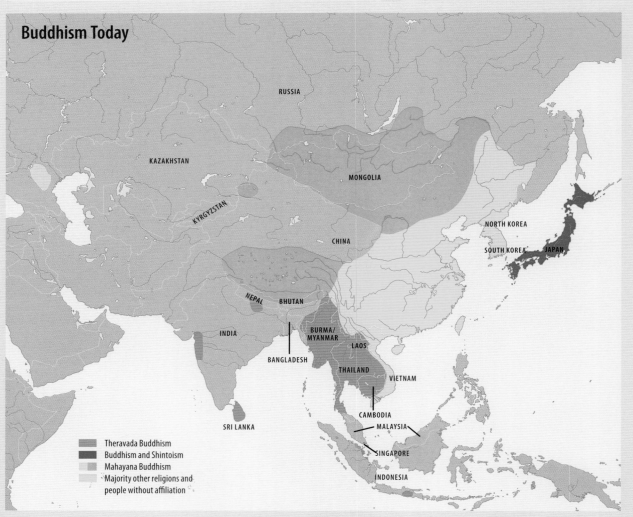

Theravada Buddhism

Buddhism and Shintoism

Mahayana Buddhism

Majority other religions and people without affiliation

Buddhism

528 BCE Siddhartha Gautama, a prince born in what is now Nepal, becomes the Buddha. Buddhism is born.

268–232 BCE Under King Ashoka, Buddhism spreads to all of India.

185 BCE The Shunga dynasty emerges in central India, leading to the persecution of Buddhists.

1st century CE The oldest recorded Buddhist teachings, the Tipitaka, appear.

67 Buddhism reaches China.

552 Buddhism spreads to Japan.

620–649 Buddhism arrives in Tibet.

11th–13th centuries Muslims suppress Indian Buddhism.

15th century Great Buddhist monasteries are founded in Tibet.

17th century Building of the Potala Palace, seat of the Dalai Lama, in Lhasa

19th century Buddhism spreads to Europe.

1959 The Fourteenth Dalai Lama flees from Tibet and goes into exile in India.

2001 The Taliban destroy ancient Buddhist statues in Afghanistan.

Buddhism is not a religion in the Western sense of the word. It is based not on revelation, but realization. Through mediation and contemplative practices, Buddhism's founder, Siddhartha Gautama, realized that all life is a cycle of suffering and rebirth, and that the struggle against greed, desire and egoism produces karma. The karma an individual accumulates influences the form of a being's reincarnation. The goal is to achieve enlightenment (nirvana) by eliminating the desire for worldly things,

and thus bringing the karmic cycle to an end. This is a particularly difficult concept for lay Buddhists, who tend to emphasize the role of good karma. Some 500 million people around the world practice Buddhism in myriad forms today.

The Buddha (Siddhartha Gautama, 563–482 BCE) The Buddha, meaning "Awakened One," came from a royal family. Surrounded by wealth and beauty from birth, he received the best education. At the age

of twenty-nine he saw an old man, a sick person and a corpse, all of which had previously been unknown to him. Aware for the first time of suffering and that nothing is permanent, he left his palace and royal identity behind to meditate in the mountains and forests of India, eventually attaining enlightenment.

Dalai Lama is the title that since 1578 has been given to the highest ranking representative of the Gelupa ("yellow hat")

Buddhist order, which is the largest in Tibet. Every new Dalai Lama is a reincarnation of the preceding one, and also the reincarnation of the Bodhisattva Avalokiteshvara, a being of limitless compassion who helps all sentient beings attain Enlightenment. After the death of a Dalai Lama, a commission of monks begins the search for his reincarnation among children. A child identified by the monks undergoes a series of tests and, if successful, he is removed from his family to be raised in a monastery.

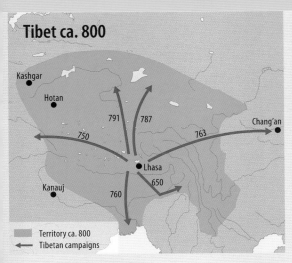

Tibet ca. 800

Kashgar
Hotan
Chang'an
791 787
750 763
Lhasa
Kanauj
650
760

Territory ca. 800
Tibetan campaigns

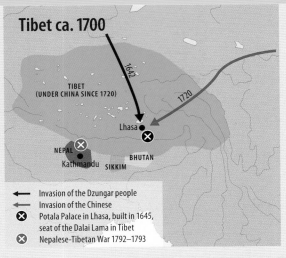

Tibet ca. 1700

TIBET
(UNDER CHINA SINCE 1720)
1642
1720
Lhasa
NEPAL
Kathmandu
BHUTAN
SIKKIM

← Invasion of the Dzungar people
← Invasion of the Chinese
⊗ Potala Palace in Lhasa, built in 1645, seat of the Dalai Lama in Tibet
⊗ Nepalese-Tibetan War 1792–1793

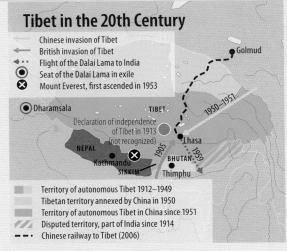

Tibet in the 20th Century

→ Chinese invasion of Tibet
→ British invasion of Tibet
⊷ Flight of the Dalai Lama to India
◉ Seat of the Dalai Lama in exile
⊗ Mount Everest, first ascended in 1953

◉ Dharamsala
Golmud
TIBET
Declaration of independence of Tibet in 1913 (not recognized)
1950–1951
NEPAL
Kathmandu
1905
Lhasa
1959
BHUTAN
SIKKIM
Thimphu

Territory of autonomous Tibet 1912–1949
Tibetan territory annexed by China in 1950
Territory of autonomous Tibet in China since 1951
Disputed territory, part of India since 1914
- - - Chinese railway to Tibet (2006)

Tibet and Bhutan

until the 7th century Era of Tibetan history celebrated in myth and legend

7th–9th centuries Golden age of the Yarlung empire, a powerful state with established borders

8th century Buddhism becomes the state religion of Tibet.

from the 9th century Tibet breaks up into numerous small principalities.

9th century Bhutan is settled and becomes independent from Tibet in the 11th century.

1253 Tibet becomes part of the Mongol Empire.

from 1578 The Dalai Lama becomes the temporal ruler of all Tibetans.

17th century The kingdom of Bhutan becomes subject to Tibetan rule; tribal unrest ensues.

1720 Tibet becomes a Chinese protectorate.

19th century China, England and Russia struggle for control of Tibet.

1865 Bhutan comes under British control.

1911 The Republic of China is formed.

1913 Tibet declares independence, but is not recognized internationally.

1949 Bhutan falls under India's control.

1950 The Chinese army occupies Tibet.

1956–1958 Anti-Chinese unrest in Tibet

1959 Tibetan uprising: The 14th Dalai Lama flees to India.

1960 Formation of the Tibetan government-in-exile

1965 Tibet becomes an autonomous region within the People's Republic of China.

2008 During the Beijing Olympic Games, supporters of the Dalai Lama demonstrate in Tibet and other places around the world to draw attention to their situation.

Hinduism integrated the old Indian religions with the beliefs of the Aryans, who immigrated to India from the north between 1500 and 600 BCE. Their holy scriptures are the four Vedas. The most important Hindu gods are Brahma, Vishnu and Shiva, who represent respectively the creation, preservation and destruction of the world. Hindus believe that all living beings follow an eternal cycle of death and rebirth, and that how a person lives determines karma, and therefore the quality of one's eventual reincarnation. The goal of Hinduism is liberation (moksha) from the karmic cycle through the union of the soul with brahma, the ultimate source of all that exists. Some 900 million people are Hindus today.

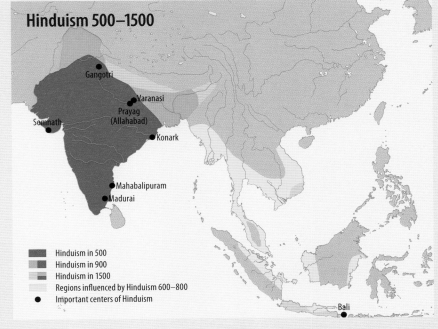

Hinduism 500–1500

Gangotri
Varanasi
Prayag (Allahabad)
Somnath
Konark
Mahabalipuram
Madurai
Bali

Hinduism in 500
Hinduism in 900
Hinduism in 1500
Regions influenced by Hinduism 600–800
● Important centers of Hinduism

*Brahma, 19th century
(from L'Inde Française)*

The caste system is a hereditary hierarchical social order that irrevocably allots all Hindus to one of four major varnas, or castes. Brahmans (priests and teachers) are the highest-ranking, closely followed by Kshatriyas (warriors and nobles), then the Vaishyas (merchants and proprietor farmers) and Sudras (artisans and laborers). Below the Sudras are the Dalit, also known as the Untouchables, who perform work that makes them ritually unclean. Modern Hinduism struggles with the gross inequalities of the caste system, which, contrary to Western perceptions, is controversial and not accepted by all Hindus.

Hinduism Today

BELIZE
TRINIDAD
GUYANA
SURINAME
AFGHANISTAN
KUWAIT
QATAR
UNITED ARAB EMIRATES
OMAN
PAKISTAN
NEPAL
BHUTAN
BURMA/MYANMAR
INDIA
THAILAND
BANGLADESH
SRI LANKA
MALAYSIA
INDONESIA
SEYCHELLES
COMOROS
MAURITIUS
RÉUNION
PAPUA NEW GUINEA
FIJI

Hinduism today
80–89%
30–79%
20–29%
10–19%
2–9%
☐ Immigration of Hindu workers

China from 6000 BCE to 960 CE

ca. 6000–1800 BCE: Yangshao and Longshan Cultures

Zhoukoudian
Lantian
Langtandong
Bailiangdong
Yunxian
Yuanmou

● Finds of the oldest *Homo erectus* remains
▨ Neolithic Yangshao culture (5000–3200 BCE)
▨ Neolithic Longshan culture (3200–1800 BCE)
▨ Region of first cultivation of rice (6000–3000 BCE)

ca. 1800–1100 BCE: Shang Dynasty

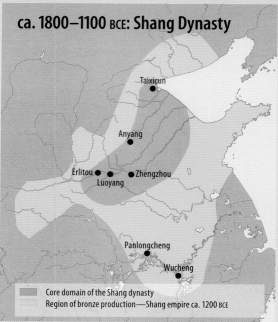

Taixicun
Anyang
Erlitou
Zhengzhou
Luoyang
Panlongcheng
Wucheng

■ Core domain of the Shang dynasty
▨ Region of bronze production—Shang empire ca. 1200 BCE

ca. 1050–256 BCE: Western and Eastern Zhou

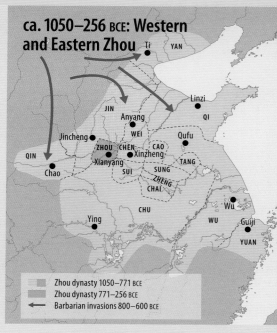

Ti   YAN
JIN   Linzi
Anyang   QI
Jincheng   WEI   Qufu
ZHOU   CHEN   CAO
QIN   Xianyang   Xinzheng   TANG
SUI   SUNG
ZHENG
CHAI
Ying   CHU   Wu
WU   Guiji
YUAN
Chao

■ Zhou dynasty 1050–771 BCE
■ Zhou dynasty 771–256 BCE
→ Barbarian invasions 800–600 BCE

5000 BCE Neolithic Yangshao culture

2700–1000 BCE Xia dynasty, the first state on Chinese territory

1600–1100 BCE Shang dynasty: Chinese writing is developed.

1100–256 BCE The Western Zhou dynasty develops a strong centralized government with ceremonial elements.

771–256 BCE During the Eastern Zhou dynasty the rulers serve mainly a religious function; genuine power rests with the local lords.

476–221 BCE Seven kingdoms vie for power at the end of the Warring States period, yet intellectual culture flourishes in the time also known as the Hundred Schools of Thought.

221–206 BCE The Qin dyansty forms the first strong central government with military power.

221 BCE Shihuangdi, the first Qin emperor, unites China and standardizes weights, measures, writing and currency. In the north, the Great Wall of China is begun.

210 BCE Shihuangdi dies. His elaborate burial includes a terra-cotta army.

206 BCE–220 CE The Han dynasty succeeds the Qin and brings further accomplishments. Paper is invented and the Silk Road opens trade with the West. Defensive wars are fought against the Xiongnu, ancestors of the Huns.

141–87 BCE Reign of Emperor Wudi: The government is remodeled on a Confucian model, and Confucianism becomes the state religion.

---

ca. 350 BCE–9 CE: The Qin and Han Dynasties

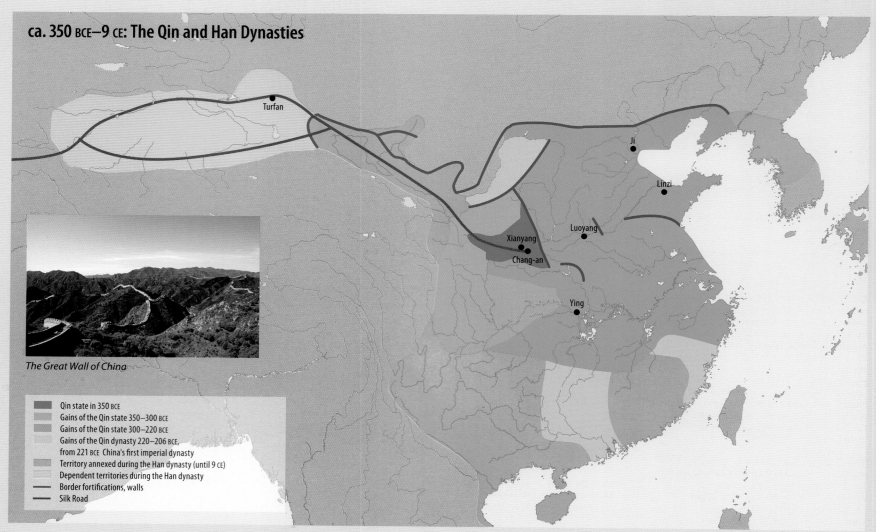

Turfan
Ji
Linzi
Luoyang
Xianyang
Chang-an
Ying

The Great Wall of China

■ Qin state in 350 BCE
■ Gains of the Qin state 350–300 BCE
■ Gains of the Qin state 300–220 BCE
■ Gains of the Qin dynasty 220–206 BCE, from 221 BCE China's first imperial dynasty
■ Territory annexed during the Han dynasty (until 9 CE)
■ Dependent territories during the Han dynasty
— Border fortifications, walls
— Silk Road

**中國 The Middle Kingdom and
Empire** As early as 3,000 years ago, the
Chinese referred to their land as the Middle
Kingdom. The name "China" comes from the
powerful, centralized military state of Qin,
which was united under the first emperor,
Shihuangdi. Much of China's development
took place in isolation: the 4,200 mile (6,700
km) long Great Wall kept out not only
foreign armies, but also foreign influences. China's restrictive policies toward
minorities and dissenters as well as its recent
precipitous rise as an economic power, are
the cause of international protests as well
as recognition.

220–280 CE The period of three
kingdoms: Shu, Wei and Wu.

265–420 The Jin dynasty is unstable;
nomads from the north invade and
the empire splits into northern and
southern dynasties.

439 The Wei dynasty takes control
of northern China. The influence of
Buddhism spreads.

581–618 The Sui dynasty reunifies
China after 300 years of separation.

618–907 The Tang dynasty presides
over China's economic and cultural
golden age.

755–763 General An Lushan leads a
rebellion against the Tang dynasty;
China is torn by civil war.

845 The last persecution of Buddhists
in China

907–960 Five Dynasties and Ten
Kingdoms period: China disintegrates
into numerous small states.

Qin Shihuangdi (260–210 BCE) The founder
of the first unified state on Chinese territory,
Qin Shihuang Di (who called himself Cheng)
was a member of the ruling family of the
military state of Qin. Within ten years of
assuming power (by 221 BCE), he had united
China with great efficiency and great
brutality. He adopted the policy of legalism,
the enforcement of political power by
means of exceptionally harsh laws. In order
to keep foreign enemies out of China, he
commissioned the construction of the
Great Wall.

Confucius (552–479 BCE) Formulating moral
laws and behavioral principles, this thinker
believed that social harmony was achieved
by respecting others and honoring one's
ancestors. The noble ideal (Junzi) permeates
all art and puts itself at the service of the
state. Confucius was opposed to hereditary
privilege, arguing that true nobility could
only be attained through developing one's
character. His short aphorisms are very
famous. With the advent of the Han dynasty,
Confucianism replaced legalism as the
state ideology.

The Great Wall of China is a fortification
4,200 miles (6,700 km) long and 20–32 feet
(6–10 m) high begun by Qin dynasty
emperor Shihuangdi. Most of what remains
today, however, was built during the 16th
century Ming dynasty. Crossing northern

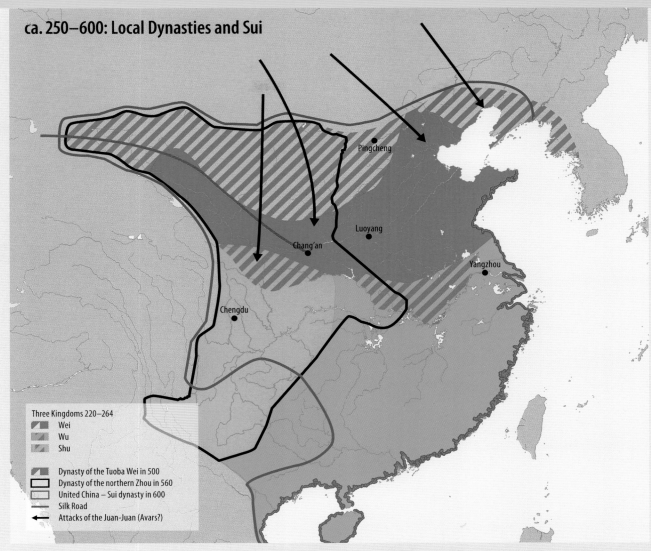

ca. 250–600: Local Dynasties and Sui

Pingcheng

Luoyang

Chang'an

Yangzhou

Chengdu

Three Kingdoms 220–264
- Wei
- Wu
- Shu

Dynasty of the Tuoba Wei in 500
Dynasty of the northern Zhou in 560
United China – Sui dynasty in 600
Silk Road
Attacks of the Juan-Juan (Avars?)

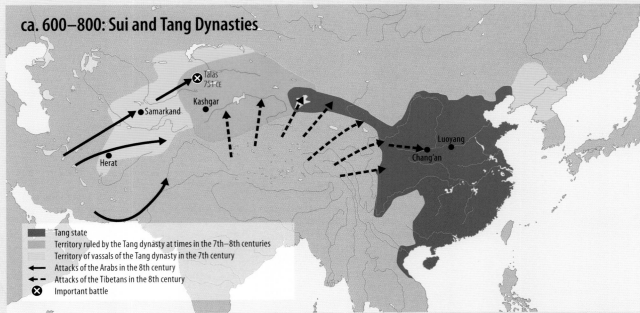

ca. 600–800: Sui and Tang Dynasties

Talas
751 CE

Samarkand

Kashgar

Herat

Luoyang

Chang'an

Tang state
Territory ruled by the Tang dynasty at times in the 7th–8th centuries
Territory of vassals of the Tang dynasty in the 7th century
Attacks of the Arabs in the 8th century
Attacks of the Tibetans in the 8th century
Important battle

China, the wall is strengthened with as many
as 25,000 watchtowers, placed every 500
feet (140 m). Military camps and garrisons
were built at regular intervals, and soldiers
stationed along the wall communicated
with each other via smoke signals. In 2007
the Great Wall was included in the list of the
Seven Wonders of the World.

The Terra-cotta Army is one of China's best
known ancient monuments. Located in
Xi'an, the warriors belong to the elaborate
burial complex of Qin Shihuangdi, the first

Chinese emperor. Discovered by chance
in 1974, the army consists of 7,000 statues
of foot soldiers, riders and wagons. Each
figure is life-sized, with individualized facial
features. The terra-cotta army was placed on
the UNESCO World Heritage list in 1987.

*Terra-cotta army,
Xi'an, China, Qin dynasty, 210–206 BCE*

China 960–1800 / Hong Kong

After 1000: Empire of the Song

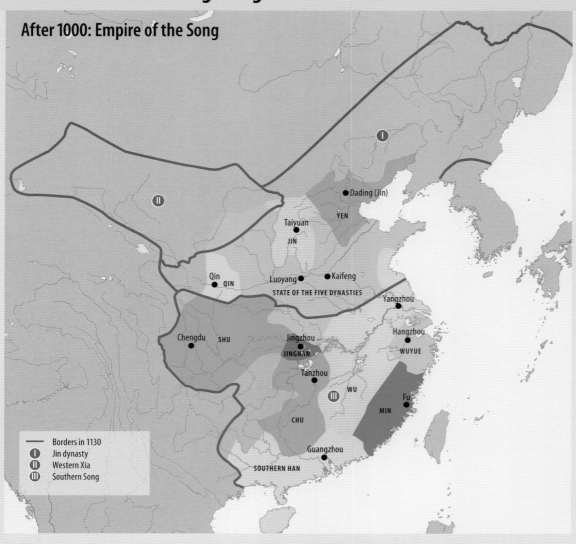

Borders in 1130
Ⅰ Jin dynasty
Ⅱ Western Xia
Ⅲ Southern Song

ca. 1259–1368: Yuan Dynasty (Mongols)

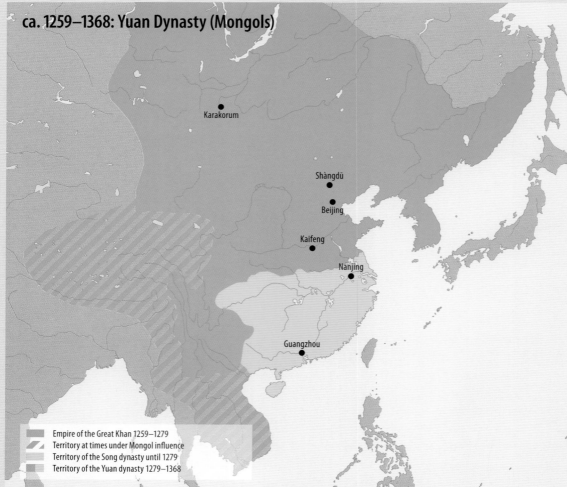

Empire of the Great Khan 1259–1279
Territory at times under Mongol influence
Territory of the Song dynasty until 1279
Territory of the Yuan dynasty 1279–1368

Genghis Khan (ca. 1162–1227)

960–1279 Under the Song dynasty, China is reunified. Paper money is introduced as part of an economic revival that includes the extensive production of iron and steel.

1126 Invading from the north, the Jin dynasty drives the Song south of the Yangtze River.

1126–1279 The southern Song dynasty is famous for its porcelain, gunpowder and publishing industry.

1211 Genghis Khan conquers the Jin state.

1261–1368 Reign of the Yuan dynasty, founded by the Mongol ruler Kublai Khan. Although the Mongols adopt Chinese customs, they are still considered foreign invaders. The Mongols rapidly overwhelm the weakened defenses at the Great Wall and advance to the Yangtze River valley.

1271–1279 The Mongols invade almost all of Eurasia and conquer the rest of China.

1352–1365 A peasant revolt led by the Chinese Red Turban movement drives out the Mongols.

1368–1644 The Ming dynasty, founded by Zhu Yuanzhang, who rules as Emperor Hongwu

1402 Foreign trade develops under the emperor Yongle.

1421 The Great Wall is extended. Peking becomes the capital, and the Forbidden City is built as an imperial palace complex.

1516 Portuguese sailors land in southern China. In 1557 they found the colony of Macao.

16th century Economic crisis in China. The Jesuits arrive and found the first missions. Led by Francis Xavier, Jesuits are the only Christian missionaries in China for the next half century.

1583 The Portuguese reach Taiwan, naming the island Formosa.

1593–1598 War with Japan

1644–1911 The Manchus occupy Peking and found the Qing dynasty.

1662 Taiwan is annexed by China.

1681 The Qing dynasty controls all of China.

until 1700 The Qing conquer Xinjiang and parts of Mongolia.

1705 Christianity is banned in China.

1720 China occupies Tibet.

1723–1735 The government is reorganized under Emperor Yongzheng.

18th century China reaches its greatest territorial extent.

1793–1803 The revolt of the White Lotus, a secret society, is put down by the Qing dynasty.

ca. 1368–1644: Ming Empire

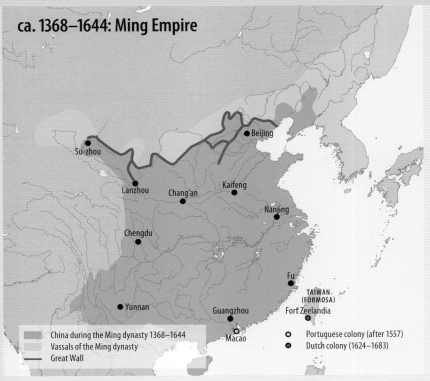

Beijing
Su-zhou
Lanzhou
Chang'an
Kaifeng
Nanjing
Chengdu
Yunnan
Guangzhou
Fu
TAIWAN (FORMOSA)
Fort Zeelandia
Macao

- China during the Ming dynasty 1368–1644
- Vassals of the Ming dynasty
- Great Wall
- Portuguese colony (after 1557)
- Dutch colony (1624–1683)

ca. 1644–1800: Early Qing (Manchus)

MANCHURIA
MONGOLIA
Shenyang
Kashgar
Beijing
TIBET
Kaifeng
Nanjing
Lhasa
Chengdu
Fuzhou
Yunnan
Canton
Macao

- Original Manchu settlements ca. 1600
- Territory under Manchu government in 1644
- Manchu empire (Qing dynasty in 1660)
- Territorial gains of the Qing dynasty by 1700
- Territorial gains of the Qing dynasty in the 18th century
- Vassal states and dependencies of China in the 18th century
- Portuguese colony

Khangxi (1654–1723)

Kangxi (1654–1723) The third Qing emperor ruled for sixty-one years and consolidated the power of the Manchu. China's economy flourished; advances in manufacturing and trade accompanied a flowering of intellectual and cultural life. The emperor also commissioned the Kangxi Dictionary, a guide to Chinese words and characters that was used into the 20th century.

The Forbidden City

The Forbidden City dates from the Ming dynasty. Located in the center of Beijing, this self-contained complex of governmental, ceremonial and residential space was said to have 888 buildings and 9999½ rooms. It was built in just fourteen years, involving the labor of 100,000 craftsmen and over a million laborers. Ordinary mortals were not permitted inside the Forbidden City; before the end of imperial China in 1911, no one could enter or leave the complex without the emperor's permission. Today the Forbidden City is open to the public as a museum.

Macao and Hong Kong, 1841

Canton
Victoria
Macao

- Macau—Portuguese after 1557
- Hong Kong—British after 1841

Macao and Hong Kong, 1860

Canton
Kowloon
Victoria
Macao

- Macau—Portuguese
- Hong Kong—British
- Area annexed by Hong Kong in 1860

Macao and Hong Kong, 1898–1999

Canton
Shenzhen
Kowloon
Victoria
Macao

- Macau—Portuguese until 1999
- Hong Kong—British until 1997
- New territory 1898–1997

- Shenzhen—Special Economic Zone of China since 1980
- Japanese occupation 1941–1945

Hong Kong was strategically important in the 19th century for the protection of British trade with China. After the Opium Wars in 1898, the English crown colony was leased to Great Britain for ninety-nine years. When this period ended in 1997, Hong Kong became one of China's two Special Administrative Regions; the other is **Macao**.

1513 Portuguese sailor Jorge Álvares is the first European to visit Hong Kong.

1553 The Portuguese acquire the right to anchor in the harbor at Macao and engage in trade.

1557 The first Portuguese settlers arrive in Macao.

1699 The East India Company of England begins trading in China.

1839–1842 British and Chinese forces face each other in the first Opium War.

1840 The Portuguese occupy the neighboring islands Taipa and Coloane.

1842 The Treaty of Nanking: China is forced to cede Hong Kong to Great Britain.

1860 The Treaty of Peking: After the second Opium War, Great Britain annexes the Kowloon Peninsula.

1887 Portugal and China sign an agreement making Macao and the neighboring islands Portuguese territory in perpetuity.

July 1, 1898 The New Territories, together with New Kowloon and the island Lantau, are leased to the British for ninety-nine years.

1987 An agreement is reached to return Macao to China in 1999.

July 1, 1997 Hong Kong is returned to China as a Special Administrative District.

China from the 19th Century to 1945

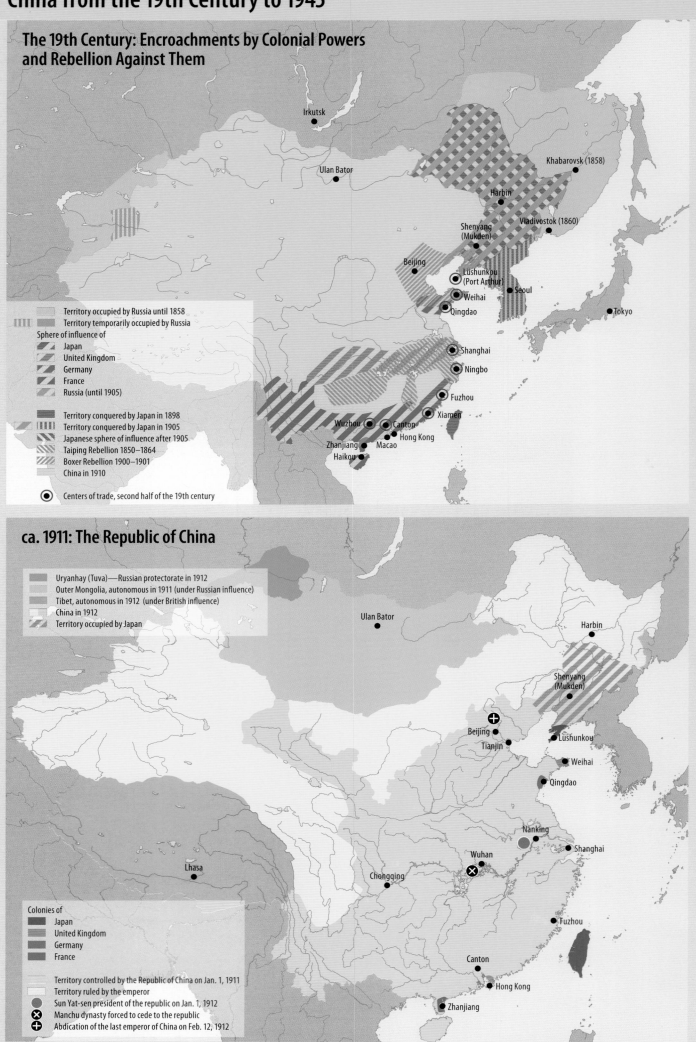

The 19th Century: Encroachments by Colonial Powers and Rebellion Against Them

Legend:
- Territory occupied by Russia until 1858
- Territory temporarily occupied by Russia

Sphere of influence of
- Japan
- United Kingdom
- Germany
- France
- Russia (until 1905)

- Territory conquered by Japan in 1898
- Territory conquered by Japan in 1905
- Japanese sphere of influence after 1905
- Taiping Rebellion 1850–1864
- Boxer Rebellion 1900–1901
- China in 1910

⊙ Centers of trade, second half of the 19th century

Map labels: Irkutsk, Ulan Bator, Khabarovsk (1858), Harbin, Vladivostok (1860), Shenyang (Mukden), Beijing, Lüshunkou (Port Arthur), Seoul, Weihai, Qingdao, Tokyo, Shanghai, Ningbo, Fuzhou, Xiamen, Wuzhou, Canton, Hong Kong, Zhanjiang, Macao, Haikou

ca. 1911: The Republic of China

Legend:
- Uryanhay (Tuva)—Russian protectorate in 1912
- Outer Mongolia, autonomous in 1911 (under Russian influence)
- Tibet, autonomous in 1912 (under British influence)
- China in 1912
- Territory occupied by Japan

Colonies of
- Japan
- United Kingdom
- Germany
- France

- Territory controlled by the Republic of China on Jan. 1, 1911
- Territory ruled by the emperor
- ⬤ Sun Yat-sen president of the republic on Jan. 1, 1912
- ⊗ Manchu dynasty forced to cede to the republic
- ⊕ Abdication of the last emperor of China on Feb. 12, 1912

Map labels: Ulan Bator, Harbin, Shenyang (Mukden), Beijing, Tianjin, Lüshunkou, Weihai, Qingdao, Nanking, Shanghai, Wuhan, Chongqing, Lhasa, Fuzhou, Canton, Hong Kong, Zhanjiang

---

By the 19th century the Qing dynasty had fallen on hard times. Great Britain and France were determined to exploit China economically, and social tensions led to a series of bloody civil wars. As the Qing dynasty lost more and more territory to colonial encroachment, Sun Yat-sen (1866–1925) founded the Revive China Society on the three principles of nationalism, the good of the Chinese people and democracy. By the early 20th century Sun Yat-sen was the central figure of the Chinese opposition. He would become the first president of the Republic of China.

1839–1842 The first Opium War breaks out when China attempts to restrict the British opium trade.

1850–1864 Taiping Rebellion: The revolt of a separatist, Christian-influenced sect against the Qing dynasty escalates to civil war. The death toll is approximately 30 million.

1853–1868 The Nien Rebellion in the north of China leads to much death and suffering, especially among China's Muslim minority.

1856–1860 The second Opium War between China and Britain

second half of the 19th century China loses its territories in Vietnam, Myanmar and Manchuria.

1898 The Hundred Days' Reform, an attempt at modernization by the young emperor Guangxu, is stifled by conservative court circles surrounding the dowager empress Cixi (Tzu Hsi).

1900 The Boxer Rebellion of peasants, supported by the Chinese government, against European and Japanese influence

1908 Death of the dowager empress Cixi (Tzu Hsi), China's de facto ruler since 1861

1911 Revolt against Emperor Puyi (1906–1967), the last emperor of China

Jan. 1, 1912 The Xinhai Revolution leads to the founding of the Republic of China.

Feb. 12, 1912 Puyi is forced to abdicate.

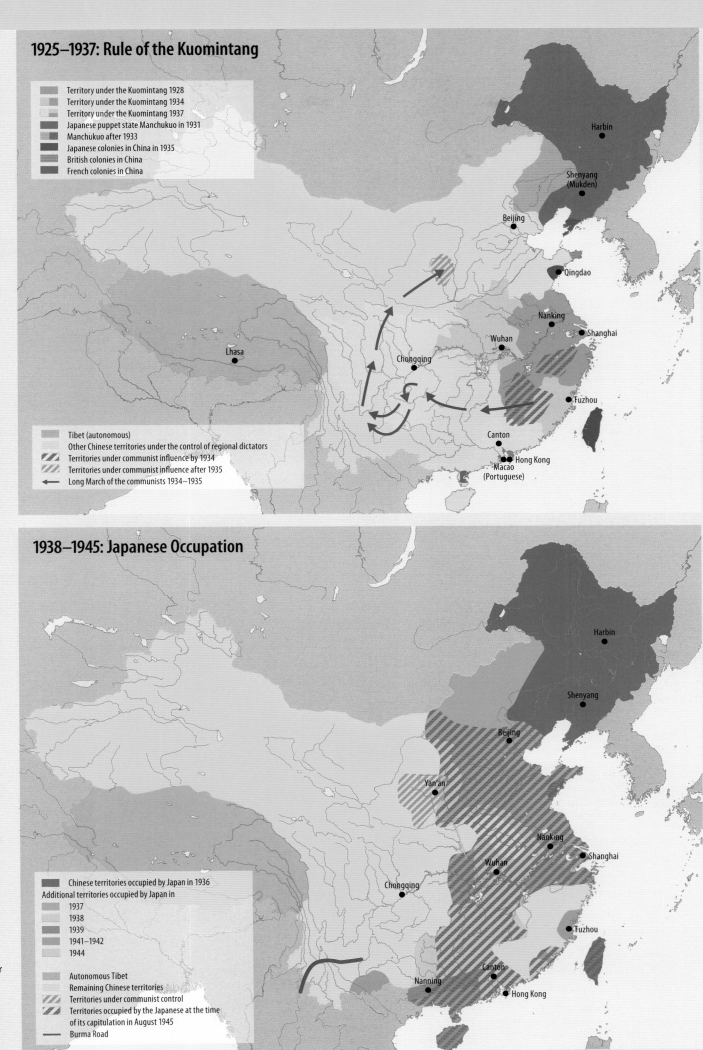

1915–1916 General Yuan Shikai tries to found a new imperial dynasty.

1917 China enters World War I on the Allied side, although as a non-combatant.

1919 The May Fourth Movement attempts to modernize China. Many of its leaders will be instrumental in the growth of communism in China.

1920 The Communist Party of China (CPC) is founded by Chen Duxiu and Li Dazhao with Soviet assistance.

1925 Chiang Kai-shek leads the Kuomintang, China's nationalist party. Despite massive support from Western nations, accusations of corruption and favoritism weaken Chinese support for Chiang, leading to the founding of more radical political movements.

1927–1949 Civil war between the communists and the Kuomintang. Sporadic fighting continues until 1955.

1931 Japanese forces occupy Manchuria and found the puppet state Manchukuo. China's last emperor, Puyi, is the nominal head of state.

1934–1935 The Long March: CPC units under Mao Zedong retreat north from Chiang Kai-shek's nationalist forces.

1937–1945 Sino-Japanese War: The communists and the Kuomintang agree to a truce.

Dec. 13, 1937 The Rape of Nanking: Japanese soldiers brutally massacre 200,000 Chinese civilians.

1945 Japan is defeated.

1945 Chiang Kai-shek arrives in Taipei, Taiwan, and sets up a provisional government.

Puyi (1906–1967) The last emperor of China ascended the throne at the age of three. He was unable to halt the disintegration of the empire, and he was forced to abdicate on Feb. 12, 1912. He lived in the Forbidden City until 1924, and later under Japanese protection. After the Japanese invasion of Manchuria, he was proclaimed ruler of Manchukuo (1934–1945). He was taken prisoner by the Soviet Red Army at the end of World War II, and in 1950 was sentenced to nine years at a reeducation camp. Released in 1959, he became a gardner, and died in 1967 at the height of the Cultural Revolution.

1925–1937: Rule of the Kuomintang

- Territory under the Kuomintang 1928
- Territory under the Kuomintang 1934
- Territory under the Kuomintang 1937
- Japanese puppet state Manchukuo in 1931
- Manchukuo after 1933
- Japanese colonies in China in 1935
- British colonies in China
- French colonies in China

Harbin
Shenyang (Mukden)
Beijing
Qingdao
Nanking
Shanghai
Wuhan
Chongqing
Lhasa
Fuzhou
Canton
Hong Kong
Macao (Portuguese)

- Tibet (autonomous)
- Other Chinese territories under the control of regional dictators
- Territories under communist influence by 1934
- Territories under communist influence after 1935
- ← Long March of the communists 1934–1935

1938–1945: Japanese Occupation

Harbin
Shenyang
Beijing
Yan'an
Nanking
Shanghai
Wuhan
Chongqing
Fuzhou
Nanning
Canton
Hong Kong

- Chinese territories occupied by Japan in 1936

Additional territories occupied by Japan in
- 1937
- 1938
- 1939
- 1941–1942
- 1944

- Autonomous Tibet
- Remaining Chinese territories
- Territories under communist control
- Territories occupied by the Japanese at the time of its capitulation in August 1945
- Burma Road

China from 1945 to the Present

1945–1951: Civil War

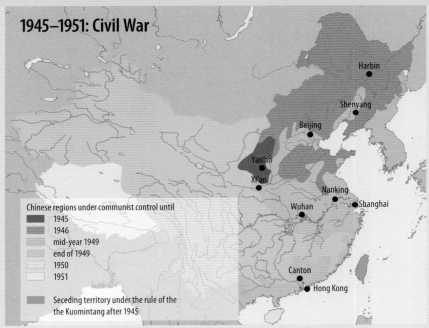

Chinese regions under communist control until
- 1945
- 1946
- mid-year 1949
- end of 1949
- 1950
- 1951

Seceding territory under the rule of the the Kuomintang after 1945

1949 The communists win the Civil War, and the People's Republic of China is proclaimed. The Kuomintang declare Taipei the new capital of the republic.

1950 China occupies Tibet, based on a centuries-old claim. Complete military takeover follows in 1959.

1950–1953 China participates in the Korean War on the side of North Korea.

1957 Brief program of cultural diversity (Let One Hundred Flowers Blossom)

1958–1961 The Great Leap Forward, a program of rapid industrialization and collectivization, leads to economic decline and devastating famine.

1960 Political and ideological split with the Soviet Union

1964 China conducts successful atomic tests.

1966–1969 The Cultural Revolution under the leadership of Mao Zedong leads to the deaths of as many as one million intellectuals and to the destruction of cultural treasures.

1971 The People's Republic of China joins the United Nations. Mao's "chosen successor" Lin Biao dies during a mysterious attempt to flee China. His health failing, Mao declares the end of the Cultural Revolution and beginning of a campaign against "deviant behavior."

1976 Mao Zedong dies. Deng Xiaoping initiates reforms.

1979 Special Economic Zones are opened.

1982 Relations with the Soviet Union are normalized.

1989 Tiananmen Square: About a thousand students are killed when the military forcibly ends a demonstration.

for democratic reform in Beijing's Square of Heavenly Peace.

1993 A socialist market economy is introduced.

1997 Hong Kong reverts to Chinese control. Deng Xiaoping dies.

1999 China resumes possession of Macao.

2008 The 2008 Summer Olympics are held in Beijing.

Dynasties

2070–1600 BCE Xia dynasty: the first larger settlements and cultural achievements. The political entity is considered largely mythical.

1600–1100 BCE During the Shang (or Yin) dynasty, the first large cities emerge, and culture becomes highly developed, even in everyday life.

~1100–256 BCE The Zhou dynasty at first establishes a strong, centralized state (Western Zhou) but is later reduced to a symbolic, religious role (Eastern Zhou).

476–221 BCE During the Warring States period (Chankuo) as many as seven different states struggle for power. It is nonetheless a time of scholarly and cultural flowering, ending with the dominance of the Qin dynasty.

221–206 BCE The Qin dynasty is characterized by a strong centralized state with policies promoting cultural unity enforced by harsh laws.

206 BCE–220 CE The Han dynasty establishes a feudal system with a highly trained bureaucratic apparatus. Confucianism becomes the state ideology (until 1912).

220–280 The Three Kingdoms period (Sanguo) is one of instability and civil wars.

265–420 During the Jin dynasty, aristocratic cliques struggle for power.

420–589 Separate Southern and Northern Dynasties (Nanbeichao): a time of foreign domination by the Xiongnu (Huns), Mongols, Tibetans and Turkic peoples

581–618 The Sui dynasty reestablishes a rigid central administration and initiates canal-building projects.

618–907 The Tang dynasty is associated with cultural achievements, centralized power and Chinese expansion in East Asia.

907–960 Five Dynasties and Ten Kingdoms period: Regional powers flourish.

916–1125 The Liao dynasty is founded by Khitan tribes and only exists in northern China.

960–1279 The Song dynasty reunites China and witnesses the first industrial production (large workshops), the introduction of rice cultivation and a flowering of art and poetry.

1032–1227 Western Xia

1115–1234 The Jurchen dynasty founded by Jurchen tribes (not native to China) in northern China

1261–1368 The Yuan dynasty is a period of foreign domination by Mongols as well as of major advances in astronomy and the sciences.

1952–1976: The People's Republic under Mao Zedong

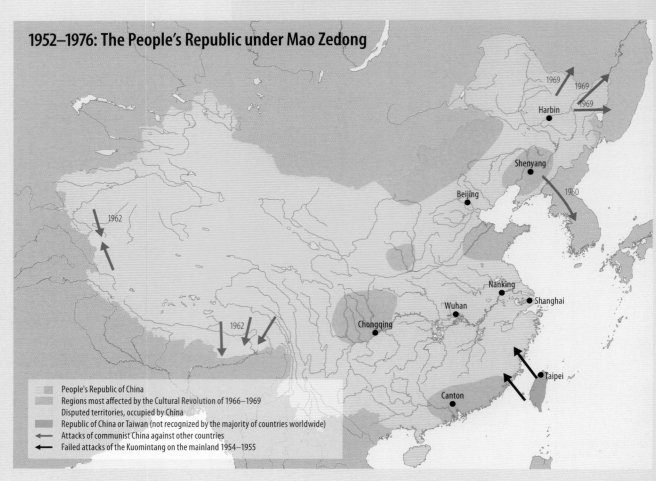

- People's Republic of China
- Regions most affected by the Cultural Revolution of 1966–1969
- Disputed territories, occupied by China
- Republic of China or Taiwan (not recognized by the majority of countries worldwide)
- Attacks of communist China against other countries
- Failed attacks of the Kuomintang on the mainland 1954–1955

1368–1644 The Ming dynasty places great emphasis on Chinese national identity. It is associated with porcelain production and fortification of the Great Wall of China. Court eunuchs wield considerable influence.

1644–1911 Qing (or Manchu) dynasty: Tibet and Mongolia are under Chinese domination. The sciences experience a late flowering. From the 19th century onward, China experiences massive pressure from foreign states and the decline of centralized government.

1915–1916 The Hongxian dynasty: a brief attempt by General Yuan Shikai to return to imperial monarchy

1912–1949 Republic of China: Political reforms are made, but the central government is weak and power fragmented. Japanese occupation causes immense suffering, a source of ongoing tension between China and Japan.

since 1949 The People's Republic of China is a strict communist state until 1976 (era of Mao Zedong). Since then economic reforms have been made despite the CPC's continued hold on power.

since 1949 Republic of China (Taiwan), not recognized by most countries: The authoritarian rule of the family of Chiang Kai-shek is followed by a return to parliamentary democracy and exponential economic growth.

Chiang Kai-shek (1887–1975) A military officer and member of the Kuomintang (Chinese National Party), he was involved in the overthrow of the Qing dynasty. After coming to the forefront of the Kuomintang (1925), he began the fight against local princes and warlords for the unification of China. In 1927 he unexpectedly attacked communists military positions with the full support of the United States, setting off a long civil war. He was president of the Republic of China from 1928–1945. After Japan's defeat in World War II, he renewed the anticommunist campaign, but lost and fled to Taiwan. There he reestablished the Republic of China (Taipei), which he ruled until his death.

Mao Zedong (1893–1976) was the leader of the Communist Party of China, and one of the 20th century's most infamous dictators. After Chiang Kai-shek's attack Mao Zedong retreated with his CPC ranks, gaining fame as the leader of what would come to be known as the Long March. After Japan's defeat in 1945 and the end of the civil war, he became president of the People's Republic of China. His time in office was marked by political and economic experiments on a grand scale in which he tried to lead China to communism through terror and enforced conformity (as laid out in his *Little Red Book*). Many millions of Chinese suffered under and fell victim to his regime.

1979–1990: The Deng Xiaoping Era

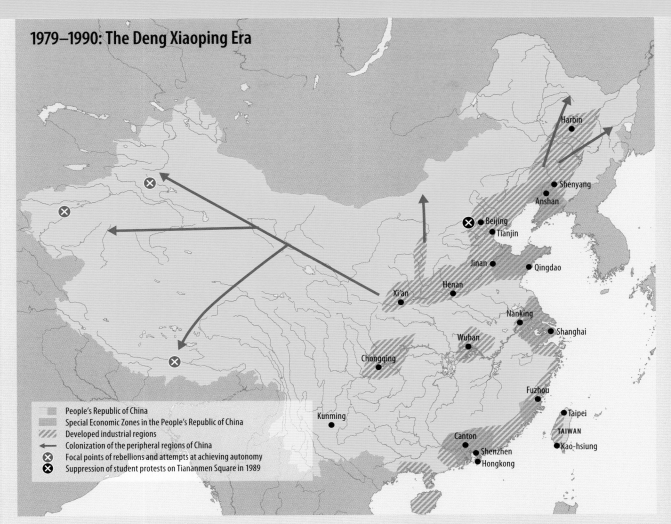

Legend:
- People's Republic of China
- Special Economic Zones in the People's Republic of China
- Developed industrial regions
- Colonization of the peripheral regions of China
- Focal points of rebellions and attempts at achieving autonomy
- Suppression of student protests on Tiananmen Square in 1989

China Today

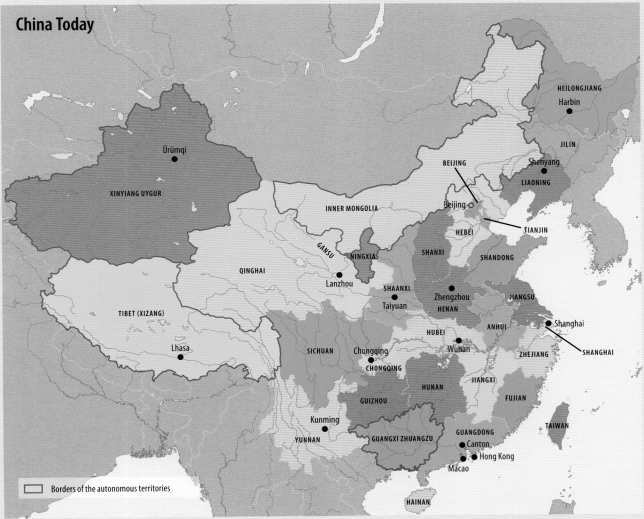

Borders of the autonomous territories

Korea

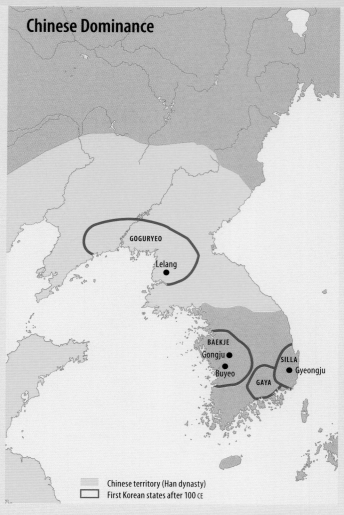

Chinese Dominance

GOGURYEO
Lelang

BAEKJE
Gongju
Buyeo
GAYA
SILLA
Gyeongju

Chinese territory (Han dynasty)
First Korean states after 100 CE

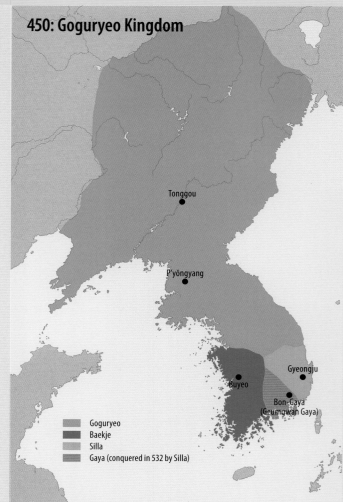

450: Goguryeo Kingdom

Tonggou

P'yŏngyang

Gyeongju

Buyeo

Bon-Gaya
(Geumgwan Gaya)

Goguryeo
Baekje
Silla
Gaya (conquered in 532 by Silla)

7th–10th Centuries: Balhae and Great Silla

Songyuan

Tonggyŏng

Changgyŏng

Sŏgyŏng

Hongwŏn

P'yŏngyang

Gyeongju
Buyeo
Busan

Kingdom of Balhae (Bohai) 694–926
Kingdom of Silla 668–918
Chinese invasion in 660
Invasion of nomads from the north in the 10th century

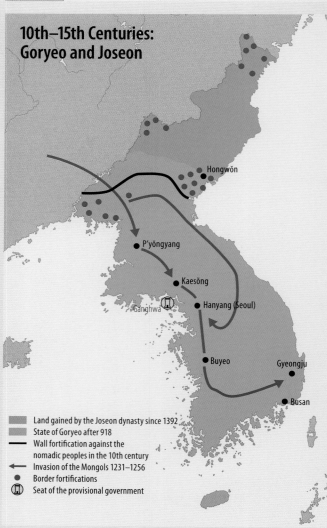

10th–15th Centuries: Goryeo and Joseon

Hongwŏn

P'yŏngyang

Kaesŏng

Hanyang (Seoul)
Ganghwa

Buyeo
Gyeongju

Busan

Land gained by the Joseon dynasty since 1392
State of Goryeo after 918
Wall fortification against the nomadic peoples in the 10th century
Invasion of the Mongols 1231–1256
Border fortifications
Seat of the provisional government

The Korean Peninsula has been inhabited since time immemorial by Korean tribes. According to legend, they were united under one ruler in 2333 BCE by Dangun, founder of the first Korean (Gojoseon) kingdom. At the Yalta Conference of 1945, the Allies divided Korea into Soviet (north) and American (south) spheres of influence, with the border between them set at the 38th parallel. One people were split into two enemy states: North Korea and South Korea.

2333 BCE Legendary founding of the Korean kingdom of Gojoseon by the demigod Dangun

500 BCE The Gojoseon (Old Joseon) empire, an advanced bronze culture, grows stronger and interacts with the Chinese.

194–108 BCE The Wiman Joseon kingdom is founded by refugees from strife in Chinese and Gojoseon natives.

100 BCE–668 CE Three kingdoms rule in Korea (Goguryeo, Baekje and Silla) along with the Gaya confederacy.

4th century Buddhism is first introduced into Korea.

532 The Silla kingdom over-runs Gaya.

660 Chinese invasion

668 Allied with the Chinese Tang Dynasty, Silla conquers large parts of Goguryeo and Baekje.

668–918 Era of the united Silla dynasty

694–926 Balhae kingdom

918–1392 Period of the Goryeo empire, which establishes its new capital at Kaesong

ca. 920 Nomadic peoples invade from the north.

1231–1256 Mongol invasion

1392–1910 Era of the Yi dynasty (Joseon)

1394 Hanyang (now Seoul) becomes the capital of Korea.

1592–1598 Japanese invasion

1610 Christianity is introduced and begins to spread.

1627 Manchu invasion

1790–1860 Anti-Christian persecution, isolationist policies

1894–1895 The Donghak Peasant Revolution leads to a second Japanese invasion.

1897 Korea becomes an empire.

1904–1905 Third Japanese invasion

1905 Korea is made a Japanese protectorate; in 1910 it becomes a colony.

1919 Korean struggle for independence: Shanghai becomes the seat of Korea's provisional government in exile.

1925 Founding of the Communist Party of Korea.

1945 Japan surrenders and World War II ends. At the Yalta Conference, the 38th parallel is identified as the boundary of a divided Korea.

1948 The Republic of Korea is south of the 38th parallel, and the Democratic People's Republic of Korea lies to the north. Kim Il-sung is dictator of North Korea, and Synman Rhee is the authoritarian leader of South Korea.

1950–1953 The Korean War breaks out between North Korea (aided by China) and South Korea (supported by US and UN troops).

1953 An armistice is signed, and new lines of demarcation are drawn.

1955 Democratic People's Republic of North Korea adopts a policy of isolation and self-reliance.

1960 In South Korea, Rhee Syng-man falls from power.

1961–1979 Dictatorship of Park Chung-Hee in South Korea.

1977 Juche (independent self-reliance) replaces Marxism as the national ideology of North Korea.

1987 After violent student protests threaten domestic stability, South Korea ratifies a democratic constitution, the first to allow for direct election of the president. New political parties form, and Roh Tae Woo becomes president of a coalition government by a narrow margin.

1500–1945: Yi Dynasty and Japanese Occupation

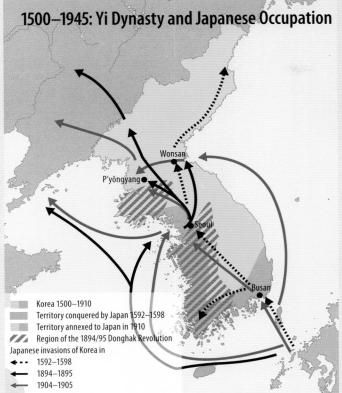

- Korea 1500–1910
- Territory conquered by Japan 1592–1598
- Territory annexed to Japan in 1910
- Region of the 1894/95 Donghak Revolution

Japanese invasions of Korea in
- 1592–1598
- 1894–1895
- 1904–1905

1950/51: The Korean War

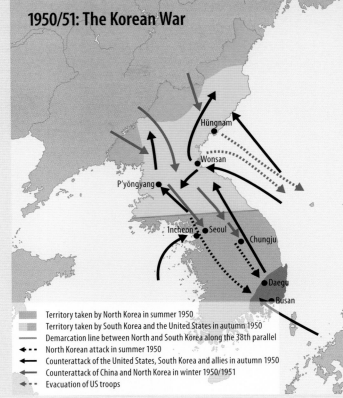

- Territory taken by North Korea in summer 1950
- Territory taken by South Korea and the United States in autumn 1950
- Demarcation line between North and South Korea along the 38th parallel
- North Korean attack in summer 1950
- Counterattack of the United States, South Korea and allies in autumn 1950
- Counterattack of China and North Korea in winter 1950/1951
- Evacuation of US troops

1951–1990: Divided Korea

- South Korean territory occupied for a time by North Korea and China in 1951
- Original demarcation line (38th parallel)
- New demarcation line since 1953
- Counterattack of US, South Korean and allied troops in autumn 1951

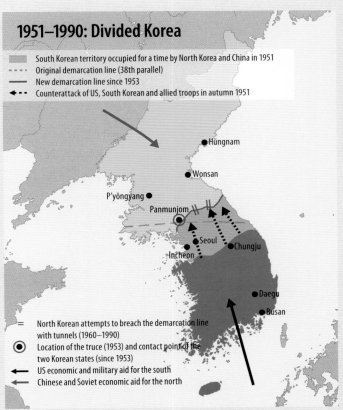

- North Korean attempts to breach the demarcation line with tunnels (1960–1990)
- Location of the truce (1953) and contact point of the two Korean states (since 1953)
- US economic and military aid for the south
- Chinese and Soviet economic aid for the north

Today

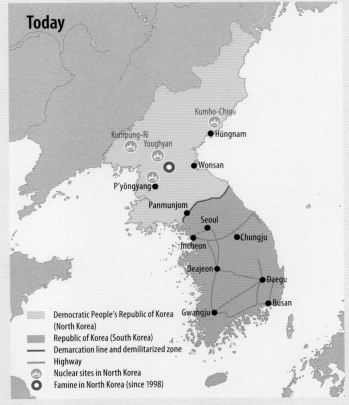

- Democratic People's Republic of Korea (North Korea)
- Republic of Korea (South Korea)
- Demarcation line and demilitarized zone
- Highway
- Nuclear sites in North Korea
- Famine in North Korea (since 1998)

1994 The United States and North Korea agree to shut down North Korea's nuclear program.

1994 Kim Il-sung's son, Kim Jong Il, assumes power in North Korea, largely continuing his father's isolationist policies and cult of personality.

2000 Korean-Korean dialogue leads to prisoner exchanges and the lifting of some trade, travel and economic sanctions.

2002–2007 North Korea revives its nuclear program and faces sanctions.

2007 Kim Jong Il meets with South Korean President Roh Moohyun.

2008 Famine threatens North Korea, and international aid programs respond.

Kim Il-sung (1912–1994)
North Korea's leader during the resistance against Japanese occupation, he was also a leading figure in the revolutionary People's Army (from 1935). He was dictator at the center of a personality cult from independence in 1948 until his death. In an attempt to unite Korea under communist rule, he provoked the Korean War by invading South Korea. After war's end, he oversaw a policy of international isolation that only increased with the fall of the USSR.

Kim Dae-jung (1925–)
A significant figure in the struggle for human rights, he fought for democracy in South Korea from 1956 onward. In 1972 he was forced into exile in Japan, where he was kidnapped by the Korean secret service in 1973. He was imprisoned, and in 1980 sentenced to death. After international protests secured his release, he was elected president of South Korea in 1998. He resumed talks with North Korea, and in 2000 was awarded the Nobel Peace Prize.

Japan Until the 17th Century

Early Period

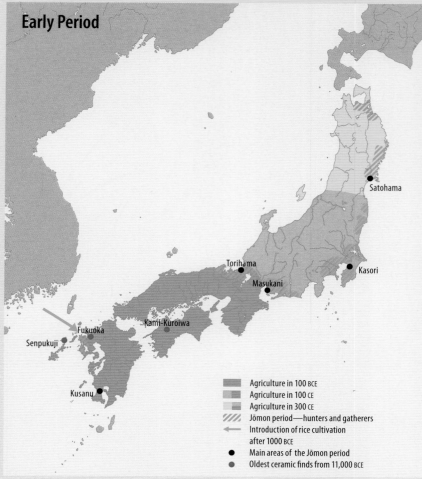

Agriculture in 100 BCE
Agriculture in 100 CE
Agriculture in 300 CE
Jōmon period—hunters and gatherers
Introduction of rice cultivation after 1000 BCE
Main areas of the Jōmon period
Oldest ceramic finds from 11,000 BCE

100–600: Yayoi and Kofun Periods

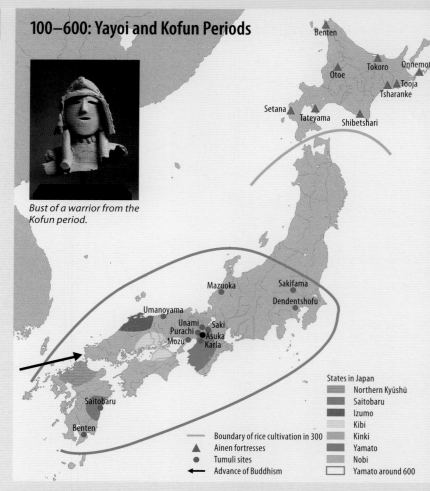

Bust of a warrior from the Kofun period.

States in Japan
Northern Kyūshū
Saitobaru
Izumo
Kibi
Kinki
Yamato
Nobi
Yamato around 600
Boundary of rice cultivation in 300
Ainen fortresses
Tumuli sites
Advance of Buddhism

700–950: Nara and Heinan Periods

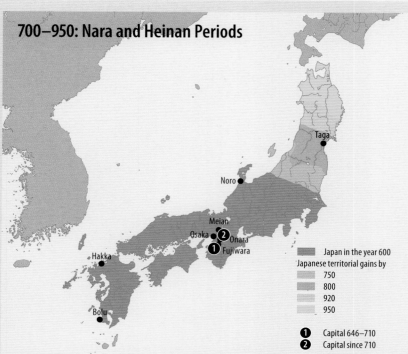

Japan in the year 600
Japanese territorial gains by
750
800
920
950
❶ Capital 646–710
❷ Capital since 710

Ni Hon or Nippon means "rising sun" and is the Japanese name of Japan. Although the island nation has gone through periods of intense isolation, it has at times readily adopted features of other cultures, such as writing from the Chinese. Japan is a land of creative innovation, but also of self-discipline, artistic culture and the samurai code known as bushido. Tragically, Japan's history is also marked by racist social policies and brutal domination of neighboring states.

10,000–300 BCE The Jomon period. Japan was first settled perhaps as early as 30,000 BCE, or even earlier.

660 BCE According to legend, this is when the first emperor, Jimmu Tenno, came to power.

300 BCE–300 CE The Yayoi period, marked by the formation of a distinctively Japanese social structure

Classical Japan

300–710 Kofun period, named for the burial mounds dating from this era

400–600 The Yamato dynasty forms the first Japanese state.

552–710 Overlapping with the Kofun period is the Asuka period, which begins the year in which Buddhism is introduced to Japan. Aspects of Chinese culture, society and technology are also adopted into Japanese culture.

604 Prince Shotoko Taishi establishes the first Japanese constitution (the Seventeen Articles).

646 The Taika reforms lead to the formation of a single centralized Japanese state following the Chinese model.

710–794 The Nara period takes its name from Heijo-kyo (Nara), the capital for most of this time.

724–756 Emperor Shomu rules Japan during a cultural golden age.

791–806 The reign of Emperor Kammu represents the height of imperial power in Japan.

794 Kyoto (Heian-kyo) becomes the new capital.

794–1185 The Heian period witnesses a decentralization of power as the emperor's influence declines. Three aristocratic clans—the Fujiwara,

Minamoto and Taira—gradually come to control most of the country.

~800 The flowing, cursive, syllabic Hiragana script develops from Chinese characters. At first used primarily by women of the court, Hiragana remains integral to Japanese writing today.

9th century The Fujiwara clan dominates.

1185 The Minamoto clan defeats the Taira clan at the naval battle of Dannoura.

12th century Period of proliferation of soldiers serving the Minamoto and Taira clans.

Feudal Japan

1185–1333 The Kamakura period sees the rise of the samurai cult.

1192 Minamoto no Yorimoto attains the title of shogun (hereditary military commander).

1274/1281 The shoguns, aided by the fortuitous arrival of two major typhoons that hinder their opponents, twice repel Mongol invaders on the southern island of Kyushu.

1318–1339 Reign of Emperor Go-Daigo, who ends the Kamakura shogunate in 1333.

1333–1336 The Kemmu Restoration, Go-Daigo's attempt to restore the older

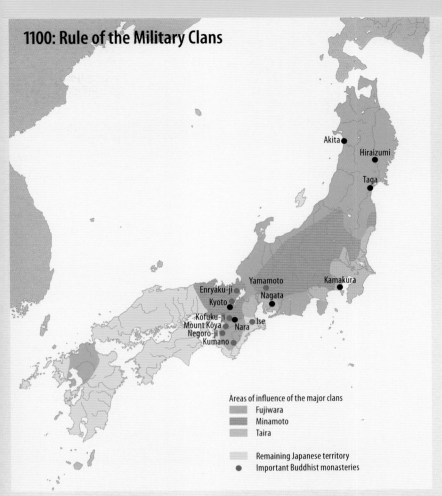

1100: Rule of the Military Clans

Akita
Hiraizumi
Taga

Enryaku-ji
Yamamoto
Kyoto
Nagata
Kōfuku-ji
Mount Kōya
Nara
Ise
Negoro-ji
Kumano
Kamakura

Areas of influence of the major clans

- Fujiwara
- Minamoto
- Taira

- Remaining Japanese territory
- ● Important Buddhist monasteries

12th and 13th Centuries: Kamakura Period

Main entrance of a Buddhist Kenchoji temple.

Hiraizumi
Azugashiyama 1189
Yokota Kawanara 1181
Shinohara 1183
Awazu 1184
Numazu 1180
Ishibashiyama 1180
Mizushima 1183
Kyoto
Dan-no-ura 1185
Nara
Osaka
Fujiwara
Yashima 1185

Areas of influence of the most important dynasties (1180)

- Taira clan
- Minamoto Yoshinaka
- Minamoto Yoritomo
- Northern Fujiwara clan
- ⌐ ⌐ Territory ruled by Yoritomo (1190)

- ← Repelled Mongolian invasions in 1274, 1281
- ⊗ Important battle

---

system of imperial rule. It is succeeded by the Ashikaga shogunate.

1333–1568 The Muromachi period

1336–1392 Japan is split into northern and southern empires.

1338 Ashikaga Takauji overthrows Emperor Go-Daigo and hands over power to the shogun.

1392 Ashikaga Yoshimutsu unifies Japan.

1467–1577 Warring States (Sengoku) period: Japan endures over a century of civil war as the armies of independent feudal lords battle for power. Thirty of what were as many as 200 autonomous warrior states take part in the conflict.

1543 Portuguese colonists arrive, bringing Christianity.

1568–1600 The Azuchi-Momoyama period unifies the Japanese empire.

1560–1616 Era of the three great unifiers: Odo Nobunaga (1560–1582), Toyotomi Hideyoshi (1582–1598) and Tokugawa Ieyasu (1598–1616)

1592 Japan fails in an attempt to conquer Korea.

1600–1867 The Edo period brings the longest period of uninterrupted peace in modern Japanese history.

1603–1867 The Tokugawa shogunate brings economic and political stability.

from 1639 Japan enters a period of strict isolation with its policy of *sakoku* (national seclusion), forbidding all European access to the country as well as any Japanese to leave the country, in part to stem the influence of Catholic missionaries.

Tokugawa Ieyasu (1543–1616) was the founder of the Tokugawa shogunate and its first shogun. He participated in the wars between rival clans from the age of seventeen. Due to his audacity, intrigues and skillful diplomacy, Tokugawa Ieyasu established his authority throughout Japan, and in 1598 he was the strongest regional ruler. In 1600 he defeated the clans hostile to him at the Battle of Sekigahara, thus becoming the most powerful man in all Japan. Taking the title of shogun in 1603, he established a tradition of strong, centralized rule that brought stability to Japan for the next 250 years.

Shoguns swere hereditary military commanders officially in service as regents of the emperor. They controlled most of Japan from 1192 to 1867.

Samurai were Japanese medieval warriors, who were educated in the arts and highly trained in combat from an early age. They were renowned for their unwavering loyalty and bravery.

Shintoism is the indigenous religion of Japan. A nature religion, its followers worship gods and spirits (called kami) associated with mountains, springs and natural phenomena in shrines and ancient sanctuaries. Shintoism, with a strong emphasis on the cult of the emperor, was the official state religion of Japan from 1868 to 1945, and it is still practiced by a majority of Japanese today.

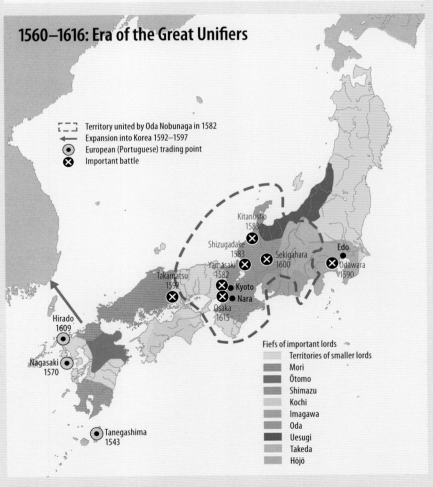

1560–1616: Era of the Great Unifiers

- ⌐ ⌐ Territory united by Oda Nobunaga in 1582
- ← Expansion into Korea 1592–1597
- ⊙ European (Portuguese) trading point
- ⊗ Important battle

Kitanoshio 1583
Shizugadake 1583
Yamasaki 1582
Sekigahara 1600
Edo
Odawara 1590
Takamatsu 1592
Kyoto
Nara
Osaka 1615

Hirado 1609

Nagasaki 1570

Tanegashima 1543

Fiefs of important lords

- Territories of smaller lords
- Mori
- Ōtomo
- Shimazu
- Kochi
- Imagawa
- Oda
- Uesugi
- Takeda
- Hōjō

Kamikaze means "divine wind," a reference to the typhoons that helped Japanese forces annihilate the Mongol navy during its attempted invasion of Japan's southernmost islands in the 13th century.

World War II suicide pilots were actually called *shimpu tokkotai* (naval air attack units). A mistranslation of the Japanese character for the unit led to its flyers' being referred to as "kamikaze pilots" in error.

Japan from the Edo Period to the Present

1700: The Edo Period

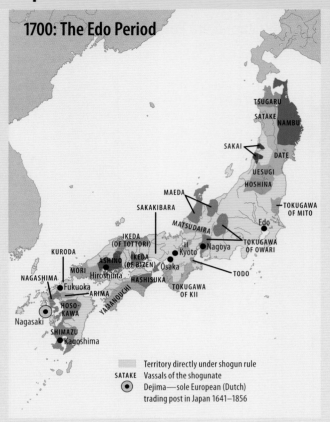

TSUGARU
SATAKE
NAMBU
SAKAI
DATE
UESUGI
HOSHINA
MAEDA
SAKAKIBARA
MATSUDAIRA
TOKUGAWA OF MITO
Edo
IKEDA (OF TOTTORI)
Nagoya
TOKUGAWA OF OWARI
KURODA
IKEDA (OF BIZEN)
II
Kyoto
MORI
ASHINO
HASHISUKA
TODO
NAGASHIMA
Hiroshima
Osaka
ARIMA
TOKUGAWA OF KII
Fukuoka
HOSO-KAWA
YAMANOUCHI
Nagasaki
SHIMAZU
Kagoshima

Territory directly under shogun rule
SATAKE Vassals of the shogunate
⊙ Dejima—sole European (Dutch) trading post in Japan 1641–1856

1853–1912: The Meiji Era and the Opening of Japan

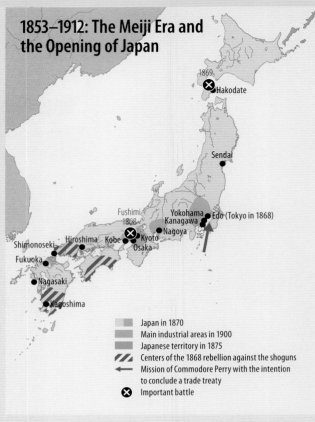

1869 ⊗ Hakodate
Sendai
Fushimi 1868
Yokohama
Kanagawa Edo (Tokyo in 1868)
Kobe Nagoya
Hiroshima Kyoto
Shimonoseki Osaka
Fukuoka
Nagasaki
Kagoshima

Japan in 1870
Main industrial areas in 1900
Japanese territory in 1875
Centers of the 1868 rebellion against the shoguns
← Mission of Commodore Perry with the intention to conclude a trade treaty
⊗ Important battle

1875–1945

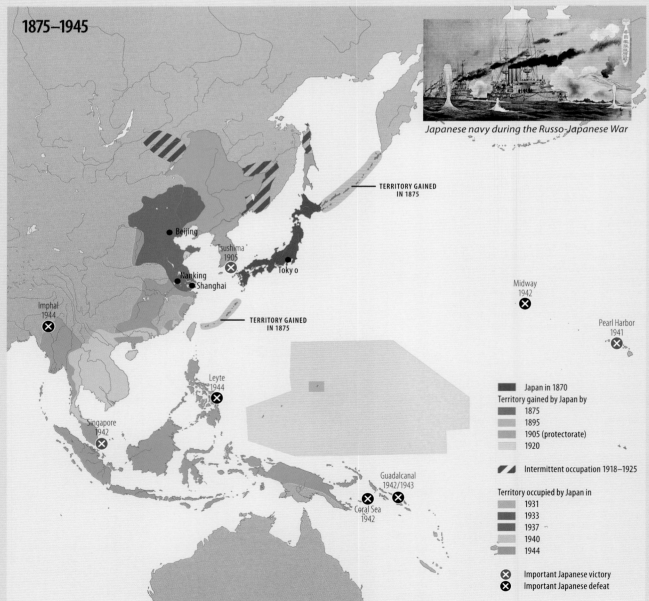

TERRITORY GAINED IN 1875

Beijing
Tsushima 1905 ⊗
Nanking
Shanghai
Tokyo
Imphal 1944 ⊗
TERRITORY GAINED IN 1875
Midway 1942 ⊗
Leyte 1944 ⊗
Pearl Harbor 1941 ⊗
Singapore 1942 ⊗
Guadalcanal 1942/1943 ⊗ ⊗
Coral Sea 1942

Japanese navy during the Russo-Japanese War

Japan in 1870
Territory gained by Japan by
■ 1875
■ 1895
■ 1905 (protectorate)
■ 1920
▨ Intermittent occupation 1918–1925
Territory occupied by Japan in
■ 1931
■ 1933
■ 1937
■ 1940
■ 1944
⊗ Important Japanese victory
⊗ Important Japanese defeat

Modern Period

1853–1854 US battleships commanded by Matthew Perry force Japan to open its ports to American commercial interests.

1868 The last shogun transfers his power to the emperor. Mutsuhito becomes the new emperor. Emperor Mutsuhito inaugurates the Meiji era, opening Japan to modernization.

1871 Feudalism is abolished.

1890–1945 Japan is ruled by a constitutional monarchy.

1894–1895 Sino-Japanese War breaks out over disagreement regarding the political status of Korea. Japan is victorious.

1902 Japan signs a treaty with Great Britain, its first with a European power.

1904–1905 The Russo-Japanese War is fought over claims to Sakhalin Island and other coastal territories. Japan wins.

1910 Japan annexes Korea.

1912 Yoshihito becomes emperor.

1914–1918 Japan fights in World War I on the side of the Allies.

1919 After World War I, the Treaty of Versailles gives Japan control over Germany's former colonies in China.

1920–1922 Japan experiences rapid economic growth.

1925 Japan holds its first general elections as the military gains increasing influence in government.

1928 Hirohito becomes emperor.

1931 Japan conquers Manchuria and establishes the puppet state of Manchukuo.

1932 The military gains authoritative control over the Japanese government.

1933 Japan withdraws from the League of Nations.

1937 Japan attacks China, brutally massacring the population of Nanking.

1940 Japan enters into the Tripartite Alliance with Germany and Italy.

1941 Japan occupies Saigon. The United States places an embargo on the export of crude oil to Japan.

Dec. 7, 1941 Japan attacks Pearl Harbor.

1942 Japanese forces occupy East Asia as far south as Australia, making use of experimental chemical and biological weapons. Japan is soundly defeated at the Battle of Midway, turning the tide of war in favor of the Allied nations.

1945 The United States conquers Iwo Jima and Okinawa.

Aug. 6–9, 1945 The United States drops atomic bombs on the cities of Hiroshima and Nagasaki. Japan surrenders on August 15, bringing World War II to an end.

1945–1952 Japan is administered by American occupation forces .

1946 Japan ratifies a democratic constitution. The emperor publicly repudiates claims to divine status.

1955 The Liberal Democrats become the strongest party, ruling until 2009.

1956 Japan becomes a member of the United Nations.

1960s Japan rapidly modernizes, becoming one of the world's leading technological powers.

1989 Hirohito dies. Akihito ascends to power. The Heisei ("peace") era begins.

from 1990 A recession batters the Japanese stock exchange (Nikkei 225), which loses as much as half of its value.

2001 Koizumi Junichiro becomes prime minster. The Japanese economy begins to recover.

2009 Yukio Hatoyama is prime minister of Japan.

Mutsuhito (1852–1912) was emperor during a period of rapid reform and modernization in Japan (the Meiji, or "enlightened" era). He broke the power of the shogunate, abolished feudalism, modernized the military, supported industrialization and reestablished the legal system. His reign transformed Japan from a rustic, undeveloped feudal state into a self-confident, modern nation. The Meiji era would serve as a model for modernization throughout Asia.

Emperor Mutsuhito

The Meiji Restoration refers to the political revolution in the second half of the 19th century that replaced the failing shogunate with a return to rule by a strong emperor with divine attributes. A samurai revolt, which was brutally suppressed by emperor Mutsuhito (over 25,000 people were killed), broke feudal control of the countryside and set Japan on the course for rapid modernization, but it also led to aggressive nationalism. The racist nationalism of the Meiji era with its emphasis on duty defined Japan during the 1930s and 1940s.

Tojo Hideki (1884–1948) The leading proponent of Japanese militarism between the world wars, he became vice minister of war in 1938, minister of war in 1940 and prime minister in 1941 (while still minister of war). Hideki concentrated power in his own hands and orchestrated Japan's entry into World War II, including the attack on Pearl Harbor in December 1941. After the island of Saipan was lost to the Allies in 1944, he was forced to resign. He attempted suicide the following year, but survived to be tried for war crimes by the International Military Tribunal for the Far East. He was condemned and hanged.

Project Manhattan was the code name for the secret atom-bomb development project of the US Army. In August 1945, two atomic bombs dropped on Hiroshima and Nagasaki killed 350,000 people, ending World War II; survivors suffered throughout their lives from the aftereffects of radiation and burns.

Hiroshima, 1945

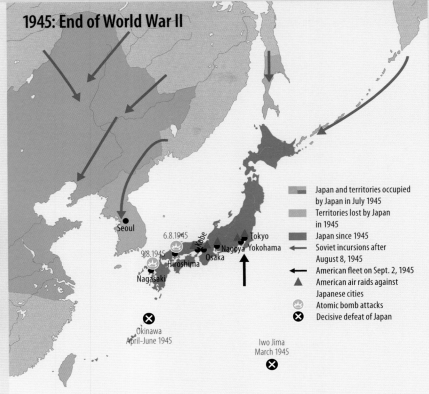

1945: End of World War II

Japan and territories occupied by Japan in July 1945
Territories lost by Japan in 1945
Japan since 1945
Soviet incursions after August 8, 1945
American fleet on Sept. 2, 1945
American air raids against Japanese cities
Atomic bomb attacks
Decisive defeat of Japan

Seoul
6.8.1945
9.8.1945
Kobe
Hiroshima
Osaka
Tokyo
Nagoya Yokohama
Nagasaki

Okinawa
April–June 1945

Iwo Jima
March 1945

Japan Today

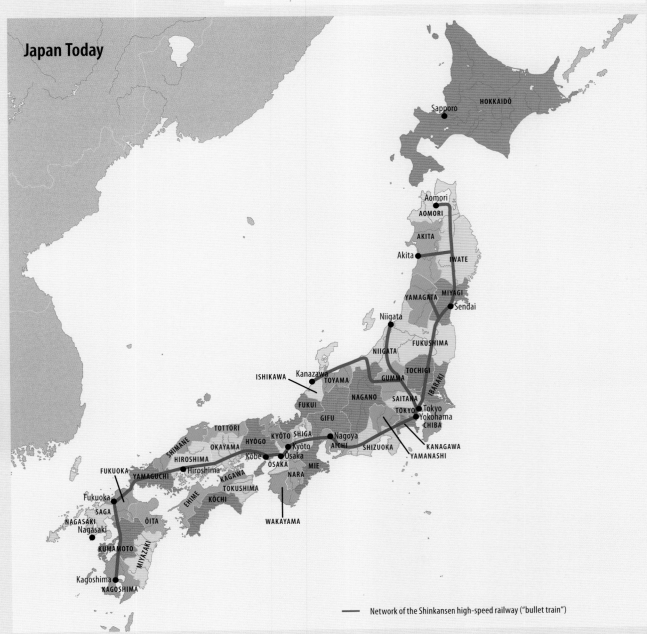

HOKKAIDŌ
Sapporo

Aomori
AOMORI
AKITA
Akita
IWATE
YAMAGATA
MIYAGI
Sendai
Niigata
NIIGATA
FUKUSHIMA
ISHIKAWA
Kanazawa
TOYAMA
TOCHIGI
GUMMA
IBARAKI
FUKUI
NAGANO
SAITAMA
TOKYO
Tokyo
Yokohama
GIFU
CHIBA
TOTTORI
KYŌTO
SHIGA
AICHI
KANAGAWA
SHIZUOKA
YAMANASHI
Nagoya
SHIMANE
OKAYAMA
HYŌGO
Kyoto
Kōbe
ŌSAKA
MIE
HIROSHIMA
Ōsaka
NARA
FUKUOKA
YAMAGUCHI
Hiroshima
KAGAWA
TOKUSHIMA
WAKAYAMA
Fukuoka
EHIME
KŌCHI
SAGA
ŌITA
NAGASAKI
Nagasaki
KUMAMOTO
MIYAZAKI
Kagoshima
KAGOSHIMA

Network of the Shinkansen high-speed railway ("bullet train")

Vietnam, Laos, Cambodia, Thailand and Myanmar

600: Early Kingdoms

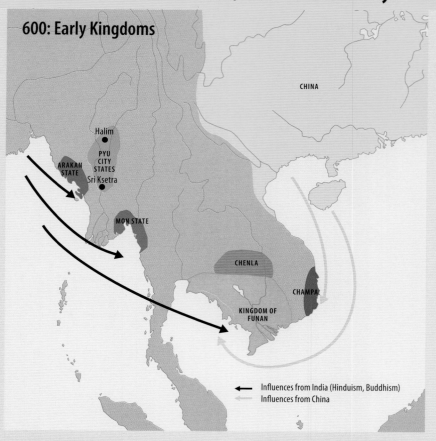

Influences from India (Hinduism, Buddhism)
Influences from China

1100: Bagan, Khmer and Dai Viet

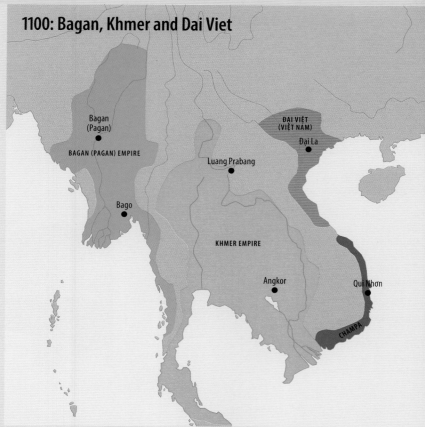

1550: Kingdoms in Southeast Asia I

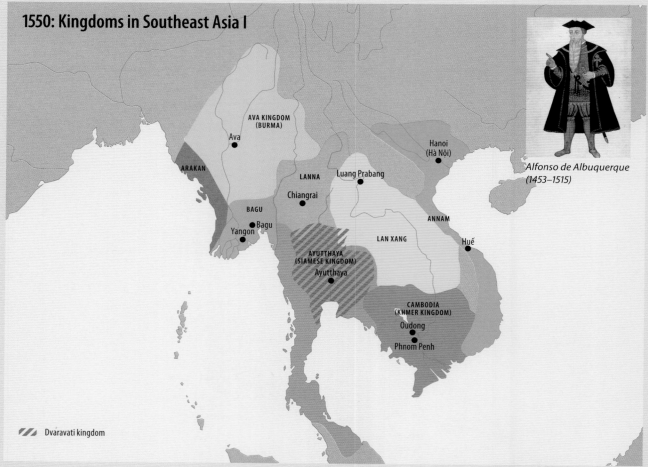

Dvaravati kingdom

Alfonso de Albuquerque (1453–1515)

400–1400 Hindu kingdom of Champa in South Vietnam

5th–8th centuries Early Khmer kingdom of Chenla (Hindu) in Cambodia

6th–11th centuries The Mon found the Buddhist Dvaravati kingdom in Thailand.

757 First Laotian state

802–1431 The Khmer empire rules from Angkor.

~ 850 Arrival of the Khmer in Thailand

931–1760 The north Vietnamese Dai Viet kingdom expands south to the southern tip of present-day Vietnam.

1113–1150 Khmer King Suryavarman II builds the temple city of Angkor Wat.

1181–1220 Jayavaraman VII reigns during the last period of Khmer empire power. He builds a new capital at Angkor Thom.

13th century The Mongols attack Indochina.

1238–1350 Period of the first Thai kingdom, Sukhothai, which means "dawn of happiness"

1259–1311 Mangrai the Great founds the kingdom of Lan Na in northern Thailand. He subjugates the rest of Thailand, conquering the Mon kingdom in 1281.

1283 The Khmer empire pays tribute to the Mongol Empire.

On the Southeast Asian peninsula lie the countries of Myanmar (Burma), Thailand (Siam), Cambodia, Laos and Vietnam. France, a regional colonial power, played an important role in their history, and in the late 20th century Cambodia, Laos and Vietnam were transformed by communist ideology and devastating wars.

1200 BCE Sa Huynh and Dong Son cultures in Vietnam (Bronze Age)

600 BCE The Thai emigrate to Southeast Asia from China.

300–100 BCE Arrival of the Mon and Khmer in Cambodia

300 BCE Founding of the first Vietnamese state, later called Nam Viet (Nanyue).

111 BCE Nam Viet becomes part of China.

1st–6th centuries Buddhist Funan empire in Cambodia

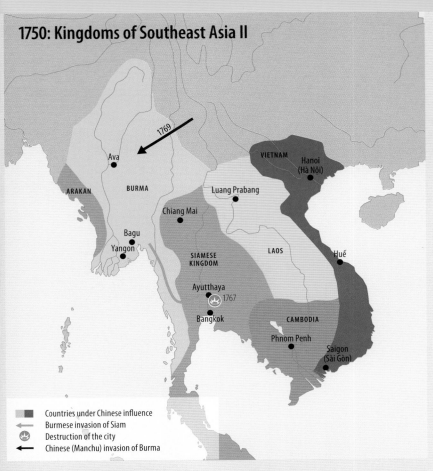

1750: Kingdoms of Southeast Asia II

1769

VIETNAM
Hanoi (Hà Nội)

ARAKAN   BURMA   Ava

Luang Prabang

Chiang Mai

Bagu

Yangon

SIAMESE KINGDOM   LAOS

Ayutthaya 1767

Bangkok

Phnom Penh

Huế

CAMBODIA

Saigon (Sài Gòn)

Countries under Chinese influence
← Burmese invasion of Siam
Destruction of the city
← Chinese (Manchu) invasion of Burma

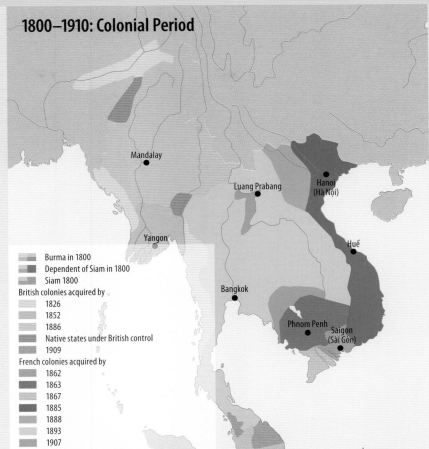

1800–1910: Colonial Period

Mandalay

Luang Prabang

Hanoi (Hà Nội)

Yangon

Huế

Bangkok

Phnom Penh

Saigon (Sài Gòn)

Burma in 1800
Dependent of Siam in 1800
Siam 1800
British colonies acquired by
1826
1852
1886
Native states under British control
1909
French colonies acquired by
1862
1863
1867
1885
1888
1893
1907

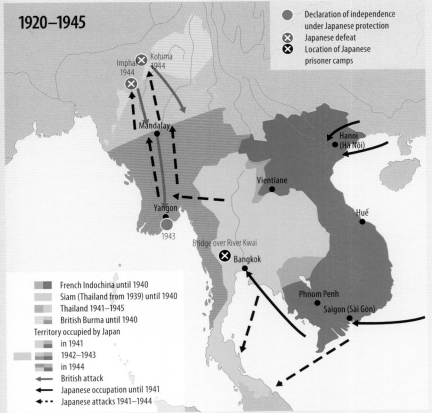

1920–1945

Declaration of independence under Japanese protection
Japanese defeat
Location of Japanese prisoner camps

Imphal 1944   Kohima 1944

Mandalay

Hanoi (Hà Nội)

Vientiane

Yangon

1943   Huế

Bridge over River Kwai

Bangkok

Phnom Penh

Saigon (Sài Gòn)

French Indochina until 1940
Siam (Thailand from 1939) until 1940
Thailand 1941–1945
British Burma until 1940
Territory occupied by Japan
in 1941
1942–1943
in 1944
← British attack
← Japanese occupation until 1941
◄-- Japanese attacks 1941–1944

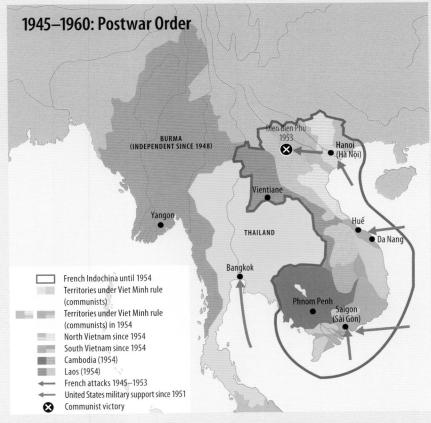

1945–1960: Postwar Order

BURMA (INDEPENDENT SINCE 1948)

Dien Bien Phu 1953

Hanoi (Hà Nội)

Vientiane

Yangon   THAILAND

Huế

Da Nang

Bangkok

Phnom Penh

Saigon (Sài Gòn)

French Indochina until 1954
Territories under Viet Minh rule (communists)
Territories under Viet Minh rule (communists) in 1954
North Vietnam since 1954
South Vietnam since 1954
Cambodia (1954)
Laos (1954)
← French attacks 1945–1953
← United States military support since 1951
Communist victory

14th century Thai rule in Cambodia

1351–1767 The long period of the kingdom of Ayutthaya in Siam (present-day Thailand)

1353–1707 The kingdom of Lan Xang, the first Laotian state

1471 The kingdom of Champa rules much of what is now Vietnam.

16th–18th centuries Vietnam fragments into feudal kingdoms, with the Nguyen dynasty ruling in the south and the Trinh dynasty holding power in the north.

1516 The Portuguese arrive in Thailand.

1549–1569 Twenty years of Burmese aggression culminate with their conquest of Ayutthaya in 1569.

by 1595 Under King Naresuan, Ayutthaya is able to expel the Burmese and regain independence.

1656–1688 King Narai of Ayutthaya engages in diplomatic relations with France.

1767 The Burmese destroy Ayutthaya. The Thonburi period begins, with its capital near Bangkok.

since 1782 The Chakri dynasty rules in Thailand.

from 1778 Laos, lacking cohesion following the end of the Lan Xang kingdom, falls under Siamese rule.

1802 Following a civil war, Gia Long becomes emperor of Vietnam. The Nguyen dynasty rules until 1945.

Vietnam, Laos, Cambodia, Thailand and Myanmar

1960–1974

- ⊙ Important cities surrounded by the Viet Cong during the January 1968 Tet Offensive
- + American bombing
- ⊕ Military coup
- ← Viet Cong supply route
- ← American offensives 1965–1973
- ⊷ American retreat

Territory controlled by the Viet Cong

Part of Cambodia ruled by dictator Lon Nol 1970–1975

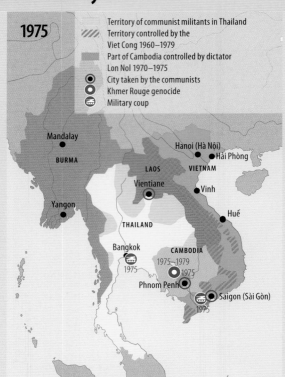

1975

- ▨ Territory of communist militants in Thailand
- ▨ Territory controlled by the Viet Cong 1960–1979
- ▨ Part of Cambodia controlled by dictator Lon Nol 1970–1975
- ⊙ City taken by the communists
- ⊙ Khmer Rouge genocide
- ⊕ Military coup

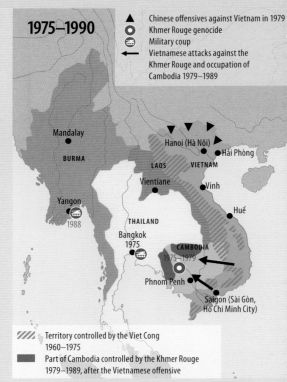

1975–1990

- ▲ Chinese offensives against Vietnam in 1979
- ⊙ Khmer Rouge genocide
- ⊕ Military coup
- ← Vietnamese attacks against the Khmer Rouge and occupation of Cambodia 1979–1989

Territory controlled by the Viet Cong 1960–1975

Part of Cambodia controlled by the Khmer Rouge 1979–1989, after the Vietnamese offensive

Today

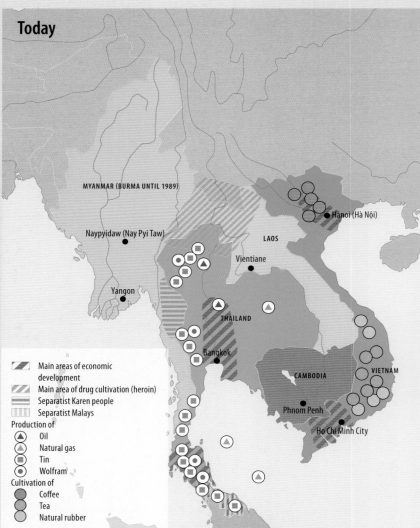

- ▨ Main areas of economic development
- ▨ Main area of drug cultivation (heroin)
- ▤ Separatist Karen people
- ▥ Separatist Malays

Production of
- ▲ Oil
- ▲ Natural gas
- ▣ Tin
- ⊙ Wolfram

Cultivation of
- ● Coffee
- ● Tea
- ● Natural rubber

1858–1862 The French attack and occupy Vietnam. The impoverished population fights back.

1868–1910 The reign of King Rama V Chulalongkorn brings political reforms, an educational system and modern infrastructure to Siam.

1884 The French bring all of Vietnam under their control.

1885–1895 Protests of French rule in Vietnam are suppressed.

1886–1907 Thailand loses control of some of its territory to France.

1887 French Indochina is created out of Vietnam and Cambodia.

1893 French occupation of Laos, which is absorbed into French Indochina

1930 Vietnamese soldiers serving in the French colonial forces lead an insurrection, the first against French colonial rule in Indochina.

from 1930 Rise of the Communist Party in Vietnam

1938 Withdrawal of the French from Cambodia

1939 Following the transition from monarchy to democracy (constitutional monarchy) made in 1935, Siam changes its name to Thailand.

1940 Japanese invasion of Indochina

1940–1941 French-Thai War over disputed territories

1945 French colonial rule is reinstated in Indochina. Ho Chi Minh founds the Democratic Republic of Vietnam in the north, becoming its first prime minister. He will serve as president from 1955 until his death in 1969.

1946 Thailand becomes a member of the United Nations. In Thailand, Bhumibol Adulyadej becomes King Rama IX; he is the longest-serving head of state currently in power in 2010.

1946–1954 First Indochina War: The French are defeated, ending French colonial rule. Indochina is divided into Cambodia, Laos, North Vietnam and South Vietnam.

1951–1957 The United States supports Thailand, which experiences rapid economic growth.

1954–1975 Civil war in Laos between leftist and rightist factions

1964–1975 A US warship is allegedly attacked in the Gulf of Tonkin off the North Vietnam coast. US President Johnson uses this as a pretext for military intervention. The Vietnam War begins.

1970 The United States supports a coup led by rightist general Lon Nol in Cambodia.

1970–1975 Civil war in Cambodia

1973 The Paris Peace Accords bring a ceasefire between the USA and North Vietnam. Fighting between North and South Vietnam ends with Viet Cong victory over the South in 1975.

1975 Monarchy is abolished in Laos and the Lao People's Democratic Republic is established.

1975–1979 Cambodia is ruled by the totalitarian Khmer Rouge regime under Pol Pot. Their policies result in depopulation of cities, forced labor and death camps known as the killing fields.

1976 Saigon is renamed Ho Chi Minh City. North and South Vietnam reunite as the Socialist Republic of Vietnam.

1977 Vietnam becomes a member of the United Nations.

1979 Vietnam repels Chinese aggression.

1979–1989 Vietnam maintains a military presence in Cambodia.

1980–1990 Vietnam occupies Laos.

1982 Cambodian government-in-exile forms in Beijing.

1986 Vietnamese reforms begin.

1991–2004 Norodom Sihanouk is king of Cambodia. He is succeeded by his son, Norodom Sihamoni.

December 2004 A tsunami ravages coastal Southeast Asia, particularly Thailand. Recovery will take years.

2006 Following a military coup, Thailand is placed under martial law. It is lifted in 2007 following ratification of a new constitution.

December 2008 Conservative circles in Thailand protest and occupy the airport, after which the elected government of Prime Minister Somchai Wongsawat resigns.

Pol Pot (1925–1998) and the Khmer Rouge
Pol Pot, born Salot Sar, was a Cambodian dictator and leader of the communist Khmer Rouge regime. His official title was "brother number one." After studying in France he returned to Cambodia in 1953, becoming leader of the Khmer Rouge communist resistance movement in 1975. His version of communist ideology rejected urbanism and industry in favor of a return to the land and massive collective agricultural projects. Under Pol Pot's terror regime, intellectuals and nearly all of Cambodia's Buddhist monks were arrested as "enemies of the proletariat," and nearly two million Cambodians were tortured, murdered or died of starvation and disease. In 1979 Vietnam's armed forces invaded Cambodia, finally putting an end to Khmer Rouge rule. Pol Pot and his followers retreated to the jungles, where they continued guerilla warfare until Pol Pot's death in 1998.

Ho Chi Minh (1890–1969) emigrated to France in 1911, when he encountered communist ideology. He continued his education in the USSR (1923) and China, where in 1930 he formed the Communist Party of Vietnam. During World War II he led his Viet Minh guerillas in a successful campaign against the Japanese occupation, and served as prime minister (1945–1955) and president (1955–1969) of the Democratic Republic of Vietnam (North Vietnam). Having led Vietnamese resistance to French colonialism in the Indochinese War (1946–1954), he continued his efforts to reunite North and South Vietnam, leading to American involvement in the Vietnam War. His modesty and integrity, as well as his benign governing style compared to other communist leaders, made him a hero of Western student movements, who called him "Uncle Ho."

Angkor Wat Angkor Wat is the largest and best-preserved Buddhist (formerly Hindu) temple complex in Angkor, the royal city of the Khmer empire. Its construction began sometime after 1113 during the reign of King Suryavarma II. Angkor Wat has become the symbol of Cambodia.

The Angkor Wat temple complex

Thailand Today

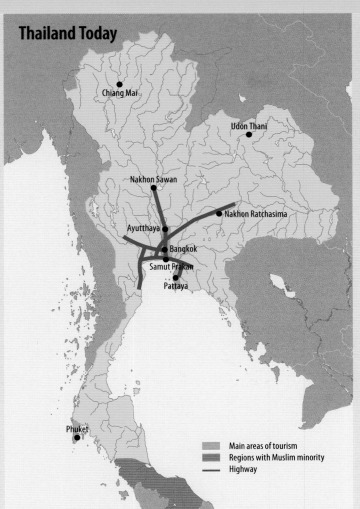

Main areas of tourism
Regions with Muslim minority
Highway

Myanmar Today

Naypyidaw New capital as of 2006

Vietnam, Laos and Cambodia Today

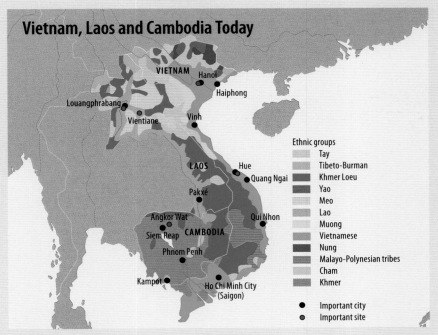

Ethnic groups
Tay
Tibeto-Burman
Khmer Loeu
Yao
Meo
Lao
Muong
Vietnamese
Nung
Malayo-Polynesian tribes
Cham
Khmer

● Important city
● Important site

Myanmar (Burma)

1st century BCE–800 CE Pyu period: Various city-states struggle for dominance of the Malay Peninsula.

9th century Burmese settle in the area.

825 The Mon kingdom of Pegu rules in southern Burma until 1757.

1044–1077 King Anawratha founds the first Burmese kingdom of Pagan in 1058.

1277–1287 Destruction of Pagan by the Mongols

1752–1760 King Alaungpaya founds the Third Burmese Empire and conquers Pegu in 1757.

1769 Victory over the invading Chinese troops

1886 Burma is annexed by British India.

late 19th century Anglo-Burmese wars

1942–1945 Japan occupies Burma.

1945–1948 Britain reoccupies Burma.

1948 Burma declares independence.

1948–1958 Democratic government under Prime Minister U Nu

1962 Socialist military coup

1962–1988 Dictatorship of General Ne Win

1987–1988 Students protest, demanding a return to democracy. Thousands of Burmese are forced into exile.

1989 The military junta renames Burma, calling it Myanmar.

1990 The National League for Democracy wins national elections, but the military regime does not recognize the election results.

1991 Activist and opponent of the regime Aung San Suu Kyi receives the Nobel Peace Prize.

2007 The Saffron Revolution, led by Buddhist monks and nuns against the military junta, is violently surpressed by the government.

2008 A tsunami kills around 130,000 people in coastal Burma. The government at first refuses international aid, then accepts it after criticism by the UN.

Malaysia, Brunei and Singapore

Early Settlement

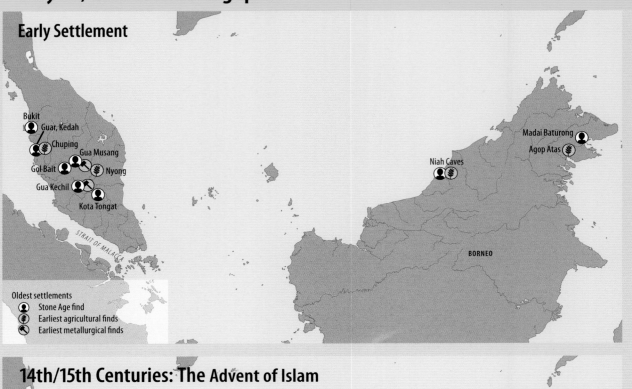

Bukit
Guar, Kedah
Chuping
Gua Musang
Gol Bait
Nyong
Gua Kechil
Kota Tongat

Niah Caves

Madai Baturong
Agop Atas

BORNEO

STRAIT OF MALACCA

Oldest settlements
- Stone Age find
- Earliest agricultural finds
- Earliest metallurgical finds

14th/15th Centuries: The Advent of Islam

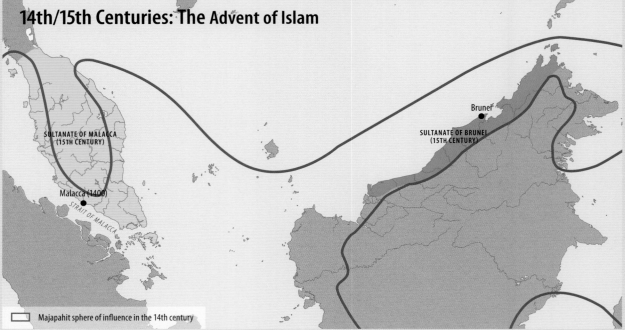

SULTANATE OF MALACCA
(15TH CENTURY)

Malacca (1409)

STRAIT OF MALACCA

Brunei

SULTANATE OF BRUNEI
(15TH CENTURY)

Majapahit sphere of influence in the 14th century

1500–1800: Colonial Period I

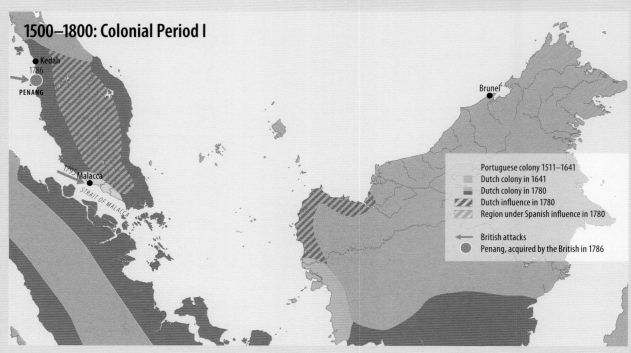

Kedah
1786
PENANG

1795
Malacca

STRAIT OF MALACCA

Brunei

- Portuguese colony 1511–1641
- Dutch colony in 1641
- Dutch colony in 1780
- Dutch influence in 1780
- Region under Spanish influence in 1780
- British attacks
- Penang, acquired by the British in 1786

Buddhism, Hinduism, Islam and Christianity have all left their mark on the multiethnic state of Malaysia. Its territory includes both the southern Malay Peninsula and northern lowlands of Borneo. Today Malaysia is a constitutional elective monarchy.

1000 BCE Malay tribes settle the region.

300–600 CE Funan empire

8th–14th centuries The Malay Peninsula forms part of the Indonesian empires of Srivijaya and Majahapit.

10th century The first Malay kingdoms, based in port cities, control coastal trade routes.

1396 The sultanate of Malacca (Melaka) is founded. Its ruling dynasty converts to Islam in 1409.

15th century Thai kingdoms rule the Malay Peninsula. The sultanate of Brunei controls Borneo.

1509 The arrival of the Portuguese

1614 The Dutch arrive.

1641 In alliance with the sultan of Johor, the Dutch expel the Portuguese.

1786/1795 The British take control of Penang in 1786 and expel the Dutch in 1795.

1819 Singapore is founded as a British trade post.

1826 The Straits Settlements (Straits of Malacca) are absorbed into the British Empire as a crown colony.

1895–1896 Unification of the Federated Malay States

1920 The Malay States become a British protectorate.

from 1930 Struggle for national independence

1941–1945 The Japanese occupy the Malay States.

1946/1948 The Malayan Union is founded in 1946 and renamed the Federation of Malaya in 1948.

from 1949 Conflict between Malays and the wealthier Chinese minority

1957 Malaya gains its independence from Great Britain.

1957–1970 Era of Abdul Rahman Putra, the Malay prime minister who negotiated independence from the British.

1959–1990 Lee Kuan Yew's rule in Singapore is one of authoritarian government and rapid modernization.

1963 Sabah, Sarawak on northern Borneo, and Singapore merge with

Lee Kuan Yew, 2004

the Federation of Malaya to form the new nation of Malaysia. The sultanate of Brunei remains independent. The eleven Malaysian states are ruled by an elective constitutional monarchy.

1964–1966 Malaysia goes to war with Indonesia over Borneo.

1965 Singapore leaves the Federation, and the current borders are established. Prime minister Lee Kuan Yew orchestrates Singapore's admission to the United Nations and membership in the British Commonwealth in October.

1970–1980 Struggles with Maoist guerillas in Malaysia lead to more authoritarian domestic social policies, particularly against non-ethnic Malays.

from 1980 Singapore and Malaysia experience rapid economic growth, but Singapore outpaces Malaysia. Disputes between them continue.

1981–2003 Malaysian prime minister Mahathir bin Mohamed's authoritarian rule modernizes Malaysia.

1997 The Petronas Twin Towers, at the time the tallest buildings in the world, open just weeks before a devastating Malaysian stock market crash.

Iskander Shah (1344–1414) This Hindu prince, originally named Parameswara, founded the sultanate of Malacca at the beginning of the 15th century. He took the name Iskander Shah after converting to Islam.

Singapore This island city-state withdrew from the Federation of Malaysia in 1965 due to persecution of its majority-Chinese population by Malay-dominated governments. Singapore first became an important port in 1819, and was a British crown colony as of 1867. Its strategic significance made it the scene of brutal fighting during World War II, ending in Japanese victory and occupation.

Brunei The sultanate of Brunei was at the center of the struggle for colonial control of the Malacca Straits, becoming a British protectorate in 1888. Britain granted it near-autonomy in 1959, followed by independence in 1971. It is one of the richest states in the world today due to vast resources of natural gas and petroleum. .

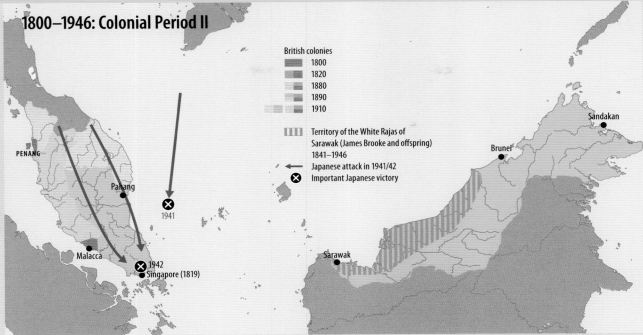

1800–1946: Colonial Period II

British colonies
- 1800
- 1820
- 1880
- 1890
- 1910

Territory of the White Rajas of Sarawak (James Brooke and offspring) 1841–1946

← Japanese attack in 1941/42
⊗ Important Japanese victory

PENANG · Pahang · Malacca · ⊗ 1941 · ⊗ 1942 Singapore (1819) · Sarawak · Brunei · Sandakan

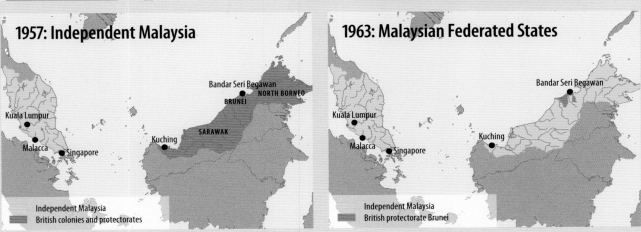

1957: Independent Malaysia

Kuala Lumpur · Malacca · Singapore · Kuching · SARAWAK · BRUNEI · Bandar Seri Begawan · NORTH BORNEO

Independent Malaysia
British colonies and protectorates

1963: Malaysian Federated States

Kuala Lumpur · Malacca · Singapore · Kuching · Bandar Seri Begawan

Independent Malaysia
British protectorate Brunei

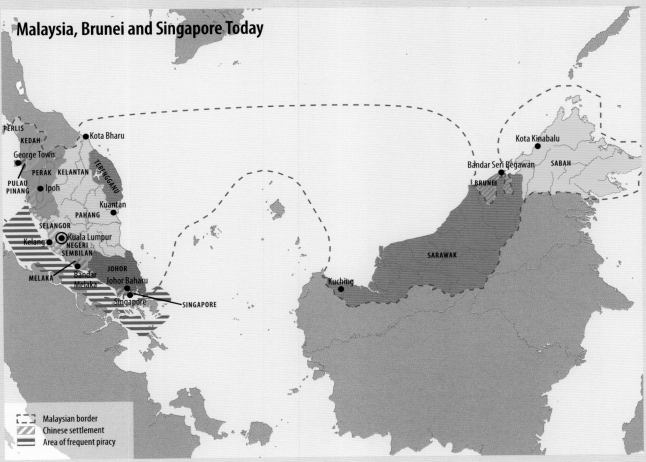

Malaysia, Brunei and Singapore Today

PERLIS · KEDAH · Kota Bharu · George Town · PULAU PINANG · PERAK · KELANTAN · TERENGGANU · Ipoh · Kuantan · PAHANG · SELANGOR · Kelang · Kuala Lumpur · NEGERI SEMBILAN · MELAKA · Bandar Melaka · JOHOR · Johor Baharu · Singapore · SINGAPORE · Kota Kinabalu · SABAH · Bandar Seri Begawan · BRUNEI · SARAWAK · Kuching

Malaysian border
Chinese settlement
Area of frequent piracy

The Philippines

Early Settlement

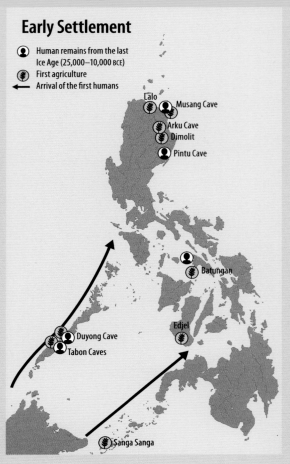

- 👤 Human remains from the last Ice Age (25,000–10,000 BCE)
- 🌿 First agriculture
- ← Arrival of the first humans

Lalo
Musang Cave
Arku Cave
Dimolit
Pintu Cave

Batungan

Duyong Cave
Tabon Caves

Edjel

Sanga Sanga

14th/15th Centuries: The Spread of Islam

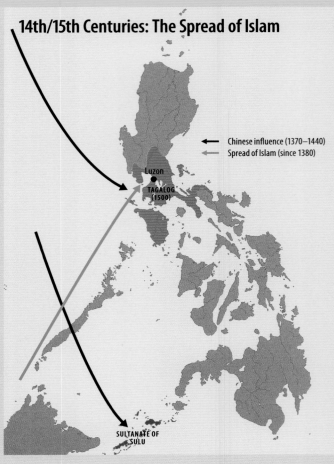

- ← Chinese influence (1370–1440)
- ← Spread of Islam (since 1380)

Luzon
TAGALOG
(1500)

SULTANATE OF
SULU

Beginning in the 14th century, Islam steadily gained influence in the Philippines until the Spanish conquest in the 16th century, which brought the islands into the Christian fold. The 20th century brought a prolonged struggle for independence and autonomy, but also the Marcos dictatorship that defined the country until it was finally able to free itself in 1986. Since then, its fragile democracy has been ever on the defensive.

25,000 BCE The Aeta are the first to settle the Philippines.

3000 BCE Austronesian tribes migrate from Taiwan.

700–1300 The Philippines fall under the influence of the Buddhist/Hindu Indonesian states of Srivijaya and Majahapit.

from 900 Direct trade with China

from 1380 The arrival of Islam

1457–1898 The Islamic sultanate of Jolo controls large parts of the Philippine archipelago. By the 19th century it controls only the southernmost islands.

16th–19th Centuries: Spanish Colonial Rule

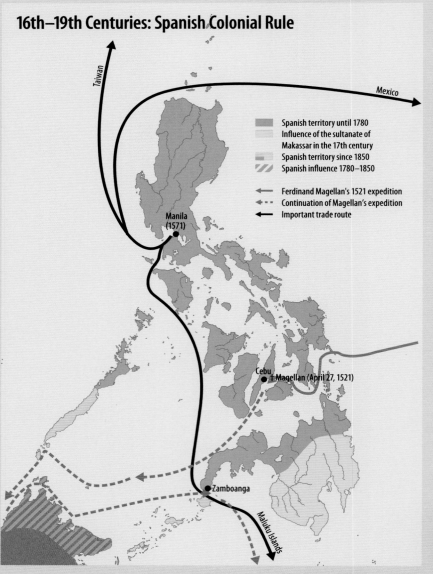

Taiwan

Mexico

- ▨ Spanish territory until 1780
- ▨ Influence of the sultanate of Makassar in the 17th century
- ▨ Spanish territory since 1850
- ▨ Spanish influence 1780–1850
- ← Ferdinand Magellan's 1521 expedition
- ⋯ Continuation of Magellan's expedition
- ← Important trade route

Manila
(1571)

Cebu
† Magellan (April 27, 1521)

Zamboanga

Maluku Islands

1898–1902: Philippine-American War

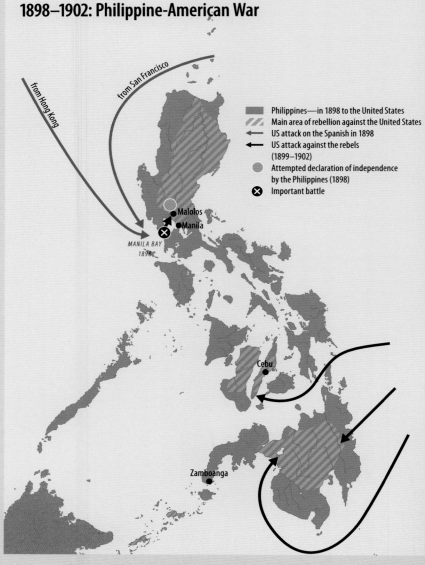

from Hong Kong

from San Francisco

- ▨ Philippines—in 1898 to the United States
- ▨ Main area of rebellion against the United States
- ← US attack on the Spanish in 1898
- ← US attack against the rebels (1899–1902)
- ⬤ Attempted declaration of independence by the Philippines (1898)
- ✕ Important battle

Malolos
Manila

MANILA BAY
1898

Cebu

Zamboanga

1521 Ferdinand Magellan claims the southern Philippines for Spain.

1565 The Spanish conquest ends the spread of Islam. The archipelago is renamed after King Philip II of Spain.

1571 The Rajas of Manila convert to Christianity, leading to rapid Christianization except in the south.

1611 Santo Tomas College (later university), the oldest university in Asia, is founded by the archbishop of Manila.

1762–1764 The British briefly occupy Manila.

until 1821 The Philippines become part of New Spain, along with the Spanish colonies in the Americas. Its trade goods include Mexican silver and Chinese silk, bringing many Chinese merchants to Manila. Trade is so heavy that the Mexican peso is practically the national currency.

from 1821 After Mexico becomes independent, the Philippines are ruled directly by Spain. Filipinos and Chinese merchants become wealthy from international trade and send their children to study in Europe. When they return, they bring 19th-century political ideas with them.

1892 The secret society Katipunan is founded with the goal of achieving Philippine independence.

1896–1898 Philippine Revolution: Katipunan fights Spanish rule.

1898 In the Battle of Manila, American ships annihilate the Spanish fleet. The Philippines now belongs to the United States.

1899–1902 Around a million people are killed in the Philippine-American War against colonial oppression.

1904–1913 The Moro Rebellion erupts after efforts by the United States to establish a provincial government in the Muslim south (the Moro province). State support for Christian settlement in Muslim territories leads to tensions that persist today.

1935 Partial autonomy is achieved when the Commonwealth of the Philippines is established.

1942–1945 Japanese occupation during World War II

1946 The Philippines achieves full independence.

1951 Filipino soldiers fight alongside US troops in the Korean War.

1963 Sabah Conflict: Muslim Malaysia lays claim to Philippine territory with support from local militant groups. Some soldiers from the Muslim south refuse to take part in an operation against the Islamic groups in 1968 and are shot.

1965 Ferdinand Marcos is elected president. Maoist groups offer resistance.

1972 Marcos declares martial law, setting up a military dictatorship. His family amasses immense wealth during a period when millions of Filipinos emigrate due to poverty and political repression.

1983 Returning from exile, opposition leader Benigno Aquino is assassinated at the airport in Manila.

1986 Aquino's widow Corazon is elected president. Marcos flees.

1992–1998 The Philippines first multi-party elections bring Fidel Ramos to power. He modernizes the economy and stabilizes the rebellious south with a combination of social programs and military strength.

since 1997 An increasingly militant Moro Islamic Liberation Front agitates for autonomy for the Muslim South. The Abu Sayyaf group and the Maoist New People's Army engage in terrorist activities against military installations, Christian missionaries and tourists.

2000 Abu Sayyaf kidnaps more than thirty tourists and missionaries. The death of American Martin Burnham during a rescue attempt by the Philippine army makes international headlines.

2004 Gloria Macapagal Arroyo is elected president. Accusations of election fraud lead to an unsuccessful coup attempt by the military in 2006.

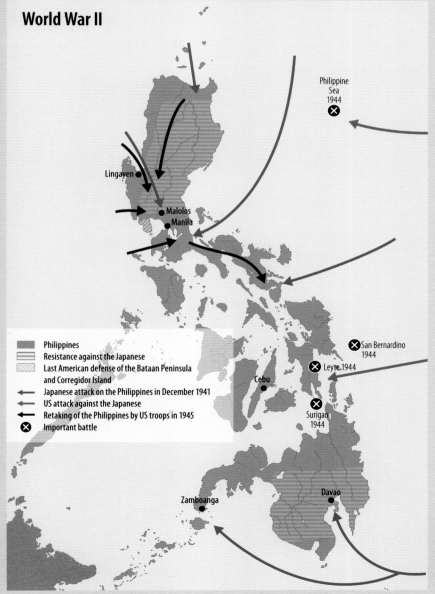

World War II

Philippines
Resistance against the Japanese
Last American defense of the Bataan Peninsula and Corregidor Island
Japanese attack on the Philippines in December 1941
US attack against the Japanese
Retaking of the Philippines by US troops in 1945
Important battle

Lingayen
Malolos
Manila
Cebu
Zamboanga
Surigao 1944
Davao
Leyte 1944
San Bernardino 1944
Philippine Sea 1944

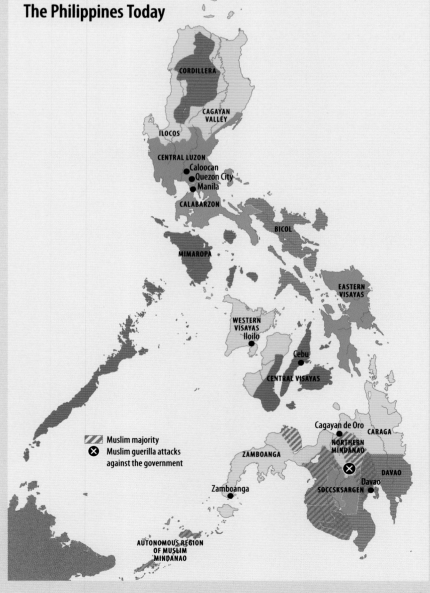

The Philippines Today

Muslim majority
Muslim guerilla attacks against the government

CORDILLERA
CAGAYAN VALLEY
ILOCOS
CENTRAL LUZON
Caloocan
Quezon City
Manila
CALABARZON
BICOL
MIMAROPA
EASTERN VISAYAS
WESTERN VISAYAS
Iloilo
Cebu
CENTRAL VISAYAS
Cagayan de Oro
CARAGA
NORTHERN MINDANAO
ZAMBOANGA
Zamboanga
DAVAO
Davao
SOCCSKSARGEN
AUTONOMOUS REGION OF MUSLIM MINDANAO

Indonesia

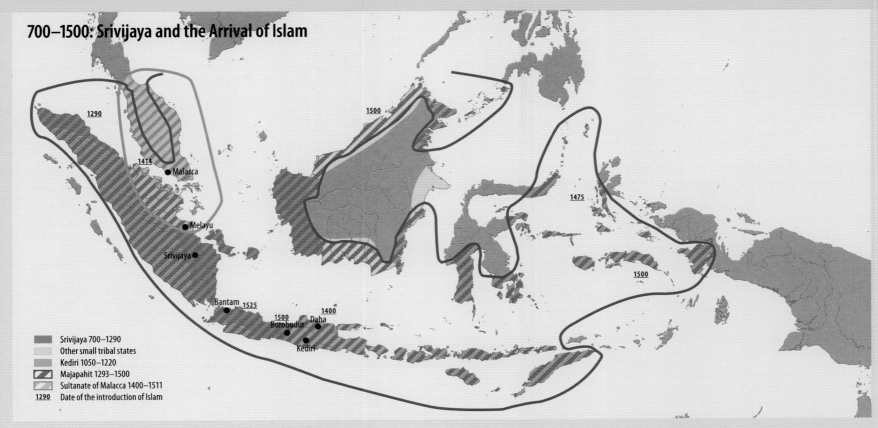

700–1500: Srivijaya and the Arrival of Islam

- Srivijaya 700–1290
- Other small tribal states
- Kediri 1050–1220
- Majapahit 1293–1500
- Sultanate of Malacca 1400–1511
- **1290** Date of the introduction of Islam

A nation of more than 17,000 islands, 6,000 of which are inhabited, Indonesia has 240 million inhabitants. Most are adherents of a moderate form of Islam; only the island of Bali has a majority Hindu population (92 percent). In the past, Portuguese, British and Dutch colonial powers have exploited Indonesia's geographic fragmentation.

200 BCE Earliest references to a Javan kingdom date from this time.

~0 Merchants and colonists spread Hinduism and Buddhism, both of which flourish alongside indigenous religious practices, and have continued to do so into the 21st century.

200–700 The first states form

700–1290 The Buddhist kingdom of Srivijaya controls Sumatra, Java and Borneo and sails the seas trading with nations including China and India.

760–840 Rule of the Shailendra dynasty in Java

from 1100 Muslim merchants and sailors bring Islam to Indonesia.

1293–1500 The Singhasari drive the Srivijaya out of Indonesia. The Majapahit become the last ruling Hindu dynasty.

1334–1389 Majapahit experiences a golden age under King Wuruk Hayam.

16th century Arrival of Portuguese, Dutch and British colonists

1602 The Dutch East India Company controls Indonesia.

1619 The Dutch found the town of Batavia, today Jakarta.

1740 Indonesians revolt, killing thousands of ethnic Chinese merchants and tax collectors.

1800 The Dutch East Indies becomes a royal colony.

1815 The volcano Tambora erupts, killing 71,000. It is the most powerful volcanic eruption in 25,000 years.

1825–1830 A revolt against the Dutch government in Java fails.

1883 The eruption of the volcano Krakatoa destroys 165 cities and towns along the coasts of Indonesia. It is the second most powerful eruption in 25,000 years.

1927 The Indonesian National Party is founded.

March 1942 The Japanese invade.

1500–1800: Colonial Domination

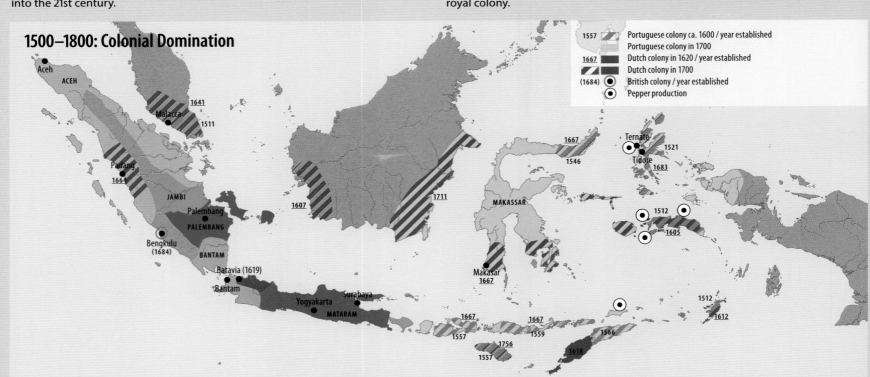

- **1557** Portuguese colony ca. 1600 / year established
- Portuguese colony in 1700
- **1667** Dutch colony in 1620 / year established
- Dutch colony in 1700
- **(1684)** British colony / year established
- Pepper production

1800–1944: Colonial Domination II

Krakatoa 1883
Batavia 1811
Ternate
Makassar
Yogyakarta 1825–1830
Surabaya
Tambora 1815
1873–1907

■ Dutch colony in 1800
■ Dutch colony in 1860
■ Dutch colony in 1910
□ Portuguese colony
▨ Rebellion against the colonial powers
← British invasion and occupation (1811–1816)
🌋 Volcanic eruption

1945 Indonesia gains its independence after World War II despite Dutch and British disapproval. Sukarno becomes the first president.

1947–1949 Indonesia revolts against the Dutch (Indonesian National Revolution).

1949 The Netherlands recognizes the Republic of Indonesia.

1955 Sukarno's Indonesian National Party wins the first national general election.

1959 Sukarno dissolves parliament, introducing a policy he calls "guided democracy."

1963 Sukarno is proclaimed president for life. Tensions with Malaysia escalate.

1965 General Suharto seizes power in a de facto military coup after a failed communist plot to overthrow Sukarno. Communist party members, as well as many ethnic Chinese demonized as communists, are deprived of civil rights, imprisoned and murdered. As many as 500,000 may have been killed across Indonesia. Sukarno is stripped of power.

1967–1998 Suharto is the dictatorial president of Indonesia.

1976 Forcible annexation of East Timor

1991 Revolt in East Timor is suppressed.

1999 Violence in East Timor leads to UN intervention. Abdurrahman Wahid becomes the first freely elected president of Indonesia. He is removed from office in 2001.

2001–2004 Sukarno's daughter Megawati Sukarnoputri assumes the presidency.

2002 East Timor gains independence. A bombing at a resort in Bali by the Islamist group Jemaah Islamiya kills over two hundred people.

2004 Indonesia's Aceh province, a stronghold of Islamic separatist activity, is devastated by a tsunami that claims 166,000 lives in Indonesia alone. The loss of life and need for aid forces an uneasy peace between the rebels and the Indonesian government.

East Timor A treaty signed in 1904 divided control of this land between the Netherlands (western part) and Portugal (eastern part). When the Portuguese dictatorship ended, East Timor declared its independence, but soon afterward was forcibly annexed by Indonesia in 1976. East Timor has been an independent island nation since 2002.

Ahmed Sukarno (1901–1970) A pioneer of Indonesian independence and the nation's first president (1949–1967), he founded the Indonesian National Party. After the Japanese invasion of Indonesia in 1942, Sukarno led the anti-Dutch resistance movement. He was elected president in 1945 (and again in 1949). In the late 1950s he dissolved parliament and sought closer ties to the Soviet Union, resulting in international isolation.

Suharto (1921–2008) A military and political leader of Indonesia, he was an army officer during the National Revolution. He was involved in suppressing the attempted communist coup in 1965, and subsequently pursued a bloody retribution. By 1967 he was president of Indonesia, exercising absolute dictatorial power. With Western support, the country experienced economic growth during his rule. Protests against his anti-democratic oppression of politial opposition forced his resignation in 1998.

1945–2007: Independence and Conflicts

■ Territory controlled by rebels against Dutch colonialists 1945–1949
■ Indonesia since 1949
■ West Irian (Western New Guinea) to Indonesia in 1963
■ East Timor occupied by Indonesia 1976–1999
■ Aceh territory—separatist movements (1976–2004)
▨ Areas threatened by deforestation
▨ Christian settlement
⊗ Violent conflicts
🌋 Terrorist attack

Banda Aceh 1976–2004
Medan
Palembang
Jakarta 1945–1949
Yogyakarta
Surabaya
Bali (2002)
Makassar (Ujung Pandang)
Ternate
Ambon
Maluku (1950, 1998–2002)
Dili 1999–2001

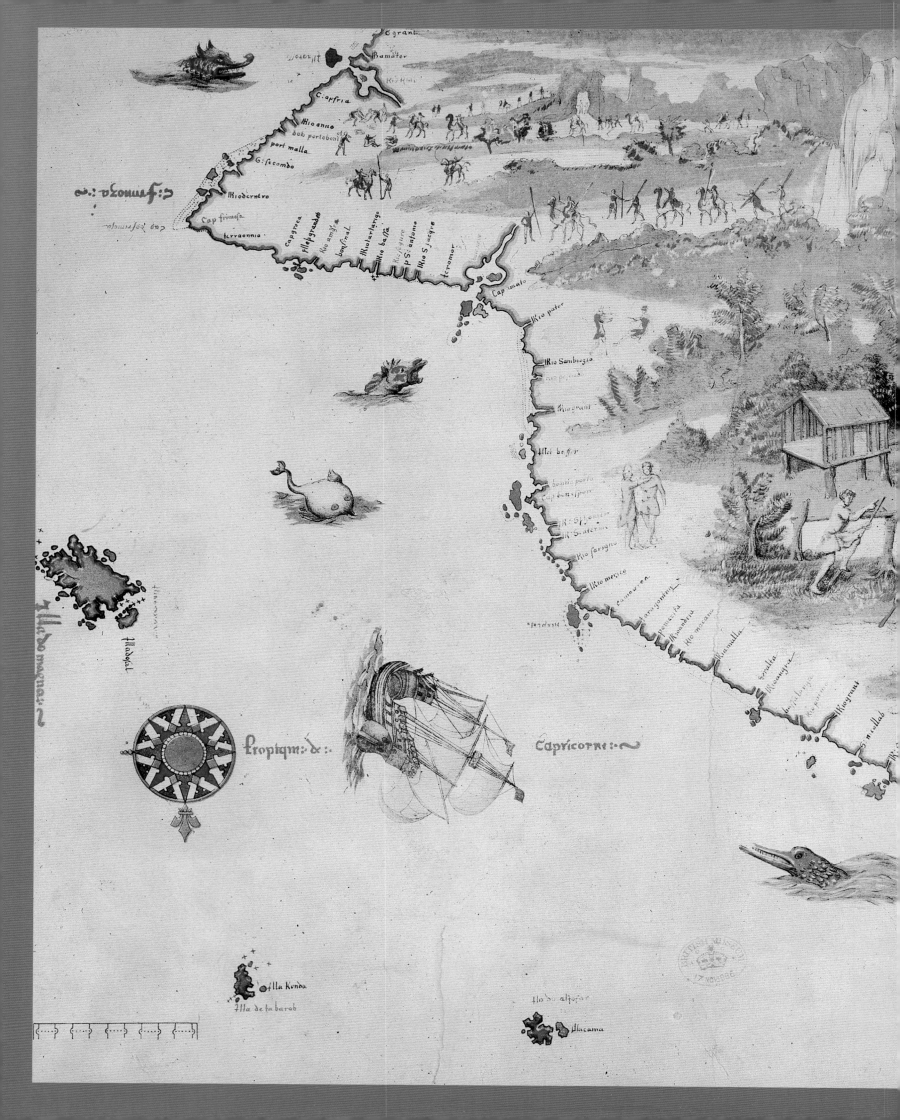

C: famoja :.

C: famoja :.

o grant
Bamator
Rio Rial
C. apfria
Rio anno
doh portobom
port malla
C: fecondo
Rio dernero
Cap frimofa
terraonnia
capgreca
fllet grando
Rio amy
bonfinal
Rio fartargo
Rio baffa
Rio giuro
P S: anfonio
Rio S: jacyra
tcraonor
Cap imato
Rio puter
Rio Sambrogio
fter pronto
Rio grant
fllet befer
bonte porto
Cap bonfpon
R: S: joner
R: S: afarm
Rio forigna
Rio mexico
cannorora
rarngonorny
pomorta
Rio anbria
Rio mocano
Rio amilla
Rio angroz
Rio pomo
Rio grant
fmallab
Hladal

Propiqm: d: .
Capricorne: .

flla Kenda
flla de la barob
flo de alfofar
flacama

AUSTRALIA AND OCEANIA

When Greek astronomer and geographer Ptolemy (100–175 CE) wrote of Terra Australis, he envisioned an enormous continent dominating the Southern Hemisphere and enclosing a gigantic sea, much like the landmasses bordering the Mediterranean Sea in the Northern Hemisphere. He was only partially correct. Oceania covers as much of the globe as Eurasia, but the ratio between land and water is exactly the opposite. Later cartographers, making free use of artistic license, added to their maps of the world a southern continent that occupied half the hemisphere. It was only after Captain James Cook circumnavigated the Antarctic in 1772 that Europeans understood that the legendary Terra Australis could not exist. The considerably smaller continental mass of Australia, which had already been circumnavigated by the Dutch captain Abel Tasman in 1642/43, was eventually given part of the name.

Melanesia, Micronesia and Polynesia	**394**
Australia Through the End of the 19th Century	**396**
Australia from the 20th Century to the Present	**398**
Aborigines / Papua New Guinea	**399**
New Zealand	**400**

The first map of Australia, from an atlas created by Nicholas Vallard in 1547

Melanesia, Micronesia and Polynesia

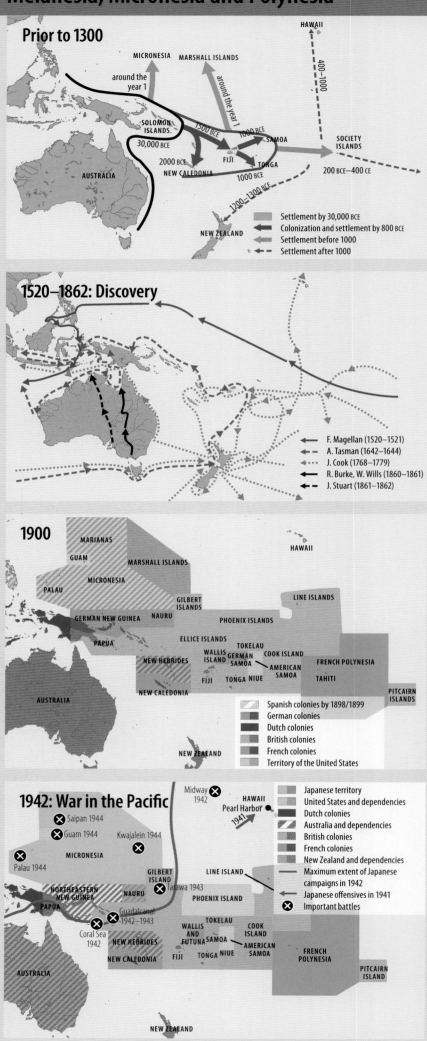

Prior to 1300

HAWAII
MICRONESIA
MARSHALL ISLANDS
around the year 1
around the year 1
400–1000
SOLOMON ISLANDS
30,000 BCE
1500 BCE
1000 BCE
SAMOA
SOCIETY ISLANDS
AUSTRALIA
2000 BCE
NEW CALEDONIA
FIJI
TONGA
200 BCE–400 CE
1000 BCE
1200–1300 BCE
NEW ZEALAND

- Settlement by 30,000 BCE
- Colonization and settlement by 800 BCE
- Settlement before 1000
- Settlement after 1000

1520–1862: Discovery

- F. Magellan (1520–1521)
- A. Tasman (1642–1644)
- J. Cook (1768–1779)
- R. Burke, W. Wills (1860–1861)
- J. Stuart (1861–1862)

1900

MARIANAS
GUAM
MARSHALL ISLANDS
HAWAII
MICRONESIA
PALAU
GILBERT ISLANDS
LINE ISLANDS
GERMAN NEW GUINEA
NAURU
PHOENIX ISLANDS
PAPUA
ELLICE ISLANDS
TOKELAU
WALLIS ISLAND
GERMAN SAMOA
COOK ISLAND
NEW HEBRIDES
FRENCH POLYNESIA
AMERICAN SAMOA
FIJI
TONGA
NIUE
TAHITI
NEW CALEDONIA
PITCAIRN ISLANDS
AUSTRALIA
NEW ZEALAND

- Spanish colonies by 1898/1899
- German colonies
- Dutch colonies
- British colonies
- French colonies
- Territory of the United States

1942: War in the Pacific

Midway 1942
HAWAII
Pearl Harbor 1941
Saipan 1944
Guam 1944
Kwajalein 1944
Palau 1944
MICRONESIA
GILBERT ISLAND
LINE ISLAND
NAURU
Tarawa 1943
NORTHEASTERN NEW GUINEA
PHOENIX ISLAND
PAPUA
Guadalcanal 1942–1943
TOKELAU
Coral Sea 1942
WALLIS AND FUTUNA
SAMOA
COOK ISLAND
NEW HEBRIDES
AMERICAN SAMOA
FRENCH POLYNESIA
NEW CALEDONIA
FIJI
TONGA
NIUE
AUSTRALIA
PITCAIRN ISLAND
NEW ZEALAND

- Japanese territory
- United States and dependencies
- Dutch colonies
- Australia and dependencies
- British colonies
- French colonies
- New Zealand and dependencies
- Maximum extent of Japanese campaigns in 1942
- Japanese offensives in 1941
- Important battles

Post-World War II to Today

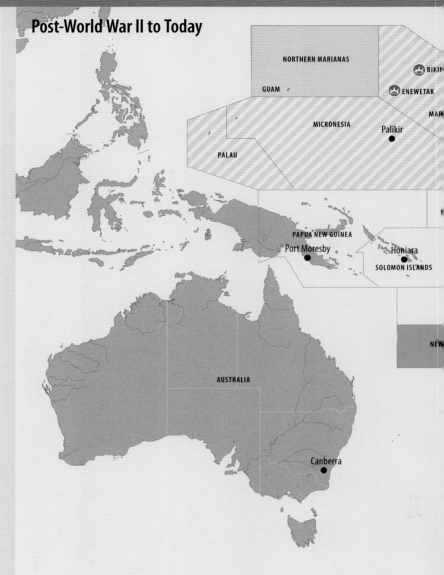

NORTHERN MARIANAS
BIKIN
GUAM
ENEWETAK
MICRONESIA
Palikir
PALAU
PAPUA NEW GUINEA
Port Moresby
Honiara
SOLOMON ISLANDS
AUSTRALIA
Canberra

The continent of Australia has been settled for 50,000 years. The aboriginal peoples arrived in small family groups, settling Australia and parts of New Guinea. The islands of Oceania and New Zealand were occupied as late as 1500 BCE by the hierarchal, chiefdom-based societies of the Polynesians. European exploration of Australia and Oceania began in earnest in the 17th century. Although the "South Sea Islands" were colonized in a relatively gentle manner, the aboriginal peoples of Australia and New Zealand were brutally oppressed, and rapidly displaced by land-hungry Europeans. Racist policies endured until the middle of the 20th century. Both government and daily life in Australia and New Zealand clearly refer back to those countries' British colonial origins.

1500/1000 BCE The Austronesia migration, probably originating near the southern China coast, begins the settlement of the South Pacific islands.

300–1300 CE Polynesian tribes settle Easter Island (ca. 300), Hawaii (ca. 400) and New Zealand (1200–1300).

500 The Malay-Polynesian migration begins.

early 16th century Spanish and Portuguese explorers arrive in the Pacific.

1524–1564 The Spanish occupy most of the Micronesian islands.

1700–1900 Christian missionaries, Catholic and Protestant, arrive in the South Pacific.

1768–1779 British Captain James Cook lands on Tahiti, Hawaii and New Caledonia. He commissions the first maps of the Marquesas and Tonga.

1800–1935 European immigrants bring viral illness to the islands; hundreds of thousands of people die.

1880 Tahiti and other Polynesian islands become French colonies.

1941 Japan attacks Pearl Harbor, Hawaii, spurring US involvement in World War II.

1942–1944 Intense fighting between Japanese and US forces in the Pacific Theater.

1946–1963 Nuclear tests take place on the American Micronesian islands.

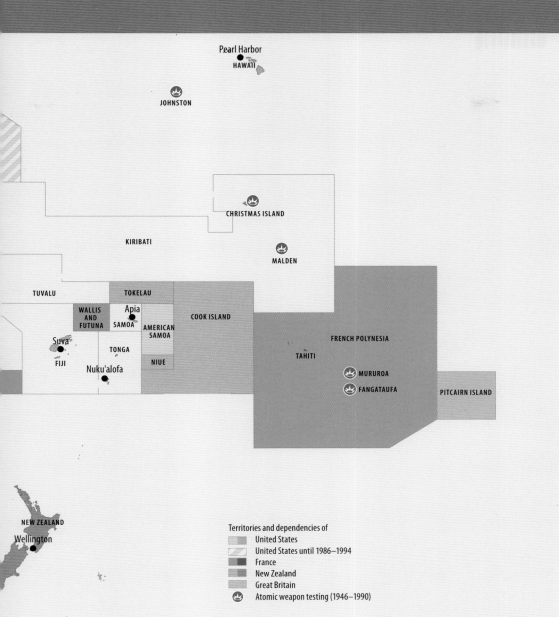

Map labels:

Pearl Harbor
HAWAII

JOHNSTON

CHRISTMAS ISLAND

KIRIBATI

MALDEN

TUVALU

TOKELAU

WALLIS AND FUTUNA
Apia
SAMOA
AMERICAN SAMOA
COOK ISLAND

FRENCH POLYNESIA

Suva
TONGA
NIUE
TAHITI
FIJI
Nuku'alofa

MURUROA
FANGATAUFA

PITCAIRN ISLAND

EASTER ISLAND

NEW ZEALAND
Wellington

Territories and dependencies of
United States
United States until 1986–1994
France
New Zealand
Great Britain
Atomic weapon testing (1946–1990)

1962 Samoa is the first Pacific island to gain independence.

1966–1996 France conducts atomic bomb tests in Mururoa Atoll, with lasting effects on the health of residents.

1987 Tension on Fiji between the native population and Indian immigrants results in a military coup.

Jakob Roggeveen (1659–1729) was a Dutch seafarer who sought Terra Australis. He discovered Easter Island instead.

George Tupou I (ca. 1797–1893) was the king of Tonga and founder of the Tupou dynasty that still rules today.

Lili'uokalani (1838–1917), the last queen of Hawaii, was deposed in 1893 when Hawaii became an American protectorate. In 1959 Hawaii became the fiftieth state.

Pomare V (1839–1891), the last king of Tahiti, ruled only three years before being forced to abdicate by the French. Tahiti's status quickly transitioned from French protectorate to colony.

The Bounty was a ship that became famous around the world after its sailors, led by Fletcher Christian, mutinied in 1789. Captain William Bligh and a few members of the crew loyal to him were set adrift

in a rowboat. Some of the mutineers returned to Tahiti in 1788. Nine of them, including Christian, six Polynesian men and twelve Polynesian women, sailed for the uninhabited Pitcairn Island. Rivalries between the men in 1793–1799 led to the death of all but one of the mutineers: John Adams. Adams led the small community until his death in 1829, and the present-day inhabitants of Pitcairn are their descendants.

Fiji
1643	Abel Tasman finds Fiji.
from 1800	European planters settle the island.
1874	Fiji becomes a crown colony of the British Empire.
1879–1916	The British import 61,000 Indians to work on sugar plantations.
1941–1945	Fiji serves as an important Allied supply base during World War II.
1970	Fiji gains its independence.
1987	Military coup by native Melanesians in the wake of elections won by the Indian Party leads to a mass exodus of ethnic Indians.

Captain William Bligh, 1792

1994	The government restores democracy, but military coups take place again in 2000 and 2006.

New Caledonia
1774	Captain James Cook discovers the islands.
1853	The French take possession.
1864–1922	New Caledonia becomes a French penal colony.
1941–1945	Capital city of Noumea is the American naval headquarters in the Pacific during World War II.
1981–1992	Competing separatist movements lead to acts of violence.
1988	Matignon Accords give New Caledonia greater autonomy.

The Solomon Islands
1568	Alvaro de Mendana de Neyra is the first European to land there, but fails to include the islands on the map of his voyage. They will not be visited again for two centuries.
1767	Carter rediscovers the islands.
1883	The Solomon Islands become a British colony.
1978	The islands gain their independence.
1998–2000	Ethnic conflict breaks out.
2007	A state of emergency is declared after a devastating earthquake and tsunami.

Vanuatu
1606	Pedro Fernandez de Quiros discovers the archipelago.
1839	The first Europeans settle the islands.
1906	A joint French-British condominium administers the islands under the name "New Hebrides."
1980	Vanuatu gains its independence.

Micronesia
ca. 1560	Portuguese explorers reach the islands of Micronesia.
1696	The Spanish occupy nearly all of Micronesia.
1885	A commission appointed by the Kaiser places the Marshall Islands under German imperial control.
1892	The Gilbert Islands become a British Protectorate.
1899	Spain sells most of the rest of Micronesia to Germany.
1914	Japan occupies Micronesia, declaring the islands Japanese Mandate territories in 1920.
1946–1954	American atomic tests take place in Bikini Atoll. The atoll is nearly completely destroyed by a hydrogen bomb in 1954.
1947	Micronesia falls under the United Nations trusteeship administered by the United States.

The Independent State of Samoa and American Samoa
1722	Jakob Roggeveen discovers Samoa.
1899/1900	Germany annexes Western Samoa. Eastern Samoa remains in the hands of the United States.
1914	New Zealand occupies Western Samoa. It falls under New Zealand trusteeship in 1946.
1929	American Samoa becomes a dependent territory of the USA.
1962	Western Samoa becomes the first Polynesian island to gain independence.

French Polynesia
1521	Magellan discovers the island of Pukapuka.
1722	Roggeveen discovers Bora Bora (Tahiti).
1836	Charles Darwin visits Tahiti during his voyage around the world.
1891–1903	French painter Paul Gauguin resides in Tahiti sporadically and dies here.
1966–1996	French atomic tests take place on Mururoa Atoll.

Society Islands (Îles de la Société)
The islands were visited by Captain James Cook, who may have named them after his sponsor, the Royal Society, or called them that because they lie so close together.

Tonga
~1200	Tu´iTonga Empire becomes known throughout the Pacific.
1845	The Tonga islands unite, forming the Kingdom of Tonga.
1875	Tonga becomes a constitutional monarchy. It is the only remaining inherited monarchy in the Pacific.
1900	Tonga becomes a British protectorate. It remains an independent member of the British Commonwealth today.
1965–2006	King Taufa´ahau Tupou IV institutes reforms, but government remains authoritarian. Efforts toward increased democracy continue today.

Australia Through the End of the 19th Century

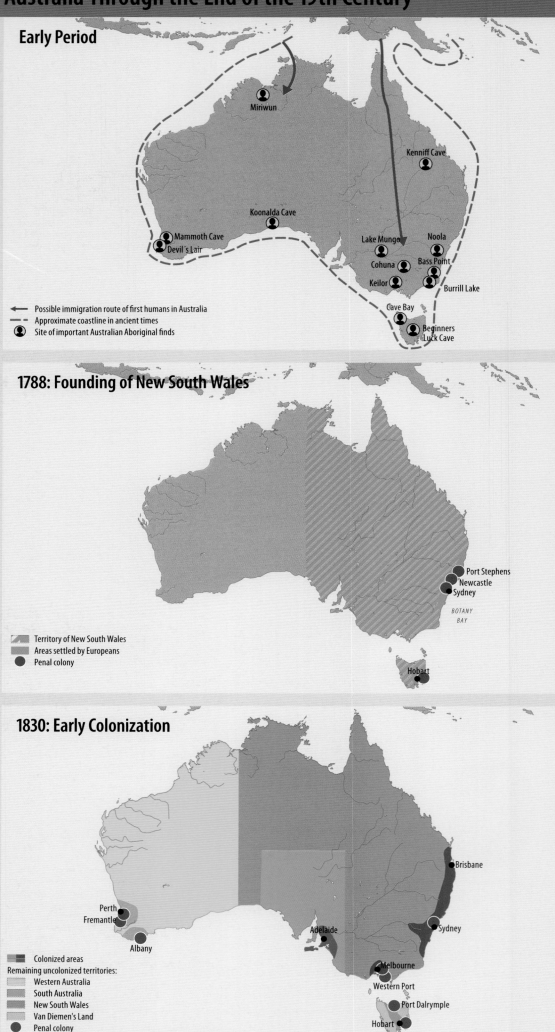

Early Period

Miriwun

Kenniff Cave

Koonalda Cave

Mammoth Cave
Devil´s Lair

Lake Mungo
Noola
Cohuna
Bass Point
Keilor
Burrill Lake
Cave Bay
Beginners
Luck Cave

→ Possible immigration route of first humans in Australia
- - - Approximate coastline in ancient times
⬤ Site of important Australian Aboriginal finds

1788: Founding of New South Wales

Port Stephens
Newcastle
Sydney

*BOTANY
BAY*

Hobart

▨ Territory of New South Wales
▨ Areas settled by Europeans
⬤ Penal colony

1830: Early Colonization

Brisbane

Perth
Fremantle

Adelaide
Sydney

Albany

Melbourne

Western Port

Port Dalrymple

Hobart

▨ Colonized areas
Remaining uncolonized territories:
▨ Western Australia
▨ South Australia
▨ New South Wales
▨ Van Diemen's Land
⬤ Penal colony

120,000 BCE The first traces of human settlement in Australia date from this time.

50,000 BCE The first Australian aboriginals arrive on the continent.

4000 BCE The Torres Strait, the land bridge connecting Australia and New Guinea, is flooded as sea levels rise.

1292 CE Marco Polo describes a land mass south of Java.

1606 The Dutchman Willem Jansz makes land in Queensland.

1642–1644 Abel Tasman circumnavigates the Australian continent and names it New Holland.

1770 James Cook finds and explores the east coast of Australia and names it New South Wales (NSW).

1788 The first ships from Britain carrying convicts arrive in Sydney, and New South Wales is founded under the leadership of Arthur Phillip.

1817 The name "Australia" is adopted in place of New Holland.

1851 Gold rush in NSW and Victoria draws fortune seekers from elsewhere in Australia and from Britain.

1854 Eureka Stockade: A revolt of discontented miners is put down by force, but leads to reforms.

from 1855 One after another, the colonies attain self-government. Victoria, South Australia and Tasmania gain independence from NSW.

1859 Queensland gains independence from NSW.

1869 The last convicts are brought to Australia; there were approximately 160,000 in all.

1872 The first telegraph connects the entire continent.

1877 The last penal colony, in Tasmania, is closed. The population of Australia exceeds two million.

1886 Gold is discovered in the colony of Western Australia.

Arthur Phillip (1738–1814) was the commander of the first fleet of convicts sent from Britain to Australia. After his arrival, he became the first governor of New South Wales and founded the city of Sydney.

Matthew Flinders (1774–1814) was a British sailor who sailed around the entire continent and named it Australia.

Ludwig Leichhardt (1813–1848?) Leichardt was a German naturalist who arrived to explore the Australian continent in 1842. He was the first to cross the continent from east to north in 1844–1845, traveling just under 3,000 miles (4,800 km) from Jimbour in Brisbane to Port Essington in Darwin. In 1846, the crossing from east to west failed. A second attempt in 1848 began northwest of Brisbane and ended in the northern Simpson Desert, with the entire party going missing.

Edward John Eyre (1815–1901) In 1841 Eyre traveled with Wylie, a native, along the coast of Adelaide to Albany. They survived with the help of the crew of a French vessel under the command of Captain Rossiter.

Robert O'Hara Burke (1820–1861) In 1860 he led the first south-north crossing of Australia by a European. For political reasons, the expedition became a race, which is why it began at the height of summer. The deputy leader of the party was William John Wills (1834–1861). On February 10, 1861, Burke and three team members reached the Flinders

River, which flows into the Carpentaria Gulf on the north coast. They had attained their goal, but John King, assisted by Aborigines, was the only participant to survive the return trip.

Ernest Giles (1835–1897) In 1875 Giles traversed the desert from Port Augusta in the south to Western Australia and became the first European to see the Kata Tjuta rock formations.

John Forrest (1847–1918) and his brother Alexander (1849–1901) explored the Western Australia Outback in 1869. They traveled through the central desert areas from Perth to Adelaide in 1874.

Edward "Ned" Kelly (1855–1880) A rancher of Irish descent who rebelled against the colonial authorities. Today he is a popular folk hero in films and novels. After an encounter with the police on his farm, he fled into the bush, but was captured and executed.

Penal Colonies

Soon after it was discovered by James Cook and through 1869, thousands of prisoners were deported from Britain to Australia. The majority of them had been convicted of petty theft. They were mostly British, but a considerable number were Irish. Hard labor awaited them in the penal colony. They could return after serving their time, but very few had the money to pay their passage to Great Britain. There were exceptions, however: some returned as wealthy individuals.

1830: Discovery and Exploration

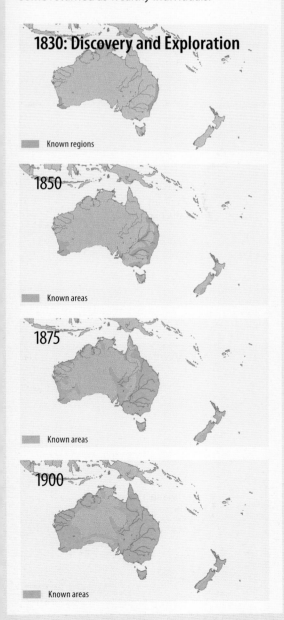

Known regions

1850

Known areas

1875

Known areas

1900

Known areas

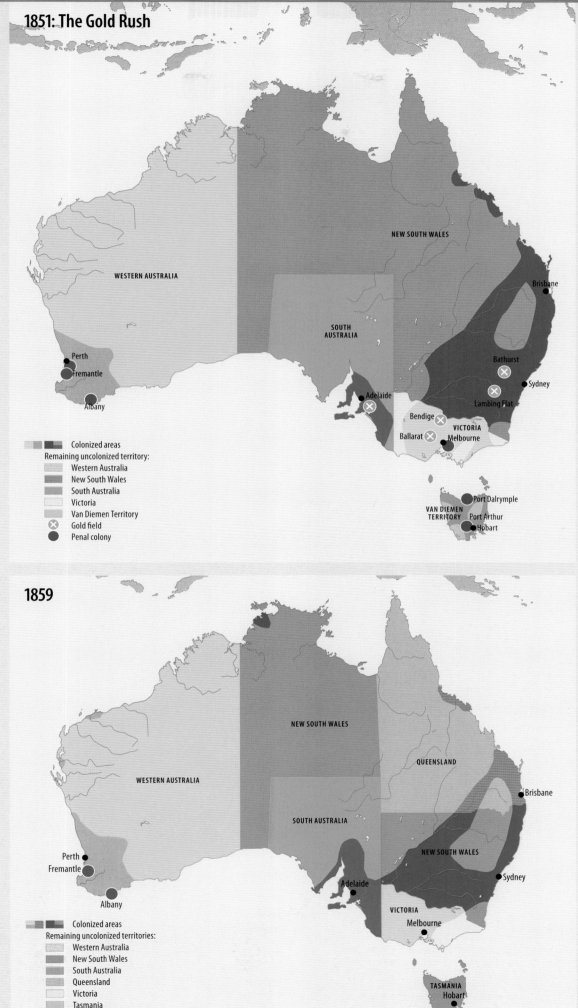

1851: The Gold Rush

WESTERN AUSTRALIA

NEW SOUTH WALES

SOUTH AUSTRALIA

Perth
Fremantle

Albany

Adelaide

Bendige

Ballarat

VICTORIA
Melbourne

Brisbane

Bathurst

Sydney

Lambing Flat

VAN DIEMEN TERRITORY

Port Dalrymple

Port Arthur

Hobart

Colonized areas
Remaining uncolonized territory:
Western Australia
New South Wales
South Australia
Victoria
Van Diemen Territory
⊗ Gold field
● Penal colony

1859

WESTERN AUSTRALIA

NEW SOUTH WALES

QUEENSLAND

SOUTH AUSTRALIA

NEW SOUTH WALES

Perth
Fremantle

Albany

Adelaide

VICTORIA
Melbourne

Brisbane

Sydney

TASMANIA
Hobart

Colonized areas
Remaining uncolonized territories:
Western Australia
New South Wales
South Australia
Queensland
Victoria
Tasmania
● Penal colony

Australia from the 20th Century to the Present

1911–1945

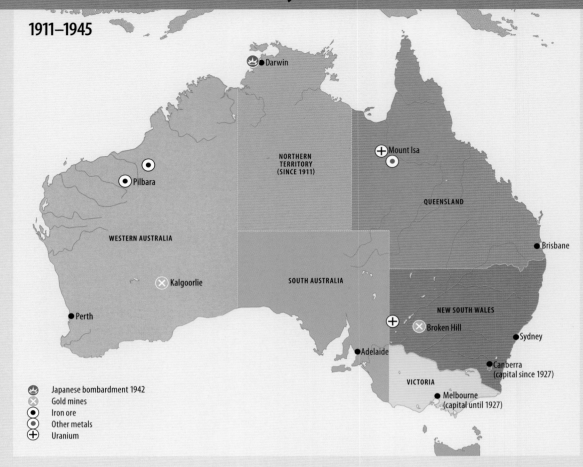

Japanese bombardment 1942
Gold mines
Iron ore
Other metals
Uranium

1901 Six Australian states form the Commonwealth of Australia.

1906 Australia gains control of New Guinea.

1915 During the World War I, ANZAC troops from Australia and New Zealand fight in Gallipoli on the side of the Allies. The day of the Gallipoli landing, April 25th, is a national holiday in both countries.

1919 Australia takes part in the Paris Peace Conference.

1927 Canberra becomes the Australian capital, which was formerly located in Melbourne.

1931 Statute of Westminster: The Dominions gain independence.

1942 The Australian Parliament agrees to independence. The Japanese Air Force bombs Darwin.

1951 ANZUS: defense agreement between Australia, New Zealand and the United States

1965–1975 Participation in the Vietnam War on the side of the United States

1994 Adoption of the Indigenous Land Rights Act

1999 The Australian republic referendum is turned down by voters.

since 2007 In 2008, Prime Minister Kevin Rudd officially apologizes to the Aborigines for the wrongs done to them.

Sir Edmund Barton (1849–1920) The first prime minister of the country (1901–1903) and founder of the Supreme Court of Australia

Robert Menzies (1894–1978) Prime minister from 1939 to 1941 and 1949 to 1966, his incumbency as prime minister was the longest in Australian history.

Arthur Calwell (1896–1973) Chairman of the Australian Labour Party from 1960 to 1967 and minister for immigration from 1945 to 1949, he encouraged mass immigration from Europe to Australia.

Eddie Mabo (1936–1992) fought for the rights of Australia's indigenous people.

Cathy Freeman (1973–) An Australian athlete, she was the first Aborigine ever to compete in the Olympics. She won a gold medal in the 400-meter dash at the Sydney Olympic Games in 2000.

Australia Today

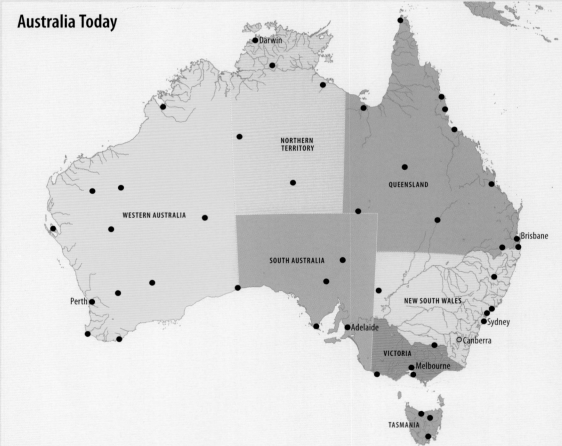

Australia

At the beginning of the 20th century, Australia gained its independence and became a dominion of the British Empire. After World War I, it also became a member of the newly founded League of Nations. Since the 1970s Australian society and the government have quarreled over the oppression of the Aborigines, whose language and culture had long been devalued. They have now been granted a high degree of autonomy, and certain sacred areas, such as Uluru (formerly Ayers Rock), are largely off limits to whites. Although their political participation has increased, the majority of Aborigines still live in impoverished conditions compared to the rest of Australians.

Uluru (Ayers Rock)

The History of the Aborigines

Australia's Aborigines, like New Zealand's Maori, are a people without written history. Oral tradition, the passing down of information about secret rituals, origin myths and other knowledge, played an important role. Unlike the class-based, aristocratic Polynesians, Australia's Aborigines lived in non-hierarchical groups organized around kinship and clans. Each clan was divided into two moieties called "skin groups." The moieties were further subdivided into two to four additional skin groups, each acting as the core family unit with generational naming conventions for referring to other members. All of a parent's generation in a skin group, for example, would call each other "sister" or "brother" as would all the children in the next generation, and so on. Strict marriage rules encouraged marriage between individuals from different skin groups, but considered marriage within a skin group to be incest.

Aborigines wandered their traditional territories as hunters and gathers. Each landscape was understood to contain features associated with ancestors and subject to taboos, such as Uluru, formerly known as Ayer's Rock. The Aborigines believe in a mythological world they call Dreamtime, where their ancestors and human-animal totems live, occasionally crossing over and leaving behind signs of their passing. The Aborigines protect the earth in their name. The oldest member of an Aboriginal group is the guardian of its knowledge.

The lack of social hierarchies and whites' unfamiliarity with the Aborigines' strict clan and marriage rules (to avoid incest) were among the factors that led white settlers to consider "Australian Negros" the most primitive people on earth. They set about destroying Aboriginal culture with no qualms whatsoever. Australia's Aborigines began to fight for reparations from the government and cultural autonomy in the 1980s.

An Aborigine with a boomerang, ca. 1860

Papua New Guinea

More than 700 Melanesian and Papuan tribes lived here before the arrival of Europeans.

1526 Discovery by Portuguese sailor Jorge de Meneses

1793 Great Britain tries to colonize the island. The Netherlands claims the western part, which is now Indonesia.

1906 The British part is ceded to Australia.

1921 The northern half becomes the Australian Mandated Territory of New Guinea.

1942–1943 The Battle of Guadalcanal, Solomon Islands: the turning point of World War II between Japan and the United States in the Pacific Theater.

1942–1944 The northern part of the island is occupied by the Japanese.

1975 Papua New Guinea gains independence.

Aborigines Today

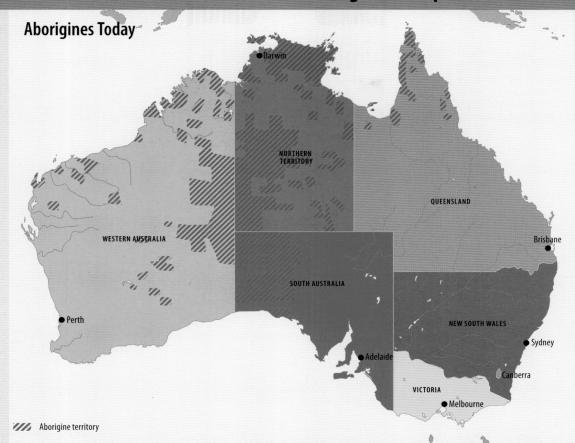

/// Aborigine territory

1942: New Guinea and the War in the Pacific

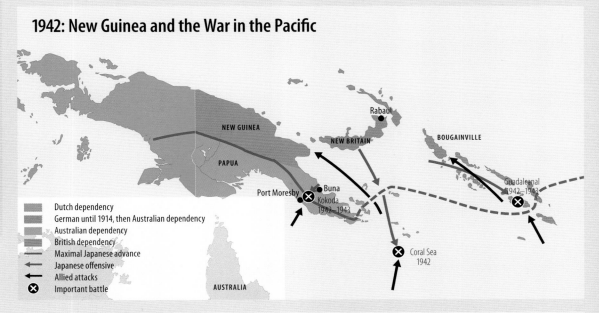

Dutch dependency
German until 1914, then Australian dependency
Australian dependency
British dependency
Maximal Japanese advance
← Japanese offensive
⊗← Allied attacks
⊗ Important battle

Papua New Guinea Today

New Zealand

New Zealand was originally inhabited by the Maoris, a warlike Polynesian tribe. The first Europeans to arrive here were the Dutch, who named the island after Zeeland, a province in the Netherlands. In the 19th century New Zealand became a British colony. Meanwhile, it has achieved the same independent nation status as Australia.

ca. 1200–1300 Colonization by Polynesians (Maori culture) arriving in several waves from the southwest Pacific islands

1642 Abel Tasman, sailing for the Dutch East Indies Company, reaches the islands.

1769 British Captain James Cook explores the coast of New Zealand.

1815 English missionaries arrive to minister to both European immigrants and Maori.

1841 The colony of New Zealand gains independence from the Australian colony of New South Wales.

1845–1872 Land wars lead to ongoing violence between the British and Maori.

1871 Long-distance postal service ("Pacific Mail") via fast steamships links Auckland and San Franscisco.

1893 New Zealand is the very first country to implement women's suffrage.

1907 New Zealand becomes a British Dominion in the Commonwealth.

1914 Thousands of New Zealanders fight alongside the British in World War I, thereby contributing to New Zealand's growing sense of national identity and pride.

1939–1945 During World War II, New Zealand troops participate in campaigns in the European, North African and Pacific theaters. Nearly 12,000 of a fighting force of 194,000 New Zealand soldiers die in combat.

1947 New Zealand becomes independent within the British Commonwealth.

1951 Pacific pact with Australia and the United States (ANZEUS)

1962 The Maori are granted equal rights under the law, leading to increased participation in local and national government.

1985 US nuclear-powered ships are banned from New Zealand's ports.

Act of 1996 The number of Maori MPs permitted to serve in Parliament is raised from six to fifteen.

2002 New Zealand officially apologizes for the "inept and incompetent early administration of Samoa" during the colonial era.

Prior to 1800: Settlement by the Maori

⬛ Maori settlements
← Arrival of the Maori in ca. 1200–1300

ca. 1830: Early Colonization

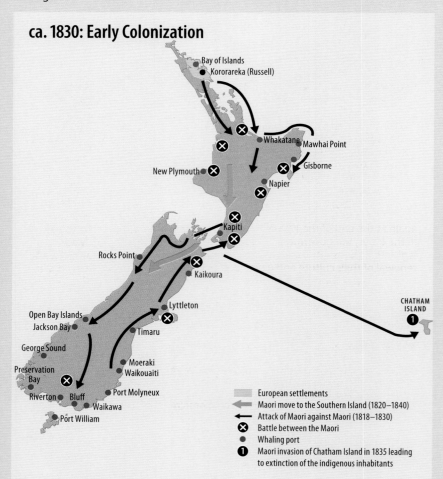

Bay of Islands
Kororareka (Russell)
Whakatang
Mawhai Point
New Plymouth
Gisborne
Napier
Kapiti
Rocks Point
Kaikoura
Lyttleton
Open Bay Islands
Jackson Bay
Timaru
George Sound
Moeraki
Waikouaiti
Preservation Bay
Riverton
Bluff
Port Molyneux
Waikawa
Port William
CHATHAM ISLAND ❶

⬛ European settlements
← Maori move to the Southern Island (1820–1840)
← Attack of Maori against Maori (1818–1830)
❌ Battle between the Maori
● Whaling port
❶ Maori invasion of Chatham Island in 1835 leading to extinction of the indigenous inhabitants

1840–1860: Larger Settlements

Waitangi
Russell
Auckland
New Plymouth
Wellington
Nelson
Christchurch
Dunedin

⬛ European settlements
▨ Movement of the Maori kings (1858)
❌ Battle of Maori against Europeans (1845–1872)

1860–1907: Later Colonial Period

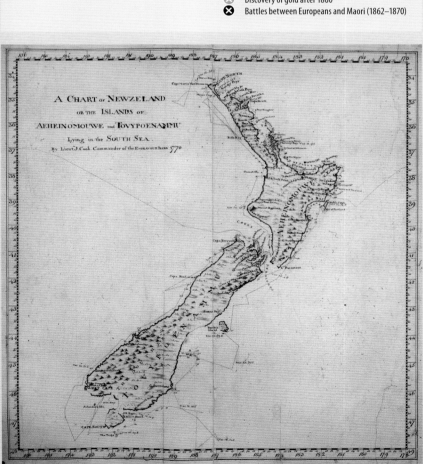

Russell
Auckland
Thames
Hamilton
Rotorua
Gisborne
New Plymouth
Napier
Marton
Castle Point
Wellington
Nelson
Greymouth
Christchurch
Dunedin
Invercargill

European settlement by 1875
European settlement by 1907
Confiscated Maori territory (1864–1867)
Discovery of gold after 1860
Battles between Europeans and Maori (1862–1870)

New Zealand Today

NORTHLAND
Whangarei
AUCKLAND
Auckland
Hamilton
Tauranga
WAIKATO
BAY OF PLENTY
GISBORNE
Gisborne
ASDSA
HAWKE'S BAY
New Plymouth
TARANAKI
Napier
WANGANUI
Palmerston North
Collingwood
Nelson
WELLINGTON
NELSON
Wellington
TASMAN
Blenheim
MARLBOROUGH
Greymouth
WEST COAST
CANTERBURY
Christchurch
OTAGO
SOUTHLAND
Dunedin
Invercargill

Sinking of the Greenpeace ship *Rainbow Warrior* in 1985

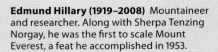

Map of New Zealand by Captain James Cook, ca. 1770

The Maori

In the 13th century, indigenous peoples came to New Zealand from Polynesia in several waves and lived in warlike *iwus* and *hapus* (tribes and sub-tribes). An *ariki* (chief) was the leader of a *hapu*. They inhabited every region and developed a unique culture. After Europeans arrived in the 19th century, they lost their rights and land. European diseases, to which the Maori had no immunity, wiped out entire tribes. The Maori population increased again at the end of the 19th century. In the 1960s, the government passed legislation that contributed to the renewal of their culture and gave Maoris equal rights within New

Maoris fighting each other

Zealand society. Dramatic facial tattooing is characteristic of Maori men and is a symbol of their social position; men without a tattoo are considered insignificant. Maori women also receive tattoos, often to commemorate important events in their lives such as the birth of a child.

Edmund Hillary (1919–2008) Mountaineer and researcher. Along with Sherpa Tenzing Norgay, he was the first to scale Mount Everest, a feat he accomplished in 1953.

David Lange (1942–2005) Member of the Labour Party and prime minister of New Zealand from 1984–1989. Essential economic reforms made during his tenure ushered in a period of growth and prosperity.

Jenny Shipley (1952–) First Chairwoman of the National Party and the first female Prime Minister (1997–1999).

Dame Te Atairangikaahu (1931–2006) Her lengthy reign of forty years makes her the longest reigning queen of the Maori.

Bruce McLaren (1937–1970) Born in Auckland, New Zealand, he was a Formula I race car driver and designer. The McLaren racing team has won the Formula 1 championship eleven times since 1974.

Harold Gilles (1882–1960) was a physician who is widely considered the father of plastic surgery.

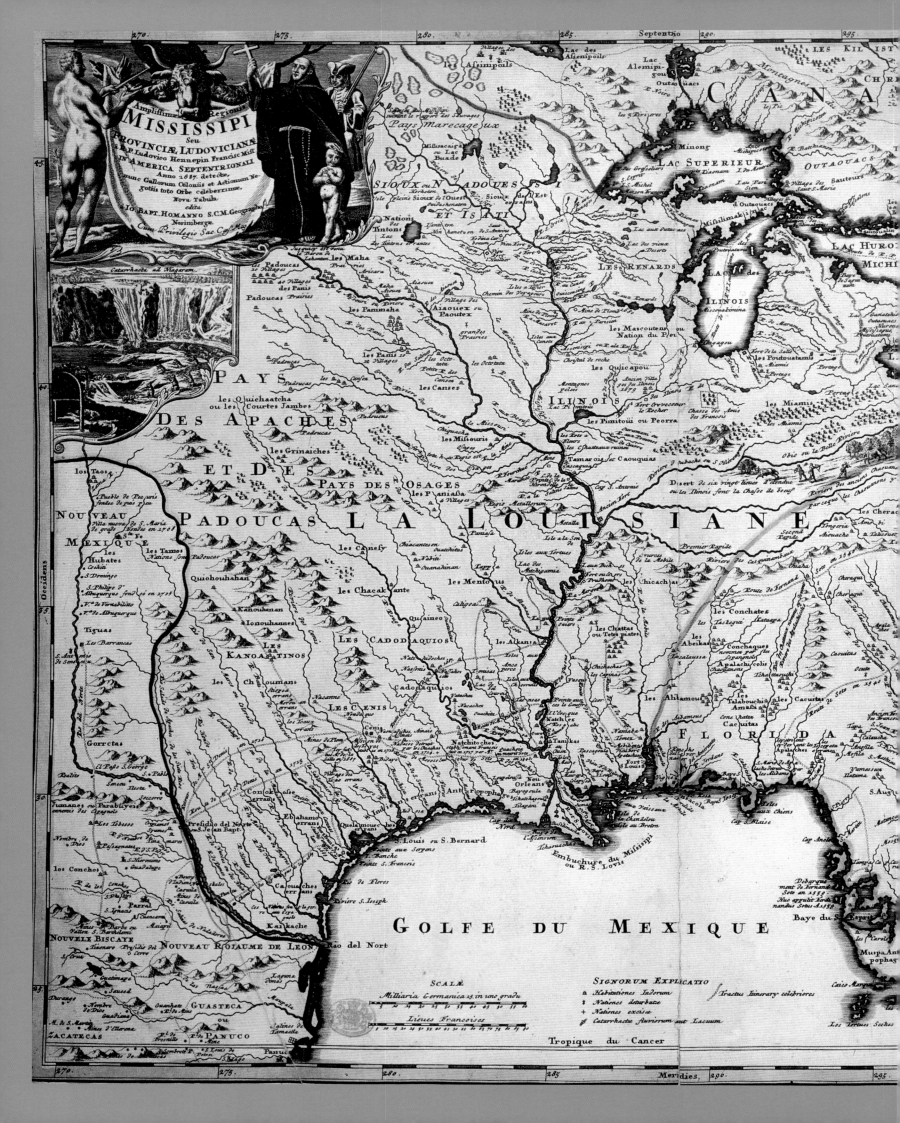

NORTH AMERICA

At the time of the first European contact in 1492, perhaps 100 million Native Americans lived in North America. Their highly developed civilizations encompassed a wide range of languages and hundreds of tribal associations. Native Americans lived in villages and cities, as hunter-gatherers or farmers and as fishermen or herders. Within 120 years of Columbus' first voyage to the New World, as many as 90 percent of all its indigenous peoples had been eradicated, many by European viral diseases including smallpox, measles and hepatitis. Rampant colonial settlement sparked by immigration and the philosophy of Manifest Destiny also played a role. Europeans moved rapidly westward, leading to near-constant and often violent conflict with the remaining native tribes. By the time of the Battle of Wounded Knee (in 1890), there were perhaps as few as 230,000 Native Americans left in the United States. Today, much of the native population of North America lives on reservations, where they struggle with poverty and other social problems, yet they take pride in their identity and there are causes for hope for the future.

Most of the more than 40 million African Americans living in North America are descendants of slaves captured by traders in Africa. Prior to 1860, up to 90 percent of the African American population lived in slavery. Even after their emancipation following the Civil War, racial segregation in "colored neighborhoods" and "black ghettos" was enforced in some states by Jim Crow laws, which remained in force well into the 20th century. Social and economic prejudices have frequently erupted into racist violence. And yet, the United States has elected its first African American president, Barack Obama, who took office in 2009.

For millions of people who saw no future in their homeland, on the other hand, and were willing to leave everything they knew behind—at first Europeans but in the meantime also from other areas of the world—the American Dream continues to offer hope and a chance for a new beginning.

North America: An Overview	404
Indigenous Peoples of North America	406
Canada from 1000 to 1870	408
Canada from 1896 to Today / Greenland	410
North America from the Colonial Period to American Independence	412
The United States from Independence to 1850	414
THE FIFTY STATES	415
The United States – The American Civil War	416
The United States – From the Civil War to Today	418
IMMIGRATION AND SETTLEMENT OF THE UNITED STATES	420
THE UNITED STATES BECOMES A WORLD POWER	422
The Caribbean	424

La Louisiane. A late 17th/early18th century print by Johann Baptista Homann showing French colonial claims in North America.

North America: An Overview

To 1500: Native Cultures and Early European Contact

Native civilizations
- Agriculture
- Mississippian culture
- Pueblo and Hohokam cultures
- Aztecs
- Maya

Colonization
- Vikings (985–1350)
- Spanish (from 1492)

West Settlement

East Settlement

Leif Eriksson (~1000)

L'Anse aux Meadows

John Cabot (1497)

Jacques Cartier (1535)

ADENA CULTURE AND HOPEWELL CULTURE

AFTER 400 BCE

MISSISSIPPIAN CULTURE

1325–1520

300–153 BCE

Christopher Columbus (1492–1493)

Santo Domingo (1498)

1504

ca. 1620: Early Colonies

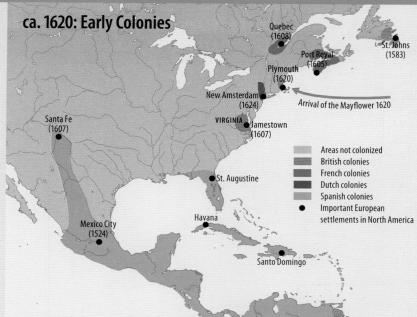

Quebec (1608)

St. Johns (1583)

Port Royal (1605)

Plymouth (1620)

New Amsterdam (1624)

Arrival of the Mayflower 1620

VIRGINIA   Jamestown (1607)

Santa Fe (1607)

St. Augustine

Mexico City (1524)

Havana

Santo Domingo

- Areas not colonized
- British colonies
- French colonies
- Dutch colonies
- Spanish colonies
- ● Important European settlements in North America

ca. 1750: French, British and Spanish Colonies

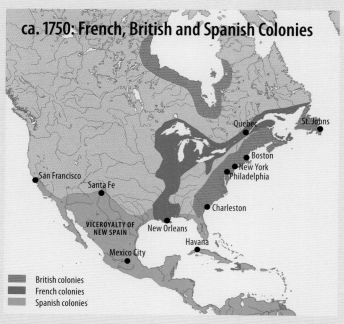

Quebec

St. Johns

Boston
New York
Philadelphia

San Francisco

Santa Fe

Charleston

VICEROYALTY OF NEW SPAIN

New Orleans

Havana

Mexico City

- British colonies
- French colonies
- Spanish colonies

1783: After the American Revolution

GREENLAND

Quebec

Montreal

Halifax

Boston
New York
Philadelphia
Richmond

San Francisco

New Orleans

Mexico City

BRITISH HONDURAS

Port-au-Prince

JAMAICA

- United States of America
- Russian colonies
- British colonies
- Danish colonies
- Spanish colonies
- French colonies

- Upper Canada
- Province of Lower Canada

The date of the first human settlement of North America is a matter of debate. The most conservative estimate is 15,000 years ago, when settlers crossed over the Bering Strait from Siberia via a now submerged land bridge called Beringia. It could only be crossed during the Ice Age, when sea levels were around 410 feet (125 m) lower than today. Others claim the settlement of North America began much earlier, citing footprints in central Mexico tentatively dated to 40,000 years ago.

before 12,000 BCE Asiatic peoples migrate to North America.

800–600 BCE The Adena and Hopewell cultures settle the Mississippi River valley and parts of the southeast.

from 400 BCE Pueblo and Hohokam cultures thrive in the southwest.

800–1500 CE The Mississippian culture brings complex civilization to the midwest and southeast.

~1000 Viking Leif Eriksson reaches Newfoundland (L'Anse aux Meadows).

1492–1504 Christopher Columbus voyages to the Americas.

1497 Italian seafarer John Cabot sails from Bristol, England, to Labrador.

1607 Virginia becomes a British colony.

1608 France settles Quebec, forming the colony of New France.

1620 The Pilgrims, a religious group split from and persecuted by the Anglican church, found Plymouth Colony in what is now Massachusetts.

1624 The Dutch found the settlement of New Amsterdam, now New York. It will be taken over by the British in 1664.

1713 The Treaty of Utrecht forces the French to cede some of their territory in the New World to Britain.

1754–1763 The Seven Years' War (French and Indian War) ends with the French losing Quebec to the British.

1773 The American colonists protest British taxes on the colonies (taxation without representation) by staging the Boston Tea Party.

1775–1783 American Revolution (or United States War of Independence)

1776 American colonial leaders representing thirteen colonies sign the Declaration of Independence.

1783 Britain recognizes the independence of the United States in the Treaty of Paris.

1789 George Washington is elected first president of the United States.

1791 Quebec is divided into English-speaking and French-speaking zones.

1803 The United States purchases the Louisiana Territory from France, doubling its size.

1812 The United States, in alliance with Napoleonic France, declares war on Great Britain.

1823 The Monroe Doctrine asserts that the Western Hemisphere is not to be further colonized by Europe, and that in return the United States will not interfere with existing European colonies or in European countries.

from 1837 Conflict intensifies between the Northern and Southern states regarding slavery and states' rights.

1846 War breaks out between the United States and Mexico. It ends with the United States in control of California and most of the Southwest.

1861 The Southern States secede from the Union in the wake of Abraham Lincoln's election to the presidency of the United States. The American Civil War begins.

1863 The Emancipation Proclamation bans slavery in the Southern states.

1865 The Southern states surrender, ending the American Civil War. Abraham Lincoln is assassinated in Washington, D.C.

1867 Canada becomes a self-governing federal dominion of the British Empire, the first British colony to do so. The United States purchases Alaska from Russia (Seward's Folly).

1876 Native Americans defeat the United States cavalry for the last time at the Battle of Little Big Horn.

1890 Revenging the defeat at Little Bighorn, the United States cavalry massacres around 140 Sioux at the Battle of Wounded Knee.

1898 Spain loses control of its last North American colonies in the Spanish-American War. The United States begins a period of expansionist policy in Latin America.

1904 The Roosevelt Corollary to the Monroe Doctrine states that the United States alone has the right to intervene in the affairs of the American continents, leading to an intensification of United States involvement in Central and South America.

1917 The United States enters World War I.

1918 US President Wilson proposes a new world order in his Fourteen Points speech to Congress, which becomes the foundation for the League of Nations.

1929 The American stock market crash sets off a worldwide economic crisis.

1931 Canada gains its independence, becoming a sovereign state of the British Commonwealth.

from 1933 Franklin Roosevelt's New Deal policies revive the United States economy.

1941 Japan bombs Pearl Harbor, Hawaii, provoking the United States's entry into World War II.

1945 Atomic bombs are dropped on Hiroshima and Nagasaki, ending World War II in the Pacific.

1950–1953 The United States enters the Korean War.

1950–1954 The McCarthy Era of attacks on intellectuals and artists suspected of communist sympathies

1959 Alaska and Hawaii gain statehood.

1962 The Cuban Missile Crisis breaks out over Soviet nuclear-armed missile launchers in Cuba.

1963 United States President John F. Kennedy is assassinated in Dallas, Texas.

1964 American intervention in Vietnam begins.

1966 Protests against the Vietnam War intensify. Peace protesters and hippies are signs of the increasing liberalization of American society.

1969 American astronauts are the first to land on the moon.

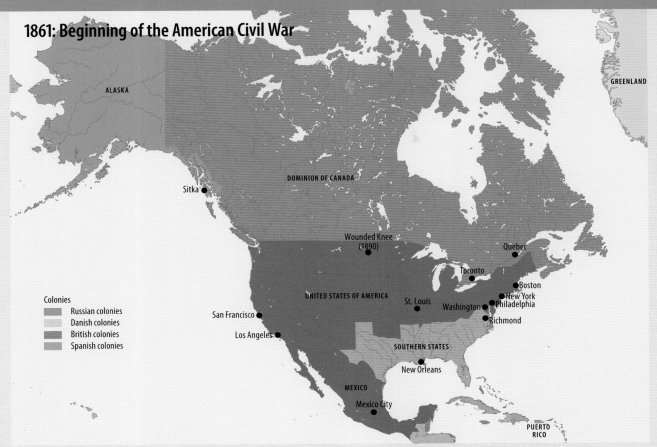

1861: Beginning of the American Civil War

ALASKA

GREENLAND

DOMINION OF CANADA

Sitka

Wounded Knee (1890)

Quebec

Toronto

Boston

New York

UNITED STATES OF AMERICA

St. Louis

Washington

Philadelphia

San Francisco

Richmond

Los Angeles

SOUTHERN STATES

New Orleans

MEXICO

Mexico City

PUERTO RICO

Colonies
- Russian colonies
- Danish colonies
- British colonies
- Spanish colonies

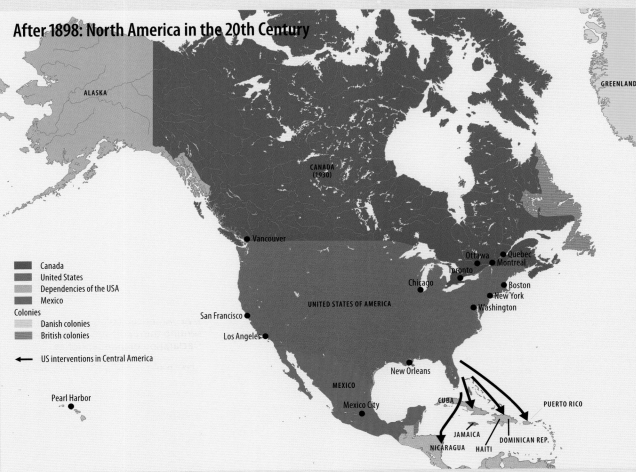

After 1898: North America in the 20th Century

ALASKA

GREENLAND

CANADA (1930)

Vancouver

Ottawa

Quebec

Montreal

Toronto

Chicago

Boston

New York

UNITED STATES OF AMERICA

Washington

San Francisco

Los Angeles

New Orleans

MEXICO

Mexico City

CUBA

PUERTO RICO

JAMAICA

NICARAGUA

HAITI

DOMINICAN REP.

Pearl Harbor

- Canada
- United States
- Dependencies of the USA
- Mexico

Colonies
- Danish colonies
- British colonies

← US interventions in Central America

1973 The United States signs a peace treaty with Vietnam.

1979 The Inuit people in Greenland, previously a colony of Denmark, are granted the right to self-government.

1981 United States President Reagan takes a confrontational stand against the USSR.

1982 The Canadian Constitution Act gives Canada complete independence from Britain.

1995 A public referendum on the question of Quebec's independence from Canada fails to pass.

2001 Terrorists attack the World Trade Center in New York City and the Pentagon near Washington, D.C.

Indigenous Peoples of North America

Language Families

Arctic Coasts

☐ **Inuit**

The Inuit hunt fish, seal, walrus, whale and polar bear from small, lightweight kayaks. They traditionally lived in huts draped with animal skins or in igloos. They believe in shamanism, the soul's ability to travel outside the body, and have close ties to the natural world. Animal spirits are invoked as protectors and guides by wearing amulets and during trance states similar to the "vision quest" of other Native American groups.

Subarctic Region

☐ **Na-Dené-Athabaskan**
☐ **Algonquin**
■ **Beotuk**

This region is home to hunter-gatherers and the classic Native American nature religion that invests cosmic power in the earth and all beings. That power, *manitou*, represents the interconnectedness of all living things.

Northwest Coasts

■ **Tlingit**
■ **Makah**
■ **Salish**

Abundant food from the ocean and a mild climate provided ideal conditions on the coast. Wood houses were built in villages. Religious life focused on totems, ancestral animal spirit guides.

California

☐ **Penutian**
☐ **Hokan-Yuma**

The central valley of California was once the most densely inhabited part of North America. Before the arrival of Europeans, natives built houses of animal skins and branches, covering the walls of the sunken rooms with clay plaster. Most tribes from this region followed the classic Native American nature religion, although some worshipped a sun god.

The Great Plains

☐ **Algonquin**
☐ **Kutenai**
☐ **Tonkawa**

These tribes were nomadic hunters who followed vast herds of bison; horses were only introduced after the Spanish imported mustangs. The hunters lived in tipis that were easily dismantled and transported. Their religion was based on shamanism and rituals associated with sacred places throughout the land.

The High Plateau and Great Basin

☐ **Aztec-Tanoan**
■ **Keres**

Hunter-gatherers flourished in this rich environment. Many tribes believed the world rose out of a primordial sea.

Southwest

☐ **Hokan-Yuma**
☐ **Aztec-Tanoan**
■ **Keres**
☐ **Na-Dené-Apaches**
☐ **Tonkawa**
☐ **Coahuiltek**
☐ **Karankawa**
■ **Zapotek**
☐ **Maya**

These tribes grew food and hunted, lived in tipis or stone houses plastered with mud, and practiced shamanism ("medicine men"), worshipping nature spirits alongside more complex deities.

Northeast

☐ **Algonquin**
☐ **Iroquois**

Skilled hunters and fishermen, the Iroquois founded a confederation of five tribes with parliamentary-style representation well before the arrival of Europeans. Their religion described human origins as the result of a union between the sun and moon.

Southeast

☐ **Siouxan-Lakota (Sioux)**
■ **Muskogee**
☐ **Timucuos**
☐ **Taino**
☐ **Carib**

Many southeastern tribes vanished in the 17th century after contact with Europeans. The natives grew corn, beans and squash, lived in villages centered around wooden longhouses, and believed the earth was an island in an endless sea.

NA-DENÉ ATHABASKEN

TLINGIT

MAKAH

KUTENAI

SALISH

PENUTIAN

HOKAN-YUMA

HOKAN-YUMA

AZTEKEN-TANOAN

PENUTIAN

HOKAN-YUMA

KERES

HOKAN-YUMA

AZTE

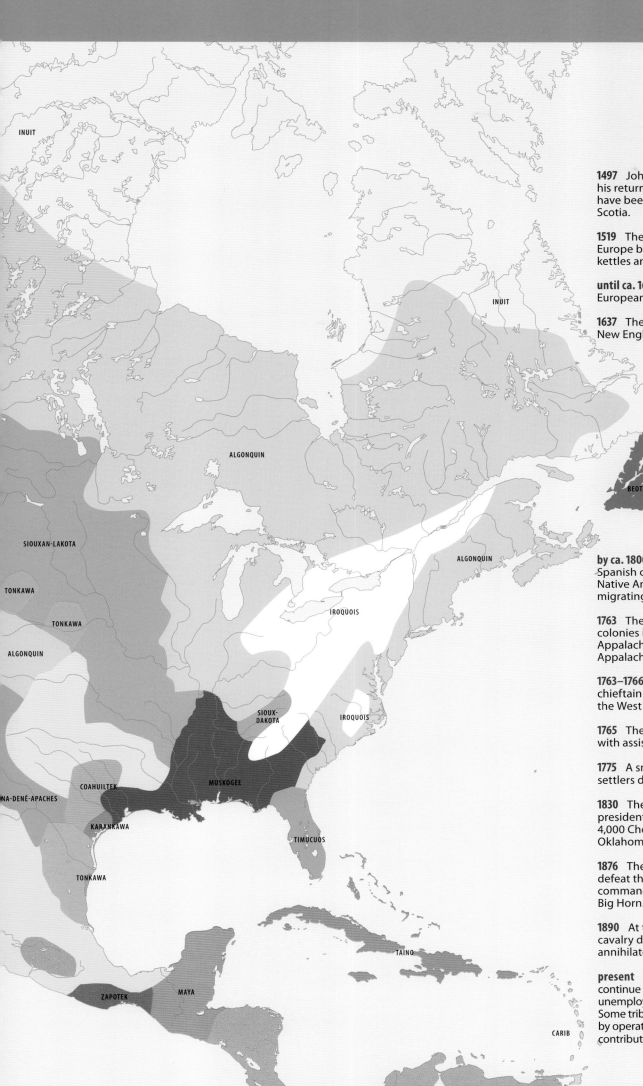

INUIT

INUIT

INUIT

ALGONQUIN

ALGONQUIN

BEOTHUK

SIOUXAN-LAKOTA

TONKAWA

TONKAWA

IROQUOIS

ALGONQUIN

ALGONQUIN

IROQUOIS

SIOUX-DAKOTA

NA-DENÉ-APACHES

COAHUILTEK

MUSKOGEE

IROQUOIS

KARANKAWA

TIMUCUOS

TONKAWA

TAINO

ZAPOTEK

MAYA

CARIB

1497 John Cabot brings three natives with him on his return journey to England. They are believed to have been members of the Mi'kmaq tribe of Nova Scotia.

1519 The fur trade between Native Americans and Europe begins; natives exchanges pelts for axes, kettles and metal goods.

until ca. 1600 Epidemics of diseases brought by Europeans ravage the native population.

1637 The Pequot War between natives and the New England colonies results in almost complete extermination of the local indigenous peoples.

1640–1701 The Iroquois use weapons obtained from Dutch settlers to devestatingly defeat the Wyandot and Erie tribes.

1756–1763 Britain and France fight the French and Indian War (Seven Years' War) with allied native tribes on both sides. France is defeated and loses most of its North American territories.

by ca. 1800 The mustang horse is introduced by Spanish colonists, radically altering the lives of Native American bison hunters. Many tribes begin migrating to the west, including the Lakota Sioux.

1763 The Proclamation Act divides the British colonies into European territory (east of the Appalachians) and native territory (west of the Appalachians).

1763–1766 Failure of a revolt led by the native chieftain Pontiac, of the Ottawa tribe, opens up the West to European settlement.

1765 The Lakota Sioux move into the Black Hills with assistance from the French.

1775 A smallpox epidemic brought by Spanish settlers decimates the tribes along the Pacific coast.

1830 The Indian Removal Act gives the United States president the power to resettle native tribes. Over 4,000 Cherokee die during their forced removal to Oklahoma (Trail of Tears).

1876 The Lakota Sioux, Arapaho and Cheyenne defeat the 7th United States Cavalry under the command of George A. Custer at the Battle of Little Big Horn.

1890 At the massacre at Wounded Knee, the same cavalry division that was defeated at Little Big Horn annihilates the last pocket of native resistance.

present Today, many First People or Native Americans continue to live on reservations that are often beset by unemployment, alcoholism and inadequate health care. Some tribes have prospered from revenue generated by operating casinos, while others feel that gambling contributes to the destruction of native culture.

Canada from 1000 to 1870

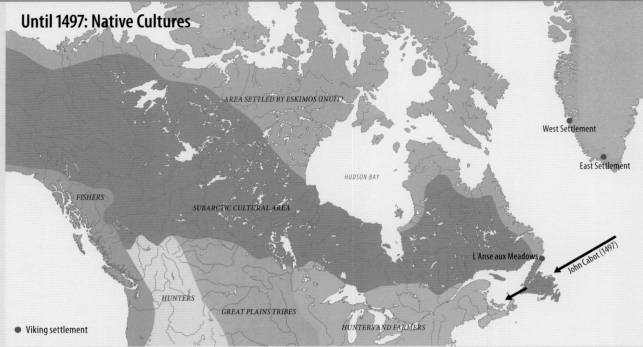

Until 1497: Native Cultures

AREA SETTLED BY ESKIMOS (INUIT)

West Settlement

East Settlement

HUDSON BAY

FISHERS

SUBARCTIC CULTURAL AREA

L'Anse aux Meadows

John Cabot (1497)

HUNTERS

GREAT PLAINS TRIBES

HUNTERS AND FARMERS

● Viking settlement

Canada quickly became the arena in which the overseas rivalry between France and Great Britain played out. After Britain's victory in the Seven Years' War (French and Indian War), the land was administered by the British in the 18th century. In 1867 Canada became the first self-governed British colony (the Dominion of Canada).

1000 The Vikings found a settlement at L'Anse aux Meadows (now in Newfoundland).

1497 John Cabot reaches the coast of Newfoundland.

1534 Jacques Cartier explores the St. Lawrence River and claims the surrounding land for the French crown.

1583 Newfoundland becomes the first British colony.

1627 The French colonies in the New World are christened New France.

1670 Hudson's Bay Company, an English trade enterprise, colonizes the area around Hudson Bay.

1713 The Treaty of Utrecht ends war between France and Britain, and Newfoundland, Acadia and the area surrounding Hudson Bay become British possessions.

1759 New France is conquered in the war with the British colonies.

1763 The Seven Years' War ends. The Treaty of Paris cedes all French colonies in North America—with the exception of the Louisiana Territory—to Great Britain.

1791 Quebec is split into Lower Canada (present-day Quebec) and Upper Canada (Ontario).

By 1710: British and French in North America I

Fort Churchill (1688)

HUDSON BAY

Fort Rupert (1668)

Quebec (1608)

Montreal (1642)

NEWFOUNDLAND

St. John's (1580)

Sault Ste. Marie (1668)

St. Lawrence River

Louisbourg (1720)

NEW FRANCE

Boston (1630)

	British colonies by 1710
	French colonies by 1650
	French colonies by 1710
●	Important city (settlement) and date of founding

ca. 1713: British and French in North America II

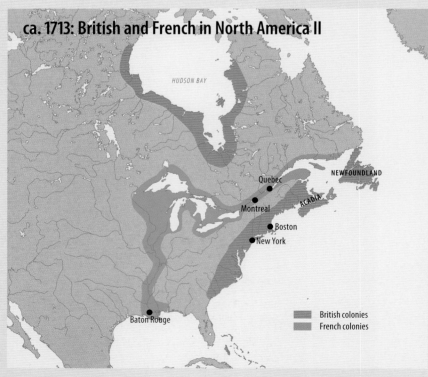

HUDSON BAY

NEWFOUNDLAND

Quebec

Montreal

ACADIA

Boston

New York

Baton Rouge

| | British colonies |
| | French colonies |

1763: Treaty of Paris

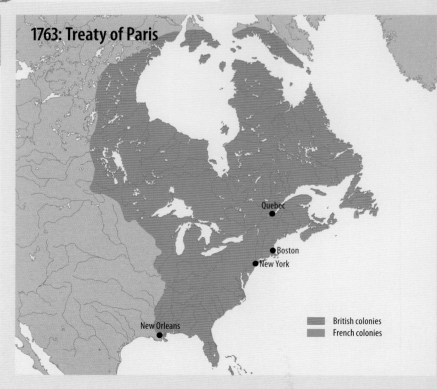

Quebec

Boston

New York

New Orleans

| | British colonies |
| | French colonies |

1867 The Dominion of Canada (consisting of the provinces of Ontario, Quebec, Nova Scotia and New Brunswick) is created.

1870 Manitoba becomes the fifth Canadian province, followed by British Columbia (1871) and Prince Edward Island (1873).

Jacques Cartier (1491–1557) was the first European to explore and map the St. Lawrence River.

Samuel de Champlain (ca. 1567–1635) founded the city of Quebec in 1608.

Jean-Baptiste Talon (1625–1694) was the first superintendent of New France under Louis XIV.

Samuel de Champlain

James Wolfe (1727–1759) was the British commander in the French and Indian War (Seven Years' War). He was killed in the battle for Quebec, which the British won, as was his opponent, the French commander Louis-Joseph Montcalm.

Dominion Designation for a self-governed state that retains the British Crown as its head of state.

ca. 1791: British Colonies

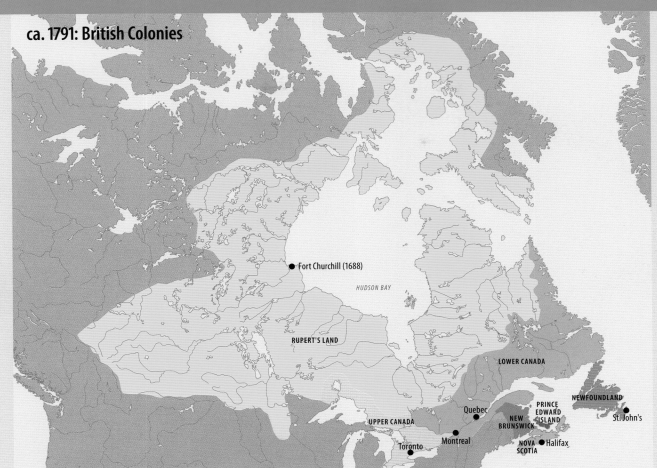

Fort Churchill (1688)

HUDSON BAY

RUPERT'S LAND

LOWER CANADA

NEWFOUNDLAND

UPPER CANADA

Quebec

PRINCE EDWARD ISLAND

NEW BRUNSWICK

St. John's

Toronto

Montreal

NOVA SCOTIA

Halifax

1870: The Five Provinces

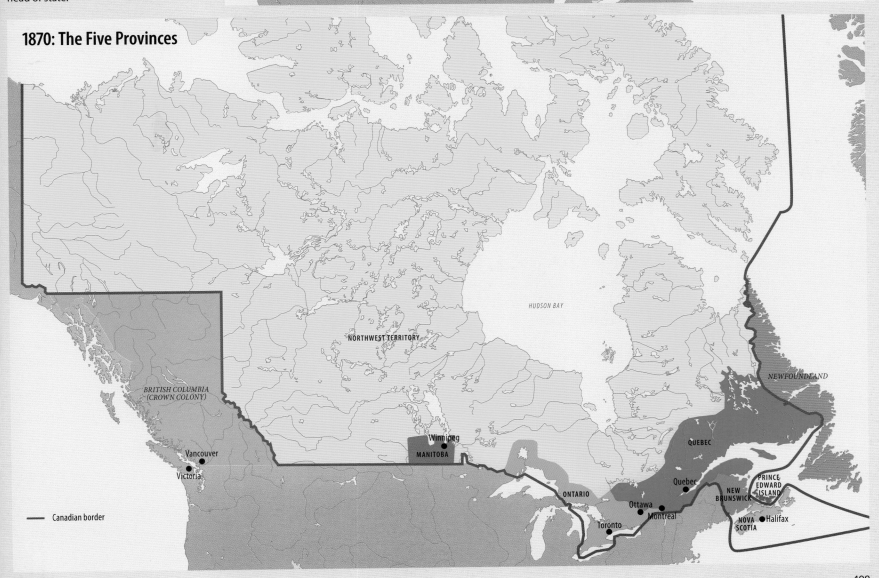

BRITISH COLUMBIA (CROWN COLONY)

HUDSON BAY

NORTHWEST TERRITORY

NEWFOUNDLAND

Vancouver

Victoria

Winnipeg

MANITOBA

QUEBEC

ONTARIO

Quebec

PRINCE EDWARD ISLAND

NEW BRUNSWICK

Ottawa

Montreal

Toronto

NOVA SCOTIA

Halifax

— Canadian border

Canada from 1896 to the Present / Greenland

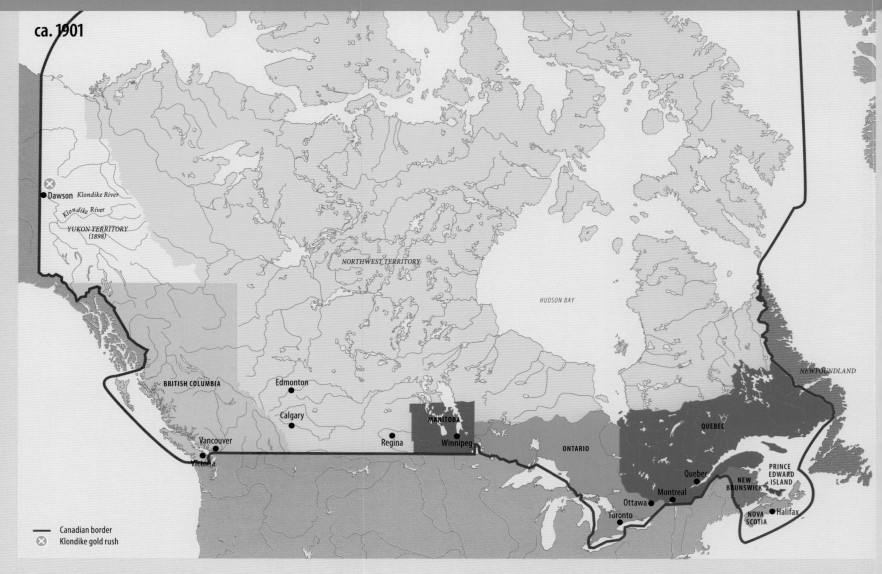

ca. 1901

Dawson
Klondike River
Klondike River
YUKON TERRITORY
(1898)

NORTHWEST TERRITORY

HUDSON BAY

NEWFOUNDLAND

BRITISH COLUMBIA

Edmonton

Calgary

Vancouver

Victoria

Regina

Winnipeg

MANITOBA

ONTARIO

QUEBEC

Quebec

Montreal

Ottawa

Toronto

NEW BRUNSWICK

PRINCE EDWARD ISLAND

NOVA SCOTIA

Halifax

— Canadian border
⊗ Klondike gold rush

In the 20th century, Canada officially attained the status of an independent country within the framework of the British Commonwealth. Economically and politically, the United

States is Canada's most important partner. In spite of political agitation toward independence for Quebec, the Franco-phone province has not seceded from the rest of Canada.

1896 Thousands flock to the Yukon Territory to seek their fortune in the gold rush along the Klondike River.

1905 The provinces of Alberta and Saskatchewan are admitted to the dominion.

1916–1918 In spite of widespread desire for independence, Canadians fight for the British Empire in World War I. They suffer heavy losses.

1919 Canadians John Alcock and Arthur Whitten Brown fly a Vickers amphibious plane from Newfoundland to Ireland, the the first to cross the Atlantic by air.

1934 Newfoundland gives up self-government and reverts to British control.

1931 Statute of Westminster officially declares the independence and equality of Canada and other British dominions.

1939 Canada declares war on Germany on September 10. More than 1.1 million Canadian volunteers serve in the war, 44,000 of whom lose their lives. In 1944 Canadian troops land on Juno Beach (Normandy) and help liberate the Netherlands in 1945.

1949 Newfoundland once again becomes part of Canada as the

ca. 1920

YUKON TERRITORY

NORTHWEST TERRITORY

HUDSON BAY

NEWFOUNDLAND

BRITISH COLUMBIA

ALBERTA

Edmonton

Calgary

SASKATCHEWAN

Regina

MANITOBA

Winnipeg

ONTARIO

QUEBEC

Vancouver

Quebec

Ottawa

Montreal

Toronto

NEW BRUNSWICK

NOVA SCOTIA

Halifax

PRINCE EDWARD ISLAND

— Canadian border

Canada Today

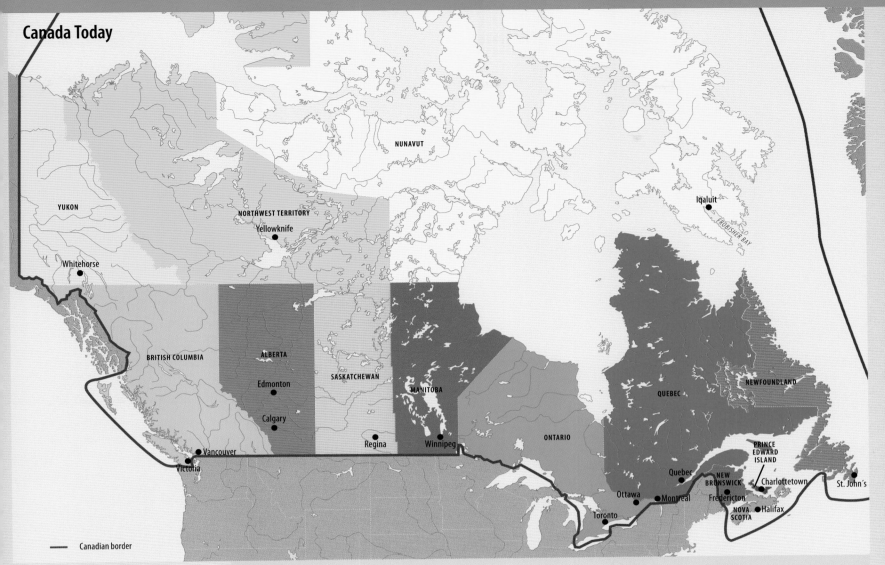

NUNAVUT

YUKON

NORTHWEST TERRITORY
• Yellowknife

• Whitehorse

BRITISH COLUMBIA

ALBERTA
• Edmonton

• Calgary

SASKATCHEWAN

• Regina

MANITOBA

• Winnipeg

ONTARIO

QUEBEC

NEWFOUNDLAND

Iqaluit
FROBISHER BAY

• Vancouver
Victoria •

• Toronto

Ottawa •
• Montreal

Quebec •

PRINCE EDWARD ISLAND

NEW BRUNSWICK
• Fredericton
• Charlottetown

NOVA SCOTIA
• Halifax

• St. John´s

— Canadian border

---

province of Newfoundland and Labrador.

1959 Agreement with the United States regarding the peaceful use of atomic energy

1963–1965 Construction of the Trans-Canada Highway

1965 The new Canadian flag, which does not include any elements of the British flag, is introduced.

1969 English and French are both recognized as official languages of Canada.

1980 The first referendum on independence for Quebec is defeated.

1982 According to the Constitution Act of 1982, amendments to the Canadian constitution no longer require British assent.

1988 The government returns some territory to First Nations (Indians) and the Inuit.

1989 Free trade agreement reached with the United States

1995 Another attempt at Quebec independence fails, but opponents of secession win the referendum by just one percentage point.

Greenland

982 The Viking Eric the Red discovers Greenland.

1721 The island is rediscovered and settled by the Danish, and is a Danish colony for the following centuries.

1979 Greenland gains autonomy within Denmark.

1985 Greenland withdraws from the European Union .

Early History

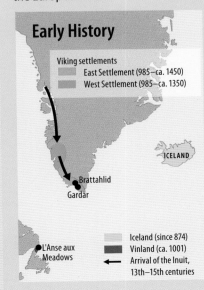

Viking settlements
▨ East Settlement (985–ca. 1450)
▨ West Settlement (985–ca. 1350)

Brattahlid
Gardar

ICELAND

L'Anse aux Meadows

▨ Iceland (since 874)
▨ Vinland (ca. 1001)
← Arrival of the Inuit, 13th–15th centuries

1700 to Today

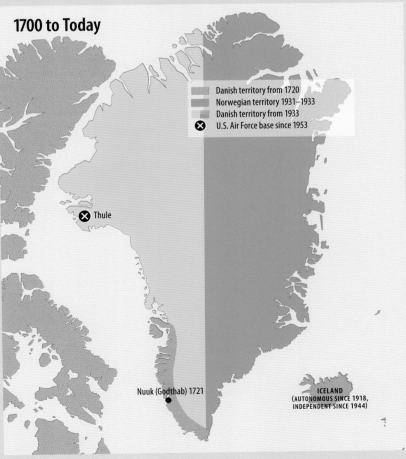

▨ Danish territory from 1720
▨ Norwegian territory 1931–1933
▨ Danish territory from 1933
⊗ U.S. Air Force base since 1953

⊗ Thule

Nuuk (Godthab) 1721

ICELAND
(AUTONOMOUS SINCE 1918, INDEPENDENT SINCE 1944)

North America from the Colonial Period to American Independence

1500: Native American Cultures

HUNTERS AND GATHERERS

FISHERS

HUNTERS, GATHERERS AND FISHERS

GREAT PLAINS TRIBES

HUNTERS AND GATHERERS

FARMERS AND HUNTERS

Mesa Verde
Pueblo Bonito
Pelos Pueblo

Angel

Shiloh

FARMERS

FARMERS

- - - Anasazi culture (700–1500)
▢ ▢ ▢ Mississippian cultures of ceremonial burial mounds (800–1500)
● Pueblos
● Mounds

The eastern regions of North America became British colonies within a short time after John Cabot's explorations. The economies of the Atlantic Coast settlements developed largely through fur trade with the Native Americans, agriculture and slave labor. The settlers' taxes went into British coffers, but they had no say in British political affairs. The Boston Tea Party (1773), a protest against this lack of influence, was followed by the American colonies' Declaration of Independence in 1776.

Less than a century later, a volatile social split focusing on the issues of slavery and states' rights led the Southern States to secede from the Union. The Civil War of 1861–1865 was the result.

In the 20th century, the United States grew into an undisputed world power in economics, politics and international leadership. Recent events have shaken these foundation into question, without diminishing American influence.

1587 A British colony is established on Roanoke Island, but all the settlers disappear by 1590 (the "Lost Colony").

1607 The British found Jamestown, creating the first permanent colony in Virginia.

1619 The first ships with African slaves arrive.

1620 The *Mayflower* reaches the East Coast; Pilgrims seeking religious tolerance found Plymouth in 1630.

1623 Founding of New Hampshire

1630 Founding of Massachusetts

1664 The British take over control of the Dutch colony of New Amsterdam (renamed New York in 1669).

1773 The Boston Tea Party initiates a boycott of British goods by the colonists.

1775–1783 The thirteen colonies fight the American Revolutionary War to gain their independence from Great Britain.

ca. 1650: Arrival of the First Settlers

Quebec (1608)
Montreal (1642)
NEW HAMPSHIRE
Port Royal (1604)
MASSACHUSETTS
Boston (1630)
Plymouth (1630)
New Amsterdam (1613)
Fort Christina (1638)
Mayflower (1620)
Jamestown (1607)
Santa Fe (1690)
St. Augustine (1565)

▨ Spanish colonies
▨ French colonies
▨ Dutch colonies
▨ British colonies
▨ Swedish colonies

← Arrival of the Mayflower in 1620

Boston Tea Party On December 17, 1773, citizens of Boston disguised as Native Americans boarded a ship of the British East India Company and dumped the ship's cargo of tea into Boston Harbor. This action was planned as a protest against the British monopoly on the tea trade, from which the American colonies also wished to profit. This originally symbolic gesture heralded the beginning of the American Revolution.

Walter Raleigh (1552–1618) This author and adventurer sought El Dorado, the legendary city of gold, and claimed Virginia for Great Britain.

Walter Raleigh

John Smith (1581–1631) This English sailor and mercenary was one of the first governors of the colony at Jamestown in Virginia.

Roger Williams (1603–1683) An English theologian, he founded Providence, Rhode Island.

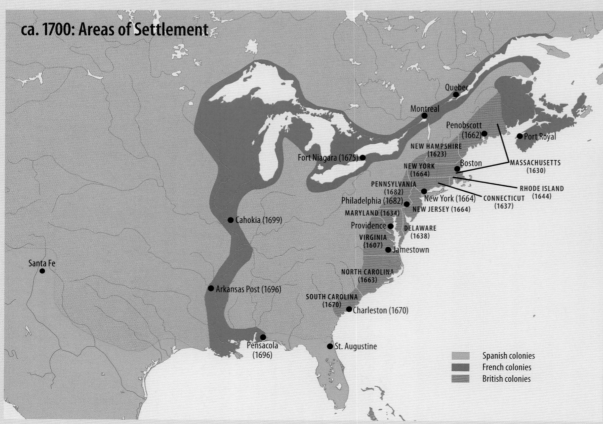

ca. 1700: Areas of Settlement

Quebec
Montreal
Penobscott (1662)
Port Royal
Fort Niagara (1675)
NEW HAMPSHIRE (1623)
NEW YORK (1664)
Boston
MASSACHUSETTS (1630)
PENNSYLVANIA (1682)
RHODE ISLAND (1644)
Philadelphia (1682)
New York (1664)
CONNECTICUT (1637)
NEW JERSEY (1664)
MARYLAND (1634)
Cahokia (1699)
Providence
DELAWARE (1638)
VIRGINIA (1607)
Jamestown
Santa Fe
Arkansas Post (1696)
NORTH CAROLINA (1663)
SOUTH CAROLINA (1670)
Charleston (1670)
Pensacola (1696)
St. Augustine

▨ Spanish colonies
▨ French colonies
▨ British colonies

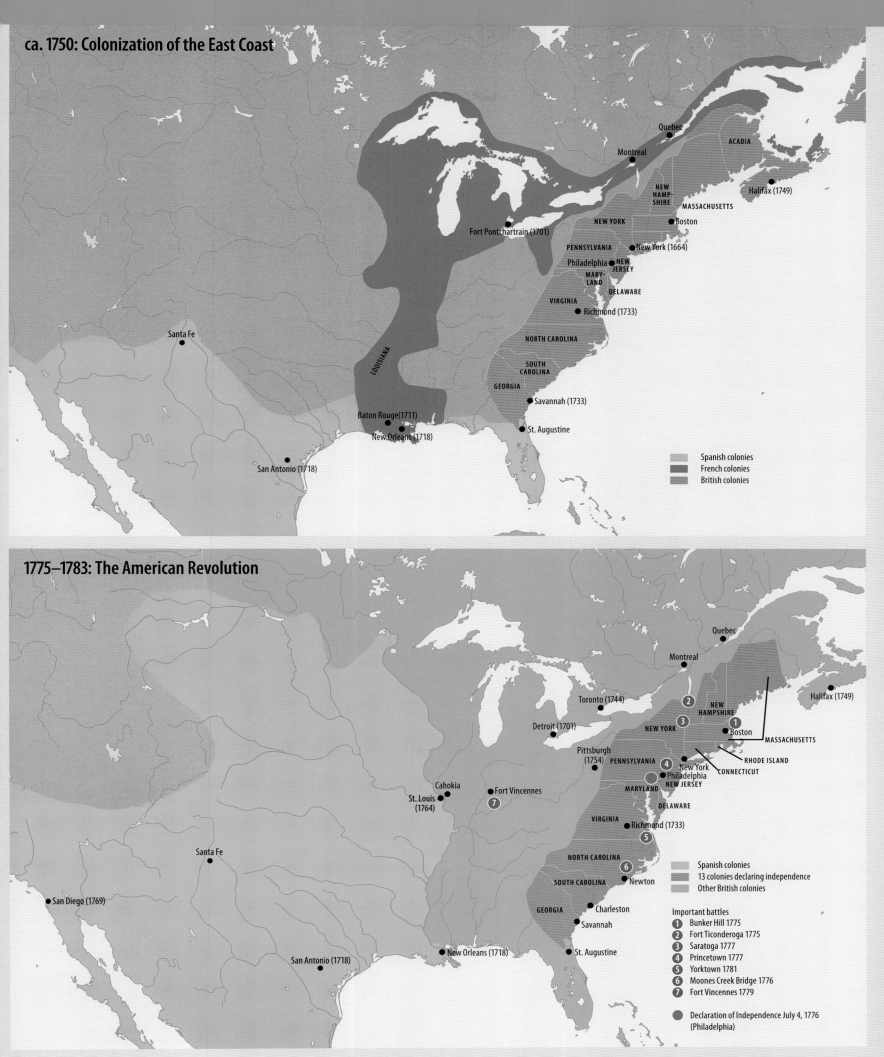

ca. 1750: Colonization of the East Coast

Quebec

ACADIA

Montreal

NEW HAMP-SHIRE

MASSACHUSETTS

Halifax (1749)

NEW YORK

Boston

Fort Pontchartrain (1701)

PENNSYLVANIA

New York (1664)

Philadelphia

NEW JERSEY

MARY-LAND

DELAWARE

VIRGINIA

Richmond (1733)

Santa Fe

NORTH CAROLINA

LOUISIANA

SOUTH CAROLINA

GEORGIA

Savannah (1733)

Baton Rouge(1711)

New Orleans (1718)

St. Augustine

San Antonio (1718)

Spanish colonies
French colonies
British colonies

1775–1783: The American Revolution

Quebec

Montreal

Toronto (1744)

NEW HAMPSHIRE

Halifax (1749)

③

①

Detroit (1701)

②

NEW YORK

Boston

MASSACHUSETTS

Pittsburgh (1754)

PENNSYLVANIA

④

New York

RHODE ISLAND

Cahokia

Fort Vincennes

MARYLAND

Philadelphia

NEW JERSEY

CONNECTICUT

St. Louis (1764)

⑦

DELAWARE

VIRGINIA

Richmond (1733)

⑤

Santa Fe

NORTH CAROLINA

⑥

SOUTH CAROLINA

Newton

Spanish colonies
13 colonies declaring independence
Other British colonies

San Diego (1769)

GEORGIA

Charleston

Savannah

San Antonio (1718)

New Orleans (1718)

St. Augustine

Important battles
① Bunker Hill 1775
② Fort Ticonderoga 1775
③ Saratoga 1777
④ Princetown 1777
⑤ Yorktown 1781
⑥ Moones Creek Bridge 1776
⑦ Fort Vincennes 1779

⬤ Declaration of Independence July 4, 1776 (Philadelphia)

The United States from Independence to 1850

Early 19th Century

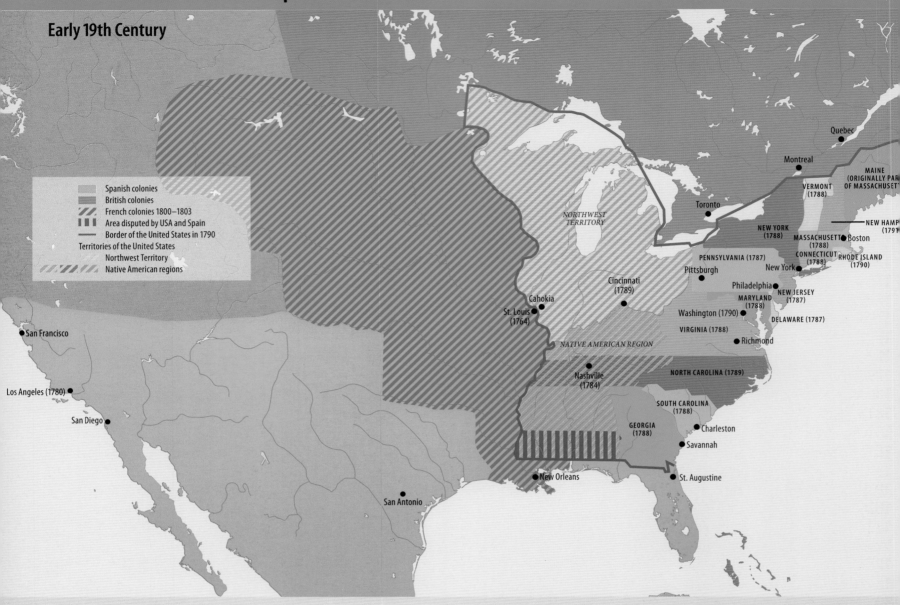

Spanish colonies
British colonies
French colonies 1800–1803
Area disputed by USA and Spain
Border of the United States in 1790
Territories of the United States
Northwest Territory
Native American regions

QuebecMontreal

MAINE (ORIGINALLY PART OF MASSACHUSETT'

VERMONT (1788)

NEW HAMP (1791

Toronto

NORTHWEST TERRITORY

NEW YORK (1788)

MASSACHUSETT (1788) Boston

CONNECTICUT (1788)

RHODE ISLAND (1790)

PENNSYLVANIA (1787)

Pittsburgh

New York

Cincinnati (1789)

Philadelphia

NEW JERSEY (1787)

Cahokia

St. Louis (1764)

Washington (1790)

MARYLAND (1788)

DELAWARE (1787)

VIRGINIA (1788)

Richmond

San Francisco

NATIVE AMERICAN REGION

Los Angeles (1780)

Nashville (1784)

NORTH CAROLINA (1789)

San Diego

SOUTH CAROLINA (1788)

GEORGIA (1788)

Charleston

Savannah

New Orleans

St. Augustine

San Antonio

1776 Representatives of 13 colonies sign the Declaration of Independence in Philadelphia on July 4.

1783 With the Treaty of Paris (not to be confused with the Treaty of Paris of 1763), Great Britain recognizes the independence of the United States of America.

1787 The United States Constitution is ratified.

1789 George Washington is elected the first president of the United States.

1803 The Louisiana Territory is purchased from France.

1812 The United States aligns itself with France, declaring war on Great Britain.

1819 Spain cedes Florida to the United States.

1823 The isolationist Monroe Doctrine (in effect until 1917) is adopted, disallowing European attempts at colonization or hegemony in North and South America.

1836 Rebellion in Texas results in its independence from Mexico.

1846–1848 Following the Mexican-American War, the United States acquires vast territories in the Southwest.

1848 The California gold rush attracts hundreds of thousands of new settlers.

1850 California becomes the thirty-first state to join the union.

An 1823 print of the Declaration of Independence

IN CONGRESS. July 4, 1776.

The unanimous Declaration of the thirteen united States of America.

Monroe Doctrine On December 2, 1823, President James Monroe reaffirmed the United States' independence from the Old World by prohibiting the United States from getting involved in intra-European conflicts. The doctrine emphasized the predominance of the United States in all questions regarding the Americas, prohibiting European colonization and thereby paving the way for future United States imperialism in Central and South America. President Theodore Roosevelt strengthened the Monroe Doctrine in 1904 with the Roosevelt Corollary, but with the entry of the United States into World War I in 1917, this policy was effectively abandoned.

George Washington (1732–1799) The supreme commander of the Continental Army during the American Revolutionary War served as the first president of the United States (1789–1797).

George Washington

Thomas Jefferson (1743–1826) The main author of the American Declaration of Independence became the third president of the United States (1801–1809).

Statehood		Abb.	Capital	Area km²	Area sq.mi.	Nickname	Population 1800	Population 1900	Population 1950	Population 2000	Flag
1787	Delaware	DE	Dover	6,452	2,490	The First State	64,273	184,735	318,085	783,600	
1787	Pennsylvania	PA	Harrisburg	119,283	46,043	Keystone State	602,365	6,302,115	10,498,012	12,281,054	
1787	New Jersey	NJ	Trenton	22,608	8,727	Garden State	211,149	1,883,669	4,835,329	8,414,350	
1788	Georgia	GA	Atlanta	153,909	59,409	Peach State	162,686	2,216,331	3,444,578	8,186,453	
1788	Connecticut	CT	Hartford	14,356	5,541	The Constitution State	251,002	908,420	2,007,280	3,405,565	
1788	Massachusetts	MA	Boston	27,336	10,552	Bay State	422,845	2,805,346	4,690,514	6,349,097	
1788	Maryland	MD	Annapolis	32,133	12,403	Old Line State	341,548	1,188,044	2,343,001	5,296,486	
1788	South Carolina	SC	Columbia	82,931	32,011	The Palmetto State	345,591	1,340,316	2,117,027	4,012,012	
1788	New Hampshire	NH	Concord	24,217	9,348	The Granite State	183,858	411,588	533,242	1,235,786	
1788	Virginia	VA	Richmond	110,785	42,763	Old Dominion	807,557	1,854,184	3,318,680	7,078,515	
1788	New York	NY	Albany	141,299	54,541	The Empire State	589,051	7,268,894	14,830,192	18,976,457	
1789	North Carolina	NC	Raleigh	139,509	53,850	Tar Heel State	478,103	1,893,810	4,061,929	8,049,313	
1790	Rhode Island	RI	Providence	3,144	1,214	The Ocean State	69,122	428,556	791,896	1,048,319	
1791	Vermont	VT	Montpelier	24,923	9,620	The Green Mountain State	154,465	343,641	377,747	608,827	
1792	Kentucky	KY	Frankfort	104,749	40,433	Bluegrass State	220,955	2,147,174	2,944,806	4,041,769	
1796	Tennessee	TN	Nashville	109,347	42,169	Volunteer State	105,602	2,020,616	3,291,718	5,689,283	
1803	Ohio	OH	Columbus	116,096	44,813	The Buckeye State	45,365	4,157,545	7,946,627	11,353,140	
1812	Louisiana	LA	Baton Rouge	134,382	51,871	Bayou State		1,381,625	2,683,516	4,468,976	
1816	Indiana	IN	Indianapolis	94,321	36,408	The Hoosier State	2,632	2,516,462	3,934,224	6,080,485	
1817	Mississippi	MI	Jackson	125,443	48,421	The Magnolia State	7,600	1,551,270	2,178,914	2,844,658	
1818	Illinois	IL	Springfield	140,998	54,425	Land of Lincoln	2,458	4,821,550	8,712,176	12,419,293	
1819	Alabama	AL	Montgomery	135,765	52,405	Yellowhammer State	1,250	1,828,697	3,061,743	4,447,100	
1820	Maine	ME	Augusta	86,542	33,405	The Pine Tree State	151,719	694,466	913,774	1,274,923	
1821	Missouri	MO	Jefferson City	180,533	69,686	The Show-Me State		3,106,665	3,954,653	5,595,211	
1836	Arkansas	AR	Little Rock	137,002	52,883	The Natural State		1,311,564	1,909,511	2,673,400	
1837	Michigan	MI	Lansing	253,793	97,964	The Wolverine State	3,757	2,420,982	6,371,766	9,938,444	
1845	Florida	FL	Tallahassee	170,304	65,737	The Sunshine State		528,542	2,771,305	15,982,378	
1845	Texas	TX	Austin	696,241	268,749	Lone Star State		3,048,710	7,711,194	20,851,820	
1846	Iowa	IA	Des Moines	145,743	56,257	The Hawkeye State		2,231,853	2,621,073	2,926,324	
1848	Wisconsin	WI	Madison	169,790	65,539	Badger State		2,069,042	3,434,575	5,363,675	
1850	California	CA	Sacramento	423,970	163,652	The Golden State		1,485,053	10,586,223	33,871,648	
1858	Minnesota	MN	Saint Paul	225,365	86,991	North Star State		1,751,394	2,982,483	4,919,479	
1859	Oregon	OR	Salem	255,026	98,440	Beaver State		413,536	1,521,341	3,421,399	
1861	Kansas	KS	Topeka	213,096	82,255	The Sunflower State		1,470,495	1,905,299	2,688,418	
1863	West Virginia	WV	Charleston	62,755	24,223	Mountain State	78,592	958,800	2,005,552	1,808,344	
1864	Nevada	NV	Carson City	286,367	110,538	Silver State		42,335	160,083	1,998,257	
1867	Nebraska	NE	Lincoln	200,520	77,401	Cornhusker State		1,066,300	1,325,510	1,711,263	
1876	Colorado	CO	Denver	269,837	104,157	The Centennial State		539,700	1,325,089	4,301,261	
1889	North Dakota	ND	Bismarck	183,272	70,743	Peace Garden State		319,146	619,636	642,200	
1889	South Dakota	SD	Pierre	199,905	77,163	The Mount Rushmore State		401,570	652,740	754,844	
1889	Montana	MT	Helena	381,156	147,126	Treasure State		243,329	591,024	902,195	
1889	Washington	WA	Olympia	184,827	71,343	The Evergreen State		518,103	2,378,963	5,894,121	
1890	Idaho	ID	Boise	216,632	83,620	Gem State		161,772	588,637	1,293,953	
1890	Wyoming	WY	Cheyenne	253,348	97,792	Equality State		92,531	290,529	493,782	
1896	Utah	UT	Salt Lake City	219,887	84,876	Beehive State		276,749	688,862	2,233,169	
1907	Oklahoma	OK	Oklahoma City	181,196	69,942	Sooner State		790,391	2,233,351	3,450,654	
1912	New Mexico	NM	Santa Fe	315,194	121,665	Land of Enchantment		195,310	681,187	1,819,046	
1912	Arizona	AZ	Phoenix	295,254	113,968	The Grand Canyon State		122,931	749,587	5,130,632	
1959	Alaska	AK	Juneau	1,717,854	663,092	The Last Frontier			128,643	626,932	
1959	Hawaii	HI	Honolulu	29,311	11,314	The Aloha State		154,001	499,794	1,211,537	

The United States – The American Civil War

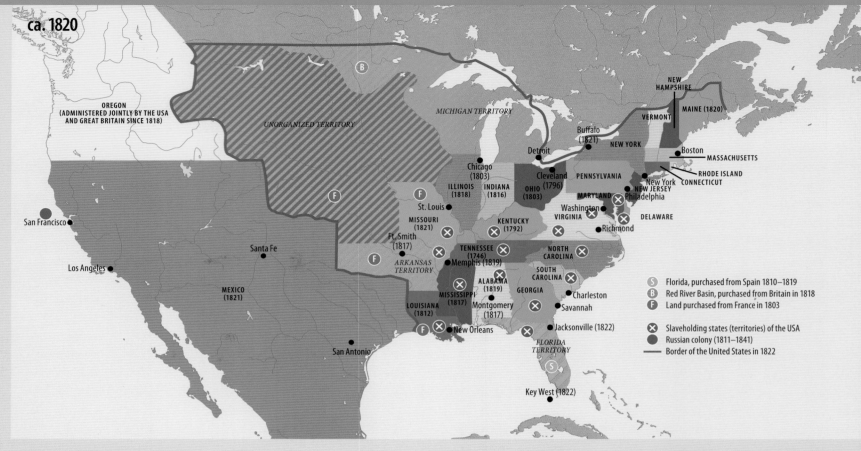

ca. 1820

OREGON
(ADMINISTERED JOINTLY BY THE USA
AND GREAT BRITAIN SINCE 1818)

UNORGANIZED TERRITORY

MICHIGAN TERRITORY

NEW HAMPSHIRE

MAINE (1820)

VERMONT

Buffalo (1821)

NEW YORK

Detroit

Boston
MASSACHUSETTS
RHODE ISLAND
CONNECTICUT

Chicago (1803)

Cleveland (1796)

PENNSYLVANIA

New York

NEW JERSEY

Philadelphia

ILLINOIS (1818)

INDIANA (1816)

OHIO (1803)

MARYLAND

DELAWARE

San Francisco

St. Louis

MISSOURI (1821)

KENTUCKY (1792)

Washington

VIRGINIA

Richmond

Santa Fe

Ft. Smith (1817)

TENNESSEE (1746)

NORTH CAROLINA

Los Angeles

ARKANSAS TERRITORY

Memphis (1819)

SOUTH CAROLINA

MEXICO (1821)

ALABAMA (1819)

GEORGIA

Charleston

MISSISSIPPI (1817)

Savannah

LOUISIANA (1812)

Montgomery (1817)

New Orleans

Jacksonville (1822)

San Antonio

FLORIDA TERRITORY

Key West (1822)

S Florida, purchased from Spain 1810–1819
B Red River Basin, purchased from Britain in 1818
F Land purchased from France in 1803

⊗ Slaveholding states (territories) of the USA
● Russian colony (1811–1841)
— Border of the United States in 1822

November 1860 Abraham Lincoln is elected president of the United States, and in December the slaveholding state of South Carolina secedes from the Union.

April 1861 The Confederate Army fires on federal troops and captures Fort Sumter, off the coast of South Carolina, setting off the Civil War.

July 1861 An unsuccessful Union offensive culminates in defeat at the First Battle of Bull Run (Manassas).

February 1862 The Battle of Fort Henry is the first significant Union victory.
April: The Battle of Shiloh is one of the bloodiest of the war. Union troops are victorious at the Battle of Fort Pulaski.
August: A Union offensive with the goal of capturing Richmond,

the Confederate capitol, ends in a Confederate victory at Second Bull Run.
September: An attempted Confederate invasion of the North is stopped at Antietam.
October: The undecided Battle of Perrysville results in tactical victory for the Confederacy but strategic victory for the Union.
December: Confederate victory at the Battle of Fredericksburg

1863 With the Emancipation Proclamation, President Lincoln declares all slaves in the Confederate States to be free.
March–July: Vicksburg Campaign: The entire Mississippi River is in Union hands.
May–July: The Union Army besieges Port Hudson.
July: The Battle of Gettysburg is a decisive defeat for the Confederacy.

ca. 1850

Olympia (1850)

OREGON COUNTRY

Portland (1845)

MINNESOTA TERRITORY

NEW HAMPSHIRE

MAINE

VERMONT

Boise (1834)

UNORGANIZED TERRITORY

WISCONSIN (1848)

Milwaukee (1839)

MICHIGAN (1837)

Detroit

NEW YORK

Boston
MASSACHUSETTS
RHODE ISLAND
CONNECTICUT

Salt Lake City (1847)

IOWA (1846)

Chicago (1803)

Cleveland (1796)

PENNSYLVANIA

Pittsburgh

New York

NEW JERSEY

Philadelphia

UTAH TERRITORY

Des Moines (1893)

ILLINOIS

INDIANA

OHIO (1796)

MARYLAND

DELAWARE

San Francisco

Sacramento (1848)

St. Louis

MISSOURI

Washington

VIRGINIA

Richmond

CALIFORNIA (1850)

KENTUCKY

Los Angeles

NEW MEXICO TERRITORY

Santa Fe

Ft. Smith (1817)

TENNESSEE

NORTH CAROLINA

San Diego

ARKANSAS (1836)

Memphis (1819)

Atlanta (1837)

SOUTH CAROLINA

TEXAS (1845)

ALABAMA (1837)

Charleston

El Paso (1850)

MISSISSIPPI

Montgomery (1817)

GEORGIA

Austin (1838)

Alamo 1836

LOUISIANA

San Antonio

Houston (1836)

New Orleans

FLORIDA (1845)

— Border of the United States
···· Border with Mexico until 1845
– – – Border with Mexico 1845–1848
— — Border of independent Texas (1836–1845)

Part of Oregon Country gained in 1846
Territory won from Mexico in 1848

⊗ Slaveholding states in the USA

1861

Chicago · Detroit
Cleveland
Pittsburgh · New York
St. Louis · Bull Run · Philadelphia
Washington
Fredericksburg
Richmond
Houston
New Orleans · Fort Sumter
Charleston
Tampa

Union states and territories
Slaveholding states that belonged to the Union
Confederate states before Lincoln's proclamation on April 15, 1861
Confederate states after Lincoln's proclamation
⊗ Important battles
— United States borders
--- Border between Union and Confederacy

1862

Chicago · Detroit
Cleveland
Pittsburgh · New York · Boston
Antietam
St. Louis · Washington
Fort Henry · Perryville · Bull Run · Norfolk
Memphis · Fredericksburg · Richmond
Atlanta · Fort Hatteras
Shiloh
Charleston
Fort Pulaski
Savannah
Houston · New Orleans

Union states and territories
Confederate areas
Confederate areas occupied by the Union
— United States border 1862
— Naval blockade of the South by the Union
--- Border between Union and Confederacy
← Union offensive against the South
⊗ Important battle

1863

Chicago · Detroit
Cleveland · Boston
Gettysburg
Pittsburgh · New York
St. Louis · Washington
Richmond
Memphis · Chattanooga
Atlanta
Vicksburg · Charleston
Port Hudson · Savannah
New Orleans
Houston

Union states and territories
Confederate areas occupied by the Union
Confederate areas 1864
Confederate areas occupied by the Union 1865
— United States border
— Naval blockade of the South by the Union
--- Border between Union and Confederacy
← Union offensive
← Confederate offensive
⊗ Important battle

1864/65

Chicago · Detroit
Cleveland
Pittsburgh · New York · Boston
Wilderness (1864) · Washington
St. Louis · Richmond (1865)
Memphis · Bentonville (1865)
Atlanta (1864) · Charleston
Savannah
Mobile Bay (1864)
New Orleans
Houston

Union states and territories
Confederate areas occupied by the Union
Confederate areas at outset of war
Confederate areas in Union control 1864
Confederate areas in Union control 1865
— United States border
— Naval blockade of the South by the Union
--- Border between Union and Confederacy
← Union offensive
● Surrender of the Confederacy on April 9, 1865 at Appomatox
⊗ Important battle

May 1864 The Battle of the Wilderness ends with no clear victor.
August: The Union navy besieges the Confederate harbor at Mobile Bay.
November: Atlanta falls to Union forces. Union victory at Chattanooga

March 1865 The Union prevails in the bloody Battle of Bentonville.

April 9, 1865 The Confederacy meets its final defeat in the Battle of Appomattox: General Robert E. Lee surrenders to General Ulysses S. Grant.

April 14, 1865 A fanatical Confederate sympathizer assassinates Abraham Lincoln.

December, 1865 Slavery is finally abolished when Congress passes an amendment to the Constitution. The Ku Klux Klan is founded.

Major Figures of the Civil War

Abraham Lincoln (1809–1865). He was the sixteenth president of the United States and the first from the ranks of the newly founded Republican Party.

Ulysses S. Grant (1822–1885). The supreme commander of the Union Army accepted the Confederate surrender after the Battle of Appomattox, and in 1869 became president of the United States.

Jefferson Davis (1808–1889) The president of the Confederate States of America from 1861–1865

Robert Edward Lee (1807–1870) A legendary Confederate general and brilliant strategist, Lee was first approached by the Union and asked to command its army, but declined in order to defend his home state of Virginia.

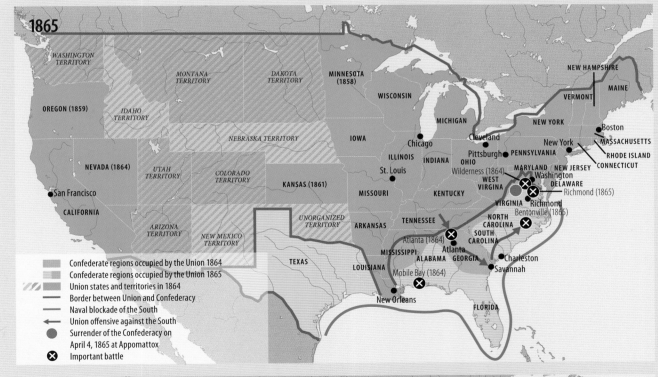

1865

WASHINGTON TERRITORY
OREGON (1859)
IDAHO TERRITORY
MONTANA TERRITORY
DAKOTA TERRITORY
MINNESOTA (1858)
NEW HAMPSHIRE
MAINE
VERMONT
WISCONSIN
MICHIGAN
NEW YORK
Boston
NEBRASKA TERRITORY
IOWA
Chicago
Cleveland
MASSACHUSETTS
RHODE ISLAND
CONNECTICUT
NEVADA (1864)
UTAH TERRITORY
COLORADO TERRITORY
KANSAS (1861)
ILLINOIS
INDIANA
OHIO
Pittsburgh · PENNSYLVANIA
New York
St. Louis
MARYLAND · NEW JERSEY
Wilderness (1864)
WEST VIRGINIA
Washington
DELAWARE
San Francisco
MISSOURI
KENTUCKY
VIRGINIA
Richmond (1865)
Bentonville (1865)
CALIFORNIA
ARIZONA TERRITORY
NEW MEXICO TERRITORY
UNORGANIZED TERRITORY
ARKANSAS
TENNESSEE
NORTH CAROLINA
SOUTH CAROLINA
Atlanta (1864)
MISSISSIPPI
ALABAMA
GEORGIA
Charleston
Savannah
TEXAS
LOUISIANA
Mobile Bay (1864)
New Orleans
FLORIDA

Confederate regions occupied by the Union 1864
Confederate regions occupied by the Union 1865
Union states and territories in 1864
— Border between Union and Confederacy
— Naval blockade of the South
← Union offensive against the South
● Surrender of the Confederacy on April 4, 1865 at Appomattox
⊗ Important battle

Pioneer Trails

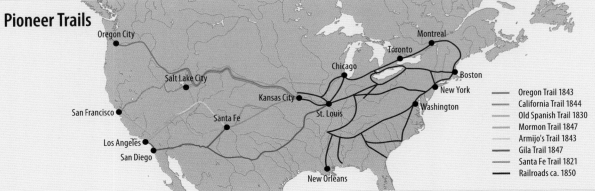

Oregon City
Montreal
Toronto
Salt Lake City
Chicago
Boston
Kansas City
New York
San Francisco
St. Louis
Washington
Santa Fe
Los Angeles
San Diego
New Orleans

— Oregon Trail 1843
— California Trail 1844
— Old Spanish Trail 1830
— Mormon Trail 1847
— Armijo's Trail 1843
— Gila Trail 1847
— Santa Fe Trail 1821
— Railroads ca. 1850

The United States – From the Civil War to Today

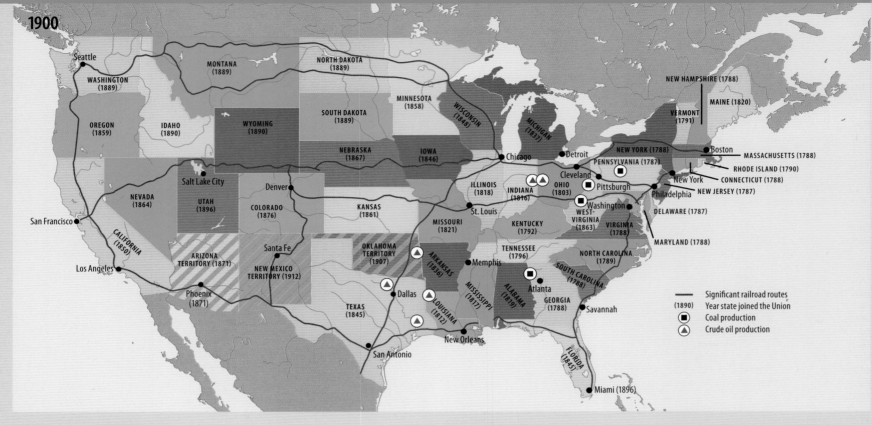

1900

Legend:
- Significant railroad routes
- (1890) Year state joined the Union
- ■ Coal production
- ▲ Crude oil production

1862 Homestead Act: Settlers willing to move westward can claim free land. The frontier moves rapidly toward the Pacific Coast.

1862–1890 Indian Wars: White hunters have practically exterminated the bison, which is the primary source of food for the Plains Indians. White settlers force the Native Americans onto reservations.

1864 Sand Creek Massacre: Cheyenne and Arapahos are murdered by the United States Army.

1867 The United States purchases Alaska from Russia for 7 million dollars.

1869 The first transcontinental railroad is completed.

1876 The Sioux win a decisive victory at the Battle of Little Big Horn, but United States troops exact a devastating revenge.

1890 Massacre at Wounded Knee; more than 150 Sioux are murdered.

1898 The Spanish-American War heralds the beginning of United States expansionist politics and interventionism.

1905 Immigration reaches its peak: Some 9 million immigrants arrive in the first decade of the 20th century.

1917 The United States enters World War I on the side of the Allies.

1918 President Wilson announces his Fourteen Points, which outline a vision for postwar order and establishment of the League of Nations.

1919 Prohibition begins; alcohol is illegal until 1933.

1920 The Nineteenth Amendment gives women the right to vote. The Ku Klux Klan has around 4 million members.

1923 The Teapot Dome Scandal, involving bribery surrounding an oil field deal in Wyoming, rocks the government of United States President Warren G. Harding. It is the most profound corruption case in US history.

1929 The stock market crash in New York heralds the Great Depression. The St. Valentine's Day Massacre in Chicago (Al Capone) marks the peak of the early gangster wars.

1930–1937 Catastrophic drought throughout much of the Great Plains

from 1933 President Franklin D. Roosevelt initiates his New Deal, a series of measures to stimulate the economy and ease unemployment.

1940 Richard and Maurice McDonald open their first hamburger restaurant in San Bernardino, California.

1941 The Japanese naval attack on Pearl Harbor results in 2,403 United States casualties. The United States enters World War II against the Axis Powers.

June 6, 1944 D-Day: The Allies land in Normandy.

1945 The United States drops atomic bombs on Hiroshima and Nagasaki; World War II ends shortly afterward.

1947 The anti-communist policy of containment begins.

1950–1953 The Korean War

1950–1954 The McCarthy Era is marked by committees investigating individuals suspected of "un-American activities."

1954 A landmark Supreme Court decision declares segregated schools unconstitutional; the African-American Civil Rights Movement begins.

1959 Alaska and Hawaii become the forty-ninth and fiftieth states.

Economic Crisis of 1929

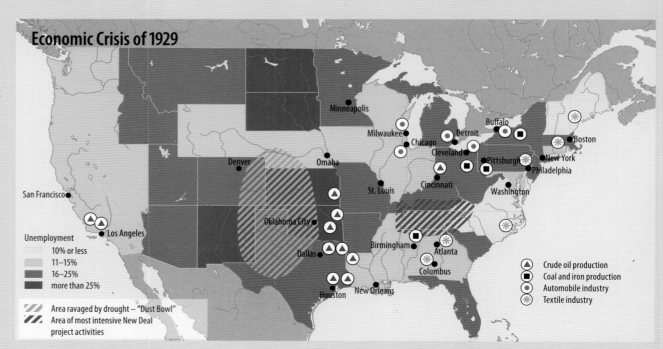

Unemployment
- 10% or less
- 11–15%
- 16–25%
- more than 25%

- ▨ Area ravaged by drought – "Dust Bowl"
- ▧ Area of most intensive New Deal project activities

Legend:
- ▲ Crude oil production
- ■ Coal and iron production
- ◉ Automobile industry
- ✳ Textile industry

1962 The United States blockade of Soviet ships delivering missiles to Cuba results in the Cuban Missile Crisis.

August 1963 The Reverend Martin Luther King Jr. leads the March on Washington.

Nov. 22, 1963 President John F. Kennedy is assassinated in Dallas.

1964 American intervention in Vietnam escalates into the Vietnam War. The Civil Rights Act outlaws the segregation of the Jim Crow era.

from 1966 Student protests against the Vietnam War find worldwide support.

1969 The Woodstock music festival takes place in New York State. Neil Armstrong is the first man to set foot on the moon. The Defense Department sets up Arpanet, a computer network connecting universities and research facilities, which will later be known as the Internet (1982). The development of the World Wide Web at CERN in Geneva spurs a dramatic boom in the technology industry.

1973 The first oil crisis occurs. The United States' involvement in the Vietnam War ends.

1974 The Watergate Affair: President Nixon's White House becomes embroiled in a scandal revolving around an illegal break-in at Democratic Party headquarters. Nixon is forced to resign.

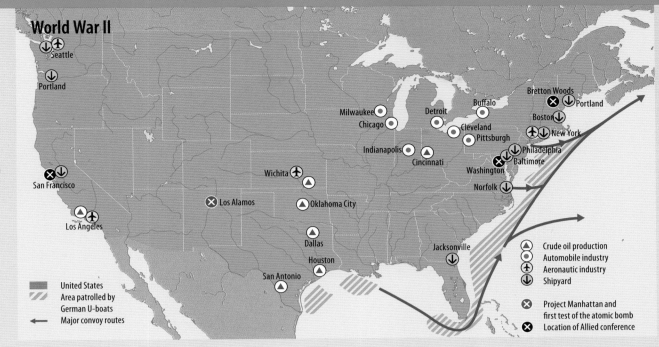

World War II

Legend:
△ Crude oil production
◉ Automobile industry
✈ Aeronautic industry
↓ Shipyard
⊗ Project Manhattan and first test of the atomic bomb
⊗↓ Location of Allied conference

United States
Area patrolled by German U-boats
→ Major convoy routes

1975 Bill Gates and Paul Allen found the Microsoft Corporation.

1978 The Camp David Accords mark a cessation of Israeli-Egyptian hostilities.

1979–1980 Second oil crisis

1981 President Reagan initiates a policy of confrontation with the Soviet Union.

1987 Disarmament talks between the United States and the USSR

1991 Operation Desert Storm in the Persian Gulf

1993–2001 The New Economy evolves under President Clinton.

1995 The United States intervenes in the Balkan War. The Murrah Federal Building in Oklahoma City is bombed by an American citizen.

2001–2008 Presidency of George W. Bush

2001 September 11: Islamist terrorists attack New York City and Washington D.C. Two hijacked airplanes crash into the World Trade Center, destroying its twin towers, and a third damages the Pentagon; a fourth crashes in rural Pennsylvania, presumably before reaching its actual target. Approximately 3,000 people died.

2005 Hurricane Katrina devastates the city of New Orleans.

2008 The United States experiences the greatest financial crisis since 1929, with worldwide repercussions.

2009 Barack Obama, the first African-American president of the United States, takes office.

Today

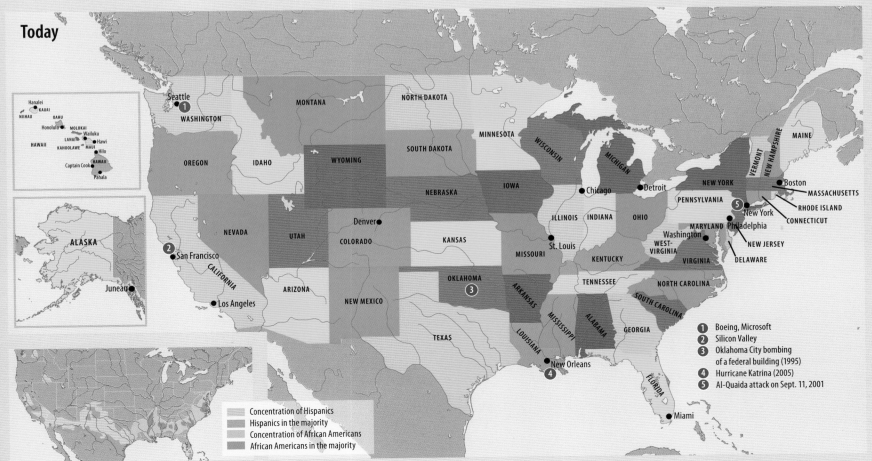

1 Boeing, Microsoft
2 Silicon Valley
3 Oklahoma City bombing of a federal building (1995)
4 Hurricane Katrina (2005)
5 Al-Quaida attack on Sept. 11, 2001

Concentration of Hispanics
Hispanics in the majority
Concentration of African Americans
African Americans in the majority

Immigration and Settlement of the United States

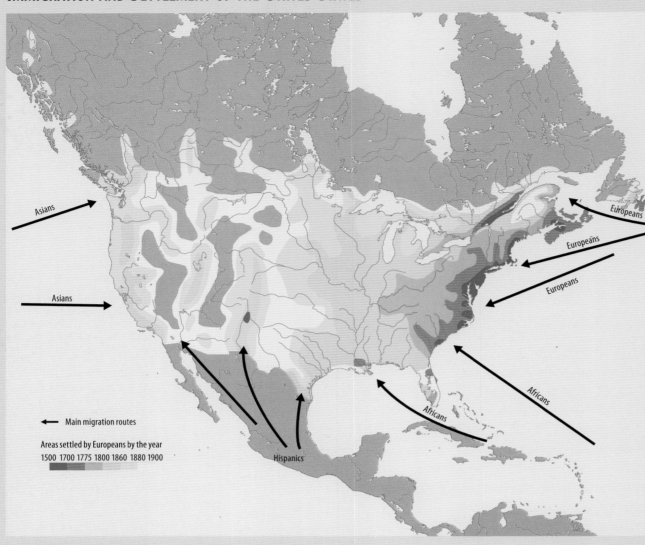

Spanish, English and French conquerers colonialized the continent from the 15th and 16th centuries, driving out and decimating the Native American peoples who had been living here. The colonies striving for their independence became the United States of America. Between 1815 and 1914, the "promised land" took in approximately 30 million immigrants from around the world.

Europeans
15th century   English and French
19th century   The greatest wave of immigrants, including large numbers of Irish, Germans, Italians, Greeks, Scandinavians, Czechs, Polish, Slovaks and Russians
1917   Congress requires an English language test as a condition for immigration and, from the 1920s, quotas.
first half of the 20th century   Immigration continues at a slower pace.

Africans
into the 19th century   Around 12 million Africans are abducted and taken to the New World.
1860   There are about 1.5 million slave families living in the United States.

Asians
1892   Limitations are placed on immigration from China.
1900 and 1908   Similar measures are passed limiting Japanese immigration.

Hispanics
The southern United States was originally settled by Mexicans of Spanish or Native American origin. Currently, Latinos are the largest immigrant group in the United States.

Naturalized Immigrants According to Ancestry

Immigrated from	1820–1829	1830–1839	1840–1849	1850–1859	1860–1869	1870–1879	1880–1889	1890–1899	1900–1909
Total	129,000	538,000	1,427,000	2,815,000	2,081,000	2,742,000	5,249,000	3,694,000	8,202,000
Europe (total)	99,000	423,000	1,369,000	2,619,000	1,877,000	2,251,000	4,639,000	3,576,000	7,573,000
Ireland	52,000	171,000	656,000	1,029,000	427,000	422,000	674,000	406,000	345,000
United Kingdom	26,000	74,000	219,000	445,000	533,000	578,000	811,000	329,000	470,000
Scandinavia	0	1,000	12,000	25,000	97,000	208,000	671,000	391,000	488,000
Germany	6,000	125,000	385,000	976,000	724,000	752,000	1,445,000	579,000	329,000
France	8,000	39,000	75,000	82,000	36,000	72,000	48,000	36,000	68,000
Spain	3,000	2,000	2,000	9,000	7,000	6,000	4,000	9,000	25,000
Portugal	0	1,000	0	1,000	2,000	14,000	15,000	26,000	65,000
Italy	0	2,000	1,000	9,000	10,000	46,000	268,000	604,000	1,930,000
Austria and Hungary	0	0	0	0	3,000	60,000	315,000	534,000	2,001,000
Russia	0	0	1,000	0	2,000	35,000	183,000	450,000	1,501,000
Asia (total)	0	0	0	36,000	54,000	134,000	71,000	61,000	230,000
China	0	0	0	36,000	54,000	133,000	66,000	15,000	20,000
Hong Kong	0	0	0	0	0	0	0	0	0
Japan	0	0	0	0	0	0	2,000	14,000	140,000
Korea	0	0	0	0	0	0	0	0	0
India	0	0	0	0	0	0	0	0	3,000
Iran	0	0	0	0	0	0	0	0	0
Israel	0	0	0	0	0	0	0	0	0
Turkey	0	0	0	0	0	0	2,000	28,000	128,000
Philippines	0	0	0	0	0	0	0	0	0
Vietnam	0	0	0	0	0	0	0	0	0
The Americas (total)	10,000	32,000	51,000	84,000	130,000	345,000	525,000	37,000	278,000
Canada	2	12,000	34,000	64,000	118,000	324,000	493,000	3000	123,000
Mexico	4	7,000	3,000	3,000	2,000	5,000	2,000	1000	31,000
Central America	0	0	0	1000	0	0	0	1,000	7,000
Caribbean	3	12,000	12,000	12,000	9,000	14,000	27,000	31,000	101,000
South America	0	1,000	1,000	4,000	4,000	1,000	2,000	1,000	15,000

Slaves brought to North America are not included in these statistics.

United States Presidents

Name	Served	Party	Vice President
1 George Washington	1789–1797	none	John Adams
2 John Adams	1797–1801	Federalist	Thomas Jefferson
3 Thomas Jefferson	1801–1809	Democratic-Republican	Aaron Burr, George Clinton
4 James Madison	1809–1817	Democratic-Republican	George Clinton, Elbridge Gerry
5 James Monroe	1817–1825	Democratic-Republican	Daniel D. Tompkins
6 John Quincy Adams	1825–1829	Democratic-Republican	John C. Calhoun
7 Andrew Jackson	1829–1837	Democrat	John C. Calhoun, Martin Van Buren
8 Martin Van Buren	1837–1841	Democrat	Richard M. Johnson
9 William Henry Harrison	1841–1841	Whig	John Tyler
10 John Tyler	1841–1845	Whig	
11 James K. Polk	1845–1849	Democrat	George M. Dallas
12 Zachary Taylor	1849–1850	Whig	Millard Fillmore
13 Millard Fillmore	1850–1853	Whig	
14 Franklin Pierce	1853–1857	Democrat	William R. King
15 James Buchanan	1857–1861	Democrat	John C. Breckinridge
16 Abraham Lincoln	1861–1865	Republican	Hannibal Hamlin, Andrew Johnson
17 Andrew Johnson	1865 1869	Democrat	
18 Ulysses S. Grant	1869 1877	Republican	Schuyler Colfax, Henry Wilson
19 Rutherford B. Hayes	1877 1881	Republican	William A. Wheeler
20 James A. Garfield	1881 1881	Republican	Chester A. Arthur
21 Chester A. Arthur	1881 1885	Republican	
22 Grover Cleveland	1885–1889	Democrat	Thomas A. Hendricks
23 Benjamin Harrison	1889–1893	Republican	Levi P. Morton
24 Grover Cleveland	1893–1897	Democrat	Adlai E. Stevenson I
25 William McKinley	1897–1901	Republican	Garret Hobart, Theodore Roosevelt
26 Theodore Roosevelt	1901–1909	Republican	Charles W. Fairbanks
27 William Howard Taft	1909–1913	Republican	James S. Sherman
28 Woodrow Wilson	1913–1921	Democrat	Thomas R. Marshall
29 Warren G. Harding	1921–1923	Republican	Calvin Coolidge
30 Calvin Coolidge	1923–1929	Republican	Charles G. Dawes
31 Herbert Hoover	1929–1933	Republican	Charles Curtis
32 Franklin D. Roosevelt	1933–1945	Democrat	John Nance Garner, Henry A. Wallace, Harry S Truman
33 Harry S. Truman	1945–1953	Democrat	Alben W. Barkley
34 Dwight D. Eisenhower	1953–1961	Republican	Richard Nixon
35 John F. Kennedy	1961–1963	Democrat	Lyndon B. Johnson
36 Lyndon B. Johnson	1963–1969	Democrat	Hubert Humphrey
37 Richard Nixon	1969–1974	Republican	Spiro Agnew, Gerald Ford
38 Gerald Ford	1974–1977	Republican	Nelson Rockefeller
39 Jimmy Carter	1977–1981	Democrat	Walter Mondale
40 Ronald Reagan	1981–1989	Republican	George H.W. Bush
41 George H. W. Bush	1989–1993	Republican	Dan Quayle
42 Bill Clinton	1993–2001	Democrat	Al Gore
43 George W. Bush	2001–2009	Republican	Dick Cheney
44 Barack Obama	2009–	Democrat	Joe Biden

Thomas Jefferson (1743–1826)

Abraham Lincoln (1809–1865)

Woodrow Wilson (1856–1924)

Franklin D. Roosevelt (1882–1945)

Harry S. Truman (1884–1972)

1910–1919	1920–1929	1930–1939	1940–1949	1950–1959	1960–1969	1970–1979	1980–1989	1990–1999		Total by ca. 2000
6,347,000	4,296,000	699,000	857,000	2,499,000	3,214,000	4,248,000	6,244,000	9,775,000		65,056,000
4,985,000	2,560,000	444,000	473,000	1,405,000	1,133,000	826,000	669,000	1,349,000		38,270,000
166,000	203,000	28,000	16,000	47,000	38,000	11,000	22,000	65,000		4,778,000
372,000	342,000	62,000	132,000	196,000	220,000	133,000	154,000	156,000		5,252,000
238,000	221,000	18,000	23,000	60,000	50,000	17,000	22,000	28,000		2,570,000
174,000	387,000	119,000	120,000	577,000	210,000	77,000	86,000	92,000		7,163,000
60,000	55,000	14,000	37,000	50,000	47,000	26,000	32,000	36,000		821,000
53,000	47,000	4,000	3,000	7,000	41,000	42,000	23,000	18,000		305,000
82,000	45,000	4,000	7,000	14,000	71,000	105,000	43,000	25,000		520,000
1,230,000	528,000	85,000	51,000	185,000	200,000	150,000	56,000	76,000		5,431,000
1,155,000	61,000	13,000	14,000	113,000	28,000	20,000	20,000	28,000		4,365,000
1,107,000	62,000	2,000	1,000	0	2,000	28,000	33,000	433,000		3,840,000
270,000	127,000	19,000	35,000	136,000	359,000	1,407,000	2,391,000	2,860,000		8,190,000
21,000	31,000	6,000	16,000	9,000	14,000	18,000	171,000	342,000		952,000
0	0	0	0	14,000	67,000	117,000	112,000	117,000		427,000
77,000	42,000	3,000	2,000	41,000	41,000	49,000	44,000	67,000		522,000
0	0	0	0	5,000	27,000	241,000	323,000	180,000		776,000
3,000	2,000	1,000	2,000	2,000	19,000	148,000	232,000	353,000		765,000
0	0	0	1,000	3,000	9,000	34,000	98,000	77,000		222,000
0	0	0	0	21,000	31,000	36,000	44,000	41,000		173,000
161,000	40,000	1,000	1,000	3,000	9,000	12,000	19,000	39,000		443,000
0	0	0	4,000	17,000	71,000	338,000	502,000	534,000		1,466,000
0	0	0	0	0	3,000	122,000	201,000	275,000		601,000
1,071,000	1,591,000	230,000	328,000	922,000	1,674,000	1,904,000	2,695,000	5,138,000		17,045,000
709,000	949,000	163,000	161,000	353,000	433,000	179,000	156,000	195,000		4,471,000
185,000	499,000	33,000	56,000	274,000	442,000	621,000	1,010,000	2,757,000		5,935,000
16,000	17,000	7000	20,000	40,000	99,000	120,000	339,000	610,000		1,277,000
121,000	83,000	18,000	46,000	116,000	427,000	709,000	790,000	1,005,000		3,536,000
40,000	43,000	10,000	20,000	78,000	251,000	274,000	400,000	571,000		1,716,000
								Total from Europe, Asia and the Americas		63,505,000

Source: Department of Homeland Security, Office of Immigration Statistics

THE UNITED STATES BECOMES A WORLD POWER

GREENLAND SINCE 1942

ICELAND SINCE 1942

NORWAY SINCE 1949

ESTONIA SINCE 2004
LATVIA SINCE 2004
LITHUANIA SINCE 2004
DENMARK SINCE 1949
GERMANY SINCE 1945
POLAND SINCE 1999
CZECH REP. SINCE 1999
SLOVAKIA SINCE 2004
HUNGARY SINCE 1999
ROMANIA SINCE 2004

UNITED KINGDOM SINCE 1917–1918
1941
1955
1948/49
1944
1945
1944
1918

FRANCE SINCE 1944
2004
BOSNIA 1995
KOSOVO 1999
SPAIN SINCE 1982
ITALY SINCE 1949
1943–1944
2004
TURKEY SINCE 1952

PORTUGAL SINCE 1949
1943
1942–1943
1955–1958
1980–1988
1981–1989
1980–1989
SINCE 2001

CANADA SINCE 1941

1916

MEXICO

1846–1848

CUBAN CRISIS 1962
1898–1933, 1940, 1961/62
1898
1961
CUBA 1915–1934
HAITI
1994/95, 1996
DOMINICAN REPUBLIC 1905–1907, 1916–1924, 1930
1961/1965
PUERTO RICO 1898

1914

GUATEMALA 1954
EL SALVADOR 1977–1992
HONDURAS 1903–1929
NICARAGUA 1854, 1909–1933, 1981–1990
PANAMA 1903–1964
1989
1981–1990
1983
GRENADA 1983
VENEZUELA 2002

COLUMBIA 1998–1999 SINCE 1990

ECUADOR

BRAZIL 1964

BOLIVIA 1964

CHILE 1973
ARGENTINA 1976

MOROCCO
1942
TUNISIA
1986
ALGERIA
LIBYA
EGYPT
1956
ISRAEL SINCE 1956
JORDAN 1970
IRAQ 1980
2003
1991
1953, 1980
1991
IRAN
1980
1990
SAUDI ARABIA SINCE 1990
PAKISTAN SINCE 1955
AFGHANISTAN

SUDAN 1998

ZAIRE (CONGO) 1965–1989
1960/61, 1965

SOMALIA 1992–1994

ANGOLA 1975–1990
1976

- ■ US military interventions
- ▲ US support of armed movements
- ◆ US military aid
- ● Current US military base

1823 President James Monroe formulate the Monroe Doctrine asserting complete US hegemony on the American continents. In exchange, the United States will refrain from intefering in European affairs.

1845 Texas, which until 1836 had been part of Mexico, is annexed by the United States.

1846–1848 The Mexican-American War: The United States annexes half of Mexico's land area (California, New Mexico, Arizona, Nevada, Utah, parts of Colorado, Kansas and Wyoming).

1853 American warships open Japan's ports for trade.

1854–1910 Multiple interventions in Nicaragua, sometimes involving military force

1898 Cuba: US troops wrest the island from Spain, and the United States exercises direct control. Intervention continues until 1933, military occupation lasts from 1906 to 1919, and a

US-dominated regime governs the island until 1959.

1898–1902 The Spanish are driven out of the Philippines, and the islands are brought under US control.

1898 The Kingdom of Hawaii is annexed, and Hawaii becomes the fiftieth state in the Union in 1959. Spain cedes Puerto Rico, which becomes an associated US commonwealth, a status it maintains today.

1903 Honduras: American Marines land to protect US interests (United Fruit Company), and many acts of intervention follow until 1929.

1904/1907 The United States and Panama sign a treaty giving the US control of the Panama Canal. US troops arrive in Panama, where they continue to intervene until 1964. Panama becomes a de facto colony of the United States

1905/07 The Dominican Republic: Military intervention leads to the

installation of a regime dependent on the United States. US military occupation lasts from 1916 to 1924.

1909–1933 Nicragua: In addition to ongoing military intervention, the United States controls the country's economy and military. Right-wing national guards are formed, and the Somoza dictatorship receives US support.

1911–1916 The United States is involved in the Mexican Revolution. A punitive expedition follows in 1916.

1915–1934 Haiti is occupied and administered as a US protectorate. From 1957–1986 the United States supports the Duvalier dictatorship.

1917 The United States enters World War I, landing in France. It remains in Europe as an occupying power until 1919.

1919 Honduras: A liberal revolution is prevented through military action. Further intervention follows in 1924/25.

1930 Intervention in the Dominican Republic helps install dictator Rafael Leonidas Trujillo, who will remain in power until 1961.

1940 Intervention in Cuba helps install the dictator Fulgencio Batista, who will remain in power, with interruptions, until 1959.

1941–1945 The United States enters World War II against Japan in the Pacific theater and against Germany in Europe. US troops land in North Africa in 1942, in Sicily and Italy in 1943, and in Normandy and pressing on into Germany in 1944. By 1945 the United States is one of the Allied powers occupying defeated Germany.

1945 The United States drops atomic bombs on Hiroshima and Nagasaki, forcing Japan's surrender. Occupation follows.

1948/49 Germany: The Berlin Airlift delivers food and supplies to Soviet-blockaded West Berlin.

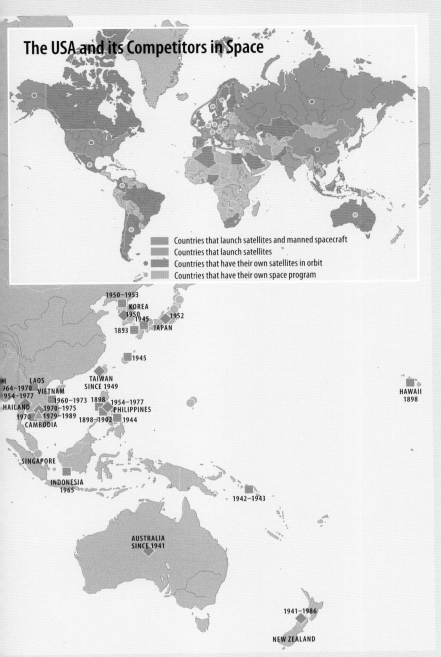

The USA and its Competitors in Space

- Countries that launch satellites and manned spacecraft
- Countries that launch satellites
- Countries that have their own satellites in orbit
- Countries that have their own space program

1950–1953
KOREA
1950 1945 1952
1853 JAPAN
1945
LAOS
1964–1970 VIETNAM
1954–1977 TAIWAN SINCE 1949
1960–1973 1898 1954–1977
THAILAND 1970–1975 PHILIPPINES
1970 1979–1989 1898–1902 1944
CAMBODIA 1898

SINGAPORE

INDONESIA
1965

HAWAII
1898

1942–1943

AUSTRALIA
SINCE 1941

1941–1986

NEW ZEALAND

1950–1953 The Korean War: US forces support the South Korean regime against the invasion of communist North Korea.

1953 Iran: The CIA sponsors the removal of the elected prime minister, Mossadegh, who plans to nationalize the oil industry. In his place, the US supports the autocratic regime of the Shah of Iran, who reigns until 1978/79.

1954 Guatemala: Aided by mercenaries, the CIA topples the government, which had initiated agrarian reform. US-supported military dictators control the country until 1996.

1956 Egypt: Warships force the end of British and French military action in the Suez Canal.

1961 Cuba: Exiled Cubans fail in their attempted invasion at the Bay of Pigs, where US aircraft bombard the Cuban air defenses.

1960/61 The Congo: The CIA orchestrates the overthrow and murder of Prime Minister Patrice Lumumba, then supports the dictatorial Mobutu regime.

1961/65 Dominican Republic: The CIA installs a hard-right military regime. In 1965, 42,000 Marines force the creation of a government obedient to the United States.

1962 The Cuban Missile Crisis: Through a blockade of Cuba, US warships force the withdrawal of Soviet missiles. A trade embargo against Cuba remains in effect to this day.

1964–1970 Laos: The military intervenes in areas loyal to the revolutionary Pathet Lao.

1964 Brazil: The CIA supports the installation of a right-wing military junta that remains in power until 1982.

1964–1975 Vietnam: The United States is involved in the prolonged and bloody Vietnam War against communist North Vietnam, sparking widespread and ongoing protests at home. At the war's

peak, 550,000 American soldiers are stationed in Vietnam.

1964–1982 Bolivia: The United States supports several hard-right regimes and juntas.

1965 Indonesia: The CIA aids the coup of right-wing General Suharto against President Sukarno.

1970 Cambodia: The United States offers support to the coup of right-wing General Lon Nol.
Jordan: US warships lend support to King Hussein II's expulsion of the Palestinian Liberation Organization.

1971 Bangladesh: The United States covertly supports Pakistan, unsuccessfully, in Bangladesh's Liberation War.

1973 Chile: The CIA aids right-wing General Augusto Pinochet in his coup against elected president Salvatore Allende, supporting Pinochet's dictatorship until 1990.

1975 East Timor: After FRETILIN rebels declare independence, the United States encourages Indonesia to occupy and annex East Timor. Civil war follows.

1976 Angola: The United States supports the UNITA rebels in their fight against the Marxist MPLA government.

1977–1992 El Salvador: The United States supports puppet governments and right-wing death squads in the fight against leftist rebels.

1980 Iran: A helicopter raid (Operation Eagle Claw) with the mission of freeing hostages taken in the US embassy fails. The hostages are later released in return for shipments of weapons.

1981–1990 Nicaragua: The United States sponsors (by way of Honduras) the right-wing Contras in opposition to the left-wing Sandinista government. A US trade embargo against Nicaragua follows in 1985.

1981–1989 Afghanistan: The Mujaheddin are supplied with weapons to resist Soviet Russian invasion and Afghanistan's communist government. After the Soviet retreat, a power vacuum leaves these weapons in the hands of the radical Taliban movement.

1982–1988 Iraq: Dictator Saddam Hussein is supplied with arms for Iraq's war against Iran.

1983 Panama: The United States installs corrupt General Manuel Noriega, but later distances itself from him.
Grenada: Unrest is followed by military occupation and the installation of a regime agreeable to the United States.

1986 Libya: In response to Libyan terrorist acts, US planes bomb targets in Tripoli and Benghazi.

1988 Iran: An Iranian passenger plane is shot down by a US cruiser in the Strait of Hormuz, resulting in 290 deaths.

1989 Panama: Military occupation and arrest of the erstwhile US ally, President Manuel Noriega

1990 Colombia: The United States begins to train paramilitary groups to combat drug lords and leftist rebels.

1991 Kuwait/Iraq: The United States leads an international coalition in operations to drive Iraqi forces out of Kuwait. Starting in 1992, no-fly zones and an economic embargo are enforced.

1992–1994 Somalia: 28,000 US troops attempt to bring Somalia's civil war to an end. The disastrous results temporarily put a hold on unilateral international intervention by the United States in favor of multilateral intervention by international coalitions.

1992–1995 Yugoslavia: NATO troops are under US leadership in the war-torn areas of the former Yugoslav states.

1993 Iraq: Twenty-three cruise missiles are fired into Baghdad.

1994/95 Haiti: US troops reinstall the exiled president, Jean-Bertrand Aristide.

1998 Sudan: In response to bomb attacks on US embassies, American planes bomb a suspected poison gas-works, which later turns out to be a pharmaceutical plant.

1999 Kosovo: Under US leadership, NATO bombs Serbian cities to force a Serbian withdrawal from Kosovo, which is subsequently occupied by NATO troops.

August 2001 Republic of Macedonia: US-sponsored NATO peacekeeping forces put down a revolt of ethnic Albanians demanding increased civil rights. Macedonia agrees to negotiate with the insurgents to improve the balance of power within the state.

2001 Afghanistan: In response to the attacks of September 11, the United States invades Afghanistan and overthrows the Taliban regime in parts of the country. The fight against the Taliban continues to this day in southern Afghanistan.

2002 Venezuela: The CIA supports a military coup against President Hugo Chávez. The coup fails after three days.

2003 Iraq: A coalition under US leadership invades Iraq and overthrows the regime of Saddam Hussein. Troops from the United States and other countries remain in Iraq today.

The Caribbean

ca. 1550: The Advent of European Exploration

Spanish colonies
1492 European arrival
1511 Beginning of colonization
● Settlements with year of founding
→ Columbus's 2nd American expedition (1493)
--→ Columbus's 3rd American expedition (1498)

ca. 1700/1750

Spanish colonies
British colonies
French colonies
Danish colonies

ca. 1840

Spanish colonies
British colonies
Danish colonies

ca. 1900/1920

United States territories and dependencies
Occupied by the USA
British colonies
French colonies
→ US military interventions
⊗ US military occupation

1492 Spanish ships reach Hispaniola (now Haiti and the Dominican Republic) and Cuba.

1493 Christopher Columbus makes his second journey to the Americas on behalf of the Spanish crown.

1497–1498 Amerigo Vespucci, an Italian explorer, travels through Honduras and the Gulf of Mexico.

1498 Columbus' third journey to the Americas.

1502 The systematic extermination of the indigenous peoples begins.

1509 Spanish troops conquer and colonize Jamaica, which is used mainly as a supply point.

1511 Diego Velázquez conquers Cuba on behalf of Spain and founds settlements, including Havana.

1555 The French corsair Jacques Sores takes Santiago de Cuba.

1586 The English admiral Sir Francis Drake raids Santo Domingo.

1626 A Dutch fleet blockades Havana.

1632 The first British settlers arrive on the island of Antigua.

1655 Jamaica becomes a British colony.

1697 Spain cedes the western part of Santo Domingo (modern-day Haiti) to France.

1763 Britain takes the island of Dominica from the French.

1791–1802 Haiti's African slaves and people of mixed race revolt under the leadership of Toussaint L'Ouverture.

1804 Haiti declares independence, after which the state of Haiti splits from the Dominican Republic.

1804–1820 Jean-Jacques Dessalines (murdered in 1806) and Henri Christophe (from 1811) reign as emperors of Haiti.

1814 France cedes St. Lucia to Britain.

1825 France recognizes Haiti's independence.

1838 The Bahamas prohibits slavery.

1844 The Dominican Republic declares independence from Haiti.

1849–1859 Faustin Soulouque becomes Emperor Faustin I and implements a reign of terror in Haiti.

1868–1878 The Ten Years' War, Cuba's first war of independence, ends in defeat for Cuba, though Spain promises greater autonomy.

1895–1898 The Republic of Cuba is declared, and the second war of independence breaks out.

1898 The short-lived Spanish-American War leads to United States control of Cuba.

1902 A Cuban republic under United States patronage is declared.

1913 Civil war erupts in Haiti.

1915–1934 The United States military occupies Haiti.

1916–1926 The United States occupies the Dominican Republic.

1930–1961 The dictator Rafael Trujillo unleashes a reign of terror in the Dominican Republic.

1933 Revolt against the Machado dictatorship in Cuba.

1937 Trujillo, motivated by racism, has 27,000 black sugarcane workers from Haiti murdered.

1940 The United States establishes a military presence in the Bahamas.

1952–1958 Fulgencio Batista is the dictator of Cuba.

1957–1986 The brutal dictatorships of François ("Papa Doc," 1957–1971) and Jean-Claude ("Baby Doc," 1971–1986) Duvalier in Haiti

Diego Velázquez de Cuéllar (1465–1524) This Spanish conquistador was the first governor of Cuba. He persecuted the native people.

William Jackson (?–1645) A privateer in British service, he led a small force that chased the Spaniards out of Spanish Town and conquered Jamaica for England.

François Mackandal (?–1758) This African slave and voodoo priest attempted to instigate a revolt in the French colony of St. Domingue by means of a large-scale poisoning of white planters.

Toussaint L'Ouverture (1743–1803) A former slave, he led the Haitian Revolution beginning in 1791. Two years later, in 1793, he prohibited slavery and declared his country

independent. He became the governor of Haiti in 1799 and was imprisoned by the French in 1802.

Toussaint L'Ouverture

Fulgencio Batista (1901–1973) A Cuban general and later president, Batista assumed dictatorial powers in 1952. He fled Cuba during the revolution of 1959 and died in Spanish exile.

Fidel Castro (1926–) The leader of the Cuban Revolution of 1959, he opted to make Cuba a communist country allied with the Soviet Union rather than the United States.

1959 Fidel Castro's Cuban Revolution is victorious and drives out Batista. Castro becomes prime minister.

1962 The presence of Soviet nuclear missiles in Cuba leads to the Cuban Missile Crisis, a tense confrontation between the United States and the Soviet Union. Jamaica gains independence from the British West Indies.

1966 Barbados declares its independence from the United Kingdom.

1978 Dominica becomes entirely independent from the United Kingdom.

1983 The United States invades Grenada.

1994 Haiti's overthrown president Jean-Bertrand Aristide is reelected.

1998 Pope John Paul II visits Cuba.

2008 Cuban president Fidel Castro cedes power to his brother, Raúl.

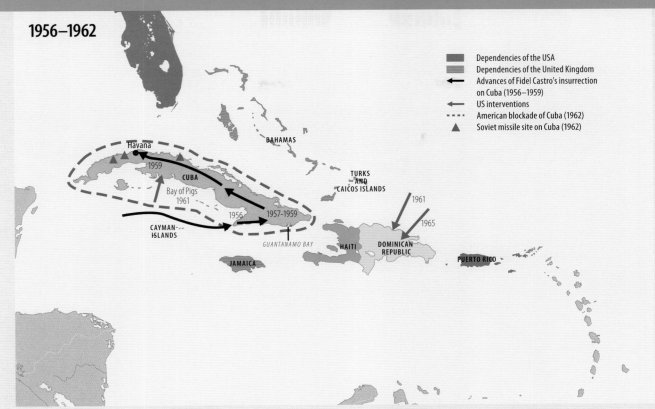

1956–1962

Dependencies of the USA
Dependencies of the United Kingdom
⟵ Advances of Fidel Castro's insurrection on Cuba (1956–1959)
⟵ US interventions
- - - American blockade of Cuba (1962)
▲ Soviet missile site on Cuba (1962)

Today

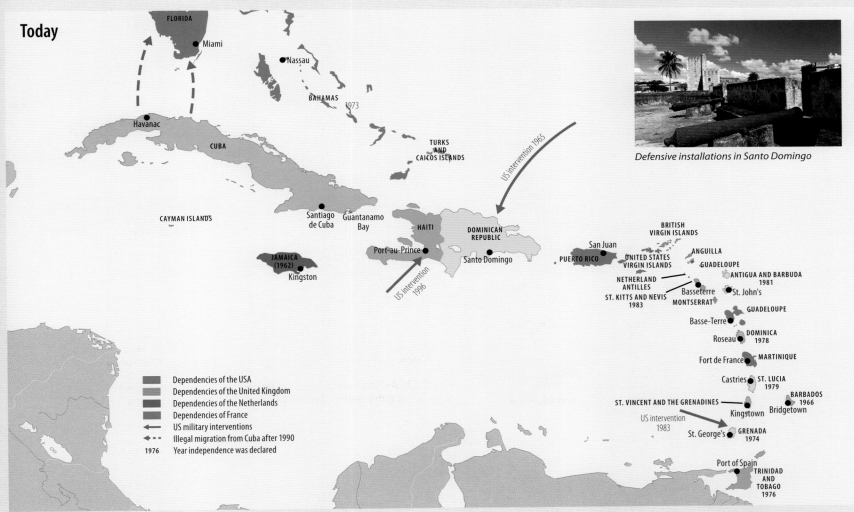

Defensive installations in Santo Domingo

Dependencies of the USA
Dependencies of the United Kingdom
Dependencies of the Netherlands
Dependencies of France
⟵ US military interventions
- - - Illegal migration from Cuba after 1990
1976 Year independence was declared

After the collapse of the Soviet Union, he continued to adhere to communism. Fidel Castro passed control of the country to his brother, Raúl, in 2008.

Rafael Trujillo (1891–1961) This general seized power in the Dominican Republic in 1930 through a US-backed coup, and established a racially-biased reign of terror.

Although he later formally relinquished his power, he remained the strong man in the background. His murder in 1961 unleashed a wave of violence.

Juan Bosch (1909–2001), A university professor and author, he was elected president of the Dominican Republic in 1963, only to be overthrown by the military that same year.

François "Papa Doc" Duvalier (1907–1971) Originally a physician and Haiti's Minister of Health, Duvalier won the presidential election of 1957. He immediately built up power with the assistance of the militia Tontons Macoutes ("bogeymen"), which was founded in 1959. Through voodoo rites and myths, he established a terror-based cult of personality with religious overtones, thereby extravagantly

enriching his family. He declared himself president for life in 1964. When he died in 1971, power was transferred to his son Jean-Claude, "Baby Doc," who was overthrown in 1986. In exile in France, Baby Doc announced his intention to run for president in Haiti's 2006 national elections. Without the support of a political party, he did not become a candidate.

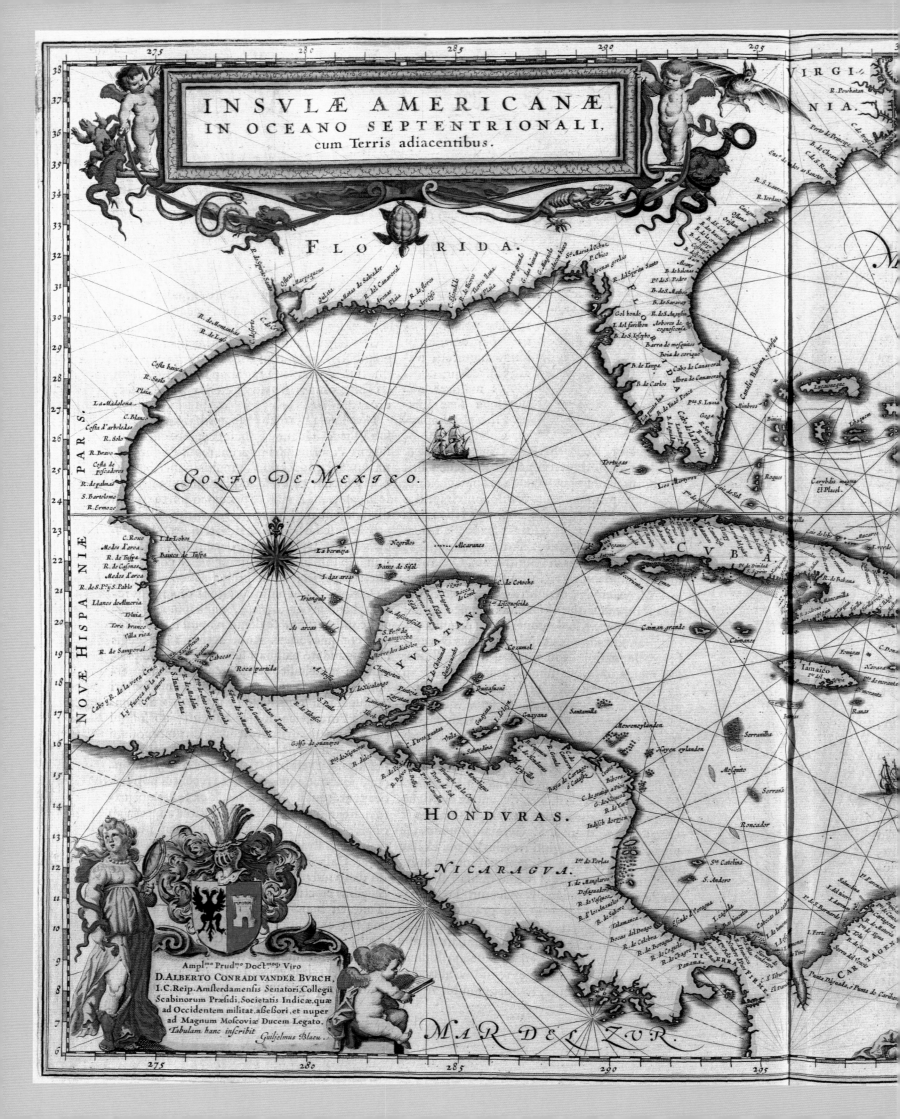

INSVLÆ AMERICANÆ
IN OCEANO SEPTENTRIONALI,
cum Terris adiacentibus.

VIRGI-
NIA.

FLO   RIDA.

GOLFO DE MEXICO.

NOVE HISPANIÆ   PARS.

CVBA

YVCATAN

HONDVRAS.

NICARAGVA.

MAR DEL ZVR.

Ampl.mo Prud.mo Doct.moq; Viro
D. ALBERTO CONRADI VANDER BVRCH,
I. C. Reip. Amsterdamensis Senatori, Collegii
Scabinorum Præsidi, Societatis Indicæ, quæ
ad Occidentem militat, aßeßori, et nuper
ad Magnum Moscoviæ Ducem Legato,
Tabulam hanc inscribit
Guilielmus Blaeu.

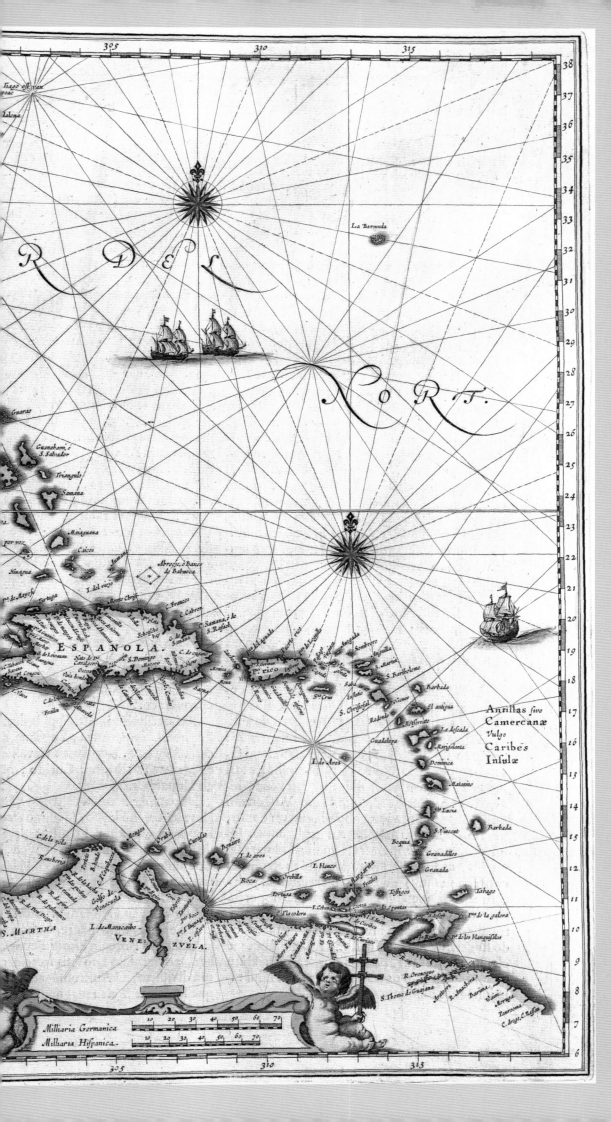

CENTRAL AMERICA

By the time the Spanish conquistadors arrived, Mexico and the Central American countries could already look back on more than 4,500 years of highly developed civilizations, among them the Olmec, Maya, Toltec and Aztec.

The latter could not defend themselves against the conquistadors. The European invaders took advantage of traditional rivalries, pitting one people against another, and overpowered indigenous peoples with firearms and imported diseases. Weakened natives of the New World, who at first thought the invaders were gods, were rapidly conquered by Spain, leaving their cultures in ruins.

The colonial empire of New Spain (1535–1822) included large parts of what is now the southwestern United States as well as Central America. Central American independence during the 19th century was followed by political instability, culminating in the 1910 Mexican Revolution. The 20th century was marked by economic trouble and government instability. Many impoverished people from Central America tried to improve their situation by immigrating, often illegally, to the United States.

Mexico – Prehistory Until the 16th Century 428

Mexico from the 16th Century Until Today 430

Central America from the Pre-Columbian Period to the Present 432

Insulæ Americanæ in Oceano Septentrionali cum Terris adiacentibus.
Albert van der Burgh, o.J.

Mexico – Prehistory Until the 16th Century

500 BCE: Olmec and Zapotec Civilizations

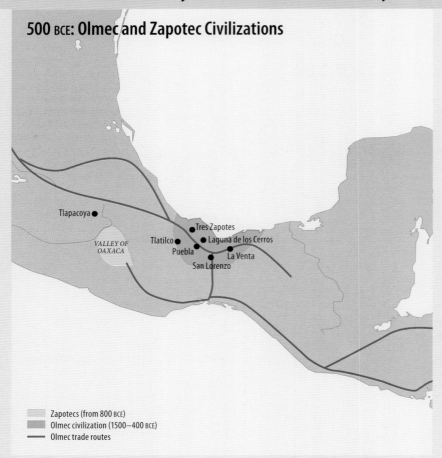

Tlapacoya

VALLEY OF OAXACA

Tres Zapotes
Tlatilco
Laguna de los Cerros
Puebla
La Venta
San Lorenzo

Zapotecs (from 800 BCE)
Olmec civilization (1500–400 BCE)
Olmec trade routes

20,000 BCE First evidence of settlement at Tlapacoya dates from this time.

~4000 BCE Beginning of maize (corn) cultivation in the Americas

1500–400 BCE Olmec civilization thrives on the southern coast of Mexico at the important site of Tlatilco. Famous for colossal stone heads, early Olmec stepped pyramids are an influence on Maya culture.

~3000 BCE–1511 CE The Maya, sophisticated architects, live in cities made of stone and pave their major roads. Brilliantly painted temples line urban plazas. They have hieroglyphic writing (only recently deciphered) and calendars more accurate than the one Europe used at the time. The Maya calculate agricultural cycles and religious holidays with surprising accuracy. Perhaps more surprising is what they do not develop: The Maya never invent the wheel, and have no real metallurgy. Pre-Columbian Maya culture is divided into three main periods.

3000 BCE–250 CE The Maya Preclassic period is defined by the archaeological sites of Duello, Lamanai (Belize), Tikal (Guatemala) and Copan (Honduras). The tallest Preclassic pyramid is El Tigre, from the 6th–3rd century BCE site of El Mirador in Guatemala: it is 180 feet (55 m) tall.

250–900 The Classic Maya period, the culture's golden age, is characterized by numerous competing city-states, among them Uxmal, Tikal and Chichen Itza.

900–1511 The Postclassic period shows increasingly strong influences from the Toltec culture moving in from the north.

1500 BCE–1500 CE Zapotec culture is the product of a sophisticated empire centered around the site of Monte Alban. Its golden age lasts 600 years (300–900 CE).

2nd–8th centuries Teotihuacan is an enormous pre-Columbian city in central Mexico. Its magnificent sun and moon pyramids frame an urban complex covering nearly 10 square miles (20 km²).

9th–12th centuries The Toltec civilization arises in central Mexico after the demise of Teotihuacan.

~1000–1521 Aztec religion centers on rituals accompanied by bloody offerings. Worship of the sun/war god Huitzilopochtli and other gods typically involves human sacrifice, usually of volunteers or prisoners of war. Victims have their hearts cut out while alive.

~1000 Aztec migration to Mexico

~1375 Settlement of Tenochtitlan (modern-day Mexico City)

Sophisticated civilizations flourished in what is now Mexico for millennia before the birth of Christ. Mayan culture was the most advanced of them, and the Aztecs, who immigrated to the region, adopted much of their knowledge. No Mesoamerican cultures used the wheel or invented firearms. All of them were utterly destroyed by the arrival of the Spanish in the 16th century.

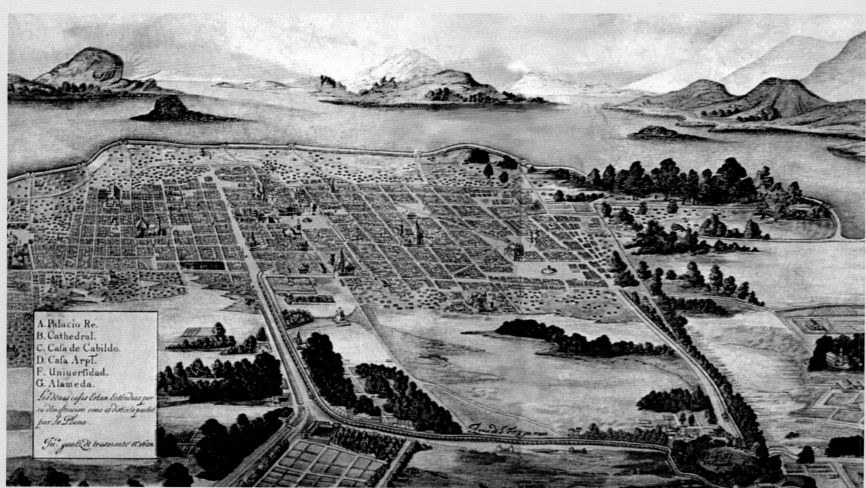

A. Palacio Re.
B. Cathedral.
C. Cafa de Cabildo.
D. Cafa Arpl.
F. Uniuerfidad.
G. Alameda.

Mexico City in 1628

1500   Golden Age: Tenochtitlan has a population of more than 300,000. Built on a series of islands bridged by paved causeways, the heart of the ancient Aztec capital lies beneath the central plaza of today's Mexico City.

1517   The Spanish arrive at the Yucatan Peninsula. After scouting Aztec cities and assessing their defenses, the conquistadors contact local peoples who are oppressed by Aztec taxation and ready to fight alongside the Spanish.

1521   The Spanish, led by Hernan Cortes, conquer Tenochtitlan. Vastly outnumbered, the Spanish instill terror in the Aztecs by massacring unarmed nobility who come to meet them. Cortes then cuts off Tenochtitlan's supply routes and, with the help of disgruntled local peoples, starves the city until it surrenders.

Cociyo, god of thunder and rain: Zapotecan urn from ca. 450, Monte Alban, Oaxaca, Mexico

Chac Mool in front of El Castillo Pyramid, Chichen Itza, Yucatan, Mexico: Toltec-Mayan culture, 11th–13th centuries

Acamapichtli (1376–1397) Aztec ruler of Tenochtitlan and founder of the ruling Aztec dynasty

Moctezuma I (1398–1469) The fifth Aztec ruler, who consolidated and expanded the empire.

Moctezuma II (1466–1520) Ruler of the Aztec empire who was taken prisoner by the Spaniards and used as a pawn in their conquest of the Spanish empire.

Cuahtemotzin (1502–1525) A nephew of Moctezuma II and the last Aztec ruler. Following the conquest of Tenochtitlan in 1521, he was taken prisoner by the Spaniards and executed four years later.

Hernan Cortes (1485–1547) Spanish conquistador whom the Aztecs at first thought was their god Quetzalcoatl.

Cortes and Moctezuma, From the New World (1509)

300–800: The Maya

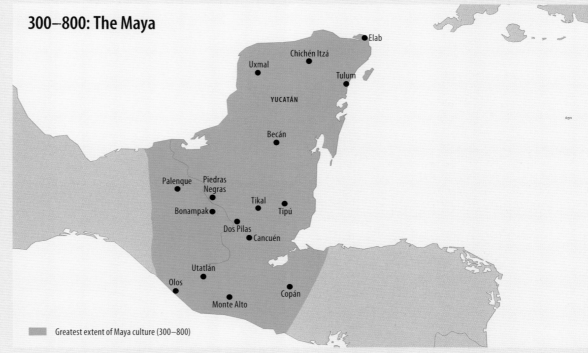

■ Greatest extent of Maya culture (300–800)

Until 1200: Early Cultures

■ Teotihuacán (2nd–8th centuries)
▨ Toltec empire (12th century)
■ Cultures along the coast of the Gulf of Mexico
■ Xochicalco (1–700)
■ Zapotec culture (1500 BCE–1500 CE)

1200–1521: The Aztecs

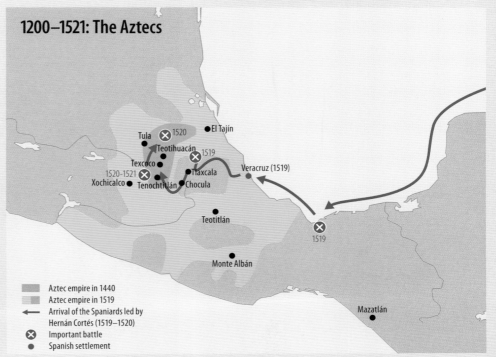

■ Aztec empire in 1440
■ Aztec empire in 1519
← Arrival of the Spaniards led by Hernán Cortés (1519–1520)
⊗ Important battle
● Spanish settlement

Mexico from the 16th Century Until Today

ca. 1750: Spanish Colonization

Legend:
- Spanish colonies by 1650
- Spanish colonies by 1750
- Viceroyalty of New Spain
- ● City with the year of its founding

Cities shown: Santa Fe (1610), Chihuahua (1691), San Antonio (1718), Monterrey (1596), La Paz (1535), Culiacán (1540), Guadalajara (1531), Mexico (1531), Veracruz (1519), Mérida (1542)

1800–1900: Spanish Loss of Territory

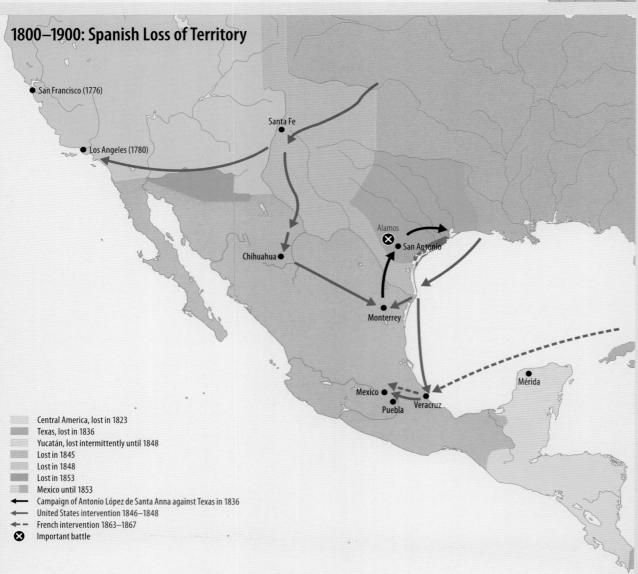

Legend:
- Central America, lost in 1823
- Texas, lost in 1836
- Yucatán, lost intermittently until 1848
- Lost in 1845
- Lost in 1848
- Lost in 1853
- Mexico until 1853
- → Campaign of Antonio López de Santa Anna against Texas in 1836
- ← United States intervention 1846–1848
- ◄- - French intervention 1863–1867
- ⊗ Important battle

Cities shown: San Francisco (1776), Santa Fe, Los Angeles (1780), Chihuahua, Alamos, San Antonio, Monterrey, Mexico, Puebla, Veracruz, Mérida

---

Mexico declared its independence from Spain at the beginning of the 19th century. This was followed by a period of wars and revolutions. Lasting democracy was first established in the second half of the 20th century.

1535 Founding of New Spain

1650 Spanish soldiers invade Native American territories in what is now Texas.

1660 Zapotec uprisings in Oaxaca

1712 Native revolt against Spanish rule led by Juan Garcia

1762 Spain acquires the Louisiana Territory from France.

1810 The Mexican War of Independence begins, led by the priest Miguel Hidalgo y Costilla. General Vicente Guerrero leads the revolt from 1814 on.

1821 Mexico achieves independence.

1822–1823 General Agustin de Iturbide crowns himself emperor.

1823 In a revolt against Iturbide, Guatemala, with the exception of the province of Chiapas, secedes from the Mexican empire.

1824 The Republic of Mexico is proclaimed.

1827 The Spanish are expelled from Mexico.

1833–1855 Presidency and dictatorship of General Antonio López de Santa Anna

1836 Texas declares independence from Mexico: Santa Anna fires on the Alamo, killing all the defenders except a few non-combatants.

1846–1848 War against the United States: Mexico loses over 500,000 square miles (1.35 million km²) of land.

1861–1867 French intervention leads to establishment of the second Mexican empire under the rule of Habsburg archduke Ferdinand Maximilian.

1861–1872 Benito Juárez opposes French intervention as president-in-exile, and serves as president of the Second Republic of Mexico after French withdrawal.

1862 French forces defeat Juárez at Puebla.

1864 The French install Austrian archduke Maximilian as emperor.

1867 Maximilian is executed after defeat at the Battle of Queretaro.

1867–1910 The Second Republic of Mexico brings separation of church and state.

1876–1880, 1884–1911 Porfirio Diaz is president of Mexico with dictatorial powers.

1910 The Mexican Revolution begins.

1911 Revolutionary guerrillas under the leadership of Pancho Villa (until 1923) overthrow Porfirio Diaz.

1911–1917 Emiliano Zapata leads a program of social revolution and agrarian reform. His followers, the Zapatistas, are still active today.

1917 Mexico adopts a liberal consti-tution. Germany tries to lure Mexico into an alliance during World War I, promising help in regaining territories lost to the United States. Under pres-sure from the United States, Mexico chooses neutrality instead.

1938 Nationalization of the oil industry

1941 Mexico joins the Allies against Germany and Japan in World War II.

1968 Student demonstrations are brutally suppressed by security forces.

1982 With Mexico on the bring of total economic collapse, many Mexicans seek their fortune in the United States, often illegally. At first welcomed as cheap labor, changing attitudes in the

ca. 1920: The Mexican Revolution

Territory controlled by local gov't and rebel groups (1910–1920)
- Pancho Villa
- Venustiano Carranza
- Francisco Madero
- Emiliano Zapata

The Mexican government
- Territory controlled by the Mexican government
- Interventions by the United States (year)

US lead to stricter border controls and deportation of many immigrants.

1994 North American Free Trade Agreement (NAFTA) between Mexico, the United States and Canada revita-lizes the Mexican economy. Uprising in the state of Chiapas leads to calls for increased agrarian reform.

Miguel Hidalgo y Costilla (1753–1811) was a Catholic priest and leader of the struggle for independence. He was executed by the Spaniards in 1811.

Porfirio Diaz (1830–1915) was president of Mexico from 1876–1880 and again

from 1884–1911. Though he took credit for an economic recovery enforced by dicta-torial measures, his social policies were so unpopular that his 1910 reelection set off the Mexican Revolution.

Emiliano Zapata (1877–1919) led the Mexican

Revolution from 1911–1917. Zapata developed revolu-tionary social programs to liberate farmers and the indigenous peoples of Mexico. The Mexican army shot and killed Zapata in 1919. His followers, the Zapatistas, continue to promote his cause today.

Today

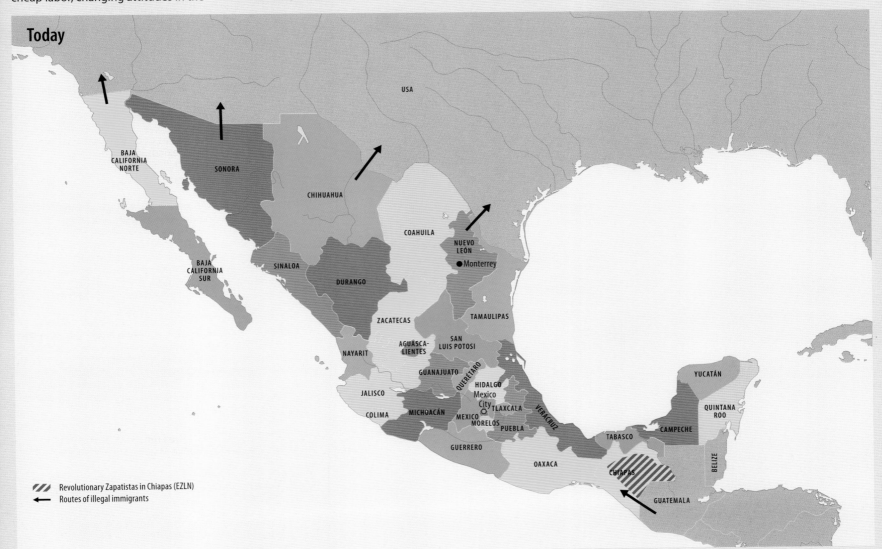

Revolutionary Zapatistas in Chiapas (EZLN)

Routes of illegal immigrants

Central America from the Pre-Columbian Period to the Present

Indigenous Cultures in the Pre-Columbian Period

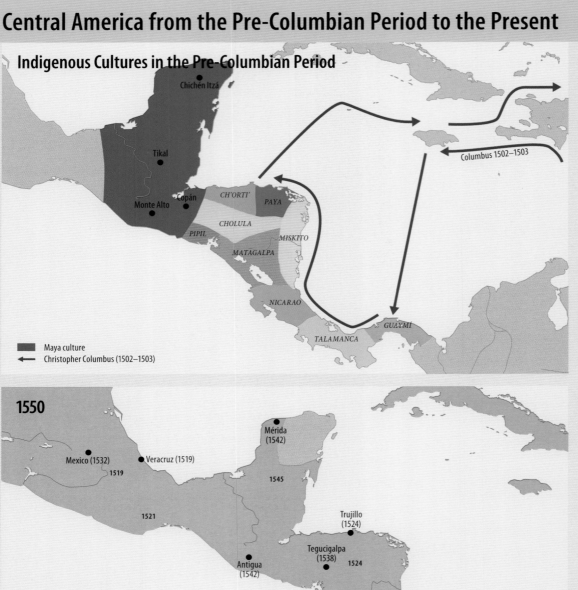

Chichén Itzá

Tikal

Copán
Monte Alto
CH'ORTI'
PAYA
CHOLULA
PIPIL
MISKITO
MATAGALPA
NICARAO
TALAMANCA
GUAYMÍ

Columbus 1502–1503

◼ Maya culture
← Christopher Columbus (1502–1503)

1550

Mérida
(1542)

Mexico (1532)
1519
Veracruz (1519)
1545

Trujillo
(1524)

1521

Tegucigalpa
(1538)
1524

Antigua
(1542)

1522
Portobelo
(1597)
Nombre de Dios
1513 Panama
(1519)
De Vios (1510)

◼ Spanish colonies
1524 Year of exploration and conquest of the region
● City with the year of its founding

1750

Mérida
(1542)

Mexico
Veracruz

JAMAICA

BELIZE

Trujillo

Guatemala

MISKITA (MOSQUITO)
COAST

San José (1738)

Panama

◼ Spanish colonies
◼ British colonies

The Spanish began colonizing Central America in the 16th century. The British arrived about a hundred years later. Like most of Latin America, Central American countries gained independence in the 19th century. The United States has long considered the region an exclusive sphere of influence and has intervened in its political affairs several times during the 20th century.

1502 Columbus lands on present-day Costa Rica.

16th century Spanish colonists arrive.

17th century British privateers and colonists settle what are now Belize and Honduras.

1821 Central America gains independence from Spain.

1823 The United Provinces of Central America are formed. The federation includes what are now Guatemala, Honduras, El Salvador, Costa Rica and Nicaragua.

1830 Panama becomes part of Colombia.

1838 All Central American countries except Belize and Panama become independent.

1862 Belize becomes the colony British Honduras.

1903 Panama secedes from Colombia.

1914 Completion of the Panama Canal

1927–1933 Guerrilla war against American military bases in Nicaragua

1937–1979 The rule of the Somoza clan in Nicaragua is supported by right-wing militias.

1948 Civil war in Costa Rica

1954 General Castillo leads a coup in Guatemala.

1960–1996 The Guatemalan civil war, the longest in Latin American history, leaves as many as a quarter of a million dead. Guatemala's indigenous peoples, many of them Maya, are particularly hard hit.

1979 Marxist-Sandinista Revolution in Nicaragua against dictator Somoza, whose family had diverted humanitarian aid intended for victims of a major earthquake to their own personal accounts.

1980–1992 Civil war in El Salvador between the military government and a coalition of leftist militias (FMLN) leads to accusations of torture and kidnapping on both sides.

1981 Belize gains independence.

1982 Some 10,000 ethnic Miskitos fighting a separatist war flee Nicaragua for Honduras.

1986 The Iran-Contra Affair comes to light: Through secret sales of weapons to Iran, the Reagan administration has supported the paramilitary war of the Contras against the Sandinistas.

1989 The United States intervenes in Panama, bringing down former ally Manuel Noriega.

1990 The Sandinistas lose the national elections to surprise candidate Violeta Chamorro, a wealthy publisher.

2006 Daniel Ortega, the Sandinistas' first leader, wins the presidential election.

Juan Rafael Mora (1814–1860) was president of Costa Rica from 1849–1859. In 1856, he led the Central American countries in an alliance against the United States-supported Nicaraguan dictatorship.

Minor Cooper (1848–1929) was an American businessman who founded the first banana plantations in Central America and marketed the fruit to the world.

Oscar Arnulfo Romero (1917–1980) was archbishop of San Salvador from 1977–1980. Romero criticized the military dictatorship in El Salvador and, as a liberation theologian, stood on the side of the poor. He was assassinated by a right-wing death squad while saying mass.

Justo Rufino Barrios (1835–1885) was president of Guatemala and a liberal reformer.

Anastasio Somoza (1896–1956) Dictator of Nicaragua from 1937. After his assassination, his sons Luis (1956–1967) and Anastasio, Jr. (1967–1979) ruled the country using right-wing death squads. Anastasio was ousted in 1979 and murdered in exile in 1980.

The Pedro Miguel lock of the Panama Canal, Panama

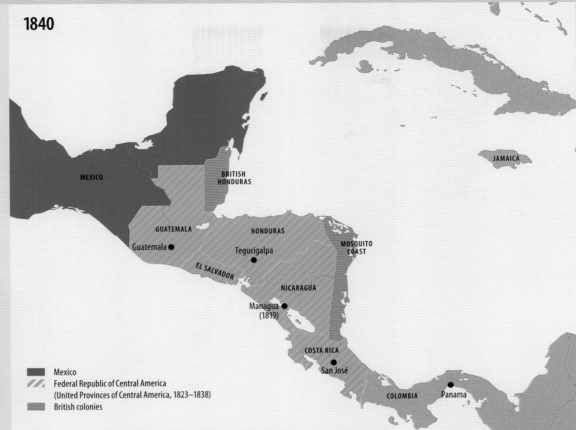

1840

Legend:
- Mexico
- Federal Republic of Central America (United Provinces of Central America, 1823–1838)
- British colonies

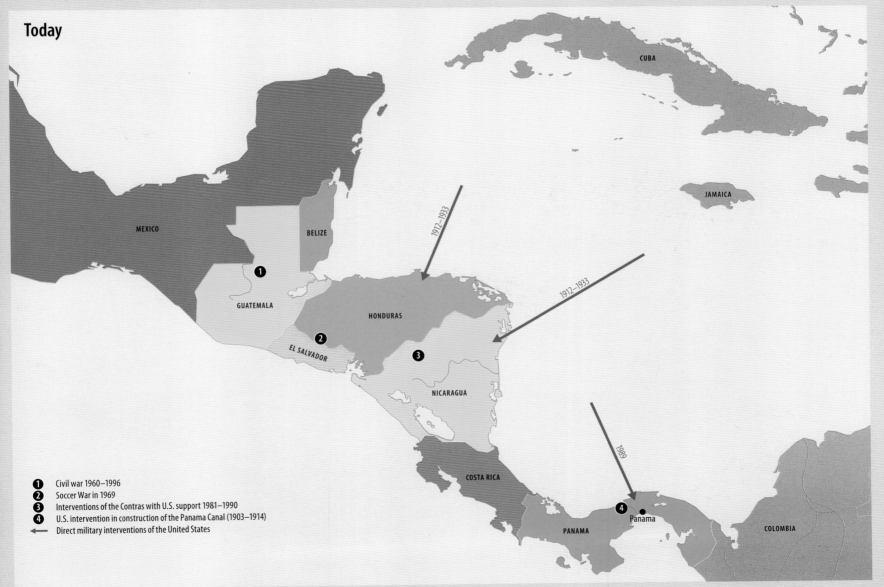

Today

- ❶ Civil war 1960–1996
- ❷ Soccer War in 1969
- ❸ Interventions of the Contras with U.S. support 1981–1990
- ❹ U.S. intervention in construction of the Panama Canal (1903–1914)
- ← Direct military interventions of the United States

SOUTH AMERICA

South America was the last continent to be colonized by *Homo sapiens*. Archaeological findings indicate that highly developed, pre-Columbian cultures already existed 6,000 years ago. In 1494, before the interior of the continent was ever explored by Europeans, the Treaty of Tordesillas established a geographical line of demarcation dividing "newly discovered" lands outside of Europe between Spain and Portugal.

After the destruction of the Inca empire in 1533, the continent experienced unprecedented colonization and exploitation. The indigenous population was forcibly Christianized. While the colonial efforts of the Dutch, French and English brought only minor territorial gains, the Spanish Viceroyalty rapidly took control of a region extending some 6,200 miles (10,000 km) from central North America to the southernmost tip of South America. In the early 19th century, revolutions led to the formation of the South American nations we know today. Dominated by dictatorships in the early 20th century, democratic government has been the norm since the century's end. Economically, many South American countries today are still considered developing nations.

South America: An Overview	**436**
The 20th Century: A Hotbed of Political Unrest	439
Venezuela	**440**
Colombia	**442**
Ecuador	**443**
Guyana, Suriname and French Guiana	**444**
Natural Resources in South America	445
Peru	**446**
Bolivia	**448**
Indigenous Peoples of South America Before Spanish Colonization	449
Brazil	**450**
Uruguay	**454**
Paraguay	**455**
Chile	**456**
Argentina	**458**

America Newly Delineated, *written by Jodocus Hondius. Engraving by H. Picard.* Published by Jean Boisseau between 1637–1640. Jodocus Hondius (1563–1612)

South America: An Overview

From 1000: Earliest Civilizations

Valdivia civilization
Tiwanaku empire (1st c. BCE–12th c. CE)
Wari empire (500–800)
Chimú culture (700–1476)

❶ Valdivia civilization 3500–1800 BCE
❷ Moche civilization 100 BCE–700 CE
❸ Nazca culture 350 BCE–450 CE

The Inca Empire

Inca empire until 1438
Pachacuti 1438–1463
Túpac Inca Yupanqui 1463–1471
Túpac Inca Yupanqui 1471–1493
Huayna Capac 1493–1527
Late Inca conquests
Spanish domain in 1525
Tordesillas line 1494
Pizarro's expedition to Peru (1531–1533)

The most sophisticated civilization in the New World developed in South America. With an efficient, well-organized administrative system, the Inca Empire has been compared to the Roman Empire. Nonetheless, the Spaniards conquered it nearly as quickly as they had the Aztec empire in Mexico. With the blessing of Pope Julius II, Spain and Portugal divided the continent.

14,000 BCE Earliest archaeological discoveries in Monte Verde, Chile, date from this time.

4,000 BCE Valdivia culture in Ecuador: ceramics and female figurines

2,600 BCE Caral in Peru is presumably the oldest city in South America (step pyramids).

500 BCE The Arawaks settle in the Orinoco delta.

4th century BCE–5th century CE The Nazca culture flourishes in Peru.

1st century BCE–12th century CE Tiahuanaco empire on Lake Titicaca

100–700 Moche culture

500–800 Wari empire in Peru

700–1476 Chimú empire in Peru

1100–1539 The Inca Empire, at its zenith stretching the entire length of South America

~ 1250 Arrival of the Incas in Cuzco

1438 Inca wars of conquest begin under Pachacutec. Within a century, the Inca Empire controls most of the western coast.

1494 Treaty of Tordesillas: America is split into Spanish and Portuguese sectors by the rulers of Spain and Portugal with the blessing of the pope.

1509 Pizarro reaches South America.

~ 1520 The first Spanish settlements are founded in the north (Venezuela and Colombia) and in Argentina.

Francisco Pizarro (1476–1541)

Atahualpa (ca. 1502–1533)

Conquest and Colonization

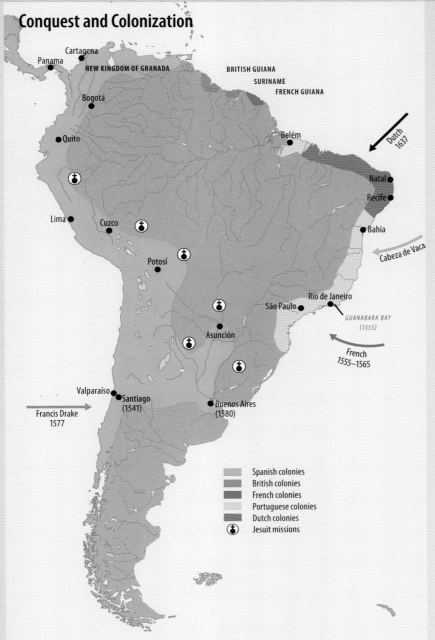

Spanish colonies
British colonies
French colonies
Portuguese colonies
Dutch colonies
Ⓣ **Jesuit missions**

ca. 1800: Before Independence

Spanish colonies
British colonies
Dutch colonies
French colonies
Portuguese colonies

Spanish Viceroyalties

Other Spanish colonies

1530 The colonization of Brazil begins.

1533 Inca ruler Atahualpa is executed.

1533–1539 The Inca Empire in Peru is conquered by the Spaniards led by Francisco Pizarro.

1535 The Viceroyalty of New Spain is founded with Venezuela.

1541 Founding of Santiago de Chile

1542 Originally called New Castile, the Viceroyalty of Peru is founded by the Spanish. Soon after, important silver deposits are discovered in Potosi.

1555 The French establish a colony in Guanabara Bay (Brazil).

1565 Rio de Janeiro is founded.

1577 British privateer Francis Drake plunders Valparaiso.

1572 The last Incan ruler, Tupac Amaru, is executed in Cuzco by the Spanish.

1580 The city of Buenos Aires is founded.

from 1604 The first Jesuit missions are founded.

1610–1767 In Paraguay, the Jesuit Reductions (self-governing native administration districts) protect the indigenous population from slave traders. As many as 150,000 natives live in forty distinct communities, each with a church, school and hospital. The success of the Reductions increases opposition to the Jesuit order among European colonists.

1616 The French are ousted from northern Brazil by the Portuguese.

1637–1639 Pedro Teixeira, a Portuguese cartographer, explores the Amazon Basin for Philip III of Spain.

1637–1654 The Netherlands briefly controls parts of Brazil.

1694 The discovery of gold in Brazil leads to economic revival of the Portuguese colony.

1700 The height of the sugar cane boom in Guayana

1717 The Viceroyalty of New Granada is founded, including the present-day countries of Colombia, Ecuador, Panama and Venezuela.

1767 The Spanish expel the Jesuits from all their New World colonies.

1776 The Viceroyalty of Rio de la Plata is founded, comprising what are now Argentina, Bolivia, Uruguay and Paraguay.

1780–1781 Tupac Amaru II, descendent of an Inca ruler, leads a failed uprising against Spanish rule in Peru. He is executed and his entire family is killed or imprisoned, ending the Inca royal line.

1807 Failed attempt by the British to take Buenos Aires

South America: An Overview

Until 1830: Independence

ca. 1880: National Borders at the End of the 19th Century

The countries of South America gained their independence in the 19th century. Widespread dissatisfaction with political systems, coupled with tense relations between different ethnic groups and regions, led to decades of civil war and military coups. In addition, the Great Depression of the 1930s increased South America's economic dependence on the United States.

1819 Simón Bolívar founds Greater Colombia, which consists of Ecuador, Gran Colombia, Panama and Venezuela.

1821 Peruvian independence marks the end of the Viceroyalty of Peru.

1822–1831 The Brazilian Empire is ruled by Pedro I.

1823 In the Monroe Doctrine, US president James Monroe promises intervention against any European attempts to found colonies in North and South America.

1830 Gran Colombia fragments into the independent nations of Venezuela, Colombia and Ecuador.

1833 Britain annexes the Falkland Islands.

1836 Unification of Peru and Bolivia

1840–1889 The reign of Emperor Pedro II is a period of progressive politics in Brazil.

1862–1870 As much as two-thirds of Paraguay's population dies during the reign of Francisco Solano Lopez after the charismatic, possibly insane, general involves the nation in a series of hopeless wars.

1864–1870 Paraguay loses most of its territory to Brazil, Argentina and Uruguay during the War of the Triple Alliance (Paraguayan War).

1879–1880 Chile and Argentina expand southward.

1879–1883 Chile defeats Peru and Bolivia during the War of the Pacific, also known as the Saltpeter War.

1888 Abolition of slavery in Brazil

1889 After a military coup, the Brazilian monarchy dissolves and the Federative Republic of Brazil is founded.

1890 Eighteen countries join forces in founding the Pan-American Union.

1941 Latin American countries side with the United States during World War II.

1946 Beginning of Juan Perón's dictatorship in Argentina

1948 Founding of the Organization of American States by twenty-one American nations

1962 After a referendum, Brazil changes from a parliamentary to a presidential form of government.

1964 Military coup in Brazil

1965 Beginning of guerrilla warfare in Colombia

1967 Marxist revolutionary Che Guevara is murdered in Bolivia.

1973 Perón returns from exile to Argentina. A military coup led by Chilean general Augusto Pinochet overthrows the democratically elected government of Salvador Allende. Given Allende's Marxist leanings, there is suspicion of US involvement.

1998 Augusto Pinochet is arrested in London and returned to Chile in 2000.

THE 20TH CENTURY: A HOTBED OF POLITICAL UNREST

NETHERLANDS ANTILLES (NETHERLANDS)

Caracas

Venezuela
1902 After calling in unpaid loans, European superpowers block Venezuelan ports.
1948 The military brings down the government of President Rómulo Gallegos.
1958 Overthrow of dictator Marcos Pérez Jimenez
1998 Popular left-wing politician Hugo Chávez is elected president. Socialist policies include nationalization of industry and the breaking up of large estates. Chávez also adopts an aggressive stance toward the United States.

VENEZUELA

Georgetown

Paramaribo

Cayenne

GUYANA

SURINAME

FRENCH GUIANA (FRANCE)

Bogotá

COLOMBIA

Colombia
1948–1957 Civil war between liberals and conservatives claims ca. 300,000 victims.
1965 Guerilla warfare by Marxist rebels continues to this day. All sides are financed by the drug cartels.
2002 Alvaro Uribe is elected president; he fights the drug cartels and Marxist insurgents.

Quito

ECUADOR

Ecuador
1963 A military junta overthrows the government of President Carlos Arosemena Monroy.
1970 After losing popular support, President José María Velasco Ibarra rules as a dictator.
1981 Defeat in the war with Peru.
2001 Luis Maldonado becomes the first minister of indigenous descent.

PERU

Lima

Peru
1948 Military coup led by General Manuel Odria.
1965 Left-wing guerrilla uprising in the province of La Concepción
1968 Civil war breaks out after a military coup led by General Velasco Alvarado Juno.
1992 Leaders of the Maoist Sendero Luminoso (Shining Path) are arrested.
2000 Corruption scandals force President Alberto Fujimori to resign.

BOLIVIA

La Paz

BRAZIL

Brasilia

Brazil
1930–1945 and 1950–1954 The era of Getúlio Dornelles Vargas brings social progress and prosperity by means of "benevolent dictatorship."
1954 The military gives Getúlio Vargas the choice between resigning or being overthrown; he commits suicide instead.
1964 Supported by big business, the army overthrows the government of President João Goulart.
1985 The end of military dictatorship. President-elect Tancredo Neves dies before taking office. Regular democratic elections resume.
2003 After more than forty years, Luiz Lula da Silva becomes the first leftist head of state. He supports a free market economy and socially equitable land reforms.

Rio de Janeiro

PARAGUAY

Asunción

Paraguay
1954 Coup led by General Alfredo Stroessner marks the beginning of his dictatorship.
1989 A military coup led by General Andrés Rodríguez ends Stroessner's dictatorship.
1992 Democratic constitution
2008 Leftist Fernando Lugo becomes president.

Bolivia
1932–1935 Bolivia loses the province of Chaco after war with Paraguay.
1964 A military coup overthrows the government of President Víctor Paz Estenssoro.
1964–1985 Military rule: officers on the right and the left struggle for power.
2005 Evo Morales becomes the first president of indigenous extraction. Social reforms modeled on Hugo Chávez's Venezuela are implemented. Land reforms beneficial to indigenous peoples lead to unrest.

URUGUAY

ARGENTINA

Santiago

CHILE

Montevideo

Buenos Aires

Uruguay
1965 The largest financial crisis in the history of the country
1973–1984 Military dictatorship and guerrilla warfare
1984 In return for immunity from prosecution, top military officials enable a gradual transition to democracy.
2006 Former dictator Juan Marío Bordaberry is arrested for crimes that took place during his dictatorship.

Chile
1970 Socialist Salvador Allende becomes president.
1973 The US Central Intelligence Agency (CIA) is suspected of supporting Chilean general Augusto Pinochet's coup against Allende. Allende is killed along with many of his followers.
1973–1990 Pinochet dictatorship
2006 Michelle Bachelet becomes the first female president.

Argentina
1946 Juan Domingo Perón becomes president.
1955 After a coup, Perón flees into exile in Europe.
1973 Perón returns. After his death in 1974, his wife Isabel continues his policies, serving as president from 1974-1976.
1976–1983 A military junta brings brutal, state-sponsored terror under Jorge Rafael Videla.
1982 Defeat by England in the Falkland War
from 1982 Severe economic crises with hyperinflation
1998 End of immunity for crimes committed by the military junta

FALKLAND ISLANDS (U.K.)/ ISLAS MALVINAS

Territory dependent on the Netherlands
Territory dependent on France
Territory dependent on the United Kingdom

Venezuela

4000–1000 BCE: Prehistory

- Tocuya civilization
- Salada civilization
- Barrancas civilization
- ○ Finds of early ceramics

Rancho Peludo (1900 BCE)

Barrancas (1000 BCE)

Orinoco

La Gruta (2100 BCE)

Parmana (1600 BCE)

Barabina (4000 BCE)

1498–1567: First Settlements and Colonies

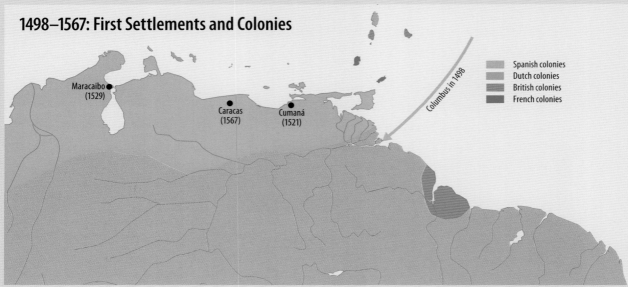

- Spanish colonies
- Dutch colonies
- British colonies
- French colonies

Maracaibo (1529)

Caracas (1567)

Cumaná (1521)

Columbus in 1498

1810–1831: The Road to Independence

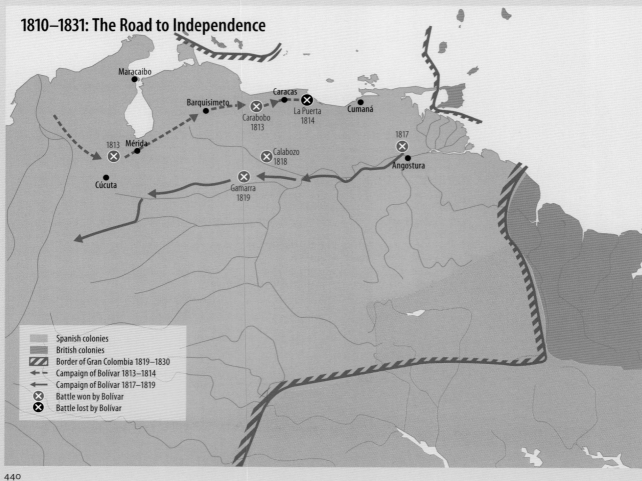

Maracaibo

Barquisimeto

Caracas

Carabobo 1813

La Puerta 1814

Cumaná

1813

Mérida

1817

Calabozo 1818

Angostura

Cúcuta

Gamarra 1819

- Spanish colonies
- British colonies
- ▨ Border of Gran Colombia 1819–1830
- ← Campaign of Bolívar 1813–1814
- ← Campaign of Bolívar 1817–1819
- ⊗ Battle won by Bolívar
- ⊗ Battle lost by Bolívar

Venezuela was the first independent state in South America. In spite of extensive oil deposits, its economic situation has steadily worsened since the early 1980s. Elected in 1998, controversial president Hugo Chávez has taken a lead role in fighting poverty within the country.

4000 BCE First settlements along the northern coast

1498 While on his third journey to the New World, Columbus lands at the mouth of the Orinoco River.

1499 Amerigo Vespucci gives Venezuela its name, meaning "little Venice," because of the stilt dwellings (palafitos) he finds there.

1521 First Spanish settlement on the northern coast

1528–1556 The Welser merchant family exploits Venezuela's resources, paying a percentage of their profits to Charles V, Habsburg emperor and king of Spain.

1535 Venezuela becomes part of New Spain (Nueva España).

15th–18th centuries Slaves are imported from Africa to work in sugarcane cultivation. Christian missionaries arrive.

1749 First stirrings of discontent with Spanish rule

1806 A revolt against Spanish rule fails to bring independence.

1810 Simón Bolívar leads a revolution in Caracas.

1811 Venezuela declares its independence from Spain.

1819 Along with New Granada (today's Colombia), Ecuador and Panama, Venezuela becomes part of Gran Colombia.

1830 The fragmentation of Gran Colombia leads to renewed independence for Venezuela.

1864 Venezuela becomes a federal republic.

1899–1908 Cipriano Castro's seizure of power marks the end of caudillismo (caudillo = "military rule" in Spanish).

1902 The great powers of Europe blockade Venezuelan harbors.

1908–1935 Under the dictatorship of Juan Vicente Gómez, Venezuela becomes the world's leading exporter of oil.

1935–1948 Democratic governments are followed in 1945 by a leftist coup led by novelist Romulo Gallegos. Romulo Betancourt takes the office of president.

1948 Romulo Gallegos is elected president, only to be overthrown by a military junta nine months later.

1958 The dictator Marcos Pérez Jiménez is overthrown.

1831–1898

Plantations
Cattle raising

1864: Venezuela Becomes a Federal Republic

☐ Border of Venezuela in 1864
■ Disputed territory, annexed by the United Kingdom in 1899
■ Disputed territory, annexed by Brazil in 1905
☐ Venezuela since 1905
■ Dutch colonies
Ⓐ Oil production since the early 20th century

1960 Venezuela is a founding member of OPEC.

1974–1979 Under the presidency of socialist Carlos Andrés Pérez (also 1989–1993), oil exports make Venezuela South America's wealthiest country.

1992 Unsuccessful coup attempt by leftist/populist leader Hugo Chávez

1998 Chávez is elected president, and is reelected in 2006.

2008 Chavez breaks off diplomatic relations with the United States, only to reestablish them in 2009 after the inauguration of Barack Obama.

Venezuela Today

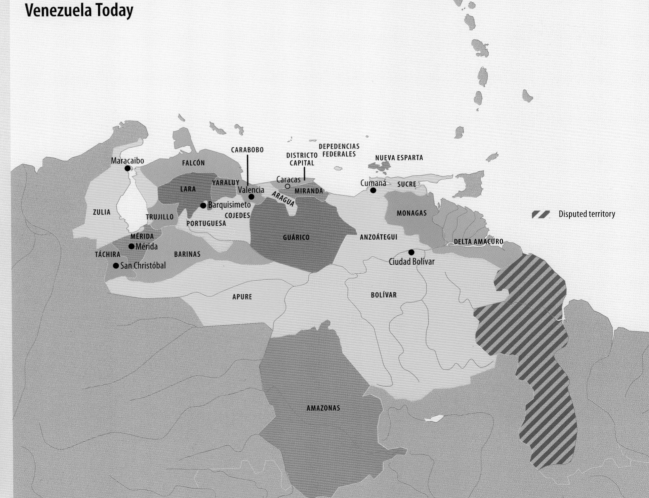

☑ Disputed territory

Simón José Antonio de la Santisima Trinidad Bolívar Palacios y Blanco

Simón Bolívar (1783–1830) A Venezuelan-born military and political leader of Latin America's resistance against Spain's colonial rule, he came to be known as "The Liberator." Bolívar eventually served as president of Gran Colombia, Venezuela, Peru and Bolivia.

Juan Vicente Gómez (1857–1935) was president and dictator of Venezuela from

1908–1935. His oil policies earned him the support of the United States.

Rómulo Gallegos (1884–1969) A famous novelist, Gallegos supported the 1945 leftist coup that put reformer Romulo Betancourt in office, and later (in 1948) was elected president himself. He was overthrown by a military coup after just nine months in office.

Wolfgang Larrazábal (1911–2003) This military officer overthrew the dictator Marcos Pérez Jiménez in 1958, but did not win the subsequent presidential election.

Hugo Chávez (1954–) An attempted coup led by General Chávez in 1992 failed, but as the leader of a leftist coalition formed in 1997 he won the 1998 presidential election.

A socialist populist, he advocates a united South America in the spirit of Simón Bolívar (Bolivarism), challenging the hegemony of the United States. His aggressive speeches and policies of socialist nationalization frequently lead to domestic unrest and criticism from abroad.

Colombia

1500: Indio Cultures

- Minca
- Betancí
- Guatavita
- San Agustín

Sinua states
Tairona states
Kimbay states
Chibcha states
San Agustín culture

1533–1803

- Santa Maria (1525)
- Nombre de Dios (1510)
- Maracaibo (1529)
- Cartagena (1533)
- Panamá (1519)
- Santa Fé de Bogotá (1538)
- Quito (1534)

Spanish colonies in 1650
Spanish colonies in 1750
The explorers
← Sebastián de Belalcázar (1533–1539)
← Gonzalo Jiménez de Quesada (1536–1537)
← Humboldt's journey (1799–1803)

1812–1851: Gran Colombia

- Santa Maria
- Maracaibo
- Caracas
- Cartagena
- Tenerife 1872
- 1823
- San Fernando de Apure
- Panamá
- Cúcuta
- Bogotá
- Boyacá 1819
- Buenaventura
- Bombona 1822
- Pichincha 1822
- Quito

Gran Colombia 1819–1830
Colombia since 1830
War of Independence
← Campaign led by Bolívar 1812–1814
← Campaign led by Bolívar 1819–1822
⊗ Important battle

ca. 1900

- Barranquilla
- Cartagena
- Panama
- Medellín
- Cúcuta
- Cali
- Bogotá
- COLOMBIA

1926

- Barranquilla
- Cartagena
- Panama
- Medellín
- Cúcuta
- Cali
- Bogotá
- Leticia

Colombia in 1926
Territory gained by Ecuador 1916–1926

Even after independence from Spain, Colombia was still often part of a larger state. Today it is plagued by aggressive drug cartels and leftist guerillas.

from 1200 BCE The first megalithic sculpture by the San Agustín appear in coastal regions.

1525 Spanish conquistadors conquer indigenous tribes.

1533 Cartagena is founded.

1717 Bogotá becomes capital of the newly founded Viceroyalty of New Granada.

1819 Simón Bolívar defeats Spanish forces, and the state of Gran Colombia is created.

1830 Great Colombia is dissolved, and the Republic of New Granada (today's Colombia and Panama) is founded.

1885–1930 Era of conservative government; the church plays a greater role.

1899–1903 A civil conflict known as the Thousand Days' War causes much bloodshed.

1903 Panama gains its independence from Colombia.

1930–1946 Liberal governments

1933 Colombia-Peru War

1946 The conservatives seize power.

1948–1957 The assassination of presidential candidate Jorge Eliécer Gaitán is followed by *La Violencia*, a civil war resulting in 300,000 deaths.

1953–1957 Military dictatorship of Gustavo Rojas Pinilla

1958–1974 Conservatives and liberals join forces to govern as the National Front.

since 1964 Guerilla wars are fought by the Marxist rebel groups FARC and ELN.

1993 Drug cartel chief Pablo Escobar is shot. The breakup of the powerful Medellín cartel brings renewed violence.

2002 Under President Alvaro Uribe, strict measures are taken to curtail guerillas and drug cartels.

2008 Franco-Colombian politician Ingrid Betancourt is rescued from FARC rebels, who have been holding her hostage for over six years.

FARC (Fuerzas Armadas Revolucionarias de Colombia)

- Medellín
- Cúcuta
- Cali
- Bogotá
- COLOMBIA
- Leticia

FARC guerilla movement (Revolutionary Armed Forces of Colombia), since 1964

ELN (Ejército de Liberación Nacional)

- Cúcuta
- Medellín
- Bogotá
- Cali
- COLOMBIA
- Leticia

ELN guerilla movement (National Liberation Army), since 1964

Coca Cultivation

- Barranquilla
- Cartagena
- Cúcuta
- Medellín
- Cali
- Bogotá
- COLOMBIA
- Leticia

Coca cultivation

~**1450** The pre-Columbian Cara culture is conquered by the Incas.

1534 Spanish forces conquer Ecuador, which becomes part of the Viceroyalty of Peru.

1535 Spanish sailors discover the Galapagos Islands, naming them after the giant land tortoises.

1822 The Battle of Pichincha near Quito results in Spanish defeat, and Ecuador becomes part of Gran Colombia.

1830 Ecuador gains full independence.

1832 Ecuador acquires the Galapagos Islands.

late 1830s Charles Darwin devises his theory of evolution after visiting the Galapagos Islands in 1835.

1859–1865 Clerical authoritarian regime of president Gabriel Garcia Moreno (also 1869–1875)

1895 General Eloy Alfaro leads a liberal revolution.

20th century Alternating civilian and military governments

1940 Discovery of oil

1941–1995 Violent border disputes with Peru repeatedly flare up.

1942 Parts of Ecuador are ceded to Peru.

2005 Congress removes President Lucio Gutiérrez from office.

since 2007 Rafael Correa is president.

Carlos Arosemena Monroy (1919–2004) Elected president in 1961, he implemented nationalist and union-friendly policies. In 1963 his regime was overthrown by a military junta back by the United States.

José Maria Velasco Ibarra (1893–1979) was a leftist-liberal politician who served five terms as president of Ecuador between 1934 and 1972. After a period of unrest in 1970, he became an authoritarian dictator. He was overthrown in 1972.

1526–1750: Spanish Colonies

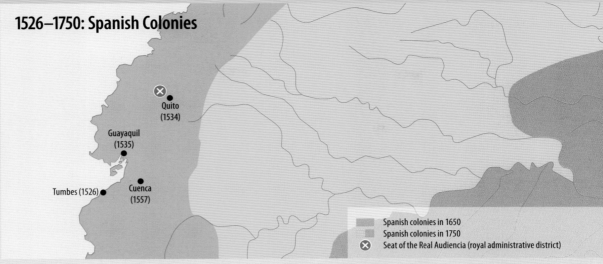

Quito (1534)

Guayaquil (1535)

Tumbes (1526)   Cuenca (1557)

Spanish colonies in 1650
Spanish colonies in 1750
⊗ Seat of the Real Audiencia (royal administrative district)

1819–1853: Ecuador as Part of Gran Colombia

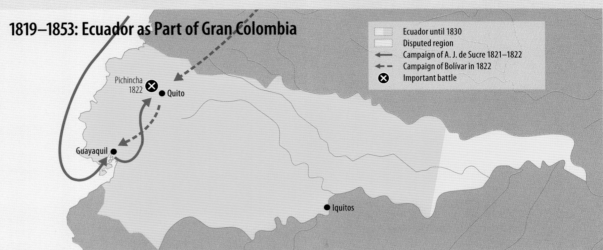

Pichincha 1822   Quito

Guayaquil

Iquitos

Ecuador until 1830
Disputed region
→ Campaign of A. J. de Sucre 1821–1822
⇢ Campaign of Bolívar in 1822
⊗ Important battle

1920 to the Present

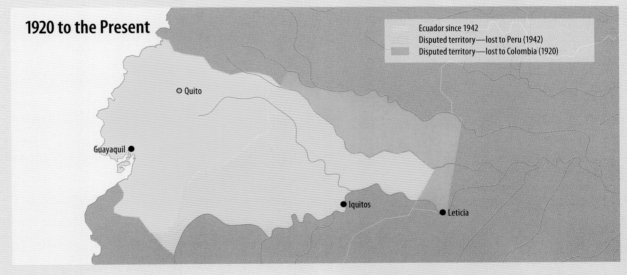

○ Quito

Guayaquil

Iquitos

Leticia

Ecuador since 1942
Disputed territory—lost to Peru (1942)
Disputed territory—lost to Colombia (1920)

The Galapagos Islands

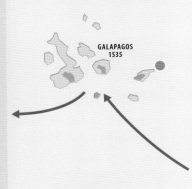

GALAPAGOS 1535

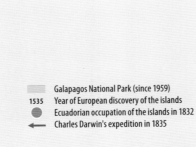

ECUADOR

Guayaquil

Galapagos National Park (since 1959)
1535 Year of European discovery of the islands
● Ecuadorian occupation of the islands in 1832
← Charles Darwin's expedition in 1835

18th-century map of the Galapagos Islands by William Ambrose Cowley

Guyana, Suriname and French Guiana

1613–1667: Spanish, British and French Settlement

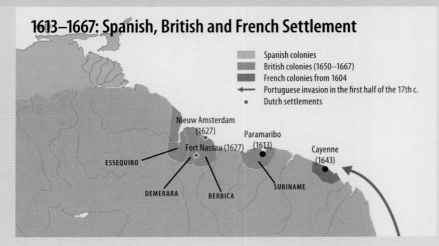

Spanish colonies
British colonies (1650–1667)
French colonies from 1604
→ Portuguese invasion in the first half of the 17th c.
• Dutch settlements

Nieuw Amsterdam (1627)
Fort Nassau (1627)
Paramaribo (1613)
Cayenne (1643)
ESSEQUIBO
DEMERARA
BERBICA
SURINAME

1750: Domination by Colonial Powers

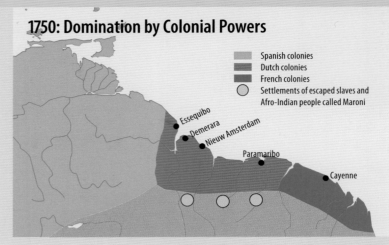

Spanish colonies
Dutch colonies
French colonies
○ Settlements of escaped slaves and Afro-Indian people called Maroni

Essequibo
Demerara
Nieuw Amsterdam
Paramaribo
Cayenne

1781–1946: Dutch, British and French Settlement

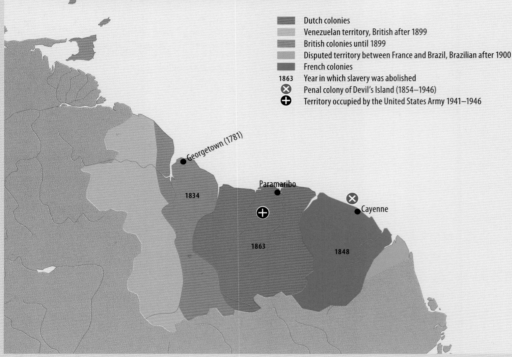

Dutch colonies
Venezuelan territory, British after 1899
British colonies until 1899
Disputed territory between France and Brazil, Brazilian after 1900
French colonies
1863 Year in which slavery was abolished
⊗ Penal colony of Devil's Island (1854–1946)
⊕ Territory occupied by the United States Army 1941–1946

Georgetown (1781)
Paramaribo
1834
⊕
1863
⊗ Cayenne
1848

1961 to the Present

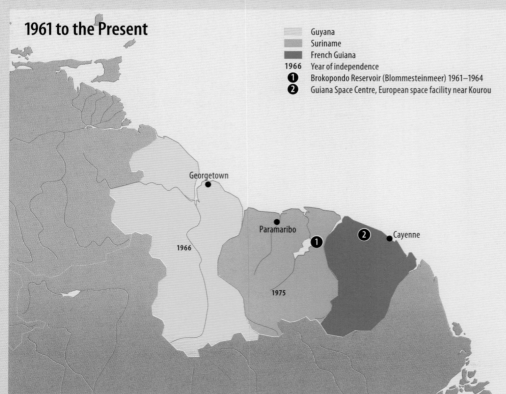

Guyana
Suriname
French Guiana
1966 Year of independence
❶ Brokopondo Reservoir (Blommesteinmeer) 1961–1964
❷ Guiana Space Centre, European space facility near Kourou

Georgetown
Paramaribo
1966
❶
❷ Cayenne
1975

These three small countries in northern South America fell under the colonial influence of Britain, the Netherlands and France. While Guyana and Suriname gained their independence in the 20th century, French Guiana remains under colonial control.

1604 The French arrive in Guiana, where they will later establish a penal colony.

1620 The Dutch begin shipping slaves to Guiana.

1651 English plantation owners are the first European settlers in present-day Suriname.

1667 England cedes its portion of what is now Suriname to the Netherlands.

1780–1813 The Dutch cede their possessions in what is now Guyana to the British.

1814 The British control Guyana.

1831 British Guiana (now Guyana) officially becomes a British colony.

1834 The British abolish slavery in British Guiana

1848 The French abolish slavery in French Guiana

1863 The Dutch abolish slavery in Dutch Guiana (Suriname).

1899 An American arbitration committee ends the border conflict between British Guiana and Venezuela that has been smoldering since 1841. Venezuela is forced to cede territory to Britain, leading to unrest.

1946 French Guiana becomes an overseas *département* of France, and its famous Devil's Island prison is closed (the rest of the penal colony remains in operation until 1952). Many of the former prison sites are now used by the European Space Agency.

1954 Suriname gains autonomy.

1966/1970 British Guiana becomes independent of Britain in 1966 and in 1970 becomes the Republic of Guyana.

1975 Suriname achieves full independence from the Netherlands.

1982 Military coup in Suriname

1986–1992 Civil war and fighting in the jungles of Suriname

Forbes Burnham (1923–1985) A descendant of African slaves, Burnham was the head of the nationalist People's National Congress in Guyana. He became the first prime minister in 1966, and in 1980 served as president.

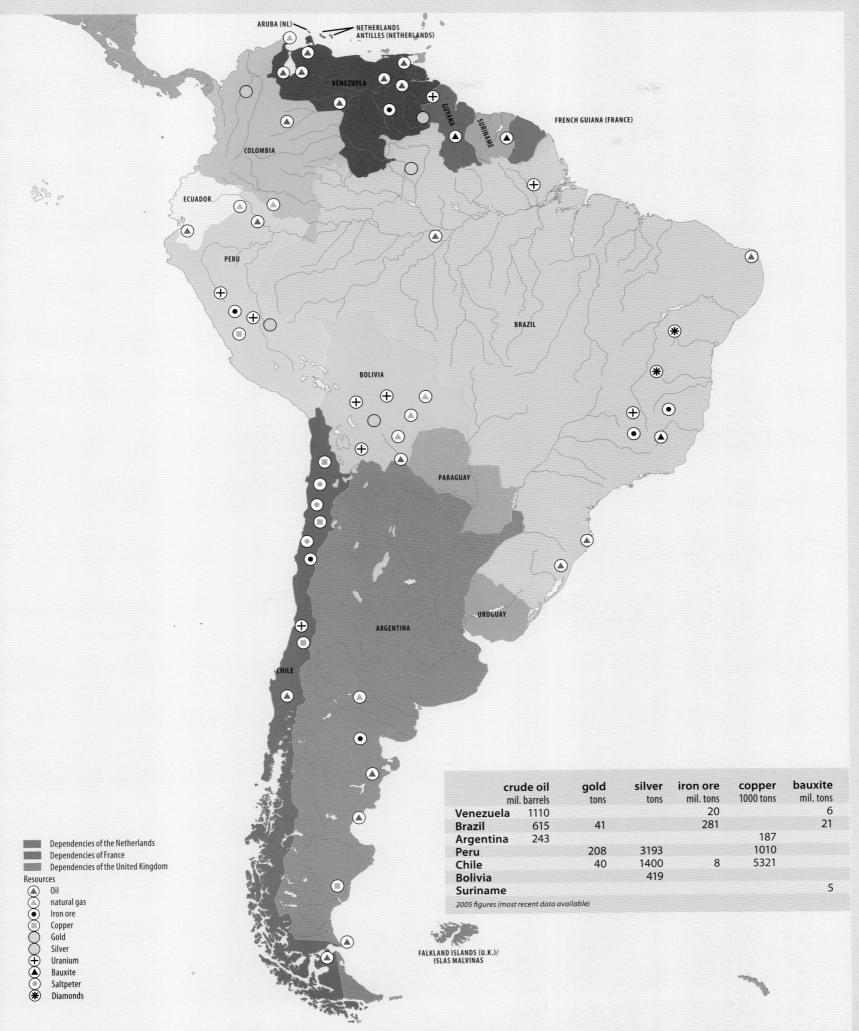

ARUBA (NL)
NETHERLANDS ANTILLES (NETHERLANDS)

VENEZUELA

GUYANA

SURINAME

FRENCH GUIANA (FRANCE)

COLOMBIA

ECUADOR

PERU

BRAZIL

BOLIVIA

PARAGUAY

CHILE

ARGENTINA

URUGUAY

FALKLAND ISLANDS (U.K.)/
ISLAS MALVINAS

Dependencies of the Netherlands
Dependencies of France
Dependencies of the United Kingdom

Resources
Oil
natural gas
Iron ore
Copper
Gold
Silver
Uranium
Bauxite
Saltpeter
Diamonds

	crude oil mil. barrels	gold tons	silver tons	iron ore mil. tons	copper 1000 tons	bauxite mil. tons
Venezuela	1110			20		6
Brazil	615	41		281		21
Argentina	243				187	
Peru		208	3193		1010	
Chile		40	1400	8	5321	
Bolivia			419			
Suriname						5

2005 figures (most recent data available)

Peru

2000 BCE–700 CE: Early Indio Cultures

Huarí

WARÍ EMPIRE (650)

Tiwanaku

TIWANAKU EMPIRE (700)

- ▬▬ Moche culture 1–600 CE
- ▨ Chavín culture 2000–200 BCE
- ▬▬ Nazca culture 350 BCE–450 CE

1400–1471: Inca Expansion

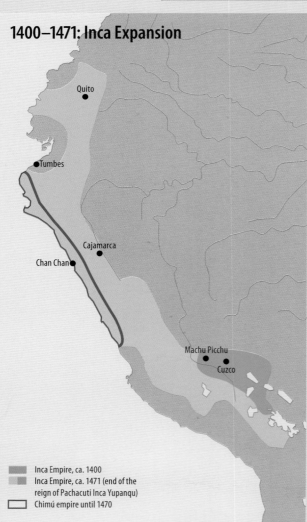

Quito

Tumbes

Cajamarca

Chan Chan

Machu Picchu

Cuzco

- ▬ Inca Empire, ca. 1400
- ▬ Inca Empire, ca. 1471 (end of the reign of Pachacuti Inca Yupanqu)
- ▭ Chimú empire until 1470

1230: Origins of the Inca Empire

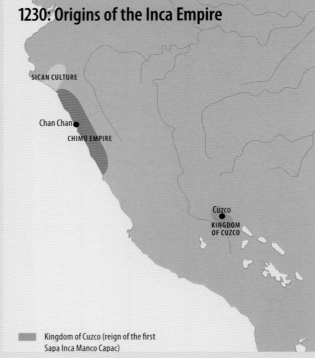

SICAN CULTURE

Chan Chan

CHIMÚ EMPIRE

Cuzco

KINGDOM OF CUZCO

- ▬ Kingdom of Cuzco (reign of the first Sapa Inca Manco Capac)

1525–1532

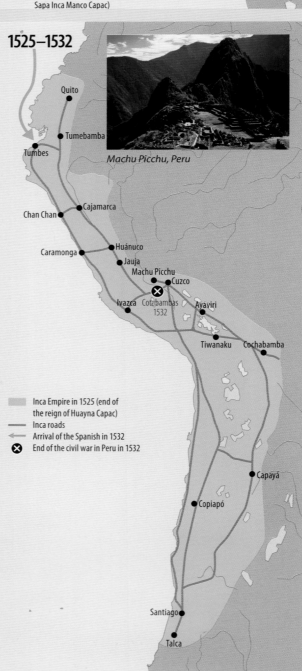

Quito

Tumebamba

Tumbes

Chan Chan

Caramonga

Huánuco

Jauja

Machu Picchu

Cuzco

Ivazca

Cotabambas 1532

Ayaviri

Tiwanaku

Cochabamba

Capayá

Copiapó

Santiago

Talca

Machu Picchu, Peru

- ▬ Inca Empire in 1525 (end of the reign of Huayna Capac)
- ▬ Inca roads
- → Arrival of the Spanish in 1532
- ✕ End of the civil war in Peru in 1532

The Incas built imposing cities with monumental stone palaces and temple complexes, connected by a sophisticated network of roads. Brilliant engineers and craftsmen, the Incas were also highly knowledgeable in medicine. They devised an administrative record system based on knots (quipu). The Inca Empire was conquered in the 16th century by a small group of Spanish conquistadors led by Francisco Pizarro. The wealth acquired through this conquest made Spain the richest nation in the world in the 16th century. Since independence, Peru has suffered through a near-unbroken string of civil wars, military coups and violent territorial conflicts with its neighboring countries.

~4000 BCE Earliest evidence of agriculture and animal husbandry

2000 BCE–700 CE Successive advanced cultures, including Chavin, Nazca, Moche and Tiwanaku

~1230 The Inca settle in the Cuzco Valley.

1438 The Inca begin their campaigns of conquest.

1527–1532 The Inca Empire is riven by a civil war between the rival factions of the brothers Huáscar and Atahualpa.

1532 Atahualpa overthrows his brother and systematically murders Huáscar's supporters among the nobility. This internal weakening contributes to Francisco Pizarro's conquest of the Inca Empire.

1533–1539 The Inca Empire is destroyed by Spanish conquistadors.

1542 The Viceroyalty of Peru is founded.

1572 The Spanish execute Inca leader Tupac Amaru I, who led a rebellion against colonial occupation and missions.

1579 Privateer Sir Francis Drake raids the port of Callao.

1739 The Viceroyalty of New Granada is founded.

1780–1781 José Gabriel, also known as Tupac Amaru II, leads an uprising.

1814–1815 Uprisings against Spanish rule resume.

1821 Peru declares independence.

1824 Spanish rule in Peru, and in South America, comes to an end with defeat at the Battle of Junin.

1828–1829 War against Gran Colombia

1836 Peruvian-Bolivian Confederation

1854 Slavery is abolished.

1860 A successful war waged against Ecuador results in territorial gains, but lack of a mutually agreed border will lead to future conflicts.

1879–1883/84 Peru loses territory in a war with Chile over the nitrate-rich region of Atacama (Saltpeter War).

1929 Some of the territory lost in the Saltpeter War is returned as part of an agreement with Chile.

1932–1934 Armed conflict with Colombia

1941–1942 The Ecuadoran-Peruvian War revives long-standing border disputes. Wars will break out between the two nations again in 1991 and 1995 before a definitive peace agreement is reached in 1996.

1968–1980 Peru is ruled by a military junta.

1985–1990 President Alán García, a social democrat, tries to undo decades of neo-liberal economic policies.

1990–2000 The government of Alberto Fujimori is marked by corruption and conflict with Marxist guerillas.

2006 Alán García is reelected president.

1526–1767: Spanish Colonies

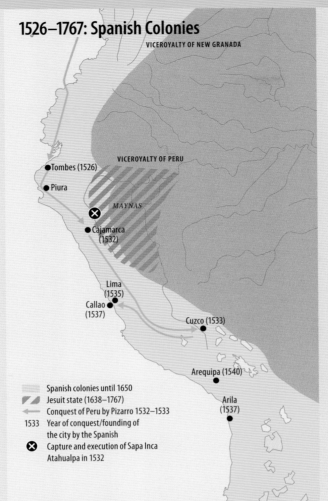

Spanish colonies until 1650
Jesuit state (1638–1767)
Conquest of Peru by Pizarro 1532–1533
1533 Year of conquest/founding of the city by the Spanish
Capture and execution of Sapa Inca Atahualpa in 1532

1820–1854: The Struggle for Independence

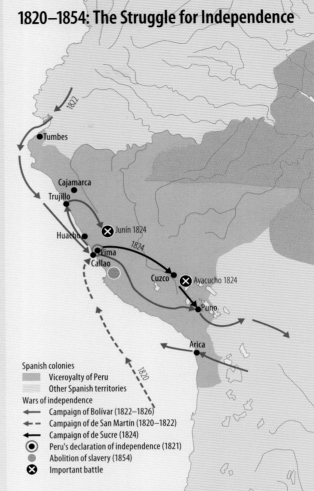

Spanish colonies
Viceroyalty of Peru
Other Spanish territories
Wars of independence
Campaign of Bolívar (1822–1826)
Campaign of de San Martín (1820–1822)
Campaign of de Sucre (1824)
Peru's declaration of independence (1821)
Abolition of slavery (1854)
Important battle

1836–1942

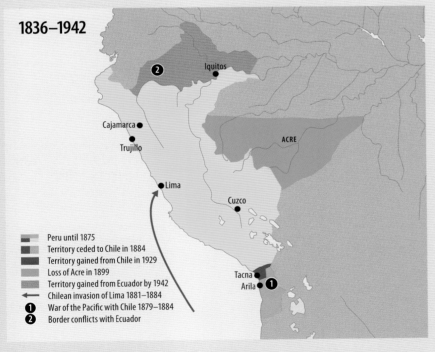

Peru until 1875
Territory ceded to Chile in 1884
Territory gained from Chile in 1929
Loss of Acre in 1899
Territory gained from Ecuador by 1942
Chilean invasion of Lima 1881–1884
① War of the Pacific with Chile 1879–1884
② Border conflicts with Ecuador

Today

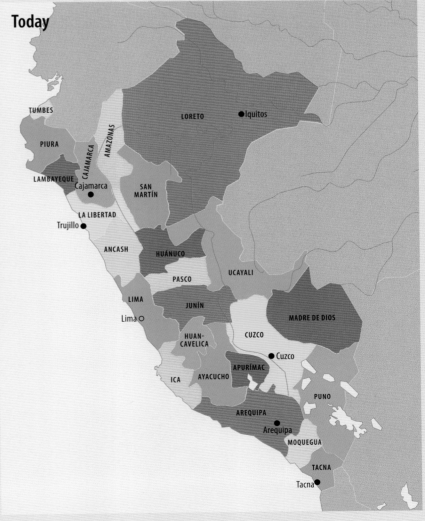

José Gabriel Condorcanqui (Tupac Amaru II, 1742–1781) A self-declared descendant of the Inca aristocracy, he led the largest insurgency of indigenous people in the history of the Americas.

Nicolás de Pierola (1839–1913) First as finance minister and then as president of Peru from 1895–1899 he introduced democratic and economic reforms.

Juan Velasco Alvarada (1909–1977) This general and dictator led the military junta from 1968–1975.

Acre The province belonged to Bolivia, but had long been settled by Brazilians. Bolivia's attempt to nationalize the culture led to uprisings. With support from the Brazilian military, Acre declared itself an independent republic in 1899. Bolivia responded with military occupation of the region from 1900 to 1903. Acre declared independence again in 1903, but formally attached itself to Brazil within months. The Treaty of Petropolis compensated Bolivia for the loss of territory and railway rights that gave the landlocked nation access to important trade ports. Acre became a federal state of Brazil in 1962.

Bolivia

600–1000: Golden Age

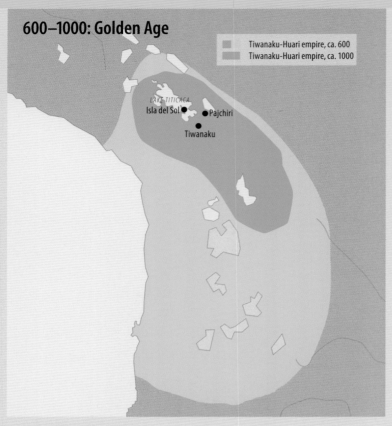

Tiwanaku-Huari empire, ca. 600
Tiwanaku-Huari empire, ca. 1000

LAKE TITICACA
Isla del Sol
Pajchiri
Tiwanaku

1537–1788: Spanish Colonies

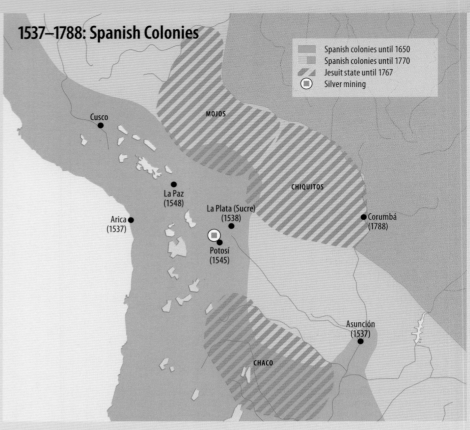

Spanish colonies until 1650
Spanish colonies until 1770
Jesuit state until 1767
Silver mining

MOJOS
Cusco
CHIQUITOS
La Paz (1548)
La Plata (Sucre) (1538)
Corumbá (1788)
Arica (1537)
Potosí (1545)
Asunción (1537)
CHACO

Bolivia was long an abundant source of silver for the Spanish empire. Territorial conflicts with neighboring states and a series of military coups marked the 19th and 20th centuries. Socialist Evo Moralaes has been president of Bolivia since 2006.

~600 Zenith of the Tiahuanaco culture around Lake Titicaca

from 800 The Tiahuanaco state disintegrates.

1460 The Inca conquer the territory around Lake Titicaca.

1538 Spanish troops conquer the region, making it part of the Viceroyalty of Peru.

1545 Discovery of silver

1825 Bolivia is liberated by Simón Bolívar.

1836–1839 The Peru-Bolivian Confederation forms. It falls apart during a war with Chile; Bolivia reclaims independence.

1869 Part of the Amazon rainforest is ceded to Brazil.

1879–1883 War of the Pacific (Saltpeter War): Bolivia loses its coastal territory to Chile.

1880 Period of unrest by indigenous peoples begins.

1903 The rubber-producing region of Acre is ceded to Brazil.

1932–1935 A territorial war is fought against Paraguay.

1953 Mines are nationalized and agrarian reforms begin.

1964 President Victor Paz Estenssoro is overthrown in a military coup.

1971–1978 Military dictatorship under General Hugo Banzer Suárez

1982 End of rule by military juntas

1992 Peru grants Bolivia the port of Ilo on the Pacific Coast.

2005 Evo Morales is the first socialist president and the first Bolivian of indigenous descent to hold a major political office. His aggressive land and social reform alienates many non-indigenous Bolivians.

Antonio José de Sucre (1795–1830) was a fighter for South American independence and a close confidant of Simón Bolívar. He defeated the Spanish on several occasions in 1824. He was the first president of Bolivia from 1826 to 1828, and was assassinated in 1830 before he could succeed Bolívar as leader of the liberation movement in South America.

Victor Paz Estenssoro (1907–2001) Father of the the Bolivian National Revolution, he was president from 1952 to 1956, 1960 to 1964 and again 1985 to 1989 after overthrowing the military junta. His nationalist-liberal policies met with some resistance. He was overthrown (1964) or voted out of office (1956, 1989) before most of these policies could be implemented.

Hugo Banzer Suárez (1926–2002) This general led a successful coup in 1971, establishing a military dictatorship with fascist overtones that remained in power until 1978. Elected president from 1997 to 2002, his term was marked by right-wing politics and an attempt to combat coca cultivation.

Evo Morales (1959–) An indigenous socialist leader and fighter for the rights of coca farmers, he won a surprisingly resounding victory in the presidential elections of 2005. As president, in 2006 he began with immediate, rigorous social reforms and comprehensive land distribution, which led to unrest in some provinces.

1824–1884: Struggle for Independence and Territorial Wars

Lima
Ayacucho 1824
La Paz
Arica
Chuquisaca (Sucre)
Potosí
Antofagasta

Bolivia since 1825
Territory lost in 1884
Territory lost in 1874
Territory of Paraguay, gained in 1874
Disputed region of Acre
Campaign of Bolívar 1824–1826
Campaign of de Sucre in 1824
Declaration of independence
Important battle

1900 to the Present

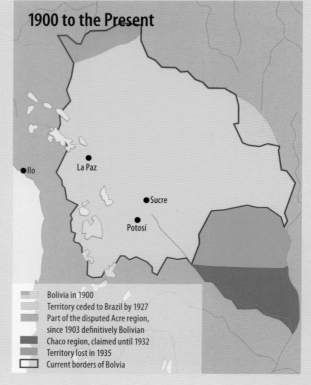

Ilo
La Paz
Sucre
Potosí

Bolivia in 1900
Territory ceded to Brazil by 1927
Part of the disputed Acre region, since 1903 definitively Bolivian
Chaco region, claimed until 1932
Territory lost in 1935
Current borders of Bolivia

Inca

Thirty percent of the population of Bolivia traces descent to the Incas, with smaller percentages in the countries of Peru, Chile, Argentina and Uruguay. The great civilizations of the New World were very different from those of the Old World. The Incas never invented the wheel and did not raise cattle. Although they understood metallurgy, they did not make iron or steel tools. Spanish conquistadors recognized their expert agricultural techniques, exporting native crops such as maize, cacao, potatoes, tomatoes, chili peppers, pineapples and peanuts to the rest of the world.

Carib

The Carib were a loosely affiliated group of related tribes living along the northern coast of South America in what is now Colombia and Venezuela. They were the first native group to come into contact with Europeans. Today, barely a trace of their existence remains.

Chibcha (Muisca)

The Chibcha, also called the Muisca, ruled an empire centered on the central Columbian plateau for at least a century before first European contact. They grew potatoes and maize, supplementing their crops with hunting and fishing. Their round houses were made of wood. They are famous for their ritual use of gold.

Quechua

Quechua refers to a language family spoken by a variety of native groups, including the Incas, who used it as a lingua franca that could be understood anywhere in the Inca Empire. It remains an important language today in Peru, Ecuador and Bolivia.

Chimú

The Chimú ruled a coastal territory known as Chimor (now Peru) between 1250 and 1460. This powerful state was made up primarily of maize farmers working in fields that were irrigated by a complex system of canals. Their efforts to expand further south were stopped by the Incas, who defeated the Chimú and laid waste to their kingdom.

Araucanian

This group of peoples, sometimes collectively called Mapuche, comes from the southern part of the continent (modern-day Chile and Argentina). They farm and raise llamas, and since contact with the Spanish in the 16th century, horses as well. The office of chief is hereditary.

Mapuche

The Mapuche are one of the Araucanian peoples, inhabiting the western Andes and part of the Pacific coast of what is now Chile. They moved into the area as late as the 17th century, and resisted Spanish rule into the late 19th century.

Aymara

The Aymara are the indigenous inhabitants of the high Andes region, which straddles the countries of Bolivia, Peru, Chile and Argentina. Most of their territory was absorbed into the Inca Empire at the end of the 15th century. They were most famous for their cultivation of the coca leaf, which is the plant used to make the narcotic cocaine. Bolivian president Evo Morales is an Aymara.

Guaraní

The Guaraní are an ethnic group native to what are now Paraguay, Argentina, southern Brazil, Uruguay and Bolivia. They were primarily farmers, with an animist religion. Many Guaraní fell prey to European slave traders in the early years of contact.

Tupí

Related to the Guaraní, the Tupí were native to the rainforests of Brazil, where they had lived for centuries before the coming of Europeans. They were the first native tribe to come in contact with the Portuguese. Many sub-groups of Tupí continue to exist in a near-constant state of warfare with each another.

Xavante

Some 10,000 Xavante still live in the Brazilian state of Mato Grosso. After an early period of devastating contact period with Europeans seeking to enslave them, the Xavante retreated deep into the rain forest and quite successfully avoided all contact with the outside world; contact was only reestablished in the 1930s. Their complex spiritual life includes ritual piercing with wooden sticks as part of an initiation ceremony for young males.

Warao

The Warao lived along the Orinoco River in what is now northeastern Venezuela and Guyana. Their traditional housing consists of tall wooden platforms set on pilings to raise floors above the level of the seasonal floods that occur in the valley. They travel the river using dugout canoes.

Puelche

The Puelche are the indigenous population of what is now Argentina. The language and culture have nearly completely died out.

Pano

The Pano language was spoken by natives living in what are now Peru, western Brazil, Bolivia, and northern Paraguay.

Tehuelche

The Tehuelche have lived in what is now Patagonia, southern Argentina, for over 12,500 years as nomadic hunter-gatherers. Early European explorers described their gigantic size, which is now considered an exaggeration.

Language families of the indigenous peoples
- Aymara
- Tupian-Guaraní
- Cariban
- Je
- Chibchan
- Quechuan
- Maipurean
- Pano-Tacanan
- Others

Agricultural peoples
Andes civilizations

Brazil

1500–1616: Arrival of the Portuguese

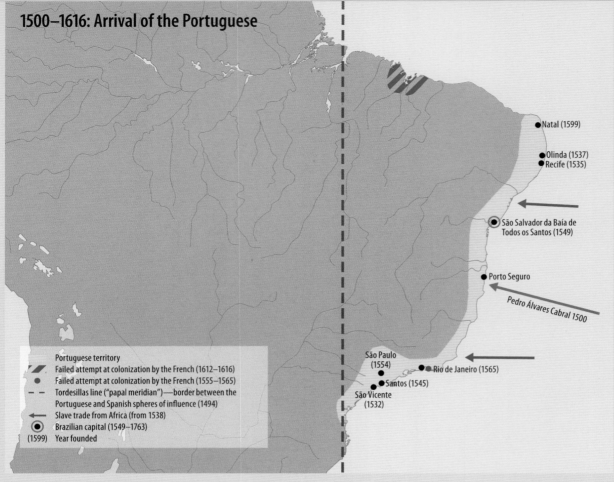

- Natal (1599)
- Olinda (1537)
- Recife (1535)
- São Salvador da Baía de Todos os Santos (1549)
- Porto Seguro
- Pedro Álvares Cabral 1500
- São Paulo (1554)
- Rio de Janeiro (1565)
- Santos (1545)
- São Vicente (1532)

Legend:
- Portuguese territory
- Failed attempt at colonization by the French (1612–1616)
- Failed attempt at colonization by the French (1555–1565)
- Tordesillas line ("papal meridian")—border between the Portuguese and Spanish spheres of influence (1494)
- Slave trade from Africa (from 1538)
- ◉ Brazilian capital (1549–1763)
- (1599) Year founded

1613–1680: Portuguese Colonies I

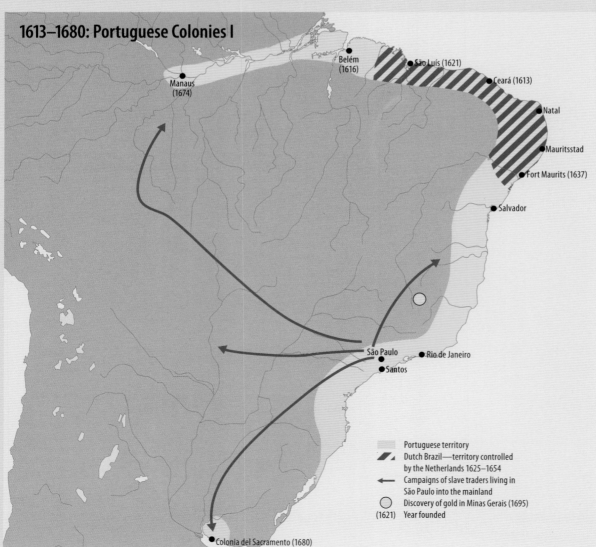

- Manaus (1674)
- Belém (1616)
- São Luís (1621)
- Ceará (1613)
- Natal
- Mauritsstad
- Fort Maurits (1637)
- Salvador
- São Paulo
- Rio de Janeiro
- Santos
- Colonia del Sacramento (1680)

Legend:
- Portuguese territory
- Dutch Brazil—territory controlled by the Netherlands 1625–1654
- Campaigns of slave traders living in São Paulo into the mainland
- ◯ Discovery of gold in Minas Gerais (1695)
- (1621) Year founded

In 1494 vast areas in the eastern part of South America were ceded to Portugal in the Treaty of Tordesillas with Spain. In the centuries that followed, the Portuguese were able to successfully ward off French and Dutch settlement of their land. Brazil gained its independence, in part because Prince Pedro of Portugal refused to return to the mother country and in 1822 was crowned emperor of Brazil.

10,000 BCE First inhabited cave sites in the Amazon Basin

1500 CE The Portuguese explorer Álvares Pedro Cabral discovers Brazil. He lands at Porto Seguro, where the Tupí Indians offer no resistance. The Portuguese keep the discovery of the new continent a secret until 1507.

1530 Portuguese colonization begins. The name Brazil comes fromm pau-brasil (ember wood), the Portuguese name for brazilwood trees, which have a reddish gloss when polished.

1538 Arrival of the first African slaves. Many of the indigenous peoples forced to work on plantations die of disease or commit suicide.

1549 Bahia becomes the capital of all fifteen *capitanias* (administrative districts) in Brazil.

1554 Founding of the city of São Paulo

1555 The French establish a colony in the Bay of Guanabara, which

1565 the Portuguese destroy a decade later. Rio de Janeiro is founded the same year.

1625 The Dutch occupy Salvador de Bahia.

1629 The Dutch establish a firm foothold in Mauritsstad, now called Recife.

1630–1694 Black fugitives from slavery found *quilombos*, settlements with up to 30,000 inhabitants, in the northeastern Brazilian state of Alagoas. The quilombos are able to resist Portuguese attacks until 1694.

1654 Treaty with the Netherlands: the Dutch leave Brazil.

1680 The Portuguese establish Colonia do Sacramento on the Rio de la Plata in present-day Uruguay.

1695 Gold is discovered in Minas Gerais.

1727 Beginning of large-scale coffee cultivation

1759 The Jesuits are expelled from Brazil.

1763 Rio de Janeiro becomes the capital.

1777 Treaty with Spain settles border disputes.

1792 Execution of Tiradentes, a rebel leader who opposed Portuguese rule

1808–1821 Portuguese King John VI flees to Brazil to escape Napoleon.

1815 Brazil declares itself an empire.

1822 Prince Pedro, son of King John VI, refuses to return to Portugal. He declares Brazilian independence and becomes emperor.

1825–1827 War with Argentina leads to the loss of what is now Uruguay. Border disputes continue into the 20th century.

1831–1889 Emperor Pedro II of Brazil, son of Pedro I, tries to modernize the country. His opposition to slavery makes him unpopular at home, but welcome in Europe, where he travels frequently to enhance Brazil's reputation internationally.

Martim Afonso de Sousa (1500–1564) Portuguese navigator, leader of the first colonial expedition to Brazil.

Mem de Sa (1500–1572) As the third governor general of Brazil, he drove the French from the Bay of Guanabara.

Martim Afonso de Sousa, ca. 1558

Pedro Teixeira (? –1640) was a Portuguese explorer who led the first Amazon expedition in 1637.

John VI (1767–1826) King of Portugal and ally of Great Britain, he fled to Brazil during the Napoleonic Wars after refusing to rule as a subordinate of Napoleon.

Pedro I (1798–1834) Portuguese prince who refused to return to the mother country. He declared Brazil's independence and was crowned its first emperor in 1822. He could not fulfill the enormous hopes placed in him and abdicated in 1831.

Pedro II (1825–1891) Son of Pedro I, he inherited the throne as a child in 1831 and was declared of legal age to rule in 1840, although he was not yet fifteen. Highly educated and capable, he made an enormous effort to modernize Brazil through the promotion of science and technology. He was not able to realize the abolition of slavery, a matter near to his heart, until 1888. This incited the hatred of wealthy landowners and led to his overthrow in 1889.

Last Portrait of Emperor Pedro I, Simplício Rodrigues de Sá, ca. 1830

1750–1800: Portuguese Colonies II

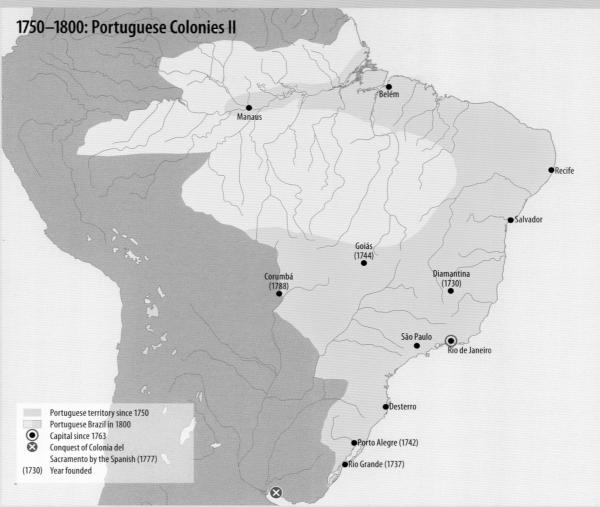

- Manaus
- Belém
- Recife
- Salvador
- Goiás (1744)
- Diamantina (1730)
- Corumbá (1788)
- São Paulo
- Rio de Janeiro
- Desterro
- Porto Alegre (1742)
- Rio Grande (1737)

Portuguese territory since 1750
Portuguese Brazil in 1800
⊙ Capital since 1763
⊗ Conquest of Colonia del Sacramento by the Spanish (1777)
(1730) Year founded

1822–1828: Fight for Independence

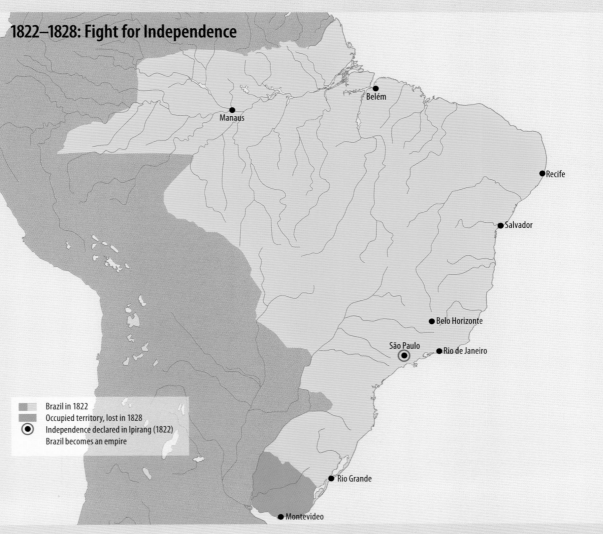

- Manaus
- Belém
- Recife
- Salvador
- Belo Horizonte
- São Paulo
- Rio de Janeiro
- Rio Grande
- Montevideo

Brazil in 1822
Occupied territory, lost in 1828
⊙ Independence declared in Ipirang (1822)
Brazil becomes an empire

451

Brazil

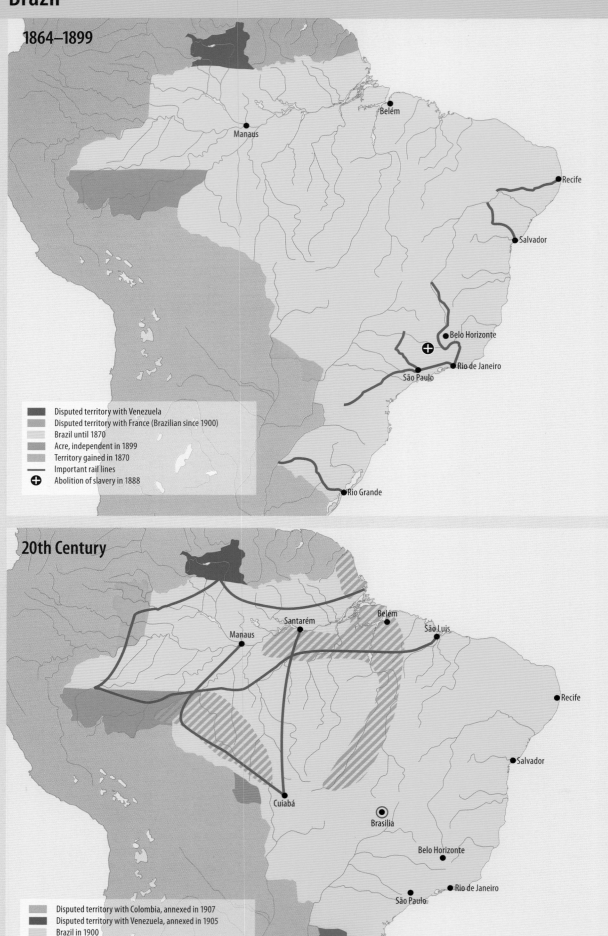

1864–1899

- Disputed territory with Venezuela
- Disputed territory with France (Brazilian since 1900)
- Brazil until 1870
- Acre, independent in 1899
- Territory gained in 1870
- Important rail lines
- ⊕ Abolition of slavery in 1888

Manaus
Belém
Recife
Salvador
Belo Horizonte
Rio de Janeiro
São Paulo
Rio Grande

20th Century

- Disputed territory with Colombia, annexed in 1907
- Disputed territory with Venezuela, annexed in 1905
- Brazil in 1900
- Acre, annexed in 1903
- Areas of deforestation in the Amazon
- Territory gained from Bolivia (1927)
- Territory gained from Argentina (1927)
- Trans-Amazonian highways
- ◉ New capital of Brasilia (1960)

Manaus
Santarém
Belém
São Luís
Recife
Salvador
Cuiabá
Brasília
Belo Horizonte
Rio de Janeiro
São Paulo
Rio Grande

Like other Latin American countries, the land so well known for coffee, samba and soccer has also been plagued by dictatorships and military juntas. After 1985 Brazil embarked on the path to democracy. The greatest problems Brazil faces today are poverty and violence in the *favelas*, sprawling shanty towns found on the outskirts of major cities.

1835–1845 Cattle breeders in the Rio Grande do Sul rebel against cheaper meats imported from Argentina and Uruguay.

1865–1870 In alliance with Argentina and Uruguay, Brazil defeats Paraguay in a war over disputed territory.

1888 Slavery is abolished, and mass immigration begins.

1889 Pedro II is overthrown. Brazil becomes a republic.

1895 Treaty with Argentina settles border disputes.

1917 Brazil opposes Germany in World War I.

1930 Getúlio Dornelles Vargas comes to power following an uprising.

1937 Vargas establishes a dictatorship, and an economic boom ensues.

1942 German U-boats sink Brazilian merchant vessels. Brazil declares war on the Axis Powers.

1945 Vargas is overthrown in a military coup.

1950 Vargas is reelected president. He lays the groundwork for the nationalized oil firm Petrobras, the largest company in Latin America.

1954 Vargas's isolationist policies worsen Brazil's precarious economy. When the military turns against him, he commits suicide.

1960 Brasilia becomes the capital of Brazil. The city is planned and developed in 1956 with Oscar Niemeyer as the principal architect.

1961 Introduction of a parliamentary system of government

1962 Following a referendum, Brazil changes from a parliamentary to a presidential system.

1964–1985 Military juntas rule the country.

2003 Inauguration of leftist President Luiz Inácio Lula da Silva, followed by a major economic upturn

Getúlio Dornelles Vargas (1882–1954) President of Brazil from 1930 to 1945 and 1950 to 1954, his "benevolent dictatorship," which had some fascist elements, instituted a broad program of social and economic reforms. Threatened by a military coup, he committed suicide in 1954.

Juscelino Kubitschek (1902–1976) A center-left president from 1956 to 1961, he integrated Brazil into the global economy. The new capital of Brasilia was his brainchild. Designed by Oscar Niemeyer, the centrally located city in Brazil's green plateau region was formally dedicated in 1960.

Kubitschek monument in front of the Palace of Justice in Brasilia.

Fernando Color de Mello (1949–) In 1990 he became the first directly elected president. In 1992 he avoided impeachment for corruption by resigning before the end of his term; he was later exonerated.

Favelas are slums made up of rudimentary huts located on the outskirts of most Brazilian cities. They have no sewage system, and usually no electricity other than what can be illegally diverted from power lines. Most were founded in the 19th century by freed slaves. Crime, disease and lack of hygiene are major problems.

Rio de Janeiro

1502 Arrival of the first Portuguese

1565 Founding of the city, which becomes the capital in 1763.

1808–1822 Rio is now the capital of the entire Portuguese Empire.

1931 Construction of Christ the Redeemer, a statue that has become the symbol of Rio.

Rio de Janeiro: Christ the Redeemer atop Sugar-loaf Mountain near the Bay of Guanabara.

Brazil Today

RORAIMA
AMAPÁ
Santarém
Belém
São Luís
Manaus
Fortaleza • RIO GRANDE DO NORTE
AMAZONAS
PARÁ
MARANHÃO
CEARÁ
Natal •
PARAIBA
PIAUÍ
PERNAMBUCO
Recife •
ACRE
ALAGOAS
SERGIPE
RONDÔNIA
TOCANTINS
BAHIA
MATO GROSSO
Salvador •
FEDERAL DISTRICT
Brasília
GOIÁS
Goiânia •
MINAS GERAIS
MATO GROSSO DO SUL
ESPÍRITO SANTO
Belo Horizonte •
Campo Grande •
RIO DE JANEIRO
SÃO PAULO
Rio de Janeiro •
São Paulo •
PARANÁ
Curitiba •
SANTA CATARINA
Florianópolis •
RIO GRANDE DO SUL
Rio Grande •

Rio de Janeiro in 1900

Magé
GUANABARA BAY
São Gonçalo
Niterói
Santa Cruz
Corcovado ▲   ▲ Sugarloaf Mountain
Copacabana

0   6 mi/10 km

Rio de Janeiro Today

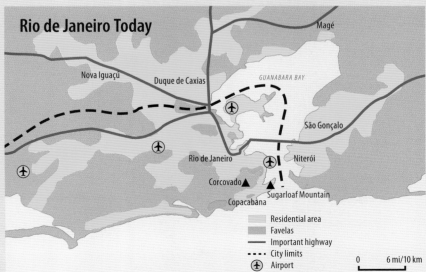

Magé
Nova Iguaçú   Duque de Caxias   GUANABARA BAY
São Gonçalo
Rio de Janeiro   Niterói
Corcovado ▲   ▲ Sugarloaf Mountain
Copacabana

Residential area
Favelas
Important highway
City limits
✈ Airport

0   6 mi/10 km

Uruguay

1600–1800: Spanish and Portuguese Colonies

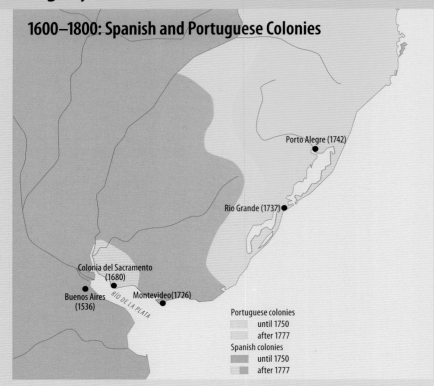

Porto Alegre (1742)

Rio Grande (1737)

Colonia del Sacramento (1680)

Buenos Aires (1536)

Montevideo (1726)

RIO DE LA PLATA

Portuguese colonies
    until 1750
    after 1777
Spanish colonies
    until 1750
    after 1777

19th Century

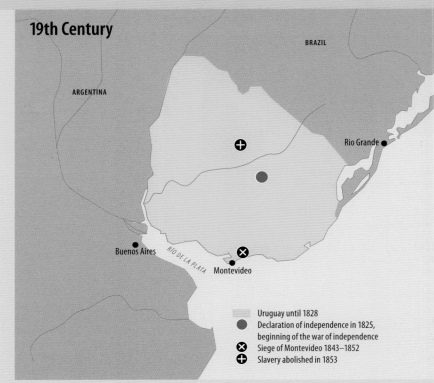

BRAZIL

ARGENTINA

Rio Grande

Buenos Aires

RIO DE LA PLATA

Montevideo

Uruguay until 1828
Declaration of independence in 1825, beginning of the war of independence
Siege of Montevideo 1843–1852
Slavery abolished in 1853

The formerly Portuguese territory of Uruguay passed into Spanish hands in the 18th century. Following the Swedish model, Uruguay developed into one of the first social welfare states in Latin America, with correspondingly high tax rates.

1516 During his exploration of the Rio de la Plata, navigator Juan Diaz de Solis is killed by indigenous people.

1726 The Spanish found the city of Montevideo and take over the territory of Uruguay from the Portuguese.

1807 The British occupy Montevideo.

1808 The La Plata Viceroyalty revolts. The Spanish Viceroyalty is driven out of Buenos Aires.

1811 Montevideo replaces Buenos Aires as the center of loyalty to the Spanish monarchy. Uruguayan national hero José Gervasio Artigas organizes opposition to Spanish rule as well as the subsequent campaign against Argentina. A long struggle for independence begins.

1812–1827 War with Portugal is followed by wars with Brazil and Argentina. Parts of Uruguay gain independence, but the rest is occupied by Portuguese and Brazilian troops.

1825 Uruguay declares independence.

1828 Convention of Rio de Janeiro between Argentina and Brazil. The Brazilians withdraw from Uruguay, which gains full independence.

1830 Uruguay ratifies its first democratic constitution.

1831 Massacre of native Charruas at Salsipuedes Creek.

1838–1865 Civil war between conservatives and liberals

1843–1852 Siege of Montevideo: Argentina occupies most of Uruguay.

1850 The Charruas cease to exist as a people.

1865–1870 War of the Triple Alliance: Uruguay, Argentina and Brazil unite against Paraguay.

1876–1890 The country modernizes under a military junta.

1903–1915 José Batlle y Ordóñez establishes a welfare state.

1930 Uruguay, the host country, wins the first Soccer World Cup (FIFA championships), beating neighboring Argentina. It will win its second World Cup in 1950 against Brazil.

1945 Uruguay declares war on Germany and Japan.

1973–1984 Military dictatorship and guerilla wars

1985 Return to democracy

2006 The Argentine-Uruguayan conflict breaks out when Argentine environmentalists object to Uruguay's plans to build two large pulp paper mills on the Uruguayan side of the Rio Uruguay.

José Gervasio Artigas (1764–1850) organized a "revolution of the poor" against Spain (1811–1814) and later against Argentina (1814–1820). After his defeat, he was forced into exile in Paraguay in 1820.

José Fructuoso Rivera (1789–1854) drove the Brazilians out of Uruguay. He twice served as president of Uruguay (1830–1834 and 1839–1843) and was a member of a ruling triumvirate from 1853–1854.

José Batlle y Ordóñez (1856–1929) created the Uruguayan social welfare state. He served as president from 1903–1907 and 1911–1915, combining remarkable social reforms with "Batllismo," the name give to his strict economic policies and successful educational policies. His family has produced three additional presidents, Jorge Batlle Ibáñez being the most recent (2000–2005).

Today

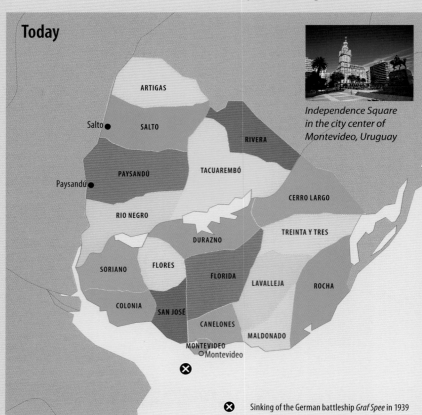

ARTIGAS

Salto

SALTO

RIVERA

PAYSANDÚ

TACUAREMBÓ

Paysandú

CERRO LARGO

RIO NEGRO

TREINTA Y TRES

DURAZNO

SORIANO

FLORES

FLORIDA

LAVALLEJA

ROCHA

COLONIA

SAN JOSÉ

CANELONES

MALDONADO

MONTEVIDEO
Montevideo

Independence Square in the city center of Montevideo, Uruguay

Sinking of the German battleship *Graf Spee* in 1939

José Batlle y Ordóñez

Paraguay

After Paraguay gained its independence, it lost a large part of its territory in the 19th-century War of the Triple Alliance. In the 20th century, dictator Alfredo Stroessner ruled the country for more than three decades.

~1500   Tupi Guarani and Arawaks live in Paraguay.

1524   Alejo Garcia travels eastward through the Gran Chaco.

1537   Juan de Salazary Espinosa founds Asunción.

1542   Paraguay becomes part of the Viceroyalty of Peru.

~1604   Founding of the first Jesuit Reductions

1776   Paraguay is now part of the Viceroyalty of La Plata.

1811   Paraguay becomes an independent nation.

1814–1840   Dictatorship under Jose Gaspar Rodriguez de Francia

1844–1862   Military dictatorship under Carlos Antonio Lopez

1862–1874   A reign of terror by Lopez's son, Francisco Solano Lopez, leads to declaration of war on Argentina, Brazil and Uruguay (War of the Triple Alliance). By war's end, Paraguay has lost more than half its territory and as much as two-thirds of its population.

1932–1935   War with Bolivia results in Paraguay's doubling its territory.

1939–1947   Paraguay is under military rule.

1954   Alfredo Stroessner leads a military coup. His fascist dictatorship receives the support of the United States.

1989   General Andres Rodriguez overthrows General Stroessner, leading to a democratic revival.

1992   A democratic constitution is adopted.

1998   General Oviedo Silva's military coup fails. The new president, Raul Cubas Grau, pardons Silva, triggering a constitutional crisis.

1999   Vice President Luis Maria Argana, a critic of the regime, is shot dead in Asunción. President Cubas Grau is removed from office and flees to Brazil. Silva flees to Argentina, which refuses to extradite him, resulting in the breakoff of diplomatic relations.

2000   Failed coup by Silva partisans

~2004   The tri-border area of Paraguay, Brazil and Argentina is repeatedly suspected of harboring Muslim terrorists.

2008   Fernando Lugo, a former Roman Catholic bishop, is elected president.

1600–1767: Jesuit State

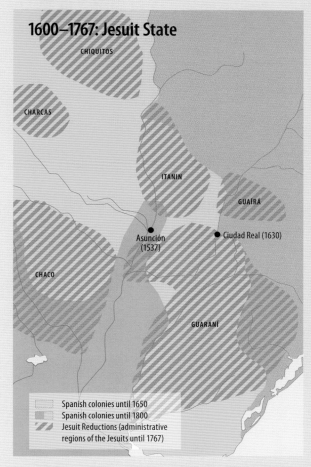

Spanish colonies until 1650
Spanish colonies until 1800
Jesuit Reductions (administrative regions of the Jesuits until 1767)

20th Century

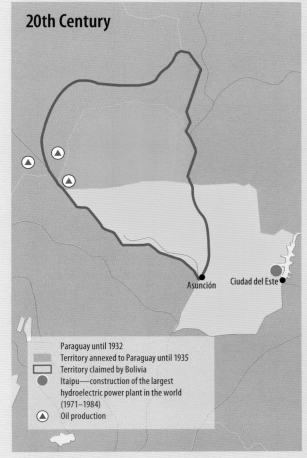

Paraguay until 1932
Territory annexed to Paraguay until 1935
Territory claimed by Bolivia
Itaipu—construction of the largest hydroelectric power plant in the world (1971–1984)
Oil production

Jesuit state in Paraguay

Beginning around 1604, the Jesuit order in Paraguay founded self-governing "reductions." These were settlements intended to protect indigenous peoples from the slave trade, annexation by large land owners and other ills. From 1610 onward they took on state-like structures. The reductions supported themselves very successfully by planting grain, sugar, tea and cotton. They were popular throughout South America, but the majority were in Paraguay. The Jesuits were driven out by the Spanish in 1767, and the reductions were abolished.

José Gaspar Rodriguez de Francia (1766–1840) led Paraguay's fight for independence from Spain. He ruled as a dictator from 1814 to 1820, observing rigorous nationalism and forcing the remaining Spaniards to intermarry with indigenous peoples. Francia also banned foreigners from his country.

Alfredo Stroessner (1912–2006) Brigadier general of German extraction who came to power in 1954 via a putsch. With the aid of the United States, he established one of the longest running dictatorships in Latin American history, a dictatorship characterized by many fascist elements. He was overthrown in 1989 and went into exile in Brazil.

Andrés Rodriguez (1923–1997) was a general and army commander. A longstanding confidant of Stroessner, he overthrew him in 1989 and, during his presidency (1989–1993), oversaw democratic reforms and free elections.

19th Century

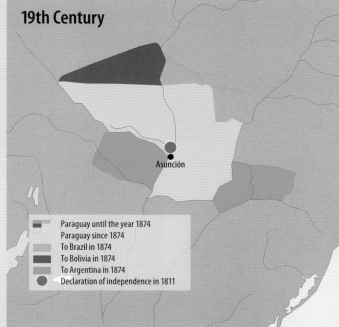

Paraguay until the year 1874
Paraguay since 1874
To Brazil in 1874
To Bolivia in 1874
To Argentina in 1874
Declaration of independence in 1811

Uruguay Today

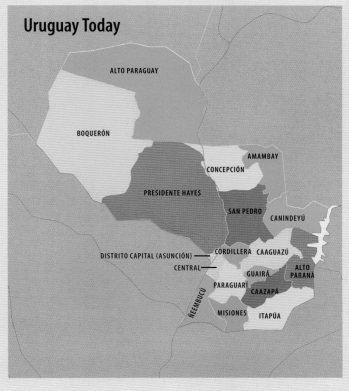

ALTO PARAGUAY
BOQUERÓN
PRESIDENTE HAYES
AMAMBAY
CONCEPCIÓN
SAN PEDRO
CANINDEYÚ
DISTRITO CAPITAL (ASUNCIÓN)
CENTRAL
CORDILLERA   CAAGUAZÚ
GUAIRÁ
ALTO PARANÁ
PARAGUARÍ
CAAZAPÁ
ÑEEMBUCÚ
MISIONES   ITAPÚA

Chile

1550: Arrival of the Spanish

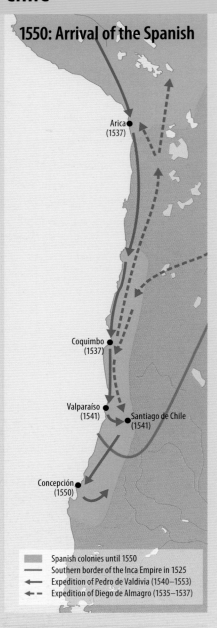

Spanish colonies until 1550
Southern border of the Inca Empire in 1525
Expedition of Pedro de Valdivia (1540–1553)
Expedition of Diego de Almagro (1535–1537)

Arica (1537)
Coquimbo (1537)
Valparaíso (1541)
Santiago de Chile (1541)
Concepción (1550)

Easter Island (Rapa Nui)

Located some 2,000 miles (3500 km) from Chile and 2,600 miles (4250 km) from Tahiti, it is one of the most isolated islands in the world. It is famous for its moai, colossal sculptures made from volcanic rock (ca. 1250–1500 CE). The culture that produced them seems to have been destroyed by internal warfare. Europeans arrived to find toppled moai and inscriptions in rongorongo, a script that remains indecipherable. The islanders

Hanga Roa

Moais
Birdman cult

followed a "birdman" cult with rituals that involved collecting bird eggs by swimming to a small islet through difficult currents, then safely swimming them back to the main island, ending with a difficult climb up a steep cliff. It is said that the one who achieved this without breaking an egg qualified as the island's next ruler. Dutch explorer Jakob Roggeveen discovered the island on Easter Sunday, 1772.

1650: Spanish Colonies I

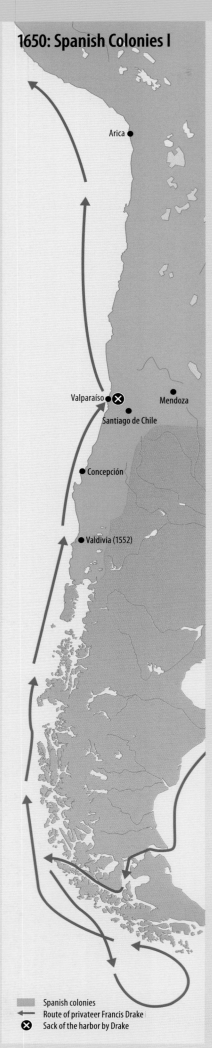

Arica
Valparaíso
Santiago de Chile
Mendoza
Concepción
Valdivia (1552)

Spanish colonies
Route of privateer Francis Drake
Sack of the harbor by Drake

Chile is one of the most stable and prosperous

Chile is one of the most stable and prosperous countries in Latin America. Unlike its neighbors, Chile was largely spared from civil wars and military coups, with the exception of General Pinochet's seventeen-year reign.

1520 Portuguese explorer Ferdinand Magellan discovers the straits that will bear his name.

1541 The Spanish conquistadors found the city of Santiago de Chile.

1647 Santiago de Chile is destroyed by an earthquake.

1779 The province of Cuyo becomes part of the Viceroyalty of La Plata.

1798 Chile becomes an independent administrative district of Peru.

1810 Beginning of patriotic resistance to Spanish rule

1817–1818 Final victory over pro-Spanish royalists brings independence. Bernardo O'Higgins becomes president.

1833–1891 Adoption of a new constitution leads to an authoritarian Conservative Party government in which the president has absolute veto power.

1879–1884 Chile defeats Peru and Bolivia during the War of the Pacific, also known as the Saltpeter War.

1880 Subjugation of the previously independent indigenous Araucanian population

1891 Around 6,000 die in a civil war.

1891–1915 Parliamentary government

1902 British king Edward VII intervenes in a territorial dispute between Chile and Argentina; the borders of Patagonia and Tierra del Fuego are redrawn.

1914–1945 Chile remains neutral in both World Wars.

1916 Chile reestablishes presidential government and direct elections.

1927–1931 Dictatorship under Carlos Ibáñez del Campo

1929 Border treaty with Peru

1931 An economic crisis sends Ibáñez into exile.

1938–1946 Rule by a left-wing coalition including the Chilean communist party.

1952–1958 Carlos Ibáñez del Campo becomes president for a second time.

1961 The notorious Colonia Dignidad cult, accused of hiding Nazis, is founded.

1964–1970 Advent of social reforms under President Eduardo Frei, a Christian Democrat.

1800: Spanish Colonies II

Arica
❶
Valparaíso
❷ Santiago de Chile
San Carlos de Ancud (1763)

Spanish colonies
Viceroyalty of Peru
Viceroyalty of the Río de la Plata
Captaincy General of Chile
❶ Sailor Alexander Selkirk was abandoned on the Juan Fernández Islands in 1704—inspiration for Daniel Defoe's *Robinson Crusoe*
❷ Founding of the university in Santiago de Chile (1747)

1970 Socialist Salvador Allende takes office as president.

1973 Allende is killed in a coup led by Chilean General Pinochet. United States support for the junta leads to suspicions of CIA involvement.

1979–1985 Conflict with Argentina over the Beagle Channel is resolved through papal intervention.

1984 End of martial law

1990 Pinochet loses in democratic elections.

1998 Pinochet resigns as commanding general.

2006 Socialist Michelle Bachelet is elected president.

Bernardo O'Higgins (1778–1842) began the Chilean fight for independence in 1810, becoming commander of the liberation army in 1813. His well-disciplined troops repeatedly defeated the Spanish forces, leading to the collapse of colonial rule. He held the title of supreme dictator from 1817 until 1823, when he was overthrown. He spent the rest of his life in exile in Peru.

Diego Portales Palazuelos (1793–1837) was a tobacco merchant and politician. As leader of the conservatives, he overthrew the government in 1830 and ruled as a dictator until 1831. He remained in the background thereafter, but remained a powerful figure. In addition, Palazuelos authored the

1820: The Fight for Independence

Chile in 1818
→ Campaign of San Martín
↞ Campaign of O´Higgins
◉ Declaration of independence 2/12/1818
✚ Slavery abolished in 1823
✖ Victory

authoritarian presidential constitution of 1833. He was assassinated in 1837.

Salvador Allende (1908–1973) trained as a medical doctor before running for president in 1964. He won in 1969 as a member of the Popular Unity Party, and began a program of comprehensive economic and social reform. His nationalization policies brought him into direct conflict with the United States, which compared Allende's government to that of communist Cuba. Allende was killed during a rightest coup led by General Pinochet. CIA involvement has long been suspected.

Augusto Pinochet (1915–2006) was a general and commander of the Chilean army. In 1973 he led a coup against Salvador Allende and began seventeen years of military dictatorship. The ruling junta is thought to have executed thousands of opposition supporters, forcing many thousands more into exile. In 1988 he called a referendum on his rule and was surprised when he lost. He fled to England, where he lived under house arrest from 1998–2000 before being deported to Chile for war crimes. Convicted, he was judged too ill to withstand imprisonment; he died shortly thereafter.

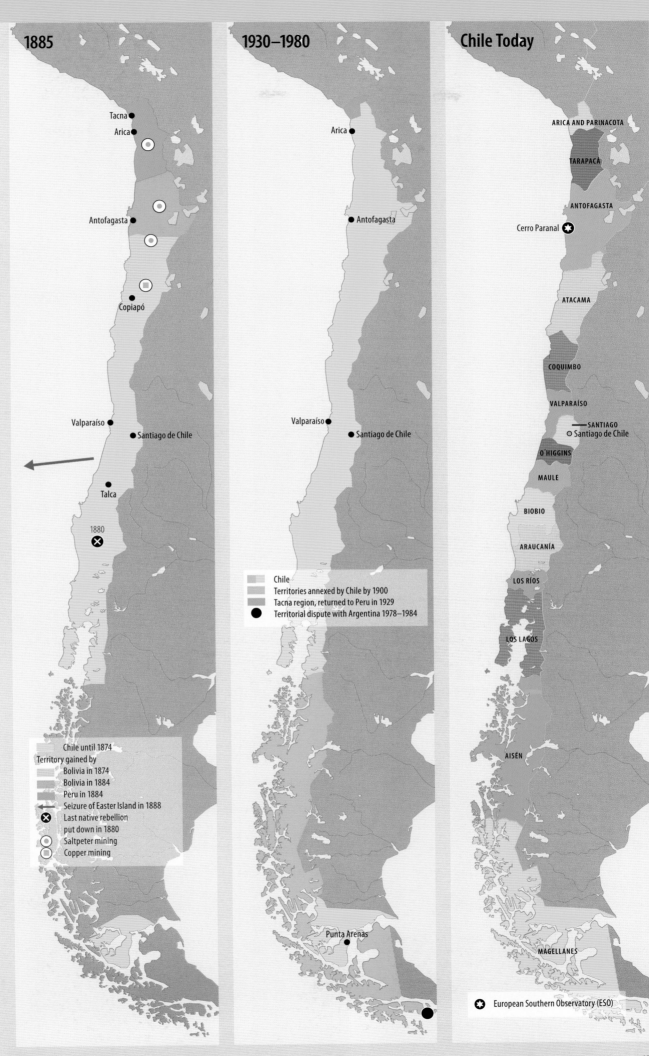

1885

Tacna
Arica
Antofagasta
Copiapó
Valparaíso
Santiago de Chile
Talca
1880 ✖

Chile until 1874
Territory gained by
Bolivia in 1874
Bolivia in 1884
Peru in 1884
Seizure of Easter Island in 1888
✖ Last native rebellion put down in 1880
◉ Saltpeter mining
▣ Copper mining

1930–1980

Arica
Antofagasta
Valparaíso
Santiago de Chile
Punta Arenas

Chile
Territories annexed by Chile by 1900
Tacna region, returned to Peru in 1929
● Territorial dispute with Argentina 1978–1984

Chile Today

ARICA AND PARINACOTA
TARAPACÁ
ANTOFAGASTA
Cerro Paranal ✖
ATACAMA
COQUIMBO
VALPARAÍSO
SANTIAGO
Santiago de Chile
O´HIGGINS
MAULE
BIOBÍO
ARAUCANÍA
LOS RÍOS
LOS LAGOS
AISÉN
MAGALLANES

✖ European Southern Observatory (ESO)

Argentina

1550: Arrival of the Spanish

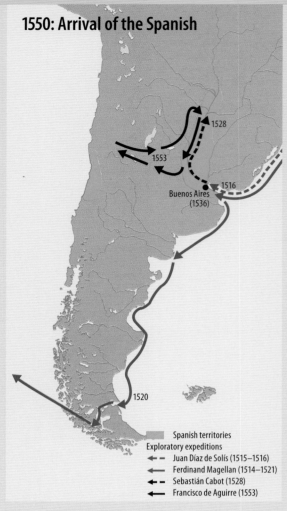

Spanish territories
Exploratory expeditions
- - - Juan Díaz de Solís (1515–1516)
——— Ferdinand Magellan (1514–1521)
- - - Sebastián Cabot (1528)
——— Francisco de Aguirre (1553)

1650: Spanish Colonies I

Mendoza (1561)
Córdoba (1573)
Buenos Aires

Spanish colonies
Guaraní Reductions
(administered by Jesuits)

1800: Spanish Colonies II

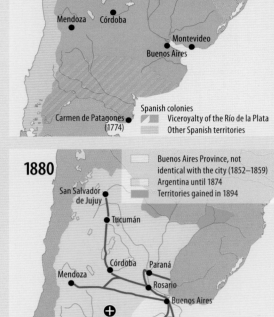

Asunción
Mendoza Córdoba
Montevideo
Buenos Aires
Carmen de Patagones (1774)

Spanish colonies
Viceroyalty of the Río de la Plata
Other Spanish territories

1820

Tucumán
Córdoba
Mendoza
Buenos Aires Montevideo

United Provinces of South America
Campaign of José de San Martín to Chile 1817–1818
Declaration of independence in 1816

1880

San Salvador de Jujuy
Tucumán
Córdoba Paraná
Mendoza Rosario
Buenos Aires
Bahía Blanca Mar del Plata

Buenos Aires Province, not identical with the city (1852–1859)
Argentina until 1874
Territories gained in 1894

——— Important rail lines
⊕ Slavery abolished in 1853

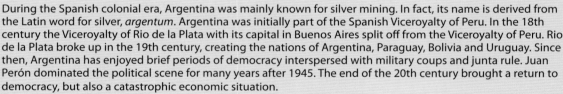

During the Spanish colonial era, Argentina was mainly known for silver mining. In fact, its name is derived from the Latin word for silver, *argentum*. Argentina was initially part of the Spanish Viceroyalty of Peru. In the 18th century the Viceroyalty of Rio de la Plata with its capital in Buenos Aires split off from the Viceroyalty of Peru. Rio de la Plata broke up in the 19th century, creating the nations of Argentina, Paraguay, Bolivia and Uruguay. Since then, Argentina has enjoyed brief periods of democracy interspersed with military coups and junta rule. Juan Perón dominated the political scene for many years after 1945. The end of the 20th century brought a return to democracy, but also a catastrophic economic situation.

1502 Amerigo Vespucci is the first European to arrive in Argentina.

1516 Juan Diaz de Solís sails along the east coast of South America to as far south as the Rio de la Plata.

1520 Ferdinand Magellan sails along the east coast of South America and discovers a strait that joins the Atlantic to the Pacific. Argentina becomes part of the Spanish Viceroyalty of Peru.

1527 Explorer Sebastián Cabot founds Sancti Spiritu, the first Spanish settlement in Argentina.

1536 Spanish settlers found Buenos Aires.

1587 Arrival of the first Jesuits

1610 Jesuits found the first Reductions to protect the indigenous people.

1767 Spain expels the Jesuits from South America.

1776 The Viceroyalty of Rio de la Plata, with its capital at Buenos Aires, splits off from the Viceroyalty of Peru. It comprises present-day Argentina, Bolivia, Paraguay and Uruguay.

1806 Great Britain attacks Buenos Aires.

1810 May Revolution: Buenos Aires declares independence, leading to a nationwide fight for emancipation.

July 7, 1816 Argentina gains independence from the previously unified provinces making up Rio de la Plata.

1817–1818 Jose San Martin organizes a campaign against the Spanish from Chile.

1826 End of the war with Brazil

1829–1852 The Argentine Federation becomes a de facto dictatorship under Governor de Rosas.

1845 Franco-British blockade of Buenos Aires

1832–1833 Rosas' campaign against the native tribes

1853 Founding of the Argentine Republic and adoption of the first democratic constitution

1861–1862 Buenos Aires joins the Republic of Argentina.

1862 Bartolomé Mitre wins the first national presidential election.

1864–1870 War of the Triple Alliance: Argentina, Brazil and Uruguay prevail against Paraguay's expansionist ambitions. The regions of present-day Misiones, Formos, and Chaco are part of the spoils.

1879–1884 Frontier campaign to gain control of the Pampas and Patagonia

1880–1886 Rigid state control under President Julio Argentino Roca (second term 1898–1904).

1880–1912 Period of heavy immigration, especially from Italy and Spain

1902 Final resolution of the border dispute with Chile, which has festered since the Saltpeter War of 1879–1884. The borders of Patagonia and Tierra del Fuego are newly established.

1916–1922 Democratic policy of national consensus under President Hipólito Irigoyen (second term 1928–1930).

1930 President Irigoyen is overthrown by the military, followed by the *decada infame* (infamous decade).

1933–1945 Argentina remains neutral during World War II. Fugitives from Nazi Germany, but also Nazi war criminals fleeing Europe after the war, immigrate to Argentina.

1946 Election of Juan Perón to the presidency

1955 A military coup ends Peronism. Perón goes into exile in Spain.

1955–1972 Periods of military dictatorship alternate with brief returns to democracy.

1973 Peronists win the election. Perón returns from exile. He dies on July 1, 1974, and his third wife, Isabel, serves out his term.

1976 The military forces President Isabel Perón to resign.

1976–1983 Bloody military regime under Jorge Rafael Videla brings state-sponsored terror in the name of

ca. 1900

- Argentina
- Patagonia, annexed in 1881
- Territory ceded to Brazil in 1927
- British territory
- (▲) Discovery and production of oil in Patagonia (since 1907)

FALKLAND ISLANDS
(ISLAS MALVINAS)

ca. 1975

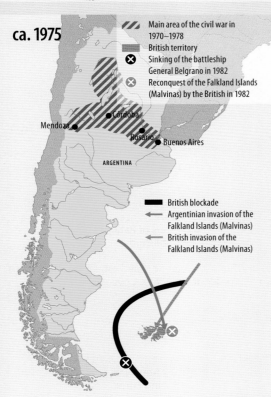

- Main area of the civil war in 1970–1978
- British territory
- ⊗ Sinking of the battleship General Belgrano in 1982
- ⊗ Reconquest of the Falkland Islands (Malvinas) by the British in 1982

- British blockade
- Argentinian invasion of the Falkland Islands (Malvinas)
- British invasion of the Falkland Islands (Malvinas)

ARGENTINA

Argentina Today

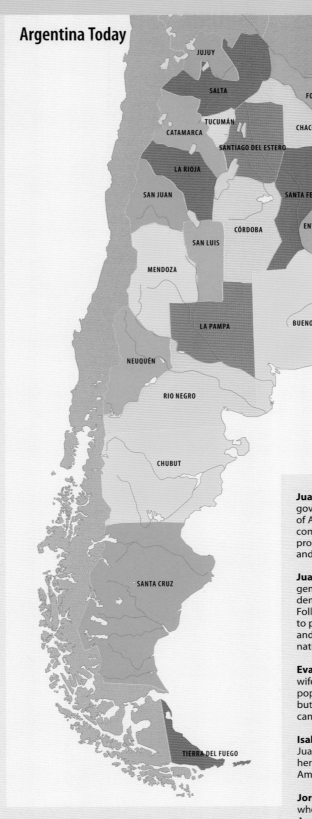

"national reorganization." Some 30,000 Argentinians disappear (*los desaparaecidos*). Many of their mothers (*las Madres de Plaza de Mayor*) continue to march for justice.

1982 Argentina loses the Falklands War to Great Britain.

1983 Raul Alfonsín is elected president, followed by a slow return to democracy.

1989 The election of Carlos Ménem to the presidency signals a return of the Peronists and neoliberal economic policy.

1998 Amnesty for crimes of the military junta is revoked.

1999–2001 Fernando de la Rúa takes over from Meném as an economic crisis unfolds.

2002 Severe economic downturn

2003–2007 Neo-Perónist government of Nestor Kirchner

2007 Kirchner's wife, Cristina Fernández de Kirchner, becomes president of Argentina in October 2007.

José de San Martín (1778–1850) was an Argentine general instrumental in the liberation of Chile, Argentina and Peru (1817–1821). In Chile, he stepped down in favor of Bernardo O'Higgins, and in 1822 stepped down again in Peru after differences with Simón Bolívar. In 1824 he was forced into exile in France.

Juan Manuel de Rosas (1793–1877) In his capacity as governor of Buenos Aires, he was the de facto dictator of Argentina from 1827 to 1852. In 1835 he also became commander of the armed forces. Having led Argentina to prosperity, he also tried to acquire the territories of Paraguay and Uruguay.

Juan Domingo Perón (1895–1974) was an Argentine general who took part in the 1943 coup d'état. He was president from 1946 to 1955, after which he was overthrown. Following exile in Spain from 1958 until 1973, he returned to power until his death in 1974. Peronism is an economic and social policy with authoritarian characteristics, as well as nationalistic and social democratic principles.

Eva ('Evita') Perón (1919–1952) was Juan Perón's second wife. Very popular among the impoverished segments of the population, she campaigned for the post of vice president but was opposed by the military. Ever since her death from cancer, she has been revered by her followers.

Isabel Martinez de Perón (1931–) was the third wife of Juan Perón. When her husband died in 1974, she continued her husband's policies as the first female president of a Latin American country. The military deposed her in 1976.

Jorge Rafael Videla (1925–) is an Argentine general who headed the military junta and became dictator of Argentina (1976–1981) after a coup. During his regime some 30,000 people disappeared, and the fate of many remains unexplained. He was sentenced to life in prison in 1985, pardoned in 1990, and taken into custody again in 1998.

Néstor Kirchner (1950–) A populist representative of a progressive Peronist spinoff party, he served as president of Argentina from 2003 to 2007. Numerous scandals cast a shadow over his government.

The Falkland Islands (*Islas Malvinas*) According to Argentine interpretation of international law, the Falkland Islands, or Islas Malvinas, are Argentine territory despite the fact that they have been occupied and governed by Great Britain since 1833. Under President Galtieri, the unpopular military junta used claims to the Falklands to increase domestic support. After invading the islands, an unexpectedly strong British military response led to the junta's collapse.

ISLANDS AND POLAR REGIONS

During the last ice age, great swaths of the northern landmasses and the poles were covered with gigantic sheets of ice. Sea level was approximately 425 feet (130 m) lower than it is today. *Homo sapiens* could reach all five continents by land, from Siberia to Alaska over the Bering Strait, and to Australia by way of the Torres Strait.

As early as 30,000 years ago, when there were no land connections between the landmasses, the first settlers had already landed on islands of the Bismarck Archipelago. Recent theories also postulate that Central and South America were reached at this time with simple boats sailing along the Pacific coast of North America.

People first settled along rivers, and the oldest surviving relics of nautical construction are river boats. People most likely began to conquer the seas in antiquity. Egyptians, Phoenicians and Greeks built seaworthy ships; the Polynesians left Melanesia (or the Philippines) to settle the South Pacific; the Arawak in Venezuela reached the islands of the Caribbean; and Indians, Malays and Chinese sailed the Indian Ocean. During the early Middle Ages the Vikings traversed the vast reaches of the North Atlantic, eventually reaching North America.

Europeans explored and dominated the world's oceans from the 15th to the 18th centuries, and finally the Arctic regions in the 20th century. They also discovered and claimed the last remaining uninhabited islands.

Atlantic Ocean	**462**
Indian Ocean	**465**
Pacific Ocean	**468**
The Arctic Region	**470**
The Antarctic Region	**472**

Nova Americae Septentrionalis Descriptio, Amsterdam, Joan Blaeu, 1659

Atlantic Ocean

Island Nations in the Atlantic Ocean

Shaped like a long, extended 'S,' the Atlantic Ocean separates the Americas from Europe and Africa. It is the second largest and second oldest of the five oceans, having formed ca. 150–200 million years ago when the supercontinent Pangaea split apart.

200 Million Years Ago

120 Million Years Ago

60 Million Years Ago

The Faroe Islands

~600 Irish monks settle the islands around what is now the town of Sumba.

~825 Beginning of conquest and colonization by the Vikings

999 Sigmundur Brestisson reintroduces Christianity to the Faroe Islands and is murdered in 1005.

1380 The Faroe Islands are taken by Denmark-Norway (Kalmar Union). Subsequently, many pirates land here.

1814 After the Treaty of Kiel, the islands remain a Danish possession.

1940 During World War II the British occupy the islands before the Germans, who occupy Denmark, can reach them.

1948 The Faroe Islands are granted a significant degree of autonomy under the authority of Denmark.

1972 The Faroese decide against joining the European Union with Denmark.

The Orkney Islands

from the 7th millennium BCE The islands are settled by people from Scotland.

2000–1500 BCE Skara Brae, a neolithic village, is inhabited.

~580 CE Christianity arrives.

before 800 The islands are conquered by the Vikings, who establish an earldom there.

1231/63 Scottish and Danish-Norwegian sovereignty

1469 The Orkney Islands belong to the Scottish throne.

1615–today The islands are under British control.

The Hebrides

from the 7th millennium BCE Settlers arrive from Scotland.

~300–572 CE The islands are part of the Irish Gaelic kingdom of Dalriada.

from 563 The island of Iona becomes the central point for the Celtic Christianizing of Europe.

572–1266 Under Norwegian rule, a Celto-Nordic hybrid culture develops.

1354–1411 The Hebrides are subject to the MacDonald clan, who bear the title "Lord of the Isles."

from 1411–today The Hebrides are governed first by Scotland, then the United Kingdom.

Newfoundland

7500–2500 BCE North American Indian cultures are present on Newfoundland.

2400 BCE The island is settled by Dorset Inuit.

1400 BCE The arrival of the Thule Inuit results in a mixed indigenous population (Beothuc, Mi'kmaq), which remains to some extent to the present day.

~1000 CE Vikings establish long-term settlements.

1497 The "newe founde islands" are officially discovered and claimed for the British crown by Italian-born John Cabot.

1610–1620 The first lasting British settlements are established.

1713 The Treaty of Utrecht: France recognizes the British claim to Newfoundland.

1882 A railway line covering the entire island is built to encourage greater economic diversity.

1907–1934 Newfoundland is a dominion of the British Empire.

1934 After unrest, Newfoundland is again a British colony.

1948/49 Residents vote for union with Canada, which goes into effect on March 31, 1949.

The Azores and Madeira

1419/27 Madeira and the Azores, presumably already known to the seafaring Phoenicians two thousand years earlier, are rediscovered by Portuguese sailors. The laurel wood (*madeira* in Portuguese) that grows there, excellently suited to shipbuilding, gives the island its name.

1427 Diogo de Silves reaches the Azores and claims them for Portugal.

from the mid-15th century Portuguese settlement of the islands begins. The toponym Azores derives from a zoological mistake: *Ilhas dos Açores* means "Hawk Islands," but the archipelago is actually inhabited by buzzards. The first settlers are also called "Flemings" (*flamengos*).

1580–1583 After Portugal loses its independence and comes under the control of the Spanish crown, the Azores put up strong resistance to Spanish domination (in part with the aid of semi-wild bulls).

1640 Portugal, and with it Madeira and the Azores, is once again independent of Spanish rule.

from ~1800 Economic prosperity on the Azores is achieved through the cultivation of oranges, tea and tobacco. Madeira wine becomes popular throughout Europe.

1801–1814 During the Napoleonic Wars, England occupies Madeira.

1957 The volcano Capelinhos erupts in the Azores, and approximately 2,000 people must be resettled.

1976 Madeira and the Azores become autonomous regions of Portugal, gaining extensive autonomy.

Bermuda

1609 Following a shipwreck, English colonists land on Bermuda.

1620 Bermuda becomes an autonomous English colony.

1815 Hamilton becomes the capital.

1941 The United States establishes two military bases on Bermuda.

1995 The population votes against independence from Great Britain.

today Bermuda, an overseas territory of the United Kingdom, is one of the largest tax havens in the world.

The Canary Islands

The history of the Canary Islands is marked by repeated waves of emigration to the Americas, caused in turn by hunger, volcanic eruptions, pirate raids and finally the Spanish Civil War.

600 BCE Phoenicians from Carthage reach the islands, beginning their settlement of Africa. The indigenous people are the Guanche, famous for their whistling language.

~40 BCE The Romans name the archipelago *Fortunatae insulae*, or the Isles of the Blessed.

1312 CE Genoese navigator Lancelotto Malocello rediscovers the Canary Islands. Lanzarote is named after him.

1402–1406 The Spanish conquest of the islands is led by Jean de Béthencourt, who becomes their king.

1478–1496 Several wars of extermination are fought against the Guanche. With the conquest of the island of Tenerife, the indigenous culture is destroyed.

1492 The island of La Gomera is Columbus's last stop before his first Atlantic crossing.

1553 The French corsair François Le Clerc (known as "Peg Leg") pillages Santa Cruz de la Palma.

from 1960 The islands' economy, historically based on agriculture, is now more dependent on tourism.

The Bahamas

400–900 Lucayan (Arawak) settle parts of the extensive archipelago.

1492 Columbus reaches the Bahamas (Guanahani or San Salvador). Their name is derived from *baja mar*, which means "flat sea." The indigenous people are shipped to Hispaniola or into slavery and largely exterminated.

1629 The islands are colonized by the English.

~1700 The Bahamas become a major base for Caribbean pirates.

1718 The infamous pirate Blackbeard (born as Englishman Edward Teach) is killed in a skirmish with the British lieutenant Robert Maynard.

1775–1932 The islands profit from crises in the United States (including the Revolutionary War, the Civil War and Prohibition), and the inhabitants of the Bahamas profit handsomely from smuggling.

1973 The Bahamas become independent of Great Britain.

today The Bahamas are a tax haven and depend heavily on tourism and banking for economic stability.

The Cayman Islands

1503 Columbus discovers the Cayman Islands, thus named in 1540 for the alligators (*caimánes*) found in their waters.

from 1666 Settlers arrive from Jamaica.

1670 Spain recognizes British sovereignty over the islands.

from 1734 Extensive settlement

from 1962 The Cayman Islands is a British colony with domestic autonomy.

Jamaica

7th century BCE The Taíno people of South America settle Jamaica.

15th century CE A wave of Carib settlers arrive.

1494 Columbus lands on the island.

1509 Spanish occupation

from 1517 The slave trade brings Africans to Jamaica as slaves.

1655 The British conquer the island, which officially becomes a British possession in 1670.

from 1730 The Maroons, former slaves who live in remote settlements, revolt intermittently.

1831 The Christmas Uprising, led by Baptist preacher Samuel Sharpe, leads to the abolition of slavery in 1834.

1865 The Morant Bay uprising

1944 Partial autonomy

1957 More extensive autonomy in domestic affairs is granted.

1962 Jamaica gains its independence and joins the British Commonwealth.

1972–1980 Democratic socialism predominates.

Atlantic Ocean

Puerto Rico

3000–2000 BCE The Ortoiroid people settle the island.

120–1000 CE The island is settled by Taíno and Arawak.

1493 Christopher Columbus lands on Puerto Rico.

from 1508 Spanish settlement brings slavery and near extermination of the native population.

from 1513 African slaves are brought to the island; Caribs conduct raids.

from 1598 British, French and Dutch forces all attempt to gain control of Puerto Rico.

16th century Pirates regularly raid the island, including Sir Francis Drake in 1595.

1815 Puerto Rico is opened to non-Spanish settlers. Sugar, coffee and tobacco plantations arise.

1835 Slavery is abolished.

1868 The struggle for independence begins; extensive autonomy is granted in 1897.

1898 Spanish-American War: Spain cedes control of Puerto Rico to the United States.

20th century Puerto Rico is an independent commonwealth of the United States.

The Virgin Islands

1st century BCE The Virgin Islands are settled by the Arawak people.

1493 CE Columbus lands.

from 1625 The Spanish take possession of some of the islands.

from 1650 Some islands are claimed by France, and some are controlled temporarily by Denmark and Brandenburg-Prussia (1689–1720).

1672 The British take control of parts of the archipelago. To this day, the British Virgin Islands are administered by a British governor.

1674 St. Croix becomes a French possession.

1733 The French Virgin Islands go to Denmark.

1917 The United States acquires the Danish Virgin Islands.

present The U.S. Virgin Islands is an unincorporated territory of the United States, administered by an American governor. Tourism is the major source of income on the islands, and the scarcity of fresh water is problematic.

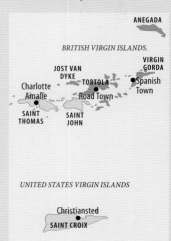

Guadeloupe

3500–3000 BCE Guadeloupe is settled by the Arawak people.

from 600 CE The Caribs settle on the islands of Guadeloupe.

1493 Columbus arrives.

from 1635 The French colonize Guadeloupe, which becomes a French colony in 1674. Slave trade is instituted to support sugar and coffee plantations.

1794 Slavery is abolished, but it is reintroduced in 1802 by Napoleon I.

1848 Slavery is abolished again, this time permanently.

20th century Guadeloupe is made an overseas *département* of France in 1946 and since 1982 is an overseas *région*.

Martinique

100 BCE Martinique is settled by the Arawak people.

10th century CE Carib settlers arrive.

1502 Columbus lands on Martinique.

1635 Frenchman Pierre Bélain claims the island. Cotton, sugar and cocoa plantations help the colony prosper.

1635 Martinique becomes a crown possession.

1787–1802 A slave revolt is followed by civil war.

1848 Slavery is abolished.

1902 The volcano Montagne Pelée erupts, resulting in more than 30,000 deaths.

1946 Martinique is a French overseas *département* (overseas *région* from 1974).

Barbados

~350 and 800 Waves of Arawak settlers land on Barbados.

13th century Carib settlers arrive.

1536 The Portuguese discover and occupy Barbados.

1625 The British take possession of the island, which they settle systematically.

1639 The first parliament meets.

1838 Slavery is abolished in the United Kingdom.

1966 Barbados becomes independent of Great Britain.

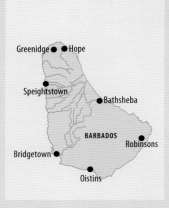

Aruba

1499 Aruba is discovered and occupied by the Spanish.

1636 The island is acquired by the Netherlands and becomes part of the Netherlands Antilles.

1825–1915 Gold is mined on Aruba, and the island is more extensively developed.

1986 Aruba separates from the Netherlands Antilles and becomes an autonomous territory within the Kingdom of the Netherlands.

Trinidad and Tobago

1498 Christopher Columbus lands on Trinidad and Tobago.

1592 Spanish settlers arrive on Trinidad, but the island is largely undeveloped.

17th century The French, British and Dutch contend for possession of Tobago; the island changes hands thirty-one times.

1704 Tobago becomes a neutral territory.

1797 Trinidad becomes a British possession. A plantation economy develops.

1814 The British acquire Tobago.

1888 The governance of Tobago is granted to Trinidad.

1958 Trinidad and Tobago gain independence as part of the West Indies Federation.

1962 Total independence is followed by membership in the British Commonwealth.

Cape Verde

1445–1461 Portuguese sailors under the command of Prince Henry the Navigator discover and settle the uninhabited Cape Verde islands.

15th–17th centuries Santiago is the central transfer point of the transatlantic slave trade, a three-way trading system with goods and slaves being exchanged between Europe, Africa and North American colonies.

1876 Slavery is abolished.

1926–1974 During the *Estado Novo*, Portuguese fascism under Salazar, an internment camp is established at Tarrafal.

1973 In Portugal, Amílcar Cabral's (1924–1973) liberation struggle leads to the Revolution of Carnations. Cabral is assasinated.

1975 Cape Verde gains independence.

Ascension, St. Helena, Tristan da Cunha

Georgetown ●
ASCENSION

Jamestown ●
SAINT HELENA

Edinburgh of the
Seven Seas
INACCESSIBLE ISLAND ● TRISTAN DA CUNHA
NIGHTINGALE
ISLAND
GOUGH ISLAND

Ascension, St. Helena and Tristan da Cunha

1501–1506 The Portuguese explore Ascension in 1501/1503, St. Helena in 1502 and Tristan da Cunha in 1506. Recognizing the islands' strategic significance, the Portuguese do not reveal their discoveries.

ca. 1600 The first English sailors arrive on St. Helena, and the Portuguese evacuate the island.

until 1651 The islands are occupied by the Dutch.

from 1659 The islands are possessions of the British East India Company.

1815 Napoleon is exiled to St. Helena, where he dies in 1821.

1815/16 The British occupy Ascension and Tristan da Cunha.

1833 Control of St. Helena reverts from the British East India Company to Great Britain.

1961 The British evacuate all inhabitants of Tristan da Cunha in anticipation of a volcanic eruption. The inhabitants eventually pressure Britain to allow their return.

today The islands remain strategically important.

The Falkland Islands (Malvinas)

1592 English navigator John Davis lands on the uninhabited Falklands, two large islands and numerous smaller ones about 300 miles (480 km) from the southern tip of Argentina.

1764 The French found the first settlement on East Falkland; the British settle West Falkland the following year.

1770 Spain acquires the Falkland Islands from France and briefly expel the British.

1820 The newly independent government of Argentina stakes its claim to the Falklands, beginning a conflict between Argentina and Great Britain that lasts into the present.

1833 The British establish a naval base.

1914 German warships are destroyed by British forces.

1982 Argentinean occupation of the islands leads to the Falklands War. British forces repel the Argentineans.

Indian Ocean

With an area of 24.9 million square miles (almost 75 million km²), the Indian Ocean is the third largest of the world's oceans. It covers much of the Southern Hemisphere and connects Africa with Asia and Australia.

Socotra

early history Socotra belongs to various states of the southern Arabian Peninsula, later becoming Christian.

1505 The island is conquered by the Portuguese.

1834 The British occupy Socotra.

1866 British protectorate

1967 The island is part of the People's Democratic Republic of Yemen (South Yemen).

1990 Socotra belongs to reunified Yemen.

Island Nations in the Indian Ocean

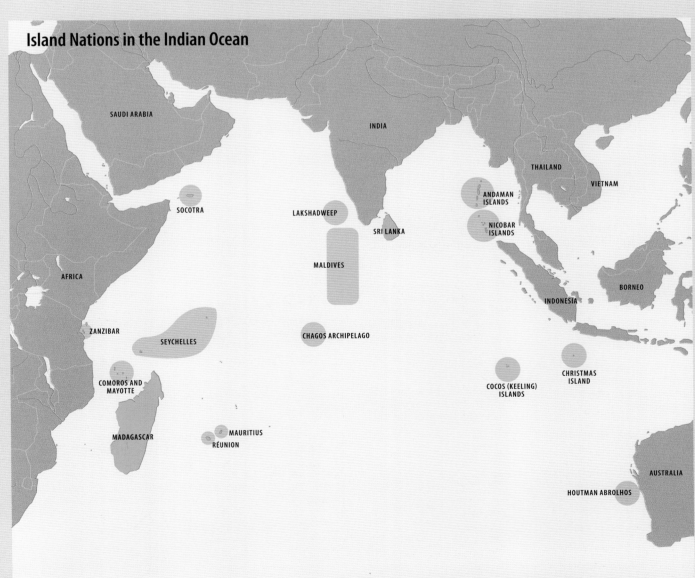

Indian Ocean

Zanzibar

8th–10th centuries Persian traders arrive on Zanzibar, introducing Islam. For centuries, the population is primarily African and Persian.

1499 Vasco da Gama lands on Zanzibar. Portuguese trade settlements are established beginning in 1503.

17th–19th centuries Arabs from Oman expel the Portuguese. Ruled by the sultans of Oman, Zanzibar becomes a center for the slave trade (75 percent of the island's population is slaves).

1832 The sultan of Oman makes Zanzibar his primary residence; the island experiences an economic boom.

1856 Zanzibar becomes an independent sultanate.

from 1870 Various colonial powers, especially Germany and Great Britain, occupy the island's coastline.

1897 The British force the abolition of slavery.

1963 The main island gains its independence from British rule.

1964 After revolution and a coup, Zanzibar enters a political union with Tanzania.

The Seychelles

from the 9th century Arab merchants land on the islands, but establish no permanent settlements.

1502 Vasco da Gama discovers the Seychelles.

from 1608 British and French expeditions explore the islands.

1756 The French annex the islands.

1811 War between France and Britain results in British control of the Seychelles.

1835 Slavery is abolished, forcing economic changes.

1903 The Seychelles are an autonomous British colony.

1976 Independence as a socialist, one-party state.

1991 A multiparty system is allowed.

Comoros and Mayotte

from 500 Bantu and Malay settlers arrive on the islands situated between Madagascar and the eastern coast of Africa.

from 800 Persian and Arab merchants land on the islands, introducing Islam. A sultanate is established.

ca. 1780–1830 Slave traders from Madagascar raid the islands.

1841 A French protectorate is established, primarily on Mayotte. The Comoros are a protectorate until 1897.

1847 Slavery is abolished.

1912 Officially a French colony, in 1947 an overseas territory

1961 Partial autonomy is granted.

1975 The predominantly Muslim islands of Comoros gain independence, but Muslim-Christian Mayotte chooses to be administered by France to this day. The political situation in Comoros is unstable.

2001 A new constitution takes effect. The nation's official name is the Union of the Comoros.

Madagascar

200–500 Madagascar's original inhabitants arrive from Southeast Asia (Indonesia).

10th–14th centuries Bantu immigrants from East Africa and Arab traders settle on Madagascar.

1500 The Portuguese are the first Europeans on Madagascar.

16th–17th centuries The British and French struggle for domination of the island.

1680–1725 Pirates use Madagascar as a base.

1745–1897 Merina kingdom

1792–1828 King Radama the Great conquers most of the island.

1890 Madagascar becomes a French protectorate.

1960 Full independence is achieved as the Malagasy Republic (now officially the Republic of Madagascar).

Mauritius

10th century Mauritius is settled by Malays and Arab merchants.

1507 The Portuguese arrive on Mauritius.

1598 Dutch forces land on the island, driving off the Portuguese.

1638–1710 The Dutch colonize Mauritius.

1710–1715 The Dutch vacate, and the island is controlled by pirates.

1715–1810 Mauritius becomes a French colony (crown colony from 1767).

1810 The British occupy Mauritius, making it a crown colony in 1814.

1968 Independent state within the British Commonwealth

1992 Mauritius is an independent parliamentary republic in the British Commonwealth.

Réunion

1507 The Portuguese explorer Diogo Dias lands on the island and calls it Santa Apolonia.

1640 The French occupy Santa Apolonia.

from 1665 The French India Company governs the island, establishing permanent settlements as well as coffee and sugar plantations.

1793 Santa Apolonia is renamed Réunion.

1848 Slavery is abolished; indentured laborers arrive.

1946 Réunion becomes a French overseas *département* (an overseas *région* from 1974).

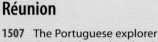

Lakshadweep

1st–2nd centuries Lakshadweep, a cluster of some thirty islands off the southwest coast of India, is first mentioned by Egyptian geographer Ptolemy.

680–720 The Pallava king Varman II conquers the islands.

from 1153 The sultans of the Maldives introduce Islam to Lakshadweep.

after 1500 After a brief occupation, the Portuguese are expelled by the Muslim rajas of Kannur.

1783 The main island of Amini revolts, placing itself under the rule of the sultan of Mysore (now Karnataka).

1799 Lakshadweep is annexed by the British East India Company.

1854–1947 The archipelago is under direct British rule.

1947 Lakshadweep becomes a possession of independent India, gaining the status of union territory in 1956.

The Maldives

5th century BCE Buddhists from India and Ceylon settle the Maldives.

1153 Arab merchants encourage conversion to Islam. A sultanate is established.

1558–1573 The Portuguese control the capital of Male for a time but are expelled.

17th century The Maldives are a sultanate under Dutch protection.

1796 British occupation

1887–1965 The Maldives are a British protectorate.

1932 The Maldives' first constitution is drafted. Domestic autonomy is granted in 1956.

1968 The sultanate becomes an independent republic.

from 1972 The Maldives are open to tourists.

1982 The Maldives join the British Commonwealth.

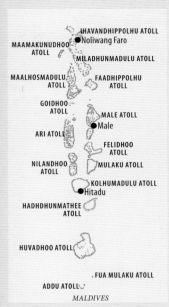

MALDIVES

IHAVANDHIPPOLHU ATOLL
Noliwang Faro
MAAMAKUNUDHOO ATOLL
MILADHUNMADULU ATOLL
MAALHOSMADULU ATOLL
FAADHIPPOLHU ATOLL
GOIDHOO ATOLL
MALE ATOLL
Male
ARI ATOLL
FELIDHOO ATOLL
NILANDHOO ATOLL
MULAKU ATOLL
KOLHUMADULU ATOLL
Hitadu
HADHDHUNMATHEE ATOLL
HUVADHOO ATOLL
FUA MULAKU ATOLL
ADDU ATOLL

The Chagos Archipelago

ca. 1500 Portuguese explorer Vasco da Gama is the first European to find the Chagos Archipelago.

17th century France claims the islands and settles them from Réunion and Mauritius.

1786 Great Britain claims the islands and settles them from the Seychelles. The French dispute this claim until Napoleon's defeat in 1814.

1903–1968 The archipelago is under direct British rule (from Mauritius).

1968 Mauritius becomes independent; the archipelago remains part of the British Indian Ocean Territory.

1971 The inhabitants of three atolls are forcibly resettled to make way for a US military base on Diego Garcia island.

from 1998 The resettled islanders sue to return to their homes. They are granted this right in 2004, but a British court forbids their return in 2008.

PEROS BANHOS ATOLL
BLENHEIM REEF
SALOMON ISLANDS
THREE BROTHERS
EAGLE ISLANDS
DANGER ISLAND
GREAT CHAGOS BANK
EGMONT ISLANDS
DIEGO GARCIA

Sri Lanka

from ca. 12,000 BCE Evidence of habitation by indigenous peoples

543–504 BCE Vijaya is the first king of Ceylon.

until 500 BCE Aryan immigrants, and later the Sinhalese, arrive from India, resulting in a mixed population.

~247 BCE Mahinda, son of Emperor Ashoka of India, introduces Theravada, a strict form of Buddhism.

~200 BCE Buddhism becomes the state religion.

2nd–9th centuries CE Immigration of Tamil people from southern India

6th–11th centuries The Sinhalese kingdom of Anuradhapura dominates the island.

13th century Various Sinhalese and Tamil kingdoms

1505 The Portuguese arrive and over the next century take control of the entire island.

17th century The Sinhalese and Dutch jointly force the Portuguese to leave. The Dutch control the coastal regions; the interior remains independent.

1796 The Dutch East India Company cedes control of the island to Britain.

1802–1947 Ceylon is a British crown colony.

1948 Political independence: The Dominion of Ceylon becomes a member state of the British Commonwealth. Solomon Bandaranaike is prime minister.

Jaffna
Trincomalee
Batticaloa
SRI LANKA
Kandy
Colombo
Galle

The Andaman and Nicobar Islands

prehistory The earliest settlements date from the Neolithic era.

17th century The Indian Maratha empire annexes parts of the Andaman Islands.

1756 Denmark claims the Andaman Islands.

1778–1784 The Nicobar Islands are an Austrian colony.

1789 The British East India Company colonizes the Andaman Islands.

1869 Nicobar is part of British India.

1943 Japan occupies the Andaman and Nicobar Islands, then transfers sovereignty to the Indian exile government "Free India."

1956–1959 Solomon Bandaranaike's term in office is characterized by repressive policies of the Sinhalese majority over the Tamil minority.

1960–1977 Sirimavo Bandaranaike continues her husband's policies, escalating ethnic conflict.

1972 Republic of Sri Lanka (Democratic Socialist Republic of Sri Lanka since 1978)

1983 Terrorist acts by the separatist Liberation Tigers of Tamil Eelam lead to civil war and government reprisals, resulting in ca. 80,000 deaths during more than two decades of fighting.

2009 Civil war is declared over.

NORTH ANDAMAN
ANDAMAN ISLANDS
MIDDLE ANDAMAN
SOUTH ANDAMAN
Wrightmyo
Port Blair
LITTLE ANDAMAN
CAR NICOBAR
NICOBAR ISLANDS
LITTLE NICOBAR
Pulokunji
GREAT NICOBAR

today The islands are administered by India (lieutenant governor) and are the site of Indian military bases. Only the Andaman Islands are accessible; visitor access to the Nicobar Islands is restricted to protect the islands' natural landscapes and indigenous peoples.

Cocos Islands

1609 The Cocos Islands are discovered by ships of the British East India Company.

1753 Dutch visitors describe the islands, which are occupied by the Dutch and the British.

1826/31 British colonial officials annex the islands.

1831–1978 Feudal rule of the Clunies-Ross family

1857 Official British occupation

1942–1945 The islands are heavily contested by the Japanese and the British.

1955 Australia claims the Cocos Islands.

1978 The Australian government buys much of the islands from the Clunies-Ross family.

1992 The Clunies-Ross family sells its last remaining property.

NORTH KEELING ISLANDS

HORSBURGH ISLAND
DIRECTION ISLAND
HOME ISLAND
SOUTH KEELING ISLANDS
WEST ISLAND
SOUTH ISLAND

Christmas Island

1643 Sailors of the British East India Company spot the island on Christmas Day.

1688 British explorer William Dampier visits the island for the first time.

1888 Great Britain annexes Christmas Island and settles it with workers from Southeast Asia.

from 1890 Phosphate mining begins.

1958 Christmas Island is placed under Australian sovereignty.

Flying Fish Cove
Drumsite
CHRISTMAS ISLAND

Houtman Abrolhos

end of the 16th century Portuguese sailors come across Houtman Abrolhos off the west coast of Australia.

1619 The islands are charted by Frederick de Houtman.

1629 Wreck of the Dutch ship *Batavia*

today The islands serve primarily as an uninhabited nature preserve, administered by Australia.

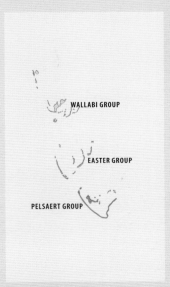

WALLABI GROUP
EASTER GROUP
PELSAERT GROUP

Pacific Ocean

With a surface area of 70 million square miles (ca. 181 million km²) and depths of up to 36,000 feet (over 11,000 meters) in the Marianas Trench, the Pacific Ocean is the largest and deepest of the world's oceans. It accounts for one half of the total ocean surface area, and 35 percent of the surface of planet Earth. The Pacific extends from Australia/Oceania and Asia in the west to the Americas in the east.

Palau

1000 BCE The first settlers arrive from Indonesia, Australia or Polynesia.

1543 CE Palau is discovered by Spanish explorers and annexed by Spain.

1899 The islands are sold to Germany and become a German protectorate.

1914 Japanese forces occupy Palau, which becomes a Japanese mandate in 1920.

1942–1945 Palau is the scene of heavy fighting during World War II.

1947 Palau becomes a United Nations Trust Territory administered by the United States.

1978 The population votes for independence, opposing the stationing of atomic weapons by the United States.

1994 The Republic of Palau is fully independent, but is pressured into entering a "Compact of Free Association" (concerted foreign policy and security) with the United States.

Papua New Guinea

60,000/50,000 BCE The northern regions are settled earliest, followed by the rest of the island.

from 8,000 BCE Extensive farming cultures

1st millennium BCE Austronesian peoples settle the coasts.

1526 CE Portuguese explorers reach Papua New Guinea.

1623 Mapping of the island is begun by the Dutch East India Company.

1828 Dutch colonization begins at a slow pace.

1884 New Guinea is divided. The Dutch control the western half of the island (part of the Dutch East Indies 1888–1949); the south is in British hands (as a protectorate 1884, annexed in 1888 and under Australian administration after 1906); and Germany obtains Kaiser-Wilhelmsland in the northeast (German New Guinea in 1899). German New Guinea is the locus of the greatest economic activity.

1914–1921 Australia takes over German New Guinea as a mandated territory. Papua is administered separately.

1920s Gold is discovered.

1945/46 Papua and New Guinea are administered by Australia, jointly, as a United Nations Trust Territory. Indonesia claims West Papua (occupation 1961, annexation 1963).

1973 Residents vote in favor of autonomy from Australia, and Papua New Guinea joins the British Commonwealth.

1975 Papua New Guinea is fully independent.

New Caledonia

1500 BCE The first settlers in New Caledonia are Lapita peoples, followed by Polynesians. The indigenous, mixed Kanak culture results from their intermingling.

17th century CE Various Europeans discover the islands, which are named by explorer James Cook in 1774.

1853 France annexes New Caledonia.

1864–1922 France establishes a penal colony.

1878 The largest of numerous Kanak uprisings occurs.

19th century British and French settlers use indigenous people as slaves to work the sugarcane plantations on Australia and Fiji.

1946 New Caledonia becomes a French overseas territory, electing its own parliament in 1953.

1988 Partial autonomy is conceded after violent unrest in the Kanak population.

1998 The Nouméa Accord provides for substantial domestic autonomy. A referendum on independence is planned for 2014.

Samoa

1000 BCE People of the Lapita culture are probably the first to settle the Samoan archipelago.

from 200 BCE Intensive trade relationships develop with Tonga and Fiji, other Polynesian peoples.

940–1250 CE Samoa rules Tonga.

1722 Jacob Roggeveen of the Netherlands arrives at Samoa.

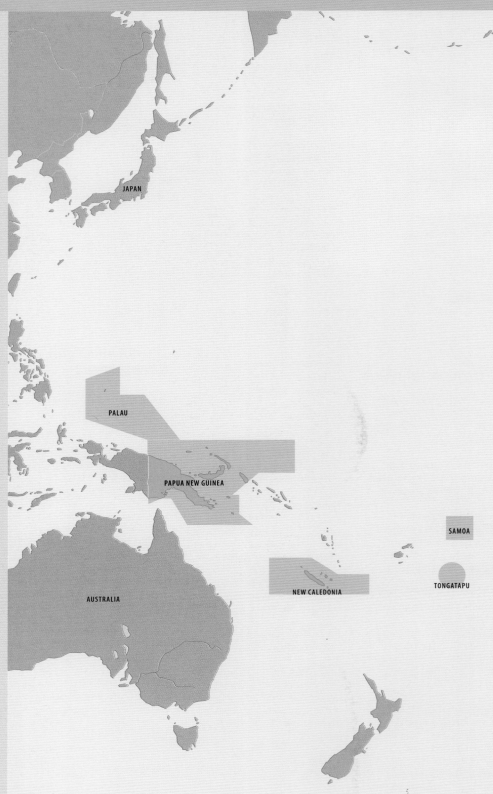

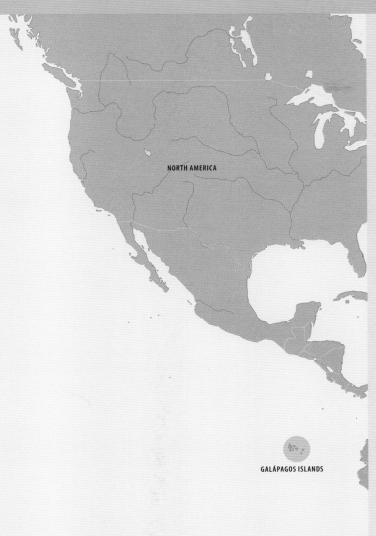

NORTH AMERICA

GALÁPAGOS ISLANDS

TAHITI

Hawaii

200–800 The Hawaiian Islands are settled by Polynesians from the Marquesas Islands.

ca. 1000 The second wave of settlers arrives from Tahiti. A strictly hierarchical tribal society develops.

1527 Spanish sailors land in Hawaii.

1750–1893 The Kingdom of Hawaii is ruled by indigenous monarchs.

1778 James Cook lands on the islands, where he is killed in 1779.

from 1820 Missionaries and plantation owners from the United States come to Hawaii, bringing major social changes.

1893/94 A coup backed by settlers from the United States overthrows the monarchy. A republic is proclaimed.

1898 The United States annexes Hawaii, which becomes a US territory in 1900.

1959 The population of Hawaii votes to become the fiftieth state in the United States of America.

Tahiti

200 BCE Settlers arrive from Tonga and Samoa. They develop a strict, hierarchical caste system.

1606 Tahiti is probably sighted by Spanish sailors.

1767–1768 British and French ships land on Tahiti, each claiming it for their country.

1769/1773/1777 Captain James Cook makes three visits to Tahiti.

1780–1803 Pomaré I is king of the entire island. British missionaries are active.

1812 King Pomaré II and much of the Tahitian nobility convert to Christianity, but there is discontent under subsequent rulers.

1842 Tahiti becomes a French protectorate.

1842 King Pomare V abdicates, and Tahiti becomes a French possession (as part of French Polynesia).

The Galápagos Islands

1535 A Panamanian ship drifting off course happens upon the Galápagos Islands. They are named the *Islas Encantadas* (Enchanted Islands).

17th century The islands serve as bases for pirates attacking Spanish gold transports passing nearby.

1832 Ecuador officially annexes the islands, which are renamed Galápagos after the giant tortoises found there.

1835 Charles Darwin visits the islands and is inspired by their unique flora and fauna to formulate his theory of natural selection.

1934–1959 Most of the islands are used as a penal colony.

1959 Ecuador declares the Galápagos Islands a national park.

1978 UNESCO names the islands a World Heritage Site (renewed in 2001).

1996 The Galápagos Marine Preserve is established.

1830 British missionaries are active in Samoa. Malietoa Vainu'upo, the Samoan ruler, is converted and the people soon follow his example.

1839 The United States establishes a consulate in Samoa, followed by Britain in 1847 and Germany in 1855. Heavy competition among the colonial powers as they establish ports.

1888/89 Samoa is divided: Germany annexes West Samoa as a German protectorate, and the United States makes East Samoa a protectorate (as it remains today).

1899/1900 The Samoan Civil War ends with the Tripartite Pact among the United States, Germany and Great Britain.

1914 New Zealand occupies West Samoa (a United Nations Trust Territory from 1946).

1928 The first mass demonstrations for independence take place in West Samoa.

1962 West Samoa becomes independent, joining the British Commonwealth in 1970 (officially the Independent State of Samoa since 1997).

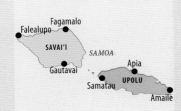

The Arctic Region

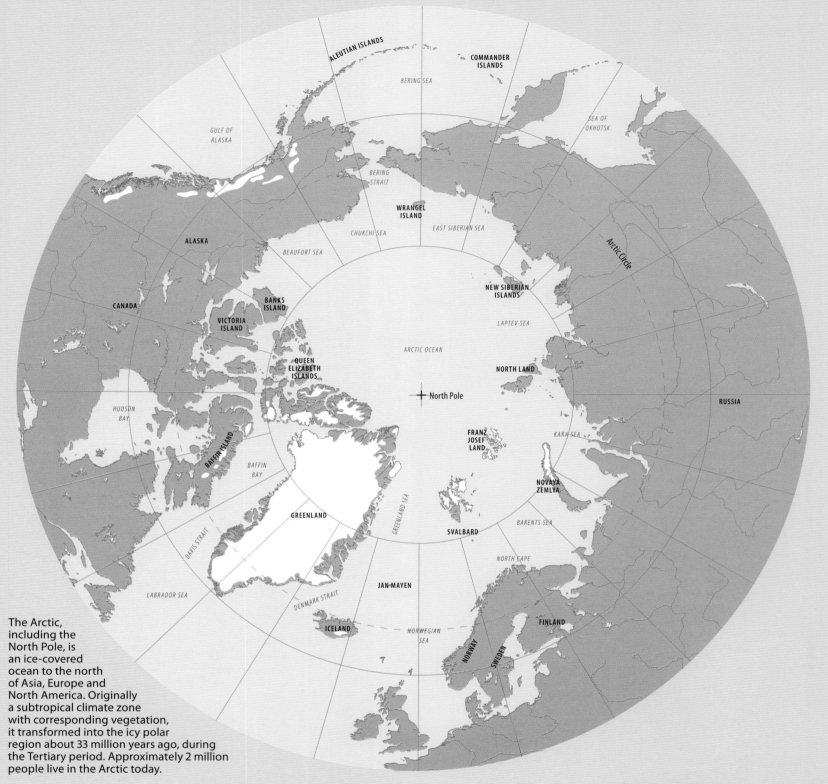

The Arctic, including the North Pole, is an ice-covered ocean to the north of Asia, Europe and North America. Originally a subtropical climate zone with corresponding vegetation, it transformed into the icy polar region about 33 million years ago, during the Tertiary period. Approximately 2 million people live in the Arctic today.

8th century/9th century The Vikings undertake the first of their northern sea voyages.

983 Norse explorer Erik the Red lands on the western coast of what is now Greenland.

1000 Leif Erikson, son of Erik the Red, lands in Labrador and Nova Scotia.

1266 For the first time, a voyage of discovery crosses the 76th parallel.

1497 John Cabot, sailing for the English crown, lands in Labrador.

1576–1578 English explorer Martin Frobisher explores the Arctic in search of the Northwest Passage and gold. Frobisher Bay is named for him.

1610 English navigator Henry Hudson discovers Hudson Bay.

1616 English explorer William Baffin discovers the Arctic islands.

1728–1741 Vitus Bering (for whom the Bering Strait is named), sailing in the service of Tsar Peter I of Russia, explores the Arctic.

1806 British explorer William Scoresby, Sr., reaches a latitude of 81° 30'.

1818–1833 A British expedition led by John and James Clark Ross, an uncle and nephew team, discovers the North Magnetic Pole in 1831.

1827 Englishman William Parry sails north of the Norwegian island of Spitsbergen (82° 40').

1845–1847 The tragic end of a British expedition led by Captain John Franklin, in which 129 men died, raises public awareness of polar exploration.

1872 The Austrian research ship *Admiral Tegethoff* under Karl Weyprecht and Julius Payer reaches Franz Josef Land, an archipelago north of Russia. Weyprecht proposes international cooperation in polar exploration.

1875/76 The first English sled expedition, under the command of George Nares, explores the possibility of overland routes to the North Pole.

1878/79 The *Vega*, captained by Adolf Erik Nordenskiöld, discovers the Northeast Passage.

1893–1896 Arctic expedition of the *Fram* under Fridtjof Nansen and Hjalmar Johansen.

1908 American physician Frederick Cook claims to be the first person to reach the Geographic North Pole; his claim is disputed.

1909 The Geographic North Pole is reached for the first time by Americans Robert Peary and Matthew Henson (disputed by scientists).

1926 Umberto Nobile and Roald Amundsen make the first flyover of the North Pole in the dirigible *Norge*.

1937 Soviet scientists under Ivan Papanin make their first flight to the North Pole.

1958 The USS *Nautilus*, a nuclear submarine, is the first seacraft to reach the North Pole.

1969 Scotsman Sir Wally Herbert reaches the North Pole by foot.

1977 The Soviet atomic icebreaker *Arktika* is the first surface craft to reach the North Pole.

1991 The Swedish *Oden* and German *Polarstern* are the first conventionally powered ships to reach it.

2007 Two Russian Mir submarines touch the sea bottom underneath the North Pole at a depth of 13,980 feet (4,261 meters).

Political Standing

According to the United Nations Convention on the Law of the Sea (1982), five nations abutting the region have a claim to the Arctic: Norway, Denmark (through Greenland), Russia, the United States (through Alaska) and Canada. An international solution is being negotiated.

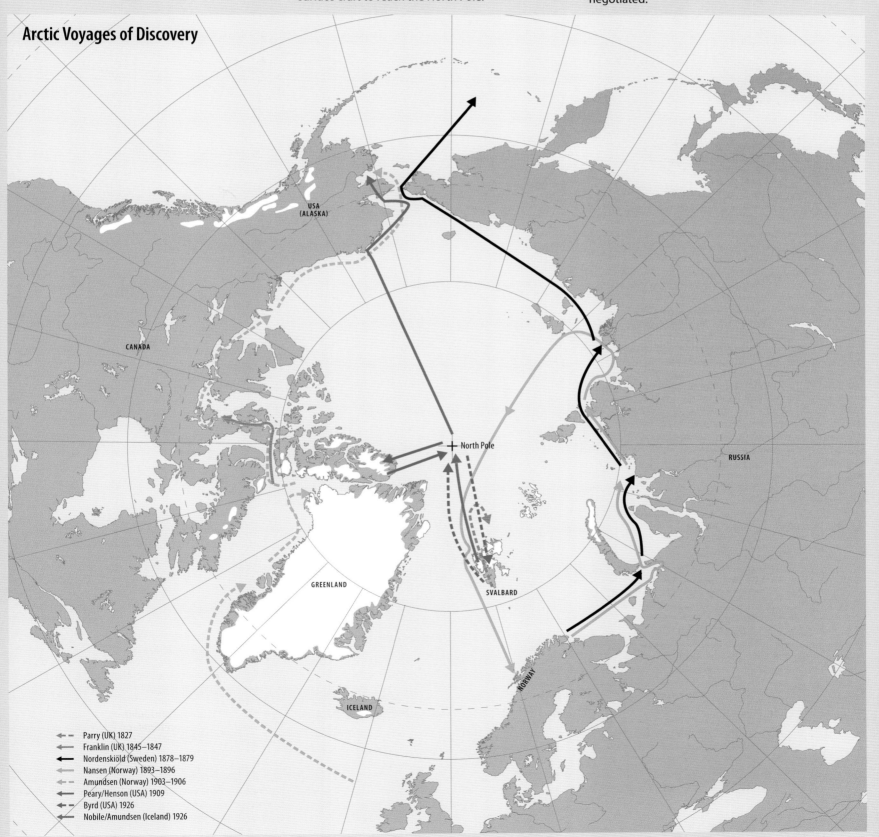

Arctic Voyages of Discovery

Parry (UK) 1827
Franklin (UK) 1845–1847
Nordenskiöld (Sweden) 1878–1879
Nansen (Norway) 1893–1896
Amundsen (Norway) 1903–1906
Peary/Henson (USA) 1909
Byrd (USA) 1926
Nobile/Amundsen (Iceland) 1926

The Antarctic Region

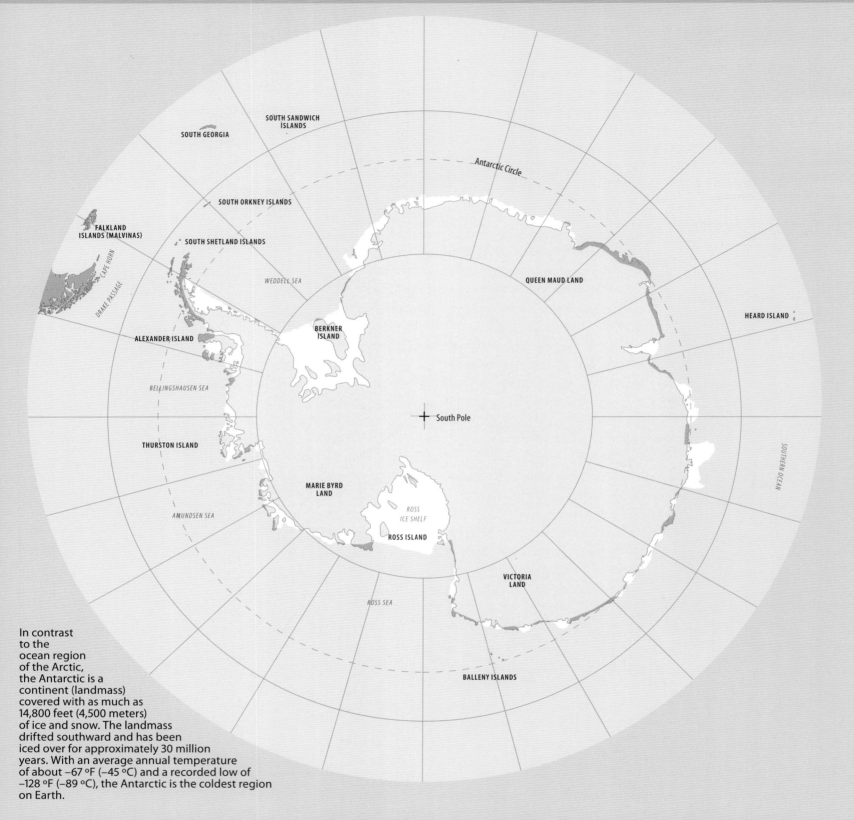

In contrast to the ocean region of the Arctic, the Antarctic is a continent (landmass) covered with as much as 14,800 feet (4,500 meters) of ice and snow. The landmass drifted southward and has been iced over for approximately 30 million years. With an average annual temperature of about –67 ºF (–45 ºC) and a recorded low of –128 ºF (–89 ºC), the Antarctic is the coldest region on Earth.

1513–1754 Maps of the world assume the existence of a gigantic southern continent called *Terra Australis Incognita*. The depictions bear some similarities to Antarctica, so an earlier discovery cannot be ruled out.

1599 Dirck Gerritszoon Pomp of the Netherlands possibly sights the South Shetland Islands.

1773 James Cook's expedition is probably the first to cross the Antarctic Circle, hitting pack ice.

1820 Antarctica is first sighted by a Russian ship under Fabian von Bellingshausen or by an English ship commanded by Edward Bransfield.

1821 The first landing of American seal hunters in the Antarctic.

1837/38 Frenchman Jules Dumont d'Urville sights Adélie Coast.

1839 The expedition of James Clark Ross attempts to reach the South Magnetic Pole (Ross Sea).

1895 The International Geographical Congress in London calls for international engagement in Antarctic research.

1901–1903 The first German Antarctic journey (the *Gauss* expedition) is led by Erich von Drygalski, who publishes extensive volumes of research afterward.

1901–1904 English naval officer Robert Falcon Scott makes his first Antarctic expedition.

1907–1909 British polar researcher Ernest Shackleton's expedition comes within 97 miles (156 km) of the South Pole.

1911 Australian geologist Douglas Mawson explores Antarctica.

1911/12 The Norwegian Roald Amundsen and the Robert Falcon Scott race to the South Pole. Amundsen reaches the pole first on December 14, 1911; Scott's party follows on January 17, 1912. Tragically, all the members of Scott's expedition die on the return journey before reaching their ships.

1914 The ship *Endurance* under Captain Ernest Henry Shackleton attempts to sail through the Antarctic, but is trapped and eventually crushed in pack ice.

1928 The tragic crash of the dirigible *Italia* piloted by Umberto Nobile is followed by a dramatic rescue of the survivors, during which Norwegian explorer Roald Amundsen dies.

1929 American pilot Richard Evelyn Byrd is the first to fly over the South Pole, making five expeditions through 1956.

1938/39 An Antarctic expedition led by Alfred Ritscher claims New Swabia for Germany.

1946/47 Operation High Jump is the largest Antarctic expedition in history. Byrd brings 4,700 people to McMurdo Sound, and Antarctica is mapped.

1956 American George Dufek is the third person (after Amundsen and Scott) to reach the South Pole.

1959 The Antarctic Treaty is signed.

1989 Reinhold Messner and Arved Fuchs are the first to cross Antarctica by foot, which they accomplish in ninety-two days.

2001 Ann Bancroft and Liv Arnesen ski across Antarctica.

The Antarctic Treaty

An international treaty signed in 1959, it went into effect in 1961 and will remain so until 2041. It provides for purely peaceful use of the Antarctic, primarily for scientific research, and contains strict controls for environmental protection. Originally agreed upon by twelve nations, thirty-three additional countries have signed since 1961.

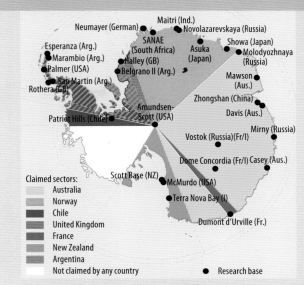

Claimed sectors:
- Australia
- Norway
- Chile
- United Kingdom
- France
- New Zealand
- Argentina
- Not claimed by any country
- ● Research base

Antarctic Voyages of Discovery, 1900

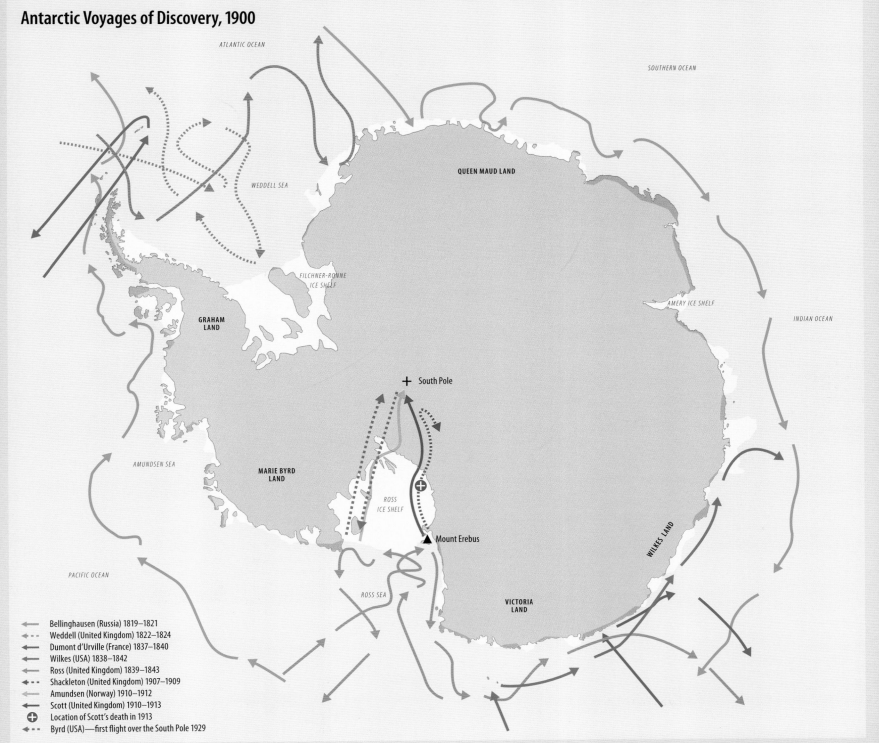

- ⟵ Bellinghausen (Russia) 1819–1821
- ⟵ Weddell (United Kingdom) 1822–1824
- ⟵ Dumont d'Urville (France) 1837–1840
- ⟵ Wilkes (USA) 1838–1842
- ⟵ Ross (United Kingdom) 1839–1843
- ⟵ Shackleton (United Kingdom) 1907–1909
- ⟵ Amundsen (Norway) 1910–1912
- ⟵ Scott (United Kingdom) 1910–1913
- ⊕ Location of Scott's death in 1913
- ⟵ Byrd (USA)—first flight over the South Pole 1929

473

Countries of the World – Europe

The following pages provide recent figures for some of the most important data about each country, arranged geographically.

Key to Symbols:

- Area (square miles/kilometers)
- Population
- **GDP** Gross Domestic Product in US$
- Language(s)
- Currency
- Infant mortality rate
- Average life expectancy
- International organizations (membership)
- Monarchs

Political parties:
- Social democratic
- Conservative
- Socialist
- Liberal
- Ecological
- Nationalist
- Unclear, or party not easily fitting into classical political categories

EUROPE

Iceland

Republic of Iceland
Independent since 1918,
Republic 1944
Constitutional republic

- 39,768 miles²/103,000 km²
- 1957 164,000
- 1993 264,000
- 2009 306,695
- **GDP** US$39,800/person
- Icelandic
- Icelandic krona
- 3.25/1,000
- 80.6 years
- UNO, NATO, OAS, WHO, WTO

President
1996– Ólafur Ragnar Grimsson

Prime ministers
2006–2008 Geir Hilmar Haarde
2009– Jóhanna Sigurdóttir

Norway

Kingdom of Norway
Independence regained 1905
Constitutional monarchy

- 125,020 miles²/323,802 km²
- 1958 3,513,000
- 1993 4,360,000
- 2009 4,660,540
- **GDP** US$59,300/person
- Norwegian
- 1 Norwegian krone = 100 øre
- 3.61/1,000
- 79.8 years
- UNO, NATO, WHO, WTO

Political parties
- Labor Party (DNA)
- Conservative Party (Høyre)
- Christian People's Party (KrF)
- Liberal Party (Venstre)
- Socialist Left Party (SV)
- Center Party (Sp)
- Progress Party (FrP)

Monarchs
1905–1957 Haakon VII

- 1957–1991 Olav V
- 1991– Harald V

Prime ministers
1945–1951, 1955–1965 Einar Gerhardsen (DNA)
1965–1971 Per Borten (Sp)
1971/72, 1973–1976 Trygve Bratteli (DNA)
1976–1981 Odvar Nordli (DNA)
1981, 1986–1989, 1990–1996 Gro Harlem Brundtland (DNA)
1981–1986 Kare Willoch (Høyre)
1996–1997 Thorbjørn Jagland (DNA)
1997–2000, 2001–2005 Kjell Magne Bondevik (KrF)
2000–2001, 2005– Jens Stoltenberg (DNA)

Sweden

Kingdom of Sweden
Established ca. 800
Constitutional monarchy

- 173,731 miles²/449,964 km²
- 1959 7,434,000
- 1993 8,830,000
- 2009 9,059,650
- **GDP** US$36,800/person
- Swedish
- 1 Swedish krone = 100 öre
- 2.75/1,000
- 80.8 years
- UNO, EU (1995), WHO, WTO

Political parties
- Swedish Social Democratic Party (SAP)
- Moderate Party (MS)
- Liberal People's Party (FL)
- Center Party (C)
- Christian Democratic Party (K)
- Environment Party the Greens
- Left Party (Vänsterpartiet/V)

Monarchs
1907–1950 Gustav V
1950–1973 Gustav VI Adolf
1973– Carl XVI Gustav

Prime ministers
1946–1969 Tage Erlander (SAP)
1969–1976, 1982–1986 Olof Palme (SAP)
1976–1978, 1979–1982 Thorbjörn Fälldin (C)
1978–1979 Ola Ullsten (FL)
1986–1991, 1994–1996 Ingvar Carlsson (SAP)
1991–1994 Carl Bildt (MS)
1996–2006 Göran Persson (SAP)
2006– Fredrik Reinfeldt (MS)

Finland

Republic of Finland
Independent since 1917
Republic

- 130,558 miles²/338,145 km²
- 1958 4,395,500
- 1993 5,090,000
- 2009 5,250,275
- **GDP** US$34,900/person
- Finnish, Swedish
- Euro (since 2002) = 5.95 Finnish marks
- 3.5/1,000
- 78.8 years
- UNO, EU (1995), WHO, WTO

Political parties
- Social Democratic Party of Finland (SDP)
- Center Party (Kesk)
- Agrarian Party
- National Coalition Party (Kok)
- Green Party (VIHR)
- Left Alliance (VAS)
- Christian Democrats (KD)
- True Finns

Presidents
1944–1946 Carl Gustaf Mannerheim
1946–1956 Juho Kusti Paasikivi
1956–1981 Urho Kekkonen (Agrarian Party)
1982–1994 Mauno Koivisto (SDP)
1994–2000 Martti Ahtisaari (SDP)
2000– Tarja Halonen (SDP)

Prime ministers
1950–1953, 1954–1956 Urho Kekkonen (Agrarian Party)
1968–1970, 1979–1982 Mauno Koivisto (SDP)
1972–1975, 1977–1979, 1982–1987 Taisto Kalevi Sorsa (SDP)
1987–1991 Harri Holkeri (Kesk)
1991–1995 Erko Aho (Kesk)
1995–2003 Paavo Lipponen (SDP)
2003 Anneli Jäätteenmäki (Kesk)
2003– Matti Vanhanen (Kesk)

Great Britain

United Kingdom of Great Britain and Northern Ireland
Act of Union 1707/1800
Constitutional monarchy

- 94,525 miles²/244,820 km²
- 1956 51,611,000
- 1993 58,390,000
- 2009 61,113,205
- GDP US$35,400/person
- English
- 1 British pound (pound sterling) = 100 pence
- 4.93/1,000
- 78.9 years
- UNO, G8, EU (1973), NATO, WHO, WTO

Political parties
- Labour Party
- Conservative Party (Tories)
- Liberal Democrats
- Additional parties in the parliaments of Scotland, Wales and Northern Ireland

Monarchs
- 1936–1952 George VI
- 1952– Elizabeth II

Prime ministers
1940–1945, 1951–1955 Winston Churchill (Con.)
1945–1951 Clement Attlee (Lab.)
1955–1957 Anthony Eden (Con.)
1957–1963 Harold Macmillan (Con.)
1963–1964 Alec Douglas-Home (Con.)
1964–1970, 1974–1976 Harold Wilson (Lab.)
1970–1974 Edward Heath (Con.)
1976–1979 James Callaghan (Lab.)
1979–1990 Margaret Thatcher (Con.)
1990–1997 John Major (Con.)
1997–2007 Tony Blair (Lab.)
2007– Gordon Brown (Lab.)

Foreign secretary
1940–1945 Anthony Eden (Con.)
1945–1951 Ernest Bevin (Lab.)
1951 Herbert Morrison (Lab.)
1951–1955 Anthony Eden (2nd term)
1955 Harold Macmillan (Con.)
1955–1960 Selwyn Lloyd (Con.)
1960–1963 Alec Douglas-Home (Con.)
1963–1964 R.A. Butler (Con.)
1964–1965 Patrick Gordon Walker (Lab.)
1965–1966 Michael Stewart (Lab.)
1966–1968 George Brown (Lab.)
1968–1970 Michael Stewart (2nd term)
1970–1974 Alec Douglas-Home (2nd term)
1974–1976 James Callaghan (Lab.)
1976–1977 Anthony Crosland (Lab.)
1977–1979 David Owen (Lab.)
1979–1982 Peter Carington (Con.)
1982–1983 Francis Pym (Con.)
1983–1989 Geoffrey Howe (Con.)

1989 John Major (Con.)
1989–1995 Douglas Hurd (Con.)
1995–1997 Malcolm Rifkind (Con.)
1997–2001 Robin Cook (Lab.)
2001–2006 Jack Straw (Lab.)
2006–2007 Margaret Beckett (Lab.)
2007– David Milliband (Lab.)

Ireland

Ireland (Eire)
Independent since 1921
Constitution 1937; Parliamentary republic

- 27,135 miles²/70,280 km²
- 1956 2,898,264
- 1993 3,530,000
- 2009 4,203,200
- GDP US$42,200/person
- Irish, English
- Euro (since 2002) = 0.79 Irish pounds
- 5.14/1,000
- 78.1 years
- UNO, EU (1973), WHO, WTO

Political parties
- Fianna Fáil (FF)
- Fine Gael (FG)
- Sinn Féin (Catholic)
- Irish Labour Party
- Progressive Democrats (1985–2009)
- Green Party

Presidents (Uachtaráin na hÉireann)
1945–1959 Seán Ó Ceallaigh
1959–1973 Eamon de Valera (FF)
1973–1974 Erskine Hamilton Childers (FF)
1974–1976 Cearbhall Ó Dálaigh
1976–1990 Patrick Hillery (FF)
1990–1997 Mary Robinson
1997– Mary McAleese (FF)

Prime ministers (Taoiseach)
1937–1948, 1951–1954, 1957–1959 Eamon de Valera (FF)
1959–1966 Seán Lemass (FF)
1966–1973, 1977–1979 Jack Lynch (FF)
1979–1981, 1982, 1987–1992 Charles J. Haughley (FF)
1981/82, 1982–1987 Garret FitzGerald (FG)
1992–1994 Albert Reynolds (FF)
1994–1997 John Bruton (FG)
1997–2008 Bertie Ahern (FF)
2008– Brian Cowen (FF)

Netherlands

Kingdom of the Netherlands
Established in 1581
Constitutional monarchy

- 16,033 miles²/41,526 km²
- 1959 11,278,700
- 1993 15,450,000
- 2009 16,716,000
- GDP US$39,000/person
- Dutch, Frisian (in Friesland province)
- Euro (since 2002) = 2.20 guilders
- 4.81/1,000
- 79.3 years
- UNO, EU (1950), NATO, WHO, WTO

Political parties
- Christian Democratic Appeal (CDA, formerly KVP)
- Labor Party (Social democrats/PvdA)

- People's Party for Freedom and Democracy (VVD)
- Party for Freedom (national/liberal, PVV)
- Socialist Party (SP)
- Green Left Party (GL)
- Christian Union Party (CU)
- Democrats 66 (D66)
- Additional parties

Monarchs
- 1890–1948 Wilhelmina
- 1948–1980 Juliana
- 1980– Beatrix

Prime ministers
1948–1958 Willem Drees (PvdA)
1967–1971 Piet de Jong (KVP)
1973–1977 Joop den Uyl (PvdA)
1977–1982 Dries van Agt (CDA)
1982–1994 Ruud Lubbers (CDA)
1994–2002 Wim Kok (PvdA)
2002– Jan Peter Balkenende (CDA)

Belgium

Kingdom of Belgium
Established in 1830
Parliamentary monarchy

- 11,787 miles²/30,528 km²
- 1958 9,026,778
- 1993 10,100,000
- 2009 10,414,335
- GDP US$36,600/person
- Dutch, French, German
- Euro (since 2002) = 40.34 Belgian francs
- 4.5/1,000
- 79.1 years
- UNO, EU (1950), NATO, WHO, WTO

Political parties
- Christian Democratic & Flemish (CD&V)
- Flemish Liberals and Democrats (VLD)
- Belgian Socialist Party (PSB)
- Social Liberal Party
- Groen!
- Reform Movement (MR)
- National Front
- Several smaller/regional parties

Monarchs
- 1934–1951 Leopold III
- 1951–1993 Baudouin I
- 1993– Albert II

Prime ministers
1945/46, 1954–1958 Achille Van Acker (PSB)
1946, 1947–1949 Paul-Henri Spaak (PSB)
1949–1950, 1958–1961, 1968–1973 Gaston Eyskens (CD&V)
1974–1978 Leo Tindemans (CD&V)
1979–1992 Wilfried Martens (CD&V)
1992–1999 Jean-Luc Dehaene (CD&V)
1999–2008 Guy Verhofstadt (VLD)
2008 Yves Leterme (CD&V)
2008 Herman Van Rompuy (CD&V)
2009– Yves Leterme (CD&V)

Luxembourg

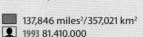

Grand Duchy of Luxembourg
Independent since 1867
Constitutional monarchy

- 998 miles²/2,586 km²
- 1955 311,633
- 1993 395,000

- 2009 491,775
- GDP US$77,600/person
- Luxembourgish, German, French
- Euro (since 2002) = 40.34 francs
- 4.62/1,000
- 79.2 years
- UNO, EU (1950), NATO, WHO, WTO

Grand Duke
2000– Henry I

Prime minister
1995– Jean-Claude Juncker

Denmark

Kingdom of Denmark
Unified state in 980
Constitutional monarchy

- 16,639 miles²/43,094 km²
- 1957 4,476,000
- 1993 5,190,000
- 2009 5,500,510
- GDP US$36,200/person
- Danish
- 1 Danish krone = 100 öre
- 4.4/1,000
- 78.1 years
- UNO, EU (1973), NATO, WHO, WTO

Political parties
- Social Democrats (S)
- Venstre (Liberal Party of Denmark)
- Det Radikale Venstre ("Radical Left")
- Conservative People's Party (KF)
- Red-Green Unity List (alliance)
- Christian Democrats (K)
- Danish People's Party (national conservative/DF)
- Liberal Alliance
- Communist Party of Denmark (DKP)
- Socialist People's Party (SF)

Monarchs
- 1912–1947 Christian X
- 1947–1972 Frederick IX
- 1972– Margrethe II

Prime ministers
1955–1960 Hans Christian Svane Hansen (S)
1962–1968, 1971/72 Jens Otto Krag (S)
1972/73, 1975–1982 Anker Jørgensen (S)
1982–1993 Poul Schlüter (KF)
1993–2001 Poul Nyrup Rasmussen (S)
2001–2009 Anders Rasmussen (Venstre)
2009– Lars Lokke Rasmussen (Venstre)

Germany

Federal Republic of Germany
Established in 1949
Federal republic

- 137,846 miles²/357,021 km²
- 1993 81,410,000
- 2009 82,329,760
- GDP US$34,200/person
- German
- Euro: since 2002 = 1.96 German marks
- 4.03/1,000
- 79.1 years
- UNO, G8, EU (1951), NATO, WHO, WTO

Political parties
- Christian Democratic Union (CDU)
- Social Democratic Party of Germany (SPD)

Countries of the World – Europe

☐ Free Democratic Party (FDP)
▨ Alliance '90/The Greens (B'90 Greens)
■ Die Linke (Left Party)
■ Christian Social Union (CSU)

Presidents
1949–1959 Theodor Heuss (FDP)
1959–1969 Heinrich Lübke (CDU)
1969–1974 Gustav Heinemann (SPD)
1974–1979 Walter Scheel (FDP)
1979–1984 Karl Carstens (CDU)
1984–1994 Richard von Weizsäcker (CDU)
1994–1999 Roman Herzog (CDU)
1999–2004 Johannes Rau (SPD)
2004– Horst Köhler (CDU)

Chancellors
1949–1963 Konrad Adenauer (CDU)
1963–1966 Ludwig Erhard (CDU)
1966–1969 Kurt Georg Kiesinger (CDU)
1969–1974 Willy Brandt (SPD)
1974–1982 Helmut Schmidt (SPD)
1982–1998 Helmut Kohl (CDU)
1998–2005 Gerhard Schröder (SPD)
2005– Angela Merkel (CDU)

Foreign ministers
1951–1955 Konrad Adenauer (CDU)
1955–1961 Heinrich von Brentano (CDU)
1961–1966 Gerhard Schröder (CDU)
1966–1969 Willy Brandt (SPD)
1969–1974 Walter Scheel (FDP)
1974–1992 Hans Dietrich Genscher (FDP)
1992–1998 Klaus Kinkel (FDP)
1998–2005 Joschka Fischer (Greens)
2005–2009 Frank-Walter Steinmeier (SPD)
2009– Guido Westerwelle (FDP)

In the GDR (East Germany, 1949–1990):
General Secretary of the Central
Committee of the Socialist Unity
Party (SED)
1950–1971 Walter Ulbricht
1971–1989 Erich Honecker
1989 Egon Krenz

Chairman of the State Council
1949–1960 Wilhelm Pieck (SED)
(president of the GDR)
1960–1973 Walter Ulbricht (SED)
1973–1976 Willi Stoph (SED)
1976–1989 Erich Honecker (SED)
1989 Egon Krenz (SED)
1989–1990 Manfred Gerlach (LDPD)

Prime ministers
1949–1964 Otto Grotewohl (SED)
1964–1973, 1976–1989 Willi Stoph (SED)
1973–1976 Horst Sindermann (SED)
1989–1990 Hans Modrow (SED)
1990 Lothar de Maizière (CDU)

Czech Republic
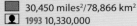
Czech Republic
Independent Czechoslovakia
from 1918, divided in 1993
Parliamentary democracy

■ 30,450 miles²/78,866 km²
👤 1993 10,330,000
👤 2009 10,211,905
GDP US$25,100/person
💬 Czech
€ Czech krone (CZK)
⊕ 3.83/1,000
👥 76.6 years
🌐 UNO, EU (2004), NATO, WHO, WTO

Political parties
Official state party 1948–1989 was the
Communist Party of Czechoslovakia (KSČ).
☐ Czech Social Democratic Party
(ČSSD)
☐ Civic Democratic Party (ODS)
■ Christian Democratic Union-
Czechoslovak People's Party
(KDU-ČSL)
▨ Green Party
■ Communist Party of Bohemia and
Moravia (KSČM)

General Secretaries of the Central
Committee of the Communist Party
1929–1953 Klement Gottwald
1953–1968 Antonin Novotny
1968–1969 Alexander Dubček
1969–1987 Gustáv Husák
1987–1989 Miloš Jakeš
Presidents
a) Czechoslovak (Socialist) Republic
1948–1953 Klement Gottwald
1953–1957 Antonin Zápotocky
1957–1968 Antonin Novotny
1968–1975 Ludvik Svoboda
1975–1989 Gustáv Husák
1989–1992 Václav Havel (Civic Forum/OF)
b) Czech Republic
1993–2003 Václav Havel (OF)
2003– Václav Klaus (ODS)
Prime ministers
a) Czechoslovak (Socialist) Republic
1946–1948 Klement Gottwald
1948–1953 Antonin Zápotocky
1953–1963 Viliam Široky
1963–1968 Jozef Lenárt
1968–1970 Oldřich Černik
1970–1988 Lubomir Štrougal
b) Czech Republic
1992–1997 Václav Klaus (ODS)
1997–1998 Jozef Tošovsky (independent)
1998–2002 Miloš Zeman (ČSSD)
2002–2004 Vladimir Špilla (ČSSD)
2004–2005 Stanislaw Gross (ČSSD)
2005–2006 Jiři Paroubek (ČSSD)
2006–2009 Mirek Topolánek (ODS)
2009– Jan Fischer (independent)

Slovakia

Slovak Republic
Founded in 1993 by splitting of
the Czech Republic (see also)
Parliamentary democracy

■ 18,933 miles²/49,036 km²
👤 1993 5,367,790
👤 2009 5,463,045
GDP US$21,100/person
💬 Slovak
€ Euro (since 2009) = 30.13 koruna (crowns)
⊕ 6.98/1,000
👥 75.2 years
🌐 UNO, EU (2004), NATO, WHO, WTO

Political parties
▐ People's Party (HZDS)
■ Movement for Democracy (HZD)
☐ Direction-Social Democracy (SMER)
■ Slovak Democratic and Christian Union-
Democratic Party (SDKU)
▐ Party of Civic Understanding (SOP;
until 2003)
■ Party of the Democratic Left (SDL)

Presidents
1993–1998 Michal Kováč (HZDS)

1999–2004 Rudolf Schuster (SOP)
2004– Ivan Gašparovič (HZD)

Prime ministers
1993–1994, 1994–1998 Vladimir Mečiar
(HZDS)
1994 Jozef Moravčik
1998–2006 Mikuláš Dzurinda (SDKU)
2006– Robert Fico (SMER)

Poland
Republic of Poland
Independence in 1918
Republic

■ 120,728 miles²/312,685 km²
👤 1958 29,000,000
👤 1993 38,600,000
👤 2009 38,482,920
GDP US$17,800/person
💬 Polish
€ 1 złoty = 100 groszy
⊕ 6.93/1,000
👥 75.4 years
🌐 UNO, EU (2004), NATO, WHO, WTO

Political parties
The Polish United Workers' Party
(PUWP) governed Poland between
1948 and 1989.
▐ Civic Platform (PO)
■ Law and Justice (PiS)
☐ Democratic Left Alliance (SLD,
previously SdRP)
☐ Polish People's Party (PSL)
☐ Social Democracy of Poland (SDPL)
☐ Democratic Party (SD)
■ Solidarity Electoral Action (AWS)
▐ League of Polish Families (LPR)

General Secretary of the Polish
United Workers' Party
1948–1956 Bolesław Bierut
1956 Edward Ochab
1956–1970 Władysław Gomułka
1970–1980 Edward Gierek
1980–1981 Stanisław Kania
1981–1989 Wojciech Jaruzelski
1989–1990 Mieczysław Rakowski

Heads of state
a) Chairman of the Polish Council of State
1952–1964 Aleksander Zawadzki
1964–1968 Edward Ochab
1972–1985 Henryk Jabłoński
1985–1989 Wojciech Jaruzelski
b) Presidents of the Republic
1989–1990 Wojciech Jaruzelski
1990–1995 Lech Wałęsa (Solidarność)
1995–2005 Aleksander Kwaśniewski
(SdRP)
2005– Lech Kaczyński (PiS)

Prime ministers
a) People's Republic
1947–1952, 1954–1970 Józef Cyrankiewicz
1952–1954 Bolesław Bierut
1970–1980 Piotr Jaroszewicz
1981–1985 Wojciech Jaruzelski
b) Republic
1989–1997 very frequent changes
1997–2001 Jerzy Buzek (AWS)
2001–2004 Leszek Miller (SLD)
2004–2005 Marek Belka (SLD)
2005–2006 Kazimierz Marcinkiewicz (PiS)
2006–2007 Jarosław Kaczyński (PiS)
2007– Donald Tusk (PO)

Lithuania
Republic of Lithuania
Independence in 1918,
again in 1990
Parliamentary republic

■ 25,174 miles²/65,200 km²
👤 1993 3,700,000
👤 2009 3,555,180
GDP US$15,000/person
💬 Lithuanian
€ 1 litas = 100 centas
⊕ 6.57/1,000
👥 74.7 years
🌐 UNO, EU (2004), NATO, WHO, WTO

President
2009– Dalia Grybauskaitė

Prime minister
2008– Andrius Kubilius

Latvia
Republic of Latvia
Independence in 1918,
again in 1991
Parliamentary republic

■ 24,938 miles²/64,589 km²
👤 1993 2,500,000
👤 2009 2,231,505
GDP US$14,500/person
💬 Latvian
€ 1 lats = 100 santims
⊕ 8.96/1,000
👥 71.9 years
🌐 UNO, EU (2004), NATO, WHO, WTO

President
2007– Valdis Zatlers

Prime minister
2007– Valdis Dombrovskis

Estonia
Republic of Estonia
Independence in 1918,
again in 1991
Parliamentary republic

■ 17,462 miles²/45,226 km²
👤 1993 1,536,000
👤 2009 1,299,370
GDP US$18,800/person
💬 Estonian
€ 1 Estonian kroon = 100 sent
⊕ 7.45/1,000
👥 72.6 years
🌐 UNO, EU (2004), NATO, WHO, WTO

President
2006– Toomas Hendrik Ilves

Prime minister
2005– Andrus Ansip

Belarus
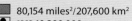

Republic of Belarus
Independence in 1991
Presidential republic

■ 80,154 miles²/207,600 km²
👤 1993 10,300,000
👤 2009 9,648,535
GDP US$11,600/person

Belarusian, Russian
1 Belarusian ruble = 100 kapeyka
6.53/1,000
70.4 years
UNO, OSCE, WHO, WTO

President
1994– Alexander Lukashenko
(de facto dictator)

Prime minister
2003– Sergei Sidorsky

Russia

Russian Federation
Soviet Union/USSR 1917–1991,
Russian Federation founded in 1991
Semi-presidential republic

6,592,735 miles²/17,075,200 km²
1993 147,860,000
2009 140,041,250
GDP US$15,200/person
Russian
1 ruble = 100 kopeks
10.81/1,000
66 years
UNO, UN Security Council, G8, ASEAN,
WHO, WTO

Political parties
*During the Soviet Union period, 1917–1991,
the CPSU was the sole governing party.*
- ☐ United Russia (centrist governing party)
- ☐ A Just Russia
- ☐ Communist Party of the Russian Federation (second-largest party)
- ☐ Liberal Democratic Party of Russia
- ☐ The Other Russia (umbrella coalition of opponents of then-President Putin)
- ☐ Right Cause (liberal)
- ☐ Patriots of Russia
- ☐ National Bolshevik Party
  The Russian United Democratic Party
- ☐ Yabloko (social liberal opposition)

General Secretaries of the Communist Party of the Soviet Union
1903/17–1922 Vladimir Ilyich Lenin
1922–1953 Joseph Stalin
1953 Georgy Maximilianovich Malenkov
1953–1964 Nikita Sergeyevich Khrushchev
1964–1982 Leonid Ilyich Brezhnev
1982–1984 Yuri Vladimirovich Andropov
1984–1985 Konstantin Ustinovich Chernenko
1985–1991 Mikhail Sergeyevich Gorbachev

Chairmen of the Central Executive Committee of the USSR/Presidents
1917 Lev Borisovich Kamenev
1917–1919 Yakov Mikhaylovich Sverdlov
1919–1946 Mikhail Ivanovich Kalinin
1946–1953 Nikolay Mikhailovich Shvernik
1953–1960 Kliment Yefremovich Voroshilov
1960–1964, 1977–1982 Leonid Brezhnev
1964–1965 Anastas Hovhannesi Mikoyan
1965–1977 Nikolai Viktorovich Podgorny
1983–1984 Yuri Vladimirovich Andropov
1984–1985 Konstantin Chernenko
1985–1988 Andrei Andreyevich Gromyko
1988–1991 Mikhail Gorbachev

President of Russia
1991–1999 Boris Nikolayevich Yeltsin
2000–2008 Vladimir Vladimirovich Putin
2008– Dmitry Anatolyevich Medvedev

Chairmen of the Council of People's Commissars of the USSR/ Premiers of the Soviet Union
1917–1924 Vladimir Ilyich Lenin
1924–1930 Alexey Ivanovich Rykov
1930–1941 Vyacheslav M. Molotov
1941–1953 Joseph Stalin
1953–1955 Georgy M. Malenkov
1955–1958 Nikolai A. Bulganin
1958–1964 Nikita S. Khrushchev
1964–1980 Aleksei N. Kosygin
1980–1985 Nikolai A. Tikhonov
1985–1990 Nikolai Ivanovich Ryzhkov
1991 Valentin Sergeyevich Pavlov
1991 Ivan Stepanovich Silayev (acting)

Prime ministers of the Russian Federation
1991–1992 Boris Nikolayevich Yeltsin
1992 Yegor Timurovich Gaidar (acting)
1992–1998 Viktor Stepanovich Chernomyrdin (in 1998 again, acting)
1998 Sergey Vladilenovich Kiriyenko
1998–1999 Yevgeny M. Primakov
1999 Sergei Vadimovich Stepashin
1999–2000, 2008– Vladimir V. Putin
2000–2004 Mikhail M. Kasyanov
2004 Viktor B. Khristenko (acting)
2004–2007 Mikhail Y. Fradkov
2007–2008 Viktor A. Zubkov

Ukraine

Ukraine
Independence in 1991
Semi-presidential republic

233,089 miles²/603,700 km²
1993 51,640,000
2009 45,700,395
GDP US$6,400/person
Ukrainian
1 hryvnia = 100 kopiyka
9.23/1,000
68.1 years
UNO, WHO, WTO

Political parties
- ■ Our Ukraine (NU)
- ☐ Social Democratic Party (United) of Ukraine (SDPU)
- ◼ Socialist Party of Ukraine (SPU)
- ☐ Fatherland Party (Batkivshchyna) (BYUT)
- ▮ Party of Industrialists and Entrepreneurs of Ukraine (PPPU)
- ☐ Party of Regions
- ☐ Liberal Democratic Party of Ukraine
- ☐ Reforms and Order Party
- ◼ Party of Greens of Ukraine (PZU)

Presidents
1990–1994 Leonid Kravchuk (SDPU)
1994–2005 Leonid Kuchma
2005– Viktor Yushchenko (NU)

Prime ministers
1991–1992 Vitold Fokin
1992–1993 Leonid Kuchma
1994–1995 Vitaliy Masol
1995–1996 Yevhen Marchuk

1996–1997 Pavlo Lazarenko
1997–1999 Valeriy Pustovoitenko
1999–2001 Viktor Yushchenko
2001–2002 Anatolij Kinach (PPPU)
2002–2005, 2006–2007 Viktor Yanukovych (Party of Regions)
2005–2006 Yuriy Yekhanurov (NU)
2005, 2007– Yulia Tymoshenko (BYUT)

Moldova

Republic of Moldova
Independence in 1991
Parliamentary republic

13,067 miles²/33,843 km²
1993 4,400,000
2009 4,320,750
GDP US$2,400/person
Moldovan (Romanian), regionally also Russian, Ukrainiaan, Gagauz
1 Moldovan leu = 100 bani
13.5/1,000
70.5 years
UNO, OSCE, WHO, WTO

President
2009– Mihai Ghimpu (acting)

Prime minister
2009– Vlad Filat

France

French Republic
Fifth French Republic 1959
Semi-presidential republic

248,427 miles²/643,427 km²
1959 44,788,000
1993 58,000,000
2009 64,057,790
GDP US$32,800/person
French
Euro since 2002 = 6.56 francs
3.36/1,000
80.9 years
UNO, EU (1950), NATO, G8, WHO, WTO

Political parties
- ■ Union for a Popular Movement (UMP)
  The UPM includes the former parties UNR, UDF and RPR.
- ☐ Socialist Party (PS)
- ◼ The Greens
- ◼ French Communist Party (PCF)
- ■ New Center (NC)
- ◼ National Front (FN)
- ☐ Democratic Movement (MoDem)

Presidents
a) Provisional Government
1944–1946 Charles de Gaulle
1946 Félix Gouin
1946 Georges Bidault
1946–1947 Léon Blum
b) Fourth French Republic
1947–1954 Vincent Auriol (PS)
1954–1959 René Coty
c) Fifth French Republic
1959–1969 Charles de Gaulle (UNR)
1969–1974 Georges Pompidou (UDR)
1974–1981 Valéry Giscard d'Estaing (UDF)
1981–1995 François Mitterand (PS)
1995–2007 Jacques Chirac (UMP)
2007– Nicolas Sarkozy (UMP)

Prime ministers/Heads of government
a) Fourth French Republic
1947 Paul Ramadier
1947–1948 Robert Schuman
1948 André Marie
1948–1949, 1950, 1951 Henri Queuille
1949–1950 Georges Bidault
1950–1951, 1951–1952 René Pleven
1952, 1955–1956 Edgar Faure
1952–1953 Antoine Pinay
1953 René Mayer
1953–1954 Joseph Laniel
1954–1955 Pierre Mendès France
1956–1957 Guy Mollet
1957 Maurice Bourgès-Maunory
1957–1958 Félix Gaillard
1958 Pierre Pflimlin
1958–1959 Charles de Gaulle

b) Fifth French Republic
1959–1962 Michel Debré (UNR)
1962–1968 Georges Pompidou (UNR)
1968–1969 Maurice Couve de Murville (UNR)
1969–1972 Jacques Chaban-Delmas (UNR/UDR)
1972–1974 Pierre Messmer (UNR/UDR)
1974–1976, 1986–1988 Jacques Chirac (RPR, cohabitation)
1976–1981 Raymond Barre (independent)
1981–1984 Pierre Mauroy (PS)
1984–1986 Laurent Fabius (PS)
1988–1991 Michel Rocard (SP)
1991–1992 Édith Cresson (SP)
1992–1993 Pierre Bérégovoy (SP)
1993–1995 Édouard Balladur (RPR/UMP; cohabitation)
1995–1997 Alain Juppé (RPR/UMP)
1997–2002 Lionel Jospin (PS; cohabitation)
2002–2005 Jean-Pierre Raffarin (UMP)
2005–2007 Dominique de Villepin (UMP)
2007– François Fillon (UMP)

Ministers of foreign affairs
a) Fourth French Republic
1944–1946, 1947–1948, 1953–1954 Georges Bidault
1946–1947 Léon Blum
1948–1953 Robert Schuman
1954–1955 Pierre Mendès-France
1955 Edgar Faure
1955–1956 Antoine Pinay
1956–1958 Christian Pineau
1958 René Pleven

b) Fifth French Republic
1958–1968 Maurice Couve de Murville (UNR)
1968–1969 Michel Debré (UNR)
1969–1973 Maurice Schumann (UDR)
1973 André Bettencourt (UDR)
1973–1974 Michel Jobert (UDR)
1974–1976 Jean Sauvagnargues (RPR)
1976–1978 Louis de Guiringaud (no party affiliation)
1978–1981 Jean François-Poncet (UDF)
1981–1984 Claude Cheysson (PS)
1984–1986, 1988–1993 Roland Dumas (PS)
1986–1988 Jean-Bernard Raimond (RPR)
1993–1995 Alain Juppé (RPR/UMP)
1995–1997 Hervé de Charette (UMP)
1997–2002 Hubert Védrine (PS)
2002–2004 Dominique de Villepin (UMP)
2004–2005 Michel Barnier (UMP)
2005–2007 Philippe Douste-Blazy (UMP)
2007– Bernard Kouchner (UMP)

Countries of the World – Europe

Andorra

Principality of Andorra
Independence in 1278
Democracy; coprincipality

- 181 miles²/468 km²
- 1954 5,664
- 1993 70,000
- 2009 83,890
- GDP US$42,500/person
- Catalan
- Euro (introduced; has no currency of its own, but uses French and Spanish)
- 3.68/1,000
- 82.7 years
- UNO, WHO, WTO

Co-princes (chiefs of state)
2003– Joan Enric Vives Sicília, bishop of Urgell
2007– Nicolas Sarkozy, president of the French Fifth Republic

Head of government (Cap de Govern)
2009– Jaume Bartumeu Cassany

Spain

Kingdom of Spain
Restored in 1975
Parliamentary monarchy

- 194,896 miles²/504,782 km²
- 1956 28,339,468
- 1993 39,200,000
- 2009 40,525,000
- GDP US$33,700/person
- Spanish
- Euro (since 2002) = 166.39 pesetas
- 4.26/1,000
- 79.9 years
- UNO, EU (1986), NATO, WHO, WTO

Political parties
- Spanish Socialist Workers Party (PSOE)
- Popular Party (PP)
- United Left (IU)
- Union, Progress and Democracy (UPyD)

Heads of state
1938–1975 Francisco Franco Bahamonde (caudillo/dictator)
1975– Juan Carlos I king)

Prime ministers
1938–1973 Francisco Franco Bahamonde (falange/dictator)
1973 Luis Carrero-Blanco (military)
1976–1981 Adolfo Suárez González (UCD/Union of the Democratic Center)
1981–1982 Leopoldo Calvo-Sotelo y Bustelo (UCD)
1982–1996 Felipe González Márquez (PSOE)
1996–2004 José María Alfredo Aznar López (PP)
2004– José Luis Rodríguez Zapatero (PSOE)

Portugal

Portuguese Republic
Republic since 1974
Parliamentary democracy

- 35,672 miles²/92,391 km²
- 1955 8,240,471
- 1993 9,900,000
- 2009 10,707,925
- GDP US$21,700/person
- Portuguese
- Euro (since 2002) = 200.48 escudos
- 4.85/1,000
- 78.1 years
- UNO, EU (1986), NATO, WHO, WTO

Political parties
- Portuguese Socialist Party (PS)
- Social Democratic Party (PSD)
- Democratic and Social Center (CDS/PP)
- Portuguese Communist Party (PCP)
- Communist Party of the Portuguese Workers (PCTP/MRPP)
- Ecologist Party (PEV)
- The Left Bloc (BE)
- People's Monarchist Party (PPM)

Presidents
a) "Estado Novo" (dictatorship of Salazar)
1926–1951 António Óscar Fragoso Carmona (UN)
1951–1958 Francisco Craveiro Lopes (UN)
1958–1974 Américo Deus Tomás (UN/ANP)
b) Carnation Revolution and Republic
1974 António Sebastião Ribeiro Spínola (MFA)
1974–1976 Francisco da Costa Gomes (MFA)
1976–1986 António dos Santos Ramalho Eanes (PRD)
1986–1996 Mário Alberto Soares (PS)
1996–2006 Jorge Branco de Sampaio (PS)
2006– Aníbal António Cavaco Silva (PSD)

Prime ministers
a) "Estado Novo" (Salazar dictatorship)
1932–1968 António de Oliveira Salazar (dictator/UN)
1968–1974 Marcelo Caetano (UN)
b) Carnation Revolution and Republic
1974–1975 Vasco dos Santos Gonçalves (National Salvation Junta)
1975–1976 José Baptista Pinheiro de Azevedo (National Salvation Junta)
1976–1978, 1983–1985 Mário Soares (PS)
1981–1983 Francisco Pinto Balsemão (PS)
1985–1995 Aníbal Cavaco Silva (PSD)
1995–2002 António Guterres (PS)
2002–2004 José Manuel Durão Barroso (PSD)
2004–2005 Pedro Santana Lopes (PSD)
2005– José Sócrates (PSD)

Switzerland

Swiss Confederation
Founded in 1291
(Swiss Confederation since 1848)
Federal republic

- 15,942 miles²/41,290 km²
- 1956 5,117,000
- 1993 7,040,000
- 2009 7,604,470
- GDP US$41,600/person
- German, French, Italian, Romansch
- 1 Swiss frank = 100 rappen/centimes/ centesimi/raps
- 4.23/1,000
- 80.8 years
- UNO, CERN, OECD, WHO, WTO

Political parties
- Swiss People's Party (SVP)
- Christian Democratic People's Party (CVP)
- Social Democratic Party of Switzerland (SP)
- Radical Free Democratic Party (FDP)
- Conservative Democratic Party (BDP)
- Evangelical People's Party (EVP)
- Green Party
- Swiss Party of Labor (PdA)

Presidents (Traditionally the duty rotates annually among the members of the Federal Council)
2001, 2006 Moritz Leuenberger (SP)
2002 Kaspar Villiger (FDP)
2003, 2008 Pascal Couchepin (FDP)
2004 Joseph Deiss (CVP)
2005 Samuel Schmid (SVP)
2007 Micheline Calmy-Rey (SP)
2009 Hans-Rudolf Merz (FDP)
2010 Doris Leuthard (CVP)

Presidents of the National Council
2004/05 Jean-Philippe Maitre (CVP)
2005 Thérèse Meyer (CVP)
2005/06 Claude Janiak (SP)
2006/07 Christine Egerszegi-Obrist (FDP)
2007/08 André Bugnon (SVP)
2008/09 Chiara Simoneschi-Cortesi (CVP)
2009/10 Pascale Bruderer Wyss (SP)

Austria

Republic of Austria
Second Republic since 1945
Parliamentary republic

- 32,382 miles²/83,870 km²
- 1956 6,983,900
- 1993 8,030,000
- 2009 8,210,280
- GDP US$39,400/person
- German, regionally also Croatian, Slovenian, Hungarian
- Euro (since 2002) = 13.76 schillings
- 4.48/1,000
- 79.4 years
- UNO, EU (1995), WHO, WTO

Political parties (National Council)
- Social Democratic Party of Austria (SPÖ)
- Austrian People's Party (ÖVP)
- Freedom Party of Austria (FPÖ)
- Alliance for the Future of Austria (BZÖ)
- The Greens—The Green Alternative

Presidents
1945–1950 Karl Renner (SPÖ)
1951–1957 Theodor Körner (SPÖ)
1957–1965 Adolf Schärf (SPÖ)
1965–1974 Franz Jonas (SPÖ)
1974–1986 Rudolf Kirchschläger (indep.)
1986–1992 Kurt Waldheim (ÖVP)
1992–2004 Thomas Klestil (ÖVP)
2004– Heinz Fischer (SPÖ)

Chancellors
1945–1953 Leopold Figl (ÖVP)
1953–1961 Julius Raab (ÖVP)
1961–1964 Alfons Gorbach (ÖVP)
1964–1970 Josef Klaus (ÖVP)
1970–1983 Bruno Kreisky (SPÖ)
1983–1986 Fred Sinowatz (SPÖ)
1986–1997 Franz Vranitzky (SPÖ)
1997–2000 Viktor Klima (SPÖ)
2000–2007 Wolfgang Schüssel (ÖVP)
2007–2008 Alfred Gusenbauer (SPÖ)
2008– Werner Faymann (SPÖ)

Liechtenstein

Principality of Liechtenstein
Independent since 1806
Parliamentary democracy under constitutional monarchy

- 62 miles²/160 km²
- 1956 15,000
- 1993 30,100
- 2009 34,760
- GDP US$122,100/person
- German
- 1 Swiss frank = 100 Rappen/centimes/ centesimi/raps
- 4.52/1,000
- 80.0 years
- UNO, OSCE, WTO

Prince
1989– Hans-Adam II, Prince of Liechtenstein (has refrained from making governmental decisions since 2004)
2004– Alois, Hereditary Prince of Liechtenstein (regent since 2004)

Prime minister
2001– Otmar Hasler

Italy

Italian Republic
Republic since 1946
Parliamentary republic

- 116,305 miles²/301,230 km²
- 1956 50,023,743
- 1993 57,200,000
- 2009 58,126,210
- GDP US$30,200/person
- Italian
- Euro (since 2002) = 1,936.27 lira
- 5.61/1,000
- 80.1 years
- UNO, G8, EU (1950), NATO, WHO, WTO

Political parties
- Forza Italia (Forward Italy/FI)
- Union of Christian and Centre Democrats (UDC, formerly DC)
- Democratic Party (PD)
- New Italian Socialist Party (NPSI, formerly PSI)
- Party of Italian Communists (PdCI)
- Italy of Values (Italia dei Valori)
- Lega Nord (North League)
- Many regional parties, new parties
- being founded and resulting from splits

Presidents
1948–1955 Luigi Einaudi (no party affiliation)
1978–1985 Sandro Pertini (PSI)
1985–1992 Francesco Cossiga (DC)
1992–1999 Oscar Luigi Scalfaro (DC)
1999–2006 Carlo Azeglio Ciampi (no party affiliation)
2006– Giorgio Napolitano (DC)

Prime ministers
1947–1953 Alcide de Gaspari (DC)
1954, 1958–63, 1982/83, 1987 Amintore Fanfani (DC)
1963–1968, 1974–1976 Aldo Moro (DC)
1972/73, 1976–1979, 1989–1992 Giulio Andreotti (DC)
1983–1987 Bettino Craxi (PSI)
1996–1998, 2006–2008 Romano Prodi (PD)
1994/95, 2001–2006, 2008– Silvio Berlusconi (FI)

Monaco

Principality of Monaco
Independent since 1297
Constitutional monarchy

- 1 mile²/2 km²
- 1956 20,422
- 1993 31,000
- 2009 32,965
- GDP US$30,000/person
- French
- Euro (since 2002)
- 5.18/1,000
- 80.0 years
- UNO, OSCE, WHO

Prince
2005– Albert II

Minister of state (head of government)
2005– Jean-Paul Proust

San Marino

Most Serene Republic
   of San Marino
Independence in 301 (world's oldest republic)
Parliamentary republic

- 24 miles²/61 km²
- 1955 14,000
- 1993 23,000
- 2009 30,165
- GDP US$41,900/person
- Italian
- Euro (since 2002)
- 5.44/1,000
- 81.9 years
- UNO, OSCE, WHO

Captains Regent
*Two are elected by the Grand Council and
General Council for a term of six months.*
2009/10 Stefano Palmieri and Francesco
Mussoni

Vatican City

The Holy See (State of the
   Vatican City)
Independence in 1929; ecclisiastical

- 0.16 miles²/0.44 km²
- 1955 1,000
- 1993 749
- 2009 825
- Italian
- Euro (since 2002)
- The Holy See has the status of a permanent observer in all organizations,
  including the United Nations.

Popes (heads of state)
1939–1958 Pius XII
1958–1963 John XXIII
1963–1978 Paul VI
1978 John Paul I
1978–2005 John Paul II
2005– Benedict XVI

Presidents of the government
Cardinal Secretary of State
2006– Cardinal Tarcisio Bertone
President of the Government
2006– Cardinal Giovanni Lajolo

Malta
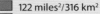

Republic of Malta
Independence since 1964
Republic

- 122 miles²/316 km²
- 1957 319,000
- 1993 363,000
- 2009 405,165
- GDP US$23,800/person
- Maltese, English
- Euro (since 2008) = 0.43 Maltese
  lira
- 3.79/1,000
- 79.3 years
- UNO, EU, OSCE, WHO, WTO

President
2009– George Abela

Prime minister
2004– Lawrence Gonzi

Slovenia
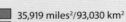

Republic of Slovenia
Independence in 1991/92
Republic

- 7,827 miles²/20,273 km²
- 1993 1,900,000
- 2009 2,005,690
- GDP US$28,200/person
- Slovene
- Euro (since 2007) = 239.64 tolars
- 4.3/1,000
- 76.7 years
- UNO, EU (2004), NATO, WHO, WTO

President
2007– Danilo Türk

Prime minister
2008– Borut Pahor

Hungary

Republic of Hungary
Third Republic since 1989
Parliamentary democracy

- 35,919 miles²/93,030 km²
- 1957 9,840,000
- 1993 10,200,000
- 2009 9,905,595
- GDP US$18,800/person
- Hungarian
- Forint
- 8.03/1,000
- 73.2 years
- UNO, EU (2004), NATO, WHO, WTO

Political parties
*From 1956 until 1989, the Hungarian
Socialist Workers' Party MSzMP was the
ruling party of Hugary.*
- Hungarian Socialist Party (MSZP)
- Alliance of Free Democrats (SZDSZ)
- Hungarian Civic Union (Fidesz)
- Hungarian Democratics Forum
  (MDF)
- Christian Democratic People's Party
  (KDNP)
- Hungarian Communist Workers' Party

General Secretaries of the Hungarian
Communist Party
1945–1956 Mátyás Rákosi
1956 Ernő Gerő

1956–1988 János Kádár
1988–1989 Károly Grósz

Heads of state
*a) Chairmen of the Presidential Council
of the People's Republic of Hungary*
1952–1967 István Dobi
1967–1987 Pál Losonczi
1987–1988 Károly Németh
b) Presidents of the Republic
1989–1990 Mátyás Szűrös (MSZP)
1990–2000 Árpád Göncz (SZDSZ)
2000–2005 Ferenc Mádl (no party affil.)
2005– László Sólyom (no party affil.)

Prime ministers
a) People's Republic
1948–1953 Mátyás Rákosi
1953–1955, 1956 (uprising) Imre Nagy
1956–1958, 1961–1965 János Kádár
1967–1975 Jenő Fock
1975–1987 György Lázár
1987–1989 Károly Grósz
b) Republic
1990–1993 József Antall (MDF)
1994–1998 Gyula Horn (MSzMP)
1998–2002 Viktor Orbán (Fidesz)
2002–2004 Péter Medgyessy (MSzMP)
2004–2009 Ferenc Gyurcsány (MSzMP)
2009– Gordon Bajnai (independent)

Croatia

Republic of Croatia
Independence in 1991
Parliamentary democracy

- 21,831 miles²/56,542 km²
- 1993 4,780,000
- 2009 4,489,410
- GDP US$17,600/person
- Croatian
- 1 kuna = 100 lipa
- 6.49/1,000
- 75.2 years
- UNO, OAS, OSCE, WHO, WTO

Political parties
Until 1990/91 (Yugoslavia): see Serbia
- Croatian Democratic Union (HDZ)
- Croatian Social Liberal Party
  (HSLS)
- Social Democratic Party of Croatia (SDP)
- Croatian People's Party—Liberal
  Democrats (HND)
- Croatian Peasant Party (HSS)
- Croatian People's Party—Liberal
  Democrats (HNS)
- Croatian Party of Right (HSP)
- Independent Democratic Serb Party
  (SDSS; party of the ethnic Serbs in
  Croatia)

Presidents
1990–1999 Franjo Tuđman (HDZ)
2000– Stjepan Mesić (HND)

Prime ministers
1990 Stjepan Mesić (HDZ)
1990–1991 Josip Manolić (HDZ)
1991–1992 Franjo Greguric (HDZ)
1992–1993 Hrvoje Šarinić (HDZ)
1993–1995 Nikica Valentić (HDZ)
1995–2000 Zlatko Mateša (HDZ)
2000–2003 Ivica Račan (SDP)
2003–2009 Ivo Sanader (HDZ)
2009– Jadranka Kosor (HDZ)

Bosnia and Herzegovina

Federation of Bosnia and Herzegovina
   together with the Republika Srpska
   and the autonomous Brčko District
Independence in 1878/1992, federal republic
since 1992
Emerging federal democratic republic

- 19,741 miles²/51,129 km²
- 1993 4,400,000
- 2009 4,613,415
- GDP US$6,300/person
- Bosnian, Serbian, Croatian
- 1 convertible mark = 100 feninga
- 9.34/1,000
- 78.3 years
- UNO, OAS, OSCE, WHO, WTO

Presidency
2006– Haris Silajdžić (Bosniak member
   of the presidency)
2006– Nebojša Radmanović (Serb
   member of the presidency)
2006– Željko Komšić (Croat member
   of the presidency)

Prime minister (chairman of the
Council of Ministers)
2007– Nikola Špirić

Serbia

Republic of Serbia
Independence in 1867/78,
Parliamentary republic since 2006

- 34,116 miles²/88,361 km²
- 2009 7,379,340 (including Kosovo)
- GDP US$10,400/person
- Serbian
- 1 dinar = 100 para
- 75.3 years
- UNO, OAS, OSCE, WHO, WTO

Political parties
a) Yugoslavia
From 1945 to 1990, the Communist Party
of Yugoslavia (KPY) was the ruling party
of the country.
b) Serbia
- Social Democratic Party of Serbia (SDPS)
- Democratic Party (DS)
- G17 Plus
- Serbian Renewal Movement (SPO)
  (monarchists)
- Liberal Democratic Party (LDP)
- Serbian Radical Party (SRS)
  (nationalists)
- Democratic Party of Serbia (DSS)
- New Serbia (NS)

Chairmen of the League of
Communists of Yugoslavia
1936–1980 Josip Broz Tito
1980–1990 Changes every year among the
members of the politburo in proportion
to the different ethnicities

Presidents
*a) Yugoslavia (Presidents of the Socialist
Federal Republic of Yugoslavia)*
1943–1953 Ivan Ribar
1953–1980 Josip Broz Tito
1980–1990 Changes every year among the
members of the national council based
on the different ethnicities

b) Serbia
1989–1997 Slobodan Milošević (SPS)
1997–1998 Dragan Tomić (SPS; acting)
1998–2002 Milan Milutinović (SPS)
2002–2004 four acting presidents
2004– Boris Tadić (DS)

Prime ministers
a) Yugoslavia
1943–1963 Josip Broz Tito
1963–1967 Petar Stambolić
1967–1969 Mika Špiljak
1969–1971 Mitja Ribičić
1971–1977 Džemal Bijedić
1977–1982 Veselin Đuranović
1982–1986 Milka Planinc
1986–1989 Branko Mikulić
1989–1990 Ante Marković
b) Serbia
1991 Dragutin Zelenović (SPS)
1991–1993 Radoman Božović (SPS)
1993–1994 Nikola Šainović (SPS)
1994–2000 Mirko Marjanović (SPS)
2001–2003 Zoran Đinđić (DS)
2003–2004 Zoran Živković (DS)
2004–2008 Vojislav Koštunica (DSS)
2008– Mirko Cvetković (independent)

Montenegro

Independence in 1878, from Serbia and Montenegro in 2006; Republic

- 16,639 miles²/14,026 km²
- 1957 4,476,000
- 1993 5,190,000
- 2009 672,180
- GDP US$9,800/person
- Montenegrin; regionally also Serbian, Bosnian, Albanian, Croatian
- Euro (since 2002, but not a member of the European Monetary Union)
- UNO, OSCE, WHO, WTO

President
2003– Filip Vujanović

Prime minister
1991–1998, 2002–2006, 2008– Milo Đukanović (president 1998–2002)

Kosovo

Republic of Kosovo
Independence from Serbia in 2008; Republic (protectorate of the UN and EU; only partial recognition internationally)

- 4,203 miles²/10,887 km²
- 2009 1,804,840
- Albanian, Serbian
- Euro (since 2002, but not a member of the European Monetary Union)

President
2006– Fatmir Sejdiu

Prime minister
2008– Hashim Thaçi

Macedonia
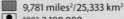
Republic of Macedonia
Independence in 1991
Parliamentary democracy

- 9,781 miles²/25,333 km²
- 1993 2,100,000
- 2009 2,066,720
- GDP US$9,000/person
- Macedonian, locally also Albanian, Turkish, Romani, Serbian
- 1 Macedonian denar = 100 deni
- 9.27/1,000
- 74.5 years
- UNO, OSCE, WHO, WTO

President
2009– Gjorge Ivanov

Prime minister
2006– Nikola Gruevski

Albania

Republic of Albania
Independence in 1912
Parliamentary republic

- 11,100 miles²/28,748 km²
- 1953 1,500,000
- 1993 3,413,000
- 2009 3,639,455
- GDP US$6,200/person
- Albanian
- 1 Albanian lek = 100 qindarkë
- 19.31/1,000
- 77.8 years
- UNO, OSCE, WHO, WTO

President
2007– Banir Topi

Prime minister
2005– Sali Berisha (president 1992–1997)

Greece

Hellenic Republic
Independence in 1829
Parliamentary republic (since 1975)

- 50,942 miles²/131,940 km²
- 1957 8,031,000
- 1993 10,430,000
- 2009 10,737,430
- GDP US$32,100/person
- Greek
- Euro (since 2002) = 100 lepta (= 340.75 drachma)
- 5.25/1,000
- 79.5 years
- UNO, EU (1981), NATO, WHO, WTO

Political parties (in parliament)
- Panhellenic Socialist Movement (PASOK)
- New Democracy (ND)
- Communist Party of Greece (KKE)
- Coalition of the Radical Left (SYRIZA)
- Popular Orthodox Rally (LAOS)

Heads of State
a) Monarchs
- 1935–1947 George II
- 1947–1964 Paul I

- 1964–1974 Constantin II (exiled in 1967)
- 1974 monarchy abolished
b) Presidents
1974–1975 Michail Stasinopoulos (ND)
1975–1980 Konstantinos Tsatsos
1980–1985, 1990–1995 Konstantinos Karamanlis (ND)
1985–1990 Christos Sartzetakis (indep.)
1995–2005 Konstantinos Stephanopoulos (indep.)
2005– Karolos Papoulias (PASOK)

Prime ministers
1945–1967 Rapidly changing governments, short periods of power
1967–1974 Military junta, Regime of the Colonels under Georgios Papadopoulos
1974–1980 Konstantinos Karamanlis (ND)
1981–1989, 1993–1996 Andreas Papandreou (PASOK)
1990–1993 Konstantinos Mitsotakis (ND)
1996–2004 Konstantinos Simitis (PASOK)
2004– Kostas Karamanlis (ND)

Bulgaria
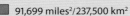
Republic of Bulgaria
Independence in 1878
Parliamentary democracy

- 42,822 miles²/110,910 km²
- 1956 7,629,254
- 1993 8,440,000
- 2009 7,204,690
- GDP US$12,600/person
- Bulgarian
- 1 lev = 100 stotinki
- 18.51/1,000
- 72.8 years
- UNO, EU (2007), NATO, WHO, WTO

Political parties
Bulgarian Communist Party (BCP) was the sole ruling party 1948–1989.
- Bulgarian Socialist Party (BSP)
- Union of Democratic Forces (SDS)
- National Movement for Stability and Progress (NDSV)
Movement for Rights and Freedoms (Turkish minority party)

Secretaries of the Central Committee
1946–1949 Georgi Dimitrov
1949–1954 Vulko Chervenkov
1954–1989 Todor Zhivkov

Presidents
a) People's Republic of Bulgaria
1950–1958 Georgi Damyanov
1958–1964 Dimitur Ganev
1964–1971 Georgi Traikov
1971–1989 Todor Zhivkov
1989–1990 Petar Mladenov
b) Republic
1990–1997 Zhelyu Zhelev (SDS)
1997–2002 Petar Stoyanov (SDS)
2002– Georgi Parvanov (BSP)

Prime ministers
a) People's Republic of Bulgaria
1950–1956 Vulko Chervenkov
1956–1962 Anton Yugov
1962–1971 Todor Zhivkov
1971–1981 Stanko Todorov
1981–1986 Grisha Filipov
1986–1990 Georgi Atanasov
b) Republic
1990–1991 Dimitar Iliev Popov
1991–1992 Philip Dimitrov (SDS)

1992–1994 Lyuben Berov
1995–1997 Zhan Videnov (BSP)
1997–2001 Ivan Kostov (SDS)
2001–2005 Simeon Saxe-Coburg-Gotha (= former Tsar Simeon II) (NDSV)
2005–2009 Sergei Stanishev (BSP)
2009– Boyko Borisov (GERB)

Romania
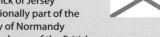
Romania
Independence in 1877
Parliamentary republic

- 91,699 miles²/237,500 km²
- 1956 17,489,794
- 1993 22,680,000
- 2009 22,215,420
- GDP US$11,500/person
- Romanian
- 1 leu = 100 bani
- 23.73/1,000
- 72.2 years
- UNO, EU (2007), NATO, WHO, WTO

Political parties
Romania was ruled 1948–1989 by the Romanian Workers' Party PMR/Romanian Communist Party PCR.
- Social Democratic Party (PSD, formerly PDSR)
- Democratic Party (PD)
- Christian-Democratic National Peasants' Party (PNT-CD)
- Democratic Liberal Party (PD-L)
- National Liberal Party (PNL)
- Democratic Union of Hungarians in Romania (UDMR)

General Secretaries of the PMR
1945–1965 Gheorghe Gheorghiu-Dej
1965–1989 Nicolae Ceaușescu

Presidents
a) Presidents of the State Council
1952–1958 Petru Groza
1958–1961 Ion Gheorghe Maurer
1961–1965 Gheorghe Gheorghiu-Dej
1965–1967 Chivu Stoica
1967–1989 Nicolae Ceaușescu (President and "Conducător")
b) Presidents
1989–1996, 2000–2004 Ion Iliescu (PDSR/PSD)
1996–2000 Emil Constantinescu (PNT-CD)
2004– Traian Băsescu (DA)

Prime ministers
a) Socialist Republic
1947–1952 Petru Groza
1955–1961 Chivu Stoica
1961–1974 Ion Gheorghe Maurer
1974–1989 Nicolae Ceaușescu
b) Republic
1989–1991 Petre Roman (PD)
1991–1992 Theodor Stolojan (PNL)
1992–1996 Nicolae Văcăroiu (PSD)
1996–1998 Victor Ciorbea (CDR)
1998–1999 Radu Vasile (PD)
1999–2000 Mugur Isărescu (independent)
2000–2004 Adrian Năstase (PSD)
2004–2008 Călin Popescu-Tăriceanu (PNL)
2008– Emil Boc (PDL)

Jersey
Bailiwick of Jersey
Traditionally part of the Duchy of Normandy
Dependency of the British crown

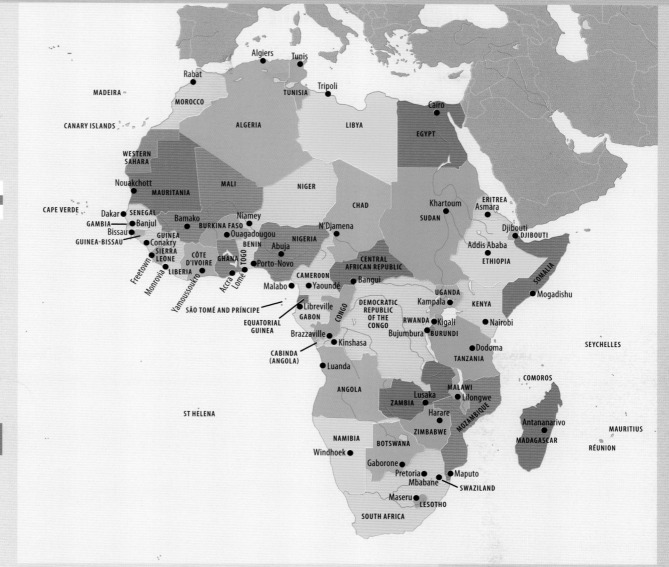

- 45 miles²/117 km²
- 2009 91,625
- English, French
- 1 pound sterling = 100 pence
- 5.01/1,000
- 79.7 years

Head of state and of government
- 1952– Queen Elizabeth II of the United Kingdom (as Duchess of Normandy)

Guernsey

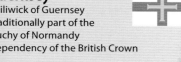

Bailiwick of Guernsey
Traditionally part of the
Duchy of Normandy
Dependency of the British Crown

- 30 miles²/78 km²
- 2009 65,485
- English, French
- 1 pound sterling = 100 pence
- 4.53/1,000
- 80.7 years

Head of state and of government
- 1952– Queen Elizabeth II of the United Kingdom (as Duchess of Normandy)

Isle of Man

Isle of Man; dependency
of British Crown since 1765

- 220 miles²/572 km²
- 2009 76,510
- Manx, English
- 1 pound sterling = 100 pence
- 5.62/1,000
- 78.8 years

Head of state
- 1952– Queen Elizabeth II of the United Kingdom (as Lord of Man)

Representative of the queen (lieutenant governor)
- 2005– Sir Paul Haddacks

Chief minister
- 2006– James Anthony (Tony) Brown

Gibraltar

Gibraltar
British occupation in 1704
British crown colony since 1780
Overseas territory of the UK

- 2 miles²/6 km²
- 2009 28,795
- English
- 1 Gibraltar pound = 100 pence
- 4.91/1,000
- 80.1 years

Head of state
- 1952– Queen Elizabeth II of the United Kingdom

Governor
- 2009– Sir Adrian Johns

Chief minister
- 1996– Peter Caruana

Faroe Islands

Faroe Islands
Autonomous since 1948
Self-governing overseas administrative
division of Danish parliamentary monarchy
(part of the Kingdom of Denmark)

- 538 miles²/1,395 km²
- 2009 48,855
- Faroese, Danish
- 1 Faroese króna = 100 oyra
- 6.46/1,000
- 79.3 years

Head of state
- 1972– Queen Margrethe II of Denmark

Prime minister
- 2008– Kaj Leo Johannessen

Greenland

Kalaallit Nunaat
Autonomy since 1979
Part of the Kingdom of Denmark

- 836,327 miles²/2,166,090 km²
- 2009 57,600
- Greenlandic (East Inuit), Danish
- 1 Danish krone = 100 øre
- 11.2/1,000
- 69.5 years

Head of state
- 1972– Queen Margrethe II of Denmark

Prime minister
- 2009– Kuupik Kleist

Canary Islands

Canady Islands
Autonomy since 1982
Autonomous community of Spain

- 2,892 miles²/7,492 km²
- 2009 2,098,595
- Spanish
- 1 Euro = 100 cents
- 79.2 years

President
- 2007– Paulino Rivero Baute

Madeira

Madeira Autonomous Region
Autonomy since 1976
Autonomous region of Portugal

- 306 miles²/794 km²
- 2009 250,000
- Portuguese
- 74.6 years

President of the regional government
- 1978– Alberto João Jardim

AFRICA

Morocco

Kingdom of Morocco
Independence in 1956
Constitutional monarchy

- 172,413 miles²/446,550 km²
- 1955 9,736,000
- 1993 27,110,000
- 2009 31,285,175
- GDP US$4,600/person
- Arabic, Berber dialects, French
- 1 dirham = 100 santim
- 38.22/1,000
- 71.5 years
- UNO, OAS, OSCE, WHO, WTO, Arab League

Political parties
The political parties have only gained political importance recently, since 1999.
- ■ Independence Party (Istiqlal)
- □ National Union of Popular Forces (UNFP)
- ◧ Socialist Union of Popular Forces (USFP)
- □ Justice and Development Party (PJO, formerly MPDC)

Monarchs
- 1927–1961 Mohammed V (first sultan, king since 1956)
- 1961–1999 Hassan II
- 1999– Mohammed VI

Countries of the World – Africa

Prime ministers
1971–1972, 1983–1986, 1992–1994 Mohammed Karim Lamrani (independent)
1972–1979 Ahmed Osman (National Rally of Independents)
1986–1992 Azzedine Laraki (independent)
1994–1998 Abdellatif Filali (independent)
1998–2002 Abderrahmane Youssoufi (USFP)
2002–2007 Driss Jettou (independent)
2007– Abbas al-Fassi (Istiqlal)

Western Sahara

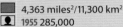

Sahrawi Arab Democratic Republic
Independence declared in 1976 by the Polisario Front
(recognized by 53 countries)
Republic

- 102,702 miles²/266,000 km²
- 2009 405,210
- Arabic, some Spanish
- 1 Moroccan dirham = 100 santim
- 71.13/1,000
- 53.9 years

President and Secretary General of the Polisario Front
1976– Mohamed Abdelaziz
(lives in exile in Algeria)

Prime minister
2003– Abdelkader Taleb Oumar
(lives in exile in Algeria)

Mauritania

The Islamic Republic of Mauritania
Independence in 1960
Military junta

- 397,953 miles²/1,030,700 km²
- 1957 624,000
- 1993 2,210,000
- 2009 3,129,485
- GDP US$2,100/person
- Arabic, French
- 1 ouguiya = 5 khoums
- 66.65/1,000
- 53.9 years
- UNO, WHO, WTO, League of Arab States

Head of state (President of the Military High Council of State)
2008– General Mohamed Ould Abdel Aziz (military commander)

Prime minister
2008– Moulaye Ould Mohamed Laghdaf

Senegal

Republic of Senegal
Independence in 1960
Republic

- 75,749 miles²/196,190 km²
- 1993 8,100,000
- 2009 13,711,600
- GDP US$1,700/person
- French

- CFA franc (currency of the West African financial union)
- 58.93/1,000
- 57.1 years
- UNO, WHO, WTO

President
2000– Abdoulaye Wade

Prime minister
2007– Soulayemane Ndene Ndiaye

The Gambia

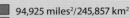

Republic of The Gambia
Independence in 1965
Republic

- 4,363 miles²/11,300 km²
- 1955 285,000
- 1993 1,080,000
- 2009 1,778,080
- GDP US$1,300/person
- English
- 1 dalasi = 100 bututs
- 68.72/1,000
- 55.0 years
- UNO, WHO, WTO

President and head of state
1994– Yahya (Abdul-Azziz Jemus Jun-kung Diliu) Jammeh (de facto dictator)

Cape Verde

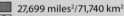

Republic of Cape Verde
Independence in 1975
Republic

- 1,557 miles²/4,033 km²
- 1955 172,000
- 1993 380,000
- 2009 429,475
- GDP US$3,900/person
- Portuguese, Crioulo
- 1 Cape Verdean escudo = 100 centavos
- 42.55/1,000
- 71.3 years
- UNO, WHO, WTO

President
2001– Pedro Verona Rodriques Pires

Prime minister
2001– José Maria Pereira Neves

Guinea-Bissau

Republic of Guinea-Bissau
Independence in 1973
Republic

- 13,946 miles²/36,120 km²
- 1993 1,050,000
- 2009 1,533,965
- GDP US$600/person
- Portuguese, Crioulo
- CFA franc (currency of the West African financial union)
- 101.64/1,000
- 47.5 years
- UNO, WHO, WTO

President
2009– Malam Bacai Sanhá

Prime minister
2009– Carlos Gomes Júnior

Guinea

Republic of Guinea
Independence in 1958
Military junta

- 94,925 miles²/245,857 km²
- 1956 2,505,000
- 1993 6,500,000
- 2009 10,057,975
- GDP US$1,100/person
- French
- 1 Guinean franc = 100 centimes
- 67.41/1,000
- 56.6 years
- UNO, WHO, WTO

Head of state (President of the National Council for Democracy and Development)
2008– Brigadier General Sékouba Konaté (acting president)

Prime minister
2010– Jean-Marie Doré

Sierra Leone

Republic of Sierra Leone
Independence in 1961
Constitutional democracy

- 27,699 miles²/71,740 km²
- 1955 2,050,000
- 1993 4,400,000
- 2009 5,132,140
- GDP US$900/person
- English
- 1 leone = 100 cents
- 156.48/1,000
- 40.9 years
- UNO, WHO, WTO

President (commander in chief) and head of government
2007– Ernest Bai Koroma

Liberia

Republic of Liberia
Founded in 1847
Presidential republic

- 43,000 miles²/111,370 km²
- 1949 1,868,000
- 1993 2,760,000
- 2009 3,441,790
- GDP US$500/person
- English
- 1 Liberian dollar = 100 cents
- 143.89/1,000
- 41.1 years
- UNO, WHO, WTO

President and head of government
2006– Ellen Johnson Sirleaf (the first elected female head of state in an African country)

Mali

Republic of Mali
Independence in 1960
Semi-presidential republic

- 478,764 miles²/1,240,000 km²
- 1993 10,460,000
- 2009 13,443,225
- GDP US$1,100/person
- French

- CFA franc (currency of the West African financial union)
- 103.83/1,000
- 49.9 years
- UNO, WHO, WTO

President
2002– Amadou Toumani Touré

Prime minister
2007– Modibo Sidibé

Algeria

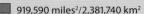

People's Democratic Republic of Algeria
Independence in 1962
Republic

- 919,590 miles²/2,381,740 km²
- 1955 9,620,000
- 1993 28,550,000
- 2009 34,178,190
- GDP US$7,100/person
- Arabic, Berber, French
- Algerian dinar
- 28.75/1,000
- 73.8 years
- UNO, OPEC, WHO, WTO, Arab League

Political parties
The FLN is the only political party to give rise to presidents and governments.
- National Liberation Front (FLN) (sole ruling party 1962–1991)
- Islamic Salvation Front (FIS; Islamist party, today mainstream)
- National Reform Movement (MNR)

Presidents
1963–1965 Mohamed Ahmed Ben Bella (also prime minister)
1965–1978 Houari Boumédienne (also prime minister)
1978–1979 Rabah Bitat
1979–1992 Chadli Bendjedid
1992 Muhammad Boudiaf
1992–1994 Ali Kafi
1994–1999 Liamine Zéroual
1999– Abdelaziz Bouteflika

Prime ministers
1979–1984 Mohamed Ben Ahmed Abdelghani
1984–1988 Abdelhamid Brahimi
1988–1995 changing every year
1995–1998, 2003–2006 Ahmed Ouyahia
1998–2000 Smail Hamdani
1999–2000 Ahmed Benbitour
2000–2003 Ali Benflis
2006–2008 Abdelaziz Belkhadem
2008– Ahmed Ouyahia

Tunisia

Tunisian Republic
Independence in 1956,
Republic since 1957
Presidential republic

- 63,170 miles²/163,610 km²
- 1956 3,782,480
- 1993 8,810,000
- 2009 10,486,340
- GDP US$8,000/person
- Arabic, French
- 1 Tunisian dinar = 1,000 millimes
- 23.43/1,000
- 75.6 years
- UNO, OAS, OSCE, WHO, WTO,

League of Arab States

Political parties

Until 1994 the party of the president, RCD (formerly Destourian Party), was the only legal party. It is still in power. Nine parties have since been officially recognized, but remain without influence.

Heads of state
1943–1957 Lamine Bey (Muhammad VIII al-Amin), last bey of Tunisia
1957–1987 Habib Bourguiba (president)
1987– Zine El Abidine Ben Ali (president)

Prime ministers
1957–1969 Habib Bourguiba
1969–1970 Bahi Ladgham
1970–1980 Hédi Amara Nouira
1980–1986 Mohamed Mzali
1986–1987 Rachid Sfar
1987 Zine El Abidine Ben Ali
1987–1989 Hédi Baccouche
1989–1999 Hamed Karoui
1999– Mohamed Ghannouchi

Libya

Great Socialist People's Libyan Arab Jamahiriya ("state of the masses")
Independence in 1951, people's republic in 1969, Islamic-socialist people's republic

- 679,358 miles²/1,759,540 km²
- 1955 1,105,000
- 1993 1,105,000
- 2009 6,324,355
- GDP US$14,600/person
- Arabic
- 1 Libyan dinar = 1,000 dirham
- 21.94/1,000
- 77.1 years
- UNO, OPEC, WHO, WTO (observer), League of Arab States

Political parties

There are no political parties in Libya; the highest legislative und executive organ is the National General People's Congress, which comprises ca. 2,700 delegates drawn from all the country's mass organizations.

Heads of state
1922–1969 Idris I (emir, in 1951 king)
1969– Muammar al-Gaddafi (leader and guide of the revolution)

Secretary General of the General People's Congress
(= de jure head of state)
1969–1979 Muammar al-Gaddafi
1979–1981 Abdul Ati al-Obeidi
1981–1984 Muhammad az-Zaruq Rajab
1984–1990 Mifta al-Usta Umar
1990–1992 Abdul Razzaq as-Sawsa
1992–2008 Muhammad al-Zanati
2008–2009 Miftah Muhammed K'eba
2009–2010 Imbarek Shamekh
2010– Mohamed Abdul Quasim al-Zwai

Niger

Republic of Niger
Independence in 1960
Presidential republic

- 489,189 miles²/1,267,000 km²
- 1957 2,415,000
- 1993 8,850,000
- 2009 15,306,250
- GDP US$700/person
- French
- CFA franc (currency of the West African financial union)
- 115.42/1,000
- 44.3 years
- UNO, WHO, WTO

President
1999– Tandja Mamadou

Prime minister
2009– Ali Badjo Gamatié

Burkina Faso

Burkina Faso (Upper Volta until 1984)
Independence in 1960
Parliamentary republic

- 105,869 miles²/274,200 km²
- 1993 10,200,000
- 2009 15,746,230
- GDP US$1,200/person
- French
- CFA franc (currency of the West African financial union)
- 86.02/1,000
- 52.6 years
- UNO, WHO, WTO

President
1987– Blaise Compaoré (periodically autocratic rule)

Prime minister
2007– Tertius Zongo

Ivory Coast

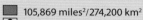

Republic of Côte d'Ivoire
Independence in 1960
Republic

- 124,502 miles²/322,460 km²
- 1957 2,485,000
- 1993 14,200,000
- 2009 20,617,070
- GDP US$1,700/person
- French
- CFA franc (currency of the West African financial union)
- 69.76/1,000
- 54.6 years
- UNO, WHO, WTO

President
2000– Laurent Koudou Gbagbo

Prime minister
2007– Guillaume Kigbafori Soro

Ghana

Republic of Ghana
Independence in 1957
Constitutional democracy

- 92,456 miles²/239,460 km²
- 1957 4,763,000
- 1993 16,940,000
- 2009 23,887,810
- GDP US$1,500/person
- English
- 1 cedi = 100 pesewa
- 52.31/1,000
- 59.5 years
- UNO, OAS, WHO, WTO

President and head of government
2009– John Evans Atta Mills

Togo

Togolese Republic
Independence in 1960
Republic

- 21,925 miles²/56,785 km²
- 1955 1,095,000
- 1993 3,930,000
- 2009 6,031,810
- GDP US$900/person
- French
- CFA franc (currency of the West African financial union)
- 57.66/1,000
- 58.3 years
- UNO, WHO, WTO

President
2005– Faure Gnassingbé

Prime minister
2008– Gilbert Houngbo

Benin

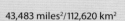

Republic of Benin
Independence in 1960
Republic

- 43,483 miles²/112,620 km²
- 1957 1,713,000
- 1993 5,560,000
- 2009 8,791,830
- GDP US$1,500/person
- French
- CFA franc (currency of the West African financial union)
- 66.2/1,000
- 58.6 years
- UNO, OAS, WHO, WTO

President and head of government
2006– Thomas Yayi Boni

Nigeria

Federal Republic of Nigeria
Independence in 1960
Presidential federal republic

- 356,667 miles²/923,768 km²
- 1955 31,254,000
- 1993 108,470,000
- 2009 149,229,090
- GDP US$2,400/person
- English
- 1 naira = 100 kobo
- 95.74/1,000
- 46.5 years
- UNO, OAS, OPEC, WHO, WTO

Political parties

The system of political parties can only partly be compared to pluralistic democracies.

- ☐ Democratic Peoples Party (DPP)
- ☐ All Nigeria Peoples Party (ANPP)
- ☐ Alliance for Democracy (AD)
- ☐ National Democratic Party (NDP)
- ☐ All Progressives Grand Alliance (APGA)
- ☐ Conference of Nigerian Political Parities (CNPP)

Presidents (most serve concurrently as prime minister)
1963–1966 Benjamin Nnamdi Azikiwe
1966 Johnson Aguiyi-Ironsi
1966–1975 Yakubu Gowon
1975–1976 Murtala Mohammed
1976–1979 Olusegun Obasanjo (military ruler)
1979–1983 Shehu Shagari
1983–1985 Muhammadu Buhari (military ruler)
1985–1993 Ibrahim Babangida (military ruler)
1993 Ernest Shonekan
1993–1998 Sani Abacha (military ruler)
1998–1999 Abdulsalami Abubakar
1999–2007 Olusegun Obasanjo (second term; DPP)
2007– Umaru Yar'Adua (DPP)

Prime minister
1960–1966 Abubakar Tafawa Balewa

Cameroon

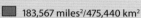

Republic of Cameroon
Independence in 1960
Republic; multiparty presidential regime

- 183,567 miles²/475,440 km²
- 1956 3,171,106
- 1993 13,280,000
- 2009 18,879,300
- GDP US$2,300/person
- French, English
- CFA franc (currency of the Central African Economic and Monetary Community)
- 64.57/1,000
- 53.3 years
- UNO, WHO, WTO

President
1982– Paul Biya (periodically autocratic rule)

Prime minister
2009– Philémon Yunji Yang

Chad

Republic of Chad
Independence in 1960
Republic

- 495,752 miles²/1,284,000 km²
- 2009 10,329,210
- GDP US$1,500/person
- French, Arabic
- CFA franc (currency of the Central African Economic and Monetary Community)
- 100.36/1,000
- 47.4 years
- UNO, WHO, WTO

President
1990– Idriss Déby

Prime minister
2008– Youssouf Saleh Abbas

Countries of the World – Africa

Egypt

Arab Republic of Egypt
Independence in 1922
Republic since 1952/53
Presidential republic

- 386,660 miles²/1,001,450 km²
- 1993 59,200,000
- 2009 78,866,635
- GDP US$6,000/person
- Arabic
- 1 Egyptian pound = 100 piaster
- 28.36/1,000
- 71.9 years
- UNO, OAS, OSCE, WHO, WTO

Political parties
*The National Democratic Party (NDP),
formerly the Arab Socialist Union,
representing Arab socialism, has been
the state party since 1952/53.
The following play a secondary role:*
- New Wafd Party
- Socialist Party
- National Progressive Unionist Party
  or Tagammu (Marxist)

Heads of state
a) Kings
1936–1952 Farouk I
1952–1953 Fuad II (formal)
b) Presidents
1953–1954 Ali Muhammad Naguib
1954–1970 Gamal Abdel Nasser
1970–1981 Anwar el-Sadat
1981– Muhammad Hosni Mubarak

Prime ministers
1952–1954 Ali Muhammad Naguib
1954–1962, 1967–1970 Gamal Abdel Nasser
1965–1966 Zakaria Mohieddin
1970–1972 Mahmoud Fawzi
1973–1974, 1980–1980 Anwar el-Sadat
1975–1978 Mamdouh Salem
1981–1982 Muhammad Hosni Mubarak
1986–1996 Atef Muhammad Naguib Sedki
1996–1999 Kamal Ganzouri
1999–2004 Atef Ebeid
2004– Ahmed Nazif

Sudan

Republic of the Sudan
Independence in 1956
Republic (Government of National Unity)

- 967,493 miles²/2,505,810 km²
- 1955 10,231,447
- 1993 28,950,000
- 2009 41,087,825
- GDP US$2,300/person
- Arabic, English
- 1 Sudanese pound = 100 qirsh
- 86.98/1,000
- 50.3 years
- UNO, WHO, WTO

Political parties
*Political parties play a limited role, but
are stable; numerous political parties are
only represented in the north or the south
of the country.*
- National Congress Party (NCP)
  (moderate Islamists; temporarily
  functions as ruling party)
- Sudan People's Liberation Movement
  (SPLM)
- Umma Party (NUP)
  (Islamists)

- Democratic Unionist Party
  (DUP)
- Sudanese Communist Party
  (SCP)

Presidents
1956–1958 Sovereignity Council
1958–1964 Ibrahim Abbud (also
prime minister)
1964 Sirr Al-Khatim Al-Khalifa (acting)
1965–1969 Ismail al-Azhari
1969–1985 Gaafar Nimeiry (also
prime minister)
1985–1986 Abdel Rahman Swar al-Dahab
1986–1989 Ahmad al-Mirghani
1989– Omar Hassan Ahmad al-Bashir

Prime ministers
1954–1956 Ismail al-Azhari
1956–1958 Sayed Abdallah Khalil
1964–1965 Sirr Al-Khatim Al-Khalifa
1965–1966, 1967–1969 Muhammad Ahmad
Mahgoub
1966–1967, 1986–1989 Sadiq al-Mahdi
1985–1986 Al-Jazuli Daf'allah
1989 Office abolished

Eritrea

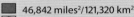

State of Eritrea
Independence (from
Ethiopia) in 1993
Provisional government

- 46,842 miles²/121,320 km²
- 1955 1,200,000
- 1993 4,003,700
- 2009 5,647,168
- GDP US$700/person
- Tigrinya, Arabic
- 1 nakfa = 100 cents
- 44.34/1,000
- 61.4 years
- UNO, WHO

**President, head of government and
secretary general of the People's Front
for Democracy and Justice**
1993– Isaias Afwerki

Djibouti

Republic of Djibouti
Independence in 1977
Semi-presidential republic

- 8,880 miles²/23,000 km²
- 1993 570,000
- 2009 724,620
- GDP US$2,800/person
- Arabic, French
- 1 Djiboutian franc = 100 centimes
- 99.13/1,000
- 43.3 years
- UNO, WHO, WTO

President
1999– Ismail Omar Guelleh

Prime minister
2001– Dileita Mohamed Dileita

Ethiopia

Federal Democratic
Republic of Ethiopia
Traditional empire until 1974,
socialist people's republic until 1991
Federal democratic republic since 1991

- 435,184 miles²/1,127,127 km²
- 1955 18,800,000
- 1993 56,200,000
- 2009 85,237,340
- GDP US$900/person
- Amarigna, Oromigna, Tigrigna
- 1 Ethiopian birr = 100 santim
- 82.64/1,000
- 55.0 years
- UNO, WHO, WTO

President
2001– Girma Wolde-Giorgis

Prime minister
1995– Meles Zenawi Asres

Somalia

Republic of Somalia
Independence in 1960
No permanent national government; transi-
tional, parliamentary federal government

- 246,199 miles²/637,657 km²
- 1993 9,080,000
- 2009 9,832,015
- GDP US$600/person
- Somali, Arabic
- Somali shilling
- 110.97/1,000
- 49.3 years
- UNO, WHO

President
2009– Sharif Sheikh Ahmed (Alliance
for the Reliberation of Somalia)

Prime minister
2009– Omar Abdirashid Ali
Sharmarke

Kenya

Republic of Kenya
Independence in 1963
Semi-presidential republic

- 224,961 miles²/582,650 km²
- 1956 6,150,000
- 1993 30,520,000
- 2008 39,002,770
- GDP US$1,200/person
- Kiswahili, English
- 1 Kenyan shilling = 100 cents
- 56.01/1,000
- 56.7 years
- UNO, WHO, WTO

President
2002– Mwai Kibaki

Prime minister
2008– Raila Amollo Odinga

Uganda

Republic of Uganda
Independence in 1962
Republic

- 91,135 miles²/236,040 km²
- 1955 5,593,000
- 1993 20,620,000
- 2009 32,369,560
- GDP US$1,300/person
- English, Ganda or Luganda
- 1 Ugandan shilling = 100 cents
- 66/1,000
- 52.3 years
- UNO, WHO, WTO

President
1986– Yoweri Kaguta Museveni

Prime minister
1999– Apolo Robin Nsibambi

Central African Republic

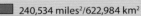

Central African Republic
Independence in 1960
Republic

- 240,534 miles²/622,984 km²
- 1956 1,134,436
- 1993 3,230,000
- 2009 4,511,490
- GDP US$700/person
- Sangho, French
- CFA franc (currency of the Economic and
  Monetary Community of Central Africa)
- 82.13/1,000
- 44.2 years
- UNO, WHO, WTO

President
2003– François Bozizé Yangouvonda
(at first in a military junta, elected
in 2005)

Prime minister
2008– Faustin-Archange Touadéra

Democratic Republic of the Congo

(Zaire 1971–1997)
Independence in 1960
Semi-presidential republic since 1978

- 905,563 miles²/2,345,410 km²
- 1956 12,956,376
- 1993 42,550,000
- 2009 68,692,540
- GDP US$300/person
- French, Kingwana, Kikongo, Tshiluba
- 1 Congolese franc = 100 centimes
- 83.11/1,000
- 54.0 years
- UNO, WHO, WTO

Political parties
*Until 1965 there were more than 200
political parties; since then a one-party
system has been established and
pluralistic democracy ended. Several of
the current political parties invoke the
heritage of Patrice Lumumba.*

Presidents
1960–1965 Joseph Kasavubu
1965–1997 Joseph-Désiré Mobutu; after
1972 Mobutu Sese Seko (dictator)
1997–2001 Laurent-Désiré Kabila
2001– Joseph Kabila

Prime ministers
1960 Patrice Lumumba
1964–1965 Moïse Kapenda Tshombe
Period of rapid turnover, short terms
2006–2008 Antoine Gizenga
2008– Adolphe Muzito

Republic of the Congo

Republic of the Congo
Independence in 1960
Republic

- 132,046 miles²/342,000 km²
- 1957 759,724
- 1993 2,520,000
- 2009 4,012,810
- **GDP** US$4,200/person
- French, Lingala and Monokutuba
- CFA franc (currency of the Economic and Monetary Community of Central Africa)
- 81.3/1,000
- 53.7 years
- UNO, WHO, WTO

President
1979–1992, 1997– Denis Sassou-Nguesso
(periodically de facto dictator)

Prime minister
2005–2009 Isidore Mvouba, position abolished thereafter

Gabon
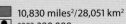

Gabonese Republic
Independence in 1960
Republic; multiparty presidential regime
(one-party system until 1990)

- 132,046 miles²/342,000 km²
- 1957 403,781
- 1993 1,280,000
- 2009 1,514,995
- **GDP** US$13,700/person
- French
- CFA franc (currency of the Economic and Monetary Community of Central Africa)
- 52.65/1,000
- 53.5 years
- UNO, WHO, WTO

President
2009– Ali-Ben Bongo Ondimba
(born Alain Bernard Bongo)

Prime ministers
2009– Paul Biyoghé Mba

Equatorial Guinea
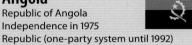

Republic of Equatorial Guinea
Independence in 1968
Presidential republic

- 10,830 miles²/28,051 km²
- 1993 390,000
- 2008 633,440
- **GDP** US$36,100/person
- Spanish, French, Fang, Bubi
- CFA franc (currency of the Economic and Monetary Community of Central Africa)
- 83.75/1,000
- 61.2 years
- UNO, OAS, WHO, WTO

President
1979– Teodoro Obiang Nguema Mbasogo (de facto dictator)

Prime minister
2008– Ignacio Milam Tang

São Tomé and Príncipe

Democratic Republic of
São Tomé and Príncipe
Independence in 1975
Democratic semi-presidential republic

- 386 miles²/1,001 km²
- 1993 125,000
- 2009 212,680
- **GDP** US$1,400/person
- Portuguese
- 1 dobra = 100 cêntimos
- 38.36/1,000
- 68 years
- UNO, WHO, WTO

President
2003– Fradique Melo de Menezes

Prime minister
2008– Joaquim Rafael Branco

Angola
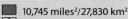

Republic of Angola
Independence in 1975
Republic (one-party system until 1992)

- 481,351 miles²/1,246,700 km²
- 1956 431,700
- 1993 10,670,000
- 2009 12,799,295
- **GDP** US$8,800/person
- Portuguese, Bantu
- 1 kwanza = 100 cêntimos
- 182.3/1,000
- 37.9 years
- UNO, OAS, OPEC, WHO, WTO

President
1979– José Eduardo dos Santos

Prime minister
2008– António Paulo Kassoma

Zambia

Republic of Zambia
Independence in 1964
Republic

- 290,584 miles²/752,614 km²
- 1993 9,370,000
- 2009 11,862,740
- **GDP** US$1,500/person
- English, Bemba, Nyanja, Tonga, Lozi
- 1 Zambian kwacha = 100 ngwee
- 101/1,000
- 38.6 years
- UNO, WHO, WTO

President and head of government
2008– Rupiah Bwezani Banda

Rwanda

Republic of Rwanda
Independence in 1962
Presidential republic

- 10,169 miles²/26,338 km²
- 1956 4,484,591
- 1993 7,750,000
- 2009 10,746,310
- **GDP** US$1,000/person
- Kinyarwanda, English, French
- 1 Rwandan franc = 100 centimes
- 83.42/1,000
- 49.7 years
- UNO, WHO, WTO

President
2000– Paul Kagame

Prime minister
2000– Bernard Makuza

Burundi

Republic of Burundi
Independence in 1962
Presidential republic

- 10,745 miles²/27,830 km²
- 1993 6,310,000
- 2009 9,511,330
- **GDP** US$300/person
- Kirundi, French, Swahili
- 1 Burundian franc = 100 centimes
- 60.77/1,000
- 51.7 years
- UNO, WHO, WTO

President and head of government
2005– Pierre Nkurunziza

Tanzania
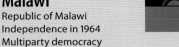

United Republic of Tanzania
Independence in 1961
Republic

- 364,898 miles²/945,087 km²
- 1993 30,340,000
- 2009 41,048,530
- **GDP** US$1,400/person
- Swahili
- 1 Tanzanian shilling = 100 senti
- 70.46/1,000
- 51.5 years
- UNO, WHO, WTO

President
2005– Jakaya Mrisho Kikwete

Prime ministers
2008– Mizengo Pinda

Malawi
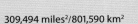

Republic of Malawi
Independence in 1964
Multiparty democracy

- 45,764 miles²/118,480 km²
- 1993 10,460,000
- 2009 15,028,755
- **GDP** US$900/person
- Chichewa
- 1 Malawian kwacha = 100 tambala
- 90.55/1,000
- 43.5 years
- UNO, WHO, WTO

President and head of government
2004– Bingu wa Mutharika

Mozambique

Republic of Mozambique
Independence in 1975
Republic

- 309,494 miles²/801,590 km²
- 1956 6,095,000
- 1993 17,420,000
- 2009 21,669,280
- **GDP** US$900/person
- Emakhuwa, Xichangana, Portuguese
- 1 Mozambican metical = 100 centavos
- 107.84/1,000
- 41.1 years
- UNO, WHO, WTO

President
2004– Armando Emilio Guebuza

Prime minister
2010– Aires Bonifácio Ali

Zimbabwe

Republic of Zimbabwe
(Rhodesia until 1980)
Independence in 1980
(de facto in 1965)
Parliamentary democracy

- 150,871 miles²/390,757 km²
- 1993 11,530,000
- 2009 11,392,630
- **GDP** US$2,100/person
- English, Shona, Sindebele
- 1 US dollar = 100 cents
- 33.86/1,000
- 44.3 years
- UNO, WHO, WTO

President
1987– Robert Mugabe

Prime minister
2009– Morgan Richard Tsvangirai

Botswana
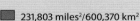

Republic of Botswana
Independence in 1966
Parliamentary republic

- 231,803 miles²/600,370 km²
- 1956 327,335
- 1993 1,460,000
- 2009 1,990,875
- **GDP** US$5,590/person
- Setswana, Kalanga, Sekgalagadi, English
- 1 pula = 100 thebe
- 44.01/1,000
- 50.2 years
- UNO, WHO, WTO

President and head of government
2008– Seretse Khama Ian Khama
(vice president 1998–2008)

Namibia

Republic of Namibia
Independence (from
South Africa) in 1990
Republic

- 318,694 miles²/825,418 km²
- 1993 1,500,000
- 2009 2,108,665
- **GDP** US$6,400/person
- English, Afrikaans, German, Oshivambo
- 1 Namibian dollar = 100 cents
- 45.64/1,000
- 49.9 years
- UNO, WHO, WTO

President
2005– Hifikepunye Lucas Pohamba

Countries of the World – Africa

Prime minister
2005– Nahas Gideon Angula

South Africa
Republic of South Africa
Independence in 1910,
republic in 1961, majority rule in 1994
Republic

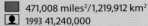

- 471,008 miles²/1,219,912 km²
- 1993 41,240,000
- 2009 49,052,490
- GDP US$10,000/person
- IsiZulu, IsiXhosa, Afrikaans, Sepedi, English, Setswana, Sesotho, Xitsonga
- 1 South African rand = 100 cents
- 45.11/1,000
- 48.9 years
- UNO, WHO, WTO

Political parties
The National Party (NP) was quasi the ruling party 1948–1994 and was responsible for the apartheid system. The United Party (UP) insisted on white supremacy yet was anti-apartheid (existed until 1977).

- African National Congress (ANC; mainly black party members)
- Democratic Alliance (DA; multicultural party)
- Inkatha Freedom Party (IFP; Zulu party) Independent Democrats (ID; social
- democratic party) United Democratic Movement (UDM;
- multicultural party) African Christian Democratic Party
- (ACDP) Freedom Front Plus (FF+; white
- conservative party)

Heads of state
a) British monarchs
1936–1952 George VI
1952–1961 Elizabeth II
b) Presidents (since 1984, also heads of government)
1961–1967 Charles Robberts Swart (NP)
1967–1968 Theophilus E. Dönges (NP)
1968–1975 Jacob Johannes Fouché (NP)
1975–1978 Nicolaas Diederichs (NP)
1978–1979 Balthazar Johannes Vorster (NP)
1979–1984 Marais Viljoen (NP)
1984–1989 Pieter Willem Botha (NP)
1989–1994 Frederik Willem de Klerk (NP)
1994–1999 Nelson Mandela (ANC)
1999–2008 Thabo Mbeki (ANC)
2008–2009 Kgalema Molanthe (ANC)
2009– Jacob Gedleyihlekisa Zuma (ANC)

Prime ministers
1939–1948 Jan Christiaan Smuts (UP)
1948–1954 Daniel François Malan (NP)
1954–1958 Johannes Gerhardus Strijdom (NP)
1958–1966 Hendrik Frensch Verwoerd (NP)
1966–1978 Balthazar J. Vorster (NP)
1978–1984 Pieter Willem Botha (NP)
1984 position abolished

Lesotho
Kingdom of Lesotho
Independence in 1966
Parliamentary constitutional monarchy

- 11,720 miles²/30,355 km²
- 1956 634,000
- 1993 2,000,000
- 2009 2,130,820
- GDP US$1,500/person
- Sesotho, English, Zulu, Xhosa
- 1 loti = 100 lisente (value tied to the South African rand)
- 78.59/1,000
- 40.2 years
- UNO, WHO, WTO

Monarch
- 1990–1995, 1996– King Letsie III (David Mohato Bereng Seeiso)

Prime minister
1998– Bethuel Pakalitha Moisili

Swaziland
Kingdom of Swaziland
Independence in 1968
Absolute monarchy

- 6,704 miles²/17,363 km²
- 1956 237,041
- 1993 910,000
- 2009 1,337,185
- GDP US$4,400/person
- English, siSwati
- 1 lilangeni = 100 cents
- 69.59/1,000
- 32 years
- UNO, WHO, WTO

Monarch
- 1986– King Mswati III Makhosetive

Prime minister
1996–2003, 2008– Barnabas Sibusiso Dlamini

Madagascar
Republic of Madagascar
Independence in 1960
Republic

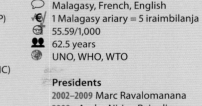

- 226,656 miles²/587,040 km²
- 1958 4,918,000
- 1993 14,300,000
- 2009 20,653,555
- GDP US$1,000/person
- Malagasy, French, English
- 1 Malagasy ariary = 5 iraimbilanja
- 55.59/1,000
- 62.5 years
- UNO, WHO, WTO

Presidents
2002–2009 Marc Ravalomanana
2009– Andry Nirina Rajoelina

Prime minister
2009– Albert Camille Vital

Comoros
Union of the Comoros
Independence in 1975 as
Federal Islamic Republic
Independent federal republic since 2001

- 838 miles²/2,170 km²
- 1955 175,552
- 1993 630,000
- 2009 752,440
- GDP US$1,000/person

- Arabic, French, Shikomoro
- 1 Comorian franc = 100 centimes
- 68.58/1,000
- 63.1 years
- UNO, WHO, WTO

President and head of government
2006– Ahmed Abdallah Mohamed Sambi

Seychelles
Republic of Seychelles
Independence in 1976
Republic

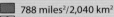

- 176 miles²/455 km²
- 1956 40,417
- 1993 71,000
- 2009 87,475
- GDP US$19,400/person
- Creole, English
- 1 Seychellois rupee = 100 cents
- 14.36/1,000
- 72.6 years
- UNO, WHO, WTO

President and head of government
2004– James Alix Michel (vice president 1996–2004)

Mauritius
Republic of Mauritius
Independence in 1968
Parliamentary democracy

- 788 miles²/2,040 km²
- 1956 586,000
- 1993 1,110,000
- 2009 1,284,265
- GDP US$12,400/person
- Creole, Bhojpuri, French, English
- 1 Mauritian rupee = 100 cents
- 12.56/1,000
- 73.8 years
- UNO, WHO, WTO

President
2003– Sir Anerood Jugnauth (prime minister 1982–1995 and 2000–2003)

Prime minister
1995–2000, 2005– Navinchandra Ramgoolam

Mayotte
Territorial Collectivity
of Mayotte
French colony in 1841
Departmental collectivity of France in 2001
French overseas department

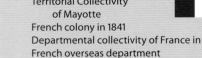

- 144 miles²/374 km²
- 2009 223,765
- French
- 1 euro = 100 cents
- 57.88/1,000
- 62.5 years

Head of State
2007– Nicolas Sarkozy, president of France

**Head of government
(president of the General Council)**
2009– Ahmed Attoumani Douchina

Saint Helena
Saint Helena including
Ascension Island and
Tristan da Cunha
British crown colony in 1833
Overseas territory of the UK
since 1981

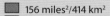

- 156 miles²/414 km²
- 2009 7,635
- English
- 1 Saint Helena pound = 100 pence
- 18.31/1,000
- 78.3 years

Head of state
- 1952– Queen Elizabeth II of the United Kingdom

Governor (head of government)
2007– Andrew Gurr

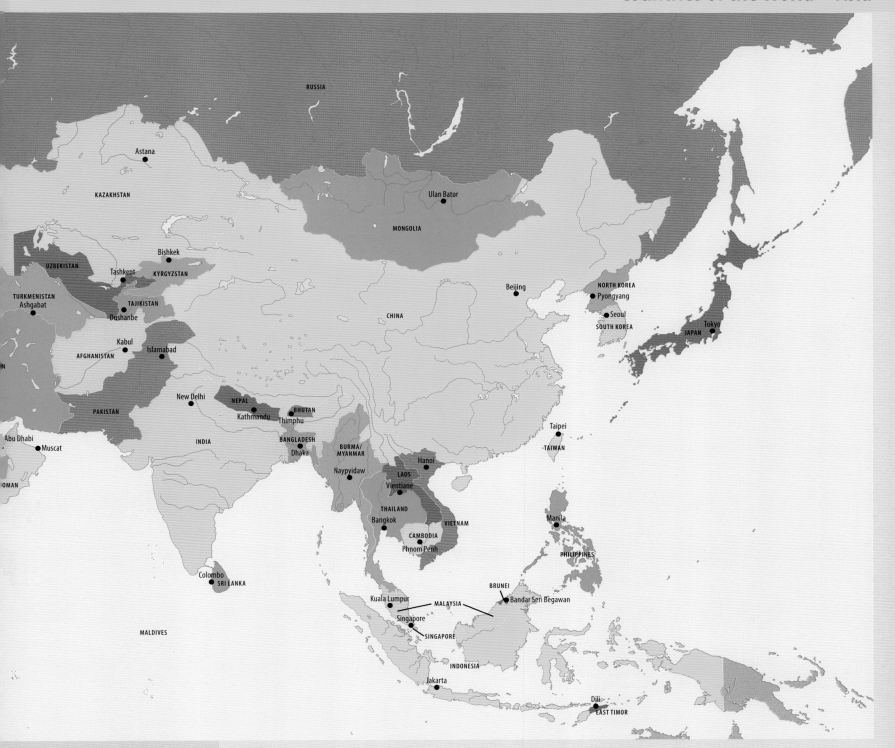

Countries of the World – Asia

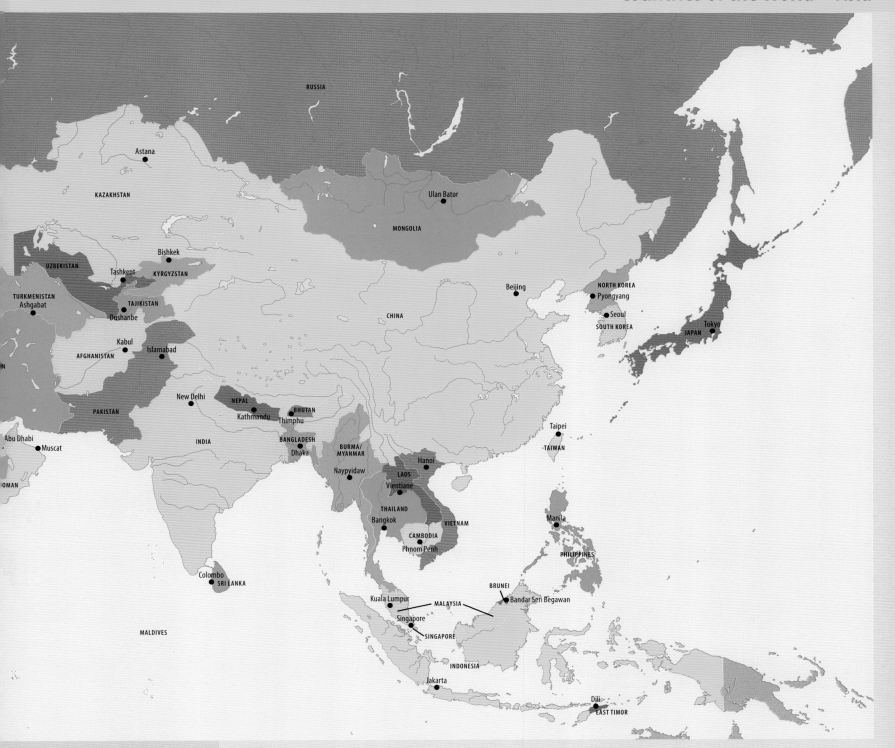

Réunion

Réunion Island
Overseas department of
France in 1946
Overseas region of France in 1982

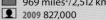 969 miles²/2,512 km²
2009 827,000
French
1 euro = 100 cents (since 2002)
73 years

Prefect
2006– Pierre-Henry Maccioni

President of the Regional Council
2004– Paul Vergès

President of the General Council
2004– Nassimah Dindar

ASIA

Turkey
Republic of Turkey
Founded as republic in 1923
Republican parliamentary democracy

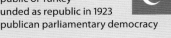 301,382 miles²/780,580 km²
1956 24,797,000
1993 61,098,000
2009 76,805,524
GDP US$11,200/person
Turkish
1 Turkish lira = 100 kuruş
36.98/1,000
73.2 years
UNO, NATO, WHO, WTO

Political parties
☐ Justice and Development Party
(AKP; moderate Islamic)

☐ Republican People's Party
(CHP; kemalists, long served quasi
as the ruling party)
☐ Democratic Party (DP)
☐ Democratic Left Party
(DSP; social democrats)
☐ Welfare Party (RP)
☐ True Path Party (DYP; successor to
the Justice Party/AP)
☐ Motherland Party (ANAP)
☐ Nationalist Movement Party
(MHP)

Presidents
1938–1950 Mustafa İsmet İnönü (CHP)
1950–1960 Mahmut Celal Bayar (DP)
1960–1966 Cemal Gürsel (military)
1966–1973 Cevdet Sunay (military)
1973–1980 Fahri Korutürk (military)
1982–1989 Kenan Evren (military)
1989–1993 Turgut Özal (ANAP)
1993–2000 Süleyman Demirel (DYP)

2000–2007 Ahmet Necdet Sezer
(judiciary)
2007– Abdullah Gül (AKP)
Prime ministers
1950–1960 Adnan Menderes
(CHP)
1965–1971, 1975–1977, 1979–1980
Süleyman Demirel (AP/DYP)
1974–1975, 1977, 1978–1979, 1999–2002
Bülent Ecevit (DSP)
1983–1989 Turgut Özal (ANAP)
1993–1996 Tansu Çiller (DYP)
1996–1997 Necmettin Erbakan (RP)
2002–2003 Abdullah Gül (AKP)
2003– Recep Tayyip Erdoğan (AKP)

Georgia
Georgia
Independence in 1991
Unitary semi-presidential republic

487

Countries of the World – Asia

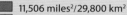

- 26,911 miles²/69,700 km²
- 1993 5,500,000
- 2009 4,615,805
- GDP US$4,500/person
- Georgian
- 1 lari = 100 tetri
- 16.78/1,000
- 76.5 years
- UNO, OAS, OSCE, WHO, WTO

President
2004– Mikheil Nikolozis dze Saak'ashvili

Prime minister
2009– Nikoloz Gilauri

Armenia
Republic of Armenia
Independence in 1991
Presidential republic

- 11,506 miles²/29,800 km²
- 1956 24,797,000
- 1993 3,700,000
- 2009 2,967,005
- GDP US$5,900/person
- Armenian
- 1 dram = 100 luma
- 19.31/1,000
- 77.8 years
- UNO, OSCE, WHO, WTO

President
2008– Serzh Azati Sargsyan

Prime minister
2008– Tigran Sargsyan

Azerbaijan
Republic of Azerbaijan
Independence in 1918,
reestablished in 1991
Parliamentary republic

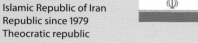

- 33,436 miles²/86,600 km²
- 1993 7,400,000
- 2009 8,238,670
- GDP US$9,900/person
- Azerbaijani (Azeri)
- 1 Azerbaijani manat = 100 qäpik
- 56.43/1,000
- 66.3 years
- UNO, OAS, OSCE, WHO, WTO

President
2003– İlham Heydar oğlu Aliyev
(prime minister in 2003)

Prime minister
2003– Artur Tahir oğlu Rasizada

Iran
Islamic Republic of Iran
Republic since 1979
Theocratic republic

- 636,293 miles²/1,648,000 km²
- 1957 19,324,000
- 1993 62,503,000
- 2009 66,429,285
- GDP US$12,900/person
- Persian
- 1 Iranian rial = 100 dinars
- 36.93/1,000
- 70.9 years
- UNO, OPEC, WHO, WTO

Political parties
Political parties and alliances regularly emerge to support presidential candidates during elections; the Guardian Council examines them to determine whether they conform with the Islamic constitution.

Heads of state
a) Shah
1941–1979 Mohammad Reza Pahlavi
b) Supreme Leader of Iran
1979–1989 Ayatollah Ruhollah Mousavi Khomeini
1989– Seyed Ali Hoseyni Khãmene'i

Presidents
1980–1981 Abolhassan Banisadr
1981 Mohammad Ali Rajai
1981–1989 Seyed Ali Hoseyni Khãmene'i
1989–1997 Ayatollah Akbar Hashemi Rafsanjani
1997–2005 Seyed Mohammad Khãtamī
2005– Mahmoud Ahmadinejad

Prime ministers
1951–1953 Mohammad Mosaddegh
1953–1955 Mohammad Fazlollah Zahedi
1962–1964 Amir Asadollah Alam
1965–1977 Amir-Abbas Hoveyda
1979 Shapour Bakhtiar
1979 Mehdi Bazargan
1980–1981 Mohammad Ali Rajai
1981 Mohammad Javad Bahonar
1981–1989 Mir-Hossein Mousavi Khameneh
1989 Position abolished

Iraq
Republic of Iraq
Founded in 1920/21
Republic in 1958
Parliamentary republic in 2004

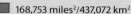

- 168,753 miles²/437,072 km²
- 1957 6,538,109
- 1993 20,021,000
- 2009 28,945,570
- GDP US$3,300/person
- Arabic, Kurdish
- 1 Iraqi dinar = 1,000 fils
- 45.43/1,000
- 69.6 years
- UNO, OPEC, WHO, WTO

Political parties
From 1968–2003 the Baath Party (= Arab Socialist Party of Resurrection) was the sole ruling party.
Seventy-three political parties and alliances participated in the 2005 elections; most were organized on the basis of religious or ethnic affiliations (Sunni, Shi'ite, Kurds, etc.).

Heads of state
a) Monarchs
1939–1958 Faisal II
1939–1953 Abdallah (regent)
b) Presidents
1958–1963 Muhammad Najib Ar-Ruba'i
1963–1966 Abdul Salam Arif
1966–1968 Abdul Rahman Arif
1968–1979 Ahmed Hassan al-Bakr
1979–2003 Saddam Hussein Abd al-Majid al-Tikriti (dictator)
2003–2004 Office for Reconstruction and Humanitarian Assistance

2004–2005 Ghazi Mashal Ajil al-Yawer (interim president)
2005– Jalal Talabani

Prime ministers
1930–1958 Nuri Pasha al-Said (eight times prime minister in these years)
1958–1963 Abd al-Karim Qasim (military junta leader)
1963, 1968–1979 Ahmed Hassan al-Bakr
1963–1964 Abdul Salam Arif
1979–1991, 1994–2003 Saddam Hussein
1991 Sa'dun Hammadi
1991–1993 Mohammed Amza az-Zubeidi
1993–1994 Ahmad Husayn Khudayir as-Samarrai
2004–2005 Ayad Allawi
2005–2006 Ibrahim al-Jaafari
2006– Nouri Jawad al-Maliki

Autonomous Kurdistan Region
Autonomous, federally recognized region of Iraq
Autonomy accord agreement signed in 1970,
Gained de facto independence in 1991 & 2005
Parliamentary republic

- ca. 30,888 miles²/80,000 km²
- 2009 8,031,630
- Kurdish
- 1 Iraqi dinar = 1,000 fils (since 2003)

President
2005– Masoud Barzani

Prime minister
2009– Barham Ahmad Salih

Northern Cyprus
Turkish Republic of Northern Cyprus
(not recognized internationally);
founded in 1983
Representative democratic republic

- 1,295 miles²/3,355 km²
- 2009 265,100
- GDP US$14,770/person
- Turkish
- 1 Turkish lira = 100 kuruş

President
2005– Mehmet Ali Talat
(prime minister 2004–2005)

Prime minister
2009– Derviş Eroğlu

Southern Cyprus
Republic of Cyprus
Independence in 1960
Presidential republic

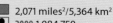

- 2,071 miles²/5,364 km²
- 2009 1,084,750
- GDP US$21,200/person
- Greek, Turkish
- Euro (since 2008) = 2.33 lira
- 6.75/1,000
- 78.2 years
- UNO, EU, OAS, WHO, WTO

President and head of government
2008– Dimitris Christofias

Syria
Syrian Arab Republic
Independence in 1946
Republic under an authoritarian regime

- 71,498 miles²/185,180 km²
- 1993 13,883,000
- 2009 21,762,980
- GDP US$4,700/person
- Arabic
- 1 Syrian pound = 100 piastres
- 26.78/1,000
- 70.9 years
- UNO, WHO

Political parties
- *National Progressive Front (NPF) includes Arab Socialist Renaissance (Ba'th) Party, the ruling party since 1963*
- *Syrian Social Nationalist Party (SSNP) (legal since 2005)*

Presidents
1943–1949, 1955–1958 Shukri al-Quwatli
1949–1951, 1954–1955 Hashim Bay Khalid al-Atassi
1953–1954 Adib ibn Hasan Shishakli
1958–1961 Part of the United Arab Republic (with Egypt)
1961–1963 Nazim al-Kudsi
1963–1966 Amin al-Hafiz
1966–1970 Noureddin Mustafa al-Atassi
1970–1971 Ahmad al-Hasan al-Khatib
1971–2000 Hafez al-Assad
2000– Bashar al-Assad

Prime ministers
1941–1966 changed almost every year
1966–1968 Yusuf Zuaiyin
1968–1970 Noureddin Mustafa al-Atassi
1970–1971 Hafez al-Assad
1980–1987 Abdul Rauf al-Kasm
1987–2000 Mahmoud Zuabi
2000–2003 Muhammad Mustafa Mero
2003– Muhammad Naji al-Otari

Lebanon
Lebanese Republic
Independence in 1943
Confessionalist, parliamentary republic

- 4,015 miles²/10,400 km²
- 1957 1,525,000
- 1993 2,958,000
- 2009 4,017,095
- GDP US$11,500/person
- Arabic, French, English, Armenian
- 1 Lebanese pound = 100 piastre
- 22.59/1,000
- 73.4 years
- UNO, OAS, WHO, WTO

Political parties
- Future Movement Bloc (Sunni)
- Progressive Socialist Party (PSP; Druse)
- Development and Resistance Bloc: Amal and Hisbollah (Shi'ite)
- Democratic Renewal Movement
- Democratic Left (DL)
- Free Patriotic Movement (Christian)
- Kataeb Party (Maronite)
- Lebanese Forces (Christian militia)
- Lebanese Communist Party (PCL)
- National Liberal Party (NLP; Maronite)

Presidents (according to the constitution always a Maronite Christian)
1943–1952 Bechara El Khoury
1952–1958 Camille Nimr Chamoun
1958–1964 Fuad Chehab
1964–1970 Charles Helou
1970–1976 Suleiman Kabalan Frangieh
1976–1982 Elias Sarkis
1982 Bachir Gemayel
1982–1988 Amine Gemayel
1989 René Moawad
1989–1998 Elias Hrawi
1998–2007 Émile Lahoud
2007–2008 Fouad Siniora
2008– Michel Suleiman

Prime ministers (according to the constitution always a Sunni Muslim)
1946–1951 Riad as-Solh
1958–1960, 1961–1964, 1965–1968, 1969–1970, 1975–1976, 1984–1987 Rashid Karami
1970–1973 Saeb Salam
1987–1990, 1998–2000 Selim Ahmed El-Hoss
1990–1992, 2004–2005 Omar Karami
1992–1998, 2000–2004 Rafic Al-Hariri
2005 Najib Azmi Mikati
2005–2009 Fuad Siniora
2009– Saad ed Deen Rafiq al-Hariri

Israel

State of Israel
Founded in 1948
Parliamentary democracy

- 8,019 miles²/20,770 km²
- 1957 1,976,000
- 1993 5,417,000
- 2009 7,233,700
- GDP US$28,400/person
- Hebrew, Arabic
- 1 Israeli new shekel = 100 agorot
- 4.28/1,000
- 80.6 years
- UNO, OSCE, CERN, WHO, WTO

Political parties
■ Likud ("The Consolidation")
□ Kadima ("Forward")
□ Avoda ("Work")
□ Schinui ("Change")
□ National Union (nationalist alliance of four parties)
□ New Movement-Meretz
■ Agudat Yisrael and Degel HaTorah—United Torah Judaism

Presidents
1948–1952 Chaim Azriel Weizmann
1952–1963 Yitzhak Ben-Zvi (Mapai/Ahdut HaAvoda—workers' party)
1963–1973 Zalman Shazar (Mapai/Ahdut HaAvoda—workers' party)
1973–1978 Ephraim Katzir (Alignment/today Avoda)
1978–1983 Yitzhak Navon (Alignment/today Avoda)
1983–1993 Chaim Herzog (Alignment/today Avoda)
1993–2000 Ezer Weizman (Kadima)
2000–2007 Moshe Katsav (Likud)
2007– Shimon Peres (Kadima)

Prime ministers
1948–1953, 1955–1963 David Ben Gurion (Mapai/Ahdut HaAvoda)
1953–1955 Moshe Sharett (Mapai/Ahdut HaAvoda—workers' party)
1963–1969 Levi Eshkol (Mapai/Alignment)
1969 Yigal Allon (Alignment)

1969–1974 Golda Meir (Alignment)
1974–1977 Yitzhak Rabin (Alignment)
1977–1983 Menachem Begin (Likud)
1983–1984 Yitzhak Shamir (Likud)
1984–1986 Shimon Peres (Alignment)
1986–1992 Yitzhak Shamir (again)
1992–1995 Yitzhak Rabin (again)
1995–1996 Shimon Peres (again)
1996–1999 Benjamin Netanyahu (Likud)
1999–2001 Ehud Barak (Avoda)
2001–2006 Ariel Sharon (Likud/Kadima)
2006–2008 Ehud Olmert (Kadima; acting prime minister in early 2009)
2009– Benjamin Netanyahu (Likud)

Foreign affairs ministers
1948–1956 Moshe Sharett (Mapai)
1956–1966 Golda Meir (Mapai)
1966–1974 Abba Eban (Alignment)
1974–1977 Yigal Allon (Alignment)
1977–1979 Moshe Dayan (independent)
1979–1980 Menachem Begin (Likud)
1980–1986 Yitzhak Shamir (Likud)
1986–1988, 1992–1995, 2001–2002 Shimon Peres (Alignment)
1988–1990 Moshe Arens (Likud)
1990–1992, 1996–1998, 1999–2000 David Levy (Gesher/One Israel)
1995 Yossi Beilin (Avoda)
1995–1996, 2000 Ehud Barak (Avoda)
1998, 2002–2003 Benjamin Netanyahu (Likud)
1998–1999, 2002 Ariel Sharon (Likud)
2000–2001 Shlomo Ben Ami (One Israel)
2003–2006 Silvan Shalom (Likud)
2006–2009 Tzipi Livni (Kadima)
2009– Avigdor Lieberman (Yisrael Beiteinu)

Jordan

Hashemite Kingdom of Jordan
Founded in 1923; kingdom in 1946
Constitutional monarchy

- 35,637 miles²/92,300 km²
- 1956 1,471,000
- 1993 3,929,000
- 2009 6,269,285
- GDP US$5,300/person
- Arabic
- 1 Jordanian dinar = 100 qirsh
- 15.57/1,000
- 78.7 years
- UNO, OSCE, WHO, WTO

Monarchs
♛ 1952–1999 King Hussein
1999– King Abdullah II

Prime minister
2009– Samir Zaid al-Rifai

Palestinian Territories

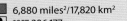

(Gaza Strip and West Bank)
Founded in 1988; currently recognized by 108 countries

- 2,432 miles²/6,300 km²
- 2009 4,013,125
- Arabic
- New Israeli shekel and Jordanian dinar

a) Gaza Strip
- 2009 1,551,860
- 19/1,000
- 73.2 years

b) West Bank
- 2009 2,461,265
- 16.5/1,000
- 74.3 years

President of the Palestinian National Authority
2005– Mahmud Abbas (prime minister in 2003)

Prime minister
2007– Salam Fayyad

Saudi Arabia

Kingdom of Saudi Arabia
Founded as a kingdom in 1932
Absolute monarchy

- 829,995 miles²/2,149,690 km²
- 1956 6,036,000
- 1993 17,608,000
- 2009 28,686,635
- GDP US$20,300/person
- Arabic
- 1 Saudi riyal = 100 halala
- 11.94/1,000
- 76.1 years
- UNO, OAS, OPEC, WHO, WTO

Political parties
None

Monarchs
♛ 1902–1953 Abdul Aziz bin Al Saud (king in 1932; all successors to date are his sons)
♛ 1953–1964 Saud bin Abdul Aziz
♛ 1964–1975 Faisal bin Abdul Aziz
♛ 1975–1982 Khalid bin Abdul Aziz
♛ 1982–2005 Fahd bin Abdul Aziz
♛ 2005– Abdullah bin Abdul Aziz

Prime ministers
Since 1953 the crown prince (brother of the king) serves as head of government.
2005– Crown Prince Sultan bin Abdul Aziz

Kuwait

State of Kuwait
Founded in 1756
Independence in 1961
Constitutional monarchy

- 6,880 miles²/17,820 km²
- 1957 206,177
- 1993 1,604,000
- 2009 2,692,525
- GDP US$55,800/person
- Arabic
- 1 Kuwaiti dinar = 1,000 fils
- 9.22/1,000
- 77.5 years
- UNO, OPEC, WHO, WTO

Monarch
♛ 2006– Sabah IV Al-Ahmad Al-Jaber Al-Sabah

Prime minister
2006– Nasser Mohammed Al-Ahmed Al-Sabah

Bahrain

Kingdom of Bahrain
Independence in 1971
Kingdom since 2002
Constitutional monarchy

- 257 miles²/665 km²
- 1957 124,000
- 1993 545,000
- 2009 728,710
- GDP US$38,400/person
- Arabic
- 1 Bahraini dinar = 1,000 fils
- 15.64/1,000
- 74.9 years
- UNO, WHO, WTO

Monarch
♛ 1999– Amir (since 2002 King) Hamad bin Isa Al Khalifa

Prime minister
1970– Shaykh Khalifa ibn Salman Al Khalifah

Qatar

State of Qatar
Independence in 1878/1971
Absolute monarchy

- 4,416 miles²/11,437 km²
- 1956 40,000
- 1993 533,000
- 2009 833,285
- GDP US$121,400/person
- Arabic
- 1 Qatari riyal = 100 dirham
- 13.1/1,000
- 75.2 years
- UNO, OAS, OPEC, WHO, WTO

Monarch
♛ 1995– Amir Hamad bin Khalifa Al Thani

Prime minister
2007– Hamad bin Jassim bin Jaber Al Thani

United Arab Emirates

United Arab Emirates (UAE)
Independence in 1971
Federation; UAE federal gov't holds certain powers, others reserved to member emirates

- 32,278 miles²/83,600 km²
- 1993 1,785,000
- 2009 4,798,490
- GDP US$41,800/person
- Arabic
- 1 UAE dirham = 100 fils
- 13.11/1,000
- 75.9 years
- UNO, OPEC, WHO, WTO

President
2004– Khalifa bin Zayed Al Nahyan (emir of Abu Dhabi; prime minister 1971–1976)

Prime minister
2006– Mohammed bin Rashid Al Maktoum (ruler of Dubai)

Countries of the World – Asia

Oman

Sultanate of Oman
Independence in 1971
Monarchy

- 82,031 miles²/212,460 km²
- 1955 550,000
- 1993 1,761,000
- 2009 3,418,085
- GDP US$20,300/person
- Arabic
- 1 Omani rial = 1,000 baizas
- 17.45/1,000
- 73.9 years
- UNO, WHO, WTO

♛ **Sultan and head of government**
1970– Sultan and Prime Minister Qaboos bin Said Al-Said

Yemen
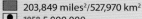
Republic of Yemen
Independence in 1918/1967,
Unification of north and south in 1990
Islamic republic

- 203,849 miles²/527,970 km²
- 1958 5,000,000
- 1993 12,938,000
- 2009 22,858,240
- GDP US$2,500/person
- Arabic
- 1 Yemeni rial = 100 fils
- 56.27/1,000
- 62.9 years
- UNO, OAS, WHO, WTO

President
1990– Ali Abdallah Salih (was president of Yemen Arab Republic [North Yemen] 1978–1990)

Prime minister
2007– Ali Muhammad Mujawwar

Afghanistan

Islamic Republic of Afghanistan
Republic since 1973; Islamic republic

- 250,000 miles²/647,500 km²
- 1953 12,000,040
- 1993 21,660,000
- 2009 28,395,715
- GDP US$800/person
- Pashto, Persian (Dari)
- 1 afghani = 100 puls
- 154.67/1,000
- 44.2 years
- UNO, OAS, WHO, WTO

Political parties
The political landscape is unclear; many interest groups and political parties are ethnically or regionally based, some of them Islamist.

Heads of state
a) Monarch
♛ 1933–1973 Mohammed Zahir Shah
b) Presidents
1973–1978 Mohammed Daoud Khan
1978–1979 Nur Muhammad Taraki (also prime minister)
1979 Hafizullah Amin (also prime minister)

1979–1986 Babrak Karmal
1986–1987 Haji Mohammad Chamkani
1987–1992 Mohammed Najibullah
c) Mujahideen
1992 Abdul Rahim Hatef (president)
1992 Sibghatullah Mojaddedi (president)
1992–1996 Burhanuddin Rabbani (president)
d) Taliban
1996–2001 Mullah Mohammed Omar (emir)
e) Islamic republic
2001 Burhanuddin Rabbani (2nd term)
2001– Hamid Karzai (also prime minister)

Prime ministers
a) Rule by the Communist Party
1979–1981 Babrak Karmal
1981–1988, 1989–1990 Sultan Ali Keshtmand
1988–1989 Mohammad Hasan Sharq
1990–1992 Fazal Haq Khaliqyar
b) Mujahideen
1992 Abdul Sabur Farid Kuhestani
1993–1994, 1996 Gulbuddin Hekmatyar
1994–1995 Arsala Rahmani
1995–1996 Ahmad Shah Ahmadzai
c) Taliban
1996–2001 Muhammad Rabbani
2001– Abdul Kabir
d) Northern Alliance
1996–1997 Gulbuddin Hekmatyar (again)
1997– Abdul Rahim Ghafoorzai
1997–2001 Abdul Ghafoor Rawan Farhadi

Turkmenistan

Turkmenistan
Independence in 1991
Presidential republic with a one-party system

- 188,455 miles²/488,100 km²
- 1993 4,000,000
- 2009 4,884,885
- GDP US$6,700/person
- Turkmen
- 1 manat = 100 tennesi
- 51.81/1,000
- 68.6 years
- UNO, OSCE, WHO

President and head of government
2006– Gurbanguly Berdimuhamedow (autocratic government)

Uzbekistan

Republic of Uzbekistan
Independence in 1991
Presidential republic

- 172,741 miles²/447,400 km²
- 1993 22,400,000
- 2009 27,606,010
- GDP US$2,800/person
- Uzbek, regionally also Karakalpak
- 1 soum (or som) = 100 tiyn
- 24.23/1,000
- 71.7 years
- UNO, OSCE, WHO, WTO

President
1990– Islom Karimov (de facto dictator)

Prime minister
2003– Shavkat Mirziyoyev

Kazakhstan

Republic of Kazakhstan
Independence in 1991
Presidential republic

- 1,049,150 miles²/2,717,300 km²
- 1993 17,000,000
- 2009 15,399,435
- GDP US$11,400/person
- Kazakh, Russian
- 1 tenge = 100 tiyn
- 26.56/1,000
- 67.6 years
- UNO, OAS, OSCE, WHO, WTO

President
1990– Nursultan Nazarbayev (authoritarian rule)

Prime minister
2007– Karim Masimov

Kyrgyzstan

Kyrgyz Republic
Independence in 1991
Presidential republic

- 76,641 miles²/198,500 km²
- 1993 4,700,000
- 2009 5,431,747
- GDP US$2,100/person
- Kyrgyz, Uzbek, Russian
- 1 soum (or som) = 100 tiyn
- 32.3/1,000
- 69.1 years
- UNO, OSCE, WHO, WTO

President
2005– Kurmanbek Bakiev (was prime minister 2000–2002)

Prime minister
2009– Daniyar Usenov

Tajikistan
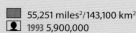
Republic of Tajikistan
Independence in 1991
Presidential republic

- 55,251 miles²/143,100 km²
- 1993 5,900,000
- 2009 7,349,145
- GDP US$1,800/person
- Tajik, Russian
- 1 somoni = 100 diram
- 42.31/1,000
- 65.0 years
- UNO, OSCE, WHO, WTO

President
1992– Emomali Rahmon

Prime minister
1999– Oqil Oqilow

Pakistan

Islamic Republic of Pakistan
Independence in 1947,
republic in 1956
Federal republic

- 310,401 miles²/803,940 km²
- 1993 131,456,000
- 2009 174,578,560

- GDP US$2,600/person
- Urdu (official language), Punjabi, English
- Pakistani rupee
- 66.94/1,000
- 64.1 years
- UNO, OAS, WHO, WTO

Political parties (selected few)
☐ Pakistan Peoples Party (PPP; laicist)
☐ Jamaat-i Islami (JI; Islamists, currently tied to other Islamist groups)
☐ Pakistan Muslim League/Nawaz group (PML-N; moderate Islamic)
☐ Pakistan Muslim League/Quaid-i-Azam group (PML-Q)
☐ Muttahida Qaumi Movement (MQM; student group/laicist)

Heads of state
a) Governor-Generals (representative of the British monarch)
1947–1948 Mohammad Ali Jinnah
1948–1951 Khwaja Nazimuddin
1951–1955 Ghulam Mohammad
1955–1956 Iskander Ali Mirza
b) Presidents
1956–1958 Iskander Ali Mirza
1958–1969 Mohammad Ayub Khan (military ruler)
1969–1971 Agha Muhammad Yahya Khan
1971–1973 Zulfikar Ali Bhutto
1973–1978 Fazal Ilahi Chaudhry
1978–1988 Mohammad Zia-ul-Haq (military ruler)
1988–1993 Ghulam Ishaq Khan
1993, 1997–1998 Wasim Sajjad (acting)
1993–1997 Farooq Ahmad Khan Leghari
1998–2001 Mohammad Rafiq Tarar
2001–2008 Pervez Musharraf (military ruler)
2008– Asif Ali Zardari

Prime ministers
1947–1951 Liaquat Ali Khan
1951–1953 Khawaja Nazimuddin
1958–1973 Military administration
1973–1977 Zulfikar Ali Bhutto (PPP)
1977–1985/88 Military administration
1985–1988 Muhammad Khan Junejo
1988–1990, 1993–1996 Benazir Bhutto (PPP)
1990–1993, 1997–1999 Nawaz Sharif (PML-N)
1999–2002 Military administration
2002–2004 Zafarullah Khan Jamali (PML-Q)
2004–2007 Shaukat Aziz (PML-Q)
2007–2008 Muhammad Mian Soomro (PML-N)
2008– Yousuf Raza Gilani (PPP)

India

Republic of India
Founded in 1947
Federal republic

- 1,269,338 miles²/3,287,590 km²
- 1955 392,440,000
- 1993 913,636,000
- 2009 1,156,897,765
- GDP US$3,100/person
- Hindi, English, 14 other official languages
- 1 Indian rupee = 100 paise
- 32.31/1,000
- 69.3 years
- UNO, ASEAN, WHO, WTO

Political parties

- Indian National Congress (INC; was long quasi "national party")
- Bharatiya Janata Party (BJP) or Indian People's Association (Hindu, conservative-nationalist)
- Bahujan Samaj Party (BSP) or Majority People's Party (party of the lower castes and other social and religious minorities)
- Communist Party of India-Marxist (CPI-M; Maoist)
- Communist Party of India (CPI) Nationalist Congress Party (NCP)

Presidents

1950–1962 Rajendra Prasad
1962–1967 Sarvepalli Radhakrishnan
1967–1969 Zakir Hussain
1969 Muhammad Hidayatullah
1969–1974 Varahagiri Venkata Giri
1974–1977 Fakhruddin Ali Ahmed
1977 Basappa Danappa Jatti
1977–1982 Neelam Sanjiva Reddy
1982–1987 Giani Zail Singh
1987–1992 Ramaswamy Venkataraman
1992–1997 Shankar Dayal Sharma
1997–2002 Kocheril Raman Narayanan
2002–2007 Avul Pakir Jainulabdeen Abdul Kalam
2007– Pratibha Patil

Prime ministers

1947–1964 Jawaharlal Nehru (INC)
1964, 1966 Gulzari Lal Nanda (INC; interim)
1964–1966 Lal Bahadur Shastri (INC)
1966–1977, 1980–1984 Indira Gandhi (INC)
1977–1979 Moraji Desai (Janata Party)
1979–1980 Choudhary Charan Singh (Janata Party)
1984–1989 Rajiv Gandhi (INC)
1989–1990 Vishwanath Pratap Singh (Janata Dal)
1990–1991 Chandra Shekhar (Janata Dal)
1991–1996 Pamulaparthi Venkata Narasimha Rao (INC)
1996 Atal Bihari Vajpayee (BJP)
1996–1997 Haradanahalli Dodde Deve Gowda (Janata Dal)
1997–1998 Inder Kumar Gujral (Janata Dal)
1998–2004 Atal Bihari Vajpayee (BJP; 2nd term)
2004– Manmohan Singh (INC)

Sri Lanka

Democratic Socialist Republic of Sri Lanka (Ceylon until 1972)
Independence in 1948; Presidential republic

- 25,332 miles²/65,610 km²
- 1957 9,000,000
- 1993 17,829,000
- 2009 21,324,790
- GDP US$4,500/person
- Sinhala, Tamil
- 1 Sri Lanka rupee = 100 cents
- 19.0/1,000
- 75.0 years
- UNO, OAS, WHO, WTO

President (also head of government)
2005– Mahinda Rajapaksa

Prime minister (largely ceremonial)
2005– Ratnasiri Wickremanayake

Maldives

Republic of Maldives
Independence in 1965
Presidential republic

- 116 miles²/300 km²
- 1956 81,950
- 1993 244,000
- 2009 396,335
- GDP US$4,200/person
- Maldivian Dhivehi
- 1 rufiyaa = 100 larees
- 30.63/1,000
- 73.7 years
- UNO, WHO, WTO

President and head of government
2008– Mohamed "Anni" Nasheed

Nepal

Federal Democratic Republic of Nepal
Traditional kingdom until 2008
Federal democratic republic

- 56,827 miles²/147,181 km²
- 1954 8,431,537
- 1993 18,120,000
- 2009 28,563,380
- GDP US$1,200/person
- Nepali
- 1 Nepalese rupee = 100 paisa
- 62/1,000
- 60.9 years
- UNO, WHO, WTO

President
2008– Ram Baran Yadav

Prime minister
2009– Madhav Kumar Nepal

Bhutan

Kingdom of Bhutan
Independence in 1949
Constitutional monarchy

- 18,147 miles²/47,000 km²
- 1955 623,000
- 1993 1,639,000
- 2009 691,140
- GDP US$6,200/person
- Dzongkha and various dialects
- 1 ngultrum = 100 chetrums (pegged to the Indian rupee)
- 51.92/1,000
- 65.5 years
- UNO, WHO, WTO

Monarch
2006– King Jigme Khesar Namgyel Wangchuck

Prime minister
1998–1999, 2003–2004, 2008– Jigme Thinley

Bangladesh

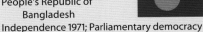

People's Republic of Bangladesh
Independence 1971; Parliamentary democracy

- 55,598 miles²/144,000 km²
- 1993 117,863,000
- 2009 156,050,885
- GDP US$1,600/person
- Bengali, English
- 1 taka = 100 poisha
- 57.45/1,000
- 63.2 years
- UNO, WHO, WTO

President
2009– Zillur Rahman

Prime minister
1996–2001, 2009– Sheik Hasina Wajed

Mongolia

Mongolia
Independence in 1911/21, people's republic until 1990
Parliamentary republic (since 1990)

- 56,827 miles²/1,564,116 km²
- 1955 100,000
- 1993 2,360,000
- 2009 3,041,140
- GDP US$3,400/person
- Mongol
- Tögrög (tugrik)
- 41.24/1,000
- 67.3 years
- UNO, OSCE, WHO, WTO

President
2009– Tsakhia Elbegdorj (prime minister 2000–2004)

Prime minister
2009– Sukhbaatar Batbold

China

People's Republic of China
Founded in 1949
People's republic (communist state)

- 3,705,386 miles²/9,596,960 km²
- 1993 1,196,520,000
- 2009 1,338,612,970
- GDP US$6,500/person
- Standard Chinese (Mandarin) and others
- 1 renminbi or yuan = 10 jiao = 100 fen
- 21.16/1,000
- 73.2 years
- UNO, UN Security Council, ASEAN, WHO, WTO

Party
The Communist Party of China (CCP), founded in 1921, has been the state party of China since 1949.

General Secretaries and Chairmen of the Communist Party of China
1927–1976 Mao Zedong
1956–1965 Deng Xiaoping (general secretary)
1976–1997 Deng Xiaoping (de facto leader of China, or "strong man")
General Secretaries:
1978–1986 Hu Yaobang
1987–1988 Zhao Ziyang
1989–2002 Jiang Zemin
2002– Hu Jintao

Presidents of China (chairman of the People's Republic of China 1949–1975, chairman of the Standing Committee of the National People's Congress 1975–1983, president since 1983)
1949–1958 Mao Zedong
1959–1965 Liu Shaoqi
1965–1968 vacant
1968–1972 Song Qingling ("Madame Sun Yat-sen")
1968–1975 Dong Biwu
1975–1976 Zhu De
1976–1978 collective leadership of the twenty vice presidents
1978–1983 Ye Jianying
1983–1988 Li Xiannian
1988–1992 Yang Shangkun
1992–2002 Jiang Zemin
2002– Hu Jintao

Premier of the People's Republic of China
1949–1976 Zhou Enlai
1976–1980 Hua Guofeng
1980–1987 Zhao Ziyang
1987–1998 Li Peng
1998–2003 Zhu Rongji
2003– Wen Jiabao

Taiwan

Republic of China on Taiwan/Taiwan
Founded in 1912 (separation from the People's Republic in 1949)
Multiparty democracy

- 13,892 miles²/35,980 km²
- 1993 21,130,000
- 2009 22,974,345
- GDP US$30,200/person
- Standard Chinese (Mandarin)
- 1 new Taiwan dollar = 100 cents
- 5.45/1,000
- 77.8 years
- WTO (not a member of UNO)

President
2008– Ma Ying-jeou

Prime minister
2009– Wu den-yih

Hong Kong

Hong Kong Special Administrative Region
British leased territory 1898–1997
Special administrative region of China 1997

- 425 miles²/1,103 km²
- 2009 7,055,070
- Chinese (Cantonese and other dialects), English
- 1 Hong Kong dollar = 100 cents
- 2.93/1,000
- 81.8 years
- WTO

Chief executive (head of government)
2005– Donald Tsang

Macau

Macau Special Administrative Region
Colonial territory of Portugal 1557–1999
Special admin. region of China since 1999

- 10 miles²/28 km²
- 2009 559,845
- Chinese (Cantonese), Portuguese
- 1 pataca = 100 avos
- 3.23/1,000
- 84.3 years
- WTO

Countries of the World – Asia

Chief executive (head of government)
2009– Fernando Chui Sai-on

North Korea

Democratic People's
Republic of Korea
Independence in 1948
Communist dictatorship

- 46,540 miles²/120,540 km²
- 1954 9,000,000
- 1993 23,029,000
- 2009 22,665,345
- **GDP** US$1,800/person
- Korean
- 1 won = 100 chon
- 21.86/1,000
- 72.2 years
- UNO, WHO

Political parties
*Since 1948 the Korean Workers' Party
(KWP) has been the sole state party.*

**General Secretary of the Korean
Workers' Party (actual ruler)**
1948–1994 Kim Il Sung (first chairman,
general secretary after 1966)
1994– Kim Jong Il (offically since 1997)

**Chairmen of the presidium of the
Supreme People's Assembly
(head of state)**
1948–1957 Kim Tu Bong
1957–1972 Choi Yong Kun
1972–1994 Kim Il Sung
1994– Kim Yong Nam

Premiers (head of government)
1948–1972 Kim Il Sung
1977–1984 Li Jong Ok
1984–1986, 1992–1997 Kang Song San
1986–1988 Li Gun Mo
1988–1992 Yon Hyang Muk
1997–2003 Hong Song Nam
2003–2007 Pak Pong Ju
2007– Kim Yong Il

South Korea
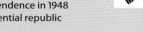
Republic of Korea
Independence in 1948
Presidential republic

- 38,023 miles²/98,480 km²
- 1993 44,352,000
- 2009 48,508,970
- **GDP** US$27,700/person
- Korean
- 1 won = 100 jeon
- 4.29/1,000
- 78.6 years
- UNO, ASEAN, OAS, WHO, WTO

Political parties
*The political parties of South Korea have
frequently changed names or changed
affiliations.*
- Grand National Party (GNP; merger of
several conservative parties including
Democratic Republicans, Democratic
Justice Party and New Korea Party)
- Our Open Party (Uri; 2004–2007)
- Democratic Party (DP), formerly
- United Democratic Party (UDP)
Democratic Labor Party (DLP)
- New Progressive Party (NPP)

Presidents
1948–1960 Rhee Syng-man
(with dictatorial powers)
1960–1962 Yun Bo-seon
1963–1979 Park Chung-hee (DRP; dictator)
1979–1980 Choi Kyu-hah
1980–1988 Chun Doo-hwan (DJP;
with dictatorial powers)
1988–1993 Roh Tae-woo (DJP)
1993–1998 Kim Young-sam (NKP)
1998–2003 Kim Dae-jung (National
Congress for New Politics)
2003–2008 Roh Moo-hyun (Uri)
2008– Lee Myung-bak (GNP/HD)

Prime ministers
Often very brief terms since 1948
1993–1994 Lee Hoi-chang (NKP)
1997–1998, 2003–2004 Goh Kun
2004–2006 Lee Hae-chan (Uri)
2006–2007 Han Myung-sook (Uri)
2007–2008 Han Duck-soo (Uri)
2008–2009 Han Seung-soo (GNP/HD)
2009– Chung Un-chan

Japan
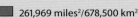
Japan
Newly founded in 1945,
constitution in 1947 (following World War II)
Parliamentary government with a
constitutional monarchy

- 145,882 miles²/377,835 km²
- 1957 90,900,000
- 1993 125,199,000
- 2009 127,078,680
- **GDP** US$32,600/person
- Japanese
- Yen
- 2.8/1,000
- 82.1 years
- UNO, ASEAN, G8, WHO, WTO

Political parties
- Liberal Democratic Party (LDP)
- Democratic Party of Japan (DPJ)
- Social Democratic Party (SDP)
- Japan Communist Party (JPC)
- Komeito ("Justice")
- People's New Party (PNP)

Emperor (tenno) of Japan
- 1926–1989 Hirohito, Emperor Showa
(regent 1921–1926; his reign is the
- Showa period)
1989– Akihito (Heisei period)

**Prime ministers (all have belonged to
the LDP since 1948 except in 1993–1996)**
1945 Prince Higashikuni Naruhiko
1945–1946 Kijuro Shidehara
1946–1947 Shigeru Yoshida
1947–1948 Tetsu Katayama
1948 Hitoshi Ashida
1948–1954 Shigeru Yoshida (2nd term)
1954–1956 Ichiro Hatoyama
1956–1957 Tanzan Ishibashi
1957–1960 Nobusuke Kishi
1960–1964 Hayato Ikeda
1964–1972 Eisaku Sato
1972–1974 Kakuei Tanaka
1974–1976 Takeo Miki
1976–1978 Takeo Fukuda
1978–1980 Masayoshi Ohira
1980–1982 Zenko Suzuki
1982–1987 Yasuhiro Nakasone
1987–1989 Noboru Takeshita
1989–1991 Toshiki Kaifu

1991–1993 Kiichi Miyazawa
1993–1994 Morihiro Hosokawa
(Japan New Party)
1994 Tsutomu Hata (Renewal)
1994–1996 Tomiichi Murayama (SDP)
1996–1998 Ryutaro Hashimoto
1998–2000 Keizo Obuchi
2000–2001 Yoshiro Mori
2001–2006 Junichiro Koizumi
2006–2007 Shinzo Abe
2007–2008 Yasuo Fukuda
2008–2009 Taro Aso
2009– Yukio Hatoyama

Myanmar/Burma

Myanmar (Union of Burma)
Independence in 1948
Military junta (since 1962)

- 261,969 miles²/678,500 km²
- 1957 20,054,000
- 1993 45,537,000
- 2009 48,137,740
- **GDP** US$1,200/person
- Burmese
- 1 kyat = 100 pyas
- 49.12/1,000
- 62.9 years
- UNO, WHO, WTO

**Chairman of the State Peace
and Development Council
(chief of state)**
1992– General Than Shwe

Prime minister
2007– General Thein Sein

Thailand

Kingdom of Thailand
Founded in 1238
Constitutional monarchy

- 198,455 miles²/514,000 km²
- 1957 2,107,600
- 1993 58,551,000
- 2009 65,998,435
- **GDP** US$8,100/person
- Thai
- 1 baht = 100 satang
- 18.23/1,000
- 72.8 years
- UNO, OAS, WHO, WTO

Monarch (chief of state)
- 1946– King Rama IX Bhumibol
Adulyadej

Prime minister
2008– Abhisit Vejjajiva

Laos

Lao People's Democratic
Republic
Independence in 1949
Republic with one-party state

- 91,428 miles²/236,800 km²
- 1955 2,000,000
- 1993 4,635,000
- 2009 6,834,345
- **GDP** US$2,100/person
- Lao
- 1 kip = 100 at
- 79.61/1,000

- 56.3 years
- UNO, WHO, WTO

**President and general secretary of the
Lao People's Revolutionary Party**
2006– Lt. General Choummali Saignason

Prime minister
2006– Bouasone Bouphavanh

Vietnam

Socialist Republic of
Vietnam
Independence in 1945,
divided 1949–1976, reunified in 1976
Socialist people's republic (communist)

- 127,243 miles²/329,560 km²
- 1993 72,318,000
- 2009 88,576,760
- **GDP** US$2,900/person
- Vietnamese
- Dong
- 23.61/1,000
- 71.3 years
- UNO, ASEAN, WHO, WTO

Political parties
*The Communist Party of Vietnam (CPV) has
been the state party of North Vietnam since
1945 and of reunited Vietnam since 1976.*

**Chairman of the Central Committee of
the Communist Party of Vietnam**
1941–1956, 1986 Truong Chinh
1951–1969 Ho Chi-Minh (CC president)
1960–1986 Le Duan
1986–1991 Nguyen Van Linh
1991–1997 Do Muoi
1997–2001 Le Kha Phieu
2001– Nong Duc Manh

Presidents
*a) North Vietnam (Democratic Republic
of Vietnam)*
1955–1969 Ho Chi Minh
1969–1976 Ton Duc Thang
b) South Vietnam (Republic of Vietnam)
1949–1955 Emperor Bao Dai
1955–1963 Ngo Dinh Diem
1967–1975 Nguyen Van Thieu
1975–1976 Huynh Tan Phat
c) Unified Vietnam
1976–1980 Ton Duc Thang
1980–1981 Nguyen Huu Tho
1981–1987 Truong Chinh
1987–1992 Vo Chi Cong
1992–1997 Le Duc Anh
1997–2006 Tran Duc Luong
2006– Nguyen Minh Triet

Prime ministers
a) North Vietnam
1945–1955 Ho Chi Minh
1955–1976 Pham Van Dong
b) Unified Vietnam
1976–1987 Pham Van Dong
1987–1988 Pham Hung
1988, 1991–1997 Vo Van Kiet
1988–1991 Do Muoi
1997–2006 Phan Van Khai
2006– Nguyen Tan Dung

Cambodia

Kingdom of Cambodia
Independence in 1953
Constitutional monarchy

- 69,900 miles²/181,040 km²
- 1958 5,040,000
- 1993 9,447,000
- 2009 14,494,295
- GDP US$1,900/person
- Khmer
- 1 riel = 100 sen (also US dollar)
- 56.6/1,000
- 61.7 years
- UNO, ASEAN, WHO, WTO

Political parties
- Cambodian People's Party (CPP) is the dominant party; as Kampuchean People's Revolutionary Party (KPRP) was the state party 1979–1991
- National United Front for Cambodia (FUNCINPEC; monarchists)
- Sam Rangsi Party (SRP; liberal)
- Norodom Ranariddh Party (NRP; nationalist)

Heads of state
- 1941–1955 Norodom II Sihanouk (king)
- 1955–1960 Norodom III Suramit (king)
- 1960–1970 Prince Norodom (II) Sihanouk (head of state)
- 1970–1972 Cheng Heng (president)
- 1972–1975 General Lon Nol (president/military dictator)
- 1975–1976 Prince Norodom (II) Sihanouk
- 1976–1979 Khieu Samphan (president of the State Presidium of Democratic Kampuchea)
- 1975–1979 Pol Pot ("Brother Nr. 1," dictator of the Khmer Rouge regime)
- 1979–1991 Heng Samrin (president, from 1981 chairman of the State Council)
- 1991–2004 Prince Norodom II Sihanouk (regent, became king in 1993)
- 2004– Norodom IV Sihamoni

Prime ministers
- 1941–1975 changed almost annually
- 1976 Khieu Samphan (Khmer Rouge)
- 1976–1979 Pol Pot (Khmer Rouge)
- 1981 Pen Sovan (CPP)
- 1981–1984 Chan Sy (CPP)
- 1985– Hun Sen (CPP)

Malaysia

Malaysia
Independence in 1957
Unique federal system with bicameral parliament headed by a monarch

- 127,316 miles²/329,750 km²
- 1957 6,276,915
- 1993 19,558,000
- 2009 25,715,820
- GDP US$14,700/person
- Bahasa Malaysia, English, Chinese
- 1 ringgit = 100 sen (cents)
- 16.39/1,000
- 73.0 years
- UNO, WHO, WTO

Monarch (elected for five-year term from among the sultans of the Malaysian states)
- 2007– Sultan Mizan Zainal Abidin (sultan of the state of Terengganu since 1998)

Prime minister
- 2009– Mohamed Najib bin Abdul Razak

Singapore

Republic of Singapore
Independence in 1965
Parliamentary republic

- 268 miles²/693 km²
- 1956 1,261,677
- 1993 2,909,000
- 2009 4,657,540
- GDP US$31,400/person
- Malay, English, Tamil, Chinese, dialects
- Singapore dollar
- 2.3/1,000
- 81.9 years
- UNO, WHO, WTO

President
- 1999– Sellapan Rama Nathan

Prime minister
- 2004– Lee Hsien Loong

Indonesia

Republic of Indonesia
Independence in 1945
Presidential republic

- 741,096 miles²/1,919,440 km²
- 1958 86,900,000
- 1993 191,588,000
- 2009 240,271,520
- GDP US$4,000/person
- Bahasa Indonesia
- 1 rupiah = 100 sen
- 31.04/1,000
- 70.5 years
- UNO, UN Security Council (currently), OPEC, WHO, WTO

Political parties
- Democratic Party (PD)
- Indonesia Democratic Party-Struggle (PDI-P)
- National Awakening Party (PKB)
- Prosperous Justice Party (PKS)
- GOLKAR (1965–1998 quasi state party, today part of the ruling coalition)

Presidents (since 1959 also heads of government/prime ministers)
- 1945–1967 Ahmed Sukarno
- 1967–1998 Suharto (military ruler from 1965)
- 1998–1999 Bacharuddin Jusuf Habibie
- 1999–2001 Abdurrahman Wahid (PKB)
- 2001–2004 Megawati Sukarnoputri (PDI-P)
- 2004– Susilo Bambang Yudhoyono (PD)

Vice presidents
- 1945–1956 Mohammed Hatta
- 1973–1978 Hamengkubuwana IX, Sultan of Yogyakarta
- 1978–1983 Adam Malik
- 1983–1988 Umar Wirahadikusumah
- 1988–1993 Sudharmono
- 1993–1998 Try Sutrisno
- 1998 Bacharuddin Jusuf Habibie
- 1999–2001 Megawati Sukarnoputri (PDI-P)
- 2001–2004 Hamzah Haz (PDI-P)
- 2004–2009 Jusuf Kalla (GOLKAR)
- 2009– Boediono (unaffiliated)

Brunei

Brunei Darussalam
Independence in 1984
Constitutional sultanate

- 2,228 miles²/5,770 km²
- 1965 71,401
- 1993 281,000
- 2009 388,190
- GDP US$50,100/person
- Malay, English, Chinese
- 1 Brunei dollar = 100 cents
- 12.69/1,000
- 75.5 years
- UNO, WHO, WTO

Sultan and prime minister
- 1967– Sultan Hassanal Bolkiah

East Timor

Democratic Republic of Timor-Leste
Independence in 1975 (internationally recognized in 2002)
Republic

- 5,794 miles²/15,007 km²
- 1993 835,000
- 2009 1,131,610
- GDP US$2,400/person
- Tetum, Portuguese
- US dollar
- 41.98/1,000
- 66.9 years
- UNO, WHO

President
- 2007– José Ramos-Horta

Prime minister
- 2007– Kay Rala Xanana Gusmão

Philippines

Republic of the Philippines
Independence in 1898,
from the USA in 1946; Presidential republic

- 115,830 miles²/300,000 km²
- 1957 22,690,000
- 1993 66,495,000
- 2009 97,976,600
- GDP US$3,300/person
- Filipino, English, 8 major dialects
- 1 peso = 100 sentimo

Political parties
Until 1965 the Liberal Party (LP) and National Party (NP) alternated power; the New Society Movement (KBL) was the ruling party 1965–1986.
- Christian Muslim Democrats (Lakas-CMD)
- Force of the Philippine Masses (PMP)
- New Patriotic Alliance (BAYAN)
- Partner of the Free Filipino (KAMPI)
- Struggle of Democratic Filipinos (LDP)
- Nationalist People's Coalition (NPC)

Presidents
- 1946–1948 Manuel Roxas (LP)
- 1948–1953 Elpidio Quirino (LP)
- 1953–1957 Ramon Magsaysay (NP)
- 1957–1961 Carlos P. Garcia (NP)
- 1961–1965 Diosdado Macapagal (LP)
- 1965–1986 Ferdinand Marcos (NP/KBL; dictator)
- 1986–1992 Corazon Aquino (united democratic umbrella group UNIDO)
- 1992–1998 Fidel V Ramos (Lakas-CMD)
- 1998–2001 Joseph Estrada (PMP)
- 2001– Gloria Macapagal-Arroyo (Lakas-CMD)

Vice presidents
- 1949–1953, 1965–1973 Fernando López
- 1953–1957 Carlos B. Garcia
- 1957–1961 Diosdado Macapagal
- 1961–1965 Emmanuel Pelaez
- 1986–1992 Salvador H. Laurel
- 1992–1998 Joseph Estrada
- 1998–2001 Gloria Macapagal-Arroyo
- 2001–2004 Teofisto Guingona
- 2004– Noli de Castro

NORTH AMERICA

Canada

Canada
Independence 1931/1982
Parliamentary democracy, federation and Commonwealth realm

- 3,851,787 miles²/9,976,139 km²
- 1958 16,887,000
- 1993 29,610,000
- 2009 33,487,210
- GDP US$38,400/person
- English, French
- 1 Canadian dollar = 100 cents
- 5.1/1,000
- 81.2 years
- UNO, NATO, G8, ASEAN, WHO, WTO

Political parties
- Progressive Conservative Party until 2003; now the Conservative Party of Canada
- Liberal Party
- New Democratic Party (social democratic)
- Bloc Québécois (social democratic and separatist)

Heads of state – monarchs of the United Kingdom
- 1936–1952 George VI
- 1952– Elizabeth II

Governor general (representatives of the monarchy)
- 1940–1946 Alexander Cambridge
- 1946–1952 Harold Alexander
- 1952–1959 Vincent Massey
- 1959–1967 Georges-Philéas Vanier
- 1967–1974 Roland Michener
- 1974–1979 Jules Léger
- 1979–1984 Edward Schreyer
- 1984–1990 Jeanne Sauvé
- 1990–1995 Ray Hnatyshyn
- 1995–1999 Roméo LeBlanc
- 1999–2005 Adrienne Clarkson
- 2005– Michaëlle Jean

Prime ministers
- 1935–1948 William Lyon Mackenzie King (L)
- 1948–1957 Louis Saint Laurent (L)
- 1957–1963 John Diefenbaker (PC)
- 1963–1968 Lester Pearson (L)
- 1968–1979, 1980–1984 Pierre Trudeau (L)
- 1979–1980 Joe Clark (PC)
- 1984 John Turner (L)
- 1984–1993 Brian Mulroney (PC)
- 1993–2003 Jean Chrétien (L)
- 2003–2006 Paul Martin (L)
- 2006– Stephen Harper (C)

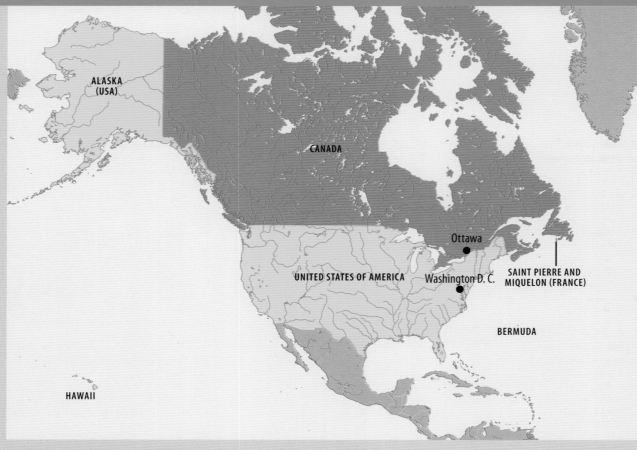

ALASKA (USA)

CANADA

Ottawa

UNITED STATES OF AMERICA

Washington D. C.

SAINT PIERRE AND MIQUELON (FRANCE)

BERMUDA

HAWAII

United States of America

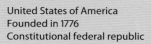

United States of America
Founded in 1776
Constitutional federal republic

- 3,718,690 miles²/9,631,418 km²
- 1957 171,438,000
- 1993 263,030,000
- 2009 307,212,100
- GDP US$46,400/person
- English
- 1 US dollar = 100 cents
- 6.3/1,000
- 78.2 years
- UNO, UN Security Council, NATO, G8, ASEAN, WHO, WTO

Political parties
- ☐ Democrats
- ■ Republicans

Presidents
1945–1953 Harry S. Truman (D)
1953–1961 Dwight D. Eisenhower (R)
1961–1963 John F. Kennedy (D)
1963–1969 Lyndon B. Johnson (D)
1969–1974 Richard M. Nixon (R)
1974–1977 Gerald Ford (R)
1977–1981 James Earl ("Jimmy") Carter (D)
1981–1989 Ronald Reagan (R)
1989–1993 George H. Bush (R)
1993–2001 William ("Bill") Clinton (D)
2001–2009 George W. Bush (R)
2009– Barack Obama (D)

Vice presidents
1945–1953 Alben W. Barkley (D)
1953–1961 Richard M. Nixon (R)
1961–1963 Lyndon B. Johnson (D)
1963–1965 office vacant
1965–1969 Hubert H. Humphrey (D)

1969–1973 Spiro Agnew (R)
1973–1974 Gerald Ford (R)
1974–1977 Nelson A. Rockefeller (R)
1977–1981 Walter Mondale (D)
1981–1989 George H. Bush (R)
1989–1993 J. Danforth Quayle (R)
1993–2001 Albert A. Gore (D)
2001–2009 Richard (Dick) B. Cheney (R)
2009– Joseph R. Biden (D)

Secretaries of state
1945–1947 James F. Byrnes (D)
1947–1949 George C. Marshall (D)
1949–1953 Dean G. Acheson (D)
1953–1959 John F. Dulles (R)
1959–1961 Christian Herter (R)
1961–1969 Dean Rusk (D)
1969–1973 William P. Rogers (R)
1973–1977 Henry Kissinger (R)
1977–1980 Cyrus Vance (D)
1980–1981 Edmund S. Muskie (D)
1981–1982 Alexander Haig (R)
1982–1989 George P. Shultz (R)
1989–1992 James Baker (R)
1992–1993 Lawrence Eagleburger (R)
1993–1997 Warren Christopher (D)
1997–2001 Madeleine Albright (D)
2001–2005 Colin Powell (R)
2005–2009 Condoleezza Rice (R)
2009– Hillary Clinton (D)

Bermuda

Bermuda
British colony in 1620
Overseas territory of the UK

- 20 miles²/53 km²
- 2009 67,837
- English
- Bermuda dollar
- 7.87/1,000
- 78.3 years

Head of state
- ♛ 1952– Queen Elizabeth II of the United Kingdom

Governor
2007– Richard Gozney

Premier
2006– Ewart Brown

Saint Pierre and Miquelon

Saint Pierre and Miquelon
Decisive French occupation in 1816,
Territorial collectivity in 1985
Overseas collectivity of France
(*collectivité d´outre-mer*) since 2003

- 93 miles²/242 km²
- 2009 7,063
- French
- Euro (since 2002)
- 7.04/1,000
- 78.9 years

Head of state
2007– Nicolas Sarkozy, president of France

Prefect
2008– Jean-Pierre Bercot

Head of government (president of the Territorial Council)
2007– Stéphane Artano

CENTRAL AMERICA

Mexico

United Mexican States
Independence in 1810
(recognized 1821)
Federal republic

- 761,602 miles²/1,972,550 km²
- 1957 31,454,190
- 1993 94,780,000
- 2009 111,211,790
- GDP US$13,200/person
- Spanish
- 1 Mexican peso = 100 centavos
- 19/1,000
- 75.8 years
- UNO, OAS, WHO, WTO

Political parties
- ☐ Institutional Revolutionary Party (PRI): was from 1929–2000 in practice the state party and appointed all important politicians and office holders
- ■ National Action Party (PAN)
- ☐ Party of the Democratic Revolution (PRD)
- ▨ Mexican Green Ecological Party (PVEM)
- ☐ Social Democratic Alternative Party (PSD)
- ▨ Labor Party (PT)
- ◧ New Alliance Party (PNA)

Presidents (also head of government)
1940–1946 Manuel Ávila Camacho
1946–1952 Miguel Alemán Valdés
1952–1958 Adolfo Ruiz Cortines
1958–1964 Adolfo López Mateos
1964–1970 Gustavo Diaz Ordaz
1970–1976 Luis Echeverría Álvarez
1976–1982 José López Portillo y Pacheco
1982–1988 Miguel de la Madrid Hurtado
1988–1994 Carlos Salinas de Gortari
1994–2000 Ernesto Zedillo Ponce de León
2000–2006 Vicente Fox Quesada (PAN)
2006– Felipe de Jesús Calderón Hinojosa (PAN)

Guatemala

Republic of Guatemala
Independence in 1821,
permanently established in 1839
Constitutional democratic republic

- 42,042 miles²/108,890 km²
- 1956 3,348,000
- 1993 10,620,000
- 2009 13,276,500
- GDP US$5,200/person
- Spanish
- 1 quetzal = 100 centavos
- 28.8/1,000
- 70.0 years
- UNO, OAS, WHO, WTO

President (also head of government)
2008– Álvaro Colom Caballeros

Belize

Belize (British Honduras until 1973)
Independence in 1981; Parliamentary democracy and Commonwealth realm

- 8,867 miles²/22,966 km²

[Belize]

- 1955 80,880
- 1993 210,000
- 2009 307,900
- GDP US$8,200/person
- English
- 1 Belize dollar = 100 cents
- 23.65/1,000
- 68.2 years
- UNO, OAS, WHO, WTO

Head of state
1952– Queen Elizabeth II

Governor general
1993– Colville Young, Sr.

Prime minister
2008– Dean Barrow

El Salvador

Republic of El Salvador
Independence in 1821,
definitive in 1838
Republic

- 8,124 miles²/21,040 km²
- 1956 2,307,659
- 1993 5,640,000
- 2009 7,185,220
- GDP US$6,000/person
- Spanish
- 1 El Salvador colón = 100 centavos;
  US dollar
- 22.2/1,000
- 72.1 years
- UNO, OAS, WHO, WTO

President and head of government
2009– Carlos Mauricio Funes Cartagena

Costa Rica

Republic of Costa Rica
Independence in 1821
Democratic republic

- 19,730 miles²/51,100 km²
- 1956 988,000
- 1993 3,070,000
- 2009 4,253,880
- GDP US$11,300/person
- Spanish
- 1 Costa Rica colón = 100 céntimos
- 9/1,000
- 77.4 years
- UNO, UN Security Council (aktuell), OAS,
  WHO, WTO

President and head of government
1986–1990, 2006– Óscar Arias Sanchez

San Andrés y Providencia

San Andrés y Providencia
Claimed by (Gran) Colombia in 1822
Department of Colombia, self-rule since 1912

- 19 miles²/44 km²
- 2009 72,740
- Spanish
- Colombian peso (COP)

Head of state
2002– Álvaro Uribe Vélez, president
of Colombia

Governor
2008– Pedro Gallardo Forbes

Honduras

Republic of Honduras
Independence from Spain
in 1821; from federation in 1838
Democratic constitutional republic

- 43,278 miles²/112,090 km²
- 1957 1,768,906
- 1993 5,950,000
- 2009 7,833,700
- GDP US$4,200/person
- Spanish
- 1 lempira = 100 centavos
- 24.6/1,000
- 69.4 years
- UNO, OAS, WHO, WTO

President and head of government
2010– Porfirio Lobo Sosa

Nicaragua

Republic of Nicaragua
Independence from Spain
in 1821; from federation in 1838
Republic

- 49,998 miles²/129,494 km²
- 1957 1,331,000
- 1993 4,540,000
- 2009 5,891,200
- GDP US$2,800/person
- Spanish
- 1 córdoba oro = 100 centavos
- 25.9/1,000
- 71.2 years
- UNO, OAS, WHO, WTO

President and head of government
1985–1990, 2006– Daniel Ortega Saavedra

Panama

Republic of Panama
Independence from Spain in
1821, from Colombia in 1903
Constitutional democracy

- 30,193 miles²/78,200 km²
- 1957 960,000
- 1993 2,630,000
- 2009 3,360,475
- GDP US$11,900/person
- Spanish
- 1 balboa = 100 centésimos; US dollar
- 13.4/1,000
- 76.9 years
- UNO, OAS, WHO, WTO

President and head of government
2009– Ricardo Martinellli Berrocal

Cayman Islands

Cayman Islands
British colony in 1670
Overseas territory of the UK with
internal administration since 1962

- 101 miles²/262 km²
- 2009 49,050
- English
- Kaiman dollar (KYD)
- 7.1/1,000
- 80.3 years

Head of state
1952– Queen Elizabeth II
of the United Kingdom

Governor
2010– Duncan Taylor

Countries of the World – Central America

Cuba

Republic of Cuba
Independence in 1898/1902,
revolution in 1958/1959
Socialist republic

- 42,803 miles²/110,860 km²
- 1956 5,926,687
- 1993 10,960,000
- 2009 11,451,650
- GDP US$9,700/person
- Spanish
- Cuban peso
- 5.93/1,000
- 77.3 years
- UNO, OAS, WHO, WTO

Political parties
*Since the revolution of 1959, the Cuban
Communist Party (PCC; so named since
1965; previously the Popular Socialist
Party) has been the only legal party.*

First Secretary of the PCC
1959– Fidel Castro

**President of the Council of State
and of the Council of Ministers**
1944–1948 Ramón Grau San Martín
(also 1933/34)
1948–1952 Carlos Prío Socarrás
1952–1958 Fulgencio Batista (dictator;
elected 1940–1944)
1959 Manuel Urrutia Lleó
1959–1976 Osvaldo Dorticós Torrado
1976–2008 Fidel Castro
2008– Raúl Castro (assumed duties
in 2006)

Prime ministers
1948–1950 Manuel Antonio de Varona
1952 Fulgencio Batista
1955–1957 Jorge García Montes
1957–1958 Andrés Rivero
1959 José Miró
1959–1976 Fidel Castro
(office officially abolished in 1976)

Heads of government
1976–2008 Fidel Castro
2008– Raúl Castro (assumed duties
in 2006)

Jamaica
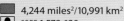
Jamaica
Independence in 1962
Parliamentary democracy

- 4,244 miles²/10,991 km²
- 1955 1,579,620
- 1993 2,530,000
- 2009 2,825,930
- GDP US$8,300/person
- English
- Jamaican dollar (JMD)
- 15.57/1,000
- 73.6 years
- UNO, OAS, WHO, WTO

Head of state
- 1952– Queen Elizabeth II
of the United Kingdom

Bahamas

Commonwealth
of the Bahamas
Independence 1973; Parliamentary monarchy

- 5,382 miles²/13,940 km²
- 1956 116,530
- 1993 266,000
- 2009 307,550
- GDP US$29,800/person
- English
- 1 Bahama dollar = 100 cents
- 23.67/1,000
- 65.7 years
- UNO, OAS, WHO, WTO

Head of state
- 1952– Queen Elizabeth II
of the United Kingdom

Governor
2006– Arthur Dion Hanna

Prime minister
1992–2002, 2007– Hubert A. Ingraham

Turks and Caicos Islands
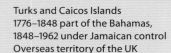

Turks and Caicos Islands
1776–1848 part of the Bahamas,
1848–1962 under Jamaican control
Overseas territory of the UK

- 155 miles²/403 km²
- 2009 22,940
- English
- US dollar
- 14.35/1,000
- 75.2 years

Head of state
- 1952– Queen Elizabeth II
of the United Kingdom

Governor
2008– Gordon Wetherell

Prime minister
2003/06–2009 Michael Eugene Misick
(office suspended 2009)

Haiti
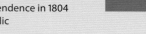
Republic of Haiti
Independence in 1804
Republic

- 10,714 miles²/27,750 km²
- 1957 3,384,000
- 1993 7,180,000
- 2009 9,035,500
- GDP US$1,300/person
- English
- 1 gourde = 100 centimes
- 62.33/1,000
- 57.6 years
- UNO, OAS, WHO, WTO

Governor general
2009– Dr. Patrick L. Allen

Prime minister
2007– Bruce Golding

Dominican Republic
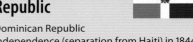
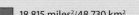
Dominican Republic
Independence (separation from Haiti) in 1844
Democratic republic

- 18,815 miles²/48,730 km²
- 1957 2,703,656
- 1993 7,770,000
- 2009 9,650,050
- GDP US$8,200/person
- Spanish
- 1 Dominican peso = 100 centavos
- 26.93/1,000
- 73.4 years
- UNO, OAS, WHO, WTO

President and head of government
1996–2000, 2004– Leonel Antonio
Fernández Reyna

Puerto Rico
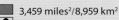
Commonwealth of Puerto Rico
U.S. colony since 1898,
U.S. citizenship for residents 1917
Unincorporated, organized territory of the
United States with commonwealth status

- 3,459 miles²/8,959 km²
- 2009 3,966,210
- Spanish, English
- US dollar
- 8.65/1,000
- 78.6 years

Head of state
2009– U.S. President Barack Obama

Governor
2009– Luis Guillermo Fortuño

United States Virgin Islands

United States Virgin
Islands
Danish rule 1733–1917
Organized, unincorporated territory
of the United States since 1917

- 134 miles²/349 km²
- 2009 109,825
- English
- US dollar
- 7.72/1,000
- 78.9 years

Head of state
2009– U.S. President Barack Obama

Governor and head of government
2007– John DeJongh

President
1996–2001, 2006– René Préval
(prime minister in 1991)

Prime minister
2009– Jean-Max Bellerive

British Virgin Islands

British Virgin Islands
British occupation in 1672
Overseas territory of the UK

- 59 miles²/153 km²
- 2009 24,490
- English
- US dollar
- 15.2/1,000
- 77.1 years

Head of state
- 1952– Queen Elizabeth II
of the United Kingdom

Governor
2006– David Pearey

Premier (chief minister until 2007)
1995–2003, 2007– Ralph Telford O´Neil

Anguilla

Anguilla
British occupation in 1650,
Associated state in 1962
Overseas territory of the UK since 1980

- 37 miles²/96 km²
- 2008 14,108
- English
- 1 East Caribbean dollar = 100 cents
- 3.54/1,000
- 80.5 years

Head of state
- 1952– Queen Elizabeth II of
the United Kingdom

Governors
2006–2009 Andrew N. George
2009– Alistair Harrison

Chief minister (head of government)
2000– Osbourne Fleming

Saint Martin
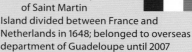
Overseas Collectivity
of Saint Martin
Island divided between France and
Netherlands in 1648; belonged to overseas
department of Guadeloupe until 2007
Overseas collectivity of France (*collectivité
d´outre-mer*) since 2007

- 36 miles²/94 km²
- 2009 29,820
- English
- Euro (since 2002)
- 78.6 years

Head of state
2007– Nicolas Sarkozy,
president of France

Prefect
2007– Dominique Lacroix

**President of the Territorial Council
(head of government)**
2008– Frantz Gumbs

Premier (head of government)
2009– McKeeva Bush

Saint Barthelemy

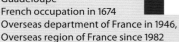

Overseas Collectivity of
  Saint Barthelemy
Swedish 1784–1877, since 1877
again under French control
Overseas collectivity of France since 2007

- 🔲 8 miles²/21 km²
- 👤 2009 7,450
- 💬 French
- 💶 Euro (since 2002)
- 👥 78.6 years

Head of state
2007– Nicolas Sarkozy,
president of France

Prefect
2007– Dominique Lacroix

**President of the Territorial Council
(head of government)**
2007– Bruno Magras

Saint Kitts and Nevis

Federation of Saint Kitts
  and Nevis
Independence in 1983
Parliamentary democracy

- 🔲 101 miles²/261 km²
- 👤 1993 41,000
- 👤 2009 40,130
- GDP US$18,800/person
- 💬 English
- 💶 1 East Caribbean dollar = 100 cents
- 🕊 14.34/1,000
- 👥 72.9 years
- 🌐 UNO, OAS, WHO, WTO

Head of state
♔ 1952– Queen Elizabeth II
of the United Kingdom

Governor general
1996– Cuthbert Montraville Sebastian

Prime minister
1995– Dr. Denzil Douglas

Antigua and Barbuda

Antigua and Barbuda
Independence in 1981
Constitutional-parliamentary monarchy

- 🔲 171 miles²/443 km²
- 👤 1993 66,000
- 👤 2009 85,630
- GDP US$18,100/person
- 💬 English
- 💶 1 East Caribbean dollar = 100 cents
- 🕊 17.5/1,000
- 👥 74.3 years
- 🌐 UNO, OAS, WHO, WTO

Head of state
♔ 1952– Queen Elizabeth II
of the United Kingdom

Governor general
2007– Louise Lake-Tack

Prime minister
2004– Winston Baldwin Spencer

Guadeloupe

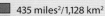

Guadeloupe
French occupation in 1674
Overseas department of France in 1946,
Overseas region of France since 1982

- 🔲 628 miles²/1,628 km²
- 👤 2009 453,750
- 💬 French
- 💶 Euro (since 2002)
- 🕊 8.4/1,000
- 👥 78.1 years

Head of state
2007– Nicolas Sarkozy,
president of France

Prefect
2004– Paul Girot de Langlade

President of the Regional Council
2004– Victorin Lurel

President of the General Council
2001– Jacques Gillot

Montserrat

Montserrat
British occupation in 1632;
belonged to the Leeward Islands 1871–1956
Overseas territory of the UK since 1962

- 🔲 39 miles²/102 km²
- 👤 2009 5,100
- 💬 English
- 💶 1 East Caribbean dollar = 100 cents
- 🕊 16.46/1,000
- 👥 72.6 years

Head of state
♔ 1952– Queen Elizabeth II
of the United Kingdom

Governor
2007– Peter A. Waterworth

Chief minister (head of government)
2009– Rueben Meade

Dominica

Commonwealth
  of Dominica
Independence in 1978
Parliamentary democracy

- 🔲 291 miles²/754 km²
- 👤 1993 73,900
- 👤 2009 72,660
- GDP US$10,200/person
- 💬 English
- 💶 1 East Caribbean dollar = 100 cents
- 🕊 14.12/1,000
- 👥 75.3 years
- 🌐 UNO, OAS, WHO, WTO

President
2003– Nicholas J. O. Liverpool

Prime minister
2004– Roosevelt Skerrit

Martinique

Martinique
French occupation in 1664
Overseas department of France
since 1946, overseas region since 1974

- 🔲 435 miles²/1,128 km²
- 👤 2009 436,130
- 💬 French
- 💶 Euro (since 2002)
- 🕊 7.0/1,000
- 👥 79.2 years

Head of state
2007– Nicolas Sarkozy,
president of France

Prefect
2007– Ange Mancini

President of the Regional Council
1998– Alfred Marie-Jeanne

President of the General Council
1992– Claude Lise

Saint Lucia

Independence in 1979
Parliamentary democracy
and a Commonwealth realm

- 🔲 238 miles²/616 km²
- 👤 1993 136,000
- 👤 2009 160,270
- GDP US$10,900/person
- 💬 English
- 💶 1 East Caribbean dollar = 100 cents
- 🕊 13.8/1,000
- 👥 76.3 years
- 🌐 UNO, OAS, WHO, WTO

Head of state
♔ 1952– Queen Elizabeth II of the
United Kingdom

Governor general
1997– Dame Pearlette Louisy

Prime minister
2007– Stephenson King

Saint Vincent and the Grenadines

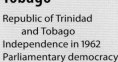

Saint Vincent and
  the Grenadines
Autonomy in 1969, independence in 1979
Parliamentary democracy

- 🔲 150 miles²/389 km²
- 👤 1993 109,000
- 👤 2009 104,575
- GDP US$18,100/person
- 💬 English
- 💶 1 East Caribbean dollar = 100 cents
- 🕊 13.62/1,000
- 👥 74.4 years
- 🌐 UNO, OAS, WHO, WTO

Head of state
♔ 1952– Queen Elizabeth II
of the United Kingdom

Governor general
2002– Fredrick Nathaniel Ballantyne

Prime minister
2001– Ralph Everard Gonsalves

Barbados

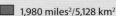

Barbados
Independence in 1966
Parliamentary democracy and
a Commonwealth realm

- 🔲 166 miles²/431 km²
- 👤 1956 229,113
- 👤 1993 260,000
- 👤 2009 284,590
- GDP US$18,500/person
- 💬 English
- 💶 1 Barbados dollar = 100 cents
- 🕊 11.05/1,000
- 👥 73.2 years
- 🌐 UNO, OAS, WHO, WTO

Head of state
♔ 1952– Queen Elizabeth II
of the United Kingdom

Governor general
1996– Clifford Straughn Husbands

Prime minister
2008– David Thompson

Grenada

Independence in 1974
Parliamentary democracy
and a Commonwealth realm

- 🔲 133 miles²/344 km²
- 👤 1993 91,000
- 👤 2009 90,740
- GDP US$12,700/person
- 💬 English
- 💶 1 East Caribbean collar = 100 cents
- 🕊 13.58/1,000
- 👥 65.6 years
- 🌐 UNO, OAS, WHO, WTO

Head of state
♔ 1952– Queen Elizabeth II of the
United Kingdom

Governor general
2008– Carlyle Arnold Glean

Prime minister
2008– Tillman Thomas

Trinidad and Tobago

Republic of Trinidad
  and Tobago
Independence in 1962
Parliamentary democracy

- 🔲 1,980 miles²/5,128 km²
- 👤 1955 754,000
- 👤 1993 1,260,000
- 👤 2009 1,229,950
- GDP US$23,300/person
- 💬 English
- 💶 Trinidad and Tobago dollar
- 🕊 31.1/1,000
- 👥 70.7 years
- 🌐 UNO, OAS, WHO, WTO

President
2003– George Maxwell Richards

Prime minister
1991–1995, 2001– Patrick Manning

Countries of the World – Central America/South America

Netherlands Antilles

(Bonaire, Curaçao, Saba, Sint Eustatius, Sint Maarten)
Autonomy in internal matters 1954; part of the Kingdom of the Netherlands. Bonaire, Saba and Sint Eustatius are "special municipalities" of the Netherlands. Dissolution of the Netherlands Antilles 2010: Curaçao and Sint Maarten become states within the kingdom (same status as Aruba).

- 370 miles²/960 km²
- 2009 227,050
- Dutch, Papiamento, English
- Antillean guilder (ANG)
- 9.36/1,000
- 76.5 years

Head of state
1980– Beatrix, Queen of the Netherlands

Governor general
2002– Frits Goedgedrag

Minister president
2006– Emily de Jongh-Elhage

Aruba

Aruba
Acquired by the Netherlands in 1636
Autonomous state within the Kingdom of the Netherlands since 1986

- 74 miles²/193 km²
- 2009 103,065
- Dutch, Papiamento
- 1 Aruba florin = 100 cents
- 14.26/1,000
- 75.1 years

Head of state
1980– Beatrix, Queen of the Netherlands

Governor general
2004– Fredis Refunjol

Prime minister
2009– Michiel (Mike) Godfried Eman

SOUTH AMERICA

Colombia

Republic of Colombia
Independence in 1810
(recognized in 1819)
Presidential republic

- 439,733 miles²/1,138,910 km²
- 1957 13,227,480
- 1993 34,520,000
- 2009 43,677,370
- GDP US$9,200/person
- Spanish
- Colombian peso (COP)
- 19.5/1,000
- 72.5 years
- UNO, OAS, WHO, WTO

Political parties
- Liberal Party (PL)
- Colombian Conservative Party (PC)
- Alternative Democratic Pole (PDA)
- Social National Unity Party

■ National Movement
Presidents (also head of government)
1946–1950 Mariano Ospina Pérez
1950–1951 Laureano Gómez
1951–1953 Roberto Urdaneta Arbeláez
1953–1957 Gustavo Rojas Pinilla (dictator)
1957–1958 Gabriel París Gordillo
1958–1962 Alberto Lleras Camargo
1962–1966 Guillermo León Valencia
1966–1970 Carlos Lleras Restrepo
1970–1974 Misael Pastrana Borrero (PC)
1974–1978 Alfonso López Michelsen (PL)
1978–1982 Julio César Turbay Ayala (PL)
1982–1986 Belisario Betancur Cuartas (PL)
1986–1990 Virgilio Barco Vargas (PL)
1990–1994 César Gaviria Trujillo (PL)
1994–1998 Ernesto Samper Pizano (PL)
1998–2002 Andrés Pastrana Arango
(NDF/New Democratic Force)
2002– Álvaro Uribe Vélez (Primero
Colombia/Colombia First)

Venezuela
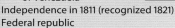
Bolivarian Republic
of Venezuela
Independence in 1811 (recognized 1821)
Federal republic

■ 352,143 miles²/912,050 km²
👤 1957 6,224,000
👤 1993 21,640,000
👤 2009 26,814,840
GDP US$13,200/person
💬 Spanish
√€ Venezuelan bolivar (VEB) = 100 céntimos
(revalued in 2008)
⊕ 22/1,000
👥 73.5 years
🌐 UNO, OPEC, OAS, WHO, WTO

Political parties
▣ Fifth Republic Movement (MVR)/
now United Socialist Party (PSUV)
☐ Democratic Action (AD)
■ Christian Democrats (COPEI)

Presidents and chiefs of state
1945–1948, 1959–1964 Rómulo Ernesto
Betancourt Bello (AD)
1948–1950 Carlos Delgado Chalbaud
(military ruler)
1950–1952 Germán Suárez Flamerich
(administrative junta)
1952–1958 Marcos Pérez Jiménez
(military dictator)
1958–1959 Edgar Sanabria
1964–1969 Raúl Leoni Otero (AD)
1969–1974, 1994–1999 Rafael Caldera
(COPEI)
1974–1979, 1989–1993 Carlos Andrés Pérez
1979–1984 Luis Herrera Campins (COPEI)
1984–1989 Jaime Lusinchi (AD)
1993–1994 Ramón José Vélasquez
1999– Hugo Chávez (PSUV)

Guyana

Cooperative Republic
of Guyana
Independence (from Great Britain) in 1966
Presidential republic

■ 83,000 miles²/214,970 km²
👤 1957 508,000
👤 1993 834,000
👤 2009 752,940
💬 English

√€ Guyanese dollar
⊕ 30.43/1,000
👥 66.4 years
🌐 UNO, OAS, WHO, WTO

President
1999– Bharrat Jagdeo

Prime minister
1997– Samuel Archibald Anthony Hinds
(president in 1997 pending elections)

Suriname

Republic of Suriname
Independence (from
the Netherlands) 1975
Constitutional democracy

■ 63,039 miles²/163,270 km²
👤 1956 225,000
👤 1993 420,000
👤 2009 481,270
GDP US$8,800/person
💬 Dutch
√€ Surinamese dollar
⊕ 19.34/1,000
👥 73.5 years
🌐 UNO, OAS, WHO, WTO

President and head of government
1991–1996, 2000– Ronald Venetiaan

French Guiana

French Guiana
Occupied by France in 1604,
penal colony 1852–1951
Overseas department of France in 1946,
overseas region of France since 1982

■ 32,252 miles²/83,534 km²
👤 2009 221,500
💬 French
√€ Euro (since 2002)
⊕ 11.8/1,000
👥 77.3 years

Head of state
2007– Nicolas Sarkozy,
president of France

Prefect
2009– Daniel Ferey

President of the Regional Council
1992– Antoine Karam

President of the General Council
2008– Alain Tien-Liong

Ecuador
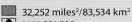
Republic of Ecuador
Independence in 1822
Republic

■ 109,483 miles²/283,560 km²
👤 1957 3,890,000
👤 1993 11,220,000
👤 2009 14,573,100
GDP US$7,300/person
💬 Spanish
√€ US dollar
⊕ 21.35/1,000
👥 76.8 years

🌐 UNO, OAS, WHO, WTO

President and head of government
2007– Rafael Vicente Correa Delgado

Peru
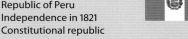
Republic of Peru
Independence in 1821
Constitutional republic

■ 496,223 miles²/1,285,220 km²
👤 1957 10,068,000
👤 1993 23,530,000
👤 2009 29,546,965
GDP US$8,600/person
💬 Spanish, Quechua, Aymara
√€ 1 nuevo sol = 100 céntimos
⊕ 29.53/1,000
👥 70.5 years
🌐 UNO, OAS, WHO, WTO

Political parties
*Alliances for a certain election or purpose,
often in flux; political parties are often
tailored to the presidential candidates.*
☐ Peruvian Aprista Party (PAP),
formerly (APRA)
☐ Peru Possible (PP)
☐ Christian People's Party (PPC)
☐ Cambio 90 (C 90)

Presidents
1945–1948 José Luis Bustamente y Rivero
1948–1956 Manuel Apolinario Odria
Amoretti
1956–1962 Manuel Prado y Ugarteche
(also 1939–1945)
1962–1963 Ricardo Pérez Godoy
(military rule)
1963–1968, 1980–1985 Fernando Belaúnde
Terry (Acción Popular)
1968–1975 Juan Velasco Alvarado
(military rule)
1975–1980 Francisco Morales Bermúdez
(military rule)
1985–1990, 2006– Alán Garcia Pérez (APRA)
1990–2000 Alberto Fujimori (C 90;
autocratic rule)
2000–2001 Valentin Paniagua
2001–2006 Alejandro Toledo (PP)
2006– Alan García Pérez

Prime ministers
Very rapid turnover since 1929
1999–2000 Alberto Bustamante Belaúnde
2000–2001 Javier Pérez de Cuellar
2001–2002 Roberto Dañino Zapata
2002–2003 Luis Solari
2003 Beatriz Merino
2003–2006 Carlos Ferrero
2006–2008 Jorge del Castillo Gálvez
2008–2009 Yehudi Simon
2009– Javier Velásquez Quesquén

Brazil
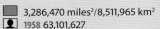
Federative Republic of Brazil
Independence in 1822
(recognized in 1825)
Federal republic

■ 3,286,470 miles²/8,511,965 km²
👤 1958 63,101,627
👤 1993 155,820,000
👤 2009 198,739,270
GDP US$10,200/person
💬 Portuguese

🌐 UNO, OAS, WHO, WTO

√€ Real
⊕ 23.33/1,000
👥 71.7 years
🌐 UNO, OAS, WHO, WTO

Political parties
*Under the Estado Novo ("New State")
of dictator Dornelles Vargas, the Social
Democratic Party was the state party.*
☐ Brazilian Labor Party (PT)
☐ Brazilian Social Democracy Party
(PSDB)
☐ Liberal Party (PL)
☐ Freedom and Socialism Party
(PSOL)
☐ Brazilian Socialist Party (PSB)
■ Party of the Republic (PR)
☐ Green Party (PV)
☐ Brazilian Democratic Movement Party
(PMDB)
☐ Liberal Front Party (PFL), now Democrats
■ Communist Party of Brazil (PCdoB)

Presidents and heads of government
1930–1945, 1951–1954 Getúlio Dornelles
Vargas (PSD; de facto dictator)
1946–1951 Enrico Gaspar Dutra (PSD)
1954–1955 João Café Filho (PSD)
1956–1961 Juscelino Kubitschek
1961–1964 João Belchior Marques Goulart
1964–1967 Humberto de Alencar Castelo
Branco (military)
1967–1969 Artur da Costa e Silva (military)
1969–1974 Emilio Garrastazu Médici
(military)
1974–1979 Ernest Geisel (military)
1979–1985 João Baptista de Oliveira
Figueiredo (military ruler; prepared
transition to democracy)
1985–1990 José Sarney
1990–1992 Fernando Collor de Mello
1992–1995 Itamar Franco (PL)
1995–2003 Fernando Henrique Cardoso
(PSDB)
2003– Luis Inácio Lula da Silva (PT)

Bolivia
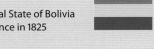
Plurinational State of Bolivia
Independence in 1825
Republic

■ 424,162 miles²/1,098,580 km²
👤 1958 63,101,627
👤 1993 155,820,000
👤 2009 9,775,245
GDP US$4,600/person
💬 Spanish, 35 indigenous languages
√€ 1 boliviano (colloquially called peso) =
100 centavos
⊕ 49.1/1,000
👥 66.5 years
🌐 UNO, OAS, WHO, WTO

Political parties
☐ Movement Toward Socialism (MAS;
party of the indigenous people)
☐ Revolutionary Nationalist Movement
(MNR)
■ Nationalist Democratic Action
(ADN)
☐ National Unity (UN)

▣ Revolutionary Left Movement - New
Majority (MIR-NM; until 2006)
■ PODEMOS (Social & Democratic Power)
☐ Free Bolivia Movement (MBL; until 2006)

Countries of the World – South America

Presidents and heads of government
(since 1825 Bolivia has experienced around 200 governments and coups)
1952–1956, 1960–1964, 1985–1989 Victor Paz Estenssoro (MNR)
1956–1960, 1982–1985 Hernán Siles Zuazo (MNR, then UDP, defunct since 1984)
1964–1965, 1966–1969 René Barrientos Ortuño
1971–1978 Hugo Banzer Suárez (military dictator)
1980–1981 Luis García Meza Tejada (military ruler)
1981–1982 Military junta
1989–1993 Jaime Paz Zamora (MIR)
1993–1997, 2002–2003 Gonzalo Sánchez de Lozada (MNR)
1997–2001 Hugo Banzer Suárez (ADN) (voted into office 2nd term)
2001–2002 Jorge Quiroga Ramírez (ADN)
2003–2005 Carlos Mesa (independent)
2005–2006 Eduardo Rodríguez (independent)
2006– Juan Evo Morales (MAS)

Chile

Republic of Chile
Independence in 1810 (recognized in 1818)
Republic

- 292,258 miles²/756,950 km²
- 1958 7,200,000
- 1993 14,200,000
- 2009 16,601,710
- GDP US$14,700/person
- Spanish
- 1 Chilean peso = 100 centavos
- 7.9/1,000
- 77.2 years
- UNO, OAS, WHO, WTO

Political parties
- Coalition of Parties for Democracy (CPD), center-left coalition
- Socialist Party (PS; in the CPD)
- Christian Democratic Party (PDC; in the CPD)
- Party for Democracy (PPD; in the CPD)
- Radical Social Democratic Party (PRSD; in the CPD)
- Independent Democratic Union (UDI)
- National Renewal (RN)

Presidents (also head of government)
1946–1952 Gabriel González Videla (Radical Party)
1952–1958 Carlos Ibáñez del Campo
1958–1964 Jorge Alessandri Rodríguez (Conservative Party)
1964–1970 Eduardo Frei Montalva (PDC)
1970–1973 Salvador Allende Gossens (Unidad Popular)
1973–1990 Augusto Pinochet Ugarte (Military dictator)
1990–1994 Patricio Aylwin Azócar (PDC/CPD)
1994–2000 Eduardo Frei Ruiz-Tagle (PDC/CPD)
2000–2006 Ricardo Lagos Escobar (PS/CPD)
2006– Michelle Bachelet (PS/CPD)

Paraguay

Republic of Paraguay
Independence in 1811
Constitutional republic

- 157,046 miles²/406,750 km²
- 1957 1,638,000
- 1993 4,830,000
- 2009 6,995,655
- GDP US$4,100/person
- Spanish, Guarani
- Guarani
- 25.55/1,000
- 75.6 years
- UNO, OAS, WHO, WTO

President (also head of government)
2008– Fernando Armindo Lugo Méndez (formerly a Catholic bishop)

Uruguay

Oriental Republic of Uruguay
Independence in 1825 (recognized in 1828)
Constitutional republic

- 68,039 miles²/176,220 km²
- 1956 2,650,000
- 1993 3,190,000
- 2009 3,494,382
- GDP US$12,600/person
- Spanish
- Uruguayan peso
- 11.66/1,000
- 76.2 years
- UNO, OAS, WHO, WTO

Political parties
- Frente Amplio (FA, "Broad Front"): coalition of left parties
- Socialist Party of Uruguay (PSU)
- Communist Party of Uruguay (PC)
- National Party (PN; formerly the *Partido Blanco*, or White Party)

Presidents (also head of government)
1943–1947 Juan José de Amezaga
1947–1951 Luis Batlle Berres
1951–1952 Andrés Martínez Trueba
1952–1967 Presidency replaced by a nine-member executive council with annually rotating leader
1967–1972 Jorge Pacheco Areco
1972–1976 Juan María Bordaberry
1973–1985 Military rule
1976–1981 Aparicio Méndez (military appointment)
1981–1985 Gregorio Álvarez Armelino (military appointment)
1985–1990, 1995–2000 Julio María Sanguinetti (PC)
1990–1995 Luis Alberto Lacalle (PN)
2000–2005 Jorge Batlle Ibáñez (PC)
2005– Tabaré Vázquez Rosas (PSU/FA)

Argentina

Argentine Republic
Independence in 1816
Republic

- 1,068,296 miles²/2,766,890 km²
- 1958 20,057,700
- 1993 34,590,000
- 2009 40,913,585
- GDP US$13,800/person
- Spanish
- Argentine peso
- 11.78/1,000
- 76.4 years
- UNO, OAS, WHO, WTO

Political parties
- Justicialist Party (PJ)/Dissident Peronists (previously the Labor Party)
- Front for Victory (FV), left spin-off of the Peronists
- Radical Civic Union (UCR)
- Socialist Party (PS)
- Support for an Egalitarian Republic (ARI), a social liberal party
- Republican Proposal (PRO), alliance of conservative-liberal political parties

Presidents (also head of government)
1946–1955 Juan Domingo Perón (PJ)
1955–1958 Pedro Eugenio Aramburu (de facto; installed by the military)
1958–1962 Arturo Frondizi (UCR)
1963–1966 Arturo Umberto Illia (UCR)
1966–1970 Juan Carlos Ongania (military dictator)
1970–1973 Presidents installed by the military
1973–1974 Juan Domingo Perón (second presidency)
1974–1976 Isabel Martinez de Perón (PJ)
1976–1981 Jorge Rafael Videla (military dictator)
1981–1982 Leopoldo Galtieri (military dictator)
1982–1983 Military rule
1983–1989 Raúl Alfonsin (UCR)
1989–1999 Carlos Menem (PJ)
1999–2001 Fernando de la Rua (UCR)
2002–2003 Eduardo Duhalde (PJ)
2003–2007 Néstor Kirchner (FV)
2007– Cristina Fernández de Kirchner (FV)

Falkland Islands

Falkland Islands (Islas Malvinas)
British colony 1837, autonomy 1985; overseas UK territory; claimed by Argentina since 1833

- 4,699 miles²/12,173 km²
- 2009 3,140
- English
- Falkland pound
- 78.3 years

Head of state
- 1952– Queen Elizabeth II of the UK

Governor (also commissioner for South Georgia and South Sandwich Islands)
2006– Alan Edden Huckle

AUSTRALIA AND OCEANIA

Australia
Commonwealth of Australia
Independence in 1901
Federal parliamentary democracy and a Commonwealth realm

- 2,967,893 miles²/7,686,850 km²
- 1957 9,591,437
- 1993 18,050,000
- 2009 21,262,640
- GDP US$38,500/person
- English
- Australian dollar
- 4.82/1,000
- 81.5 years
- UNO, ASEAN, WHO, WTO

Political parties
- Country Liberal Party (LP)
- Australian Labour Party (ALP)
- Australian Democrats (AD)
- Australian Greens
- Christian Democratic Party (CDP)

Chiefs of state (monarchs of the United Kingdom)
- 1936–1952 George VI
- 1952– Elizabeth II

CHRISTMAS ISLAND

COCOS (KEELING) ISLAND

NORTHERN MARIANA ISLANDS

GUAM

MARSHALL ISLANDS

Palikir •

PALAU

FEDERATED STATES OF MICRONESIA

Yaren •

NAURU

KIRIBATI

PAPUA NEW GUINEA

Port Moresby •

Honiara •

SOLOMON ISLANDS

TUVALU

TOKELAU

WALLIS AND FUTUNA

Apia •

SAMOA

AMERICAN SAMOA

COOK ISLANDS

FRENCH POLYNESIA

VANUATU

Port Vila •

Suva •

TONGA

Nuku'alofa •

NIUE

NEW CALEDONIA

FIJI

PITCAIRN ISLANDS

AUSTRALIA

NORFOLK ISLAND

EASTER ISLAND

Canberra •

Wellington •

NEW ZEALAND

Governors general
1947–1953 William John McKell
1953–1960 William Joseph Slim
1969–1974 Paul Hasluck
1977–1982 Zelman Cowen
1982–1989 Ninian Martin Stephen
1989–1996 William George Hayden
1996–2001 William Patrick Deane
2001–2003 Archbishop Peter Hollingworth
2003–2008 Michael Jeffery
2008– Quentin Bryce

Prime ministers
1945–1949 Ben Chifley (ALP)
1949–1966 Robert Menzies (LP;
also previously 1939–1941)
1966–1967 Harold Holt (LP)
1967–1968 John McEwen (LP)

1968–1971 John Gorton (LP)
1971–1972 William McMahon (LP)
1972–1975 Gough Whitlam (ALP)
1975–1983 Malcolm Fraser (LP)
1983–1991 Bob Hawke (ALP)
1991–1996 Paul Keating (ALP)
1996–2007 John Howard (LP)
2007– Kevin Rudd (ALP)

New Zealand

New Zealand
Founded in 1840,
independence from the
United Kingdom in 1907
Parliamentary democracy and
a Commonwealth realm

103,737 miles^2/268,680 km^2
1957 2,229,000
1993 3,540,000
2009 4,213,420
GDP US$27,700/person
English, Maori
New Zealand dollar
4.99/1,000
80.2 years
UNO, ASEAN, WHO, WTO

Political parties
■ National Party (NP)
□ Labour Party (LP)
■ Green Party
□ Maori Party
■ ACT New Zealand (ACT)
■ United Future (UF)

Chiefs of state (monarchs of the United Kingdom)
♛ 1936–1952 George VI
♛ 1952– Elizabeth II

Governors general
1946–1952 Bernard Freyberg
1957–1962 Charles Lyttelton
1967–1972 Arthur Porritt
1980–1985 David Beattie
1985–1990 Paul Reeves
1990–1996 Catherine Tizard
1996–2001 Michael Hardie Boys
2001–2006 Silvia Cartwright
2006– Anand Satyanand

Prime ministers
1940–1949 Peter Fraser (LP)
1949–1957 Sidney Holland (NP)
1957, 1960–1972 Keith Holyoake (NP)
1957–1960 Walter Nash (LP)
1972 Jack Marshall (NP)
1972–1974 Norman Kirk (LP)
1974–1975 Bill Rowling (LP)
1975–1984 Robert Muldoon (NP)
1984–1989 David Lange (LP)
1989–1990 Geoffrey Palmer (LP)
1990 Mike Moore (LP)
1990–1997 Jim Bolger (NP)
1997–1999 Jenny Shipley (NP)
1999–2008 Helen Clark (LP)
2008– John Key (NP)

Northern Marianas

Commonwealth of the
Northern Mariana
Islands
United States territory in 1899
Commonwealth in political union with
the United States since 1975

- 184 miles²/477 km²
- 2009 51,485
- English, Chamorro, Chinese
- US dollar
- 6.72/1,000
- 76.5 years

Head of state
2009– U.S. President Barack Obama

Governor (head of government)
2006– Benigno Repeki Fitial

Guam

Territory of Guam
United States territory
in 1899, autonomous
since 1949
Unincorporated territory of the United States

- 211 miles²/549 km²
- 2009 178,430
- English, Chamorro
- US dollar
- 6.55/1,000
- 78.9 years

Head of state
2009– U.S. President Barack Obama

Governor
2003– Felix Perez Camacho

Marshall Islands

Republic of the Marshall
Islands; independence 1986
Republic in association with United States

- 4,577 miles²/11,854 km²
- 1993 60,000
- 2009 64,520
- GDP US$2,500/person
- English, Marshallese
- US dollar
- 26.36/1,000
- 70.9 years
- UNO, WHO

Presidents (also head of government)
2008–2009 Litokwa Tomeing
2009– Jurelang Zedkaia

Micronesia

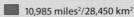

Federated States of
Micronesia
Independence in 1986; Federal republic
in association with the United States

- 271 miles²/702 km²
- 1993 103,000
- 2009 107,434
- GDP US$2,200/person
- English
- US dollar
- 27/1,000
- 70.7 years
- UNO, WHO

President and head of government
2007– Manny (Emanuel) Mori

Palau

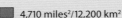

Republic of Palau
Independence in 1994
Republic in free association
with the United States

- 177 miles²/458 km²
- 1993 16,000
- 2009 20,795
- GDP US$8,100/person
- English, Palauan
- US dollar
- 13.7/1,000
- 71 years
- UNO, WHO

President (also head of government)
2008– Johnson Toribiong

Papua New Guinea

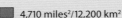

Independent State of
Papua New Guinea
Independence in 1975; Parliamentary
democracy and a Commonwealth realm

- 178,703 miles²/462,840 km²
- 1993 4,070,000
- 2009 5,940,775
- GDP US$2,300/person
- English, Tok Pisin
- 1 kina = 100 toea
- 46.67/1,000
- 66 years
- UNO, ASEAN, WHO, WTO

Head of state
1952– Queen Elizabeth II of the UK

Governor general (representative)
2004– Paulias Matane

Prime minister
1975–1980, 1982–1985, 2002– Michael Somare

Solomon Islands

Solomon Islands
Independence in 1978
Parliamentary democracy

- 10,985 miles²/28,450 km²
- 1993 399,000
- 2009 595,610
- GDP US$2,600/person
- English
- Solomon Island dollar
- 19.67/1,000
- 73.4 years
- UNO, WHO, WTO

Head of state
1952– Queen Elizabeth II of
the United Kingdom

Governor general
2009– Frank Kabui

Prime minister
2007– Derek Sikua

Vanuatu

Republic of Vanuatu
Independence in 1980
Parliamentary republic

- 4,710 miles²/12,200 km²
- 1993 173,600
- 2009 218,520
- GDP US$4,800/person
- English, French, Bislama
- 1 vatu = 100 centimes
- 50.77/1,000
- 63.6 years
- UNO, OAS, WHO, WTO

President
2009– Iolu Johnson Abil

Prime minister
2001–2004, 2008– Edward Natapei
(was president in 1999)

New Caledonia

French colony in 1853,
overseas territory of France
1946–2003; Nouméa Accord charted
greater independence in 1998; currently
a self-governing territory of France

- 7,359 miles²/19,060 km²
- 2009 227,435
- French
- CFP franc (franc of the
French Pacific colonies)
- 7.2/1,000
- 74.8 years

Head of state
2007– Nicolas Sarkozy,
president of France

High commissioner (representative)
2007– Yves Dassonville

President of the government
2009– Philippe Gomes

Fiji

Republic of the Fiji Islands
Independence in 1970
Republic

- 7,054 miles²/18,270 km²
- 1956 345,737

- 1993 770,000
- 2009 944,720
- GDP US$3,800/person
- Fijian, English, Hindustani
- 1 Fiji dollar = 100 cents
- 11.9/1,000
- 70.4 years
- UNO, WHO, WTO

President
2009– Ratu Epeli Nailatikau

Prime minister
2007– Frank Bainimarama (interim prime
minister, commander of military forces
and de facto ruler)

Tuvalu

Tuvalu
Independence in 1978
Parliamentary democracy and
a Commonwealth realm

- 10 miles²/26 km²
- 1993 9,900
- 2009 12,373
- GDP US$1,600/person
- Tuvaluan, English
- Australian dollar (also have
own currency)
- 19/1,000
- 69.0 years
- UNO, WHO

Head of state
1952– Queen Elizabeth II of
the United Kingdom

Governor general
2005– Filoimea Telito

Prime minister
2006– Apisai Ielemia

Nauru

Republic of Nauru
Independence in 1968
Republic

- 8 miles²/21 km²
- 1956 4,303
- 1993 10,000
- 2009 14,220
- GDP US$5,000/person
- Nauruan, English
- Australian dollar
- 9.43/1,000
- 63.8 years
- UNO, WHO

President (also head of government)
2007– Marcus Stephen

Kiribati

Republic of Kiribati
Independence in 1979
Republic

- 313 miles²/811 km²
- 1993 76,900
- 2009 112,850
- GDP US$5,300/person
- I-Kiribati, English
- Australian dollar

44.7/1,000
62.9 years
UNO, WHO

President (also head of government)
2003– Anote Tong

Tokelau

Colonial occupation by
New Zealand in 1925,
administered by New Zealand after 1948
Self-administering territory of New Zealand

4 miles²/12 km²
2009 1,415
Tokelauan, English
New Zealand dollar
69 years

Head of state
1952– Queen Elizabeth II of the UK

Administrator
2006– David Bruce Payton

**Head of government (rotates
annually among the three Faipule,
the most important village leaders)**
2009– Foua Toloa

Wallis and Futuna

Territory of the Wallis
and Futuna Islands
French protectorate in 1842,
colony in 1888; overseas territory of France
with partial autonomy since 1961

105 miles²/274 km²
2009 15,290
French
CFP franc (franc of the French
Pacific colonies)
74.3 years

Head of state
2007– Nicolas Sarkozy, president
of France

High administrator
2008– Philippe Paolantoni

President of the Territorial Assembly
2007– Pesamino Taputai

Samoa

Independent State of
Samoa
Independence in 1962
Parliamentary democracy

1,137 miles²/2,944 km²
1993 163,000
2009 219,990
GDP US$4,700/person
Samoan, English
1 tala = 100 sene
25/1,000
71.6 years
UNO, WHO, WTO

Head of state (President)
2007– Tupua Tamasese Tupuola Taisi
Tufuga Efi (prime minister 1976–1982)

Prime minister
1998– Sailele Malielegaoi Tuila'epa

Tonga

Kingdom of Tonga
Independence in 1970
Constitutional monarchy

289 miles²/748 km²
1956 56,838
1993 100,000
2009 120,900
GDP US$4,600/person
Tongan, English
Pa'anga, also Tonga dollar
11.88/1,000
70.4 years
UNO, WHO, WTO

Monarch
2006– King George Tupou V

Prime minister
2006– Dr. Feleti Sevele

American Samoa

Territory of American Samoa
Dependent territory in 1929
Unincorporated and unorganized territory
of the United States

76 miles²/199 km²
2009 65,630
Samoan, English
US dollar
10.46/1,000
73.5 years

Head of state
2009– U.S. President Barack Obama

Governor
2003– Togiola Talalelei Tulafono

Niue

Niue
Annexed by New Zealand
in 1901
Self-governing in free association
with New Zealand since 1974

100 miles²/260 km²
2009 1,400
Niuean, English
New Zealand dollar
71 years

Head of state
1952– Queen Elizabeth II
of the United Kingdom

Governor general (of New Zealand)
2006– Anand Satyanand

Prime minister
2008– Toke Tufukia Talagi

Cook Islands

Cook Islands
Self-governing since 1965
Self-governing parliamentary democracy in
free association with New Zealand

92 miles²/240 km²
2009 11,870
Cook Islands Maori, English
1 Cook Island dollar = 100 cents
72 years

Head of state
1952– Queen Elizabeth II
of Great Britain

Queen's representative
2001– Sir Frederick Goodwin

**High commissioner
(representative of New Zealand)**
2008–2009 Tia Barrett
2009– (acting) Nicola Ngawati

Prime minister
2004– Jim Marurai

French Polynesia

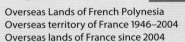

Overseas Lands of French Polynesia
Overseas territory of France 1946–2004
Overseas lands of France since 2004

1,608 miles²/4,167 km²
2009 287,030
French, Polynesian
CFP franc (franc of the French
Pacific colonies)
7.7/1,000
76.5 years

Head of state
2007– Nicolas Sarkozy, president
of France

High commissioner of the republic
2008– Adolphe Colrat

President and head of government
2008– Gaston Tong Sang

Pitcairn Islands

Pitcairn Islands
British crown colony in 1838
Local self-administration since 1964
Overseas territory of the UK

18 miles²/47 km²
2009 48
English, Pitkern
New Zealand dollar

Head of state
1952– Queen Elizabeth II
of the United Kingdom

Governor
2006– George Fergusson

Mayor and chair of the Island Council
2004– Mike Warren

Norfolk Island

Territory of Norfolk Island
Occupied by Australia in 1856
Australian region in 1914
Self-governing territory of Australia since 1979

1,608 miles²/4,167 km²
2009 2,140

English, Norfolk
Australian dollar
64.8 years

Head of state
1952– Queen Elizabeth II
of the United Kingdom

Administrator
2007– Owen Walsh

Chief minister
2007– Andre Neville Nobbs

Cocos Islands

Territory of Cocos (Keeling)
Islands
Owned by the Clunie-Ross family 1831–1978
Administered by Australia from 1978
External territory of Australia since 1955

5 miles²/14 km²
2009 596
English
Australian dollar

Head of state
1952– Queen Elizabeth II of the UK

Administrator (head of government)
2009– Brian Lacy

Easter Island

Rapa Nui
Annexed by Chile in 1888
(1914–1967 under martial law)
Part of Chilean region of Valparaiso 1966–
2007; special territory of Chile since 2007

62 miles²/163 km²
2009 4,780
Spanish, Rapanui
Chilean peso

Head of state
2006– Michelle Bachelet, president
of Chile

Provincial governor
2006– Melania Carolina Hotu Hey

Christmas Island

Territory of Christmas Island
British occupation in 1888,
sovereignty transferred to Australia in 1958
Non-self-governing territory of Australia

52 miles²/135 km²
2009 1,400
English, Chinese, Malay
Australian dollar
64.8 years

Head of state
1952– Queen Elizabeth II of the UK

Australian governor general
2008– Quentin Bryce

Administrator (head of government)
2009– Brian Lacy

Index

A

Abbas, Mahmoud, 341
Abbasid Caliphate, 17, 332–333, 335–336, 342, 350–351, 354
Abbas the Great, 327, 333, 335, 354
Abdallah I (Jordan), 328, 334, 344
Abdallah II (Jordan) 345
Abd ar-Rahman III, 244
Abdulhamid II, 121, 272, 297
Abdullah (Saudi Arabia), 347
Abdul Rahman Putra, 386
Abkhazia, 331, 356–357
Aborigines, 399
Abraham, 84
Abdullah (Saudi Arabia), 347
Abu Bakr, 332, 336
Abu Sayyaf, 389
Acampichtli, 429
Achaean League, 75
Achaemenid dynasty, 16, 24, 59, 63, 71, 325, 350, 354
Acre, 447
Act of Settlement, 148
Act of Union, 147
Adams, John (Bounty sailor), 395
Adams, John (US President), 421
Adenauer, Konrad, 180
Adrianople, Treaty of, 272, 290, 356
  See also Hadrianopolis
Aeschylus, 77
Aetius (bishop), 81
Afghanistan, 18–19, 34, 43, 54, 74, 235, 239, 297, 329–330, 332, 335, 337, 347, 354, 358–359, 423, 490
Afghanistan, war in, 34, 43, 229, 235, 322, 329–330, 423
Aflaq, Michel, 353
Agincourt (battle), 118–119, 144, 232
Agis IV (Sparta), 75
Ahmadinejad, Mahmoud, 335, 355
Ahmose (pharaoh), 308
Akhenaton (pharaoh), 309
Alaric I, 93, 252
Alaric II, 244
Alaungpaya (Burma), 385
Alba, 3rd duke of (Fernando Alvarez de Toledo), 158
Albania, 101, 126, 131, 135, 137, 206, 258, 266, 268, 271, 275, 278–279, 281–283, 295, 423, 480
Albigensian crusade, 232
Albrecht II (Germany), 192
Alcock, John, 410
Alemanni, 90–91
Alexander I (Yugoslavia), 206, 276
Alexander I (Russia), 217–219
Alexander II (Russia), 217–219
Alexander III (Russia), 217–219
Alexander Nevsky (Russia), 107, 217–218
Alexander the Great, 23–25, 59, 69–76, 84, 118, 292–293, 309, 324–325, 338, 342, 350, 354, 358, 362, 292, 296, 309, 325, 338, 342, 350, 362
Alexandria, 76, 85, 95, 106, 260, 309, 342
Alexius I Comnenus, 260
Alfaro, Eloy, 443
Alfonso I (Portugal), 250
Alfonso X the Wise (Castile), 245
Alfonso XIII (Spain), 121, 249
Alfred the Great (England), 143
Algeria, 35, 42, 95, 178, 238, 240–242, 272, 306, 311–312, 321, 333–3335, 482
Algerian War, 272, 311, 334–335, 337, 482

Alia, Ramiz, 283
Allen, Paul, 419
Allende, Salvador, 439, 456–457
Allied Powers (WW II), 125, 238, 258, 290, 421
Alp-Arslan, 296
Alps, 79, 90, 154, 162, 182, 251
Altamira cave, 20, 244
Alvarado, Juno Velasco, 439
Álvares, Jorge, 371
Alves, Cabral, Pedro, 450
American Samoa, 395, 503
American Virgin Islands, 496
Amselfeld (battle), 199, 271, 275, 280
Amundsen, Roald, 471–472
Anatolia, ancient, 10, 16, 22, 58–59, 72–73, 75–76, 79, 90, 291, 296–297, 324
Anatolia, Ottoman, 271, 297, 334–335, 350
Anawratha (Burma), 385
Anaximander, 77
Anaximenes of Miletus, 77
al-Andalus, 244–245
Andaman and Nicobar islands, 467
Andorra, 478
Andrew II (Hungary), 63
Andropov, Yuri, 217, 225
Angevin dynasty, 100, 144, 195, 201, 253
Angkor Wat, 17, 26–27, 382, 385
Anglican Church, 49, 64, 88–89, 112, 145, 404
Anglo-German Naval Agreement, 172–173
Anglo-Saxons, 60–61, 88, 90, 116, 118, 142–144, 154
Angola, 35, 43, 251, 318–319, 321, 423, 485
Anguilla, 496
An Lushan (general), 369
Annan, Kofi, 51
Anschluss (of Austria), 190, 195
Antarctic, 472–473
Antarctic Treaty, 473
Antigonus I (Macedonia), 293
Antigonus III (Macedonia), 75
Antigua and Barbuda, 497
Antiochus I, 90
Antiochus III the Great, 79, 84
Antiochus IV Epiphanes, 84
Antonius Pius, 252
Aquino, Benigno, 389
Aquino, Corazon, 389
Arab League, 332, 334, 347, 352
Arabian Peninsula, 273, 317, 332, 346–349, 465
Arabic, 296, 298, 481–484
Arabs, 11–12, 16–17, 24, 27, 32, 34, 54, 60, 86–87, 96–97, 164, 231, 244–245, 253, 267, 275, 298–299, 303, 305, 310–313, 323, 327, 329, 332–333, 335, 342–353, 356, 363, 369, 465–466
Aradiphithecus ramidus, 20
Arafat, Yasir, 53, 341
Aramis (Ethiopia), 20
Arctic, 30, 242, 406, 461, 470–471
Arelet, 183
Aretas III (Nabataean), 342
Argentinia, 42, 340, 346–347, 438–439, 445, 449, 452, 454–459, 465, 473, 498–500
Arianism, 88
Aristarchus of Samos, 11
Aristide, Jean-Bertrand, 421
Aristophanes, 77
Aristotle, 72–73, 77

Arius, 88
Armada, Spanish, 247–248
Armenia, 77, 80, 228–229, 273, 296–298, 334–336, 343–344, 356–357, 488
Armenian genocide, 297–298, 336, 357
Arminus (Hermann), 90–91, 162
Armstrong, Neil, 419
Arnesen, Liv, 473
Árpád dynasty, 101
Arroyo, Gloria Macapagal, 389
Artigas, José Gervasio, 454
Aruba, 160, 464, 498
ASEAN See Association of Southeast Asian Nations
Ashikaga, Takauji, 379
Ashikaga, Yoshimitsu, 379
Ashoka, 362, 366
Asia Minor, 58, 61, 70–76, 80, 267–268, 273, 293, 296–297, al-Assad, Bashar, 330, 345
Association of Southeast Asian Nations (ASEAN), 328
Assyria, 22–24, 58, 70–71, 77, 84–86, 299, 309, 324, 338, 342, 350
Atahualpa, 86, 350
Atatürk, Mustafa Kemal, 273, 297–298
Athens, 25, 60, 72–79, 127, 281, 292–294
Atlantic Ocean, 462–463
Attalos III, 296
Attila the Hun, 59, 91
Augustine of Hippo, 88
Augustus (Roman emperor), 80–81, 244, 252, 309
Augustus II the Strong (Poland), 170, 209
Augustus III (Poland), 209
Aurangzeb, 363
Aurelian, 252, 288, 332
Austerlitz (battle), 202
Australia, 11, 15–16, 30–31, 49, 122, 151, 297, 315, 380, 393, 396–398, 461, 466–468, 472, 500–503
Australopithecus africanus, 16, 20–21, 303, 316, 318
Austria, 34, 36–37, 41–42, 63, 65–68, 87, 93–94, 112, 114, 124, 144, 156–158, 164, 167–175, 177, 180–182, 186–199, 200–202, 205–212, 218, 221, 234, 236, 241, 246, 248, 254, 256–258, 260, 270, 272, 276–281, 283–290, 333, 351, 430, 467, 471, 478
Austro-Hungarian Compromise (1867) 189, 198, 202
Austrofascism, 124, 195
Avars, 61, 187, 196, 200–201, 274
Axis Powers (WWII), 127, 258, 452
Ayutthaya kingdom, 326, 382–385
Azerbaijan, 49, 229, 271, 333–334, 349, 351, 356–357, 488
Azores and Madeira, 463
Aztecs, 18, 25, 29, 246, 427–430, 436

B

Baath party, 352–353
Babylon, 10–11, 22–25, 58, 70–71, 74–75, 324–325, 338, 348–350
Babylonian Exile, 84, 86
Bachelet, Michelle, 439, 456
Baffin, William, 470
Baghdad, 173, 332, 335–336, 346, 351–354, 423
Bagrat III (Georgia), 356
Bahadur II (Shah), 364

Bahamas, 35, 246, 424, 463, 496
Bahrain, 49, 346–347, 489
Baikal-Amur Magistral (railway), 360
Balfour Declaration, 339
Balkan region, 7, 19, 28, 59, 66, 115–117, 120, 127, 179, 195, 205–207, 220, 266–295, 326, 333
Balkan wars, 66, 120, 188, 195, 205–207, 273, 276–277, 281–282, 286, 290, 294, 297, 419
Balliol College (Oxford), 155
Baltic region, 57, 62, 65, 118, 138–139, 168, 187, 201, 212– 213, 215
Baltic states, 67, 201, 212–215
Bancroft, Ann, 473
Bandaranaike, Sirimavo, 467
Bandaranaike, Solomon, 467
Bangladesh, 323, 329, 337, 364–365, 423, 491
Bannockburn (battle), 144, 147
Banzer Suárez, Hugo, 448
Baptists, 111
Baranov, Alexander, 31
Barbados, 35, 304, 425, 464, 497
Barents, Willem, 30
Barrios, Justo Rufino, 433
Barth, Heinrich, 305
Barton, Edmund
Basil II Bulgaroktonos, 267, 293
Basques, 137, 244, 248–249
Basra, 352
Bastille, storming of 114, 131, 234
Batavian Republic, 114, 158, 161, 236
Batista, Fulgencio, 420, 424
battles, list of, 118–120
  Adrianople, 266
  Agincourt, 232
  Amselfeld, 199, 271, 275, 280
  Austerlitz, 202
  Bannockburn, 144, 147
  Catalaunian Plains, 93
  Crécy, 232
  Culloden, 147
  Gettysburg, 416
  Hastings, 60, 138, 143
  Kosovo, 199, 271, 275, 280, 282, 297, 337
  Legnano, 253
  Lepanto, 112, 246, 272, 294, 296
  Manzikert , 268, 296
  Marathon, 73
  Marengo, 236
  Marignano, 184
  Mohács , 187, 197, 199, 202, 271
  Morgarten, 182
  Nikopolis, 271
  Pavia, 254
  Poltava, 107, 216
  Sedan, 117, 169, 173
  Sempach, 182
  Skagerrak, 175
  Solferino, 66
  Tannenberg, 106, 208, 212
  Teutoburg Forest, 162
  Trafalgar, 114, 236, 248
  Verdun, 238
  Zenta, 198, 272
Battle y Ordonez, José, 454
Batu Khan, 107
Baudouin I (Belgium), 159
Bavaria, 112–113, 156, 163–164, 166–167, 170, 173, 176, 186, 192–194, 200, 294,
Bavarian Succession, War of, 170, 192–194
Beatrix (Queen of Netherlands), 159
Becket, Thomas, 144
Bedouins, 332, 346–347

Begin, Menachem, 340
Behaim, Martin, 11
Belarus, 69, 126, 210, 214, 221–222, 476
Belgian Congo See Congo, Belgian
Belgian revolution, 159
Belgium, 34–36, 53, 65, 104, 116, 126, 135, 137, 156–158, 161–164, 172, 174–176, 179, 475
Belize, 428–429, 432, 494–495
Bellinghausen, Fabian von, 472
Benedict of Nursia, 89, 104
Benedictines, 104
Ben Gurion, David, 340
Benelux nations, 156–161, 178
Benelux Treaty, 159
Benin, 483
Benin empire, 303, 314
Bering, Vitus, 31, 470
Berisha, Sali, 283
Berlin, 32, 42, 68, 110, 128–129, 131, 168–170, 180–181, 222, 224, 236, 422
Berlin Airlift, 32, 42, 68, 180, 224, 422
Berlin, Congress of, 35, 42, 160, 272, 276, 281, 286–287, 290, 297, 333
Berlin Wall, 19, 42, 68–69, 132, 134, 181, 225
Berlusconi, Silvio, 259
Bermuda, 31, 63, 463, 494
Bermúdez, Juan de, 31
Bernadotte, Jean-Baptiste, 139
Bernard de Clairvaux, 63, 104
Bern, miracle of, 180
Bessarabia, 126, 128, 218, 222, 272, 291–294
Betancourt, Ingrid, 442
Bethlen, Gábor, 198
Beyazit I (sultan), 271
Bhutan, 49, 323, 366–367, 491
Bhutto, Benazir, 365
Bhutto, Zulfikar Ali, 364
Biafran War, 19, 42
Bible, Hebrew, 84
Bierut, Boleslaw, 210
Bismarck, Otto von, 65, 117–120, 169, 172–173
Black September, 181, 328, 345
Blaeu, Jan, 461
Blaeuw, Guilielmo, 57
Blair, Tony, 148
Bligh, William, 395
Blix, Hans, 353
Bloody Sunday (Ireland), 152–153
Bloody Sunday (St. Petersburg), 220
Bloody Sunday (Vilnius), 213
Blum, Léon, 240
Bocskay, István, 198
Boers, 120, 306, 318–319
Boer Wars, 306, 318–319
Bogdan (Moldavia), 288
Bohemia, 28, 61, 64, 87, 89, 98–99, 102, 107, 112, 118, 126, 164, 166, 169, 177–178, 186–187, 189, 200–204, 208, 349
Boisseau, Jean, 435
Boleslav I (Bohemia), 200
Boleslaw Chrobry, 208
Bolivarism, 441
Bolivar, Simón, 440–442, 448
Bolivia, 423, 437–439, 446–448, 455, 457–458, 499
Bolsheviks, 210, 220
Bonaparte, Joseph, 236, 248, 256
Boniface VIII (pope), 89
Bordaberry, Juan Mario, 439
Boris III (Bulgaria), 286
Bosch, Juan, 421

Bosnia (historical region), 66, 205–206, 272, 275–276, 280–281
Bosnia and Herzegovina, 69, 110, 135, 188, 195, 208, 278–282, 479
Bosnian war, 207, 278, 281
Boston Tea Party, 404, 412
Botswana, 35, 485
Botticelli, Sandro, 255
Bounty mutiny, 395
Bourbon dynasty, 65, 100, 118, 232–233, 235, 248–249, 257, 262–263
Boutros-Ghali, Boutros, 51
Boxer Rebellion, 35, 327, 372
Brabant Revolution, 159
Brahmin (caste), 367
Brandenburg, 65, 69, 113, 166–168, 170, 201, 218, 464
Brandt, Willy, 181
Bransfield, Edward, 472
Brazil, 30, 43, 50, 250–251, 304, 423, 435, 437–439, 441, 443, 447–459, 499
Brazilian Empire, 437–438, 450
Brazza, Pierre Savorgnan de, 305
Brennus, 78
Brezhnev, Leonid, 217, 225
Brest-Litowsk, Treaty of, 67, 122, 174, 211, 221
Brian Boru, 146
Briand, Aristide, 125
British East India Company, 18, 151, 363–364, 371, 412, 465–467
British Empire, 130, 150–155, 299, 343, 358, 364, 386, 405, 410, 463
British Virgin Islands, 496
Bronze Age, 10, 16, 21, 58, 142, 186, 214, 288, 296, 382
Brown, Arthur Whitten, 410
Brown, Gordon, 148
Brunei, 323, 386–387
Buddhism, 15–17, 23–24, 48–49, 323–325, 359, 366–369, 376–379, 382, 385–386, 388–390, 466–467
Bukovina (Ukraine), 291
Bulgaria, 60–61, 66, 68, 89, 116, 120, 123, 126–131, 133,   186, 206, 214, 219, 267–268, 270–279, 282–291, 480
Bulgarian empire, 186, 214, 267–268, 270, 274, 282, 285, 288
Burgh, Albert van der, 427
Burgundian Netherlands, 157
Burgundy, house of, 61, 99, 106
Burgundy, kingdom of, 31, 93, 96–98, 144, 155–158, 163, 182–183, 231–233, 235, 246
Burke, Robert O'Hara, 396–397
Burma (Myanmar), 26, 45, 49, 327, 372–373, 382–385, 492 See also Myanmar
Burnham, Forbes, 444
Burundi, 151, 317, 485
Bush, George W., 349, 353, 419
Byrd, Richard Edwyn, 473
Byzantine Empire, 17–18, 28, 60–61, 64, 78, 81, 88, 93, 106, 118, 186–187, 204, 214, 252–253, 260–261, 266–268, 274, 280, 282–288, 296–299, 311, 313, 317, 326, 332, 336, 342, 353–356
Byzantine Iconoclastic Controversy, 293

C

Cabot, John (Giovanni Caboto), 150, 404, 407–408, 470
Caboto, Sebastian, 458

Cabral, Amilcar, 464
Caesar, Gaius Julius, 25, 59, 79–82, 90, 142, 156, 162, 182, 230, 252, 309
Caillié, René, 305
Calicut, 326
Calvin, John, 89, 111, 184
Calwell, Arthur, 398
Cambodia, 27, 43, 49, 323, 325, 328–329, 382–385, 423, 492
Cambodian genocide, 43, 385
Cambrai, League of, 254, 260
Cambyses II, 309
Cameroon, 35, 306, 314–315, 337, 483
Canada, 30, 34–35, 42, 68, 150, 173, 359, 403–411, 431, 463, 471, 493
Canary Islands, 35, 463, 481
Canossa, 60, 164–165
Canute (England), 138, 143
Cape Colony, 160
Cape Verde islands, 464, 482
Capetian dynasty, 99–100, 106, 231–233, 235
Capone, Al, 418
Carausius, Marcus Aurelius, 257
Carbonari, 257
Carnations, Revolution of, 251
Carol I (Romania), 290
Carol II (Romania), 290
Caribbean Sea, 304, 317, 403, 416, 424, 461, 463
Carlowitz, treaty of, 272
Carolingian dynasty, 17, 96–98, 156, 163, 169, 183, 230–231, 235
Carthage, 16, 24–25, 58, 73, 79, 82, 95, 244, 252, 299, 310–313, 343, 463
Cartier, Jacques, 408
Casablanca Conference, 128
Casmir III the Great (Poland), 208
Cassini de Thury, Jacques und César, 13
Castro, Cipriano, 440
Castro, Fidel, 424–425, 496
Castro, Raúl, 425
Catalaunian Plains (battle), 93
Çatal Hüyük, 10, 23, 58–59, 296
Catherine II the Great, 65, 209, 217–219
Catholic League, 65, 112–113, 117, 165–166
Caucasus, 65, 238, 335, 356,
Cavour, Camillo Benso di, 257
Cayman Islands, 463, 495
Celts, 10, 16–17, 21, 90, 142–143, 146–147, 156–157, 162, 182, 186–187, 230, 244, 252, 280, 284, 462
Central Africa, 304, 314–315 See also individual countries
Central African Republic, 484
Central America, 23, 27, 29, 32, 427–435, 496 See also individual countries
Central Asia, 7, 323–326, 331, 333, 335–336, 358–359 See also individual countries
Central Powers, 123, 126, 211, 277, 286
Ceslav Klonimirovič (Grand Župan), 274
Chad, 305, 337, 483
Chagos Archipelago, 467
Chalcedon, Council of, 88–89
Chamberlain, Neville, 148
Champlain, Samuel de, 409
Champollion, Jean-François, 309
Charlemagne, 17, 26, 60, 89, 96–98, 156, 163, 182, 186, 192, 231, 244, 253, 267
Charles I (Anjou), 245

Charles I (England), 100, 113, 144
Charles I (Hungary), 201
Charles I (England), 144
Charles II (Spain) 247
Charles IV (Holy Roman emperor), 118, 164, 201
Charles IV (Spain), 248
Charles V (Holy Roman emperor), 64, 99, 111–113, 158, 160, 164, 184, 193, 246, 440
Charles VI (Holy Roman emperor), 185, 194
Charles VII (France), 233
Charles VII (Holy Roman emperor), 99, 170
Charles VIII (France), 254
Charles X (France), 238
Charles XII (Sweden), 139
Charles XIV (Sweden), 139
Charles Martell, 96, 231
Charles of Anjou, 245
Charles of Provence, 156
Charles Robert of Anjou, 196
Charles the Bald (West Francia), 96, 98, 163, 231–232
Charles the Bold (Burgundy), 156–157, 183, 232
Charles Thopia (Albania), 282
Chávez, Hugo, 425, 439, 441
Chechnya, 200, 226, 228, 331, 476
Chechnya, war in, 226, 228, 331
Chernenko, Konstantin, 217, 225
Chernobyl, 225
Cherusci, 91
Chiang Kai-shek, 373, 375
Chile, 181, 423, 434–439, 445, 447–449, 456–459, 500
China, 10–11, 15–18, 23, 25, 28, 31, 43, 46, 50, 54, 105, 117, 151, 175, 220, 224–225, 260, 283, 323–331, 360–361, 368–375, 377, 380, 382, 385, 388, 420, 491
Chirac, Jacques, 241
Chlochilaicus, 138
Chlotar I, 96, 98
Chlotar II, 60, 96, 98
Chmelnitzki, Bogdan, 216
Chola dynasty, 362–363
Christian II (Denmark), 138
Christian IV (Denmark), 166
Christian IX (Denmark), 139
Christian, Fletcher, 395
Christianity, 16, 23–25, 48–49, 57, 59–60, 81–82, 85, 89–90, 92, 97, 138, 143, 145, 208, 212, 231, 252, 283–284, 303, 314, 316–317, 323, 327, 356, 370, 376, 379, 386, 389, 462, 469
Christianity, Coptic, 317
Christmas Island, 467, 503
Churchill, Winston, 68, 128, 148–149, 178–179, 355, 475
Cicero, Marcus Tullius, 81
Çiller, Tansu, 298
Cinna, 79
Cistercians, 104
Cixi (Tzu Hsi, China), 372
Classical period, 17, 24–25, 72–81
Cleisthenes, 73
Clemenceau, Georges, 123
Clementis, Vladimir, 202
Cleomenes III (Sparta), 75
Cleopatra, 309
Clinton, Bill, 419
Clovis (Chlodwig), 89, 93, 96–98, 231
Clovis points, 20
Cocos Islands, 467, 503
Codex Iustinianus, 267

Cold War, 68, 207, 279
Colombia, 42, 432–433, 436–443, 446–447, 452, 498
Color de Mello, Fernando, 453
Columbus, Christopher, 9, 30, 110, 246, 404, 420, 432, 440, 463
Comecon See Council for Mutual Economic Assistance
Committee of Public Safety (France), 235
Commodus, 162
Commonwealth, British, 145, 387
Commonwealth of Nations, 151
Communist Manifesto, 18, 117
Comnenian dynasty, 260, 268, 288
Comoros, 466, 486
Confucius, 325, 369
Congo, Belgian, 160–161, 315
Congo Conference, 120, 306
Congo, Democratic Republic of (DRC), 42, 54, 423, 484
Congo Free State, 160
Congo, French, 315
Congo, Republic of (Brazzaville), 315
Congo River, 305–306
Congo, war in, 42, 54, 321
Conrad II (Holy Roman emperor), 164
Conrad III (Germany), 164
Constantine I (Greece), 295
Constantine I the Great, 59, 80–81, 88, 252, 264, 269
Constantine II (antipope), 264
Constantine II (Greece), 295
Constantine IX (Byzantine emperor), 268
Constantine XI (Byzantine emperor), 268
Constantinople, 18, 28, 63–64, 76, 81, 88, 90, 106, 110, 119, 260, 266–272, 274, 277, 284–286, 290–296, 326, 332, 336
Cook, Frederick, 471
Cook, James, 30, 151, 394–395, 400, 469, 472
Cook Islands, 503
Cooper, Minor, 433
Copernicus, Nicolaus, 10, 12
Córdoba (caliphate and emirate), 60–61, 87, 92, 95, 196, 244–245, 311, 332, 336
Corinth, 59, 74–75, 95, 292
Correa, Rafael, 443
Cortés, Hernán, 30, 429
Costa Rica, 53, 432–433, 495
Côte d'Ivoire See Ivory Coast
Council for Mutual Economic Assistance (Comecon), 42, 68
Counter-Reformation, 18, 64, 89, 104, 111–112, 165, 199
Couthon, Georges, 234
Crassus, Marcus Licinius, 80
Crécy (battle), 232
Crimean War, 19, 66, 116–117, 214, 218, 271–272, 290, 333, 356
Croatia, 60, 94, 101, 135, 137, 186–187, 191–194, 204–207, 276–281, 478–479
Croesus of Lydia, 296
Cro-Magnon (France), 20
Cromwell, Oliver, 113, 144–147
Crusades, 62–64, 339–341
Cuba, 35, 42, 249, 319, 422–424, 457, 496
Cuban missile crisis, 42, 224, 405,419, 421, 425
Culloden (battle), 147

Cultural Revolution (China), 43, 328, 369, 374
Custer, George, 407
Cyprus, 88, 107, 137, 260, 272, 298, 332, 488
Cyrillic, 89
Cyrus the Great, 84, 338, 354
Czechia (historical region), 177, 203
Czechoslovakia, 38, 77–79, 124–125, 130–134, 149, 175–176, 188–191, 199, 200–204, 210–211, 221–222, 225, 240, 266, 276, 283, 291, 476
Czechoslovak Legion, 221
Czech Republic, 3, 20, 61, 79, 91, 114, 186–187, 191, 200– 204, 240, 476

D

Dacians, 94, 288
Dagobert I, 96, 201, 231
Daladier, Édouard, 240
Dalai Lama (Tenzin Gyatso), 53, 328, 331, 366–367
Dame Te Atairangikaahu, 401
Danelaw, 138, 142–143
Dangung (Korea), 376
Danton, Georges, 113, 235
Danube monarchy, 189
Danube River, 63, 90–91, 93, 124, 162, 186–187, 266–267, 274, 280, 284, 288–290
Daoud Khan, Muhammad, 359
Darius I, 284, 354
Darius III, 350, 354
Darwin, Charles, 443, 469
Davis, Jefferson, 417
Dawes, Charles, 124
D-Day, 39, 67, 119, 128, 178, 418,
Decembrists, 218
Decius, 88
Declaration of Arbroath, 147
De Gaulle, Charles, 240–241
Delian League, 73, 75, 118, 292–293,
Demirel, Süleyman, 298
Democratic Unionist Party (DUP), 152
Deng Xiaoping, 374–375
Denmark, 38, 52, 64, 67, 91, 101, 107, 112, 118, 126, 133, 138–141, 154, 166–167, 172–174, 176, 178, 212, 405, 408, 462, 464, 467, 471, 475
Diaz, Bartolomeo, 30, 110, 250, 318
Diaz de Solis, Juan, 454, 458
Diaz, Porfirio, 430–431
Dimitrov, Georgi, 287
Dink, Hrant, 298
Diocletian, 80, 88
Dionysius I (Syracuse), 73
Djibouti, 484
Djindić, Zoran, 278
Doges, 260
Dollfuss, Engelbert, 124, 195
Dolni Verstonice, 20
Dominica, 422–425, 496
Dominican Republic, 496
Dominicans (monastic order), 104
Dominicus de Guzmán (St. Dominic), 409
Don Juan d'Austria, 246
Donskoy, Dmitry, 107
Dorian migrations, 72, 293
Dornelles Vargas, Getúlio, 439, 452
Drago (Moldova), 288
Drake, Edwin, 348
Drake, Francis, 31, 150, 420, 437, 446, 464
Dresden, bombing of, 128
Dreyfus Affair, 238–239
Dreyfus, Alfred, 238–239

Drygalski, Erich von, 472
Dubček, Alexander, 203
Dudayev, Dzhokhar, 226
Dufek, George, 473
Duma, 220
Dumont d'Urville, Jules, 472
Dunkirk, 154
Dutch East India Company, 30, 160–161, 390–391, 467–468
Duvalier, François (Papa Doc), 421, 424
Duvalier, Jean-Claude (Baby Doc), 421, 424

E

East Africa, 16, 35, 40, 173, 259, 303, 316–317, 466 See also individual countries
East Asia (Far East), 18, 25, 27, 32, 34, 223, 374, 380 See also individual countries
Easter Island (Rapa Nui), 456, 503
Eastern Bloc, 19, 42, 54, 68–69, 132–135, 181, 202, 251, 283, 291, 299
Eastern Bloc, collapse of, 68, 134, 224–225
East Timor, 35, 43, 330, 391, 423, 493
Ebert, Friedrich, 176
Ecuador, 23, 436–443, 447–449, 469, 499
Edict of Fontainebleu, 233
Edict of Milan, 81, 88, 252
Edict of Nantes, 65, 112–113, 233
Edict of Potsdam, 168
Edict of Restitution, 166
Edward I (England), 87, 100, 144–147, 154
Edward II (England), 100, 144, 154, 232
Edward III (England), 118, 144, 154
Edward IV (England), 144
Edward VII (England), 154, 456
Edward the Confessor, 143, 154
EFTA See European Free Trade Association
Egypt, 22, 34–35, 51–53, 58–59, 63, 70–71, 74, 127, 151, 187, 236–237, 266, 271–272, 279, 303, 306, 311–313, 317, 325, 328, 332–335, 339–344, 356, 421, 484
Egypt, ancient, 5, 9, 16–25, 76–84, 86–87, 95, 301–302, 308–309, 313, 338–339
Eichmann, Adolf, 340
Ejército de Liberación Nacional (ELN), 442
Elam, 22, 33, 71, 324, 350
Elcano, Juan Sebastian, 110
El Cid, 245
Eleanor of Aquitaine, 144, 232
Elizabeth I (England), 101, 112, 144–147, 154
Elizabeth II (England), 148, 154, 481, 494–502
Elizabethan Age, 145–147
Elizabeth Petrovna (Russia), 168–170, 217–218
El Salvador, 421, 432–433, 495
Engels, Friedrich, 116
England See Great Britain
English Civil War, 113, 118, 145, 148
Entente Cordial, 120, 123, 173–174, 239
Ephesus, Artemis of, 76
Equatorial Guinea, 485
Eratosthenes, 11
Erhard, Louis, 181

Erik I (Jorvik), 143
Erikson, Leif, 470
Erik the Red, 138, 411, 470
Eritrea, 258–259, 321, 484
Escobar, Pablo, 442
Estonia, 89, 126, 138, 212–213, 222, 476
Ethiopia, 20, 25, 29, 67, 69, 88, 131, 259, 303, 305–306, 316–317, 346, 484
Ethiopia, war in, 259, 316
Ethiopian Orthodox Church, 88
Euripides, 77
Europe, 15–54, 56–69, 78, 83, 87, 90–301, 305, 311, 317, 321, 325, 332–333, 336, 349, 361, 404–405, 416–418 See also individual countries
European Atomic Energy Community (Euratom), 133
European Free Trade Association (EFTA), 141, 185
European Union (EU), 19, 68–69, 132–133, 136–137, 141, 146, 151, 153, 185, 191, 194, 206, 211, 213, 228, 242, 249–251, 259, 283, 295, 298–299, 411, 462
Evren, Kenan, 298
Exodus, 84, 86
Eyre, Edward John, 396
Ezana of Aksum, 316

F

Fahd (Saudi Arabia), 347
Faisal I (Iraq), 352
Faisal I (Saudi Arabia), 329, 347
Faisal II (Iraq), 352
Faisal-Weizmann Agreement, 339
Falange, 249
Falkland Islands (Malvinas), 42, 148, 438–439, 459, 465, 500
Falklands War, 42
Faroe Islands, 462, 481
Fatima, 336
Ferdinand I (Bulgaria), 286
Ferdinand I (Holy Roman emperor), 113, 169, 187, 189, 197, 202, 204, 262, 286
Ferdinand I (Naples), 255
Ferdinand II (Aragon and Spain), 101, 110, 112, 246
Ferdinand II (Holy Roman emperor), 112, 166, 169, 262
Ferdinand III (Castile), 245
Ferdinand VII (Spain), 248–249
Ferdinand Maximilian (archduke), 430
Fernandez de Quiros, Pedro, 395
Ferrara, Council of, 268
Ferrara, kingdom of, 106, 255
Ficino, Marsilio, 255
Fiji, 395, 468, 502
Finland, 53, 65–66, 68, 126, 128, 130–131, 133, 138–141, 218–219, 222–224, 474
Fleet Acts (Germany), 120
Flemish states, 156, 159
Flinders, Matthew, 396
Florence (Italy), 64, 107, 157, 170, 253–258, 261, 268
Forbidden City (Beijing), 28, 370–371, 373
Forma Urbis Romae, 11
Forrest, John, 397
Fortuyn, Pim, 159
Fossey, Dian, 321
France, 10, 13, 15, 17–20, 35, 37–44, 47, 59–67, 87, 90–97, 99–100, 104, 106,

(France, continued) 112–128, 136, 143–146, 148–149, 154, 156, 159, 166–174, 176, 178, 181, 184, 190, 194–196, 202, 207, 218, 230–247, 254–261, 272–273, 283, 294, 297, 299, 305–306, 311, 313, 332–334, 340, 343, 346–347, 354, 359, 363, 373, 382–384, 404, 407–408, 414–415, 422, 424–425, 430, 439, 441, 452, 459, 464–468, 473, 477, 494, 496–499, 502–503
Francis I (Austria), 194, 262
Francis I (France), 169, 232, 235
Francis I (Holy Roman emperor), 169, 194
Francis II (France), 147, 235
Francis II Rákóczi, 198, 202
Franciscans, 104
Francis Ferdinand (archduke), assassination of, 36, 65–66, 120, 122, 174, 276, 281
Francis Joseph I (Austria), 99, 121, 194
Francis Joseph II (Austria), 185
Francis of Assisi (St. Francis), 104
Franco, Francisco, 249
Franco-Prussian War, 66–67, 117–118, 173–174
Franklin expedition, 470
Franks, 59, 61, 89–91, 94–95, 98, 118, 143, 156, 162–163, 182, 204, 230–231, 244, 253
Franz Josef Land, 470
Frederick I Barbarossa, 63, 98, 164, 169, 253
Frederick I (III) of Prussia, 168
Frederick II (Holy Roman emperor), 63, 164
Frederick II the Great (Prussia), 65, 100, 168, 170
Frederick III (Holy Roman emperor), 118, 173, 183
Frederick V (elector of Palatine), 112, 166
Frederick VI of Hohenzollern, 168
Frederick IX (Denmark), 475
Frederick William, elector of Brandenburg, 65, 168
Frederick William I (Prussia), 65, 168
Frederick William III (Prussia), 168
Frederick William IV (Prussia), 169
Freeman, Cathy, 398
Frei, Eudardo, 456
French Guiana, 239, 242, 435, 443–444, 499
French Polynesia, 35, 242, 395, 469, 503
French Revolution, 15, 18, 34, 65, 87, 114–115, 118–119, 166, 171, 184, 234–237
French Southern and Antarctic Lands, 242
French vassal states, 158, 188, 236, 255
Frisia, 91, 97, 142, 156, 163, 231, 475
Frobisher, Martin, 470
Fuchs, Arved, 473
Fuerzas Armadas Revolucionarias de Colombia (FARC), 442
Fujimori, Alberto, 439, 447

G

Gabon, 485
Gagarin, Yuri, 224
Gaitán, Jorge Eliécer, 442
Galapagos, 443, 469
Galilei, Galileo, 12
Gallegos, Rómulo, 440–441
Gama al-Islamiyya al-, 321

Gama, Vasco da, 30, 110, 250, 318, 326, 363, 466–467
Gambia, 306, 482
Gamsakhurdia, Zviad, 228
Gandhi, Indira, 328–329, 364–365
Gandhi, Mahatma, 328, 364–365
Gandhi, Rajiv, 365
Garcia, Alán, 447
Garcia, Juan, 430
Garcia Morenos, Gabriel, 443
Gardar, Svavarsson, 138
Garibaldi, Giuseppe, 257
Gates, Bill, 419
Gautama Buddha, 325, 359, 362, 366
Gediminas of Lithuania, 212
Gelugpa, 366
Genghis Khan, 326, 358, 360–362, 370
George II (Greece), 295
George Tupou I, 395
Georgia, 137, 223, 228, 331, 356–357, 487–488
Georgia, civil war in, 357
German confederacies, 125
German Customs Union (Zollverein), 116–117, 172
German Democratic Republic (East Germany), 42, 68, 132–135, 171, 224, 476
German Empire (Reich), 169, 173
German Federal Republic (West Germany), 68, 132–135, 171, 475
German federal states, 181
Germanic kingdoms, 26
Germanic tribes, 17, 61, 78–81, 90–93, 96, 142, 156, 162–163, 188–189, 192, 212, 244, 266, 288
German-Soviet Nonaggression Pact, 210
Germany, 10, 17, 19–20, 34–42, 48–50, 54, 57, 65–68, 83–91, 93–94, 96, 102, 104–107, 110, 112, 114, 122–131, 148–150, 162–181, 187, 188, 190–191, 195–198, 201–203, 206, 208, 210–211, 213, 218–225, 236, 238–242, 249, 258–259, 272–273, 276–281, 283, 287, 290, 294–295, 297, 306, 315, 336, 340, 348, 355, 380, 410, 422, 431, 452, 454, 466, 468–469, 473, 475
Germany, Nazi, 3, 38, 67–68, 86–87, 113, 125, 127–132, 177–181, 195, 202, 206–210, 220–223, 239–240, 283, 315, 355, 456, 458
Germany, reunification of, 181, 225
Gerritz, Dirk, 472
Gestapo, 177
Getty, Jean Paul, 348
Gettysburg (battle), 416–417
Ghana, 27, 51, 303, 314, 483
Ghaznavids, 297, 332, 335, 354, 358, 362–363
Gheorghiu-Dej, Gheorge, 291
Ghibellines, 118, 261
Gia Long (Vietnam), 383
Gibraltar, 481
Gierek, Edward, 211
Giles, Ernest, 397
Gilgamesh, 70
Gilles, Harold, 401
Giscard d'Estaing, Valéry, 242
Giza, pyramids of, 22, 76, 309
Glencoe, massacre of, 146
Glorious Revolution, 148
Göbekli Tepe, 59, 296
Go-Daigo, 378
Godoy, Manuel de, 248
Goebbels, Joseph, 177
Gogh, Theo van, 159

Golan Heights, 330, 340–341, 343
Golden Horde, 212, 214–215
Gömbös, Gyula 198
Gómez, Juan Vicente, 440 f
Gomulka, Wladyslaw, 211
Good Friday (Belfast) Agreement, 152
Gorbachev, Mikhail, 132, 134, 181, 225
gods, Egyptian, list of, 76
gods, Greek, list of, 76–77
gods, Hindu, list of, 367
gods, Roman, list of, 76
Gottwald, Klement, 202
Goulart, João, 439
Gracchus, Gaius Sempronius, 79
Gracchus, Tiberius, Sempronius, 79
Grand Župan, 275
Grant, Ulysses S., 417
Grau, Raúl Cubas, 455
Great Britain, 34–35, 38, 42–43, 48, 52, 65, 94, 100, 120–123, 125–127, 130, 133, 135,146–161, 173–174, 190–192, 218, 235, 238–240, 248, 258–259, 273, 287, 297, 299, 306, 313, 319, 327–329, 334, 339–340, 347, 352, 371, 380, 386, 404, 408, 412, 414, 451, 458–459, 463–467, 469, 475, 481, 495–503
Great Leap Forward (China), 43, 475
Great Powers, European, 34, 42, 67, 115, 120, 159, 172, 208, 212, 273, 277, 282, 287, 290, 297, 440
Great Schism, 60, 88–89, 106, 268
Great Wall of China, 9, 23, 368–370, 374
Greece, ancient, 24–25, 58–59, 72–74, 77–78, 95, 286, 292–295, 309, 324
Greece, Byzantine, 293
Greece, modern, 24, 26, 65–67, 116, 125, 127–133, 178, 199, 246, 272, 277, 281–287, 294–299, 333, 336, 480
Greece, Ottoman, 273, 293–294
Greek alphabet, 77
Greek colonies, 24–25, 59, 73, 78, 204, 266, 293, 312
Greek-Macedonian conflict, 281, 295
Greenland, 138–139, 141, 405, 410–411, 470, 481
Gregory VII (pope), 89, 164, 264
Grenada, 423, 497
Guadaloupe, 242, 464, 497
Guam, 35, 249, 502
Guatemala, 53, 423, 428, 433, 494
Guelf and Ghibelline Wars, 118
Guelfs, 118, 261 See also Welfs
Guernsey, 481
Guevara, Ernesto Che, 438
Guinea-Bissau, 482
Gulf War, First (Iran-Iraq War), 43, 335, 352
Gulf War, Second, 43, 330, 335, 352
Gulf War, Third, 43, 330
Gupta dynasty, 17, 27, 325, 362
Gürsel, Cemal, 298
Gustav I Wasa, 112, 138
Gustav II (Sweden), 112, 138, 166
Gustav III (Sweden), 139
Gutenberg, Johannes, 110
Guttierez, Lucio, 443
Guyana, 35, 435, 443–444, 499

H

Haakon IV, 138
Haakon VII, 139
Habsburg-Lothringen, 99
Habsburg Bohemia, 187
Habsburg dynasty, 18, 34, 65, 99, 113, 158, 164–166, 169–171, 186–192,

(Habsburg dynasty, continued) 198–200, 202, 204–205, 233, 237, 239, 246–247, 276, 430, 440
Hasburg dynasty, Spanish, 65, 165, 247, 255
Habsburg Hungary, 202
Habsburg Netherlands, 168
Habsburg Wars, 171, 184
Hadar (Ethiopia), 20
Hadrian, 80, 95, 142
Hadrianopolis (battle) 80–81, 118–119, 186, 266, 285 See also Adrianopolis
Hadrian's Wall, 142
Hague Convention, 50
Haile Selassie, 317
Haiti, 304, 422, 424, 496
Halicarnassus, Mausoleum of, 76
Hallstadt culture, 186
Hallstein Doctrine, 180
Hamas, 340–341
Hammarskjöld, Dag, 51
Hammurabi, 71, 324, 350
Hanging Gardens of Babylon, 76
Hannibal, 25, 79
Hannover, 154
Hanseatic League, 27, 107, 138, 214
Hanukka, 87
ul-Haq, Zia, 364
Harald I Bluetooth (Denmark), 138
Harald I Fairhair (Norway), 138
Harding, Warren G., 418
al-Hariri, Rafiq, 345
Harold II Godwinson (England), 143
Harun ar-Rashid, 332, 336
Hasmonean dynasty, 84, 338
Hassan II (Morocco), 311
Hastings (battle), 60, 138, 143
Hatshepsut, 309
Hattusilis III, 309
Havel, Václav, 203
Hawaii, 35, 405, 418–419, 469, 494
Hébert, Jacques, 235
Hebrides, 462
Hellenism, 59, 74, 78, 295
Hellenistic kingdoms (Diadochi), 75, 82, 94, 286, 309
Hellenistic period, 25, 73, 286, 324
Helsinki Conference, 68
Helvetian Republic, 184
Henry I (England), 144
Henry I (Germany), 464
Henry, II (England), 144, 232
Henry III (Holy Roman emperor), 164
Henry IV (France), 233
Henry IV (Holy Roman emperor), 60, 87, 164
Henry V (Holy Roman emperor), 164
Henry VI (Holy Roman emperor), 164
Henry VII (England), 144, 150
Henry VII (Holy Roman emperor), 154
Henry VIII (England), 64, 112, 144–146
Henry the Navigator (Portugal), 163
Henson, Matthew, 471
Heraclitus, 77
Herbert, Wally, 471
Herod Agrippa I, 338
Herod Agrippa II, 338
Herod Antipas, 84
Herodotus, 10, 77
Herod the Great, 84, 338
Herzl, Theodor, 339
Hesiod, 77
Heydrich, Reinhard, 179
Hidalgo y Costilla, Miguel, 430
Hillary, Edmund, 401
Himalaya, 43, 323, 325, 362
Hindenburg, Paul von, 123, 175

Hinduism, 15, 17, 25, 49, 323, 325, 362–363, 366–367
Hipparchus, 11
Hippocrates, 77
Hirohito, 380–382
Hiroshima, 39, 381, 405, 418, 424
Hitler-Stalin Pact, 124
Hitler, Adolf, 9, 124, 128, 177, 179, 240, 315
Hittite empire, 58, 70, 296
Ho Chi Minh, 384–386
Hohenstaufen dynasty, 98, 164, 169, 253
Hohenzollern dynasty, 99, 165, 168–169
Holocaust, 38–39, 69, 86–87, 178, 340
Holy Alliance, 117, 169, 218
Homann, Johann Baptista, 403
Homer, 77
Homo erectus, 16, 20–21, 301, 303, 316
Homo habilis, 21, 316
Homo heidelbergensis, 20–21, 162
Homo rudolfensis, 20–21
Homo sapiens, 7–8, 20–21, 288, 301, 303, 316–318, 435, 461
Hondius, Jodocus, 435
Honduras, 422–424, 432, 495
Honecker, Erich, 134, 181
Hong Kong, 151, 370, 374, 491
Horthy, Miklós, 198–199
Houtman-Abrolhos, 467
Houtman, Frederick de, 467
Hoxha, Enver, 283
Huang River, 323
Huáscar, 446
Hudson, Henry, 470
Huguenots, 64, 89, 102, 112, 168, 232–233
Huitzilopochtli, 428
Hülägü Khan, 351
Hundred Days of Reform (China), 372
Hundred Years' War, 64–65, 106, 144–145, 232–233
Hungarian crisis, 163, 196
Hungarian Revolution, 42–43, 68, 190
Hungary, 61, 64–65, 67–68, 89, 93, 100, 102, 110, 112, 118, 125–128, 131, 180, 186–206, 208, 220–221, 255, 271–272, 275–277, 280–281, 283, 286, 288–289, 294, 333, 420, 479
Huns, 26–27, 59, 91–93, 266, 270, 288, 368
Huns, White (Hephthalites), 325, 354, 361–362
Hus, Jan, 201
Husak, Gusav, 134, 203
Husein Gradaščević, 281
Hussein II (Jordan), 329, 3334, 344
Hussein, Saddam, 329, 335, 341, 352, 425
Hussite wars, 106, 118, 201
Hyksos, 308

I

Ibánez del Campo, Carlos, 456
Iberian Peninsula, 26, 60, 91, 244–245, 250, 266, 332
Ibn Ali, Hussein, 332, 336
Ibn Ali Talib, Ali, 336
Ibn Saud, 334, 347
Iceland, 9, 61, 93, 138–141, 145, 471, 474
Idi Amin, 43, 317
Ignatius Loyola, 89, 104, 111
Illiescu, Ion, 135
Illyria, 116, 188, 204–206, 274, 282–284
Illyrian wars, 204, 206
Inca, 29, 246, 435–437, 446–449

India, 4, 9–10, 16–18, 22–25, 27–35, 43–44, 48–50, 52, 59, 73, 77, 151, 161, 235, 237, 239, 250, 279, 305, 318–319, 323–336, 362–367, 382, 385, 390, 461, 465–468, 490
Indian Ocean, 10, 161, 242, 461
indigenous peoples of Africa, 315
indigenous peoples of Central America, 427, 431–432
indigenous peoples of India, 23–25
indigenous peoples of North America, 403, 406–407, 424 See also Native Americans
indigenous peoples of South America, 435–437, 439, 443, 447–449, 454, 459–461, 463, 499
indigenous peoples of the South Pacific, 463, 468–469
Indonesia, 8, 20, 45, 160–161, 327, 336–337, 386–391, 421, 466, 468, 493
Indus River, 323–324, 362
Industrial Revolution, 3, 19, 116, 119, 148, 158
Indus Valley civilization, 16, 23–25, 323–324, 362
International Atomic Energy Agency (IAEA), 51
International Court of Justice (ICJ), 50, 278
International Security Assistance Force (ISAF), 359
Investiture Controversy, 164–165
IRA See Irish Republican Army
Iran, 18, 24, 43, 59, 71, 74, 127, 181, 297–298, 324, 328–329, 333–337, 340, 351–354, 357–358, 362, 423, 432, 488 See also Persia
Iran-Contra Affair, 423, 432
Iran-Iraq War (First Gulf War), 329, 335, 351–55, 423
Iraq, 9, 18–20, 43, 49, 54, 71, 273, 299, 328–330, 333–335, 347–357, 423, 488
Ireland (Eire), 67, 89–90, 100, 124, 137, 142, 144–155, 475, 410, 420, 475 See also Northern Ireland (Ulster)
Irian Jaya, 371 See also New Guinea, Western
Irigoyen, Hipólito 458
Irish Republican Army (IRA), 137, 151–152
Iron Age, 21, 24, 58–59, 186, 214, 252
Isabella I (Spain), 64, 101 See also Isabella of Castile
Isabella II (Spain), 248
Isabella of Castile, 110, 246 See also Isabella I
Iskander Shah, 387
Islam, 6, 15, 17, 26–27, 48–49, 57, 63, 146, 159, 283, 302–303, 311, 313, 317, 323, 325–326, 332, 336–337, 346, 386–390, 466
Islamic dynasties, list of, 335
Islamic Salvation Front (Algeria), 321
Isle of Man, 481
Ismaili (Shi'ite sect), 337
Israel, 42, 52–54, 58, 70–71, 84–87, 95, 180–181, 313, 317, 324, 328–330, 334, 338–345, 352–353, 355, 419, 489
Israelites, 71, 84–87
Istanbul, 18, 95, 266, 271, 273, 295, 298 See also Constantinople
Italy, 9, 16, 19, 27–28, 38–45, 52, 57–58, 60–61, 63–69, 78–79, 89–91, 93, 98, 108–109, 118, 120–121, 123–128, 130, 137, 164, 174, 187–191, 195, 202, 206–207, 236–237, 248–249,

(Italy, continued) 252–261, 266, 273, 277, 283, 287, 305–306, 317, 334–335, 380, 422, 458, 478
Italo-Ethiopian War, 257–259, 317
Iturbide, Agustin de, 430
Ivan I Kalita, 107, 214, 217
Ivan II the Red, 217
Ivan III the Great, 107, 214
Ivan IV the Terrible, 214, 327
Ivan Asen II (Bulgaria), 285
Ivory Coast, 306, 483

J

Jackson, William, 420
Jacob, 84
Jacobaa of Bavaria, 156
Jacobins, 234
Jacobites, 147
Jagiellon dynasty, 101, 208
Jahyavarman VII (Khmer), 382
Jamaica, 31, 35, 247, 304, 317, 463–464, 496
James (apostle), 84–85
James I of Aragon, 245
James I (England), 144, 147
James II (England), 113, 148, 151, 154
James (duke) of York, 151
James Stuart (Scotland) See James I of England
Jansz, Willem, 396
Jankowitsch, Wiktor, 227
Japan, 15, 19, 25, 27, 29, 31–32, 34–41, 49–50, 52, 54, 67, 104, 125, 161, 175, 178, 219–220, 287, 323, 326–327, 360, 366, 370–373, 377–381, 385, 431, 454, 467, 492
Jaruzelski, Wojciech, 134, 211
Jasenovac, 277
Jeanne d'Arc, 106, 144, 232
Jeddah, Treaty of, 347
Jefferson, Thomas, 414
Jelačič, Joseph, 205
Jelling dynasty, 154
Jersey, 480
Jerusalem, 58, 63, 70–71, 80–81, 84–88, 93–94, 97, 110–111, 213, 266, 271, 328–329, 332–334, 338–342, 344
Jerusalem, Council of, 84
Jesuit Reductions, 437, 455
Jesuits, 64, 89, 104, 111, 250, 327, 437, 447, 455
Jesus Christ, 9, 84–87, 129, 325, 338
Jimmu , 378
John II (France), 232
John III Sobieski (Poland), 108, 118, 209
John IV (Portugal), 250
John VI (Portugal), 251, 451
John Hunyadi (Hungary), 275, 289
John of Austria, 173
John Paul I (pope), 255
John Paul II (pope), 211, 255, 479
Johansen, Hjalmar, 470
John Zápolya (Hungary) 187, 197
Jordan, 328–329, 332, 334, 338–345, 489
Joseph I (Portugal), 250
Joseph II (Holy Roman emperor), 189, 194, 202
Juan Carlos I (Spain), 249
Juárez, Benito, 430
Judaea, 84, 338
Judaism, 15, 84, 86, 177, 323
Julian the Apostate, 81, 88
Juliana (Netherlands), 159
Julius II (pope), 183, 261
Junker, Wilhelm, 305

Justinian I, 60, 93, 266, 293
Jutes, 59, 91, 142

K

Kaaba, 337
Kabul Khan, 325, 361
Kádár, János, 134, 198
Kammu, 378
Kapp-Lüttwitz Putsch, 176
Karadžič, Radovan, 278
Karakoram, 323, 361
Karbala, 332, 336, 351
Karim Khan Zand, 327, 355
Karzai, Hamid, 359
Kashmir, 43–44, 235, 362–364
Katyn, massacre of, 210–211
Kazakhstan, 368–369, 490
Kelly, Edward "Ned," 397
Kemmu Restoration, 378
Kenya, 317, 484
Kepler, Johannes, 12
Kerensky, Aleksandr, 221
Khagan Kuvrat (Bulgaria), 284
Khang-si (China), 371
Khatami, Mohammad, 329, 355
Khazar, 214
Kherat, 284, 358
Khmer, 17, 27, 325, 382–383, 385
Khmer Rouge, 43, 384–385
Khodorkovsky, Mikhail, 217, 226
Khomeini, Ayatollah Ruhollah, 329, 335, 337, 355
Khosrau I (Persia), 354
Khrushchev, Nikita, 181, 224–225, 279, 477
Kiel, Treaty of, 139
Kievan Rus, 60, 89, 107, 118, 128, 208, 214
Kim Dae-jung, 377
Kim Jong-il, 377
Ki-moon, Ban, 51
Kirchner, Cristina Fernández de, 459
Kirchner, Néstor, 459
Kiribati, 502
Kirov, Sergei, 222
Klasis River caves (South Africa), 20
Knesset, 340
Kohl, Helmut, 135, 181
Koizumi, Junichiro, 381
Koobi Fora (Kenya), 20
Koran, 336
Korea, 25, 43–44, 376–377, 379–380 See also South Korea and North Korea
Korean War, 19, 43–44, 325, 328, 374, 377, 389, 424
Kosciuszko, Tadeusz, 209
Kosovo, 54, 135, 137, 197–199, 271, 275, 278, 280, 282, 297, 335, 479–480
Kosovo Polje (battle), 106, 110, 119, 121, 197
Kossuth, Lájos, 198
Kostov, Traicho, 287
Kraków, 200, 208, 210–211
Kremlin, 132, 217
Kristallnacht, 129, 177
Kruger dispatch, 120
Krum (Bulgaria), 28
Kubitschek, Juscelino, 452
Kublai Khan, 260, 326, 361
Kuchma, Leonid, 226
Ku Klux Klan, 417
Kuomintang, 373–374
Kurdish Autonomous Region, 330, 353, 357, 488
Kurds, 133, 298, 325, 328, 330, 333, 342, 352–353, 357
Kutusov, Michail, 115

507

Kuwait, 323, 329–330, 335, 346–347, 350–352, 489
Kyrgyzstan, 358, 490

L

Lakshadweep, 466
Lange, David, 401
Laos, 328, 382–384, 480, 492
Laozi, 324
La Pérouse, Jean-François de, 30
Larrazabal, Wolfgang, 441
La Réunion, 242, 467, 487
Lascaux, cave of, 10, 20, 230
Las Navas de Tolosa (battle), 245
La Tène culture, 182
Latin alphabet, 77
Latin America, 18–19, 34, 42, 44, 48, 54, 304, 348, 432, 438, 441, 452, 454–456 See also individual countries
Lateran treaties, 258, 261
Latvia, 67, 69, 89, 212–213, 476
Laval, Pierre, 240
Lebanese Civil War, 42, 335, 344
Lebanon, 24, 42, 49, 58, 328, 334–335, 340–345, 488
Lebrun, Albert, 240
Lee Kuan Yew (Singapore), 386
Lee, Robert Edward, 417
Legnano (battle), 253
Leichhardt, Louis, 396
Leif Eriksson, 404, 470
Leipzig, Battle of, 115, 218, 236–237
Le Moustir (France), 20
Lenin, Vladimir Ilich, 19, 165, 217, 220–221, 360, 477
Leo the Great (pope), 88
Leonidas of Sparta, 73
Leopold I (Belgium), 159
Leopold I (Holy Roman emperor), 118, 194
Leopold II (Belgium), 160–161, 315
Leopold III (Austria), 182
Leopold III (Belgium), 159
Leopold VI (Austria), 63
Lepanto (naval battle) 112, 246, 272, 294, 296
Lepidus, 80
Lesotho, 318, 486
Lesseps, Ferdinand de, 313
Levant, 323, 342–344
Liberia, 35, 314, 321, 482
Liberian civil war, 321
Libya, 94–95, 120, 127, 273, 299, 303, 306, 309, 312–313, 333–335, 483
Lie, Trygve, 51
Liebknecht, Karl, 176
Liechtenstein, 184–185, 478
Liechtenstein, Johann Adam Andreas, 185
Lili'uokalani (Hawaii), 395
Lin Biao, 374
Lincoln, Abraham, 404, 416
Lindisfarne, 138, 143
Lithuania, 57, 65, 67, 89, 99, 101, 105, 126, 176, 187–188, 208–210, 212–214, 476
Little Big Horn (battle), 405, 407, 418
Litvinenko, Alexander 227
Liudolf, house of, 98
Livingstone, David, 304
Livy, (Titus Livius), 81
Locarno, Pact of, 124, 240
Lockerbie terrorist attack, 313, 335
Lombard League, 164
Lombards, 60–61, 91, 93, 96–97, 164, 186, 252–254, 266, 288, 352
Lombardy, 61, 194, 254, 256–257

Longshan culture, 368
L'Ouverture, Toussaint, 420
London, 94, 117, 130, 144–145, 149, 152, 268, 313, 364, 438, 472
London Convention, 294
London, Great Fire of, 144
London Protocol, 294
London, Treaty of, 103, 276–277, 282
López, Carlos Antonio, 455
López, Francisco Solano, 455
Lothar I, 96, 156, 231
Lothar II, 96, 156, 231
Lothringen 157, 231
Louis I of Anjou, 196, 208
Louis II (Holy Roman emperor), 95, 156
Louis II (Hungary), 64, 101, 110, 187, 189, 199
Louis II of Bavaria, 98, 164, 169, 173
Louis III (Bavaria), 169
Louis IV (Bavaria), 169
Louis VI the Great (France), 232, 235
Louis VII (France), 232, 235
Louis VIII (France), 232, 235
Louis IX the Pious (France), 63, 95–96, 169, 231–232, 235
Louis XI (France), 157, 232, 235
Louis XII (France), 98, 235
Louis XIII (France), 233, 235, 242
Louis XIV (France), 65, 101, 113–114, 233, 235, 247
Louis XV (France), 233, 235
Louis XVI (France), 114, 235, 238
Louis XVIII (France), 235, 238
Louisiana Territory, 236, 430
Louis of Baden, 272
Louis the German, 95–96, 98, 163, 169, 231
Louis-Philippe of Orléans, 101, 235, 238
Lublin, Union of, 209, 212
"Lucy" (Australopithecus), 8, 20, 303
Ludendorff, Erich, 175
Lüderitz, Adolf, 173
Lueger, Karl, 195
Lugo, Fernando, 439, 455
Lukashenko, Alexander, 226
Lula da Silva, Luis, 439, 452
Lusitania, 122, 174
Luther, Martin, 48, 64, 89, 111, 164
Luxembourg, 69, 98, 159, 164–166, 187, 201, 246, 475
Luxembourg, House of, 98, 164–166, 187, 201
Luxembourg, Rosa, 176
Lycurgus, 73
Lysimachus, 74

M

Mabo, Eddie, 398
Macao, 251, 371, 374, 491
Macbeth, 146–147
Maccabees, 84, 338
Macedonia, 25, 59, 70, 72, 74, 79, 95, 98, 275–277, 280–282, 284, 286, 293–295, 480
Macedonia, former Yugoslavian Republic of (FYROM), 135, 281, 295, 480
Macedonia, Greek, 281
Macedonia, kingdom of, 25, 59, 70, 72, 74, 79, 98, 284
Macedonia, Ottoman province, 276
Macedonia, Roman province, 75
Macedonia, Serbian, 281
Macedonian dynasty, 267, 281, 293
Mackandal, François, 420
Madagascar, 466, 486

Madeira, 463, 481
Mafia, 137
Magellan, Ferdinand, 30, 110, 388, 395, 456, 458
Maghreb, 242, 310–311
Magna Carta, 106, 144
Magnus I the Good, 138
Magyars, 60–61, 164, 195–197, 200, 202, 288
Mahathir Muhammad (Malaysia), 387
Mahdi revolt, 333
Mahmud II, 272
Mahmud of Ghazna, 332, 362
Makarios III, 299
Malawi, 485
Malaysia 30, 328, 337, 386–387, 389, 401, 493
Maldonado, Luis, 439
Maldives, 466–467, 491
Mali, 17, 303–304, 314, 482
Malta, 298–299, 479
Malta, Knights of, 76, 299
al-Mamun, 332, 336, 351
Mandela, Nelson, 319
Mangrai the Great (Thailand), 382
Manhattan Project, 381
Mannerheim, Carl Gustav, 140
Manzikert (battle), 268, 296
Manuel I, 250
Maoist guerillas, 387, 389, 439
Mao Zedong, 9, 43, 225, 328, 373–375
Maori, 400, 501, 503
Mappa Mundi, 11
Marat, Jean-Paul, 235
Marathon (battle), 73, 120
Marcomanni, 91, 162, 186
Marco Polo, 107, 260, 361, 396
Marcos, Ferdinand, 329, 388
March on Rome, 258
Marcus Aurelius, 80, 91, 162, 186
Marengo (battle), 236
Margaret I, 138
Margaret of Flanders, 156
Maria Luisa (Spain), 248
Maria Theresa, Empress 188, 194, 202
Marie Antoinette (France), 114, 235
Marignano (battle), 184
Marius, 79
Mark (evangelist), 81, 260
Mark Antony, 80, 309
Markham, Clements, 470
Marshall, George, 180
Marshall Islands, 502
Marshall Plan, 180, 224
Martinique, 242, 497
Marx, Karl, 116
Mary Stuart (Mary Queen of Scots), 144, 147
Masada, 87, 338
Masaryk, Tomáš Garrigue, 202
massacres
    Bogside, 153
    Glencoe, 146–147
    Greysteel, 153
    Katyn Forest, 210–211
    Kingsmill, 153
    Leipzig, 115, 236
    Munich, 181
    Nanking, 373, 380
    Sicilian Vespers, 253
    Sabra and Shatila, 345
    Salsipuedes Creek, 454
    Sebrenica, 54, 135, 281
    St. Bartholomew's Day, 64, 112, 232
    Wounded Knee, 405, 407, 418
Matthias (Holy Roman emperor), 194

Matthias Corvinus, 197
Maurya dynasty, 16, 17, 23, 325, 362
Mauretania, 482
Mauritius, 466
Maximian (Roman emperor), 80
Maximilian I (Holy Roman emperor), 158, 183
Maximilian I (Mexico), 430
Maximilian II Emanuel of Bavaria, 170
Maya, 17, 23–25, 27, 29, 427–429, 432
Mayflower, 412
Mayotte, 242, 486
Mazzini, Giuseppe, 257
McCarthy era, 405, 418
McDonald, Richard and Maurice, 418
McLaren, Bruce, 401
Mecca, 271, 273, 303, 329, 332–337, 347
Medici, Cosimo de, 261
Medici, Lorenzo de, 254, 261
Medvedev, Dmitry, 227
Meerssen, Treaty of, 96, 163, 231
Mehmed I, 271
Mehmed II, 281, 327
Mehmet Ali See Muhammad Ali
Meiji Restoration, 327, 380
Meir, Golda, 340
Melanesia, 394, 461
Mendana de Neyra, Alvaro de, 395
Menderes, Adnan, 298
Menem, Carlos, 459
Menes (pharaoh), 303, 308
Mensheviks, 221
Mentuhotep II, 308
Menzies, Robert, 398
Mercator, Gerhard, 12
Merenptah (pharaoh), 84
Merkel, Angela, 181
Merovingian dynasty, 60, 97–98, 163, 230
Mesolithic Period, 20, 58, 318,
Mesopotamia, 10, 15–16, 22–24, 57–58, 70–71, 74, 271, 324, 332, 335, 348, 350–351, 354, 356, 339,
Messner, Reinhold, 473
Metaxas, Ioannis, 295
Methodism, 88–89
Metternich, Klemens von, 117, 188, 194
Mexican-American War, 424
Mexican Revolution, 427, 431
Mexico, 17, 21–23, 27, 30, 40–41, 52, 221, 246–247, 388, 427–433, 436–437, 494
Michael the Brave (prince) 289
Michelangelo, 255
Micronesia, 394, 502
Middle Ages, 61, 64, 102
Middle East conflicts, 330
Mieszko I, 208
Mikhail Romanov, 216
Milan, 31, 254–261
Milan, Edict of, 252
Milošević, Slobodan, 278
Milutinovic, Milan, 480
Minamoto, Yoritomo, 378
Mindaugas of Lithuania, 212
Minoan culture, 16, 23–24, 58, 72–73, 292–293
Mintoff, Dom, 299
Mirabeau, Comte de, 235
Miracle of the House of Brandenburg, 170
Mircea the Old (Walachia), 288
Mitanni, 22, 70
Mithridates VI of Pontos, 79

Mitterrand, François, 242
Mladeč (Czech Republic), 20
Mobutu, Joseph Sese Seko, 315, 425
Moctezuma, 429
Mohács (battle), 187, 197, 199, 202, 271
Mohammad Reza Pahlavi (Iran), 328, 355
Mohammed VI (Morocco), 311
Mojmir I (Moravia), 200
Moldavia, 147, 272–276, 288–291
Moldova, 291, 477
Monaco, 479
monastic orders
    Benedictines, 60, 104
    Cistercians, 104, 144
    Dominicans, 104, 144
    Franciscans, 104, 144
Mongke Khan, 361
Mongolia, 17, 297, 329, 361–362, 372, 375
Mongol invasion, 118, 200, 208, 214, 288, 296–297, 333, 351, 361–362, 376–379
Mongols, 15, 17–18, 26–27, 212–216, 260, 285, 288, 296, 325–326, 333, 336, 339, 351, 354, 356, 360–363, 367, 370, 376–379, 382, 386, 491
Monophysite heresy, 88
Monroe Doctrine, 404, 414, 424, 438
Monroe, James, 414
Monroy, Carlos Arosemena, 439, 443
Monte Cassino, 104
Montenegro, 274, 480
Montserrat, 497
Mora, Juan Rafael, 433
Morales, Evo, 439, 448
Moreau de Séchelles, Jean, 31
Morgarten (battle), 182
Morocco, 18, 20–21, 108, 120, 173, 240, 249–250, 303, 310–311, 321, 332–336, 481
Morocco Crisis, 120
Morocco, Spanish, 21, 249
Moro, Aldo, 259
Moroto (Uganda), 20
Morotopithecus bishopi, 20
Moscow, 68–69, 119, 127, 137, 203, 214–229, 267, 279, 283, 361, 430
Moscow Peace Treaty, 140, 222
Moscow show trials, 222
Moses, 84
Mossadegh, Mohammed, 355
Mountbatten, Louis. 364
Mozambique, 35, 251, 318–319, 351, 485
Mugabe, Robert, 321
Muhammad (Prophet), 325, 332, 336–337, 346
Muhammad Ali (Egypt), 272, 313, 343
Munich accord, 124, 191, 198, 202
Münster, Sebastian, 11
Müntzer, Thomas, 111
Murad IV, 272
Musharraf, Pervez, 365
Muslim Africa, 48
Muslim League (India), 336, 364
Mussolini, Benito, 124, 128, 258
Mutsuhito (Tenno), 380
Myanmar, 49, 327, 372, 382, 384–385, 492 See also Burma
Mycenaean culture, 22–23, 25, 58, 72–73, 292–293, 299

N

Nachtigall, Gustav, 305
Nader Shah, 327, 333, 355
NAFTA see North American Free Trade Agreement

Nagasaki, 49–51, 379, 381, 405, 418, 424
Nagorno-Karabakh, 229
Namibia, 173, 318–319, 485
Nanking, massacre of, 373, 380
Nansen, Fridtjof, 470
Nantes, Edict of, 64, 112–113, 233
Napoleon I Bonaparte, 65, 114–115, 169, 184, 205, 218, 234, 236, 248, 254–255, 260–261, 299, 465
Napoleon III, 116, 238
Narai of Ayutthaya, 383
Nares, George, 470
Narodniki, 219
National Socialists (Germany) See Germany, Nazi
NATO See North Atlantic Treaty Organization
Nasir ad-Din (shah), 355
Nasser, Gamal Abd el, 328, 334
Native Americans, 404–408, 412
See also indigenous peoples of North America
Nauru, 502
Nazi Party (Nationalsozialistische Deutsche Arbeiterpartei), 86, 125 See also Germany, Nazi
Neanderthals, 9, 20, 162
Neander Valley (Germany), 20
Nebra disk, 10, 162
Nebuchadnezzar II, 58, 70, 84, 86, 350
Nehru, Jawaharlal, 364
Nelson, Horatio, 115
Neo-absolutism, 189, 195
Neo-Assyrian empire, 58, 70–71, 324, 341, 350
Neo-Babylonian period, 58, 71, 350
Neolithic Period, 9–10, 15, 18, 20, 74, 142, 296, 308, 368, 462, 468
Neolithic revolution, 16, 58
Neolithic sites, 296, 462
Nepal, 491
Nero (emperor), 80, 252
Nestorians, 88
Netherlands, 15, 18, 30–36, 52, 61, 65, 67, 69, 112–113, 119, 126, 151, 156–160, 233, 236, 246–250, 319, 391, 437, 439, 441–442, 446, 450, 464, 468, 472, 475
Netherlands Antilles, 35, 160, 464, 498
Netherlands, Austrian, 158–159, 236
Netherlands, Burgundian, 156–157
Netherlands, Habsburg, 158
Netherlands, Spanish, 158, 233, 246–247
Neves, Tancredo, 439
New Amsterdam, 151, 160
Ne Win, (Burma) 385
New Caledonia, 242, 395, 468, 502
Newfoundland, 31, 35, 463
New Guinea, German, 35, 469
New Guinea, Papua, 35, 399, 469, 503
New Guinea, Western, 371
See also Irian Jaya
New Netherlands, 151, 160
New Testament, 84
New York, 35, 37, 151, 160, 314, 340, 359
New Zealand, 35, 400, 501–503
Nibelungenlied, 93
Nicaea, 10, 293, 296
Nicaea, Council of, 88, 267, 293
Nicaragua, 432–435, 495
Niemeyer, Oscar, 452
Niger, 483

Niger River, 306, 316, 322
Nigeria, 19, 35, 42, 304, 306, 322, 483
Nikitin, Afanassi, 31
Nicholas I, 218, 273
Nicholas II, 121, 140, 219, 221
Nicopolis (battle), 271
Ninoslav, Matej, 280
Niue, 503
Nixon, Richard M., 291
Nobel Prize for Literature, 149
Nobel Prize for Peace, 52
Nobile, Umberto, 471, 473
nonaligned states, 279
Noort, Olivier van, 30
Norbert of Xanten, 104
Nordenskiöld, Adolf Erik, 470
Nordic Seven Years' War, 139, 212
Norfolk Island, 503
Noriega, Manuel, 425, 432
Norman Conquest, 143
Normans, House of Hauteville, 100
Normans, Rollonids, 100, 154
Norodom Sihanouk, 385
North America, 29, 32, 48, 133, 138, 151, 160, 236–237, 301, 305, 402–425, 431, 435, 461–465, 471, 494 See also individual countries
North America, colonies in, 65, 151
North American Free Trade Agreement (NAFTA), 431
North Atlantic Treaty Organization, (NATO), 3, 19, 39, 68, 119, 132–134, 137, 159, 204, 207, 212–213, 226–229, 243, 249, 259, 278, 281, 287, 295, 298
Northern Ireland (Ulster), conflict in, 137, 153
Northern Mariana Islands, 502
North German Confederation, 173
North Korea, 328–329, 376–377, 492
See also Korea
Norway, 50–52, 67, 126, 133, 138–141, 149, 341, 462, 471, 474, 494
Novotny, Antonin, 202
Nuremburg race laws, 124, 177
Nuremburg trials, 130, 180
Nuzi, clay tablets from, 10
Nystad, Peace of, 139, 212, 216

O
Obama, Barack, 317, 419
Occupied territories (Palestine), 180
October Revolution, 195, 220
Oda Nobunaga, 379
Odria, Manuel, 439
O'Higgins, Bernardo, 456
Oldenburg, 101
Olof Skötkonung, 138
Olduvai Gorge (Tanzania), 20
Olmecs, 428
Olympia, 76
Olympic Games, 58, 73, 291–292, 340, 367, 374
Oman, 332, 334, 346–347, 466, 490
OPEC See Organization of Petroleum Exporting Countries
Operation Desert Fox, 351
Operation Desert Storm, 330, 353
Operation Dragon, 128
Operation Eagle Claw, 355
Operation Gomorrah, 178
Operation High Jump, 479
Operation Husky, 128, 178, 258
Operation Overlord, 240
Operation Solomon, 317
Operation Torch, 240
Operation Valkyrie, 179
Operation Weserübung, 126, 140

Opium wars, 371
Orange and Nassau, House of, 154
Orange Revolution, 226
Orda Khan, 360
Organization of Petroleum Exporting Countries (OPEC), 328, 334, 349, 352, 441, 451
Orkney, 462
Orrorin tugenensis, 20
Ortega, Daniel, 432
Ortelius, Abraham, 12, 323
Orthodox Church (Greek), 48, 60, 65, 69, 207, 209, 267–268, 283, 299, 339, 344
Orthodox Church (Russian), 48–49, 209, 219
Osman I Gazi, 107, 270, 296
Ostrogoths, 60–61, 90–93, 186, 252–253266, 280, 299
Ota Benga (Benin), 315
Ottoman Empire, 15, 18–19, 27, 31–34, 64–67, 110, 198, 202–205, 209, 214–218, 237–238, 246, 260, 266, 268–293 295, 297, 299, 307, 310–313, 316, 326–327, 332–333, 336, 339, 343, 346–347, 351, 354–356
Otto I the Great, 60, 164
Otto II (Holy Roman emperor), 164
Otto of Bavaria (Greece), 294
Ottokar II of Bohemia, 164, 192, 200
Ottonian period, 98, 169
Ötzi (glacier mummy), 252
Özal, Turgut, 298

P
Pacific Ocean, 30, 468–469
Pacific, War of (Saltpeter War), 438, 448–449, 456, 458
Pacific War (World War II), 38–40, 67, 328, 394, 399
Pacta Conventa, 205, 207
Pahlavi dynasty, 328, 354–355
Pakistan, 5, 43, 54, 229, 305, 323, 328–330, 335, 358–365, 490
Paksas, Rolandas, 213
Palatine, 102
Palatine War of Succession, 170
Palau, 468, 502
Paleolithic Period, 10, 20, 58, 288
Palestine, 6, 71, 84, 86, 323, 326, 328, 331–333, 338–343
Palestinian autonomous regions, 42, 329, 331, 489
Palestinian Liberation Organization (PLO), 328, 340–341
Palestinians, 42, 54, 313, 330, 341
Palme, Olof, 141
Palmyra, 332, 342
Panama, 30, 432–433, 442, 469, 495
Panama Canal, 432–433
Papandreou, Georgios, 295
Papanin, Ivan, 471
Papen, Franz von, 177
Paraguay, 5, 435, 437–439, 448–449, 452–456, 459–460, 500
Paranthropus, 20
Paris, 66, 218, 233–240, 243–245, 261
Paris Commune, 238, 241
Paris Peace Accords (1973), 329, 384
Paris Peace Conference (1919–1920), 283
Paris Peace Conference (1947), 198, 259, 261, 295
Paris, Treaty of (1763), 29, 235, 363
Paris, Treaty of (1856), 290, 408
Park Chung-Hee, 377
Park, Mungo, 305

Parmenides, 77
Parry, William Edward, 470
Passarowitz, Treaty of, 272, 290
Passover See Pesach
Patkul, Johann Reinhold von, 212
Patrick (saint), 89, 147
Päts, Konstantin, 213
Paul (saint), 84, 88
Paul I (czar), 218
Pavelič, Ante, 206
Pavia (battle), 254
Payer, Julius von, 470
Paz Estenssoro, Victor, 439, 448
Pearl Harbor, 380, 394, 405, 418
Peary, Robert, 471
Peasant Revolt (England), 221, 249, 405
Peasant Revolt (Germany), 111
Pedro I, 438, 450
Pedro II, 438, 451
Peisistratus, 73
Peking man, 20
Pelayo, 244
Peloponnesian League, 293
Peloponnesian War, 73, 293
Peres, Shimon, 341
Perestroika, 225
Pérez de Cuéllar, Javier, 51
Pérez Jimenez, Marcos, 441
Pérez, Carlos Andrés, 441
Pergamum, 75, 95
Pericles, 73
Perón, Evita, 459
Perón, Isabel, 439, 458–459
Perón, Juan, 438, 458–459
Perry, Matthew, 380
Persia, 23–24, 71, 266, 271, 284, 287, 290, 324–327, 332–338, 342, 345–346, 350–358, 361–362, 466
See also Iran
Persian Empire, 325, 327, 343, 350–351, 362, 368 See also Achaemenid dynasty
Persian Wars, 73, 354
Perseus (Macedon), 75
Peru, 246, 436–440, 442–443, 446–448, 458–459, 499
Pesach (Passover), 87
Pétain, Henri Philippe, 123, 178, 240
Peter (saint), 84, 88
Peter I the Great (tsar), 216, 218,
Peter III (tsar), 218
Peter III of Aragon, 245
Petra (Jordan), 332, 342–343
petroleum, 267, 334, 348–349, 356, 387
Petrovič, George (Karadjordje), 276
Philhellenes, 295
Philip the Good (Burgundy), 156
Philip the Bold (Burgundy) 156
Philip I the Fair (France), 246
Philip II (Macedon), 74, 284
Philip II (Spain), 31, 112,158, 246, 389
Philip II August (France), 63, 232
Philip III (Spain), 192
Philip IV the Fair, (France), 232
Philip V (Macedon), 75
Philip V (Spain), 248
Philip VI (France), 232
Philippines, 327, 329, 388–389, 461, 493
Phillip, Arthur, 396
philosophers, ancient, 77, 325
philosophers, modern, 202, 255–256
Phoenician alphabet, 77
Phoenicians, 24, 244, 291, 324, 338, 340, 342–343, 461, 463–464

Pierola, Nicolas de, 447
Pilsudski, Józef, 210
Pindar, 77
Pinochet, Augusto, 438, 456
Pippin III the Younger, 96, 231
Pippin, Donation of, 261
Pitcairn Island, 503
Pizarro, Francisco, 30, 436–437, 446–447
plague epidemics, 4, 109, 266
Plantagenet, House of, 100, 154
plantations, 147
Plato, 77
PLO See Palestinian Liberation Organization
Poincaré, Raymond, 239
Poland, 37, 47–48, 52, 56–57, 61, 65, 67–68, 88, 200, 203, 208–213, 218–219, 240, 288, 476
Poland, partition of, 37, 47–48, 65, 88, 209, 212, 218
Polar regions, 460–461
Polisario Front, 311
Politovskaya, Anna, 227
Polo, Marco 107, 260, 361, 396
Pol Pot, 43, 329, 384
Poltava (battle), 107, 216
Polynesia, 34, 242, 385, 394–395, 461, 468–469, 503
Pomare V, 395
Pombal, Marquis of, 250
Pommern, Erich von, 138
Pompey the Great, 80
Pompeii, 80
Pompidou, Georges, 242
Poniatowski, Stanislaus August, 209
popes, list of, 264–265
Poppo von Schleswig 138
Portales Palazuelos, Diego 457
portolan charts, 11
Portugal, 15, 18, 29–30, 33–36, 236, 241, 244–251, 311– 312, 371, 391, 435–436, 450–451, 463–464, 471, 478
postwar period, 4, 38, 161, 259, 383
Potemkin (battleship), 220
Potemkin, Grigory, 219
Potsdam Conference, 128
Pragmatic Sanction of Bourges, 194
Prague, Defenestration of, 65, 166, 201
Prague Spring, 203, 225, 291
Přemyslid dynasty, 101
presidents, list of United States, 421–422
prime ministers of Great Britain, list of, 155
Primo de Rivera, 249
principate (Rome), 252–253
Privilegium maius, 192
Protestant Union, 65, 112, 165
Protestants, North American, 48
Prüm, partition of, 97, 156, 163, 231
Prussia, 13, 33, 65–66, 168, 209–210, 213, 218, 234–238, 464
Prussians, 208, 212, 238
Ptolemaeus, Claudius, 10
Ptolemy I, 309
Ptolemy's map, 11
Puerto Rico, 35, 249, 464, 496
Punic Wars, 79, 244, 252
Punjab, 325, 327, 335, 364–365
Purim, 87
Putin, Vladimir, 226–227
Puyi, 325, 327, 372
pyramids, Egyptian, 9, 309

pyramids, Mesoamerican, 428–429, 436
Pyrrhos of Epirus, 79
Pythagoras 77
Pythias of Marseilles, 10

Q

al-Qaddafi, Muammar, 335
qadi, 91
al-Qaeda, 321, 329–330, 335, 337, 347, 353, 359
Qatar, 347, 489
Qajar dynasty, 333, 354–355
Qin Shihuangdi, 325, 368
Qing dynasty, 18, 32, 327, 361, 370–372, 375
qipu (knot-writing), 446

R

Rabin, Yitzhak, 341
Radetzky, Josef Wenzel, 257
radiocarbon dating, 21
Rafael, 72
Rafsanjani, Ali Akbar, 355
Rákóczi, György, 198
Rákosi, Mátyás, 198
Raleigh, Walter, 412
Rama IX Bhumipol (Thailand), 384
Rama V Chulalongkorn (Siam), 384
Ramos, Fidel, 389
Ramses II the Great, 309
Rasputin, Grigory, 219
Ravenna, 61, 266–267, 293
Ravenna, exarchate of, 266–267
Reagan, Ronald, 225, 405, 423
Reconquista, 245–246, 249, 336
Red Army (USSR), 203, 210, 221–223, 373
Reformation, 4, 15, 18, 64, 89, 138, 209–211
regnum Noricum, 187
religious wars, list of, 112–113
Republic of the Seventeen Provinces, 158
résistance (France), 130
Restoration period (England), 65–66
reunification of Germany, 135
Revolutions of 1848, 36–37, 52, 65, 195, 202, 238
Reza Shah (Iran), 328, 355
Rhee Syng-man, 377
Rhine, League of, 172
Rhine Franks, 19
Rhine (river and region), 19, 230
Rhodes, 271, 332
Rhodes, Cecil, 319
Rhodes, Colossus of, 76
Rhodri Mawr, 147
Richard I Lion-heart (England), 63, 144
Richard II (England), 144
Richelieu, Cardinal, 65, 112, 233
Ringmann, Matthias, 12
Rio de Janeiro, 437, 450–454
Ritscher, Alfred, 473
Rivera, José Fructuoso, 454
Robert of Molesme, 104
Robert the Bruce, 147, 155
Robespierre, Maximilien de, 114, 234
Roca, Julio Argentino, 458
Rockefeller, John, 348
Rodriguez de Francia, José Gaspar, 455
Rodriguez, Andrés. 439, 455
Roggeveen, Jakob, 395, 468

Roh Moo-hyun, 377
Röhm, Ernst, 177
Rojas Pinilla, Gustavo, 442
Rollo (duke of Normandy), 138
Roman Empire, 11, 59, 204, 230–231, 244, 252, 255, 264, 266, 274, 280, 282, 284, 287, 290, 297, 299, 338, 342, 356, 436
Romania, 54, 65, 68, 222–223, 277, 288–291, 298, 477, 480
Romanov dynasty, 216–217
Roman provinces, ancient, 82, 205, 230, 252, 267, 274, 282, 284, 288, 292, 296, 338
Roman Republic, ancient, 238, 252–253
Roman Republic, 19th century, 257, 261
Rome-Berlin Axis, 258
Romero, Oscar Arnulfo, 433
Rommel, Erwin, 179
Romulus and Remus, 79, 252
Romulus Augustulus, 81, 253
Roosevelt, Franklin D., 178, 355, 405
Rosas, Juan Manuel de, 458
Rosh Hashana, 87
Roses, War of, 144
Rosetta Stone, 77, 309
Ross, James Clark, 470, 472
Ross, John Clark, 470
royal houses of Europe, list of, 98–101
Rúa, Fernando de la, 459
Rudd, Kevin, 398
Rudolf I of Habsburg, 107, 164, 192, 200
Rudolf II (Holy Roman emperor), 194
Rurik (Viking), 214
Rurikid princes, 217
Rushdie, Salman, 337
Russia, 4, 65, 107, 203, 207–221, 224, 226–229, 237–238, 272–273, 285, 287, 291, 294–295, 297–298, 326–327, 333, 339, 349, 352, 355–358, 360–361, 367, 372, 471, 473, 477 See also Soviet Union
Russian-Chechnya conflict, 226, 228, 331
Russian Federation, 217–219, 228, 331, 477–478
Russian Orthodox Church, 209–210, 220
Russian rulers, list of, 217–218
Russo-Georgia War, 137, 227, 331, 357
Russo-Japanese War, 220, 380
Russo-Turkish Wars, 219–220, 272, 287–289, 297, 356
Rwanda, 19, 43, 318, 321, 485
Rwanda genocide, 43, 318, 321

S

de Sa, Mem, 451
Saakashvili, Micheil, 228
Al-Sabah dynasty, 346, 352
Sabbath (Shabbat) 87
Sadat, Anwar, 313, 340
Safavid dynasty, 18, 22, 327, 333, 335, 354–356
Saffron Revolution (Myanmar), 385
Sahara Desert, 302–306, 311, 482
Sahara, Spanish, 25
Sahir Shah (Afghanistan), 358
Saigon, 325, 327, 380, 383–385
Saint-Barthélemy (Lesser Antilles), 242, 497
Saint-Germain, Treaty of, 258
Saint-Just, Antoine de 235

Saint-Pierre and Miquelon 242, 494
Saladin, 333, 339, 342
Salazar y Espinosa, Juan de, 455
Salazar, António de Oliveira, 124, 251
Saltpeter War, 447, 458
Samaritans, 91
Samo, kingdom of, 201
Samoa, 395, 468–469, 503
Samoa, American, 25, 469, 503
Samoa, German, 25, 469
Samuel (biblical prophet) 84
samurai, 28, 30, 377–381
San Andrés y Providencia, 495
Sandinista, 432
Sangiran, (Java) 20
San Marino, 479
San Martin, José de, 458
Sans-culottes, 234
Santa Anna, António López de, 430
São Tomé and Principe, 485
Sappho, 77
Sargon I of Akkad, 70, 324
Sarkozy, Nicolas, 242
Saudi Arabia, 305, 328–329, 334–335, 346–347, 353, 465, 489
Saul (Israel), 84, 338
Sava of Serbia (saint), 275
SAVAK (Iranian security organization), 355
Savoy, House of, 32, 64, 101, 231, 246, 248, 254–261, 264, 267, 272
Saxe-Coburg-Gotha, House of, 154, 251, 287, 480
Saxony, 10, 61, 91, 202, 209, 212
Scaliger, Joseph, Justice, 261
Scandinavia, 48, 61, 68, 138–141
schisms, religious, 15, 60, 88, 106, 268, 332, 336
Schleyer, Hanns Martin, 181
Schlieffen, Alfred von, 174
Schmalkaldic League, 165
Schuschnigg, Kurt, 195
Schwarzenberg, Felix (prince), 189
Scipio Africanus, Publius Cornelius, 79
Scoresby, William, 470
Scotland, 9, 146–155, 362–363, 475
Scott, Robert Falcon, 472
Sebastian I (Portugal), 250
Sea Peoples, 59, 72, 296, 338
secretaries-general of the UN, 159
Seljuq Turks, 26, 296–297, 332–338, 351, 353, 356, 358
Seleucid dynasty, 24, 59, 74, 338, 342, 350, 354, 356, 358
Selim I (sultan), 271, 313, 333, 343, 346
Selim III (sultan), 272
Senegal, 30, 307, 482
Sepoy (Indian) Mutiny, 34, 364
Septimius Severus, 80
Serbia, 36, 66, 206, 217, 220, 274–281, 479
Serbs, 42, 69, 206–211
Serbs, Croats and Slovenes, Kingdom of, 206, 276, 282, 287
Seven Wonders of the World, 76
Seven Years' War, 65, 218, 235, 363
Seventeen Provinces, 158
Seychelles, 31, 467–468, 486
Shackleton, Ernest, 472
Shaka Zulu, 318
Shakespeare, William, 145
Shanidar cave, 20
Shapur I (Persia), 354
sharia, 337, 347, 359
Shevardnadze, Eduard, 228, 357

Shi'ites, Ismaili, 337
Shi'ites, Twelver, 336, 355
Shinto, 379
Shipley, Jenny, 401
shoguns, 327, 379–380
Shomu (Tenno), 378
Shotoku Taishi, 378
Siam, 326, 382–384 See also Thailand
Siberia, 214, 219–224, 227, 335, 360–361, 461
Sierra Leone, 306, 315, 321, 325, 482
Sigismund (Holy Roman Emperor), 168
Sigismund of Tirol, 183
Sigmundur Brestisson, 462
signoria (Italy), 253
Sikhs, 365
Silk Road, 324–325, 368–369
Silurian Period, 8
Silva, Oviedo, 455
Simeon I (Bulgaria), 285, 288
Simeon II (Bulgaria), 287
Simon Bar-Kokhba, 87, 339
Singapore, 386, 493
Sinn Féin, 153
Sino-Tibetan conflict, 331
Six-Day War, 340
Sicilian Vespers massacre, 253
Skanderbeg (George Kastrioti), 282
Slánsky, Rudolf 202
slavery, 236, 304–305, 313–315, 318, 333, 347–348, 350, 444, 446–458, 463–468
Slavs, 61, 91, 274
Slovaks, 200, 476
Slovenia, 204–207, 258, 278, 478–479
Smetona, Antanas, 213
Smith, John, 412
Society Islands, 395
Socotra (Yemen), 465
Socrates, 77
Solferino (battle), 66
Solidarność (Solidarity), 134, 211
Solomon (biblical king), 70, 84, 338
Solomon Islands, 395, 502
Solon, 73
Somalia, 258–259, 303, 317, 320, 337, 484
Somalia, civil war in, 42, 321
Somoza Debayle, Anastasio, 433
Somoza Garcia, Anastasio, 432
Somoza, Luis, 433
Sonderbund War, 184
Sophocles 77
Sores, Jacques, 420
Souflouque, Faustin, 420
Sousa, Martim Afonso de, 451
South Africa, 318–321, 365, 473, 486
South America, 23, 27, 29, 32, 304, 348, 434–459, 461, 463, 499–502 See also individual countries
Southeast Asia, 7, 25, 27, 32, 34, 328, 330, 382, 385, 466–467 See also individual countries
southeastern Europe, 186, 266–272, 336 see also Balkans
South Korea, 328–329, 376–377, 492 see also Korea
South Ossetia, 331
Soviet Union, 206, 211, 213, 217, 222–229, 241, 287–291, 298, 355–358, 374, 391, 477 see also Russia
Spain, 7, 9, 64, 233, 236–237, 244–250, 254–255, 264, 272, 294, 296, 299, 303, 311–312, 327, 332–332,

(Spain, continued) 335–336, 341, 346, 379, 427, 430, 432, 435–437, 440, 442, 456–459, 463–465, 468, 478, 496
Spanish Armada, 247
Spanish Civil War, 249
Spanish colonies, 247
Spanish Inquisition, 246
Spanish Netherlands, 246
Spanish Succession, War of 233, 247
Sparta, 75, 293
Spartacus, 79
Sputnik I, 224
Srebrenica massacre, 281
Sri Lanka, 467, 491
Stalin, Joseph, 9, 67, 124, 178–80, 209–210, 220–225, 279, 283, 355–356, 360, 477
Stalingrad, 127, 178, 222
Stalinism, 220
Stanley, Henry Morton, 304, 315
Stauffenberg, Claus Graf Schenk von, 128, 178
St. Bartholomew's massacre, 112, 232
Stefan I (Serbia), 275
Stefan II Kotromanić (Bosnia), 280
Stefan Tomašević (Bosnia), 281
Stefan Uroš I (Serbia), 275
Stefan Uroš II Milutin (Serbia), 275
Stefan Uroš IV Dušan, (Serbia), 275, 282
Stefan Uroš V (Serbia), 275
Stenka Razin, 216
Stephen I (saint; king of Hungary), 60, 196
Stephen the Great (Moldavia), 289
Stewart, House of, See Stuart
St. Helena, 465, 486
St. Kitts and Nevis, 497
St. Lucia, 497
St. Martin, 242, 496
Stockholm Bloodbath (massacre), 138
Stone Age, 20
Stonehenge, 10, 142
St. Petersburg, 216–219
Strabo, 11
Stresemann, Gustav, 176
Stroessner, Alfredo, 439, 455
Struensee, Johann Friedrich, 139
Stuart, House of, 100, 144, 147, 154–155
St. Vincent and the Grenadines, 495, 497
succession, wars of, 254–255
Sucre, Antonio José de, 448
Sudan, 42, 303, 311, 317, 321–322, 333–335, 484
Sudan, civil war in, 321
Sudetenland, 67, 177
Suebi, 91
Suez Canal, 313, 340
Suez Crisis, 340
Suharto, 391, 425
Sukarno, Achmed, 391, 425
Sukarnoputri, Megawati, 391
Süleyman I the Magnificent, 271, 333
Sulla, 79, 253
Sumer, 22
Sumerians, 8–9, 71, 332, 350
Sun Yat-sen, 372
Sunni, 303, 332–333, 337, 353
Supplinburger dynasty, 169
Suriname, 435, 444–445, 466, 499
Suryavarman II (Khmer), 382

Svatopluk I, 200
Sven Gabelbart, 138
Swanscombe (England), 20
Swartkrans (South Africa), 20
Swaziland, 318, 486
Sweden, 141, 209, 212–216, 218, 242, 471, 474
Swiss Guards, 183
Swiss Habsburg Wars, 184
Switzerland, 12, 182, 184, 230, 232–233, 236–237, 345, 478
Sword, fraternal orders of the, 212
Sviatoslav I (Russia), 285
Syagrius, 93, 96, 230
synods, 88
Synod of Whitby, 143
Syria, 266, 277, 309, 313, 324, 328, 332–335, 339–344, 353, 357, 488
Szálasi, Ferenc, 198

T

Taborites, 201
Tabula Peutingeriana (Peutinger Table), 11
Tahiti, 456, 469
Taiwan, 370, 374–375, 388, 491
Tajikistan, 354, 358–359, 490
Taj Mahal, 363
Taliban, 330, 335–337, 359, 366
Talon, Jean-Baptiste, 409
Tambora (volcano), 390
Tamerlane *See* Timur
Tamil Tigers, 467
Tang dynasty, 324–325, 376
Tannenberg (battle), 106, 208, 212
Tanzania, 317, 466, 485
Tanzimat reforms, 272, 297
Tarquinius Superbus, 78, 252
Tasman, Abel, 31, 395, 400
Tassilo III of Bavaria, 97, 163
Taufa'ahau Tupou IV, 395
Taung skull, 20
Tehran Conference, 128, 178
Teixeira, Pedro, 437, 451
Tejero, Antonio, 249
temples, Egyptian, list of, 309
Tervel (Bulgaria), 284
Teutoburg Forest (battle), 162
Teutonic Order, 138, 168, 208f, 212, 214
Thaçi, Hashim, 279
Thailand, 382, 492 see also Siam
Thales of Miletus, 10, 77
Thatcher, Margaret, 148
thaw, glacial, 224
Theodoric the Great, 93, 253
Theodosius I the Great, 81, 88, 93, 252, 266
Thiers, Adolphe, 239
Third Reich, 177, 202, 213, 222
    See also German Empire
Thirty Years' War, 89, 113, 166
Thopia, Karl, 282
Thucydides, 77
Thutmose I, 309
Thutmose III, 309
Tiananmen Square, 329, 374
Tibet, 323–324, 326–331, 366–367, 370–371, 374–375
Tigranes II the Great, 296, 356
Timur (Timur Lenk, Tamerlane) 268, 271, 326, 333, 351, 356, 358, 363
Tiradentes, 450
Tiridates I (Armenia), 356
Tito, Josip Broz, 206, 224, 276, 283
Titoism, 206, 278
Titus, 84, 338
Toba (volcano), 9

Togo, 483
Tojo Hideki, 381
Tokelau, 503
Tokugawa Ieyasu, 376
Tokugawa shogunate, 327, 379
Tomislav I (Croatia), 204
Tonga, 395, 503
Toqtamish Khan, 360
Tordesillas, Treaty of, 30, 110, 435
Tories, 148
Toyotomi Hideyoshi, 379
Trafalgar (battle), 114, 236, 248
Trajan, 81, 288, 339
Transcaucasia, 324, 356–357
Transnistria, 137
Trans-Siberian Railroad, 219, 360–361
Trastámara, 101
Trent, Council of, 89, 111
Trianon, Treaty of, 189
Trinidad und Tobago, 464, 497
Triple Alliance, 174
Triple Entente, 66, 120, 123, 148
Tristan da Cunha, 465
Trojan War, 72, 293
Trotsky, Leo, 221
Trujillo, Rafael, 420, 424
Tsarist rule, 215
Tudor, House of 100, 145, 154
Tugen Hills (Kenya), 20
Tughril Beg, 354
Tunesia, 311, 482
Tupac Amaru I, 437, 446
Tupac Amaru II, 437, 446–447
Turkey, 296–299, 487
Turkic peoples, 214, 285, 287, 297, 356–357, 359, 374
Turkmenbasi (Saparmyrat Nyyazov), 359
Turkmenistan, 354, 358–359, 490
Turks and Caicos, 496
Turks, wars against, 187, 219
Tuvalu, 502
Tvrtko I (Bosnia), 280
two-party system, 148
Tymoschenko, Julia, 227
Tzu Hsi *See* Cixi

U

U Thant, 51
Uganda, 303, 305, 317, 484
Ukraine, 209, 214, 216, 218,-219, 222, 224–228–229, 291, 477
Ulbricht, Walter, 181
Ulmanis, Karlis, 213
Ulster Unionist Party (UPP), 152
Ultraquists 201
Umar ibn al-Khattab (caliph), 332, 336
Umayyad dynasty, 244, 267, 299, 302–303, 310–311, 332, 336, 342, 351, 354
UN *See* United Nations
UNESCO *See* United Nations Educational, Scientific and Cultural Organization
UNICEF *See* United Nations Children's Fund
unification of Europe, 69
Union of Krewo, 212
Union of Lublin, 209
United Arab Emirates (UAE), 346–347, 489
United Nations (UN), 12, 50, 278–279, 306, 330, 339, 353–354, 361, 377, 384, 391, 476, 494
United Nations Children's Fund (UNICEF), 51

United Nations Educational, Scientific and Cultural Organization (UNESCO), 51
United Nations High Commissioner for Refugees (UNHCR), 51
United Provinces (Netherlands), 158
United States of America (USA), 13, 18–19, 29, 34–53, 65, 67–69, 88, 119, 122, 124–125, 134, 138–139, 174–175, 195, 219, 224–225, 236, 238, 242, 249, 270, 280, 282, 287, 291, 298, 304–305, 313–317, 320, 328–330, 334, 337, 341–358, 377, 380–381, 383–384, 388, 392, 404, 412–423, 427, 430–433, 438–439, 441, 444, 455–457, 463–471, 494–502
U Nu (Burma), 385
Ur, 71, 324, 332, 350
Uribe, Alvaro, 439, 442
Uruguay, 438–439, 449–452, 454–455, 458–459, 499–501
Uruk, 324, 350
Ustashe, 206
Uthman ibn Affan, 336
Utrecht, Treaty of 248
Uzbekistan, 219, 354, 490

V

Valck, Gerard, 15
Valentinian I, 81
Valentinian III, 81
Valera, Eamon de, 152
Valerian, 80
Vallard, Nicholas, 393
Valmy, Kanonade of, 236
Valois dynasty, 99
Vanatu, 395, 503
Vandals, 61, 91
Vanuatu, 502
Vasa era, 101
Vatican City, 479
Vatican Council, Second, 89
Vedas, 362, 367
Velasco Alvarada, Juan, 447
Velasco Ibarra, José Maria, 443
Velázquez, Diego de, 420
Venice, 63, 87, 107, 114, 204–205, 252–258, 260, 272, 276, 294, 299,
Venezuela, 305, 428, 435–445, 449, 452, 461, 499
Vercingetorix, 90, 230–231
Verdun (battle), 238
Verdun, Treaty of, 96, 156, 163, 183, 231
Versailles, Treaty of, 124, 175, 240
Vespucci, Amerigo, 12, 31, 440, 458
Vesuvius (volcano), 80
Vichy regime, 178, 240
Victoria (England), 121, 151, 364
Videla, Jorge Rafael, 439, 459
Vienna Awards, 191
Vienna, Congress of, 65, 115, 168, 184, 188, 194, 210, 218, 238, 256
Vietnam, 327–329, 372, 382–385, 492
Vietnam War, 43, 384, 405, 419, 425
Victor Emanuel II (Italy), 257
Victor Emanuel III (Italy), 258
Vikings, 61, 138, 142, 212, 214, 461–463, 470
Villa, Pancho, 431
Virgin Islands, 396, 464
Visconti, Gian Galeazzo, 261
Visigoths, 59–61, 81, 90–93, 118, 231, 252, 266, 280,
Vlad III Dracul, 289
Vlastimir I, 274
Vogelweide, Walther von der, 102

Völkerbund resolution, 50, 124
Voronin, Vladimir, 291
Vratislav II, 200
Vytautas the Great, 212

W

Wahhabism, 346–347
Wajdak skulls (Java), 20
Walachia, 288
Waldemar IV, 138
Waldheim, Kurt, 51
Waldseemüller, Martin, 12
Wales, 146
Walesa, Lech, 132, 211
Wallace, William, 147
Wallenstein, Albrecht von, 113, 166
Wallis and Futuna, 242, 503
Walloons, 159
Wannsee Conference, 127, 178
Warsaw, 210–211, 224, 236–237
Warsaw ghetto, 128, 178
Warsaw Pact, 5, 68, 132, 203, 210, 279, 289
Warsaw Uprising, 210
Wartburg Festival, 172
Washington, George, 404, 414
Watergate Scandal, 419
Waterloo, 65, 236
Weimar Republic, 124, 176
Welf dynasty, 164, 169 *See also* Guelfs
Wellington, Duke of, 148, 248
Wenzel II (Austria), 208
West Africa, 314
Westphalia, Peace of, 113, 139, 166, 170, 184, 247
Western Sahara, 311–312, 322, 482
Weyprecht, Carl, 470
Whigs, 148
Whitby, Synod of, 89, 142
White Lotus (secret society), 370
WHO *See* World Health Organization
William I (Germany), 117, 173
William I (Orange), 158
William I (Netherlands), 159
William II (England), 144
William II (Germany) 120, 173, 176
William III (Orange), 147–148, 158
William the Conqueror, 143
Williams, Roger, 412
Wilson, Woodrow, 122, 405
Windsor, House of, 154
Wittelsbach, House of, 98, 165
Wolfe, James, 409
Woodstock music festival 419
World Health Organization (WHO), 51
World Trade Center (New York), 330, 335, 405
World War I, 36, 67, 122–124, 149, 159, 174, 190, 206, 211, 220, 238–240, 258, 277, 287, 294–296, 357
World War II, 38, 67, 124, 126, 130, 140, 149, 159, 178, 190–191, 207, 211, 213, 222, 240–243, 258–261, 277, 287, 291, 294–301 *See also* Pacific War
Worms, Concordat of, 89, 106, 164
Wounded Knee (battle), 405, 407, 418
Wudi (China), 368

X

Xoxe, Koci (Albania), 283

Y

Yahya Muhammad, Iman, 347
Yalta Conference, 69, 128, 179, 222

Yangshao culture, 368
Yeltsin, Boris, 226
Yemen, 271, 305, 317, 328–329, 332, 335–336, 346–347, 465, 490
Yermak (Cossack), 214
Yeschov, Nikolai, 222
Yom Kippur, 87
Yom Kippur War, 340
Yongzheng (China), 370
York, House of, 154
Yoshihito (Tenno), 380
Yuan dynasty, 326, 361
Yuan Shikai, 373
Yugoslavia, 206–207, 224, 259, 276–281, 283, 286–287, 479
Yugoslavia, wars in, 42, 69, 135, 207, 278
Yung-fu, Liu (China) 370
Yushchenko, Viktor, 226–227

Z

Zaydi (Fiver Shi'ites), 337, 346–347
Zambia, 485
Zanzibar, 303, 317, 466–467
Zapata, Emiliano, 431, 499
Zapatistas, 431
Zapotecs, 428–431
Zealots, 86, 338
Zenta (battle), 198, 272
Zhoukoudian (China) 20
Zhou dynasty, 325, 368–369, 375
Zhu Yuanzhang, 370
Zimbabwe, 303, 318–319, 485
Živkov, Todor, 135
Zog I (Albania), 283
Zollverein *See* German Customs Union
Zweibund (German-Austrian alliance), 66, 120, 172
Zwingli, Ulrich, 111, 184

Picture Credits

2009 © Photo SCALA, Florence
9 c.l.; 22 l., 22 c.r., 72, 75, 76 nr. 6, 78, 80 b., 94 b.l., 95 t.l., 97, 98 t.l., 104 b., 105 c., 165, 193 b., 275 l.;
HIP 10 c., 12 t.c., 12 b.c., 12 t.r., 39, 68, 79, 80, 91 r., 94 t.l., 100 t., 107, 109, 110, 116 c., 116 r., 119, 121 t.l., 151, 154 t.c., 155 l., 155 t.r., 160, 206, 221 r., 223 b., 248, 269 t., 271 t., 304, 305 b., 365 t., 365 c., 382, 392/393, 395, 399, 401 l., 401 r., 402/403, 412, 429 l., 436 l., 443;
Ann Ronan/HIP 63 b.l., 63 r., 76 nr. 1, 85 b., 91 l., 121 r.c., 121 b.r., 123 c., 125, 126, 147 b., 154 t.l., 154 b.l., 169 t., 239, 241, 246 l., 259 b., 267, 292, 305 r., 319 t., 365 b., 367, 380, 381 b., 409, 421 (Roosevelt), 421 (Truman), 436 r., 441;
CM Dixon/HIP 9 c., 70 t.;
Spectrum/HIP 94 r., 95 t.r., 95 b.r., 122 t., 122 b., 150, 154 t.r., 155 b.r., 281, 363, 369, 398, 433, 454 l.;
DeAgostini Picture Library 10 l., 13 l., 76 nr. 2, 85 l., 94 c., 113, 132, 180, 222, 223 t., 291, 385, 425, 429 r., 446, 453 t., 453 b.;
Austrian Archive 12 b.l., 38, 99 t.l., 121 t.r., 123 t., 116 b.c., 169 b., 177, 199;
White Images 22 r., 63 t.l., 99 t.r., 99 r.c., 100 b., 116 t., 121 l.c., 147 t., 171, 194, 216, 221 l., 234 t., 234 b., 237, 255 r., 271 b., 273, 277, 283 l., 283 r., 286, 297, 337, 370, 381 t., 424;
Werner Forman Archive 70 b., 80 t., 90, 269 b., 311 b., 324, 325, 368, 371 r., 379;
Luciano Romano 108;
DUfoto 259 t.;
AGF 295, 298, 319 b., 341, 353, 359;
© 1990 Courtesy of the Ministero Beni e Att. Culturali 11 r., 74, 82, 83, 193 t., 246 r., 255 l.; © 1996 Courtesy of the Ministero Beni e Att. Culturali 300/301; © 2004 Courtesy of the Ministero Beni e Att. Culturali 370 l.; © 2008 Courtesy of the Ministero Beni e Att. Culturali 22 c.l.;
© 1990 Fondo Edifici de Culto – Min. dell'Interno 105 t.;
© 2008 Museum of Fine Arts, Boston. Henry Lillie Pierce Fund Inv. 99.22. All rights reserved 314;
© 2007 The Metropolitan Museum of Art/Art Resource/The Harry G.C. Packard Collection of Asian Art, Gift of Harry G.C. Packard, and Purchase, Fletcher, Rogers, Harris Brisbane Dick, and Louis V. Bell Funds, Joseph Pulitzer Bequest, and The Annenberg Fund Inc. Gift, 1975. Acc.n.: 1975.268.414 Image copyright 378; © 2007 The Metropolitan Museum of Art/Art Resource/ Bequest of Charles Allen Munn, 1924. Acc.n.: 24.90.185 Image copyright 414 r.;
© 2008 Photo National Portrait Gallery/Smithsonian/Art Resource 421 (Jefferson – Bequest of Charles Francis Adams); © 2009 Photo National Portrait Gallery/Smithsonian/Art Resource 421 (Lincoln), 421 (Wilson);
© 2008 Kimbell Art Museum, Fort Worth, Texas (AP 1985.09)/Art Resource, NY 429 c.;
© 2004 The Pierpoint Morgan Library (M.525, f.10. New York)/Art Resource 451 t.

Achim Bednorz 102/103 all, 104 t., 104 c., 105 b.

University Library, Bratislava, Slovakia 14/15, 56/57, 322/323, 426/427, 460/461

Vladimír Vanko 20

Front and back end papers:
Typus Orbis Terrarum. London, British Library (2009 © Photo SCALA, Florence/HIP)
Pages 2/3:
World map, 1657. London, British Library (2009 © Photo SCALA, Florence/HIP)

Published in 2010

Copyright © Parragon Books Ltd 2010
Queen Street House
4 Queen Street
Bath BA1 1HE, U.K.

Original edition produced by Frechmann Kolón GmbH
Project management: Sally Bald (for Frechmann), Katarina Halčinová (for Slovart)
Map templates: Geoatlas
Maps: Daniel Gurňák for Slovart (World, Europe, Africa, Asia, Americas, Australia, Oceania, Polar regions), Martin Štefánik for Slovart (Europe), Peter Draškaba (Europe), Anton Šteger for Slovart (Europe), Gerhard Pastircák for Slovart (Europe), Nagy Béla for Slovart (Europe)
Cartography: Sabine Meyerding
Text: Ludwig Könemann, Markus Hattstein, Martin Štefánik for Slovart (Europe), Matej Hanula for Slovart (World, Africa, America, Australia, Oceania), Róbert Beutelhauser for Slovart (Asia), Ladislav Tolmáči for Slovart (Countries of the World)
Editing: Markus Hattstein, Nikolaus Wolters, Hartmut Lehbrink
Design & Layout: Rheinische Umbrechereien, Werk Düsseldorf-Süd

English edition produced by APE International, LLC
Translation from German: Dr. Maureen Basedow, Nina Gettler, Linda Marianiello & Franz Vote, Jennifer Taylor, Heustis P. Whiteside
Editing of English edition: Dr. Maureen Basedow, Mary Dobrian, Tammi Reichel, Susan Shepard

ISBN 978–1–4075–8333–4

Printed in United Arab Emirates

Acknowledgments

Bringing together all the conceptual elements, historical maps, chronologies and glossaries into a harmonious whole on each spread demanded great effort from everyone involved in this project. We are grateful to all of you.

Sándor Kotyrba took thousands of conceptual building blocks and put them together into a unifying sructure. Juraj Heger and Katarína Halčinová organized a team of cartographers and historians, and tirelessly wrestled this project through to the very end. Laurent Lafitte of Geoatlas provided helpful tips and laid the foundation for creating the maps, work that was executed by Daniel Gurňák, Martin Štefánik and the team at Slovart. Queen Sabine, Sabine Meyerding, a virtuoso of graphics in Illustrator, realized them in that format.

To Daniel, Martin and the many other contributors goes our gratitude for your contributions to the text and numerous corrections to the Editor in Chief's efforts.

Rheinische Umbrechereien, Werk Düsseldorf-Süd and Birgit Beyer were responsible for creating the layout.

Markus Hattstein corrected text and maps with great diligence, contributing his thorough kowledge of history to them.

Sabine Gerber and Susanne Könemann read the book to make sure everything is understandable and plausible.

We would also like to express our gratitude to countless historians who have published their knowledge in books and on the Internet. For every entry in the *Historical Atlas of the World*, entire volumes have been written, which we were able to consult.

We thank you all.

Sally Bald (Project Manager)   Ludwig Könemann (Editor in Chief)

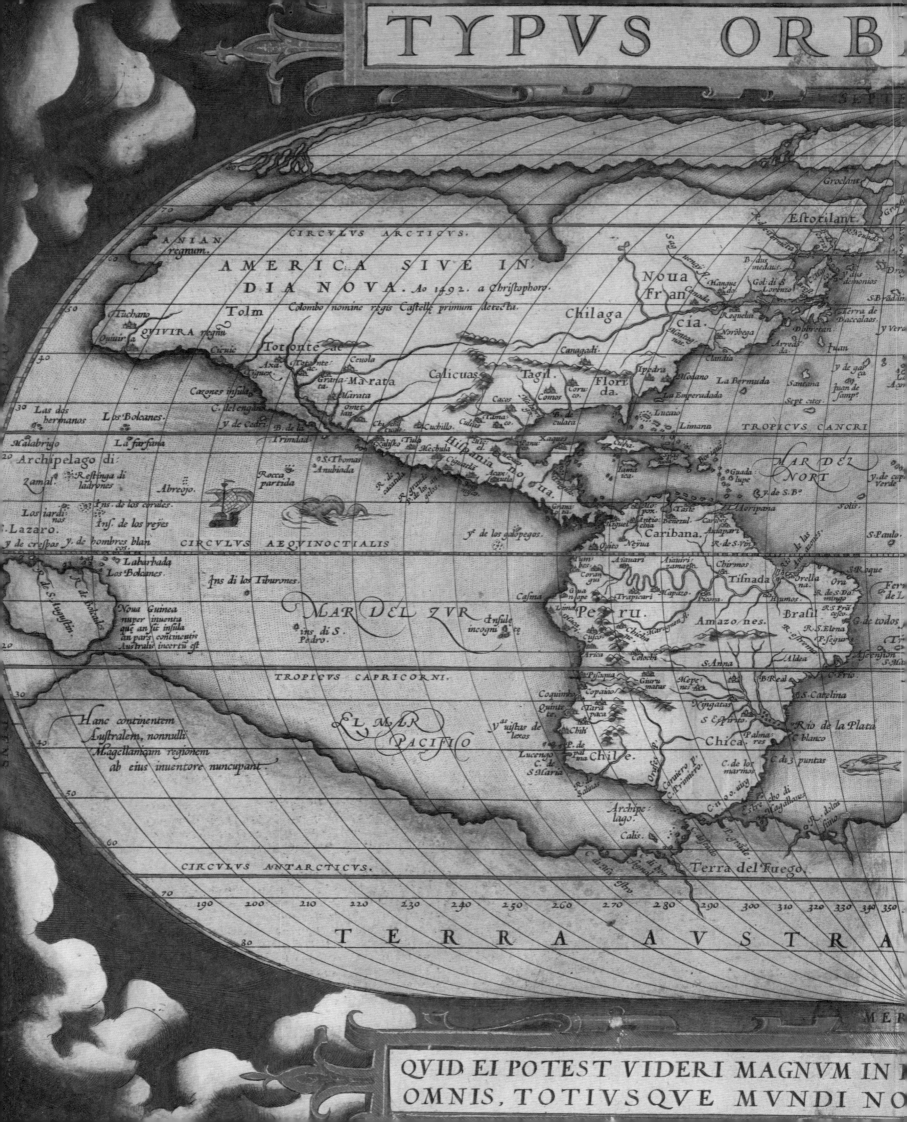

TYPVS ORB

SEPTE

QVID EI POTEST VIDERI MAGNVM IN
OMNIS, TOTIVSQVE MVNDI N